P9-AFP-908

Film Review Index

Volume 1: 1882-1949

Edited by
Patricia King Hanson
Stephen L. Hanson

ORYX PRESS
1986

The rare Arabian Oryx is believed to have inspired the myth of the unicorn. This desert antelope became virtually extinct in the early 1960s. At that time several groups of international conservationists arranged to have 9 animals sent to the Phoenix Zoo to be the nucleus of a captive breeding herd. Today the Oryx population is over 400, and herds have been returned to reserves in Israel, Jordan, and Oman.

Copyright © 1986 by
The Oryx Press
2214 North Central at Encanto
Phoenix, AZ 85004-1483

Published simultaneously in Canada

All rights reserved
No part of this publication may be reproduced or transmitted in any form or by any means, electronic or mechanical, including photocopying, recording, or by any information storage and retrieval system, without permission in writing from The Oryx Press.

Printed and Bound in the United States of America

∞ The paper used in this publication meets the minimum requirements of American National Standard for Information Science—Permanence of Paper for Printed Library Materials, ANSI Z39.48, 1984.

Library of Congress Cataloging-in-Publication Data

Film review index, volume 1: 1882–1949

  Bibliography: p.
  Includes Indexes.
  Contents: v. 1. 1882–1949.
  1. Moving-pictures—Reviews—Indexes. I. Hanson, Patricia King. II. Hanson, Stephen L.
  25784.M9F513 1986 [PN1995] 016.79143'75 85-43369
  ISBN 0-89774-153-6 (v. 1)

We dedicate this book to our son,
David Grant Hanson,
who went from Blessed Event to
Forty Pounds of Trouble
during its preparation.

Table of Contents

Ref.
PN
1995Z
Z99
F48
v. 1

EB

Contributors to Volume I

Glenna Dunning, University of Southern California Library

Marva Felchlin, Alhambra Public Library

Alan Gevinson, American Film Institute

Julia Johnson, University of Southern California Library

Carolyn McIntosh, University of Southern California Library

Lindy Narver, University of Southern California Library

Marsha Maguire, Library of Congress, Washington D.C

Sue Ellen Picker, American Film Institute

6-25-87

Introduction

The evolution of the motion picture from scientific experiment to simple entertainment and its ultimate development into a complex art form worthy of serious scholarship in less than a century has created a body of critical writng that is inordinately diverse for a recognized discipline. Its literature has quickly grown to encompass not only the primary source material of the films themselves but also, at one remove, the reminiscences of its practitioners, the opinions of its critics, and, finally, the analyses of modern historians and scholars. However, even as the motion picture has gained recognition as a subject worthy of serious scholarship, it has continually outrun even the most ambitious efforts to acheive a measure of bibliographical control over the body of knowledge it represents.

Although the origin of what we now recognize as the "movie review," is shrouded in obscurity, at least one film historian, George C. Pratt, author of *Spellbound in Darkness*, attributes it to Nathaniel Hawthorne, already famous as the "father of American Literature," who was apparently the first writer to critique an instance of projected moving images. Describing a "faux-pas" ridden Diorama presentation in his 1838 *American Notebooks*, Hawthorne wrote:

> There were views of cities and edifices in Europe, of Napoleon's battles and Nelson's sea-fights, in the midst of which would be seen a gigantic, brown, hairy hand (the Hand of Destiny) pointing at the principle points of conflict, while the old Dutchman explained. He gave a good deal of dramatic effect to his descriptions, but his accent and intonation cannot be written. He seemed to take interest and pride in his exhibition, yet when the utter and ludicrous miserability thereof made us laugh, he joined in the joke very readily. When the last picture had been shown, he caused a country boor, who stood gaping beside the machine, to put his head within it, and thrust out his tongue. The head becoming gigantic, a singular effect was produced.

A rudimentery prototype for the film review was thus established —it only remained for the motion picture to be invented.

In 1872, when an English photographer, Eadweard Muybridge, performed his famous "Animals in Motion" experiment utilizing 12 single-frame cameras to record a galloping horse, and then re-created its motion by projecting the resultant images with a Zoopraxiscope and magic lantern, the acheivement was purely scientific and the writers of the period treated it accordingly. The invention of "series photography" was properly thought to be of primary interest to journals like the *Scientific American* or the news section of *The New York Times*, both of which debated the merits of Muybridge's 12-camera method vs. Etiene-Jules Morey's technique of taking all of the photographs, sequentially, with one camera. Any artistic considerations centered simply on whether or not all of the horse's feet were ever off of the ground at the same time—the issue that had prompted Muybridge's original experiment. Although the single-camera achievement ultimately earned Muybridge's French competitor the accolade as "the father of the motion picture," the greater press coverage gained by the English photographer's demonstrations in the 1880s should certainly allow Muybridge at least a certain "midwife" recognition in the birth of what would finally become the motion picture review.

By the turn of the century, as interest in Muybridge's Zoopraxiscope was supplanted by the newer Kinetoscope and the Cinematographe, with their numerous entertainment possibilities, the subject matter to be photographed and projected became every bit as important as the process itself. The rise of Nickelodeons indicated that the motion picture was arriving as a powerful new mass medium for the working class and so *The New York Times* shifted its coverage of the phenomena to its entertainment pages and began to print reviews regularly as early as 1913. Even the staid *New York Dramatic Mirror* began to intersperse film reviews with its theatrical criticism around the same period.

Yet, prior to 1910, "one-reelers" were usually exhibited in clusters under the headings of their producer and called by such titles as Edison Program Number One or Lumiere Program Number 2. Consequently, local newspaper film reviews more closely resembled the collective type employed for variety shows and vaudeville entertainments than they did more traditional modes of literary and dramatic criticism. Early reviewers rarely singled out individual directors or performers. Florence Lawrence, for example, was routinely called "the Vitagraph Girl" before her immense popularity caused audiences to demand her real name and establish her as the first real "movie star."

During the teens, when motion pictures became big business, a number of trade journals including *Variety* and *Moving Picture World* began to publish a different kind of review. Their critiques were aimed at exhibitors and consequently predated more popular treatments and placed major emphasis on credits and production information. (A tradition continued at present by *The Hollywood Reporter, Motion Picture Herald Product Digest* and, *Variety*). Today when many of the films they discussed no longer exist, these appraisals are often the scholar's only indication of what a particular film was about or who was in it. Unfortunately, however, the majority of these reviews were never comprehensively indexed beyond the brief listings done at irregular intervals by some of the publications while others were not indexed at all.

Historically, the few attempts that have been made to provide a systematic approach to indexing film reviews have usually adopted the arbitrary stance of selecting a fixed universe of anywhere from five to fifteen film journals and then listing citations for every film reviewed by them. Such approaches have, of necessity, ignored a wide range of deserving films and valuable critical perspectives.

Today, as film scholarship approaches the century mark, most researchers still consider the *Readers' Guide to Periodical Literature* as the most comprehensive single index of film reviews. For more scholarly approaches to individual films, there are, of course, *The International Index to Film Periodicals* and *The Film Literature Index*, but they are both highly selective as well as relative newcomers to the field. *The Film Review Index* is an attempt to fill the gap left by traditional indexes and to provide a retrospective bibliography of articles about specific films which have, over the years, established themselves as being of the highest interest to researchers and students. It is thus designed to be a latchkey for scholars, critics, film buffs, librarians, film critics, students and anyone else who is primarily interested in obtaining information on specific films. Accordingly, we have avoided what we consider to be nonessential references to biographical, technical, and other types of material having but a peripheral relationship to the films we have selected for inclusion. All articles, chapters and book citations listed under each film in *The Film Review Index* deal primarily with that film either as a review, as history, or as critical commentary.

Coverage begins in 1882 with some citations to Muybridge's pre-cinema experiments with "Animals in Motion" and a number of other notable nineteenth century landmarks such as Thomas A. Edison's "The Kiss" (1896) which are regarded as still being of significant importance to scholars. However, the primary focus of the volumes concentrates on the period 1903 (the date of "The Great Train Robbery") to 1986. This affords coverage of almost 8000 feature films or an average of 75 films a year for each of the high production years between 1914 and 1986. We have obviously not attempted to include every film produced within those years, but primarily those pictures that have established themselves as being of continuing importance to film researchers. At the same time, we have not ignored "programmers" or minor films that could, at some point, become the object of certain highly specialized types of research due to their reflection of certain sociological trends or simply because they were extremely popular for a variety of reasons.

The overriding consideration in the selection of titles was: "Would anyone, at some point in time, ever conceivably want citations to this film?" If the answer was affirmative, we then had to determine "What, if anything can be found?" Often, the options were limited. But in most cases, the basic sources such as *The New York Times, Variety, Film Daily, Hollywood Reporter* and *Moving Picture World* or *Motion Picture Herald* could be counted on to provide a respectable number of citations.

This film-centered approach admittedly places us well out on the proverbial limb, as it is the antithesis of the traditional procedures employed by existing indices which attempt to index journals rather than films. However, it is of more importance to the objectives of *The Film Review Index* to provide a variety of unique, "hard to find" materials for each individual film than it is to provide "in-depth" documentation of various critics, anthologies, histories, and journals which appeal to a small number of film scholars and which are readily available only in a limited number of libraries. Admittedly, in some cases, though, we simply had to settle for what we could find. While this approach may anger some specialists who may find their favorite treatise excluded in favor of a "trade" review or a chapter from a film history, it does provide other advantages. Paramount among these is the fact that the wide variety of entries provided for the most significant films should include some citations that are in reach of users of even the smallest libraries. Individual libraries might not have *Variety* or *The History of Narrative Film* but they certainly will have access to *Saturday Review, Newsweek* or, in the case of the early silents, one of the reprint series or histories cited. Small public or special libraries which cannot afford the major film literature indices will find *The Film Review Index* invaluable as its broad coverage allows it to supplant a variety of more expensive reference works. We have hopefully provided something practical and accessible to both the scholar and the interested nonprofessional alike.

Each of the film entries includes as many references as are available to the film, with four primary reasons for exclusion: redundancy, foreign language sources, lack of common accessibility, and lack of substance. Thus, an article by French director Francois Truffaut on one of Alfred Hitchcock's films is included if it is in English, but omitted if it is in French. At the same time, a minor film review in a popular magazine like *Glamour* or *Family Circle* will not be found here while those in *Time* and *The New Yorker* will be. One determining factor is often whether or not the popular review includes background or production information that is not commonly available in more critical sources. This is particularly important in reviews of foreign language films where contemporary treatments may contain production details omitted by later historical studies and philosophical critiques.

Great emphasis has also been placed on including references to trade publications—long the most important source of film reviews. Such publications as *The Hollywood Reporter, Variety, The Motion Picture Herald Product Digest* and their antecedents have heretofore never been included in any index. These sources, as mentioned earlier, normally provide the earliest reviews of a film, the most extensive production information and the most complete credits. Yet, they are, historically, the most inaccessible and least indexed avenue of film research. In most cases, the inclusion of citations to these reviews in *The Film Review Index* mandated a page by page examination of the complete runs of each journal. In addition to journal, newspaper, and trade reviews, *The Film Review Index* also lists articles in important, freely available books which deal with specific films, such as *The Films of.........* books and *Magill's Survey of Cinema*.

Films in *The Film Review Index* are listed in alphabetical order with cross references for title changes. The bibliographic format was designed for librarians and laypeople alike and thus avoids illogical or complicated abbreviations. The information for each selection includes the film's title, any alternate or foreign title, the country of origin, director, and year produced. Books are listed by title and page number with full bibliographical information provided separately in an extensive "Books Consulted" section. Periodical titles are cited in full under each film and list the date, volume and page on which the review can be found. One interesting and unforseen result of *The Film Review Index's*

alphabetical arrangement was the discovery of a surprising number of films that have been made and remade a number of times during the relatively short history of cinema. For example, the famous version of "Oliver Twist" is the 1949 David Lean version but that was at least the fifth film adaptation of the Dickens novel. Similarly, Walt Disney's "Snow White" was predated by a 1916 version. We hope that such discoveries will be an equally pleasant surprise to users of this book.

Because of the confines of time and space, we were unable to cite every source of value on each film, try as we might. To researchers, then, we would strongly urge a careful perusal of the Books Consulted Section at the end of the book. Many of the more theoretical studies provide general background information on a variety of topics beyond those sections cited under particular films elsewhere in *The Film Review Index*. Similarly, if certain books on Howard Hawks or John Ford do not discuss a specific film in depth, it might still offer invaluable insights into the directors' works as a whole.

During the course of production of this book, many people offered their help and assistance. We would particularly like to thank Lisa Mosher, Steve Ambers, Dan Sallitt, Eric Smoodin, and Mickey and Margaret King. We would also like to express our appreciation to the staffs of the following libraries: The Louis B. Mayer Library of the American Film Institute, The Margaret Herrick Library of the Academy of Motion Picture Arts and Sciences, The Reference and Special Collections Departments of the University of Southern California Library, the Theater Arts Library at the University of California at Los Angeles, and the Beverly Hills Public Library.

Among our contributors, we would particularly like to thank Julia Johnson who never stopped giving us citations to "King Kong" and "Gone with the Wind" and Sue Ellen Picker, who waded her way through "Citizen Kane." At Oryx Press, we would like to thank Jim Thomas for his encouragement and support in the early stages of the project, Anne Thompson who was very patient and supportive in the development of the specifics of the text's format and computerization, and to Sam Mongeau and his staff who had the rather thankless task of reading through the material citation-by-citation.

Patricia King Hanson
Stephen L. Hanson

Film Listings

Abe Lincoln in Illinois (US; Cromwell, John; 1940)
Commonweal. Feb 19, 1940,, v31, p367.
Film Daily. Jan 17, 1940, p7.
Hollywood Reporter. Jan 9, 1940, p3.
Life. Feb 12, 1940, v8, p74-79.
Magill's Survey of Cinema. Series I. v1, p1-5.
The Nation. March 16, 1940, v150, p372.
The New Republic. Mar 4, 1940, v102, p308.
The New York Times. Feb 23, 1940, p19.
The New Yorker. Feb 24, 1940, v16, p67.
Newsweek. Jan 29, 1940, v15, p32-33.
Photoplay. Apr 1940, v54, p68.
Scholastic. Dec 11, 1940,, v35, p30-31.
Time. Feb 5, 1940, v35, p60.
Variety. Jan 24, 1940, p14.

Abie's Irish Rose (US; Fleming, Victor; 1928)
Film Daily. Apr 22, 1928, p8.
The Film Spectator. Mar 31, 1928, v5, p18-19.
The New York Times. Apr 20, 1928, p26.
Variety. Apr 25, 1928, p29.
Variety. Dec 26, 1928, p27.

Abilene Town (US; Marin, Edwin L.; 1946)
Commonweal. Jan 4, 1946, v43, p309.
Film Daily. Jan 11, 1946, p16.
Hollywood Reporter. Jan 9, 1946, p3.
Motion Picture Herald Product Digest. Jan 12, 1946, p2793.
The New York Times. Mar 4, 1946, p16.
The New Yorker. Mar 16, 1946, v22, p89.
Time. Jan 28, 1946, v47, p99.
Variety. Jan 9, 1946, p76.

Above Suspicion (US; Thorpe, Richard; 1943)
Basil Rathbone: His Life and His Films. p274-77.
Commonweal. Sep 10, 1943, v38, p514.
Film Daily. Apr 28, 1943, p8.
The Films of Joan Crawford. p152-54.
The Great Spy Pictures. p43-45.
Hollywood Reporter. Apr 28, 1943, p3.
Motion Picture Herald Product Digest. May 1, 1943, p1289.
The New York Times. Aug 6, 1943, p10.
Time. Aug 23, 1943, v42, p94.
Variety. Apr 28, 1943, p8.

Abraham Lincoln (US; Rosen, Phil; 1924)
BFI/Monthly Film Bulletin. Sep 1974, v41, p208-09.
Film Daily. Jan 27, 1924, p6.
The Moving Picture World. Feb 2, 1924, p415.
The New York Times. Jan 22, 1924, p17.
Photoplay. Mar 1924, v25, p60.
Selected Film Criticism, 1921-1930. p3.
Variety. Jan 24, 1924, p26.

Abraham Lincoln (US; Griffith, D.W.; 1930)
American Film Criticism. p238-40.
BFI/Monthly Film Bulletin. Sep 1974, v41, p208.
The Civil War on the Screen. p75-79.
Commonweal. Sep 17, 1930, v 12, p498.

Film Daily. Aug 31, 1930, p10.
The Films of D.W. Griffith. p241-52.
The Films of the Thirties. p37-38.
Judge. Oct 11, 1930, v99, p21.
Judge. Sep 19, 1931, v101, p20.
Life. Sep 12, 1930, v96, p17.
Literary Digest. Sep 20, 1930, v106, p15-16.
The Nation. Sep 17, 1930, v131, p305.
National Board of Review Magazine. Oct 1930, v5, p9.
National Magazine. Dec 1930, v59, p144.
The New Republic. Sep 10, 1930, v64, p101-02.
The New York Times. Aug 26, 1930, p24.
The New York Times. Aug 13, 1930, p5.
The New Yorker. Sep 6, 1930, v6, p61-62.
Outlook and Independent. Sep 10, 1930, v156, p72.
Rob Wagner's Script. Feb 5, 1938, v18, p10.
Saturday Review (London). Feb 28, 1931, v151, p303.
Selected Film Criticism, 1921-1930. p3-5.
Sociology and Social Research. Jan 1931, v15, p298.
Take One. Nov-Dec 1971, v3, p8-12.
Theatre Magazine. Nov 1930, v52, p47.
Time. Sep 8, 1930, v16, p25.
Variety. Aug 27, 1930, p21.
Vogue. Oct 13, 1930, v76, p126.

Abus de Confiance (Also titled: Abused Confidence) (FR; Decoin, Henri; 1938)
Hollywood Reporter. Sep 25, 1939, p3.
Motion Picture Herald. Dec 10, 1938, p48-49.
The New York Times. Dec 1, 1938, p29.
Variety. Dec 24, 1938, p15.

Abyssinia (USSR; Soyuzfilmnews; 1936)
Commonweal. Jan 1, 1937, v25, p276.
Film Daily. Dec 10, 1936, p7.
Garbo and the Night Watchman. p169-70.
The New Masses. Dec 22, 1936, v21, p29.
The Spectator. Jul 5, 1935, v155, p14.
Variety. Jul 22, 1936, p34.
Variety. Dec 12, 1936, p15.

Accent on Youth (US; Ruggles, Wesley; 1935)
Film Daily. Aug 10, 1935, p4.
Graham Greene on Film. p37.
Literary Digest. Aug 17, 1935, v120, p28.
Motion Picture Herald. Jul 13, 1935, p57.
The New Statesman and Nation. Sep 7, 1935, v10, p306.
The New York Times. Aug 12, 1935, p10.
The New Yorker. Aug 17, 1935, v11, p46.
Rob Wagner's Script. Aug 24, 1935, v13, p8.
The Spectator. Nov 22, 1935, v155, p863.
Stage. Sep 1935, v12, p2.
Time. Jul 29, 1935, v26, p42.
Variety. Aug 14, 1935, p15.

Accused (GB; Freeland, Thornton; 1936)
Film Daily. Dec 17, 1936, p4.
Hollywood Reporter. Feb 10, 1937, p3.
Motion Picture Herald. Aug 8, 1936, p43.

The New York Times. Dec 17, 1936, p35.
Variety. Aug 12, 1936, p19.
Variety. Dec 30, 1936, p11.

The Accused (US; Dieterle, William; 1948)
Commonweal. Jan 21, 1949, v49, p377.
Film Daily. Nov 17, 1948, p5.
Hollywood Reporter. Nov 17, 1948, p3.
Motion Picture Herald Product Digest. Nov 20, 1948, p4389.
The New York Times. Jan 13, 1949, p26.
The New Yorker. Jan 17, 1949, v33, p73.
Time. Jan 24, 1949, v53, p82+.
Variety. Nov 17, 1948, p13.

Across the Pacific (US; Huston, John; Sherman, Vincent; 1942)
Commonweal. Aug 28, 1942, v36, p448.
The Complete Films of Humphrey Bogart. p103-05.
Film Daily. Aug 18, 1942, p6.
The Films of World War II. p80-81.
Hollywood Reporter. Aug 14, 1942, p3.
Humphrey Bogart: The Man and His Films. p118-19.
The London Times. Nov 2, 1942, p6.
Magill's Survey of Cinema. Series II. v1, p8-10.
Motion Picture Exhibitor. Aug 26, 1942, v28, n16, sec2, p1080.
The New York Times. Sep 5, 1942, p9.
The New York Times. Oct 19, 1942, p19.
Newsweek. Sep 7, 1942, v20, p80.
Theatre Arts. Nov 1942, v26, p693.
Time. Aug 17, 1942, v40, p42.
Variety. Aug 19, 1942, p8.

Act of Violence (US; Zinnemann, Fred; 1949)
Commonweal. Feb 4, 1949, v49, p424.
Film Daily. Dec 21, 1948, p6.
Hollywood Reporter. Dec 21, 1948, p3.
Motion Picture Herald Product Digest. Dec 25, 1948, p4433.
The New York Times. Jan 24, 1949, p16.
The New Yorker. Feb 5, 1949, v24, p76.
Newsweek. Jan 31, 1949, v33, p75.
Rotarian. May 1949, v74, p34.
Sequence. Sum 1949, v8, p86-88.
Time. Jan 31, 1949, v53, p68.
Variety. Dec 22, 1948, p6.

Action for Slander (GB; Saville, Victor; 1937)
Canadian Magazine. Feb 1938, v89, p29.
Film Daily. Jan 24, 1938, p7.
Graham Greene on Film. p167.
Great Britain and the East. Jul 22, 1937, v49, p128.
Hollywood Reporter. Aug 11, 1937, p8.
Motion Picture Herald. Aug 14, 1937, p63-64.
The New Statesman and Nation. Sep 4, 1937, v14, p339.
Variety. Aug 4, 1937, p25.

Action in the North Atlantic (US; Bacon, Lloyd; 1943)
Cinema, the Magic Vehicle. v1, p377.
Commonweal. Jun 11, 1943, v38, p203.
The Complete Films of Humphrey Bogart. p110-11.
Film Daily. May 17, 1943, p6.
The Films of World War II. p126-27.
Hollywood Reporter. May 17, 1943, p3.
Humphrey Bogart: The Man and His Films. p123.
Magill's Survey of Cinema, Series II. v1, p14.
Motion Picture Herald Product Digest. May 22, 1943, p1325.
The New Republic. Jun 14, 1943, v108, p794.
The New York Times. May 22, 1943, p10.
The New York Times. May 30, 1943, sec2, p3.
The New Yorker. May 29, 1943, v19, p38.
Newsweek. Jun 7, 1943, v21, p94.
Variety. May 19, 1943, p8.

The Actress (US; Franklin, Sidney; 1928)
Film Daily. Jun 15, 1928, p8.
The Film Spectator. Jun 23, 1928, v5, p12-13, 18.

The Films of Norma Shearer. p144-51.
Life. Jul 26, 1928, v92, p26.
The New York Times. Jul 9, 1928, p25.
Variety. Jul 11, 1928, p25.

Adam Had Four Sons (US; Ratoff, Gregory; 1941)
Commonweal. Apr 11, 1941, v33, p623.
Film Daily. Feb 24, 1941, p5.
The Films of Ingrid Bergman. p75-77.
The Films of Susan Hayward. p59-61.
Hollywood Reporter. Feb 17, 1941, p3.
The London Times. Aug 4, 1941, p8.
Magill's Survey of Cinema. Series II. v1, p21-23.
Motion Picture Exhibitor. Mar 5, 1941, p699.
Motion Picture Herald Product Digest. Jan 11, 1941, p38.
The New York Times. Mar 28, 1941, p26.
The New York Times. Mar 30, 1941, sec9, p5.
Variety. Feb 19, 1941,, p16.

Adam's Rib (US; Cukor, George; 1949)
Commonweal. Dec 23, 1949, v51, p319.
The Films of Katharine Hepburn. p143-46.
The Films of Spencer Tracy. p199-201.
George Cukor (Phillips). p81-85+.
Hollywood Reporter. Nov 2, 1949, p3.
The International Dictionary of Films and Filmmakers. v1, p11-12.
Magill's Survey of Cinema. Series I. v1, p6-8.
Motion Picture Herald. Nov 5, 1949, p73.
The New Republic. Jan 9, 1950, v122, p23.
The New York Times. Dec 26, 1949, p33.
The New Yorker. Jan 7, 1950, v25, p48.
Newsweek. Dec 26, 1949, v34, p56-57.
Rotarian. Feb 1950, v76, p38.
Time. Nov 28, 1949, v54, p84.
Variety. Nov 2, 1949, p10.

Adorable (US; Dieterle, William; 1933)
Canadian Magazine. Aug 1933, v80, p35-36.
Film Daily. May 19, 1933, p6.
Hollywood Reporter. May 11, 1933, p3.
Motion Picture Herald. May 20, 1933, p29, 32.
The New York Times. May 19, 1933, p20.
Newsweek. May 27, 1933, v1, p31.
Rob Wagner's Script. May 20, 1933, v9, p8.
Time. May 29, 1933, v21, p33.
Variety. May 23, 1933, p19.

Adventure (US; Fleming, Victor; 1945)
Commonweal. Feb 8, 1946, v43, p430.
Film Daily. Dec 28, 1945, p7.
The Films of Clark Gable. p208-10.
Hollywood Reporter. Dec 17, 1945, p3.
The New York Times. Feb 8, 1946, p23.
The New Yorker. Feb 16, 1946, v22, p87.
Newsweek. Feb 18, 1946, v27, p98.
Scholastic. Mar 18, 1946, v48, p33.
Theatre Arts. Mar 1946, v30, p159.
Time. Feb 11, 1946, v47, p94.
Variety. Dec 19, 1945, p18.

Adventure in Baltimore (Also titled: Bachelor Bait) (US; Wallace, Richard; 1949)
Commonweal. May 13, 1949, v50, p121.
Film Daily. Mar 29, 1949 , p8.
The Films of Shirley Temple. p244-45.
Hollywood Reporter. Mar 22, 1949, p3.
Motion Picture Herald Product Digest. Mar 26, 1949, p4549.
The New Republic. May 9, 1949, v120, p30.
The New York Times. Apr 29, 1949, p27.
Newsweek. May 9, 1949, v33, p90.
Rotarian. July 1949, v75, p36.
Time. Apr 18, 1949, v53, p102.
Variety. Mar 23, 1949, p8.

Adventure in Manhattan (US; Ludwig, Edward; 1936)
Canadian Magazine. Nov 1936, v86, p38.
Film Daily. Oct 23, 1936, p7.
Motion Picture Herald. Oct 31, 1936, p45.
The New York Times. Oct 23, 1936, p27.
Stage. Dec 1936, v14 p12.
Time. Oct 26, 1936, v28, p71.
Variety. Oct 28, 1936, p14.

The Adventures of Chico (GB; Woodard, Stacy; Woodard, Horace; 1938)
Film Daily. Mar 3, 1938, p4.
Hollywood Reporter. Nov 23, 1937, p3.
Lorentz on Film. p153-54.
Motion Picture Herald. Nov 27, 1937, p55.
The Nation. Mar 12, 1938, v146, p310.
National Board of Review Magazine. Apr 1938, v13, p18.
The New Masses. Mar 8, 1938, v23, p29.
The New Republic. Mar 23, 1938, v94, p195.
The New York Times. Feb 26, 1938, p9.
The New Yorker. Mar 5, 1938, v14, p48.
Scholastic. Apr 23, 1938, v32, p12.
Time. Mar 7, 1938, v31, p47.
Variety. Feb 23, 1938, p14.

The Adventures of Dolly (US; Griffith, D.W.; 1908)
American Silent Film. p42.
D.W. Griffith, His Biograph Films in Perspective. p1-4, 12, 170.
The Emergence of Film Art. p40-41.
A History of Narrative Film. p62-63.
A Million and One Nights. p457-58.
Spellbound in Darkness. p55.

The Adventures of Don Juan (US; Sherman, Vincent; 1949)
Film Daily. Dec 24, 1948, p4.
The Films of Errol Flynn. p154-59.
The Films of the Forties. p246-49.
Hollywood Reporter. Dec 24, 1948, p3.
Motion Picture Herald Product Digest. Jan 1, 1949, p4443.
The New York Times. Dec 25, 1948, p10.
Newsweek. Jan 10, 1949, v33, p76.
Rotarian. Mar 1949, v74, p38.
Time. Jan 3, 1949, v53, p58+.
Variety. Dec 29, 1948, p6.

The Adventures of Happy Hooligan (US; 1900)
Film Before Griffith. p61-62.
The New York Clipper. Oct 13, 1900, p740.

The Adventures of Huckleberry Finn *See* Huckleberry Finn

The Adventures of Kathlyn (US; Grandon, F.J.; 1913)
The Moving Picture World. Jan 17, 1914, p266.
Selected Film Criticism, 1912-1920. p3-4.

The Adventures of Marco Polo (US; Mayo, Archie; 1938)
Basil Rathbone: His Life and His Films. p191-93.
Canadian Magazine. Feb 1938, v89, p28-29.
Commonweal. Mar 18, 1938, v27, p581.
Commonweal. Apr 22, 1938, v27, p728.
Esquire. Jun 1938, v9, p89, 149-50.
Film Daily. Feb 15, 1938, p8.
The Films of Gary Cooper. p153-55.
The Films of Lana Turner. p64-66.
Great Britain and the East. Sep 22, 1938, v51, p323-24.
Hollywood Reporter. Feb 12, 1938, p3.
Motion Picture Herald. Feb 19, 1938, p38.
The New Masses. Apr 19, 1938, v27, p27-29.
The New York Times. Apr 8, 1938, p17.
Newsweek. Jan 3, 1938, v11, p34-35.
Newsweek. Mar 7, 1938, v11, p20.
Rob Wagner's Script. Apr 16, 1938, v19, p9.
Samuel Goldwyn Presents. p191-93.

Scholastic. Apr 2, 1938, v32, p35.
The Spectator. Sep 2, 1938, v161, p368.
Stage. Dec 1937, v15, p66-68.
Stage. Mar 1938, v15, p39.
Time. Mar 7, 1938, v31, p37.
Variety. Feb 16, 1938, p15.
World Film News. May-Jun 1938, v3, p58-59, 87.
World Film News. Oct 1938, v3, p265, 267-68.

The Adventures of Mark Twain (US; Rapper, Irving; 1944)
Christian Science Monitor Magazine. Apr 15, 1944, p8-9.
Commonweal. May 5, 1944, v40, p63.
Film Daily. May 3, 1944, p5.
The Films of Fredric March. p181-84.
The Films of the Forties. p116-18.
Hollywood Reporter. May 3, 1944, p3.
Life. May 8, 1944, v49, p150.
Musician. Aug 1944, v49, p150.
The New York Times. May 4, 1944, p25.
Newsweek. May 8, 1944, v23, p98-99.
Scholastic. Apr 17, 1944, v44, p18-19.
Time. May 8, 1944, v43, p56+.
Variety. May 3, 1944, p23.

The Adventures of Robin Hood (US; Curtiz, Michael; 1938)
America's Favorite Movies. p61-86.
Basil Rathbone: His Life and His Films. p194-98.
Chestnuts in Her Lap. p41-43.
Collier's. Aug 6, 1938, v102, p17+.
Commonweal. May 27, 1938, v28, p133.
A Companion to the Movies. p195-96.
Esquire. Aug 1938, v10, p82.
Film Daily. Apr 29, 1938, p8.
Film Quarterly. Wint 1969-70, v23, p42-47.
Film Quarterly. Fall 1970, v24, p27-30.
The Films of Errol Flynn. p60-67.
The Films of Olivia de Havilland. p109-16.
The Films of the Thirties. p208-10.
From Quasimodo to Scarlett O'Hara. p285-87.
The Great Adventure Films. p74-81.
Halliwell's Hundred. p1-4.
Hollywood Reporter. Apr 26, 1938, p3.
The Hollywood Spectator. May 7, 1938, v13, p6.
Kiss Kiss Bang Bang. p280-81.
A Library of Film Criticism: American Film Directors. p73.
Life. May 23, 1938, v4, p60-62.
Magill's Survey of Cinema. Series I. v1, p9-14.
Motion Picture Herald. Apr 30, 1938, p44.
Motion Picture Herald. Dec 25, 1937, p14-15.
Motion Picture Herald. May 7, 1938, p25.
The Nation. Jun 4, 1938, v146, p653-54.
National Board of Review Magazine. Jun 1938, v13, p13-15.
The New Masses. May 24, 1938, v27, p29.
The New Republic. Jun 8, 1938, v95, p131.
The New York Times. May 13, 1938, p17.
The New Yorker. May 21, 1938, v14, p55-56.
Newsweek. May 9, 1938, v11, p22-23.
Photoplay. Mar 1938, v52, p39-41.
Photoplay. Jul 1938, v52, p23.
Rob Wagner's Script. May 14, 1938, v19, p8.
Saint Nicholas. Feb 1938, v65, p37+.
Scholastic. May 14, 1938, v32, p30-33.
Selected Film Criticism, 1931-1940. p3-4.
Time. May 16, 1938, v31, p57.
Variety. Apr 27, 1938, p22.
Warner Brothers Presents. p157-59.
World Film News. Aug 1938, v3, p172.
World Film News. Nov 1938, v3, p313.

The Adventures of Sherlock Holmes (US; Werker, Alfred L.; 1939)
Basil Rathbone: His Life and His Films. p220-25.
The Film Criticism of Otis Ferguson. p271.

Film Daily. Sep 5, 1939, p6.
The Films of Sherlock Holmes. p75-87.
Graham Greene on Film. p273-74.
Hollywood Reporter. Aug 19, 1939, p3.
Hollywood Spectator. Sep 2, 1939, v14, p14.
Motion Picture Herald. Aug 26, 1939, p55.
The New Republic. Sep 20, 1939, v100, p190.
The New York Times. Sep 2, 1939, p20.
The New Yorker. Sep 9, 1939, v15, p61.
Rob Wagner's Script. Sep 30, 1939, v22, p17.
Sherlock Holmes on the Screen. p174-75.
The Spectator. Mar 8, 1940, v164, p328.
Variety. Sep 6, 1939, p14.

Adventures of Tartu (US; Bucquet, Harold S.; 1943)
Agee on Film. v1, p53, 66.
Commonweal. Oct 15, 1943, p634.
Film Daily. Aug 4, 1943, p8.
The Great Spy Pictures. p49-50.
Hollywood Reporter. Aug 3, 1943, p3.
Motion Picture Herald Product Digest. Aug 7, 1943, p1546.
The Nation. Sep 25, 1943, v157, p360.
The New Republic. Oct 25, 1943, v109, p573.
The New York Times. Sep 24, 1943, p26.
The New Yorker. Sep 25, 1943, v19, p26.
Newsweek. Oct 11, 1943, v19, p78.
Time. Sep 25, 1943, v42, p94.

The Adventures of Tom Sawyer (US; Taurog, Norman; 1938)
The Classic American Novel and the Movies. p73-82.
The Film Criticism of Otis Ferguson. p213-15.
Film Daily. Feb 15, 1938, p8.
The Great Adventure Films. p82-85.
Hollywood Reporter. Feb 11, 1938, p3.
Judge. Apr 1938, v114, p35.
Life. Mar 7, 1938, v4, p44-47.
Magill's Survey of Cinema. Series I. v1, p15-17.
Motion Picture Herald. Feb 19, 1938, p38.
Motion Picture Herald. Oct 9, 1937, p16-17.
The New Masses. Mar 1, 1938, v26, p29-30.
The New Republic. Mar 2, 1938, v94, p102.
The New Statesman and Nation. May 14, 1938, v15, p833.
The New York Times. Feb 18, 1938, p23.
The New Yorker. Feb 26, 1938, v14, p52-53.
Newsweek. Feb 28, 1938, v11, p31.
Publishers Weekly. Feb 5, 1938, v33, p727.
Rob Wagner's Script. Mar 26, 1938, v19, p11.
Saint Nicholas. Feb 1938, v65, p37.
Scholastic. Feb 19, 1938, v32, p30-31.
Scholastic. Jan 15, 1938, v31, p30-31.
Scribner's Magazine. May 1938, v103, p63.
Time. Feb 28, 1938, v31, p63.
Variety. Feb 16, 1938, p15.
World Film News. Jul 1938, v3, p128.

The Adventuress *See* I See a Dark Stranger

Aerograd *See* Frontier

The Affair Blum (German title: Affaire Blum) (WGER; Engel, Erich; 1949)
Christian Century. Dec 21, 1949, v66, p1527.
Commonweal. Nov 11, 1949, v51, p159.
Film Daily. Oct 20, 1949, p6.
Hollywood Reporter. Nov 10, 1949, p3.
The New Republic. Oct 24, 1949, v121, p23.
The New York Times. Oct 18, 1949, p35.
The New Yorker. Oct 22, 1949, v25, p115.
Newsweek. Oct 31, 1949, v34, p67-68.
Rotarian. Feb 1950, v76, p38.
Variety. Sep 21, 1949, p8.

The Affairs of Anatol (US; DeMille, Cecil B.; 1921)
Film Daily. Sep 18, 1921, p4.
The Films of Cecil B. DeMille. p195-200.

The Films of Gloria Swanson. p99-103.
Magill's Survey of Cinema. Silent Films. v1, p133-36.
Motion Picture Classic. Sep 1921, v13, p89.
The New York Times. Sep 12, 1921, p16.
Selected Film Criticism, 1921-1930. p5.
Variety. Aug 26, 1921, p36.

The Affairs of Annabel (US; Stoloff, Benjamin; 1938)
Commonweal. Sep 23, 1938, v28, p561.
Film Daily. Jul 13, 1938, p.
Hollywood Reporter. Jul 8, 1938, p3.
Motion Picture Herald. Jul 16, 1938, p58.
The New York Times. Oct 13, 1938, p29.
Variety. Aug 10, 1938, p12.

The Affairs of Annabelle (Also titled: Annabelle's Affairs) (US; Werker, Alfred L.; 1931)
Film Daily. Jun 28, 1931, p10.
The Films of Jeanette MacDonald and Nelson Eddy. p79-83.
Hollywood Reporter. May 13, 1931, p2.
Hollywood Spectator. Aug 15, 1931, v12, p11-12.
Judge. Jul 18, 1931, v101, p21.
Motion Picture Herald. May 30, 1931, p53.
The New York Times. Jun 14, 1931, p4.
The New York Times. Jul 5, 1931, p3.
The New York Times. Jun 29, 1931, p20.
The New Yorker. Jul 4, 1931, v7, p48.
Time. Jul 6, 1931, v18, p20.
Variety. Jun 30, 1931, p15.

Africa Speaks (US; Hoefler, Paul L.; 1930)
Close-Up. Mar 1931, v8, p81.
Exhibitors Herald-World. Sep 27, 1930, p39.
Exhibitors Herald-World. Oct 4, 1930, p32.
Film Daily. Sep 21, 1930, p31.
Life. Oct 10, 1930, v96, p20.
The New York Times. Sep 20, 1930, p15.
The New York Times. Sep 28, 1930, p3.
The New Yorker. Sep 27, 1930, v6, p63-64.
Outlook and Independent. Oct 1, 1930, v156, p192.
Time. Oct 6, 1930, v16, p34.
Variety. Sep 24, 1930, p23.

After Many Years (US; Griffith, D.W.; 1908)
The Emergence of Film Art. p43.
The Moving Picture World. Nov 1, 1908, p379.
The New York Dramatic Mirror. Nov 14, 1908, p10.
Selected Film Criticism, 1896-1911. p4.

After Office Hours (US; Leonard, Robert Z.; 1935)
Film Daily. Feb 16, 1935, p7.
The Films of Clark Gable. p161-62.
Hollywood Reporter. Jan 30, 1935, p3.
Judge. Apr 1935, v108, p16.
Motion Picture Herald. Feb 16, 1935, p7.
The New York Times. Mar 9, 1935, p19.
The New Yorker. Mar 16, 1935, v11, p71.
Rob Wagner's Script. Mar 23, 1935, v13, p8.
Time. Mar 4, 1935, v25, p16.
Variety. Mar 13, 1935, p15.

After the Thin Man (US; Van Dyke, W.S.; 1936)
Canadian Magazine. Mar 1937, v87, p23.
Commonweal. Jan 1, 1937, v25, p276.
The Detective in Film. p94, 96.
The Film Criticism of Otis Ferguson. p159-61.
Film Daily. Dec 7, 1936, p11.
The Films of James Stewart. p41-43.
The Films of Myrna Loy. p201-02.
Garbo and the Night Watchman. p216-21.
Hollywood Reporter. Dec 3, 1936, p2.
Hollywood Spectator. Dec 19, 1936, v11, p8-9.
Judge. Feb 1937, v112, p24.
Lorentz on Film. p139-40.
Lunatics and Lovers. p166.
Motion Picture Herald. Dec 12, 1936, p52.

The Nation. Jan 16, 1937, v144, p81.
The New Masses. Jan 12, 1937, v22, p27-28.
The New York Times. Dec 25, 1936, p19.
The New Yorker. Jan 2, 1937, v12, p50.
Newsweek. Jan 2, 1937, v9, p24.
Rob Wagner's Script. Jan 2, 1937, v16, p12-13.
Scribner's Magazine. Apr 1937, v101, p61.
The Spectator. Apr 9, 1937, v158, p663.
Stage. Jan 1937, v14, p63-64.
Time. Jan 4, 1937, v29, p21-22.
Variety. Dec 30, 1936, p10.

Age d'Or, L' (Also titled: The Golden Age) (FR; Buñuel, Luis; 1930)
American Film Criticism. p288-90.
Buñuel (Higgenbotham). p39-47+.
The Cinema of Luis Buñuel. p14-29.
Cinemage. 1955, v1, p18-25, 27-29.
Classics of the Foreign Film. p62-63.
Dictionary of Films. p4.
Eighty Years of Cinema. p83.
The Essential Cinema. p118-22.
Figures of Desire: a Theory and Analysis of Surrealist Film. p106-50.
Films and Filming. Apr 1962, v8, p13-15, 38-41.
The International Dictionary of Films and Filmmakers. v1, p15.
Luis Buñuel: A Critical Biography. p68-84.
Luis Buñuel (Durgnat). p38-45.
Magill's Survey of Cinema. Foreign Language Films. v1, p29-33.
The Nation. Apr 5, 1933, v136, p382-84.
The New York Times. Sep 22, 1964, p44.
Surrealism and the Cinema. p59-78.
Vanity Fair. May 1933, v40, p50-51.
Variety. Sep 23, 1964, p6.
The World of Luis Buñuel. p154-79.

The Age of Consent (US; La Cava, Gregory; 1932)
Film Daily. Aug 25, 1932, p8.
Judge. Oct 1932, v103, p20.
Motion Picture Herald. Jul 30, 1932, p31-32.
The New York Times. Sep 3, 1932, p16.
Rob Wagner's Script. Jul 23, 1932, v7, p9.
Time. Aug 1, 1932, v20, p23.
Variety. Sep 6, 1932, p21.

The Age of Innocence (US; Moeller, Philip; 1934)
Film Daily. Sep 1, 1934, p4.
Hollywood Reporter. Aug 24, 1934, p3.
Motion Picture Herald. Sep 8, 1934, p39.
The New York Times. Oct 19, 1934, p19.
Time. Oct 8, 1934, v24, p36.
Variety. Oct 23, 1934, p18.

Ah, Wilderness! (US; Brown, Clarence; 1935)
Canadian Magazine. Feb 1936, v85, p38.
Commonweal. Jan 10, 1936, v23, p301.
Esquire. Feb 1936, v5, p99.
The Film Criticism of Otis Ferguson. p107-09.
Film Daily. Nov 15, 1935, p4.
The Films of the Thirties. p154-55.
Hollywood Reporter. Nov 11, 1935, p4.
Hollywood Spectator. Nov 23, 1935, v10, p6.
Judge. Jan 1936, v109, p27.
Literary Digest. Dec 28, 1935, v120, p22.
Magill's Survey of Cinema. Series I. v1, p26-30.
Motion Picture Herald. Nov 23, 1935, p70.
The Nation. Jan 15, 1936, v142, p84.
The New Republic. Dec 25, 1935, v85, p198.
The New York Times. Dec 25, 1935, p30.
Newsweek. Dec 14, 1935, v6, p38.
Rob Wagner's Script. Dec 7, 1935, v14, p10.
Scholastic. Jan 18, 1936, v27, p28+.
Time. Dec 9, 1935, v26, p44.

Variety. Jan 1, 1936, p44.
Will Rogers in Hollywood. p171-72.

Air Force (US; Hawks, Howard; 1943)
Cinema, the Magic Vehicle. v1, p366.
Commonweal. Feb 12, 1943, v37, p423.
Film Daily. Feb 3, 1943, p6.
The Films of Howard Hawks (Willis). p162-65.
The Films of John Garfield. p109-10.
The Films of World War II. p99-100.
Guts & Glory. p25-33+.
Hollywood Reporter. Feb 3, 1943, p3.
Motion Picture Herald Product Digest. Feb 6, 1943, p1145.
The Nation. Feb 20, 1943, v156, p283.
The New Republic. Feb 22, 1943, v108, p254.
The New York Times. Feb 4, 1943, p29.
The New Yorker. Feb 6, 1943, v18, p52.
Newsweek. Feb 8, 1943, v21, p84.
Time. Feb 8, 1943, v41, p85.
Variety. Feb 3, 1943, p14.

Air Mail (US; Ford, John; 1932)
Hollywood Reporter. Sep 26, 1932, p3.
Motion Picture Herald. Oct 8, 1932, p91.
The New Outlook. Dec 1932, v161, p47.
The New York Times. Nov 7, 1932, p20.
The Non-Western Films of John Ford. p228-29.
Rob Wagner's Script. Oct 15, 1932, v8, p8.
Time. Nov 14, 1932, v20, p33.
Variety. Nov 8, 1932, p17.

Air-City *See* Frontier

Alcatraz Island (US; McGann, William; 1937)
Film Daily. Jan 21, 1938, p15.
Motion Picture Herald. Oct 23, 1937, p56.
The New Statesman and Nation. Mar 5, 1938, v15, p368.
The New York Times. Oct 14, 1937, p22.
Variety. Oct 13, 1937, p16.

Alexander Hamilton (US; Adolfi, John; 1931)
Commonweal. Sep 30, 1931, v14, p525.
Film Daily. Sep 20, 1931, p10.
Films in Review. Nov 1985, v36, p521.
Hollywood Reporter. Jun 3, 1931, p3.
Judge. Oct 10, 1931, v101, p18.
Life. Oct 9, 1931, v98, p18.
Literary Digest. Oct 3, 1931, v111, p20-21.
Motion Picture Herald. Jun 13, 1931, p31.
The New Statesman and Nation. Oct 31, 1931, v2, p545.
The New York Times. Sep 17, 1931, p21.
The New York Times. Sep 27, 1931, p5.
The New Yorker. Sep 26, 1931, v7, p57-58.
Outlook and Independent. Sep 16, 1931, v159, p87.
Rob Wagner's Script. Oct 17, 1931, v6, p8-9.
Time. Jan 19, 1931, v17, p24.
Time. Sep 28, 1931, v18, p30.
Variety. Sep 22, 1931, p22.

Alexander Nevsky (USSR; Eisenstein, Sergei; Vasiliev, D.I.; 1938)
American Film Criticism. p368-70.
Cineaste. Fall 1968, v2, p16-17.
Cinema, the Magic Vehicle. v1, p284-85.
Classic Film Collector. Wint 1973, n41, p6-7.
Classics of the Foreign Film. p122-27.
The Complete Films of Eisenstein. p99-123.
Dictionary of Films. p6-7.
Eighty Years of Cinema. p114-16.
Eisenstein at Work. p97-103.
The Film Criticism of Otis Ferguson. p250.
Film Daily. Mar 29, 1939, p9.
Film Propaganda. p116-30.

From Quasimodo to Scarlett O'Hara. p299-301.
The International Dictionary of Films and Filmmakers. v1, p18-20.
Kino. p348-51.
Life. Apr 10, 1939, v6, p48-49.
Life and Letters To-day. May 1939, v21, p126-27.
Magill's Survey of Cinema. Foreign Language Films. v1, p50-55.
The Nation. Apr 8, 1939, v148, p413-14.
National Board of Review Magazine. Apr 1939, v14, p18.
The New Masses. Apr 4, 1939, v31, p29-30.
The New Republic. Apr 12, 1939, v98, p279.
The New Republic. Mar 29, 1939, v98, p222-23.
The New Statesman and Nation. Apr 29, 1939, v17, p648.
The New York Times. Mar 23, 1939, p27.
The New Yorker. Apr 1, 1939, v15, p67.
North American Review. Jun 1939, v247, p381-82.
Rob Wagner's Script. May 27, 1939, v21, p22.
Selected Film Criticism: Foreign Films, 1930-1950. p4-5.
Sight and Sound. Spr 1939, v8, p6-7.
Sight and Sound. Sum 1939, v8, p77-78.
Time. Apr 3, 1939, v33, p40-41.
Variety. Mar 29, 1939, p16.

Alexander's Ragtime Band (US; King, Henry; 1938)
Commonweal. Aug 12, 1938, v28, p411.
The Film Criticism of Otis Ferguson. p231-32.
Film Daily. May 28, 1938, p3.
Films and Filming. Mar 1963, v9, p41.
The Films of Alice Faye. p101-04.
The Films of Tyrone Power. p73-75.
Hollywood Reporter. May 25, 1938, p3.
Hollywood Spectator. Jun 4, 1938, v13, p6-7.
Magill's Survey of Cinema, Series II. v1, p33-36.
Motion Picture Herald. May 28, 1938, p51.
The New York Times. Aug 6, 1938, p7.
The New Yorker. Aug 13, 1938, v14, p39.
Newsweek. Aug 1, 1938, v12, p19.
Rob Wagner's Script. Aug 16, 1938, v19, p22.
Stage. Sep 1938, v16, p48.
Time. Aug 15, 1938, v32, p35.
Variety. Jun 1, 1938, p12.
World Film News. Aug 1938, v3, p144-45.
World Film News. Nov 1938, v3, p314.

Algiers (US; Cromwell, John; 1938)
Canadian Magazine. Sep 1938, v90, p58.
Commonweal. Jul 29, 1938, v28, p370.
Esquire. Nov 1938, v10, p92, 171.
The Film Criticism of Otis Ferguson. p225-27.
Film Daily. Jun 28, 1938, p6.
The Films of the Thirties. p216-17.
The Foremost Films of 1938. p97-113.
The Great Gangster Pictures. p18-19.
Hedy Lamarr. p99-105.
Hollywood Reporter. Jun 24, 1938, p3.
Magill's Survey of Cinema, Series II. v1, p37-40.
Motion Picture Herald. Jul 2, 1938, p40.
The New Republic. Aug 3, 1938, v95, p363.
The New York Times. Jul 15, 1938, p13.
The New Yorker. Jul 16, 1938, v14, p44.
Newsweek. Jul 11, 1938, v12, p27.
Rob Wagner's Script. Jul 9, 1938, v19, p18.
Time. Jul 25, 1938, v32, p22.
Variety. Jun 29, 1938, p12.
World Film News. Sep 1938, v3, p224.

Ali Baba Goes to Town (US; Butler, David; 1937)
Film Daily. Oct 21, 1937, p18.
Hollywood Reporter. Oct 16, 1937, p3.
Motion Picture Herald. Oct 23, 1937, p50.
The New Statesman and Nation. Dec 18, 1937, v14, p1064.
The New York Times. Oct 23, 1937, p14.
The New Yorker. Oct 30, 1937, v13, p89.
Newsweek. Nov 1, 1937, v10, p29.

Rob Wagner's Script. Nov 6, 1937, v18, p8.
Scholastic. Nov 13, 1937, v31, p36.
Time. Nov 1, 1937, v30, p44.
Variety. Oct 20, 1937, p12.
World Film News. Dec 1937, v2, p29.

Alias Jimmy Valentine (US; Tourneur, Maurice; 1915)
Motion Picture News. Feb 6, 1915, p29.
Motion Picture News. Feb 27, 1915, p42, 51.
Motography. Feb 27, 1915, p315-16.
Motography. Mar 6, 1915, p384.
The Moving Picture World. Mar 6, 1915, p1459, 1520.
The New York Dramatic Mirror. Feb 24, 1915, p28.

Alias Jimmy Valentine (US; Conway, Jack; 1928)
Exhibitor's Herald-World and Moving Picture World. Dec 1, 1928, p59.
Film Daily. May 5, 1929, p8.
Film Daily. Nov 18, 1928, p4.
The New York Times. Nov 16, 1928, p28.
Photoplay. Oct 1928, v34, p54.
Selected Film Criticism, 1921-1930. p5-6.
Variety. Nov 21, 1928, p13.

Alias Nick Beal (US; Farrow, John; 1949)
Film Daily. Jan 19, 1949, p7.
Hollywood Reporter. Jan 18, 1949, p3.
Magill's Survey of Cinema. Series II. v1, p41-43.
Motion Picture Herald Product Digest. Jan 22, 1949, p4469.
The New Republic. Mar 21, 1949, v120, p30.
The New York Times. Mar 10, 1949, p35.
The New Yorker. Mar 19, 1949, v25, p83.
Newsweek. Mar 14, 1949, v33, p82.
Rotarian. Oct 1949, v75, p38.
Time. Mar 14, 1949, v53, p105.
Variety. Jan 19, 1949, p10.

Alias the Deacon (US; Sloman, Edward; 1927)
Film Daily. Jun 26, 1927, p9.
Moving Picture World. Jun 25, 1927, p611.
The New York Times. Jun 21, 1927, p29.
The New Yorker. Jun 25, 1927, v3, p51.
Selected Film Criticism, 1921-1930. p6.
Variety. Jun 22, 1927, p30.

Alias the Doctor (US; Curtiz, Michael; 1932)
Film Daily. Mar 6, 1932, p10.
Hollywood Reporter. Feb 6, 1932, p3.
Judge. Apr 2, 1932, v102, p22.
The New York Times. Mar 3, 1932, p22.
The New Yorker. Mar 12, 1932, v8, p56.
Time. Mar 14, 1932, v19, p26.
Variety. Mar 8, 1932, p23.

Alibi (US; West, Roland; 1929)
BFI/Monthly Film Bulletin. Jul 1979, v46, p156-57.
Cinema, the Magic Vehicle. v1, p169.
Exhibitor's Herald-World. Sep 21, 1929, p21.
Film Daily. Apr 14, 1929, p12.
The New York Times. Apr 9, 1929, p29.
Variety. Apr 10, 1929, p16.

Alibi, L' (Also titled: The Alibi) (FR; Chenal, Pierre; 1936)
Film Daily. Apr 14, 1939, p13.
Graham Greene on Film. p192.
London Mercury. Jul 1938, v38, p256.
Motion Picture Herald. Feb 26, 1938, p39.
The New Masses. Apr 25, 1939, v31, p30.
The New Statesman and Nation. Jun 11, 1938, v15, p991.
The New York Times. Apr 10, 1939, p13.
The New Yorker. Apr 22, 1939, v15, p67.
Rob Wagner's Script. Sep 23, 1939, v22, p16.
The Spectator. Jun 17, 1938, v160, p1096.
The Tatler. Jun 15, 1938, v148, p482.
Variety. Apr 19, 1939, p23.

Alice Adams (US; Stevens, George; 1935)
BFI/Monthly Film Bulletin. Mar 1979, v41, p57-58.
Commonweal. Aug 30, 1935, v22, p427.
Esquire. Oct 1935, v4, p97.
Film Comment. Wint 1971-72, v7, p66-69.
The Film Criticism of Otis Ferguson. p89-90.
Film Daily. Aug 14, 1935, p14.
The Films of Katharine Hepburn. p67-70.
The Great Romantic Films. p38-41.
Hollywood Reporter. Aug 3, 1935, p3.
Kiss Kiss Bang Bang. p282-83.
Life. Oct 1935, v102, p36.
Literary Digest. Aug 24, 1935, v120, p26.
Magill's Survey of Cinema. Series I. v1, p33-36.
Motion Picture Herald. Aug 10, 1935, p47.
The New Republic. Sep 4, 1935, v84, p104.
The New York Times. Aug 16, 1935, p11.
The New Yorker. Aug 24, 1935, v11, p45.
Newsweek. Aug 24, 1935, v6, p29.
Rob Wagner's Script. Oct 12, 1935, v14, p11.
Selected Film Criticism, 1931-1940. p5.
Time. Aug 26, 1935, v26, p26.
Variety. Aug 21, 1935, p21.

Alice in Wonderland (US; McLeod, Norman Z.; 1933)
Children's Novels and the Movies. p15-27.
Film Daily. Dec 11, 1933, p7.
The Films of Cary Grant. p68-69.
The Films of Gary Cooper. p117-18.
The Films of W.C. Fields. p86-88.
Hollywood Reporter. Nov 27, 1933, p3.
Literary Digest. Jan 6, 1934, v117, p31.
Motion Picture Herald. Dec 16, 1933, p3.
The Nation. Jan 17, 1934, v138, p84.
The New York Times. Dec 23, 1933, p19.
The New Yorker. Dec 30, 1933, v9, p42.
Newsweek. Dec 30, 1933, v2, p30.
Pictures Will Talk. p59-60.
Rob Wagner's Script. Dec 23, 1933, v10, p11-12.
The Spectator. Dec 22, 1933, v151, p931.
Time. Dec 25, 1933, v22, p20-22.
Vanity Fair. Feb 1934, v41, p46.
Variety. Dec 26, 1933, p10.
W.C. Fields: A Life on Film. p125-26.

The Alien (US; Ince, Thomas H.; 1915)
Motion Picture News. Feb 6, 1915, p35.
Motion Picture News. Feb 27, 1915, p41.
Motion Picture News. Mar 6, 1915, p42.
Motion Picture News. Mar 27, 1915, p45.
Motion Picture News. Apr 3, 1915, p150.
Motion Picture News. May 1, 1915, p43.
Motography. Apr 10, 1915, p572.
Motography. May 1, 1915, 691.
Motography. Jun 12, 1915, p957.
Motography. Jun 19, 1915, p1035.
The Moving Picture World. Feb 27, 1915, p1300.
The Moving Picture World. Apr 24, 1915, p535, 561.
The Moving Picture World. May 1, 1915, p740-41.
The Moving Picture World. Jun 12, 1915, p1789.
The Moving Picture World. Jul 24, 1915, p732.
The New York Dramatic Mirror. Jun 2, 1915, p28.
Variety. Jun 4, 1915, p18.

Alimony (US; Collins, James W. Horne; 1924)
Film Daily. Jan 20, 1924, p7.
The Moving Picture World. Feb 2, 1924, p415.

All My Sons (US; Reis, Irving; 1948)
Agee on Film. v1, p300.
The Cinema of Edward G. Robinson. p169-71.
Film Daily. Feb 19, 1948, p8.
The Films of Burt Lancaster. p37-38.
Hollywood Reporter. Feb 19, 1948, p3.
Magill's Survey of Cinema. Series II. v1, p50.
Motion Picture Herald Product Digest. Feb 21, 1948, p4065.
The New Republic. Mar 27, 1948, v118, p33.
The New York Times. Mar 29, 1948, p17.
The New Yorker. Apr 3, 1948, v24, p58.
Newsweek. Apr 12, 1948, v31, p89.
Time. Apr 12, 1948, v51, p100.
Variety. Feb 25, 1948, p8.

All on Account of the Milk (US; Powell, Frank; 1910)
The New York Dramatic Mirror. Jan 22, 1910, p17.
Selected Film Criticism, 1896-1911. p4-5.

All Quiet on the Western Front (US; Milestone, Lewis; 1930)
American Cinematographer. Sep 1985, v66, p34-43.
American Film Criticism. p235-36.
Celluloid: The Film To-Day. p120-34.
Cinema. Jun 1930, v1, p37-38.
Cinema, the Magic Vehicle. v1, p177-78.
Close-Up. Mar 1930, v6, p171-73.
Commonweal. May 21, 1930, v12, p81.
A Companion to the Movies. p173.
Dictionary of Films. p7-8.
Eighty Years of Cinema. p82.
Exhibitors Herald-World. May 3, 1930, p32.
Exhibitors Herald-World. May 10, 1930, p31.
Film Daily. Apr 27, 1930, p12.
The Film Spectator. May 10, 1930, v9, p6-7.
The Film Spectator. Jun 7, 1930, v9, p16-17.
Films and Filming. Apr 1963, v9, p55-58.
The Films of the Thirties. p24-26.
From Quasimodo to Scarlett O'Hara. p120-22.
The Great Films. p77-82.
The International Dictionary of Films and Filmmakers. v1, p21-22.
Judge. May 24, 1930, v98, p23.
Kiss Kiss Bang Bang. p284-85.
Lewis Milestone (Millichap). p37-53+.
Life. May 23, 1930, v95, p18.
Literary Digest. May 17, 1930, v105, p19-20.
Literary Digest. Aug 30, 1930, v106, p17.
Lorentz on Film. p43-45.
Magill's Survey of Cinema, Series I. v1, p43-45.
The Nation. Jun 11, 1930, v130, p688.
The Nation. Jul 2, 1930, v131, p7-8.
The Nation. Apr 15, 1931, v132, p430.
National Board of Review Magazine. May-Jun 1930, v5, p5.
The New Republic. Jul 31, 1950, v123, p23.
The New York Times. Apr 30, 1930, p29.
The New York Times. May 4, 1930, p5.
The New York Times. Oct 9, 1939, p15.
The New Yorker. Aug 5, 1950, v26, p38.
The New Yorker. May 10, 1930, v6, p98-99.
Outlook and Independent. May 14, 1930, v155, p72.
Quarterly of Film, Radio and Television. Spr 1954, v8, p273-89.
Rob Wagner's Script. Jun 21, 1930, v3, p10.
Saturday Review. May 19, 1956, v39, p50.
Saturday Review (London). Jun 14, 1930, v149, p754.
Selected Film Criticism, 1921-1930. p6-8.
Sequence. 1952, n14, p12-16.
Shots in the Dark. p237-40.
Souvenir Programs of 12 Classic Movies, 1927-1944. p61-80.
The Spectator. Jun 28, 1930, v144, p1045.
Theatre Arts. Sep 1941, v25, p620.
Theatre Magazine. Jul 1930, v52, p44.
Those Fabulous Movie Years: The 30s. p13.
Time. Oct 2, 1939, v34, p49.
Time. May 18, 1931, v17, p54.
Time. May 5, 1930, v15, p30, 32.
Variety. May 7, 1930, p21.
The War, the West and the Wilderness. p214-19.
World Film News. Feb 1937, v1, p25.
50 Classic Motion Pictures. p200-05.

All That Money Can Buy *See* The Devil and Daniel
Webster

All the King's Men (US; Rosson, Richard; 1949)
Christian Century. Jan 4, 1950, v67, p31.
Commonweal. Nov 18, 1949, v51, p181.
Film Daily. Nov 7, 1949, p7.
Films in Review. Feb 1950, v1, p28-29.
The Films of the Forties. p271-73.
Hollywood Reporter. Nov 4, 1949, p3.
Library Journal. Feb 1, 1950, v75, p180.
Life. Nov 28, 1949, v27, p111-12.
Magill's Survey of Cinema. Series I. v1, p57-61.
Motion Picture Herald. Nov 5, 1949, p73.
The New Republic. Nov 21, 1949, v121, p21.
The New York Times. Nov 9, 1949, p37.
The New Yorker. Nov 12, 1949, v25, p101.
Newsweek. Nov 21, 1949, v34, p91-93.
Rotarian. Mar 1950, v76, p36.
Senior Scholastic. Dec 14, 1949, v55, p22.
Sequence. Sum 1950, v11, p3.
Seventy Years of Cinema. p176-77.
Sight and Sound. Jun 1950, v29, p163-64.
Time. Dec 5, 1949, v54, p102.
Variety. Nov 9, 1949, p6.
Vintage Films. p105-08.

All This and Heaven Too (US; Litvak, Anatole; 1940)
Bette Davis: Her Films and Career. p101-03.
Film Daily. June 17, 1940, p13.
Hollywood Reporter. Jun 14, 1940, p3.
Life. Jul 1, 1940, v9, p35-36.
The London Times. Dec 19, 1940, p6.
Magill's Survey of Cinema. Series II. v1, p65-67.
The New York Times. July 5, 1940, p10.
Newsweek. Jun 24, 1940, v15, p48.
Photoplay. Jul 1940, v104, p35-36.
Photoplay. Aug 1940, v104, p61.
Selected Film Criticism, 1941-1950. p4-5.
Time. Jun 24, 1940, v35, p89.
Variety. Jun 12, 1940, p14.

Allegheny Uprising (US; Seiter, William A.; 1939)
Commonweal. Nov 17, 1939, v31, p97.
The Complete Films of John Wayne. p95-96.
Film Daily. Oct 20, 1939, p6.
Film Daily. Oct 24, 1939, p10.
The Great Western Pictures. p4-5.
Hollywood Reporter. Oct 21, 1939, p3.
Hollywood Spectator. Oct 28, 1939, v14, p10.
Motion Picture Herald. Oct 28, 1939, p43.
The New York Times. Sep 28, 1939, p29.
Photoplay. Jan 1940, v54, p59.
Rob Wagner's Script. Dec 16, 1939, v22, p16.
Theatre Arts. Nov 1939, v23, p802.
Variety. Nov 8, 1939, p14.

Aloma of the South Seas (US; Tourneur, Maurice; 1926)
Film Daily. May 23, 1926, p22.
The New York Times. May 17, 1926, p19.
Photoplay. Jul 1926, v30, p59.
Selected Film Criticism, 1921-1930. p10.
Variety. May 19, 1926, p16.

Aloma of the South Seas (US; Santell, Alfred; 1940)
Chestnuts in Her Lap. p80-81.
Commonweal. Sep 12, 1941, v34, p496.
Film Daily. Aug 28, 1941, p6.
The London Times. Nov 21, 1941, p6.
Motion Picture Exhibitor. Sep 3, 1941, p831.
The New York Times. Aug 28, 1941, p23.
The New Yorker. Aug 30, 1941, p49.
Newsweek. Sep 1, 1941, v18, p49.
Scribner's Commentator. Nov 1941, v11, p106-07.
Variety. Aug 27, 1941, p8.

Along Came Jones (US; Heisler, Stuart; 1945)
Commonweal. Jun 8, 1945, v42, p192.
Film Daily. Jun 18, 1945, p5.
The Films of Gary Cooper. p199-200.
Hollywood Reporter. Jun 13, 1945, p3.
The New York Times. Jul 19, 1945, p8.
The New Yorker. Jul 28, 1945, v21, p51.
Newsweek. Jul 30, 1945, v26, p84.
Time. Jul 9, 1945, v46, p85.
Variety. Jun 13, 1945, p17.

Always Goodbye (US; Lanfield, Sidney; 1938)
Film Daily. Jun 27, 1938, p6.
The Films of Barbara Stanwyck. p123.
Hollywood Reporter. Jun 24, 1938, p3.
Motion Picture Herald. Jul 2, 1938, p40.
The New York Times. Jun 25, 1938, p7.
Rob Wagner's Script. Jul 9, 1938, v19, p17-18.
Starring Miss Barbara Stanwyck. p115.
Time. Jul 4, 1938, v32, p18.
Variety. Jun 29, 1938, p12.

Always Good-Bye (US; McKenna, Kenneth; Menzies,
William Cameron; 1931)
Film Daily. May 24, 1931, p10.
Hollywood Spectator. Aug 29, 1931, v12, p22.
Judge. Jun 13, 1931, v100, p22.
Life. Jun 12, 1931, v97, p20.
Motion Picture Herald. Apr 25, 1931, p40.
The New York Times. May 23, 1931, p13.
The New York Times. May 31, 1931, p5.
Outlook and Independent. Jun 17, 1931, v158, p218.
Variety. May 27, 1931, p57.

Always Leave Them Laughing (US; Del Ruth, Roy; 1949)
Commonweal. Dec 9, 1949, v51, p269.
Film Daily. Nov 23, 1949, p6.
Hollywood Reporter. Nov 22, 1949, p3.
Motion Picture Herald. Nov 26, 1949, p97.
The New York Times. Nov 24, 1949, p48.
The New Yorker. Dec 3, 1949, v25, p74.
Newsweek. Dec 12, 1949, v34, p87.
Time. Dec 5, 1949, v54, p102.
Variety. Nov 23, 1949, p8.

Amants Diaboliques, Les *See* Ossessione

Amarilly of Clothes-Line Alley (US; Neilan, Marshall;
1918)
Exhibitor's Trade Review. Mar 23, 1918, p1299.
Motion Picture News. Mar 23, 1918, p1762.
The Moving Picture World. Mar 9, 1918, p1412.
The Moving Picture World. Mar 23, 1918, p1703.
Variety. Mar 8, 1918, p41.
Wid's Daily. Mar 21, 1918, p1018-19.

The Amateur Gentleman (GB; Freeland, Thornton; 1936)
Canadian Magazine. Apr 1936, v85, p59.
Commonweal. Mar 20, 1936, v23, p580.
Film Daily. Apr 27, 1936, p8.
Hollywood Reporter. Feb 8, 1936, p6.
Motion Picture Herald. Feb 22, 1936, p64.
The New Statesman and Nation. Feb 1, 1936, v11, p151.
The New York Times. Apr 27, 1936, p19.
Rob Wagner's Script. Jun 27, 1936, v15, p10-11.
The Spectator. Jan 31, 1936, v156, p170.
Stage. Feb 1936, v13, p8.
The Tatler. Feb 5, 1936, v139, p246.
Time. Apr 13, 1936, v27, p32.
Variety. Feb 5, 1936, p12.
Variety. Apr 29, 1936, p15.

The Amazing Dr. Clitterhouse (US; Litvak, Anatole; 1938)
The Cinema of Edward G. Robinson. p115-17.
Classics of the Gangster Film. p59-62.
Commonweal. Aug 5, 1938, v28, p390.

The Complete Films of Humphrey Bogart. p58-59.
Crime Movies. p147-49.
Esquire. Nov 1938, v10, p171-72.
The Film Criticism of Otis Ferguson. p228-29.
Film Daily. Jun 21, 1938, p5.
The Great Gangster Pictures. p20-22.
Hollywood Reporter. Jun 28, 1938, p3.
Humphrey Bogart: The Man and His Films. p80-82.
Lunatics and Lovers. p277, 280.
Motion Picture Herald. Jun 25, 1938, p47, 50.
The New Masses. Jul 5, 1938, v28, p29-30.
The New Republic. Aug 10, 1938, v96, p18.
The New York Times. Jul 21, 1938, p14.
The New Yorker. Jul 23, 1938, v14, p53.
Newsweek. Jul 4, 1938, v12, p26.
Rob Wagner's Script. Aug 16, 1938, v19, p22.
The Spectator. Dec 2, 1938, v161, p945.
The Tatler. Nov 30, 1938, v150, p378.
Those Fabulous Movie Years: The 30s. p144.
Time. Jul 18, 1938, v32, p20.
Variety. Jun 22, 1938, p14.
World Film News. Oct 1938, v3, p266-67.

America (US; Griffith, D.W.; 1924)
Film Daily. Mar 2, 1924, p9.
The Films of D.W. Griffith. p195-204.
Life. Mar 13, 1924, p26.
Magill's Survey of Cinema. Silent Films. v1, p137-41.
The New York Times. Feb 22, 1924, p20.
The New York Times. Jan 13, 1924, sec7, p5.
Photoplay. May 1924, v25, p55.
Selected Film Criticism, 1921-1930. p11-12.
Spellbound in Darkness. p258-59.
Variety. Feb 28, 1924, p22.

American Biograph First Program (US; 1896)
The Illustrated American. Nov 28, 1896, v20, p735.
The New York Dramatic Mirror. Oct 24, 1896, p17.
Selected Film Criticism, 1896-1911. p5.
Spellbound in Darkness. p20.

An American Citizen (US; Dawley, J. Searle; 1914)
The Moving Picture World. Jan 17, 1914, p292, 342.
The New York Dramatic Mirror. Jan 7, 1914, p29.
Selected Film Criticism, 1912-1920. p5-6.
Variety. Jan 9, 1914, p12.

American Madness (US; Capra, Frank; 1932)
American Film Criticism. p268.
Commonweal. Aug 17, 1932, v16, p392.
Film Daily. Jul 1, 1932, p6.
The Films of Frank Capra (Scherle and Levy). p107-10.
The Films of Frank Capra (Willis). p131-35.
Frank Capra (Maland). p70-74.
Frank Capra: The Man and His Films. p57-67.
Great Film Directors: A Critical Anthology. p153-59.
Judge. Oct 1932, v103, p20.
Judge. Sep 1932, v103, p23.
Motion Picture Herald. Jul 9, 1932, p36.
The Name Above the Title. p137-40.
The Nation. Aug 31, 1932, v135, p199.
The New York Times. Aug 6, 1932, p14.
The New Yorker. Aug 13, 1932, v8, p37.
Photoplay. Sep 1932, v42, p52.
Rob Wagner's Script. Sep 13, 1932, v8, p8.
Selected Film Criticism, 1931-1940. p6-7.
Time. Aug 15, 1932, v20, p25.
Variety. Aug 9, 1932, p17.

An American Tragedy (US; Sternberg, Josef von; 1931)
BFI/Monthly Film Bulletin. Nov 1975, v42, p272.
Cinema, the Magic Vehicle. v1, p197-98.
The Classic American Novel and the Movies. p239-56.
Close-Up. Dec 1931, v8, p268-79.
Dictionary of Films. p9.
Film Daily. Aug 9, 1931, p10.

The Films of Josef von Sternberg. p32-34.
Hollywood Spectator. Sep 12, 1931, v12, p22.
Judge. Aug 15, 1931, v101, p22.
Life. Aug 31, 1931, v98, p18.
Literary Digest. Sep 5, 1931, v110, p18-19.
Lorentz on Film. p76-78.
Make It Again, Sam: A Survey of Movie Remakes. p27-31.
Motion Picture Herald. Jun 6, 1931, p32.
The Nation. Sep 2, 1931, v133, p237.
The New Republic. Aug 19, 1931, v68, p21-22.
The New Republic. Jun 3, 1931, v67, p73.
The New York Times. Aug 6, 1931, p22.
Outlook and Independent. Aug 19, 1931, v158, p502.
Rob Wagner's Script. Aug 22, 1931, v6, p8-9.
Rob Wagner's Script. Nov 21, 1931, v6, p6-7.
Selected Film Criticism, 1931-1940. p7-10.
Time. Aug 17, 1931, v18, p17.
Variety. Aug 11, 1931, p19.

America's Answer (Also titled: America's Answer to the Hun) (US; 1918)
Exhibitor's Trade Review. Aug 10, 1918, p838-39.
The Moving Picture World. Nov 30, 1918, p992.
Variety. Aug 2, 1918, p38.
Wid's Daily. Aug 4, 1918, p23-24.

Amour Guide, L' *See* The Way to Love

Amours de la Reine Elisabeth *See* Queen Elizabeth

Amphitryon (Also titled: The Gods at Play) (GER; Schunzel, Reinhold; Valentin, Albert; 1936)
Architectural Record. Feb 1937, v81, p15.
Film Daily. Mar 30, 1937, p11.
Hollywood Reporter. Oct 29, 1936, p3.
Motion Picture Herald. Apr 3, 1937, p41.
The New York Times. Mar 24, 1937, p29.
The New Yorker. Oct 31, 1936, v12, p61.
The New Yorker. Apr 3, 1937, v13, p71-72.
Rob Wagner's Script. Jan 30, 1937, v16, p11.
Saint Cinema: Selected Writings, 1929-1970. p46-47.
The Spectator. Dec 31, 1937, v159, p1177.
Variety. Mar 31, 1937, p19.

Anchors Aweigh (US; Sidney, George; 1945)
Commonweal. Aug 3, 1941, p382.
Film Daily. Jul 9, 1945, p7.
The Films of Frank Sinatra. p42-45.
The Films of Gene Kelly. p60-66.
The Films of the Forties. p146-48.
The Hollywood Musical. p261, 300+.
Hollywood Musicals. p179-80.
Hollywood Reporter. Jul 18, 1945, p3.
Life. Aug 13, 1945, v19, p61-62.
The London Times. Jan 7, 1946, p6.
Magill's Survey of Cinema. Series II. v1, p79-81.
Motion Picture Exhibitor. Jul 25, 1945, v34, n12, p1749.
Motion Picture Herald Product Digest. Jul 21, 1945, p2553.
The New Republic. Aug 27, 1945, v113, p256.
The New York Times. Jul 20, 1945, p15.
The New Yorker. Jul 28, 1945, v21, p51.
Newsweek. Jul 30, 1945, v24, p84.
Photoplay. Sep 1945, v29, p587.
Rob Wagner's Script. Aug 11, 1945, p23.
Selected Film Criticism, 1941-1950. p7.
Theatre Arts. Oct 1945, v29, p587.
Time. Jul 30, 1945, v46, p96.
Variety. Jul 18, 1945, p34.

And Baby Makes Three (US; Levin, Henry; 1949)
Christian Century. Dec 28, 1949, v66, p1559.
Film Daily. Jan 5, 1950, p6.
Hollywood Reporter. Nov 28, 1949, p3.
Motion Picture Herald. Nov 3, 1949, p105.
The New York Times. Dec 23, 1949, p17.
Rotarian. Feb 1950, v66, p38.

Time. Jan 23, 1950, v55, p76.
Variety. Nov 30, 1949, p6.

And So They Were Married (US; Nugent, Elliott; 1936)
  Film Daily. May 14, 1936, p6.
  Hollywood Reporter. Apr 10, 1936, p2.
  Motion Picture Herald. Apr 18, 1936, p36.
  The New York Times. May 14, 1936, p29.
  Time. May 25, 1936, v27, p48.
  Variety. May 20, 1936, p23.

And Then There Were None (US; Clair, René; 1945)
  Canadian Forum. Feb 1946, v25, p265.
  Commonweal. Nov 9, 1945, v43, p94-95.
  Film Daily. Jul 11, 1945, p7.
  Hollywood Reporter. Jul 11, 1945, p3.
  Life. Oct 29, 1945, v19, p89-90+.
  Magill's Survey of Cinema. Series I. v1, p68-71.
  Motion Picture Exhibitor. Jul 25, 1945, v34, n12, sec2, p1721.
  Motion Picture Herald Product Digest. Jul 14, 1945, p2626.
  The New York Times. Nov 1, 1945, p20.
  The New Yorker. Nov 10, 1945, v21, p61.
  Newsweek. Oct 29, 1945, v26, p104.
  René Clair (McGerr). p150-57.
  Scholastic. Oct 15, 1945, v47, p29.
  Time. Oct 15, 1945, v46, p54.
  Variety. Jul 11, 1945, p14.

An Andalusian Dog *See* Chien Andalou, Un

Andy Hardy Gets Spring Fever (US; Van Dyke, W.S.;
    1939)
  Commonweal. Jul 28, 1939, v30, p340.
  Film Daily. Jul 12, 1939, p5.
  Motion Picture Herald. Jul 15, 1939, p53-54.
  The New Statesman and Nation. Sep 30, 1939, v18, p455.
  The New York Times. Jul 19, 1939, p23.
  The New Yorker. Jul 22, 1939, v15, p64.
  Time. Jul 24, 1939, v34, p43.
  Variety. Jul 12, 1939, p12.

Angel (US; Lubitsch, Ernst; 1937)
  Chestnuts in Her Lap. p18-20.
  The Comic Mind. p223.
  Ernst Lubitsch: A Guide to References and Resources. p133-37.
  Ernst Lubitsch's American Comedy. p133-55.
  Film Daily. Sep 17, 1937, p13.
  Film Society Review. Sep 1965, p15.
  The Films of Marlene Dietrich. p137-39.
  From Quasimodo to Scarlett O'Hara. p259-60.
  Hollywood Reporter. Sep 14, 1937, p3.
  Life. Oct 11, 1937, v3, p118-19.
  Literary Digest. Oct 30, 1937, v124, p34.
  Magill's Survey of Cinema, Series II. v1, p82-85.
  Motion Picture Herald. Sep 25, 1937, p44, 49.
  National Board of Review Magazine. Oct 1937, v12, p12.
  The New Statesman and Nation. Nov 13, 1937, v14, p795.
  The New York Times. Nov 4, 1937, p29.
  The New Yorker. Nov 6, 1937, v13, p75.
  Newsweek. Nov 8, 1937, v10, p22.
  Rob Wagner's Script. Nov 13, 1937, v18, p9.
  Sight and Sound. Wint 1937, v6, p188.
  The Spectator. Nov 26, 1937, v159, p949.
  Talking Pictures. p169-71.
  Time. Nov 8, 1937, v30, p48.
  Variety. Sep 15, 1937, p13.
  World Film News. Dec 1937, v2, p30.

The Angel and the Badman (US; Grant, James Edward;
    1947)
  The Complete Films of John Wayne. p151-53.
  Film Daily. Feb 7, 1947, p6.
  Hollywood Reporter. Feb 6, 1947, p3.
  Motion Picture Herald Product Digest. Feb 15, 1947, p3474.
  The New York Times. Mar 3, 1947, p28.
  Variety. Feb 19, 1947.

Angel on My Shoulder (US; Mayo, Archie; 1946)
  Film Daily. Sep 18, 1946, p8.
  Hollywood Reporter. Sep 16, 1946, p3.
  Motion Picture Herald Product Digest. Sep 21, 1946, p3210.
  The New York Times. Oct 21, 1946, p27.
  The New Yorker. Oct 19, 1946, v22, p114.
  Newsweek. Nov 4, 1946, v28, p92.
  Paul Muni: His Life and His Films. p211-15.
  Time. Oct 19, 1946, p104.
  Variety. Sep 18, 1946, p16.

Angele *See* Heartbeat

Angels Over Broadway (US; Hecht, Ben; Garmes, Lee;
    1940)
  Commonweal. Jul 26, 1940, v33, p292.
  The Film Criticism of Otis Ferguson. p321-22.
  Film Daily. Nov 22, 1940, p6.
  The Films of Rita Hayworth. p114-16.
  Hollywood Reporter. Oct 3, 1940, p3.
  Magill's Survey of Cinema, Series II. v1, p86-88.
  Motion Picture Exhibitor. Oct 16, 1940, p619.
  The New Republic. Dec 9, 1940, p789.
  The New York Times. Nov 18, 1940, p23.
  The New York Times. Nov 24, 1940, sec9, p5.
  Talking Pictures. p18-21.
  Time. Nov 4, 1940, v36, p78.
  Variety. Oct 9, 1940, p16.

Angels Wash Their Faces (US; Enright, Ray; 1939)
  Film Daily. Sep 8, 1939, p7.
  The Films of Ronald Reagan. p86-88.
  The Great Gangster Pictures. p24.
  Hollywood Reporter. Oct 6, 1939, p3.
  Motion Picture Herald. Sep 9, 1939, p46-48.
  The New York Times. Sep 4, 1939, p16.
  Rob Wagner's Script. Oct 14, 1939, v22, p17.
  Variety. Sep 6, 1939, p14.

Angels With Dirty Faces (US; Curtiz, Michael; 1938)
  America in the Dark. p169-70.
  Classics of the Gangster Film. p55-58.
  Commonweal. Nov 25, 1938, v29, p133.
  The Complete Films of Humphrey Bogart. p62-63.
  Crime Movies. p152-55.
  Esquire. Mar 1939, v11, p153-54.
  Film Daily. Oct 24, 1938, p7.
  The Films of James Cagney. p129-33.
  The Great Gangster Pictures. p24-26.
  Hollywood Genres. p100-01.
  Hollywood Reporter. Oct 21, 1938, p3.
  Hollywood Spectator. Oct 29, 1938, v13, p14, 16.
  Magill's Survey of Cinema, Series I. v1, p72-74.
  Motion Picture Herald. Oct 29, 1938, p42.
  The Nation. Dec 10, 1938, v147, p639.
  National Board of Review Magazine. Dec 1938, v13, p21-22.
  The New Statesman and Nation. Jan 21, 1939, v17, p85.
  The New York Times. Nov 26, 1938, p18.
  The New Yorker. Nov 26, 1938, v14, p75.
  Newsweek. Nov 7, 1938, v12, p28-29.
  Photoplay. Jan 1939, v53, p44.
  Rob Wagner's Script. Nov 26, 1938, v20, p12.
  Selected Film Criticism, 1931-1940. p11-12.
  Sight and Sound. Spr 1939, v8, p31.
  The Spectator. Feb 3, 1939, v162, p176.
  Stage. Dec 1938, v16, p57.
  Time. Oct 31, 1938, v32, p26.
  Time. Dec 5, 1938, v32, p28+.
  Variety. Oct 26, 1938, p13.
  Warner Brothers Presents. p62-63.

Animal Crackers (US; Heerman, Victor; 1930)
  American Film Criticism. p144.
  Dictionary of Films. p12.
  Exhibitors Herald-World. Sep 6, 1930, p38-39.

Film Daily. Aug 3, 1930, p11.
Hooray for Captain Spaulding! 1973.
Judge. Sep 20, 1930, v99, p21.
Life. Sep 26, 1930, v96, p20.
Magill's Survey of Cinema, Series I. v1, p75-77.
The Marx Brothers. p47-54.
The Nation. Oct 1, 1930, v131, p355.
The New York Times. May 4, 1930, p6.
The New York Times. Aug 29, 1930, p30.
The New York Times. Sep 7, 1930, p5.
The New Yorker. Sep 6, 1930, v6, p62-63.
Outlook and Independent. Sep 17, 1930, v156, p112.
Selected Film Criticism, 1921-1930. p12-14.
Time. Sep 8, 1930, v16, p25.
Variety. Sep 3, 1930, p19.

The Animal Kingdom (US; Griffith, Edward H.; 1932)
Film Daily. Dec 23, 1932, p6.
The Films of Myrna Loy. p145-47.
Hollywood Reporter. Nov 29, 1932, p3.
The New York Times. Dec 30, 1932, p14.
The New Yorker. Dec 31, 1932, v8, p40.
Rob Wagner's Script. Dec 24, 1932, v8, p8.
Time. Jan 9, 1933, v21, p37.
Vanity Fair. Feb 1933, v39, p48+.
Variety. Jan 3, 1933, p19.

Animals in Motion (US; Muybridge, Eadweard; 1882)
American Silent Film. p17-18.
A Million and One Nights. p21-49.
The New York Times. Nov 18, 1882, p2.
The Scientific American Supplement. Jan 28, 1882, p5058-59.
The Scientific American Supplement. July 29, 1882, p5469-70.
Spellbound in Darkness. p4-6.

Ann Vickers (US; Cromwell, John; 1933)
Film Daily. Sep 29, 1933, p6.
Hollywood Reporter. Sep 18, 1933, p3.
Motion Picture Herald. Sep 30, 1933, p38.
The New York Times. Sep 29, 1933, p24.
The New Yorker. Oct 7, 1933, v9, p57.
Newsweek. Oct 7, 1933, v2, p30.
Rob Wagner's Script. Dec 23, 1933, v10, p11-12.
Time. Oct 9, 1933, v22, p30.

Anna (Also titled: The Party Ticket) (USSR; Piriev, Ivan; 1936)
Motion Picture Herald. Aug 1, 1936, p57.
The New Masses. Jul 28, 1936, v20, p30.
The New York Times. Jul 17, 1936, p20.
Variety. Jul 22, 1936, p34.

Anna and the King of Siam (US; Cromwell, John; 1946)
Commonweal. Jul 5, 1946, v44, p285.
Film Daily. Jun 3, 1946, p10.
The Films of the Forties. p170-73.
Hollywood Reporter. Jun 3, 1946, p3.
Life. Jun 24, 1946, v20, p81-84.
Magill's Survey of Cinema, Series I. v1, p78-81.
Motion Picture Herald Product Digest. Jun 8, 1946, p3029.
The Nation. Jul 6, 1946, v163, p25.
The New York Times. Jun 21, 1946, p20.
The New Yorker. Jul 6, 1946, v22, p43.
Newsweek. Jun 24, 1946, v27, p94.
Theatre Arts. Aug 1946, v30, p442.
Time. Jun 24, 1946, v47, p98.
Variety. Jun 5, 1946, p13.

Anna Christie (US; Wray, John Griffith; 1923)
Exceptional Photoplays. Oct-Nov 1923, v4, p1-2.
Film Daily. Nov 25, 1923, p9.
The Films of Greta Garbo. p87-90.
The Films of the Twenties. p83-85.
Magill's Survey of Cinema. Silent Films. v1, p142-45.
A Million and One Nights. p728-29.
The New York Times. Dec 10, 1923, p20.

Photoplay. Jan 1924, v25, p68.
Selected Film Criticism, 1921-1930. p14-17.
Variety. Dec 6, 1923, p23.

Anna Christie (US; Brown, Clarence; 1930)
American Film Criticism. p232-33.
BFI/Monthly Film Bulletin. Jul 1977, v44, p178.
Cinema. Apr 1930, v1, p37.
Close-Up. Jun 1930, v6, p461-62.
Commonweal. Mar 26, 1930, v11, p590-91.
Exhibitors Herald-World. Feb 15, 1930, p28.
Film Daily. Feb 9, 1930, p12.
The Film Spectator. Jan 18, 1930, v9, p6.
The Film Spectator. Feb 15, 1930, v9, p19-20.
The Films of Greta Garbo. p87-91.
The Films of the Thirties. p20-23.
From Quasimodo to Scarlett O'Hara. p117-19.
Garbo: A Portrait (Walker). p109-10.
Hound and Horn: Essays on Cinema. p572-73.
Judge. Apr 5, 1930, v98, p23.
A Library of Film Criticism: American Film Directors. p19.
Life. Mar 21, 1930, v95, p20.
Lorentz on Film. p39-41.
Magill's Survey of Cinema, Series II. v1, p92-95.
The Nation. Apr 2, 1930, v130, p406.
National Board of Review Magazine. Feb 1930, v5, p12.
The New York Times. Mar 15, 1930, p22.
The New York Times. Mar 23, 1930, p5.
The New York Times. Jan 6, 1931, p25.
The New Yorker. Mar 22, 1930, v6, p52-53.
Outlook and Independent. Feb 26, 1930, v154, p355.
Rob Wagner's Script. Mar 29, 1930, v3, p10.
Saturday Review (London). May 17, 1930, v149, p614.
Selected Film Criticism, 1921-1930. p17-18.
Time. Mar 3, 1930, v15, p28.
Variety. Mar 19, 1930, p34.
Vintage Films. p13-15.

Anna Karenina (US; Brown, Clarence; 1935)
Basil Rathbone: His Life and His Films. p150-53.
Canadian Magazine. Nov 1935, v84, p34-35.
Esquire. Nov 1935, v4, p107.
Film Daily. Aug 31, 1935, p7.
The Films of Fredric March. p130-33.
The Films of Greta Garbo. p129-34.
From Quasimodo to Scarlett O'Hara. p205-07.
Garbo: A Portrait (Walker). p145-48.
Garbo and the Night Watchman. p120-23.
Graham Greene on Film. p25-26.
Hollywood Reporter. Jun 29, 1935, p3.
Judge. Nov 1935, v109, p18, 29.
Life. Nov 1935, v102, p24.
Literary Digest. Aug 31, 1935, v120, p29.
London Mercury. Nov 1935, v33, p63.
Magill's Survey of Cinema. Series I. v1, p82-85.
Motion Picture Herald. Jul 6, 1935, p72.
The Nation. Oct 2, 1935, v141, p391.
National Board of Review Magazine. Sep-Oct 1935, v10, p10.
The New Masses. Sep 24, 1935, v16, p28.
New Theatre. Oct 1935, v2, p22.
The New York Times. Aug 31, 1935, p16.
The New Yorker. Sep 7, 1935, v11, p61-62.
Newsweek. Aug 31, 1935, v6, p26.
Rob Wagner's Script. Oct 12, 1935, v14, p10.
Saturday Review (London). Oct 12, 1935, v160, p320.
Selected Film Criticism, 1931-1940. p13-14.
The Spectator. Oct 11, 1935, v155, p547.
Time. Sep 9, 1935, v26, p46.
Vanity Fair. Oct 1935, v45, p46-47.
Variety. Sep 4, 1935, p14.

Anna Lucasta (US; Laven, Arnold; 1949)
Commonweal. Aug 26, 1950, v50, p490.
Film Daily. Jul 11, 1949 , p8.
Hollywood Reporter. Jun 29, 1949, p3.

Motion Picture Herald Product Digest. Jul 16, 1949, p4682.
The New Republic. Aug 22, 1949, v121, p22.
The New York Times. Aug 12, 1949, p13.
The New Yorker. Aug 20, 1949, v25, p49.
Newsweek. Aug 22, 1949, v34, p70-71.
Theatre Arts. Oct 1949, v33, p96.
Time. Aug 15, 1949, v54, p78.
Variety. Jul 13, 1949, p16.

Annapolis Salute (US; Cabanne, Christy; 1937)
Film Daily. Aug 17, 1937, p4.
Hollywood Reporter. Aug 13, 1937, p3.
Motion Picture Herald. Aug 21, 1937, p55.
The New York Times. Oct 2, 1937, p18.
Variety. Oct 6, 1937, p12.

Anne Boleyn (Also titled: Deception) (GER; Lubitsch, Ernst; 1920)
Ernst Lubitsch: A Guide to References and Resources. p64-66.
The Moving Picture World. Apr 30, 1921, p989.
The New York Times. Apr 18, 1921, p8.
Variety. Jan 21, 1921, p45.
Variety. Apr 22, 1921, p40.
Wid's Daily. Apr 24, 1921, p3.

Anne of Green Gables (US; Taylor, William Desmond; 1919)
Exhibitor's Trade Review. Nov 22, 1919, p2137.
Exhibitor's Trade Review. Feb 28, 1920, p1329.
Fifty Great American Silent Films, 1912-1920. p112-13.
Magill's Survey of Cinema. Silent Films. v1, p146-48.
Motion Picture News. Nov 15, 1919, p3599.
Motion Picture News. Nov 29, 1919, p3975.
The Moving Picture World. Nov 22, 1919, p438, 455.
The Moving Picture World. Dec 6, 1919, p685.
The Moving Picture World. Jan 10, 1920, p222.
The New York Times. Dec 22, 1919, p18.
Selected Film Criticism, 1912-1920. p6.
Variety. Nov 14, 1919, p59.
Wid's Daily. Nov 23, 1919, p20.

Annie Laurie (US; Robertson, John S.; 1927)
Film Daily. Jun 5, 1927, p18.
The Moving Picture World. May 21, 1927, p211.
The New York Times. May 12, 1924, p3.
Photoplay. Jul 1927, p55.
Selected Film Criticism, 1921-1930. p20.
Variety. May 18, 1927, p20.

Annie Oakley (US; Stevens, George; 1935)
Esquire. Jan 1936, v5, p156.
Film Daily. Oct 29, 1935, p6.
The Films of Barbara Stanwyck. p102-03.
Hollywood Reporter. Oct 26, 1935, p3.
Hollywood Spectator. Nov 9, 1935, v10, p11-12.
Literary Digest. Jan 4, 1936, v121, p23.
Motion Picture Herald. Nov 9, 1935, p60-61.
The Nation. Jan 15, 1936, v142, p84.
The New York Times. Dec 24, 1935, p10.
The New Yorker. Jan 4, 1936, v11, p49.
Rob Wagner's Script. Nov 30, 1935, v14, p8.
Scholastic. Dec 7, 1935, v27, p12.
Starring Barbara Stanwyck. p75, 77.
Time. Nov 25, 1935, v26, p50.
Variety. Dec 25, 1935, p15.
The Velvet Light Trap. 1973, n8, p11-13.

Another Dawn (US; Dieterle, William; 1937)
Commonweal. May 28, 1937, v26, p132.
Film Daily. Jun 18, 1937, p12.
Garbo and the Night Watchman. p251-52.
Hollywood Reporter. Apr 1, 1937, p3.
Hollywood Spectator. Apr 10, 1937, v12, p13-14.
Motion Picture Herald. Apr 10, 1937, p66.
Motion Picture Herald. Mar 6, 1937, p16-17.
The New York Times. Jun 18, 1937, p25.

Rob Wagner's Script. Jun 26, 1937, v17, p13.
Time. Jul 5, 1937, v30, p26.
Variety. Jun 23, 1937, p12.

Another Language (US; Griffith, Edward H.; 1933)
Film Daily. Aug 5, 1933, p3.
Hollywood Reporter. Jul 14, 1933, p3.
Motion Picture Herald. Aug 5, 1933, p38.
The Nation. Aug 30, 1933, v137, p250.
The Nation. Sep 20, 1933, v137, p326.
New Outlook. Sep 1933, v162, p44.
The New York Times. Aug 5, 1933, p9.
The New Yorker. Aug 12, 1933, v9, p43.
Newsweek. Aug 12, 1933, v2, p30.
Photoplay. Aug 14, 1933, v44, p12.
Rob Wagner's Script. Sep 9, 1933, v10, p10.
Time. Aug 14, 1933, v22, p22.
Vanity Fair. Oct 1933, v41, p40.
Variety. Aug 8, 1933, p19.

Another Part of the Forest (US; Gordon, Michael; 1948)
Agee on Film. v1, p305.
Commonweal. Jun 4, 1948, v48, p185-86.
Film Daily. Apr 19, 1948, p9.
The Films of Fredric March. p192-94.
Hollywood Reporter. Apr 15, 1948, p3.
Life. May 31, 1948, v24, p63-64+.
Motion Picture Herald Product Digest. Apr 17, 1948, p4125.
The New Republic. Jun 7, 1948, v118, p29.
The New York Times. May 19, 1948, p30.
The New Yorker. May 29, 1948, v24, p66.
Newsweek. May 31, 1948, v31, p72.
Time. May 31 1948, v51, p86.
Variety. Apr 21, 1948, p13.

Another Thin Man (US; Van Dyke, W.S.; 1939)
Film Daily. Nov 14, 1939, p7.
The Films of Myrna Loy. p215-16.
Hollywood Reporter. Nov 10, 1939, p3.
Hollywood Spectator. Nov 25, 1939, v14, p6-7.
Motion Picture Herald. Nov 18, 1939, p44.
The New York Times. Nov 24, 1939, p29.
The New Yorker. Dec 2, 1939, v15, p93.
Newsweek. Nov 27, 1939, v14, p33-34.
Photoplay. Dec 1939, v53, p20+.
Photoplay. Jan 1940, v54, p59+.
Rob Wagner's Script. Nov 25, 1939, v22, p17.
Time. Dec 11, 1939, v34, p78.
Variety. Nov 15, 1939, p18.

Anthony Adverse (US; LeRoy, Mervyn; 1936)
Canadian Magazine. Aug 1936, v86, p34-35.
Commonweal. Aug 14, 1936, v24, p387.
Esquire. Sep 1936, v6, p98, 174.
The Film Criticism of Otis Ferguson. p143-46.
Film Daily. May 12, 1936, p12.
The Films of Fredric March. p143-46.
The Films of Olivia de Havilland. p75-80.
Graham Greene on Film. p103-04.
Hollywood Reporter. May 9, 1936, p3.
Hollywood Spectator. May 23, 1936, v11, p7-8.
Life. Oct 1936, v103, p32.
Literary Digest. Jun 13, 1936, v121, p22.
Magill's Survey of Cinema. Series II. v1, p96-99.
Motion Picture. Apr 1936, v51, p34-35+.
Motion Picture Herald. May 23, 1936, p41.
Motion Picture Herald. Aug 22, 1936, p15.
The New Republic. Aug 5, 1936, v87, p381-82.
The New York Times. Aug 27, 1936, p16.
The New York Times. Sep 13, 1936, p3.
The New Yorker. Aug 29, 1936, v12, p46.
Newsweek. Aug 29, 1936, v8, p24-25.
Saturday Review (London). Sep 26, 1936, v162, p377.
Scholastic. Sep 19, 1936, v29, p17.
Selected Film Criticism, 1931-1940. p17-18.

The Spectator. Sep 25, 1936, v157, p495.
Stage. Apr 1936, v13, p44-45.
Stage. Jul 1936, v13, p32-33.
Those Fabulous Movie Years: The 30s. p112-13.
Time. Aug 17, 1936, v28, p43.
Variety. Sep 2, 1936, p18.
World Film News. Nov 1936, v1, p20.

Anthony and Cleopatra (IT; 1913)
The New York Dramatic Mirror. Jan 21, 1914, p32.
Variety. May 15, 1914, p22.

Antoine et Antoinette (FR; Becker, Jacques; 1947)
Film Daily. Apr 19, 1948, p9.
Hollywood Reporter. Feb 24, 1949, p3.
The New York Times. Apr 16, 1948, p29.
The New Yorker. Dec 20, 1947, v23, p56.
The New Yorker. Aug 24, 1948, v24, p59.
Sequence. Wint 1948, n6, p42-43.
Variety. Nov 12, 1947, p24.

Antony and Cleopatra (US; Griffith, D.W.; 1908)
The New York Dramatic Mirror. Nov 14, 1908, p10.
Selected Film Criticism, 1896-1911. p8.

Any Number Can Play (US; LeRoy, Mervyn; 1949)
Commonweal. Jul 8, 1949, v50, p319.
Film Daily. Jun 2, 1949, p7.
The Films of Clark Gable. p217.
Hollywood Reporter. Jun 1, 1949, p3.
Motion Picture Herald Product Digest. Jun 4, 1949, p4633.
The New York Times. Jul 1, 1949, p14.
The New Yorker. Jul 9, 1949, v25, p38.
Newsweek. Jul 11, 1949, v34, p68.
Rotarian. Aug 1949, v75, p42.
Time. Jul 25, 1949, v54, p78.
Variety. Jun 8, 1949, p18.

Anything Goes (Also titled: Tops Is the Limit) (US; Milestone, Lewis; 1936)
Esquire. Apr 1936, v5, p104.
Film Daily. Feb 6, 1936, p9.
The Films of Bing Crosby. p75-76.
The Films of the Thirties. p162-63.
Graham Greene on Film. p53.
Hollywood Reporter. Jan 4, 1936, p3.
Hollywood Spectator. Feb 1, 1936, v10, p12-13.
Motion Picture. Feb 1936, v51, p29.
Motion Picture Herald. Feb 22, 1936, p62, 64.
The New York Times. Feb 6, 1936, p23.
Rob Wagner's Script. Feb 11, 1936, v14, p11.
The Spectator. Feb 21, 1936, v156, p300.
Time. Feb 3, 1936, v27, p57.
Variety. Feb 12, 1936, p16.

Apartment for Peggy (US; Seaton, George; 1948)
Commonweal. Oct 22, 1948, v49, p41.
Film Daily. Sep 8, 1948, p8.
The Films of William Holden. p85-87.
Motion Picture Herald Product Digest. Sep 18, 1948, p4318.
National Education Association Journal. Dec 1948, v37, p608.
The New Republic. Nov 15, 1948, v119, p31.
The New York Times. Oct 16, 1948, p9.
Newsweek. Oct 18, 1948, v32, p108.
Rotarian. Jan 1949, v74, p11.
Scholastic. Sep 29, 1948, v52, p37.
Scholastic. Nov 3, 1948, v53, p22.
Time. Oct 25, 1948, v52, p106.
Variety. Sep 15, 1948, p15.

Applause (US; Mamoulian, Rouben; 1929)
Cinema. Jan 1930, p36-37.
Film Daily. Oct 13, 1929, p8.
The Films of the Twenties. p251-53.
The Hollywood Musical. p33.
Hollywood Musicals. p59-61.

Magill's Survey of Cinema. Series II. v1, p100-03.
Mamoulian (Milne). p17-28.
The Nation. Oct 30, 1929, v129, p503.
The New York Times. Oct 8, 1929, p24.
Selected Film Criticism, 1921-1930. p20-22.
Variety. Oct 9, 1929, p31.

The Arab (US; Ingram, Rex; 1924)
Film Daily. Jul 6, 1924, p8.
The New York Times. Jul 14, 1924, p11.
Photoplay. Sep 1924, v26, p43.
Rex Ingram: Master of the Silent Cinema. p216.
Selected Film Criticism, 1921-1930. p22-23.
Variety. Jul 16, 1924, p22.

Arabian Nights (US; Rawlins, John; 1942)
Commonweal. Jan 15, 1943, v37, p328.
Film Daily. Dec 23, 1942, p6.
Hollywood Reporter. Dec 18, 1942, p3.
Life. Sep 28, 1942, v13, p69-70.
The London Times. Jan 25, 1943, p8.
Motion Picture Exhibitor. Dec 30, 1942, v29, n8, p1181.
The New York Times. Dec 26, 1942, p15.
Time. Jan 11, 1943, v41, p88.
Variety. Dec 23, 1942, p8.

Arch of Triumph (US; Milestone, Lewis; 1948)
Commonweal. May 7, 1948, v48, p80.
Film Daily. Feb 18, 1948, p10.
The Films of Ingrid Bergman. p117-20.
Hollywood Reporter. Feb 18, 1948, p3.
Life. May 3, 1948, v24, p65-66+.
Magill's Cinema Annual. 501-05.
Motion Picture Herald Product Digest. Feb 21, 1948, p4065.
The New Republic. May 3, 1948, v118, p31.
The New York Times. Apr 21, 1948, p33.
The New Yorker. Apr 24, 1948, v24, p59.
Newsweek. Apr 26, 1948, v31, p91.
Time. May 10, 1948, v51, p100+.
Variety. Feb 15, 1948, p8.

Are Parents People? (US; St. Clair, Malcolm; 1925)
Film Daily. Jul 14, 1925, p6.
Magill's Survey of Cinema. Silent Films. v1, p149-51.
The Moving Picture World. Jun 20, 1925, p857.
The New York Times. Jun 9, 1985, p16.
Photoplay. Aug 1925, v28, p50.
Selected Film Criticism, 1921-1930. p23.

Are You a Mason? (US; Heffron, Thomas N.; 1915)
The Moving Picture World. Apr 3, 1915, p70.
The New York Dramatic Mirror. Mar 31, 1915, p28.
Variety. Mar 26, 1915, p24.

Aren't We All? (GB; Lachman, Harry; 1932)
Film Daily. Jul 1, 1932, p6.
Motion Picture Herald. Apr 9, 1932, p24.
Motion Picture Herald. Jul 9, 1932, p36.
The New York Times. Jul 1, 1932, p19.
Time. Jul 11, 1932, v20, p22.
Variety. Jul 5, 1932, p14.

Argent, L' (FR; Herbier, Marcel L'; 1929)
French Cinema. p28-29.
The International Dictionary of Films and Filmmakers. v1, p28-29.
The New York Times. Sep 23, 1968, p42.

Arise My Love (Also titled: Arise, My Love) (US; Leisen, Mitchell; 1940)
The Bright Side of Billy Wilder, Primarily. p65-66.
Commonweal. Nov 8, 1940, v33, p81.
The Film Career of Billy Wilder. p59-61.
Film Daily. Oct 17, 1940, p7.
Halliwell's Hundred. p13-16.
Journey Down Sunset Boulevard. p210-11.
The London Times. Feb 13, 1941, p6.

Magill's Survey of Cinema. Series II. v1, p107-09.
Motion Picture Exhibitor. Oct 30, 1940, p627.
Motion Picture Herald Product Digest. Mar 23, 1941, p76.
The New York Times. Oct 17, 1940, p33.
Photoplay. Oct 1940, v54, p69.
Scribner's Commentator. Dec 1940, v9, p106-07.
Time. Oct 28, 1940, v36, p84.
Variety. Oct 23, 1940, p14.

Arizona (US; Parker, Albert; 1918)
Exhibitor's Trade Review. Dec 21, 1918, p245.
Motion Picture News. Dec 28, 1918, p3957.
The Moving Picture World. Dec 28, 1918, p1559.
Variety. Dec 20, 1918, p36.
Wid's Daily. Dec 15, 1918, p21.

The Arizona Kid (US; Santell, Alfred; 1930)
Commonweal. May 28, 1930, v12, p110.
Film Daily. May 8, 1930, p13.
The Films of Carole Lombard. p73-74.
Life. Jun 6, 1930, v95, p20.
The New York Times. May 17, 1930, p21.
The New York Times. May 25, 1930, p5.
The New Yorker. May 24, 1930, v6, p91.
Time. Jun 2, 1930, v15, p63.
Variety. May 21, 1930, p25.

Arms and the Girl *See* Red Salute

Arroseur Arrose, L' (Also titled: Jardinier, Le) (FR; Lumiere, Louis; 1895)
Behind the Screen. p90-91.
Dictionary of Films. p200-01.
A History of Films. p24, 34, 347.
A Million and One Nights. p238, 320.

Arrowsmith (US; Ford, John; 1931)
Around Cinemas. p62-65.
Cinema, the Magic Vehicle. v1, p210.
Film Daily. Dec 13, 1931, p10.
The Films of Myrna Loy. p127-28.
The Films of Ronald Colman. p143-48.
Hollywood Reporter. Oct 26, 1931, p3.
Hollywood Spectator. Feb 1932, v12, p10.
Hollywood Spectator. Mar 1932, v12, p8-9.
Hygeia. Mar 1932, v10, p224-25.
Judge. Feb 13, 1932, v102, p24.
A Library of Film Criticism: American Film Directors. p118-19.
Lorentz on Film. p85-87.
Magill's Survey of Cinema. Series II. v1, p110-12.
Motion Picture Herald. Nov 21, 1931, p48-49.
The Nation. Dec 23, 1931, v133, p706+.
National Board of Review Magazine. Jan 1932, v7, p10.
The New York Times. Dec 8, 1931, p36.
The New York Times. Dec 13, 1931, p6.
The New Yorker. Dec 19, 1931, v7, p62.
The Non-Western Films of John Ford. p244-46.
Outlook and Independent. Dec 16-23, 1931, v159, p503, 515.
Photoplay. Jan 1932, v41, p47.
Rob Wagner's Script. Apr 30, 1932, v7, p10.
Samuel Goldwyn Presents. p113-15.
Saturday Review (London). Apr 2, 1932, v153, p346.
Selected Film Criticism, 1931-1940. p18-20.
Time. Dec 14, 1931, v18, p26.
Variety. Dec 15, 1931, p14.

Arsenal (Russian title: Vufku; Also titled: The January Uprising in Kiev in 1918) (USSR; Dovzhenko, Alexander; 1929)
BFI/Monthly Film Bulletin. Sep 1977, v44, p200-01.
Film Daily. Nov 17, 1929, p8.
The International Dictionary of Films and Filmmakers. v1, p39-40.
Kino. p252-56.
Magill's Survey of Cinema. Silent Films. v1, p152-54.

The Nation. Nov 27, 1929, v129, p640.
The New York Times. Nov 11, 1929, p20.
Variety. Nov 13, 1929, p18.

Arsene Lupin (US; Conway, Jack; 1932)
Film Daily. Feb 28, 1932, p10.
Hollywood Reporter. Jan 6, 1932, p3.
Judge. Apr 9, 1932, v102, p22.
Magill's Survey of Cinema. Series II. v1, p113-15.
Motion Picture Herald. Jan 16, 1932, p35, 38.
The Nation. Mar 16, 1932, v134, p321.
The New York Times. Feb 27, 1932, p22.
The New Yorker. Mar 5, 1932, v8, p63.
The Spectator. Mar 12, 1932, v148, p365.
Time. Mar 7, 1932, v19, p28.
Variety. Mar 1, 1932, p20.

Arsene Lupin Returns (US; Fitzmaurice, George; 1938)
Film Daily. Jan 25, 1938, p9.
Hollywood Reporter. Jan 21, 1938, p3.
Motion Picture Herald. Jan 29, 1938, p56, 61.
The New York Times. Mar 9, 1938, p21.
Variety. Feb 23, 1938, p14.

Arsenic and Old Lace (US; Capra, Frank; 1944)
Commonweal. Sep 22, 1944, v40, p548.
Film Daily. Sep 1, 1944, p8.
The Films of Cary Grant. p177-79.
The Films of Frank Capra (Scherle and Levy). p187-94.
The Films of Frank Capra (Willis). p114-20.
The Films of Peter Lorre. p168-70.
Hollywood Reporter. Sep 1, 1944, p3.
The London Times. Feb 15, 1945, p6.
Magic and Myth of the Movies. p121-31.
Magill's Survey of Cinema. Series I. v1, p105-08.
Motion Picture Exhibitor. Sep 6, 1944, v32, n17, sec2, p1577-78.
Motion Picture Herald Product Digest. Sep 2, 1944, p2081.
The New York Times. Sep 2, 1944, p17.
Newsweek. Sep 11, 1944, v24, p110.
Photoplay. Nov 1944, v25, p21.
Rob Wagner's Script. Oct 7, 1944, v30, p15.
Scholastic. Sep 18, 1944, v45, p30.
Selected Film Criticism, 1941-1950. p7-8.
Theatre Arts. Oct 1944,, v28, p596.
Time. Sep 11, 1944, v44, p95+.
Variety. Sep 6, 1944, p10.

Artists and Models (US; Walsh, Raoul; 1937)
Film Daily. Aug 5, 1937, p15.
Hollywood Reporter. Aug 3, 1937, p3.
Hollywood Spectator. Aug 14, 1937, v12, p8-9.
Motion Picture Herald. Aug 7, 1937, p45.
The New York Times. Aug 5, 1937, p19.
The New Yorker. Aug 7, 1937, v13, p34.
Rob Wagner's Script. Aug 14, 1937, v17, p18.
Time. Aug 16, 1937, v30, p36.
Variety. Aug 4, 1937, p18.
World Film News. Oct 1937, v2, p23.

Artists and Models Abroad (US; Leisen, Mitchell; 1938)
Commonweal. Jan 13, 1939, v29, p330.
Film Daily. Nov 2, 1938, p4.
Hollywood Director. p123-25.
Hollywood Reporter. Nov 26, 1938, p3.
Hollywood Spectator. Nov 12, 1938, v13, p9-10.
The New York Times. Dec 22, 1938, p25.
Rob Wagner's Script. Jan 7, 1939, v20, p17-18.
Time. Jan 2, 1939, v33, p17.
Variety. Nov 2, 1938, p15.

As You Desire Me (US; Fitzmaurice, George; 1932)
Commonweal. Jun 15, 1932, v16, p188.
Film Daily. Jun 5, 1932, p10.
The Films of Greta Garbo. p115-18.
London Mercury. Oct 1932, v26, p563-64.

Motion Picture Herald. Jun 11, 1932, p29.
The Nation. Jun 22, 1932, v134, p708.
National Board of Review Magazine. Jun 1932, v7, p9.
The New York Times. Jun 3, 1932, p23.
The New Yorker. Jun 11, 1932, v8, p53.
Rob Wagner's Script. Jul 30, 1932, v7, p8.
Time. Jun 6, 1932, v19, p23.
Variety. Jun 7, 1932, p21.
The Village Voice. Jun 10, 1971, v16, p69-70, 73.

As You Like It (US; Griffith, D.W.; 1908)
The Moving Picture World. Oct 3, 1908, p253.
Selected Film Criticism, 1896-1911. p11.

As You Like It (US; Czinner, Paul; 1936)
Around Cinemas. p124-26.
Canadian Magazine. Nov 1936, v86, p36.
Esquire. Mar 1937, v7, p111.
Film Daily. Nov 6, 1936, p13.
The Films of Laurence Olivier. p70-71.
Graham Greene on Film. p98-100.
Hollywood Reporter. Sep 4, 1936, p3.
Hollywood Spectator. Dec 5, 1936, v11, p6-7.
Laurence Olivier (Hirsch). p40-42.
Laurence Olivier: Theater and Cinema. p49-52.
Motion Picture Herald. Sep 19, 1936, p45.
Motion Picture Herald. Jun 13, 1936, p16-17.
The Nation. Nov 21, 1936, v143, p613-14.
National Board of Review Magazine. Dec 1936, v11, p11.
The New Masses. Nov 17, 1936, v21, p29.
The New Statesman and Nation. Sep 12, 1936, v12, p352.
The New York Times. Nov 6, 1936, p29.
The New Yorker. Nov 14, 1936, v12, p96-97.
The Pleasure-Dome. p98-100.
Rob Wagner's Script. Dec 12, 1936, v16, p12-13.
Saturday Review (London). Sep 19, 1936, v162, p377.
Shakespeare and the Film. p30-36.
The Spectator. Sep 11, 1936, v157, p416.
Stage. Dec 1936, v14, p12.
The Tatler. Sep 16, 1936, v141, p516.
Time. Nov 9, 1936, v28, p45.
Variety. Sep 16, 1936, p16.
Variety. Nov 11, 1936, p14.
World Film News. Oct 1936, v1, p22.

The Assassination of the Duke de Guise (French title: Assassinat du Duc de Guise, L') (FR; Le Bargy, Charles; 1908)
Behind the Screen. p108.
Dictionary of Films. p16.
A History of Narrative Film. p52-54.
Magill's Survey of Cinema. Silent Films. v1, p155-57.
The Moving Picture World. Feb 20, 1909, p200.
The Moving Picture World. Mar 13, 1909, p294-95.
Selected Film Criticism, 1896-1911. p11-13.

Astor Battery on Parade (US; 1899)
Film Before Griffith. p48-49.
Mahatma. Feb 1899, p81.

At the Circus (Also titled: The Marx Brothers at the Circus) (US; Buzzell, Edward; 1939)
Film Daily. Nov 17, 1939, p7.
Graham Greene on Film. p257.
Hollywood Reporter. Oct 13, 1939, p3.
Hollywood Spectator. Oct 28, 1939, v14, p8-9.
Life. Dec 4, 1939, v7, p57.
Magill's Survey of Cinema. Series II. v1, p127-30.
Motion Picture Herald. Oct 21, 1939, p36.
The New Statesman and Nation. Dec 16, 1939, v18, p892-93.
The New York Times. Nov 17, 1939, p17.
The New Yorker. Nov 25, 1939, v15, p71.
Newsweek. Oct 30, 1939, v14, p39.
Photoplay. Nov 1939, v53, p64.
Rob Wagner's Script. Oct 28, 1939, v22, p16.

The Spectator. Dec 15, 1939, v163, p864.
Time. Dec 4, 1939, v34, p57.
Variety. Oct 18, 1939, p14.
Why a Duck? p273-76.

At the Rink *See* The Rink

Atalante, L' (Also titled: Chaland qui passe, Le) (FR; Vigo, Jean; 1934)
Cinema Quarterly. Aut 1934, v3, p46-49.
Cinema, the Magic Vehicle. v1, p222-23.
Eighty Years of Cinema. p101.
Film Quarterly. Fall 1985, v29, p21-26.
The Films of Jean Vigo. p97-118.
The Films of My Life. p23-26.
The Golden Age of French Cinema 1929-39. p99-105, 130-31, 139-40.
The Great French Films. p54-57.
Hollywood Reporter. Oct 2, 1947, p3.
The International Dictionary of Films and Filmmakers. v1, p40-41.
Jean Vigo (Sales Gomes). p149-94.
The Nation. Jul 12, 1947, v165, p51-52.
The New York Times. Jun 23, 1947, p14.

Atlantic (German title: Atlantik) (GB; GER; Dupont, E.A.; 1929)
The International Dictionary of Films and Filmmakers. v1, p40-41.
The New York Times. Oct 6, 1929, p21.
Variety. Nov 20, 1929, p12.
Variety. Dec 4, 1929, p15.
Variety. Oct 8, 1930, p22.

Atlantide, L' (FR; Feyder, Jacques; 1921)
BFI/Monthly Film Bulletin. Aug 1979, v46, p185.
Close-Up. Jun 1929, v4, p5-9.

Atlantide, L' (Also titled: Atlantis; German title: Herrin von Atlantis, Die) (GER; Pabst, G.W.; 1932)
Close-Up. Sep 1932, v9, p153-59.
Dictionary of Films. p17-18.
French Film (Sadoul). p62-63.
From Caligari to Hitler. p242-43.
G.W. Pabst. p105-09.
Magill's Survey of Cinema. Foreign Language Films. v1, p170-73.
The New Statesman and Nation. Dec 24, 1932, v4, p833.
The New York Times. Aug 7, 1932, p2.
Variety. Jun 21, 1932, p14.

The Atonement of Gösta Berling (Swedish title: Gösta Berling's Saga) (SWED; Stiller, Mauritz; 1923)
Close-Up. Dec 1933, p327.
Dictionary of Films. p133.
The Films of Greta Garbo. p36-40.
The Great Films. p31-34.
A History of Films. p130.
The History of World Cinema. p82-83, 102.
The International Dictionary of Films and Filmmakers. v1, p181-82.
Magill's Survey of Cinema. Silent Films. v1, p158-61.
Photoplay. Jan 1929, v35, p92.
Selected Film Criticism, 1921-1930. p116.

Attack on a China Mission (GB; Williamson, James; 1901)
Behind the Screen. p106.

Auberge Rouge, L' (FR; Epstein, Jean; 1922)
Cinema, the Magic Vehicle. v1, p82-83.
Variety. Nov, 28, 1951, p6.

Autour D'Une Cabine (FR; Reynaud, Emile; 1894)
Dictionary of Films. p19.

The Avalanche (US; Fitzmaurice, George; 1919)
Exhibitor's Trade Review. Jul 12, 1919, p469.
Motion Picture News. Jul 12, 1919, p593.
The Moving Picture World. Jul 12, 1919, p285.
The New York Times. Jun 30, 1919, p16.
Variety. Jul 4, 1919, p43.
Wid's Daily. Jul 6, 1919, p15.

Avalanche (German title: Sturme Uber Dem Montblanc; Also titled: Storms Over Mont Blanc) (GER; Fanck, Arnold; 1930)
Film Daily. Mar 27, 1932, p23.
From Caligari to Hitler. p257-58.
Leni Riefenstahl (Berg-Pan). p63-64.
The New York Times. Mar 26, 1932, p17.

Avec le Sourire (Also titled: With a Smile) (FR; Tourneur, Maurice; 1939)
Chevalier. p139-41.
Film Daily. Feb 9, 1939, p8.
Motion Picture Herald. Feb 18, 1939, p50, 52.
The New York Times. Feb 6, 1939, p8.
Rob Wagner's Script. Apr 22, 1939, v21, p16.
Variety. Feb 8, 1939, p19.

The Avenging Conscience (US; Griffith, D.W.; 1914)
The Films of D.W. Griffith. p42-45.
Magill's Survey of Cinema. Silent Films. v1, p162-64.
The Moving Picture World. Aug 15, 1914, p936.
The Moving Picture World. Aug 22, 1915, p1150.
The New York Dramatic Mirror. Aug 12, 1914, p28.
Selected Film Criticism, 1912-1920. p7-9.
Variety. Aug 7, 1914, p18.

Avocate d'Amour (Also titled: Counsel for Love; Counsel for Romance) (FR; Ploquin, Raoul; 1938)
Commonweal. Sep 30, 1938, v28, p590.
Film Daily. Sep 14, 1938, p7.
Hollywood Reporter. Sep 14, 1938, p12.
Motion Picture Herald. Sep 24, 1938, p43.
The New York Times. Sep 8, 1938, p27.
Time. Sep 19, 1938, v32, p26.
Variety. Sep 14, 1938, p23.

The Awful Truth (US; McCarey, Leo; 1937)
The Comic Mind. p254.
Commonweal. Nov 5, 1937, v27, p48.
Film Comment. Sep-Oct 1973, v9, p10-11.
The Film Criticism of Otis Ferguson. p205-06.
Film Daily. Oct 11, 1937, p8.
Film Society Review. Oct 1965, p29.
The Films of Cary Grant. p113-15.
The Films of the Thirties. p200-01.
Hollywood Reporter. Oct 6, 1937, p3.
A Library of Film Criticism: American Film Directors. p299-300.
Lunatics and Lovers. p53-58.
Magill's Survey of Cinema, Series I. v1, p109-11.
Motion Picture Herald. Oct 9, 1937, p44.
The Nation. Nov 20, 1937, v145, p567.
The New Republic. Dec 1, 1937, v93, p102.
The New York Times. Nov 5, 1937, p19.
The New Yorker. Nov 13, 1937, v13, p77-78.
Pursuits of Happiness. p229-63.
Reruns. p41-45.
Scholastic. Dec 18, 1937, v31, p36.
Selected Film Criticism, 1931-1940. p20.
The Spectator. Jan 28, 1938, v160, p132.
Stage. Dec 1937, v15, p87.
Stage. May 1938, v15, p26.
Those Fabulous Movie Years: The 30s. p130.
Time. Nov 1, 1937, v30, p45.
Variety. Oct 20, 1937, p12.
World Film News. Mar 1938, v3, p34.

Babbitt (US; Keighley, William; 1934)
The Classic American Novel and the Movies. p226-38.
Film Daily. Dec 15, 1934, p3.
Hollywood Reporter. Nov 7, 1934, p3.
Motion Picture Herald. Nov 17, 1934, p49.
The New York Times. Dec 17, 1934, p24.
Variety. Dec 18, 1934, p13.

The Babe Ruth Story (US; Del Ruth, Roy; 1948)
Film Daily. July 20, 1948, p6.
Motion Picture Herald Product Digest. Jul 24, 1948, p4249.
The New Republic. Aug 9, 1948, v119, p28.
The New York Times. Jul 29, 1948, p17.
The New Yorker. Aug 7, 1948, v24, p63.
Newsweek. Aug 9, 1948, v32, p65.
Variety. Jul 21, 1948, p10.

Babes in Arms (US; Berkeley, Busby; 1939)
Around Cinemas. p171-73.
The Busby Berkeley Book. p124-25.
Commonweal. Oct 27, 1939, v30, p14.
Film Daily. Sep 19, 1939, p7.
Hollywood Reporter. Sep 15, 1939, p3.
Hollywood Spectator. Oct 28, 1939, v14, p7-8.
Judy: The Films and Career of Judy Garland. p73-77.
Life. Nov 6, 1939, v7, p8.
Motion Picture Herald. Sep 23, 1939, p45, 48.
The New Masses. Nov 14, 1939, v33, p30.
The New York Times. Oct 20, 1939, p27.
The New Yorker. Oct 28, 1939, v15, p63-64.
Newsweek. Oct 16, 1939, v14, p43.
Photoplay. Nov 1939, v53, p65.
Rob Wagner's Script. Oct 21, 1939, v22, p16.
Saint Nicholas. Oct 1939, v66, p41.
Scholastic. Oct 30, 1939, v35, p30+.
The Tatler. Jan 24, 1939, v155, p100.
Variety. Sep 20, 1939, p15.

Babes in Toyland (US; Meins, Gus; Rogers, Charles; 1934)
Film Daily. Nov 12, 1934, p11.
The Films of Laurel and Hardy. p160-62.
The Hollywood Musical. p97.
Laurel and Hardy. p277-92.
Life. Feb 1935, v102, p35.
Magill's Survey of Cinema. Series II. v1, p137-40.
Motion Picture Herald. Nov 24, 1934, p36.
The New York Times. Dec 13, 1934, p28.
Rob Wagner's Script. Dec 22, 1934, v12, p8-9.
Selected Film Criticism, 1931-1940. p23.
Time. Dec 10, 1934, v24, p28.
Variety. Dec 18, 1934, p12.

Baby Face (US; Green, Alfred E.; 1933)
Film Daily. Jun 24, 1933, p7.
The Films of Barbara Stanwyck. p88-90.
The Films of the Thirties. p106-07.
Hollywood Reporter. Mar 22, 1933, p3.
Motion Picture Herald. Apr 1, 1933, p24-25.
New Outlook. Aug 1933, v162, p45.
The New York Times. Jun 24, 1933, p16.
The New Yorker. Jul 1, 1933, v9, p45.
Rob Wagner's Script. May 6, 1933, v9, p10.
Starring Miss Barbara Stanwyck. p54-55.
Time. Jul 3, 1933, v22, p30.
Variety. Jun 27, 1933, p15.

Baby Mine (US; Robertson, John S.; Ballin, Hugo; 1917)
Magill's Survey of Cinema. Silent Films. v1, p165-67.
Motion Picture News. Oct 13, 1917, p2581.
The Moving Picture World. Oct 13, 1917, p248.
The New York Dramatic Mirror. Oct 6, 1917, p18.
Selected Film Criticism, 1912-1920. p9.
Variety. Sep 28, 1917, p37.
Wid's Daily. Oct 4, 1917, p633.

The Bachelor and the Bobby Soxer (US; Reis, Irving; 1947)
Canadian Forum. Feb 1948, v27, p255.
Commonweal. Jul 25, 1947, v23, p82.
Film Daily. Jun 4, 1947, p10.
The Films of Cary Grant. p187-89.
The Films of Myrna Loy. p233-34.
The Films of Shirley Temple. p234-37.
Hollywood Reporter. Jun 3, 1947, p3.
Life. Jul 7, 1947, v23, p82.
Magill's Survey of Cinema, Series II. v1, p146-48.
Motion Picture Herald Product Digest. Jun 7, 1947, p3665.
New Republic. Aug 18, 1947, v117, p38.
The New York Times. Jul 25, 1947, p12.
The New Yorker. Aug 2, 1947, v23, p47.
Newsweek. Aug 11, 1947, v30, p88.
Time. Aug 11, 1947, v50, p95.
Variety. Jun 4, 1947, p16.

Bachelor Apartment (US; Sherman, Lowell; 1931)
BFI/Monthly Film Bulletin. May 1981, v48, p98-99.
Film Daily. Mar 8, 1931, p11.
Judge. Jun 6, 1931, v100, p20.
Motion Picture Herald. Feb 28, 1931, p49.
The New York Times. May 16, 1931, p13.
The New York Times. May 24, 1931, p5.
Variety. May 20, 1931, p17.

Bachelor Bait *See* Adventure in Baltimore

The Bachelor Father (US; Leonard, Robert Z.; 1931)
Exhibitors Herald-World. Dec 30, 1930, p31.
Film Daily. Feb 1, 1931, p10.
Judge. Feb 21, 1931, v100, p23.
The New York Times. Feb 2, 1931, p23.
The New York Times. Feb 8, 1931, p5.
Variety. Feb 4, 1931, p16.

Bachelor Mother (US; Kanin, Garson; 1939)
Commonweal. Jul 14, 1939, v30, p300.
The Film Criticism of Otis Ferguson. p261-62.
Film Daily. Jul 3, 1939, p8.
The Films of David Niven. p60-62.
The Films of Ginger Rogers. p152-53.
Hollywood Reporter. Jun 28, 1939, p3.
Life. Jul 3, 1939, v7, p27-29.
Magill's Survey of Cinema. Series II. v1, p149-52.
Motion Picture Herald. Jul 1, 1939, p42.
The Nation. Aug 5, 1939, v149, p155.
The New Republic. Jul 19, 1939, v99, p307.
The New Statesman and Nation. Sep 2, 1939, v18, p342-43.
The New York Times. Jun 30, 1939, p17.
The New Yorker. Jul 1, 1939, v15, p64.
Newsweek. Jul 10, 1939, v14, p32.
Photoplay. Sep 1939, v53, p63.
Rob Wagner's Script. Jul 29, 1939, v21, p16-17.
Talking Pictures. p67-70.
The Tatler. Sep 27, 1939, v153, p542.
Time. Jul 10, 1939, v34, p27.
Variety. Jul 5, 1939, p14.

Back Door to Heaven (US; Howard, William K.; 1939)
Commonweal. May 5, 1939, v30, p49.
Esquire. Aug 1939, v12, p79, 137-38.
Film Daily. Apr 12, 1939, p9.
Hollywood Reporter. Feb 20, 1939, p3.
Motion Picture Herald. Apr 15, 1939, p57, 60.
The New Masses. May 16, 1939, v31, p29-30.
The New York Times. Apr 20, 1939, p21.
The New Yorker. Apr 22, 1939, v15, p67.
Newsweek. Apr 24, 1939, v13, p33.
Time. May 1, 1939, v33, p69.
Variety. Apr 12, 1939, p13.

Back in Circulation (US; Enright, Ray; 1937)
Film Daily. Jul 30, 1937, p10.
Fortune. Dec 1937, v16, p111.
Hollywood Reporter. Jul 27, 1937, p3.
Motion Picture Herald. Aug 7, 1937, p52.
The New York Times. Oct 4, 1937, p17.
The New Yorker. Oct 2, 1937, v13, p60.
Rob Wagner's Script. Oct 9, 1937, v18, p8-9.
Time. Oct 4, 1937, v30, p51.
Variety. Jul 28, 1937, p27.

Back Street (US; Stevenson, Robert; 1941)
Commonweal. Feb 14, 1941, v33, p424.
Film Daily. Feb 5, 1941, p5.
Hollywood Reporter. Feb 5, 1941, p3.
The London Times. May 5, 1941, p8.
Magill's Survey of Cinema. Series II. v1, p153-56.
Motion Picture Exhibitor. Feb 5, 1941, p685.
The New York Times. Feb 12, 1941, p25.
The New York Times. Feb 16, 1941, sec9, p5.
The New Yorker. Feb 8, 1941, v16, p63.
Newsweek. Feb 17, 1941, v17, p65-66.
Scribner's Commentator. Apr 1941, v9, p105.
Time. Feb 24, 1941, v37, p96.
Variety. Feb 12, 1941, p14.

Back Street (US; Stahl, John M.; 1932)
Canadian Forum. Nov 1932, v13, p78-79.
Judge. Oct 1932, v103, p20.
Motion Picture Herald. Jul 23, 1932, p42, 48.
The New York Times. Aug 29, 1932, p9.
Photoplay. Sep 1932, v42, p52.
Rob Wagner's Script. Aug 13, 1932, v8, p8.
Selected Film Criticism, 1931-1940. p24-25.
Time. Aug 8, 1932, v20, p18.
Variety. Aug 30, 1932, p14.

Backstairs (German title: Hintertreppe) (GER; Jessner, Leopold; Leni, Paul; 1921)
Cinema, the Magic Vehicle. v1, p75-76.

Bad Company (US; Garnett, Tay; 1931)
BFI/Monthly Film Bulletin. Jul 1977, v44, p155.
Film Daily. Nov 8, 1931, p10.
Hollywood Reporter. Aug 24, 1931, p3.
Judge. Dec 5, 1931, v100, p20.
Life. Nov 27, 1931, v98, p21.
Motion Picture Herald. Sep 12, 1931, p26.
The New York Times. Nov 7, 1931, p16.
Variety. Nov 10, 1931, p23.

Bad Girl (US; Borzage, Frank; 1931)
Film Daily. Aug 9, 1931, p10.
Hollywood Reporter. Jul 9, 1931, p4.
Hollywood Spectator. Aug 29, 1931, v12, p10-11.
Hollywood Spectator. Sep 26, 1931, v12, p24.
Life. Oct 24, 1930, v96, p18-19.
Motion Picture Herald. Jul 18, 1931, p38.
National Board of Review Magazine. Dec 1931, v6, p8.
National Magazine. Oct-Nov 1931, v59, p453.
The New Statesman and Nation. Sep 26, 1931, v2, p374.
The New York Times. Aug 26, 1937, p25.
The New Yorker. Aug 22, 1931, v7, p44.
Outlook and Independent. Sep 2, 1931, v159, p21.
Rob Wagner's Script. Sep 26, 1931, v6, p10.
Time. Aug 24, 1931, v18, p21.
Vanity Fair. Dec 1930, v35, p46.
Variety. Aug 18, 1931, p30.

The Baker's Wife *See* Femme du Boulanger, La

Balalaika (US; Schunzel, Reinhold; 1939)
Commonweal. Dec 29, 1939, v31, p227.
Film Daily. Dec 15, 1939, p4.
The Films of Jeanette MacDonald and Nelson Eddy. p268-77.
Hollywood Reporter. Dec 14, 1939, p3.

Motion Picture Herald. Dec 23, 1939, p40-41.
The New York Times. Dec 15, 1939, p33.
Time. Jan 1, 1940, v35, p29.
Variety. Dec 20, 1939, p14.

Balked at the Altar (US; Griffith, D.W.; 1908)
D.W. Griffith, His Biograph Films in Perspective. p10-11.
The First Twenty Years. p134-35.

Ball of Fire (US; Hawks, Howard; 1941)
Commonweal. Jan 30, 1942, v35, p369.
The Film Career of Billy Wilder. p63-64.
Film Daily. Dec 2, 1941, p5.
The Films of Barbara Stanwyck. p143-45.
The Films of Gary Cooper. p184-86.
The Films of Howard Hawks (Willis). p30-35.
Hollywood Reporter. Dec 2, 1941, p3.
Life. Dec 15, 1941, v11, p89-92.
The London Times. Mar 20, 1942, p6.
Magill's Survey of Cinema. Series I. v1, p119-22.
Motion Picture Exhibitor. Dec 10, 1941, v17, n5, p904-05.
Motion Picture Herald Product Digest. Dec 6, 1941, p393.
The Nation. Jan 24, 1942, v154, p101.
The New York Times. Jan 16, 1942, p25.
The New York Times. Jan 25, 1942, sec9, p5.
Newsweek. Jan 19, 1942, v19, p58.
Photoplay. Feb 1942, v20, p24.
Rob Wagner's Script. Jan 3, 1942, v27, p16-17.
Samuel Goldwyn (Epstein). p116-17.
Samuel Goldwyn Presents. p220-22.
Selected Film Criticism, 1941-1950. p11.
Starring Miss Barbara Stanwyck. p155-82.
Talking Pictures. p143-45.
Theatre Arts. Feb 1942, v26, p132.
Time. Jan 12, 1942, p70.
Variety. Dec 3, 1941, p8.

Ballerina (FR; Benoit-Levy, Jean; 1938)
Commonweal. Dec 2, 1938, v29, p161.
Current History. Jan 1939, v49, p46.
Film Daily. Nov 9, 1938, p5.
Motion Picture Herald. Dec 3, 1938, p38.
The Nation. Nov 26, 1938, v147, p574.
National Board of Review Magazine. Dec 1938, v13, p18.
The New Masses. Nov 22, 1938, v29, p28-29.
The New Republic. Nov 16, 1938, v97, p46.
The New York Times. Nov 15, 1938, p27.
The New Yorker. Nov 19, 1938, v14, p86-87.
Rob Wagner's Script. May 30, 1939, v21, p18.
Scholastic. Dec 17, 1938, v33, p29.
Time. Nov 28, 1938, v32, p51.
Time. Dec 12, 1938, v32, p39.

Baltic Deputy (Russian title: Deputat Baltiki) (USSR;
   Zarkhi, Alexander; Heifetz, Joseph; 1936)
Cinema, the Magic Vehicle. v1, p258-59.
Film Criticism and Caricatures, 1943-53. p35.
The Film Criticism of Otis Ferguson. p196-97.
Film Daily. Sep 16, 1937, p14.
Kino. p336-37.
Motion Picture Herald. Sep 18, 1937, p44.
National Board of Review Magazine. Oct 1937, v12, p15.
The New Masses. Sep 14, 1937, v24, p28-29.
The New York Times. Sep 4, 1937, p8.
Time. Sep 13, 1937, v30, p32.
Variety. Sep 8, 1937, p19.

Bambi (US; Hand, David; Pearce, Perce; 1942)
The Art of Walt Disney. p255-70.
Commonweal. Aug 7, 1942, v36, p374.
The Disney Films. p49-52.
Film Daily. May 27, 1942, p5.
Hollywood Reporter. May 26, 1942, p3.
Magill's Cinema Annual, 1985. p543-48.
Motion Picture Herald Product Digest. May 30, 1942, p685.
Nature. Aug 1942, v35, p350-52.

Nature. Oct 1942, v35, p441.
The New Republic. Jun 29, 1942, v106, p893.
The New York Times. Aug 14, 1942, p13.
The New York Times Magazine. Jul 12, 1942, p16-17.
The New Yorker. Aug 15, 1942, v18, p53.
Newsweek. Aug 17, 1942, v20, p70.
Selected Film Criticism, 1941-1950. p11-12.
Time. Aug 24, 1942, v40, p78.
Variety. May 27, 1942, p8.
Walt Disney: A Guide to References and Resources. p24-25.

Bandera, La *See* Escape from Yesterday

The Bandit of Sherwood Forest (US; Sherman, George;
   Sanforth, Clifford; 1946)
Commonweal. Mar 29, 1946, v43, p600.
Film Daily. Feb 19, 1946, p10.
Hollywood Reporter. Feb 18, 1946, p3.
The New York Times. Mar 23, 1946, p8.
Newsweek. Apr 8, 1946, v27, p89.
Variety. Feb 20, 1946, p8.

The Bandit Queen *See* Belle Starr

Banjo on My Knee (US; Cromwell, John; 1936)
Film Daily. Dec 1, 1936, p17.
The Films of Barbara Stanwyck. p109-11.
The Hollywood Professionals. v5, p78-80.
Hollywood Reporter. Nov 28, 1936, p3.
Hollywood Spectator. Dec 5, 1936, v11, p8-9.
Motion Picture Herald. Dec 5, 1936, p42.
The New York Times. Dec 12, 1936, p15.
The New Yorker. Dec 19, 1936, v12, p88.
Rob Wagner's Script. Dec 12, 1936, v16, p12.
Starring Miss Barbara Stanwyck. p90.
Time. Dec 21, 1936, v28, p23.
Variety. Dec 16, 1936, p14.

The Bank (US; Chaplin, Charles; 1915)
Chaplin's Films. p93-95.
Charles Chaplin: A Guide to References and Resources. p57.
Essanay News. Aug 28, 1915, p1.
The Films of Charlie Chaplin. p103-05.
Motion Picture News. Aug 28, 1915, p79.
The Moving Picture World. Aug 28, 1915, p1538.
The Silent Clowns. p79-80.
Variety. Aug 20, 1915, p21.

The Bank Dick (US; Cline, Edward; 1940)
American Film Criticism. p406-08.
The Film Criticism of Otis Ferguson. p326-27.
Film Daily. Dec 3, 1940, p11.
The Films of W. C. Fields. p148-53.
Hollywood Reporter. Nov 29, 1940, p3.
Magill's Survey of Cinema. Series I. v1, p129-31.
Motion Picture Exhibitor. Dec 11, 1940, p653.
The New Republic. Dec 20, 1940, v103, p900.
The New York Times. Dec 13, 1940, p29.
The New Yorker. Jun 25, 1949, v25, p77.
Time. Dec 30, 1940, v36, p35.
Variety. Dec 12, 1940, p12.
W.C. Fields: A Life on Film. p217-29.
50 Classic Motion Pictures. p116-21.

Bank Holiday (Also titled: Three on a Weekend) (GB;
   Reed, Carol; 1938)
Cinema, the Magic Vehicle. v1, p299.
The Film Criticism of Otis Ferguson. p232-33.
Film Daily. Jun 1, 1938, p7.
Motion Picture Herald. Mar 26, 1938, p42-43.
The New Republic. Sep 14, 1938, v96, p160.
The New Statesman and Nation. Mar 19, 1938, v15, p479.
The New York Times. Jun 2, 1938, p19.
Variety. Feb 9, 1938, p15.
World Film News. May-Jun 1938, v3, p89.

The Bank Robbery (US; 1908)
The First Twenty Years. p134-35.

Barbara Frietchie (US; Hillyer, Lambert; 1924)
Film Daily. Oct 5, 1924, p4.
Photoplay. Dec 1924, v27, p53.
Selected Film Criticism, 1921-1930. p24.
Variety. Oct 1, 1924, p53.

Barbary Coast (US; Hawks, Howard; 1935)
Canadian Magazine. Oct 1935, v84, p42.
The Cinema of Edward G. Robinson. p105-06.
Film Daily. Sep 24, 1935, p12.
The Films of David Niven. p30.
The Films of Howard Hawks (Willis). p108-09.
Graham Greene on Film. p32.
Hollywood Reporter. Sep 20, 1935, p3.
Howard Hawks (Poague). p88-94.
Howard Hawks, Storyteller. p64-65.
Magill's Cinema Annual, 1984. p506-11.
Motion Picture Herald. Oct 5, 1935, p38.
The New York Times. Oct 14, 1935, p21.
The New Yorker. Oct 26, 1935, v11, p72-73.
Newsweek. Oct 19, 1935, v6, p25.
Rob Wagner's Script. Oct 5, 1935, v14, p14.
Samuel Goldwyn (Epstein). p138-40.
Samuel Goldwyn Presents. p152-54.
Scholastic. Nov 2, 1935, v27, p28.
The Spectator. Nov 1, 1935, v155, p718.
Time. Oct 21, 1935, v26, p45.
Vanity Fair. Nov 1935, v45, p48.
Variety. Oct 16, 1935, p22.

Barbary Sheep (US; Tourneur, Maurice; 1917)
Fifty Great American Silent Films, 1912-1920. p84-85.
Magill's Survey of Cinema. Silent Films. v1, p168-71.
Motion Picture News. Sep 29, 1917, p2205.
The Moving Picture World. Sep 29, 1917, p2004.
The New York Dramatic Mirror. Sep 22, 1917, p18.
The New York Dramatic Mirror. Sep 15, 1917, p16.
Photoplay. Oct 1917, v12, p35.
Selected Film Criticism, 1912-1920. p9-11.
Variety. Sep 14, 1917, p37.
Wid's Daily. Sep 20, 1917, p606.

Bardeleys the Magnificent (US; Vidor, King; 1926)
Film Daily. Oct 17, 1926, p8.
The Moving Picture World. Nov 13, 1926, p103.
The New York Times. Nov 1, 1926, p28.
Photoplay. Nov 1926, v30, p53.
Selected Film Criticism, 1921-1930. p24.
Variety. Oct 13, 1926, p20.

The Bargain (US; Barker, Reginald; 1914)
The Complete Films of William S. Hart. p3-6.
Fifty Great American Silent Films. p15-17.
Magill's Survey of Cinema. Silent Films. v1, p172-74.
The Moving Picture World. Dec 5, 1914, p1390.
The Moving Picture World. Dec 19, 1914, p1746.
The New York Dramatic Mirror. Nov 18, 1914, p32.
Selected Film Criticism, 1912-1920. p11-13.
Variety. Nov 14, 1914, p25.

The Barkleys of Broadway (US; Walters, Charles; 1949)
Commonweal. May 13, 1949, v50, p121.
Film Daily. Apr 11, 1949, p7.
The Films of Ginger Rodgers. p224-25.
The Fred Astaire and Ginger Rodgers Book. p168-80.
The Hollywood Musical. p302.
Hollywood Reporter. Apr 11, 1949, p3.
Life. May 16, 1949, v26, p113.
Motion Picture Herald Product Digest. Apr 16, 1949, p4573.
The New Republic. May 16, 1949, v120, p23.
The New York Times. May 5, 1949, p34.
The New Yorker. May 14, 1949, v25, p106.
Newsweek. May 2, 1949, v33, p83.

Rotarian. Aug 1949, v75, p42.
Starring Fred Astaire. p319-31.
Theatre Arts. Jun 1949, v33, p7.
Time. Apr 25, 1949, v53, p96.
Variety. Apr 13, 1949, p11.

The Barretts of Wimpole Street (US; Franklin, Sidney; 1934)
Christian Century. Mar 6, 1934, v52, p295-97.
Film Daily. Sep 8, 1934, p3.
The Films of Fredric March. p119-22.
The Films of Norma Shearer. p197-201.
Hollywood Reporter. Jul 13, 1934, p3.
Life. Dec 1934, v101, p34-35.
Literary Digest. Oct 13, 1934, v118, p26.
Magill's Survey of Cinema. Series II. v1, p181-83.
Motion Picture Herald. Aug 4, 1934, p30-32.
The Nation. Oct 10, 1934, v139, p419-20.
The New York Times. Sep 29, 1934, p12.
Newsweek. Sep 29, 1934, v4, p28.
Time. Oct 1, 1934, v24, p22.
Variety. Oct 2, 1934, p37.

Barricade (US; Ratoff, Gregory; 1939)
Film Daily. Dec 14, 1939, p8.
The Films of Alice Faye. p119-22.
Hollywood Reporter. Dec 9, 1939, p3.
Hollywood Spectator. Dec 23, 1939, v14, p13.
Motion Picture Herald. Dec 9, 1939, p28.
The New York Times. Dec 9, 1939, p18.
The New Yorker. Dec 16, 1939, v15, p59.
Rob Wagner's Script. Jan 20, 1940, v23, p18.
Variety. Dec 13, 1939, p11.

Bas-Fonds, Les *See* The Lower Depths

The Bat (US; West, Roland; 1926)
Film Daily. Mar 21, 1926, p7.
The New York Times. Mar 15, 1926, p18.
Photoplay. May 1926, v24, p48.
Selected Film Criticism, 1921-1930. p25.
Variety. Mar 17, 1926, p38.

The Bat Whispers (US; West, Roland; 1931)
The Detective in Film. p57, 59.
Exhibitors Herald-World. Nov 15, 1930, p40-41.
Film Daily. Jan 18, 1931, p10.
Life. Feb 6, 1931, v97, p20.
The New Statesman and Nation. Apr 11, 1931, v1, p254.
The New York Times. Jan 16, 1931, p27.
The New York Times. Jan 25, 1931, p5.
The New Yorker. Jun 24, 1931, v6, p55.
Outlook and Independent. Jan 28, 1931, v157, p151.
Time. Jan 26, 1931, v17, p26.
Variety. Jan 21, 1931, p17.

Bataan (US; Garnett, Tay; 1943)
Agee on Film. v1, p43-44+.
Commonweal. Jun 11, 1943, v38, p202.
Film Daily. May 28, 1943, p7.
The Films of Robert Taylor. p101-02.
The Films of World War II. p132-34.
Guts & Glory. p45-48.
Hollywood Reporter. May 26, 1943, p3.
Motion Picture Herald Product Digest. May 29, 1943, p1337.
The New Republic. Jun 21, 1943, v108, p829.
The New York Times. Jun 4, 1943, p17.
The New Yorker. Jun 5, 1943, v19, p48.
Time. Jun 7, 1943, v41, p94.
Variety. May 26, 1943, p8.

Bathing Beauty (US; Sidney, George; 1944)
Basil Rathbone: His Life and His Films. p291-92.
Commonweal. Jul 28, 1944, v40, p353.
Film Daily. May 31, 1944, p7.
Hollywood Reporter. May 26, 1944, p3.

Life. Apr 17, 1944, v16, p77-82.
The Nation. Jul 1, 1944, v159, p24.
The New Republic. Jul 31, 1944, v111, p133.
The New York Times. Jun 28, 1944, p20.
Newsweek. Jul 3, 1944, v24, p81.
Time. Jul 3, 1944, v44, p88.
Variety. May 31, 1944, p20.

The Battle (US; Griffith, D.W.; 1911)
A Million and One Nights. p613.
The Moving Picture World. Nov 4, 1911, p367.
Selected Film Criticism, 1896-1911. p13-14.

The Battle at Elderbush Gulch (Also titled: The Battle of Elderbush Gulch) (US; Griffith, D.W.; 1913)
American Silent Film. p45-46, 72-73.
The Films of D.W. Griffith. p20-23.
Spellbound in Darkness. p105-06.
The Western. p63-66.

The Battle Cry of Peace (US; North, Wilfred; 1915)
Magill's Survey of Cinema. Silent Films. v1, p175-78.
A Million and One Nights. p726-27.
Motion Picture News. Jul 31, 1915, p49.
Motion Picture News. Aug 7, 1915, p19-22.
Motion Picture News. Aug 21, 1915, p82.
Motography. Jul 31, 1915, p216.
Motography. Aug 21, 1915, p361-62.
Motography. Nov 20, 1915, p1089.
The Moving Picture World. Aug 21, 1915, p1291.
The New York Dramatic Mirror. Aug 4, 1915, p24.
The New York Dramatic Mirror. Aug 11, 1915, p28.
The New York Times. Aug 7, 1915, p8.
The New York Times. Sep 15, 1915, p11.
Photoplay. Nov 1915, v8, p80-81.
The Rise of the American Film. p251-52.
Selected Film Criticism, 1912-1920. p13-15.
Variety. Aug 13, 1915, p17.

The Battle Cry of War *See* Whom the Gods Destroy

The Battle in the Clouds (GB; 1909)
The Moving Picture World. Jan 15, 1910, p56.
Selected Film Criticism, 1896-1911. p15.

Battle of Broadway (US; Marshall, George; 1938)
Commonweal. May 6, 1938, v28, p49.
Film Daily. Apr 27, 1938, p24.
Hollywood Reporter. Mar 26, 1938, p3.
Motion Picture Herald. Apr 2, 1938, p40.
The New York Times. Apr 25, 1938, p19.
Time. Apr 25, 1938, v31, p29.
Variety. Apr 27, 1938, p22.

The Battle of Gallipoli *See* Tell England

The Battle of Gettysburg (US; Ince, Thomas H.; 1913)
Motography. Jul 12, 1913, p18.
The Moving Picture World. Apr 26, 1913, p346-47.
The New York Clipper. Nov 29, 1913, p17.
The New York Dramatic Mirror. Jun 4, 1913, p26.
The New York Dramatic Mirror. Jun 11, 1913, p27.
Variety. Jun 27, 1913, p16.

The Battle of Shiloh (US; Smiley, Joseph; Ince, John; 1913)
The Moving Picture World. Nov 22, 1913, p877.
The Moving Picture World. Jan 17, 1914, p334.
The New York Clipper. Jan 17, 1914, p16.
The New York Dramatic Mirror. Jan 7, 1914, p32.

The Battle of the Sexes (Also titled: The Single Standard) (US; Griffith, D.W.; 1914)
The Films of D.W. Griffith. p31-33.
The Moving Picture World. Apr 18, 1914, p424.
The New York Dramatic World. Apr 15, 1914, p50.
Variety. Apr 17, 1914, p21.

The Battle of the Sexes (US; Griffith, D.W.; 1928)
Exhibitor's Herald-World and Moving Picture World. Oct 13, 1928, p46.
Film Daily. Oct 14, 1928, p4.
The Film Spectator. Aug 18, 1928, v6, p6.
The Films of D.W. Griffith. p232-34.
Life. Nov 2, 1928, v92, p28.
The New York Times. Oct 15, 1928, p16.
Outlook. Nov 7, 1928, v150, p1121.
Photoplay. Sep 1928, v34, p56.
Selected Film Criticism, 1921-1930. p26-27.
Variety. Oct 17, 1928, p16.

The Battle of Trafalgar (US; Dawley, J. Searle; 1911)
The Moving Picture World. Sep 9, 1911, p695.
Selected Film Criticism, 1896-1911. p15-16.

Battlefield Scenes (US; 1898)
The George Kleine Collection Catalog. p9.
The New York Clipper. Oct 7, 1899, p652.
The New York Dramatic Mirror. May 7, 1898, p18.

Battleground (US; Wellman, William A.; 1949)
Christian Century. Mar 1, 1950, v67, p287.
Commonweal. Nov 25, 1949, v51, p213.
Film Daily. Sep 28, 1949, p8.
Guts & Glory. p74-81.
Hollywood Reporter. Sep 28, 1949, p3.
Life. Nov 21, 1949, v27, p91-93.
Magill's Survey of Cinema. Series II. v1, p184-86.
Motion Picture Herald. Oct 1, 1949, p33.
The New Republic. Nov 28, 1949, v121, p38.
The New York Times. Nov 12, 1949, p8.
The New Yorker. Nov 19, 1949, v25, p110.
Newsweek. Nov 14, 1949, v34, p88.
Parents Magazine. Nov 1949, v24, p21.
Rotarian. Apr 1950, v76, p38.
Sequence. Sum 1950, v11, p10-11.
Sight and Sound. May 1950, v19, p125-26.
Theatre Arts. Nov 1949, v33, p2.
Time. Nov 14, 1949, v54, p102.
Variety. Sep 28, 1949, p6.
William A. Wellman (Thompson). p224-26.

Battleship Potemkin (Russian title: Bronenosets Potyomkin; Potemkin) (USSR; Eisenstein, Sergei; 1925)
The Cinema 1952. p157-83.
Cinema, the Magic Vehicle. v1, p110-11.
Classic Movies. p14-15.
Close-Up. Nov 1928, p10-12.
Close-Up. Dec 1928, p21-26.
Close-Up. Jul 1928, p213-14.
Close-Up: A Critical Perspective on Film. p23-25.
Eisenstein. p90-113.
Eisenstein's Potemkin. 2304-16.
Film Daily. Dec 19, 1926, p10.
From Quasimodo to Scarlett O'Hara. p75-78.
The International Dictionary of Films and Filmmakers. v1, p69-71.
Kino. p193-199.
Landmark Films. p32-43.
Magill's Survey of Cinema. Silent Films. v2, p880-82.
Masters of the Soviet Cinema. p210-11.
Motion Picture Herald. Apr 15, 1933, v111, p30.
Motion Picture News. Nov 27, 1926, p2025-26.
The Nation. Sep 15, 1926, v123, p252.
The New Republic. Oct 20, 1926, v48, p243-44.
Notes of a Film Director. p18-31.
Presentation of the Best Films of All Time; Universal and International Exhibition of Brussels, 1958. v1, p1-37.
Selected Film Criticism, 1921-1930. p228-30.
Sergei M. Eisenstein: A Biography. p73-95.
S.M. Eisenstein. p77-103.
Spellbound in Darkness. p433.

Variety. Dec 8, 1926, p17.
Variety. Jun 16, 1926, p19.

Battling Butler (US; Keaton, Buster; 1926)
Buster Keaton. p136-42.
Cinema, the Magic Vehicle. v1, p123-24.
The Comic Mind. p134-36.
The Film Career of Buster Keaton. p62-64.
Life. Sep 16, 1926, v88, p24.
Magill's Survey of Cinema. Silent Films. v1, p179-82.
The Moving Picture World. Sep 4, 1926, p43.
The New York Times. Aug 23, 1926, p9.
The Silent Clowns. p143-44.
Variety. Aug 25, 1926, p18.

Be Mine Tonight (GB; Litvak, Anatole; 1933)
Film Daily. Mar 16, 1933, p4.
Hollywood Reporter. Feb 4, 1933, p3.
Life. Jun 1933, v100, p39.
Motion Picture Herald. Feb 18, 1933, p30-31.
The New York Times. Apr 14, 1933, p22.
The New Yorker. Apr 22, 1933, v9, p51.
Rob Wagner's Script. Apr 15, 1933, v9, p8.
Selected Film Criticism, 1931-1940. p10-11.
Time. Apr 24, 1933, v21, p44.
Variety. Apr 18, 1933, p21.

Be Yourself (US; Freeland, Thornton; 1930)
Cinema. May 1930, v1, p37-38.
Exhibitors Herald-World. Mar 15, 1930, p35.
Film Daily. Mar 9, 1930, p4.
The Film Spectator. May 10, 1930, v9, p22.
Judge. Apr 12, 1930, v98, p21.
The New York Times. Mar 7, 1930, p20.
The New Yorker. Mar 15, 1930, v6, p87.
Outlook and Independent. Mar 26, 1930, v154, p513.
Selected Film Criticism, 1921-1930. p28.
Time. Mar 17, 1930, v15, p54.
Variety. Mar 12, 1930, p21.

The Beachcomber (Also titled: Vessel of Wrath) (GB;
    Pommer, Erich; 1938)
Commonweal. Jan 6, 1939, v29, p302.
The Film Criticism of Otis Ferguson. p244-45.
Film Daily. Dec 1, 1938, p5.
Grierson on Documentary. p79-81.
Hollywood Reporter. Nov 23, 1938, p3.
Hollywood Reporter. Apr 1, 1938, p5.
Hollywood Spectator. Dec 10, 1938, v13, p11-12.
Life. Dec 5, 1938, v5, p34-37.
Magill's Survey of Cinema. Series II. v1, p187-89.
Motion Picture Herald. Nov 26, 1938, p24.
Motion Picture Herald. Mar 26, 1938, p42.
Motion Picture Herald. Mar 26, 1938, p42.
The Nation. Jan 7, 1939, v148, p44.
National Board of Review Magazine. Dec 1938, v13, p16.
The New Masses. Dec 27, 1938, v30, p28.
The New Republic. Dec 28, 1938, v97, p231.
The New Statesman and Nation. Mar 5, 1938, v15, p368.
The New York Times. Dec 26, 1938, p29.
The New Yorker. Dec 31, 1938, v14, p48-49.
Newsweek. Dec 26, 1938, v12, p23.
Photoplay. Mar 1939, v53, p52.
Rob Wagner's Script. Feb 11, 1939, v21, p18.
Selected Film Criticism: Foreign Films, 1930-1950. p12-13.
The Spectator. Mar 11, 1938, v160, p426.
The Tatler. Mar 9, 1938, v147, p420.
Time. Jan 2, 1939, v33, p17.
Variety. Nov 30, 1938, p12.
Variety. Mar 16, 1938, p15.
Variety. Mar 16, 1938, p15.
World Film News. Apr 1938, v3, p32, 37.

The Beast of the City (US; Brabin, Charles; 1932)
Crime Movies (Clarens). p76-78.
Film Daily. Mar 13, 1932, p10.

The Films of Jean Harlow. p64-67.
From Quasimodo to Scarlett O'Hara. p154-56.
The Great Gangster Pictures. p31-32.
Hollywood Reporter. Dec 16, 1931, p3.
Judge. Apr 2, 1932, v102, p22.
Motion Picture Herald. Mar 5, 1932, p66.
The Nation. Mar 30, 1932, v134, p380.
National Board of Review Magazine. Mar 1932, v7, p9-13.
The New York Times. Mar 14, 1932, p13.
The New Yorker. Mar 19, 1932, v8, p76-77.
Rob Wagner's Script. May 21, 1932, v7, p10.
Time. Mar 21, 1932, v19, p39.
Variety. Mar 15, 1932, p14.

Beasts of Berlin (Also titled: Hitler, the Beast of Berlin)
    (US; Scott, Sherman; 1939)
Film Daily. Nov 22, 1939, p6.
Motion Picture Herald. Nov 25, 1939, p42.
The New York Times. Nov 20, 1939, p15.
The New Yorker. Nov 25, 1939, v15, p71.
Newsweek. Dec 4, 1939, v14, p37-38.
The Spectator. Apr 5, 1940, v164, p481.
Time. Dec 4, 1939, v34, p82.
Variety. Nov 22, 1939, p16.

Beating Back (US; Fleming, Caryl S.; 1914)
The First Twenty Years. p70.
The Moving Picture World. Jun 12, 1915, p1791.
The New York Dramatic World. Apr 15, 1914, p31.
The War, the West, and the Wilderness. p281-82.

Beau Brummel (US; Beaumont, Harry; 1924)
Film Daily. Apr 13, 1924, p6.
Magill's Survey of Cinema. Silent Films. v1, p183-86.
The New York Times. Mar 31, 1924, p20.
Photoplay. v25, p54.
Selected Film Criticism, 1921-1930. p28-29.
Variety. Apr 24, 1924, p22.

Beau Geste (US; Brenon, Herbert; 1926)
Film Daily. Aug 15, 1926, p6.
The Films of Ronald Colman. p97-102.
Magill's Survey of Cinema. Silent Films. v1, p187-90.
Motion Picture News. Nov 20, 1926, v34, p1933-34.
The Moving Picture World. Sep 4, 1926, p40.
The New York Times. Aug 26, 1926, p17.
Photoplay. Nov 1926, v30, p52.
Selected Film Criticism, 1921-1930. p29.
Spellbound in Darkness. p428-29.
Variety. Sep 1,1926, p14.

Beau Geste (US; Wellman, William A.; 1939)
Commonweal. Aug 11, 1939, v30, p380.
Esquire. Nov 1939, v12, p101.
The Film Criticism of Otis Ferguson. p263-64.
Film Daily. Jul 24, 1939, p7.
The Films of Gary Cooper. p162-65.
The Films of Susan Hayward. p52-54.
Graham Greene on Film. p237-38.
The Great Adventure Films. p96-99.
Hollywood Reporter. Jul 19, 1939, p3.
Hollywood Spectator. Aug 5, 1939, v14, p7-8.
Magill's Survey of Cinema, Series I. v1, p135-40.
Motion Picture Herald. Jul 22, 1939, p48.
Nation. Aug 19, 1939, v149, p205.
The New Republic. Aug 9, 1939, v100, p20.
The New Statesman and Nation. Aug 12, 1939, v18, p244.
The New York Times. Aug 3, 1939, p15.
The New Yorker. Aug 5, 1939, v15, p59-60.
Newsweek. Aug 7, 1939, v14, p40-41.
Photoplay. Oct 1939, v53, p64.
Rob Wagner's Script. Sep 9, 1939, v22, p22.
Saint Nicholas. Sep 1939, v61, p39.
The Spectator. Aug 11, 1939, v163, p217.
The Tatler. Sep 6, 1939, v153, p420.
Time. Aug 14, 1939, v34, p33.

Variety. Jul 26, 1939, p15.
William A. Wellman (Thompson). p181-88.

The Beautiful Blonde From Bashful Bend (US; Sturges, Preston; 1949)
Between Flops. p226-27, 238-41.
Film Daily. May 31, 1949, p6.
The Hollywood Musical. p30.
Hollywood Reporter. May 25, 1949, p3.
Motion Picture Herald Product Digest. May 28, 1949, p4626.
The New York Times. May 28, 1949, p11.
The New Yorker. Jun 11, 1949, v25, p85.
Newsweek. Jun 6, 1949, v33, p80.
Preston Sturges: A Guide to References and Resources. p80-81.
Rotarian. Sep 1949, v75, p37.
Time. Jun 6, 1949, v53, p94.
Variety. May 25, 1949, p8.

Beauty and the Beast (French title: Belle et la Bête, La) (FR; Cocteau, Jean; 1947)
Classics of the Foreign Film. p170-71.
Commonweal. Dec 12, 1947, v47, p227.
Film Daily. Jan 15, 1948, p9.
Films and Filming. Jun 1964, v10, p27-28.
Films and Filming. Jun 1964, v10, p27-28.
The Great French Films. p114-17.
Hollywood Reporter. Dec 5, 1947, p3.
The International Dictionary of Films of Filmmakers. v1, p48-49.
Jean Cocteau (Gilson). p44-63.
Jean Cocteau: Three Screenplays. p.
Life. Dec 29, 1947, v23, p61.
Magill's Survey of Cinema. Foreign Language Films. v1, p243-47.
New Republic. Dec 29, 1947, v117, p35.
The New York Times. Dec 24, 1947, p12.
The New Yorker. Dec 20, 1947, v23, p56.
Newsweek. Dec 29, 1947, v30, p68.
Sequence. Spr 1948, n3, p28-30.
Theatre Arts. Jan 1948, v32, p20-26.
Time. Dec 29, 1947, v50, p62.
Variety. Dec 24, 1947, p13.

Beauty for the Asking (US; Tryon, Glenn; 1939)
Commonweal. Feb 24, 1939, v29, p497.
Film Daily. Feb 16, 1939, p6.
Hollywood Reporter. Jan 20, 1939, p3.
Hollywood Spectator. Feb 4, 1939, v13, p15-16.
The New York Times. Feb 10, 1939, p19.
Variety. Feb 15, 1939, p13.

Becky Sharp (US; Mamoulian, Rouben; 1935)
American Cinematographer. Nov 1984, v65, p99-108.
Catholic World. Sep 1935, v141, p727-28.
Cinema Quarterly. Sum 1935, v3, p231-33.
Commonweal. Jun 28, 1935, v22, p243.
Commonweal. Jul 26, 1935, v22, p316.
The English Novel and the Movies. p108-20.
Esquire. Aug 1935, v4, p153, 162.
The Film Criticism of Otis Ferguson. p80-81.
Film Daily. Jun 14, 1935, p11.
Garbo and the Night Watchman. p55-56.
Graham Greene on Film. p8.
Hollywood Reporter. Jun 14, 1935, p3.
Judge. Aug 1935, v109, p12, 30.
Life. Aug 1935, v102, p43, 45.
Literary Digest. Jun 8, 1935, v119, p26.
London Mercury. Aug 1935, v32, p376.
Magill's Cinema Annual, 1982. p403-07.
Mamoulian (Milne). p91-100.
Motion Picture. Apr 1935, v49, p37.
Motion Picture Herald. Jun 22, 1935, p70.
Movie Classic. Sep 1935, v9, p18.
The Nation. Jul 3, 1935, v141, p28.
The New Masses. Jul 2, 1935, v16, p44.

The New Republic. Jun 26, 1935, v83, p194.
The New York Times. Jun 14, 1935, p27.
The New Yorker. Jun 22, 1935, v11, p53.
Newsweek. Jun 22, 1935, v5, p22-23.
Photoplay. Aug 1935, v48, p24-25+.
Rob Wagner's Script. Jun 29, 1935, v13, p10.
Scholastic. May 11, 1935, v26, p28.
Selected Film Criticism, 1931-1940. p26-28.
The Spectator. Nov 22, 1935, v155, p864.
Stage. Jul 1935, v12, p36-40.
The Tatler. Jun 9, 1937, v144, p468.
Time. May 27, 1935, v25, p28.
Vanity Fair. Aug 1935, v44, p44.
Variety. Jun 19, 1935, p21.

Bed of Roses (US; La Cava, Gregory; 1933)
BFI/Monthly Film Bulletin. Mar 1977, v44, p55-56.
Film Daily. Jul 1, 1933, p3.
Hollywood Reporter. May 31, 1933, p3.
Motion Picture Herald. Jul 8, 1933, p42.
New Outlook. Aug 1933, v162, p45.
The New York Times. Jun 30, 1933, p20.
Newsweek. Jul 8, 1933, v1, p32.
Rob Wagner's Script 3b Jul 22, 1933. v9, p8.
Time. Jul 10, 1933, v22, p41.
Variety. Jul 4, 1933, p16.

Bedelia (GB; Comfort, Lance; 1946)
Around Cinemas, Second Series. p269-70.
Commonweal. Feb 21, 1947, v45, p469.
Film Daily. Jan 30, 1947, p3.
Hollywood Reporter. Jan 29, 1947, p3.
Motion Picture Herald Product Digest. Feb 1, 1947, p3445.
The New York Times. Feb 8, 1947, p10.
The New Yorker. Feb 22, 1947, v22, p87.
Newsweek. Feb 10, 1947, v29, p92.
Time. Jan 27, 1947, v49, p97.
Variety. Jun 5, 1946, p13.

Bedlam (GB; Robson, Mark; 1946)
Agee on Film. v1, p192.
BFI/Monthly Film Bulletin. Nov 1974, v41, p260.
Boris Karloff and His Films. p135-36, 143-46.
Film Daily. May 9, 1946, p6.
The Films of Boris Karloff. p194-97.
Hollywood Reporter. Apr 19, 1946, p3.
Motion Picture Herald Product Digest. Apr 27, 1946, p2962.
The Nation. Mar 23, 1946, v162, p354.
The New York Times. Apr 20, 1946, p16.
Time. May 27, 1946, p97.
Variety. Apr 24, 1946, p8.

Bedside (US; Florey, Robert; 1934)
Film Daily. Mar 6, 1934, p11.
The New York Times. Mar 7, 1934, p23.
Variety. Mar 13, 1934, p16.

A Bedtime Story (US; Taurog, Norman; 1933)
Chevalier. p114-17.
Film Daily. Apr 22, 1933, p4.
Hollywood Reporter. Apr 4, 1933, p3.
Motion Picture Herald. Apr 27, 1933, p28.
The New York Times. Apr 20, 1933, p20.
The New Yorker. Apr 29, 1933, v9, p44.
Newsweek. Apr 29, 1933, v1, p26.
Rob Wagner's Script. Apr 15, 1933, v9, p8.
Time. May 1, 1933, v21, p36.
Vanity Fair. Jun 1933, v40, p38.
Variety. Apr 25, 1933, p15.

Beethoven *See* Grande Amour de Beethoven, Une

Beethoven Concerto (USSR; Schmidthof, V.; Gavronsky, M.; 1937)
Commonweal. Apr 30, 1937, v26, p20.
Film Daily. Mar 30, 1937, p11.

Motion Picture Herald. Apr 10, 1937, p68, 70.
The New Masses. Apr 6, 1937, v23, p27.
The New York Times. Mar 24, 1937, p29.
Rob Wagner's Script. May 8, 1937, v17, p8-9.
Scholastic. Apr 24, 1937, v30, p28.
Variety. Mar 31, 1937, p19.

Beethoven's Great Love *See* Grande Amour de Beethoven, Une

Beggar on Horseback (US; Cruze, James; 1925)
Film Daily. Jun 14, 1925, p6.
Life. Jun 1925, v85, p24.
Magill's Survey of Cinema. Silent Films. v1, p191-94.
The Moving Picture World. Jun 20, 1925, p859.
The New York Times. Jun 6, 1925, p9.
Photoplay. Jul 1925, p50.
Selected Film Criticism, 1921-1930. p29-31.
Variety. Jun 10, 1925, p37.

Beggars of Life (US; Wellman, William A.; 1928)
Exhibitor's Herald-World and Moving Picture World. Oct 20, 1928, p51.
Film Daily. Sep 30, 1928, p8.
The Film Spectator. Oct 27, 1928, v6, p6-7.
The Films of the Twenties. p206-08.
Magill's Survey of Cinema. Silent Films. v1, p195-98.
The New York Times. Sep 24, 1928, p25.
Selected Film Criticism, 1921-1930. p31-32.
Variety. Sep 26, 1928, p14.
William A. Wellman (Thompson). p79-84, 92-94.

The Beggar's Opera *See* The Three Penny Opera

Behind Office Doors (US; Brown, Melville; 1931)
Film Daily. Mar 22, 1931, p10.
Judge. Apr 18, 1931, v100, p20, 22.
The New York Times. Mar 21, 1931, p5.
Variety. Mar 25, 1931, p24.

Behind the Door (US; Willat, Irvin; 1920)
Fifty Great American Silent Films, 1912-1920. p118-20.
The Moving Picture World. Jan 10, 1920, p300.
Selected Film Criticism, 1912-1920. p15-16.
Variety. Jan 31, 1920, p56.
Wid's Daily. Jan 4, 1920, p11.

Behold My Wife (US; Leisen, Mitchell; 1935)
Film Daily. Feb 16, 1935, p7.
Hollywood Director. p83-86.
Motion Picture Herald. Feb 23, 1935, p59.
The New York Times. Feb 18, 1935, p19.
Variety. Feb 20, 1935, p15.

A Bell for Adano (US; King, Henry; 1945)
Commonweal. Jul 27, 1945, v42, p358.
Film Daily. Jun 21, 1945, p8.
Hollywood Reporter. Jun 20, 1945, p3.
The New York Times. Jul 6, 1945, p8.
The New York Times Magazine. May 20, 1945, p17.
The New Yorker. Jul 14, 1945, v21, p35.
Newsweek. Jul 16, 1945, v26, p101.
Theatre Arts. Oct 1945, v29, p582-83.
Time. Jul 2, 1945, v46, p86.
Variety. Jun 20, 1945, p11.

Bella Donna (US; Porter, Edwin S.; Ford, Hugh; 1915)
Motion Picture News. Sep 18, 1915, p66.
Motion Picture News. Nov 27, 1915, p94.
Motography. Nov 13, 1915, p1022.
Motography. Dec 4, 1915, p1193, 1211.
The Moving Picture World. Nov 20, 1915, p1510.
The Moving Picture World. Nov 27, 1915, p1730.
The New York Dramatic Mirror. Nov 27, 1915, p28.
The New York Times. Nov 15, 1915, p11.
Photoplay. Feb 1916, v9, p105.

Selected Film Criticism, 1912-1920. p16.
Variety. Nov 19, 1915, p23.

Bella Donna (US; Fitzmaurice, George; 1923)
Film Daily. Apr 22, 1923, p2.
Magill's Survey of Cinema. Silent Films. v1, p199-201.
The New York Times. Apr 16, 1923, p20.
Photoplay. Jun 1923, v24 p64.
Selected Film Criticism, 1921-1930. p33-34.
Variety. Apr 19, 1923, p35.

Belle Équipe, La (Also titled: They Were Five) (FR; Duvivier, Julien; 1936)
Cinema, the Magic Vehicle. v1, p264-65.
Commonweal. Jun 24, 1938, v28, p245.
Dictionary of Films. p28.
Film Daily. Jun 8, 1938, p6.
The Golden Age of French Cinema, 1929-1939. p115-18.
Motion Picture Herald. Jun 18, 1938, p39.
The New Masses. Jun 14, 1938, v27, p31.
The New Statesman and Nation. Jan 15, 1938, v15, p82-83.
The New York Times. Jun 1, 1938, p19.
Time. Jun 13, 1938, v31, p24.
Variety. Oct 7, 1936, p15.

Belle et la Bête, La *See* Beauty and the Beast

Belle Nivernaise, La (FR; Epstein, Jean; 1923)
Cinema, the Magic Vehicle. v1, p92.

Belle of the Nineties (Also titled: Belle of the 90's) (US; McCarey, Leo; 1934)
Film Daily. Sep 6, 1934, p7.
The Films of Mae West. p91-103.
The Hollywood Musical. p92.
Hollywood Reporter. Aug 18, 1934, p3.
Literary Digest. Oct 6, 1934, v118, p32.
Motion Picture Herald. Aug 25, 1934, p31-35.
The New Republic. Oct 24, 1934, v80, p310.
The New York Times. Sep 22, 1934, p12.
Newsweek. Sep 29, 1934, v4, p28.
Time. Sep 24, 1934, v24, p34.
Variety. Sep 25, 1934, p13.

Belle Starr (Also titled: The Bandit Queen) (US; Cummings, Irving; 1941)
Film Daily. Aug 22, 1941, p5.
Hollywood Reporter. Aug 22, 1941, p3.
The London Times. Feb 16, 1942, p8.
Motion Picture Exhibitor. Sep 3, 1941, p835.
Motion Picture Herald Product Digest. Jun 14, 1941, p161.
The New York Times. Nov 1, 1941, p20.
Newsweek. Sep 29, 1941, v18, p55-56.

The Bells of St. Mary's (US; McCarey, Leo; 1945)
Commonweal. Dec 28, 1945, v43, p288.
Film Daily. Nov 23, 1945, p6.
The Films of Bing Crosby. p153-56.
The Films of Ingrid Bergman. p101-04.
Harper's Bazaar. Jun 1945, v79, p65.
Hollywood Reporter. Nov 23, 1945, p3.
Hollywood Review. Nov 26, 1945, v32, p1+.
The London Times. Mar 22, 1946, p6.
Magill's Survey of Cinema. Series II. v1, p196-98.
Motion Picture Exhibitor. Nov 28, 1945, v35, n4, sec2, p1836-87.
Motion Picture Herald Product Digest. Dec 1, 1945, p2734.
The New York Times. Dec 7, 1945, p26.
The New Yorker. Dec 8, 1945, v21, p87.
Newsweek. Dec 17, 1945, v26, p118-19.
Photoplay. Feb 1946, v28, p22.
Rob Wagner's Script. Jan 5, 1945, v32, p14-15.
Scholastic. Dec 10, 1945, v47, p36.
Selected Film Criticism, 1941-1950. p12-14.
Talking Pictures. p233-34.
Theatre Arts. Jan 1946, v30, p48-50.

Time. Dec 10, 1945, v46, p94+.
Variety. Nov 28, 1945, p10.
Visions of Yesterday. p260-62.

The Beloved Bachelor (US; Corrigan, Lloyd; 1931)
Film Daily. Oct 18, 1931, p10.
Hollywood Reporter. Sep 29, 1931, p4.
Life. Nov 6, 1931, v98, p19.
Motion Picture Herald. Oct 3, 1931, p33.
The New York Times. Oct 17, 1931, p20.
Variety. Oct 20, 1931, p27.

The Beloved Brat (US; Lubin, Arthur; 1938)
Film Daily. May 5, 1938, p6.
Hollywood Reporter. Feb 10, 1938, p2.
The New York Times. May 2, 1938, p13.
The New Yorker. May 7, 1938, v14, p66-67.

The Beloved Brute (US; Blackton, J. Stuart; 1924)
Film Daily. Nov 16, 1924, p7.
The Moving Picture World. Nov 2, 1924, p359.
The New York Times. Nov 10, 1924, p20.
Variety. Nov 12, 1924, p25.

Beloved Enemy (US; Potter, H.C.; 1936)
Canadian Magazine. Mar 1937, v87, p25.
Commonweal. Jan 15, 1937, v25, p333.
Esquire. Mar 1937, v7, p111, 188-89.
Film Daily. Dec 12, 1936, p3.
The Films of David Niven. p40-41.
Hollywood Reporter. Dec 9, 1936, p2.
Hollywood Spectator. Dec 19, 1936, v11, p10-11.
Life. Dec 21, 1936, v1, p48-49.
Motion Picture Herald. Dec 19, 1936, p54.
The New Masses. Jan 5, 1937, v22, p27-28.
The New York Times. Dec 26, 1936, p15.
Newsweek. Jan 2, 1937, v9, p23.
Rob Wagner's Script. Jan 23, 1937, v16, p10.
Samuel Goldwyn Presents. p172-74.
Scholastic. Jan 16, 1937, v29, p24.
Time. Jan 4, 1937, v29, p21.
Variety. Dec 30, 1936, p10.
World Film News. Mar 1937, v1, p25.

The Beloved Rogue (US; Crosland, Alan; 1927)
Magill's Cinema Annual, 1984. p522-25.
The Moving Picture World. Apr 2, 1927, p503-06.
The New York Times. Mar 14, 1927, p16.
Photoplay. June 1927, v32, p139.
Selected Film Criticism, 1921-1930. p33.
Variety. Mar 16, 1927, p17.

The Beloved Vagabond (French title: Vagabond Bien-Aimé, Le) (GB; Bernhardt, Curtis; 1936)
Chevalier. p142-45.
Film Daily. Feb 9, 1937, p8.
Motion Picture Herald. Nov 26, 1936, p42-43.
The New York Times. Feb 8, 1937, p12.
Variety. Sep 9, 1936, p17.
Variety. Feb 10, 1937, p15.

Ben-Hur (US; Niblo, Fred; 1925)
A Dictionary of Film. p29-30.
Film Daily. Jan 24, 1926, p4.
Film Daily. Dec 6, 1931, p10.
The Films of the Twenties. p133-35.
A History of Narrative Film. p221, 246.
The History of World Cinema. p109.
Life. Apr 8, 1926, v85, p32.
Literary Digest. Feb 6, 1926, v88, p29.
Magill's Survey of Cinema. Silent Films. v1, p202-08.
A Million and One Nights. p462, 463, 757.
The New York Times. Dec 31, 1925, Addenda p10.
The New York Times. Nov 1, 1925, sec8, p5.
The New Yorker. Jan 9, 1926, v1, p30.
Photoplay. Mar 1926, v24, p54.

Spellbound in Darkness. p404-05.
Variety. Jan 6, 1926, p38.

Berge in Flammen *See* The Doomed Battalion

Berkeley Square (US; Lloyd, Frank; 1933)
The Age of the Dream Palace. p239-40.
Canadian Magazine. Nov 1933, v80, p34-35.
Commonweal. Nov 24, 1933, v19, p103.
Film Daily. Sep 15, 1933, p11.
Hollywood Reporter. Jun 24, 1933, p3.
Literary Digest. Sep 30, 1933, v116, p32.
Love in the Film. p108-10.
Motion Picture Herald. Jul 22, 1933, p53.
The Nation. Sep 27, 1933, v137, p363-64.
National Board of Review Magazine. Nov 1933, v8, p8.
New Outlook. Oct 1933, v162, p48.
The New York Times. Sep 14, 1933, p26.
The New Yorker. Sep 23, 1933, v9, p58-59.
Newsweek. Sep 23, 1933, v2, p32.
Photoplay. Oct 1933, v44, p11+.
Rob Wagner's Script. Nov 25, 1933, v10, p8.
Sociology and Social Research. Jan 1934, v18, p298.
Time. Sep 25, 1933, v22, p32.
Vanity Fair. Nov 1933, v41, p56.
Variety. Sep 19, 1933, p13.

Berlin Express (US; Tourneur, Jacques; 1948)
Film Daily. Apr 6, 1948, p8.
Motion Picture Herald Product Digest. Apr 10, 1948, p4118.
The New Republic. May 31, 1948, v118, p37.
The New York Times. May 21, 1948, p19.
Newsweek. May 31, 1948, v31, p72.
Time. May 3, 1948, v50, p105.
Variety. Apr 7, 1948, p10.

The Best Years of Our Lives (US; Wyler, William; 1946)
Agee on Film. v1, p229-37, 255.
American Film and Society Since 1945. p18-21.
Cinema. Jun 1947, v1, p15.
Cinema, the Magic Vehicle. v1, p422-23.
Classic Movies. p150-52.
Commonweal. Dec 13, 1946, v45, p230.
Film Daily. Nov 22, 1946, p7.
The Films of Fredric March. p188-91.
The Films of Myrna Loy. p227-30.
The Films of World War II. p244-46.
Fortnight. Dec 2, 1946, v1, p42.
The Great Films. p177-80.
The Great Hollywood Movies. p114-15.
Hollywood Quarterly. Apr 1947, v2, p257-60.
Hollywood Reporter. Nov 22, 1946, p3.
The Hollywood Social Problem Films. p230-33.
The International Dictionary of Films and Filmmakers. v1, p50-51.
Life. Dec 16, 1946, v21, p71-73.
Magill's Survey of Cinema. Series I. v1, p155-58.
Motion Picture Herald Product Digest. Nov 30, 1946, p335.
The Nation. Dec 7-14, 1946, v163, p672-73, 708-710.
The New Republic. Dec 2, 1946, v115, p723.
The New York Times. Nov 22, 1946, p27.
The New York Times Magazine. Nov 17, 1946, p26-27.
The New Yorker. Nov 23, 1946, v22, p75.
Newsweek. Nov 25, 1946, v28, p104+.
Partisan Review. May-Jun 1947, v14, p305-09.
Samuel Goldwyn. p150-65.
Samuel Goldwyn Presents. p246-50.
Saturday Review. Mar 13, 1954, v37, p28.
Selected Film Criticism, 1941-1950. p15-19.
Sight and Sound. Wint 1946-47, v15, p140.
Theatre Arts. Jan 1947, v31, p38-40.
Time. Nov 25, 1946, v48, p103.
Variety. Nov 27, 1946, p14.
The Village Voice. Jul 15, 1965, p11.
When Hollywood Ruled the Skies. p119-22.

William Wyler: A Guide to References and Resources. p117-21.
William Wyler (Anderegg). p126-46.
William Wyler (Madsen). p266-69, 257-58+.

Bête Humaine, La (Also titled: The Human Beast; Judas Was a Woman) (FR; Renoir, Jean; 1938)
Cinema, the Magic Vehicle. v1, p296-97.
Commonweal. Mar 8, 1940, v31, p435.
Dictionary of Films. p31-32.
Films and Filming. Feb 1964, v10, p4.
Films and Filming. Feb 1964, v10, p14.
Films in Review. Apr 1963, v14, p200-01.
The Films of My Life. p40-42.
From Quasimodo to Scarlett O'Hara. p348-50.
Graham Greene on Film. p220.
The Great French Films. p245-46.
Jean Renoir (Durgnat). p172-84.
Jean Renoir: My Life and My Films. p137-39.
Jean Renoir: The French Films, 1924-1939. p351-77.
Life and Letters To-day. Jul 1939, v22, p116-18.
Magill's Survey of Cinema. Foreign Language Films. v1, p272-76.
Motion Picture Herald. Apr 1, 1939, p30.
National Board of Review Magazine. Mar 1940, v15, p15.
The New Masses. Mar 12, 1940, v24, p28-29.
The New Republic. Mar 11, 1940, v102, p346.
The New York Times. Feb 26, 1939, p5.
Saturday Review. May 11, 1940, v22, p21.
Selected Film Criticism: Foreign Films, 1930-1950. p80.
Sight and Sound. Sum 1939, v8, p79.
The Spectator. May 5, 1939, v162, p760.
The Tatler. Apr 26, 1939, v152, p148.
Time. Mar 4, 1940, v35, p68.
Variety. Feb 15, 1939, p13.

Betrayal (US; Milestone, Lewis; 1929)
Film Daily. May 12, 1929, p8.
The Films of Gary Cooper. p65-67.
The New York Times. Apr 29, 1929, p29.
Variety. May 8, 1929, p17.

Betrayal (FR; Ozep, Fedor; 1939)
Film Daily. Sep 21, 1939, p7.
Motion Picture Herald. Sep 23, 1939, p48.
The New York Times. Sep 16, 1939, p20.
The New Yorker. Sep 30, 1939, v15, p57.
Variety. Sep 20, 1939, p27.

The Better 'Ole (Also titled: Carry On) (GB; Pearson, George; 1918)
Motion Picture News. Mar 8, 1919, p1541.
The Moving Picture World. Mar 8, 1919, p1392-93.
The New York Times. Feb 24, 1919, p11.
Photoplay. Jul 1919, v16, p119-20.
Selected Film Criticism, 1912-1920. p16-17.
Variety. Feb 28, 1919, p58-59.
Wid's Daily. Mar 9, 1919, p23-24.

Between Two Women (US; Seitz, George B.; 1937)
Film Daily. Jun 29, 1937, p10.
Hollywood Reporter. Jun 25, 1937, p3.
Motion Picture Herald. Jul 3, 1937, p45.
The New York Times. Aug 6, 1937, p21.
Rob Wagner's Script. Aug 14, 1937, v17, p17.
Variety. Aug 11, 1937, p19.

Beyond the Forest (US; Vidor, King; 1949)
Bette Davis: Her Films and Her Career. p121-24.
Film Daily. Oct 19, 1949, p4.
Hollywood Reporter. Oct 18, 1949, p3.
Motion Picture Herald. Oct 22, 1949, p59.
The New York Times. Oct 22, 1949, p11.
The New Yorker. Oct 29, 1949, v25, p100.
Newsweek. Oct 31, 1949, v34, p67.
Rotarian. Feb 1950, v76, p38.

Senior Scholastic. Nov 9, 1949, v55, p29.
Time. Oct 31, 1949, v54, p76.
Variety. Oct 19, 1949, p8.

Beyond the Rocks (US; Wood, Sam; 1922)
Film Daily. May 14, 1922, p3.
The New York Times. May 8, 1922, p14.
Photoplay. Jul 1922, v22, p54.
Selected Film Criticism, 1921-1930. p35.
Variety. May 12, 1922, p32.

Beyond Victory (US; Robertson, John S.; 1931)
BFI/Monthly Film Bulletin. Sep 1978, v45, p184-85.
Film Daily. Apr 12, 1931, p32.
Hollywood Reporter. Apr 10, 1931, p6.
Motion Picture Herald. Apr 18, 1931, p40.
The New York Times. Apr 6, 1931, p24.
Time. Apr 20, 1931, v17, p28.
Variety. Apr 8, 1931, p19.

Bezhin Meadow (Russian title: Bezhin Lug) (USSR; Eisenstein, Sergei; 1937)
Cinema, the Magic Vehicle. v1, p271-73.
The Complete Films of Eisenstein. p89-97.
Eisenstein at Work. p85-95.
Film Society Review. Oct 1967, p15-17.
Kino. p327-34, 338-39.
Sight and Sound. Spr 1959, v28, p74-77.
Sight and Sound. Wint 1967-68, v37, p33-37.
Time. Mar 29, 1937, v29, p52.

B.F.'s Daughter (US; Leonard, Robert Z.; 1948)
Film Daily. Feb 17, 1948, p6.
The Films of Barbara Stanwyck. p186-89.
Hollywood Reporter. Feb 17, 1948, p3.
Motion Picture Herald Product Digest. Feb 21, 1948, p4066.
The New Republic. Apr 12, 1948, v118, p21.
The New York Times. Mar 25, 1948, p35.
The New Yorker. Apr 3, 1948, v24, p59.
Newsweek. Apr 12, 1948, v31, p88.
Starring Miss Barbara Stanwyck. p203-07.
Time. Apr 26, 1948, v51, p99.
Variety. Feb 18, 1948, p8.

Bicycle Thief (Italian title: Ladri di Biciclette; Also titled: The Bicycle Thieves) (IT; Da Sica, Vittorio; 1949)
Bicycle Thieves. p28+.
Christian Century. Mar 15, 1950, v67, p351.
Cinema, the Magic Vehicle. v1, p465-66.
Classic Movies. p153.
Classics of the Foreign Film. p178-81.
Commonweal. Dec 23, 1949, v51, p319.
Cue. Dec 17, 1949, p24.
Dictionary of Films. p183-84.
Film Daily. Dec 21, 1949, p7.
Films in Review. Feb 1950, v1, p31-32.
Fortnight. Jan 6, 1950, v8, p30.
Hollywood Reporter. Dec 27, 1949, p3.
The International Dictionary of Films and Filmmakers. v1, p247-249.
The Italian Cinema (Bindanella). p109-10.
The Italian Cinema: From Neorealism to the Present. p56-62.
Journal of Aesthetic Education. Apr 1975, v9, p50-61.
Library Journal. Mar 15, 1950, v75, p503.
Life. Jan 9, 1950, v28, p43-44.
Magill's Survey of Cinema. Foreign Language Films. v1, p287-91.
The New Republic. Dec 19, 1949, v121, p23.
The New York Times. Dec 13, 1949, p49.
The New York Times Magazine. Dec 4, 1949, p24-25.
The New Yorker. Dec 10, 1949, v25, p139.
Newsweek. Dec 26, 1949, v34, p56.
Rotarian. May 1950, v76, p40.
Saturday Review of Literature. Jan 7, 1950, v33, p30-32.
Selected Film Criticism, 1941-1950. p15-16.

Sequence. New Year 1950, v10, p174-75.
Sight and Sound. Mar 1950, v19, p26-28.
Theatre Arts. Feb 1950, v34, p38-39.
Time. Dec 12, 1949, v54, p98.
Time. Jan 16, 1950, v55, p86.
Variety. Dec 15, 1949, p6.
Variety. Dec 7, 1949, p6.

Big Boy (US; Crosland, Alan; 1930)
Exhibitors Herald-World. Sep 20, 1930, p40.
Film Daily. Sep 14, 1930, p12.
Life. Oct 17, 1930, v96, p20.
The New York Times. Sep 13, 1930, p9.
The New York Times. Sep 21, 1930, p5.
The New Yorker. Sep 20, 1930, v6, p84.
Outlook and Independent. Sep 24, 1930, v156, p150.
Time. Sep 22, 1930, v16, p30.
Variety. Sep 17, 1930, p21.

The Big Brain (US; Archainbaud, George; 1933)
Film Daily. Aug 5, 1933, p3.
Hollywood Reporter. May 20, 1933, p3.
Motion Picture Herald. Jun 3, 1933, p34.
New Outlook. Sep 1933, v162, p44.
The New York Times. Aug 5, 1933, p9.
Variety. Aug 8, 1933, p19.

The Big Broadcast (US; Tuttle, Frank; 1932)
Film Daily. Oct 15, 1932, p4.
The Films of Bing Crosby. p48-49.
Hollywood Reporter. Oct 1, 1932, p3.
Motion Picture Herald. Oct 8, 1932, p91.
The New Outlook. Nov 1932, v161, p46.
The New York Times. Oct 15, 1932, p13.
The New Yorker. Oct 22, 1932, v8, p57.
Rob Wagner's Script. Oct 22, 1932, v8, p8.
Variety. Oct 18, 1932, p14.

The Big Broadcast of 1936 (US; Taurog, Norman; 1935)
Canadian Magazine. Nov 1935, v84, p40.
Film Daily. Sep 14, 1935, p7.
Hollywood Reporter. Sep 10, 1935, p3.
Motion Picture Herald. Sep 21, 1935, p41.
The New York Times. Sep 16, 1935, p151.
The New Yorker. Sep 21, 1935, v11, p59-60.
Newsweek. Sep 21, 1935, v6, p17.
Rob Wagner's Script. Sep 21, 1935, v14, p10.
Time. Sep 23, 1935, v26, p45.
Variety. Sep 18, 1935, p35.

The Big Broadcast of 1937 (US; Leisen, Mitchell; 1936)
Commonweal. Nov 20, 1936, v25, p104.
Esquire. Jan 1937, v7, p109.
Film Daily. Oct 6, 1936, p12.
Hollywood Director. p100-04.
Hollywood Reporter. Oct 2, 1936, p3.
Hollywood Spectator. Oct 10 1936, v11, p17, 19.
Motion Picture Herald. Oct 10, 1936, p52-53.
The New Masses. Nov 3, 1936, v21, p29.
The New Republic. Oct 28, 1936, v88, p351.
The New Statesman and Nation. Nov 7, 1936, v12, p710.
The New York Times. Oct 22, 1936, p31.
Rob Wagner's Script. Oct 17, 1936, v16, p10.
Stage. Dec 1936, v14, p14.
Time. Oct 19, 1936, v28, p67.
Variety. Oct 28, 1936, p14.

The Big Broadcast of 1938 (US; Leisen, Mitchell; 1938)
Collier's. Apr 1938, v101, p51+.
Film Daily. Feb 11, 1938, p12.
The Films of W.C. Fields. p128-33.
Hollywood Director. p119-22.
Hollywood Reporter. Feb 8, 1938, p3.
Motion Picture Herald. Feb 12, 1938, p46.
Motion Picture Herald. Nov 20, 1937, p14-15.
The New York Times. Mar 10, 1938, p16.

The New Yorker. Mar 12, 1938, v14, p56.
Rob Wagner's Script. Mar 5, 1938, v19, p6.
Scholastic. Apr 2, 1938, v32, p35.
The Tatler. Mar 16, 1938, v147, p466.
Variety. Feb 9, 1938, p14.
W.C. Fields: A Life on Film. p190-95.

Big Brown Eyes (US; Walsh, Raoul; 1936)
Esquire. Jul 1936, v6, p97.
Film Daily. May 2, 1936, p3.
The Films of Cary Grant. p91-93.
Graham Greene on Film. p82.
Hollywood Reporter. Apr 1, 1936, p3.
Hollywood Spectator. Apr 11, 1936, v11, p31.
Motion Picture Herald. Apr 11, 1936, p54.
The New York Times. May 2, 1936, p11.
The New Yorker. May 9, 1936, v12, p71.
Rob Wagner's Script. May 9, 1936, v15, p10.
The Spectator. Jun 19, 1936, v156, p1131.
Time. Apr 13, 1936, v27, p32.
Variety. May 6, 1936, p18.

The Big Cage (US; Neumann, Kurt; 1933)
Film Daily. May 10, 1933, p9.
Hollywood Reporter. Feb 24, 1933, p3.
Motion Picture Herald. Mar 4, 1933, p46.
The New York Times. May 9, 1933, p20.
The New Yorker. May 20, 1933, v9, p50.
Rob Wagner's Script. Mar 11, 1933, v9, p8.
Stage. Jun 1933, v10, p43-44.
Variety. May 16, 1933, p17.

Big City (US; Borzage, Frank; 1937)
Esquire. Dec 1937, v8, p271-72.
Film Daily. Aug 30, 1937, p9.
Graham Greene on Film. p173.
Hollywood Reporter. Aug 25, 1937, p3.
Hollywood Spectator. Sep 11, 1937, v12, p15-16.
Motion Picture Herald. Sep 4, 1937, p40, 43.
The New Masses. Sep 28, 1937, v25, p29.
The New York Times. Sep 17, 1937, p29.
The New Yorker. Sep 25, 1937, v13, p65.
Newsweek. Sep 17, 1937, v10, p29.
Rob Wagner's Script. Sep 18, 1937, v18, p12.
Variety. Sep 15, 1937, p13.
World Film News. Nov 1937, v2, p18-19.
World Film News. Dec 1937, v2, p28.

Big City (US; Taurog, Norman; 1948)
Film Daily. Mar 29, 1948, p7.
Motion Picture Herald Product Digest. Apr 3, 1948, p4111.
The New York Times. May 21, 1948, p19.
Newsweek. May 31, 1948, v31, p72.
Variety. Mar 24, 1948, p8.

Big City Blues (US; LeRoy, Mervyn; 1932)
The Complete Films of Humphrey Bogart. p22-23.
Film Daily. Sep 10, 1932, p6.
Humphrey Bogart: The Man and His Films. p44-46.
Motion Picture Herald. Jun 18, 1932, p31.
The New York Times. Sep 10, 1932, p18.
Time. Sep 19, 1932, v20, p21.
Variety. Sep 13, 1932, p29.

The Big Clock (US; Farrow, John; 1948)
Film Daily. Sep 16, 1948, p8.
Hollywood Reporter. Feb 16, 1948, p3.
Life. Apr 19, 1948, v24, p133-34.
Magill's Survey of Cinema. Series II. v1, p209.
Motion Picture Herald Product Digest. Feb 21, 1948, p4065.
The New Republic. May 3, 1948, v118, p30.
The New York Times. Apr 22, 1948, p34.
The New Yorker. May 1, 1948, v24, p83.
Newsweek. Apr 19, 1948, v31, p91.
Scholastic. May 10, 1948, v52, p35.

Time. Apr 19, 1948, v51, p92.
Variety. Feb 18, 1948, p8.

Big Fella (GB; Wills, J. Elder; 1937)
Motion Picture Herald. Jul 10, 1937, p54.
Variety. Jul 7, 1937, p25.

The Big House (US; Hill, George; 1930)
Cinema, the Magic Vehicle. v1, p180.
Close-Up. Oct 1930, v7, p244-47.
Crime Movies. p49-51.
Dictionary of Films. p33.
Exhibitors Herald-World. Jul 5, 1930, p35.
Film Daily. Jun 29, 1930, p10.
The Great Gangster Pictures. p37.
Judge. Jul 19, 1930, v99, p23.
Life. Jul 11, 1930, v96, p17.
Literary Digest. Aug 2, 1930, v106, p15.
Magill's Survey of Cinema. Series II. v1, p220-22.
The Nation. Aug 6, 1930, v131, p161.
New York Times. Jun 22, 1930, p4.
The New York Times. Jun 25, 1930, p31.
The New York Times. Jun 29, 1930, v8, p3.
The New Yorker. Jul 5, 1930, v6, p46.
Outlook and Independent. Jul 9, 1930, v155, p390.
Selected Film Criticism, 1921-1930. p35-36.
The Spectator. Oct 11, 1930, v145, p489-90.
Theatre Magazine. Aug-Sep 1930, v52, p48.
Time. Jul 7, 1930, v16, p62.
Variety. Jul 2, 1930, p25.

The Big Parade (US; Vidor, King; 1925)
American Silent Film. p292-93.
Cinema, the Magic Vehicle. v1, p113-14.
Classics of the Silent Screen. p64-65.
Dictionary of Films. p34.
Film Daily. Nov 22, 1925, p6.
Guts ı& Glory. p14-24.
A History of Films. p112.
The History of World Cinema. p107.
Life. Dec 10, 1925, v24, p24-25.
Literary Digest. Mar 6, 1926, v88, p38-42.
Literary Digest. Jun 12, 1926, v89, p29.
Magill's Survey of Cinema. Silent Films. v1, p212-15.
The Moving Picture World. Dec 5, 1925, p481.
The New York Times. Nov 20, 1925, p18.
Outlook. Jan 6, 1926, v144, p307-08.
Photoplay. Jun 1, 1926, v30, p117.
Selected Film Criticism, 1921-1930. p36-38.
The Spectator. Jun 5, 1926, v136, p946-47.
Spellbound in Darkness. p398-404.
Variety. Nov 11, 1925, p36.
Variety. Dec 2, 1925, p40.
The War, the West, and the Wilderness. p187-93.

The Big Pond (US; Henley, Hobart; 1930)
Exhibitors Herald-World. May 24, 1930, p35.
Film Daily. Apr 13, 1930, p10.
The Film Spectator. May 24, 1930, v9, p23-24.
Judge. Jul 19, 1930, v99, p23.
Life. Jun 6, 1930, v95, p20.
The New York Times. May 19, 1930, p21.
The New York Times. Jan 5, 1930, p5.
The New York Times. May 25, 1930, p5.
The New Yorker. May 24, 1930, v6, p89.
Outlook and Independent. May 28, 1930, v155, p151.
Rob Wagner's Script. Jul 12, 1930, v3, p10.
The Spectator. Aug 23, 1930, v145, p247.
Time. May 26, 1930, v15, p56.
Variety. May 21, 1930, p25.

The Big Sleep (US; Hawks, Howard; 1946)
Agee on Film. v1, p215, 238.
BFI/Monthly Film Bulletin. Sep 1978, v45, p185.
The Big Sleep. 1985.
Cinema, the Magic Vehicle. v1, p424-25.

Commonweal. Sep 6, 1946, p504.
The Complete Films of Humphrey Bogart. p125-28.
The Dark Side of the Screen: Film Noir. p33-34, 168-69+.
The Detective in Hollywood. p314-21.
Film Daily. Aug 14, 1946, p5.
Film Heritage. Sum 1970, v5, p7-15.
Film Journal. Sum 1971, v 1, p3-10.
The Films of Howard Hawks. p119-30.
The Films of the Forties. p174-76.
The Great Movies. p60-63.
Halliwell's Hundred. p21-23.
Hawks on Hawks. p102-05.
Hollywood Quarterly. Jan 1947, v2, p161-63.
Hollywood Reporter. Aug 13, 1946, p3.
Howard Hawks (Poague). p127-28+.
Howard Hawks: Storyteller. p243-96.
Howard Hawks (Wood). p168-70+.
Humphrey Bogart: The Man and His Films. p135-36.
The International Dictionary of Films and Filmmakers. v1,
   p53-54.
Magill's Survey of Cinema. Series I. v1, p162-64.
The Modern American Novel and the Movies. p80-94.
Motion Picture Herald Product Digest. Aug 17, 1940, p3149.
The Nation. Aug 31, 1946, v163, p250.
The New Republic. Sep 23, 1946, v115, p351.
The New York Times. Aug 24, 1946, p6.
The New Yorker. Sep 7, 1946, v22, p48.
Newsweek. Sep 2, 1946, v28, p78.
Raymond Chandler and Film. p121-53.
Raymond Chandler in Hollywood. p65-73.
Raymond Chandler on Screen. p38-62.
Rob Wagner's Script. Sep 28, 1946, v32, p12-13.
Selected Film Criticism, 1941-1950. p20-22.
Seventy Years of Cinema. p160.
Sight and Sound. Wint 1974-75, v44, p34-39.
Theatre Arts. Sep 1946, v30, p520.
Time. Aug 26, 1946, v48, p95.
Variety. Aug 14, 1946, p10.

The Big Steal (US; Siegal, Don; 1949)
BFI/Monthly Film Bulletin. Feb 1984, v51, p60-61.
Christian Century. Jul 20, 1949, v66, p879.
Commonweal. Jul 22, 1949, v50, p368.
Film Daily. Jun 17, 1949, p6.
Hollywood Reporter. Jun 14, 1949, p3.
Motion Picture Herald Product Digest. Jun 18, 1949, p4649.
The New Republic. Jul 25, 1949, v121, p23.
The New York Times. Jul 11, 1949, p13.
Newsweek. Jul 25, 1949, v34, p76.
Robert Mitchum on the Screen. p108-09.
Rotarian. Sep 1949, v75, p6.
Sight and Sound. Dec 1949, v28, p21.
Theatre Arts. Sep 1949, v33, p6.
Time. Jul 25, 1949, v54, p80.
Variety. Jun 15, 1949, p13.

The Big Trail (US; Walsh, Raoul; 1930)
The Complete Films of John Wayne. p35-36.
Each Man in His Own Time. p239-47.
Film Daily. Oct 12, 1930, p15.
Films and Filming. Jan 1973, v19, p40.
The Great Western Pictures. p24-26.
Judge. Nov 15, 1930, v99, p19.
Life. Nov 14, 1930, v96, p18.
Literary Digest. Nov 22, 1930, v107, p34.
The Nation. Nov 12, 1930, v131, p534, 536.
New York Times. Oct 25, 1930, p20.
The New Yorker. Nov 1, 1930, v6, p70.
Outlook and Independent. Nov 5, 1930, v156, p393.
Photoplay. Nov 1930, v38, p52.
Selected Film Criticism, 1921-1930. p38-41.
Theatre Magazine. Jan 1931, v53, p48.
Time. Oct 13, 1930, v16, p26.
Variety. Oct 29, 1930, p17, 27.
The War, the West and the Wilderness. p39.

Bill Henry (US; Storm, Jerome; 1919)
The Bioscope. Dec 25, 1919, p56.
Exhibitor's Trade Review. Aug 30, 1919, p1085.
Motion Picture News. Aug 30, 1919, p1867.
The Moving Picture World. Aug 30, 1919, p1372.
Variety. Aug 22, 1919, p77.
Wid's Daily. Sep 7, 1919, p5.

A Bill of Divorcement (US; Cukor, George; 1932)
Bookman (London). Apr 1933, v84, p29.
Film Daily. Sep 17, 1932, p22.
The Films of Katharine Hepburn. p39-41.
The Films of the Thirties. p84-85.
From Quasimodo to Scarlett O'Hara. p166-69.
George Cukor (Phillips). p61-63.
Hollywood Reporter. Aug 31, 1932, p3.
Magill's Survey of Cinema, Series II. v1, p239-41.
Motion Picture Herald. Sep 10, 1932, p40.
The Nation. Oct 26, 1932, v135, p409.
National Board of Review Magazine. Sep-Oct 1932, v7, p21.
National Board of Review Magazine. Nov 1932, v7, p12.
The New Outlook. Nov 1932, v161, p47.
The New York Times. Oct 3, 1932, p15.
The New Yorker. Oct 8, 1932, v8, p57-58.
On Cukor. p59-62.
Photoplay. Nov 1932, v42, p56.
Rob Wagner's Script. Sep 10, 1932, v8, p8.
Selected Film Criticism, 1931-1940. p28-29.
Time. Oct 10, 1932, v20, p32.
Vanity Fair. Nov 1932, v39, p58.
Variety. Oct 4, 1932, p15.

Billy the Kid (US; Miller, David; 1941)
Commonweal. Jun 13, 1941, v43, p186.
Film Daily. May 1941, p9.
The Filming of the West. p194-97.
The Films of Robert Taylor. p87-90.
Focus on Film. Sum 1973, n15, p9.
Hollywood Reporter. May 22, 1941, p3.
Life. Aug 4, 1941, v11, p65-69.
The London Times. Sep 25, 1941, p6.
Motion Picture Exhibitor. Jun 11, 1940, p763.
The New York Times. Jun 20, 1941, p28.
The New York Times. Jun 22, 1941, sec9, p3.
Newsweek. Jun 2, 1941, v17, p51-53.
Variety. May 28, 1941, p16.

Billy the Kid (US; Vidor, King; 1930)
Around Cinemas. p41-43.
Close-Up. Dec 1930, v7, p386-90.
Exhibitors Herald-World. Oct 25, 1930, p41.
Exhibitors Herald-World. Sep 13, 1930, p41.
Film Daily. Oct 19, 1930, p11.
The Great Western Pictures. p26-30.
Judge. Nov 8, 1930, v99, p23.
The Nation. Nov 12, 1930, v131, p534, 536.
New York Times. Jul 6, 1930, p2.
New York Times. Oct 8, 1930, p23.
New York Times. Oct 26, 1930, p5.
The New Yorker. Oct 25, 1930, v6, p77.
Outlook and Independent. Oct 29, 1930, v156, p353.
Time. Nov 3, 1930, v16, p44.
Variety. Oct 22, 1930, p23.

Billy the Kid Returns (US; Kane, Joseph; 1938)
Film Daily. Sep 16, 1938, p8.
Hollywood Reporter. Aug 26, 1938, p4.
Hollywood Spectator. Sep 3, 1938, v13, p14-15.
Motion Picture Herald. Sep 24, 1938, p43.
Variety. Sep 21, 1938, p13.

Biography of a Bachelor Girl (US; Griffith, Edward H.; 1934)
Film Daily. Dec 18, 1934, p8.
Hollywood Reporter. Dec 15, 1934, p3.

Motion Picture Herald. Dec 29, 1934, p59.
The New York Times. Mar 2, 1934, p18.
Variety. Mar 6, 1935, p20.

Bird of Paradise (US; Vidor, King; 1932)
The Busby Berkeley Book. p45.
Film Daily. Aug 12, 1932, p3.
The Films of the Thirties. p78-79.
The International Photographer. Aug 1932, v4, p31.
Literary Digest. Oct 1, 1932, v114, p17.
Motion Picture Herald. Jun 25, 1932, p25.
The New Outlook. Oct 1932, v161, p39.
The New York Times. Sep 10, 1932, p18.
The New Yorker. Sep 24, 1932, v8, p52-53.
Photoplay. Oct 1932, v42, p54.
Selected Film Criticism, 1931-1940. p29-30.
Those Fabulous Movie Years: The 30s. p36.
Time. Aug 22, 1932, v20, p20.
Vanity Fair. Oct 1932, v39, p44+.
Variety. Sep 13, 1932, p19.

The Birth of a Nation (Also titled: The Clansman; The Birth of the Nation) (US; Griffith, D.W.; 1915)
Adventures With D.W. Griffith. p80-90+.
American Cinematographer. Jan 1969, v50, p86-91, 148-53, 172-73.
American Quarterly. Fall 1960, v11 p347-57.
American Silent Film. p77-89.
The Art of the Moving Picture. p74-77.
BFI/Monthly Film Bulletin. May 1975, v46, p105-06.
Billy Bitzer: His Story. p102-29.
The Birth of a Nation: Shot Analysis.
The Birth of a Nation Story.
Black Films and Film-makers. p75-83.
Black Images in American Films, 1896-1954. p27-42.
The Crisis. May-Jun 1915, p33, 40-42, 87-88.
D.W. Griffith: American Film Master. p20-22.
D.W. Griffith: An American Life. p212-302.
D.W. Griffith: His Life and Work. p141-65.
Fifty Great American Silent Films, 1912-1920. p29-33.
Fighting a Vicious Film.
Film Culture. Spr-Summ 1965, v36, p1-210.
Film Daily. Dec 21, 1930, p10.
The Films of D.W. Griffith. p46-61.
Focus on D.W. Griffith. p27-29, 39-42, 80-102, 116-18.
Focus on The Birth of a Nation.
From Sambo to Superspade. p23-39.
Griffith: First Artist of the Movies. p61-78.
The Historian. 1963, p344-62.
Landmark Films. p14-23.
Lillian Gish: The Movies, Mr. Griffith, and Me. p131-47.
Magill's Survey of Cinema. Silent Films. v1, p216-22.
The Man Who Invented Hollywood. p88-97.
A Million and One Nights. p635-44.
Motion Picture News. Jan 2, 1915, p33.
Motion Picture News. Feb 6, 1915, p74.
Motion Picture News. Feb 13, 1915, p34.
Motion Picture News. Mar 13, 1915, p49-50.
Motion Picture News. Mar 27, 1915, p32.
Motion Pictures: The Development of an Art Form. p89-101.
Motography. Feb 20, 1915, p272.
Motography. Mar 20, 1915, p431.
Motography. Jun 19, 1915, p1009.
The Movies in the Age of Innocence. p87-97.
Movies of the Silent Years. p32-33.
The Moving Picture World. Feb 20, 1915, p1121.
The Moving Picture World. Mar 13, 1915, p1586-87.
The Negro in Films. p33-43.
The Negro in Hollywood Films. p18-20.
The New York American. Feb 28, 1915, City Life and Dramatic sec, p9.
The New York Dramatic Mirror. Mar 10, 1915, p28.
The New York Republic. Mar 20, 1915, p185.
The New York Times. Mar 4, 1915, p9.
The North Carolina Historical Review. 1962, v , p519-40.

Outlook. Jan 7, 1931, v157, p32.
The Parade's Gone By. p46-50.
Photoplay. Jan 1915, v8, p57-62.
Photoplay. Oct 1916, v10, p86-94.
The Rise of the American Film. p171-88.
Selected Film Criticism, 1912-1920. p17-24.
The Silent Picture. p18-20.
Slow Fade to Black. p41-69.
Stage to Screen. p223-25.
Toms, Coons, Mulattoes, Mammies,& Bucks. p10-18.
Variety. Mar 12, 1915, p23.
The Village Voice. Jul 17, 1969, p45.
The Village Voice. Jul 24, 1969, p37, 45.
When the Movies Were Young. p249-55.

The Birth of a Race (US; Noble, John W.; 1918)
Exhibitor's Trade Review. May 10, 1918, p1761.
Motion Picture News. May 3, 1918, p2891.
The Moving Picture World. May 10, 1918, p938.
Selected Film Criticism, 1912-1920. p24-25.
Variety. Dec 6, 1918, p38.

The Birth of the Blues (US; Schertzinger, Victor; 1941)
Commonweal. Dec 12, 1941, v35, p199.
The Film Criticism of Otis Ferguson. p387-88.
Film Daily. Sep 3, 1041, p6.
The Films of Bing Crosby. p120-23.
Hollywood Reporter. Sep 3, 1941, p3.
Life. Nov 17, 1941, v11, p96-97.
The London Times. Dec 15, 1941, p8.
Motion Picture Exhibitor. Sep 17, 1941, p848-49.
Motion Picture Herald Product Digest. Sep 13, 1941, p231.
The New Republic. Oct 6, 1941, v105, p437.
The New York Times. Oct 19, 1941, sec9, p4.
The New York Times. Dec 11, 1941, p39.
The New York Times. Dec 14, 1941, sec9, p7.
Newsweek. Nov 10, 1941, v18, p69.
Scholastic. Nov 17, 1941, v39, p28.
Theatre Arts. Dec 1941, v25, p885.
Variety. Sep 3, 1941, p8.

The Birth of the Nation *See* The Birth of a Nation

The Biscuit Eater (US; Heisler, Stuart; 1940)
The Film Criticism of Otis Ferguson. p297.
The Golden Age of "B" Movies. p41-44.
Life. May 6, 1940, v8, p71-72+.
Lorentz on Film. p196-97.
Magill's Survey of Cinema. Series II. v1, p253-55.
The New Republic. Apr 22, 1940, v102, p536.
The New York Times. May 23, 1940, p28.
The New York Times. May 26, 1940, sec9, p3.
Newsweek. May 6, 1940, v15, p32.
Photoplay. Jun 1940, v54, p68.
Scholastic. Apr 15, 1940, v36, p36.
Variety. Apr 10, 1940, p14.

The Bishop Misbehaves (US; Dupont, E.A.; 1935)
Film Daily. Sep 28, 1935, p7.
Hollywood Reporter. Sep 13, 1935, p3.
Motion Picture Herald. Nov 9, 1935, p64.
Rob Wagner's Script. Oct 26, 1935, v114, p10.
Time. Sep 30, 1935, v26, p26.
Variety. Oct 2, 1935, p16.

The Bishop's Wife (US; Koster, Henry; 1947)
Commonweal. Jan 2, 1948, v47, p303.
Film Daily. Nov 18, 1947, p8.
The Films of Cary Grant. p190-93.
The Films of David Niven. p84-85.
Fortnight. Dec 19, 1947, v3, p28-29.
Hollywood Reporter. Nov 17, 1947, p3.
Life. Jan 12, 1948, v24, p71-72.
Magill's Survey of Cinema, Series II. v1, p256-58.
Motion Picture Herald Product Digest. Nov 22, 1947, p3941.
New Movies. Dec 1947, v22, p8.

New Republic. Dec 15, 1947, v117, p31.
The New York Times. Dec 10, 1947, p44.
Newsweek. Dec 22, 1947, v30, p81-82.
Samuel Goldwyn Presents. p255-57.
Selected Film Criticism, 1941-1950. p23-24.
Theatre Arts. Dec 1947, v31, p48-50.
Time. Dec 8, 1947, v50, p104.
Variety. Nov 19, 1947, p8.

The Bitch *See* Chienne, La

Bitter Rice (Italian title: Riso Amaro) (IT; De Santis, Giuseppe; 1949)
Cinema, the Magic Vehicle. v1, p499-500.
Commonweal. Oct 6, 1950, v52, p632.
Film Daily. Sep 21, 1950, p3.
Hollywood Reporter. Nov 16, 1950, p3.
The Italian Cinema (Bondanella). p105-06.
Magill's Survey of Cinema. Foreign Language Films. v1, p311-15.
The New Republic. Oct 9, 1950, v123, p30.
The New Yorker. Sep 30, 1950, v26, p60.
Newsweek. Sep 18, 1950, v36, p92.
Rotarian. Mar 1951, v78, p36.
Sequence. Sum 1950, n2, p12.
Time. Nov 6, 1950, v56, p104.
Variety. Nov 16, 1949, p29.

Bitter Sweet (GB; Wilcox, Herbert; 1933)
Cinema Quarterly. Aut 1933, v2, p48.
Film Daily. Aug 25, 1933, p9.
Hollywood Reporter. Aug 24, 1933, p3.
Life. Oct 1933, v100, p25.
Motion Picture Herald. Aug 19, 1933, p40.
The Nation. Sep 13, 1933, v137, p308.
The New York Times. Aug 24, 1933, p18.
Newsweek. Sep 2, 1933, v2, p30.
Rob Wagner's Script. Oct 7, 1933, v10, p10.
Selected Film Criticism: Foreign Films, 1930-1950. p16-17.
Time. Sep 4, 1933, v22, p22.
Variety. Aug 29, 1933, p14.

The Bitter Tea of General Yen (US; Capra, Frank; 1933)
BFI/Monthly Film Bulletin. Jan 1974, v41, p56-57.
Film Daily. Jan 12, 1933, p6.
The Films of Barbara Stanwyck. p82-85.
The Films of Frank Capra (Scherle and Levy). p111-16.
The Films of Frank Capra (Willis). p88-98.
Frank Capra (Maland). p74-78.
Hollywood Reporter. Nov 16, 1932, p2.
Magill's Survey of Cinema. Series I. v1, p172-76.
Motion Picture Herald. Nov 26, 1932, p5.
Motion Picture Herald. Dec 3, 1932, p22.
Movie-Made America. p206-07.
The New York Times. Jan 12, 1933, p20.
The New York Times. Jan 22, 1933, p5.
The New Yorker. Jan 21, 1933, v8, p47.
Starring Miss Barbara Stanwyck. p47, 50, 54.
Time. Jan 23, 1933, v21, p34.
Variety. Jan 17, 1933, p14.

Bizarre, Bizarre (FR; Carné, Marcel; 1939)
Film Daily. Apr 14, 1939, p13.
Motion Picture Herald. Apr 1, 1939, p30.
The New Masses. Apr 4, 1939, v31, p30.
The New York Times. Mar 21, 1939, p27.
The New Yorker. Apr 1, 1939, v15, p68.
Variety. Mar 29, 1939, p14.

Black Beauty (US; Smith, David; 1921)
Film Daily. Jan 9, 1921, p3.
The New York Times. Feb 21, 1921, p16.
Photoplay. Apr 1921, v19, p53.
Selected Film Criticism, 1921-1930. p41-42.
Variety. Feb 25, 1921, p42.

The Black Book *See* Reign of Terror

The Black Cat (US; Ulmer, Edgar G.; 1934)
American Cinematographer. Oct 1984, v65, p34-48.
Film Daily. May 19, 1934, p33.
The Films of Bela Lugosi. p96-101.
Hollywood Reporter. May 4, 1934, p3.
An Illustrated History of the Horror Film. p74-75.
Motion Picture Herald. May 26, 1934, p42.
The New York Times. May 19, 1934, p18.
Time. May 24, 1934, v23, p36.
Variety. May 22, 1934, p15.

Black Eyes *See* Dark Eyes

Black Fury (US; Curtiz, Michael; 1935)
Canadian Magazine. Jun 1935, v83, p32.
Cinema Quarterly. Sum 1935, v3, p238, 241.
Esquire. Jun 1935, v3, p144, 181-82.
The Film Criticism of Otis Ferguson. p73-74.
Film Daily. Mar 28, 1935, p4.
From Quasimodo to Scarlett O'Hara. p198-200.
Hollywood Reporter. Mar 26, 1935, p3.
Hollywood Reporter. Apr 19, 1935, p2.
Literary Digest. Apr 27, 1935, v119, p34.
Motion Picture Herald. Apr 6, 1935, p50.
The Nation. Apr 24, 1935, v140, p491-92.
National Board of Review Magazine. May 1935, v10, p13.
The New Masses. Apr 23, 1935, v15, p28-29.
The New Republic. Apr 24, 1935, v82, p313.
New Theatre. May 1935, v2, p8-9.
The New York Times. Apr 11, 1935, p27.
The New Yorker. Apr 20, 1935, v11, p72.
Newsweek. Apr 13, 1935, v5, p25.
Paul Muni: His Life and His Films. p135-40.
Rob Wagner's Script. May 25, 1935, v13, p6.
Theatre Arts Monthly. Jun 1935, v19, p34.
Time. Apr 22, 1935, v25, p60.
Vanity Fair. Apr 1935, v44, p47.
Variety. Apr 17, 1935, p14.
Warner Brothers Presents. p75, 78.
We're in the Money. p105-07.

The Black Legion (US; Mayo, Archie; 1937)
Black Images in American Films, 1896-1954. p192.
Commonweal. Jan 22, 1937, v25, p360.
The Complete Films of Humphrey Bogart. p37-39.
The Film Criticism of Otis Ferguson. p165-67.
Film Daily. Dec 30, 1936, p11.
Fortune. Dec 1937, v16, p113.
Graham Greene on Film. p151-54.
Hollywood Reporter. Jan 5, 1937, p3.
Hollywood Spectator. Jan 16, 1937, v11, p8.
Humphrey Bogart: The Man and His Films. p63.
Literary Digest. Jan 16, 1937, v123, p23.
Motion Picture Herald. Jan 9, 1937, p44.
The Nation. Jan 30, 1937, v144, p137.
National Board of Review Magazine. Feb 1937, v12, p8.
The New Masses. Jan 26, 1937, v22, p37.
The New Republic. Feb 17, 1937, v90, p47-48.
The New Statesman and Nation. Jul 3, 1937, v14, p15-16.
New Theatre. Mar 1937, v4, p58.
The New York Times. Jan 18, 1937, p21.
The New Yorker. Jan 23, 1937, v12, p61.
Rob Wagner's Script. Feb 20, 1937, v17, p6.
Scholastic. Feb 6, 1937, v30, p22.
The Spectator. Jul 9, 1937, v159, p60.
Time. Jan 25, 1937, v29, p46.
Variety. Jan 20, 1937, p14.
Warner Brothers Presents. p78-79.
World Film News. Aug 1937, v2, p11.

Black Magic (US; Ratoff, Gregory; 1949)
The Cinema of Orson Welles. p209.
Commonweal. Dec 30, 1949, v51, p342.
Film Daily. Aug 22, 1949, p6.

Hollywood Reporter. Aug 18, 1949, p3.
Motion Picture Herald Product Digest. Aug 20, 1949, p4721.
The New York Times. Nov 9, 1949, p37.
Newsweek. Aug 8, 1949, v34, p69.
Orson Welles (Leaming). p348-50.
Time. Sep 5, 1949, v54, p62.
Variety. Aug 24, 1949, p18.

Black Narcissus (GB; Powell, Michael; Pressburger,
    Emeric; 1946)
Commonweal. Aug 22, 1947, v46, p455.
Film Daily. Jul 17, 1947, p6.
The Great British Films. p110-12.
Hollywood Reporter. Jul 8, 1947, p3.
Life. Sep 1, 1947, v23, p55-56.
Magill's Survey of Cinema, Series I. v1, p177-79.
Motion Pitcure Herald Product Digest. Jul 12, 1947, p3725.
The Nation. Aug 30, 1947, v165, p209.
New Republic. Sep 15, 1947, v117, p37.
The New York Times. Aug 14, 1947, p29.
The New Yorker. Aug 23, 1947, v23, p42.
Newsweek. Aug 18, 1947, v30, p77-78.
Theatre Arts. Oct 1947, v31, p51-52.
Time. Aug 25, 1947, v50, p88+.
Variety. May 5, 1947, p18.

Black Orchids (US; Ingram, Rex; 1917)
The Moving Picture World. Jan 6, 1917, p98-99, 136.
The New York Dramatic Mirror. Dec 30, 1916, p26.
Photoplay. Mar 1917, v11, p120.
Rex Ingram: Master of the Silent Cinema. p44, 50.
Selected Film Criticism, 1912-1920. p25-26.
Variety. Dec 29, 1916, p22.

Black Oxen (US; Lloyd, Frank; 1924)
Film Daily. Jan 13, 1924, p5.
Magill's Survey of Cinema. Silent Films. v1, p223-25.
The Moving Picture World. Jan 19, 1924, p216.
The New York Times. Jan 7, 1924, p23.
Photoplay. Mar 1924, v25, p61.
Selected Film Criticism, 1921-1930. p42.
Variety. Jan 3, 1924, p23.
Variety. Jan 10, 1924, p26.

The Black Pirate (US; Parker, Albert; 1926)
BFI/Monthly Film Bulletin. Apr 1986, v53, p126-27.
Classics of the Silent Screen. p82-83.
Film Daily. Mar 21, 1926, p6.
His Majesty the American. p145-54.
Life. Mar 25, 1926, v87, p26.
Literary Digest. Apr 10, 1926, v89, p34-42.
Magill's Survey of Cinema. Silent Films. v1, p226-31.
A Million and One Nights. p572.
Motion Picture News. Dec 4, 1926, v34, p2141-42.
The New York Times. Mar 9, 1926, p21.
Outlook. Apr 14, 1926, v142, p560-62.
Photoplay. May 1926, v24, p48.
Selected Film Criticism, 1921-1930. p42-44.
Spellbound in Darkness. p435.
Variety. Mar 10, 1926, p21.

Black Sheep (US; Dwan, Allan; 1935)
Film Daily. Jun 28, 1935, p6.
Hollywood Reporter. May 3, 1935, p3.
Motion Picture Herald. May 18, 1935, p47.
The New York Times. Jun 28, 1935, p34.
Time. May 27, 1935, v25, p28.
Variety. Jul 3, 1935, p15.

The Black Swan (US; King, Henry; 1942)
Commonweal. Jan 1, 1943, v37, p280.
Film Daily. Oct 16, 1942, p7.
The Films of Anthony Quinn. p90-91.
The Films of Tyrone Power. p130-33.
Hollywood Reporter. Oct 19, 1942, p3.
The London Times. Apr 29, 1943, p6.

Motion Picture Exhibitor. Oct 21, 1942, v28, n24, sec2, p1138.
Motion Picture Herald Product Digest. Oct 17, 1942, p958.
The New York Times. Dec 24, 1942, p18.
Newsweek. Dec 7, 1942, v20, p86.
Photoplay. Jan 1943, p4.
Scholastic. Jan 18, 1943, v41, p33.
Time. Dec 7, 1942, v40, p109.
Variety. Oct 21, 1942, p8.

The Black Watch (US; Ford, John; 1929)
Exhibitor's Herald-World. Jul 6, 1929, p116.
Film Daily. May 26, 1929, p8.
The New York Times. May 23, 1929, p26.
Variety. May 15, 1929, p20.

Blackmail (GB; Hitchcock, Alfred; 1929)
The Art of Alfred Hitchcock. p18-25.
BFI/Monthly Film Bulletin. Oct 1974, v41, p234.
Film Daily. Oct 6, 1929, p9.
The Films of Alfred Hitchcock. p27-33.
Hitch. p85-90.
Hitchcock: The First Forty-Four Films. p20-24.
Hitchcock's British Films. p99-113.
The International Dictionary of Films and Filmmakers. v1, p58-59.
Magill's Survey of Cinema. Series I. v1, p181-83.
The New York Times. Jul 14, 1929, sec9, p4.
Photoplay. Dec 1929, v37, p54.
Selected Film Criticism, 1921-1930. p44-45.
Variety. Jul 10, 1929, p24.
Variety. Oct 9, 1929, p34.

Blackmail (US; Potter, H.C.; 1939)
The Cinema of Edward G. Robinson. p121-24 .
Film Daily. Sep 15, 1939, p5.
Hollywood Reporter. Sep 7, 1939, p3.
Hollywood Spectator. Sep 16, 1939, v14, p7.
Motion Picture Herald. Sep 9, 1939, p46.
The New Statesman and Nation. Oct 21, 1939, v18, p549.
The New York Times. Sep 15, 1939, p26.
The New Yorker. Sep 23, 1939, v15, p58.
Newsweek. Sep 25, 1939, v14, p44.
Rob Wagner's Script. Oct 21, 1939, v22, p16.
Variety. Sep 13, 1939, p12.

Blaue Engel, Der *See* The Blue Angel

Blaue Licht, Das *See* The Blue Light

Blaue Licht, Der *See* The Blue Light

Blessed Event (US; Del Ruth, Roy; 1932)
Film Daily. Aug 23, 1932, p9.
Magill's Survey of Cinema, Series II. v1, p267-69.
Motion Picture Herald. Sep 10, 1932, p38, 40.
The New York Times. Sep 3, 1932, p16.
The New Yorker. Sep 10, 1932, v8, p50-51.
Rob Wagner's Script. Sep 10, 1932, v8, p8.
Time. Sep 12, 1932, v20, p29.
Variety. Sep 6, 1932, p15.

Blind Husbands (US; Stroheim, Erich von; 1919)
The Bioscope. Jun 17, 1920, p57-58.
Exhibitor's Trade Review. Oct 11, 1919, p1658.
Hollywood Scapegoat. p30-32.
Magill's Survey of Cinema. Silent Films. v1, p232-36.
Motion Picture News. Oct 11, 1919, p3044.
The Moving Picture World. Sep 27, 1919, p1966.
The New York Times. Dec 8, 1919, p20.
Selected Film Criticism, 1912-1920. p26-27.
Stroheim. p8-10.
Stroheim: A Pictorial Record of His Nine Films. p2-19.
Variety. Dec 12, 1919, p46.
Wid's Daily. Oct 19, 1919, p7.

Blithe Spirit (GB; Lean, David; 1945)
Agee on Film. v1, p178.
The Cinema of David Lean. p47-50.
Cinema, the Magic Vehicle. v1, p412-13.
Commonweal. Oct 12, 1945, v42, p624.
David Lean and His Films. p33-35.
Film Daily. Sep 25, 1945, p10.
The Great British Films. p79-81.
Halliwell's Hundred. p24-27.
Hollywood Reporter. Jan 8, 1946, p3.
Life. Oct 22, 1945, v19, p77-80.
Magill's Survey of Cinema. Series I. v1, p188-90.
Motion Picture Herald Product Digest. Sep 22, 1945, p2798.
The Nation. Oct 27, 1945, v161, p441.
The New Republic. Oct 29, 1945, v113, p573-74.
The New York Times. Oct 4, 1945, p27.
The New Yorker. Oct 6, 1945, v21, p95.
Newsweek. Oct 15, 1945, v26, p102.
Rob Wagner's Script. Feb 2, 1946, v32, p14.
Selected Film Criticism: Foreign Films, 1930-1950. p18-19.
Theatre Arts. Nov 1945, v29, p639-40.
Time. Oct 15, 1945, v46, p54.
Variety. Apr 25, 1945, p14.

Blockade (US; Lawson, John Howard; 1938)
Commonweal. Jul 1, 1938, v28, p273.
Film Daily. Jun 9, 1938, p4.
The Films of Henry Fonda. p70-71.
The Fondas (Springer). p79-80.
Hollywood Reporter. Jun 4, 1938, p3.
Hollywood Spectator. Jun 11, 1938, v13, p5-6.
Life. Jun 13, 1938, v4, p60-62.
Motion Picture Herald. Jun 11, 1938, p35, 38.
The Nation. Jun 18, 1938, v146, p688.
The Nation. Jul 9, 1938, v147, p38-40.
National Board of Review Magazine. Jun 1938, v13, p15.
The New Masses. Aug 2, 1938, v28, p30-31.
The New Masses. Jun 28, 1938, v28, p27-29.
The New Republic. Jun 29, 1938, v95, p217.
The New Statesman and Nation. Jun 11, 1938, v15, p991.
The New York Times. Jun 17, 1938, p25.
The New Yorker. Jun 18, 1938, v14, p53.
Newsweek. Jun 20, 1938, v11, p23.
Rob Wagner's Script. Jun 18, 1938, v19, p14-15.
Time. Jun 20, 1938, v31, p37-38.
Variety. Jun 8, 1938, p17.
World Film News. Jul 1938, v3, p127.

Block-Heads (US; Blystone, John G.; 1938)
The Film Criticism of Otis Ferguson. p222-23.
Film Daily. Aug 19, 1938, p6.
Hollywood Reporter. Aug 12, 1938, p3.
Laurel and Hardy. p365-73.
Motion Picture Herald. Aug 20, 1938, p47.
The New York Times. Aug 30, 1938, p14.
The Spectator. Sep 16, 1938, v161, p439.
Variety. Aug 31, 1938, p18.
World Film News. Oct 1938, v3, p265.
World Film News. Nov 1938, v3, p315.

Blonde Venus (US; Sternberg, Josef von; 1932)
The Cinema of Josef von Sternberg. p101-12.
Cinema Quarterly. Wint 1932, v1, p116.
Close-Up. Sep 1932, v9, p192-95.
Film Daily. Sep 24, 1932, p6.
The Films of Cary Grant. p41-44.
The Films of Josef von Sternberg. p35-37.
The Films of Marlene Dietrich. p104-07.
Hollywood Reporter. Sep 1, 1932, p3.
Magill's Survey of Cinema. Series II. v1, p273-76.
Motion Picture Herald. Sep 10, 1932, p38.
The New Outlook. Nov 1932, v161, p47.
The New York Times. Sep 24, 1932, p18.
The New Yorker. Oct 1, 1932, v8, p54-55.
Photoplay. Nov 1932, v42, p58.

Rob Wagner's Script. Sep 24, 1932, v8, p8.
Selected Film Criticism, 1931-1940. p30-32.
Sublime Marlene. p54-60.
Time. Oct 3, 1932, v20, p36.
Vanity Fair. Nov 1932, v39, p58.
Variety. Sep 27, 1932, p17.
We're in the Money. p53.

Blondie (US; Strayer, Frank R.; 1938)
Film Daily. Nov 7, 1938, p10.
Hollywood Reporter. Oct 29, 1938, p3.
Hollywood Spectator. Nov 12, 1938, v13, p14.
Motion Picture Herald. Nov 5, 1938, p38.
The New York Times. Dec 22, 1938, p25.
Photoplay. Jan 1939, v53, p45.
Rob Wagner's Script. Dec 10, 1938, v20, p10-11.
Variety. Nov 2, 1938, p22.

Blondie of the Follies (US; Goulding, Edmund; 1932)
Film Daily. Sep 2, 1932, p4.
Fortune. Dec 1932, v6, p56.
Hollywood Reporter. Aug 27, 1932, p3.
Motion Picture Herald. Sep 10, 1932, p40.
The New Outlook. Oct 1932, v161, p39.
The New York Times. Sep 2, 1932, p19.
The New Yorker. Sep 10, 1932, v8, p51.
Time. Sep 5, 1932, v20, p40.
Variety. Sep 13, 1932, p19.

Blondie on a Budget (US; Strayer, Frank R.; 1940)
Film Daily. Apr 10, 1940, p5.
The Films of Rita Hayworth. p107-08.
Magill's Survey of Cinema. Series II. v1, p276-79.
Variety. Feb 28, 1940, p16.

Blood and Sand (US; Niblo, Fred; 1922)
Exceptional Photoplays. Nov 1922, p4.
Film Daily. Aug 13, 1922, p2.
Magill's Survey of Cinema. Silent Films. v1, p237-39.
The New York Times. Aug 7, 1927, p14.
Photoplay. Oct 1922, v22, p58.
Selected Film Criticism, 1921-1930. p45-46.
Variety. Aug 11, 1922, p32.

Blood and Sand (US; Mamoulian, Rouben; 1941)
Commonweal. Jun 6, 1941, v34, p160.
Film Daily. May 22, 1941, p5.
The Films of Anthony Quinn. p77-78.
The Films of Rita Hayworth. p122-24.
The Films of Tyrone Power. p114-17.
Hollywood Reporter. May 19, 1941, p3.
The Hollywood Spectator. Jul 1, 1941, v16, p11-12.
The London Times. Jan 26, 1942, p8.
Magill's Survey of Cinema. Series II. v1, p280-82.
Motion Picture Exhibitor. May 23, 1941, p757.
Motion Picture Herald Product Digest. Apr 19, 1941, p111.
The Moving Image. p392-94.
The Nation. Jun 7, 1941, v152, p677.
The New York Times. May 23, 1941, p25.
Newsweek. Jun 2, 1941, v17, p51.
Rob Wagner's Script. May 31, 1941, v25, p16.
Scribner's Commentator. Aug 1941, v10, p108.
Selected Film Criticism, 1941-1950. p25-27.
Surrealism and the Cinema. p39-42.
Time. Jun 9, 1941, v37, p8+.
Variety. May 21, 1941, p15.

Blood Money (US; Brown, Rowland; 1933)
Cinema Quarterly. Sum 1934, v2, p249-50.
Crime Movies. p70-71.
Film Daily. Nov 11, 1933, p3.
Hollywood Reporter. Nov 9, 1933, p2.
Motion Picture Herald. Nov 18, 1933, p36.
The New York Times. Nov 16, 1933, p30.
Rob Wagner's Script. Nov 18, 1933, v10, p9.
Time. Nov 27, 1933, v22, p31.

Vanity Fair. Jan 1933, v41, p46.
Variety. Nov 21, 1933, p20.

The Blood of a Poet (French title: Sang d'un Poète, Le)
 (FR; Cocteau, Jean; 1930)
BFI/Monthly Film Bulletin. May 1977, v44, p112.
Classics of the Foreign Film. p58-61.
Dictionary of Films. p325-26.
French Literary Filmmakers. p3-5.
Kiss Kiss Bang Bang. p295.
Magill's Survey of Cinema. Foreign Language Films. v1, p340-44.
The Nation. Aug 30, 1933, v137, p250.
National Board of Review Magazine. Feb 19, 1934, v9, p4.
The New Masses. Jan 9, 1934, v10, p29-30.
The New Statesman and Nation. Apr 8, 1933, v5, p446-47.
New York Times. Nov 3, 1933, p23.
The New Yorker. May 27, 1933, v9, p44.
The New Yorker. Nov 11, 1933, v9, p59.
Time. Nov 20, 1933, v22, p38.
Variety. Nov 7, 1933, p23.
Yale French Studies. Sum 1956, v17, p14-28.

Blossoms in the Dust (US; LeRoy, Mervyn; 1941)
Commonweal. Jul 11, 1941,, v34, p278.
Film Daily. Jun 23, 1941, p6.
Hollywood Reporter. Jun 24, 1941, p3.
The London Times. Oct 20, 1941, p8.
Motion Picture Exhibitor. Jul 9, 1941, p781-82.
The New Republic. Aug 4, 1941, v105, p155.
The New York Times. Jun 27, 1941, p14.
The New York Times. Jul 6, 1941, sec9, p3.
Newsweek. Jul 7, 1941, v18, p51.
Photoplay. Sep 1941, v19, p24.
Scribner's Commentator. Sep 1941, v10, p105-06.
Time. Jul 7, 1941, v38, p66.
Variety. Jun 25, 1941, p16.

Blossoms on Broadway (US; Wallace, Richard; 1937)
Motion Picture Herald. Nov 20, 1937, p35, 38.
Motion Picture World. Sep 25, 1937, p16-17.
The New York Times. Dec 3, 1937, p29.
Rob Wagner's Script. Jan 8, 1938, v18, p15.
Variety. Nov 17, 1937, p16.

The Blot (US; Weber, Lois; 1921)
Film Daily. Aug 21, 1921, p2.
Magill's Survey of Cinema. Silent Films. v1, p240-43.
Photoplay. Nov 1921, v20, p113.
Selected Film Criticism, 1921-1930. p46.
Variety. Aug 19, 1921, p35.

The Blue Angel (German title: Blaue Engel, Der) (GER;
 Sternberg, Josef von; 1930)
Authors on Film. p123-28.
The Blue Angel.
Canadian Forum. Jun 1931, v11, p357-58.
The Cinema of Josef von Sternberg. p101-12+.
Cinema, the Magic Vehicle. v1, p173-75.
Classics of the Foreign Film. p52-53.
Close-Up. Feb 1930, v6, p99.
Commonweal. Dec 31, 1930, v13, p242.
Dictionary of Films. p38.
Eighty Years of Cinema. p82-83.
Film Daily. Nov 16, 1930, p11.
Film Journal. Fall-Wint 1972, v1, p53-61.
The Films of Josef von Sternberg. p24-28.
The Films of Marlene Dietrich. p87-91.
From Caligari to Hitler. p215-18.
From Quasimodo to Scarlett O'Hara. p127-29.
Great Film Directors. p697-700.
Halliwell's Hundred. p28-32.
The Haunted Screen. p314.
The International Dictionary of Films and Filmmakers. v1,
 p60-61.

Judge. Dec 27, 1930, v99, p20.
Kiss Kiss Bang Bang. p296.
Life. Jan 2, 1931, v97, p20.
London Mercury. Aug 1930, v22, p361.
Magill's Survey of Cinema. Foreign Language Films. v1, p355-60.
Movie. Sum 1965, no13, p26-27.
Movies and Methods. p263-65.
National Board of Review Magazine. Jan 1931, v6, p9.
The New York Times. Dec 26, 1930, p21.
The New York Times. Dec 14, 1930, p4.
The New Yorker. Dec 13, 1930, v6, p97.
The New Yorker. Dec 20, 1930, v6, p79-80.
The Novel and the Cinema. p121-31.
Outlook and Independent. Dec 17, 1930, v156, p630.
Quarterly of Film, Radio and Television. Fall 1951, v6, p48-53.
Rob Wagner's Script. Feb 21, 1931, v5, p8.
Saturday Review (London). Aug 16, 1930, v150, p201.
Selected Film Criticism, 1921-1930. p47-48.
Sight and Sound. Aug-Sep 1951, v21, p42-44.
The Sociology of Film Art. p63-66.
The Spectator. Aug 16, 1930, v145, p214.
Sternberg. p24-27.
Sublime Marlene. p30-34.
Time. Dec 15, 1930, v16, p32.
Variety. Apr 30, 1930, p35.
Variety. Dec 10, 1930, p15.

The Blue Bird (US; Tourneur, Maurice; 1918)
Fifty Great American Silent Films, 1912-1920. p93-95.
Magill's Survey of Cinema. Silent Films. v1, p244-49.
Motion Picture News. Apr 13, 1918, p2307.
The Moving Picture World. Apr 6, 1918, p134.
The Moving Picture World. Apr 13, 1918, p283.
The New York Times. Apr 1, 1918, p9.
Photoplay. May 1918, v13, p80.
The Rivals of D.W. Griffith. p40-42.
Selected Film Criticism, 1912-1920. p27-30.
Variety. Apr 5, 1918, p43.
Wid's Daily. Apr 4, 1918, p1053-54.

Blue Blazes Rawden (US; Hart, William S.; 1918)
The Complete Films of William S. Hart. p84-85.
Motion Picture News. Mar 2, 1918, p1315.
The Moving Picture World. Feb 16, 1918, p1007.
The Moving Picture World. Mar 2, 1918, p1269.
The New York Times. Feb 18, 1918, p9.
Selected Film Criticism, 1912-1920. p30-31.
Variety. Mar 15, 1918, p46.
Wid's Daily. Feb 21, 1918, p964.

The Blue Dahlia (US; Marshall, George; 1946)
Agee on Film. v1, p202-03.
The Blue Dahlia.
Commonweal. May 24, 1946, v44, p143.
The Detective in Hollywood. p312-14.
Film Daily. Feb 6, 1946, p10.
The Films of Alan Ladd. p97-101.
Hollywood Reporter. Jan 28, 1946, p3.
Magill's Survey of Cinema. Series II. v1, p283-86.
Motion Picture Herald Product Digest. Feb 2, 1946, p2829.
The Nation. Jun 8, 1946, v162, p701.
The New Republic. Jun 3, 1946, v114, p806.
The New York Times. May 9, 1946, p27.
The New Yorker. May 18, 1946, v22, p91.
Newsweek. Apr 22, 1946, v27, p98+.
Raymond Chandler and Film. p44-56.
Raymond Chandler in Hollywood. p56-64.
Rob Wagner's Script. Jul 20, 1946, v32, p13.
Selected Film Criticism, 1941-1950 p27-30.
Time. May 13, 1946, v47, p98+.
Variety. Jan 30, 1946, p12.

The Blue Danube (GB; Wilcox, Herbert; 1934)
Film Daily. Nov 7, 1934, p9.
The New York Times. Nov 8, 1934, p27.
Variety. Nov 20, 1934, p17.

The Blue Express *See* China Express

Blue Jeans (US; Collins, John H.; 1918)
Exhibitor's Trade Review. Dec 29, 1918, p370.
Magill's Survey of Cinema. Silent Films. v1, p250-52.
Motion Picture News. Dec 29, 1917, p4587.
The Moving Picture World. Dec 29, 1917, p1959, 2003-04.
The Moving Picture World. Jan 5, 1918, p132.
The Rivals of D.W. Griffith. p46-49.
Variety. Mar 22, 1918, p50.
Wid's Daily. Mar 28, 1918, p1036.

The Blue Lagoon (GB; Launder, Frank; 1949)
Agee on Film. v1, p394.
Commonweal. Sep 30, 1949, v50, p608.
Film Daily. Aug 2, 1949, p6.
Hollywood Reporter. Jul 28, 1949, p3.
Motion Picture Herald Product Digest. Aug 6, 1949, p4706.
The New York Times. Oct 3, 1949, p13.
Newsweek. Aug 15, 1949, v34, p80.
Time. Sep 26, 1949, v54, p100.
Variety. Mar 9, 1949, p20.

The Blue Light (German title: Blaue Licht, Das) (GER; Riefenstahl, Leni; 1932)
BFI/Monthly Film Bulletin. Apr 1983, v49, p72.
Cinema Quarterly. Wint 1932, v1, p114.
Close-Up. Jun 1932, v9, p119-22.
Film Comment. Wint 1965, v3, p24-25.
Film Daily. May 8, 1934, p8.
Film Quarterly. Fall 1960, v14, p12-13.
From Caligari to Hitler. p258-59.
The German Cinema. p56-57.
The Haunted Screen. p313.
Leni Riefenstahl (Berg-Pan). p71-95.
Leni Riefenstahl: The Fallen Film Goddess. p29-35.
Magill's Survey of Cinema. Foreign Language Films. v1, p361-63.
The New Statesman and Nation. Nov 5, 1932, v4, p547.
The New York Times. May 9, 1934, p23.
Photoplay. Aug 1934, v46, p126.
Selected Film Criticism: Foreign Films, 1930-1950. p19.
Variety. Apr 29, 1932, p25.

Blue Skies (US; Werker, Alfred L.; 1929)
Film Daily. Jul 7, 1929, p8.
Variety. Jul 29, 1929, p53.

Blue Skies (US; Heisler, Stuart; 1946)
Commonweal. Oct 4, 1946, v44, p597.
Film Daily. Sep 26, 1946, p8.
The Films of Bing Crosby. p163-68.
The Hollywood Musical. p277.
Hollywood Musicals. p202, 208.
Hollywood Reporter. Sep 26, 1946, p3.
Life. Oct 7, 1946, v21, p116-19.
Motion Picture Herald Product Digest. Sep 28, 1946, p3221.
The New York Times. Oct 17, 1946, p28.
The New Yorker. Oct 12, 1946, v22, p66+.
Newsweek. Sep 30, 1946, v28, p90.
Starring Fred Astaire. p289-301.
Theatre Arts. Oct 1946, v30, p602.
Time. Oct 14, 1946, v48, p103.
Variety. Sep 25, 1946, p10.

Bluebeard's Eighth Wife (US; Lubitsch, Ernst; 1938)
The American Films of Ernst Lubitsch. p168-71.
The Cinema of Ernst Lubitsch. p102-04+.
Claudette Colbert (Quirk). p101-03.
Ernst Lubitsch: A Guide to References and Resources. p137-40.
The Film Career of Billy Wilder. p52-54.

The Film Criticism of Otis Ferguson. p218.
Film Daily. Mar 18, 1938, p4.
Film Society Review. Jan 1969, p30.
The Films of David Niven. p47-48.
The Films of Gary Cooper. p156-58.
Hollywood Reporter. Mar 17, 1938, p3.
Magill's Survey of Cinema. Series II. v1, p290-93.
Motion Picture Herald. Mar 26, 1938, p39, 42.
National Board of Review Magazine. Apr 1938, v13, p19.
The New Republic. Apr 6, 1938, v94, p275.
The New Statesman and Nation. Apr 23, 1938, v15, p688-89.
The New York Times. Mar 24, 1938, p21.
The New Yorker. Mar 26, 1938, v14, p60.
Newsweek. Mar 28, 1938, v11, p25-26.
Photoplay. Mar 1938, v52, p46-47.
Rob Wagner's Script. Mar 26, 1938, v19, p10-11.
The Spectator. Apr 29, 1938, v160, p747.
Stage. May 1938, v15, p27.
The Tatler. May 11, 1938, v148, pxxviii, 244.
Time. Mar 28, 1938, v31, p38.
Variety. Mar 23, 1938, p16.
World Film News. May-Jun 1938, v3, p83, 86-87.

Blues in the Night (US; Litvak, Anatole; 1941)
Commonweal. Dec 12, 1941, v35, p199.
Film Daily. Oct 30, 1941, p15.
Films in Review. Mar 1980, v31, p160-62.
The Hollywood Musical Goes to War. p40-41.
Hollywood Reporter. Oct 30, 1941, p3.
The London Times. Jun 29, 1942, p8.
Magill's Survey of Cinema. Series II. v1, p294-97.
Motion Picture Exhibitor. Nov 12, 1941, v27, n1, p889.
Motion Picture Herald Product Digest. Nov 1, 1941, p343.
The New York Times. Dec 12, 1941, p35.
The New York Times. Dec 14, 1941, sec9, p7.
Variety. Nov 5, 1941, p8.

Blushing Brides *See* Our Blushing Brides

Body and Soul (US; Santell, Alfred; 1931)
The Complete Films of Humphrey Bogart. p17.
Film Daily. Mar 15, 1931, p10.
The Films of Myrna Loy. p113-14.
Fortune. Aug 1931, v4, p114+.
Humphrey Bogart: The Man and His Films. p36-38.
Life. Apr 3, 1931, v97, p21.
Motion Picture Herald. Mar 7, 1931, p61.
The New York Times. Mar 14, 1931, p23.
The New York Times. Mar 22, 1931, p5.
The New Yorker. Mar 21, 1931, v7, p71, 73.
Time. Mar 23, 1931, v17, p46.
Variety. Mar 18, 1931, p14.

Body and Soul (US; Rosson, Richard; 1947)
BFI/Monthly Film Bulletin. Jan 1986, v86, p25-26.
Film Daily. Aug 13, 1947, p6.
Film Quarterly. Spr 1968, v21, p56.
The Films of John Garfield. p149-55.
Fortnight. Sep 12, 1947, v3, p30.
Hollywood Quarterly. Fall 1947, v3, p63-65.
Hollywood Reporter. Aug 13, 1947, p3.
The Hollywood Social Problem Films. p273-78.
Life. Sep 29, 1947, v23, p141-42.
Magill's Survey of Cinema, Series I. v1, p195-97.
Motion Picture Herald Product Digest. Aug 16, 1947, p3781.
The Nation. Nov 8, 1947, v165, p511.
New Movies. Nov 1947, v22, p9-10.
New Republic. Dec 1, 1947, v117, p55.
The New York Times. Nov 10, 1947, p21.
The New Yorker. Nov 15, 1947, v23, p118.
Newsweek. Sep 29, 1947, v30, p94.
Selected Film Criticism, 1941-1950. p30-31.
Theatre Arts. Oct 1947, v31, p52-54.
Time. Oct 20, 1947, v50, p101.
Variety. Aug 13, 1947, p15.

The Body Snatcher (US; Wise, Robert; 1945)
Classics of the Horror Film. p178-80.
Commonweal. Jun 15, 1941, v42, p214.
Film Daily. Feb 20, 1945, p8.
The Films of Bela Lugosi. p211-13.
The Films of Boris Karloff. p186-90.
Hollywood Reporter. Feb 14, 1941, p3.
Literature/Film Quarterly. 1982, v10, n1, p25-37.
Magic Moments from the Movies. 142-43.
Magill's Survey of Cinema. Series I. v1, p198-201.
Motion Picture Exhibitor. Feb 21, 1945, v33, n16, sec2, p1669.
Motion Picture Herald Product Digest. Feb 17, 1945, p2318.
The New York Times. May 26, 1945, p18.
Newsweek. Apr 30, 1945, v25, p96.
Time. May 21, 1945, v45, p94.
Val Lewton. p75-78, 153-59.
Variety. Feb 21, 1945, p8.

Bogataya Nevesta *See* The Country Bride

Boheme, La (US; Vidor, King; 1926)
Film Daily. Mar 7, 1926, p8.
Life. Apr 8, 1926, v87, p32.
Lillian Gish: The Movies, Mr. Griffith, and Me. p277-82.
Magill's Survey of Cinema. Silent Films. v1, p253-55.
Photoplay. May 1926, v24, p48.
Selected Film Criticism, 1921-1930. p160.
Variety. Mar 3, 1926, p34.

The Bohemian Girl (US; Horne, James; 1935)
Film Daily. Feb 6, 1936, p9.
Hollywood Reporter. Dec 12, 1935, p3.
Laurel and Hardy. p319-27.
Motion Picture Herald. Mar 7, 1936, p51.
The New York Times. Feb 17, 1936, p21.
Variety. Feb 19, 1936, p12.

Bolero (US; Ruggles, Wesley; 1934)
Film Daily. Feb 17, 1934, p3.
The Films of the Thirties. p131-32.
The Hollywood Musical. p85.
Hollywood Reporter. Feb 7, 1934, p3.
Motion Picture Herald. Feb 17, 1934, p35.
The New York Times. Feb 17, 1934, p20.
Variety. Feb 20, 1934, p25.

Bombshell (US; Fleming, Victor; 1933)
Film Daily. Oct 11, 1933, p2.
The Films of Jean Harlow. p88-95.
Hollywood Reporter. Sep 28, 1933, p3.
Judge. Jan 1934, v106, p12, 26.
Literary Digest. Nov 4, 1933, v116, p35.
Lunatics and Lovers. p259, 262.
Magill's Survey of Cinema. Series I. v1, p202-04.
Motion Picture Herald. Oct 7, 1933, p35.
The New York Times. Oct 21, 1933, p11.
The New York Times. Oct 29, 1933, p3.
The New Yorker. Oct 28, 1933, v9, p49-50.
Newsweek. Oct 28, 1933, v2, p28.
Rob Wagner's Script. Oct 28, 1933, v10, p10.
Time. Oct 23, 1933, v22, p43.
Variety. Oct 24, 1933, p17.

Bonaparte et la Revolution *See* Napoleon

Bonds of Honor (US; Worthington, William; 1919)
Motion Picture News. Feb 8, 1919, p919.
The Moving Picture World. Jan 25, 1919, p541-42.
The New York Times. Oct 5, 1919, sec4, p5.
Variety. Jan 31, 1919, p53.
Wid's Daily. Jan 26, 1919, p23.

Bonheur, Le (FR; Herbier, Marcel L'; 1936)
Film Daily. Feb 29, 1936, p7.
Hollywood Reporter. Jun 6, 1936, p3.
Hollywood Reporter. Apr 3, 1935, p3.

Motion Picture Herald. Mar 21, 1936, p41.
The New York Times. Feb 28, 1936, p18.
Variety. Mar 6, 1935, p21.
Variety. Mar 4, 1936, p31.

Bonne Chance (FR; Guitry, Sacha; 1935)
Garbo and the Night Watchman. p86-87.
Graham Greene on Film. p55-56.
The New Statesman and Nation. Feb 29, 1936, v11, p308.
The Spectator. Feb 28, 1936, v156, p343.
Variety. Oct 30, 1935, p15.

Boom Town (US; Conway, Jack; 1940)
Commonweal. Sep 13, 1940, v32, p429.
Film Daily. Aug 6, 1940, p8.
The Films of Clark Gable. p198-99.
The Films of Hedy Lamarr. p118-23.
The Films of Spencer Tracy. p161-64.
The London Times. May 9, 1941, p6.
Magill's Survey of Cinema. Series II. v1, p305-08.
The New Republic. Aug 19, 1940, v103, p246.
The New York Times. Sep 6, 1940, p25.
The New York Times. Sep 8, 1940, sec9, p3.
Newsweek. Sep 9, 1940, v16, p62.
Photoplay. Oct 1940, v54, p67.
Time. Aug 26, 1940, v36, p48.
Variety. Aug 7, 1940, p14.

Boomerang (US; Kazan, Elia; 1947)
Commonweal. Mar 21, 1947, v45, p566.
Film Daily. Jan 24, 1947, p6.
The Films of the Forties. p188-90.
Hollywood Reporter. Jan 24, 1947, p3.
Life. Mar 24, 1947, 22, p87-88.
Magill's Survey of Cinema, Series II. v1, p309-11.
Motion Picture Herald Product Digest. Feb 1, 1947, p3446.
The Nation. Mar 22, 1947, v164, p340.
New Republic. Feb 17, 1947, v116, p39.
The New York Times. Mar 6, 1947, p36.
The New Yorker. Mar 15, 1947, v23, p64.
Newsweek. Mar 17, 1947, v29, p100.
Photoplay. Mar 1948, v32, p41.
Time. Mar 10, 1947, v49, p97.
Variety. Jan 29, 1947, p8.

Boots (US; Clifton, Elmer; 1919)
Exhibitor's Trade Review. Mar 8, 1919, p1065.
Motion Picture News. Mar 1, 1919, p1349-51.
Motion Picture News. Mar 15, 1919, p1712.
The Moving Picture World. Mar 8, 1919, p1390.
The New York Times. Mar 10, 1919, p9.
Variety. Mar 14, 1919, p46, 48.
Wid's Daily. Mar 2, 1919, p11.

Bordertown (US; Mayo, Archie; 1935)
Bette Davis: Her Films and Career. p59-60.
Film Daily. Jan 24, 1935, p3.
Hollywood Reporter. Jan 14, 1935, p3.
Motion Picture Herald. Feb 2, 1935, p58.
The Nation. Feb 6, 1935, v140, p168.
The New Masses. Feb 5, 1935, v14, p30.
The New York Times. Jan 24, 1935, p22.
The New Yorker. Feb 2, 1935, v10, p57.
Newsweek. Jan 12, 1935, v5, p32.
Paul Muni: His Life and His Films. p130-34.
Time. Jan 14, 1935, v25, p36.
Variety. Jan 29, 1935, p14.

Borinage (Also titled: Misere au Borinage) (BELGIUM; Ivens, Joris; 1933)
Dictionary of Films. p40.
The Documentary Tradition. p164.
Film on the Left. p119-21.
Joris Ivens, Film-Maker. p68-75.
Non-Fiction Film: A Critical History. p88-91.

Born Reckless (US; Ford, John; 1930)
Exhibitors Herald-World. Jun 21, 1930, p70.
Film Daily. May 25, 1930, p16.
The Great Gangster Pictures. p53.
Life. Jun 29, 1930, v95, p17.
New York Times. Jun 7, 1930, p10.
New York Times. Jun 5, 1930, p5.
The New Yorker. Jun 14, 1930, v6, p71-72.
Variety. Jun 11, 1930, p19.

Born Reckless (US; St. Clair, Malcolm; 1937)
Film Daily. Jun 22, 1937, p20.
Hollywood Reporter. Jun 19, 1937, p3.
Hollywood Spectator. Jul 3, 1937, v12, p12-13.
Motion Picture Herald. Jun 26, 1937, p89, 92.
The New York Times. Jul 30, 1937, p22.
Variety. Jul 21, 1937, p18.

Born to Dance (US; Del Ruth, Roy; 1936)
Film Daily. Nov 17, 1936, p9.
The Films of James Stewart. p39-40.
The Films of the Thirties. p175-77.
Garbo and the Night Watchman. p137-38.
Hollywood Reporter. Nov 14, 1936, p3.
Hollywood Spectator. Nov 7, 1936, v11, p9-10.
Motion Picture Herald. Nov 21, 1936, p51.
The New Masses. Dec 22, 1936, v21, p29.
The New York Times. Dec 5, 1936, p16.
The New Yorker. Dec 12, 1936, v12, p97.
Newsweek. Dec 12, 1936, v8, p32+.
Rob Wagner's Script. Nov 28, 1936, v16, p10.
The Spectator. Jan 8, 1937, v158, p47.
Time. Dec 7, 1936, v28, p26.
Variety. Dec 9, 1936, p12.
World Film News. Feb 1937, v1, p25.

Boudu Savé Des Eaux (Also titled: Boudu Saved from Drowning) (FR; Renoir, Jean; 1932)
Cahiers du Cinema in English. Mar 1967, n9, p53.
The Comic Mind. p238-42.
Dictionary of Films. p41.
Eighty Years of Cinema. p91.
Film Daily. Feb 24, 1967, p8.
Film Society Review. Feb 1967, p23-24.
Film Society Review. Nov 1967, p24, 32.
Films and Filming. Apr 1962, v8, p13-15, p38-41.
Films and Filming. Nov 1965, v12, p32.
French Film (Sadoul). p67.
The International Dictionary of Films and Filmmakers. v1, p66.
Jean Renoir: A Guide to References and Resources. p82-84.
Jean Renoir (Bazin). p30-33.
Jean Renoir (Durgnat). p85-91.
Jean Renoir (Gilliatt). p41-42.
Jean Renoir: My Life and My Films. p116-17.
Jean Renoir: The French Films, 1924-1939. p112-39.
Jean Renoir: The World of His Films. p49-50, 112-16.
Jump Cut. Jan-Feb 1975, n5, p20-21.
Magill's Survey of Cinema. Foreign Language Films. v1, p398-401.
Movie Man. p82-83, 144-45.
New Left Review. May-Jun 1964, n25, p58-59.
The New York Times. Feb 24, 1967, p26.
Variety. Mar 1, 1967, p6.
The Village Voice. Feb 23, 1967, v12, p23.
Wide Angle. n4 1981, v4, p4-11.

Bought (US; Mayo, Archie; 1931)
Film Daily. Aug 16, 1931, p10.
Hollywood Reporter. Jul 9, 1931, p3.
Hollywood Spectator. Sep 12, 1931, v12, p23.
Motion Picture Herald. Jul 18, 1931, p38, 40.
The New York Times. Aug 15, 1931, p18.
Outlook and Independent. Sep 16, 1931, v159, p87.
Rob Wagner's Script. Sep 12, 1931, v6, p10-11.

Time. Aug 24, 1931, v18, p21.
Variety. Aug 18, 1931, p17.

The Bowery (US; Walsh, Raoul; 1933)
Each Man in His Own Time. p248-53.
Film Daily. Oct 7, 1933, p4.
Films and Filming. Jul 1973, v19, p32-33.
Hollywood Reporter. Sep 25, 1933, p1, 3.
Motion Picture Herald. Oct 7, 1933, p35.
New Outlook. Nov 1933, v162, p42.
The New York Times. Oct 5, 1933, p24.
The New Yorker. Oct 14, 1933, v9, p54.
Rob Wagner's Script. Oct 7, 1933, v10, p11-12.
Time. Oct 9, 1933, v22, p32.
Variety. Oct 10, 1933, p17.

The Boy From Barnardos *See* Lord Jeff

Boy Meets Girl (US; Bacon, Lloyd; 1938)
Commonweal. Sep 9, 1938, v28, p505.
Film Daily. Jul 22, 1938, p7.
The Films of James Cagney. p125-28.
The Films of Ronald Reagan. p53-54.
Hollywood Reporter. Jul 19, 1938, p3.
Motion Picture Herald. Jul 23, 1938, p39.
The New Masses. Sep 6, 1938, v28, p30.
The New York Times. Aug 27, 1938, p7.
The New Yorker. Sep 3, 1938, v14, p44.
Newsweek. Sep 5, 1938, v12, p22-23.
Rob Wagner's Script. Aug 20, 1938, v20, p14.
Time. Sep 5, 1938, v31, p32.
Variety. Aug 31, 1938, p18.
World Film News. Sep 1938, v3, p222.
World Film News. Nov 1938, v3, p312.

Boy of the Streets (US; Nigh, William; 1937)
Film Daily. Dec 2, 1937, p7.
Hollywood Reporter. Dec 2, 1937, p3.
Literary Digest. Dec 25, 1937, v124, p34.
Motion Picture Herald. Dec 14, 1937, p40-41.
National Board of Review Magazine. Dec 1937, v12, p9.
The New Masses. Jan 18, 1938, v26, p29.
The New Republic. Jan 5, 1938, v93, p256-57.
The New York Times. Jan 24, 1938, p17.
The New Yorker. Jan 22, 1938, v13, p56.
Scholastic. Dec 18, 1937, v31, p36.
Time. Dec 20, 1937, v30, p51.
Variety. Dec 1, 1937, p14.

The Boy with Green Hair (US; Losey, Joseph; 1948)
Collier's. Jan 15, 1949, v123, p36.
Commonweal. Jan 21, 1949, v49, p378.
Film Daily. Nov 16, 1948, p6.
Hollywood Reporter. Nov 16, 1948, p3.
Joseph Losey (Hirsch). p31-36.
Life. Dec 6, 1948, v25, p82-84.
Magill's Survey of Cinema. Series I. v1, p212-14.
Motion Picture Herald Product Digest. Nov 20, 1948, p4389.
The New Republic. Jan 17, 1949, v24, p55.
The New York Times. Jan 13, 1949, p26.
Newsweek. Jan 17, 1949, v33, p74.
Rotarian. Apr 1949, v74, p36.
Time. Jan 10, 1949, v53, p84.
Variety. Nov 17, 1948, p13.

Boys' School *See* Disparus de Saint-Agil, Les

Boys Town (US; Taurog, Norman; 1938)
Canadian Magazine. Oct 1938, v90, p55.
Commonweal. Sep 23, 1938, v28, p561.
Esquire. Jan 1939, v11, p82.
The Film Criticism of Otis Ferguson. p235.
Film Daily. Sep 6, 1938, p11.
The Films of Spencer Tracy. p147-49.
Hollywood Reporter. Sep 2, 1938, p3.
Hollywood Spectator. Sep 17, 1938, v13, p7.

Magill's Survey of Cinema, Series II. v1, p325-27.
Motion Picture Herald. Sep 10, 1938, p55.
National Board of Review Magazine. Oct 1938, v13, p18.
The New Republic. Sep 21, 1938, v96, p188.
The New York Times. Sep 9, 1938, p25.
The New Yorker. Sep 10, 1938, v14, p59.
Newsweek. Sep 19, 1938, v12, p23.
Photoplay. Nov 1938, v52, p22-23+.
Rob Wagner's Script. Sep 17, 1938, v20, p13.
Scholastic. Oct 1, 1938, v33, p13.
The Tatler. Oct 5, 1938, v150, p6.
Time. Sep 12, 1938, v32, p45.
Variety. Sep 7, 1938, p12.
World Film News. Nov 1938, v3, p312.

The Brasher Doubloon (Also titled: The High Window)
(US; Brahm, John; 1947)
Film Daily. Feb 6, 1947, p8.
Motion Picture Herald Product Digest. Feb 8, 1947, p3458.
The New Republic. Jun 16, 1947, v116, p32.
The New York Times. May 22, 1947, p34.
Newsweek. Apr 21, 1947, v29, p96.
Raymond Chandler and Film. p121-53.
Raymond Chandler in Hollywood. p95-102.
Raymond Chandler on Screen. p86-114.
Time. Jun 2, 1947, v49, p97.
Variety. Feb 5, 1947, p12.

The Brat (US; Ford, John; 1931)
Film Daily. Aug 2, 1931, p11.
Hollywood Reporter. Jul 14, 1931, p3.
John Ford. p55.
Motion Picture Herald. Jul 25, 1931, p34.
The New York Times. Aug 24, 1931, p13.
Variety. Aug 25, 1931, p20.

Break of Hearts (US; Moeller, Philip; 1935)
Film Daily. May 16, 1935, p10.
The Films of Katharine Hepburn. p63-66.
Graham Greene on Film. p20-21.
Hollywood Reporter. May 10, 1935, p3.
Literary Digest. Jun 1, 1935, v119, p25.
Motion Picture Herald. May 25, 1935, p54.
The Nation. May 29, 1935, v140, p640.
The New Statesman and Nation. Sep 14, 1935, v10, p343.
The New York Times. May 17, 1935, p24.
The New Yorker. May 25, 1935, v11, p69-70.
Newsweek. May 25, 1935, v5, p34.
Rob Wagner's Script. Jun 1, 1935, v13, p10.
The Spectator. Sep 13, 1935, v155, p390.
Time. May 27, 1935, v25, p34.
Variety. May 22, 1935, p16.

Break the News (GB; Clair, René; 1938)
Chevalier. p146-49.
Film Daily. Jan 10, 1941, p8.
Motion Picture Herald. May 14, 1938, p52.
The Nation. Mar 17, 1945, v160, p314.
The New Statesman and Nation. May 21, 1938, v15, p872.
The New York Times. Jan 2, 1941, p24.
René Clair. p132-34.
The Spectator. May 27, 1938, v160, p960.
Variety. Jan 8, 1941, p24.
World Film News. Jul 1938, v3, p130.

Breaking the Ice (US; Cline, Edward; 1938)
Film Daily. Sep 1, 1938, p7.
Hollywood Reporter. Aug 23, 1938, p3.
Hollywood Spectator. Sep 3, 1938, v13, p10-11.
Motion Picture Herald. Aug 27, 1938, p53.
The New York Times. Sep 23, 1938, p35.
Time. Sep 12, 1938, v32, p46.
Time. Oct 3, 1938, v32, p36.
Variety. Sep 7, 1938, p12.

The Breath of Araby (US; Gaskill, Charles; 1915)
Motion Picture News. Apr 10, 1915, p59.
The Moving Picture World. Apr 10, 1915, p241.
The Moving Picture World. May 1, 1915, p780.
The New York Dramatic Mirror. Apr 7, 1915, p28, 33.
Vitagraph Life Portrayals. May 1915, p17.

Breccia di Porta Pia, La *See* Presa di Roma

Brewster's Millions (US; DeMille, Cecil B.; Apfel, Oscar C.; 1914)
The Moving Picture World. Apr 18, 1914, p336, 428.
The New York Dramatic World. Apr 15, 1914, p40.
The New York Dramatic World. Apr 22, 1914, p30.
Variety. May 1, 1914, p21.

Brewster's Millions (GB; Freeland, Thornton; 1935)
Film Daily. Apr 5, 1935, p6.
Hollywood Reporter. Apr 19, 1935, p3.
Motion Picture Herald. Apr 13, 1935, p50.
The New York Times. Apr 8, 1935, p23.
Variety. Feb 5, 1935, p31.
Variety. Apr 10, 1935, p17.

The Bride Came C.O.D. (US; Keighley, William; 1941)
Bette Davis: Her Films and Career. p108-09.
Commonweal. Aug 1, 1941, v34, p352.
Film Daily. Jul 2, 1941, p10.
The Films of James Cagney. p162-64.
Hollywood Reporter. Jun 26, 1941, p3.
The London Times. Jul 1, 1942, p6.
Motion Picture Exhibitor. Jul 9, 1941, p784.
The New Republic. Jul 21, 1941, v105, p85.
The New York Times. Jul 26, 1941, p18.
Newsweek. Jul 21, 1941, v18, p53.
Scribner's Commentator. Oct 1941, v10, p105-06.
Time. Jul 28, 1941, v38, p74.
Variety. Jul 2, 1941, p12.

The Bride Comes Home (US; Ruggles, Wesley; 1935)
Canadian Magazine. Feb 1936, v85, p38.
Claudette Colbert (Quirk). p86-87.
Commonweal. Dec 27, 1935, v23, p244.
Film Daily. Dec 27, 1935, p4.
Graham Greene on Film. p45-46.
Hollywood Reporter. Nov 11, 1935, p3.
Hollywood Spectator. Dec 21, 1935, v10, p12-13.
Judge. Feb 1936, v110, p14.
Lunatics and Lovers. p30-31.
Motion Picture Herald. Nov 23, 1935, p74-75.
The New York Times. Dec 25, 1935, p30.
The New Yorker. Jan 4, 1936, v11, p49.
Time. Jan 6, 1936, v27, p28.
Variety. Jan 1, 1936, p44.

Bride for Sale (US; Russell, William D.; 1949)
Claudette Colbert (Quirk). p157-58.
Film Daily. Oct 19, 1949, p4.
Hollywood Reporter. Oct 19, 1949, p3.
Motion Picture Herald. Oct 22, 1949, p58.
The New York Times. Nov 21, 1949, p29.
Newsweek. Dec 5, 1949, v34, p83.
Rotarian. Feb 1950, v76, p38.
Time. Apr 25, 1949, v53, p100.
Variety. Oct 19, 1949, p8.

The Bride Goes Wild (US; Taurog, Norman; 1948)
Commonweal. Apr 30, 1948, v48, p675.
Film Daily. Mar 3, 1948, p6.
Motion Picture Herald Product Digest. Feb 28, 1948, p4077.
The New York Times. Jun 4, 1948, p8.
Time. Jun 21, 1948, v51, p96.
Variety. Jun 4, 1948, p27.

The Bride of Frankenstein (US; Whale, James; 1935)
Cinema of the Fantastic. p89-106.
Classics of the Horror Film. p36-61.
A Companion to the Movies. p36.
Esquire. Jun 1935, v3, p144.
The Film Criticism of Otis Ferguson. p79.
Film Daily. Apr 11, 1935, p9.
The Films of the Thirties. p144-45.
Focus on the Horror Film. p74-82.
Graham Greene on Film. p5-6.
Halliwell's Hundred. p33-36.
Hollywood Reporter. Apr 8, 1935, p3.
Horror! p126-30.
James Whale (Curtis). pxvi-ii, 120-27.
Judge. Jun 1935, v108, p23.
Magill's Survey of Cinema. Series I. v1, p222-24.
Motion Picture Herald. Apr 20, 1935, p34.
Movie Monsters and Their Masters: The Birth of the Horror Film. p43.
The New Republic. May 29, 1935, v83, p75.
The New York Times. May 11, 1935, p21.
The New Yorker. May 25, 1935, v11, p70.
Newsweek. May 4, 1935, v5, p25.
Rob Wagner's Script. Apr 20, 1935, v13, p8.
Selected Film Criticism, 1931-1940. p32-33.
The Spectator. Jul 5, 1935, v155, p14.
Terrors of the Screen. p70-72.
Time. Apr 29, 1935, v25, p52.
Variety. May 15, 1935, p19.

Bride of the Regiment (US; Dillon, John Francis; 1930)
Exhibitors Herald-World. May 31, 1930, p124.
Exhibitors Herald-World. Jun 14, 1930, p108.
Film Daily. May 26, 1930, p16.
The New York Times. May 22, 1930, p32.
The New Yorker. May 31, 1930, v6, p61-62.
Outlook and Independent. Jun 4, 1930, v155, p192.
Theatre Magazine. Jul 1930, v52, p47.
Time. Jun 2, 1930, v15, p64.
Variety. May 28, 1930, p21.

The Bride Walks Out (US; Jason, Leigh; 1936)
Film Daily. Jul 1, 1936, p8.
The Films of Barbara Stanwyck. p107-08.
Garbo and the Night Watchman. p68, 71.
Hollywood Spectator. Jul 4, 1936, v11, p19.
Motion Picture Herald. Jul 11, 1936, p105, 108.
The New York Times. Jul 10, 1936, p15.
The New Yorker. Jul 18, 1936, v12, p45.
Rob Wagner's Script. Jul 11, 1936, v15, p12-13.
Starring Miss Barbara Stanwyck. p77, 80.
Time. Jul 20, 1936, v28, p36.
World Film News. Jan 1937, v1, p26-27.

The Bride Wore Boots (US; Pichel, Irving; 1946)
Commonweal. May 31, 1946, v44, p167.
Film Daily. Mar 19, 1946, p11.
The Films of Barbara Stanwyck. p166-67.
Hollywood Reporter. Mar 19, 1946, p3.
Motion Picture Herald Product Digest. Mar 23, 1946, p2905.
The New York Times. Jun 6, 1946, p16.
Newsweek. Jun 10, 1946, v27, p93.
Starring Miss Barbara Stanwyck. p185-92.
Time. Jun 3, 1946, v47, p98+.
Variety. Mar 20, 1946, p8.

The Bride Wore Red (US; Arzner, Dorothy; 1937)
Chestnuts in Her Lap. p25-28.
Commonweal. Oct 15, 1937, v26, p580.
Film Daily. Oct 12, 1937, p6.
The Films of Joan Crawford. p126-27.
Hollywood Reporter. Sep 23, 1937, p3.
Motion Picture Herald. Oct 2, 1937, p36.
The New York Times. Oct 15, 1937, p18.
The New Yorker. Oct 16, 1937, v13, p7.

Rob Wagner's Script. Oct 23, 1937, v18, p12.
Scholastic. Oct 23, 1937, v31, p37.
Time. Oct 18, 1937, v30, p29.
Variety. Sep 29, 1937, p14.

The Bridge at San Luis Rey (US; Brabin, Charles; 1929)
Film Daily. Oct 27, 1928, p12.
Film Daily. Apr 28, 1929, p9.
Magill's Cinema Annual, 1982. p408-11.
The New York Times. May 20, 1929, p22.
Outlook. Jun 5, 1929, v152, p235.
Variety. May 22, 1929, p16.

The Bridge of San Luis Rey (US; Lee, Rowland V.; 1944)
Film Daily. Feb 3, 1944, p4.
Hollywood Reporter. Feb 1, 1944, p7.
The New York Times. Mar 4, 1944, p11.
The New Yorker. Mar 4, 1944, v20, p46+.
Scholastic. Mar 27, 1944, v44, p38.
Variety. Feb 2, 1944, p18.

Brief Encounter (GB; Lean, David; 1945)
Around Cinemas, Second Series. p261-62.
The Cinema of David Lean. p51-59.
Cinema, the Magic Vehicle. v1, p400-01.
Classic Movies. p97-99.
Commonweal. Sep 13, 1946, v44, p526-27.
David Lean and His Films. p39-52.
David Lean (Anderegg). p25-36.
Fifty Classic British Films. p58-60.
Film Daily. Aug 23, 1946, p10.
The Great British Films. p91-93.
Halliwell's Hundred. p37-39.
Magill's Survey of Cinema. Series I. v1, p230-33.
Motion Picture Herald Product Digest. Aug 31, 1946, p3174.
The Nation. Aug 31, 1946, v163, p249.
The New Republic. Oct 21, 1946, v115, p518-19.
The New York Times. Aug 26, 1946, p21.
The New Yorker. Sep 7, 1946, v22, p48.
Newsweek. Sep 2, 1946, v28, p76.
Reruns: Fifty Memorable Films. p65-67.
Rob Wagner's Script. Nov 9, 1946, v32, p742.
Saturday Review. Oct 12, 1946, v29, p36-37.
Selected Film Criticism: Foreign Films, 1930-1950. p19-21.
Seventy Years of Cinema. p155-56.
Theatre Arts. Oct 1946, v30, p596, 604.
Time. Sep 9, 1946, v48, p102+.
Variety. Nov 28, 1945, p17.

Brigham Young—Frontiersman (US; Hathaway, Henry; 1940)
Commonweal. Sep 20, 1940, v32, p449.
Film Daily. Aug 27, 1940, p7.
The Films of Tyrone Power. p106-09.
Hollywood Reporter. Aug 26, 1940, p3.
Life. Sep 23, 1940, v9, p59-67.
Motion Picture Herald. Aug 31, 1940, p42.
The New York Times. Sep 21, 1940, p13.
Newsweek. Sep 23, 1940, v16, p51-52.
Time. Oct 7, 1940, v32, p63.
Variety. Aug 28 1940, p16.

Bright Eyes (US; Butler, David; 1934)
Film Daily. Dec 11, 1934, p6.
The Films of Shirley Temple. p142-45.
Hollywood Reporter. Nov 22, 1934, p3.
Motion Picture Herald. Dec 15, 1934, p40.
The New York Times. Dec 21, 1934, p31.
Time. Dec 31, 1934, v24, p14.
Variety. Dec 25, 1934, p12.

Bright Lights (US; Curtiz, Michael; 1931)
Film Daily. Feb 15, 1931, p10.
Judge. Mar 7, 1931, v100, p20.
The New York Times. Feb 10, 1931, p24.

Time. Feb 23, 1931, v17, p62.
Variety. Mar 3, 1931, p21.

Bright Shawl (US; Robertson, John S.; 1923)
Film Daily. Apr 22, 1923, p3.
Magill's Survey of Cinema. Silent Films. v1, p256-58.
The New York Times. Apr 23, 1923, p18.
Photoplay. Jul 1923, v24, p68.
Selected Film Criticism, 1921-1930. p49-50.
Variety. Apr 26, 1923, p18.

Brillantenschiff, Das *See* The Spiders

Bring 'Em Back Alive (US; Elliott, Clyde; 1932)
Commonweal. Aug 3, 1932, v16, p351.
Film Daily. Jun 5, 1932, p10.
Motion Picture Herald. Jun 4, 1932, p35.
The Nation. Jul 6, 1932, v135, p18.
National Board of Review Magazine. Jun 1932, v7, p9.
The New Statesman and Nation. Sep 17, 1932, v3, p314.
The New York Times. Jun 18, 1932, p9.
The New Yorker. Jun 25, 1932, v8, p49.
Time. Jun 27, 1932, v19, p24.
Variety. Jun 21, 1932, p14.

Bringing Up Baby (US; Hawks, Howard; 1938)
The Comic Mind. p253-56.
Commonweal. Mar 4, 1938, v27, p524.
Dictionary of Films. p42-43.
The Film Criticism of Otis Ferguson. p215-16.
Film Daily. Feb 11, 1938, p12.
The Films of Cary Grant. p116-19.
The Films of Howard Hawks (Willis). p3-9.
The Films of Katharine Hepburn. p91-95.
Halliwell's Hundred. p40-43.
Hollywood Reporter. Feb 10, 1938, p3.
Howard Hawks. p249-72.
Howard Hawks, Storyteller. p133-61.
The International Dictionary of Films and Filmmakers. v1, p67-68.
Kiss Kiss Bang Bang. p297-98.
Life. Feb 28, 1938, v4, p22-23.
Lunatics and Lovers. p111-15.
Magill's Survey of Cinema, Series I. v1, p237-42.
Motion Picture Herald. Feb 19, 1938, p39, 46.
The New Masses. Mar 15, 1938, v26, p28.
The New Republic. Mar 16, 1938, v94, p165.
The New Statesman and Nation. Mar 26, 1938, v15, p527-28.
The New York Times. Mar 4, 1938, p17.
The New Yorker. Mar 5, 1938, v14, p47-48.
Pursuits of Happiness. p111-32.
Rob Wagner's Script. Feb 19, 1938, v19, p10-11.
Saint Nicholas. Apr 1938, v65, p42.
The Spectator. Apr 8, 1938, v160, p627.
Stage. May 1938, v15, p27.
Theatre Arts. Jun 1938, v22, p417.
Time. Mar 7, 1938, v31, p38.
Variety. Feb 16, 1938, p15.
World Film News. May-Jun 1938, v3, p88-89.

Britannia Mews *See* The Forbidden Street

British Agent (US; Curtiz, Michael; 1934)
Film Daily. Aug 2, 1934, p11.
Hollywood Reporter. Aug 1, 1934, p3.
Literary Digest. Sep 29, 1934, v118, p29.
Motion Picture Herald. Jun 23, 1934, p107.
Motion Picture Herald. Aug 11, 1934, p31-34.
The New York Times. Sep 20, 1934, p20.
Time. Sep 17, 1934, v24, p40.
Variety. Sep 25, 1934, p13.

Broadway Bill (US; Capra, Frank; 1934)
Film Daily. Nov 9, 1934, p7.
The Films of Frank Capra (Scherle and Levy). p131-32.
The Films of Frank Capra (Willis). p151-55.

The Films of Myrna Loy. p179-81.
Frank Capra (Maland). p83-86.
Hollywood Reporter. Oct 25, 1934, p3.
Literary Digest. Dec 15, 1934, v118, p36.
Motion Picture Herald. Jul 14, 1934, p48.
Motion Picture Herald. Nov 10, 1934, p38.
The Name Above the Title. p405-06.
The New Republic. Dec 19, 1934, v81, p167.
The New York Times. Nov 30, 1934, p22.
Newsweek. Dec 8, 1934, v4, p26.
Time. Dec 10, 1934, v24, p28.
Variety. Dec 4, 1934, p12.

Broadway Gondolier (US; Bacon, Lloyd; 1935)
Film Daily. Jul 11, 1935, p8.
The Hollywood Musical. p105.
Hollywood Musicals. p82-83.
Hollywood Reporter. Jun 26, 1935, p3.
Motion Picture Herald. Jul 6, 1935, p72.
The New York Times. Jul 18, 1935, p15.
Rob Wagner's Script. Aug 10, 1935, v13, p8.
Time. Jul 29, 1935, v26, p42.
Variety. Jul 24, 1935, p21.

The Broadway Melody (US; Beaumont, Harry; 1929)
Film Daily. Feb 17, 1929, p10.
The Film Mercury. Feb 22, 1929, v9, p6.
The Films of the Twenties. p224-27.
The Hollywood Musical. p22.
Hollywood Musicals. p33-44.
Magill's Survey of Cinema. Series I. v1, p243-44.
The New York Times. Feb 9, 1929, p15.
Selected Film Criticism, 1921-1930. p51-53.
Variety. Feb 13, 1929, p13.

Broadway Melody of 1936 (US; Del Ruth, Roy; 1935)
Canadian Magazine. Nov 1935, v84, p41.
Esquire. Dec 1935, v4, p118.
The Film Criticism of Otis Ferguson. p94.
Film Daily. Aug 29, 1935, p4.
The Films of Robert Taylor. p41-42.
The Hollywood Musical. p102, 106+.
Hollywood Musicals. p119-21.
Hollywood Reporter. Aug 26, 1935, p3.
Motion Picture Herald. Sep 7, 1935, p12.
The New Republic. Oct 2, 1935, v84, p216.
The New Statesman and Nation. Dec 21, 1935, v10, p980.
The New York Times. Sep 19, 1935, p28.
The New Yorker. Sep 28, 1935, v11, p63-64.
Rob Wagner's Script. Sep 21, 1935, v14, p10.
Selected Film Criticism, 1931-1940. p34-35.
Stage. Oct 1935, v13, p6.
Time. Sep 23, 1935, v26, p46.
Variety. Sep 25, 1935, p12.

Broadway Melody of 1938 (US; Del Ruth, Roy; 1937)
Film Daily. Aug 17, 1937, p4.
Hollywood Reporter. Aug 14, 1937, p3.
Hollywood Spectator. Aug 28, 1937, v12, p8-9.
Judy: The Films and Career of Judy Garland. p47-50.
Motion Picture Herald. Aug 21, 1937, p54.
The New York Times. Sep 3, 1937, p12.
The New Yorker. Sep 4, 1937, v13, p60.
Rob Wagner's Script. Aug 28, 1937, v17, p10.
Sight and Sound. Aut 1937, v6, p142.
Time. Aug 30, 1937, v30, p23-24.
Variety. Aug 18, 1937, p27.
World Film News. Oct 1937, v2, p20.
World Film News. Nov 1937, v2, p23.

Broadway Melody of 1940 (US; Taurog, Norman; 1940)
Commonweal. Mar 1, 1940, v31, p413.
Film Daily. Feb 14, 1940, p5.
The Hollywood Musical. p173, 209.
The Hollywood Musical Goes to War. p128-29.
Hollywood Musicals. p167-69.

The London Times. Jul 29, 1940, p6.
Magill's Survey of Cinema. Series I. v1, p245-47.
The MGM Years. p34-35.
The New York Times. Mar 29, 1940, p25.
The New York Times. Mar 31, 1940, sec9, p5.
Photoplay. Apr 1940, v54, p68.
Starring Fred Astaire. p200-11.
Time. Mar 4, 1940, v35, p69.
Variety. Feb 7, 1940, p14.

Broadway Thru a Keyhole (US; Sherman, Lowell; 1933)
Film Daily. Nov 2, 1933, p6.
The Great Gangster Pictures. p60-61.
Hollywood Reporter. Oct 7, 1933, p3.
Motion Picture Herald. Oct 21, 1933, p39.
The New York Times. Nov 2, 1933, p18.
The New Yorker. Nov 11, 1933, v9, p59.
Newsweek. Nov 11, 1933, v2, p29.
Rob Wagner's Script. Oct 14, 1933, v10, p8.
Time. Nov 6, 1933, v22, p42.
Variety. Nov 7, 1933, p16.

Broken Blossoms (US; Griffith, D.W.; 1919)
Adventures with D.W. Griffith. p223-27, 239-43.
BFI/Monthly Film Bulletin. Nov 1975, v43, p246.
Billy Bitzer: His Story. p197-217.
Classics of the Silent Screen. p25-26.
D.W. Griffith: American Film Master. p28-29.
D.W. Griffith: An American Life. p389-95.
D.W. Griffith: His Life and Work. p200-06.
Exhibitor's Trade Review. May 24, 1919, p1896.
Fifty Great American Silent Films, 1912-1920. p104-06.
The Films of D.W. Griffith. p126-32.
Griffith: First Artist of the Movies. p109-15.
Lillian Gish: The Movies, Mr. Griffith, and Me. p217-22.
Magill's Survey of Cinema. Silent Films. v1, p259-61.
The Man Who Invented Hollywood. p123-24.
Motion Picture Classic. Aug 1919, p46-47, 60.
Motion Picture News. May 24, 1919, p3461.
The Movies in the Age of Innocence. p106-12.
The Moving Picture World. May 24, 1919, p1158.
The Moving Picture World. May 31, 1919, p1321-22.
The New York Times. May 14, 1919, p15.
Photoplay. Aug 1919, v16, p50.
Selected Film Criticism, 1912-1920. p32-36.
Variety. May 16, 1919, p50.
Wid's Daily. May 18, 1919, p5.

Broken Blossoms (GB; Brahm, John; 1936)
Film Daily. Jan 15, 1937, p6.
Hollywood Reporter. Jun 4, 1936, p12.
Motion Picture Herald. Jun 6, 1936, p60.
The New Statesman and Nation. Jun 27, 1936, v11, p1029.
The New York Times. Jan 14, 1937, p16.
Variety. Jun 10, 1936, p18.
Variety. Jan 20, 1937, p27.
World Film News. Aug 1936, v1, p18.

Broken Lullaby *See* The Man I Killed

Bronenosets Potyomkin *See* Battleship Potemkin

Brother Orchid (US; Bacon, Lloyd; 1940)
The Cinema of Edward G. Robinson. p127-29.
Classics of the Gangster Film. p81-84.
Commonweal. Jun 14, 1940, v32, p170.
The Complete Films of Humphrey Bogart. p84-85.
Film Daily. May 31, 1940, p6.
Hollywood Reporter. May 28, 1940, p3.
Humphrey Bogart: The Man and His Films. p104-07.
Motion Picture Herald Product Digest. Apr 27, 1940, p62-64.
The New York Times. Jun 8, 1940, p18.
Time. Jun 17, 1940, v35, p86-87.
Variety. May 29, 1940, p14.

Brother Rat (US; Keighley, William; 1938)
Commonweal. Nov 18, 1938, v29, p105.
Film Daily. Oct 17, 1938, p7.
The Films of Ronald Reagan. p59-63.
Hollywood Reporter. Oct 12, 1938, p3.
Hollywood Spectator. Oct 29, 1938, v13, p12-13.
Lunatics and Lovers. p277.
Magill's Survey of Cinema. Series II. v1, p349-52.
Motion Picture Herald. Oct 15, 1938, p36.
The New Masses. Nov 15, 1938, v29, p29.
The New York Times. Nov 5, 1938, p15.
Newsweek. Oct 24, 1938, v12, p33.
Photoplay. Jan 1939, v53, p81.
Rob Wagner's Script. Oct 22, 1938, v20, p12.
Scholastic. Nov 5, 1938, v33, p38.
Variety. Oct 19, 1938, p12.

The Brothers (GB; MacDonald, David; 1947)
BFI/Monthly Film Bulletin. Sep 1985, v52, p295.
Commonweal. May 21, 1948, v48, p140.
Film Daily. May 7, 1948, p8.
Motion Picture Herald Product Digest. May 8, 1948, p4154.
The New Republic. May 31, 1948, v118, p38.
The New York Times. May 5, 1948, p30.
The New Yorker. May 8, 1948, v24, p91.
Newsweek. May 17, 1948, v31, p98+.
Time. May 24, 1948, v51, p99.
Variety. May 14, 1947, p15.

The Brothers Karamazov *See* Karamazov

Brute Force (US; Dassin, Jules; 1947)
Commonweal. Aug 8, 1947, v46, p405.
Film Daily. Jun 18, 1947, p8.
Hollywood Quarterly. Fall 1947, v3, p63-65.
Hollywood Reporter. Jun 18, 1947, p3.
Life. Aug 11, 1947, v23, p69.
Magill's Survey of Cinema, Series II. v1, p360-62.
Motion Picture Herald Product Digest. Jun 28, 1947, p3702.
The Nation. Sep 13, 1947, v165, p264.
New Republic. Aug 18, 1947, v117, p38.
The New York Times. Jul 17, 1947, p16.
Newsweek. Jul 28, 1947, v30, p84.
Photoplay. Sep 1947, v31, p4.
Time. Aug 4, 1947, v50, p76.
Variety. Jun 18, 1947, p8.

The Buccaneer (US; DeMille, Cecil B.; 1938)
Canadian Magazine. Feb 1938, v89, p28-29.
Commonweal. Feb 4, 1938, v27, p414.
Film Daily. Feb 4, 1938, p10.
The Films of Anthony Quinn. p50-51.
The Films of Cecil B. De Mille. p308-13.
The Films of Fredric March. p154-56.
The Foremost Films of 1938. p63-78.
Life. Jan 10, 1938, v4, p54-57.
Literary Digest. Jan 29, 1938, v125, p22.
Motion Picture Herald. Jan 15, 1938, p47, 50.
Motion Picture Herald. Oct 23, 1937, p14-15.
The New Masses. Mar 1, 1938, v26, p30.
The New Statesman and Nation. Feb 5, 1938, v15, p208.
The New York Times. Feb 17, 1938, p17.
The New Yorker. Feb 26, 1939, v14, p53.
Rob Wagner's Script. Feb 5, 1938, v18, p11.
Saint Nicholas. Jan 1938, v65, p37+.
Scholastic. Feb 22, 1938, v32, p27S.
The Spectator. Feb 11, 1938, v160, p223.
Stage. Feb 1938, v15, p10.
The Tatler. Feb 9, 1938, v147, p236.
Time. Jan 17, 1938, v31, p44.
Variety. Jan 12, 1938, p14.

Büchse der Pandora, Die *See* Pandora's Box

Buck Privates (US; Lubin, Arthur; 1941)
Commonweal. Mar 7, 1941, v33, p498.
Film Daily. Feb 3, 1941, p9.
Magill's Survey of Cinema. Series I. v1, p252-54.
Motion Picture Exhibitor. Feb 5, 1941, p685.
Motion Picture Herald Product Digest. Mar 22, 1941, p88.
The New York Times. Feb 2, 1941, sec9, p5.
The New York Times. Feb 14, 1941, p15.
Newsweek. Feb 10, 1941, v27, p62.
Time. Mar 24, 1941, v37, p89.
Variety. Feb 5, 1941, p12.

Buffalo Bill (US; Wellman, William A.; 1944)
Commonmweal. May 5, 1944, v40, p62.
Film Daily. Mar 17, 1944, p6.
The Films of Anthony Quinn. p95-96.
Hollywood Reporter. Mar 15, 1944, p3.
Life. Apr 10, 1944, v16, p109-12+.
The New York Times. Apr 20, 1944, p32.
Newsweek. Apr 24, 1944, v23, p84+.
Time. Aug 24, 1944, v43, p94+.
Variety. Mar 15, 1944, p32.
William A. Wellman (Thompson). p215-17.

Bugle Ann *See* The Voice of Bugle Ann

Bukhta Smerti *See* Death Bay

Bulldog Drummond (US; Jones, F. Richard; 1929)
Exhibitor's Herald-World. Oct 19, 1929, p45.
Famous Movie Detectives. p19-21+.
Film Daily. May 5, 1929, p9.
The Films of Ronald Colman. p127-36.
Magill's Survey of Cinema. Series II. v1, p363-66.
The New York Times. May 3, 1929, p23.
Outlook. May 22, 1929, v152, p155.
Photoplay. Jul 1929, v36, p54.
Samuel Goldwyn (Epstein). p34-36.
Samuel Goldwyn Presents. p82-84.
Selected Film Criticism, 1921-1930. p53-54.
Variety. May 8, 1929, p20.

Bulldog Drummond Comes Back (US; King, Louis; 1937)
Film Daily. Sep 7, 1937, p7.
Hollywood Reporter. Sep 1, 1937, p3.
Motion Picture Herald. Sep 11, 1937, p51.
The New York Times. Sep 4, 1937, p8.
Variety. Sep 8, 1937, p18.

Bulldog Drummond Escapes (US; Hogan, James; 1937)
Film Daily. Apr 6, 1937, p9.
Hollywood Spectator. Feb 13, 1937, v11, p11.
Motion Picture Herald. Mar 13, 1937, p47.

Bulldog Drummond Strikes Back (US; Del Ruth, Roy; 1934)
Film Daily. May 4, 1934, p9.
The Films of Ronald Colman. p159-63.
Hollywood Reporter. May 3, 1934, p3.
Literary Digest. Sep 1, 1934, v118, p118.
Motion Picture Herald. May 19, 1934, p65.
The New York Times. Aug 16, 1934, p20.
Time. Aug 6, 1934, v24, p32.
Variety. Aug 21, 1934, p17.

Bulldog Drummond Strikes Back (US; McDonald, Frank; 1947)
Hollywood Reporter. Sep 19, 1947, p3.
Motion Picture Herald Product Digest. Nov 1, 1947, p3906.

Bulldog Drummond's Revenge (US; King, Louis; 1937)
Film Daily. Dec 22, 1937, p6.
Hollywood Reporter. Oct 29, 1937, p3.
Motion Picture Herald. Nov 6, 1937, p33.
The New York Times. Dec 17, 1937, p33.
Rob Wagner's Script. Jan 3, 1938, v18, p15.

Bullets or Ballots (US; Keighley, William; 1936)
The Cinema of Edward G. Robinson. p106-08.
Classics of the Gangster Film. p42-45.
Commonweal. Jan 12, 1936, v24, p190.
The Complete Films of Humphrey Bogart. p29-30.
Esquire. Aug 1936, v6, p99.
Film Daily. May 18, 1936, p10.
The Gangster Film. p107-10.
Graham Greene on Film. p121.
The Great Gangster Pictures. p68-70.
Hollywood Reporter. May 14, 1936, p3.
Hollywood Spectator. May 23, 1936, v11, p12.
Humphrey Bogart: The Man and His Films. p55.
Motion Picture Herald. May 23, 1936, p44.
The New York Times. May 27, 1936, p27.
The New Yorker. May 30, 1936, v12, p58-59.
The Pleasure-Dome. p121.
Rob Wagner's Script. May 30, 1936, v15, p11.
The Spectator. Nov 27, 1936, v157, p945.
Time. Jun 1, 1936, v27, p26.
Variety. Jun 3, 1936, p15.
World Film News. Jan 1937, v1, p25.

Bureau of Missing Persons (US; Del Ruth, Roy; 1933)
Bette Davis: Her Films and Career. p44-45.
Film Daily. Sep 2, 1933, p3.
Hollywood Reporter. Aug 15, 1933, p3.
Motion Picture Herald. Sep 2, 1933, p35.
New Outlook. Oct 1933, v162, p49.
The New York Times. Sep 9, 1933, p9.
The New Yorker. Sep 16, 1933, v9, p56.
Newsweek. Sep 16, 1933, v2, p38.
Rob Wagner's Script. Sep 9, 1933, v10, p10.
Time. Sep 18, 1933, v22, p32.

The Burlesque Queen (US; 1910)
The New York Dramatic Mirror. Sep 10, 1910, p28.
Selected Film Criticism, 1896-1911. p16-17.

The Busher (US; Storm, Jerome; 1919)
Exhibitor's Trade Review. Jun 7, 1919, p57.
Motion Picture News. May 31, 1919, p3625.
Motion Picture News. Jun 7, 1919, p3856.
The Moving Picture World. Jun 7, 1919, p1529.
The New York Times. May 26, 1919, p20.
Variety. May 30, 1919, p77.
Wid's Daily. Jun 1, 1919, p23.

By Candlelight (US; Whale, James; 1933)
Film Daily. Jan 6, 1934, p6.
Hollywood Reporter. Dec 16, 1933, p2.
James Whale. p110-12.
Literary Digest. Jan 20, 1934, v117, p32.
Motion Picture Herald. Dec 23, 1933, p47.
The New York Times. Jan 6, 1934, p18.
The New Yorker. Jan 13, 1934, v9, p68.
Newsweek. Jan 13, 1934, v3, p33.
Rob Wagner's Script. Dec 9, 1933, v10, p8.
Sight and Sound. Sum 1973, v42, p168-69.
Time. Jan 15, 1934, v23, p32.
Variety. Jan 9, 1934, p17.

Byeleyet Parus Odinoky *See* The Lone White Sail

Cabin in the Cotton (US; Curtiz, Michael; 1932)
Bette Davis: Her Films and Career. p32-33.
Close-Up. Mar 1933, v10, p34-36.
Film Daily. Oct 1, 1932, p8.
Hollywood Reporter. Aug 10, 1932, p3.
Motion Picture Herald. Sep 10, 1932, p38.
The Nation. Oct 26, 1932, v135, p409.
The New Outlook. Nov 1932, v161, p47.
The New York Times. Sep 30, 1932, p17.
Time. Oct 10, 1932, v20, p34.
Variety. Oct 4, 1932, p19.

Cabin in the Sky (US; Minnelli, Vincente; 1943)
Commonweal. Jun 18, 1943, v38, p225.
Film Daily. Feb 15, 1943, p5.
The Hollywood Musical. p216, 320.
Hollywood Reporter. Feb 10, 1943, p3.
Motion Picture Herald Product Digest. Feb 13, 1943, p1157.
The New Republic. Jul 5, 1943, v109, p20.
The New York Times. May 28, 1943, p19.
The New Yorker. May 29, 1943, v19, p39.
Newsweek. April 26, 1943, v21, p88.
Rob Wagner's Script. May 15, 1943, v29, p14.
Selected Film Criticism, 1941-1950. p33-34.
Time. Apr 26, 1943, v41, p96.
Toms, Coons, Mulattoes, Mammies & Bucks. p180-84+.
Variety. Feb 10, 1943, p8.
Vincente Minnelli and the Film Musical. p37-42+.

The Cabinet of Dr. Caligari (German titles: Cabinet des Dr. Caligari, Das; Kabinett des Doktors Caligari, Das) (GER; Wiene, Robert; 1920)
American Cinematographer. Jul 1962, v43, p420-44, 441-45.
BFI/Monthly Film Bulletin. Jun 1979, v46, p135.
Classic Movies. p10-11.
From Caligari to Hitler. p17-27+.
German Expressionist Film. p29-65.
The Great Films. p21-23.
The Haunted Screen. p61-79+.
The International Dictionary of Films and Filmmakers. v1, p73-74.
Magill's Survey of Cinema. Silent Films. v1, p262-65.
The New York Times. Mar 20, 1921, sec6, p2.
The New York Times. Apr 4, 1921, p4.
Quarterly of Film, Radio and Television. Sum 1954, v8, p375-92.
Quarterly of Film, Radio and Television. Wint 1956, v11, p136-48.
Variety. Apr 8, 1921, p40.
Wid's Daily. Apr 10, 1921, p4.

Cabiria (IT; Fosco, Piero (Pastrone, Giovanni); 1913)
Cabiria.
The Green Book Magazine. Sep 1914, v12, p495-96.
Magill's Survey of Cinema. Silent Films. v1, p266-76.
The Moving Picture World. May 23, 1914, p1090-91.
The New York Dramatic Mirror. May 13, 1914, p40.
Selected Film Criticism, 1912-1920. p37-39.
Variety. May 15, 1914, p22.

Caduta di Troia, La *See* The Fall of Troy

Caesar and Cleopatra (GB; Pascal, Gabriel; 1945)
Agee on Film. v1, p212-13.
Around Cinemas. Second Series. p262-64.
Chestnuts in Her Lap. p166-68.
The Collected Screenplays of Bernard Shaw. p125-47.
Commonweal. Aug 16, 1941, v44, p433-34.
Film Daily. Aug 6, 1946, p7.
The Great British Films. p97-101.
Harper. Apr 1947, v194, p382.
Hollywood Reporter. Aug 6, 1946, p3.
Life. Jul 29, 1946, v21, p44-46.
The London Times. Nov 23, 1945, p10.
Magill's Survey of Cinema. Series II. v1, p383-85.
Modern Music. Oct 1946, v23, n4, p313-14.
Motion Picture Exhibitor. Aug 7, 1946, v36, n14, sec2, p1983.
Motion Picture Herald Product Digest. Dec 22, 1945, p2766.
The Nation. Aug 17, 1941, v163, p193.
The Nation. Aug 31, 1946, v163, p251.
The New York Times. Jul 16, 1944, sec2, p3.
The New York Times. Sep 6, 1946, p18.
The New York Times Magazine. Jul 21, 1946, p18-19.
The New Yorker. Sep 7, 1946, v22, p48.
Newsweek. Aug 26, 1946, v28, p77.
Rob Wagner's Script. Aug 31, 1945, v32, p14.
Scholastic. Sep 23, 1946, v49, p36-37.

Selected Film Criticism: Foreign Films, 1930-1950. p23-24.
The Serpent's Eye. p113-46.
Theatre Arts. Feb 1946, v30, p97.
Theatre Arts. Sep 1946, v30, p517-18.
Time. Dec 31, 1945, v46, p88.
Time. Aug 19, 1946, v48, p98.
Variety. Jan 2, 1946, p8.
Variety. Aug 7, 1946, p12.
Vogue. Jan 15, 1945, v105, p64-65.

Café Metropole (US; Griffith, Edward H.; 1937)
Canadian Magazine. Jun 1937, v87, p51.
Film Daily. Apr 29, 1937, p4.
The Films of Tyrone Power. p60-62.
Graham Greene on Film. p171-72.
Hollywood Reporter. Apr 28, 1937, p3.
Hollywood Spectator. May 8, 1937, v12, p10-11.
Literary Digest. May 15, 1937, v123, p20.
The New Masses. May 18, 1937, v23, p31.
The New York Times. Apr 29, 1937, p17.
The New Yorker. May 8, 1937, v13, p64.
Rob Wagner's Script. May 29, 1937, v17, p10-11.
Sight and Sound. Aut 1937, v6, p141.
Time. May 10, 1937, v29, p69.
Variety. May 5, 1937, p16.
World Film News. Nov 1937, v2, p23.

Cain and Artem (USSR; Petrov-Bytov, P.P.; 1930)
Film Daily. Jun 8, 1930, p10.
The Nation. Jun 25, 1930, v130, p739-40.
National Board of Review Magazine. Jun 1931, v6, p14.
The New York Times. Jun 7, 1930, p10.
Time. Jun 23, 1930, v15, p62.
Variety. Jun 11, 1930, p19.

Cain and Mabel (US; Bacon, Lloyd; 1936)
Film Daily. Oct 19, 1936, p7.
The Films of Clark Gable. p177.
Hollywood Reporter. Aug 7, 1936, p3.
Hollywood Spectator. Aug 29, 1936, v11, p7-8.
Judge. Oct 1936, v111, p20.
Motion Picture Herald. Oct 31, 1936, p45.
Motion Picture Herald. Aug 29, 1936, p36-37.
The New York Times. Oct 19, 1936, p22.
The New Yorker. Oct 24, 1936, v12, p59.
Rob Wagner's Script. Nov 7, 1936, v16, p10-11.
Stage. Oct 1936, v14, p24.
Time. Oct 26, 1936, v28, p70.
Variety. Oct 21, 1936, p15.
World Film News. Mar 1937, v1, p26-27.

Calamity Jane and Sam Bass (US; Sherman, George; 1949)
Commonweal. Jul 22, 1949, v50, p367.
Film Daily. Jun 3, 1949, p7.
Hollywood Reporter. Jun 3, 1949, p3.
Motion Picture Herald Product Digest. Jun 4, 1949, p4633.
The New York Times. Jul 18, 1949, p14.
Newsweek. Aug 1, 1949, v34, p65.
Variety. Jun 8, 1949, p18.

California (US; Farrow, John; 1947)
Commonweal. Jun 24, 1946, v45, p376.
Film Daily. Dec 19, 1946, p10.
The Films of Anthony Quinn. p108-09.
The Films of Barbara Stanwyck. p172-74.
Hollywood Reporter. Dec 16, 1946, p6.
Motion Picture Herald Product Digest. Dec 21, 1946, p3373.
The New Republic. Feb 3, 1946, v116, p42.
The New York Times. Jan 15, 1947, p31.
The New Yorker. Jan 25, 1947, v22, p71.
Starring Miss Barbara Stanwyck. p198-200.
Variety. Dec 18, 1946, p14.

California Straight Ahead (US; Lubin, Arthur; 1937)
Film Daily. Apr 16, 1937, p10.
Motion Picture Herald. Apr 3, 1937, p40, 41.
Rob Wagner's Script. Apr 10, 1937, v17, p10.
Variety. Jul 14, 1937, p21.

Call Her Savage (US; Dillon, John Francis; 1932)
Film Daily. Nov 26, 1932, p4.
Hollywood Reporter. Nov 14, 1932, p3.
Motion Picture Herald. Dec 3, 1932, p27.
The New York Times. Nov 25, 1932, p19.
The New Yorker. Dec 3, 1932, v8, p72.
Rob Wagner's Script. Dec 17, 1932, v8, p8.
Time. Dec 5, 1932, v20, p32.
Variety. Nov 29, 1932, p18.

Call It a Day (US; Mayo, Archie; 1937)
Canadian Magazine. Jun 1937, v87, p52.
Film Daily. Mar 6, 1937, p3.
Graham Greene on Film. p155-56.
Hollywood Reporter. Mar 3, 1937, p3.
Literary Digest. Apr 24, 1937, v123, p20+.
Motion Picture Herald. Mar 13, 1937, p43, 46.
The New York Times. May 7, 1937, p29.
Newsweek. May 1, 1937, v9, p30.
Rob Wagner's Script. Apr 24, 1937, v17, p10.
Scholastic. Apr 17, 1937, v30, p27.
The Spectator. Jul 16, 1937, v159, p104.
The Tatler. Jul 21, 1937, v145, p102.
Time. May 17, 1937, v29, p58.
Variety. May 12, 1937, p12.
World Film News. Aug 1937, v2, p11.
World Film News. Oct 1937, v2, p25.

Call Northside 777 (US; Hathaway, Henry; 1948)
Commonweal. Feb 27, 1948, v47, p495.
Film Daily. Jan 21, 1948, p6.
The Films of James Stewart. p109-12.
The Films of the Forties. p219-21.
Hollywood Reporter. Jan 21, 1948, p3.
Life. Mar 1, 1948, v24, p57-59.
Magill's Survey of Cinema. Series I. v1, p280.
Motion Picture Herald Product Digest. Jan 24, 1948, p4029.
The New York Times. Feb 19, 1948, p29.
The New Yorker. Feb 28, 1948, v24, p62.
Newsweek. Feb 23, 1948, v31, p90.
Scholastic. Feb 9, 1948, v52, p29.
Time. Feb 16, 1948, v51, p99.
Variety. Jun 21, 1948, p8.

Call of the Wild (US; Wellman, William A.; 1935)
Esquire. Sep 1935, v4, p144.
Film Daily. Apr 30, 1935, p8.
The Films of Clark Gable. p162-63.
The Great Adventure Films. p48-53.
Hollywood Reporter. Apr 27, 1935, p3.
Hollywood Reporter. Aug 20, 1935, p11.
Literary Digest. Aug 24, 1935, v120, p26.
Motion Picture Herald. May 4, 1935, p35.
The New York Times. Aug 15, 1935, p15.
The New Yorker. Aug 24, 1935, v11, p46.
Rob Wagner's Script. Jul 27, 1935, v13, p10.
Time. Aug 26, 1935, v26, p26.
Vanity Fair. Jul 1935, v44, p39.
Variety. Aug 21, 1935, p21.
William A. Wellman (Thompson). p150-53.

The Calling of Dan Matthews (US; Rosen, Phil; 1936)
Film Daily. Jan 25, 1936, p3.
Hollywood Reporter. Nov 20, 1935, p10.
Motion Picture Herald. Feb 1, 1936, p48.
The New York Times. Jan 25, 1936, p18.
Variety. Jan 29, 1936, p16.

Cameo Kirby (US; Ford, John; 1923)
Film Daily. Oct 21, 1923, p5.
The New York Times. Feb 8, 1930, p12.
Photoplay. Dec 1923, v25, p73.
Selected Film Criticism, 1921-1930. p58.
Variety. Feb 12, 1930, p19.

Cameo Kirby (US; Cummings, Irving; 1930)
Film Daily. Feb 9, 1930, p12.
The Films of Myrna Loy. p92.
Judge. Mar 1, 1930, v98, p32.
Life. Feb 21, 1930, v95, p20, 31.
The New York Times. Feb 8, 1930, p12.
The New York Times. Feb 16, 1930, p5.
Outlook and Independent. Feb 19, 1930, v154, p313.
Time. Feb 24,1930, v15, p24.
Variety. Feb 12, 1930, p19.

The Cameraman (US; Sedgwick, Edward; 1928)
Buster Keaton (Lebel). p137-53.
Buster Keaton (Robinson). p169-74.
The Cameraman.
Cinema, the Magic Vehicle. v1, p154-55.
The Comic Mind. p141-43+.
The Film Career of Buster Keaton. p73-75.
Film Daily. Sep 23, 1928, p9.
The Film Spectator. Nov 24, 1928, v6, p11.
Life. Oct 5, 1928, v92, p25.
Lorentz on Film. p29-30.
Magill's Survey of Cinema. Silent Films. v1, p277-79.
Motion Picture Classic. Nov 28, 1928, p53.
National Board of Review Magazine. Sep 1928, v3, p9.
The New York Times. Sep 17, 1928, p27.
Photoplay. Oct 1928, v34, p54.
Selected Film Criticism, 1921-1930. p58.
The Silent Clowns. p235, 244.
Variety. Sep 19, 1928, p12.

Camille (FR; 1909)
The Moving Picture World. Jan 22, 1910, p93.
Selected Film Criticism, 1896-1911. p18.

Camille (US; Smallwood, Roy C.; 1921)
Film Daily. Sep 11, 1921, p2.
Photoplay. Dec 1921, v21, p62.
Selected Film Criticism, 1921-1930. p58-59.
Variety. Sep 16, 1921, p35.

Camille (US; Niblo, Fred; 1927)
Film Daily. May 1, 1927, p6.
Magill's Survey of Cinema. Silent Films. v1, p280-83.
The Moving Picture World. May 2, 1927, p848.
The New York Times. Apr 22, 1927, p19.
Photoplay. Jun 1927, v32, p54.
Selected Film Criticism, 1921-1930. p59.
Variety. Apr 27, 1927, p16.

Camille (US; Cukor, George; 1936)
American Film Criticism. p353-55.
Around Cinemas. p142-44.
Classic Movies. p84-85.
Commonweal. Jan 29, 1937, v25, p388.
The Film Criticism of Otis Ferguson. p170-71.
Film Daily. Dec 15, 1936, p8.
The Films of Greta Garbo. p135-40.
The Films of Robert Taylor. p54-56.
From Quasimodo to Scarlett O'Hara. p234-36.
Garbo: A Portrait (Walker). p148-53.
Garbo and the Night Watchman. p242-44.
George Cukor (Phillips). p96-98.
The Great Films. p114-20.
The Great Romantic Films. p46-51.
Hollywood Reporter. Dec 12, 1936, p4.
Hollywood Spectator. Dec 19, 1936, v11, p5.
Independent Woman. Jan 1937, v16, p1+.

The International Dictionary of Films and Filmmakers. v1, p76-77.
Kiss Kiss Bang Bang. p300.
Literary Digest. Jan 2, 1937, v123, p23.
London Mercury. Apr 1937, v35, p625.
Look. May 3, 1955, v19, p99-101.
Magill's Survey of Cinema. Series I. v1, p285-88.
Motion Picture Herald. Dec 19, 1936, p54.
Motion Picture Herald. Oct 24, 1936, p16-17.
The Nation. Feb 19, 1955, v180, p167.
National Board of Review Magazine. Feb 1937, v12, p13.
The New Masses. Jan 19, 1937, v22, p30-31.
The New Republic. Mar 24, 1937, v90, p211-12.
The New Statesman and Nation. Mar 13, 1937, v13, p408.
New Theatre. Mar 1937, v4, p58.
The New York Times. Jan 23, 1937, p13.
The New Yorker. Jan 16, 1937, v12, p49, 51.
Newsweek. Jan 9, 1937, v9, p32.
On Cukor. p108-15.
Photoplay. Dec 1936, v50, p48-49.
Rob Wagner's Script. Jan 30, 1937, v16, p10.
Scribner's Magazine. Apr 1937, v101, p61-62.
Selected Film Criticism, 1931-1940. p35-36.
Sight and Sound. Sum 1955, v25, p35.
The Spectator. Mar 12, 1937, v158, p471.
Star Acting. p186-206.
Those Fabulous Movie Years: The 30s. p82-83.
Time. Jan 18, 1937, v29, p25.
Variety. Jan 27, 1937, p12.
Vogue. Nov 15, 1936, v88, p70-71.
World Film News. Mar 1937, v1, p24.

The Campbells Are Coming (US; Ford, Francis; 1915)
Motion Picture News. May 29, 1915, p68.
Motography. Oct 23, 1915, p857, 882.
The Moving Picture World. May 29, 1915, p1439.
The Moving Picture World. Oct 23, 1915, p621, 671.
The New York Dramatic Mirror. May 19, 1915, p28.
Variety. Oct 1, 1915, p19.

The Canterville Ghost (US; Dassin, Jules; 1944)
Commonweal. Aug 11, 1944, v40, p400.
Film Daily. May 31, 1944, p10.
Hollywood Reporter. May 26, 1944, p3.
The London Times. Jul 26, 1944, p7.
Magill's Survey of Cinema. Series II. v1, p396-99.
Motion Picture Exhibitor. May 31, 1944, v32, n3, sec2, p1518.
Motion Picture Herald Product Digest. May 27,, p1909.
The New York Times. Jul 29, 1944, p16.
The New Yorker. Aug 5, 1944, v20, p32.
Newsweek. Jul 31, 1944, v24, p82.
Time. Aug 14, 1944, v44, p96.
Variety. May 31, 1944, p20.

Canyon Passage (US; Tourneur, Jacques; 1946)
Commonweal. Aug 30, 1946, v44, p479.
Film Daily. Jul 17, 1946, p4.
The Films of Susan Hayward. p109-12.
Hollywood Reporter. Jul 15, 1946, p3.
The New York Times. Aug 8, 1946, p18.
The New Yorker. Aug 17, 1946, v22, p86.
Newsweek. Jul 29, 1946, v28, p77.
Time. Aug 5, 1946, v48, p98.
Variety. Jul 24, 1946, p14.

Caprice (US; Dawley, J. Searle; 1913)
Motion Picture News. Nov 22, 1913, p34-35.
The Moving Picture World. Nov 15, 1913, p718, 786.
The Moving Picture World. Dec 14, 1918, p1254.
The New York Clipper. Nov 8, 1913, p4-5.
The New York Dramatic Mirror. Nov 19, 1913, p32.

Captain Blood (US; Smith, David; 1924)
Film Daily. Sep 14, 1924, p4.
Magill's Survey of Cinema. Silent Films. v1, p284-86.
The Moving Picture World. Sep 20, 1924, p243.

The New York Times. Sep 9, 1924, p19.
Photoplay. Nov 1924, v26, p60.
Selected Film Criticism, 1921-1930. p59.
Variety. Sep 10, 1924, p27.

Captain Blood (US; Curtiz, Michael; 1936)
Canadian Magazine. Jan 1936, v85, p33.
Canadian Magazine. Feb 1936, v85, p36.
Casablanca and Other Major Films of Michael Curtiz. p1-28.
Cinema, the Magic Vehicle. v1, p245.
Commonweal. Jan 3, 1936, v23, p272.
Film Daily. Dec 19, 1935, p5.
The Films of Basil Rathbone. p164-68.
The Films of Errol Flynn. p30-32.
The Films of Olivia de Havilland. p67-74.
Fortune. Dec 1937, v16, p112.
Graham Greene on Film. p54.
Hollywood Reporter. Dec 31, 1935, p4.
Hollywood Spectator. Jan 18, 1936, v10, p11-12.
Magill's Survey of Cinema. Series II. v1, p400-04.
Motion Picture. Feb 1936, v51, p50.
Motion Picture Herald. Jan 11, 1936, p53.
The New York Times. Dec 27, 1935, p14.
Newsweek. Dec 28, 1935, v6, p24-25.
Rob Wagner's Script. Jan 11, 1936, v14, p13.
Scholastic. Jan 25, 1936, v27, p28.
The Spectator. Feb 21, 1936, v156, p300.
Stage. Jan 1936, v13, p32.
Talking Pictures. p286-88.
Those Fabulous Movie Years: The 30s. p70-71.
Time. Dec 30, 1935, v26, p16.
Variety. Jan 1, 1936, p44.
The Velvet Light Trap. Jun 1971, v1, p26-32.
Warner Brothers Presents. p150.

Captain Courtesy (US; Weber, Lois; 1915)
Motion Picture News. Apr 17, 1915, p47.
Motion Picture News. Apr 24, 1915, p71.
Motography. Apr 17, 1915, p611.
Motography. Apr 24, 1915, p661-62, 682.
The Moving Picture World. Apr 24, 1915, p566.
The Moving Picture World. Jan 25, 1919, p541.
The New York Dramatic Mirror. Apr 14, 1915, p28.
Variety. Apr 16, 1915, p19.

Captain Eddie (US; Bacon, Lloyd; 1945)
Commonweal. Aug 17, 1945, v42, p431.
Film Daily. Jun 19, 1945, p7.
Hollywood Reporter. Jun 19, 1945, p3.
Life. Aug 20, 1945, v19, p47-48+.
The New York Times. Aug 9, 1945, p24.
The New Yorker. Aug 18, 1945, v21, p57.
Newsweek. Aug 13, 1945, v26, p86.
Scholastic. Sep 17, 1945, v47, p32.
Time. Aug 6, 1945, v46, p98.
Variety. Jun 20, 1945, p11.

The Captain from Castile (US; King, Henry; 1947)
Commonweal. Dec 19, 1947, v47, p256.
Film Daily. Nov 26, 1947, p6.
The Films of Tyrone Power. p147-50.
Hollywood Reporter. Nov 26, 1947, p3.
Motion Picture Herald Product Digest. Nov 29, 1947, p3953.
New Republic. Jan 5, 1948, v118, p32.
The New York Times. Dec 26, 1947, p22.
Newsweek. Jan 5, 1948, v31, p68.
Scholastic. Jan 12, 1948, v51, p36.
Time. Jan 5, 1948, 51, p71.
Variety. Nov 26, 1947, p11.

The Captain Hates the Sea (US; Milestone, Lewis; 1934)
Close Up: The Contract Director. p314-15.
Film Daily. Nov 30, 1934, p15.
Motion Picture Herald. Oct 27, 1934, p41-46.
The New York Times. Nov 29, 1934, p33.

Time. Nov 12, 1934, v24, p44.
Variety. Dec 4, 1934, p12.

Captain January (US; Butler, David; 1936)
Commonweal. Apr 3, 1936, v23, p636.
Film Daily. Mar 17, 1936, p9.
The Films of Shirley Temple. p164-69.
Graham Greene on Film. p92.
Hollywood Reporter. Jan 30, 1936, p3.
Hollywood Spectator. Mar 28, 1936, v10, p6.
Motion Picture Herald. Mar 21, 1936, p38.
The New York Times. Apr 25, 1936, p21.
Rob Wagner's Script. May 2, 1936, v15, p10.
Scholastic. Apr 4, 1936, v28, p26.
The Spectator. Aug 7, 1936, v157, p235.
Time. Apr 27, 1936, v27, p36.
Variety. Apr 29, 1936, p15.

Captain Kidd (US; Lee, Rowland V.; 1945)
Commonweal. Nov 16, 1945, v43, p117.
Film Daily. Jul 31, 1945, p6.
Hollywood Reporter. Jul 30, 1945, p3.
The New York Times. Nov 23, 1945, p26.
Newsweek. Oct 22, 1945, v26, p104.
Time. Oct 15, 1945, v46, p54+.
Variety. Aug 1, 1945, p16.

The Captain of Koepenick *See* Hauptmann von Koepenick, Der

Captain of the Guard (French title: Marseillaise, La) (US; Robertson, John S.; 1930)
Commonweal. Oct 29, 1930, v12, p670.
Film Daily. Mar 30, 1930, p8.
The Film Spectator. Apr 12, 1930, v9, p21.
Life. Apr 18, 1930, v95, p20.
The New York Times. Mar 29, 1930, p23.
The New Yorker. Apr 5, 1930, v6, p91.
Outlook and Independent. Apr 9, 1930, v154, p594.
Time. Apr 14, 1930, v15, p38.
Variety. Apr 2, 1930, p19.

Captains Courageous (US; Fleming, Victor; 1937)
Canadian Magazine. Jun 1937, v87, p46.
Child Life. Jul 1937, v16, p46.
Cinema Arts. Jul 1937, p32.
Commonweal. Apr 23, 1937, v25, p726.
Esquire. Jul 1937, v8, p97.
Fifty Classic Motion Pictures. p56-61.
The Film Criticism of Otis Ferguson. p182-83.
Film Daily. Mar 29, 1937, p5.
The Films of Spencer Tracy. p136-39.
From Quasimodo to Scarlett O'Hara. p251-53.
Hollywood Reporter. Mar 24, 1937, p3.
Hollywood Spectator. Apr 10, 1937, v12, p13.
Independent Woman. Jun 1937, v16, p178.
A Library of Film Criticism: American Film Directors. p112.
Life. Apr 26, 1937, v2, p32-35.
Literary Digest. May 22, 1937, v123, p28.
London Mercury. Jun 1937, v36, p187.
Magill's Survey of Cinema. Series I. v1, p289-91.
Motion Picture. Mar 1937, v53, p56-57+.
Motion Picture Herald. Apr 3, 1937, p37.
Motion Picture Herald. Apr 24, 1937, p12.
The Nation. Jun 12, 1937, v144, p685.
National Board of Review Magazine. Jun 1937, v12, p11.
The New Masses. Jul 6, 1937, v24, p27.
The New Republic. Jun 16, 1937, v91, p160.
The New York Times. May 12, 1937, p27.
The New Yorker. May 15, 1937, v13, p85.
Newsweek. Apr 24, 1937, v9, p23.
Photoplay. May 1938, v52, p28.
Rob Wagner's Script. May 15, 1937, v17, p8.
Saint Nicholas. Dec 1936, v64, p52.
Sight and Sound. Sum 1937, v6, p79-80.

Souvenir Programs of Twelve Classic Movies, 1927-1941. p121-40.
Stage. Jun 1937, v14, p53.
Time. Apr 19, 1937, v29, p65.
Variety. May 19, 1937, p22.
Woman's Home Companion. Apr 1937, v64, p13-14+.
World Film News. Jul 1937, v2, p25.
World Film News. Dec 1937, v2, p18-19.

Captains of the Clouds (US; Curtiz, Michael; 1942)
Commonweal. Feb 20, 1942, v35, p438.
Film Daily. Jan 20, 1942, p7.
The Films of James Cagney. p165-67.
Hollywood Reporter. Jan 20, 1942, p3.
The London Times. Feb 16, 1942, p2.
Motion Picture Exhibitor. Jan 29, 1942, p939.
Motion Picture Herald Product Digest. Jan 24, 1942, p473.
The Nation. Mar 14, 1942, v154, p320.
The New York Times. Feb 13, 1942, p24.
The New York Times. Feb 15, 1942, sec8, p5.
Newsweek. Feb 23, 1942, p54.
Scholastic. Mar 2, 1942, v40, p29.
Time. Mar 2, 1942, v39, p74.
Variety. Jan 21, 1942, p8.
When Hollywood Ruled the Skies. p41-46.

The Captive (US; DeMille, Cecil B.; 1915)
The Autobiography of Cecil B. DeMille. p127-28.
The Films of Cecil B. DeMille. p66-69.
Motion Picture News. Apr 10, 1915, p49.
Motion Picture News. May 1, 1915, p67.
Motography. May 8, 1915, p765.
The Moving Picture World. Apr 10, 1915, p248.
The Moving Picture World. May 1, 1915, p743.
The Moving Picture World. May 8, 1915, p986, 988.
The New York Dramatic Mirror. Apr 28, 1915, p26.
Selected Film Criticism, 1912-1920. p41-42.
Variety. Apr 30, 1915, p18.

Captured (US; Del Ruth, Roy; 1933)
Canadian Magazine. Sep 1933, v80, p34.
Film Daily. Aug 19, 1933, p7.
Hollywood Reporter. Jun 14, 1933, p3.
Motion Picture Herald. Jun 24, 1933, p42-43.
The New York Times. Aug 18, 1933, p18.
Newsweek. Aug 26, 1933, v2, p31.
Rob Wagner's Script. Sep 2, 1933, v10, p10-11.
Time. Aug 28, 1933, v22, p20.
Vanity Fair. Sep 1933, v41, p45.
Variety. Feb 28, 1933, p15.

Car 99 (US; Barton, Charles; 1935)
Film Daily. Feb 23, 1935, p3.
Hollywood Reporter. Feb 8, 1935, p3.
Hollywood Reporter. Mar 7, 1935, p2.
Motion Picture Herald. Feb 16, 1935, p46-47.
The New York Times. Feb 23, 1935, p14.
Rob Wagner's Script. Apr 6, 1935, v13, p8.
Variety. Feb 27, 1935, p26.

Caravan (US; Charell, Erik; 1934)
Film Daily. Sep 28, 1934, p19.
The Hollywood Musical. p95.
Hollywood Reporter. Aug 3, 1934, p3.
Motion Picture Herald. Sep 8, 1934, p34.
The New York Times. Sep 28, 1934, p27.
Time. Oct 8, 1934, v24, p36.
Variety. Oct 2, 1934, p37.

Caravan (GB; Crabtree, Harold; 1946)
Hollywood Reporter. Sep 9, 1947, p3.
Newsweek. Sep 22, 1947, v30, p90.
Variety. Apr 17, 1946, p32.

Cardinal Richelieu (Also titled: Richelieu) (US; Lee, Rowland V.; 1935)
Canadian Magazine. Jun 1935, v83, p33.
Commonweal. May 3, 1935, v22, p20.
Film Daily. Mar 26, 1935, p7.
Films in Review. Nov 1935, v36, p524-25.
Hollywood Reporter. Mar 23, 1935, p3.
Hollywood Reporter. Apr 20, 1935, p2.
Literary Digest. May 4, 1935, v119, p24.
Motion Picture Herald. Mar 30, 1935, p41.
The Nation. May 8, 1935, v140, p556.
The New York Times. Apr 19, 1935, p24.
The New Yorker. Apr 27, 1935, v11, p70.
Rob Wagner's Script. May 4, 1935, v13, p8.
The Spectator. Jun 28, 1935, v154, p1102.
Theatre Arts Monthly. Jun 1935, v 19, p407.
Time. Apr 29, 1935, v25, p53-54.

Career Woman (US; Seiler, Lewis; 1936)
Film Daily. Nov 24, 1936, p7.
Hollywood Reporter. Nov 20, 1936, p3.
Motion Picture Herald. Nov 28, 1936, p66.
Rob Wagner's Script. Jan 16, 1937, v16, p12.
Variety. Dec 16, 1936, p21.

Carefree (US; Sandrich, Mark; 1938)
Carefree. 1984.
Commonweal. Sep 9, 1938, v28, p505.
Esquire. Dec 1938, v10, p141-42.
Film Daily. Aug 30, 1938, p6.
The Films of Ginger Rogers. p145-47.
The Fred Astaire & Ginger Rogers Book. p138-51.
The Hollywood Musical. p140.
Hollywood Reporter. Aug 25, 1938, p3.
Hollywood Spectator. Sep 3, 1938, v13, p9-10.
The Journal of Popular Film and Television. Fall 1980, v8, p15-24.
Life. Aug 22, 1938, v5, p28-30.
Magill's Survey of Cinema. Series I. v2, p292-94.
Motion Picture Herald. Sep 3, 1938, p38.
The New York Times. Sep 23, 1938, p35.
The New Yorker. Sep 24, 1938, v14, p65.
Newsweek. Sep 12, 1938, v12, p20-21.
Rob Wagner's Script. Sep 3, 1938, v20, p10.
Starring Fred Astaire. p173-85.
Time. Sep 5, 1938, v32, p32.
Variety. Aug 31, 1938, p18.
World Film News. Nov 1938, v3, p315.

Carmen (US; DeMille, Cecil B.; 1915)
The Autobiography of Cecil B. DeMille. p139-43.
DeMille. p36-46.
Exhibitor's Trade Review. Oct 5, 1918, p1531.
Fifty Great American Silent Films, 1912-1920. p37-38.
The Films of Cecil B. DeMille. p86-89.
Magill's Survey of Cinema. Silent Films. v1, p287-88.
A Million and One Nights. p712.
Motion Picture News. Oct 16, 1915, p43-44.
Motion Picture News. Nov 13, 1915, p84.
Motography. Aug 21, 1915, p350.
Motography. Oct 2, 1915, p667.
The Moving Picture World. Nov 6, 1915, p1208.
The Moving Picture World. Oct 12, 1918, p273, 278.
The New York Dramatic Mirror. Nov 16, 1918, p743.
The New York Times. Nov 1, 1915, p7.
Photoplay. Nov 1915, v8, p77-80.
Selected Film Criticism, 1912-1920. p42-45.
Variety. Nov 5, 1915, p22.

Carnet de Bal, Un (Also titled: Life Dances On; Christine) (FR; Duvivier, Julien; 1937)
Cinema, the Magic Vehicle. v1, p276-77.
Commonweal. Apr 15, 1938, v27, p692.
Dictionary of Films. p54.
Esquire. Feb 1938, v9, p113.

Film Daily. Mar 31, 1938, p7.
From Quasimodo to Scarlett O'Hara. p282-84.
The Golden Age of French Cinema, 1929-1939. p123-27, 130-31.
Graham Greene on Film. p184.
The Great French Films. p244-45.
Hollywood Reporter. Oct 22, 1937, p8.
Hollywood Spectator. Mar 18, 1939, v13, p13.
Kiss Kiss Bang Bang. p301-02.
Life. May 2, 1938, v4, p46-47.
London Mercury. Jan 1938, v37, p334.
Motion Picture Herald. Jan 29, 1938, p61.
The Nation. Apr 9, 1938, v146, p421-22.
National Board of Review Magazine. Apr 1938, v13, p14.
The New Republic. Apr 20, 1938, v94, p333.
The New Statesman and Nation. Dec 4, 1937, v14, p919.
The New York Times. Mar 26, 1938, p12.
The New Yorker. Apr 2, 1938, v14, p50-51.
Rob Wagner's Script. Mar 4, 1939, v21, p16.
Saint Cinema: Selected Writings, 1929-1970. p77-78.
Selected Film Criticism: Foreign Films, 1930-1950. p98-99.
The Spectator. Dec 10, 1937, v159, p1049.
Studio. May 1939, v117, p200.
Time. Apr 4, 1938, v31, p29.
Variety. Oct 20, 1937, p27.
Variety. Mar 30, 1938, p15.
World Film News. Dec 1937, v2, p31.

Carnival in Flanders (French title: Kermesse Héroïque, La) (FR; Feyder, Jacques; 1935)
American Film Criticism. p346-47.
Cinema, the Magic Vehicle. v1, p241-42.
Classics of the Foreign Film. p96-97.
Commonweal. Apr 15, 1938, v27, p692.
Commonweal. Nov 6, 1936, v25, p52.
The Film Criticism of Otis Ferguson. p153-55.
Film Daily. Sep 24, 1936, p11.
From Quasimodo to Scarlett O'Hara. p228-31.
The Golden Age of French Cinema, 1929-1939. p69-73.
The Great French Films. p58-62.
The Great French Films. p58-62.
Hollywood Reporter. Oct 5, 1936, p9.
Hollywood Reporter. Dec 21, 1935, p6.
Hollywood Spectator. Jan 30, 1937, v11, p7-9.
The International Dictionary of Films and Filmmakers. v1, p236-37.
Kiss Kiss Bang Bang. p302.
Motion Picture Herald. Oct 3, 1936, p47-48.
The Nation. Oct 10, 1936, v143, p428-29.
National Board of Review Magazine. Nov 1936, v11, p10.
The New Masses. Oct 6, 1936, v21, p29.
The New Republic. Oct 14, 1936, v88, p281.
The New Statesman and Nation. Oct 24, 1936, v12, p628.
The New York Times. Sep 23, 1936, p29.
The New Yorker. Oct 3, 1936, v12, p61.
Newsweek. Oct 3, 1936, v8, p34.
The Pleasure-Dome. p111-13.
Selected Film Criticism: Foreign Films, 1930-1950. p98-99.
Sight and Sound. Aut 1936, v5, p85-86.
Sight and Sound. Sum 1937, v5, p85-86.
The Spectator. Oct 30, 1936, v157, p747.
Stage. Jun 1937, v14, p42-43.
Theatre Arts Magazine. Sep 1941, v25, p657.
Time. Oct 5, 1936, v28, p30.
Variety. Dec 18, 1935, p13.
Variety. Sep 30, 1936, p29.
World Film News. Nov 1936, v1, p21.

Carnival of Sinners (French title: Main du Diable, La) (FR; Torneur, Maurice; 1947)
Hollywood Reporter. Jun 28, 1947, p3.
The New York Times. Apr 8, 1947, p34.
Newsweek. Apr 21, 1947, v29, p96.
Variety. Apr 2, 1947, p16.

Carry On *See* The Better 'Ole

Casablanca (US; Curtiz, Michael; 1942)
American Film. Jun 1976, v1, p10-16.
American Film. Oct 1976, v2, p3-4.
America's Favorite Movies. p154-76.
Best Film Plays of 1943-1944. p631-94.
Beyond Formula. p278-81.
Casablanca. 1974.
Casablanca and Other Major Films of Michael Curtiz. p77-95.
Casablanca: Script and Legend. 1973.
Cineaste. Sum 1977, v8, p34-35.
Classic Film Collector. Spr 1974, n42, p43.
Classic Film Collector. Sep 1979, n65, p65.
Classic Movies. p92-93.
Commonweal. Dec 11, 1942, v37, p207.
The Complete Films of Humphrey Bogart. p106-09.
Esquire. Nov 1980, v94, p130.
Favorite Movies: Critics' Choice. p114-25.
Film Comment. Nov/Dec 1982, v18, p15-19.
Film Culture. Fall 1964, v34, p35-37.
Film Daily. Nov 27, 1942, p7.
Films and Filming. Aug 1974, v20, p20-24.
The Films of Ingrid Bergman. p86-89.
The Films of Peter Lorre. p151-55.
The Films of World War II. p86-88.
Focus on Film. Jun 1978, n30, p4-6.
Focus on Film. Apr 1979, n32, p7-17.
The Great Movies. p132-37.
Halliwell's Hundred. p44-47.
Hollywood Reporter. Dec 8, 1942, p3.
Hollywood Studio. 1984, v17, n2, p8-27.
Humphrey Bogart (Barbour). p89-92.
Humphrey Bogart: The Man and His Films. p120-21.
Ingrid Bergman. p46-50.
The International Dictionary of Films and Filmmakers. v1, p78-79.
The London Times. Jan 13, 1943, p6.
Magic Moments from the Movies. p109.
Magill's Survey of Cinema. Series I. v1, p305-07.
Media Montage. 1976, v1, n1, p12-24.
Motion Picture Exhibitor. Dec 2, 1942, v29, n4, sec2, p1161.
Motion Picture Herald Product Digest. Nov 28, 1942, p1029.
The Movies on Your Mind. p79-105.
New Movies. Jan 1943, v18, p10-11.
The New Republic. Dec 14, 1942, v107, p793.
The New York Magazine. Apr 30, 1973, v6, p74-81.
The New York Times. Nov 27, 1942, p27.
The New York Times. Nov 29, 1942, sec8, p3.
Newsweek. Nov 30, 1942, v20, p78.
Persistence of Vision. p103-07.
Photoplay. Feb 1943, v22, p4.
Rob Wagner's Script. Feb 6, 1943, v29, p24.
Running Away from Myself. p10-37.
Saturday Review. Feb 27, 1943, v26, p18.
Selected Film Criticism, 1941-1950. p35-36.
Selected Film Criticism, 1941-1950. p34-35.
Talking Pictures. p103-16.
Theatre Arts. Jan 1943, v27, p7.
Time. Nov 30, 1942, v40, p94+.
Time. Dec 27, 1982, v120, p7.
Variety. Dec 2, 1942, p8.
The Village Voice. Jan 8, 1970, v15, p51+.
Vintage Films. p64-67.
You Must Remember This... 1980.
50 Classic Motion Pictures. p274-79.

Casanova Brown (US; Wood, Sam; 1944)
Agee on Film. v1, p113-14.
Commonweal. Sep 22, 1944, v40, p547-48.
Film Daily. Aug 3, 1944, p7.
The Films of Gary Cooper. p197-98.
Hollywood Reporter. Aug 1, 1944, p3.
Life. Sep 18, 1944, v17, p87-88.
The Nation. Sep 16, 1944, v159, p334.

The New York Times. Sep 15, 1944, p16.
The New Yorker. Sep 23, 1944, v20, p54.
Newsweek. Aug 28, 1944, v24, p97-99.
Theatre Arts. Oct 1944, v28, p597.
Time. Sep 18, 1944, v44, p92+.
Variety. Aug 2, 1944, p10.

Casbah (US; Charell, Eric; 1948)
Commonweal. Apr 30, 1948, v48, p675.
Film Daily. Mar 4, 1948, p8.
The Films of Peter Lorre. p193-95.
Motion Picture Herald Product Digest. Mar 6, 1948, p4085.
The New York Times. May 3, 1948, p27.
Newsweek. May 17, 1948, v31, p96.
Time. Jun 14, 1948, v51, p98.
Variety. Mar 10, 1948, p10.

The Case Against Mrs. Ames (US; Seiter, William A.; 1936)
Film Daily. May 5, 1936, p9.
Hollywood Reporter. May 1, 1936, p3.
Literary Digest. May 16, 1936, v121, p20+.
Motion Picture Herald. May 9, 1936, p42.
The New York Times. May 28, 1936, p19.
Newsweek. May 16, 1936, v7, p42.
Rob Wagner's Script. Jun 27, 1936, v15, p8.
Time. May 18, 1936, v27, p62.
Variety. Jun 3, 1936, p15.

The Case of Becky (US; Reicher, Frank; 1915)
Motion Picture News. Sep 25, 1915, p120.
Motography. Aug 7, 1915, p240.
Motography. Oct 2, 1915, p713.
The Moving Picture World. Sep 25, 1915, p2198, 2252.
The New York Dramatic Mirror. Sep 22, 1915, p30.

The Case of Lena Smith (US; Sternberg, Josef von; 1929)
The New York Times. Jan 15, 1929, p22.
Variety. Jan 16, 1929, p14.

The Case of Sergeant Grischa (US; Brenon, Herbert; 1930)
Around Cinemas. p37.
Commonweal. Sep 17, 1930, v12, p499.
Exhibitors Herald-World. Mar 8, 1930, p39.
Film Daily. Mar 2, 1930, p10.
Judge. Mar 29, 1930, v98, p21.
Life. Apr 11, 1930, v95, p22.
New York Times. Mar 8, 1930, p21.
The New Yorker. Mar 15, 1930, v6, p85, 87.
Outlook and Independent. Mar 19, 1930, v154, p471.
Rob Wagner's Script. Apr 19, 1930, v3, p11-12.
The Spectator. Jun 7, 1930, v144, p936.
Time. Mar 17, 1930, v15, p54.
Variety. Mar 12, 1930, p21.

The Case of the Curious Bride (US; Curtiz, Michael; 1935)
Film Daily. Apr 4, 1935, p11.
The Films of Errol Flynn. p26-27.
Hollywood Reporter. Apr 9, 1935, p3.
Motion Picture Herald. Apr 13, 1935, p48.
The New York Times. Apr 5, 1935, p21.
The New Yorker. Apr 13, 1935, v11, p64.
Time. Apr 15, 1935, v25, p38.

The Case of the Lucky Legs (US; Mayo, Archie; 1935)
Film Daily. Nov 1, 1935, p7.
Garbo and the Night Watchman. p173-74.
Graham Greene on Film. p48-49.
Hollywood Reporter. Sep 14, 1935, p4.
Motion Picture Herald. Sep 21, 1935, p44.
The New York Times. Nov 1, 1935, p25.
Rob Wagner's Script. Oct 5, 1935, v14, p14.
The Spectator. Jan 31, 1936, v156, p170.
Variety. Nov 13, 1935, p17.

Casino de Paree *See* Go Into Your Dance

Cass Timberlaine (US; Sidney, George; 1947)
Film Daily. Nov 7, 1947, p10.
The Films of Lana Turner. p151-54.
The Films of Spencer Tracy. p193-94.
Hollywood Reporter. Nov 4, 1947, p3.
Motion Picture Herald Product Digest. Nov 15, 1947, p3930.
The New York Times. Nov 7, 1947, p20.
Variety. Nov 5, 1947, p8.

Castle in Flanders (German title: Schloss im Flandern, Das) (GER; von Bolvary, Geza; 1936)
Film Daily. Aug 18, 1937, p11.
The New York Times. Aug 7, 1937, p7.
Sight and Sound. Aut 1937, v6, p143.
The Spectator. Aug 27, 1937, v159, p347.
The Tatler. Sep 8, 1937, v145, p424.
Variety. Sep 23, 1936, p17.
World Film News. Oct 1937, v2, p25.

Castle of Doom *See* Vampyr, ou L'Étrange Adventure de David Gray

The Cat and the Canary (US; Leni, Paul; 1927)
BFI/Monthly Film Bulletin. Nov 1976, v43, p239.
Film Daily. May 15, 1927, p7.
The Films of the Twenties. p174-75.
Magill's Survey of Cinema. Silent Films. v1, p289-91.
The Moving Picture World. May 14, 1927, p133.
The New York Times. Sep 10, 1927, p10.
Photoplay. Jul 1927, v32, p55.
Selected Film Criticism, 1921-1930. p59-60.
Spellbound in Darkness. p460-61.
Variety. Sep 14, 1927, p22.

Cat People (US; Tourneur, Jacques; 1942)
Classics of the Horror Film. p182-87.
Film. Wint 1965-66, n44, p27.
Film Comment. Sum 1972, v8, p64-70.
Film Daily. Nov 16, 1942, p5.
Hollywood Reporter. Nov 13, 1942, p3.
Horror Movies. p138-40.
The International Dictionary of Films and Filmmakers. v1, p80-81.
Magic Moments from the Movies. p108.
Magill's Survey of Cinema. Series I. v1, p312-15.
Motion Picture Exhibitor. Nov 18, 1942, v29, n2, sec2, p1154.
Motion Picture Herald Product Digest. Nov 14, 1942, p1005.
The New York Times. Dec 7, 1942, p22.
Personal Views. p209-23.
Post Script. Autumn 1982, v2, p59.
Rob Wagner's Script. Nov 21, 1942, v27, p18.
Selected Film Criticism, 1941-1950. p36-37.
Time. Jan 4, 1943, v41, p86.
Val Lewton. p30-40, 101-06.
Variety. Nov 18, 1942, p8.

Catherine the Great (GB; Korda, Alexander; 1934)
Cinema Quarterly. Spr 1934, v2, p186-87.
Film Daily. Feb 2, 1934, p8.
From Quasimodo to Scarlett O'Hara. p179-82.
Hollywood Reporter. Feb 10, 1934, p3.
Literary Digest. Mar 3, 1934, v117, p40.
Motion Picture Herald. Feb 10, 1934, p43-44.
The New Republic. Mar 7, 1934, v78, p102-03.
The New York Times. Feb 15, 1934, p15.
Newsweek. Feb 24, 1934, v3, p34.
Variety. Jan 30, 1934, p12.
Variety. Feb 20, 1934, p14.

Caught (US; Sloman, Edward; 1931)
Film Daily. Oct 4, 1931, p8.
Hollywood Reporter. Jun 26, 1931, p3.
Hollywood Spectator. Sep 26, 1931, v12, p23-24.
Variety. Oct 6, 1931, p29.

Caught (US; Ophuls, Max; 1949)
Commonweal. Mar 4, 1949, v49, p521.
Film Daily. Mar 4, 1949, p8.
The Films Of James Mason. p86-87.
Hollywood Reporter. Feb 16, 1949, p4.
Motion Picture Herald Product Digest. Feb 19, 1949, p4506.
The New Republic. Mar 7, 1949, v120, p30.
The New York Times. Feb 18, 1949, p26.
The New Yorker. Feb 26, 1949, v25, p73.
Newsweek. Feb 28, 1949, v33, p79.
Theatre Arts. May 1949, v33, p93.
Time. Mar 7, 1949, v53, p103.
Variety. Feb 23, 1949, p10.

Caught in the Draft (US; Butler, David; 1941)
Commonweal. Jul 11, 1941, v34, p278.
Film Daily. May 29, 941, p9.
The Films of World War II. p50.
Hollywood Reporter. May 23, 1941, p3.
The London Times. Aug 4, 1941, p8.
Motion Picture Exhibitor. Jun 11, 1941, p764.
Motion Picture Herald Product Digest. Apr 19, 1941, p110.
The New York Times. Jun 26, 1941, p27.
Newsweek. Jul 7, 1941, v18, p50.
Scribner's Commentator. Sep 1941, v10, p105.
Time. Jul 7, 1941, v38, p61+.
Variety. Apr 28, 1941, p16.

Caught Short (US; Riesner, Charles F.; 1930)
Film Daily. Jun 22, 1930, p14.
The Film Spectator. Apr 12, 1930, v9, p24-25.
Judge. Jul 26, 1930, v99, p23.
Life. Jul 18, 1930, v95, p17.
The New York Times. Jun 21, 1930, p20.
The New York Times. Jun 29, 1930, p3.
The New Yorker. Jun 28, 1930, v6, p36.
Outlook and Independent. Jul 2, 1930, v155, p351.
Time. Jul 7, 1930, v16, p62.
Variety. Jun 25, 1930, p109.

Cavalcade (US; Lloyd, Frank; 1933)
American Film Criticism. p277-78.
Around Cinemas. p78-80.
Canadian Magazine. Dec 1932, v78, p37.
Canadian Magazine. Mar 1933, v79, p42.
Catholic World. May 1933, v137, p206-07.
Cinema Quarterly. Spring 1933, v1, p178-79.
Commonweal. Jan 25, 1933, v17, p357.
Dictionary of Films. p57.
English Review. May 1933, v56, p576-77.
Film Daily. Jan 7, 1933, p6.
Film Notes. p87-88.
Judge. Mar 1933, v104, p20.
A Library of Film Criticism: American Film Directors. p271.
Literary Digest. Jan 28, 1933, v115, p15-16.
Literary Digest. Apr 8, 1933, v115, p12.
Lorentz on Film. p105-07.
Magill's Survey of Cinema. Series I. v1, p316-19.
Motion Picture. Feb 1933, v45, p40-41+.
Motion Picture Herald. Jan 14, 1933, p16.
Motion Picture Herald. Feb 11, 1933, p20-21.
The Nation. Feb 1, 1933, v136, p130-31.
National Board of Review Magazine. Feb 1933, v8, p11.
New Outlook. Feb 1933, v161, p49.
The New Republic. Apr 19, 1933, v74, p282.
The New Statesman and Nation. Feb 25, 1933, v5, p223.
The New York Times. Jan 6, 1933, p23.
The New York Times. Sep 25, 1933, p4.
The New York Times. Jan 12, 1933, p20.
The New York Times. Jan 15, 1933, p5.
Review of Reviews. Dec 10, 1932, v82, p53-57.
Rob Wagner's Script. Jan 21, 1933, v8, p8.
Saturday Review. Apr 8, 1933, v9, p527.
Saturday Review (London). Feb 25, 1933, v155, p195.
Selected Film Criticism: Foreign Films, 1931-1940. p8.

Stage. Feb 1933, v10, p40.
Those Fabulous Movie Years: The 30s. p46.
Time. Jan 16, 1933, v21, p19.
Vanity Fair. Mar 1933, v40, p48.
Variety. Jan 10, 1933, p15.

Cecilia of the Pink Roses (US; Steger, Julius; 1918)
Motion Picture News. Jun 15, 1918, p3548.
The Moving Picture World. Jun 8, 1918, p1473.
The Moving Picture World. Jun 15, 1918, p1620.
The New York Times. Jun 3, 1918, p9.
Variety. Jun 7, 1918, p34.
Wid's Daily. May 26, 1918, p13-14.

Ceiling Zero (US; Hawks, Howard; 1936)
Esquire. Apr 1936, v5, p104.
The Film Criticism of Otis Ferguson. p115-17.
Film Daily. Dec 24, 1935, p7.
The Films of Howard Hawks (Willis). p89-92.
The Films of James Cagney. p115-17.
The Gangster Film. p163-65.
Hollywood Reporter. Dec 20, 1935, p3.
Hollywood Spectator. Jan 4, 1936, v10, p12.
Motion Picture Herald. Dec 28, 1935, p64-65.
National Board of Review Magazine. Feb 1936, v11, p17.
The New Republic. Feb 5, 1936, v85, p369.
The New York Times. Jan 20, 1936, p22.
The New Yorker. Feb 1, 1936, v11, p46.
Newsweek. Jan 18, 1936, v7, p41.
Rob Wagner's Script. Jan 4, 1936, v14, p10.
Time. Jan 27, 1936, v27, p46.
Variety. Jan 22, 1936, p14.

Centennial Summer (US; Preminger, Otto; 1946)
The Cinema of Otto Preminger. p84-85.
Commonweal. Aug 2, 1946, v44, p384.
Film Daily. May 29, 1946, p7.
The Hollywood Musical. p272.
Hollywood Musicals. p219.
Hollywood Reporter. May 27, 1946, p3.
Motion Picture Herald Product Digest. Jun 8, 1946, p3030.
The New York Times. Jul 18, 1946, p20.
The New Yorker. Jul 27, 1946, v22, p49.
Newsweek. Jul 29, 1946, v28, p78-79.
Time. Jul 29, 1946, v48, p88+.
Variety. May 29, 1946, p10.

Central Airport (US; Wellman, William A.; 1933)
Film Daily. Mar 29, 1933, p8.
Hollywood Reporter. Mar 21, 1933, p3.
Motion Picture Herald. Apr 1, 1933, p22, 24.
New Outlook. May 1933, v161, p47.
The New York Times. May 4, 1933, p20.
Rob Wagner's Script. Apr 22, 1933, v9, p8.
Variety. May 9, 1933, p14.
William A. Wellman (Thompson). p133-36.

César (FR; Pagnol, Marcel; 1936)
Cinema, the Magic Vehicle. v1, p261-62.
Dictionary of Films. p210-11.
Esquire. Feb 1938, v9, p110-11.
Film Society Review. Oct 1967, p11-13.
Film Society Review. Oct 1967, p11-13.
Fortnight. Oct 28, 1949, v7, p31.
The Great French Films. p67-70.
The New York Times. Oct 28, 1948, p36.
Selected Film Criticism: Foreign Films, 1930-1950. p28-29.
Variety. Nov 25, 1936, p19.

Chad Hanna (US; King, Henry; 1940)
Film Daily. Dec 18, 1940, p5.
The Films of Henry Fonda. p98-99.
The Fondas (Springer). p106-07.
Hollywood Reporter. Dec 11, 1940, p3.
The New York Times. Dec 26, 1940, p23.
Newsweek. Jan 6, 1941, v17, p53.

Time. Jan 6, 1941, v37, p48.
Variety. Dec 18, 1940, p16.

Chained (US; Brown, Clarence; 1934)
Film Daily. Aug 31, 1934, p4.
The Films of Clark Gable. p157.
The Films of Joan Crawford. p112-13.
Hollywood Reporter. Aug 13, 1934, p3.
Motion Picture Herald. Sep 1, 1934, p33-36.
The New York Times. Sep 1, 1934, p16.
Time. Sep 10, 1934, v24, p40.
Variety. Sep 4, 1934, p19.

Chaland qui passe, Le *See* L'Atalante

The Champ (US; Vidor, King; 1931)
BFI/Monthly Film Bulletin. Feb 1976, v43, p36-37.
Film Daily. Nov 15, 1931, p10.
Hollywood Reporter. Oct 6, 1931, p3.
Judge. Dec 12, 1931, v101, p18.
Life. Nov 27, 1931, v98, p21.
Magill's Survey of Cinema, Series II. v1, p421-23.
Make It Again, Sam. p42-44.
Motion Picture Herald. Oct 17, 1931, p38.
The Nation. Dec 9, 1931, v133, p652.
The New York Times. Nov 10, 1931, p29.
The New Yorker. Nov 21, 1931, v7, p70-71.
Outlook and Independent. Nov 25, 1931, v159, p406.
Photoplay. Dec 1931, v41, p47.
Rob Wagner's Script. Nov 21, 1931, v6, p6.
Selected Film Criticism, 1931-1940. p39-41.
Time. Nov 23, 1931, v18, p40.
Variety. Nov 17, 1931, p14.

Champagne Waltz (US; Sutherland, Edward; 1936)
Commonweal. Feb 5, 1937, v25, p418.
Film Daily. Feb 5, 1937, p9.
Harper's Bazaar. Jan 1945, v79, p64.
Hollywood Reporter. Dec 5, 1936, p3.
Hollywood Spectator. Dec 19, 1936, v11, p9-10.
Motion Picture Herald. Dec 12, 1936, p53, 56.
The New York Times. Feb 4, 1937, p17.
The New Yorker. Feb 13, 1937, v12, p60-61.
Time. Jan 25, 1937, v29, p45.
Variety. Feb 10, 1937, p14.

Champion (US; Robson, Mark; 1949)
Commonweal. Apr 29, 1949, v50, p69.
Film Daily. Mar 14, 1949, p7.
The Films of Kirk Douglas. p57-61.
Hollywood Reporter. Mar 14, 1949, p3.
Life. Apr 11, 1949, v26, p68-70.
Magill's Survey of Cinema. Series II. v1, p424-26.
Motion Picture Herald Product Digest. Mar 19, 1949, p4537.
The Nation. May 7, 1949, v168, p538-39.
The New Republic. Apr 25, 1949, v120, p30.
The New York Times. Apr 11, 1949, p29.
The New Yorker. Apr 9, 1949, v25, p60.
Newsweek. Apr 11, 1949, v33, p102.
Rotarian. Sep 1949, v75, p36.
Selected Film Criticism, 1941-1950. p37-39.
Sequence. Aut 1949, v9, p132-34.
Theatre Arts. May 1949, v33, p92.
Time. Apr 11, 1949, v53, p102.
Variety. Mar 16, 1949, p11.

Champs Élysees (Also titled; Remontons Les Élysées)
(FR; Guitry, Sacha; 1938)
Commonweal. Mar 10, 1939, v29, p552.
Film Daily. Mar 2, 1939, p6.
Graham Greene on Film. p259.
Motion Picture Herald. Mar 4, 1939, p42.
The Nation. Mar 11, 1939, v148, p302.
The New Statesman and Nation. Dec 23, 1939, v18, p927.
The New York Times. Feb 28, 1939, p17.
The New Yorker. Mar 1939, v15, p65.

The New Yorker. Mar 4, 1939, v15, p65.
Rob Wagner's Script. May 6, 1939, v21, p12-13.
Selected Film Criticism: Foreign Films, 1930-1950. p2.
The Spectator. Dec 29, 1939, v163, p932.
Time. Mar 13, 1939, v33, p32.
Variety. Dec 21, 1938, p15.

A Chance at Heaven (US; Seiter, William A.; 1933)
Film Daily. Dec 23, 1933, p3.
Hollywood Reporter. Sep 22, 1933, p3.
Motion Picture Herald. Oct 14, 1933, p36.
The New York Times. Dec 26, 1933, p19.
Rob Wagner's Script. Apr 22, 1933, v9, p8.
Variety. Dec 26, 1933, p26.

Chances (US; Dwan, Allan; 1931)
Film Daily. Jun 14, 1931, p16.
Hollywood Reporter. Apr 29, 1931, p3.
Hollywood Spectator. Aug 1, 1931, v12, p16-17.
Hollywood Spectator. Aug 15, 1931, v12, p12-13.
Judge. Jul 4, 1931, v101, p20.
Life. Jul 17, 1931, v98, p18.
Motion Picture Herald. May 9, 1931, p37.
The New York Times. Jun 12, 1931, p27.
The New York Times. Jun 21, 1931, p3.
The New Yorker. Jun 20, 1931, v7, p54.
Time. Jun 22, 1931, v17, p26.
Variety. Jun 16, 1931, p21.

Chandu, the Magician (US; Varnel, Marcel; 1932)
Film Daily. Sep 16, 1932, p7.
Hollywood Reporter. Sep 3, 1932, p3.
Motion Picture Herald. Sep 17, 1932, p40.
The New York Times. Oct 1, 1932, p10.
Rob Wagner's Script. Oct 22, 1932, v8, p9.
Time. Oct 10, 1932, v20, p32.
Variety. Oct 4, 1932, p19.

Chang (US; Cooper, Merian C.; Schoedsack, Ernest B.; 1928)
Close-Up. Oct 1927, v1, p82-84.
Film Daily. Apr 17, 1927, p8.
The New York Times. Apr 30, 1927, p25.
Photoplay. Jun 1927, v32, p20.
Selected Film Criticism, 1921-1930. p60.
Variety. May 4, 1927, p20.

Chapayev (USSR; Vasiliev, Sergei; Vasiliev, Georgi; 1934)
Cinema, the Magic Vehicle. v1, p223-24.
Dictionary of Films. p59.
Eighty Years of Cinema. p103-04.
Esquire. Jun 1935, v3, p144.
Film Daily. Jan 15, 1935, p15.
Filmfront. Jan 28, 1935, v1, p18.
Filmfront. Jan 28, 1935, v1, p18.
Garbo and the Night Watchman. p152-56.
Hollywood Reporter. Jan 24, 1935, p3.
The International Dictionary of Films and Filmmakers. v1, p82-83.
Kino. p314-17.
Motion Picture Herald. Jan 26, 1935, p42.
The Nation. Jan 30, 1935, v140, p140.
National Board of Review Magazine. Feb 1935, v10, p6.
The New Masses. Jan 22, 1935, v14, p29-30.
The New Masses. Feb 12, 1935, v14, p29-30.
The New Republic. Feb 6, 1935, v81, p360.
The New Statesman and Nation. Feb 2, 1935, v9, p139-40.
The New Yorker. May 4, 1935, v11, p58.
Partisan Review. Aug-Sep 1938, v5, p41.
Rob Wagner's Script. Mar 30, 1935, v13, p6.
Selected Film Criticism: Foreign Films, 1930-1950. p29-31.
Time. Jan 28, 1935, v25, p32.
Variety. Jan 22, 1935, p15.

Chapeau de Paille d'Itailie, Un *See* An Italian Straw Hat

The Charge of the Light Brigade (US; Curtiz, Michael; 1936)
Around Cinemas. p139-41.
Canadian Magazine. Oct 1936, v86, p46.
Casablanca and Other Major Films of Michael Curtiz. p61-65.
Chestnuts in Her Lap. p22.
Commonweal. Nov 13, 1936, v25, p76.
Esquire. Jan 1937, v7, p187.
The Fifty-Year Decline and Fall of Hollywood. p211.
Film Daily. Oct 20, 1936, p8.
Film Society Review. Mar 1969, v4, p14-34.
The Films of David Niven. p37-39.
The Films of Errol Flynn. p44-50.
The Films of Olivia de Havilland. p81-88.
Garbo and the Night Watchman. p108-10.
Hollywood Reporter. Oct 17, 1936, p4.
Hollywood Spectator. Oct 24, 1936, v11, p7-8.
Judge. Dec 1936, v111, p32.
A Library of Film Criticism: American Film Directors. p75-76.
Literary Digest. Oct 17, 1936, v122, p30.
Magill's Survey of Cinema. Series II. v1, p427-32.
Motion Picture Herald. Oct 24, 1936, p54.
Movie Classic. Jan 1937, v11, p12.
The New Statesman and Nation. Jan 9, 1937, v13, p49.
The New York Times. Nov 2, 1936, p24.
Newsweek. Oct 31, 1936, v8, p24-25.
Rob Wagner's Script. Jan 23, 1937, v16, p12.
Scholastic. Sep 19, 1936, v29, p29-36.
Selected Film Criticism, 1931-1940. p41-42.
Stage. Nov 1936, v14, p69.
Stage. Dec 1936, v14, p14.
The Tatler. Jan 6, 1937, v143, p6.
Time. Nov 2, 1936, v28, p21.
Variety. Nov 4, 1936, p18.
World Film News. Feb 1937, v1, p26.

Charley's Aunt (US; Mayo, Archie; 1941)
Commonweal. Aug 29, 1941, v34, p448.
Film Daily. Jul 23, 1941, p6.
Hollywood Reporter. Jul 23, 1941, p3.
Motion Picture Herald Product Digest. Jul 26, 1941, p262.
The New York Times. Aug 2, 1941, p18.
Newsweek. Aug 11, 1941, v18, p60.
Scribner's Commentator. Oct 1941, v10, p60.
Time. Aug 18, 1941, v38, p71.
Variety. Jul 23, 1941, p8.

Charlie Chan at the Olympics (US; Humberstone, Bruce; 1937)
Film Daily. Mar 29, 1937, p5.
Hollywood Reporter. Mar 24, 1937, p4.
The New York Times. May 24, 1937, p23.
Variety. May 26, 1937, p14.

Charlie Chan Carries On (US; MacFadden, Hamilton; 1931)
Film Daily. Mar 22, 1931, p10.
Motion Picture Herald. Mar 28, 1931, p37.
The New York Times. Mar 21, 1931, p15.
Rob Wagner's Script. Jul 4, 1931, v5, p10.
Variety. Mar 25, 1931, p24.

Charlie Chan in Egypt (US; King, Louis; 1935)
Film Daily. Jun 4, 1935, p6.
Hollywood Reporter. May 31, 1935, p2.
Motion Picture Herald. Jun 8, 1935, p73, 76.
The New York Times. Jun 24, 1935, p12.
The New Yorker. Jun 29, 1935, v11, p55.
Time. Jul 1, 1935, v26, p35.
Variety. Jun 26, 1935, p23.

Charlie Chan in Panama (US; Foster, Norman; 1940)
Magill's Survey of Cinema. Series II. v1, p437-41.
The New York Times. Feb 23, 1940, p19.
Variety. Feb 21, 1940, p12.

Charlie Chan in Paris (US; Seiler, Lewis; 1935)
Film Daily. Jan 22, 1935, p4.
Films and Filming. Aug 11, 1957, v3, p16.
Hollywood Reporter. Jan 29, 1935, p2.
Hollywood Reporter. Dec 22, 1934, p3.
Motion Picture Herald. Jan 5, 1935, p35.
The New York Times. Jan 22, 1935, p23.
Time. Feb 4, 1935, v25, p40-41.
Variety. Jan 29, 1935, p14.

Charlie Chaplin's Burlesque on Carmen (Also titled: Charlie Chaplin's Carmen) (US; Chaplin, Charles; 1916)
Charles Chaplin: A Guide to References and Resources. p58-59.
The Films of Charlie Chaplin. p109-11.
The Moving Picture World. Apr 22, 1916, p639, 699.
The Moving Picture World. Jul 8, 1916, p236.
The New York Dramatic Mirror. Apr 8, 1916, p25.
The New York Dramatic Mirror. Apr 15, 1916, p29.
Variety. Apr 14, 1916, p24.
Wid's Daily. Jun 1, 1916, p617.

Charlie's Aunt (US; Scott, Sidney; 1925)
Film Daily. Feb 15, 1925, p6.
Magill's Survey of Cinema. Silent Films. v1, p292-94.
The Moving Picture World. Feb 21, 1925, p785.
The New York Times. Feb 9, 1925, p15.
The Silent Clowns. p292-95.
Variety. Feb 11, 1925, p31.

The Cheat *See* Roman d'un Tricheur, Le

The Cheat (US; DeMille, Cecil B.; 1915)
The Autobiography of Cecil B. DeMille. p149-50.
Cecil B. DeMille. p43-45.
DeMille. p46-48.
Fifty Great American Silent Films, 1912-1920. p39-41.
The Films of Cecil B. DeMille. p94-97.
Magill's Survey of Cinema. Silent Films. v1, p295-97.
Motion Picture News. Dec 25, 1915, p127.
The Moving Picture World. Dec 18, 1915, p2206, 2260.
The Moving Picture World. Dec 25, 1915, p2384.
The Moving Picture World. Nov 9, 1918, p691.
The Moving Picture World. Nov 30, 1918, p990-91.
The New York Times. Dec 18, 1915, p13.
The Rivals of D.W. Griffith. p43-46.
Selected Film Criticism, 1912-1920. p45-47.
Variety. Dec 17, 1915, p18.

The Cheat (US; Abbott, George; 1931)
Film Daily. Dec 13, 1931, p10.
Judge. Jan 9, 1931, v101, p29.
Motion Picture Herald. Dec 19, 1931, p50.
The New York Times. Dec 12, 1931, p23.
The New Yorker. Dec 19, 1931, v7, p62.
Rob Wagner's Script. Dec 12, 1931, v6, p8.
Time. Dec 21, 1931, v18, p25.
Variety. Dec 15, 1931, p14.

Check and Double Check (US; Brown, Melville; 1930)
Exhibitors Herald-World. Oct 4, 1930, p29.
Film Daily. Oct 12, 1930, p14.
Judge. Nov 22, 1930, v99, p20.
Life. Nov 28, 1930, v96, p20.
Magill's Survey of Cinema. Series II. v1, p446-48.
The New York Times. Jul 12, 1930, p16.
The New York Times. Nov 1, 1930, p23.
The New York Times. Nov 9, 1930, p5.
The New Yorker. Nov 8, 1930, v6, p93.
Outlook and Independent. Nov 12, 1930, v156, p431.
Time. Nov 17, 1930, v16, p51.
Variety. Oct 8, 1930, p22.

Cheers for Miss Bishop (US; Garnett, Tay; 1941)
Commonweal. Mar 21, 1941, v33, p543-44.
Film Daily. Jan 14, 1941, p5.
Hollywood Reporter. Jan 13, 1941, p3.
Motion Picture Herald Product Digest. Jan 11, 1941, p37.
The New Republic. Mar 17, 1941, v104, p372.
The New York Times. Mar 14, 1941, p17.
Newsweek. Jan 27, 1941, v17, p47-48.
Scholastic. Feb 10, 1941, v38, p36.
Scholastic. Mar 3, 1941, v38, p17-19.
Scribner's Commentator. May 1941, v10, p107.
Time. Feb 3, 1941, v37, p70.
Variety. Jan 15, 1941, p14.

A Chess Maniac (Hungarian title: Sakkjatek Orultje, A)
(HUNG; Nagy, Endre; 1898)
Film Before Griffith. p77.

Chicago-Michigan Football Game (US; 1903)
The George Kleine Collection Catalog. p18.

Chicken Every Sunday (US; Seaton, George; 1949)
Film Daily. Dec 9, 1948, p7.
Hollywood Reporter. Dec 8, 1949, p3.
Motion Picture Herald Product Digest. Dec 11, 1948, p4273.
The New York Times. Jan 19, 1949, p34.
Newsweek. Jan 31, 1949, v33, p75.
Rotarian. May 1949, v74, p34.
Senior Scholastic. Jan 12, 1949, v53, p37.
Time. Jan 24, 1949, v53, p86.
Variety. Dec 8, 1948, p10.

Chien Andalou, Un (Also titled: An Andalusian Dog) (FR;
Buñuel, Luis; Dali, Salvador; 1928)
American Film. Sep 1982, v7, p34-40.
The Cinema of Luis Buñuel. p9-15+.
Dictionary of Films. p390-91.
Film Culture. Sum 1963, v29, p22-27.
Films and Filming. Apr 1962, v8, p13-15, 38-41.
Films and Filming. Jan 1969, v15, p45, 48.
The International Dictionary of Films and Filmmakers. v1,
p87-88.
Luis Buñuel: A Critical Biography. p56-67+.
Luis Buñuel: An Introduction. p18-20.
Luis Buñuel (Durgnat). p22-37.
Luis Buñuel (Higginbotham). p30-40.
Magill's Survey of Cinema. Silent Films. v1, p298-300.
Screen. Aut 1977, v18, p55-120.
The Secret Life of Salvador Dali. p20-48+.
Surrealism and the Cinema. p13-14, 59-69+.
The World of Luis Buñuel. p149-53.

Chienne, La (Also titled: The Bitch; Isn't Life a Bitch?)
(FR; Renoir, Jean; 1931)
Dictionary of Films. p61.
Films and Filming. Jun 1960, v6, p13-14.
French Film (Sadoul). p66-67.
The Golden Age of French Cinema, 1929-1939. p40-43.
Jean Renoir: A Guide to References and Resources. p75-79.
Jean Renoir (Bazin). p24-29.
Jean Renoir (Durgnat). p67-75.
Jean Renoir: My Life and My Films. p104-19.
Jean Renoir: The French Films, 1924-1939. p77-101.
Jean Renoir: The World of His Films. p84-85, 201.
Sight and Sound. Sum 1960, v29, p133.
Variety. Jun 12, 1932, p28.

The Childhood of Maxim Gorky (Russian title: Detstvo
Gorkovo; Also titled: The Childhood of Gorky)
(USSR; Donskoy, Mark; 1938)
Cinema, the Magic Vehicle. v1, p286-87.
Classics of the Foreign Film. p114-17.
Dictionary of Films. p82-83.
Film Daily. Oct 5, 1938, p6.
Kino. p374+.

The New Masses. Oct 4, 1938, v29, p28-30.
The New Masses. Jan 3, 1939, v30, p29-30.
The New York Times. Sep 28, 1938, p29.
The New Yorker. Oct 8, 1938, v14, p55.
Variety. Sep 28, 1938, p21.

Children of Paradise (French title: Enfants du Paradis,
Les) (FR; Carné, Marcel; 1945)
Agee on Film. v1, p246-47, 275.
American Film. Jul-Aug, 1979, v4, p42-49.
Canadian Forum. Aug 1948, v28, p112.
Children of Paradise/Les Enfants du Paradis.
Cinema, the Magic Vehicle. v1, p394-95.
Classic Movies. p94-96.
Classics of the Foreign Film. p142-47.
Commonweal. Jan 3, 1947, v45, p304.
Dictionary of Films. p101-02.
Film Daily. Nov 13, 1946, p14.
Film Quarterly. Sum 1959, v12, p26-35.
Films and Filming. Oct 1965, v12, p33.
French Cinema of the Occupation and Resistance. p107-09+.
French Film (Sadoul). p102-04+.
The Great Films. p169-72.
The Great French Films. p103-10.
Hollywood Quarterly. Jul 1946, v1, p420-21.
Hollywood Reporter. Oct 31, 1946, p3.
The International Dictionary of Films and Filmmakers. v1,
p141-42.
Life. May 14, 1945, v18, p113-15.
Magill's Survey of Cinema. Foreign Language Films. v2, p532-
35.
Motion Picture Herald Product Digest. Nov 9, 1946, p3298.
The Nation. Apr 12, 1947, v164, p433.
The New York Times. Feb 20, 1947, p32.
The New York Times Magazine. Dec 1, 1946, p22-29.
The New Yorker. Feb 15, 1947, v22, p86.
Newsweek. Dec 9, 1946, v28, p101.
Rob Wagner's Script. Dec 7, 1946, v32, p744.
Selected Film Criticism: Foreign Films, 1930-1950. p31-32.
Seventy Years of Cinema. p153.
Sight and Sound. Spr 1946, v15, p4-6.
Theatre Arts. Dec 1946, v30, p713-14.
Time. Nov 25, 1946, v48, p103+.
Variety. Feb 26, 1947, p11.
The Village Voice. Nov 23, 1955, p6.

Chimmie Fadden (US; DeMille, Cecil B.; 1915)
Motion Picture News. May 29, 1915, p46.
Motion Picture News. Jul 10, 1915, p70.
Motography. Jul 17, 1915, p139.
The Moving Picture World. Jul 10, 1915, p322, 398, 400.
The New York Dramatic Mirror. Jul 7, 1915, p28.
Variety. Jul 2, 1915, p16.

China (US; Farrow, John; 1943)
Around Cinemas, Second Series. p227.
Commonweal. May 7, 1943, v38, p74.
Film Daily. Mar 27, 1943, p6.
The Films of Alan Ladd. p85-87.
Hollywood Reporter. Mar 22, 1943, p3.
Motion Picture Herald. Mar 20, 1943, p18.
Motion Picture Herald Product Digest. Mar 27, 1943, p1226.
The New York Times. Apr 22, 1943, p31.
The New Yorker. May 1, 1943, v19, p36.
Newsweek. May 3, 1943, v21, p31.
Time. May 3, 1943, v41, p96.
Variety. Mar 24, 1943, p20.

China Clipper (US; Enright, Ray; 1936)
Canadian Magazine. Oct 1936, v86, p46.
Commonweal. Sep 11, 1936, v24, p467.
The Complete Films of Humphrey Bogart. p33-34.
Film Daily. Aug 12, 1936, p9.
Hollywood Reporter. Jul 31, 1936, p3.
Hollywood Spectator. Aug 15, 1936, v11, p9.

Humphrey Bogart: The Man and His Films. p56-58.
Literary Digest. Aug 22, 1936, v122, p24.
Motion Picture Herald. Aug 15, 1936, p62.
The New York Times. Aug 12, 1936, p14.
The New Yorker. Aug 22, 1936, v12, p38.
Scholastic. Oct 3, 1936, v29, p32.
Time. Aug 24, 1936, v28, p32.
Variety. Aug 19, 1936, p16.
World Film News. Dec 1936, v1, p22-23.

China Express (Russian title: Goluboi Express; Also
    titled: The Blue Express) (USSR; Trauberg, Ilya;
    1929)
Close-Up. Dec 1930, v7, p433-36.
Dictionary of Films. p132.
Film Daily. Mar 16, 1930, p8.
Judge. Apr 12, 1930, v98, p21.
Kino. p272.
The New York Times. Mar 10, 1930, p24.
The New Yorker. Mar 16, 1930, v6, p85.
Outlook and Independent. Mar 19, 1930, v154, p471.
The Spectator. Oct 31, 1931, v147, p567-68.
Variety. Mar 12, 1930, p33.

China Seas (US; Garnett, Tay; 1935)
A Companion to the Movies. p207-08.
Esquire. Oct 1935, v4, p97.
Film Daily. Jul 25, 1935, p6.
The Films of Clark Gable. p164-66.
The Films of Jean Harlow. p118-23.
Hollywood Reporter. Jun 24, 1935, p3.
Judge. Sep 1935, v109, p14, 30.
Literary Digest. Aug 17, 1935, v120, p28.
Motion Picture Herald. Aug 3, 1935, p59.
The New Statesman and Nation. Sep 21, 1935, v10, p375.
The New York Times. Aug 10, 1935, p16.
The New Yorker. Aug 3, 1935, v11, p41-42.
Rob Wagner's Script. Aug 31, 1935, v14, p12.
Time. Aug 19, 1935, v26, p26.
Variety. Aug 14, 1935, p15.

China's Four Hundred Million *See* The Four Hundred
    Million

The Chocolate Soldier (US; Del Ruth, Roy; 1941)
Chestnuts in Her Lap. p69-71.
Commonweal. Nov 14, 1941, v35, p94.
Film Daily. Oct 15, 1941, p6.
Films and Filming. Mar 1972, v18, p19-22.
The Films of Jeanette MacDonald and Nelson Eddy. p179-83.
Hollywood Reporter. Oct 15, 1941, p3.
The London Times. Jan 12, 1941, p8.
Motion Picture Exhibitor. Oct 29, 1941, p879.
Motion Picture Herald Product Digest. Oct 18, 1941, p317-18.
The New York Times. Nov 1, 1941, p20.
The New York Times. Nov 9, 1941, sec9, p5.
Newsweek. Nov 10, 1941, v18, p68.
Time. Nov 17, 1941, v38, p92.
Variety. Oct 15, 1941, p8.

Chotard et Compagnie (FR; Renoir, Jean; 1933)
Jean Renoir: A Guide to References and Resources.
Jean Renoir (Bazin). p33-34.
Jean Renoir (Durgnat). p92-93.
Jean Renoir: The French Films, 1924-1939. p140-41.
Jean Renoir: The World of His Films. p112-13, 202.

The Christian (US; Thomson, Frederick; 1914)
Magill's Survey of Cinema. Silent Films. v1, p301-03.
The Moving Picture World. Mar 28, 1914, p1656-57.
The Moving Picture World. Jun 6, 1914, p1452.
The New York Dramatic Mirror. Mar 18, 1914, p34.
Selected Film Criticism, 1912-1920. p47-49.
Variety. May 22, 1914, p22.

Christine *See* Carnet de Bal, Un

A Christmas Carol (US; Marin, Edwin L.; 1938)
Commonweal. Dec 30, 1938, v29, p273.
Film Daily. Dec 12, 1938, p10.
Hollywood Reporter. Dec 9, 1938, p3.
Hollywood Spectator. Dec 24, 1938, v13, p11-12.
Life. Dec 26, 1938, v5, p17.
Motion Picture Herald. Dec 17, 1938, p49.
The New York Times. Dec 23, 1938, p16.
The New Yorker. Dec 24, 1938, v14, p45-46.
Photoplay. Jan 1939, v53, p74.
Rob Wagner's Script. Dec 17, 1938, v20, p18.
Saint Nicholas. Jan 1939, v66, p35.
Scholastic. Jan 7, 1939, v33, p32.
The Tatler. Dec 28, 1938, v150, p570.
Time. Dec 19, 1938, v32, p21.
Variety. Dec 14, 1938, p14.

Christmas in July (US; Sturges, Preston; 1940)
Between Flops. p99-101, 138-43.
Commonweal. Nov 15, 1940, v33, p104.
Film Daily. Sep 20, 1940, p5.
The London Times. Mar 17, 1941, p6.
Magill's Survey of Cinema. Series II. v1, p454-57.
Motion Picture Exhibitor. Oct 2, 1940, p611-12.
The New Republic. Jan 20, 1941, v104, p85.
The New York Times. Nov 6, 1940, p35.
The New York Times. Nov 10, 1940, sec9, p5.
Newsweek. Oct 14, 1940, v16, p73.
Photoplay. Dec 1940, v54, p62.
Preston Sturges: A Guide to References. p50-52.
Scholastic. Nov 18, 1940, v37, p33.
Time. Oct 21, 1940, v36, p91.
Variety. Sep 18, 1940, p14.

Christopher Bean (US; Wood, Sam; 1933)
Film Daily. Nov 22, 1933, p10.
Hollywood Reporter. Oct 27, 1933, p2.
Motion Picture Herald. Nov 18, 1933, p38.
The New York Times. Nov 25, 1933, p10.
The New Yorker. Dec 2, 1933, v9, p60-61.
Newsweek. Dec 2, 1933, v2, p33.
Rob Wagner's Script. Dec 2, 1933, v10, p10.
Time. Dec 4, 1933, v22, p37.

Christopher Columbus (GB; MacDonald, David; 1949)
Commonweal. Oct 21, 1949, v51, p36.
Coronet. Oct 1949, v26, p61-68.
Film Daily. Oct 11, 1949, p8.
The Films of Fredric March. p198-200.
Hollywood Reporter.
Motion Picture Herald. Oct 15, 1949, p49.
The New York Times. Oct 13, 1949, p33.
Newsweek. Oct 17, 1949, v34, p94.
Rotarian. Dec 1949, v75, p38.
Senior Scholastic. Sep 28, 1949, v55, p35.
Time. Nov 7, 1949, v54, p98.
Variety. Jun 22, 1949, p6.

Christopher Strong (US; Arzner, Dorothy; 1933)
BFI/Monthly Film Bulletin. Aug 1980, v47, p163.
Camera Obscura. Sum 1979, n3-4, p21-31.
Film Daily. Mar 11, 1933, p4.
The Films of Katharine Hepburn. p42-45.
The International Dictionary of Films and Filmmakers. v1,
    p92.
Judge. May 1933, v104, p23-24.
Motion Picture Herald. Mar 18, 1933, p32, 34.
The Nation. Mar 29, 1933, v136, p354.
The New York Times. Mar 10, 1933, p19.
The New Yorker. Mar 18, 1933, v9, p62-63.
Newsweek. Mar 18, 1933, v1, p28.
Popcorn Venus. p150-51.
Rob Wagner's Script. May 13, 1933, v9, p9, 19.
Selected Film Criticism, 1931-1940. p42-43.
Time. Mar 20, 1933, v21, p42.

Vanity Fair. May 1933, v40, p49-50.
Variety. Mar 4, 1933, p14.
The Velvet Light Trap. Fall 1973, n10, p16.

Chute de la Maison d'Usher, La *See* Fall of the House of Usher

Cimarron (US; Ruggles, Wesley; 1931)
Celluloid: The Film To-Day. p154-68.
Close-Up. Jun 1931, v8, p148.
Commonweal. Feb 18, 1931, v13, p440-41.
Exhibitors Herald-World. Dec 27, 1930, p20.
Film Daily. Jan 18, 1931, p10.
The Great Western Pictures. p59-60.
Hollywood Reporter. Dec 20, 1930, p1, 3.
Judge. Mar 28, 1931, v100, p22, 32.
Life. Mar 27, 1931, v97, p23.
Literary Digest. Feb 21, 1931, v108, p28.
Magill's Survey of Cinema. Series I. v1, p339-42.
Motion Picture Herald. Jan 3, 1931, p71.
The Nation. Feb 18, 1931, v132, p199-200.
National Board of Review Magazine. Feb 1931, v6, p11.
The New Statesman and Nation. Mar 14, 1931, v1, p109.
The New York Times. Jan 27, 1931, p20.
The New Yorker. Feb 7, 1931, v6, p67.
Outlook and Independent. Feb 11, 1931, v157, p233.
Photoplay. Feb 1931, v39, p54.
Photoplay. Jul 1932, v42, p66-67+.
Rob Wagner's Script. Apr 18, 1931, v5, p8.
Saturday Review (London). Mar 14, 1931, p378.
Selected Film Criticism, 1931-1940. p44-45.
The Spectator. Mar 28, 1931, v146, p499.
Theatre Magazine. Jan 1931, v53, p48.
Those Fabulous Movie Years: The 30s. p32-33.
Time. Feb 2, 1931, v17, p40.

Cinderella (FR; Melies, Georges; 1899)
The Emergence of Film Art. p12-13.
The Moving Picture World. Dec 2, 1911, p704-05.
Selected Film Criticism, 1896-1911. p18-20.

Cinderella (US; 1911)
A Million and One Nights. p474.
The Moving Picture World. Dec 2, 1911, v10, p704-05.
Selected Film Criticism, 1896-1911. p18-20.

Cinderella (US; Kirkwood, James; 1915)
The New York Dramatic World. Jan 6, 1915, p33.
Selected Film Criticism, 1912-1920. p49-50.
Variety. Jan 1, 1915, p29.

Circe, the Enchantress (US; Leonard, Robert Z.; 1924)
Film Daily. Sep 14, 1924, p6.
Magill's Survey of Cinema. Silent Films. v1, p304-06.

The Circus (US; Chaplin, Charles; 1928)
American Film Criticism. p201-04.
Chaplin: The Mirror of Opinion. p71-72, 80-81+.
Charles Chaplin: A Guide to References and Resources. p72-73.
Charlie Chaplin. p164-69.
The Comic Mind. p102-06+.
Dial. Mar 1928, v84, p257-259.
Dial. May 1928, v84, p413-414.
Exhibitor's Herald-World and Moving Picture World. Mar 3, 1928, p49.
Film Daily. Jan 22, 1928, p6.
The Film Spectator. Dec 10, 1927, v4, p7-8.
The Films of Charlie Chaplin. p177-80.
Focus on Chaplin. p130-32+.
Literary Digest. Mar 24, 1928, v96, p36.
Magill's Survey of Cinema. Silent Films. v1, p307-09.
Motion Picture Classic. Oct 1927, v26, p28-29.
The Nation. Feb 29, 1928, v126, p247-48.
The New York Times. Jan 9, 1928, p20.
Selected Film Criticism, 1921-1930. p61-63.

The Silent Clowns. p339-43+.
Theatre Arts. Fall 1948, v32, p50.
Vanity Fair. Mar 1928, v30, p68-69.
Variety. Jan 11, 1928, p16.

The Cisco Kid (US; Cummings, Irving; 1931)
Film Daily. Oct 25, 1931, p10.
The Great Western Pictures. p60-62.
Judge. Nov 21, 1931, v101, p18.
Motion Picture Herald. Oct 10, 1931, p46.
The New York Times. Oct 24, 1931, p20.
Variety. Oct 27, 1931, p19.

The Citadel (US; Vidor, King; 1938)
The Age of the Dream Palace. p230-31.
Cinema, the Magic Vehicle. v1, p298.
Commonweal. Nov 11, 1938, v29, p77.
Education. Nov 1938, v59, p157-63.
Film Daily. Oct 25, 1938, p5.
The Films of the Thirties. p218-19.
The Foremost Films of 1938. p147-63.
Hollywood Reporter. Oct 22, 1938, p3.
Hollywood Spectator. Oct 29, 1938, v13, p13-14.
A Library of Film Criticism: American Film Directors. p457-58.
Life. Nov 7, 1938, v5, p35-36.
Lorentz on Film. p158-61.
Magill's Survey of Cinema. Series I. v1, p343-45.
Motion Picture Herald. Oct 29, 1938, p42, 44.
The Nation. Nov 12, 1938, v147, p516.
The New Masses. Nov 8, 1938, v29, p29.
The New Republic. Nov 16, 1938, v97, p46.
The New Statesman and Nation. Dec 24, 1938, v16, p1088.
The New York Times. Nov 4, 1938, p27.
The New York Times. Dec 17, 1938, p11.
The New York Times. Jan 3, 1939, p18.
The New Yorker. Nov 5, 1938, v14, p57.
Newsweek. Oct 31, 1938, v12, p28.
Rob Wagner's Script. Nov 19, 1938, v20, p12.
Scholastic. Oct 22, 1938, v33, p8-9.
Selected Film Criticism, 1931-1940. p47-48.
The Spectator. Jan 6, 1939, v162, p16.
Stage. Dec 1938, v16, p57.
The Tatler. Jan 4, 1939, v151, p6.
Theatre Arts. Mar 1939, v23, p188.
Time. Nov 7, 1938, v32, p41.
Variety. Oct 26, 1938, p13.

The Citadel of Silence *See* Citadelle du Silence

Citadelle du Silence (Also titled: The Citadel of Silence) (FR; Herbier, Marcel L'; 1937)
Film Daily. Jan 2, 1940, p11.
Hollywood Reporter. Nov 5, 1937, p13.
Motion Picture Herald. Dec 30, 1939, p50-51.
The New York Times. Dec 25, 1939, p29.
Variety. May 19, 1937, p22.

Citizen Kane (US; Welles, Orson; 1941)
Afterimage. Spr 1974, v5, p40-66.
The Age of the American Novel. p26-32.
America in the Dark. p125-56.
American Cinematographer. Feb 1941, v22, p54-55.
American Film. Sep 1985, v10, p42-49+.
American Film Criticism. p409-10, 413-15.
The American Film Heritage. p127-33.
Around Cinemas. p227-31.
Australian Journal of Screen Theory. 1981, n8, p34-45.
California Arts and Architecture. Jul 1941, v58, p16+.
Chestnuts in Her Lap. p62-63, 152-53.
Cinema 81. Jul/Aug 1981, n271/272, p167.
Cinema Journal. Fall 1973, v12, p11-25.
Cinema Journal. 1977, v16, n2, p51-58.
The Cinema of Orson Welles (Bogdanovich). p4-6.
The Cinema of Orson Welles (Cowie). p21-48.
The Citizen Kane Book. 1971.

Classic Film Collector. Sum 1975, n47, p22-23.
Classic Film/Video Images. Nov 1981, n78, p26-28.
Classic Images. Nov 1982, n89, p42-44.
Classic Images. Jan 1984, n103, p37-38.
Classic Movies. p173-76.
Commonweal. May 9, 1941, v34, p65.
Commonweal. May 28, 1971, v94, p286-87.
Commonweal. Jun 22, 1979, v106, p369-71.
A Critical Inquiry. Wint 1975, v2, p307-25.
Critical Inquiry. 1978, v5, n2, p369-400.
Critical Inquiry. 1982, v8, n4, p651-74.
Directors in Action. p1-17.
Esquire. Oct 1972, v78, p99-105+.
The Film and the Public. p140-43.
Film Art. p60-72, 221-30.
Film as Film. p136-54.
Film Comment. Sum 1971, v7, p38-47.
Film Comment. Nov/Dec 1978, v14, p42-48.
Film Criticism. Spr 1981, v5, p12-20.
The Film Criticism of Otis Ferguson. p363-70.
Film Culture. 1956, v2, n3, p14-16.
Film Culture Reader. p29-36.
Film Daily. Apr 11, 1941, p5.
Film Heritage. Fall 1968, v4, p7-18.
Film Heritage. Fall 1971, v7, p13-16+.
Film & Literature: An Introduction. p118-28.
Film Making. Apr 1977, v15, p54-55.
Film Notes. p114-17.
Film Quarterly. Fall 1985, v29, p10-20.
Film Quarterly. Sum 1982, v35, p2-12.
Film Reader. 1975, n1, p9-54.
Film Study Guide. p28-45.
Films and Film. Dec 1963, v10, p15-19.
The Films of My Life. p278-85.
The Films of Orson Welles. p9-47.
Focus on Citizen Kane. 1971.
Focus on Orson Welles. p28-53, 103-22.
Great Film Directors: a Critical Analogy. p754-59.
The Great Films. p147-52.
The Great Movies. p148-54.
Halliwell's Hundred. p44-47.
A History of Narrative Film. p347-67.
Hollywood Spectator. May 1, 1941, v15, p6-7.
In the Dark. p70-74.
The International Dictionary of Films and Filmmakers. v1,
    p95-97.
Introduction to the Art of the Movies. p247-52.
Journal of Aesthetic Education. Apr 1975, n2, p32-47.
Journal of Aesthetics and Art Criticism. 1980, v38, n4, p419-
    26.
Journal of Popular Film. 1973, v2, p152-53.
Landmark Films. p176-87.
Life. Mar 17, 1941, v10, p53-56.
Life. May 26, 1941, v10, p108-16.
Literature/Film Quarterly. Sum 1974, v2, p196-215.
Literature/Film Quarterly. Spr 1977, v5, p118-24.
Literature/Film Quarterly. Spr 1979, v7, p99-111.
The London Times. Oct 13, 1941, p8.
Magic Moments from the Movies. p96-99.
The Magic World of Orson Welles. p65-101.
Magill's Survey of Cinema. Series I. v1, p346-51.
The Making of Citizen Kane. 1985.
Mank. p77-79, 249-75.
Marion Davies. p312-20.
Metro. Nov 1980, n53, p14-17.
Mindscreen. p23-44.
Motion Picture Exhibitor. Apr 16, 1941, p731.
Motion Picture Exhibitor. Sep 3, 1941, v26, n17, sec2, p833-
    34.
Motion Picture Herald Product Digest. Feb 22, 1941, p61.
Movies and Methods. p273-90.
Movietone News. Jan 1975, n38, p27.
The Nation. Apr 26, 1941, v152, p508.
A Neglected Art. p53-57.

New Masses. Feb 4, 1941, v38, p26-27.
The New Republic. Feb 24, 1941, v104, p270-71.
The New Republic. Jun 2, 1941, v104, p760-61.
The New Republic. Jun 16, 1941, v104, p824-25.
The New York Times. May 2, 1941, p25.
The New York Times. Oct 31, 1971, sec7, p3.
The New Yorker. May 3, 1941, v17, p79.
The New Yorker. Feb 27, 1971, v97, p44-50+.
Newsweek. Mar 17, 1941, v17, p60.
The Novel and the Cinema. p47-58.
On Film: Unpopular Essays on a Popular Art. p408-09.
Orson Welles; A Critical View. p53-59.
Orson Welles, Actor and Director. p27-35.
Orson Welles (Bessy). p127-38.
Orson Welles (Leaming). p184-86+.
Orson Welles (McBride). p33-51.
Photoplay. Jul 1941, v19, p24.
The Primal Screen. p111-36.
The Primal Screen. p111-36.
Quarterly Review of Film Studies. 1976, v1, p388-93.
Raising Kane. 1971.
Readings and Writings. p49-61.
Renaissance of the Film. p60-70.
A Ribbon of Dreams. p27-62.
Rob Wagner's Script. Apr 19, 1941, v25, p16.
Run Through. p448-61.
Scholastic. May 5, 1941, v38, p33.
Screen Writer. Sep 1945, v1, p42-50.
Scribner's Commentator. Jul 1941, v10, p103-04.
Selected Film Criticism, 1941-1950. p41-44.
Sight and Sound. Spr 1972, v41, p71-73.
Sound and the Cinema. p125-30, 202-09.
Souvenir Programs of Twelve Classic Movies, 1927-1941. p217-
    36.
Stage. Dec 1940, v1, p54-55.
Storytelling and Mythmaking. p157-62.
Take One. Jul-Aug 1971, v3, p10-14.
Take One. 1978, v7, n2, p12-13+.
Talking Pictures. p250-53.
Ten Film Classics. p18-32.
Theatre Arts. Jun 1941, v25, p427-29, 431-32.
Time. Jan 27, 1941, v37, p69.
Time. Mar 17, 1941, v37, p90+.
University Film Association Journal. 1975, v27, p1-29.
University Film Study Center Newsletter. 1977, v7, n3, p5-10.
Variety. Apr 16, 1941, p16.
The Village Voice. Mar 7, 1956, v1, p6+.
The Village Voice. Apr 15, 1971, v16, p65+.
The Village Voice. Apr 29, 1971, v16, p71+.
The Village Voice. May 27, 1971, v16, p67+.
The Village Voice. Jun 3, 1971, v16, p59+.
The Village Voice. Apr 25, 1974, v19, p75-76.
The Village Voice. May 5, 1980, v25, p26.
World. Jan 16, 1973, v2, p66-69+.
50 Classic Motion Pictures. p236-43.

City Across the River (US; Shane, Maxwell; 1949)
The Big Book of B Movies. p178-79.
Film Daily. Feb 25, 1949, p6.
Hollywood Reporter.
Motion Picture Herald Product Digest. Mar 5, 1949, p4523.
The New Republic. Apr 25, 1949, v120, p30.
The New York Times. Apr 8, 1949, p31.
The New Yorker. Apr 16, 1949, v25, p95.
Rotarian. Jul 1949, v75, p36.
Time. Apr 25, 1949, v53, p96.
Variety. Feb 23, 1949, p10.

City Lights (US; Chaplin, Charles; 1931)
American Film Criticism. p253-54.
Around Cinemas. p50-51.
The Bookman. Apr 1931, v73, p184-85.
Celluloid: The Film To-Day. p85-104.
Charles Chaplin: A Guide to References and Resources. p73-
    74.

Charles Chaplin's City Lights: Its Production and Dialectical Structure. p.
Cinema, the Magic Vehicle. v1, p172-73.
Classic Movies. p34-35.
Classics of the Silent Screen. p114-15.
Commonweal. Mar 18, 1931, v13, p553.
Dictionary of Films. p65.
Eighty Years of Cinema. p87-88.
Film Criticism and Caricatures, 1943-1953. p115-16.
Film Daily. Feb 15, 1931, p10.
Films in Review. May-Jun 1950, v1, p33-34, 45-46.
The Films of Charles Chaplin. p191-97.
From Quasimodo to Scarlett O'Hara. p133-35.
The Great Movies. p67-70.
Hollywood as Historian. p53-57.
The International Dictionary of Films and Filmmakers. v1, p98-99.
Judge. Feb 28, 1931, v100, p22.
Judge. Sep 19, 1931, v101, p20.
Life. Feb 27, 1931, v97, p20.
Life. Sep 5, 1949, v27, p76.
Life. May 8, 1950, v28, p81-82+.
Literary Digest. Feb 28, 1931, v108, p28.
Lorentz on Film. p65-67.
Magic and Myth of the Movies. p35-38.
Magill's Survey of Cinema. Series I. v1, p352-55.
Motion Picture Herald. May 16, 1931, p22, 43.
Movie Comedy. p31-32.
The Nation. Mar 4, 1931, v132, p250-51.
National Board of Review Magazine. Mar 1931, v6, p5.
The New Republic. Feb 25, 1931, v66, p46-47.
The New Republic. May 1, 1950, v122, p21.
The New Republic. Dec 21, 1963, v149, p29.
The New Statesman and Nation. Mar 7, 1931, v1, p65-66.
The New York Times. Feb 7, 1931, p11.
The New York Times. Mar 19, 1950, p5.
The New York Times. Apr 16, 1950, p1.
The New York Times. Dec 4, 1963, p56.
The New Yorker. Feb 21, 1931, v6, p52-53.
Newsweek. May 1, 1950, v35, p75.
Outlook and Independent. Feb 18, 1931, v157, p271.
Reruns. p17-20.
Rob Wagner's Script. Feb 7, 1931, v4, p6.
Saturday Review (London). Mar 7, 1931, v151, p340.
Scrutiny of Cinema. p42-45.
Selected Film Criticism, 1931-1940. p49-51.
Shots in the Dark. p230-31.
The Spectator. Mar 7, 1931, v146, p344-45.
Those Fabulous Movie Years: The 30s. p24-25.
Time. Apr 17, 1950, v55, p105.
Variety. Feb 11, 1934, p14.
Variety. Mar 22, 1950, p6.
50 Classic Motion Pictures. p134-39.

City Streets (US; Rogell, Albert S.; 1938)
Film Daily. Jul 29, 1938, p11.
Hollywood Reporter. Jun 17, 1938, p3.
Hollywood Spectator. Jun 25, 1938, v13, p9.
The New York Times. Jul 25, 1938, p18.
Variety. Jul 27, 1938, p17.

City Streets (US; Mamoulian, Rouben; 1931)
Cinema, the Magic Vehicle. v1, p195-96.
Dark Cinema. p138-39.
Dictionary of Films. p65.
Film Daily. Apr 19, 1931, p10.
Films and Filming. Jan 1964, v10, p10.
The Films of Gary Cooper. p92-94.
From Quasimodo to Scarlett O'Hara. p146-48.
The Great Gangster Pictures. p80-81.
Judge. May 9, 1931, v100, p22.
Life. May 8, 1931, v97, p20.
Motion Picture Herald. Apr 11, 1931, p34.
National Board of Review Magazine. May 1931, v6, p7-12.
The New York Times. Apr 18, 1931, p17.

The New Yorker. Apr 25, 1931, v7, p79, 81.
Rob Wagner's Script. Apr 18, 1931, v5, p11-12.
Rouben Mamoulian. p29-38.
The Spectator. Aug 22, 1931, v147, p240.
Time. Apr 27, 1931, v17, p38.
Variety. Apr 22, 1931, p19.

The City That Never Sleeps (US; Cruze, James; 1924)
Film Daily. Oct 5, 1924, p7.
The Moving Picture World. Oct 11, 1924, p520.
The New York Times. Sep 29, 1924, p10.
Variety. Oct 1, 1924, p22.

Civilization (US; Barker, Reginald; West, Raymond B.; 1916)
BFI/Monthly Film Bulletin. Apr 1975, v42, p91.
Fifty Great American Silent Films, 1912-1920. p48-50.
The International Dictionary of Films and Filmmakers. v1, p99-100.
Magill's Survey of Cinema. Silent Films. v1, p318-21.
The Moving Picture World. Jun 17, 1916, p2056.
The New York Dramatic Mirror. Jun 10, 1916, p27.
The New York Times. Jun 3, 1916, p11.
Photoplay. Aug 1916, v10, p135-37.
Selected Film Criticism, 1912-1920. p50-54.
Variety. Jun 9, 1916, p23.
The War, the West, and the Wilderness. p72-77.
Wid's Daily. Jun 8, 1916, p628.

The Clairvoyant (GB; Elvey, Maurice; 1935)
Canadian Forum. Jan 1936, v15, p15.
Film Daily. Jun 8, 1935, p8.
Hollywood Reporter. Jun 17, 1935, p3.
London Mercury. Sep 1935, v32, p475.
Motion Picture Herald. Jun 15, 1935, p83.
The New Statesman and Nation. Aug 17, 1935, v10, p223.
The New York Times. Jun 8, 1935, p12.
Time. Jun 17, 1935, v25, p41.
Variety. Jun 12, 1935, p41.

The Clansman *See* The Birth of a Nation

Claudia (US; Goulding, Edmund; 1943)
Commonweal. Nov 26, 1943, v39, p145.
Film Daily. Aug 19, 1943, p6.
Hollywood Reporter. Aug 18, 1943, p3.
Motion Picture Herald Product Digest. Aug 21, 1943, p1493.
The New York Times. Nov 5, 1943, p5.
Newsweek. Sep 27, 1943, v22, p98.
Scholastic. Oct 4, 1943, v43, p35.
Time. Sep 13, 1943, v42, p96.
Variety. Aug 18, 1943, p10.

Cleopatra (US; Edwards, J. Gordon; 1917)
Magill's Survey of Cinema. Silent Films. v1, p322-25.
Motion Picture News. Nov 3, 1917, p3134.
Motography. Nov 3, 1917, p940.
The Moving Picture World. Nov 3, 1917, p708.
The New York Times. Oct 15, 1917, p11.
Selected Film Criticism, 1912-1920. p54-55.
Wid's Daily. Oct 18, 1917, p663-64.

Cleopatra (US; DeMille, Cecil B.; 1934)
Claudette Colbert (Quirk). p67-70.
Film Daily. Jul 25, 1934, p13.
The Films of Cecil B. DeMille. p292-97.
Hollywood Reporter. Jul 23, 1934, p3.
Life. Oct 1934, v101, p30.
Magill's Survey of Cinema. Series I. v1, p356-61.
Motion Picture Herald. Aug 25, 1934, p35-38.
The New York Times. Aug 17, 1934, p12.
Newsweek. Aug 25, 1934, v4, p25.
Pictorial Review. Nov 1934, v36, p78.
Rob Wagner's Script. Oct 20, 1934, v12, p10.
Selected Film Criticism, 1931-1940. p52.

Time. Aug 27, 1934, v24, p36.
Variety. Aug 21, 1934, p17.

Clive of India (US; Boleslavski, Richard; 1935)
Esquire. Mar 1935, v3, p142.
Film Daily. Jan 17, 1935, p4.
The Films of Ronald Colman. p163-68.
Great Britain and the East. Apr 4, 1935, v44, p415.
Hollywood Reporter. Jan 16, 1935, p3.
Hollywood Reporter. Jan 21, 1935, p2.
Judge. Mar 1935, v108, p30.
Motion Picture Herald. Jan 26, 1935, p42.
The Nation. Jan 30, 1935, v140, p139-40.
The New York Times. Jan 18, 1935, p29.
Newsweek. Jan 26, 1935, v5, p27.
Rob Wagner's Script. Feb 23, 1935, v13, p8.
Scholastic. Feb 9, 1935, p29.
The Spectator. Mar 29, 1935, v154, p529.
Time. Jan 28, 1935, v25, p33.
Variety. Jan 22, 1935, p14.

Cloak and Dagger (US; Lang, Fritz; 1946)
The Cinema of Fritz Lang. p160-64.
Commonweal. Oct 18, 1946, v45, p17.
Film Daily. Sep 11, 1946, p10.
Films and Filming. Feb 1969, v15, p74-75.
The Films of Fritz Lang. p218-20.
The Films of Gary Cooper. p204-05.
The Films of World War II. p242-43.
Fritz Lang: A Guide to References and Resources. p95-97.
Fritz Lang (Eisner). p267-74.
Fritz Lang in America. p69-73.
Hollywood Reporter. Sep 5, 1946, p3.
Motion Picture Herald Product Digest. Sep 14, 1946, p3197.
The New York Times. Oct 5, 1946, p13.
The New Yorker. Oct 12, 1946, v22, p66.
Newsweek. Oct 7, 1946, v28, p94+.
Theatre Arts. Nov 1946, v30, p670-71.
Time. Oct 21, 1946, v48, p102.
Variety. Sep 11, 1946, p10.

The Clock (US; Minnelli, Vincente; 1945)
Commonweal. Aug 27, 1945, v42, p48.
Film Daily. Mar 22, 1945, p8.
Hollywood Reporter. Mar 22, 1945, p3.
Judy: The Films and Career of Judy Garland. p123-26.
Life. May 28, 1945, v18, p75-76+.
Magic and Myth of the Movies. p169-70.
Magill's Survey of Cinema. Series II. v1, p472-74.
Motion Picture Exhibitor. Apr 24, 1945, v33, n22, sec2, p1689-90.
Motion Picture Herald Product Digest. Mar 24, 1945, p2374.
The Nation. May 26, 1945, v160, p608-09.
The New Republic. May 21, 1945, v112, p709.
The New York Times. May 4, 1945, p23.
The New Yorker. May 12, 1945, v21, p77-78.
Newsweek. May 14, 1945, v25, p110-11.
Photoplay. Jun 1945, v27, p20.
Theatre Arts. May 1945, v29, p278.
Time. May 14, 1945, v45, p93-94+.
Variety. Mar 28, 1945, p19.
The World of Entertainment. p146-51.

The Clodhopper (US; Schertzinger, Victor; 1917)
Motion Picture News. Jul 7, 1917, p114.
Photoplay. Sep 1917, v12, p105.
Selected Film Criticism, 1912-1920. p55-56.
Variety. Jun 29, 1917, p31.
Wid's Daily. Jun 28, 1917, p403.

The Closed Road (US; Tourneur, Maurice; 1916)
The Moving Picture World. p980, 1046.
The New York Dramatic Mirror. Apr 29, 1916, p31.
Photoplay. Jul 1916, v16, p116.
Variety. Apr 21, 1916, p29.
Wid's Daily. Apr 27, 1916, p540.

A Clown Must Laugh *See* Pagliacci

Club des Femmes (Also titled: Women's Club) (FR; Deval, Jacques; 1936)
Film Daily. Oct 26, 1937, p7.
Hollywood Reporter. Jun 19, 1936, p10.
Motion Picture Herald. Oct 23, 1937, p58.
The Nation. Oct 30, 1937, v145, p486.
The New York Times. Oct 20, 1937, p27.
The New Yorker. Oct 23, 1937, v13, p66-67.
Rob Wagner's Script. Dec 11, 1937, v18, p12.
Time. Oct 25, 1937, v30, p26+.
Variety. Jul 1, 1936, p23.
Variety. Oct 13, 1937, p17.

Cluny Brown (US; Lubitsch, Ernst; 1946)
Agee on Film. v1, p203.
The Cinema of Ernst Lubitsch. p134-41.
Commonweal. Jun 14, 1946, v44, p216.
Ernst Lubistch's American Comedy. p259-328.
Ernst Lubitsch: A Guide to References and Resources. p167-70.
Film Daily. May 1, 1946, p6.
The Films of Jennifer Jones. p59-64.
Hollywood Reporter. May 1, 1946, p3.
Life. May 27, 1946, v20, p125-28.
Magill's Survey of Cinema. Series II. v1, p480-84.
Motion Picture Herald Product Digest. Apr 27, 1946, p2961.
The Nation. Jun 8, 1946, v162, p701.
The New Republic. Jul 29, 1946, v115, p103.
The New York Times. Jun 3, 1946, p27.
The New Yorker. Jun 15, 1946, v22, p59.
Newsweek. May 6, 1946, v27, p90.
Sight and Sound. Aut 1946, v15, p97-98.
Theatre Arts. Jun 1946, v30, p349-50.
Time. May 20, 1946, v47, p90.
Variety. May 1, 1946, p8.

The Coast of Folly (US; Dwan, Allan; 1925)
Allan Dwan: The Last Pioneer. p76-78.
Film Daily. Sep 13, 1925, p6.
The Films of Gloria Swanson. p183-88.
The Films of the Twenties. p118-20.
Magill's Survey of Cinema. Silent Films. v1, p326-28.
The Moving Picture World. Sep 12, 1925, p171-72.
The New York Times. Aug 31, 1925, p19.
Variety. Sep 2, 1925, p36.

Cobra Woman (US; Siodmak, Robert; 1944)
Film Daily. Jun 16, 1944, p6.
Hollywood Reporter. Apr 21, 1944, p3.
Magill's Survey of Cinema. Series II. v2, p485-88.
Motion Picture Exhibitor. May 3, 1944, v31, n25, sec2, p1502.
Motion Picture Herald Product Digest. Apr 27, 1944, p1866.
The New York Times. May 18, 1941, p17.
Newsweek. May 29, 1944, v23, p72.
Time. May 29, 1944, v43, p96.
Variety. Apr 26, 1944, p12.

The Cock-Eyed World (Also titled: Cockeyed World) (US; Walsh, Raoul; 1929)
Exhibitor's Herald-World. Oct 5, 1929, p44-45.
Film Daily. Aug 4, 1929, p9.
The Hollywood Musical. p30.
The New York Times. Aug 5, 1929, p25.
Variety. Aug 7, 1929, p208.

The Cocktail Hour (US; Schertzinger, Victor; 1933)
Film Daily. Jun 3, 1933, p3.
Motion Picture Herald. Jun 10, 1933, p38.
The Nation. Jun 21, 1933, v136, p707.
New Outlook. Jul 1933, v162, p43.
The New York Times. Jun 5, 1933, p18.
The New Yorker. Jun 10, 1933, v9, p49.
Newsweek. Jun 10, 1933, v1, p29.
Time. Jun 12, 1933, v21, p30.
Variety. Jun 6, 1933, p14.

Cocoanut Grove (US; Santell, Alfred; 1938)
Film Daily. May 18, 1938, p8.
Hollywood Reporter. May 7, 1938, p3.
Motion Picture Herald. May 14, 1938, p47.
The New York Times. Jun 16, 1938, p21.
The New Yorker. Jun 25, 1938, v14, p53.
Rob Wagner's Script. May 21, 1938, v19, p9.
Time. May 30, 1938, v31, p49.
Variety. May 18, 1938, p12.

The Cocoanuts (US; Florey, Robert; Santley, Joseph; 1929)
Exhibitor's Herald-World. Jul 20, 1929, p90.
Film Daily. Jun 2, 1929, p9.
The Film Spectator. Jul 27, 1929, v8, p4.
The Films of the Twenties. p241-43.
The Hollywood Musical. p24.
The Marx Brothers. p39, 42-48+.
The New York Times. May 25, 1929, p17.
Selected Film Criticism, 1921-1930. p63-64.
Variety. May 29, 1929, p14.
Why a Duck? p15-51.

The Codfish *See* Merlusse

Coeur Fidele (FR; Epstein, Jean; 1923)
Cinema, The Magic Vehicle. v1, p87-88.

The Cohens and Kellys in Trouble (US; Stevens, George; 1933)
Film Daily. Apr 15, 1933, p3.
Hollywood Reporter. Mar 8, 1933, p3.
Motion Picture Herald. Apr 22, 1933, p36-37.
The New York Times. Apr 17, 1933, p16.
Variety. Apr 18, 1933, p4.

Colleen (US; Green, Alfred E.; 1936)
Film Daily. Mar 6, 1936, p9.
Hollywood Reporter. Jan 21, 1936, p3.
Motion Picture Herald. Feb 1, 1936, p46.
The New York Times. Mar 9, 1936, p20.
Rob Wagner's Script. Mar 14, 1936, v15, p10.
Time. Mar 16, 1936, v27, p58.
Variety. Mar 11, 1936, p15.

The Colleen Bawn (US; 1911)
The Moving Picture World. Sep 30, 1911, p954-56.
Selected Film Criticism, 1896-1911. p20-23.

College (US; Horne, James; 1927)
American Silent Film. p270.
BFI/Monthly Film Bulletin. Oct 1974, v41, p234.
Buster Keaton. p154-59.
The Film Career of Buster Keaton. p68-70, 104-19.
Film Daily. Sep 18, 1927, p5.
Magill's Survey of Cinema. Silent Films. v1, p329-32.
The Moving Picture World. Sep 17, 1927, p183.
The New York Times. Sep 12, 1927, p29.
Photoplay. Nov 1927, v32, p55.
Selected Film Criticism, 1921-1930. p64.
The Silent Clowns. p241-42.
Variety. Sep 14, 1927, p22.

College Coach (US; Wellman, William A.; 1933)
Film Daily. Nov 10, 1933, p12.
Hollywood Reporter. Oct 9, 1933, p3.
Motion Picture Herald. Nov 18, 1933, p42.
The New York Times. Nov 11, 1933, p10.
Rob Wagner's Script. Nov 11, 1933, v10, p9-10.
Time. Nov 6, 1933, v22, p42.
Variety. Nov 14, 1933, p30.
William A. Wellman (Thompson). p141-42+.

College Holiday (US; Tuttle, Frank; 1936)
Film Daily. Dec 19, 1936, p3.
Hollywood Reporter. Dec 16, 1936, p3.
Motion Picture Herald. Dec 26, 1936, p54.

The New Statesman and Nation. Jan 23, 1937, v13, p119.
The New York Times. Dec 24, 1936, p21.
The New Yorker. Jan 2, 1937, v12, p50.
Rob Wagner's Script. Jan 2, 1937, v16, p13.
The Spectator. Jan 22, 1937, v158, p122.
Time. Jan 4, 1937, v29, p22.
Variety. Dec 30, 1936, p10.

College Humor (US; Ruggles, Wesley; 1933)
Film Daily. Jun 14, 1933, p6.
The Films of Bing Crosby. p50-52.
Hollywood Reporter. Jun 6, 1933, p11.
Motion Picture Herald. Jun 17, 1933, p34.
New Outlook. Aug 1933, v162, p44.
The New York Times. Jun 23, 1933, p15.
Newsweek. Jul 1, 1933, v1, p31.
Time. Jul 3, 1933, v22, p30.
Variety. Jun 27, 1933, p14.

College Rhythm (US; Taurog, Norman; 1934)
Film Daily. Nov 1, 1934, p7.
The Hollywood Musical. p97.
Hollywood Reporter. Oct 31, 1934, p3.
Motion Picture Herald. Nov 10, 1934, p39-42.
The New York Times. Nov 24, 1934, p19.
Time. Dec 3, 1934, v24, p46.
Variety. Nov 27, 1934, p15.

College Swing (US; Walsh, Raoul; 1938)
Film Daily. Apr 28, 1938, p4.
Hollywood Reporter. Apr 12, 1938, p3.
Motion Picture Herald. Apr 16, 1938, p33.
The New York Times. Apr 28, 1938, p27.
Rob Wagner's Script. Apr 30, 1938, v19, p8.
Variety. Apr 27, 1938, p22.

Colonel Blimp (Also titled: The Life and Death of Colonel Blimp) (GB; Powell, Michael; Pressburger, Emeric; 1943)
Agee on Film. v1, p152-53.
BFI/Monthly Film Bulletin. Aug 1985, v52, p156-57.
Commonweal. Mar 30, 1945, v41, p590.
A Critical History of the British Cinema. p220-21.
Fifty Classic British Films. p46-48.
Film Daily. Mar 21, 1945, p6.
The Great British Films. p69-71.
Hollywood Reporter. Mar 21, 1945, p6.
Magill's Survey of Cinema. Series II. v2, p489.
A Mirror for England. p27-28.
Motion Picture Herald Product Digest. Jul 10, 1943, p1413-14.
The Nation. Mar 31, 1945, v160, p370.
The New Republic. Apr 30, 1945, v112, p587.
The New York Times. Mar 30, 1945, p18.
The New Yorker. Apr 7, 1945, v21, p65.
Newsweek. Mar 26, 1945, v25, p114.
Rob Wagner's Script. Nov 17, 1945, v31, p14.
Selected Film Criticism: Foreign Films, 1930-1950. p33-34.
Time. Jun 21, 1943, v41, p31.
Time. Apr 2, 1945, v45, p90.
Variety. Jun 23, 1943, p24.

Colorado Territory (US; Walsh, Raoul; 1949)
Commonweal. Jul 22, 1949, v50, p367.
Film Daily. May 18, 1949 , p8.
Hollywood Reporter. May 17, 1949, p3.
Motion Picture Herald Product Digest. May 21, 1949, p4617.
The New York Times. Jun 25, 1949, p8.
Newsweek. Jun 27, 1949, v33, p88.
Rotarian. Sep 1949, v75, p36.
Time. Jun 20, 1949, v53, p84.
Variety. May 18, 1949, p8.

Come and Get It (US; Hawks, Howard; Wyler, William; 1936)
Esquire. Jan 1937, v7, p109.

Film Daily. Oct 29, 1936, p11.
The Films of Howard Hawks (Willis). p110-12.
Hollywood Reporter. Oct 27, 1936, p3.
Hollywood Spectator. Nov 7, 1936, v11, p7-8.
Magill's Cinema Annual 1982. p412-15.
Motion Picture Herald. Nov 7, 1936, p54.
The New Masses. Nov 24, 1936, v21, p29.
The New Statesman and Nation. Dec 5, 1936, v12, p895.
The New York Times. Nov 12, 1936, p31.
The New Yorker. Nov 7, 1936, v12, p69-70.
Newsweek. Nov 14, 1936, v8, p60.
Rob Wagner's Script. Nov 14, 1936, v16, p12.
Samuel Goldwyn (Epstein). p140-43.
Samuel Goldwyn Presents. p168-71.
Stage. Dec 1936, v14, p14.
Time. Nov 16, 1936, v28, p37.
Variety. Nov 18, 1936, p12.
William Wyler: A Guide to References and Resources. p90-92.
World Film News. Jan 1937, v1, p25-26.

Command Decision (US; Wood, Sam; 1949)
Commonweal. Jan 28, 1949, v49, p400.
Film Daily. Dec 23, 1948, p6.
The Films of Clark Gable. p215-16.
Hollywood Reporter. Dec 23, 1948, p3.
Magill's Survey of Cinema. Series II. v2, p498-502.
Motion Picture Herald Product Digest. Dec 25, 1948, p4433.
The New Republic. Feb 7, 1949, v120, p30.
The New York Times. Jan 20, 1949, p34.
The New Yorker. Jan 29, 1949, v24, p53.
Newsweek. Jan 24, 1949, v33, p73.
Theatre Arts. Apr 1949, v33, p86.
Time. Jan 24, 1949, v53, p82.
Variety. Dec 29, 1948, p6.

Common Clay (US; Fleming, Victor; 1930)
Commonweal. Aug 20, 1930, v12, p406.
Exhibitors Herald-World. Aug 16, 1930, p32.
Film Daily. Aug 3, 1930, p10.
Judge. Sep 6, 1930, v99, p23.
Life. Aug 29, 1930, v96, p18.
The New York Times. Aug 2, 1930, p16.
The New York Times. Aug 10, 1930, p3.
The New Yorker. Aug 9, 1930, v6, p55-56.
Theatre Magazine. Oct 1930, v52, p47.
Time. Aug 18, 1930, v16, p46.
Variety. Aug 6, 1930, p21.

The Common Law (US; Stein, Paul; 1931)
Film Daily. Jul 19, 1931, p11.
Hollywood Reporter. Jun 12, 1931, p3.
Hollywood Spectator. Aug 15, 1931, v12, p5-6.
Hollywood Spectator. Aug 29, 1931, v12, p22.
Life. Aug 14, 1931, v98, p18.
Motion Picture Herald. Jul 25, 1931, p34.
The Nation. Aug 19, 1931, v133, p192.
The New York Times. Jul 20, 1931, p20.
The New York Times. Jul 26, 1931, p3.
The New Yorker. Jul 25, 1931, v7, p54.
Rob Wagner's Script. Sep 12, 1931, v6, p9-10.
Time. Jul 27, 1931, v18, p30.
Variety. Jul 21, 1931, p34.

Compliments of Mr. Flow *See* Mr. Flow

Comrade X (US; Vidor, King; 1940)
Film Daily. Dec 11, 1940, p5.
The Films of Clark Gable. p200-01.
The Films of Hedy Lamarr. p124-27.
The London Times. Apr 14, 1941, p8.
Motion Picture Exhibitor. Dec 25, 1940, p659.
The New Republic. Jan 13, 1941, v106, p54.
The New York Times. Dec 26, 1940, p23.
Time. Jan 6, 1941, v37, p48.
Variety. Dec 11, 1940, p16.

Comrades of 1918 *See* Westfront 1918

Comradeship *See* Kameradschaft

Confessions of a Cheat *See* Roman d'un Tricheur, Le

Confessions of a Co-Ed (US; Burton, David; Murphy, Dudley; 1931)
Film Daily. Jun 21, 1931, p10.
Hollywood Reporter. Jun 9, 1931, p3.
Judge. Jul 11, 1931, v101, p24.
Life. Jul 10, 1931, v98, p22.
The New York Times. Jun 20, 1931, p20.
The New York Times. Jun 28, 1931, p3.
The New Yorker. Jun 27, 1931, v7, p57.
Rob Wagner's Script. Jul 4, 1931, v5, p8-9.
Time. Jun 29, 1931, v17, p22.
Variety. Jun 23, 1931, p18.

Confidential Agent (US; Shumlin, Herman; 1945)
Agee on Film. v1, p178-79.
Film Daily. Nov 2, 1945, p10.
The Films of Peter Lorre. p177-78.
Graham Greene on Film. p31-35.
Hollywood Reporter. Nov 2, 1945, p3.
The London Times. Dec 31, 1945, p8.
Magill's Survey of Cinema. Series II. v2, p507-10.
Motion Picture Exhibitor. Nov 13, 1945, v35, n2, sec2, p1827.
Motion Picture Herald Product Digest. Nov 3, 1945, p2701.
The Nation. Nov 10, 1945, v161, p506.
The New York Times. Nov 3, 1945, p11.
The New Yorker. Nov 10, 1945, v21, p59.
Newsweek. Nov 12, 1945, v26, p100.
Saint Cinema. p136-39.
Scholastic. Dec 3, 1945, v47, p35.
The Spanish Civil War in American and European Films. p45-56.
Storytelling and Mythmaking. p183.
Time. Nov 19, 1945, v46, p98.
Variety. Oct 7, 1945, p25.

The Congress Dances (German title: Kongress Tanzt, Der) (GER; Charell, Eric; 1931)
Around Cinemas. p57-60.
Canadian Magazine. Aug 1932, v78, p27.
Cinema, the Magic Vehicle. v1, p188-89.
Close-Up. Dec 1931, v8, p283.
Dictionary of Films. p178-79.
Film Daily. May 15, 1932, p10.
Gotta Sing Gotta Dance. p73-75.
Judge. Jun 11, 1932, v102, p24.
Motion Picture Herald. May 14, 1932, p18-19.
Motion Picture Herald. May 28, 1932, p88.
The New Statesman and Nation. Dec 12, 1931, v2, p748.
The New York Times. Nov 22, 1931, p6.
The New York Times. Mar 27, 1932, p6.
The New York Times. May 12, 1932, p23.
The New Yorker. May 21, 1932, v8, p62-63.
Rob Wagner's Script. Aug 6, 1932, v7, p8.
Selected Film Criticism: Foreign Films, 1930-1950. p36-37.
Time. May 23, 1932, v19, p30.
Variety. Nov 10, 1931, p14.
Variety. May 17, 1932, p15.

A Connecticut Yankee (US; Butler, David; 1931)
Film Daily. Apr 12, 1931, p32.
The Films of Myrna Loy. p115-17.
From Quasimodo to Scarlett O'Hara. p142-43.
Motion Picture Herald. Mar 21, 1931, p39.
National Board of Review Magazine. Apr 1931, v6, p15.
The New York Times. Apr 13, 1931, p17.
The New Yorker. Apr 18, 1931, v7, p75, 77.
Outlook and Independent. Apr 15, 1931, v157, p539.
Rob Wagner's Script. May 30, 1931, v5, p10-11.
Time. Apr 20, 1931, v17, p28.

Variety. Apr 15, 1931, p20.
Will Rogers in Hollywood. p111-12.

A Connecticut Yankee in King Arthur's Court (US; Flynn, Emmett J.; 1921)
Film Daily. Feb 6, 1921, p3.
Life. May 5, 1921, v77, p652.
The New York Times. Mar 15, 1921, p14.
Photoplay. Jun 1921, v20, p51.
Selected Film Criticism, 1921-1930. p64-65.
Variety. Jan 28, 1921, p40.

A Connecticut Yankee in King Arthur's Court (Also titled: A Yankee in King Arthur's Court) (US; Garnett, Tay; 1949)
Collier's. Mar 19, 1949, v123, p36.
Commonweal. Apr 22, 1949, v50, p48.
Film Daily. Feb 24, 1949, p6.
The Films of Bing Crosby. p183-86.
The Hollywood Musical. p301.
Hollywood Reporter. Feb 1, 1949, p3.
Motion Picture Herald Product Digest. Feb 26, 1949, p4513.
The New Republic. Apr 18, 1949, v120, p31.
The New York Times. Apr 8, 1949, p31.
The New Yorker. Apr 16, 1949, v25, p95.
Newsweek. Apr 18, 1949, v33, p89.
Rotarian. Aug 1949, v75, p42.
Senior Scholastic. Apr 13, 1949, v54, p25.
Time. Apr 25, 1949, v53, p99.
Variety. Feb 23, 1949, p10.

The Conquering Power (US; Ingram, Rex; 1921)
Film Daily. Jul 10, 1921, p2.
Motion Picture Classic. Oct 1921, v13, p65, 86.
Moving Picture World. Jul 16, 1921, v51, p339.
The New York Times. Jul 10, 1921, sec6, p2.
Selected Film Criticism, 1921-1930. p67.
Variety. Jul 8, 1921, p27.

The Conquerors (US; Wellman, William A.; 1932)
Film Daily. Nov 19, 1932, p4.
The Great Western Pictures. p65-66.
Hollywood Reporter. Oct 29, 1932, p3.
The Nation. Dec 7, 1932, v135, p576.
The New York Times. Nov 21, 1932, p21.
The New Yorker. Nov 26, 1932, v8, p50.
Time. Nov 28, 1932, v20, p21.
Variety. Nov 22, 1932, p17.
William A. Wellman (Thompson). p128-30+.

Conquest (Also titled: Marie Walewska) (US; Brown, Clarence; 1937)
Commonweal. Nov 12, 1937, v27, p78.
Film Daily. Oct 26, 1937, p6.
The Films of Greta Garbo. p141-43.
Graham Greene on Film. p187, 190.
Hollywood Reporter. Oct 23, 1937, p3.
Independent Woman. Dec 1937, v16, p398.
Life. Nov 8, 1937, v3, p40-43.
Literary Digest. Nov 20, 1937, v124, p34.
Motion Picture Herald. Oct 30, 1937, p47.
National Board of Review Magazine. Nov 1937, v12, p14.
The New Masses. Nov 9, 1937, v25, p28.
The New Statesman and Nation. Dec 25, 1937, v14, p1102.
The New York Times. Nov 5, 1937, p19.
The New Yorker. Nov 6, 1937, v13, p74-75.
Newsweek. Nov 8, 1937, v10, p22.
Rob Wagner's Script. Dec 11, 1937, v18, p12.
Scholastic. Dec 4, 1937, v31, p10.
Sight and Sound. Wint 1937-38, v6, p187-88.
The Spectator. Dec 24, 1937, v159, p1145.
Stage. Oct 1937, v15, p50-52.
The Tatler. Dec 29, 1937, v146, p574.
Time. Nov 8, 1937, v30, p48.

Variety. Oct 27, 1937, p18.
World Film News. Apr 1938, v3, p34.

Conquete du Pole, A La (FR; 1912)
Dictionary of Films. p6.

Conrad in Quest of His Youth (US; Mille, William C. de; 1920)
Motion Picture News. Nov 20, 1920, p3989.
The Moving Picture World. Nov 20, 1920, p388-89.
The New York Dramatic Mirror. Nov 13, 1920, p914.
The New York Times. Nov 8, 1920, p20.
Selected Film Criticism, 1912-1920. p56-57.
Variety. Nov 12, 1920, p35.
Wid's Daily. Nov 14, 1920, p5.

The Constant Nymph (GB; Dean, Basil; 1934)
Film Daily. Apr 7, 1934, p19.
Motion Picture Herald. Apr 14, 1934, p42.
The New Republic. May 2, 1934, v78, p338.
The New York Times. Apr 7, 1934, p7.
Rob Wagner's Script. Apr 28, 1934, v11, p9.
Selected Film Criticism: Foreign Films, 1930-1950. p37-38.
Time. Apr 16, 1934, v23, p48.

The Constant Nymph (US; Goulding, Edmund; 1943)
Commonweal. Aug 13, 1943, v38, p421.
Film Daily. Jun 30, 1943, p6.
The Films of Peter Lorre. p157-59.
The Films of the Forties. p88-89.
Hollywood Reporter. Jun 29, 1943, p3.
Magill's Survey of Cinema. Series II. v2, p511.
Motion Picture Herald Product Digest. Jul 13, 1943, p1401.
The New Republic. Aug 23, 1943, v109, p255.
The New York Times. Jul 24, 1943, p8.
Newsweek. Aug 9, 1943, v22, p85.
Time. Aug 9, 1943, v42, p96.
Variety. Jun 6, 1943, p8.

Convoy (GB; Tennyson, Pen; 1940)
Commonweal. Jan 24, 1941, v33, p352.
Film Daily. Jan 8, 1941, p6.
Life. Sep 22, 1941, v11, p24.
The London Times. Jul 8, 1940, p6.
Motion Picture Exhibitor. Jan 8, 1941, p670.
Motion Picture Herald Product Digest. Mar 22, 1941, p88.
The New York Times. Jan 17, 1940, p21.
Rob Wagner's Script. Apr 5, 1941, v25, p16.
Selected Film Criticism: Foreign Films, 1930-1950. p36.
Time. Jan 27, 1941, v37, p70.
Variety. Jun 26, 1940, p16.

Coquette (US; Taylor, Sam; 1929)
Film Daily. Apr 14, 1929, p12.
Magill's Survey of Cinema. Series II. v2, p524-27.
The New York Times. Apr 6, 1929, p14.
Variety. Apr 19, 1929, p25.

The Corn Is Green (US; Rapper, Irving; 1945)
Agee on Film. v1, p157.
Bette Davis: Her Films and Career. p131-33.
Commonweal. May 6, 1945, v41, p626-27.
Film Daily. Mar 29, 1945, p8.
Hollywood Reporter. Mar 29, 1945, p3.
The London Times. Mar 21, 1945, p6.
Magill's Survey of Cinema. Series I. v1, p387-89.
Motion Picture Exhibitor. Apr 4, 1945, v33, n22, sec2, p1693.
Motion Picture Herald Product Digest. Mar 31, 1945, p2381.
The Nation. Apr 14, 1945, v160, p425.
The New York Times. Mar 30, 1945, p18.
The New Yorker. Mar 24, 1945, v21, p76.
Newsweek. Apr 9, 1945, v25, p91-93.
Photoplay. Jul 1945, v27, p19.
Scholastic. Apr 16, 1945, v46, p30.
Time. Apr 30, 1945, v45, p89.
Variety. Apr 4, 1945, p10.

A Corner in Wheat (US; Griffith, D.W.; 1909)
The Bioscope. Jan 20, 1910, p52.
Dictionary of Films. p70.
The Moving Picture World. Dec 25, 1909, p921.
Moving Pictures. p57.
The New York Dramatic Mirror. Dec 25, 1909, p15.
The New York Dramatic Mirror. Jan 15, 1910, p13.
Selected Film Criticism, 1896-1911. p23-25.
Spellbound in Darkness. p67-68.

Cornered (US; Dmytryk, Edward; 1945)
Commonweal. Jan 25, 1946, v43, p383.
Film Daily. Dec 26, 1945, p15.
Hollywood Reporter. Nov 14, 1945, p3.
Life. Dec 10, 1945, v19, p71-72+.
The Nation. Feb 16, 1946, v162, p206.
The New York Times. Dec 26, 1945, p15.
The New Yorker. Dec 29, 1945, v21, p59.
Newsweek. Dec 17, 1945, v26, p114+.
Saturday Review of Literature. Feb 2, 1946, v29, p18.
Theatre Arts. Feb 1946, v30, p102-03.
Time. Dec 17, 1945, v46, p93.
Variety. Nov 14, 1945, p12.

The Corsican Brothers (US; Ratoff, Gregory; 1941)
Commonweal. Dec 26, 1941, v35, p249-50.
Film Daily. Dec 19, 1941, p7.
Hollywood Reporter. Dec 17, 1941, p6.
Motion Picture Herald Product Digest. Dec 20, 1941, p431.
The New York Times. Jan 16, 1942, p25.
Newsweek. Dec 15, 1941, v18, p71+.
Time. Jan 5, 1942, v39, p66.
Variety. Dec 24, 1941, p18.

Corvette K-225 (US; Rosson, Richard; 1943)
Commonweal. Nov 12, 1943, v38, p421.
Film Daily. Sep 27, 1943, p8.
The Films of the Forties. p98-99.
Hollywood Reporter. Sep 27, 1943, p3.
Motion Picture Herald Product Digest. Oct 2, 1943, p1565.
The New Republic. Nov 15, 1943, v109, p687.
The New York Times. Oct 21, 1943, p30.
The New Yorker. Oct 30, 1943, v19, p83.
Newsweek. Oct 18, 1943, v22, p110.
Variety. Sep 29, 1943, p8.

A Cottage on Dartmoor (GB; Asquith, Anthony; 1929)
BFI/Monthly Film Bulletin. Jan 1976, v42, p14.
The Films of Anthony Asquith. p53-56.

Counsel for Love *See* Avocate d'Amour

Counsel for Romance *See* Avocate d'Amour

Counsellor-at-Law (US; Wyler, William; 1933)
Esquire. Feb 1934, v1, p131.
Film Daily. Nov 28, 1933, p4.
Hollywood Reporter. Nov 18, 1933, p3.
Kiss Kiss Bang Bang. p311-12.
Literary Digest. Dec 23, 1933, v116, p31.
Motion Picture Herald. Nov 25, 1933, p35.
The Nation. Dec 27, 1933, v137, p744.
New Outlook. Jan 1934, v163, p43.
The New York Times. Dec 8, 1933, p31.
The New Yorker. Dec 16, 1933, v9, p71-72.
Newsweek. Dec 16, 1933, v2, p30.
Rob Wagner's Script. Jan 6, 1934, v10, p8.
Time. Dec 18, 1933, v22, p34.
Variety. Dec 12, 1933, p19.
William Wyler: A Guide to References and Resources. p74-77.
William Wyler (Anderegg). p37-39.

The Count of Monte Cristo (US; Porter, Edwin S.; 1913)
Fifty Great American Silent Films, 1912-1920. p4-6.
Magill's Survey of Cinema. Silent Films. v1, p336-38.
The Moving Picture World. Nov 1, 1913, p500, 534.

The Count of Monte Cristo (US; Lee, Rowland V.; 1934)
Film Daily. Aug 29, 1934, p7.
Hollywood Reporter. Aug 20, 1934, p3.
Magill's Survey of Cinema. Series II. v2, p531-33.
Motion Picture Herald. Sep 8, 1934, p38.
The New Republic. Oct 24, 1934, v80, p311.
The New York Times. Sep 27, 1934, p25.
Time. Oct 1, 1922, v24, p22.
Variety. Oct 2, 1934, p37.

Counterplan (Russian title: Vstrechnyi; Also titled: Counter-Plan; Turbine 50,000) (USSR; Ermler, Friedrich; Yutkevich, Sergei; 1932)
Cinema, the Magic Vehicle. v1, p209-10.
Dictionary of Films. p409-10.
Kino. p289-90.
Variety. Dec 6, 1932, p15.

The Countess Charming (US; Eltinge, Julian; 1917)
Fifty Great American Silent Films, 1912-1920. p86-88.
The Moving Picture World. Oct 6, 1917, p70.
The New York Dramatic Mirror. Sep 29, 1917, p24.
The New York Times. Sep 17, 1917, p11.
Selected Film Criticism, 1912-1920. p57-58.
Variety. Sep 21, 1917, p44.
Wid's Daily. Sep 27, 1917, p616.

The Country Bride (Russian title: Bogataya Nevesta; Also titled: The Rich Bride) (USSR; Piriev, Ivan; 1938)
Film Daily. Jun 8, 1938, p6.
Graham Greene on Film. p236-37.
Kino. p342.
The New Masses. Jun 21, 1938, v27, p30-31.
The New Statesman and Nation. Aug 5, 1939, v18, p214.
The New York Times. Jun 4, 1938, p18.
Partisan Review. Sep-Oct 1938, v5, p53-54.
The Spectator. Aug 4, 1939, v163, p180.
Variety. Jun 15, 1938, p15.

A Country Cupid (US; Griffith, D.W.; 1911)
The Moving Picture World. Aug 12, 1911, p375.
Selected Film Criticism, 1896-1911. p25-26.

The Country Doctor (US; King, Henry; 1936)
Canadian Magazine. Apr 1936, v85, p56.
Collier's. Apr 4, 1936, v97, p17+.
Esquire. May 1936, v5, p115.
Film Daily. Mar 2, 1936, p6.
Garbo and the Night Watchman. p65.
Graham Greene on Film. p80-81.
Hollywood Reporter. Feb 27, 1936, p3.
Hollywood Spectator. Mar 14, 1936, v10, p7-8.
Hygeia. Jun 1936, v14, p518-19.
Literary Digest. Dec 14, 1935, v120, p21.
Literary Digest. Mar 14, 1936, v121, p22.
Motion Picture. Mar 1936, v31, p30-31+.
Motion Picture Herald. Mar 21, 1936, p38, 40.
Movie Classic. Mar 1936, v10, p31+.
National Board of Review Magazine. Apr 1936, v11, p14.
The New Masses. Apr 7, 1936, v19, p45-46.
The New York Times. Mar 13, 1936, p27.
The New York Times. Mar 21, 1936, v12, p63.
Newsweek. Mar 21, 1936, v7, p22-24.
Photoplay. Mar 1936, v49, p21-23+.
Rob Wagner's Script. Mar 7, 1936, v15, p10.
Scholastic. Mar 28, 1936, v28, p26.
The Spectator. Jun 12, 1936, v156, p1080.
The Tatler. Jun 17, 1936, v140, p524.
Time. Mar 16, 1936, v27, p57.
Variety. Mar 18, 1936, p17.

The County Chairman (US; Blystone, John G.; 1935)
Film Daily. Jan 3, 1935, p22.
Hollywood Reporter. Dec 17, 1934, p3.
Hollywood Reporter. Feb 5, 1935, p2.
Magill's Survey of Cinema. Series II. v2, p538-40.

Motion Picture Herald. Dec 29, 1934, p54.
The New York Times. Jan 19, 1935, p8.
Rob Wagner's Script. Feb 2, 1935, v12, p8-9.
Scholastic. Feb 9, 1935, p29.
Time. Jan 28, 1935, v25, p32.
Variety. Jan 22, 1935, p14.
Will Rogers in Hollywood. p152-53.

The Courier of Lyons (FR; Lehmann, Maurice; 1938)
Film Daily. Jun 8, 1938, p6.
Hollywood Spectator. Apr 1, 1939, v13, p14.
Motion Picture Herald. Jun 18, 1938, p39.
The New Masses. Jun 14, 1938, v27, p31.
The New York Times. Jun 3, 1938, p17.
The New Yorker. Jun 11, 1938, v14, p51.
Variety. Jun 15, 1938, p15.

Courrier-Sud (Also titled: Southern Mail) (FR; Billon, Pierre; 1937)
Motion Picture Herald. Feb 20, 1937, p42, 46.
Variety. Feb 24, 1937, p19.

Cover Girl (US; Vidor, Charles; 1944)
Agee on Film. v1, p86-88.
Commonweal. Apr 21, 1944, v40, p16.
Film Daily. Mar 7, 1944, p7.
The Films of Gene Kelly. p48-55.
The Films of Rita Hayworth. p146-50.
The Hollywood Musical. p234, 238.
Hollywood Reporter. Mar 2, 1944, p3.
The Nation. Apr 8, 1944, v158, p428.
The New York Times. Mar 31, 1944, p26.
Newsweek. Apr 10, 1944, v23, p79.
Selected Film Criticism, 1941-1950. p45-46.
Time. Apr 10, 1944, v43, p94.
Variety. Mar 8, 1944, p14.

The Covered Wagon (US; Cruze, James; 1923)
American Silent Film. p250-56.
The Best Moving Pictures of 1922-1923. p71-77.
Cameras West. p66-70, 73-74.
Cinema, the Magic Vehicle. v1, p89-90.
Film Daily. Mar 25, 1923, p8.
Film Heritage. Spr 1969, v4, p17-22.
Films and Filming. May 1960, v6, p12-14.
From Quasimodo to Scarlett O'Hara. p21-23.
The Great Films. p27-30.
The International Dictionary of Films and Filmmakers. v1, p107-08.
Magill's Survey of Cinema. Silent Films. v1, p339-43.
The New York Times. Mar 17, 1923, p9.
Photoplay. May 1923, v23, p64.
A Pictorial History of the Western Film. p70-75.
Selected Film Criticism, 1921-1930. p67-72.
Spellbound in Darkness. p292-93.
Variety. Mar 22, 1923, p28.
The War, the West, and the Wilderness. p368-81.
The Western: From Silents to the Seventies. p131-36, 138-40.

The Coward (US; Ince, Thomas H.; Barker, Reginald; 1915)
Fifty Great American Silent Films, 1912-1920. p37-38.
Magill's Survey of Cinema. Silent Films. v1, p344-46.
Motion Picture News. Oct 16, 1915, p83.
Motography. Oct 16, 1915, p803.
Motography. Oct 23, 1915, p856.
Motography. Nov 20, 1915, p1106.
The Moving Picture World. Oct 30, 1915, p862, 864.
Photoplay. Dec 1915, v8, p84.
Selected Film Criticism, 1912-1920. p58-59.

The Cowboy and the Lady (US; Potter, H.C.; 1938)
Commonweal. Dec 2, 1938, v29, p161.
The Film Criticism of Otis Ferguson. p241.
Film Daily. Nov 11, 1938, p4.
The Films of Gary Cooper. p159-61.

Hollywood Reporter. Nov 8, 1938, p3.
Hollywood Spectator. Nov 26, 1938, v13, p10.
Life. Nov 21, 1938, v5, p38-40.
Motion Picture Herald. Nov 12, 1938, p35.
The New Republic. Dec 14, 1938, v97, p174.
The New Statesman and Nation. Jan 7, 1939, v17, p13.
The New York Times. Nov 25, 1938, p19.
Newsweek. Nov 28, 1938, v12, p19.
Rob Wagner's Script. Nov 19, 1938, v20, p12-13.
Samuel Goldwyn Presents. p194-96.
The Spectator. Jan 20, 1939, v162, p88.
Stage. Sep 1938, v15, p26.
Time. Nov 21, 1938, v32, p53.
Variety. Nov 9, 1938, p16.

Cowboy from Brooklyn (US; Bacon, Lloyd; 1938)
Commonweal. Jul 22, 1938, v28, p351.
Film Daily. Jun 14, 1938, p5.
The Films of Ronald Reagan. p49-52.
Hollywood Reporter. Jun 8, 1938, p3.
Motion Picture Herald. Jun 11, 1938, p35.
The New York Times. Jul 14, 1938, p17.
Rob Wagner's Script. Jul 23, 1938, v19, p10.
Time. Jul 25, 1938, v32, p22.
Variety. Jun 15, 1938, p14.

Crack-Up (US; St. Clair, Malcolm; 1937)
Film Daily. Dec 14, 1936, p6.
Hollywood Reporter. Dec 10, 1936, p3.
Hollywood Spectator. Dec 19, 1936, v11, p11.
Motion Picture Herald. Jan 16, 1937, p32.
The New Statesman and Nation. Feb 27, 1937, v13, p328.
The New York Times. Jan 4, 1937, p20.
Rob Wagner's Script. Dec 19, 1936, v16, p11.
The Spectator. Mar 12, 1937, v158, p471.
Variety. Jan 13, 1937, p13.

Cradle Song (US; Leisen, Mitchell; 1933)
Film Daily. Nov 18, 1933, p4.
Hollywood Director. p62-65.
Hollywood Reporter. Oct 23, 1933, p3.
Literary Digest. Dec 2, 1933, v116, p38.
Motion Picture Herald. Nov 4, 1933, p37.
The Nation. Nov 29, 1933, v137, p631.
The New York Times. Nov 20, 1933, p18.
Newsweek. Nov 4, 1933, v2, p30.
Rob Wagner's Script. Nov 11, 1933, v10, p6.
Time. Nov 6, 1933, v22, p43.
Variety. Nov 21, 1933, p20.

Craig's Wife (US; Arzner, Dorothy; 1936)
Canadian Magazine. Nov 1936, v86, p37.
Film Daily. Oct 2, 1936, p10.
The Films of the Thirties. p178-79.
From Reverence to Rape. p135-36.
Hollywood Reporter. Sep 11, 1936, p3.
Hollywood Spectator. Sep 26, 1936, v11, p6-7.
Literary Digest. Oct 10, 1936, v122, p28.
Motion Picture Herald. Sep 19, 1936, p48, 50.
The Nation. Oct 24, 1936, v143, p502.
The New York Times. Oct 2, 1936, p29.
The New Yorker. Oct 10, 1936, v12, p70-71.
Newsweek. Sep 26, 1936, v8, p27.
Rob Wagner's Script. Sep 26, 1936, v16, p12-13.
The Tatler. Jan 20, 1937, v143, p98.
Time. Oct 12, 1936, v28, p32.
Variety. Oct 7, 1936, p15.
World Film News. Mar 1937, v1, p26.

Crainquebille (FR; Feyder, Jacques; 1922)
Cinema, the Magic Vehicle. v1, p81-82.
Variety. Aug 4, 1954, p6.

Crash Dive (US; Mayo, Archie; 1943)
Commonweal. May 14, 1943, v38, p100.
Film Daily. Apr 22, 1943, p7.

The Films of Tyrone Power. p134-37.
The Films of World War II. p120-21.
Hollywood Reporter. Apr 21, 1943, p3.
Motion Picture Herald Product Digest. Apr 24, 1943, p1273.
The New York Times. Apr 29, 1943, p25.
The New Yorker. May 1, 1943, v19, p36.
Time. May 10, 1943, v41, p98.
Variety. Apr 21, 1943, p8.

The Crazy Ray (French title: Paris qui Dort) (FR; Clair, René; 1931)
The New Statesman and Nation. Jun 27, 1931, v1, p649.
René Clair (McGerr). p33-38+.
The Spectator. Jun 27, 1931, v146, p1007.

Crime and Punishment (Russian title: Raskolnikov) (USSR; Weine, Robert; 1923)
Film Daily. Apr 28, 1929, p6.
The New York Times. Jul 13, 1927, p21.
Variety. Jul 20, 1927, p19.

Crime and Punishment (US; Sternberg, Josef von; 1935)
Canadian Magazine. Jan 1936, v85, p32.
Commonweal. Dec 6, 1935, v23, p162.
Esquire. Feb 1936, v5, p99, 170.
Film Daily. Nov 22, 1935, p8.
The Films of Josef von Sternberg. p44-45.
Garbo and the Night Watchman. p97-101.
Graham Greene on Film. p60-61.
Hollywood Reporter. Nov 12, 1935, p3.
Hollywood Spectator. Nov 9, 1935, v10, p7.
Kiss Kiss Bang Bang. p312.
Masters of Menace: Greenstreet and Lorre. p31-32.
Motion Picture Herald. Nov 30, 1935, p64.
The Nation. Dec 4, 1935, v141, p659.
The New Masses. Dec 17, 1935, v17, p46.
The New York Times. Nov 22, 1935, p18.
The New Yorker. Nov 30, 1935, v11, p74.
Newsweek. Nov 30, 1935, v6, p27.
Rob Wagner's Script. Dec 14, 1935, v14, p10.
Stage. Nov 1935, v13, p64-65.
Time. Dec 2, 1935, v26, p39.
Variety. Nov 20, 1935, p16.
Variety. Nov 27, 1935, p14.

Crime de Monsieur Lange, Le (Also titled: The Crime of Monsieur Lange) (FR; Renoir, Jean; 1935)
Cineaste. Sum 1980, v10, p28-31.
Cinema, the Magic Vehicle. v1, p242-43.
Dictionary of Films. p71-72.
Eighty Years of Cinema. p108-09.
Films and Filming. Jul 1960, v6, p14.
Films and Filming. Jul 1965, v11, p32.
The Golden Age of the French Cinema, 1929-1939. p113-15.
Hollywood Reporter. Mar 4, 1936, p3.
The International Dictionary of Films and Filmmakers. v1, p109-10.
Jean Renoir: A Guide to References and Resources. p89-92.
Jean Renoir: The French Films, 1924-1939. p185-220.
Jean Renoir: The World of His Films. p116-20, 203-04.
Journal of Aesthetic Education. n1, 1974, v8, p5-26.
Movie. Sum 1965, n13, p37-38.
The New York Times. Apr 4, 1964, p15.
Sight and Sound. Sum 1960, v29, p134-35.
Sight and Sound. Wint 1979-80, v49, p36-41.
Village Voice. Apr 9, 1964, v9, p15, 17.
Wide Angle. n2, 1979, v3, p54-61.

Crime et Châtiment (Also titled: Crime and Punishment) (FR; Chenal, Pierre; 1935)
Esquire. Jan 1936, v5, p156.
Film Daily. Nov 14, 1935, p12.
Garbo and the Night Watchman. p78-89.
Graham Greene on Film. p57-58.
The Great French Films. p242.

Hollywood Reporter. Jun 1, 1935, p6.
Hollywood Spectator. Dec 21, 1935, v10, p10-11.
Kiss Kiss Bang Bang. p312.
London Mercury. Jan 1936, v33, p327-28.
The Nation. Dec 4, 1935, v141, p659.
National Board of Review Magazine. Dec 1935, v10, p10.
The New Masses. Dec 17, 1935, v17, p46.
The New Statesman and Nation. Nov 30, 1935, v10, p812.
The New York Times. Nov 13, 1935, p25.
The New Yorker. Nov 23, 1935, v11, p79-80.
Newsweek. Nov 30, 1935, v6, p27.
Rob Wagner's Script. Dec 14, 1935, v14, p10.
Saturday Review (London). Mar 21, 1936, v161, p378.
The Spectator. Mar 13, 1936, v156, p467.
Time. Dec 25, 1935, v26, p40.
Variety. Jun 12, 1935, p12.

The Crime of Dr. Crespi (US; Auer, John H.; 1936)
Film Daily. Sep 24, 1935, p12.
Hollywood Reporter. Sep 27, 1935, p3.
The New York Times. Jan 13, 1936, p14.
The New Yorker. Jan 25, 1936, v11, p56.
Variety. Jan 15, 1936, p18.

The Crime of Dr. Forbes (Also titled: Mercy Killer) (US; Marshall, George; 1936)
Commonweal. Jul 17, 1936, v24, p307.
Film Daily. Jun 16, 1936, p24.
Hollywood Reporter. Jun 8, 1936, p3.
Motion Picture Herald. Jun 20, 1936, p66.
The New Masses. Jul 21, 1936, v20, p28.
The New York Times. Jul 6, 1936, p11.
Rob Wagner's Script. Jul 11, 1936, v15, p14.
Variety. Jul 8, 1936, p15.

Crime School (US; Seiler, Lewis; 1938)
Commonweal. May 27, 1938, v28, p133.
The Complete Films of Humphrey Bogart. p54-55.
The Film Criticism of Otis Ferguson. p220-21.
Film Daily. May 11, 1938, p10.
Hollywood Reporter. May 3, 1938, p3.
Hollywood Spectator. May 14, 1938, v13, p7, 10.
Humphrey Bogart: The Man and His Films. p79.
Motion Picture Herald. May 7, 1938, p36.
National Board of Review Magazine. Jun 1938, v13, p17.
The New Republic. May 25, 1938, v95, p76.
The New York Times. May 11, 1938, p17.
The New Yorker. May 14, 1938, v14, p72-73.
Rob Wagner's Script. Jun 11, 1938, v19, p10-11.
The Tatler. Oct 5, 1938, v150, p6.
Time. May 23, 1938, v31, p40.
We're in the Money. p160.

Crime Without Passion (US; Hecht, Ben; MacArthur, Charles; 1934)
American Cinematographer. Oct 1985, v66, p34-41.
Ben Hecht: Hollywood Screenwriter. p109-40.
Film Daily. Aug 18, 1934, p4.
Film Society Review. Jan, 1966, p10.
Hollywood Reporter. Jul 28, 1934, p3.
Magill's Survey of Cinema. Series II. v2, p541-44.
Motion Picture Herald. Aug 25, 1934, p35.
The New Republic. Sep 26, 1934, v80, p184.
The New York Times. Sep 1, 1934, p16.
Time. Sep 10, 1934, v24, p40.
Variety. Sep 4, 1934, p34.

The Criminal Code (US; Hawks, Howard; 1930)
BFI/Monthly Film Bulletin. Oct 1984, v51, p313-14.
Crime Movies. p50-51.
Exhibitors Herald-World. Dec 27, 1930, p22.
Film Daily. Jan 4, 1931, p10.
The Films of Howard Hawks. p152-53.
The Great Gangster Pictures. p91.
Hawks on Hawks. p46-47, 164-65+.

Howard Hawks (Poague). p86-87+.
Judge. Jan 31, 1931, v100, p22.
Life. Jan 30, 1931, v97, p20.
The Nation. Jan 21, 1931, v132, p80.
The New York Times. Jan 5, 1931, p21.
The New York Times. Jan 11, 1931, p5.
The New Yorker. Jan 10, 1931, v6, p57.
Outlook and Independent. Jan 21, 1931, v157, p113.
Rob Wagner's Script. Feb 21, 1931, v5, p8.
Selected Film Criticism, 1931-1940. p53-55.
The Spectator. May 16, 1931, v146, p768.
Time. Jan 19, 1931, v17, p24.

The Crisis (US; Campbell, Colin; 1916)
The Moving Picture World. Oct 14, 1916, p218-19.
Selected Film Criticism, 1912-1920. p59-63.
Variety. Oct 6, 1916, p25.
Wid's Daily. Oct 5, 1916, p1010.

Criss Cross (US; Siodmak, Robert; 1949)
Burt Lancaster: A Pictorial Treasury of His Films. p37-38.
Cinema, the Magic Vehicle. v1, p481-82.
Film Daily. Jan 12, 1949, p8.
Hollywood Reporter. Jan 12, 1949, p3.
Motion Picture Herald Product Digest. Jan 15, 1949, p4461.
The New York Times. Mar 12, 1949, p10.
Time. Feb 28, 1949, v53, p89.
Variety. Jan 12, 1949, p8.

The Cross of Lorraine (US; Garnett, Tay; 1943)
Agee on Film. v1, p62, 67.
Commonweal. Dec 3, 1943, v34, p176.
Film Daily. Nov 12, 1943, p11.
The Films of Gene Kelly. p44-47.
The Films of Peter Lorre. p160-61.
Hollywood Reporter. Nov 10, 1943, p4.
Motion Picture Herald Product Digest. Nov 13, 1943, p1625.
The New Republic. Dec 20, 1943, v109, p885.
The New York Times. Dec 3, 1943, p27.
The New Yorker. Dec 4, 1943, v19, p82.
Newsweek. Dec 13, 1943, v22, p102.
Time. Dec 6, 1943, v42, p35.
Variety. Nov 10, 1943, p34.

Crossfire (US; Dmytryk, Edward; 1947)
Agee on Film. v1, p269-70.
Canadian Forum. May 1948, v28, p39.
Commonweal. Aug 1, 1947, v46, p386.
Film Daily. Jun 27, 1947, p8.
The Films of the Forties. p210-11.
Hollywood Quarterly. Fall 1947, v3, p63-65.
Hollywood Reporter. Jun 25, 1947, p3.
The International Dictionary of Films and Filmmakers. v1, p110-11.
Life. Jun 30, 1947, v22, p71-72.
Magill's Survey of Cinema, Series II. v2, p548-60.
Motion Picture Herald Product Digest. Jun 28, 1947, p3701.
The Nation. Aug 2, 1947, v165, p129.
New Republic. Aug 11, 1947, v117, p34.
The New York Times. Jul 23, 1947, p19.
The New Yorker. Jul 19, 1947, v23, p46.
Newsweek. Jul 28, 1947, v30, p84.
Photoplay. Oct 1947, v31, p4.
Robert Mitchum on The Screen. p93-94.
Saturday Review. Dec 6, 1947, v30, p69-70.
Theatre Arts. Sep 1947, v31, p15.
Time. Aug 4, 1947, v50, p76.
Variety. Jun 25, 1947, p8.

The Crowd (US; Vidor, King; 1928)
AFFS Newsletter. Nov 1964, p11-12.
American Film Criticism. p205-11.
American Silent Film. p330-31+.
Cinema, the Magic Vehicle. v1, p143.
Classic Movies. p146-47.
Classics of the Silent Screen. p112-13.

Dictionary of Films. p73-74.
Film Comment. Jul-Aug 1973, v9, p15-16.
Film Daily. Feb 26, 1928, p6.
The Film Spectator. Apr 14, 1928, v5, p6-7.
The Films of the Twenties. p189-92.
From Quasimodo to Scarlett O'Hara. p102-03.
The Great Films. p66-70.
The International Dictionary of Films and Filmmakers. v1, p111-12.
King Vidor (Baxter). p30-34.
King Vidor on Filmmaking. p70-71, 163-65.
Lorentz on Film. p13-14.
Magill's Survey of Cinema. Silent Films. v1, p347-49.
The New Republic. Mar 7, 1928, v54, p98-99.
The New York Times. Feb 20, 1928, p14.
Photoplay. Dec 1927, v33, p52.
Selected Film Criticism, 1921-1930. p73-76.
Sight and Sound. Aut 1981, v56, p224.
Variety. Feb 22, 1928, p20.

The Crowd Roars (US; Thorpe, Richard; 1938)
Canadian Magazine. Sep 1938, v90, p58.
Commonweal. Aug 19, 1938, v28, p430.
Esquire. Nov 1938, v10, p172.
Film Daily. Aug 2, 1938, p7.
The Films of Robert Taylor. p69-70.
Hollywood Reporter. Jul 28, 1938, p3.
Hollywood Spectator. Aug 6, 1938, v13, p11-12.
Motion Picture Herald. Aug 6, 1938, p44, 46.
The New York Times. Aug 5, 1938, p11.
The New Yorker. Aug 13, 1938, v14, p39-40.
Newsweek. Aug 15, 1938, v12, p27.
Rob Wagner's Script. Aug 16, 1938, v19, p22-23.
Time. Aug 15, 1938, v32, p35.
Variety. Aug 3, 1938, p15.
The Velvet Light Trap. Jun 1971, v1, p12-17.
World Film News. Sep 1938, v3, p220.
World Film News. Oct 1938, v3, p268.

The Crowd Roars (US; Hawks, Howard; 1932)
Film Daily. Mar 27, 1932, p22.
Films and Filming. Jul 1962, v8, p22.
The Films of Howard Hawks. p93-97.
The Films of James Cagney. p61-63.
The Films of the Thirties. p73-74.
The Gangster Film. p153-54.
Hollywood Reporter. Mar 1, 1932, p4.
Judge. Apr 16, 1932, v102, p22.
Motion Picture Herald. Apr 2, 1932, p38.
The Nation. Apr 13, 1932, v134, p444-45.
The New Statesman and Nation. May 28, 1932, v3, p705.
The New York Times. Apr 3, 1932, p4.
The New Yorker. Apr 2, 1932, v8, p56.
Time. Apr 4, 1932, v19, p24.
Variety. Mar 29, 1932, p24.
The Velvet Light Trap. Jun 1971, n1, p12-14.

The Crusades (US; DeMille, Cecil B.; 1935)
Catholic World. Oct 1935, v142, p83-88.
Commonweal. Sep 13, 1935, v22, p472.
Esquire. Dec 1935, v4, p118, 198-99.
Film Daily. Aug 5, 1935, p16.
The Films of Cecil B. DeMille. p298-303.
Garbo and the Night Watchman. p75-76.
Graham Greene on Film. p16-18.
The Great Adventure Films. p54-57.
Hollywood Reporter. Aug 1, 1935, v28, p3.
Literary Digest. Aug 31, 1935, v120, p29.
Motion Picture. Sep 1935, v50, p34-35+.
Motion Picture Herald. Aug 10, 1935, p47.
Motion Picture Herald. Aug 31, 1935, p33.
The Nation. Oct 2, 1935, v141, p391-92.
The New Statesman and Nation. Aug 31, 1935, v10, p279.
The New York Times. Aug 22, 1935, p21.
The New Yorker. Aug 31, 1935, v11, p43.

Newsweek. Aug 31, 1935, v6, p26-27.
Photoplay. Jul 1935, v48, p94.
Rob Wagner's Script. Nov 2, 1935, v14, p10.
Scientific American. Aug 1935, v153, p61-63.
Sight and Sound. Jan-Mar 1955, v24, p152-56.
The Spectator. Aug 30, 1935, v155, p322.
Stage. Oct 1935, v13, p8.
Time. Sep 2, 1935, v26, p38.
Vanity Fair. Oct 1935, v45, p46.
Variety. Aug 28, 1935, p12.

Cry of the City (US; Siodmak, Richard; 1948)
Commonweal. Oct 15, 1948, v49, p13.
Film Daily. Sep 10, 1948, p10.
Motion Picture Herald Product Digest. Sep 18, 1948, p4317.
The New York Times. Sep 30, 1948, p32.
Newsweek. Oct 11, 1948, v32, p94-95.
Rotarian. Jan 1949, v74, p11+.
Time. Oct 18, 1948, v52, p105.
Variety. Sep 15, 1948, p15.

The Cuban Love Song (US; Van Dyke, W.S.; 1931)
Film Daily. Dec 6, 1931, p10.
Hollywood Reporter. Oct 16, 1931, p3.
Motion Picture Herald. Oct 24, 1931, p30.
The New York Times. Dec 5, 1931, p21.
The New Yorker. Dec 12, 1931, v7, p80.
Outlook and Independent. Dec 16, 1931, v159, p503.
Variety. Dec 8, 1931, p15.

The Cup of Life (US; West, Raymond B.; Ince, Thomas H.; 1915)
Motion Picture News. Jan 23, 1915, p35.
Motion Picture News. Feb 20, 1915, p42.
Motion Picture News. Mar 27, 1915, p38.
Motion Picture News. Apr 3, 1915, p147.
Motion Picture News. May 1, 1915, p30.
Motion Picture News. May 8, 1915, p72.
Motography. May 8, 1915, p741, 765.
The Moving Picture World. Apr 17, 1915, p393.
The Moving Picture World. May 1, 1915, p740, 806.
The New York Dramatic Mirror. Apr 21, 1915, p26.

Curly Top (US; Cummings, Irving; 1935)
Commonweal. Aug 16, 1935, v22, p387.
Esquire. Oct 1935, v4, p97.
Film Daily. Aug 2, 1935, p11.
The Films of Shirley Temple. p156-59.
Hollywood Reporter. Jul 15, 1935, p3.
Literary Digest. Aug 10, 1935, v120, p29.
Motion Picture Herald. Jul 27, 1935, p48.
The New York Times. Aug 2, 1935, p22.
Time. Aug 12, 1935, v26, p32.
Variety. Aug 7, 1935, p21.

Curse of the Cat People (US; Wise, Robert; Fristch, Gunther von; 1944)
Classics of the Horror Film. p181-87.
Film Daily. Feb 21, 1944, p8.
Hollywood Reporter. Feb 17, 1944, p4.
The Nation. Apr 1, 1944, v158, p40.
The New Republic. Mar 20, 1944, v110, p380-81.
The New York Times. Mar 4, 1944, p11.
Val Lewton: The Reality of Terror. p59-63+.
Variety. Feb 23, 1944, p10.

The Curtain Pole (US; Griffith, D.W.; 1909)
D.W. Griffith, His Biograph Films in Perspective. p26-29.
The Moving Picture World. Feb 20, 1909, p202.
The New York Dramatic Mirror. Feb 20, 1909, p13.
Selected Film Criticism, 1896-1911. p27.

Cynara (US; Vidor, King; 1932)
Around Cinemas. p83-85.
Film Daily. Nov 12, 1932, p6.
The Films of Ronald Colman. p149-52.

Hollywood Reporter. Oct 27, 1932, p2.
The New York Times. Dec 26, 1932, p26.
The New Yorker. Dec 31, 1932, v8, p40.
Rob Wagner's Script. Nov 5, 1932, v8, p8.
Samuel Goldwyn (Epstein). p39-41.
Samuel Goldwyn Presents. p125-27.
Time. Dec 26, 1932, v20, p36.
Vanity Fair. Jan 1933, v39, p48.
Variety. Jan 3, 1933, p19.

Cytherea (US; Fitzmaurice, George; 1924)
Magill's Survey of Cinema. Silent Films. v1, p350-53.
Variety. May 28, 1924, p27.

D.O.A. (US; Mate, Rudolph; 1949)
The Big Book of B Movies. p20+.
Commonweal. Apr 21, 1950, v52, p45.
Film Daily. Dec 27, 1949, p8.
Hollywood Reporter. Dec 23, 1949, p3.
Magill's Survey Of Cinema. Series II. v2, p560-63.
Motion Picture Herald. Dec 31, 1949, p137.
The New Yorker. May 6, 1950, v26, p72.
Newsweek. May 8, 1950, v35, p87.
Time. May 15, 1950, v55, p96.

Daddy-Long-Legs (US; Neilan, Marshall; 1919)
Exhibitor's Trade Review. May 24, 1919, p1933.
Motion Picture News. May 24, 1919, p3466.
The Moving Picture World. May 24, 1919, p1159-60.
The New York Times. May 12, 1919, p11.
Selected Film Criticism, 1912-1920. p63-64.
Variety. May 16, 1919, p54.
Wid's Daily. May 18, 1919, p7.

Daddy Long Legs (US; Santell, Alfred; 1931)
Film Daily. Jun 7, 1931, p10.
Hollywood Reporter. May 13, 1931, p2.
Hollywood Spectator. Jun 20, 1931, v12, p8, 19.
Judge. Jun 27, 1931, v100, p24.
Life. Jun 26, 1931, v97, p18.
Love in the Film. p82-84.
Motion Picture Herald. May 23, 1931, p36.
The New York Times. Jun 6, 1931, p15.
The New Yorker. Jun 13, 1931, v7, p64.
Outlook and Independent. Jun 17, 1931, v158, p218.
Rob Wagner's Script. May 30, 1931, v5, p9.
Time. Jun 15, 1931, v17, p61.
Variety. Jun 9, 1931, p18.

Daisy Kenyon (US; Preminger, Otto; 1947)
The Cinema of Otto Preminger. p87-88+.
Film Daily. Nov 24, 1947, p6.
The Films of Henry Fonda. p135-36.
The Films of Joan Crawford. p168-69.
The Fondas (Springer). p143-44.
Hollywood Reporter. Nov 24, 1947, p3.
Motion Picture Herald Product Digest. Nov 29, 1947, p3593.
The New York Times. Dec 25, 1947, p32.
Newsweek. Jan 12, 1948, v31, p78.
Time. Dec 29, 1947, v50, p62.
Variety. Nov 26, 1947, p11.

Dames (US; Enright, Ray; Berkeley, Busby; 1934)
The Busby Berkeley Book. p82-84.
Film Daily. Aug 16, 1934, p6.
Hollywood Musicals. p74-77.
Hollywood Reporter. Aug 31, 1934, p3.
Motion Picture Herald. Aug 25, 1934, p3.
The New York Times. Aug 16, 1934, p20.
Time. Aug 27, 1934, v24, p42.
Variety. Aug 21, 1934, p17.

A Damsel in Distress (US; Stevens, George; 1937)
Commonweal. Dec 3, 1937, v27, p160.
Film Daily. Nov 20, 1937, p7.
The Fred Astaire and Ginger Rogers Book. p134-35.

The Hollywood Musical. p120-21.
Hollywood Reporter. Nov 18, 1937, p3.
Life. Nov 29, 1937, v3, p74-75.
Motion Picture Herald. Nov 27, 1937, p52, 54.
The Nation. Dec 18, 1937, v145, p697.
The New Masses. Nov 30, 1937, v25, p27.
The New York Times. Nov 25, 1937, p37.
The New Yorker. Nov 27, 1937, v13, p73.
Newsweek. Dec 10, 1937, v10, p33.
Rob Wagner's Script. Dec 25, 1937, v18, p5.
Scholastic. Dec 11, 1937, v31, p19.
The Spectator. Apr 15, 1938, v160, p671.
Starring Fred Astaire. p163-71.
Time. Dec 6, 1937, v30, p49.
Variety. Nov 24, 1937, p16.
World Film News. May-Jun 1938, v3, p83.

Dance, Fools, Dance (US; Beaumont, Harry; 1931)
Film Daily. Feb 1, 1931, p10.
The Films of Clark Gable. p114-15.
The Films of Joan Crawford. p82-83.
The Great Gangster Pictures. p97-98.
Life. Mar 27, 1931, v97, p23.
Motion Picture Herald. Jan 3, 1931, p74.
The New York Times. Mar 21, 1931, p15.
The New York Times. Mar 29, 1931, p5.
The New York Times. Feb 14, 1931, p6.
The New Yorker. Mar 28, 1931, v7, p77.
Outlook and Independent. Apr 1, 1931, v157, p475.
Rob Wagner's Script. Apr 25, 1931, v5, p11-12.
Variety. Mar 25, 1931, p24.

Dance, Girl, Dance (US; Strayer, Frank; 1933)
Film Daily. Oct 26, 1933, p7.
Hollywood Reporter. Oct 6, 1933, p4.
Motion Picture Herald. Nov 11, 1933, p30.
The New York Times. Oct 25, 1933, p23.
Variety. Oct 31, 1933, p25.

Dancers in the Dark (US; Burton, David; 1932)
Film Daily. Mar 20, 1932, p10.
Hollywood Reporter. Feb 18, 1932, p3.
Judge. Apr 9, 1932, v102, p22.
Motion Picture Herald. Mar 26, 1932, p35, 38.
The New York Times. Mar 19, 1932, p11.
The New Yorker. Mar 26, 1932, v8, p52-53.
Rob Wagner's Script. Mar 12, 1932, v7, p10.
Time. Mar 21, 1932, v19, p38.
Variety. Mar 22, 1932, p13.

Dancing in the Dark (US; Reis, Irving; 1949)
Christian Century. Feb 8, 1950, v68, p191.
Film Daily. Nov 4, 1949, p6.
The Hollywood Musical. p307.
Hollywood Reporter. Nov 4, 1949, p3.
Motion Picture Herald. Nov 5, 1949, p74.
The New York Times. Dec 3, 1949, p8.
Newsweek. Dec 12, 1949, v34, p90.
Time. Dec 19, 1949, v54, p90.
Variety. Nov 9, 1949, p6.

Dancing Lady (US; Leonard, Robert Z.; 1933)
Film Daily. Dec 2, 1933, p3.
The Films of Clark Gable. p149-50.
The Films of Joan Crawford. p105-07.
The Fred Astaire & Ginger Rogers Book. p19-21.
The Hollywood Musical. p88-90.
Hollywood Reporter. Nov 9, 1933, p3.
Judge. Jan 1934, v106, p26.
Literary Digest. Dec 16, 1933, v116, p47.
Motion Picture Herald. Nov 25, 1933, p39.
The New York Times. Dec 1, 1933, p23.
The New Yorker. Dec 9, 1933, v9, p90-91.
Newsweek. Dec 9, 1933, v2, p33.
Rob Wagner's Script. Dec 9, 1933, v10, p8.
The Spectator. Dec 29, 1933, v151, p963.

Starring Fred Astaire. p47-55.
Time. Dec 11, 1933, v22, p30.
Variety. Dec 5, 1933, p16.

Dancing Mothers (US; Brenon, Herbert; 1926)
Film Daily. Feb 28, 1926, p6.
Life. Apr 8, 1926, v87, p32.
Magill's Survey of Cinema. Silent Films. v1, p354-56.
The New York Times. Feb 18, 1926, p21.
Photoplay. Apr 1926, v24, p54.
Selected Film Criticism, 1921-1930. p76-77.
Variety. Feb 17, 1926, p40.

Danger—Love At Work (US; Preminger, Otto; 1937)
Film Daily. Sep 30, 1937, p10.
Hollywood Reporter. Sep 27, 1937, p3.
Lunatics and Lovers. p144.
The New York Times. Dec 11, 1937, p22.
Rob Wagner's Script. Oct 2, 1937, v18, p13.
Time. Nov 15, 1937, v30, p42+.
Variety. Dec 1, 1937, p14.

Dangerous (US; Green, Alfred E.; 1935)
Bette Davis: Her Films and Career. p64-65.
Esquire. Mar 1936, v5, p105.
Film Daily. Nov 6, 1935, p4.
Graham Greene on Film. p81-82.
Hollywood Reporter. Nov 18, 1935, p3.
Hollywood Spectator. Dec 7, 1935, v10, p9.
Magill's Survey of Cinema. Series II. v2, p564-66.
Motion Picture Herald. Nov 30, 1935, p63.
The New Statesman and Nation. Jun 20, 1936, v11, p968-69.
The New York Times. Dec 27, 1935, p14.
The New Yorker. Jan 4, 1936, v11, p49.
Newsweek. Jan 4, 1936, v7, p25.
Rob Wagner's Script. Dec 28, 1935, v14, p11.
The Spectator. Jun 19, 1936, v156, p1131.
Time. Jan 6, 1936, v27, p28.
Variety. Jan 1, 1936, p44.
Warner Brothers Presents. p127.

The Dangerous Flirt (US; Browning, Tod; 1924)
Film Daily. Dec 15, 1924, p7.
The Moving Picture World. Nov 29, 1924, p544.
Variety. Dec 17, 1924, p37.

Dangerous Money (US; Tuttle, Frank; 1924)
Film Daily. Oct 19, 1924, p6.
The Moving Picture World. Oct 25, 1924, p72.
The New York Times. Oct 14, 1924, p21.
Variety. Oct 15, 1924, p30.

Dangerous Nan McGrew (US; St. Clair, Malcolm; 1930)
Exhibitors Herald-World. Jul 19, 1930, p32.
Film Daily. Jun 22, 1930, p14.
Judge. Jul 19, 1930, v99, p23.
Life. Jul 18, 1930, v95, p17.
The New York Times. Jun 21, 1930, p20.
Outlook and Independent. Jul 9, 1930, v154, p390.
Rob Wagner's Script. Aug 9, 1930, v3, p8-9.
Variety. Jun 25, 1930, p115.

Dangerous Paradise (US; Wellman, William A.; 1930)
Exhibitors Herald-World. Feb 22, 1930, p37.
Film Daily. Feb 16, 1930, p9.
The Films of Nancy Carroll. p98-101.
The New York Times. Feb 16, 1930, p8.
Rob Wagner's Script. Apr 19, 1930, v3, p10-11.
Time. Mar 3, 1930, v15, p28.
Variety. Feb 19, 1930, p33.
William A. Wellman (Thompson). p94-98.

Dangerously Yours (US; St. Clair, Malcolm; 1937)
Film Daily. Sep 21, 1937, p5.
Hollywood Reporter. Sep 17, 1937, p5.
The New York Times. Oct 18, 1937, p14.
Variety. Oct 20, 1937, p12.

Dangerously Yours (US; Tuttle, Frank; 1933)
Film Daily. Feb 24, 1933, p7.
Hollywood Reporter. Jan 25, 1933, p3.
Motion Picture Herald. Feb 4, 1933, p39.
The New York Times. Feb 23, 1933, p20.
Variety. Feb 28, 1933, p39.

Dante's Inferno (US; Lachman, Harry; 1935)
Film Daily. Aug 1, 1935, p10.
The Films of Spencer Tracy. p118-20.
Garbo and the Night Watchman. p39-40.
Hollywood Reporter. Aug 1, 1935, p4.
Motion Picture Herald. Aug 10, 1935, p53.
The New York Times. Aug 1, 1935, p15.
The New Yorker. Aug 3, 1935, v11, p42.
Newsweek. Aug 10, 1935, v6, p27-28.
Photoplay. Mar 1940, v54, p42.
Rob Wagner's Script. Aug 10, 1935, v13, p9-10.
Time. Aug 12, 1935, v26, p32-33.
Variety. Aug 7, 1935, p21.

Danton (GER; Behrendt, Hans; 1931)
Film Daily. Sep 13, 1931, p10.
From Caligari to Hitler. p253-54.
The New Masses. Nov 8, 1938, v29, p29.
The New Republic. Sep 30, 1931, v68, p182.
The New York Times. Sep 7, 1931, p19.
Variety. Feb 18, 1931, p78.
Variety. Sep 1, 1931, p33.

Dark Angel (US; Fitzmaurice, George; 1925)
Film Daily. Oct 18, 1925, p6.
Magill's Survey of Cinema. Silent Films. v1, p357-60.
The Moving Picture World. Sep 19, 1925, p256.
The New York Times. Oct 12, 1925, p19.
Spellbound in Darkness. p418, 420.
Variety. Oct 14, 1925, p42.

The Dark Angel (US; Franklin, Sidney; 1935)
Canadian Magazine. Oct 1935, v84, p41.
Commonweal. Sep 20, 1935, v22, p499.
Esquire. Nov 1935, v4, p106.
Film Daily. Aug 30, 1935, p6.
The Films of Fredric March. p134-36.
Hollywood Reporter. Sep 4, 1935, v29, p3.
Literary Digest. Sep 14, 1935, v120, p33.
Motion Picture Herald. Sep 14, 1935, p35.
The New Statesman and Nation. Oct 5, 1935, v10, p447.
The New York Times. Sep 6, 1935, p12.
The New Yorker. Sep 7, 1935, p62.
Newsweek. Sep 7, 1935, v6, p22-23.
Rob Wagner's Script. Sep 14, 1935, v14, p8.
Samuel Goldwyn Presents. p149-51.
The Spectator. Oct 4, 1935, v155, p506.
Stage. Oct 1935, v13, p6.
Time. Sep 16, 1935, v26, p61.
Vanity Fair. Oct 1935, v45, p47.
Variety. Sep 11, 1935, p17.

Dark Command (US; Walsh, Raoul; 1940)
Commonweal. Apr 26, 1940, v32, p20.
The Complete Films of John Wayne. p97-99.
Film Daily. Apr 5, 1940, p7.
Hollywood Reporter. Apr 5, 1940, p3.
Motion Picture Herald. Apr 13, 1940, p38.
Motion Picture Herald. Mar 9, 1940, p63.
The New York Times. May 11, 1940, p15.
Newsweek. Apr 15, 1940, v15, p30.
Scholastic. Apr 22, 1940, v36, p36.
Variety. Apr 10, 1940, p14.

Dark Eyes (French title: Yeux Noirs, Les; Also titled:
 Black Eyes) (FR; Tourjansky, Victor; 1935)
Commonweal. Apr 29, 1938, v28, p21.
Film Daily. Apr 21, 1938, p4.
Graham Greene on Film. p211.

Motion Picture Herald. May 7, 1938, p39.
The New Statesman and Nation. Apr 1, 1939, v17, p493.
The New York Times. Apr 19, 1938, p24.
The Spectator. Apr 7, 1939, v162, p592.
Variety. Apr 27, 1938, p23.

Dark Hazard (US; Green, Alfred E.; 1933)
The Cinema of Edward G. Robinson. p98-99.
Film Daily. Feb 23, 1934, p6.
The Gangster Film. p106.
Hollywood Reporter. Nov 15, 1933, p3.
Motion Picture Herald. Nov 25, 1933, p38.
The New York Times. Feb 23, 1934, p23.
Time. Mar 5, 1934, v23, p61.
Variety. Feb 27, 1934, p17.

The Dark Horse (US; Green, Alfred E.; 1932)
Bette Davis: Her Films and Career. p30-31.
Film Daily. Jun 11, 1932, p18.
Motion Picture Herald. Jun 18, 1932, p35, 38.
The Nation. Jul 16, 1932, v135, p18.
The New York Times. Jun 9, 1932, p27.
The New Yorker. Jun 18, 1932, v8, p53.
Rob Wagner's Script. Jul 16, 1932, v7, p8.
Time. Jun 20, 1932, v19, p24.
Variety. Jun 14, 1932, p17.
We're in the Money. p27.

Dark Journey (GB; Saville, Victor; 1937)
Film Daily. Aug 24, 1937, p4.
Graham Greene on Film. p141.
The Great Spy Films. p132-33.
Hollywood Reporter. Feb 18, 1937, p15.
Motion Picture Herald. Mar 6, 1937, p44.
The New Statesman and Nation. Mar 27, 1937, v13, p523.
The New York Times. Aug 23, 1937, p22.
The Spectator. Apr 2, 1937, v158, p619.
Variety. Mar 17, 1937, p23.

Dark Manhattan (US; Fraser, Harry; 1937)
Hollywood Reporter. Feb 13, 1937, p4.
Variety. Mar 17, 1937, p15.

The Dark Mirror (US; Siodmak, Robert; 1946)
Agee on Film. v1, p226-27.
Commonweal. Nov 1, 1946, v45, p71.
Film Daily. Oct 7, 1946, p7.
The Films of Olivia de Havilland. p212-13.
Hollywood Reporter. Oct 2, 1946, p3.
Life. Oct 21, 1946, v21, p131-34+.
Magill's Survey of Cinema. Series II. v2, p567-69.
Motion Picture Herald Product Digest. Oct 5, 1946, p3237.
The Nation. Nov 9, 1946, v163, p536.
The New Republic. Nov 18, 1946, v115, p661.
The New York Times. Oct 19, 1946, p19.
The New Yorker. Oct 26, 1946, v22, p109.
Newsweek. Nov 4, 1946, v28, p92.
Theatre Arts. Dec 1946, v20, p714.
Time. Oct 21, 1946, v48, p99.
Variety. Oct 2, 1946, p8.

Dark Passage (US; Daves, Delmer; 1947)
Commonweal. Sep 26, 1947, v46, p574.
The Complete Films of Humphrey Bogart. p134-35.
Film Daily. Sep 3, 1947, p6.
Hollywood Reporter. Sep 3, 1947, p3.
Humphrey Bogart: The Man and His Films. p140-42.
Motion Picture Herald Product Digest. Sep 6, 1947, p3817.
New Republic. Sep 29, 1947, v117, p37.
The New York Times. Sep 6, 1947, p11.
The New Yorker. Sep 13, 1947, v23, p113.
Newsweek. Sep 15, 1947, v30, p90.
Surrealism and American Feature Films. p101-22.
Time. Sep 22, 1947, v50, p97.
Variety. Sep 3, 1947, p16.

Dark Rapture (US; Armand, Denis; 1938)
Commonweal. Oct 14, 1938, v28, p645.
The Film Criticism of Otis Ferguson. p240.
Film Daily. Oct 11, 1938, p6.
Graham Greene on Film. p270.
Hollywood Reporter. Oct 21, 1938, p3.
Motion Picture Herald. Oct 15, 1938, p37.
The New Masses. Oct 25, 1938, v29, p29-30.
The New Statesman and Nation. Feb 10, 1940, v19, p171.
The New York Times. Oct 10, 1938, p14.
The New Yorker. Oct 22, 1938, v14, p56.
Newsweek. Oct 3, 1938, v12, p23.
Rob Wagner's Script. Dec 3, 1938, v20, p18.
The Spectator. Feb 16, 1940, v164, p213.
Theatre Arts. Jan 1939, v23, p59.
Time. Oct 17, 1938, v32, p32.
Variety. Oct 12, 1938, p15.

Dark Sands *See* Jericho

A Dash Through the Clouds (US; 1912)
The First Twenty Years. p161-65.

A Date With Judy (US; Thorpe, Richard; 1948)
Commonweal. Aug 6, 1948, v48, p42.
Film Daily. Jun 21, 1948, p6.
The Films of Elizabeth Taylor. p64-67.
Hollywood Reporter. Jun 18, 1948, p3.
Motion Picture Herald Product Digest. Jun 19, 1948, p4317.
The New York Times. Aug 7, 1948, p8.
The New Yorker. Aug 14, 1948, v32, p81.
Newsweek. Jul 13, 1948, v32, p81.
Time. Sep 6, 1948, v52, p86.
Variety. Jun 23, 1948, p6.

A Daughter of the Gods (US; Brenon, Herbert; 1916)
Fifty Great American Silent Films, 1912-1920. p56-57.
Magill's Survey of Cinema. Silent Films. v1, p361-63.
The Moving Picture World. Nov 4, 1916, p673.
The New York Dramatic Mirror. Oct 21, 1916, p34.
The New York Dramatic Mirror. Oct 28, 1916, p24.
The New York Times. Oct 18, 1916, p9.
Photoplay. Aug 1916, v10, p133-35.
Selected Film Criticism, 1912-1920. p65-69.
Variety. Oct 20, 1916, p27.
Wid's Daily. Oct 19, 1916, p1038-39.

Daughters Courageous (US; Curtiz, Michael; 1939)
Commonweal. June 10, 1939,, v30, p259.
Film Daily. Jun 16, 1939, p6.
The Films of John Garfield. p65-67.
Graham Greene. p250.
Hollywood Reporter. Jun 15, 1939, p3.
Hollywood Spectator. Jun 24, 1939, v14, p6.
Motion Picture Herald. Jun 24, 1939, p39.
The New Masses. Jul 25, 1939, p29.
The New Statesman and Nation. Nov 4, 1939, v18, p644.
The New York times. Jun 24, 1939, p14.
The New Yorker. Jun 24, 1939, v14 p64-65.
Newseek. Jul 3, 1939, v14 p35.
Photoplay. Aug 1939, v53, p45.
Rob Wagner's Script. Jul 4, 1939, v21, p18.
The Spectator. Nov 10, 1939, v163, p648.
The Tatler. Nov 15, 1939, v154, p210.
Time. Jul 3, 1939, v34, p35.
Variety. Jun 21, 1939,, p6.

David Copperfield (US; 1911)
The Moving Picture World. Sep 30, 1911, p952-53.
Selected Film Criticism, 1896-1911. p27-29.

David Copperfield (US; Cukor, George; 1935)
Around Cinemas. p134-37.
Basil Rathbone: His Life and His Films. p147-49.
Canadian Magazine. Apr 1935, v83, p41.
Cinema Quarterly. Spr 1935, v3, p173-75.

Commonweal. Feb 1, 1935, v21, p403.
Dickens and Film. p265-68.
The English Novel and the Movies. p132-42.
Esquire. Apr 1935, v3, p144.
The Film Criticism of Otis Ferguson. p67.
Film Daily. Jan 8, 1935, p8.
The Films of W. C. Fields. p106-11.
From Quasimodo to Scarlett O'Hara. p191-95.
George Cukor (Phillips). p130-32.
Hollywood Reporter. Jan 7, 1935, p3.
Judge. Mar 1935, v108, p18, 30.
Library Journal. Mar 1, 1951, v76, p418.
Life. Mar 1935, v102, p35-36.
Literary Digest. Feb 2, 1935, v119, p30.
London Mercury. Apr 1935, v31, p580.
Magill's Survey of Cinema. Series II. v2, p574-77.
Motion Picture. Feb 1935, v49, p22-23.
Motion Picture Herald. Jan 19, 1935, p58.
Movie Classic. Feb 1935, v7, p40-42+.
The Nation. Feb 6, 1935, v140, p168.
National Board of Review Magazine. Feb 1935, v10, p7.
The New Statesman and Nation. Mar 16, 1935, v9, p380.
The New York Times. Jan 19, 1935, p8.
The New Yorker. Jan 26, 1935, v10, p56-57.
Newsweek. Jan 26, 1935, v5, p27.
On Cukor. p82-87.
Photoplay. Mar 1935, v47, p52-53.
Rob Wagner's Script. Jan 19, 1935, v12, p8.
Scholastic. Jan 26, 1935, v25, p9-10+.
Selected Film Criticism, 1931-1940. p57-58.
Sight and Sound. Oct-Dec 1953, v23, p78-82.
The Spectator. Mar 15, 1935, v154, p434.
The Spectator. Nov 22, 1935, v154, p864.
Time. Jan 28, 1935, v25, p32.
Variety. Jan 22, 1935, p14.
W. C. Fields: A Life on Film. p162-67.

David Golder (FR; Duvivier, Julien; 1932)
Film Daily. Oct 21, 1932, p7.
Motion Picture Herald. Oct 29, 1932, p34.
The New Statesman and Nation. Nov 12, 1932, v4, p579.
The New York Times. Oct 20, 1932, p24.
The New Yorker. Oct 29, 1932, v8, p52.
Variety. Oct 25, 1932, p54.

Dawn *See* Morgenrot

Dawn (GB; Wilcox, Herbert; 1928)
Film Daily. Jun 13, 1928, p9.
Literary Digest. Apr 14, 1928, v97, p24-26.
Living Age. Apr 1, 1928, v334, p646-47.
The New York Times. Jun 3, 1928, sec8, p5.
Outlook. Apr 25, 1928, v148, p655.
Variety. Mar 14, 1928, v25.
Variety. Jun 6, 1928, p12.

The Dawn of a Tomorrow (US; Kirkwood, James; 1915)
Motion Picture News. Jun 19, 1915, p70.
Motography. Jun 19, 1915, p1035.
The Moving Picture World. Jun 12, 1915, p1792.
The Moving Picture World. Jan 25, 1919, p541.
The New York Dramatic Mirror. Jun 16, 1915, p28.
Variety. Jun 11, 1915, p18.

The Dawn Patrol (US; Hawks, Howard; 1930)
Commonweal. Jul 30, 1930, v12, p345.
Dictionary of Films. p79.
Exhibitors Herald-World. Jul 19, 1930, p32.
Film Daily. Jul 13, 1930, p10.
The Films of Howard Hawks. p166-67.
Hawks on Hawks. p25-27, 10-12+.
Judge. Aug 1, 1930, v99, p23.
Life. Aug 8, 1930, v96, p17.
Magill's Survey of Cinema. Series II. v2, p578-82.
The Nation. Aug 20, 1930, v131, p209.
The New York Times. Jul 11, 1930, p22.

The New York Times. Dec 27, 1933, p23.
The New York Times. Jul 20, 1930, p4.
The New Yorker. Jul 19, 1930, v6, p54.
Outlook and Independent. Jul 30, 1930, v155, p510.
Time. Jul 21, 1930, v16, p44.
Variety. Jul 16, 1930, p15.

Dawn Patrol (US; Goulding, Edmund; 1938)
Basil Rathbone: His Life and His Films. p202-05.
Canadian Magazine. Feb 1939, v91, p44.
Commonweal. Dec 30, 1938, v29, p273.
Esquire. Apr 1939, v11, p164.
Film Daily. Dec 14, 1938, p7.
The Films of David Niven. p54-55.
The Films of Errol Flynn. p73-76.
Graham Greene on Film. p207-10.
Hollywood Reporter. Dec 13, 1938, p3.
Hollywood Spectator. Dec 24, 1938, v13, p14.
Life. Dec 26, 1938, v5, p33-35.
Motion Picture Herald. Dec 17, 1938, p49.
The New Masses. Jan 17, 1939, v30, p29-30.
The New Statesman and Nation. Feb 18, 1939, v17, p245.
The New York Times. Dec 24, 1938, p12.
The New Yorker. Dec 24, 1938, v14, p46.
Newsweek. Dec 12, 1938, v12, p25.
Photoplay. Feb 1939, v53, p48.
Rob Wagner's Script. Dec 24, 1938, v20, p10.
The Spectator. Mar 3, 1939, v162, p349.
Stage. Jan 1939, v16, p42.
The Tatler. Mar 1, 1939, v151, p374.
Time. Jan 2, 1939, v33, p17.
Variety. Dec 14, 1938, p14.

A Day at the Races (US; Wood, Sam; 1937)
Cinema Journal. Spr 1969, v8, p2-9.
Commonweal. Jul 3, 1937, v26, p267.
The Film Criticism of Otis Ferguson. p183-84.
Film Daily. Jun 15, 1937, p9.
Garbo and the Night Watchman. p252.
Graham Greene on Film. p160-61.
Hollywood Reporter. Jun 11, 1937, p4.
Hollywood Spectator. Jun 19, 1937, v12, p11-12.
Life. Jun 21, 1937, v2, p30-33.
Literary Digest. Jun 26, 1937, v123, p22-23.
Magill's Survey of Cinema, Series II. v2, p583-85.
Motion Picture Herald. Jun 19, 1937, p56.
The Nation. Jul 10, 1937, v145, p53.
The New Masses. Jul 6, 1937, v24, p27.
The New Republic. Jun 30, 1937, v91, p222.
The New Statesman and Nation. Jul 31, 1937, v14, p186.
The New York Times. Jun 18, 1937, p25.
The New Yorker. Jun 19, 1937, v13, p63-64.
Newsweek. Jun 19, 1937, v9, p20.
Rob Wagner's Script. Jun 19, 1937, v17, p10.
Sight and Sound. Aut 1937, v6, p140.
The Spectator. Aug 6, 1937, v159, p240.
The Tatler. Aug 11, 1937, v145, p240.
Time. Jun 21, 1937, v29, p45-46.
Variety. Jun 23, 1937, p12.
Why a Duck? p237-71.
World Film News. Sep 1937, v2, p24, 26.

A Day in the Country *See* Partie de Campagne, Une

Day of Wrath (Danish title: Vredens Dag) (DEN; Dreyer, Carl-Theodor; 1943)
Agee on Film. v1, p303-05.
Carl Theodor Dreyer: Four Screenplays. p131-36.
The Cinema of Carl Dreyer. p130-45.
Cinema, the Magic Vehicle. v1, p363-64.
Classics of the Foreign Film. p138-41.
Dictionary of Films. p409.
The Films of Carl-Theodor Dreyer (Boardwell). p117-43, 217-19.
Hollywood Reporter. Mar 4, 1949, p3.

The International Dictionary of Films and Filmmakers. v1, p513-14.
Life. Sep 6, 1948, v25, p61-62.
Magill's Survey of Cinema. Foreign Language Films. v2, p739-45.
The Nation. May 22, 1948, v166, p584.
The New York Times. Apr 26, 1948, p27.
The New Yorker. May 1, 1948, v24, p82.
Saturday Review of Literature. Aug 14, 1948, v31, p35.
Selected Film Criticism: Foreign Films, 1930-1950. p39-40.
Sight and Sound. Wint 1946-47, v15, p154+.
Time. May 24, 1948, v51, p96.
Variety. Apr 28, 1948, p22.

Daybreak *See* Jour se Lève, Le

Daybreak (US; Feyder, Jacques; 1931)
Film Daily. May 31, 1931, p10.
Hollywood Reporter. Apr 9, 1931, p3.
Motion Picture Herald. Apr 18, 1931, p42.
The New York Times. May 24, 1931, p5.
The New York Times. Jun 1, 1931, p15.
The New York Times. Jun 7, 1931, p5.
Variety. Jun 2, 1931, p15.

Day-Time Wife (US; Ratoff, Gregory; 1939)
Film Daily. Nov 16, 1939, p6.
Hollywood Reporter. Nov 11, 1939, p3.
Hollywood Spectator. Nov 25, 1939, v14, p7-8.
Motion Picture Herald. Nov 18, 1939, p48.
The New York Times. Nov 24, 1939, p29.
Rob Wagner's Script. Nov 18, 1939, v22, p18.
Variety. Nov 15, 1939, p18.

Dead End (US; Wyler, William; 1937)
American Film Criticism. p357-58.
Around Cinemas. p147-49.
Cinema, the Magic Vehicle. v1, p278-79.
Classics of the Gangster Film. p51-54.
Commonweal. Aug 20, 1937, v26, p406.
The Complete Films of Humphrey Bogart. p48-50.
Crime Movies. p145-47.
Dictionary of Films. p79-80.
Esquire. Aug 1938, v10, p82.
The Film Criticism of Otis Ferguson. p192-93.
Film Daily. Aug 3, 1937, p7.
The Gangster Film. p182-86.
Graham Greene on Film. p180-81.
The Great Gangster Pictures. p104-05.
Hellman in Hollywood. p50-57.
Hollywood Reporter. Jul 30, 1937, p3.
The Hollywood Social Problem Films. p36-43.
Hollywood Spectator. Aug 14, 1937, v12, p7-8.
Humphrey Bogart: The Man and His Films. p71.
A Library of Film Criticism: American Film Directors. p509-10.
Life. Jan 11, 1937, v2, p40.
Life. Aug 30, 1937, v3, p62-64.
Literary Digest. Sep 4, 1937, v124, p30.
Literary Digest. Dec 11, 1937, v124, p4.
Magill's Survey of Cinema. Series II. v2, p592-94.
Motion Picture Herald. Aug 7, 1937, p48.
National Board of Review Magazine. Oct 1937, v12, p12.
The New Republic. Sep 1, 1937, v92, p103.
The New Statesman and Nation. Nov 20, 1937, v14, p836.
The New York Times. Aug 25, 1937, p25.
The New Yorker. Aug 28, 1937, v13, p46.
Newsweek. Aug 28, 1937, v10, p24.
Rob Wagner's Script. Sep 11, 1937, v18, p10.
Samuel Goldwyn (Epstein). p52-56.
Samuel Goldwyn Presents. p181-83.
Scholastic. Sep 25, 1937, v31, p36.
Scribner's Magazine. Nov 1937, v102, p63-64.
Selected Film Criticism, 1931-1940. p59.
Sight and Sound. Wint 1937-38, v6, p186-87.

Sociology and Social Research. Nov 1937, v22, p198.
The Spectator. Dec 3, 1937, v159, p992.
Stage. Sep 1937, v14, p41.
The Tatler. Dec 1, 1937, v146, p378.
Time. Sep 6, 1937, v30, p61.
Variety. Aug 4, 1937, p18.
Vogue. Nov 1, 1937, v90, p91.
We're in the Money. p153-60.
William Wyler: A Guide to References and Resources. p93-95.
William Wyler (Anderegg). p61-64.
World Film News. Apr 1938, v3, p34.
World Film News. Nov 1937, v2, p22.
World Film News. Apr 1938, v3, p34.

Dead of Night (GB; Cavalcanti, Alberto; Dearden, Basil; Hamer, Robert; Crichton, Charles; 1946)
Agee on Film. v1, p213.
Classic Film Collection. Spr 1974, n42, p31+.
Classics of the Foreign Film. p168-70.
Classics of the Horror Film. p161-70.
Commonweal. Jul 19, 1946, v44, p335.
Fifty Classic British Films. p55-57.
Film Comment. May-Jun 1974, v10, p21.
Film Daily. Jul 1, 1946, p8.
The Great British Films. p55-58.
Halliwell's Hundred. p61-64.
Hollywood Reporter. Jun 28, 1946, p3.
Horror Films. p145.
Magic Moments from the Movies. p134-35.
Magill's Survey of Cinema. Series II. v2, p595-99.
Motion Picture Herald Product Digest. Jul 6, 1946, p3077.
The Nation. Aug 17, 1946, v163, p194.
The New York Times. Jun 29, 1946, p22.
The New Yorker. Jul 13, 1946, v22, p77.
Newsweek. Jul 15, 1946, v28, p98.
Theatre Arts. Aug 1946, v30, p441.
Time. Jul 15, 1946, v48, p98.
Variety. Sep 19, 1945, p10.
Variety. Jul 3, 1946, p10.

Dead Reckoning (US; Cromwell, John; 1947)
Bette Davis: Her Films and Career. p138-41.
The Complete Films of Humphrey Bogart. p129-30.
Film Daily. Jan 2, 1947, p16.
Hollywood Reporter. Jan 17, 1947, p3.
Humphrey Bogart: The Man and His Films. p139.
Motion Picture Herald Product Digest. Jan 4, 1947, p3397.
The New York Times. Jan 23, 1947, p31.
Variety. Jan 29, 1947, p8.

Deadly as the Female *See* Gun Crazy

Deadly Is the Female *See* Gun Crazy

The Deadly Ray from Mars *See* Flash Gordon's Trip to Mars

Dear Ruth (US; Russell, William D.; 1947)
Commonweal. Jun 20, 1947, v46, p240.
Film Daily. May 28, 1947, p9.
The Films of William Holden. p76-78.
Hollywood Reporter. May 28, 1947, p3.
Motion Picture Herald Product Digest. May 31, 1947, p3653.
New Republic. Jun 30, 1947, v116, p35.
The New York Times. Jun 11, 1947, p33.
The New Yorker. Jun 14, 1947, v23, p88+.
Newsweek. Jun 16, 1947, v29, p98.
Time. Jun 16, 1947, v49, p63.
Variety. May 28, 1947, p15.

Death Bay (Russian title: Bukhta Smerti) (USSR; Room, Abram; 1926)
Cinema, the Magic Vehicle. v1, p125.
Kino. p214-15.

Death Takes a Holiday (US; Leisen, Mitchell; 1933)
American Review. May 1934, v3, p153-54.
Canadian Magazine. Jun 1934, v81, p43.
Esquire. Apr 1934, v1, p121.
Film Daily. Feb 23, 1934, p6.
The Films of Fredric March. p109-11.
Great Horror Movies. p79-81.
The Great Romantic Films. p26-29.
Hollywood Director. p65-75.
Horror Movies (Clarens). p111-12.
Literary Digest. Mar 10, 1934, v117, p38.
Magill's Survey of Cinema. Series I. v1, p424-26.
The Nation. Mar 21, 1934, v138, p342.
The New York Times. Feb 24, 1934, p18.
The New York Times. Aug 12, 1934, p2.
The New Yorker. Mar 3, 1934, v10, p58-59.
Newsweek. Mar 3, 1934, v3, p34.
Newsweek. Nov 11, 1933, v2, p29.
Rob Wagner's Script. Mar 10, 1934, v11, p8.
The Spectator. Apr 6, 1934, v152, p538.
Time. Mar 5, 1934, v23, p60.
Vanity Fair. Apr 1934, v42, p49.
Variety. Feb 27, 1934, p17.
50 Classic Motion Pictures. p262-67.

Deception *See* Anne Boleyn

Deception (US; Rapper, Irving; 1946)
Bette Davis: Her Films and Career. p136-37.
Commonweal. Nov 1, 1946, v45, p71.
Film Daily. Oct 24, 1946, p8.
Hollywood Reporter. Oct 17, 1946, p3.
Motion Picture Herald Product Digest. Oct 19, 1946, p3261.
The New York Times. Oct 19, 1946, p15.
The New Yorker. Oct 26, 1946, v22, p108.
Newsweek. Oct 28, 1946, v28, p93.
Theatre Arts. Dec 1946, v30, p715.
Time. Nov 4, 1946, v48, p104+.
Variety. Oct 23, 1946, p10.

The Defense of Volochayevsk (Russian title: Volochayevskiye Dni; Also titled: Volochayevsk Days) (USSR; Vasiliev, Sergei; Vasiliev, Georgi; 1938)
Film Daily. Sep 1, 1938, p7.
Kino. p343.
The New Masses. Aug 23, 1938, v28, p29-30.
The New York Times. Aug 11, 1938, p13.
Time. Aug 29, 1938, v32, p23.

The Delhi Dunbar (US; 1912)
The Moving Picture World. Mar 2, 1912, p774.
Selected Film Criticism, 1912-1920. p69-71.

Delicious (US; Butler, David; 1931)
Film Daily. Dec 27, 1931, p10.
The Hollywood Musical. p66-68.
Hollywood Reporter. Dec 1, 1931, p3.
Motion Picture Herald. Dec 12, 1931, p35-36.
The New York Times. Dec 26, 1931, p15.
Outlook and Independent. Jan 13, 1932, v160, p55.
Time. Jan 4, 1932, v19, p19.
Variety. Dec 29, 1931, p166.

Deliverance (US; Platt, George Foster; 1919)
Exhibitor's Trade Review. Aug 30, 1919, p1089.
The George Kleine Collection Catalog. p29-30.
Motion Picture News. Aug 30, 1919, p1873.
The Moving Picture World. Aug 30, 1919, p1369.
The New York Times. Aug 19, 1919, p10.
Variety. Aug 22, 1919, p76.
Wid's Daily. Aug 24, 1919, 22.

The Deluge (US; 1911)
The Moving Picture World. Feb 18, 1911, v8, p371.
Selected Film Criticism, 1896-1911. p29-30.

Deputat Baltiki *See* Baltic Deputy

Dernier Milliardaire, Le (Also titled: The Last Multi-
Millionaire) (FR; Clair, René; 1934)
Cinema Quarterly. Aut 1934, v3, p112.
Film Daily. Oct 22, 1935, p8.
From Quasimodo to Scarlett O'Hara. p216-17.
Hollywood Reporter. Nov 9, 1934, p2.
The Nation. Nov 6, 1935, v141, p548.
National Board of Review Magazine. Dec 1935, v10, p13.
New Theatre. Feb 1936, v3, p13.
The New York Times. Oct 30, 1935, p16.
The New Yorker. Nov 2, 1935, v11, p76.
René Clair (McGerr). p117-21.
The Spectator. Nov 9, 1934, v153, p714.
Time. Nov 11, 1935, v26, p28.
Variety. Nov 6, 1934, p17.
Variety. Nov 6, 1935, p21.

The Descendant of Genghis Khan *See* Storm Over Asia

The Desert Song (US; Del Ruth, Roy; 1929)
The Hollywood Musical. p24.
Hollywood Musicals. p44-45.
The New York Times. May 2, 1929, p20.
Variety. Apr 10, 1929, p19.

Deserter (USSR; Pudovkin, Vsevolod; 1933)
Cinema Quarterly. Wint 1933-34, v2, p116-17.
Film Daily. Oct 15, 1934, p17.
Graham Greene on Film. p132-33.
Kino. p295-97.
The New Statesman and Nation. Nov 11, 1933, v6, p583.
The New York Times. Oct 13, 1934, p10.
Rotha on the Film. p132-34.
Sight and Sound. Spr 1937, v6, p26.
The Spectator. Nov 10, 1933, v151, p660.
The Spectator. Feb 19, 1937, v158, p312.

Design for Living (US; Lubitsch, Ernst; 1933)
The American Films of Ernst Lubitsch. p154-58.
Ben Hecht: Hollywood Screenwriter. p57-78.
BFI/Monthly Film Bulletin. Dec 1978, v45, p251.
The Cinema of Ernst Lubitsch. p41-42+.
Cinema Quarterly. Spr 1934, v2, p188.
The Comic Mind. p222.
Ernst Lubitsch: A Guide to References and Resources. p121-24.
Ernst Lubitsch's American Comedy. p34-86.
Esquire. Feb 1933, v1, p131.
Film Daily. Nov 17, 1933, p1.
Film Society Review. Jan 1969, v4, p25, 29.
The Films of Fredric March. p102-05.
The Films of Gary Cooper. p115-16.
Hollywood Reporter. Oct 23, 1933, p3.
Literary Digest. Dec 9, 1933, v 116, p29.
The Lubitsch Touch. p133-35.
Magill's Survey of Cinema. Series II. v2, p609-11.
Motion Picture Herald. Nov 25, 1933, p35.
The Nation. Dec 6, 1933, v137, p660-61.
New Outlook. Jan 1934, v163, p43.
The New York Times. Nov 23, 1933, p24.
The New York Times. Dec 3, 1933, p9.
Newsweek. Dec 2, 1933, v2, p33.
Rob Wagner's Script. Dec 2, 1933, v10, p8.
The Spectator. Jan 26, 1934, v152, p119.
Talking Pictures. p11-15.
Those Fabulous Movie Years: The 30s. p52.
Time. Nov 27, 1933, v22, p30.
Vanity Fair. Jan 1934, v41, p45-46.
Variety. Nov 28, 1933, p20.
We're in the Money. p59.
World Film News. Aug 1938, v3, p175.

Desirable Woman *See* Woman On the Beach

Desire (US; Lee, Rowland V.; 1923)
BFI/Monthly Film Bulletin. Jul 1980, v47, p141.
Film Daily. Sep 23, 1923, p6.
Variety. Oct 11, 1923, p30.

Desire (US; Borzage, Frank; 1936)
BFI/Monthly Film Bulletin. Jul 1980, v47, p141-42.
Esquire. May 1936, v5, p115.
Film Daily. Feb 4, 1936, p10.
Film Notes. p97-98.
Film Society Newsletter. Nov 1964, p14.
The Films of Gary Cooper. p136-38.
The Films of Marlene Dietrich. p119-24.
Garbo and the Night Watchman. p83-86.
Graham Greene on Film. p64.
Hollywood Reporter. Jan 31, 1936, p3.
Hollywood Spectator. Feb 15, 1936, v10, p3-4.
A Library of Film Criticism: American Film Directors. p5.
Literary Digest. Mar 7, 1936, v121, p21.
Love in the Film. p127-28.
Motion Picture Herald. Feb 8, 1936, p55.
National Board of Review Magazine. Apr 1936, v11, p14.
The New Republic. Apr 1, 1936, v86, p222.
The New Statesman and Nation. Apr 4, 1936, v11, p528.
New Theatre. Apr 1936, v3, p35.
The New York Times. Apr 13, 1936, p15.
The New Yorker. Apr 18, 1936, v12, p64.
Newsweek. Mar 7, 1936, v7, p32.
Rob Wagner's Script. Mar 14, 1936, v15, p10-11.
Saturday Review (London). Apr 4, 1936, v161, p448.
Sight and Sound. Spr 1936, v5, p25.
The Spectator. Apr 3, 1936, v156, p616.
Talking Pictures. p300-03.
The Tatler. Apr 15, 1936, v140, p98.
Time. Mar 9, 1936, v27, p47.
Variety. Apr 15, 1936, p16.
World Film News. Aug 1936, v1, p19.

Desperate Journey (US; Walsh, Raoul; 1942)
Commonweal. Sep 4, 1942, v36, p473.
Film Daily. Aug 18, 1942, p6.
The Films of Errol Flynn. p112-14.
The Films of Ronald Reagan. p137-40.
Hollywood Reporter. Aug 14, 1942, p3.
Motion Picture Herald Product Digest. Aug 22, 1942, p915.
The New York Times. Sep 26, 1942, p11.
The New Yorker. Sep 26, 1942, v18, p74.
Newsweek. Sep 21, 1942, v20, p80+.
Time. Aug 17, 1942, v40, p44.
Variety. Aug 19, 1942, p8.

Destination Tokyo (US; Daves, Delmer; 1943)
Agee on Film. v1, p68, 70.
Commonweal. Jan 21, 1944, v39, p352.
Film Daily. Dec 21, 1943, p6.
The Films of Cary Grant. p167-69.
The Films of John Garfield. p111-12.
The Films of World War II. p164-67.
Guts & Glory. p54-57.
Hollywood Reporter. Dec 21, 1943, p3.
Magill's Survey of Cinema. Series II. v2, p625.
Motion Picture Herald Product Digest. Dec 25, 1943, p1685.
The Nation. Jan 1, 1944, v158, p23.
The New York Times. Jan 1, 1944, p3.
The New Yorker. Jan 1, 1944, v19, p53.
Newsweek. Jan 10, 1944, v23, p82.
Variety. Dec 22, 1943, p12.

Destination Unknown (US; Garnett, Tay; 1933)
Film Daily. Apr 8, 1933, p7.
Hollywood Reporter. Feb 8, 1933, p3.
Motion Picture Herald. Jan 28, 1933, p25.
The New York Times. Apr 8, 1933, p16.
The New Yorker. Apr 15, 1933, v9, p54-55.

Newsweek. Apr 15, 1933, v1, p27.
Variety. Apr 11, 1933, p17.

Destiny (German title: Mude Tod, Der) (GER; Lang, Fritz; 1921)
BFI/Monthly Film Bulletin. Feb 1974, v41, p36.
Cinema, the Magic Vehicle. v1, p65-67.
The Films of Fritz Lang. p87-97.
From Caligari to Hitler. p88-91.
The Haunted Screen. p89-94.

Destry Rides Again (US; Marshall, George; 1939)
Commonweal. Dec 15, 1939, v31, p187.
Film Daily. Nov 30, 1939, p10.
The Filming of the West. p390-91.
The Films of James Stewart. p76-79.
The Films of Marlene Dietrich. p140-43.
The Films of the Thirties. p250-52.
From Quasimodo to Scarlett O'Hara. p335.
The Great Western Pictures. p83-86.
Halliwell's Hundred. p65-68.
Hollywood Reporter. Nov 29, 1939, p3.
Hollywood Spectator. Dec 9, 1939, v14, p6.
Kiss Kiss Bang Bang. p317-18.
Magill's Survey of Cinema. Series I. v1, p436-40.
Make It Again, Sam. p45-49.
Motion Picture Herald. Dec 2, 1939, p41.
The Nation. Dec 9, 1939, v149, p662.
National Board of Review Magazine. Jan 1940, v15, p23.
The New Masses. Dec 19, 1939, v33, p29-30.
The New York Times. Nov 30, 1939, p25.
The New Yorker. Dec 9, 1939, v15, p97.
Newsweek. Dec 11, 1939, v14, p33.
Reruns. p46-50.
Rob Wagner's Script. Jan 13, 1940, v21, p16.
The Spectator. Feb 16, 1940, v164, p213.
Time. Dec 18, 1939, v34, p76.
Variety. Dec 6, 1939, p14.

Detstvo Gorkovo *See* The Childhood of Maxim Gorky

Deuxieme Bureau *See* Second Bureau

The Devil and Daniel Webster (Also titled: All That Money Can Buy; Here Is a Man) (US; Dieterle, William; 1941)
Around Cinemas. Second Series. p198-200.
BFI/Monthly Film Bulletin. Oct 1979, v46, p214-15.
Commonweal. Oct 31, 1941, v35, p51.
Film Daily. Jul 16, 1941, p7.
Halliwell's Hundred. p9-12.
Life. Oct 27, 1941, v11, p87-90+.
The London Times. Mar 16, 1941, p8.
Magic Moments from the Cinema. p102.
Magill's Survey of Cinema. Series II. v2, p632-35.
Motion Picture Exhibitor. Jul 23, 1941, p792-93.
Motion Picture Exhibitor. Sep 3, 1941, v26, n17, sec2, p833.
Motion Picture Herald Product Digest. Jul 26, 1941, p197.
The New York Times. Oct 17, 1941, p27.
The New York Times. Oct 19, 1941, sec9, p5.
The New Yorker. Oct 18, 1941, v17, p89.
Newsweek. Oct 20, 1941, v18, p75.
Scholastic. Oct 13, 1941, v39, p32.
Time. Oct 20, 1941, v38, p98+.

The Devil and Miss Jones (US; Wood, Sam; 1941)
Child Life. Jun 1941, v20, p268.
Commonweal. May 2, 1941, v34, p39.
The Film Criticism of Otis Ferguson. p357-59.
Film Daily. Apr 8, 1941, p7.
Hollywood Reporter. Apr 7, 1941, p3.
Life. Apr 28, 1941, v10, p53-54+.
The London Times. Jul 14, 1941, p8.
Magill's Survey of Cinema. Series II. v2, p636-38.
Motion Picture Exhibitor. Apr 16, 1941, p727.
Motion Picture Herald Product Digest. Feb 22, 1941, p62.

The New Republic. May 12, 1941, v104, p665.
The New York Times. May 16, 1941, p21.
The New York Times. May 18, 1941, sec9, p3.
Newsweek. Apr 21, 1941, v17, p60.
Scholastic. Apr 28, 1941, v38, p34.
Time. Apr 21, 1941, v37, p98.
Variety. Apr 9, 1941, p16.

The Devil and the Deep (US; Gering, Marion; 1932)
Film Daily. Aug 4, 1932, p4.
The Films of Cary Grant. p38-40.
The Films of Gary Cooper. p101-03.
Hollywood Reporter. Jul 27, 1932, p3.
Motion Picture Herald. Aug 6, 1932, p35-36.
The New Outlook. Oct 1932, v161, p39.
The New York Times. Aug 20, 1932, p7.
The New Yorker. Aug 27, 1932, v8, p37-38.
Rob Wagner's Script. Aug 13, 1932, v8, p8-9.
Time. Aug 29, 1932, v20, p26.
Variety. Aug 23, 1932, p15.

Devil Dogs of the Air (US; Bacon, Lloyd; 1935)
Film Daily. Feb 7, 1935, p6.
The Films of James Cagney. p93-97.
The Gangster Film. p166-67.
Hollywood Reporter. Jan 30, 1935, p3.
Hollywood Reporter. Feb 16, 1935, p2.
Motion Picture Herald. Feb 9, 1935, p58.
The New York Times. Feb 7, 1935, p23.
The New Yorker. Feb 16, 1935, v11, p65.
The Spectator. Aug 9, 1935, v155, p222.
Time. Feb 18, 1935, v25, p71.
Variety. Feb 12, 1935, p19.

The Devil Doll (US; Browning, Tod; 1936)
Canadian Magazine. Aug 1936, v86, p36.
Classics of the Horror Film. p143-46.
Commonweal. Jul 31, 1936, v24, p347.
Film Daily. Jul 7, 1936, p6.
Literary Digest. Jul 18, 1936, v122, p19.
Motion Picture Herald. Jul 11, 1936, p109.
The New York Times. Aug 8, 1936, p5.
The New Yorker. Aug 8, 1936, v12, p49.
Rob Wagner's Script. Aug 8, 1936, v15, p12.
Time. Jul 20, 1936, v28, p36.
Variety. Aug 24, 1936, p18.
World Film News. Oct 1936, v1, p24.

The Devil Is A Sissy (Also titled: The Devil Takes the Count) (US; Van Dyke, W.S.; 1936)
Canadian Magazine. Nov 1936, v86, p38.
Commonweal. Sep 25, 1936, v24, p504.
Esquire. Dec 1936, v6, p136, 139.
The Film Criticism of Otis Ferguson. p155-57.
Film Daily. Sep 9, 1936, p11.
From Quasimodo to Scarlett O'Hara. p227-28.
Garbo and the Night Watchman. p105-08.
Hollywood Spectator. Sep 26, 1936, v11, p9-10.
Literary Digest. Sep 26, 1936, v122, p24.
National Board of Review Magazine. Sep-Oct 1936, v11, p7.
The New Masses. Oct 27, 1936, v21, p27.
The New Republic. Oct 21, 1936, v88, p310.
The New York Times. Oct 17, 1936, p21.
The New Yorker. Oct 24, 1936, v12, p59.
Rob Wagner's Script. Nov 14, 1936, v16, p12-13.
Stage. Sep 28, 1936, v28, p31.
Time. Sep 28, 1936, v28, p31.
Variety. Oct 21, 1936, p15.
We're in the Money. p154.

The Devil Is a Woman (US; Sternberg, Josef von; 1935)
Cinema Quarterly. Sum 1935, v3, p241.
Esquire. Jun 1935, v3, p144.
Film Daily. Apr 17, 1935, p6.
Film Notes. p97.
The Films of Josef von Sternberg. p40-42.

The Films of Marlene Dietrich. p16-18.
Hollywood Reporter. Feb 23, 1935, p3.
Hollywood Reporter. May 10, 1935, p4.
International Dictionary of Films and Filmmakers. v1, p120-21.
Motion Picture Herald. Mar 2, 1935, p55.
The Nation. May 29, 1935, v140, p640.
The New Statesman and Nation. May 11, 1935, v9, p67.
The New York Times. May 4, 1935, p17.
The New Yorker. May 11, 1935, v11, p67.
The Spectator. May 10, 1935, v154, p780.
Sublime Marlene. p71-77.
Surrealism and the Cinema. p87-96.
Time. May 13, 1935, v25, p38.
Vanity Fair. Jun 1935, v44, p48.
Variety. May 8, 1935, p16.

The Devil Is Driving (US; Lachman, Harry; 1937)
Film Daily. Jul 20, 1937, p11.
Hollywood Reporter. Jul 1, 1937, p3.
Motion Picture Herald. Jul 24, 1937, p50.
The New Masses. Jul 27, 1937, v24, p29.
The New York Times. Jul 16, 1937, p22.
Variety. Jul 7, 1937, p13.

The Devil Is Driving (US; Stoloff, Benjamin; 1932)
Film Daily. Dec 16, 1932, p4.
Hollywood Reporter. Nov 29, 1932, p3.
The New York Times. Dec 16, 1932, p25.
The New Yorker. Dec 24, 1932, v8, p42.
Rob Wagner's Script. Dec 10, 1932, v8, p8.
Time. Dec 26, 1932, v20, p36.
Variety. Dec 20, 1932, p16.

Devil May Care (Also titled: Devil-May-Care) (US; Franklin, Sidney; 1929)
Film Daily. Dec 29, 1929, p8.
Life. Jan 31, 1930, v95, p22.
The Nation. Jan 8, 1930, v130, p54.
The New York Times. Dec 23, 1929, p18.
The New York Times. Dec 29, 1929, p6.
The New Yorker. Jan 4, 1930, v5, p48.
Outlook and Independent. Jan 8, 1930, v154, p74.
Rob Wagner's Script. Feb 8, 1930, v2, p12-13.
Rob Wagner's Script. Jun 7, 1930, v3, p10.
Variety. Dec 25, 1929, p20.

The Devil Stone (Also titled: The Devil's Stone) (US; DeMille, Cecil B.; 1917)
The Films of Cecil B. DeMille. p140-43.
The Moving Picture World. Dec 29, 1917, p1996.
The New York Dramatic Mirror. Nov 24, 1917, p25.
Variety. Dec 21, 1917, p46.
Wid's Daily. Dec 20, 1917, p813.

The Devil to Pay (US; Fitzmaurice, George; 1930)
Film Daily. Dec 21, 1930, p10.
The Films of Myrna Loy. p111-12.
The Films of Ronald Colman. p135-38.
Judge. Jan 10, 1931, v100, p23.
Life. Jan 30, 1931, v97, p20.
The New Statesman and Nation. Feb 28, 1931, v1, p17.
The New York Times. Dec 19, 1930, p30.
Outlook and Independent. Dec 31, 1930, v156, p712.
Samuel Goldwyn Presents. p98-100.
Theatre Magazine. Feb 1931, v53, p48.
Time. Dec 29, 1930, v16, p17.
Variety. Dec 24, 1930, p20.

The Devil's Brother (Also titled: Fra Diavolo) (US; Roach, Hal; 1933)
Commonweal. Jun 23, 1933, v18, p214.
Film Daily. Jun 10, 1933, p18.
Hollywood Reporter. Mar 31, 1933, p3.
Laurel & Hardy. p233-43.
Literary Digest. Jul 8, 1933, v116, p25.

Lorentz on Film. p114-15.
Motion Picture Herald. Apr 8, 1933, p23.
New Outlook. Jul 1933, v162, p43.
The New York Times. Jun 10, 1933, p16.
The New Yorker. Jun 17, 1933, v9, p48.
Newsweek. Jun 17, 1933, v1, p31.
Rob Wagner's Script. Jul 22, 1933, v9, p10.
Vanity Fair. Aug 1933, v40, p37.
Variety. Jun 13, 1933, p15.

The Devil's Envoys *See* Visiteurs du Soir, Les

The Devil's Holiday (US; Goulding, Edmund; 1930)
Exhibitors Herald-World. May 17, 1930, p41.
Film Daily. May 11, 1930, p10.
The Films of Nancy Carroll. p110-15.
The Films of the Thirties. p29-30.
Life. May 30, 1930, v95, p20.
National Board of Review Magazine. May-Jun 1930, v5, p15.
The New York Times. May 10, 1930, p25.
The New York Times. May 18, 1930, p5.
The New Yorker. May 17, 1930, v6, p85.
Outlook and Independent. May 28, 1930, v155, p151.
Rob Wagner's Script. Jun 7, 1930, v3, p12.
Time. May 19, 1930, v15, p62.
Variety. May 14, 1930, p39.

The Devil's in Love (US; Dieterle, William; 1933)
Film Daily. Jul 28, 1933, p8.
Hollywood Reporter. Jul 10, 1933, p3.
Motion Picture Herald. Aug 5, 1933, p40.
New Outlook. Sep 1933, v162, p45.
The New York Times. Jul 28, 1933, p18.
Time. Aug 7, 1933, v22, p24.
Variety. Aug 1, 1933, p14.

Devil's Lottery (US; Taylor, Sam; 1932)
Film Daily. Apr 3, 1932, p10.
Hollywood Reporter. Feb 25, 1932, p3.
Judge. Apr 23, 1932, v102, p26.
Motion Picture Herald. Apr 9, 1932, p23.
The New York Times. Apr 2, 1932, p13.
The New Yorker. Apr 9, 1932, v8, p67.
Rob Wagner's Script. May 28, 1932, v7, p10.
Time. Apr 11, 1932, v19, p29.
Variety. Apr 5, 1932, p23.

The Devil's Pass-Key (US; Stroheim, Erich von; 1920)
The Moving Picture World. Apr 17, 1920, p2290.
The New York Times. Aug 9, 1920, p6.
Photoplay. Jul 1920, v18, p71-72.
Selected Film Criticism, 1912-1920. p71-72.
Stroheim: A Pictorial Record of His Nine Films. p21-32.
Stroheim (Finler). p6-12.
Variety. Aug 13, 1920, p36.
Wid's Daily. Apr 11, 1920, p2.

The Devil's Playground (US; Kenton, Erle C.; 1937)
Film Daily. Feb 16, 1937, p7.
Hollywood Reporter. Feb 11, 1937, p3.
Motion Picture Herald. Feb 27, 1937, p60.
The New York Times. Feb 15, 1937, p12.
Time. Feb 15, 1937, v29, p58.
Variety. Feb 27, 1937, p14.

The Diamond From the Sky (US; Taylor, William Desmond; 1915)
A Million and One Nights. p668-69.
The Moving Picture World. Apr 24, 1915, p533-34.
The Moving Picture World. May 1, 1915, 738.

Diamond Jim (US; Sutherland, Edward; 1935)
Canadian Magazine. Nov 1935, v84, p38.
Esquire. Oct 1935, v4, p97.
Film Daily. Aug 24, 1935, p4.
Hollywood Reporter. Jul 10, 1935, p3.
Literary Digest. Sep 7, 1935, v120, p30.

Motion Picture Herald. Jul 20, 1935, p85.
The New York Times. Aug 24, 1935, p18.
The New Yorker. Aug 31, 1935, v11, p43.
Newsweek. Aug 31, 1935, v6, p26.
Rob Wagner's Script. Sep 7, 1935, v14, p12.
Stage. Sep 1935, v12, p3.
Talking Pictures. p34-37.
Time. Aug 12, 1935, v26, p32.
Variety. Aug 28, 1935, p12.

Diamond Ship *See* The Spiders

Diana of the Follies (US; Cabanne, Christy; 1916)
The Moving Picture World. Sep 23, 1916, p1959, 2036.
The New York Dramatic Mirror. Sep 16, 1916, p24.
Variety. Oct 6, 1916, p25.
Wid's Daily. Sep 14, 1916, p913.

Diary of a Chambermaid (US; Renoir, Jean; 1946)
BFI/Monthly Film Bulletin. Feb 1978, v45, p76.
Commonweal. Mar 8, 1946, v43, p526.
Film Daily. Jan 28, 1946, p6.
Film Quarterly. Wint 1970-71, v24, p48-51.
Hollywood Reporter. Jan 28, 1946, p10.
Jean Renoir: A Guide to References and Resources. p138-39.
Jean Renoir (Bazain). p93-97+.
Jean Renoir (Durgnat). p252-60+.
Motion Picture Herald Product Digest. Feb 2, 1946, p2829.
The New York Times. Jun 23, 1946, p28.
Newsweek. Mar 18, 1946, v27, p102.
Seventy Years of Cinema. p160-61.
Sight and Sound. Aut 1964, v33, p174-78.
Theatre Arts. Mar 1946, v30, p159-60.
Time. Mar 11, 1946, v47, p97.
Variety. Jan 30, 1946, p12.

The Diary of a Lost Girl (German title: Tagebuch einer
  Verlorenen, Das) (GER; Pabst, G.W.; 1929)
BFI/Monthly Film Bulletin. Dec 1982, v49, p302.
Cinema, the Magic Vehicle. v1, p161-62.
From Caligari to Hitler. p179-80.
G.W. Pabst (Atwell). p64-71.
The Haunted Screen. p303-06+.

The Dictator (GB; Saville, Victor; 1935)
Film Daily. Mar 11, 1935, p4.
Hollywood Reporter. Feb 26, 1935, p3.
Motion Picture Herald. Feb 16, 1935, p47, 51.
The New Statesman and Nation. Feb 6, 1935, v9, p214.
The New York Times. Mar 24, 1935, p3.
Rob Wagner's Script. Mar 9, 1935, v13, p9.
Saturday Review (London). Feb 16, 1935, v159, p218.
The Spectator. Feb 15, 1935, v154, p246.
Variety. Dec 12, 1935, p19.

Dimples (US; Jones, Edgar; 1916)
The Moving Picture World. Feb 26, 1916, p1311, 1370.
The New York Dramatic Mirror. Feb 19, 1916, p28.
Variety. Feb 18, 1916, p21.

Dimples (US; Seiter, William A.; 1936)
Child Life. Dec 1936, v15, p567.
Film Daily. Sep 26, 1936, p7.
The Films of Shirley Temple. p174-77.
Hollywood Reporter. Sep 23, 1936, p3.
Hollywood Spectator. Oct 10, 1936, v11, p19.
Judge. Nov 1936, v111, p22.
Motion Picture Herald. Oct 17, 1936, p47.
The New York Times. Oct 10, 1936, p21.
The New Yorker. Oct 17, 1936, v12, p77.
Rob Wagner's Script. Oct 31, 1936, v16, p10.
Time. Oct 19, 1936, v28, p64.
Variety. Oct 14, 1936, p15.

Dinner at Eight (US; Cukor, George; 1933)
Around Cinemas. p90-92.
Canadian Magazine. Nov 1933, v80, p34.

Canadian Magazine. Mar 1934, v81, p28.
Commonweal. Sep 29, 1933, v18, p509.
Dictionary of Films. p85.
Film Daily. Aug 25, 1933, p9.
The Films of Jean Harlow. p96-103.
The Films of the Thirties. p108-09.
George Cukor (Phillips). p39-41.
Hollywood Reporter. May 29, 1933, p3.
Judge. Oct 1933, v104, p16.
A Library of Film Criticism: American Film Directors. p64-65.
Literary Digest. Sep 9, 1933, v116, p35.
Lorentz on Film. p120-23.
Lunatics and Lovers. p262-63.
Magill's Survey of Cinema. Series I. v1, p444-47.
Motion Picture. Sep 1933, v46, p54-55+.
Motion Picture Herald. Jun 10, 1933, p36.
The Nation. Sep 13, 1933, v137, p308.
National Board of Review Magazine. Dec 1933, v8, p9-10.
New Outlook. Oct 1933, v162, p48.
The New Statesman and Nation. Sep 16, 1933, v6, p326.
The New York Times. Aug 24, 1933, p18.
The New York Times. Aug 20, 1933, p3.
The New York Times. Sep 3, 1933, p3.
The New Yorker. Sep 2, 1933, v9, p42-43.
Newsweek. Sep 2, 1933, v2, p30.
On Cukor. p62-66.
Photoplay. Aug 1933, v44, p55.
Rob Wagner's Script. Sep 2, 1933, v10, p8.
Selected Film Criticism, 1931-1940. p61-63.
Souvenir Programs of Twelve Classic Movies, 1927-1944. p101-
  20.
Those Fabulous Movie Years: The 30s. p50-51.
Time. Sep 4, 1933, v22, p22.
Vanity Fair. Oct 1933, v41, p39.
Variety. Aug 29, 1933, p14.
50 Classic Motion Pictures. p26-31.

Dinner at the Ritz (US; Schuster, Harold; 1937)
Film Daily. Dec 9, 1937, p7.
The Films of David Niven. p46.
Hollywood Reporter. Nov 4, 1937, p9.
Motion Picture Herald. Nov 13, 1937, p47.
The New Statesman and Nation. Feb 5, 1938, v15, p209.
The New York Times. Dec 4, 1937, p21.
Variety. Nov 10, 1937, p19.

Diplomaniacs (US; Seiter, William A.; 1933)
Film Daily. Apr 29, 1933, p3.
Hollywood Reporter. Apr 8, 1933, p2.
Motion Picture Herald. Apr 15, 1933, p29-30.
The New York Times. Apr 29, 1933, p14.
Pictures Will Talk. p55-57.
Variety. May 4, 1933, p12.

Dirigible (US; Capra, Frank; 1931)
Film Daily. Apr 12, 1931, p32.
The Films of Frank Capra (Scherle and Levy). p91-94.
Frank Capra (Maland). p49-52.
Life. Apr 24, 1931, v97, p22.
Motion Picture Herald. Mar 14, 1931, p45.
The New Statesman and Nation. Jun 20, 1931, v1, p613.
The New York Times. Apr 6, 1931, p24.
The New Yorker. Apr 11, 1931, v7, p91.
Outlook and Independent. Apr 15, 1931, v157, p539.
Rob Wagner's Script. Apr 11, 1931, v5, p10.
Saturday Review (London). Jun 20, 1931, v151, p901.
The Spectator. Jun 27, 1931, v146, p1007.
Time. Jun 8, 1931, v17, p30.
Variety. Apr 8, 1931, p18.

Disbarred (US; Florey, Robert; 1939)
Film Daily. Jan 10, 1939, p6.
Hollywood Reporter. Jan 5, 1939, p3.
Motion Picture Herald. Jan 14, 1939, p49.

The New York Times. Jan 19, 1939, p17.
Variety. Jan 11, 1939, p13.

Dishonored (US; Sternberg, Josef von; 1931)
Film Daily. Mar 8, 1931, p10.
The Films of Josef von Sternberg. p30-32.
The Films of Marlene Dietrich. p96-99.
The Films of the Thirties. p51.
From Quasimodo to Scarlett O'Hara. p140-42.
The Great Spy Films. p153-54.
Judge. Mar 28, 1931, v100, p22.
Life. Apr 17, 1931, v97, p22.
Lorentz on Film. p67-68.
Motion Picture Herald. Mar 7, 1931, p60.
Movies and Methods. p266-67.
National Board of Review Magazine. Apr 1931, v6, p12.
The New York Times. Mar 6, 1931, p26.
The New York Times. Mar 15, 1931, p5.
The New Yorker. Mar 14, 1931, v7, p75.
Outlook and Independent. Mar 18, 1931, v157, p412.
Rob Wagner's Script. Jul 4, 1931, v5, p8.
Sublime Marlene. p42-48.
Time. Mar 16, 1931, v17, p63.
Variety. Mar 11, 1931, p14.

Disparus de Saint-Agil, Les (Also titled: Boys' School)
(FR; Christian-Jacque; 1938)
Film Daily. Jun 29, 1939, p6.
French Film (Sadoul). p93.
Graham Greene on Film. p239-40.
Motion Picture Herald. Jun 17, 1939, p50, 52.
The New Masses. Jun 20, 1939, v31, p30-31.
The New Statesman and Nation. Aug 19, 1939, v18, p277.
The New York Times. Jun 6, 1939, p26.
The Spectator. Aug 25, 1939, v163, p289.
Time. Jun 26, 1939, v33, p46.
Variety. May 25, 1938, p13.

Disputed Passage (US; Borzage, Frank; 1939)
Commonweal. Nov 10, 1939, v31, p79.
Film Daily. Oct 20, 1939, p6.
Graham Greene on Film. p257-58.
Hollywood Reporter. Oct 12, 1939, p3.
Motion Picture Herald. Oct 21, 1939, p36.
Movies and Methods. p339-44.
The New Statesman and Nation. Dec 2, 1939, v18, p788.
The New York Times. Oct 26, 1939, p27.
Photoplay. Dec 1939, v53, p63.
Sociology and Social Research. Jan 1940, v24, p297.
The Spectator. Dec 15, 1939, v163, p864.
Time. Nov 13, 1939, v34, p65.
Variety. Oct 18, 1939, p14.

Disraeli (US; Kolker, Henry; 1921)
Film Daily. Aug 28, 1921, p3.
The New York Times. Aug 22, 1921, p13.
Photoplay. Nov 1921, v20, p61.
Selected Film Criticism, 1921-1930. p77.
Variety. Aug 26, 1921, p36.

Disraeli (US; Green, Alfred E.; 1929)
Cinema. Jan 1930, v1, p42.
Commonweal. Feb 5, 1930, v11, p399.
Exhibitor's Herald-World. Dec 14, 1929, p44.
Film Daily. Oct 13, 1929, p8.
The Film Mercury. Nov 1, 1929, v10, p6.
Literary Digest. Apr 12, 1929, v105, p19.
Magill's Cinema Annual, 1982. p429-31.
The New York Times. Oct 3, 1929, p27.
Outlook. Oct 16, 1929, v153, p273.
Selected Film Criticism, 1921-1930. p77-79.
Variety. Oct 9, 1929, p46.

Dive Bomber (US; Curtiz, Michael; 1941)
Commonweal. Sep 12, 1941, v34, p497.
The Film Criticism of Otis Ferguson. p386-87.

Film Daily. Aug 15, 1941, p7.
The Films of Errol Flynn. p103-05.
The Films of World War II. p53.
Guts & Glory. p37-38.
Hollywood Reporter. Aug 21, 1941, p3.
The London Times. Mar 2, 1942, p2.
Motion Picture Exhibitor. Sep 3, 1941, p838-39.
Motion Picture Herald Product Digest. May 31, 1941, p145.
The New Republic. Sep 29, 1941, v105, p405.
The New York Times. Aug 30, 1941, p10.
The New Yorker. Aug 30, 1941, v17, p49.
Newsweek. Sep 1, 1941, v18, p48.
Scholastic. Sep 22, 1941, v99, p30.
Time. Sep 8, 1941, v38, p67.
Variety. Aug 13, 1941, p8.
When Hollywood Ruled the Skies. p25-30.

The Divine Woman (US; Sjostrom, Victor; 1928)
Exhibitor's Herald-World. Feb 4, 1928, p52.
Film Daily. Jan 22, 1928, p7.
The Film Spectator. Jun 9, 1928, v5, p8-9.
The Films of Greta Garbo. p61-64.
The New York Times. Jan 16, 1928, p24.

The Divorce of Lady X (GB; Whelan, Tim; 1938)
Film Daily. Jan 14, 1938, p8.
The Films of Laurence Olivier. p74-75.
Hollywood Reporter. Jan 18, 1938, p3.
Hollywood Spectator. May 14, 1938, v13, p11.
Laurence Olivier: Theater and Cinema. p57-60.
Literary Digest. Dec 11, 1937, v124, p34.
Motion Picture Herald. Jan 15, 1938, p52.
The New York Times. Apr 1, 1938, p17.
Newsweek. Feb 14, 1938, v11, p25.
Rob Wagner's Script. Apr 23, 1938, v19, p15.
The Tatler. Jan 19, 1938, v147, p98.
Time. Apr 11, 1938, v31, p23.
Variety. Jan 19, 1938, p19.

The Divorcee (US; Leonard, Robert Z.; 1930)
Exhibitors Herald-World. Apr 22, 1930, p56.
Film Daily. Apr 20, 1930, p10.
The Films of Norma Shearer. p166-68.
The Films of the Thirties. p26-27.
Judge. Jun 14, 1930, v98, p23.
Life. May 30, 1930, v95, p20.
Magill's Cinema Annual, 1982. p429-31.
The New York Times. May 10, 1930, p25.
The New York Times. May 18, 1930, p5.
The New Yorker. May 17, 1930, v6, p84-85.
Outlook and Independent. May 21, 1930, v155, p110.
Rob Wagner's Script. Jul 19, 1930, v3, p10.
Time. May 26, 1930, v15, p56.
Variety. May 14, 1930, p3.

Dixie (US; Sutherland, Edward; 1943)
Commonweal. Jul 9, 1943, v38, p302.
Film Daily. Jun 24, 1943, p6.
The Films of Bing Crosby. p138-42.
Hollywood Reporter. Jun 24, 1943, p3.
Life. Jul 5, 1943, v15, p80.
Motion Picture Herald Product Digest. Jun 26, 1943, p1385.
The New York Times. Jun 24, 1943, p26.
The New Yorker. Jul 3, 1943, v19, p28.
Newsweek. Jul 5, 1943, v22, p108.
Time. Jul 12, 1943, v42, p94.

The Docks of New York (US; Sternberg, Josef von; 1928)
Cinema, the Magic Vehicle. v1, p148-49.
Close-Up. p48.
Exhibitors Herald World and Moving Picture World. Oct 27, 1928, p52.
Film Daily. Sep 23, 1928, p6.
Film Mercury. Oct 26, 1928, v8, p6.
The Film Spectator. Sep 29, 1928, v6, p13-14.
The Films of Josef von Sternberg. p19-22.

The Great Gangster Films. p118-19.
Magill's Survey of Cinema. Silent Films. v1, p364-69.
The New York Times. Sep 17, 1928, p28.
The New York Times. Apr 20, 1930, sec8, p6.
The Parade's Gone By. p200-201+.
Selected Film Criticism, 1921-1930. p79-81.
Variety. Sep 19, 1928, p12.

The Docks of San Francisco (US; Seitz, George B.; 1932)
Film Daily. Jan 24, 1932, p10.
Motion Picture Herald. Jan 30, 1932, p48.
Variety. Mar 15, 1932, p60.

Doctor and the Girl (US; Bernhardt, Curtis; 1949)
Film Daily. Sep 12, 1949, p6.
Hollywood Reporter. Sep 8, 1949, p3.
Motion Picture Herald. Sep 17, 1949, p17.
The New York Times. Oct 31, 1949, p20.
Newsweek. Oct 24, 1949, v33, p87.
Rotarian. Jan 1950, v76, p40.
Senior Scholastic. Dec 7, 1949, v55, p30.
Time. Dec 12, 1949, v54, p102.
Variety. Sep 14, 1949, p8.

Dr. Cyclops (US; Schoedsack, Ernest B.; 1940)
Classics of the Horror Film. p157-60.
Film Daily. Mar 8, 1940, p6.
Hollywood Reporter. Mar 5, 1940, p3.
Motion Picture Herald. Mar 9, 1940, p56.
Motion Picture Herald. Sep 23, 1939, p58.
The New York Times. Apr 11, 1940, p32.
Newsweek. Apr 8, 1940, v15, p35.
Time. Apr 8. 1940, v35, p33.
Variety. Mar 6, 1940, p16.

Dr. Ehrlich's Magic Bullet (Also titled: The Story of Dr. Ehrlich's Magic Bullet) (US; Dieterle, William; 1940)
The Cinema of Edward G. Robinson. p124-26.
Commonweal. Mar 1, 1940, v31, p412.
The Film Criticism of Otis Ferguson. p291-93.
Film Daily. Feb 2, 1940, p6.
Hollywood Reporter. Feb 2, 1940, p3.
Hygeia. Feb 1940, v18, p138-39.
Life. Mar 4, 1940, v8, p74-77.
Lorentz on Film. p187-89.
Magill's Survey of Cinema. Series I. v1, p454-56.
The Nation. Mar 9, 1940, v150, p346.
The New Republic. Mar 25, 1940, v102, p409.
The New York Times. Feb 24, 1940, p9.
The New York Times. Feb 15, 1940, sec9, p5.
The New Yorker. Feb 24, 1940, v16, p67.
Newsweek. Feb 26, 1940, v15, p30+.
Photoplay. May 1940, v54, p69.
Scholastic. Feb 19, 1940, v36, p38.
Time. Feb 19, 1940, v35, p80+.
Variety. Feb 7, 1940, p14.

Doctor Fu Manchu *See* The Mysterious Dr. Fu Manchu

Dr. Jack (US; Newmeyer, Fred; 1922)
Film Daily. Dec 31, 1922, p6.
Harold Lloyd. p50-55.
Harold Lloyd: The Shape of Laughter. p154-55.
The New York Times. Dec 31, 1922, Addenda sec7, p2.
Variety. Jan 5, 1923, p41.

Doctor Jekyll and Mr. Hyde (US; 1910)
The Moving Picture World. Sep 24, 1910, p685.
Selected Film Criticism, 1896-1911. p30-31.

Dr. Jekyll and Mr. Hyde (US; 1912)
The Moving Picture World. Jan 27, 1912, p305.
Selected Film Criticism, 1912-1920. p72.

Dr. Jekyll and Mr. Hyde (US; Robertson, John S.; 1920)
Fifty Great American Silent Films, 1912-1920. p121-22.
Magill's Survey of Cinema. Silent Films. v1, p370-72.

The Moving Picture World. Apr 10, 1920, p300.
The New York Times. Mar 29, 1920, p18.
Photoplay. Jun 1920, v18, p66-67.
Selected Film Criticism, 1912-1920. p72-74.
Variety. Oct 17, 1919, p65.
Variety. Apr 2, 1920, p95, 97.
Wid's Daily. Apr 3, 1920, p2.

Dr. Jekyll and Mr. Hyde (US; Fleming, Victor; 1941)
Authorship and Narrative in the Cinema. p250-64.
Cinema: the Novel into Film. p83-86.
Commonweal. Sep 5, 1941, v34, p473-74.
Film Daily. Jul 22, 1941, p7.
The Films of Ingrid Bergman. p82-85.
The Films of Lana Turner. p102-05.
The Films of Spencer Tracy. p168-71.
Hollywood Reporter. Jul 21, 1941, p3.
Ingrid Bergman. p38-43.
Life. Aug 25, 1941, v11, p14-16.
The London Times. Feb 16, 1942, p16.
Magill's Survey of Cinema. Series I. v1, p461-64.
Make It Again, Sam. p50-58.
Motion Picture Exhibitor. Aug 6, 1941, p801.
Motion Picture Exhibitor. Sep 4, 1941, v26, n17, sec2, p1941.
Motion Picture Herald Product Digest. May 17, 1941, p134.
The New York Times. Aug 13, 1941, p13.
The New York Times. Aug 17, 1941, sec9, p3.
The New Yorker. Aug 23, 1941, v17, p63.
Newsweek. Aug 25, 1941, v18, p53.
Rob Wagner's Script. Sep 13, 1941, v26, p14-15.
Selected Film Criticism, 1941-1950. p46-47.
Time. Sep 1, 1941, v38, p86.
Variety. Jul 23, 1941, p8.

Dr. Jekyll and Mr. Hyde (US; Mamoulian, Rouben; 1932)
Authorship and Narrative in the Cinema. p221-49.
Caligari's Children. p85-107.
Cinefantastique. Sum 1971, v1, p36-38.
Classic Movie Monsters. p89-95.
Classics of the Horror Film. p73-76.
The English Novel and the Movies. p165-79.
Filament. 1984, n4, p2-13.
Film Daily. Jan 3, 1932, p9.
The Film Journal. Jan-Mar 1973, v2, p36-44.
The Films of Fredric March. p78-81.
The Films of the Thirties. p71-72.
Halliwell's Hundred. p69-71.
Hollywood Reporter. Dec 9, 1931, p3.
Horror! p207-08.
Horror in the the Cinema. p46-48.
Horror Movies (Clarens). p106-08.
Horrors. p230.
The International Dictionary of Films and Filmmakers. v1, p123-24.
Judge. Feb 27, 1932, v102, p24.
Life. Mar 1932, v99, p38.
Magill's Survey of Cinema. Series I. v1, p457-60.
Make It Again, Sam. p50-58.
Mamoulian (Milne). p39-50.
Monsters from the Movies. p56-57.
Motion Picture Herald. Dec 26, 1931, p27, 30.
The Nation. Jan 20, 1932, v134, p82.
The New Statesman and Nation. Feb 20, 1932, v3, p230-31.
The New York Times. Jan 2, 1932, p14.
The New Yorker. Jan 9, 1932, v7, p71.
Outlook and Independent. Jan 6, 1932, v160, p23.
Rob Wagner's Script. Jan 2, 1932, v6, p9-10.
Rouben Mamoulian's Dr. Jekyll and Mr. Hyde.
Selected Film Criticism, 1931-1940. p63-65.
Sight and Sound. Sum 1961, v30, p125.
Time. Jan 11, 1932, v19, p25.
Variety. Jan 5, 1932, p19.
Wide Angle. n3, 1983, v5, p59-63.

Dr. Kildare's Strange Case (US; Bucquet, Harold S.;
   1940)
   Film Daily. Apr 16, 1940, p9.
   Hollywood Reporter. Apr 10, 1940, p3.
   The London Times. Sep 11, 1940, p6.
   Magill's Survey of Cinema. Series II. v2, p650-53.
   The New York Times. May 12, 1940, p19.
   Variety. Apr 17, 1940, p13.

Dr. Mabuse, the Gambler (German title: Dr. Mabuse, der
   Spieler) (GER; Lang, Fritz; 1922)
   Cinema, the Magic Vehicle. v1, p78-79.
   The Films of Fritz Lang. p98-105.
   Fritz Long (Eisner). p139-48.
   From Caligari to Hitler. p81-84.
   The Haunted Screen. p240-46.
   A History of Narrative Film. p118.
   The New York Times. Aug 10, 1927, p21.
   Variety. June 2, 1922, p34.

Doctor Rhythm (US; Tuttle, Frank; 1938)
   Commonweal. Jun 3, 1938, v28, p161.
   Film Daily. Apr 30, 1938, p4.
   The Films of Bing Crosby. p87-90.
   Hollywood Reporter. Apr 23, 1938, p3.
   Motion Picture Herald. Apr 30, 1938, p44, 46.
   The New Masses. Aug 13, 1940, v36, p21-22.
   The New Statesman and Nation. May 28, 1938, v15, p912.
   The New York Times. May 19, 1938, p25.
   The New Yorker. May 28, 1938, v14, p59-60.
   Rob Wagner's Script. Apr 30, 1938, v19, p8.
   Time. May 9, 1938, v31, p44.
   Variety. Apr 27, 1938, p22.

Dr. Socrates (US; Dieterle, William; 1935)
   Canadian Magazine. Nov 1935, v84, p39.
   Film Daily. Oct 3, 1935, p8.
   Graham Greene on Film. p50-51.
   The Great Gangster Pictures. p120-21.
   Motion Picture Herald. Oct 19, 1935, p86-87.
   The New York Times. Oct 3, 1935, p29.
   The New Yorker. Oct 12, 1935, v11, p68.
   Paul Muni: His Life and His Films. p141-45.
   The Spectator. Feb 7, 1936, v156, p211.
   Variety. Oct 9, 1935, p14.

Doctor Syn (GB; Neill, Roy William; 1937)
   Film Daily. Oct 21, 1937, p18.
   Great Britain and the East. Jul 22, 1937, v49, p127.
   Hollywood Reporter. Oct 8, 1937, p3.
   Literary Digest. Nov 3, 1937, v124, p34.
   Motion Picture Herald. Sep 18, 1937, p46.
   The New York Times. Nov 15, 1937, p15.
   The New Yorker. Nov 20, 1937, v13, p88.
   Scholastic. Nov 6, 1937, v31, p36.
   Time. Nov 15, 1937, v30, p44.
   Variety. Sep 8, 1937, p18.

Doctor X (Also titled: Dr. X) (US; Curtiz, Michael; 1932)
   Classics of the Horror Film. p94-96.
   Commonweal. Aug 24, 1932, v16, p411.
   Film Daily. Jul 8, 1932, p22.
   Horror Movies (Clarens). p104.
   Motion Picture Herald. Jun 11, 1932, p29-30.
   The New Outlook. Oct 1932, v161, p39.
   The New York Times. Aug 4, 1932, p17.
   The New Yorker. Aug 13, 1932, v8, p37.
   Time. Aug 15, 1932, v20, p26.
   Variety. Aug 9, 1932, p17.

Dodge City (US; Curtiz, Michael; 1939)
   Casablanca and Other Major Films of Michael Curtiz. p65-68.
   Commonweal. Apr 14, 1939, v29, p693.
   Film Daily. Apr 5, 1939, p6.
   The Films of Errol Flynn. p77-81.
   The Films of Olivia De Havilland. p131-36.

The Great Western Pictures. p87-89.
Hollywood Reporter. Apr 3, 1939, p3.
Hollywood Spectator. Apr 15, 1939, v14, p29.
Motion Picture Herald. Apr 8, 1939, p60.
The Nation. Apr 22, 1939, v148, p478.
The New Masses. Apr 18, 1939, v31, p30-31.
The New Statesman and Nation. Aug 26, 1939, v18, p309.
The New York Times. Apr 8, 1939, p19.
The New Yorker. Apr 15, 1939, v15, p80.
Newsweek. Apr 17, 1939, v13, p26.
North American Review. Jun 1939, v247, p384.
Photoplay. Jun 1939, v53, p59.
Rob Wagner's Script. Apr 15, 1939, v21, p18-19.
The Spectator. Sep 1, 1939, v163, p325.
Time. Apr 17, 1939, v33, p50.
Variety. Apr 12, 1939, p13.

Dodsworth (US; Wyler, William; 1936)
   Canadian Magazine. Oct 1936, v86, p44.
   Canadian Magazine. Nov 1936, v86, p36.
   The Classic American Novel and the Movies. p272-85.
   Commonweal. Oct 2, 1936, v24, p532.
   Esquire. Dec 1936, v6, p133.
   Film Daily. Sep 19, 1936, p3.
   The Films of David Niven. p36.
   The Films of the Thirties. p173-74.
   Graham Greene on Film. p113-15.
   Hollywood Reporter. Sep 16, 1936, p3.
   Hollywood Spectator. Sep 26, 1936, v11, p8-9.
   Judge. Nov 1936, v111, p23.
   Literary Digest. Oct 3, 1936, v122, p20.
   Magill's Survey of Cinema. Series I. v1, p471-73.
   Motion Picture Herald. Aug 8, 1936, p16-17.
   Motion Picture Herald. Sep 26, 1936, p39.
   The Nation. Oct 24, 1936, v143, p502.
   The New Masses. Oct 6, 1936, v21, p29.
   The New Statesman and Nation. Oct 31, 1936, v12, p672.
   The New York Times. Sep 24, 1936, p29.
   The New Yorker. Oct 3, 1936, v12, p61.
   Newsweek. Oct 3, 1936, v8, p34.
   Rob Wagner's Script. Oct 3, 1936, v16, p10.
   Samuel Goldwyn (Epstein). p74-80.
   Samuel Goldwyn Presents. p161-63.
   Selected Film Criticism, 1931-1940. p65-67.
   The Spectator. Nov 6, 1936, v157, p808.
   The Tatler. Nov 4, 1936, v142, p198.
   Time. Sep 28, 1936, v28, p31.
   Variety. Sep 30, 1936, p17.
   William Wyler: A Guide to References and Resources. p87-90.
   William Wyler (Anderegg). p56-61.
   World Film News. Dec 1936, v1, p22.

A Dog's Life (US; Chaplin, Charles; 1918)
   Charles Chaplin: A Guide to References and Resources. p66.
   The Films of Charlie Chaplin. p152-53.
   Variety. Apr 19, 1918, p45.

The Dollar Mark (US; Lund, O.A.C.; 1914)
   The Moving Picture World. Sep 19, 1914, p1616.
   The Moving Picture World. Oct 3, 1914, p106.
   The New York Dramatic Mirror. Sep 16, 1914, p28.
   Variety. Sep 11, 1914, p32.

A Doll's House (US; 1911)
   The Moving Picture World. Aug 5, 1911, p295.
   Selected Film Criticism, 1896-1911. p31-33.

The Dolly Sisters (US; Cummings, Irving; 1945)
   Commonweal. Nov 30, 1945, v43, p170.
   Film Daily. Sep 29, 1945, p6.
   The Hollywood Musical. p264, 266.
   Hollywood Reporter. Sep 26, 1945, p3.
   Motion Picture Herald Product Digest.
   The New York Times. Nov 15, 1945, p24.
   Newsweek. Nov 26, 1945, v26, p109-10.
   Scholastic. Oct 15, 1945, v47, p29.

Time. Oct 29, 1945, v46, p98.
Variety. Sep 26, 1945, p14.

Dolwyn *See* The Woman of Dolwyn

Don Juan (US; Crosland, Alan; 1926)
Classics of the Silent Screen. p83-84.
Film Daily. Aug 15, 1926, p6.
Life. Aug 26, 1926, v88, p26.
Magill's Survey of Cinema. Silent Films. v1, p373-77.
The New York Times. Aug 7, 1926, Addenda p6.
The New Yorker. Aug 14, 1926, v2, p33-34.
Photoplay. Oct 1926, v30, p52.
Selected Film Criticism, 1921-1930. p81-84.
Spellbound in Darkness. p416-17.
Variety. Aug 11, 1926, p11.

Don Q., Son of Zorro (US; Crisp, Donald; 1925)
Film Daily. Jun 21, 1925, p3.
His Majesty the American. p119-32.
The Moving Picture World. Jun 27, 1925, p961.
The New York Times. Jun 16, 1925, p24.
Outlook. Jul 8, 1925, v140, p350-51.
Photoplay. Aug 1925, v28, p51.
Selected Film Criticism, 1921-1930. p84-85.
Variety. Jun 17, 1925, p35.

Don Quixote (French title: Don Quichotte) (FR; Pabst, G.W.; 1933)
Arts and Decoration. Jun 1933, v39, p32-33.
Bookman (London). Jul 1933, v84, p194.
Cinema Quarterly. Sum 1933, v1, p209-11, 239-40.
Cinema, the Magic Vehicle. v1, p220.
Classics of the Foreign Film. p80-83.
Close-Up. Dec 1932, v9, p275-80.
Dictionary of Films. p90-91.
Film Daily. Dec 26, 1934, p6.
G.W. Pabst (Atwell). p109-13.
Hollywood Reporter. Jan 7, 1935, p4.
Kiss Kiss Bang Bang. p322.
Literary Digest. Jan 12, 1935, v119, p31.
Living Age. Feb 1933, v343, p555.
Magill's Survey of Cinema. Foreign Language Films. v2, p862-64.
Motion Picture Herald. Jul 8, 1933, p42.
The Nation. Jan 2, 1935, v140, p27-28.
The New Masses. Jan 1, 1935, v14, p45.
The New Republic. Jan 9, 1935, v81, p246.
The New Statesman and Nation. Jun 3, 1933, v5, p733-34.
The New York Times. Dec 24, 1934, p17.
Newsweek. Dec 29, 1934, v4, p21.
Rob Wagner's Script. Jun 22, 1935, v13, p10.
Saturday Review (London). Jun 3, 1933, v155, p538.
Selected Film Criticism: Foreign Films, 1930-1950. p41-42.
Sight and Sound. Sum 1933, v2, p50-51.
Time. Dec 31, 1934, v24, p14.
Variety. Apr 11, 1933, p20.
Variety. Jun 6, 1933, p14.

The Doomed Battalion (German title: Berge in Flammen) (GER; Trenker, Luis; 1931)
From Caligari to Hitler. p260-61.
Motion Picture Herald. Jun 18, 1932, p34.
Motion Picture Herald. Jan 9, 1932, p40.
The New York Times. Jun 11, 1932, p9.
Photoplay. Jun 1932, v42, p48.
Rob Wagner's Script. Apr 9, 1932, v7, p10-11.
Selected Film Criticism: Foreign Films, 1930-1950. p42-43.
Stage. Jul 1933, v10, p34.
Time. Apr 11, 1932, v19, p29.
Variety. Jun 14, 1932, p16.

Dorothy Vernon of Haddon Hall (US; Neilan, Marshall; 1924)
The American Films of Ernst Lubitsch. p46.
Film Daily. May 25, 1924, p8.

Photoplay. Jul 1924, v26, p44.
Selected Film Criticism, 1921-1930. p85-86.
Variety. May 7, 1924, p24.

Double Crime sur la Ligne Maginot (Also titled: Double Crime in the Maginot Line) (FR; Gandera, Felix; 1938)
Film Daily. Apr 13, 1939, p10.
Motion Picture Herald. Apr 22, 1938, p39.
The New Statesman and Nation. Mar 19, 1938, v15, p478-79.
The Spectator. Mar 25, 1938, v160, p514.
Variety. Apr 19, 1939, p23.

Double Harness (US; Cromwell, John; 1933)
Film Daily. Jul 13, 1933, p26.
Hollywood Reporter. Jun 29, 1933, p11.
Motion Picture Herald. Jul 8, 1933, p40.
New Outlook. Sep 1933, v162, p44.
The New York Times. Jul 21, 1933, p20.
Rob Wagner's Script. Jul 22, 1933, v9, p10.
Time. Jul 31, 1933, v22, p19.
Variety. Jul 25, 1933, p14.

Double Indemnity (US; Wilder, Billy; 1944)
Agee on Film. v1, p119-20.
Billy Wilder (Dick). p42-50.
Billy Wilder in Hollywood. p111-23.
Billy Wilder (Madsen). p87-91.
The Bright Side of Billy Wilder, Primarily. p80-85.
The Cinema of Edward G. Robinson. p150-53.
Commonweal. May 26, 1944, v40, p132-33.
Dark City. p12-16.
The Film Career of Billy Wilder. p69-71.
Film Daily. Apr 24, 1944, p14.
Film Noir. p92-94.
The Films of Barbara Stanwyck. p157-60.
The Films of the Forties. p111-12.
The Great Hollywood Movies. p207-09.
Hollywood Reporter. Apr 24, 1944, p3.
The International Dictionary of Films and Filmmakers. v1, p131-32.
Journey Down Sunset Boulevard. p255-70.
Life. Jul 10, 1944, v17, p55+.
Literature/Film Quarterly. Spr 1978, v6, p116-24.
Literature/Film Quarterly. 1984, v7, n3, p160-70.
The London Times. Sep 18, 1944, p8.
Magic Moments from the Movies. p175-89, 266-70.
Magill's Survey of Cinema. Series I. v1, p478-81.
Motion Picture Exhibitor. May 3, 1944, v31, n25, sec2, p1500.
Motion Picture Herald Product Digest. Apr 29, 1944, p1866.
The Moving Image. p351-52.
The Nation. Oct 14, 1944, v159, p445.
The New Captain George's Whizzbang. 1974, v3, p20-26+.
The New Republic. July 24, 1944, v111, p103.
The New York Times. Sep 7, 1941, p21.
The New Yorker. Sep 16, 1944, v20, p53.
Newsweek. May 29, 1944, v23, p70.
Photoplay. Aug 1944, v25, p24.
Rob Wagner's Script. Aug 26, 1941, v30, p10.
Running Away from Myself. p172-81.
Scholastic. Sep 25, 1944, v45, p36.
Selected Film Criticism, 1941-1950. p47-48.
Starring Miss Barbara Stanwyck. p169-77.
Time. Jul 10, 1944, v44, p94.
Variety. Apr 26, 1944, p12.

A Double Life (US; Cukor, George; 1948)
Commonweal. Mar 12, 1948, v47, p546.
Film Daily. Jun 6, 1948, p10.
The Films of Ronald Colman. p237-40.
The Films of the Forties. p222-25.
Fortnight. Jan 16, 1948, v4, p25.
George Cukor. p53-57+.
Hollywood Reporter. Dec 24, 1947, p3.
Magill's Survey of Cinema, Series II. v2, p663-65.

Motion Picture Herald Product Digest. Jan 3, 1948, p4001.
New Movies. Feb-Mar 1948, v23, p7-8.
New Republic. Mar 15, 1948, v118, p27.
The New York Times. Feb 20, 1948, p20.
The New Yorker. Feb 28, 1948, v24, p62.
Newsweek. Feb 9, 1948, v31, p74.
Photoplay. Apr 1948, v32, p23.
Selected Film Criticism, 1941-1950. p48-50.
Theatre Arts. Dec 1947, v31, p30-35.
Time. Feb 23, 1948, v51, p99-101.
Variety. Dec 31, 1947, p10.

Double or Nothing (US; Reed, Theodore; 1937)
Film Daily. Aug 16, 1937, p7.
Hollywood Reporter. Aug 10, 1937, p2.
Motion Picture Herald. Aug 21, 1937, p54.
The New York Times. Sep 2, 1937, p17.
Rob Wagner's Script. Sep 4, 1937, v18, p13.
Variety. Aug 18, 1937, p27.

Double Wedding (US; Thorpe, Richard; 1937)
Film Daily. Sep 23, 1937, p9.
The Films of Myrna Loy. p204-05.
Hollywood Reporter. Sep 20, 1937, p3.
Motion Picture Herald. Sep 25, 1937, p49, 52.
The New York Times. Oct 22, 1937, p27.
Rob Wagner's Script. Oct 30, 1937, v18, p10.
Time. Oct 25, 1937, v30, p25-26.
Variety. Sep 22, 1937, p18.
World Film News. Dec 1937, v2, p29.

Doubling for Romeo (US; Badger, Clarence; 1921)
Exceptional Photoplays. Nov 1921, v10, p9-10.
Film Daily. Oct 30, 1921, p2.
The New York Times. Oct 24, 1921, p13.
Photoplay. Sep 1921, v20, p57.
Selected Film Criticism, 1921-1930. p86-87.
Variety. Oct 28, 1921, p34.
Will Rogers in Hollywood. p37-38.

Doubting Thomas (US; Butler, David; 1935)
The Film Criticism of Otis Ferguson. p91.
Film Daily. Jul 11, 1935, p8.
The Films of the Thirties. p146-47.
Hollywood Reporter. Apr 2, 1935, p3.
Motion Picture Herald. Apr 20, 1935, p34.
The New York Times. Jul 11, 1935, p24.
The New Yorker. Jul 20, 1935, v11, p47-48.
Time. Jun 10, 1935, v25, p24.
Variety. Jul 17, 1935, p27.
Will Rogers in Hollywood. p160-61.

Dough Boys (US; Sedgwick, Edward; 1930)
Exhibitors Herald-World. Sep 27, 1930, p40.
Film Daily. Sep 21, 1930, p31.
Judge. Oct 11, 1930, v99, p21.
Life. Oct 10, 1930, v96, p20.
The New York Times. Sep 22, 1930, p23.
The New York Times. Sep 28, 1930, p5.
The New Yorker. Sep 27, 1930, v6, p64.
Variety. Sep 24, 1930, p30.

Down Argentine Way (US; Cummings, Irving; 1940)
Commonweal. Nov 8, 1940, v30, p81.
Film Daily. Oct 4, 1940, p10.
The Hollywood Musical. p178-79+.
Hollywood Musicals. p171-73.
Hollywood Reporter. Oct 2, 1940, p3.
The London Times. Mar 24, 1941, p6.
Motion Picture Exhibitor. Oct 2, 1940, p616.
Motion Picture Herald Product Digest. Apr 5, 1941, p100.
The New York Times. Oct 18, 1940, p25.
Newsweek. Oct 28, 1940, v16, p59.
Photoplay. Dec 1940, v54, p62.
Variety. Oct 9, 1940, p16.

Down in Paris *See* Paris Commune

Down to Earth (US; Hall, Alexander; 1947)
Commonweal. Sep 19, 1947, v46, p554.
Film Daily. Jul 30, 1947, p8.
The Films of Rita Hayworth. p164-68.
Harpers. Aug 1947, v195, p189-90.
Magill's Survey of Cinema, Series II. v2, p666-68.
Motion Picture Herald Product Digest. Aug 2, 1947, p3757.
New Republic. Oct 6, 1947, v117, p33.
The New York Times. Sep 12, 1947, p18.
The New Yorker. Sep 20, 1947, v23, p53.
Newsweek. Aug 25, 1947, v30, p81.
Publisher's Weekly. Jul 16, 1949, v156, p221.
Theatre Arts. Jun 1947, v31, p50-51.
Time. Sep 1, 1947, v50, p80.
Variety. Jul 30, 1947, p8.

Down to the Sea in Ships (US; Clifton, Elmer; 1922)
The Best Moving Pictures of 1922-1923. p63-70.
Film Daily. Feb 18, 1923, p65.
The Films of the Twenties. p69-70.
Magill's Survey of Cinema. Silent Films. v1, p380-83.
The New York Times. Feb 19, 1923, p10.
Photoplay. Feb 1923, v23, p64.
Selected Film Criticism, 1921-1930. p87-92.
Variety. Dec 8, 1922, p23.
Variety. Jan 25, 1923, p42.

Down to the Sea in Ships (US; Hathaway, Henry; 1949)
Commonweal. Mar 11, 1949, v49, p543.
Film Daily. Feb 16, 1949, p6.
Hollywood Reporter. Feb 16, 1949, p3.
Life. Mar 28, 1949, v26, p81-82.
Motion Picture Herald Product Digest. Feb 19, 1949, p4505.
The New York Times. Feb 23, 1949, p31.
The New Yorker. Mar 5, 1949, v25, p60.
Newsweek. Mar 7, 1949, v33, p88-90.
Rotarian. Jul 1949, v75, p36.
Time. Jul 5, 1949, v52, p62.
Variety. Feb 26, 1949, p13.

Down to Their Last Yacht (British title: Hawaiian Nights)
   (US; Sloane, Paul; 1934)
Film Daily. Sep 22, 1934, p4.
The Hollywood Musical. p95.
Hollywood Reporter. Aug 27, 1934, p4.
Motion Picture Herald. Sep 29, 1934, p38.
The New York Times. Sep 24, 1934, p14.
Variety. Sep 25, 1934, p13.

Dracula (US; Browning, Tod; 1931)
The Celluloid Vampires. p33-34.
Dictonary of Films. p92.
Film Daily. Feb 15, 1931, p11.
Films in Review. Jan 1954, v5, p15.
The Films of Bela Lugosi. p50-60+.
Films of the Thirties. p47-49.
Focus on the Horror Film. p50-57.
Great Horror Movies. p19-22.
The Hollywood Professionals. v4, p33-35.
Horror. p47-48.
Horror in the Cinema. p28-29, 40-42.
Horror Movies (Clarens). p79-80.
Horrors! p58-61.
The International Dictionary of Films and Filmmakers. v1,
   p132-33.
Journal of Popular Film. Fall 1973, v2, p361-63.
A Library of Film Criticism: American Film Directors. p26-28.
Magill's Survey of Cinema. Series I. v1, p482-84.
Monsters from the Movies. p100-02.
Motion Picture Herald. Jan 3, 1931, p71-72.
*Movie Monsters and Their Masters: The Birth of the Horror
   Film.* p28.
The New York Times. Feb 13, 1931, p21.

Photoplay. Mar 1931, v39, p57.
The Seal of Dracula. p15-18.
Terrors of the Screen. p61-64.
Time. Feb 23, 1931, v17, p62.
The Vampire Cinema. p50, 52-53.
The Vampire Film. p65-68.
Variety. Feb 18, 1931, p14.
50 Classic Motion Pictures. p176-81.

Dracula's Daughter (US; Hillyer, Lambert; 1936)
Film Daily. May 18, 1936, p10.
Hollywood Reporter. May 2, 1936, p3.
Motion Picture Herald. May 9, 1936, p42.
National Board of Review Magazine. Jun 1936, v11, p12.
The New York Times. May 18, 1936, p14.
Rob Wagner's Script. Jun 6, 1936, v15, p12.
Variety. May 20, 1936, p12.

The Dragon Painter (US; Worthington, William; 1919)
Exhibitor's Trade Review. Oct 4, 1919, p1585.
Motion Picture News. Oct 4, 1919, p2877.
The Moving Picture World. Oct 4, 1919, p161.
The New York Times. Oct 5, 1919, sec4, p5.
Variety. Oct 3, 1919, p56.
Wid's Daily. Oct 12, 1919, p3.

Dragon Seed (US; Conway, Jack; 1944)
Asia. Sep 1944, v44, p424.
Best Film Plays, 1943-44. p357-450.
Commonweal. Aug 11, 1944, v40, p400.
Film Daily. Jul 18, 1944, p7.
The Films of Katharine Hepburn. p118-21.
The Films of World War II. p195-97.
Hollywood Reporter. Jul 17, 1944, p3.
Nation. Aug 5, 1944, v159, p165.
The New Republic. Aug 7, 1944, v111, p161.
The New York Times. Jul 21, 1944, p16.
The New Yorker. Jul 29, 1944, v20, p42.
Newsweek. Jul 24, 1944, v24, p106.
Saturday Review of Literature. Jul 29, 1944, v27, p16.
Scholastic. Sep 11, 1944, v45, p33.
Scholastic. Sep 25, 1944, v45, p22-23.
Theatre Arts. Oct 1944, v25, p594.
Time. Jul 21, 1944, v44, p50+.
Variety. Jul 19, 1944, p13.

Dragonwyck (US; Mankiewicz, Joseph L.; 1946)
Commonweal. Apr 5, 1946, v43, p623.
Ernst Lubitsch: A Guide to References and Resources. p163-67.
Film Daily. Feb 28, 1946, p5.
Films in Review. Mar 1951, v2, p32-36.
Hollywood Reporter. Feb 18, 1946, p3.
Joseph L. Mankiewicz (Dick). p31-36.
Life. Mar 18, 1946, v20, p121-22+.
Motion Picture Herald Product Digest. Feb 23, 1946, p2857.
The New York Times. Apr 11, 1946, p35.
The New Yorker. Apr 13, 1946, v22, p107.
Newsweek. Apr 22, 1946, v27, p94+.
Sight and Sound. Aut 1946, v15, p97.
Time. Apr 1, 1946, v47, p96.
Variety. Feb 20, 1946, p8.
Vincent Price Unmasked. p170-71.

Dramatic School (US; Sinclair, Robert; 1938)
Chestnuts in Her Lap. p45-46.
Commonweal. Dec 23, 1938, v29, p245.
Film Daily. Dec 6, 1938, p9.
The Films of Lana Turner. p75-77.
Hollywood Reporter. Dec 2, 1938, p3.
Motion Picture Herald. Dec 10, 1938, p48.
The New York Times. Dec 9, 1938, p31.
The New Yorker. Dec 10, 1938, v14, p96.
Rob Wagner's Script. Jan 28, 1939, v20, p16.
Time. Dec 12, 1938, v32, p39.
Variety. Dec 7, 1938, p12.

Drame de Shanghai, Le (Also titled: Shanghai Drama) (FR; Pabst, G.W.; 1938)
Graham Greene on Film. p235-36.
The Nation. Feb 3, 1945, v160, p137.
The New Statesman and Nation. Jul 29, 1939, v18, p177.
The New York Times. Jan 11, 1945, p19.
Variety. Nov 16, 1938, p15.

The Dream Girl (US; DeMille, Cecil B.; 1916)
The Films of Cecil B. DeMille. p118-21.
The Moving Picture World. Jul 22, 1916, p800.
The Moving Picture World. Jul 29, 1916, p851.
The New York Dramatic Mirror. Jul 22, 1916, p24.
Variety. Jul 14, 1916, p19.
Wid's Daily. Jul 27, 1916, p742.

Dream Girl (US; Leisen, Mitchell; 1948)
Commonweal. Jul 23, 1948, v48, p356.
Film Daily. May 6, 1948, p8.
Life. Jul 12, 1948, v25, p84.
Motion Picture Herald Product Digest. May 15, 1948, p4163.
The New York Times. Jun 17, 1948, p29.
New Yorker. Jun 26, 1948, v24, p55.
Newsweek. Jun 28, 1948, v31, p88-90.
Time. Jul 5, 1948, v52, p62.
Variety. May 5, 1948, p8.

The Dream of a Rarebit Fiend (US; Porter, Edwin S.; 1906)
The Emergence of Film Art. p32-33.
The Silent Clowns. p50.
Spellbound in Darkness. p33.

A Dream or Two Ago (US; Kirkwood, James; 1916)
The Moving Picture World. Dec 2, 1916, p1381.
The Moving Picture World. Dec 16, 1916, p1655.

Dream Street (US; Griffith, D.W.; 1921)
Film Daily. Apr 17, 1921, p3.
The Films of D.W. Griffith. p162-68.
Life. May 12, 1921, v77, p692.
Magill's Survey of Cinema. Silent Films. v1, p384-87.
Motion Picture Classic. Aug 1921, v12, p50-51.
Photoplay. Jul 1921, v20, p58.
Selected Film Criticism, 1921-1930. p93-94.
Variety. Apr 15, 1921, p40.

Dreaming Lips (GB; Czinner, Paul; 1937)
Around Cinemas. p85-87.
Film Daily. May 20, 1937, p8.
Graham Greene on Film. p133.
Hollywood Reporter. Feb 23, 1937, p7.
Kiss Kiss Bang Bang. p322-23.
London Mercury. Mar 1937, v35, p505.
Motion Picture Herald. Mar 6, 1937, p42, 44.
The New Statesman and Nation. Feb 6, 1937, v13, p203.
The New York Times. May 20, 1937, p17.
The New Yorker. May 29, 1937, v13, p57.
Scholastic. Apr 24, 1937, v30, p29.
The Spectator. Feb 19, 1937, v158, p312.
Time. May 31, 1937, v29, p30+.
Variety. Feb 10, 1937, p14.
Variety. May 26, 1937, p14.
World Film News. Mar 1937, v1, p26.

The Dreaming Mouth *See* Traumende Mund, Der

Drei von der Tankstelle, Die (Also titled: Three Men and Lilian; The Three Men from the Gas Station) (GER; Thiele, William; 1930)
BFI/Monthly Film Bulletin. Dec 1978, v45, p251-52.
Dictionary of Films. p93.
Film Daily. Jun 21, 1931, p10.
From Caligari to Hitler. p207.
Hollywood Reporter. Dec 31, 1931, p3.
The New York Times. Jun 20, 1931, p20.

Rob Wagner's Script. Jan 9, 1932, v6, p8.
Variety. Oct 15, 1930, p29.

Dreigroschenoper *See* The Three Penny Opera

Dressed to Kill (US; Neill, Roy William; 1946)
Basil Rathbone: His Life and His Films. p314-16.
Film Daily. May 20, 1946, p10.
The Films of Sherlock Holmes. p181-88.
Hollywood Reporter. May 16, 1946, p3.
Motion Picture Herald Product Digest. May 25, 1946, p3007.
The New York Times. May 25, 1946, p12.
Sherlock Holmes on the Screen. p164-72.
Variety. May 22, 1946, p10.

Dressing Room Scenes-Adolf Zinc (US; 1900)
The George Kleine Collection Catalog. p31.

The Dreyfus Case (Also titled: Dreyfus) (GB; Kraemer,
    F.W.; Rosmer, Milton; 1931)
Commonweal. Oct 7, 1931, v14, p556.
Film Daily. Aug 30, 1931, p11.
Motion Picture Herald. May 2, 1931, p44.
The New Republic. Sep 16, 1931, v68, p128.
The New Statesman and Nation. May 2, 1931, v1, p359-60.
The New York Times. Aug 31, 1931, p11.
The New Yorker. Sep 5, 1931, v7, p54.
Outlook and Independent. Sep 16, 1931, v159, p87.
Saturday Review (London). Apr 25, 1931, v151, p603.
The Spectator. Apr 25, 1931, v146, p662.
Time. Sep 14, 1931, v18, p50.
Variety. Sep 1, 1931, p31.

Driven (US; Brabin, Charles; 1923)
Film Daily. Nov 26, 1922, p6.
Magill's Survey of Cinema. Silent Films. v1, p388-90.
The New York Times. Feb 12, 1923, p13.
Variety. Dec 1, 1922, p35.

Drole de Drame (FR; Carné, Marcel; 1932)
Cinema, the Magic Vehicle. v1, p273-74.
Eighty Years of Cinema. p112-13.
French Film (Sadoul). p82.

Drums (Also titled: The Drum) (GB; Korda, Zoltan;
    1938)
Commonweal. Oct 14, 1938, v28, p645.
Esquire. Jan 1939, v11, p110.
Film Daily. Jul 20, 1938, p6.
Great Britain and the Far East. Apr 21, 1938, v50, p432.
Hollywood Reporter. Aug 24, 1938, p2.
London Mercury. May 1938, v38, p69.
Motion Picture Herald. Apr 30, 1938, p46.
The New Masses. Oct 11, 1938, v29, p30.
The New Republic. Nov 2, 1938, v96, p363.
The New Statesman and Nation. Apr 9, 1938, v15, p612+.
The New York Times. Sep 30, 1938, p24.
The New Yorker. Oct 1, 1938, v14, p49.
Newsweek. Sep 19, 1938, v12, p22-23.
Rob Wagner's Script. Oct 8, 1938, v20, p13.
Scholastic. Sep 24, 1938, v33, p29.
The Spectator. Apr 15, 1938, v160, p671.
Time. Sep 19, 1938, v32, p24.
Variety. Apr 20, 1938, p25.
World Film News. May-Jun 1938, v3, p83, 87.

Drums Along the Mohawk (US; Ford, John; 1939)
American History/American Film. p97-119.
Claudette Colbert (Quirk). p111-12.
Commonweal. Nov 17, 1939, v31, p97.
The Film Criticism of Otis Ferguson. p277.
Film Daily. Nov 6, 1939, p5.
The Films of Henry Fonda. p87-88.
The Films of the Thirties. p236-38.
The Fondas (Springer). p95-96.
From Quasimodo to Scarlett O'Hara. p329-31.

The Great Western Pictures. p90-92.
Hollywood Reporter. Nov 3, 1939, p3.
Hollywood Spectator. Nov 11, 1939, v14, p8.
John Ford (Bogdanovich). p74-75.
Journal of Popular Film and Television. Spr 1980, v8, p35.
Magill's Survey of Cinema. Series I. v1, p485-88.
The Making of the Great Westerns. p77-92.
Motion Picture Herald. Nov 11, 1939, p38.
National Board of Review Magazine. Dec 1939, v14, p12.
The New Republic. Nov 22, 1939, v101, p142.
The New York Times. Nov 4, 1939, p11.
The New Yorker. Nov 11, 1939, v15, p69.
Newsweek. Nov 13, 1939, v14, p33.
Photoplay. Jan 1940, v54, p58.
Rob Wagner's Script. Nov 11, 1939, v22, p16-18.
Scholastic. Nov 20, 1939, v35, p33-34.
Selected Film Criticism, 1931-1940. p68-70.
The Spectator. Mar 29, 1940, v164, p448.
Time. Nov 20, 1939, v34, p80.
Variety. Nov 8, 1939, p14.
The Western Films of John Ford. p42-57.
World Horizons. Nov 1939, v4, p22-23.

Drums of Love (US; Griffith, D.W.; 1928)
Exhibitor's Herald-World and Moving Picture World. Jul 21,
    1928, p53.
Film Daily. Feb 5, 1928, p6.
The Film Spectator. Feb 18, 1928, v5, p8-9.
The Film Spectator. Mar 3, 1928, v5, p15.
The Films of D.W. Griffith. p227-31.
The New York Times. Jan 25, 1928, p20.
Variety. Feb 2, 1928, p22.

A Drunkard's Reformation (US; Griffith, D.W.; 1908)
American Silent Film. p48.
D.W. Griffith, His Biograph Films in Perspective. p71-73.
The Emergence of Film Art. p44-45.

Du Barry (Also titled: Madame Du Barry) (US; Edwards,
    J. Gordon; 1917)
Exhibitor's Trade Review. Jan 12, 1918, p518, 522.
Motion Picture News. Jan 12, 1918, p185.
Motion Picture News. Jan 19, 1918, p443.
The Moving Picture World. Jan 12, 1918, p273.
The Moving Picture World. Jan 19, 1918, p379.
Wid's Daily. Jan 31, 1918, p911-12.

Du Barry Was a Lady (US; Del Ruth, Roy; 1943)
Film Daily. May 5, 1943, p7.
The Films of Gene Kelly. p37-39.
The Films of Lana Turner. p208-11.
Hollywood Reporter. May 5, 1943, p3.
Motion Picture Herald Product Digest. May 8, 1943, p1301.
The New York Times. Aug 20, 1943, p13.
The New Yorker. Aug 21, 1943, v19, p58+.
Newsweek. Jun 28, 1943, v21, p108.
Variety. May 5, 1943, p8.

Dubrovsky (USSR; Ivanovsky, A.V.; 1936)
Motion Picture Herald. Apr 11, 1936, p57, 60.
The Nation. Apr 15, 1936, v142, p492.
The New York Times. Mar 30, 1936, p17.
Variety. Apr 1, 1936, p16.

Duck Soup (US; McCarey, Leo; 1933)
American Film Criticism. p292-93.
Cinema Quarterly. Spr 1934, v2, p189.
The Comic Mind. p284-85.
Dictionary of Films. p94.
Eighty Years of Cinema. p96.
Esquire. Feb 1934, v1, p131.
Film Comment. Sept-Oct 1973, v9, p8-9.
Film Daily. Nov 17, 1933, p11.
Film Notes. p89-90.
The Great Movies. p73-76.
Halliwell's Hundred. p72-76.

The Hollywood Musical. p138-39.
Hollywood Reporter. Nov 2, 1933, p3.
The International Dictionary of Films and Filmmakers. v1,
    p135-36.
Landmark Films. p82-91.
Magill's Survey of Cinema. Series II. v2, p673-75.
The Marx Brothers. p64, 67, 71-75.
Motion Picture Herald. Nov 11, 1933, p27.
Movie-Made America. p182-84.
The Nation. Dec 13, 1933, v137, p688.
The New Republic. Nov 20, 1976, v175, p42-44.
The New York Times. Nov 23, 1933, p24.
The New York Times. Dec 10, 1933, p7.
The New Yorker. Dec 2, 1933, v9, p61.
Newsweek. Dec 2, 1933, v2, p33.
Rob Wagner's Script. Nov 18, 1933, v10, p8.
Selected Film Criticism, 1931-1940. p70-71.
The Spectator. Feb 16, 1934, v152, p235.
Surrealism and American Feature Films. p37-58.
Take One. Sep-Oct 1970, v3, p18-21.
Time. Nov 20, 1933, v22, p38.
Variety. Nov 28, 1933, p20.
We're in the Money. p34-38.
Why a Duck? p141-84.

Duel in the Sun (US; Vidor, King; 1947)
Commonweal. May 23, 1947, v46, p142.
David O. Selznick's Hollywood. p352-59.
Film Daily. Dec 31, 1946, p4.
The Filming of the West. p498-507.
The Films of Gregory Peck. p63-79.
The Films of Jennifer Jones. p65-72.
Hollywood Reporter. Dec 31, 1946, p3.
King Vidor (Baxter). p66-69.
King Vidor on Filmmaking. p76-77, 178-79+.
Life. Oct 1947, v22, p68-71.
Magill's Survey of Cinema. Series II. v2, p676-79.
The Making of the Great Westerns. p139-56.
Motion Picture Herald Product Digest. Jan 11, 1947, p3409.
The New Republic. May 19, 1947, v116, p33.
The New York Times. May 8, 1947, p8.
Newsweek. Mar 3, 1947, v29, p81-82.
Rob Wagner's Script. Jan 18, 1947, v33, p14-15.
Selected Film Criticism, 1941-1950. p50-53.
Seventy Years of Cinema. p163-64.
Theatre Arts. Jun 1947, v31, p49.
Time. Jan 27, 1947, v49, p86.
Time. Mar 17, 1947, v49, p99-100.
A Tree Is a Tree. p260-67.
Variety. Jan 1, 1947, p14.

The Duke of West Point (US; Green, Alfred E.; 1938)
Commonweal. Jan 13, 1939, v29, p330.
Film Daily. Dec 16, 1938, p9.
Hollywood Reporter. Dec 14, 1938, p3.
Hollywood Spectator. Dec 24, 1938, v13, p18-19.
Motion Picture Herald. Dec 17, 1938, p52.
The New Statesman and Nation. May 6, 1939, v17, p680.
The New York Times. Dec 16, 1938, p33.
The New Yorker. Dec 24, 1938, v14, p46.
Photoplay. Feb 1939, v53, p48.
Rob Wagner's Script. Mar 4, 1939, v21, p17.
Variety. Dec 21, 1938, p14.

Dulcimer Street (Also titled: London Belongs to Me) (GB;
    Gilliatt, Sidney; 1948)
Commonweal. Dec 3, 1948, v49, p198.
Film Daily. Nov 8, 1948, p6.
Fortnight. Feb 18, 1949, v6, p29.
Hollywood Reporter. Nov 5, 1948, p3.
New Republic. Nov 29, 1948, v119, p30.
The New York Times. Nov 8, 1947, p24.
The New Yorker. Nov 20, 1948, v24, p107.
Selected Film Criticism: Foreign Films, 1930-1950. p43.
Sight and Sound. Aut 1948, v17, p143.

Time. Dec 6, 1948, v52, p108.
Variety. Aug 25, 1948, p18.

Dulcy (US; Franklin, Sidney; 1923)
Film Daily. Sep 23, 1923, p6.
Magill's Cinema Annual 1982. p432-34.
The New York Times. Sep 17, 1923, p18.
Variety. Aug 27, 1923, p3.

The Dumb Girl of Portici (US; Weber, Lois; Smalley,
    Phillips; 1916)
Magill's Survey of Cinema. Silent Films. v1, p391-94.
The Moving Picture World. Apr 22, 1916, p640.
The Moving Picture World. May 20, 1916, p1391.
The New York Dramatic Mirror. Apr 15, 1916, p28.
The New York Times. Apr 4, 1916, p11.
Photoplay. Apr 1916, v9, p102-04.
Selected Film Criticism, 1912-1920. p75-77.
Variety. Apr 7, 1916, p21.
Wid's Daily. Apr 13, 1916, p500.

Dumbo (US; Sharpsteen, Ben; 1941)
The Art of Walt Disney. p255-70.
Commonweal. Nov 7, 1941, v35, p72.
The Disney Films. p49-53.
The Disney Version. p264-67.
The Film Criticism of Otis Ferguson. p392-93.
Film Daily. Oct 1, 1940, p4.
Films and Filming. Sep 1962, v8, p39.
Hollywood Reporter. Oct 1, 1941, p3.
Life. Dec 8, 1941, v11, p72-73.
The London Times. Dec 18, 1941, p6.
Magill's Survey of Cinema. Series II. v2, p680-83.
Modern Plastics. Sep 1941, v19, p31-37.
Motion Picture Exhibitor. Oct 15, 1941, v26, n23, sec2, p869-
    70.
Motion Picture Herald Product Digest. Oct 4, 1941, p247.
The Nation. Nov 8, 1941, v153, p463.
The New Republic. Oct 27, 1941, v105, p551.
The New York Times. Oct 24, 1941, p27.
The New York Times. Oct 26, 1941, sec9, p5.
Newsweek. Oct 27, 1941, v18, p61.
PM. Oct 24, 1941, p23.
Rob Wagner's Script. Dec 20, 1941, v26, p14.
Scholastic. Nov 3, 1941, v39, p30.
Selected Film Criticism, 1941-1950. p53-55.
Theatre Arts. Dec 1941, v25, p907.
Time. Oct 27, 1941, v38, p97-98.
Time. Sec 29, 1941, v38, p27-28.
Variety. Oct 1, 1941, p9.
Walt Disney: A Guide to References and Resources. p22-24.

The Dupe (US; Reicher, Frank; 1916)
The Moving Picture World. Jul 15, 1916, p475.
The New York Dramatic Mirror. Jul 8, 1916, p30.
Variety. Jun 30, 1916, p19.
Wid's Daily. Jul 16, 1916, p718.

Dust Be My Destiny (US; Seiler, Lewis; 1939)
Film Daily. Oct 10, 1939, p10.
The Films of John Garfield. p68-74.
Hollywood Reporter. Aug 12, 1939, p3.
The Hollywood Social Problem Films. p148-51.
Motion Picture Herald. Aug 19, 1939, p50.
The New Masses. Oct 24, 1939, v33, p29.
The New York Times. Oct 7, 1939, p11.
The New Yorker. Sep 9, 1939, v15, p60-61.
The Spectator. Feb 9, 1940, v164, p179.
Variety. Aug 16, 1939, p14.

The Dybbuk (POL; Waszynsky, Michael; 1938)
Classics of the Foreign Film. p120-21.
Film Daily. Feb 1, 1938, p12.
Magic and Myth of the Movies. p88-90.
Motion Picture Herald. Mar 19, 1938, p47.
The New Masses. Feb 8, 1938, v26, p27-28.

The New York Times. Jan 28, 1938, p17.
Time. Feb 7, 1938, v31, p58.
Variety. Feb 2, 1938, p17.

The Dying Swan *See* Mort du Cygne, La

Dynamite (US; DeMille, Cecil B.; 1929)
Film Daily. Dec 13, 1929, p8.
The Films of Cecil B. DeMille. p262-65.
Magill's Survey of Cinema. Series II. v2, p684-87.
The New York Times. Dec 28, 1929, p11.
Photoplay. Oct 1929, v36, p53.
Selected Film Criticism, 1921-1930. p95.
Time. Jan 25, 1930, v98, p23.
Variety. Jan 1, 1930, p24.

Dynamite Smith (US; Ince, Ralph; 1924)
Film Daily. Sep 7, 1924, p6.
The Moving Picture World. Sep 13, 1924, p139.

Each Dawn I Die (US; Keighley, William; 1939)
Commonweal. Aug 4, 1939, v30, p359.
Crime Movies (Clarens). p152-54.
Esquire. Nov 1939, v12, p102.
The Film Criticism of Otis Ferguson. p264-65.
Film Daily. Jul 18, 1939, p7.
The Films of James Cagney. p183-92.
The Great Gangster Pictures. p130-31.
Hollywood Reporter. Jul 18, 1939, p3.
Hollywood Spectator. Aug 5, 1939, v14, p10.
Motion Picture Herald. Jul 22, 1939, p48.
The New Republic. Aug 9, 1939, v100, p20.
The New Statesman and Nation. Dec 30, 1939, v18, p956.
The New York Times. Jul 22, 1939, p12.
The New Yorker. Jul 29, 1939, v15, p57.
Newsweek. Jul 31, 1939, v14, p30.
Photoplay. Oct 1939, v53, p65.
Rob Wagner's Script. Aug 26, 1939, v22, p18.
The Spectator. Jan 5, 1940, v164, p16.
Time. Jul 31, 1939, v34, p22.
Variety. Jul 19, 1939, p12.

The Eagle (US; Brown, Clarence; 1925)
BFI/Monthly Film Bulletin. May 1976, v43, p111-12.
Film Daily. Nov 22, 1925, p7.
The Films of the Twenties. p126-28.
Magill's Survey of Cinema. Silent Films. v1, p395-97.
The Moving Picture World. Nov 21, 1925, p60.
The New York Times. Nov 9, 1925, p25.
Photoplay. Jan 1926, v24, p46.
Rudolph Valentino. p105, 116.
Selected Film Criticism, 1921-1930. p95.
Variety. Nov 11, 1925, p36.

The Eagle and the Hawk (US; Walker, Stuart; 1933)
Film Daily. May 6, 1933, p4.
The Films of Carole Lombard. p109-10.
The Films of Cary Grant. p59-61.
The Films of Fredric March. p99-101.
Hollywood Reporter. Apr 25, 1933, p3.
Motion Picture Herald. May 6, 1933, p27, 30.
New Outlook. Jun 1933, v161, p49.
The New York Times. May 13, 1933, p16.
The New Yorker. May 20, 1933, v9, p49-50.
Rob Wagner's Script. May 30, 1933, v9, p8.
Time. May 22, 1933, v21, p24.
Variety. May 16, 1933, p21.

Eagle Squadron (US; Lubin, Arthur; 1941)
Commonweal. Jul 17, 1942, v36, p304.
Film Daily. Jun 16, 1942, p6.
Hollywood Reporter. Jun 15, 1942, p3.
Life. Jun 29, 1942, v12, p62-64.
The London Times. Aug 3, 1942, p8.
Motion Picture Exhibitor. Jul 1, 1942, p1042.
Motion Picture Herald Product Digest. Jun 20, 1942, p725.

The New York Times. Jul 3, 1942, p12.
Newsweek. Jul 6, 1942, v20, p59.
Photoplay. Sep 1942, v21, p24.
Photoplay. Jun 1942, v21, p42-44+.
Time. Jul 13, 1942, p40, p86-87.
Variety. Jun 17, 1942, p8.
When Hollywood Ruled the Skies. p49-51.

The Earl of Chicago (US; Thorpe, Richard; 1939)
Commonweal. Jan 26, 1940, v31, p307.
Film Daily. Jan 3, 1940, p10.
The Great Gangster Pictures. p131-32.
Hollywood Reporter. Dec 27, 1939, p3.
Hollywood Spectator. Jan 6, 1940, v14, p3-4.
Motion Picture Herald. Dec 30, 1939, p46.
The New York Times. Mar 14, 1940, p29.
Newsweek. Jan 15, 1940, v15, p33.
The Spectator. Apr 12, 1940, v164, p524.
Time. Feb 12, 1940, v35, p73+.
Variety. Jan 3, 1940, p40.

Early to Bed (US; McLeod, Norman Z.; 1936)
Film Daily. May 25, 1936, p9.
Hollywood Reporter. May 21, 1936, p2.
Literary Digest. Jun 6, 1936, v121, p21.
Motion Picture Herald. Jul 25, 1936, p64.
The New Masses. Jul 28, 1936, v20, p29.
The New York Times. Jul 16, 1936, p20.
The New Yorker. Jul 25, 1936, v12, p56.
Rob Wagner's Script. Jul 11, 1936, v15, p14.
Time. Jun 8, 1936, v27, p40.
Variety. Jul 22, 1936, p17.

Earth (Russian title: Zemlya; Zimlia; Zemla) (USSR; Dovzhenko, Alexander; 1930)
Celluloid: The Film To-Day. p135-53.
Cinema, the Magic Vehicle. v1, p171-72.
Classics of the Foreign Film. p54-57.
Close-Up. Sep 1930, v7, p171-75.
Dictionary of Films. p428-29.
Film Culture. Wint 1963-64, v31, p44-46.
Kino. p275-76.
Kiss Kiss Bang Bang. p323.
Rotha on the Film. p113-22.

The Earth Thirsts *See* The Soil is Thirsty

Earthworm Tractors (US; Enright, Ray; 1936)
Film Daily. Jun 16, 1936, p24.
Hollywood Reporter. Jun 11, 1936, p3.
Motion Picture Herald. Jun 20, 1936, p66-67.
The New York Times. Jul 25, 1936, p16.
Time. Jul 27, 1936, v28, p41.
Variety. Jul 29, 1936, p14.

East Lynne (US; Lloyd, Frank; 1931)
Film Daily. Feb 22, 1931, p14.
Motion Picture Herald. Feb 28, 1931, p49.
National Board of Review Magazine. Mar 1931, v6, p10.
The New York Times. Feb 21, 1931, p15.
The New Yorker. Feb 28, 1931, v6, p59.
Outlook and Independent. Mar 4, 1931, v157, p348.
Rob Wagner's Script. Feb 14, 1931, v5, p8.
Sociology and Social Research. Mar 1931, v15, p398.
Time. Mar 2, 1931, v17, p26.
Variety. Feb 25, 1931, p12.

East of Borneo (US; Melford, George; 1931)
Film Daily. Aug 23, 1931, p18.
Hollywood Reporter. Jun 17, 1931, p3.
Hollywood Spectator. Sep 26, 1931, v12, p9, 24.
Judge. Oct 17, 1931, v101, p18.
Life. Oct 16, 1931, v98, p18.
Motion Picture Herald. Oct 3, 1931, p32.
The New York Times. Sep 26, 1931, p25.
The New Yorker. Oct 3, 1931, v7, p71.

Outlook and Independent. Oct 7, 1931, v159, p183.
Time. Oct 5, 1931, v18, p21.
Variety. Sep 29, 1931, p22.

East of Shanghai *See* Rich and Strange

East Side of Heaven (US; Butler, David; 1939)
Commonweal. May 5, 1939, v30, p49.
Film Daily. Apr 10, 1939, p6.
The Films of Bing Crosby. p99-100.
Hollywood Reporter. Apr 5, 1939, p3.
Hollywood Spectator. Apr 15, 1939, v14, p35.
Motion Picture Herald. Apr 8, 1939, p64.
The New York Times. May 5, 1939, p29.
Newsweek. Apr 24, 1939, v13, p33-34.
Photoplay. Jun 1939, v53, p59.
Rob Wagner's Script. May 13, 1939, v21, p17.
Variety. Apr 12, 1939, p13.

Easter Parade (US; Walters, Charles; 1948)
Agee on Film. v1, p310.
Commonweal. Jun 25, 1948, v48, p260.
Film Daily. Jun 1, 1948, p4.
The Hollywood Musical. p238, 290.
Judy: The Films and Career of Judy Garland. p143-47.
Life. Jun 21, 1948, v24, p71.
Magill's Survey of Cinema. Series I. v2, p491.
Motion Picture Herald Product Digest. May 29, 1948, p4181.
The New Republic. Jul 12, 1948, v118, p30.
The New York Times. Jul 1, 1948, p19.
The New York Times Magazine. Jun 6, 1948, p54-55.
The New Yorker. Jul 10, 1948, v24, p39.
Newsweek. Jul 5, 1948, v32, p70.
Starring Fred Astaire. p303-18.
Time. Jul 5, 1948, v52, p60.
Variety. May 26, 1948, p8.

Easy Living (US; Leisen, Mitchell; 1937)
Film Daily. Jul 7, 1937, p6.
Film Notes. p103-04.
Hollywood Director. p115-18.
Hollywood Reporter. Jul 2, 1937, p3.
Hollywood Spectator. Jul 17, 1937, v12, p4-5.
Lunatics and Lovers. p31-36.
Magill's Survey of Cinema. Series II. v2, p688-91.
Motion Picture Herald. Jul 10, 1937, p51, 54.
The New Masses. Jul 20, 1937, v24, p28.
The New Statesman and Nation. Aug 14, 1937, v14, p252.
The New York Times. Jul 8, 1937, p20.
The New Yorker. Jul 17, 1937, v13, p56.
Preston Sturges: A Guide to References and Resources. p40-45.
Rob Wagner's Script. Jul 17, 1937, v17, p16.
The Spectator. Aug 13, 1937, v159, p275.
The Tatler. Aug 18, 1937, v145, p286.
Variety. Jul 7, 1937, p12.
World Film News. Sep 1937, v2, p25.

Easy Street (US; Chaplin, Charles; 1917)
Charles Chaplin: A Guide to References and Resources. p64.
The Comic Mind. p81-84.
The Films of Charlie Chaplin. p140-42.
The Moving Picture World. Feb 17, 1917, p1037.
Photoplay. Apr 1917, v11, p172.
Selected Film Criticism, 1912-1920. p78.
Variety. Feb 2, 1917, p24.

Easy to Wed (US; Buzzell, Edward; 1946)
Commonweal. May 3, 1946, v44, p73.
Film Daily. Apr 10, 1946, p6.
The Hollywood Musical. p271.
Hollywood Musicals. p219.
Hollywood Reporter. Apr 9, 1946, p3.
Life. Jul 8, 1946, v21, p64-66.
Motion Picture Herald Product Digest. Apr 13, 1946, p2937.
The New York Times. Jul 12, 1946, p14.
The New Yorker. Jul 20, 1946, v22, p52.

Time. Jul 15, 1946, v48, p97.
Variety. Apr 10, 1946, p16.

Ebb Tide (US; Hogan, James; 1937)
Film Daily. Sep 28, 1937, p8.
Hollywood Reporter. Sep 23, 1937, p2.
Literary Digest. Dec 11, 1937, v124, p34.
Motion Picture. Nov 1937, v54, p42-43+.
The New York Times. Nov 18, 1937, p27.
Rob Wagner's Script. Nov 20, 1937, v18, p20-21.
Saint Nicholas. Nov 1937, v65, p41.
Saturday Review. Feb 12, 1938, v17, p21.
Scholastic. Dec 4, 1937, v31, p10.
The Tatler. Nov 3, 1937, v146, p194.
Time. Nov 29, 1937, v30, p42.
Variety. Oct 13, 1937, p16.
World Film News. Dec 1937, v2, p29.

Ecstasy (Czechoslovakian title: Extase) (CZECH; Machaty, Gustav; 1933)
Classics of the Foreign Film. p90-91.
Close-Up. Jun 1933, v10, p196-97.
Dictionary of Films. p107.
The Films of Hedy Lamarr. p92-98.
Hollywood Spectator. May 23, 1936, v11, p14-15.
Love in the Film. p111-16.
The New Statesman and Nation. Feb 19, 1938, v15, p287.
The New York Times. Dec 25, 1940, p33.
Newsweek. Jan 19, 1935, v5, p26.
Newsweek. Jul 6, 1935, v6, p18.
Rob Wagner's Script. Jul 25, 1936, v15, p10.
Selected Film Criticism: Foreign Films, 1930-1950. p44-47.
Time. Jul 25, 1938, v32, p22.
Variety. Jan 8, 1941, p24.
Variety. Apr 11, 1933, p20.
World Film News. Apr 1938, v2, p39.

The Edge of the World (GB; Powell, Michael; 1937)
Commonweal. Sep 30, 1938, v28, p590.
Film Daily. Sep 9, 1938, p15.
Great Britain and the East. Jul 15, 1937, v49, p86.
The Nation. Sep 17, 1938, v147, p278.
National Board of Review Magazine. Oct 1938, v13, p16.
The New Republic. Sep 14, 1938, v96, p160.
The New Statesman and Nation. Sep 18, 1937, v14, p407.
The New York Times. Sep 12, 1938, p13.
The New Yorker. Sep 3, 1938, v14, p62.
Scholastic. Oct 29, 1938, v33, p29.
Sight and Sound. Aut 1937, v6, p120-21.
The Spectator. Sep 17, 1937, v159, p459.
The Tatler. Sep 22, 1937, v145, p516.
Variety. Jul 21, 1937, p13.
Variety. Sep 14, 1938, p15.
World Film News. Oct 1937, v2, p21.

Edison First Program (US; 1896)
Behind the Screen. p87.
The First Twenty Years. p14.
The New York Clipper. May 2, 1896, p136.
The New York Dramatic Mirror. May 2, 1896, p19.
The New York Times. Apr 24, 1896, p5.
Selected Film Criticism, 1896-1911. p33-35.

Edison, the Man (US; Brown, Clarence; 1940)
Commonweal. May 31 1940, v32, p130.
Film Daily. May 17, 1940, p8.
The Films of Spencer Tracy. p158-60.
Hollywood Reporter. May 17, 1940, p3.
Motion Picture Herald. Mar 30, 1940, p53.
Motion Picture Herald. May 25, 1940, p44.
The New York Times. Jun 7, 1940, p27.
Newsweek. May 27, 1940, v15, p48.
Popular Science Monthly. Jul 1940, v137, p102-05.
Time. Jun 10, 1940, v35, p100+.
Variety. May 22, 1940, p14.

The Egg and I (US; Erskine, Chester; 1947)
Claudette Colbert (Quirk). p151-53.
Commonweal. May 23, 1947, v46, p142.
Film Daily. Mar 24, 1947, p6.
Hollywood Reporter. Mar 24, 1947, p3.
Magill's Survey of Cinema, Series II. v2, p695-97.
Motion Picture Herald Product Digest. Mar 29, 1947, p3549.
The Nation. May 10, 1949, v164, p553.
New Republic. May 12, 1947, v116, p39.
The New York Times. Apr 25, 1947, p29.
The New Yorker. May 3, 1947, v23, p95.
Newsweek. Apr 21, 1947, v29, p96.
Photoplay. Mar 1948, v32, p42.
Time. Apr 28, 1947, v49, p99.
Variety. Mar 26, 1947, p12.

The Egg Crate Wallop (US; Storm, Jerome; 1919)
Exhibitor's Trade Review. Oct 18, 1919, p1723.
Motion Picture News. Oct 11, 1919, p2899.
The Moving Picture World. Oct 20, 1919, p1013.
The New York Times. Sep 29, 1919, p16.
Variety. Oct 3, 1919, p57.
Wid's Daily. Oct 12, 1919, p19.

Eldorado (FR; Herbier, Marcel L'; 1921)
Cinema, the Magic Vehicle. v1, p74-75.
French Cinema. p305-12.

Elephant Boy (GB; Flaherty, Robert; Korda, Zoltan; 1937)
Asia. Dec 1936, v36, p799-800.
Asia. Jun 1937, v37, p463.
Asiatic Review. Jul 1937, v33, p657-58.
Canadian Magazine. Jan 1937, v87, p42-43.
Commonweal. Apr 30, 1937, v26, p20.
Esquire. Jul 1937, v8, p97.
The Film Criticism of Otis Ferguson. p172-74.
Film Daily. Apr 6, 1937, p8.
From Quasimodo to Scarlett O'Hara. p240-43.
Graham Greene on Film. p143-44.
Hollywood Reporter. Mar 6, 1937, p8.
Life. Apr 12, 1937, v2, p32-38.
Literary Digest. Apr 17, 1937, v123, p21.
London Mercury. May 1937, v36, p72.
Motion Picture Herald. Mar 13, 1937, p46.
The Nation. Apr 24, 1937, v144, p489.
National Board of Review Magazine. Apr 1937, v12, p9.
The New Masses. Apr 13, 1937, v23, p27.
The New Republic. Apr 21, 1937, v90, p323.
The New Statesman and Nation. Apr 10, 1937, v13, p593.
The New York Times. Apr 6, 1937, p20.
The New Yorker. Apr 3, 1937, v13, p71.
Rob Wagner's Script. May 29, 1937, v17, p10.
Robert Flaherty: A Guide to References and Resources. p104-05.
Scholastic. Apr 3, 1937, v30, p20.
Selected Film Criticism: Foreign Films, 1930-1950. p47-48.
Sociology and Social Research. Sep 1937, v22, p96.
The Spectator. Apr 16, 1937, v158, p707.
The Tatler. Apr 21, 1937, v144, p102.
Time. Apr 12, 1937, v29, p48+.
Variety. Feb 24, 1937, p17.
Variety. Apr 7, 1937, p14.
Vogue. Jun 15, 1937, v89, p56.
World Film News. Mar 1937, v1, p5.
World Film News. May 1937, v2, p23.
World Film News. Feb 1937, v1, p10-11.
The World of Robert Flaherty. p109-35.

Elizabeth the Queen *See* The Private Lives of Elizabeth and Essex

Ella Cinders (US; Green, Alfred E.; 1926)
Film Daily. Jun 13, 1926, p12.
The Films of the Twenties. p139-40.

The New York Times. Jun 7, 1926, p23.
Photoplay. Aug 1926, v30, p56.
Selected Film Criticism, 1921-1930. p95-96.
Variety. Jun 9, 1926, p16.

Elmer the Great (US; LeRoy, Mervyn; 1933)
Film Daily. May 26, 1933, p6.
Hollywood Reporter. Mar 23, 1933, p3.
Motion Picture Herald. Apr 1, 1933, p24.
The New York Times. May 26, 1933, p24.
The New Yorker. Jun 3, 1933, v9, p58.
Time. Apr 24, 1933, v21, p24.
Variety. May 30, 1933, p15.

Elopement on Horseback (US; 1898)
The First Twenty Years. p8.

Elsa Maxwell's Hotel for Women *See* Hotel for Women

Elstree Calling (GB; Hitchcock, Alfred; 1930)
BFI/Monthly Film Bulletin. Oct 1975, v42, p246-47.
Hitchcock's British Films. p114-17.
The New Statesman. Feb 15, 1930, v34, p602.
The New York Times. Mar, 9, 1930, p6.
Variety. Feb 26, 1930, p42.

Elusive Isabel (US; Paton, Stuart; 1916)
The Moving Picture World. May 13, 1916, p1179.
The Moving Picture World. May 20, 1916, p1404.
Variety. May 5, 1916, p26.
Wid's Daily. May 4, 1916, p547.

Emil and the Detectives (German title: Emil und die Detektiv) (GER; Lamprecht, Gerhard; 1931)
Cinema Quarterly. Spr 1933, v1, p183.
Cinema, the Magic Vehicle. v1, p196-97.
Close-Up. Mar 1932, v9, p58-59.
Dictionary of Films. p101.
Film Daily. Dec 20, 1931, p11.
From Caligari to Hitler. p224-26.
Motion Picture Herald. Jan 9, 1932, p40.
The New Statesman and Nation. Dec 23, 1933, v6, p845.
The New Statesman and Nation. Mar 18, 1933, v5, p322-23.
The New York Times. Dec 21, 1931, p28.
Review of Reviews (London). Apr 1933, v83, p74.

Emma (US; Brown, Clarence; 1932)
Film Daily. Jan 3, 1932, p8.
The Films of Myrna Loy. p129.
Hollywood Reporter. Dec 5, 1931, p3.
Motion Picture Herald. Jan 2, 1932, p30.
The New York Times. Feb 6, 1932, p14.
The New Yorker. Feb 13, 1932, v7, p57-58.
Outlook. Mar 1932, v160, p188.
Rob Wagner's Script. Mar 19, 1932, v7, p10.
Time. Feb 15, 1932, v19, p28.
Variety. Feb 9, 1932, p15.

The Emperor Jones (US; Murphy, Dudley; 1933)
American Film Heritage. p71-74.
Black Images in American Films, 1896-1954. p164.
Bookman (London). Jun 1934, v86, p149.
Canadian Magazine. Nov 1933, v80, p35.
Close-Up. Dec 1933, v10, p351-52.
Commonweal. Oct 6, 1933, v18, p532.
Film Comment. Spr 1971, v7, p74.
Film Daily. Sep 16, 1933, p4.
Film Library Quarterly. Spr 1971, v4, p48-49.
Forgotten Horrors: Early Talkie Chillers From Poverty Row. p105-07.
Hollywood Reporter. Sep 15, 1933, p3.
Kiss Kiss Bang Bang. p325.
Lorentz on Film. p123-26.
Magill's Survey of Cinema. Series II. v2, p709-11.
Motion Picture Herald. Sep 23, 1933, p33.
The Nation. Oct 11, 1933, v137, p419.
National Board of Review Magazine. Sep-Oct 1933, v8, p10.

Negro History Bulletin. Nov 1971, v34, p160-62.
The New York Times. Sep 20, 1933, p26.
The New York Times. Sep 24, 1933, p3.
The New York Times. May 26, 1933, p42.
The New York Times. Jun 11, 1933, p3.
The New York Times. Jul 16, 1933, p2.
The New Yorker. Sep 23, 1933, v9, p59.
Newsweek. Sep 23, 1933, v2, p32.
Rob Wagner's Script. Nov 25, 1933, v10, p8.
The Spectator. Mar 23, 1934, v152, p448.
Stage. Aug 1933, v10, p40.
Time. Sep 25, 1933, v22, p31.
Vanity Fair. Nov 1933, v41, p47+.
Variety. Sep 26, 1933, p15.
The Village Voice. Jun 24, 1971, v16, p69.
The Village Voice. Jul 1, 1971, v16, p57.

The Emperor Waltz (US; Wilder, Billy; 1948)
Billy Wilder. p124-27.
Collier's. Jan 24, 1948, v121, p20.
Commonweal. Jun 25, 1948, v48, p260.
The Film Career of Billy Wilder (Dick). p73-75.
Film Daily. May 3, 1948, p8.
The Films of Bing Crosby. p179-82.
Hollywood Reporter. May 3, 1948, p3.
Life. Jan 12, 1948, v24, p44-45.
Life. Jun 21, 1948, v24, p72.
Motion Picture Herald Product Digest. May 8, 1948, p4153.
The Nation. Jul 24, 1948, v167, p108.
New Republic. Jun 28, 1948, v118, p29.
The New York Times. Jun 18, 1948, p19.
The New Yorker. Jun 26, 1948, v52, p98+.
Variety. May 5, 1948, p8.

The Emperor's Candlesticks (US; Fitzmaurice, George; 1937)
Film Daily. Jun 29, 1937, p10.
Hollywood Reporter. Jun 24, 1937, p3.
Hollywood Spectator. Jul 3, 1937, v12, p6.
Motion Picture Herald. Jul 3, 1937, p45, 48.
The New Masses. Jul 13, 1937, v24, p28.
The New York Times. Jul 9, 1937, p18.
The New Yorker. Jul 10, 1937, v13, p51.
Newsweek. Jul 17, 1937, v10, p38.
Rob Wagner's Script. Jul 3, 1937, v17, p11.
The Tatler. May 27, 1936, v140, p378.
Time. Jul 19, 1937, v30, p44.
Variety. Jun 30, 1937, p21.
World Film News. Oct 1937, v2, p23-24.

Enchanted April (US; Beaumont, Harry; 1935)
Film Daily. Jan 16, 1935, p10.
Hollywood Reporter. Mar 20, 1935, p2.
Hollywood Reporter. Dec 6, 1934, p3.
Motion Picture Herald. Dec 16, 1934, p40-41.
The New York Times. Mar 9, 1935, p19.
Variety. Mar 13, 1935, p15.

The Enchanted Cottage (US; Robertson, John S.; 1924)
Film Daily. Apr 20, 1924, p6.
The Moving Picture World. Apr 19, 1924, p665.
The New York Times. Apr 14, 1924, p14.
Variety. Apr 16, 1924, p23.

The Enchanted Cottage (US; Cromwell, John; 1945)
Commonweal. Mar 23, 1945, v41, p567.
Cosmopolitan. Mar 1945, v118, p90+.
Film Daily. Feb 15, 1945, p8.
The Great Romantic Films. p112-15.
Hollywood Reporter. Feb 14, 1945, p3.
Life. Apr 9, 1945, v18, p49-50.
The London Times. Jun 4, 1945, p8.
Magill's Survey of Cinema. Series I. v2, p502-05.
Motion Picture Exhibitor. Feb 21, 1945, v33, n16, sec2, p1669.
Motion Picture Herald Product Digest. Feb 17, 1945, p2317.

The Nation. Apr 14, 1945, v160, p425.
The New Republic. May 28, 1945, v112, p753.
The New York Times. Apr 28, 1945, p19.
The New Yorker. Apr 28, 1945, v21, p63.
Newsweek. Apr 23, 1945, v25, p102.
Photoplay. Apr 1945, v22, p18.
Running Away from Myself. p121-28.
Theatre Arts. Apr 1945, v29, p232.
Time. Apr 16, 1945, v45, p94.
Variety. Feb 14, 1945, p14.

Enchantment (US; Reis, Irving; 1948)
Collier's. Dec 11, 1948, v122, p46+.
Commonweal. Dec 24, 1948, v49, p282.
Film Daily. Dec 7, 1948, p8.
The Films of David Niven. p90-91.
Hollywood Reporter. Dec 7, 1948, p3.
Motion Picture Herald Product Digest. Dec 11, 1948, p4417.
The New Republic. Jan 10, 1949, v120, p23.
The New York Times. Dec 27, 1948, p16.
The New York Times Magazine. Dec 5, 1948, p66-67.
The New Yorker. Dec 25, 1948, v24, p57.
Newsweek. Jan 3, 1949, v33, p57.
Time. Dec 27, 1948, v52, p58.
Variety. Dec 8, 1948, p10.

The End of St. Petersburg (Russian title: Konyets Sankt-Peterburga) (US; Pudovkin, Vsevolod; 1927)
Cinema, the Magic Vehicle. v1, p127-28.
Close-Up. Apr 1928, v2, p30-35.
Dictionary of Film. p179.
Eisenstein. p116-17.
Film Daily. Jun 10, 1928, p6.
A History of Films. p195.
A History of Narrative Film. p187-88.
Kino. p233-36.
Magill's Survey of Cinema. Silent Films. v1, p401-05.
Masters of the Soviet Cinema. p39.
National Board of Review Magazine. Jun 1928, v3, p7-9.
The New Republic. Jun 13, 1928, v55, p97-98.
The New Republic. Jul 3, 1929, v59, p179-80.
The New York Times. May 31, 1928, p31.
Spellbound in Darkness. p516-21.
Variety. Apr 25, 1928, p28.
Variety. Jun 6, 1928, p12.

The End of the Day *See* Fin du Jour, La

Enfants du Paradis, Les *See* Children of Paradise

An Englishman's Home (Also titled: Madmen of Europe) (GB; De Courville, Albert; 1939)
Motion Picture Herald. Nov 11, 1939, p43.
The Spectator. Oct 6, 1939, v163, p471.
The Tatler. Oct 18, 1939, v154, p70.
Variety. Oct 18, 1939, p20.

Enoch Arden (US; Cabanne, Christy; 1915)
Motion Picture News. Apr 24, 1915, p70.
Motography. Apr 17, 1915, p603, 633.
The Moving Picture World. Apr 10, 1915, p310.
The Moving Picture World. Apr 24, 1915, p557, 568.
The New York Dramatic Mirror. May 5, 1915, p38.
Selected Film Criticism, 1912-1920. p78-79.

Enoch Arden, Part 1 (US; Griffith, D.W.; 1911)
D.W. Griffith, His Biograph Films in Perspective. p164-65.
The Emergence of Film Art. p52-53.
The First Twenty Years. p14.
Motography. Jul 1911, v6, p38.
The Moving Picture World. Jun 24, 1911, p1454.
Selected Film Criticism, 1896-1911. p35-36.

Enoch Arden, Part 2 (US; Griffith, D.W.; 1911)
The Emergence of Film Art. p52-53.
The Moving Picture World. Jul 1, 1911, p1519.
Selected Film Criticism, 1896-1911. p36-37.

Entente Cordiale (FR; Herbier, Marcel L'; 1939)
Film Daily. Jan 2, 1940, p11.
Hollywood Reporter. May 19, 1939, p5.
Life. Jan 15, 1940, v8, p36-37.
Motion Picture Herald. Jan 6, 1940, p44.
The Nation. Jan 6, 1940, v150, p25.
National Board of Review Magazine. Jan 1940, v15, p24.
The New York Times. Dec 26, 1939, p23.
Time. Jan 1, 1940, v35, p29.
Variety. May 17, 1939, p14.

Entr'acte (FR; Clair, René; 1924)
French Cinema. p377-82.
The International Dictionary of Films and Filmmaking. v1, p143-44.
Magill's Survey of Cinema. Silent Films. v1, p406-08.
The New Republic. Sep 15, 1926, v48, p95-96.
A Nous la Liberte/Entr'acte: Films by René Clair. p108-40+.
René Clair (McGerr). p37-40.
Spellbound in Darkness. p497-99.

Equipage, L' (FR; Litvak, Anatole; 1938)
The New York Times. May 20, 1938, p5.
The Spectator. May 13, 1938, v160, p867.
Variety. Oct 26, 1938, p15.
World Film News. Jul 1938, v3, p131.

Escapade (US; Leonard, Robert Z.; 1935)
Commonweal. Jul 19, 1935, v22, p307.
Esquire. Sep 1935, v4, p144.
Film Daily. Jul 6, 1935, p7.
Hollywood Reporter. Jul 2, 1935, p3.
Judge. Sep 1935, v109, p14.
Literary Digest. Jul 20, 1935, v120, p24.
Motion Picture Herald. Jul 13, 1935, p57.
The Nation. Jul 24, 1935, v141, p112.
The New Statesman and Nation. Nov 9, 1935, v10, p676.
The New York Times. Jul 6, 1935, p16.
The New Yorker. Jul 13, 1935, v11, p51-52.
Rob Wagner's Script. Jul 13, 1935, v13, p8.
Time. Jul 15, 1935, v26, p40.
Variety. Jul 10, 1935, p19.

The Escape (US; Griffith, D.W.; 1914)
The Films of D.W. Griffith. p34-36.
The Moving Picture World. Jun 13, 1914, p1515.
The New York Dramatic Mirror. Jun 10, 1914, p42.
The New York Times. Jun 2, 1914, p11.
Selected Film Criticism, 1912-1920. p79-81.
Variety. Jun 5, 1914, p19.

Escape (US; LeRoy, Mervyn; 1940)
Commonweal. Nov 15, 1940, v33, p104.
Film Daily. Oct 31, 1940, p4.
The Films of Norma Shearer. p235-40.
The Films of Robert Taylor. p85-86.
The Films of World War II. p42-43.
Hollywood Reporter. Oct 31, 1940, p3.
Life. Sep 22, 1941, v11, p23.
The London Times. Jan 20, 1941, p6.
Motion Picture Exhibitor. Nov 13, 1940, p635.
The New Republic. Nov 25, 1940, v103, p724.
The New York Times. Nov 1, 1940, p33.
Newsweek. Nov 11, 1940, v16, p58.
Photoplay. Aug 1940, v54, p44.
Scholastic. Nov 11, 1940, v37, p34.
Scribner's Commentator. Jan 1941, v9, p106-07.
Time. Nov 18, 1940, v36, p86.
Variety. Oct 30, 1940, p14.

Escape (US; Dean, Basil; 1930)
Exhibitors Herald-World. Nov 8, 1930, p40.
Film Daily. Nov 2, 1930, p10.
The New York Times. Nov 1, 1930, p23.
The New York Times. Nov 9, 1930, p5.
Outlook and Independent. Nov 19, 1930, v156, p473.
Variety. Sep 10, 1930, p17.

Escape from Yesterday (French title: Bandera, La) (FR; Duvivier, Julien; 1935)
Dictionary of Films. p23-24.
Film Daily. May 11, 1939, p6.
French Film. p74-75.
Garbo and the Night Watchman. p123, 125.
Graham Greene on Film. p38-39.
Motion Picture Herald. May 13, 1939, p42.
The New York Times. May 3, 1939, p27.
Variety. Oct 2, 1935, p17.

Escape Me Never (GB; Czinner, Paul; 1935)
Cinema Quarterly. Spr 1935, v3, p176-77.
Commonweal. Jun 7, 1935, v22, p160.
Film Daily. May 24, 1935, p4.
Hollywood Reporter. Apr 3, 1935, p3.
Literary Digest. Jun 8, 1935, v119, p26.
Motion Picture Herald. Apr 20, 1935, p38.
The Nation. Jun 5, 1935, v140, p668.
National Board of Review Magazine. Jul 1935, v10, p10.
The New York Times. May 24, 1935, p24.
The New Yorker. Jun 1, 1935, v11, p55-56.
Newsweek. Jun 1, 1935, v5, p24.
Rob Wagner's Script. Jun 22, 1935, v13, p8.
Selected Film Criticism: Foreign Films, 1930-1950. p48-49.
The Spectator. Apr 5, 1935, v154, p566.
Time. Jun 3, 1935, v25, p50.
Variety. Apr 17, 1935, p14.
Variety. May 29, 1935, p14.

Escape to Happiness *See* Intermezzo, a Love Story

Eskimo (US; Van Dyke, W.S.; 1933)
Film Daily. Nov 16, 1933, p6.
From Quasimodo to Scarlett O'Hara. p182-84.
Hollywood Reporter. Oct 16, 1933, p3.
Judge. Jan 19, 1934, v106, p12.
Motion Picture Herald. Nov 18, 1933, p36.
Movie Classic. Nov 1933, v5, p34-35.
The Nation. Nov 29, 1933, v137, p631.
New Outlook. Dec 1933, v162, p47.
The New York Times. Nov 15, 1933, p25.
The New Yorker. Nov 25, 1933, v9, p57.
Newsweek. Nov 25, 1933, v2, p32.
Rob Wagner's Script. Jan 20, 1934, v10, p8.
Time. Nov 27, 1933, v22, p31.
Variety. Nov 21, 1933, p14.

Espionage (US; Neumann, Kurt; 1937)
Film Daily. Mar 6, 1937, p3.
The Great Spy Pictures. p165.
Hollywood Reporter. Feb 25, 1937, p3.
Motion Picture Herald. Mar 6, 1937, p39, 42.
The New York Times. Mar 9, 1937, p27.
Rob Wagner's Script. Apr 24, 1937, v17, p10.
Variety. Mar 17, 1937, p14.

Espionage Agent (US; Bacon, Lloyd; 1939)
Commonweal. Oct 6, 1939, v30, p539.
Film Daily. Sep 25, 1939, p5.
The Great Spy Pictures. p165-66.
Hollywood Reporter. Sep 21, 1939, p3.
Motion Picture Herald. Sep 30, 1939, p39.
The Nation. Oct 14, 1939, v149, p422.
The New Republic. Oct 18, 1939, v100, p301.
The New York Times. Sep 23, 1939, p22.
The New Yorker. Sep 30, 1939, v15, p57.
Rob Wagner's Script. Sep 30, 1939, v22, p16-17.

The Spectator. Dec 22, 1939, v163, p900.
Time. Oct 2, 1939, v34, p49.
Variety. Sep 27, 1939, p12.

The Eternal City (US; Porter, Edwin S.; Ford, Hugh; 1915)
A Million and One Nights. p639-40.
Motion Picture News. Jan 9, 1915, p45.
Motography. Jan 16, 1915, p112.
The Moving Picture World. Jan 9, 1915, p194, 199.
The Moving Picture World. Dec 21, 1918, p1388.
The Moving Picture World. Dec 28, 1918, p1552.
The New York Dramatic Mirror. Jan 6, 1915, p26.
The New York Times. Apr 13, 1915, p11.
Selected Film Criticism, 1912-1920. p81-83.
Variety. Jan 1, 1915, p29.

The Eternal Grind (US; O'Brien, John B.; 1916)
The Moving Picture World. Apr 22, 1916, p642, 696.
The New York Dramatic Mirror. Apr 15, 1916, p25.
The New York Times. Apr 10, 1916, p11.
Variety. Apr 14, 1916, p24.
Wid's Daily. Apr 13, 1916, p509.

Eternal Love (US; Lubitsch, Ernst; 1929)
Ernst Lubitsch: A Guide to References and Resources. p96-98.
Film Daily. May 19, 1929, p9.
The New York Times. May 13, 1929, p27.
Variety. May 15, 1929, p23.

The Eternal Mask (German title: Ewige Maske, Die) (SWITZ; Hochbaum, Werner; 1936)
Classics of the Foreign Film. p102-03.
Film Daily. Jan 12, 1937, p6.
Hollywood Reporter. Jun 9, 1936, p15.
Literary Digest. Jan 16, 1937, v123, p24.
Motion Picture Herald. Jan 23, 1937, p38, 40.
National Board of Review Magazine. Feb 1937, v12, p10.
New Theatre. Mar 1937, v4, p46.
The New York Times. Jan 13, 1937, p20.
The New Yorker. Jan 9, 1937, v12, p65.
Rob Wagner's Script. Apr 10, 1937, v17, p10.
Saturday Review (London). May 30, 1936, v161, p704.
Scholastic. Feb 6, 1937, v30, p22.
Sight and Sound. Spr 1936, v5, p27.
Time. Jan 25, 1937, v29, p45.
Variety. Jan 20, 1937, p14.

Eternally Yours (US; Garnett, Tay; 1939)
Commonweal. Oct 20, 1939, v30, p587.
Film Daily. Oct 3, 1939, p6.
The Films of David Niven. p63-64.
Hollywood Reporter. Oct 10, 1939, p4.
Hollywood Spectator. Oct 28, 1939, v14, p8.
Motion Picture Herald. Oct 7, 1939, p38.
The New York Times. Oct 7, 1939, p11.
The New Yorker. Oct 14, 1939, v15, p89.
Photoplay. Nov 1939, v53, p64.
Time. Oct 16, 1939, v34, p101-02.
Variety. Oct 4, 1939, p12.

Evangeline (US; Walsh, Raoul; 1919)
Exhibitor's Trade Review. Aug 23, 1919, p991.
Motion Picture News. Aug 23, 1919, p1697.
The Moving Picture World. Aug 23, 1919, p1177.
The New York Times. Aug 20, 1919, p12.
Selected Film Criticism, 1912-1920. p83-84.
Variety. Aug 15, 1919, p71.
Variety. Aug 22, 1919, p77.
Wid's Daily. Aug 24, 1919, p3.

The Eve of St. Mark (US; Stahl, John M.; 1944)
Commonweal. Jun 16, 1944, v40, p205.
Film Daily. May 22, 1944, p6.
Hollywood Reporter. May 17, 1944, p3.
Nation. Jun 3, 1944, v158, p661.

The New Republic. Jun 19, 1944, v110, p816.
The New York Times. May 31, 1944, p22.
The New Yorker. Jun 3, 1944, v20, p61.
Newsweek. Jun 12, 1944, v23, p72.
Variety. May 17, 1944, p10.

Evelyn Prentice (US; Howard, William K.; 1934)
Film Daily. Nov 10, 1934, p4.
Hollywood Reporter. Oct 27, 1934, p3.
Motion Picture Herald. Nov 3, 1934, p36.
The New York Times. Nov 10, 1934, p19.
Time. Nov 19, 1934, v24, p26.
Variety. Nov 13, 1934, p15.

Evensong (GB; Saville, Victor; 1934)
Film Daily. Nov 14, 1934, p7.
Hollywood Reporter. Nov 20, 1934, p3.
Literary Digest. Dec 1, 1934, v118, p30.
Motion Picture Herald. Nov 3, 1934, p37.
The New York Times. Nov 17, 1934, p12.
Time. Nov 26, 1934, v24, p35.
Variety. Sep 25, 1934, p13.
Variety. Nov 20, 1934, p15.

Ever in My Heart (US; Mayo, Archie; 1933)
Film Daily. Oct 13, 1933, p10.
The Films of Barbara Stanwyck. p91-92.
Hollywood Reporter. Sep 22, 1933, p3.
Motion Picture Herald. Oct 21, 1933, p40.
The New York Times. Oct 13, 1933, p25.
Rob Wagner's Script. Oct 21, 1933, v10, p9-10.
Starring Miss Barbara Stanwyck. p58.
Time. Oct 23, 1933, v22, p44.
Variety. Oct 17, 1933, p19.

Ever Since Eve (US; Bacon, Lloyd; 1937)
Film Daily. Jun 22, 1937, p20.
Hollywood Reporter. Jun 18, 1937, p3.
Motion Picture Herald. Jun 26, 1937, p89.
The New York Times. Jun 25, 1937, p25.
Rob Wagner's Script. Jul 17, 1937, v17, p14.
Time. Jul 5, 1937, v30, p20.
Variety. Jun 30, 1937, p20.

Evergreen (GB; Saville, Victor; 1934)
The Age of the Dream Palace. p215-17.
Canadian Magazine. Oct 1934, v82, p38.
Esquire. Mar 1935, v3, p142.
Film Daily. Jan 11, 1935, p8.
The Great British Films. p19-20.
Hollywood Reporter. Jan 14, 1935, p3.
Jessie Matthews. p110-17+.
Magill's Survey of Cinema. Series II. v2, p728-30.
The Nation. Jan 23, 1935, v140, p112.
The New York Times. Jan 11, 1935, p29.
The New Yorker. Jan 19, 1935, v10, p59.
Photoplay. Mar 1935, v47, p94.
Selected Film Criticism: Foreign Films, 1930-1950. p49.
Time. Jan 21, 1935, v25, p32.
Vanity Fair. Feb 1935, v43, p43.
Variety. May 8, 1934, p14.
Variety. Jan 15, 1935, p13.

Every Day's a Holiday (US; Sutherland, Edward; 1937)
Film Daily. Dec 27, 1937, p8.
Films and Filming. Nov 1970, v17, p40.
Hollywood Reporter. Dec 20, 1937, p2.
Life. Jan 10, 1938, v4, p2-3.
Motion Picture Herald. Dec 25, 1937, p36+.
The New York Times. Jan 27, 1938, p17.
The New Yorker. Jan 29, 1938, v13, p48.
Newsweek. Jan 31, 1938, v11, p24-25.
Rob Wagner's Script. Jan 29, 1938, v18, p10.
Time. Jan 24, 1938, v31, p35.
Variety. Dec 22, 1937, p16.

Every Night at Eight (US; Walsh, Raoul; 1935)
Film Daily. Jul 30, 1935, p8.
The Films of Alice Faye. p49-52.
Hollywood Reporter. Jul 26, 1935, p3.
Motion Picture Herald. Aug 10, 1935, p52.
The New York Times. Aug 3, 1935, p16.
Rob Wagner's Script. Aug 10, 1935, v13, p10.
Time. Aug 12, 1935, v26, p34-35.
Variety. Aug 7, 1935, p21.

Everybody Sing (US; Marin, Edwin L.; 1938)
Canadian Magazine. Mar 1938, v89, p33.
Film Daily. Jan 26, 1938, p9.
Hollywood Reporter. Jan 19, 1938, p3.
Judy: The Films and Career of Judy Garland. p55-58.
Motion Picture Herald. Jan 22, 1938, p38.
The New York Times. Mar 11, 1938, p15.
The New Yorker. Mar 19, 1938, v14, p58.
Rob Wagner's Script. Feb 19, 1938, v19, p11.
Variety. Jan 26, 1938, p14.

Everybody's Old Man (US; Flood, James; 1936)
Film Daily. Mar 27, 1936, p9.
Hollywood Reporter. Mar 7, 1936, p3.
Motion Picture Herald. Mar 14, 1936, p56, 58.
The New York Times. Mar 26, 1936, p27.
Rob Wagner's Script. Apr 4, 1936, v15, p13.
Time. Mar 2, 1936, v27, p34+.
Variety. Apr 1, 1936, p16.

Everybody's Sweetheart (US; Trimble, Laurence; 1920)
Variety. Oct 8, 1920, p996.
Wid's Daily. Oct 24, 1920, p4.

Everything Happens at Night (US; Cummings, Irving; 1939)
Film Daily. Dec 18, 1939, p5.
Hollywood Reporter. Dec 16, 1939, p3.
Hollywood Spectator. Jan 6, 1940, v14, p6.
Motion Picture Herald. Dec 23, 1939, p41.
The New York Times. Dec 16, 1939, p12.
The Spectator. Jun 14, 1940, v164, p808.
Time. Jan 1, 1940, v35, p29.
Variety. Dec 30, 1939, p47.

Everything Is Thunder (GB; Rosmer, Milton; 1936)
Canadian Magazine. Nov 1936, v86, p38.
Film Daily. Nov 20, 1936, p9.
Graham Greene on Film. p94-95.
Hollywood Reporter. Aug 5, 1936, p6.
Motion Picture Herald. Sep 12, 1936, p48.
Rob Wagner's Script. Sep 26, 1936, v16, p11-12.
The Spectator. Aug 21, 1936, v157, p307.
Variety. Aug 5, 1936, p17.

Ewige Maske, Die *See* The Eternal Mask

Exclusive (US; Hall, Alexander; 1937)
Esquire. Oct 1937, v8, p121.
Film Daily. Jul 22, 1937, p12.
Graham Greene on Film. p175-76.
Hollywood Reporter. Jul 20, 1937, p3.
Hollywood Spectator. Jul 31, 1937, v12, p10.
Motion Picture Herald. Jul 31, 1937, p36.
The New Statesman and Nation. Oct 15, 1937, v14, p604.
The New York Times. Jul 22, 1937, p15.
Rob Wagner's Script. Jul 31, 1937, v17, p13-14.
Time. Jul 26, 1937, v30, p26.
Variety. Jul 21, 1937, p13.
World Film News. Dec 1937, v2, p31.

Exclusive Story (US; Seitz, George B.; 1936)
Film Daily. Jan 18, 1936, p7.
Hollywood Reporter. Jan 6, 1936, p3.
Hollywood Spectator. Jan 18, 1936, v10, p14.
Motion Picture Herald. Jan 18, 1936, p44.

The New York Times. Jan 18, 1936, p19.
The New Yorker. Jan 25, 1936, v11, p56.
Rob Wagner's Script. Feb 29, 1936, v15, p9.
Time. Jan 27, 1936, v27, p46.
Variety. Jan 22, 1936, p14.

The Ex-Convict (US; Porter, Edwin S.; 1906)
The Emergence of Film Art. p31.

Excursion (French title: Promenade en Bicyclette) (GER; Messter, Oskar; 1898)
Behind the Screen. p105-06.

Excuse My Dust (US; Wood, Sam; 1920)
The Moving Picture World. Mar 20, 1920, p2003.
Photoplay. Jun 1920, v18, p68.
Selected Film Criticism, 1912-1920. p84.
Variety. Mar 26, 1920, p51.
Wid's Daily. Mar 28, 1920, p5.

The Exile (US; Ophuls, Max; 1947)
Film Daily. Oct 17, 1947, p8.
Hollywood Reporter. Oct 15, 1947, p3.
Motion Picture Herald Product Digest. Oct 25, 1947, p3893.
The New York Times. Dec 26, 1947, p22.
Time. Dec 8, 1947, v50, p103.
Variety. Oct 15, 1947, p10.

Exit Smiling (US; Taylor, Sam; 1926)
The Films of the Twenties. p147-49.
Magill's Survey of Cinema. Silent Films. v1, p409-11.
The Moving Picture World. Nov 20, 1926, p166.
Selected Film Criticism, 1921-1930. p96.
Variety. Nov 10, 1926, p14.

Ex-Lady (US; Florey, Robert; 1933)
Bette Davis: Her Films and Career. p42-43.
Film Daily. May 13, 1933, p3.
Hollywood Reporter. Feb 7, 1933, p5.
Motion Picture Herald. Feb 18, 1933, p30.
The New York Times. May 15, 1933, p16.
Rob Wagner's Script. Jun 24, 1933, v9, p8.
Variety. May 16, 1933, p21.

The Ex-Mrs. Bradford (US; Roberts, Stephen; 1936)
Film Daily. Apr 23, 1936, p7.
Hollywood Reporter. Apr 20, 1936, p3.
Hollywood Spectator. Apr 25, 1936, v11, p10.
Literary Digest. Jun 6, 1936, v121, p20-21.
Lunatics and Lovers. p171-72.
Motion Picture Herald. May 2, 1936, p47.
The New Statesman and Nation. Jun 13, 1936, v11, p931.
The New York Times. May 28, 1936, p19.
The New Yorker. Jun 6, 1936, v12, p62-63.
Rob Wagner's Script. May 2, 1936, v15, p10.
Saturday Review (London). Jun 13, 1936, v161, p768.
Sight and Sound. Sum 1936, v5, p24-25.
The Spectator. Jun 12, 1936, v156, p1080.
Time. May 25, 1936, v27, p50.
Variety. Jun 3, 1936, p15.

The Exploits of Elaine (US; Goddard, Charles L.; 1914)
The Moving Picture World. Jan 2, 1915, p80.
Selected Film Criticism, 1912-1920. p84-85.

Extra Girl (US; Jones, F. Richard; 1923)
Film Daily. Jan 27, 1924, p7.
Magill's Survey of Cinema. Silent Films. v1, p412-14.
The New York Times. Jan 21, 1924, p20.
Variety. Jan 24, 1924, p26.

Eyes of Youth (US; Parker, Albert; 1919)
Exhibitor's Trade Review. Nov 15, 1919, p2049.
Fifty Great American Silent Films, 1912-1920. p110-11.
Magill's Survey of Cinema. Silent Films. v1, p415-17.
The Moving Picture World. Nov 15, 1919, p362.
Selected Film Criticism, 1912-1920. p85-86.

Variety. Nov 7, 1919, p98.
Wid's Daily. Nov 16, 1919, p3.

Faithless (US; Beaumont, Harry; 1932)
Film Daily. Nov 19, 1932, p4.
Hollywood Reporter. Oct 5, 1932, p2.
Motion Picture Herald. Oct 15, 1932, p64-65.
The New York Times. Nov 19, 1932, p20.
Time. Oct 31, 1932, v20, p21.
Variety. Nov 22, 1932, p17.
We're in the Money. p51-53.

The Fall of Babylon *See* Intolerance

The Fall of Babylon (US; 1910)
The Moving Picture World. Apr 16, 1910, p597.
Selected Film Criticism, 1896-1911. p37-38.

Fall of the House of Usher (French title: Chute de la
  Maison d'Usher, La) (FR; Epstein, Jean; 1928)
Cinema, the Magic Vehicle. v1, p144.
Magill's Survey of Cinema. Silent Films. v1, p418-21.

The Fall of the Romanoffs (US; Brenon, Herbert; 1917)
The Moving Picture World. Sep 22, 1917, p1859.
The New York Dramatic Mirror. Jul 28, 1917, p17.
The New York Dramatic Mirror. Aug 11, 1917, p13.
The New York Times. Sep 7, 1917, p9.
The New York Times. Sep 24, 1917, p11.
Selected Film Criticism, 1912-1920. p88-89.
Variety. Sep 14, 1917, p35.
Wid's Daily. Oct 11, 1917, p647.

The Fall of Troy (Italian title: Caduta di Troia, La) (IT;
  Pastrone, Giovanni; 1911)
The Bioscope. Feb 23, 1911, p55.
The Italian Cinema. p21.
Selected Film Criticism, 1896-1911. p36-37.

The Fallen Idol (GB; Reed, Carol; 1949)
Commonweal. Dec 2, 1949, v51, p238.
Film Daily. Oct 4, 1949, p8.
Films in Review. Feb 1950, v1, p37.
The Great British Films. p125-27.
Hollywoood Reporter. Nov 17, 1949, p4.
Library Journal. Feb 1, 1950, v75, p181.
Literature/Film Quarterly. Fall 1974, v2, p324-31.
Magill's Survey of Cinema. Series II. v2, p745-48.
Motion Picture Herald Product Digest. Jul 9, 1949, p4675.
The New Republic. Nov 21, 1949, v121, p22.
The New York Times. Nov 16, 1949, p39.
The New Yorker. Nov 19, 1949, v25, p110.
Newsweek. Oct 31, 1949, v34, p66.
Rotarian. Feb 1950, v76, p38.
Sequence. Wint 1948-49, v6, p40-41.
Sight and Sound. Wint 1948-49, v17, p182.
Theatre Arts. Aug 1949, v33, p97.
Variety. Oct 6, 1949, p11.

False Faces (US; Sherman, Lowell; 1932)
Film Daily. Nov 3, 1932, p6.
Hollywood Reporter. Sep 24, 1932, p3.
Motion Picture Herald. Dec 3, 1932, p30-31.
The New York Times. Nov 25, 1932, p19.
The New Yorker. Dec 3, 1932, v8, p73.
Variety. Nov 29, 1932, p19.

A Family Affair (US; Seitz, George B.; 1937)
Film Daily. Apr 22, 1937, p14.
Hollywood Reporter. Mar 6, 1937, p3.
Hollywood Spectator. Mar 13, 1937, v11, p10.
Magill's Survey of Cinema, Series II. v2, p749-52.
Motion Picture Herald. Mar 20, 1937, p49.
The New York Times. Apr 20, 1937, p29.
Variety. Apr 21, 1937, p14.

Family Honeymoon (US; Binyon, Claude; 1949)
Claudette Colbert (Quirk). p155-57.
Commonweal. Mar 25, 1949, v99, p592.
Film Daily. Dec 13, 1949, p8.
Motion Picture Herald Product Digest. Dec 18, 1949, p4425.
The New York Times. Feb 25, 1949, p28.
Time. Feb 14, 1949, v53, p92.
Variety. Dec 8, 1950, p11.

The Famous Ferguson Case (US; Bacon, Lloyd; 1932)
Film Daily. Apr 24, 1932, p10.
Hollywood Reporter. Mar 12, 1932, p3.
Judge. May 28, 1932, v102, p22.
Motion Picture Herald. Apr 30, 1932, p40, 42.
The New York Times. Apr 25, 1932, p18.
Variety. Apr 26, 1932, p13.

The Fan (Also titled: Lady Windermere's Fan) (US;
  Preminger, Otto; 1949)
The Cinema of Otto Preminger. p89-91+.
Commonweal. Apr 22, 1949, v50, p46.
Film Daily. Apr 7, 1949, p6.
Hollywood Reporter. Mar 31, 1949, p3.
Motion Picture Herald Product Digest. Apr 2, 1949, p4557.
The New Republic. Apr 18, 1949, v120, p31.
The New York Times. Apr 2, 1949, p12.
Newsweek. Apr 18, 1949, v33, p90.
Rotarian. Jul 1949, v125, p50.
Time. Apr 11, 1949, v53, p102.
Variety. Apr 6, 1949, p8.

Fanny *See* Port of Seven Seas

Fanny (FR; Allégret, Marc; 1932)
Cinema, the Magic Vehicle. v1, p212-13.
Classics of the Foreign Film. p84-87.
Commonweal. Feb 13, 1948, v47, p448.
Dictionary of Films. p210-11.
Film Daily. Mar 22, 1948, p8.
Film Society Review. Oct 1967, p11-13.
The Great French Films. p42-46.
Hollywood Reporter. Jan 22, 1948, p3.
The New Republic. Feb 2, 1948, v118, p34.
The New York Times. Feb 13, 1948, p26.
Newsweek. Feb 2, 1948, v31, p73.
Selected Film Criticism: Foreign Films, 1930-1950. p50-51.
Variety. Jan 21, 1948, p20.

Fantasia (US; 1940)
American Cinematographer. Dec 1940, v21, p558.
American Film Criticism. p391-96.
Around Cinemas. p222-24.
Art Digest. Dec 1, 1940, v15, p3, 10-11.
The Art of Walt Disney. p227-54.
Child Life. Jan 1941, v20, p21.
Classic Images. May 1982, n83, p54.
Classic Movies. p62-64.
Commonweal. Nov 29, 1940, v33, p152-53.
Commonweal. Jun 4, 1976, v103, p367-68.
The Disney Films. p38-45.
The Disney Version. p239-47.
The Film Criticism of Otis Ferguson. p317-18.
Film Daily. Nov 14, 1940, p5.
Filmmakers Monthly Newsletter. Mar 1980, v13, p62.
Films. Aug 1982, v2, p35.
Films and Filming. Apr 1979, v25, p40.
Films in Review. Nov 1968, v16, p529-35.
The Great Films. p143-46.
Halliwell's Hundred. p81-84.
Hollywood Spectator. Feb 15, 1941, v15, p13.
Independent Woman. Jan 1941, v20, p15.
The International Dictionary of Films and Filmmakers. v1,
  p149-52.
Journal of Aesthetics and Art Criticism. 1942, v2, n1, p27-31.
Landmark Films. p164-75.

Life. Apr 3, 1940, v68, p15.
The London Times. Jul 25, 1941, p6.
Lorentz on Film. p204-08.
Magic Moments from the Movies. p80-81.
Magill's Survey of Cinema. Series I. v2, p513-16.
Mickey Mouse: 50 Happy Years. p177-83.
Millimeter. Feb 1976, v4, p18-24+.
Motion Picture Exhibitor. Nov 27, 1940, p647-48.
Motion Picture Exhibitor. Jan 28, 1941, v27, n12, sec2, p938.
Motion Picture Herald Product Digest. Nov 16, 1940, p2.
Movie Maker. May 1983, v17, p282-83.
Musician. Dec 1940, v45, p217.
The Nation. Nov 23, 1940, v151, p513+.
The Nation. Nov 30, 1940, v151, p543.
The Nation. Jan 11, 1941, v152, p53-54.
The Nation. May 10, 1941, v152, p566.
The Nation. Nov 8, 1941, v153, p465.
The New Republic. Nov 25, 1945, v103, p724.
New Statesman. Mar 30, 1979, v97, p456-57.
The New York Times. Nov 14, 1940, p28.
The New York Times. Nov 17, 1940, sec9 p7.
The New York Times. Nov 17, 1963, sec2, p1.
The New York Times. May 28, 1978, sec2 p11.
The New York Times. Nov 5, 1982, pC4.
The New York Times Magazine. Nov 3, 1940, p6-7+.
The New York Times Magazine. Nov 24, 1940, sec9, p7.
The New Yorker. Nov 23, 1940, v16, p63-64+.
Newsweek. Nov 25, 1940, v106, p50-51.
Popular Mechanics. Jan 1942, v77, p34-37.
Popular Science. Jan 1941, v138, p65-67.
Scholastic. Dec 9, 1940, v37, p34.
Scientific American. Jan 1941, v164, p28-30.
Scribner's Commentator. Jan 1941, v9, p105-06.
Selected Film Criticism, 1941-1950. p55-56.
Stage. Nov 1940, v1, p78-81.
Surrealism and the Cinema. p140-41.
Theatre Arts. Dec 1940, v24, p870-71.
Theatre Arts. Jan 1941, v25, p55-61.
Time. Nov 18, 1940, v36, p52-55.
Variety. Nov 13, 1940, p16.
Walt Disney: A Guide to References and Resources. p19-21.
Walt Disney's Fantasia. 1983.

Farewell Again (GB; Whelan, Tim; 1937)
Hollywood Reporter. Jun 8, 1937, p10.
Hollywood Reporter. Oct 12, 1937, p3.
Literary Digest. Nov 13, 1937, v124, p34.
London Mercury. Jun 1937, v36, p188.
Motion Picture Herald. May 22, 1937, p60.
The New Statesman and Nation. May 15, 1937, v13, p812.
Rob Wagner's Script. Oct 16, 1937, v18, p9.
Sight and Sound. Aut 1937, v6, p138-39.
The Spectator. May 14, 1937, v158, p903.
Variety. May 19, 1937, p22.
World Film News. Jul 1937, v2, p22.

Farewell, My Lovely *See* Murder, My Sweet

A Farewell to Arms (US; Borzage, Frank; 1932)
America in the Dark. p214-15.
The Classic American Novel and the Movies. p297-304.
Classic Film Collector. Wint 1973, n41, p9.
Film Daily. Dec 10, 1932, p18.
The Films of Gary Cooper. p106-08.
Hemingway on Film. p6-16.
Judge. Jan 1933, v104, p15, 29.
Lorentz on Film. p104-05.
Love in the Film. p92-94.
Magill's Survey of Cinema, Series I. v2, p524-26.
The Nation. Jan 4, 1933, v136, p28.
The New Outlook. Jan 1933, v161, p47.
The New York Times. Dec 9, 1932, p26.
The New Yorker. Dec 17, 1932, v8, p57-58.
Rob Wagner's Script. Dec 31, 1932, v8, p8.
Selected Film Criticism, 1931-1940. p72.

Stage. Jan 1933, v10, p42.
Time. Dec 19, 1932, v20, p28.
Vanity Fair. Jan 1933, v39, p62.
Variety. Dec 13, 1932, p14.
World Film News. Aug 1938, v3, p174.

The Farmer Takes a Wife (US; Fleming, Victor; 1935)
Commonweal. Aug 30, 1935, v22, p427.
Film Daily. Jun 11, 1935, p10.
The Films of Henry Fonda. p35-39.
The Fondas (Springer). p52-54.
Hollywood Reporter. Jun 10, 1935, p3.
Literary Digest. Aug 17, 1935, v120, p28.
Motion Picture Herald. Jul 20, 1935, p85.
Movie Classic. Sep 1935, v9, p18+.
The New York Times. Aug 9, 1935, p21.
The New Yorker. Aug 17, 1935, v11, p46.
Time. Aug 19, 1935, v26, p27.

The Farmer's Daughter (US; Potter, H.C.; 1947)
Film Daily. Feb 24, 1947, p7.
The Films of the Forties. p191-93.
Hollywood Reporter. Feb 27, 1947, p3.
Life. May 5, 1947, v22, p67-68.
Motion Picture Herald Product Digest. Mar 1, 1947, p3502.
The Nation. Apr 12, 1947, v164, p433.
New Republic. Apr 14, 1947, v116, p40.
The New York Times. Mar 26, 1947, p31.
The New Yorker. Apr 5, 1947, v23, p83.
Newsweek. Apr 7, 1947, v29, p87.
Time. Apr 7, 1947, v49, p100.
Variety. Feb 29, 1947, p6.

Farrebique (FR; Rouquier, Georges; 1948)
Agee on Film. v1, p296-99.
Commonweal. Mar 5, 1948, v47, p522.
Film Daily. Mar 22, 1948, p9.
Hollywood Reporter. Mar 1, 1948, p3.
The International Dictionary of Films and Filmmakers. v1, p153.
Museum of Modern Art Film Notes. Apr 4, 1978, p4.
The Nation. Mar 13, 1948, v166, p312-13.
The New Republic. Mar 1, 1948, v118, p26-27.
The New York Times. Feb 24, 1948, p21.
The New Yorker. Mar 6, 1948, v24, p74.
Newsweek. Mar 8, 1948, v31, p83.
Sight and Sound. Wint 1946-47, p67.
Time. Mar 15, 1948, v51, p100+.

Fashions of 1934 (Also titled: The Fashions of 1934) (US; Dieterle, William; 1934)
The Busby Berkeley Book. p78-81.
Film Daily. Jan 9, 1934, p7.
Hollywood Reporter. Dec 29, 1933, p3.
Motion Picture Herald. Jan 13, 1934, p38.
The New York Times. Jan 20, 1934, p12.
Newsweek. Jan 20, 1934, v3, p34.
Variety. Jan 23, 1934, p13.

Fast and Furious (US; Berkeley, Busby; 1939)
The Busby Berkeley Book. p126.
Film Daily. Oct 20, 1939, p6.
Hollywood Reporter. Oct 4, 1939, p3.
Hollywood Spectator. Oct 14, 1939, v14, p9.
Motion Picture Herald. Oct 7, 1939, p39.
The New York Times. Oct 12, 1939, p33.
Variety. Oct 18, 1939, p14.

Fast and Loose (US; Newmeyer, Fred; 1930)
Exhibitors Herald-World. Nov 29, 1930, p32-33.
Film Daily. Nov 30, 1930, p10.
The Films of Carole Lombard. p78-80.
Life. Dec 26, 1930, v96, p21.
The Nation. Dec 14, 1930, v131, p713-14.
The New York Times. Dec 1, 1930, p21.

Time. Dec 15, 1930, v16, p34.
Variety. Dec 3, 1930, p14.

Fast and Loose (US; Marin, Edwin L.; 1939)
Commonweal. Mar 3, 1939, v29, p525.
Film Daily. Feb 17, 1939, p6.
Hollywood Reporter. Feb 11, 1939, p3.
Hollywood Spectator. Feb 18, 1939, v13, p10.
Motion Picture Herald. Feb 18, 1939, p48.
The New York Times. Mar 9, 1939, p18.
Rob Wagner's Script. Mar 25, 1939, v21, p16.
Time. Feb 27, 1939, v33, p30.
Variety. Feb 15, 1939, p12.

Fast Company (US; Buzzell, Edward; 1938)
Film Daily. Jun 30, 1938, p7.
Hollywood Reporter. Jun 25, 1938, p3.
Motion Picture Herald. Jul 2, 1938, p40+.
The New York Times. Jul 6, 1938, p21.
Variety. Jun 29, 1938, p12.
World Film News. Sep 1938, v3, p222.

Fast Life (US; Pollard, Harry; 1932)
Film Daily. Dec 24, 1932, p4.
The New York Times. Dec 24, 1932, p11.
Rob Wagner's Script. Dec 10, 1932, v8, p8.
Time. Dec 26, 1932, v20, p36.
Variety. Dec 27, 1932, p54.

Father Was a Fullback (US; Stahl, John M.; 1949)
Commonweal. Oct 28, 1949, v51, p70.
Film Daily. Aug 15, 1949, p8.
Hollywood Reporter. Aug 15, 1949, p3.
Motion Picture Herald Product Digest. Aug 20, 1949, p4721.
The New York Times. Oct 13, 1949, p33.
Newsweek. Oct 24, 1949, v34, p88.
Rotarian. Dec 1949, v75, p38.
Senior Scholastic. Oct 12, 1949, v55, p19.
Time. Oct 31, 1949, v54, p76.
Variety. Aug 17, 1949, p8.

Faust (GER; Murnau, F.W.; 1926)
Film Daily. Dec 12, 1926, p9.
From Caligari to Hitler. p148-49.
From Quasimodo to Scarlett O'Hara. p69-72.
The Haunted Screen. p105-06.
Magill's Survey of Cinema. Silent Films. v1, p422-24.
The Moving Picture World. Dec 11, 1926, p440.
Murnau (Eisner). p154-166.
The New York Times. Dec 7, 1926, p21.
Photoplay. Jan 1927, v31, p52.
Selected Film Criticism, 1921-1930. p96-97.
Spellbound in Darkness. p450.
Variety. Nov 17, 1926, p16.
Variety. Dec 8, 1926, p16.

Fazil (US; Hawks, Howard; 1928)
Exhibitor's Herald-World and Moving Picture World. Dec 1, 1928, p58-59.
Film Daily. May 10, 1928, p8.
The Film Spectator. Jul 7, 1928, v5, p6.
Hawks on Hawks. p22-23.
The New York Times. Jun 5, 1928, p21.
Variety. Jun 6, 1928, p13.

The Feast of Life (US; Capellani, Albert; 1916)
The Moving Picture World. May 13, 1916, p1176, 1230.
The New York Dramatic Mirror. May 6, 1916, p32.
Variety. Apr 28, 1916, p29.
Wid's Daily. May 4, 1916, p553.

A Feather in Her Hat (US; Santell, Alfred; 1935)
Film Daily. Oct 25, 1935, p10.
Hollywood Reporter. Nov 1, 1935, p3.
The New York Times. Oct 25, 1935, p24.
Variety. Oct 30, 1935, p14.

Feet First (US; Lloyd, Harold; 1930)
Exhibitors Herald-World. Oct 18, 1930, p44.
Exhibitors Herald-World. Nov 8, 1930, p41.
Film Daily. Nov 2, 1930, p10.
Harold Lloyd: The King of Daredevil Comedy. p114-19.
Harold Lloyd: The Shape of Laughter. p196-203.
Judge. Nov 29, 1930, v99, p19.
Life. Nov 28, 1930, v96, p20.
The New Republic. Dec 10, 1930, v65, p103.
The New Statesman and Nation. Mar 28, 1931, v1, p186.
The New York Times. Oct 31, 1930, p20.
The New York Times. Nov 9, 1930, p5.
Outlook and Independent. Nov 12, 1930, v156, p431.
Time. Nov 10, 1930, v16, p68.
Variety. Nov 5, 1930, p23.

Female (US; Curtiz, Michael; 1933)
Canadian Magazine. Dec 1933, v80, p38.
Film Daily. Nov 4, 1933, p4.
Hollywood Reporter. Oct 11, 1933, p3.
Literary Digest. Nov 18, 1933, v116, p37.
Motion Picture Herald. Oct 21, 1933, p39.
The New York Times. Nov 14, 1933, p18.
The New Yorker. Nov 11, 1933, v9, p58-59.
Variety. Nov 7, 1933, p16.

Femme du Boulanger, La (Also titled: The Baker's Wife)
(FR; Pagnol, Marcel; 1938)
Around Cinemas. p166-68.
Canadian Forum. Jun 1946, v26, p63+.
Cinema, the Magic Vehicle. v1, p315-16.
Classics of the Foreign Film. p118-19.
Commonweal. Mar 8, 1940, v31, p436.
Dictionary of Films. p113.
The French Literary Filmmakers. p60-61.
The Golden Age of French Cinema, 1929-1939. p99-104.
Graham Greene on Film. p227.
The Great French Films. p84-87.
Hollywood Spectator. Jun 1, 1940, v15, p11.
Kiss Kiss Bang Bang. p287-88.
Magill's Survey of Cinema. Foreign Language Films. v1, p203-06.
Marcel Pagnol. p105-10.
Motion Picture Herald. Mar 2, 1940, p35.
National Board of Review Magazine. Mar 1940, v15, p17.
The New Republic. Apr 8, 1940, v102, p474.
The New Statesman and Nation. Feb 25, 1939, v17, p281.
The New York Times. Feb 27, 1940, p17.
The New Yorker. Mar 2, 1940, v16, p55.
Rob Wagner's Script. May 25, 1940, v23, p17.
Saint Cinema: Selected Writings, 1929-1970. p91-92.
Selected Film Criticism: Foreign Films, 1930-1950. p9-10.
The Spectator. Feb 24, 1939, v162, p301.
The Spectator. Jun 9, 1939, v162, p997.
The Tatler. Jun 7, 1939, v152, p428.
Theatre Arts. May 1940, v24, p321.
Variety. Oct 12, 1938, p19.

Fifth Avenue Girl (US; La Cava, Gregory; 1939)
Commonweal. Sep 1, 1939, v30, p439.
The Film Criticism of Otis Ferguson. p268.
Film Daily. Aug 22, 1939, p17.
Hollywood Reporter. Aug 17, 1939, p3.
Hollywood Spectator. Sep 2, 1939, v14, p11.
Motion Picture Herald. Aug 26, 1939, p50.
The New Masses. Aug 29, 1939, v32, p31.
The New Republic. Sep 6, 1939, v100, p132.
The New York Times. Aug 25, 1939, p12.
The New Yorker. Aug 26, 1939, v15, p55-56.
Rob Wagner's Script. Sep 16, 1939, v22, p14.
The Spectator. Feb 9, 1940, v164, p179.
Time. Aug 28, 1939, v34, p47.
Variety. Aug 23, 1939, p14.

Fifty Million Frenchmen (US; Bacon, Lloyd; 1931)
Film Daily. Mar 29, 1931, p10.
Life. Apr 10, 1931, v97, p20.
Motion Picture Herald. Jan 3, 1931, p74.
The New York Times. Mar 26, 1931, p31.
The New Yorker. Apr 4, 1931, v7, p73, 75.
Time. Apr 6, 1931, v17, p55.
Variety. Apr 1, 1931, p16.

Fifty Roads to Town (US; Taurog, Norman; 1937)
Film Daily. Mar 29, 1937, p5.
Hollywood Reporter. Mar 25, 1937, p3.
Motion Picture Herald. Apr 3, 1937, p40.
The New York Times. Jun 5, 1937, p21.
The New Yorker. Jun 5, 1937, v13, p62.
Rob Wagner's Script. May 1, 1937, v17, p8.
Scholastic. Apr 24, 1937, v30, p28.
Time. Apr 12, 1937, v29, p46.
Variety. Jun 9, 1937, p15.

Fifty-Second Street (US; Young, Harold; 1937)
Film Daily. Nov 17, 1937, p8.
Hollywood Reporter. Oct 2, 1937, p3.
Life. Nov 29, 1937, v3, p64-67.
Motion Picture Herald. Oct 9, 1937, p39.
The New York Times. Nov 15, 1937, p15.
The Tatler. Dec 8, 1937, v146, p432.
Time. Nov 22, 1937, v30, p52.
Variety. Oct 6, 1937, p12.

Fighter Squadron (US; Walsh, Raoul; 1948)
Commonweal. Dec 17, 1948, v49, p259.
Film Daily. Nov 19, 1948, p8.
Motion Picture Herald Product Digest. Nov 20, 1948, p4389.
The New York Times. Nov 20, 1948, p9.
Newsweek. Dec 6, 1948, v32, p94+.
Rotarian. Feb 1949, v74, p35.
Time. Dec 6, 1948, v52, p107.
Variety. Nov 24, 1948, p6.

Fighting Blood (US; Griffith, D.W.; 1911)
The Moving Picture World. Jul 8, 1911, p1575.
Selected Film Criticism, 1896-1911. p39-40.

Fighting Father Dunne (US; Tetzlaff, Ted; 1948)
Agee on Film. v1, p310.
Commonweal. Jun 18, 1948, v48, p235.
Film Daily. May 12, 1948, p8.
Hollywood Reporter. May 12, 1948, p3.
Motion Picture Herald Product Digest. May 15, 1948, p4161.
The New York Times. Jun 25, 1948, p26.
The New Yorker. Jul 3, 1948, v24, p58.
Time. Aug 2, 1948, v52, p74.
Variety. May 12, 1948, p20.

The Fighting O'Flynn (US; Pierson, Arthur; 1949)
Commonweal. Mar 11, 1949, v69, p543.
Film Daily. Jan 5, 1949, p8.
Hollywood Reporter. Jan 5, 1949, p3.
Motion Picture Herald Product Digest. Jan 8, 1949, p4449.
The New York Times. Feb 28, 1949, p16.
Rotarian. May 1949, v74, p34.
Time. Feb 21, 1949, v53, p105.
Variety. Jan 5, 1949, p58.

The Fighting Seabees (US; Ludwig, Edward; 1944)
Commonweal. Feb 25, 1944, v39, p471.
The Complete Films of John Wayne. p135.
Film Daily. Jan 19, 1944, p6.
The Films of Susan Hayward. p91-94.
The New York Times. Mar 20, 1944, p14.
Newsweek. Mar 6, 1944, v23, p80.
Scholastic. Mar 27, 1944, v44, p38.
Variety. Jan 19, 1944, p30.

The Fighting Sixty-Ninth (US; Keighley, William; 1939)
Commonweal. Dec 29, 1939, v30, p227.
Commonweal. Feb 9, 1940, v31, p348.
Film Daily. Jan 5, 1940, p5.
Film Daily. Jan 25, 1940, p9.
The Films of World War II. p29-30.
Hollywood Reporter. Jan 4, 1940, p3.
Life. Jan 20, 1940, v8, p32-34.
Motion Picture Herald. Jan 13, 1940, p36.
The Nation. Feb 17, 1940, v150, p262.
The New Masses. Feb 13, 1939, v34, p29.
The New York Times. Jan 27, 1940, p9.
The New Yorker. Jan 27, 1939, v15, p49.
Photoplay. Mar 1940, v54, p62.
Time. Feb 12, 1940, v35, p73.
Variety. Jan 10, 1940, p14.

Fille de l'Eau, La *See* Miracle of the Wolves

Fille du Puisatier *See* The Well-Digger's Daughter

Fin du Jour, La (Also titled: The End of the Day) (FR;
    Duvivier, Julien; 1939)
Cinema, the Magic Vehicle. v1, p312-13.
Commonweal. Sep 15, 1939, v30, p481.
Film Daily. Sep 18, 1939, p19.
From Quasimodo to Scarlett O'Hara. p325-26.
Hollywood Reporter. Nov 4, 1939, p3.
Motion Picture Herald. Sep 16, 1939, p28.
The Nation. Sep 23, 1939, v149, p329-30.
National Board of Review Magazine. Nov 1939, v14, p16.
The New Masses. Sep 19, 1939, v32, p29.
The New York Times. Sep 12, 1939, p28.
The New Yorker. Sep 16, 1939, v15, p62.
Rob Wagner's Script. Nov 18, 1939, v22, p16-17.
Time. Sep 25, 1939, v33, p33.
Variety. May 3, 1939, p16.

The Finger Points (US; Dillon, John Francis; 1931)
Film Daily. Mar 29, 1931, p10.
The Great Gangster Pictures. p140-41.
Hollywood Spectator. Jun 20, 1931, v12, p10.
Judge. Apr 26, 1931, v100, p28.
Life. May 1, 1931, v97, p22.
Motion Picture Herald. Mar 21, 1931, p42.
The New Statesman and Nation. Aug 1, 1931, v2, p141.
The New York Times. Mar 28, 1931, p15.
The New York Times. Apr 5, 1931, p5.
The New Yorker. Apr 4, 1931, v7, p73.
Outlook and Independent. Apr 15, 1931, v157, p539.
Time. Apr 6, 1931, v17, p55.
Variety. Apr 8, 1931, p18.

Finn and Hattie (US; Taurog, Norman; McLeod, Norman
    Z.; 1931)
Film Daily. Feb 1, 1931, p10.
Life. Feb 13, 1931, v97, p18.
Motion Picture Herald. Feb 7, 1931, p51-52.
The New York Times. Jan 31, 1931, p15.
The New York Times. Apr 5, 1931, p5.
The New Yorker. Feb 7, 1931, v6, p67, 69.
Outlook and Independent. Feb 11, 1931, v157, p233.
Photoplay. Nov 1931, v40, p124.
Pictures Will Talk. p36-37.
Rob Wagner's Script. Apr 25, 1931, v5, p12.
Time. Feb 9, 1931, v17, p26.
Variety. Feb 4, 1931, p16.

Fire Over England (GB; Howard, William K.; 1937)
The Age of the Dream Palace. p166.
Canadian Magazine. May 1937, v87, p31.
Commonweal. Feb 26, 1937, v25, p502.
Film Daily. Jan 14, 1937, p9.
The Films of James Mason. p46.
The Films of Laurence Olivier. p72-73.
Graham Greene on Film. p135-36.

The Great British Films. p36-38.
Hollywood Reporter. Jan 9, 1937, p3.
Hollywood Spectator. Jan 16, 1937, v11, p7-8.
Judge. Mar 1937, v112, p21.
Laurence Olivier: Theater and Cinema. p53-56.
Life. Feb 1, 1937, v2, p46-49.
Literary Digest. Mar 13, 1937, v123, p24.
London Mercury. Apr 1937, v35, p624.
Lorentz on Film. p140-41.
Magill's Survey of Cinema. Series I. v2, p534-37.
Motion Picture Herald. Jan 16, 1937, p28.
The New Statesman and Nation. Mar 6, 1937, v13, p369.
The New York Times. Mar 5, 1937, p16.
The New Yorker. Mar 6, 1937, v13, p61.
Newsweek. Feb 27, 1937, v9, p22.
Photoplay. Jan 1937, v51, p78.
Rob Wagner's Script. Jun 12, 1937, v37, p8.
Scholastic. Apr 3, 1937, v30, p21.
Selected Film Criticism: Foreign Films, 1930-1950. p51-54.
The Spectator. Mar 5, 1937, v158, p403.
Stage. Apr 1937, v14, p58-59.
Time. Mar 15, 1937, v29, p36+.
Variety. Mar 10, 1937, p14.
Variety. Jan 27, 1937, p12.

The Firefly (US; Leonard, Robert Z.; 1937)
Film Daily. Sep 2, 1937, p9.
The Films of Jeanette MacDonald and Nelson Eddy. p205-12.
The Great Spy Films. p176-77.
The Hollywood Musical. p131-32.
Hollywood Reporter. Jul 21, 1937, p3.
Hollywood Spectator. Jul 31, 1937, v12, p9-10.
McCall's. Nov 1937, v64, p19, 38.
Motion Picture Herald. Jul 24, 1937, p46.
The New Masses. Sep 14, 1937, v24, p29.
The New York Times. Sep 2, 1937, p17.
The New Yorker. Sep 4, 1937, v13, p60.
Rob Wagner's Script. Aug 14, 1937, v17, p14.
Saint Nicholas. Jul 1937, v64, p37.
Time. Aug 23, 1937, v30, p50.
Variety. Jul 28, 1937, p16.

Fireman Save My Child (US; Sutherland, Edward; 1927)
Film Daily. Oct 16, 1927, p7.
The New York Times. Oct 10, 1927, p24.
Variety. Aug 31, 1927, p24.

Fireman, Save My Child (US; Bacon, Lloyd; 1932)
Film Daily. Feb 21, 1932, p10.
Hollywood Reporter. Jan 27, 1932, p3.
Motion Picture Herald. Feb 27, 1932, p36, 40.
The New York Times. Feb 18, 1932, p25.
Rob Wagner's Script. Mar 26, 1932, v7, p12-13.
Variety. Feb 23, 1932, p19.

Fires of Faith (US; José, Edward; 1919)
Exhibitor's Trade Review. May 17, 1919, p1837.
Motion Picture News. May 17, 1919, p3282.
The Moving Picture World. May 17, 1919, p1069.
The New York Times. May 6, 1919, p16.
Variety. May 9, 1919, p52.
Wid's Daily. May 11, 1919, p17.

First a Girl (GB; Saville, Victor; 1935)
Canadian Magazine. Feb 1936, v85, p37.
Hollywood Reporter. Dec 13, 1935, p4.
Literary Digest. Dec 28, 1935, v120, p22.
Motion Picture Herald. Nov 30, 1935, p64.
The New York Times. Jan 4, 1936, p19.
The New Yorker. Jan 11, 1936, v11, p63-64.
Rob Wagner's Script. Jan 25, 1936, v14, p8.
Time. Jan 13, 1936, v27, p43.
Variety. Nov 20, 1935, p39.
Variety. Jan 8, 1936, p12.

The First Hundred Years (US; Thorpe, Richard; 1938)
Film Daily. Feb 14, 1938, p6.
Hollywood Reporter. Mar 9, 1938, p3.
Motion Picture Herald. Mar 12, 1938, p42-43.
The New Yorker. Apr 16, 1938, v14, p54.
Rob Wagner's Script. Apr 2, 1938, v19, p11.
Variety. Mar 16, 1938, p15.

First Lady (US; Logan, Stanley; 1937)
Film Daily. Sep 3, 1937, p9.
Hollywood Reporter. Aug 31, 1937, p3.
Hollywood Spectator. Sep 11, 1937, v12, p18-19.
Motion Picture Herald. Sep 11, 1937, p51.
The New York Times. Dec 23, 1937, p25.
The New Yorker. Dec 25, 1937, v13, p45.
Newsweek. Dec 13, 1937, v10, p30.
Rob Wagner's Script. Dec 11, 1937, v18, p13.
Scholastic. Dec 11, 1937, v31, p19.
Time. Dec 13, 1937, v30, p24.
Variety. Sep 1, 1937, p22.

First Love (US; Koster, Henry; 1939)
Commonweal. Nov 24, 1939, v31, p119.
Film Daily. Nov 3, 1939, p6.
Graham Greene on Film. p258.
Hollywood Reporter. Nov 1, 1939, p3.
Hollywood Spectator. Nov 11, 1939, v14, p6.
Love in the Film. p155-58.
Motion Picture Herald. Nov 4, 1939, p46.
The New Statesman and Nation. Dec 16, 1939, v18, p893.
The New York Times. Sep 12, 1939, p13.
The New Yorker. Nov 11, 1939, v15, p69.
Newsweek. Nov 13, 1939, v14, p33.
Rob Wagner's Script. Nov 25, 1939, v22, p16-17.
Scholastic. Nov 20, 1939, v35, p33.
The Spectator. Dec 22, 1939, v163, p900.
Time. Nov 20, 1939, v34, p80.
Variety. Nov 8, 1939, p14.

First of the Few *See* Spitfire

Five Came Back (US; Farrow, John; 1939)
Commonweal. Jun 30, 1939, v30, p259.
Film Daily. Jun 12, 1939, p11.
Hollywood Reporter. Jun 7, 1939, p3.
The New York Times. Jul 5, 1939, p20.
The New Yorker. Jul 8, 1939, v15, p69-70.
Rob Wagner's Script. Jun 17, 1939, v21, p17.
Time. Jun 26, 1939, v33, p45.
Variety. Jun 21, 1939, p16.

Five Graves to Cairo (US; Wilder, Billy; 1943)
Billy Wilder (Dick). p39-42.
Commonweal. Jun 11, 1943, v38, p203.
The Film Career of Billy Wilder. p67-69.
Film Daily. May 4, 1943, p8.
The Films of World War II. p128-29.
Hollywood Reporter. May 4, 1943, p3.
Magill's Survey of Cinema. Series II. v2, p789-91.
Motion Picture Herald Product Digest. May 8, 1943, p1301.
The New York Times. May 27, 1943, p21.
The New York Times. May 30, 1943, sec2, p3.
The New Yorker. Jun 5, 1943, v19, p48.
Newsweek. May 31, 1943, v21, p87-88.
Rob Wagner's Script. Jun 12, 1943, v29, p14.
Selected Film Criticism, 1941-1950. p59-60.
Time. May 24, 1943, v41, p98.
Variety. May 5, 1943, p8.

Five of a Kind (US; Leeds, Herbert I.; 1938)
Commonweal. Nov 11, 1938, v29, p77.
Film Daily. Oct 14, 1938, p6.
Hollywood Reporter. Oct 8, 1938, p3.
Motion Picture Herald. Oct 15, 1938, p37.
The New York Times. Oct 31, 1938, p12.
The New Yorker. Oct 29, 1938, v14, p58.

Rob Wagner's Script. Nov 26, 1938, v20, p13-14.
Time. Oct 31, 1938, v32, p26+.
Variety. Oct 12, 1938, p15.

Five Star Final (US; LeRoy, Mervyn; 1931)
Commonweal. Sep 30, 1931, v14, p525.
Film Daily. Sep 13, 1931, p10.
The Hollywood Professionals. v5, p138-40.
Life. Oct 2, 1931, v98, p18.
Motion Picture Herald. Jun 27, 1931, p35.
The New York Times. Sep 11, 1931, p24.
The New York Times. Sep 20, 1931, p5.
The New Yorker. Sep 19, 1931, v7, p67.
Outlook and Independent. Sep 30, 1931, v159, p153.
Rob Wagner's Script. Nov 7, 1931, v6, p8.
Scrutiny. May 1932, v1, p63-64.
Time. Sep 21, 1931, v18, p41.
Variety. Sep 15, 1931, p14.

The Flame of New Orleans (US; Clair, René; 1941)
Film Daily. Apr 24, 1941, p7.
The Films of Marlene Dietrich. p148-51.
Hollywood Reporter. Apr 24, 1941, p3.
Motion Picture Herald Product Digest. Apr 26, 1941, p53.
The New York Times. Apr 26, 1941, p20.
René Clair (McGerr). p138-42.
Scribner's Commentator. Jul 1941, v10, p106.
Variety. Apr 13, 1941, p16.

The Flame Within (US; Goulding, Edmund; 1935)
Film Daily. Jun 1, 1935, p4.
Hollywood Reporter. May 2, 1935, p3.
Motion Picture Herald. May 18, 1935, p47.
The New York Times. Jun 1, 1935, p18.
The New Yorker. Jun 8, 1935, v11, p62.
Rob Wagner's Script. May 25, 1935, v13, p7-8.
Time. Jun 10, 1935, v25, p26.
Variety. Jun 5, 1935, p15.

Flamingo Road (US; Curtiz, Michael; 1949)
Commonweal. Apr 29, 1949, v50, p69.
Film Daily. Apr 7, 1949, p8.
The Films of Joan Crawford. p170-71.
Hollywood Reporter. Apr 5, 1949, p3.
Motion Picture Herald Product Digest. Apr 9, 1949, p4565.
The New Republic. May 16, 1949, v120, p22.
The New York Times. May 7, 1949, p10.
Newsweek. May 16, 1949, v33, p84.
Rotarian. Jul 1949, v75, p36.
Time. May 2, 1949, v53, p90.
Variety. Apr 6, 1949, p8.

Flamme, Die (GER; Lubitsch, Ernst; 1924)
Ernst Lubitsch: A Guide to References and Resources. p.
Exceptional Photoplays. Feb-Mar 1924, p5.
Film Daily. Jul 6, 1924, p11.
The Moving Picture World. Oct 11, 1924, p523.
Variety. Jul 9, 1924, p25.

Flash Gordon (US; Stephani, Frederick; 1936)
Album of Great Science Fiction Films. p43-49.
Cinema of the Fantastic. p125-30.
Fifty Years of Serial Thrills. p133-45.
The Great Science Fiction Pictures. p125-27.
Magill's Survey of Cinema. Series II. v2, p796-99.
Motion Picture Herald. Mar 14, 1936, p60-61.
The Serials. p97-106.
Variety. Mar 11, 1936, p27.
50 Classic Motion Pictures. p104-09.

Flash Gordon's Trip to Mars (Also titled: The Deadly Ray from Mars) (US; Beebe, Ford; Hill, Robert; 1938)
Film Daily. Feb 16, 1938, p7.
Hollywood Reporter. Mar 7, 1938, p3.
Motion Picture Herald. Feb 19, 1938, p47.

Time. Mar 28, 1938, v31, p36+.
Variety. Feb 16, 1938, p17.

Flesh (US; Ford, John; 1932)
Film Daily. Dec 10, 1932, p18.
Hollywood Reporter. Dec 1, 1932, p3.
Motion Picture Herald. Dec 17, 1932, p34.
The New York Times. Dec 10, 1932, p19.
The Non-Western Films of John Ford. p230-31.
Time. Dec 19, 1932, v20, p28.
Variety. Dec 13, 1932, p14.

Flesh and Blood (US; Cummings, Irving; 1922)
Film Daily. Aug 27, 1922, p9.
Variety. Mar 21, 1951, p7.

Flesh and the Devil (US; Brown, Clarence; 1927)
Exceptional Photoplays. Feb 1927, v2, p11-13.
Film Daily. Jan 16, 1927, p6.
The Film Mercury. Dec 24, 1926, v5, p19.
The Films of Greta Garbo. p52-56.
From Quasimodo to Scarlett O'Hara. p82-85.
Magill's Survey of Cinema. Silent Films. v2, p431-33.
The Moving Picture World. Jan 15, 1927.
The New York Times. Jan 10, 1927, p20.
Photoplay. Feb 1927, v31, p52.
Selected Film Criticism, 1921-1930. p97-98.
Spellbound in Darkness. p450-52.
Variety. Jan 12, 1927, p14.

Flight for Freedom (US; Mendes, Lothar; 1943)
Commonweal. Apr 16, 1943, v37, p643.
Film Daily. Feb 4, 1943, p8.
The Films of World War II. p118-20.
Hollywood Reporter. Feb 2, 1943, p3.
Motion Picture Herald Product Digest. Feb 6, 1943, p1145.
The New York Times. Apr 16, 1943, p24.
The New Yorker. Apr 17, 1943, v19, p41.
Newsweek. Apr 19, 1943, v21, p74.
Time. Apr 5, 1943, v41, p56.

The Flirt (US; Weber, Lois; Smalley, Phillips; 1916)
The Moving Picture World. Mar 25, 1916, p2025, 2091.
Variety. Mar 31, 1916, p24.
Wid's Daily. Apr 6, 1916, p486.

Flirtation Walk (US; Borzage, Frank; 1934)
Film Daily. Nov 2, 1934, p8.
The Hollywood Musical. p95.
Hollywood Reporter. Nov 1, 1934, p3.
Life. Jan 1935, v102, p34.
Motion Picture Herald. Nov 10, 1934, p38.
The New York Times. Nov 29, 1934, p33.
Time. Oct 10, 1934, v24, p28.
Variety. Dec 4, 1934, p12.

Flirting with Fate (US; Cabanne, Christy; 1916)
The Moving Picture World. Jul 8, 1916, p263, 306.
The New York Dramatic Mirror. Jul 1, 1916, p48.
Selected Film Criticism, 1912-1920. p90-91.
Variety. Jun 30, 1916, p20.
Wid's Daily. Jul 8, 1916, p105.

The Floradora Girl (US; Beaumont, Harry; 1930)
Exhibitors Herald-World. Jun 7, 1930, p90.
Film Daily. Jun 1, 1930, p10.
Judge. Jun 28, 1930, v98, p23.
Life. Jun 20, 1930, v95, p20.
The New York Times. May 31, 1930, p19.
The New Yorker. Jun 7, 1930, v6, p71.
Outlook and Independent. Jun 11, 1930, v155, p229.
Rob Wagner's Script. Jul 5, 1930, v3, p10-12.
Time. Jun 9, 1930, v15, p52.
Variety. Jun 1, 1930, p25.

The Florentine Dagger (US; Florey, Robert; 1935)
Film Daily. Apr 26, 1935, p5.
Hollywood Reporter. May 4, 1935, p4.
Motion Picture Herald. May 4, 1935, p38.
The New York Times. Apr 27, 1935, p20.
The New Yorker. May 4, 1935, v11, p59.
Variety. May 1, 1935, p17.

A Florida Enchantment (US; Drew, Sidney; 1914)
The Big V. p86.
The Moving Picture World. Sep 19, 1914, p1696.
The New York Dramatic Mirror. Aug 19, 1914, p26.
Variety. Aug 14, 1914, p21.

The Flying Deuces (US; Sutherland, Edward; 1939)
Commonweal. Nov 24, 1939, v31, p119.
Film Daily. Oct 10, 1939, p6.
Hollywood Reporter. Oct 6, 1939, p4.
Laurel & Hardy. p273-78.
Motion Picture Herald. Oct 14, 1939, p38, 42.
The New York Times. Nov 24, 1939, p29.
Time. Dec 4, 1939, v34, p83.
Variety. Oct 11, 1939, p13.

Flying Down to Rio (US; Freeland, Thornton; 1933)
Film Daily. Dec 20, 1933, p9.
Film Notes. p78-79.
Films in Review. Jan 1966, v17, p27-28.
The Films of Ginger Rogers. p88-89.
The Fred Astaire & Ginger Rogers Book. p23-29.
The Hollywood Musical. p70-71.
Hollywood Reporter. Dec 7, 1933, p3.
The Journal of Popular Film and Television. Fall 1980, v8, p15-24.
Magill's Survey of Cinema. Series I. v2, p545-48.
Motion Picture Herald. Dec 16, 1933, p30.
Movie Classic. Jan 1934, v5, p38-39.
The New York Times. Dec 22, 1933, p25.
The New Yorker. Dec 30, 1933, v9, p42.
Newsweek. Dec 30, 1933, v2, p31.
Rob Wagner's Script. Dec 30, 1933, v10, p10.
Selected Film Criticism, 1931-1940. p73-74.
The Spectator. May 25, 1934, v152, p813.
Starring Fred Astaire. p57-67.
Time. Jan 1, 1934, v23, p16.
Vanity Fair. Feb 1934, v41, p46.
Variety. Dec 26, 1933, p10.

Flying High (US; Riesner, Charles F.; 1931)
The Busby Berkeley Book. p42-43.
Film Daily. Dec 13, 1931, p10.
Hollywood Reporter. Oct 5, 1931, p4.
Hollywood Spectator. Feb 1932, v12, p11.
Motion Picture Herald. Oct 24, 1931, p30.
The New York Times. Dec 12, 1931, p23.
The New York Times. Dec 20, 1931, p4.
Outlook and Independent. Dec 9, 1931, v159, p471.
Variety. Dec 15, 1931, p14.

The Flying Irishman (US; Jason, Leigh; 1939)
Commonweal. Apr 7, 1939, v29, p665.
Film Daily. Mar 17, 1939, p17.
Hollywood Reporter. Mar 1, 1939, p3.
Lorentz on Film. p173-74.
Motion Picture Herald. Mar 4, 1939, p39.
The New Masses. Apr 25, 1939, v31, p30.
The New York Times. Apr 12, 1939, p27.
The New Yorker. Apr 15, 1939, v15, p80.
Newsweek. Mar 27, 1939, v13, p29.
Photoplay. May 1939, v53, p62.
Time. Mar 27, 1939, v33, p67.
Variety. Mar 8, 1939, p18.

The Foggy Quay *See* Quai des Brumes

Folies Bergere (US; Del Ruth, Roy; 1935)
Chevalier (Ringgold and Badeen). p130-35.
Film Daily. Feb 20, 1935, p9.
The Hollywood Musical. p98-100+.
Hollywood Reporter. Feb 16, 1935, p3.
Hollywood Reporter. Mar 4, 1935, p2.
Judge. Apr 1935, v108, p16-17.
Motion Picture Herald. Feb 23, 1935, p54-55.
The New York Times. Feb 25, 1935, p13.
The New Yorker. Mar 9, 1935, v11, p61.
Rob Wagner's Script. Mar 30, 1935, v13, p6.
Time. Mar 4, 1935, v25, p17.
Variety. Feb 27, 1935, p12.
Variety. Apr 22, 1936, p19.

The Follies Girl (US; Dillon, Jack; 1919)
Exhibitor's Trade Review. Apr 19, 1919, p1521.
Magill's Survey of Cinema. Silent Films. v2, p434-36.
Motion Picture News. Apr 26, 1919, p2715.
The Moving Picture World. Apr 19, 1919, p311.
Variety. Apr 25, 1919, p83.

Follow the Boys (US; Sutherland, Edward; 1944)
Commonweal. Apr 21, 1944, v40, p17.
Film Daily. Mar 27 1944, p6.
The Films of Jeanette MacDonald and Nelson Eddy. p354-56.
The Films of Marlene Dietrich. p168-69.
Hollywood Reporter. Mar 23, 1944, p3.
The New York Times. Apr 26, 1944, p24.
The New Yorker. Apr 29, 1944, v20, p50+.
Newsweek. May 1, 1944, v23, p93.
Time. Apr 24, 1944, v43, p94.
Variety. Mar 29, 1944, p21.

Follow the Fleet (US; Sandrich, Mark; 1936)
Canadian Magazine. Apr 1936, v85, p57.
Commonweal. Feb 28, 1936, v23, p497.
Esquire. May 1936, v5, p115.
Film Daily. Feb 19, 1936, p4.
The Films of Ginger Rogers. p125-28.
The Fred Astaire & Ginger Rogers Book. p81-97.
Graham Greene on Film. p67-69.
The Hollywood Musical. p116-17.
Hollywood Musicals. p112, 115.
Hollywood Reporter. Feb 10, 1936, p3.
Hollywood Spectator. Feb 15, 1936, v10, p4-5.
Literary Digest. Feb 29, 1936, v121, p20.
Magill's Survey of Cinema. Series I. v2, p549-52.
Motion Picture Herald. Feb 22, 1936, p62.
The Nation. Mar 18, 1936, v142, p360.
The New Statesman and Nation. Apr 18, 1936, v11, p601.
The New York Times. Feb 21, 1936, p21.
The New Yorker. Feb 29, 1936, v12, p50.
Rob Wagner's Script. Feb 29, 1936, v15, p8.
The Spectator. Apr 24, 1936, v156, p744.
Starring Fred Astaire. p119-31.
Time. Mar 2, 1936, v27, p26.
Variety. Feb 26, 1936, p15.

Follow Thru (US; Schwab, Laurence; Corrigan, Lloyd; 1930)
Exhibitors Herald-World. Sep 20, 1930, p39.
Film Daily. Sep 14, 1930, p12.
The Films of Nancy Carroll. p116-19.
Life. Oct 3, 1930, v96, p20.
The New York Times. Sep 13, 1930, p9.
The New York Times. Sep 21, 1930, p5.
The New Yorker. Sep 20, 1930, v6, p83-84.
Time. Sep 28, 1930, v16, p32.
Variety. Sep 17, 1930, p30.

A Fool There Was (US; Powell, Frank; 1915)
Exhibitor's Trade Review. Jun 22, 1918, p197.
Exhibitor's Trade Review. Jun 29, 1918, p320.
Fifty Great American Silent Films, 1912-1920. p18-19.

Magill's Survey of Cinema. Silent Films. v2, p437-39.
A Million and One Nights. p701-02.
Motion Picture News. Jan 16, 1915, p6.
Motion Picture News. Apr 17, 1915, p5.
Motion Picture News. Jun 22, 1918, p3741.
Motography. Jan 23, 1915, p134, 151.
The Moving Picture World. Jan 30, 1915, p677.
The Moving Picture World. Jun 22, 1918, p1756.
The Moving Picture World. Jul 13, 1918, p253.
The New York Dramatic Mirror. Jan 20, 1915, p31.
Selected Film Criticism, 1912-1920. p91-93.
Variety. Mar 12, 1915, p24.

Foolish Wives (US; Stroheim, Erich von; 1922)
BFI/Monthly Film Bulletin. Aug 1976, v67, p34-39.
Film Daily. Jan 15, 1922, p3.
Magill's Survey of Cinema. Silent Films. v2, p440-45.
Motion Picture Classic. Apr 1922, v14, p48, 49, 87.
The New York Times. Jan 12, 1922, p15.
The New York Times. Dec 14, 1924, sec8, p7.
Photoplay. Mar 1922, v21, p70.
Selected Film Criticism, 1921-1930. p99-102.
Spellbound in Darkness. p326-30.
Stroheim: A Pictorial Record of His Nine Films. p33-72.
Variety. Jan 20, 1922, p35.

The Fool's Awakening (US; Shaw, Harold; 1924)
Film Daily. Feb 3, 1924, p6.
The Moving Picture World. Feb 16, 1924, p581.
Variety. Mar 19, 1924, p26.

Fools for Scandal (US; LeRoy, Mervyn; 1938)
Film Daily. Mar 29, 1938, p6.
The Films of Carole Lombard. p156-57.
Graham Greene on Film. p200.
Hollywood Reporter. Mar 15, 1938, p3.
Motion Picture Herald. Mar 19, 1938, p40-41.
The New York Times. Mar 25, 1938, p15.
Newsweek. Apr 4, 1938, v11, p24.
Rob Wagner's Script. Apr 30, 1938, v19, p8.
The Spectator. Aug 26, 1938, v161, p335.
Stage. May 1938, v15, p26.
Time. Apr 4, 1938, v31, p29.
Variety. Mar 30, 1938, p15.

A Fool's Revenge (US; Griffith, D.W.; 1909)
The New York Dramatic Mirror. Mar 13, 1909, p16.
Spellbound in Darkness. p57.

Footlight Parade (US; Bacon, Lloyd; Berkeley, Busby; 1933)
The Busby Berkeley Book. p65-71.
Cinema Quarterly. Wint 1933-34, v2, p125.
Film Daily. Sep 30, 1933, p3.
The Films of John Garfield. p47-48.
The Genius of Busby Berkeley. p170-71.
Genre: The Musical. p41-56.
Hollywood Reporter. Sep 30, 1933, p2.
Literary Digest. Oct 21, 1933, v116, p31.
Magill's Survey of Cinema. Series II. v2, p800-04.
Motion Picture Herald. Oct 7, 1933, p35, 38.
New Outlook. Nov 1933, v162, p43.
The New York Times. Oct 6, 1933, p21.
The New York Times. Oct 15, 1933, p3.
The New Yorker. Oct 7, 1933, v9, p57-58.
Rob Wagner's Script. Nov 11, 1933, v10, p6-7.
Time. Oct 9, 1933, v22, p30.
Variety. Oct 10, 1933, p17.
The Velvet Light Trap. Jun 1971, n1, p20-25.
Warner Brothers Presents. p97, p102-03.
We're in the Money. p63-65.

For Heaven's Sake (US; Taylor, Sam; 1926)
Film Daily. Apr 11, 1926, p5.
Harold Lloyd. p86-91.
Harold Lloyd: The Shape of Laughter. p188-89.

The New York Times. Apr 5, 1926, p24.
Photoplay. Jun 1926, v30, p53.
Selected Film Criticism, 1921-1930. p103.
Variety. Apr 7, 1926, p36.

For Love of Gold (Also titled: For the Love of Gold) (US; Griffith, D.W.; 1908)
D.W. Griffith, His Biograph Films in Perspective. p7-9, 33-34.
The Emergence of Film Art. p42-43.

For the Defense (US; Cromwell, John; 1930)
Exhibitors Herald-World. Jul 12, 1930, p35.
Exhibitors Herald-World. Jul 26, 1930, p28.
Film Daily. Jul 20, 1930, p14.
Judge. Aug 9, 1930, v98, p23.
Life. Aug 8, 1930, v96, p17.
The New York Times. Jul 19, 1930, p7.
The New York Times. Jul 27, 1930, p3.
The New Yorker. Jul 26, 1930, v6, p53-54.
Outlook and Independent. Jul 30, 1930, v155, p510.
Time. Aug 4, 1930, v16, p25.
Variety. Jul 23, 1930, p3.

For the Term of His Natural Life (AUST; Dawn, Norman; 1927)
Australian Silent Film. p155-62+.
Film Daily. Jun 16, 1929, p9.
Variety. Jun 12, 1929, p31.

For Whom the Bell Tolls (US; Wood, Sam; 1943)
Agee on Film. v1, p46-49.
Commonweal. Jul 30, 1943, v38, p371.
Film Daily. Jul 15, 1943, p7.
The Films of Gary Cooper. p190-93.
The Films of Ingrid Bergman. p92-96.
The Films of World War II. p139-40.
Hemingway on Film. p33-47.
Hollywood Reporter. Jul 14, 1943, p3.
Magill's Survey of Cinema. Series I. v2, p553-55.
Motion Picture Herald. Jul 17, 1943, p37.
Motion Picture Herald Product Digest. Jul 24, 1943, p1441-42.
The Nation. Jul 24, 1943, v157, p108.
The New Republic. Jul 19, 1943, v109, p77.
The New York Times. Jul 15, 1943, p25.
Newsweek. Jul 26, 1943, v22, p66.
Rob Wagner's Script. Aug 28, 1943, v29, p14.
Saturday Review. Jul 31, 1943, v26, p18.
Selected Film Criticism, 1941-1950. p60-61.
Time. Aug 2, 1943, v42, p55.
Variety. Jul 21, 1943, p22.

For You Alone *See* When You're in Love

Forbidden (US; Capra, Frank; 1931)
Film Daily. Jan 17, 1932, p8.
The Films of Barbara Stanwyck. p74-75.
Frank Capra (Maland). p57-58.
Hollywood Reporter. Dec 12, 1931, p3.
Judge. Jan 30, 1932, v102, p22.
Motion Picture Herald. Jan 16, 1932, p40, 42.
The New York Times. Jan 11, 1932, p28.
The New Yorker. Jan 16, 1932, v7, p53-54.
Outlook and Independent. Jan 20, 1932, v160, p87.
Rob Wagner's Script. Mar 19, 1932, v7, p11-12.
Starring Miss Barbara Stanwyck. p34, 39.
Variety. Jan 12, 1932, p24.

The Forbidden City (US; Franklin, Sidney; 1918)
Exhibitor's Trade Review. Oct 19, 1918, p1696-97.
Motion Picture News. Oct 19, 1918, p2607.
Motion Picture News. Oct 26, 1918, p2712.
The Moving Picture World. Oct 19, 1918, p445.
The Moving Picture World. Oct 26, 1918, p549.
The New York Times. Oct 7, 1918, p11.
Selected Film Criticism, 1912-1920. p95-96.

Variety. Oct 11, 1918, p45.
Wid's Daily. Oct 13, 1918, p23-24.

Forbidden Paradise (US; Lubitsch, Ernst; 1924)
Ernst Lubitsch: A Guide to References and Resources. p80-82.
Film Daily. Nov 30, 1924, p13.
The Films of the Twenties. p103-04.
The Lubitsch Touch. p72-76.
The Moving Picture World. Nov 29, 1924, p448.
The New York Times. Nov 17, 1924, p16.
Variety. Nov 19, 1924, p31.

The Forbidden Street (Also titled: Britannia Mews) (GB; Negulesco, Jean; 1949)
Film Daily. May 3, 1949, p6.
Hollywood Reporter. Apr 29, 1949, p3.
Motion Picture Herald Product Digest. May 7, 1949, p4597.
The New York Times. May 14, 1949, p9.
Newsweek. May 30, 1949, v33, p83.
Rotarian. Oct 1949, v75, p38.
Time. May 30, 1949, v53, p82.
Variety. Mar 9, 1949, p6.

Force of Evil (US; Polonsky, Abraham; 1948)
Film Daily. Dec 8, 1948, p6.
The Films of John Garfield. p158-61.
Hollywood Reporter. Dec 27, 1948, p3.
Motion Picture Herald Product Digest. Jan 1, 1949, p4442.
The New Republic. Jan 10, 1949, v120, p23.
The New York Times. Dec 27, 1948, p16.
Newsweek. Jan 3, 1949, v33, p57.
Time. Jan 10, 1949, v53, p84.
Variety. Dec 29, 1948, p6.

A Foreign Affair (US; Wilder, Billy; 1948)
Agee on Film. v1, p310-11.
Billy Wilder. p63-66.
Canadian Forum. Sep 1948, v28, p137.
Commonweal. Aug 6, 1948, v48, p401.
The Film Career of Billy Wilder. p75-78.
Film Daily. Jun 14, 1948, p8.
The Films of Marlene Dietrich. p180-83.
The Films of the Forties. p234-38.
Independent Woman. Feb 1949, v28, p40+.
Life. Aug 9, 1949, v25, p59-60.
Magill's Survey of Cinema. Series II. v2, p812-14.
The New Republic. Jul 12, 1948, v119, p29.
The New York Times. Jul 1, 1948, p19.
The New Yorker. Jul 10, 1948, v24, p39.
Newsweek. Jul 12, 1948, v32, p82.
Time. Jul 26, 1948, v52, p65-66.
Variety. Jun 16, 1948, p8.

Foreign Correspondent (US; Hitchcock, Alfred; 1940)
American Mercury. Nov 1940, v51, p358-62.
The Art of Alfred Hitchcock. p97-107.
Christian Century. Oct 16, 1940, v57, p1284-85.
Commonweal. Aug 30, 1940, v32, p390.
Film Comment. May-Jun 1974, v10, p22.
The Film Criticism of Otis Ferguson. p308-09.
Film Daily. Aug 29, 1940, p6.
Films and the Second World War. p35-36.
The Films of Alfred Hitchcock. p94-98.
The Films of World War II. p37-38.
Hitchcock: The First Forty-Four Films. p60-63.
Hollywood Reporter. Aug 28, 1940, p3.
Life. Aug 25, 1940, v9, p42-45.
The London Times. Oct 10, 1940, p6.
The London Times. Aug 29, 1940, p3.
Magic Moments from the Movies. p83-85.
Magill's Survey of Cinema. Series I. p556-60.
Motion Picture Exhibitor. 1940, p587.
The New Republic. Sep 16, 1940, v103, p385-86.
The New York Times. Apr 14, 1940, sec9, p5.
The New York Times. Aug 28, 1940, p15.
The New York Times. Sep 1, 1940, sec9, p3.

The New Yorker. Aug 31, 1940, v16, p51.
Newsweek. Aug 26, 1940, v16, p49.
Photoplay. Oct 1940, v54, p66.
Rob Wagner's Script. Sep 28, 1940, v24, p16.
Scholastic. Sep 16, 1940, v37, p38.
Selected Film Criticism, 1931-1940. p75-77.
Theatre Arts. Oct 1940, v24, p727.
Theatre Arts. Sep 1941, v25 p628.
Theatre Arts. May 1949, v33, p37.
Time. Sep 2, 1940, v36, p31.
Variety. Aug 28, 1940, p16.

Forever (US; Fitzmaurice, George; 1921)
Film Daily. Oct 23, 1921, p4.
Magill's Survey of Cinema. Silent Films. v2, p446-48.
The New York Times. Oct 17, 1921, p18.

Forever Amber (US; Preminger, Otto; 1947)
The Cinema of Otto Preminger. p86-87+.
Commonweal. Oct 31, 1947, v47, p71.
Film Daily. Oct 10, 1947, p8.
Hollywood Reporter. Oct 10, 1947, p3.
Life. Nov 3, 1947, v23, p66-68+.
Motion Picture Herald Product Digest. Oct 18, 1947, p3885.
New Republic. Oct 27, 1947, v117, p36.
The New York Times. Oct 23, 1947, p31.
The New York Times Magazine. Jul 20, 1947, p12.
The New Yorker. Oct 25, 1947, v23, p95.
Newsweek. Nov 3, 1947, v30, p87.
Time. Nov 3, 1947, v50, p99.
Variety. Oct 15, 1947, p10.

Forever and a Day (US; Clair, René; Lloyd, Frank; Saville, Victor; Goulding, Edmund; Stevenson, Robert; Wilcox, Herbert; Hardwicke, Sir Cedric; 1943)
Around Cinemas, Second Series. p226.
Commonweal. Mar 19, 1943, v27, p544.
Film Daily. Mar 19, 1943, p7.
Hollywood Reporter. Jan 20, 1943, p7.
Magill's Survey of Cinema. Series II. v2, p815.
Motion Picture Herald Product Digest. Jan 23, 1943, p1125.
The New York Times. Mar 13, 1943, p9.
Newsweek. Mar 29, 1943, v21, p65.
René Clair. p147-48.
Time. Mar 29, 1943, v41, p40.
Variety. Jan 20, 1943, p9.

Forsaking All Others (US; Van Dyke, W.S.; 1934)
Film Daily. Dec 19, 1934, p8.
The Films of Clark Gable. p158-60.
The Films of Joan Crawford. p114-15.
Hollywood Reporter. Nov 26, 1934, p3.
Motion Picture Herald. Dec 8, 1934, p46.
The New Republic. Mar 13, 1934, v82, p132.
The New York Times. Dec 21, 1934, p18.
Variety. Jan 1, 1934, p18.

Fort Apache (US; Ford, John; 1948)
About John Ford. p123-26+.
Agee on Film. v1, p311.
The Complete Films of John Wayne. p157-59.
Film Daily. Mar 10, 1948, p10.
The Films of Henry Fonda. p139-41.
The Films of Shirley Temple. p240-43.
The Fondas (Springer). p147-49.
Hollywood Reporter. Mar 10, 1948, p3.
Magill's Cinema Annual, 1984. p530-34.
Motion Picture Herald Product Digest. Mar 13, 1948, p4094.
The Nation. Jul 24, 1948, v167, p109.
New Republic. Jul 12, 1948, v119, p29.
The New York Times. Jun 25, 1948, p26.
The New Yorker. Jul 3, 1948, v24, p58.
Newsweek. May 17, 1948, v31, p95.
Time. May 10, 1948, v51, p102+.

Variety. Mar 10, 1948, p10.
The Western Films of John Ford. p74-91.

Forty Little Mothers *See* Mioche, Le

49th Parallel (Also titled: The Invaders) (GB; Powell, Michael; 1941)
BFI/Monthly Film Bulletin. Nov 1984, v51, p356-57.
Commonweal. Mar 20, 1942, v35, p536.
Film Daily. Feb 18, 1942, p8.
Films and the Second World War. p67-69.
The Films of Laurence Olivier. p92-93.
The Great Adventure Films. p112-15.
Life. Mar 23, 1942, v12, p57-58+.
The London Times. Oct 9, 1941, p6.
Motion Picture Exhibitor. Feb 25, 1942, p953.
Motion Picture Herald Product Digest. Nov 8, 1941, p349.
Motion Picture Herald Product Digest. Mar 7, 1941, p537.
The Nation. Mar 14, 1942, v154, p320.
The New Republic. Mar 23, 1942, v106, p399.
The New York Times. Jan 5, 1941, sec9, p4.
Newsweek. Mar 16, 1942, v19, p72-73.
Newsweek. Sep 21, 1942, v20, p80.
Photoplay. May 1942, v20, p24.
Time. Mar 16, 1942, v39, p90+.
Variety. Nov 5, 1941, p8.

Forty-Second Street (Also titled: 42nd Street) (US; Bacon, Lloyd; 1933)
The Busby Berkeley Book. p50-55.
A Companion to the Movies. p109-10.
Dictionary of Films. p117.
Film Daily. Feb 4, 1933, p3.
Film News. Oct 1973, v30, p17-18.
Film Notes. p78.
Films and Filming. Jan 1962, v8, p13-15, 41, 46.
The Genius of Busby Berkeley. p168-69.
Genre: The Musical. p41-56.
The Hollywood Musical. p43-49.
Hollywood Reporter. Jan 12, 1933, p2.
The International Dictionary of Films and Filmmakers. v1, p158-59.
Journal of Popular Film. 1975, n1, p33-46.
Life. May 1933, v100, p39.
Magill's Survey of Cinema. Series I. v2, p561-65.
Motion Picture. Mar 1933, v45, p40-41+.
Motion Picture Herald. Mar 18, 1933, p34.
Movie. Spr 1977, n24, p36-43.
Movie Classic. Mar 1933, v4, p42-43.
The New York Times. Mar 10, 1933, p19.
The New York Times. Mar 19, 1933, p3.
The New Yorker. Mar 18, 1933, v9, p62.
Newsweek. Mar 18, 1933, v1, p28.
Rob Wagner's Script. Feb 11, 1933, v9, p9.
Rob Wagner's Script. Mar 25, 1933, v9, p10.
Selected Film Criticism, 1931-1940. p78.
Time. Feb 13, 1933, v21, p30.
Vanity Fair. Apr 1933, v40, p43.
Variety. Mar 14, 1933, p14.
The Velvet Light Trap. Jun 1971, n1, p20-25.
The Velvet Light Trap. Wint 1977, n17, p1-7.
Warner Brothers Presents. p90-91.
We're in the Money. p63-64.
42nd Street. p9-37.
50 Classic Motion Pictures. p244-49.

The Fountainhead (US; Vidor, King; 1949)
Commonweal. Jul 29, 1949, v50, p390.
Film Daily. Jun 27, 1949, p7.
The Films of Gary Cooper. p214-17.
King Vidor (Baxter). p70-72.
King Vidor on Film Making. p231-32.
Magill's Survey of Cinema. Series II. v2, p828-31.
Motion Picture Herald Product Digest. Jun 25, 1949, p4658.
The New Republic. Jul 18, 1949, v121, p22.

The New York Times. Jul 9, 1949, p3.
The New Yorker. Jul 16, 1949, v25, p46.
Newsweek. Jul 25, 1949, v34, p76.
Rotarian. Oct 1949, v75, p38.
Senior Scholastic. Oct 26, 1949, v55, p2.
Sequence. New Year 1950, v10, p157.
Time. Jul 11, 1949, v54, p95.
Variety. Jun 29, 1949, p14.

Four Daughters (US; Curtiz, Michael; 1938)
Casablanca and Other Major Films of Michael Curtiz. p115-16.
Commonweal. Sep 2, 1938, v28, p477.
Esquire. Jan 1939, v11, p110.
Film Daily. Aug 10, 1938, p7.
The Films of John Garfield. p49-53.
Hollywood Reporter. Aug 9, 1938, p3.
Life. Sep 12, 1938, v5, p62-63.
Magill's Survey of Cinema. Series II. v2, p832-35.
Motion Picture Herald. Aug 13, 1938, p59.
The New Masses. Aug 30, 1938, v28, p31.
The New York Times. Aug 19, 1938, p13.
The New Yorker. Aug 27, 1938, v14, p52.
Newsweek. Aug 29, 1938, v12, p20-21.
Rob Wagner's Script. Sep 10, 1938, v20, p8.
Scholastic. Sep 17, 1938, v33, p12.
The Tatler. Jan 11, 1939, v151, p52, viii.
Time. Aug 29, 1938, v32, p23.
Variety. Aug 17, 1938, p22.

Four Devils (US; Murnau, F.W.; 1928)
Film Daily. Jun 30, 1929, p6.
Literary Digest. Oct 20, 1928, v99, p28-29.
Murnau (Eisner). p186-201.
The New York Times. Oct 4, 1928, p26.
Photoplay. Dec 1928, v35, p52.
Selected Film Criticism, 1921-1930. p103-04.
Variety. Oct 10, 1928, p15.
Variety. Jun 19, 1929, p24.

Four Faces West (US; Green, Alfred E.; 1948)
Film Daily. May 10, 1948, p8.
The Films of the Forties. p232-34.
Hollywood Reporter. May 10, 1948, p3.
Motion Picture Herald Product Digest. May 15, 1948, p4162.
The New York Times. Aug 4, 1948, p18.
The New Yorker. Aug 14, 1948, v24, p71.
Newsweek. Aug 16, 1948, v32, p76.
Time. May 31, 1948, v51, p86+.
Variety. May 12, 1948, p8.

The Four Feathers (US; Cooper, Merian C.; Schoedsack, Ernest B.; Mendes, Lothar; 1929)
Film Daily. Jun 16, 1929, p8.
The New York Times. Jun 13, 1929, p23.
Variety. Jun 19, 1929, p24.

Four Feathers (GB; Korda, Zoltan; 1939)
Commonweal. Aug 18, 1939, v30, p400.
Esquire. Nov 1939, v12, p101-02.
The Film Criticism of Otis Ferguson. p264.
Film Daily. Jul 24, 1939, p7.
Focus on Film. Spr 1971, n6, p52-54.
Graham Greene on Film. p218.
The Great Adventure Films. p92-95.
Hollywood Reporter. Jul 21, 1939, p3.
Hollywood Spectator. Aug 5, 1939, v14, p6-7.
Magill's Survey of Cinema. Series I. v2, p566-69.
Motion Picture Herald. May 6, 1939, p36.
The Nation. Aug 19, 1939, v149, p204.
National Board of Review Magazine. Oct 1939, v14, p12.
The New Masses. Aug 22, 1939, v32, p31.
The New Republic. Aug 9, 1939, v100, p20.
The New York Times. Aug 4, 1939, p11.
The New Yorker. Aug 12, 1939, v15, p47.
Newsweek. Aug 7, 1939, v14, p40.

North American Review. Sep 1939, v247, p195.
Photoplay. Sep 1939, v53, p63.
Rob Wagner's Script. Aug 26, 1939, v22, p16.
Selected Film Criticism: Foreign Films, 1930-1950. p54.
Sight and Sound. Sum 1939, v8, p76.
The Spectator. Apr 28, 1939, v162, p708.
The Tatler. May 3, 1939, v152, p194.
Time. Aug 14, 1939, v34, p32.
Variety. Apr 26, 1939, p12.

Four Girls in White (US; Simon, S. Sylvan; 1939)
Film Daily. Jan 24, 1939, p6.
Hollywood Reporter. Jan 19, 1939, p4.
Motion Picture Herald. Feb 4, 1939, p61, 64.
The New York Times. Feb 23, 1939, p19.
Photoplay. Apr 1939, v53, p53.
Variety. Jan 25, 1939, p11.

The Four Horsemen of the Apocalypse (US; Ingram, Rex; 1921)
American Silent Film. p168.
Exceptional Photoplays. Mar 1921, v4, p5, 7.
Film Daily. Feb 20, 1921, p3.
Films and Filming. May 1956, v2, p15.
From Quasimodo to Scarlett O'Hara. p15-16.
The International Dictionary of Films and Filmmakers. v1, p159-60.
Life. Mar 24, 1921, v77, p433.
Magill's Survey of Cinema. Silent Films. v2, p450-53.
The New York Times. Mar 7, 1921, p8.
The New York Times. Oct 3, 1926, sec8, p5.
Photoplay. May 1921, v19, p52.
Rex Ingram: Master of the Silent Cinema. p72-86+.
Selected Film Criticism, 1921-1930. p104-08.
Spellbound in Darkness. p282-85.
Variety. Feb 18, 1921, p40.

Four Hours to Kill (US; Leisen, Mitchell; 1935)
Film Daily. Apr 11, 1935, p9.
Hollywood Director. p86-91.
Motion Picture Herald. Apr 6, 1935, p46, 48.
The New York Times. Apr 11, 1935, p27.
The New Yorker. Apr 20, 1935, v11, p71.
Rob Wagner's Script. Jun 1, 1935, v13, p10-11.
The Spectator. Jun 28, 1935, v154, p1102.
Time. Apr 22, 1935, v25, p61.
Variety. Apr 17, 1935, p14.

The Four Hundred Million (Also titled: China's Four Hundred Million) (US; Ivens, Joris; 1939)
Commonweal. Mar 31, 1939, v29, p640.
Dictionary of Films. p118.
Film on the Left. p190-94.
Hollywood Spectator. Apr 1, 1939, v13, p10-11.
Joris Ivens, Film-Maker. p51-53.
Lorentz on Film. p164-65.
The Nation. Mar 25, 1939, v148, p358.
The New Masses. Mar 21, 1939, v30, p30-31.
The New Masses. Mar 14, 1939, v30, p30.
The New Masses. Mar 28, 1939, v31, p31.
The New Republic. Mar 22, 1939, v98, p194.
The New Statesman and Nation. Feb 10, 1940, v19, p172.
The New York Times. Mar 8, 1939, p19.
The New Yorker. Mar 18, 1939, v15, p65-66.
Time. Mar 20, 1939, v33, p45.

Four Infantry Men *See* Westfront 1918

Four Men and a Prayer (US; Ford, John; 1938)
Commonweal. May 20, 1938, v28, p106.
The Film Criticism of Otis Ferguson. p226-27.
Film Daily. Apr 26, 1938, p8.
Hollywood Reporter. Apr 20, 1938, p3.
Hollywood Spectator. Apr 30, 1938, v13, p6.
Motion Picture Herald. Apr 23, 1938, p45.
The New Republic. Aug 3, 1938, v95, p363.

The New York Times. May 7, 1938, p18.
The New Yorker. May 14, 1938, v14, p73.
Newsweek. May 2, 1938, v11, p23.
The Non-Western Films of John Ford. p232-33.
Rob Wagner's Script. Jun 11, 1938, v19, p10.
Time. May 2, 1938, v31, p43.
Variety. Apr 27, 1938, p22.

Four Sons (US; Ford, John; 1928)
Film Daily. Feb 19, 1928, p8.
John Ford (Bogdanovich). p49-50.
Magill's Survey of Cinema. Silent Films. v2, p454-56.
The New York Times. Feb 21, 1928, p11.
Variety. Feb 15, 1928, p24.

Four Sons (US; Ford, John; 1940)
Commonweal. Jun 21, 1940, v32, p192.
Film Daily. Jun 4, 1940, p6.
The Films of World War II. p31-33.
Hollywood Reporter. May 28, 1940, p3.
Motion Picture Herald Product Digest. May 31, 1940, p4.
The New York Times. Jun 8, 1940, p18.
Newsweek. Jun 17, 1940, v15, p50.
Time. Jun 24, 1940, v35, p90.
Variety. Apr 29, 1940, p14.

Four Wives (US; Curtiz, Michael; 1939)
Canadian Forum. Jan 1940, v19, p327.
Commonweal. Dec 29, 1939, v31, p227.
Film Daily. Nov 28, 1939, p10.
Hollywood Reporter. Nov 21, 1939, p3.
Hollywood Spectator. Dec 9, 1939, v14, p7.
Motion Picture Herald. Nov 25, 1939, p40.
The New York Times. Dec 23, 1939, p9.
The New Yorker. Dec 23, 1939, v15, p52-53.
Rob Wagner's Script. Dec 9, 1939, v22, p14-15.
Time. Dec 18, 1939, v34, p78.
Variety. Nov 22, 1939, p14.

Four's a Crowd (US; Curtiz, Michael; 1938)
Canadian Magazine. Sep 1938, v90, p58.
Commonweal. Aug 26, 1938, v28, p451.
Film Daily. Aug 12, 1938, p6.
The Films of Errol Flynn. p68-69.
The Films of Olivia de Havilland. p117-20.
Hollywood Reporter. Jul 13, 1938, p3.
Motion Picture Herald. Jul 16, 1938, p58, 61.
The New York Times. Aug 12, 1938, p11.
Rob Wagner's Script. Sep 10, 1938, v20, p8.
Time. Aug 22, 1938, v32, p42.
Variety. Aug 17, 1938, p22.

Fourteenth of July *See* Quatorze Juillet

The Foxes of Harrow (US; Stahl, John M.; 1947)
Film Daily. Sep 23, 1947, p8.
Hollywood Reporter. Sep 22, 1947, p3.
Motion Picture Herald Product Digest. Sep 27, 1947, p3849.
The New York Times. Sep 25, 1947, p35.
The New Yorker. Oct 4, 1947, v23, p85.
Newsweek. Oct 6, 1947, v30, p80.
Time. Oct 13, 1947, v50, p105.
Variety. Sep 24, 1947, p11.

F.P.1 Antwortet Nicht (Also titled: No Answer from F.P.1; F.P.1) (GER; GB; Pommer, Erich; 1933)
BFI/Monthly Film Bulletin. Aug 1979, v46, p185.
Film Daily. Sep 16, 1933, p4.
Motion Picture Herald. May 20, 1933, p32.
The New York Times. Sep 16, 1933, p9.
Rob Wagner's Script. May 29, 1937, v17, p10.
Rob Wagner's Script. Sep 9, 1933, v10, p12.
Science Fiction Studies in Film. p74-77.
Selected Film Criticism: Foreign Films, 1930-1950. p50.
Time. Aug 14, 1933, v22, p21.
Variety. Sep 19, 1933, p13.

Fra Diavolo *See* The Devil's Brother

Francesca da Rimini (US; 1910)
The Bioscope. Feb 23, 1911, p31.
Selected Film Criticism, 1896-1911. p40.

Frankenstein (US; Dawley, J. Searle; 1910)
The Film Index. Mar 12, 1910, v5, p6.
The Moving Picture World. Apr 2, 1910, p508.
The New York Dramatic Mirror. Mar 26, 1910, p18.
Selected Film Criticism, 1896-1911. p40-42.

Frankenstein (US; Whale, James; 1931)
America's Favorite Movies. p1-21.
Boris Karloff and His Films. p23-45.
Classic Movies. p77-78.
Classics of the Horror Film. p37-43.
A Companion to the Movies. p33.
Dictionary of Films. p118-19.
The English Novel and the Movies. p52-66.
Film Comment. Fall 1970, v6, p42-46.
Film Daily. Dec 6, 1931, p10.
The Films of Boris Karloff. p58-63.
The Frankenstein Legend. p90-120.
Great Horror Movies. p2-27.
Hollywood Reporter. Nov 3, 1931, p3.
Horror Films. p11-32.
Horror in the Cinema. p36-39.
Horror Movies (Clarens). p80-84.
Horrors! p136-42.
The International Dictionary of Films and Filmmakers. v1, p160-61.
James Whale. p70-89.
James Whale: Ace Director. p3-4.
James Whale's Frankenstein.
Journal of Popular Film. Fall 1973, v2, p358-61.
Landmark Films. p72-81.
Magill's Survey of Cinema. Series I. v2, p570-73.
Monsters From the Movies. p29-34.
Motion Picture Herald. Nov 14, 1931, p40, 42.
Movie Monsters and Their Masters: The Birth of the Horror Film. p30.
The New Statesman and Nation. Jan 30, 1932, v3, p120.
The New York Times. Dec 5, 1931, p21.
The New Yorker. Dec 12, 1931, v7, p79-80.
Outlook and Independent. Dec 9, 1931, v159, p471.
Photoplay. Jan 1932, v41, p47.
Rob Wagner's Script. Feb 20, 1932, v7, p10.
Science Fiction Studies in Film. p58-62.
Selected Film Criticism, 1931-1940. p79-80.
Sight and Sound. Aut 1957, v27, p96.
Terrors of the Screen. p64-68.
Time. Dec 14, 1931, v18, p25.
Variety. Dec 8, 1931, p14.
50 Classic Motion Pictures. p182-87.

Frankenstein Meets the Wolfman (US; Neill, Roy William; 1943)
Classics of the Horror Film. p213-17.
Film Daily. Mar 1, 1943, p8.
The Films of Bela Lugosi. p192-95.
Hollywood Reporter. Mar 1, 1943, p3.
Horror Movies (Clarens). p101, 128+.
An Illustrated History of the Horror Film. p78, 102, 195.
Motion Picture Herald Product Digest. Feb 27, 1943, p1181.
The New York Times. Mar 6, 1943, p8.

Frankie and Johnny (US; Erskine, Chester; 1936)
Film Daily. Jun 25, 1935, p11.
Motion Picture Herald. May 23, 1936, p45.
The New York Times. May 25, 1936, p23.
Variety. May 27, 1936, p14.

Fraternally Yours *See* Sons of the Desert

Frau im Mond (Also titled: The Woman in the Moon) (GER; Lang, Fritz; 1929)
Celluloid: The Film To-Day. p235-38.
Close-Up. Nov 1929, v5, p442-44.
Discovery. Nov 1929, v10, p369-72.
Film Daily. Feb 8, 1931, p10.
The Films of Fritz Lang. p147-54.
Fritz Lang (Eisner). p106-10.
Horror Movies (Clarens). p50-52.
Motion Picture Herald. Feb 14, 1931, p69.
The New York Times. Feb 7, 1931, p11.
The New Yorker. Feb 21, 1931, v7, p55.
Outlook and Independent. Feb 25, 1931, v157, p312.
Saturday Review (London). Jul 26, 1930, v150, p110.
Time. Feb 16, 1931, v17, p21.
Variety. Feb 11, 1931, p29.
Variety. Nov 13, 1929, p32.
Variety. Aug 6, 1930, p38.
Variety. Feb 7, 1931, p11.

Freaks (US; Browning, Tod; 1932)
Cinema of the Fantastic. p33-48.
Classic Film Collector. Fall 1976, n52, p57.
Classic Images. Nov 1983, n101, p66-67.
Classics of the Horror Film. p77-79.
Dictionary of Films. p119.
Eighty Years of Cinema. p91-92.
Film Daily. Jul 9, 1932, p6.
Film Quarterly. Spr 1964, v17, p59-61.
Film Society Newsletter. Apr 1965, p15-16.
Films and Filming. Aug 1963, v9, p22-23.
Freaks: Cinema of the Bizarre. p50-59.
The Hollywood Professionals. v4, p13-14, 35-38, 50.
Hollywood Reporter. Jan 12, 1932, p3.
Horror in the Cinema. p48-50.
Horror Movies (Clarens). p90-94.
The International Dictionary of Films and Filmmakers. v1, p161-62.
Judge. Aug 1932, v102, p22.
Magill's Survey of Cinema. Series II. v2, p842-46.
Motion Picture. Apr 1932, v43, p30-32+.
Motion Picture Herald. Jul 23, 1932, p48.
Movie. Jul-Aug 1963, v11, p32.
National Board of Review Magazine. Mar 1932, v7, p9-13.
The New York Times. Jul 9, 1932, p7.
The New Yorker. Jul 16, 1932, v8, p45-46.
Outlook. Apr 1932, v160, p229.
Photon. 1973, n23, p25-35.
Rob Wagner's Script. Feb 20, 1932, v7, p8-9.
Sight and Sound. Sum 1963, v32, p145.
Stories Into Film. p11-31.
Time. Apr 18, 1932, v19, p17.
Variety. Jul 12, 1932, p16.

Free and Easy (US; Sedgwick, Edward; 1930)
Exhibitors Herald-World. Apr 26, 1930, p28.
Film Daily. Apr 20, 1930, p9.
The Film Spectator. May 24, 1930, v9, p22.
Judge. May 17, 1930, v98, p25.
Life. May 16, 1930, v95, p18.
The New York Times. Apr 19, 1930, p15.
The New Yorker. Apr 26, 1930, v6, p83.
Outlook and Independent. May 7, 1930, v155, p32.
Rob Wagner's Script. May 10, 1930, v3, p13.
Time. May 5, 1930, v15, p32.
Variety. Apr 23, 1930, p36.

A Free Soul (US; Brown, Clarence; 1931)
The Age of the Dream Palace. p240.
Film Daily. Jun 7, 1931, p10.
The Films of Clark Gable. p120-22.
The Films of Norma Shearer. p174-78.
The Films of the Thirties. p61-63.
The Great Gangster Pictures. p143-45.
Hollywood Reporter. Apr 20, 1931, p3.

Hollywood Spectator. Aug 1, 1931, v12, p9, 20.
Life. Jun 19, 1931, v97, p19.
Motion Picture Herald. Apr 25, 1931, p40.
The New York Times. Jun 3, 1931, p29.
The New Yorker. Jun 13, 1931, v7, p61, 63.
Outlook and Independent. Jun 3, 1931, v158, p154.
Rob Wagner's Script. Aug 15, 1931, v6, p8.
Time. Jun 15, 1931, v17, p60.
Variety. Jun 9, 1931, p18.

Free to Live *See* Holiday

French Without Tears (GB; Asquith, Anthony; 1939)
Commonweal. May 3, 1940, v32, p43.
Film Daily. May 7, 1940, p16.
The Films of Anthony Asquith. p96-98.
Graham Greene on Film. p248.
Motion Picture Herald. Nov 11, 1939, p42.
The New Statesman and Nation. Oct 28, 1939, v18, p609.
The New York Times. Apr 29, 1940, p12.
The Spectator. Oct 27, 1939, v163, p584.
The Tatler. Nov 1, 1939, v154, p140.
Variety. Nov 15, 1939, p20.

Frenchman's Creek (US; Leisen, Mitchell; 1944)
Commonweal. Oct 13, 1944, v40, p614.
Film Daily. Sep 20, 1944, p6.
Hollywood Reporter. Sep 20, 1944, p3.
The Nation. Oct 14, 1944, v159, p445.
The New York Times. Sep 21, 1944, p26.
The New Yorker. Sep 30, 1944, v20, p54.
Newsweek. Oct 2, 1944, v24, p106.
Scholastic. Oct 16, 1944, v45, p23.
Time. Oct 9, 1944, v44, p94+.
Variety. Sep 20, 1944, p10.

The Freshman (US; Taylor, Sam; 1925)
The Comic Mind. p154-55, 161-63.
Film Daily. Jul 12, 1925, p6.
Harold Lloyd. p79-85.
Harold Lloyd: The Shape of Laughter. p182-87.
The International Dictionary of Films and Filmmakers. v1, p162-63.
Life. Dec 3, 1925, v28, p51.
Magill's Survey of Cinema. Silent Films. v1, 395-97.
The New York Times. Sep 21, 1925, p12.
Photoplay. Sep 1925, v28, p51.
Selected Film Criticism, 1921-1930. p109.
The Silent Clowns. p208-10.
Spellbound in Darkness. p396-97.
Variety. Jul 15, 1925, p34.

Freshman Year (US; McDonald, Frank; 1938)
Film Daily. Aug 23, 1938, p7.
Hollywood Reporter. Aug 17, 1938, p3.
Hollywood Spectator. Sep 3, 1938, v13, p11.
Motion Picture Herald. Aug 20, 1938, p50.
The New York Times. Jul 10, 1938, p3.
Variety. Sep 21, 1938, p12.

Freudlose Gasse, Die *See* The Joyless Street

Frieda (GB; Dearden, Basil; 1947)
Commonweal. Aug 29, 1947, v46, p476.
Film Daily. Aug 18, 1947, p9.
Hollywood Reporter. Nov 6, 1947, p3.
Life. Sep 8, 1947, v23, p67-68.
Motion Picture Herald Product Digest. Aug 23, 1947, p3793.
New Republic. Sep 22, 1947, v117, p39.
The New York Times. Aug 15, 1947, p12.
The New Yorker. Aug 30, 1947, v23, p38.
Newsweek. Aug 25, 1947, v30, p81-82.
Sight and Sound. Aut 1947, v16, p120.
Theatre Arts. Oct 1947, v31, p52.
Time. Sep 22, 1947, v50, p98+.

Variety. Jun 25, 1947, p8.
Variety. Aug 20, 1947, p16.

Friends and Lovers (US; Schertzinger, Victor; 1931)
BFI/Monthly Film Bulletin. Oct 1979, v46, p216.
Film Daily. Nov 8, 1931, p10.
The Films of Laurence Olivier. p57-58.
Laurence Olivier: Theater and Cinema p37-38.
Life. Nov 27, 1931, v98, p21.
Magill's Survey of Cinema. Series II. v2, p847-48.
Motion Picture Herald. Aug 15, 1931, p31.
The New York Times. Nov 7, 1931, p16.
The New Yorker. Nov 14, 1931, v7, p69.
Variety. Nov 10, 1931, p15.

Frisco Jenny (US; Wellman, William A.; 1932)
Film Daily. Jan 7, 1933, p6.
Hollywood Reporter. Dec 3, 1932, p3.
The New York Times. Jan 7, 1933, p11.
Rob Wagner's Script. Dec 17, 1932, v8, p8.
Time. Jan 16, 1933, v21, p19.
Variety. Jan 10, 1933, p15.
William A. Wellman (Thompson). p130-32.

The Frisco Kid (US; Bacon, Lloyd; 1935)
Film Daily. Oct 30, 1935, p10.
The Films of James Cagney. p111-14.
Hollywood Reporter. Oct 23, 1935, p4.
Hollywood Spectator. Dec 21, 1935, v10, p11.
Literary Digest. Dec 7, 1935, v120, p24.
Motion Picture. Jan 1936, v50, p50.
Motion Picture Herald. Nov 2, 1935, p62.
The Nation. Dec 18, 1935, v141, p724.
The New York Times. Nov 25, 1935, p22.
Newsweek. Nov 30, 1935, v6, p27.
Rob Wagner's Script. Nov 30, 1935, v14, p8.
Variety. Nov 27, 1935, p14.

From the Manger to the Cross (US; Olcott, Sidney; 1912)
Magill's Survey of Cinema. Silent Films. v2, p461-63.
The Moving Picture World. Oct 26, 1912, p324.
The New York Dramatic Mirror. Oct 23, 1912, p28.
Selected Film Criticism, 1912-1920. p96-101.

From This Day Forward (US; Berry, John; 1946)
Commonweal. Apr 26, 1946, v44, p47.
Film Daily. Mar 1, 1946, p6.
Hollywood Reporter. Feb 26, 1946, p3.
Motion Picture Herald Product Digest. Mar 2, 1946, p2869.
The Nation. Apr 27, 1946, v162, p516.
The New York Times. Apr 20, 1946, p16.
The New Yorker. Apr 20, 1946, v22, p86.
Newsweek. Apr 29, 1946, v27, p89.
Scholastic. Apr 15, 1946, v48, p33.
Theatre Arts. Jun 1946, v30, p350.
Time. Apr 22, 1946, v47, p96+.
Variety. Feb 27, 1946, p8.

The Front Page (US; Milestone, Lewis; 1931)
Ben Hecht: Hollywood Screenwriter. p41-56.
Cinema, the Magic Vehicle. v1, p192.
Commonweal. May 6, 1931, v14, p17.
Dictionary of Films. p121.
Film Comment. Spr 1971, v7, p72-73.
Film Daily. Mar 22, 1931, p10.
Film Quarterly. Mar 22, 1931, p10.
Judge. Apr 11, 1931, v100, p19, 28.
Life. Apr 10, 1931, v97, p20.
London Mercury. Jun 1931, v24, p171-72.
Lorentz on Film. p69-71.
Magill's Survey of Cinema. Series I. v2, p586-88.
Motion Picture Herald. Mar 28, 1931, p6.
Movie Comedy. p60-63.
The Nation. Apr 15, 1931, v132, p429-30.
National Board of Review Magazine. Apr 1931, v6, p14.
The New Republic. Apr 29, 1931, v66, p303.

The New York Times. Mar 20, 1931, p29.
The New Yorker. Mar 28, 1931, v7, p75.
Outlook and Independent. Apr 1, 1931, v157, p475.
Rob Wagner's Script. Jun 27, 1931, v5, p9-10.
Saturday Review (London). May 9, 1931, v151, p678.
The Spectator. May 16, 1931, v146, p768.
Talking Pictures. p315-19.
Time. Mar 30, 1931, v17, p33.
Variety. Mar 25, 1931, p17.
World Film News. May-Jun 1938, v3, p87.

Front Page Woman (US; Curtiz, Michael; 1935)
Bette Davis: Her Films and Career. p62.
Film Daily. Jul 11, 1935, p8.
Hollywood Reporter. Jul 2, 1935, p3.
Literary Digest. Jul 27, 1935, v120, p27.
Motion Picture Herald. Jul 20, 1935, p88.
The New York Times. Jul 12, 1935, p15.
The New Yorker. Jul 20, 1935, v11, p47.
Newsweek. Jul 20, 1935, v6, p29.
Popcorn Venus. p145.
Rob Wagner's Script. Aug 24, 1935, v13, p8.
Time. Jul 22, 1935, v26, p30.
Variety. Jul 17, 1935, p27.

Frontier (Russian title: Aerograd; Also titled: Air-City)
     (USSR; Dovzhenko, Alexander; 1935)
Film Daily. Dec 30, 1935, p5.
The Nation. Jan 15, 1936, v142, p84.
The New Masses. Dec 31, 1935, v18, p29.
The New Masses. Jan 7, 1936, v18, p29-30.
New Theatre. Jan 1936, v3, p24, 42.
The New York Times. Dec 28, 1935, p10.
The New Yorker. Jan 11, 1936, v11, p64.
Partisan Review. Aug-Sep 1938, v5, p48-49.
Variety. Jan 8, 1936, p12.
Variety. Jan 1, 1936, p58.

Frontier Marshall (US; Seiler, Lewis; 1934)
Film Daily. Jan 31, 1934, p6.
Motion Picture Herald. Feb 11, 1934, p42.
The New York Times. Jan 31, 1934, p20.
Variety. Feb 6, 1934, p34.

Frontier Marshall (US; Dwan, Allan; 1939)
Commonweal. Aug 11, 1939, v30, p380.
Film Daily. Jul 31, 1939, p12.
The Great Western Pictures. p107-08.
Hollywood Reporter. Jul 22, 1939, p3.
Motion Picture Herald. Jul 29, 1939, p50.
The New York Times. Jul 29, 1939, p18.
The New Yorker. Aug 5, 1939, v15, p64.
Photoplay. Oct 1939, v53, p89.
Variety. Jul 26, 1939, p15.

The Fugitive (US; 1910)
The New York Dramatic Mirror. Nov 16, 1910, p30.
Selected Film Criticism, 1896-1911. p42.

The Fugitive (Also titled: On the Night of the Fire) (US;
     Hurst, Brian Desmond; 1940)
Commonweal. Aug 9, 1940, v32, p331.
Film Daily. Jul 25, 1940, p7.
The London Times. Nov 27, 1939, p4.
The New York Times. Jul 23, 1940, p22.
Variety. Nov 22, 1939, p14.

The Fugitive (US; Ford, John; 1947)
Commonweal. Dec 26, 1947, v47, p277-78.
Film Daily. Nov 7, 1947, p8.
The Films of Henry Fonda. p133-34.
The Fondas (Springer). p140-42.
The Hollywood Reporter. Nov 5, 1947, p3.
Life. Oct 6, 1947, v23, p51.
Magill's Survey of Cinema, Series II. v2, p855-57.
Motion Picture Herald Product Digest. Nov 8, 1947, p3917.

New Republic. Dec 29, 1947, v117, p34.
The New York Times. Dec 26, 1947, p22.
The New Yorker. Dec 27, 1947, v23, p38.
Newsweek. Jan 12, 1948, v31, p78.
The Non-Western Films of John Ford. p262-71.
Religion in Film. p62-65+.
Theatre Arts. Nov 1947, v31, p48.
Time. Dec 1, 1947, v50, p105.
Variety. Nov 5, 1947, p8.

Full Confession (US; Farrow, John; 1939)
Commonweal. Oct 6, 1939, v30, p539.
Film Daily. Sep 19, 1939, p5.
Hollywood Reporter. Aug 19, 1939, p4.
The New York Times. Sep 28, 1939, p29.
Variety. Aug 23, 1939, p14.

Fury (US; Lang, Fritz; 1936)
America in the Dark. p171-74.
American Film Criticism. p339-40.
Black Images in American Films, 1896-1954. p191-92.
Canadian Magazine. Aug 1936, v86, p36.
Cinema, the Magic Vehicle. v1, p256-57.
Commonweal. Jun 26, 1936, v24, p246.
Crime Movies. p159-60.
Dark Cinema. p143-44.
Dictionary of Films. p122.
Eighty Years of Cinema. p110.
Esquire. Aug 1936, v6, p99, 108.
The Film Criticism of Otis Ferguson. p135-37.
Film Daily. May 22, 1936, p8.
The Films of Fritz Lang. p172-76.
The Films of Spencer Tracy. p126-28.
Fritz Lang (Eisner). p160-76.
Garbo and the Night Watchman. p132-35, 206-08.
Graham Greene on Film. p84-85.
Great Film Directors. p600-01.
Hollywood Reporter. May 19, 1936, p3.
Hollywood Spectator. Jun 6, 1936, v11, p8-9.
A Library of Film Criticism: American Film Directors. p244-
     45.
Literary Digest. May 30, 1936, v121, p28.
London Mercury. Aug 1936, v34, p349.
Magill's Survey of Cinema. Series I. v2, p596-99.
Motion Picture Herald. May 30, 1936, p37.
The Nation. Jun 24, 1936, v142, p821.
The New Masses. Jun 16, 1936, v19, p28.
The New Republic. Jun 10, 1936, v87, p130.
New Theatre. Jul 1936, v3, p11-12.
The New York Times. Jun 6, 1936, p21.
The New Yorker. Jun 13, 1936, v12, p66-67.
Newsweek. Jun 13, 1936, v7, p39-40.
Sight and Sound. Aut 1936, v5, p78-79.
Sight and Sound. Sum 1955, v25, p15-21+.
The Spectator. Jul 3, 1936, v157, p15.
The Tatler. Jul 8, 1936, v141, p52.
Time. Jun 8, 1936, v27, p40.
Vanity Fair. Apr 1936, v40, p43.
Variety. Jun 10, 1936, p18.
We're In the Money. p120-22.
World Film News. Aug 1936, v1, p17.

G Men (US; Keighley, William; 1935)
America in the Dark. p168-69.
Classics of the Gangster Film. p31-35.
The Film Criticism of Otis Ferguson. p76-77.
Film Daily. Apr 18, 1935, p4.
The Films of James Cagney. p98-101.
The Gangster Film. p122-25.
The Great Gangster Pictures. p148-50.
Hollywood Genres. p101-02.
Hollywood Reporter. Apr 17, 1935, p3.
Hollywood Reporter. May 7, 1935, p4.
Judge. Jul 1935, v108, p16-17.
Literary Digest. May 11, 1935, v119, p30.

Motion Picture Herald. Apr 20, 1935, p48.
The Nation. Jun 12, 1935, v140, p694+.
The New Republic. May 15, 1935, v83, p19.
The New York Times. May 2, 1935, p17.
The New Yorker. May 4, 1935, v11, p59.
Newsweek. May 4, 1935, v5, p25.
Rob Wagner's Script. Apr 27, 1935, v13, p11.
The Spectator. Jun 21, 1935, v154, p1062.
Theatre Arts Monthly. Jun 1935, v19, p406.
Time. May 13, 1935, v25, p39.
Vanity Fair. Jun 1935, v44, p49.
Variety. May 8, 1935, p16.
We're in the Money. p84-88.

Gabriel Over the White House (US; La Cava, Gregory; 1933)
Cinema Examined. p202-21.
Cinema Quarterly. Sum 1933, v1, p241-42.
Commonweal. May 5, 1933, v18, p20.
Crime Movies. p106-08.
Film Daily. Apr 1, 1933, p3.
Judge. May 20, 1933, v104, p20, 23.
Literary Digest. Apr 22, 1933, v115, p13.
Lorentz on Film. p112-13.
Motion Picture Herald. Apr 8, 1933, p26.
Movie Classic. May 1933, v4, p30-31+.
The Nation. Apr 26, 1933, v136, p482-83.
The New Masses. May 1933, v8, p24-25.
New Outlook. May 1933, v161, p47.
The New Republic. Apr 19, 1933, v74, p280-82.
The New York Times. Apr 1, 1933, p18.
The New Yorker. Apr 8, 1933, v9, p56-57.
Newsweek. Apr 8, 1933, v1, p25.
Time. Apr 10, 1933, v21, p27.
Vanity Fair. Jun 1933, v40, p37.
Variety. Apr 4, 1933, p15.
We're in the Money. p115-18.

Gallant Lady (US; La Cava, Gregory; 1933)
Esquire. Mar 1934, v1, p127.
Film Daily. Dec 7, 1933, p6.
Hollywood Reporter. Dec 2, 1933, p3.
Motion Picture Herald. Dec 9, 1933, p38.
The New York Times. Jan 22, 1934, p12.
Newsweek. Jan 13, 1934, v3, p34.
Rob Wagner's Script. Dec 30, 1933, v10, p11-12.
Time. Jan 15, 1934, v23, p34.
Vanity Fair. Feb 1934, v41, p45.
Variety. Jan 23, 1934, p13.

The Gamblers (US; Curtiz, Michael; 1929)
Film Daily. Aug 25, 1929, p9.
The New York Times. Aug 24, 1929, p11.
Variety. Sep 18, 1929, p18.

Gambling Ship (US; Gasnier, Louis; Marcin, Max; 1933)
Film Daily. Jul 13, 1933, p26.
The Films of Cary Grant. p62-64.
Hollywood Reporter. Jun 3, 1933, p3.
Motion Picture Herald. Jun 17, 1933, p36-37.
New Outlook. Aug 1933, v162, p45.
The New York Times. Jul 13, 1933, p17.
Rob Wagner's Script. Jul 8, 1933, v9, p9-10.
Variety. Jul 18, 1933, p37.

The Gang Buster (US; Sutherland, Edward; 1931)
Film Daily. Jan 25, 1931, p11.
The Great Gangster Pictures. p151-52.
Judge. Feb 14, 1931, v100, p22.
The New York Times. Jan 24, 1931, p15.
The New York Times. Feb 1, 1931, p5.
Pictures Will Talk. p35-36.
Time. Feb 2, 1931, v17, p40.
Variety. Jan 28, 1931, p15.

The Gang's All Here (US; Berkeley, Busby; 1943)
Busby Berkeley and the Movie Musical. p151-55.
The Busby Berkeley Book. p151-55.
Commonweal. Dec 10, 1943, v39, p206.
Film Daily. Nov 29, 1943, p5.
The Films of Alice Faye. p165-68.
The Films of the Forties. p100-01.
The Hollywood Musical. p232-34.
Hollywood Reporter. Nov 26, 1943, p3.
Motion Picture Herald Product Digest. Dec 4, 1943, p1653.
The New York Times. Dec 23, 1943, p26.
Selected Film Criticism, 1941-1950. p62-63.
Variety. Dec 1, 1943, p10.

Gangs of New York (US; Cruze, James; 1938)
Film Daily. May 23, 1938, p10.
Motion Picture Herald. May 28, 1938, p54.
The New York Times. May 28, 1938, p9.
The New Yorker. May 28, 1938, v14, p60.
Variety. May 25, 1938, p13.

Gangster's Boy (US; Nigh, William; 1938)
Film Daily. Nov 8, 1938, p4.
The Great Gangster Pictures. p159-60.
Motion Picture Herald. Nov 12, 1938, p38, 40.
The New Statesman and Nation. Mar 4, 1939, v17, p322.
The New York Times. Nov 7, 1938, p23.
The New Yorker. Nov 12, 1938, v14, p95.
Time. Nov 14, 1938, v32, p43.
Variety. Nov 9, 1938, p16.

Gangway (GB; Hale, Sonnie; 1937)
The Age of the Dream Palace. p221.
Film Daily. Aug 18, 1937, p11.
Graham Greene on Film. p173.
Great Britain and the East. Jul 8, 1937, v49, p51.
Hollywood Reporter. Aug 17, 1937, p3.
Motion Picture Herald. Aug 28, 1937, p50.
The New York Times. Aug 21, 1937, p7.
Time. Aug 30, 1937, v30, p23.
Variety. Aug 18, 1937, p27.
World Film News. Nov 1937, v2, p22-24.

The Garden of Allah (US; Campbell, Colin; 1917)
Motion Picture News. Aug 18, 1917, p1150.
The New York Dramatic Mirror. Jul 28, 1915, p22.
Selected Film Criticism, 1912-1920. p101-02.

The Garden of Allah (US; Ingram, Rex; 1927)
Film Daily. Sep 11, 1927, p6.
The Moving Picture World. Sep 10, 1927, p113.
The New York Times. Sep 11, 1927, sec8, p5.
The New York Times. Sep 3, 1927, p13.
Photoplay. Nov 1927, v32, p54.
Rex Ingram: Master of the Silent Cinema. p169-73.
Selected Film Criticism, 1921-1930. p109-12.
Variety. Sep 7, 1927, p20.

The Garden of Allah (US; Boleslavski, Richard; 1936)
Canadian Magazine. Oct 1936, v86, p44-45.
Commonweal. Nov 27, 1936, v25, p134.
Esquire. Jan 1937, v7, p109.
Film Daily. Nov 3, 1936, p6.
The Films of Marlene Dietrich. p127-31.
Garbo and the Night Watchman. p192.
Graham Greene on Film. p125-26.
Hollywood Reporter. Oct 31, 1936, p3.
Hollywood Spectator. Nov 7, 1936, v11, p6-7.
Literary Digest. Nov 14, 1936, v122, p11.
Motion Picture Herald. Nov 7, 1936, p54.
Motion Picture Herald. Jun 6, 1936, p14-15.
The New Masses. Dec 1, 1936, v21, p28.
The New York Times. Nov 20, 1936, p27.
The New Yorker. Nov 21, 1936, v12, p79.
Newsweek. Nov 21, 1936, v8, p21-22.
Rob Wagner's Script. Jan 16, 1937, v16, p10.

Selected Film Criticism, 1931-1940. p80-81.
The Spectator. Dec 25, 1936, v157, p1122.
Stage. Dec 1936, v14, p16.
Time. Nov 30, 1936, v28, p39-40.
Variety. Nov 25, 1936, p14.
World Film News. Feb 1937, v1, p27.

The Garden of Eden (US; Milestone, Lewis; 1928)
Exhibitor's Herald-World. Jul 28, 1928, p47.
Film Daily. Mar 25, 1928, p6.
The New York Times. Mar 19, 1928, p26.
Variety. Mar 21, 1928, p18.

Garden of the Moon (US; Berkeley, Busby; 1938)
The Busby Berkeley Book. p118.
Commonweal. Aug 26, 1938, v28, p451.
Film Daily. Sep 16, 1938, p7.
Hollywood Reporter. Jul 21, 1938, p3.
Hollywood Spectator. Aug 20, 1938, v13, p10-11.
The New York Times. Sep 24, 1938, p13.
Rob Wagner's Script. Oct 1, 1938, v20, p10-11.
Time. Oct 3, 1938, v32, p36.
Variety. Aug 17, 1938, p12.

Gaslight (US; Cukor, George; 1944)
Collier's. Mar 18, 1944, v108, p4.
Commonweal. May 26, 1944, v40, p132.
Film Comment. May-Jun 1976, v12, p23-25.
Film Daily. May 11, 1944, p7.
Film Heritage. Sum 1973, v8, p19-25.
The Films of Ingrid Bergman. p97-100.
The Films of the Forties. p113-15.
George Cukor (Phillips). p47-51.
Halliwell's Hundred. p89-92.
Hollywood Reporter. May 8, 1944, p3.
Ingrid Bergman. p61-67.
Life. May 22, 1944, v16, p75-78.
Magill's Survey of Cinema. Series I. v2, p600-04.
Motion Picture Exhibitor. May 17, 1944, v32, n1, sec2, p1507.
Motion Picture Herald Product Digest. May 16, 1944, p1885.
The Nation. May 20, 1944, v158, p605.
The New Republic. May 22, 1944, v110, p711.
The New York Times. May 5, 1944, p17.
The New Yorker. May 13, 1944, v20, p66.
Newsweek. May 22, 1944, v23, p102.
Rob Wagner's Script. Jul 15, 1944, v30, p24.
Selected Film Criticism, 1941-1950. p63-65.
Time. May 22, 1944, v43, p94+.
Variety. May 10, 1944, p10.
Women's Film and Female Experience. p176-85.

The Gaucho (US; Jones, F. Richard; 1927)
Film Daily. Nov 27, 1927, p6.
His Majesty the American. p155-62.
Literary Digest. Dec 31, 1927, v95, p26.
Magill's Survey of Cinema. Silent Films. v2, p464-66.
The Moving Picture World. Nov 26, 1927, p25.
The New York Times. Nov 22, 1927, p32.
Variety. Nov 9, 1927, p18.

The Gay Deception (US; Wyler, William; 1935)
Hollywood Reporter. Aug 5, 1935, p3.
Motion Picture Herald. Aug 24, 1935, p58.
The New York Times. Oct 11, 1935, p31.
Newsweek. Sep 21, 1935, v6, p17.
Rob Wagner's Script. Sep 14, 1935, v14, p8.
Time. Sep 16, 1935, v26, p63.
Variety. Oct 16, 1935, p21.
William Wyler: A Guide to References and Resources. p82-84.
William Wyler (Anderegg). p39-42.

The Gay Desperado (US; Mamoulian, Rouben; 1936)
Commonweal. Oct 23, 1936, v24, p617.
Esquire. Dec 1936, v6, p133.
Esquire. Dec 1937, v8, p166, 268.
The Film Criticism of Otis Ferguson. p157-59.

Film Daily. Oct 3, 1936, p3.
Garbo and the Night Watchman. p87-88.
Graham Greene on Film. p116-17.
The Hollywood Musical. p103-04.
Hollywood Reporter. Sep 30, 1936, p3.
Mamoulian (Milne). p101-05.
Motion Picture Herald. Oct 10, 1936, p52.
Motion Picture Herald. Sep 5, 1936, p32-33.
The New Masses. Oct 20, 1936, v21, p28.
The New Republic. Oct 28, 1936, v88, p351.
The New Statesman and Nation. Nov 14, 1936, v12, p773.
The New York Times. Oct 9, 1936, p31.
The New Yorker. Oct 10, 1936, v12, p70.
Newsweek. Oct 10, 1936, v8, p30.
Rob Wagner's Script. Nov 7, 1936, v16, p10.
The Spectator. Nov 13, 1936, v157, p851.
Time. Oct 19, 1936, v28, p66.
Variety. Oct 14, 1936, p15.
World Film News. Dec 1936, v1, p22.

The Gay Divorcee (US; Sandrich, Mark; 1934)
Film Daily. Oct 3, 1934, p10.
The Films of Ginger Rogers. p104-08.
The Films of the Thirties. p133-35.
Fred Astaire. p90-98.
The Fred Astaire & Ginger Rogers Book. p31-44.
The Hollywood Musical. p34.
Hollywood Musicals. p85, 88-91.
Hollywood Reporter. Oct 1, 1934, p3.
Life. Jan 1935, v102, p30-31.
Literary Digest. Dec 1, 1934, v118, p30.
Magill's Survey of Cinema. Series I. v2, p605-09.
Motion Picture Herald. Oct 13, 1934, p60-64.
The New Republic. Nov 21, 1934, v81, p46.
The New York Times. Nov 16, 1934, p27.
Rob Wagner's Script. Oct 20, 1934, v12, p18.
Selected Film Criticism, 1931-1940. p84.
Starring Fred Astaire. p69-81.
Time. Oct 22, 1934, v24, p44.
Variety. Nov 20, 1934, p15.

The Gay Shoe Clerk (US; Porter, Edwin S.; 1903)
Film Before Griffith. p285.
The First Twenty Years. p36.
Spellbound in Darkness. p27, 32, 33.

Geheimnisse Einer Seele *See* Secrets of a Soul

The General (US; Keaton, Buster; Bruckman, Clyde; 1927)
Buster Keaton (Robinson). p143-54.
Cinema Journal. Spr 1970, v9, p24-30.
Cinema, the Magic Vehicle. v1, p119-20.
Classic Movies. p16-18.
Classics of the Silent Screen. p89-92.
The Comic Mind. p8, 12, 23.
Dictionary of Films. p124-25.
The Film Career of Buster Keaton. p64-68.
Film Daily. Feb 20, 1927, p10.
Films and Filming. Oct 1963, v10, p31.
Films and Filming. Sep 1961, v7, p14-16.
The International Dictionary of Films and Filmmakers. v1, p167-68.
Landmark Films. p44-51.
Life. Feb 1927, v89, p26.
Magill's Survey of Cinema. Silent Films. v2, p467-71.
Motion Picture Classic. Apr 1927, v25, p80.
The Moving Picture World. Feb 12, 1927, p513.
The New York Times. Feb 8, 1927, p8, 21.
Photoplay. Mar 1927, v31, p52.
Selected Film Criticism, 1921-1930. p110.
Sight and Sound. Apr-Jun 1953, v22, p198-99.
The Silent Clowns. p253-63.
Spellbound in Darkness. p450.
Variety. Feb 9, 1927, p16.

General Crack (US; Crosland, Alan; 1929)
Film Daily. Dec 28, 1929, p10.
The Film Spectator. Jan 18, 1930, v9, p23.
National Board of Review Magazine. Jan 1930, v5, p7.
The New York Times. Dec 4, 1929, p36.
The New Yorker. Dec 14, 1929, v5, p68.
Time. Dec 16, 1929, v14, p58.
Variety. Dec 11, 1929, p35.

The General Died at Dawn (US; Milestone, Lewis; 1936)
Commonweal. Sep 25, 1936, v24, p504.
Esquire. Nov 1936, v6, p125.
The Film Criticism of Otis Ferguson. p150-52.
Film Daily. Sep 3, 1936, p6.
The Films of Gary Cooper. p144-46.
The Films of the Thirties. p169-70.
Hollywood Reporter. Sep 1, 1936, p3.
Hollywood Spectator. Sep 12, 1936, v11, p11-12.
Judge. Nov 1936, v111, p12.
Motion Picture Herald. Aug 15, 1936, p16-17.
Motion Picture Herald. Sep 12, 1936, p45.
The Nation. Sep 26, 1936, v143, p375.
National Board of Review Magazine. Sep-Oct 1936, v11, p8.
The New Masses. Jul 28, 1936, v20, p12-13.
The New Masses. Sep 8, 1936, v20, p29.
The New Republic. Sep 16, 1936, v88, p156-57.
The New Statesman and Nation. Oct 17, 1936, v12, p588-89.
New Theatre. Oct 1936, v3, p18.
The New York Times. Sep 3, 1936, p17.
The New Yorker. Sep 12, 1936, v12, p74-75.
Newsweek. Sep 12, 1936, v8, p42.
Photoplay. Sep 1936, v50, p10-11.
The Pleasure-Dome. p112-13.
Rob Wagner's Script. Sep 19, 1936, v16, p10.
Scholastic. Oct 3, 1936, v29, p32.
The Spectator. Oct 30, 1936, v157, p747.
Stage. Oct 1936, v14, p24, 42-43.
Time. Sep 14, 1936, v28, p28.
Variety. Sep 9, 1936, p16.
World Film News. Nov 1936, v1, p19.

The General Line *See* The Old and the New

Generals Without Buttons (FR; Daroy, Jacques; 1938)
The Film Criticism of Otis Ferguson. p216-17.
Film Daily. Feb 1, 1938, p12.
Hollywood Reporter. Jan 25, 1938, p7.
Motion Picture Herald. Jan 29, 1938, p56.
The Nation. Mar 26, 1938, v146, p366.
National Board of Review Magazine. Apr 1938, v13, p19.
The New Masses. Mar 22, 1938, v26, p27-28.
The New Republic. Mar 16, 1938, v94, p165-66.
The New York Times. Mar 8, 1938, p23.
The New Yorker. Mar 12, 1938, v14, p57.
Scholastic. Mar 5, 1938, v32, p23.
Time. Mar 21, 1938, v31, p40.
Variety. Jan 26, 1938, p15.
World Film News. May-Jun 1938, v3, p89.

A Generation of Conquerors *See* Revolutionists

Gens du Voyage, Les (FR; Feyder, Jacques; 1938)
French Film (Sadoul). p85.
London Mercury. Apr 1939, v39, p632-33.
The New Statesman and Nation. Mar 11, 1939, v17, p357.
The Spectator. Mar 17, 1939, v162, p444.
Variety. Apr 6, 1938, p15.

Gentle Julia (US; Blystone, John G.; 1936)
Canadian Magazine. Apr 1936, v85, p59.
Film Daily. Feb 19, 1936, p4.
Hollywood Reporter. Feb 15, 1936, p3.
Motion Picture Herald. Feb 29, 1936, p40-41.
The New York Times. Apr 11, 1936, p19.
Scholastic. Feb 8, 1936, v28, p30.

Time. Apr 27, 1936, v27, p36.
Variety. Apr 15, 1936, p4.

Gentleman Jim (US; Walsh, Raoul; 1942)
Commonweal. Dec 18, 1942, v37, p231.
Each Man in His Own Time. p333-34.
Film Daily. Oct 30, 1942, p7.
The Films of Errol Flynn. p115-18.
Hollywood Reporter. Oct 30, 1942, p3.
The London Times. Oct 18, 1942, p8.
Magill's Survey of Cinema. Series II. v2, p868-73.
Motion Picture Exhibitor. Nov 4, 1942, v27, n26, sec2, p1145.
Motion Picture Herald Product Digest. Oct 31, 1942, p981.
Movietone News. Nov 1975, n45, p24-30.
The New York Times. Nov 26, 1942, p40.
The New York Times. Nov 29, 1942, sec8, p3.
Newsweek. Nov 9, 1942, v20, p68.
Time. Dec 14, 1942, v40, p110+.
Variety. Nov 4, 1942, p8.

A Gentleman of Paris (US; D'Arrast, Harry D'Abbadie; 1927)
Film Daily. Oct 9, 1927, p6.
Magill's Survey of Cinema. Silent Films. v2, p472-74.
The Moving Picture World. Oct 8, 1927, p381.
The New York Times. Oct 3, 1927, p20.
Variety. Oct 5, 1927, p22.

Gentleman's Agreement (US; Kazan, Elia; 1947)
Canadian Forum. May 1948, v28, p39.
Commentary. Jan 1948, v5, p51-56.
Commentary. Mar 1949, v7, p278-80.
Commonweal. Nov 21, 1947, v47, p144.
Film Daily. Nov 11, 1947, p8.
The Films of Gregory Peck. p70-77.
The Films of John Garfield. p156-57.
Fortnight. Dec 19, 1947, v3, p28.
Hollywood Reporter. Nov 10, 1947, p3.
The Hollywood Social Problem Films. p238-41.
Life. Dec 1, 1947, v23, p95-96.
Magill's Survey of Cinema, Series I. v2, p610-12.
Motion Picture Herald Product Digest. Nov 15, 1947, p3929.
New Movies. Dec 1947, v22, p4-5.
New Republic. Nov 17, 1947, v117, p38.
The New York Times. Nov 12, 1947, p36.
The New Yorker. Nov 15, 1947, v23, p117.
Newsweek. Nov 17, 1947, v30, p98.
Photoplay. Feb 1948, v32, p20.
Saturday Review. Dec 6, 1947, v30, p68-71.
Selected Film Criticism, 1941-1950. p64-66.
Theatre Arts. Jan 1948, v32, p32-33.
Time. Nov 17, 1947, v50, p105.
Variety. Nov 12, 1947, p8.

A Gentleman's Fate (US; LeRoy, Mervyn; 1931)
Film Daily. Jun 23, 1931, p10.
The Hollywood Professionals: King Vidor, John Cromwell. p137.
Motion Picture Herald. Jan 31, 1931, p54.
The New York Times. Jun 27, 1931, p20.
The New Yorker. Jul 4, 1931, v7, p48.
Variety. Jun 30, 1931, p15.

Gentlemen Prefer Blondes (US; St. Clair, Malcolm; 1928)
Exhibitor's Herald-World and Moving Picture World. Feb 18, 1928, p47-48.
Film Daily. Jan 22, 1928, p6.
The Film Spectator. Dec 10, 1927, v4, p8-9.
The New York Times. Jan 16, 1928, p24.
Selected Film Criticism, 1921-1930. p110-113.
Variety. Jan 18, 1928, p13.

George Washington Slept Here (US; Keighley, William; 1942)
Commonweal. Nov 13, 1942, v37, p97.
Film Daily. Sep 18, 1942, p6.

Hollywood Reporter. Sep 18, 1942, p3.
Life. Nov 30, 1942, v13, p57-59.
Motion Picture Herald Product Digest. Sep 19, 1942, p909.
Musician. Jan 1943, v47, p184.
The New York Times. Oct 31, 1942, p11.
Newsweek. Nov 9, 1942, v20, p66.
Time. Nov 30, 1942, v40, p94.
Variety. Sep 23, 1942, p8.

Germany, Year Zero (Italian title: Germania, Anno Zero)
(IT; Rossellini, Roberto; 1947)
BFI/Monthly Film Bulletin. Nov 1980, v47, p225-26.
Christian Century. Jan 25, 1950, v67, p127.
Commonweal. Oct 7, 1949, v50, p632.
Dictionary of Films. p126.
Film Daily. Oct 28, 1949, p6.
Films in Review. Feb 1950, v6, p35-36.
Fortnight. Jan 6, 1950, v8, p31.
Harpers. Oct 1949, v199, p100-02.
The Italian Cinema (Leprohon). p116-17.
Magill's Survey of Cinema. Foreign Language Films. v3,
    p1211-15.
New Republic. Oct 3, 1949, v121, p22.
The New York Times. Sep 20, 1947, p35.
The New Yorker. Sep 24, 1949, v25, p52.
Newsweek. Sep 26, 1949, v34, p90.
Rossellini: The War Trilogy. p349-467.
Saturday Review. Oct 15, 1949, v33, p7.
Selected Film Criticism: Foreign Films, 1930-1950. p55.
Sequence. Sum 1949, n8, p84-85.
Theatre Arts. Oct 1949, v33, p7.
Variety. Jun 9, 1948, p12.

Gestapo *See* Night Train

Getting Gertie's Garter (US; Hopper, E. Mason; 1927)
Film Daily. Feb 13, 1927, p8.
The Moving Picture World. Feb 19, 1927, p591.
The New York Times. Feb 9, 1927, p17.
Variety. Feb 9, 1927, p16.

The Ghost and Mrs. Muir (US; Mankiewicz, Joseph L.;
    1947)
Commonweal. Jul 11, 1947, v46, p311.
Film Daily. May 20, 1947, p6.
The Films of the Forties. p198-200.
Hollywood Reporter. May 16, 1947, p3.
Joseph L. Mankiewicz. p49-54.
Magill's Survey of Cinema, Series II. v2, p877-79.
Motion Picture Herald Product Digest. May 24, 1947, p3641.
New Republic. May 26, 1947, v116, p36.
The New York Times. Jun 27, 1947, p17.
The New Yorker. Jul 5, 1947, v23, p42.
Newsweek. Jun 30, 1947, v29, p76.
Time. Jun 23, 1947, v49, p93.
Variety. May 21, 1947, p20.

The Ghost Breaker (US; DeMille, Cecil B.; Apfel, Oscar
    C.; 1914)
The Moving Picture World. Dec 19, 1914, p1692, 1747.
The New York Dramatic Mirror. Dec 9, 1914, p38.
Variety. Dec 11, 1914, p28.

The Ghost Breaker (US; Green, Alfred E.; 1922)
Film Daily. Sep 17, 1922, p8.
The New York Times. Sep 11, 1922, p20.
Variety. Sep 15, 1922, p42.

The Ghost Goes West (GB; Clair, René; 1935)
The Age of the Dream Palace. p229.
Commonweal. Jan 24, 1936, v23, p356.
Esquire. Apr 1936, v5, p104, 162-65.
Film Daily. Jan 11, 1936, p3.
Graham Greene on Film. p40-41.
Great Horror Movies. p81-82.
Hollywood Reporter. Dec 18, 1935, p3.

Hollywood Spectator. Feb 1, 1936, v10, p10-11.
Judge. Mar 1936, v110, p14.
Kiss Kiss Bang Bang. p336.
Life. Mar 1936, v103, p28.
Literary Digest. Jan 18, 1936, v121, p20.
London Mercury. Feb 1936, v33, p434.
Lorentz on Film. p130-32.
Motion Picture Herald. Jan 4, 1936, p48.
The Nation. Jan 29, 1936, v142, p138, 140.
The New Masses. Jan 28, 1936, v18, p29.
The New York Times. Jan 11, 1936, p9.
The New Yorker. Jan 18, 1936, v11, p52.
Newsweek. Jan 18, 1936, v7, p40.
The Pleasure-Dome. p40-41.
René Clair (McGerr). p123-30.
Rob Wagner's Script. Feb 1, 1936, v14, p10.
Saturday Review (London). Dec 28, 1935, v160, p672.
Scholastic. Feb 1, 1936, v28, p26.
Selected Film Criticism: Foreign Films, 1930-1950. p55-56.
The Spectator. Dec 27, 1935, v155, p1068.
Stage. Feb 1936, v13, p9.
The Tatler. Jan 1, 1936, v139, p6.
Time. Jan 20, 1936, v27, p57.
Variety. Jan 15, 1936, p18.

Ghosts (US; Nicholls, George, Jr; 1915)
Motion Picture News. May 29, 1915, p67.
Motography. Jun 5, 1915, p923-24, 953.
The Moving Picture World. May 29, 1915, p1439, 1510.
Variety. Jun 11, 1915, p19.

G.I. Joe *See* The Story of G.I. Joe

Gilda (US; Vidor, Charles; 1946)
Ben Hecht: Hollywood Screenwriter. p166-67.
Commonweal. Apr 5, 1946, v43, p623.
Film Daily. Mar 14, 1946, p10.
The Films of Rita Hayworth. p156-63.
Halliwell's Hundred. p104-07.
Hollywood Reporter. Mar 13, 1946, p3.
Magill's Survey of Cinema. Series I. v2, p627-29.
Motion Picture Herald Product Digest. Mar 23, 1946, p2907.
The New York Times. Mar 15, 1946, p27.
The New Yorker. Mar 23, 1946, v22, p77.
Newsweek. Mar 25, 1946, v27, p94.
Selected Film Criticism, 1941-1950. p66-69.
Time. Apr 1, 1946, v47, p94.
Variety. Mar 20, 1946, p8.

The Gilded Lily (US; Ruggles, Wesley; 1935)
Claudette Colbert (Quirk). p71-74.
Film Daily. Feb 9, 1935, p4.
The Films of the Thirties. p142-43.
The Films of the Thirties. p42-43.
Hollywood Reporter. Feb 13, 1935, p2.
Hollywood Reporter. Dec 26, 1934, p4.
Literary Digest. Feb 23, 1935, v119, p33.
Lunatics and Lovers. p24-26.
Motion Picture Herald. Jan 5, 1935, p35, 38.
National Board of Review Magazine. Feb 1935, v10, p9.
The New Masses. Feb 19, 1935, v14, p27.
The New Republic. Feb 6, 1935, v81, p361.
The New York Times. Feb 9, 1935, p11.
The New Yorker. Feb 16, 1935, v11, p64-65.
Rob Wagner's Script. Feb 9, 1935, v12, p8-9.
Time. Feb 4, 1935, v25, p38.
Vanity Fair. Mar 1935, v44, p54.
Variety. Feb 12, 1935, p19.

Girl Crazy (US; Seiter, William A.; 1932)
Film Daily. Mar 27, 1932, p22.
Hollywood Reporter. Mar 9, 1932, p5.
Judge. Apr 16, 1932, v102, p22.
Motion Picture Herald. Apr 2, 1932, p35.
The New York Times. Mar 25, 1932, p23.

Time. Apr 4, 1932, v19, p22.
Variety. Mar 29, 1932, p25.

Girl Crazy (US; Taurog, Norman; 1943)
The Busby Berkeley Book. p150-51.
Commonweal. Dec 17, 1943, v39, p233.
Film Daily. Aug 3, 1943, p6.
The Hollywood Musical. p233-34.
Hollywood Reporter. Aug 3, 1943, p3.
Judy: The Films and Career of Judy Garland. p109-12.
Magill's Survey of Cinema. Series I. v2, p630.
Motion Picture Herald Product Digest. Aug 7, 1943, p1469.
The New York Times. Dec 3, 1943, p27.
Time. Dec 27, 1943, v42, p90.

The Girl from Calgary (US; Whitman, Phil; D'Usseau, Leon; 1932)
Film Daily. Nov 17, 1932, p7.
Hollywood Reporter. Sep 9, 1932, p2.
Variety. Nov 22, 1932, p36.

The Girl from Jones Beach (US; Godfrey, Peter; 1949)
Commonweal. Aug 5, 1949, v50, p415.
Film Daily. Jun 27, 1949, p6.
The Films of Ronald Reagan. p163-66.
Hollywood Reporter. Jun 21, 1949, p3.
Motion Picture Herald Product Digest. Jun 25, 1949, p4658.
The New York Times. Jul 30, 1949, p9.
Newsweek. Aug 1, 1949, v34, p66.
Rotarian. Oct 1949, v75, p39.
Time. Jul 25, 1949, v54, p79.
Variety. Jun 22, 1949, p6.

The Girl from Outside (US; Barker, Reginald; 1919)
Exhibitor's Trade Review. Nov 22, 1919, p2139.
Motion Picture News. Nov 22, 1919, p3792.
The Moving Picture World. Nov 22, 1919, p454.
The New York Times. Nov 10, 1919, p18.
Variety. Nov 14, 1919, p61.
Wid's Daily. Aug 24, 1919, p7.

The Girl From 10th Avenue (US; Green, Alfred E.; 1935)
Bette Davis: Her Films and Career. p61.
Film Daily. Apr 5, 1935, p6.
Motion Picture Herald. Jun 1, 1935, p50-51.
The New Statesman and Nation. Jan 11, 1936, v11, p49.
The New York Times. May 27, 1935, p20.
The New Yorker. Jun 1, 1935, v11, p56.
Time. Jun 3, 1935, v25, p50.
Variety. May 29, 1935, p14.

The Girl from the Marsh Croft (Swedish title: Tösen från Stormytorpet; Also titled: the Girl from Stormycroft) (SWED; Sjostrom, Victor; 1917)
The New York Times. Mar 30, 1919, sec4, p6.
Swedish Cinema. p22-24.

The Girl I Loved (US; De Grasse, Joseph; 1923)
Film Daily. Feb 18, 1923, p70.
Magill's Survey of Cinema. Silent Films. v2, p475-77.
Variety. May 24, 1923, p23.
Variety. Mar 29, 1923, p36.

A Girl in Every Port (US; Hawks, Howard; 1928)
BFI/Monthly Films Bulletin. Jul 1980, v47, p142.
Film Daily. Feb 26, 1928, p6.
The Films of Howard Hawks. p102-04.
The Films of Myrna Loy. p68.
Hawks on Hawks. p24-25, 152-53+.
Howard Hawks (Poague). p73-79.
The New York Times. Feb 20, 1928, p14.
Photoplay. Mar 1928, v33, p55.
Selected Film Criticism, 1921-1930. p113.
Variety. Feb 22, 1928, p20.

A Girl Must Live (GB; Reed, Carol; 1939)
Around Cinemas. p168-70.
Hollywood Reporter. Aug 10, 1939, p5.
Motion Picture Herald. May 13, 1939, p43.
The New York Times. Mar 24, 1942, p25.
The Tatler. Aug 16, 1939, v153, p282, viii.
Variety. May 10, 1939, p23.

Girl of the Golden West (US; Leonard, Robert Z.; 1938)
Commonweal. Apr 1, 1938, v27, p636.
Film Daily. Mar 17, 1938, p4.
The Films of Jeanette MacDonald and Nelson Eddy. p221-30.
Hollywood Reporter. Mar 12, 1938, p3.
Motion Picture Herald. Mar 19, 1938, p40.
Motion Picture Herald. Feb 5, 1938, p16-17.
The New York Times. Mar 25, 1938, p15.
The New Yorker. Mar 26, 1938, v14, p61.
Rob Wagner's Script. Mar 19, 1938, v19, p13.
Saint Nicholas. Apr 1938, v65, p37+.
Variety. Mar 16, 1938, p15.
World Film News. Jul 1938, v3, p130.

The Girl Philippa (US; Drew, Sidney; 1917)
The Moving Picture World. Jan 20, 1917, p356.
The Moving Picture World. Jan 27, 1917, p584.
The New York Dramatic Mirror. Jan 13, 1917, p26.
The New York Dramatic Mirror. Jan 20, 1917, p29.
Variety. Jan 5, 1917, p27.
Wid's Daily. Jan 4, 1917, p5.

The Girl Said No (US; Wood, Sam; 1930)
Exhibitors Herald-World. Apr 12, 1930, p36.
Film Daily. Apr 6, 1930, p40.
The Film Spectator. Feb 15, 1930, v9, p18-19.
Judge. Apr 29, 1930, v98, p23.
Life. Apr 25, 1930, v95, p18.
The New York Times. Apr 5, 1930, p23.
The New York Times. Apr 13, 1930, p4.
The New Yorker. Apr 12, 1930, v6, p99.
Outlook and Independent. Apr 16, 1930, v154, p632.
Rob Wagner's Script. Apr 12, 1930, v3, p11.
Time. Apr 21, 1930, v15, p68.
Variety. Apr 9, 1930, p22.

The Girl Said No (US; Stone, Andrew L.; 1937)
Film Daily. May 21, 1937, p10.
Hollywood Reporter. May 17, 1937, p3.
Motion Picture Herald. May 29, 1937, p46.
The New York Times. Oct 18, 1937, p14.
Rob Wagner's Script. Jun 19, 1937, v17, p10.
Scholastic. Nov 6, 1937, v31, p36.
Time. Jun 21, 1937, v29, p45.

Girl Shy (US; Newmeyer, Fred; Taylor, Sam; 1924)
Film Daily. Apr 6, 1924, p6.
Harold Lloyd. p68-73.
Harold Lloyd: The Shape of Laughter. p166-75.
The Moving Picture World. Apr 12, 1924, p584.
The New York Times. Apr 21, 1924, p21.
The Silent Clowns. p200-02.
Variety. Apr 2, 1924, p23.

The Girl Was Young *See* Young and Innocent

The Girl Who Stayed at Home (US; Griffith, D.W.; 1919)
D.W. Griffith: An American Life. p386-88.
D.W. Griffith: His Life and Work. p198-200.
Exhibitor's Trade Review. Apr 5, 1919, p1359, 1371.
The Films of D.W. Griffith. p111-14.
Motion Picture Classic. Jun 1919, p46-47.
Motion Picture News. Apr 5, 1919, p2188.
The Moving Picture World. Apr 5, 1919, p77-78, 121.
The New York Times. Mar 24, 1919, p11.
Selected Film Criticism, 1912-1920. p102-03.
Variety. Mar 28, 1919, p93.
Wid's Daily. Mar 30, 1919, p9.

Girls About Town (US; Cukor, George; 1931)
Film Daily. Nov 1, 1931, p10.
George Cukor (Phillips). p32-33.
Hollywood Reporter. Oct 9, 1931, p3.
Motion Picture Herald. Oct 17, 1931, p40.
The New York Times. Nov 2, 1931, p27.
The New York Times. Nov 8, 1931, p5.
On Cukor. p40-41.
Rob Wagner's Script. Oct 31, 1931, v6, p9-10.
Rob Wagner's Script. Dec 5, 1931, v6, p11.
Variety. Nov 3, 1931, p17.

Girls' Dormitory (US; Cummings, Irving; 1936)
Canadian Magazine. Aug 1936, v86, p36.
Film Daily. Aug 29, 1936, p7.
The Films of Tyrone Power. p47-48.
Graham Greene on Film. p124.
Hollywood Reporter. Jul 25, 1936, p3.
Hollywood Spectator. Aug 1, 1936, v11, p8.
Literary Digest. Aug 29, 1936, v122, p20.
Motion Picture Herald. Aug 1, 1936, p56.
The New Masses. Sep 8, 1936, v20, p29.
The New York Times. Aug 29, 1936, p16.
The New Yorker. Sep 5, 1936, v12, p59.
Newsweek. Aug 8, 1936, v8, p31.
Rob Wagner's Script. Sep 12, 1936, v16, p10.
The Spectator. Dec 18, 1936, v157, p1081.
The Tatler. Feb 24, 1937, v143, p328.
Time. Aug 24, 1936, v28, p30.
Variety. Sep 2, 1936, p18.
World Film News. Nov 1936, v1, p20.

A Girl's Folly (US; Tourneur, Maurice; 1917)
The Moving Picture World. Mar 3, 1917, p1369, 1410.
Selected Film Criticism, 1912-1920. p103.
Variety. Feb 16, 1917, p22.
Wid's Daily. Mar 1, 1917, p137.

Girls in Uniform *See* Maedchen in Uniform

Girls' School (US; Brahm, John; 1938)
The Film Criticism of Otis Ferguson. p239-40.
Film Daily. Sep 27, 1938, p6.
Hollywood Reporter. Sep 21, 1938, p3.
Motion Picture Herald. Sep 24, 1938, p38.
The New Masses. Nov 15, 1938, v29, p29-30.
The New Republic. Nov 2, 1938, v96, p362.
The New York Times. Nov 3, 1938, p27.
The New Yorker. Nov 12, 1938, v14, p94-95.
Rob Wagner's Script. Dec 24, 1938, v20, p10.
Variety. Sep 28, 1938, p14.

Give Me a Sailor (US; Nugent, Elliott; 1938)
Commonweal. Aug 26, 1938, v28, p451.
Film Daily. Jul 26, 1938, p9.
Hollywood Reporter. Jul 22, 1938, p3.
The New York Times. Aug 11, 1938, p31.
The New Yorker. Aug 13, 1938, v14, p40.
Rob Wagner's Script. Aug 20, 1938, v20, p15-16.
Time. Aug 15, 1938, v32, p36.
Variety. Jul 27, 1938, p17.

Give Me Your Heart (US; Mayo, Archie; 1936)
Canadian Magazine. Oct 1936, v86, p45.
Esquire. Dec 1936, v6, p133.
Film Daily. Jul 14, 1936, p11.
Hollywood Reporter. Jul 10, 1936, p3.
Motion Picture Herald. Jul 18, 1936, p52.
The New York Times. Sep 17, 1936, p18.
Newsweek. Aug 8, 1936, v8, p31.
Rob Wagner's Script. Sep 26, 1936, v16, p11.
Time. Sep 28, 1936, v28, p31.
Variety. Sep 16, 1936, p16.

The Glass Key (US; Tuttle, Frank; 1935)
Film Daily. Jun 15, 1935, p3.
Hollywood Reporter. May 15, 1935, p3.
Literary Digest. Jun 29, 1935, v119, p28.
Motion Picture Herald. May 25, 1935, p54.
The New York Times. Jun 15, 1935, p20.
The New Yorker. Jun 22, 1935, v11, p53.
Rob Wagner's Script. Jun 8, 1935, v13, p8.
Time. Jun 24, 1935, v25, p51.
Variety. Jun 19, 1935, p21.

The Glorious Adventure (US; Blackton, J. Stuart; 1922)
Film Daily,. Apr 30, 1922, p2.
Magill's Survey of Cinema. Silent Films. v2, p478-80.
Motion Picture News. May 6, 1922, v25, p2592.
Photoplay. Jul 1922, v22, p54.
Selected Film Criticism, 1921-1930. p113-14.

Go Chase Yourself (US; Cline, Edward; 1938)
Film Daily. Apr 19, 1938, p6.
Hollywood Reporter. Apr 8, 1938, p3.
Motion Picture Herald. Apr 16, 1938, p36.
The New York Times. Jun 15, 1938, p27.
Rob Wagner's Script. Jun 18, 1938, v19, p15.
Variety. Apr 20, 1938, p15.

Go Into Your Dance (French title: Casino de Paree) (US; Mayo, Archie; 1935)
Esquire. Jun 1935, v3, p144.
Film Daily. Mar 19, 1935, p4.
Garbo and the Night Watchman. p59-60.
The Hollywood Musical. p77-78.
Hollywood Musicals. p82-83.
Hollywood Reporter. Mar 13, 1935, p3.
Hollywood Reporter. May 14, 1935, p6.
Motion Picture Herald. Mar 23, 1935, p42.
The New York Times. May 4, 1935, p17.
Rob Wagner's Script. May 25, 1935, v13, p6.
Time. Apr 29, 1935, v25, p56.
Variety. May 8, 1935, p16.

Go West (US; Keaton, Buster; 1925)
Buster Keaton. p128-35.
Cinema, the Magic Vehicle. v1, p117.
The Comic Mind. p130, 134.
The Film Career of Buster Keaton. p60-62.
Film Daily. Nov 1, 1925, p5.
The Moving Picture World. Nov 7, 1925, p59.
The New York Times. Oct 26, 1925, p25.
Photoplay. Jan 1926, v24, p49.
Selected Film Criticism, 1921-1930. p114-15.
The Silent Clowns. p225-26, 240-41.
Variety. Nov 28, 1925, p36.

Go West, Young Man (US; Hathaway, Henry; 1936)
Film Daily. Nov 6, 1936, p13.
The Films of Mae West. p125-32.
Graham Greene on Film. p124-25.
Hollywood Reporter. Nov 3, 1936, p3.
Hollywood Spectator. Nov 21, 1936, v11, p14.
Literary Digest. Nov 21, 1936, v122, p26.
Motion Picture Herald. Nov 14, 1936, p58.
The New Masses. Dec 1, 1936, v21, p28.
The New York Times. Nov 19, 1936, p31.
The New Yorker. Nov 21, 1936, v12, p79, 81.
Newsweek. Nov 28, 1936, v8, p20.
Rob Wagner's Script. Dec 5, 1936, v16, p10.
The Spectator. Dec 18, 1936, v157, p1081.
Time. Nov 23, 1936, v28, p25.
Variety. Nov 25, 1936, p14.

Gobsek (Also titled: Gobseck) (USSR; Eggert, Konstantin; 1935)
Film Daily. Jul 20, 1937, p11.
Motion Picture Herald. Aug 14, 1937, p63.
The New Masses. Jul 27, 1937, v24, p29.

The New York Times. Jul 16, 1937, p22.
Variety. Jul 21, 1937, p19.

God Is My Co-Pilot (US; Florey, Robert; 1945)
Film Daily. Feb 21, 1945, p4.
The Films of World War II. p220-22.
Hollywood Reporter. Feb 22, 1945, p3.
The New York Times. Mar 24, 1945, p22.
The New Yorker. Mar 24, 1945, v21, p76.
Newsweek. Apr 2, 1945, v25, p78.
Scholastic. Mar 26, 1945, v46, p46.
Time. Apr 2, 1945, v45, p90+.
Variety. Feb 21, 1945, p8.

The Gods at Play *See* Amphitryon

God's Country and the Woman (US; Keighley, William; 1936)
Film Daily. Dec 19, 1936, p3.
Graham Greene on Film. p154-55.
Hollywood Reporter. Dec 15, 1936, p3.
Hollywood Spectator. Jan 2, 1937, v11, p13-14.
Motion Picture Herald. Dec 26, 1936, p52.
The New York Times. Jan 11, 1937, p15.
Rob Wagner's Script. Feb 13, 1937, v17, p8-9.
The Spectator. Jul 16, 1937, v159, p104.
Time. Jan 18, 1937, v29, p25.
Variety. Jan 13, 1937, p13.
World Film News. Sep 1937, v2, p27.

The Go-Getter (US; Berkeley, Busby; 1937)
The Busby Berkeley Book. p108.
Film Daily. Apr 27, 1937, p10.
Hollywood Reporter. Apr 23, 1937, p3.
Hollywood Spectator. May 8, 1937, v12, p14-15.
Motion Picture Herald. Jun 19, 1937, p56.
The New York Times. Jun 4, 1937, p27.
The New Yorker. Jun 5, 1937, v13, p62.
Time. Jun 14, 1937, v29, p26+.
Variety. Jun 9, 1937, p15.

Goin' to Town (US; Hall, Alexander; 1935)
Esquire. Jul 1935, v3, p152.
Film Daily. Apr 25, 1935, p11.
The Films of Mae West. p104-14.
Hollywood Reporter. Apr 23, 1935, p3.
Judge. Jul 1935, v109, p17.
Motion Picture Herald. May 11, 1935, v54.
The New York Times. May 11, 1935, p21.
The New Yorker. May 18, 1935, v11, p67.
Rob Wagner's Script. May 18, 1935, v13, p9.
Time. May 20, 1935, v25, p32.
Variety. May 15, 1935, p19.

Going Hollywood (US; Walsh, Raoul; 1933)
Film Daily. Dec 22, 1933, p14.
Films and Filming. Jul 1973, v19, p33-34.
The Films of Bing Crosby. p55-58.
Hollywood Reporter. Dec 9, 1933, p3.
Literary Digest. Jan 6, 1934, v117, p31.
Motion Picture Herald. Dec 16, 1933, p30, 34.
The New York Times. Dec 23, 1933, p19.
The New Yorker. Dec 30, 1933, v9, p42.
Rob Wagner's Script. Jan 27, 1934, v10, p9.
Time. Jan 1, 1934, v23, p16.
Variety. Dec 26, 1933, p10.

Going My Way (US; McCarey, Leo; 1944)
Best Film Plays of 1943-1944. p149-222.
Catholic World. Sep 1944, v159, p554.
Chestnuts in Her Lap. p126-27.
Christian Century. Oct 4, 1944, v61, p1132.
Commonweal. Apr 28, 1944, v40, p41.
Film Daily. Feb 28, 1944, p12.
The Films of Bing Crosby. p143-47.
The Films of the Forties. p109-10.

Hollywood Reporter. Feb 28, 1944, p3.
Ingrid Bergman. p74-76.
Life. May 1, 1944, v16, p69-70+.
Life. Apr 2, 1945, v18, p37-38+.
The London Times. Jul 27, 1944, p6.
Magill's Survey of Cinema. Series I. v2, p648-50.
Motion Picture Exhibitor. Mar 8, 1944, v31, n17, sec2, p1468.
Motion Picture Herald Product Digest. Feb 26, 1944, p1773.
The New Captain George's Whizzbang. 1974, v3, p20-26+.
New Movies. Apr-May 1944, v19, p5-6.
The New Republic. May 8, 1944, v110, p629.
The New York Times. May 3, 1944, p25.
The New York Times. May 7, 1944, sec2, p3.
The New Yorker. May 13, 1944, v20, p66.
Newsweek. May 15, 1944, v23, p78+.
Photoplay. Mar 1945, v26, p28-29.
Rob Wagner's Script. Aug 30, 1944, v19, p5-6.
Selected Film Criticism, 1941-1950. p69-71.
Time. May 1, 1944, v43, p90.
Variety. Mar 8, 1944, p14.

Going Places (US; Enright, Ray; 1938)
Film Daily. Dec 28, 1938, p4.
The Films of Ronald Reagan. p64-66.
Hollywood Reporter. Dec 17, 1938, p3.
Hollywood Spectator. Dec 24, 1938, v13, p20-21.
Motion Picture Herald. Dec 24, 1938, p41.
The New York Times. Jan 7, 1939, p6.
Time. Jan 16, 1939, v31, p26.
Variety. Jan 11, 1939, p12.

Going Wild (US; Seiter, William A.; 1931)
Film Daily. Feb 1, 1931, p10.
Motion Picture Herald. Jan 31, 1931, p54.
The New York Times. Jan 26, 1931, p21.
The New York Times. Feb 1, 1931, p5.
Time. Feb 9, 1931, v17, p28.
Variety. Jan 28, 1931, p15.

Gold and the Woman (US; Vincent, James; 1916)
The Moving Picture World. Mar 18, 1916, p1902.
The Moving Picture World. Apr 1, 1916, p99, 105.
The New York Times. Mar 13, 1916, p5.
Variety. Mar 17, 1916, p31.
Wid's Daily. Mar 23, 1916, p459.

Gold Diggers in Paris (US; Enright, Ray; 1938)
Commonweal. Jun 10, 1938, v28, p188.
Film Daily. May 17, 1938, p11.
The New York Times. Jun 2, 1938, p19.
Rob Wagner's Script. Jun 25, 1938, v19, p13.
Time. Jun 13, 1938, v31, p24.
Variety. May 25, 1938, p12.

Gold Diggers of 1933 (US; LeRoy, Mervyn; 1933)
Beyond Formula: American Film Genres. p80-83.
The Busby Berkeley Book. p57-63.
Dictionary of Films. p129-30.
Film Daily. May 25, 1933, p7.
Film Notes. p78.
The Films of the Thirties. p99-101.
The Genius of Busby Berkeley. p169-70.
Genre: The Musical. p41-56.
Gold Diggers of 1933. p9-31.
The Hollywood Musical. p81-85.
Hollywood Reporter. May 19, 1933, p3.
The International Dictionary of Films and Filmmakers. v1, p178-79.
Journal of Popular Film. Sum 1981, v9, p95-97.
Journal of Popular Film. Wint 1975, v4, p33-46.
Judge. Jul 1933, v104, p20.
Kiss Kiss Bang Bang. p339-40.
A Library of Film Criticism: American Film Directors. p261-62.
Magill's Survey of Cinema. Series II. v2, p900-03.
Motion Picture. July 1933, v45, p42-43+.

Motion Picture Herald. May 27, 1933, p31.
Movie Classic. June 1933, v4, p38-39.
New Outlook. Jul 1933, v162, p43.
The New York Times. June 8, 1933, p22.
The New York Times. June 18, 1933, p3.
The New York Times. June 4, 1933, p3.
The New Yorker. Jun 17, 1933, v9, p47.
Photoplay. Aug 1933, v44, p54.
Rob Wagner's Script. June 3, 1933, v9, p8.
Selected Film Criticism, 1931-1940. p85-86.
Time. Jun 5, 1933, v21, p19.
Variety. June 13, 1933, p15.
The Velvet Light Trap. Jun 1971, no1, p20-25.
Warner Brothers Presents. p91-97.

Gold Diggers of 1935 (US; Berkeley, Busby; 1935)
The Busby Berkeley Book. p88-93.
Film Daily. Mar 15, 1935, p17.
Film Notes. p78.
The Hollywood Musical. p87-88.
Hollywood Musicals. p2-3, 80-81.
Hollywood Reporter. Mar 22, 1935, p2.
Hollywood Reporter. Apr 18, 1935, p3.
Literary Digest. Mar 30, 1935, v119, p32.
Motion Picture Herald. Mar 23, 1935, p39.
The New York Times. Mar 15, 1935, p25.
The New Yorker. Mar 23, 1935, v11, p61.
Time. Mar 25, 1935, v25, p46.
Variety. Mar 20, 1935, p17.
Warner Brothers Presents. p105-06, 109.

Gold Diggers of 1937 (US; Bacon, Lloyd; 1936)
The Busby Berkeley Book. p102-07.
Film Daily. Dec 2, 1936, p7.
The Genius of Busby Berkeley. p173-74.
Hollywood Spectator. Dec 19, 1936, v11, p6.
Motion Picture Herald. Dec 12, 1936, p56.
The New York Times. Dec 25, 1936, p19.
The New Yorker. Dec 26, 1936, v12, p51.
Newsweek. Dec 19, 1936, v8, p23.
Rob Wagner's Script. Jan 9, 1937, v16, p12-13.
Stage. Dec 1936, v14, p15.
Time. Jan 4, 1937, v29, p21.
Variety. Dec 30, 1936, p10.
Warner Brothers Presents. p110-11.

Gold Is Not All (US; Griffith, D.W.; 1910)
The Moving Picture World. Apr. 9, 1910, p553.
Selected Film Criticism, 1896-1911. p43.

Gold Is Where You Find It (US; Curtiz, Michael; 1938)
Film Daily. Jan 25, 1938, p8.
The Films of Olivia de Havilland. p103-08.
London Mercury. Sep 1938, v38, p459.
Motion Picture Herald. Jan 22, 1938, p38.
The New Masses. Mar 1, 1938, v26, p30.
The New York Times. Feb 14, 1938, p20.
The New Yorker. Feb 12, 1938, v13, p59-60.
Rob Wagner's Script. Mar 12, 1938, v19, p9.
Scholastic. Feb 5, 1938, v32, p31-32.
The Spectator. Aug 12, 1938, v161, p264.
Time. Feb 21, 1938, v31, p58.
Variety. Feb 16, 1938, p17.
World Film News. Sep 1938, v3, p221, 225.

The Gold Rush (US; Chaplin, Charles; 1925)
American Film Criticism. p162-65.
Authors on Film. p57-58.
BFI/Monthly Film Bulletin. 1956, v23, p113.
Charles Chaplin: A Guide to References and Resources. p72.
Cinema. Sum 1968, v4, p16-44.
Cinema Journal. Spr 1970, v9, p24-30.
Cinema, the Magic Vehicle. v1, p111-12.
Classic Film Collector. Sum 1978, n59, p4.
Classic Film Collector. Sum 1977, p32.
Classics of the Silent Screen. p66-67.

Film Comment. Sep-Oct 1972, v8, p16-18.
Film Daily. Aug 30, 1925, p4.
Film News. Jan-Feb 1942, v1, p6-8.
Film Quarterly. Fall 1959, v13, p31-37.
Films and Filming. Feb 1960, v6, p5.
The Films of Charlie Chaplin. p180-86.
The Films of the Twenties. p110-14.
Focus on Chaplin. p113-23.
The Great Films. p49-53.
Hollywood Reporter. Mar 3, 1942, p3.
In the Dark. p33-35.
The International Dictionary of Films and Filmmakers. v1, p177-78.
Let's Go to the Movies. p129-36.
Literature/Film Quarterly. 1980, v8, n3, p170-81.
Literature/Film Quarterly. Spr 1975, v3, p182-86.
Living Images. p298-306.
The London Times. Jan 14, 1947, p7.
The London Times. Sep 15, 1925, p10.
Modern Music. May-Jun 1942, v19, p275-76.
Motion Picture Exhibitor. Mar 11, 1942, p964-65.
Motion Picture Herald Product Digest. Mar 14, 1942, p551.
Motion Picture News. Nov 6, 1926, v34, p1755-56.
The Moving Picture World. Aug 29, 1925, p917.
Musician. Apr 1942, v47, p58.
My Autobiography. p303-05.
The New York Times. Aug 17, 1925, p10.
The New Yorker. May 2, 1942, v18, p10.
Newsweek. Apr 20, 1942, v19, p74.
North Dakota Quarterly. Aut 1963, v31, p63-69.
Photoplay. Sep 1925, v28, p50.
Saturday Review. Jan 19, 1935, v12, p440.
Selected Film Criticism, 1921-1930. p115.
Spellbound in Darkness. p417-18.
Theatre Arts. Jun 1942, p399-400.
Time. Apr 6, 1942, v39, p80.
Variety. Jul 1, 1925, p32.
Variety. Aug 19, 1925, p36.
Variety. Mar 4, 1942, p8.
Wide Angle. 1979, v3, n2, p42-49.

The Golden Age *See* Age d'Or, L'

The Golden Arrow (US; Green, Alfred E.; 1936)
Bette Davis: Her Films and Career. p68.
Film Daily. May 4, 1936, p7.
Hollywood Reporter. May 1, 1936, p3.
Motion Picture Herald. May 9, 1936, p42-43.
The New York Times. May 4, 1936, p16.
Time. May 11, 1936, v27, p58.
Variety. May 6, 1936, p18.

Golden Boy (US; Mamoulian, Rouben; 1939)
Commonweal. Sep 8, 1939, v30, p459.
Film Daily. Aug 21, 1939, p4.
The Films of Barbara Stanwyck. p130-31.
The Films of William Holden. p38-42.
Graham Greene on Film. p255-56.
Hollywood Reporter. Aug 15, 1939, p3.
Hollywood Spectator. Sep 2, 1939, v14, p10-11.
Magill's Survey of Cinema. Series I. v2, p651-53.
Mamoulian (Milne). p116-20.
Motion Picture Herald. Aug 19, 1939, p50.
The Nation. Sep 16, 1939, v149, p301.
National Board of Review Magazine. Oct 1939, v14, p11.
The New Masses. Sep 5, 1939, v32, p29-30.
The New Statesman and Nation. Nov 25, 1939, v18, p756.
The New York Times. Sep 8, 1939, p28.
The New Yorker. Sep 9, 1939, v15, p60.
Newsweek. Sep 4, 1939, v14, p28.
Rob Wagner's Script. Sep 9, 1939, v22, p22-23.
The Spectator. Dec 1, 1939, v163, p776.
Starring Miss Barbara Stanwyck. p128, 133.
The Tatler. Dec 6, 1939, v154, p316.
Those Fabulous Movie Years: The 30s. p157.

Time. Sep 18, 1939, v34, p51.
Variety. Aug 16, 1939, p14.

The Golden Chance (US; DeMille, Cecil B.; 1916)
The Films of Cecil B. DeMille. p99-102.
The Moving Picture World. Jan 8, 1916, p255.
The Moving Picture World. Jan 22, 1916, p674.
The New York Dramatic Mirror. Dec 18, 1915, p26.
The New York Times. Jan 17, 1916, p20.
Variety. Dec 31, 1916, p20.

Golden Earrings (US; Leisen, Mitchell; 1947)
Commonweal. Dec 19, 1947, v47, p256.
Film Daily. Aug 27, 1947, p6.
The Films of Marlene Dietrich. p176-79.
The Great Spy Films. p151-70.
Hollywood Reporter. Aug 26, 1947, v47, p256.
Motion Picture Herald Product Digest. Aug 30, 1947, p3805.
The New York Times. Dec 4, 1947, p41.
Newsweek. Nov 3, 1947, v30, p88.
Scholastic. Nov 17, 1947, v51, p35.
Time. Dec 15, 1947, v50, p103.
Variety. Aug 27, 1947, p16.

The Golden Lake *See* The Spiders

Golden See, Der *See* The Spiders

Goldie (US; Stoloff, Benjamin; 1931)
Film Daily. Jun 28, 1931, p10.
The Films of Jean Harlow. p50-53.
The Films of Spencer Tracy. p74-75.
Motion Picture Herald. Jul 11, 1931, p26.
The New York Times. Jun 29, 1931, p20.
Variety. Jun 30, 1931, p20.

The Goldwyn Follies (US; Marshall, George; 1938)
Commonweal. Feb 18, 1938, v27, p468.
Film Daily. Jan 27, 1938, p5.
Hollywood Reporter. Jan 26, 1938, p3.
Life. Feb 7, 1938, v4, p20-23.
Literary Digest. Feb 19, 1938, v125, p23.
Motion Picture Herald. Jan 29, 1938, p48.
The New Statesman and Nation. Mar 19, 1938, v15, p479.
The New Yorker. Feb 19, 1938, v14, p58.
Newsweek. Feb 14, 1938, v11, p25.
Rob Wagner's Script. Feb 19, 1938, v19, p10.
Samuel Goldwyn (Epstein). p110-14.
Samuel Goldwyn Presents. p188-90.
The Spectator. Mar 25, 1938, v160, p514.
Stage. Dec 1937, v15, p86.
Time. Feb 7, 1938, v31, p58.
Variety. Feb 2, 1938, p15.
World Film News. Apr 1938, v3, p33.

The Golem (German title: Golem, Der) (GER; Wegner,
   Paul; Boese, Carl; 1920)
BFI/Monthly Film Bulletin. Jul 1979, v46 p157-58.
Film Daily. Jun 26, 1921, p2.
From Caligari to Hitler. p112-13.
The Haunted Screen. p56-59.
A History of Narrative Film. p109.
An Illustrated History of the Horror Film. p20-21.
Magill's Survey of Cinema. Silent Films. v2, p488-93.
The New York Times. Jun 20, 1921, p17.
Photoplay. Sep 1921, v20, p57.
Selected Film Criticism, 1921-1930. p116.
Spellbound in Darkness. p362-63.
Variety. June 24, 1921, p34.
Wide Angle. Nov 21, 1983, v5, p14-25.

The Golem (French title: Golem, Le; Also titled: The
   Legend of Prague) (FR/CZECH; Duvivier, Julien;
   1935)
BFI/Monthly Film Bulletin. Jul 1979, v46, p156-57.
Dictionary of Films. p131-32.

Film Daily. Mar 24, 1937, p6.
Graham Greene on Film. p144-45.
Hollywood Reporter. Oct 25, 1937, p3.
Hollywood Reporter. Mar 3, 1936, p15.
Motion Picture Herald. Mar 27, 1937, p43, 45.
National Board of Review Magazine. Apr 1937, v12, p10.
The New Masses. Mar 30, 1937, v23, p28.
The New York Times. Mar 22, 1937, p27.
The New Yorker. Mar 27, 1937, v13, p55.
Rob Wagner's Script. Oct 30, 1937, v18, p10.
Saint Cinema: Selected Writings, 1929-1970. p65-67.
Selected Film Criticism: Foreign Films, 1930-1950. p58-59.
Sight and Sound. Spr 1937, v6, p26.
The Spectator. Apr 23, 1937, v158, p759.
Time. Mar 29, 1937, v29, p48.
Variety. Feb 26, 1936, p37.
Variety. Mar 24, 1937, p16.
World Film News. May 1937, v2, p25.

Golgotha (FR; Duvivier, Julien; 1935)
Commonweal. Jan 15, 1937, v25, p332-33.
Commonweal. May 17, 1935, v22, p76.
Film Daily. Feb 10, 1937, p6.
National Board of Review Magazine. Apr 1937, v12, p10.
Variety. Apr 24, 1935, p12.
Variety. Feb 17, 1937, p14.
World Film News. Nov 19, 1936, v1, p21.

Goluboi Express *See* China Express

Gone With the Wind (US; Fleming, Victor; 1939)
American Cinematographer. Nov 1967, v48, p788-91+.
American Classic Screen. Dec 1981, v5, p14-16.
American Classic Screen. Sep-Oct 1982, v6, p16-22.
American Film Criticism. p370-77.
Atlanta Historical Journal. Sum 1978, v22, p7-131.
The Atlanta Journal Sunday Magazine. Nov 19, 1939, p1-2.
The Atlantic. Feb 1973, v231, p37-51.
The Atlantic. Mar 1973, v231, p56-72.
Beyond Formula. p270-74.
Black Film Stars. p72-74.
Catholic World. Aug 1954, v179, p385.
Chestnuts in Her Lap. p81-82.
The Civil War on the Screen. p88-100.
Classic Film Collector. Fall 1976, n52, p41.
Classic Film Collector. Fall 1978, n60, p18-20.
Classic Film Collector. Sum 1977, n55, p37.
Classic Film/Video Images. Nov 1981, n78, p61.
Classic Images. Jul 1983, n97, p72.
Classic Images. Mar 1984, n105, p36.
Collier's. Dec 16, 1939, v104, p20+.
Commonweal. Jan 5, 1940, v31, p246.
David O. Selznick's Hollywood. p236-312.
*David O. Selznick's Production of Margaret Mitchell's Gone
   With The Wind.*
Dictionary of Films. p132.
Esquire. Nov 1961, v56, p62-63.
The Film Criticism of Otis Ferguson. p280-81, 297-98.
Film Culture. May-Jun 1955, v1, p26-27.
Film Daily. Dec 13, 1939, p11.
Film Reader. 1982, n5, p76-82.
The Film Story of Gone With the Wind. 1984.
Films and Filming. Dec 1967, v14, p12-17.
Films and Filming. Nov 1968, v15, p54.
Films and Filming. Jun 1984, n357, p18.
Films Illustrated. Oct 1975, v5, p52.
Films in Review. May 1961, v12, p293-95.
Films in Review. May 1957, v8, p205-10.
Films in Review. Nov 1967, v18, p577-79.
Films in Review. Dec 1967, v18, p652-53.
The Films of Clark Gable. p190-95.
The Films of Olivia De Havilland. p137-46.
The Films of the Thirties. p253-56.
From Quasimodo to Scarlett O'Hara. p331-34.
From the Old South to the New. p143-51.

Gable (Williams). p75-79.
George Cukor (Phillips). p132-37.
Georgia Review. n1 1948, v38, p146-64.
Gone With The Wind: A Legend Endures.
Gone With the Wind as Book and Film. p127-83.
Good Housekeeping. Jan 1950, v130, p10.
The Great Films. p130-36.
GWTW: The Making of Gone With the Wind. 1973.
GWTW: The Screenplay. p7-44.
Halliwell's Hundred. p108-10.
Harpers Magazine. Feb 1949, v p97-98.
Hi Fidelity. Jun 1974, v24, p114-15.
Hollywood Reporter. Dec 13, 1939, p3.
Hollywood Spectator. Dec 23, 1939, v14, p10-12.
House and Garden. Nov 1939, v76, p36-40+.
The International Dictionary of Films and Filmmakers. v1,
   p179-80.
Journal of Popular Film. 1973, v2, p366-71.
Journal of Popular Film. 1974, v3, p202-18.
Landmark Films. p140-51.
Life. Dec 25, 1939, v7, p9-13.
Life. Aug 29, 1949, v27, p54-55.
Light of a Star. p68-78.
The Lion's Share. p261-69.
Lorentz on Film. p180-83.
Magill's Survey of Cinema. Series I. v2, p654-59.
Margaret Mitchell of Atlanta. p169-88, 190-200.
Margaret Mitchell's Gone With the Wind Letters, 1936-1949.
Memo from David O. Selznick. p135-47.
Motion Picture Herald. Dec 16, 1939, p24.
The Nation. Dec 30, 1939, v149, p740.
National Board of Review Magazine. Jan 1940, v15, p19.
The New Masses. Jan 2, 1940, v34, p28-30.
The New Masses. Jan 23, 1940, v34, p28-30.
The New Masses. Jan 30, 1940, v34, p28-30.
New Orleans Review. 1983, n2-3 v10, p91-98.
The New Republic. Jan 8, 1940, v102, p53.
The New Republic. Jan 25, 1975, v172, p19-22.
The New York Times. Dec 20, 1939, p31.
The New Yorker. Dec 30, 1939, v15, p47.
Newsweek. Dec 25, 1939, v14, p26-29.
The Oliviers. p179-90.
On Cukor. p88-90.
Photoplay. Mar 1937, v51, p21-23+.
Photoplay. May 1940, v54, p68.
Rob Wagner's Script. Dec 23, 1939, v22, p16.
Saturday Evening Post. Jun 3, 1939, v211, p14-15, 75-81.
Saturday Review. Dec 23, 1939, v21, p10-12.
Scarlett Fever. 1977.
*Scarlett, Rhett and a Cast of Thousands: The Filming of Gone
   With the Wind.* 1975.
Scholastic. Jan 8, 1940, v35, p32-33.
Selected Film Criticism, 1931-1940. p86-90.
Selznick (Thomas). p139-75.
Southern World. Jan-Feb 1981, v2, p32-36, 38.
Souvenir Programs of Twelve Classic Movies, 1927-1941. p181-
   200.
The Spectator. Apr 26, 1940, v164, p594.
The Story of Gone With The Wind (Thomas).
Tara Revisited. 1976.
The Tara Treasury. 1980.
Theatre Arts. Feb 1940, v24, p128-29.
Those Fabulous Movie Years: The 30s. p158-61.
Time. Oct 5, 1983, v122, p31.
Time. Dec 25, 1939, v34, p30-32.
Variety. Dec 20, 1939, p14.
The Village Voice. Oct 26, 1967, v13, p31, 39.
The Village Voice. Nov 29, 1976, v21, p11.
*White Columns in Hollywood: Reports from the Gone With the
   Wind Sets.* 1982.

The Good Companions (GB; Saville, Victor; 1933)
The Age of the Dream Palace. p213-14, 319.
Cinema Quarterly. Sum 1933, v1, p224-25.

Cinema Quarterly. Spr 1933, v1, p180-81.
Film Daily. Oct 10, 1933, p8.
Motion Picture Herald. Apr 29, 1933, p30.
The New York Times. Oct 10, 1933, p24.
Newsweek. Oct 21, 1933, v2, p30.
Photoplay. Dec 1933, v45, p92.
Rob Wagner's Script. Sep 30, 1933, v10, p12.
Selected Film Criticism: Foreign Films, 1930-1950. p59.
Variety. Mar 14, 1933, p15.
Variety. Oct 17, 1933, p19.

The Good Earth (US; Franklin, Sidney; 1937)
Asia. Apr 1937, v37, p314-15.
Canadian Magazine. Sep 1937, v86, p29.
Commonweal. Feb 19, 1937, v25, p472-73.
Esquire. May 1937, v7, p182, 184.
Fifty Classic Motion Pictures. p152-57.
The Film Criticism of Otis Ferguson. p167-69.
Film Daily. Feb 3, 1937, p9.
The Films of the Thirties. p187-89.
From Quasimodo to Scarlett O'Hara. p236-38.
Graham Greene on Film. p140-41.
Hollywood Reporter. Dec 7, 1936, p3.
Hollywood Spectator. Feb 13, 1937, v11, p2-4.
Independent Woman. Mar 1937, v16, p65+.
Life. Jan 18, 1937, p50-56.
Literary Digest. Feb 13, 1937, v123, p19.
London Mercury. May 1937, v36, p71.
Magill's Survey of Cinema. Series II. v2, p907-10.
McCall's. May 1937, v64, p112.
Motion Picture. Oct 1936, v52, p40-41+.
Motion Picture Herald. Feb 6, 1937, p46.
Motion Picture Herald. Jul 11, 1936, p16-17.
Movie Classic. Oct 1936, v11, p34-35+.
The Nation. Feb 13, 1937, v144, p194.
National Board of Review Magazine. Feb 1937, v12, p15.
The New Masses. Feb 16, 1937, v22, p29.
New Republic. Mar 17, 1937, v90, p167.
The New Statesman and Nation. Apr 3, 1937, v13, p555.
The New York Times. Feb 3, 1937, p27.
The New Yorker. Feb 6, 1937, v12, p59-60.
Newsweek. Feb 13, 1937, v9, p23-24.
Paul Muni: His Life and His Films. p152-59.
Photoplay. Aug 1936, v50, p38-39.
Rob Wagner's Script. Feb 6, 1937, v16, p8.
Scholastic. Feb 10, 1937, v30, p22-23.
Selected Film Criticism, 1931-1940. p92-93.
Sight and Sound. Spr 1937, v6, p12-14, 20.
Sociology and Social Research. May 1937, v21, p496.
Souvenir Programs of Twelve Classic Movies, 1927-1941. p141-
   60.
The Spectator. Apr 2, 1937, v158, p619.
Stage. Apr 1937, v14, p54-56.
Stage. Jun 1937, v14, p54-55.
Studio. May 1939, v17, p196-97.
Those Fabulous Movie Years: The 30s. p114-15.
Time. Feb 15, 1937, v29, p55-56.
Variety. Feb 10, 1937, p14.
World Film News. May 1937, v2, p22.

The Good Fairy (US; Wyler, William; 1935)
Between Flops. p98-102.
Esquire. Apr 1935, v3, p144.
Film Daily. Feb 1, 1935, p13.
Filmfront. Feb 15, 1935, v1, p11-12.
Hollywood Reporter. Jan 31, 1935, p3.
Hollywood Reporter. Feb 6, 1935, p2.
Literary Digest. Feb 16, 1935, v119, p22.
Lunatics and Lovers. p24.
Motion Picture Herald. Feb 9, 1935, p59, 62.
Movie Classic. Feb 1935, v74, p44-49+.
The New York Times. Feb 1, 1935, p18.
Rob Wagner's Script. Feb 23, 1935, v13, p8.
Time. Feb 11, 1935, v25, p48.
Variety. Feb 5, 1935, p14.

William Wyler: A Guide to References and Resources. p79-81.
William Wyler (Anderegg). p39-42.

Good Girls Go to Paris (US; Hall, Alexander; 1939)
Commonweal. Jul 7, 1939, v30, p278.
Film Daily. Jun 20, 1939, p14.
Hollywood Reporter. Jun 17, 1939, p3.
Hollywood Spectator. Jun 24, 1939, v14, p7.
Motion Picture Herald. Jun 24, 1939, p42-43.
The New York Times. Jun 23, 1939, p23.
The New Yorker. Jul 1, 1939, v15, p56-57.
Rob Wagner's Script. Jul 4, 1939, v21, p16.
Time. Jul 3, 1939, v33, p36.
Variety. Jun 28, 1939, p14.

A Good Little Devil (US; Porter, Edwin S.; 1914)
The Moving Picture World. Jul 26, 1913, p407.
The Moving Picture World. Mar 7, 1914, p1249.
The New York Dramatic Mirror. Dec 24, 1913, p32.
The New York Dramatic Mirror. Mar 4, 1914, p31, 33.
Selected Film Criticism, 1912-1920. p104-06.
Variety. Mar 13, 1914, p23.

Good News (US; Walters, Charles; 1947)
Commonweal. Jan 2, 1948, v47, p304.
Film Daily. Dec 2, 1947, p8.
Hollywood Reporter. Dec 2, 1947, p3.
Magill's Survey of Cinema, Series II. v2, p911-13.
Motion Picture Herald Product Digest. Dec 6, 1947, p3965.
The New York Times. Dec 5, 1947, p53.
Newsweek. Dec 15, 1947, v30, p88.
Time. Dec 22, 1947, v50, p79.
Variety. Dec 3, 1947, p11.

The Good Old Soak (US; Ruben, J. Walter; 1937)
Canadian Magazine. Jun 1937, v87, p52.
Film Daily. Apr 20, 1937, p8.
Hollywood Reporter. Apr 15, 1937, p3.
Hollywood Spectator. Apr 24, 1937, v12, p12-13.
Motion Picture Herald. Apr 24, 1937, p43.
The New York Times. Apr 20, 1937, p25.
The New Yorker. May 1, 1937, v13, p63.
Rob Wagner's Script. May 22, 1937, v17, p8.
Time. May 3, 1937, v29, p32.
Variety. Apr 28, 1937, p15.

Good Time Charlie (US; Curtiz, Michael; 1927)
The New York Times. Nov 21, 1927, p20.
Variety. Nov 23, 1927, p24.

Goodbye Again (US; Curtiz, Michael; 1933)
Film Daily. Sep 2, 1933, p3.
Hollywood Reporter. Jun 10, 1933, p3.
Motion Picture Herald. Jun 17, 1933, p34.
New Outlook. Oct 1933, v162, p49.
The New York Times. Sep 2, 1933, p15.
The New Yorker. Sep 9, 1933, v9, p54.
Rob Wagner's Script. Sep 2, 1933, v10, p8.
Time. Sep 11, 1933, v22, p47.
Vanity Fair. Sep 1933, v41, p46+.
Variety. Sep 5, 1933, p23.

Goodbye, Mr. Chips (GB; Wood, Sam; 1939)
Commonweal. May 26, 1939, v30, p132.
Esquire. Sep 1939, v12, p96, 114.
The Film Criticism of Otis Ferguson. p255-56.
Film Daily. May 16, 1939, p6.
From Quasimodo to Scarlett O'Hara. p313-16.
Graham Greene on Film. p227-28.
Hollywood Reporter. May 16, 1939, p3.
Hollywood Spectator. May 27, 1939, v14, p8.
Kiss Kiss Bang Bang. p341-42.
Lorentz on Film. p171-73.
Magill's Survey of Cinema. Series I. v2, p663-66.
Make It Again, Sam. p63-68.
Motion Picture Herald. May 20, 1939, p42-43.

The Nation. Jun 3, 1939, v148, p654.
National Board of Review Magazine. Jul 1939, v14, p28.
The New Masses. May 30, 1939, v31, p29-30.
The New Republic. May 31, 1939, v99, p102.
The New Republic. Jul 1, 1978, v179, p28-29.
The New Statesman and Nation. Jun 17, 1939, v17, p934.
The New York Times. May 16, 1939, p27.
The New Yorker. May 20, 1939, v15, p76-77.
Newsweek. May 22, 1939, v13, p34-35.
Rob Wagner's Script. May 27, 1939, v21, p20-21.
Scholastic. May 27, 1939, v34, p31.
Selected Film Criticism, 1931-1940. p93-96.
Selected Film Criticism: Foreign Films, 1930-1950. p60-61.
Sight and Sound. Spr 1939, v8, p27-28.
Sight and Sound. Sum 1939, v8, p75.
The Spectator. Jun 16, 1939, v162, p1036.
The Tatler. Jun 21, 1939, v152, p524.
Time. May 22, 1939, v33, p56.
Variety. May 17, 1939, p12.
The Village Voice. Jul 14, 1974, v20, p61-63.

Goodnight, Vienna *See* Magic Night

The Goose and the Gander (US; Green, Alfred E.; 1935)
Film Daily. Sep 12, 1935, p4.
Hollywood Reporter. Jul 31, 1935, p3.
Motion Picture Herald. Oct 5, 1935, p42.
The New York Times. Sep 12, 1935, p29.
Newsweek. Sep 21, 1935, v6, p18.
Rob Wagner's Script. Oct 19, 1935, v14, p11.
Time. Sep 23, 1935, v26, p47.
Variety. Sep 18, 1935, p15.

The Goose Girl (US; Thomson, Frederick; 1915)
Marguerite Clark. p58, 62.
Motion Picture News. Jan 9, 1915, p35, 42, 57.
Motion Picture News. Jan 30, 1915, p1.
Motion Picture News. Feb 6, 1915, p44.
Motography. Feb 6, 1915, p212, 230.
The Moving Picture World. Feb 6, 1915, p809.
The Moving Picture World. Feb 13, 1915, p1048.
The Moving Picture World. Dec 7, 1918, p1117.
The New York Dramatic Mirror. Feb 3, 1915, p26.
Variety. Jan 29, 1915, p24.
Variety. Nov 29, 1918, p41.

The Goose Woman (US; Brown, Clarence; 1925)
Film Daily. Jul 26, 1925, p5.
Magill's Survey of Cinema. Silent Films. v2, p494-96.
The Moving Picture World. Aug 1, 1925, p532.
The New York Times. Aug 4, 1925, p14.
Selected Film Criticism, 1921-1930. p116.
Variety. Aug 5, 1925, p31.

The Gorgeous Hussy (US; Brown, Clarence; 1936)
Canadian Magazine. Oct 1936, v86, p45.
Commonweal. Sep 18, 1936, v24, p487.
Film Daily. Sep 1, 1936, p7.
The Films of Joan Crawford. p120-21.
The Films of Robert Taylor. p52-53.
Hollywood Reporter. Aug 28, 1936, p3.
Judge. Nov 1936, v111, p12, 22.
Literary Digest. Sep 12, 1936, v122, p17.
Motion Picture Herald. Sep 5, 1936, p41.
Motion Picture Herald. Aug 1, 1936, p16-17.
The New Masses. Sep 8, 1936, v20, p29.
The New Statesman and Nation. Oct 17, 1936, v12, p589.
The New York Times. Sep 5, 1936, p7.
The New Yorker. Sep 12, 1936, v12, p75.
Rob Wagner's Script. Sep 5, 1936, v16, p10.
Stage. Oct 1936, v14, p24.
Time. Sep 7, 1936, v28, p19.
Variety. Sep 8, 1936, p16.
World Film News. Dec 1936, v1, p22.

The Gorilla (US; Dwan, Allan; 1939)
Film Daily. May 24, 1939, p6.
Hollywood Reporter. May 18, 1939, p3.
Hollywood Spectator. May 27, 1939, v14, p11-12.
Motion Picture Herald. May 27, 1939, p32.
The New York Times. May 28, 1939, p6.
Newsweek. Jun 5, 1939, v13, p35.
Time. Jun 5, 1939, v33, p67.
Variety. May 24, 1939, p14.

Gösta Berling's Saga *See* The Atonement of Gösta
   Berling

Goupi Mains Rouge (Also titled: It Happened at the Inn)
   (FR; Becker, Jacques; 1942)
Agee on Film. v1, p189.
Commonweal. Feb 1, 1946, v43, p407.
The London Times. Oct 12, 1944, p6.
The London Times. Mar 7, 1949, p7.
Motion Picture Herald Product Digest. Jan 19, 1946, p2806.
The Nation. Feb 16, 1946, v162, p205.
The New Republic. Jun 10, 1946, v114, p836.
The New York Times. Dec 22, 1945, p16.
The New York Times. Jan 12, 1946, sec2, p3.
The New Yorker. Jan 5, 1946, v21, p61.
Newsweek. Dec 31, 1945, v26, p94.
Rob Wagner's Script. Apr 13, 1946, v32, p19.
Selected Film Criticism: Foreign Films, 1930-1950. p83-84.
Theatre Arts. Feb 1946, v30, p101.
Time. Jan 21, 1946, v47, p97.
Variety. Dec 26, 1945, p14.

The Gracie Allen Murder Case (US; Green, Alfred E.;
   1939)
Commonweal. Jun 9, 1939, v30, p189.
Film Daily. May 17, 1939, p5.
Hollywood Reporter. May 13, 1939, p3.
Motion Picture Herald. May 20, 1939, p43.
The New York Times. Jun 8, 1939, p31.
The New Yorker. Jun 10, 1939, v15, p75.
Newsweek. May 29, 1939, v13, p28.
Photoplay. Jul 1939, v53, p62.
Rob Wagner's Script. Jul 15, 1939, v21, p18.
Stage. Jun 1939, v16, p34-35.
Time. Jun 12, 1939, v33, p78.
Variety. May 17, 1939, p12.

Grain (USSR; Preobrazhenskaya, Olga; 1936)
Film Daily. Jan 17, 1936, p8.
The New Masses. Jan 28, 1936, v18, p29-30.
The New York Times. Jan 16, 1936, p25.

The Grand Duchess and the Waiter (US; St. Clair,
   Malcolm; 1926)
Film Daily. Feb 21, 1926, p6.
Magill's Survey of Cinema. Silent Films. v2, p497-501.
The New York Times. Feb 9, 1926, p22.
Photoplay. Apr 1926, v24, p54.
Selected Film Criticism, 1921-1930. p117.
Variety. Feb 10, 1926, p40.

Grand Hotel (US; Goulding, Edmund; 1932)
Canadian Forum. Jul 1932, v12, p399.
Cinema Quarterly. Wint 1932, v1, p112.
Commonweal. Aug 3, 1932, v16, p351.
Film Daily. Apr 17, 1932, p10.
The Films of Greta Garbo. p108-14.
The Films of Joan Crawford. p92-96.
The Films of the Thirties. p75-76.
From Quasimodo to Scarlett O'Hara. p156-58.
Garbo: A Portrait (Walker). p124-29.
Hollywood Reporter. Mar 12, 1932, p1, 3.
Hollywood Reporter. Mar 14, 1932, p3.
Judge. May 7, 1932, v102, p20, 27.
Kiss Kiss Bang Bang. p342-43.

Literary Digest. May 7, 1932, v113, p15.
Magill's Survey of Cinema. Series I. v2, p672-74.
Motion Picture. May 1932, v43, p52-53+.
The Nation. Apr 27, 1932, v134, p498.
National Board of Review Magazine. May 1932, v7, p7.
The New Republic. Apr 27, 1932, v70, p301.
The New York Times. Apr 13, 1932, p23.
The New Yorker. Apr 16, 1932, v8, p56.
The New Yorker. Apr 23, 1932, v8, p56-57.
Reruns. p21-25.
Rob Wagner's Script. May 7, 1932, v7, p10.
Saturday Review (London). Oct 1, 1932, v154, p346.
Souvenir Programs of Twelve Classic Movies, 1927-1941. p81-
   100.
Star Acting. p134-66.
Those Fabulous Movie Years: The 30s. p38-39.
Time. Apr 25, 1932, v19, p29.
Tynan Right and Left. p236.
Vanity Fair. Jun 1932, v38, p24-25.
Variety. Apr 19,1932, p14.

Grand Jeu, Le (Also titled: The Great Game) (FR;
   Feyder, Jacques; 1934)
Dictionary of Films. p135-36.
French Film (Sadoul). p72-73.
The Golden Age of French Cinema, 1929-1939. p48-51, 61-64.
The New Statesman and Nation. Oct 26, 1946, v32, p300.
Variety. May 15, 1934, p14.

Grand Slam (US; Dieterle, William; 1933)
Film Daily. Feb 23, 1933, p7.
Garbo and the Night Watchman. p231.
Hollywood Reporter. Jan 5, 1933, p3.
Motion Picture Herald. Jan 14, 1933, p30.
The New York Times. Feb 22, 1933, p25.
Rob Wagner's Script. Jan 14, 1933, v8, p8.
Variety. Feb 28, 1933, p15.

Grande Amour de Beethoven, Une (Also titled:
   Beethoven's Great Love; The Life and Loves of
   Beethoven; Beethoven) (FR; Gance, Abel; 1936)
Film Daily. Jan 29, 1937, p8.
From Quasimodo to Scarlett O'Hara. p270-71.
Graham Greene on Film. p230.
The Great French Films. p244.
Hollywood Reporter. Mar 23, 1938, p6.
Hollywood Spectator. Apr 9, 1938, v12, p6-8.
National Board of Review Magazine. Dec 1937, v12, p10.
The New Masses. Dec 28, 1937, v26, p27.
The New Statesman and Nation. Jun 24, 1939, v17, p975-76.
The New York Times. Nov 22, 1937, p15.
Rob Wagner's Script. Apr 9, 1938, v19, p10-11.
Selected Film Criticism: Foreign Films, 1930-1950. p95-98.
The Spectator. Jun 30, 1939, v162, p1128.
Variety. Nov 24, 1937, p16.

Grande Illusion, La (Also titled: Grand Illusion) (FR;
   Renoir, Jean; 1937)
American Film Criticism. p358-62.
Cinema, the Magic Vehicle. v1, p269-70.
Classic Film Collector. Wint 1973, n41, p9.
Classic Film Collector. Fall 1975, n48, p22-23.
Classic Movies. p102-03.
Classics of the Foreign Film. p108-11.
Commonweal. Sep 30, 1938, v28, p590.
Current History. Dec 1938, v49, p45-46.
Dictionary of Films. p134-35.
Eighty Years of Cinema. p112.
The Film Criticism of Otis Ferguson. p236-37.
Film Daily. Sep 16, 1938, p8.
Film Quarterly. Winter 1960, v14, p10-17.
Film Society Review. Nov 1968, p17-23.
Films and Filming. Feb 1964, v10, p14.
From Quasimodo to Scarlett O'Hara. p287-89.
The Great Films. p121-24.

The Great French Films. p75-79.
The Great Movies. p104-06.
Hollywood Reporter. Sep 19, 1938, p6.
Hollywood Reporter. Jun 23, 1937, p3.
Horizon. Sum 1972, v14, p48-55.
I Lost It At the Movies. p96-99.
The International Dictionary of Films and Filmmakers. v1, p182-84.
Jean Renoir: A Guide to References and Resources.
Jean Renoir: My Life and My Films. p145-53, 159-68.
Jean Renoir: The French Films, 1924-1939. p282-322.
Landmark Films. p120-29.
Life. Oct 10, 1938, v5, p35-36.
Literature/Film Quarterly. Wint 1977, v5, p50-56.
Lorentz on Film. p157-58.
Motion Picture Herald. Jul 3, 1937, p48-49.
The Nation. Oct 22, 1938, v147, p433-34.
National Board of Review Magazine. Oct 1938, v13, p15.
The New Masses. Jan 17, 1939, v30, p28-29.
The New Masses. Sep 27, 1938, v29, p28-30.
The New Masses. Jan 3, 1939, v30, p29.
The New Republic. Oct 19, 1938, v96, p307.
The New Statesman and Nation. Jan 15, 1938, v15, p82.
The New York Times. Sep 13, 1938, p28.
The New York Times. Dec 17, 1938, p11.
The New York Times. Jan 3, 1939, p18.
The New Yorker. Sep 24, 1938, v14, p66.
Photoplay. Jan 1939, v58, p45.
Rob Wagner's Script. Nov 12, 1938, v20, p15-16.
Saint Cinema: Selected Writings, 1929-1970. p79-83.
Screen. Wint 1972-73, v13, p37-38.
Selected Film Criticism: Foreign Films, 1930-1950. p61-65.
The Spectator. Jan 14, 1938, v160, p51.
The Tatler. Jan 26, 1938, v147, p144.
Theatre Arts. Sep 1941, v25, p656.
Time. Sep 26, 1938, v32, p50.
Variety. Sep 14, 1938, p23.
A World on Film. p3-5.

Grandma's Boy (US; Newmeyer, Fred; 1922)
Exceptional Photoplays. Mar-May 1922, p6, 7.
Film Daily. Sep 10, 1922, p2.
Harold Lloyd. p44-49.
The New York Times. Sep 4, 1922, p14.
Photoplay. Jul 1922, v22, p52.
Selected Film Criticism, 1921-1930. p118-19.
Variety. Jun 16, 1922, p40.

Grandma's Reading Glass (GB; Smith, G.A.; 1900)
Behind the Screen. p105.

The Grapes of Wrath (US; Ford, John; 1940)
American Film Criticism. p383-90.
America's Favorite Movies. p119-34.
Awake in the Dark. p320-25.
Before My Eyes. p349-50.
Collier's. Jan 27, 1940, v105, p23+.
Commonweal. Feb 9, 1940, v31, p348.
English Journal. Jan 1977, v66, p82-86.
Film and Literature. p107-17.
Film Comment. Sep-Oct 1976, v12, p46-51.
The Film Criticism of Otis Ferguson. p282-85.
Film Daily. Jan 24, 1940, p4.
Films and Filming. Mar 1973, v19, p58.
The Films of Henry Fonda. p89-93.
The Fondas (Springer). p97-101.
Fortnightly. Oct 1940, v154, p409-16.
The Great Films. p137-42.
Halliwell's Hundred. p111-15.
Hollywood Reporter. Jan 23, 1940, p3.
In the Dark. p181-200.
The International Dictionary of Films and Filmmakers. v1, p184-85.
Journal of Popular Film. Sum 1974, v3, p202-18.
Landmark Films. p154-63.

Life. Jan 22, 1940, v8, p29-31+.
Life. Feb 19, 1940, v8, p10-11.
Literature/Film Quarterly. 1981, v9, n4, p207-12.
The London Times. Jul 19, 1940, p6.
Lorentz on Film. p183-86.
Magic and Myth of the Movies. p230-47, 274-78.
Magill's Survey of Cinema. Series I. v2, p675-77.
The Modern American Novel and the Cinema. p107-18.
The Motion Picture and the Teaching of English. p103-11.
The Nation. Feb 3, 1940, v150, p137-38.
National Board of Review Magazine. Feb 1940, v15, p16-18.
The New Republic. Feb 12, 1940, v102, p212.
The New York Times. Jan 25, 1940, p17.
The New York Times. Jan 28, 1940, sec9, p5.
Newsweek. Feb 12, 1940, v15, p37-38.
The Non-Western Films of John Ford. p59-70.
Novels into Film. p147-69.
On Film: Unpopular Essays on a Popular Art. p90-92.
Photoplay. Nov 1939, v53, p22-23+.
Photoplay. Mar 1940, v54, p44-45, 68.
Quarterly Review of Film Studies. Wint 1978, v3, p49-71.
Rob Wagner's Script. Mar 9, 1940, v23, p16.
Saturday Review. Feb 10, 1940, v21, p16.
Scholastic. Feb 5, 1940, v36, p36.
Selected Film Criticism, 1931-1940. p98-102.
Theatre Arts. Mar 1940, v24, p214.
Theatre Arts. Sep 1941, v25, p619.
Time. Feb 12, 1940, v35, p70+.
Variety. Jan 31, 1940, p14.
The Village Voice. Oct 18, 1973, v18, p77-78.
50 Classic Motion Pictures. p188-93.

Grass (US; Cooper, Merian C.; 1925)
Exceptional Photoplays. Feb-Mar 1925, p1-2.
Film Daily. April 12, 1925, p8.
Life. Jun 4, 1925, v85, p35.
Literary Digest. Apr 25, 1925, v85, p27-28.
Magill's Survey of Cinema. Silent Films. v2, p502-04.
A Million and One Nights. p600.
The Moving Picture World. Apr 11, 1925, p581.
The New York Times. Mar 31, 1925, p17.
Outlook. May 6, 1925, v140, p10.
Selected Film Criticism, 1921-1930. p119-22.

Graustark (US; Wright, Fred E.; 1915)
Essanay News. Apr 24, 1915.
Motion Picture News. May 8, 1915, p66.
Motography. Dec 19, 1914, p842.
Motography. May 8, 1915, p742.
The Moving Picture World. May 8, 1915, p918, 988.
The New York Dramatic Mirror. May 5, 1915, p26.

The Great Barrier (GB; Rosmer, Milton; 1937)
Graham Greene on Film. p132.
Hollywood Reporter. Feb 23, 1937, p7.
London Mercury. Mar 1937, v35, p504.
Motion Picture Herald. Feb 27, 1937, p56.
Motion Picture Herald. Feb 6, 1937, p20-21.
The New York Times. Feb 5, 1937, p17.
The Spectator. Feb 12, 1937, v158, p267.
Variety. Feb 27, 1937, p14.
World Film News. Mar 1937, v1, p24-25.

A Great Citizen (Russian title: Velikii Grazhdanin)
(USSR; Ermler, Friedrich; 1938; 1939)
Cinema, the Magic Vehicle. v1, p313-14.
Dictionary of Films. p400.
Film Daily. Jan 26, 1939, p12.
Kino. p343-44.
The New Masses. Jan 24, 1939, v30, p27-29.
The New Masses. Jan 31, 1939, v30, p27-28.
The New York Times. Jan 16, 1939, p11.
Variety. Jan 18, 1939, p19.

The Great Dictator (US; Chaplin, Charles; 1940)
American Film Criticism. p201-04, 396-99, 400-04-04.
Atlantic. Aug 1939, p196-85.
Canadian Forum. Aug 1941, v21, p149-50.
Catholic World. Dec 1940, v152, p333.
Charles Chaplin: A Guide to References and Resources. p75-76.
Chestnuts in Her Lap. p54-56.
Christian Science Monitor Magazine. Sep 7, 1940, p7+.
Commonweal. Nov 8, 1940, v33, p80.
Confessions of a Cultist. p124-28.
Current History. Sep 1939, v51, p52.
Encounter. Jun 1978, v50, p25-33.
Film Comment. Sep-Oct 1972, v8, p20-22.
The Film Criticism of Otis Ferguson. p314-16.
Film Daily. Oct 16, 1940, p6.
Film News. Mar-Apr 1979, v36, p30.
The Films of Charles Chaplin. p204-10.
The Films of My Life. p54-57.
The Films of World War II. p39-41.
Focus on Chaplin. p136-39.
Hollywood Reporter. Oct 15, 1940, p3.
The International Dictionary of Films and Filmmakers. v1, p186-87.
Life. Sep 2, 1940, v9, p53-56.
Life. Sep 22, 1941, v11, p24-25.
Living Age. Mar 1941, v360, p53.
The London Times. Oct 16, 1940, p3.
The London Times. Oct 17, 1940, p3.
The London Times. Dec 12, 1940, p6.
Magic Moments from the Movies. p73-74.
Magill's Survey of Cinema. Series I. v2, p678-81.
Modern Music. Nov-Dec 1940, v18, p15-17.
Motion Picture Exhibitor. Oct 30, 1940, p628-29.
Motion Picture Herald Product Digest. Mar 8, 1941, p76.
Moviegoer. Wint 1964, v1, p58-64.
My Autobiography. p392-93, 398-400.
The Nation. Oct 26, 1940, v151, p401+.
The Nation. Oct 4, 1941, v103, p310.
National Board of Review Magazine. Nov 1940, v15, p10-12.
The National Society of Film Critics on Movie Comedy. p32-33.
The New Masses. Dec 17, 1940, 37, p30-31.
The New Republic. Nov 4, 1940, v103, p629-30.
The New Republic. Mar 28, 1940, v150, p30+.
New Statesman. Aug 6, 1982, v104, p24-25.
The New York Times. Oct 16, 1940, p29.
The New York Times. Oct 20, 1940, sec9, p5.
The New York Times. Oct 20, 1940, sec4, p8.
The New York Times. Jun 18, 1972, sec2, p1.
The New York Times. Jul 30, 1973, p22.
The New York Times. May 13, 1976, p3.
The New York Times Magazine. Sep 8, 1940, p8-9.
The New Yorker. Oct 26, 1940, v16, p78.
The New Yorker. Jun 17, 1972, v98, p69.
Newsweek. Oct 28, 1940, v16, p60.
Notes of a Film Director. p199-201.
Photoplay. Jan 1941, v18, p14.
Popular Culture. 1979, v13, n1, p55-66.
Saint Cinema. p95-99.
Saturday Evening Post. Apr 1978, v250, p18+.
Saturday Review. Nov 9, 1940, v21, p8+.
Saturday Review. Dec 21, 1940, v21, p9.
Scholastic. Sep 16, 1940, v37, p32.
Scholastic. Oct 28, 1940, v37, p39.
Scribner's Commentator. Dec 1940, v9, p104-05.
Selected Film Criticism, 1931-1940. p102-04.
Sight and Sound. Aut 1940, v9, p43.
Sight and Sound. Wint 1940, v9, p67.
Souvenir Programs of Twelve Classic Movies. 1927-1941. p201-16.
Theatre Arts. Dec 1940, v24, p862-65.
Time. Aug 7, 1939, v34, p24.
Time. Nov 4, 1940, v36, p76.

University Film Association Journal. Wint 1979, v31, p23-46.
Variety. Oct 16, 1944, p16.
The Village Voice. Mar 12, 1964, v9, p12+.
Vintage Films. p48-52.
Wide Angle. 1979, v3, n2, p50-53.
A World on Film. p162-64.

The Great Divide (US; Barker, Reginald; 1930)
Exhibitors Herald-World. Mar 1, 1930, p36.
Film Daily. Feb 23, 1930, p8.
The Film Spectator. Jan 4, 1930, v9, p21.
The New York Times. Feb 17, 1930, p17.
Variety. Feb 19, 1930, p33.

Great Expectations (US; Walker, Stuart; 1934)
Dickens and Film. p261-64.
Film Daily. Dec 26, 1934, p6.
Hollywood Reporter. Oct 10, 1934, p3.
Motion Picture Herald. Oct 20, 1934, p45.
The New York Times. Mar 24, 1935, sec8, p3.
Time. Oct 29, 1934, v24, p58.
Variety. Jan 29, 1935, p14.

Great Expectations (GB; Lean, David; 1946)
Agee on Film. v1, p266-69+.
The Cinema of David Lean. p59-72.
Cinema, the Magic Vehicle. v1, p420-21.
David Lean. p37-46.
David Lean and His Films. p53-72.
Dickens and Film. p279-97.
The English Novel and the Movies. p143-54.
Fifty Classic British Films. p64-66.
Film Daily. Mar 25, 1947, p8.
Film & Literature: An Introduction. p146-55.
Fortnight. Apr 21, 1947, v2, p28.
The Great British Films. p102-05.
Halliwell's Hundred. p254-57.
Hollywood Quarterly. Fall 1947, v3, p87-89.
Hollywood Reporter. Mar 26, 1947, p3.
Hollywood Review. Apr 22, 1947, v39, p8-9.
The International Dictionary of Films and Filmmakers. v1, p187-88.
Life. Jun 2, 1947, v22, p61-64+.
Literature/Film Quarterly. Spr 1974, v2, p140-53.
Magill's Survey of Cinema. Series I. v2, p685-87.
A Mirror for England. p21-23+.
Motion Picture Herald Product Digest. Dec 28, 1946, p3385.
The Nation. Jul 19, 1947, v165, p79-81.
The New Republic. Mar 10, 1947, v116, p41.
The New York Times. May 23, 1947, p31.
The New York Times Magazine. May 11, 1947, p22-23.
The New Yorker. Jan 24, 1947, v22, p63.
Newsweek. May 26, 1947, v29, p95.
Selected Film Criticism, 1941-1950. p69.
Selected Film Criticism: Foreign Films, 1930-1950. p66-69.
Theatre Arts. Jun 1947, v31, p48.
Time. May 26, 1947, v49, p100+.
Variety. Dec 25, 1946, p24.
Vintage Films. p89-92.

The Great Flamarion (US; Mann, Anthony; 1945)
Film Daily. Feb 5, 1945, p5.
Hollywood Reporter. Apr 13, 1945, p3.
The London Times. Jul 2, 1945, p6.
Magill's Survey of Cinema. Series II. v2, p923-25.
Motion Picture Exhibitor. Jan 24, 1945, v33, n2, p1654.
Motion Picture Herald Product Digest. Jan 20, 1945, p2277.
The New York Times. Jan 15, 1945, p15.
Variety. Jan 17, 1945, p14.

The Great Gabbo (US; Cruze, James; 1929)
American Cinematographer. Mar 1985, v67, p34-39.
BFI/Monthly Film Bulletin. Apr 1977, v44, p84.
Film Daily. Sep 15, 1929, p13.
The Film Mercury. Oct 4, 1929, v10, p4.
The Films of the Twenties. p248-50.

The Hollywood Musical. p31.
Magill's Survey of Cinema. Series II. v2, p926-28.
The New York Times. Sep 13, 1929, p33.
Selected Film Criticism, 1921-1930. p122-24.
Variety. Sep 18, 1929, p15.

The Great Gambini (US; Vidor, Charles; 1937)
Film Daily. Jun 7, 1937, p9.
Hollywood Reporter. Jun 3, 1937, p3.
Motion Picture Herald. Jul 24, 1937, p50.
The New York Times. Jul 12, 1937, p20.
Rob Wagner's Script. Jul 17, 1937, v17, p15.
Variety. Jul 14, 1937, p20.

The Great Game *See* Grande Jeu, Le

The Great Garrick (Also titled: Ladies and Gentlemen)
(US; Whale, James; 1937)
Commonweal. Oct 29, 1937, v27, p20.
Film Daily. Sep 28, 1937, p8.
The Films of Lana Turner. p61-63.
The Films of Olivia De Havilland. p61-63.
Hollywood Reporter. Sep 25, 1937, p3.
James Whale: Ace Director. p7-8.
James Whale (Curtis). p159-61.
Motion Picture Herald. Oct 2, 1937, p32.
The New York Times. Oct 25, 1937, p23.
The New Yorker. Oct 30, 1937, v13, p89-90.
Rob Wagner's Script. Nov 13, 1937, v18, p8.
Saturday Review (London). Sep 12, 1936, v162, p352.
Scholastic. Oct 23, 1937, v31, p37.
Stage. Oct 1937, v15, p95.
Time. Nov 1, 1937, v30, p44.
Variety. Sep 29, 1937, p14.

The Great Gatsby (US; Davis, Owen; 1926)
Film Daily. Nov 28, 1926, p13.
The Films of the Twenties. p150-51.
The Moving Picture World. Dec 4, 1926, p365.
The New York Times. Nov 22, 1926, p28.
Variety. Nov 24, 1926, p14.

The Great Gatsby (US; Nugent, Elliott; 1949)
The Classic American Novel and the Movies. p257-61.
Commonweal. Jul 1, 1949, v50, p296.
Film Daily. Apr 27, 1949, p7.
The Films of Alan Ladd. p137-42.
Films of the Forties. p255-56.
Hollywood Reporter. Apr 26, 1949, p3.
Literature/Film Quarterly. Spr 1974, v2, p216-28.
Magill's Survey of Cinema. Series II. v2, p929-32.
Motion Picture Herald Product Digest. Apr 30, 1949, p4591.
The Nation. Aug 13, 1949, v169, p162.
The New Republic. Jul 25, 1949, v121, p22.
The New York Times. Jul 14, 1949, p20.
The New Yorker. Jul 23, 1949, v25, p69.
Newsweek. Aug 1, 1949, v34, p64.
Rotarian. Nov 1949, v75, p34.
Theatre Arts. Jul 1949, v33, p9.
Time. Jul 25, 1949, v54, p78.
Variety. Apr 27, 1949, p11.

Great Guy (Also titled: Pluck of the Irish) (US; Blystone,
John G.; 1936)
Canadian Magazine. Apr 1937, v87, p38.
The Film Criticism of Otis Ferguson. p198-200.
Film Daily. Dec 9, 1936, p8.
The Films of James Cagney. p118-20.
Graham Greene on Film. p137-38.
The Great Gangster Pictures. p173.
Hollywood Reporter. Dec 7, 1936, p4.
Hollywood Spectator. Dec 19, 1936, v11, p10.
Judge. Feb 1937, v112, p24.
Literary Digest. Jan 16, 1937, v123, p23.
Motion Picture Herald. Dec 19, 1936, p58.
The Nation. Jan 16, 1937, v144, p80.

The New Masses. Jan 19, 1937, v22, p30.
New Theatre. Nov 1936, v3, p58.
The New York Times. Jan 1, 1937, p19.
The New Yorker. Jan 9, 1937, v12, p64-65.
Newsweek. Dec 26, 1936, v8, p37.
Rob Wagner's Script. Jan 16, 1937, v16, p10-11.
Scholastic. Jan 16, 1937, v29, p24.
Time. Jan 11, 1937, v29, p56.
Variety. Jan 6, 1937, p40.

The Great Jasper (US; Ruben, J. Walter; 1933)
Film Daily. Feb 17, 1933, p7.
Hollywood Reporter. Jan 31, 1933, p3.
Motion Picture Herald. Feb 11, 1933, p30.
The New York Times. Feb 17, 1933, p5.
The New Yorker. Feb 25, 1933, v9, p54-55.
Rob Wagner's Script. Mar 4, 1933, v9, p8-9.
Time. Feb 27, 1933, v21, p35.
Variety. Feb 21, 1933, p14.

The Great K and A Train Robbery (US; Seiler, Lewis;
1926)
Film Daily. Oct 10, 1926, p6.
Magill's Survey of Cinema. Silent Films. v2, p505-07.
The Moving Picture World. Oct 16, 1926, p443.
Photoplay. Dec 1926, v25, p57.
Variety. Oct 27, 1926, p40.

The Great Lie (US; Goulding, Edmund; 1941)
Bette Davis: Her Films and Career. p106-07.
Commonweal. Apr 25, 1941, v34, p16.
Film Daily. Apr 4, 1941, p6.
Hollywood Reporter. Apr 3, 1941, p3.
The London Times. Oct 2, 1941, p6.
Magill's Survey of Cinema. Series II. v2, p933-35.
Motion Picture Exhibitor. Apr 16, 1941, p728-29.
Motion Picture Herald Product Digest. Feb 8, 1941, p54.
The New York Times. Apr 12, 1941, p19.
The New Yorker. Apr 12, 1941, v17, p78.
Newsweek. Apr 21, 1941, v17, p60.
Scribner's Commentator. Jul 1941, v10, p105-06.
Time. Apr 21, 1941, v37, p98+.
Variety. Apr 16, 1941, p728-29.

The Great Love *See* Grosse Liebe, Die

The Great Love (US; Griffith, D.W.; 1918)
Exhibitor's Trade Review. Jul 13, 1918, p470.
Exhibitor's Trade Review. Aug 24, 1918, p1018.
The Films of D.W. Griffith. p97-101.
Motion Picture News. Aug 24, 1918, p1211, 1232.
Motion Picture News. Aug 31, 1918, p1425.
The Moving Picture World. Jul 27, 1918, p593.
The Moving Picture World. Aug 24, 1918, p1155.
The New York Times. Aug 12, 1918, p7.
Photoplay. May 1918, v13, p85.
Selected Film Criticism, 1912-1920. p106.
Variety. May 31, 1918, p33.
Variety. Jul 26, 1918, p32-33.
Variety. Aug 16, 1918, p36.
Wid's Daily. Aug 18, 1918, p15.

The Great Lover (US; Beaumont, Harry; 1931)
Film Daily. Aug 30, 1931, p10.
Hollywood Reporter. Jun 25, 1931, p3.
Hollywood Spectator. Sep 12, 1931, v12, p22.
Motion Picture Herald. Jul 4, 1931, p35.
The New York Times. Aug 24, 1931, p13.
The New York Times. Aug 30, 1931, p5.
Outlook and Independent. Jul 29, 1931, v158, p407.
Variety. Aug 25, 1931, p20.

The Great Man Votes (US; Kanin, Garson; 1939)
Commonweal. Jan 27, 1939, v29, p386.
Film Daily. Jan 11, 1939, p7.
Hollywood Reporter. Jan 7, 1939, p3.

Hollywood Spectator. Jan 21, 1939, v13, p9-10.
Motion Picture Herald. Jan 14, 1939, p43, 46.
The New Masses. Jan 31, 1939, v30, p27.
The New York Times. Jan 20, 1939, p15.
Preston Sturges: A Guide to References and Resources. p70-74.
Time. Jan 23, 1939, v33, p26.
Variety. Jan 11, 1939, p12.

The Great Man's Lady (US; Wellman, William A.; 1942)
Commonweal. May 8, 1942, v36, p63.
Film Daily. Mar 18, 1942, p6.
The Films of Barbara Stanwyck. p145-48.
Hollywood Reporter. Mar 17, 1942, p4.
Motion Picture Herald Product Digest. Mar 21, 1942, p561.
The New York Times. Apr 30, 1942, p14.
Starring Miss Barbara Stanwyck. p147-55.
Time. May 25, 1942, v39, p50.
Variety. Mar 18, 1942, p8.
William A. Wellman (Thompson). p199-202.

The Great McGinty (US; Sturges, Preston; 1940)
American Film. May 1982, v7, p44-45+.
American Film Criticism. p408-09.
Between Flops. p92-93, 126-38+.
Commonweal. Aug 16, 1940, v32, p352.
Commonweal. Nov 1, 1940, v33, p58.
Film Daily. Jul 23, 1940, p6.
Focus on Film. Apr 1980, v35, p44-46.
Hollywood Reporter. Jul 22, 1940, p3.
Lorentz on Film. p194-96.
Magic Moments from the Movies. p79.
Magill's Survey of Cinema. Series I. v2, p693-96.
The New Republic. Sep 30, 1940, v103, p448.
The New York Times. Aug 15, 1940, p23.
The New York Times. Aug 18, 1940, sec9, p3.
The New York Times. Aug 25, 1940, sec9, p3.
The New York Times. Nov 6, 1949, sec2, p1.
The New Yorker. Aug 24, 1940, v16, p60.
Newsweek. Aug 19, 1940, v16, p44.
Photoplay. Oct 1940, v54, p66.
Preston Sturges: A Guide to References and Resources. p47-50.
Time. Aug 26, 1940, v36, p48.
Variety. Jul 24, 1940, p14.
Vintage Films. p53-56.

The Great Meadow (US; Brabin, Charles; 1931)
Close-Up. Jun 1931, v8, p95.
Exhibitors Herald-World. Dec 6, 1930, p27.
Film Daily. Mar 15, 1931, p10.
Life. Apr 10, 1931, v97, p20.
The New York Times. Mar 14, 1931, p23.
The New York Times. Mar 15, 1931, p6.
The New York Times. Mar 22, 1931, p5.
The New Yorker. Mar 21, 1931, v7, p73.
Outlook and Independent. Apr 1, 1931, v157, p475.
Variety. Mar 18, 1931, p14.

The Great Moment (US; Wood, Sam; 1921)
Film Daily. Jul 28, 1921, p2.
The Films of Gloria Swanson. p93-98.
Magill's Survey of Cinema. Silent Films. v2, p508-10.
The New York Times. Jul 25, 1921, p8.

The Great Moment (US; Sturges, Preston; 1944)
Between Flops. p168-74+.
Commonweal. Aug 25, 1944, v40, p446.
Film Daily. Jun 9, 1944, p7.
Hollywood Reporter. Jun 9, 1944, p3.
The New Republic. Nov 27, 1944, v111, p692.
The New York Times. Nov 13, 1944, p15.
The New Yorker. Nov 25, 1944, v20, p79.
Newsweek. Nov 27, 1944, v24, p109.
Preston Sturges: A Guide to References and Resources. p70-74.
Time. Dec 4, 1944, v44, p94+.
Variety. Jun 7, 1944, p19.

The Great O'Malley (US; Dieterle, William; 1937)
The Complete Films of Humphrey Bogart. p40-41.
Film Daily. Mar 9, 1937, p10.
Hollywood Reporter. Dec 3, 1936, p3.
Humphrey Bogart: The Man and His Films. p60-62.
Motion Picture Herald. Dec 5, 1936, p56.
The New York Times. Mar 6, 1937, p10.
The New Yorker. Mar 13, 1937, v13, p78.
Rob Wagner's Script. Mar 20, 1937, v17, p8.
Variety. Mar 10, 1937, p14.
We're in the Money. p162-63.

The Great Sinner (US; Siodmark, Robert; 1949)
Commonweal. Jul 15, 1949, v50, p342.
Film Daily. Jul 7, 1949, p8.
The Films of Gregory Peck. p86-89.
Hollywood Reporter. Jun 30, 1949, p3.
Motion Picture Herald Product Digest. Jul 2, 1949, p4665.
The New York Times. Jun 30, 1949, p19.
The New Yorker. Jul 9, 1949, v25, p38.
Newsweek. Jul 11, 1949, v34, p68.
Rotarian. Oct 1949, v75, p38.
Time. Jul 18, 1949, v54, p76.
Variety. Jun 29, 1949, p14.

The Great Train Robbery (US; Porter, Edwin S.; 1903)
American Silent Film. p238-39.
Behind the Screen. p114-16.
The Emergence of Film Art. p27-30.
Film Before Griffith. p320-21.
A History of Films. p48-49.
A History of Narrative Film. p24-28.
Magill's Survey of Cinema. Silent Films. v2, p511-13.
A Million and One Nights. p416-19.
Motion Pictures. p37-42.
Spellbound in Darkness. p34-36.

The Great Victor Herbert (US; Stone, Andrew L.; 1939)
Commonweal. Dec 15, 1939, v31, p187.
Film Daily. Dec 1, 1939, p8.
Hollywood Reporter. Nov 28, 1939, p3.
Hollywood Spectator. Dec 9, 1939, v14, p6-7.
Motion Picture Herald. Dec 2, 1939, p41.
The New York Times. Dec 7, 1939, p35.
The New Yorker. Dec 9, 1939, v15, p98.
Newsweek. Dec 18, 1939, v14, p35-36.
Photoplay. Feb 1940, v54, p62.
Rob Wagner's Script. Jan 13, 1939, v21, p16.
Time. Dec 18, 1939, v34, p78.
Variety. Nov 29, 1939, p14.

The Great Waltz (US; Duvivier, Julien; 1938)
Commonweal. Nov 25, 1938, v29, p133.
Film Daily. Nov 4, 1938, p6.
The Films of the Thirties. p222-23.
The Hollywood Musical. p102-03.
Hollywood Reporter. Nov 2, 1938, p3.
Hollywood Spectator. Nov 12, 1938, v13, p10.
Motion Picture Herald. Nov 5, 1938, p36.
The Nation. Dec 10, 1938, v147, p638.
The New Masses. Dec 6, 1938, v29, p31.
The New Statesman and Nation. Dec 24, 1938, v16, p1089.
The New York Times. Nov 25, 1938, p19.
The New Yorker. Nov 26, 1938, v14, p73.
Newsweek. Nov 14, 1938, v12, p29.
Photoplay. Jan 1939, v53, p45.
Rob Wagner's Script. Nov 12, 1938, v20, p14.
Scholastic. Dec 3, 1938, v33, p32.
Time. Nov 14, 1938, v32, p42.
Variety. Nov 2, 1938, p15.

The Great Ziegfeld (US; Leonard, Robert Z.; 1936)
Canadian Magazine. May 1936, v85, p59.
Canadian Magazine. Jun 1936, v85, p40.
Commonweal. Apr 17, 1936, v23, p698.
Esquire. Jun 1936, v5, p110.

The Film Criticism of Otis Ferguson. p131-32.
Film Daily. Apr 9, 1936, p10.
The Films of Myrna Loy. p194-96.
Graham Greene on Film. p100-01.
The Hollywood Musical. p100-02.
Hollywood Reporter. Mar 23, 1936, p1-2.
Hollywood Spectator. Apr 25, 1936, v11, p13-14.
Hollywood Spectator. May 9, 1936, v11, p3.
Literary Digest. Apr 4, 1936, v121, p22.
Magill's Survey of Cinema. Series II. v2, p936-41.
Motion Picture. Mar 1936, v51, p28-29.
Motion Picture Herald. Apr 4, 1936, p34.
The Nation. Apr 29, 1936, v142, p560.
National Board of Review Magazine. May 1936, v11, p12.
The New Masses. Apr 28, 1936, v19, p29.
The New Republic. May 13, 1936, v87, p18.
The New Statesman and Nation. Sep 5, 1936, v12, p320.
The New York Times. Apr 9, 1936, p21.
The New York Times. Mar 5, 1937, p17.
The New Yorker. Apr 18, 1936, v12, p63-64.
Newsweek. Apr 18, 1936, v7, p29.
Photoplay. Feb 1936, v49, p42-43.
Rob Wagner's Script. Apr 25, 1936, v15, p12.
Scholastic. May 16, 1936, v28, p22.
Selected Film Criticism, 1931-1940. p105-06.
The Spectator. Sep 18, 1936, v157, p455.
Stage. Mar 1936, v13, p62.
Those Fabulous Movie Years: The 30s. p98-99.
Time. Apr 20, 1936, v27, p47-48.
Variety. Apr 15, 1936, v27, p16.
World Film News. Oct 1936, v1, p24.

The Greatest Question (US; Griffith, D.W.; 1919)
D.W. Griffith: An American Life. p413-14.
Exhibitor's Trade Review. Jan 10, 1920, p613.
The Films of D.W. Griffith. p133-37.
Motion Picture News. Jan 10, 1920, p691.
The Moving Picture World. Jan 10, 1920, p298-99.
The New York Times. Dec 29, 1919, p7.
Photoplay. Mar 1920, v17, p64.
Selected Film Criticism, 1912-1920. p107-08.
Variety. Jan 2, 1920, p74.
Wid's Daily. Jan 4, 1920, p5.

The Greatest Thing in Life (US; Griffith, D.W.; 1918)
Exhibitor's Trade Review. Jan 4, 1919, p38.
Motion Picture News. Jan 4, 1919, p149.
The Moving Picture World. Dec 28, 1918, p1558.
The Moving Picture World. Jan 4, 1919, p115.
The New York Times. Dec 23, 1918, p9.
Selected Film Criticism, 1912-1920. p108.
Variety. Jan 3, 1919, p38.
Wid's Daily. Jan 2, 1919, p4.

Greed (US; Stroheim, Erich von; 1924)
Bianco e Nero. No.2, 1959, Entire Issue.
Carl Sandburg at the Movies. p121-24.
Cinema Texas Program Notes. Sep 1975, v29.
Cinema, the Magic Vehicle. v1, p97-98.
Classic Movies. p12-13.
Classics of the Film. p41-49.
Classics of the Silent Screen. p48.
The Complete Greed by Erich von Stroheim.
Exceptional Photoplays. Dec-Jan 1925, v5, p23.
The Film and the Public. p109-112.
Film Culture. No.3, 1958, Entire Issue.
Film Daily. Dec 7, 1924, p4.
Films in Review. Jun-Jul 1955, v6, p263-68.
From Quasimodo to Scarlett O'Hara. p37-39.
The Great Films. p39-43.
The International Dictionary of Films and Filmmakers. v1, p188-89.
Life. Jan 1, 1925, v85, p24.
Magill's Survey of Cinema. Silent Films. v2, p514-26.
Motion Picture Classic. Aug 1926, v23, p66.

Motion Picture Magazine. Aug 1923, v26, p69-70.
Motion Picture Magazine. Apr 1924, v27, p76.
The Moving Picture World. Dec 30, 1924, p726, 737.
The New York Times. Jan 25, 1920, sec8, p6.
The New York Times. Dec 5, 1924, p28.
The Novel and the Cinema. p116-20.
Photoplay. Feb 1925, v27, p55.
Photoplay. Jan 1925, v27, p27.
Presentation of the Best Films of All Time: Universal and International Exhibition of Brussels, 1958. p1-8.
Selected Film Criticism, 1921-1930. p124-27.
Spellbound in Darkness. p330-37.
Stroheim. p23-76.
Stroheim: A Pictorial Record of his Nine Films. p95-135.
This Film Business. p132-145.
Variety. Dec 10, 1924, p34.

The Greeks Had a Word for Them (Also titled: Three Broadway Girls) (US; Sherman, Lowell; 1932)
Film Daily. Feb 7, 1932, p10.
Hollywood Reporter. Nov 17, 1931, p2.
Motion Picture Herald. Nov 28, 1931, p43-44.
The New York Times. Feb 4, 1932, p25.
The New Yorker. Feb 13, 1932, v7, p58.
Rob Wagner's Script. Apr 23, 1932, v7, p10.
Samuel Goldwyn Presents. p118-20.
Time. Feb 15, 1932, v19, p28.
Variety. Feb 9, 1932, p15.

Green Dolphin Street (US; Saville, Victor; 1947)
Commonweal. Oct 31, 1947, v47, p71.
Film Daily. Oct 16, 1947, p8.
The Films of Lana Turner. p145-50.
Hollywood Reporter. Oct 16, 1947, p3.
Motion Picture Herald Product Digest. Oct 25, 1947, p3894.
New Republic. Oct 27, 1947, v117, p36.
The New York Times. Oct 16, 1947, p34.
The New Yorker. Oct 25, 1947, v23, p94.
Newsweek. Oct 27, 1947, v30, p96.
Time. Nov 3, 1947, v50, p100.
Variety. Oct 22, 1947, p12.

The Green Goddess (US; Green, Alfred E.; 1930)
Exhibitors Herald-World. Feb 22, 1930, p36.
Film Daily. Feb 16, 1930, p8.
The Film Spectator. Mar 29, 1930, v9, p22.
Films in Review. Nov 1985, v36, p518.
Judge. Mar 15, 1930, v98, p25.
Life. Mar 7, 1930, v95, p20.
The Nation. Mar 5, 1930, v130, p280.
The New York Times. Feb 14, 1930, p20.
The New York Times. Feb 23, 1930, p5.
The New Yorker. Feb 22, 1930, v6, p80.
Outlook and Independent. Feb 26, 1930, v154, p355.
Variety. Feb 19, 1930, p21.

Green Light (US; Borzage, Frank; 1937)
Canadian Magazine. Apr 1937, v87, p36-38.
Commonweal. Mar 5, 1937, v25, p528.
Esquire. Apr 1937, v7, p117.
Film Daily. Jan 5, 1937, p4.
The Films of Errol Flynn. p51-52.
Hollywood Reporter. Dec 31, 1936, p2.
Hollywood Spectator. Jan 16, 1937, v11, p6-7.
Motion Picture Herald. Jan 9, 1937, p44, 46.
The New Masses. Feb 23, 1937, v22, p30-31.
The New York Times. Feb 13, 1937, p9.
The New Yorker. Feb 20, 1937, v13, p60-61.
Newsweek. Feb 20, 1937, v9, p21.
Rob Wagner's Script. Mar 6, 1937, v17, p11.
Scholastic. Feb 20, 1937, v30, p22.
Time. Feb 22, 1937, v29, p25.
Variety. Feb 17, 1937, p14.

Hollywood Reporter. Dec 16, 1939, p3.
Hollywood Spectator. Jan 6, 1940, v14, p6-7.
Motion Picture Herald. Dec 16, 1939, p25.
The New Masses. Dec 26, 1939, v34, p29-30.
The New York Times. Dec 21, 1939, p29.
The New Yorker. Dec 23, 1939, v15, p52.
Newsweek. Jan 1, 1940, v15, p30-31.
Photoplay. Jan 1940, v54, p19.
Photoplay. Feb 1940, v54, p62.
Rob Wagner's Script. Jan 6, 1940, v23, p17.
Scholastic. Jan 8, 1940, v35, p37.
Time. Jan 1, 1940, v35, p29.
Variety. Dec 20, 1939, p14.

Gun Crazy (Also titled: Deadly as the Female; Deadly Is the Female) (US; Lewis, Joseph H.; 1949)
BFI/Monthly Film Bulletin. Feb 1980, v47, p56-57.
The Big Book of B Movies. p42+.
Film Daily. Nov 2, 1949, p8.
Hollywood Reporter.
Magill's Survey of Cinema. Series II. v2, p949-51.
Motion Picture Herald. Nov 5, 1949, p74.
Sequence. Aut 1950, v12, p14-15.
Variety. Nov 2, 1949, p10.

Gung Ho (Also titled: Gung Ho!) (US; Enright, Ray; 1943)
Commonweal. Jan 21, 1944, v39, p353.
Film Daily. Dec 20, 1943, p6.
Hollywood Reporter. Dec 17, 1943, p3.
Life. Feb 7, 1944, v16, p77-78+.
Motion Picture Herald Product Digest. Dec 25, 1943, p1686.
The New York Times. Jan 26, 1944, p23.
The New Yorker. Jan 29, 1944, v19, p46+.
Newsweek. Jan 17, 1944, v23, p68+.
Variety. Dec 22, 1943, p12.

Gunga Din (US; 1911)
The New York Dramatic Mirror. May 24, 1911, p32.
Selected Film Criticism, 1896-1911. p43.

Gunga Din (US; Stevens, George; 1939)
American Cinematographer. Sep 1982, v63, p895-99+.
America's Favorite Movies. p87-103.
Commonweal. Feb 10, 1939, v29, p441.
Country Life. Apr 1939, v75, p26.
Dialogue. May-Jun 1975, v4, p2-32.
The Film Criticism of Otis Ferguson. p246-47.
Film Daily. Jan 25, 1939, p8.
The Films of Cary Grant. p124-28.
The Films of the Thirties. p224-26.
The Great Adventure Films. p86-91.
Hollywood Reporter. Jan 25, 1939, p3.
Hollywood Spectator. Feb 4, 1939, v13, p10-11.
Kiss Kiss Bang Bang. p345-46.
Magill's Survey of Cinema. Series II. v2, p959-62.
Motion Picture Herald. Jan 28, 1939, p32.
The Nation. Feb 4, 1939, v148, p158-59.
National Board of Review Magazine. Feb 1939, v14, p17.
The New Masses. Feb 7, 1939, v30, p28-29.
The New Republic. Feb 22, 1939, v98, p73.
The New Statesman and Nation. Mar 4, 1939, v17, p322.
The New York Times. Jan 28, 1939, p19.
The New Yorker. Feb 4, 1939, v14, p52-53.
Newsweek. Feb 6, 1939, v13, p25.
Photoplay. Jan 1939, v53, p38-39.
Rob Wagner's Script. Feb 4, 1939, v20, p16-17.
Scholastic. Feb 11, 1939, v34, p33.
Sight and Sound. Spr 1939, v8, p4-5.
Stage. Mar 15, 1939, v16, p7.
The Tatler. Mar 8, 1939, v151, p420.
Those Fabulous Movie Years: The 30s. p178.
Time. Feb 6, 1939, v33, p36.
Variety. Jan 25, 1939, p11.
World Horizons. Feb 1939, v3, p14-15.

A Guy Named Joe (US; Fleming, Victor; 1943)
Agee on Film. v1, p89-90.
Film Daily. Dec 24, 1943, p5.
The Films of Spencer Tracy. p180-83.
The Films of World War II. p162-63.
Hollywood Reporter. Dec 24, 1943, p3.
The Los Angeles Times. Mar 17, 1944, p23.
Magill's Survey of Cinema Annual, 1982. p435-38.
Motion Picture Herald Product Digest. Dec 25, 1943, p1686.
The New Republic. Jan 14, 1944, v110, p84.
The New York Times. Dec 24, 1943, p17.
The New Yorker. Jan 1, 1944, v19, p53.
Newsweek. Jan 10, 1944, v23, p82.
Time. Jan 10, 1944, v43, p92.
Variety. Dec 29, 1943, p8.

Gypsies (USSR; Schneider, Evgeni; Goldblatt, M.; 1936)
Motion Picture Herald. Aug 22, 1937, p52.
New Theatre. Sep 1936, v3, p23.
The New York Times. Jul 30, 1936, p22.
Variety. Aug 5, 1936, p16.

Hail the Conquering Hero (US; Sturges, Preston; 1944)
Agee on Film. v1, p114-16, 352-53.
Best Film Plays of 1943-1944. p561-630.
Between Flops. p185-92.
Canadian Forum. Jan 1945, v24, p234-35.
Commonweal. Aug 25, 1944, v40, p446-47.
Film Daily. Jun 7, 1944, p9.
Films and the Second World War. p202-03.
The Films of World War II. p200-01.
Hollywood Reporter. Jun 8, 1944, p3.
Life. Aug 28, 1944, v17, p45-46.
The London Times. Oct 26, 1944, p6.
Magill's Survey of Cinema. Series II. v2, p963-65.
Motion Picture Exhibitor. Jun 14, 1944, v32, n5, sec2, p1521.
Motion Picture Herald Product Digest. Jun 10, 1944, p1933.
The Nation. Sep 23, 1944, v159, p361-62.
New Movies. Oct 1944, v19, p5.
The New Republic. Aug 21, 1944, v111, p220.
The New York Times. Aug 10, 1944, p14.
The New York Times. Aug 13, 1944, sec2, p1.
The New Yorker. Aug 19, 1944, v20, p34.
Newsweek. Aug 7, 1944, v24, p98-99.
Preston Sturges: A Guide to References and Resources. p67-70.
Reruns. p61-64.
Rob Wagner's Script. Sep 23, 1944, v30, p20.
Running Away from Myself. p88-92.
Scholastic. Sep 11, 1944, v45, p33.
Selected Film Criticism, 1941-1950. p72-74.
Talking Pictures. p50-52.
Theatre Arts. Oct 1944, v28, p595-96.
Time. Aug 21, 1944, v44, p94.
Variety. Jun 7, 1944, p19.
50 Classic Motion Pictures. p230-35.

The Hairy Ape (US; Santell, Alfred; 1944)
Commonweal. Jun 30, 1944, v40, p256.
Film Daily. May 18, 1944, p6.
The Films of Susan Hayward. p95-97.
Hollywood Reporter. May 17, 1944, p3.
The Nation. Jun 17, 1944, v158, p716.
The New York Times. Jul 3, 1944, p8.
The New Yorker. Jul 8, 1944, v20, p44.
Newsweek. Jul 3, 1944, v24, p82-83.
Time. Jun 19, 1944, v43, p94.
Variety. May 17, 1944, p10.

The Half-Naked Truth (US; La Cava, Gregory; 1932)
Film Daily. Dec 31, 1932, p4.
Hollywood Reporter. Nov 16, 1932, p3.
Judge. Feb 1933, v104, p19.
Motion Picture Herald. Jan 7, 1933, p23, 26.
The New York Times. Dec 31, 1932, p10.

Rob Wagner's Script. Dec 10, 1932, v8, p9.
Variety. Jan 3, 1933, p27.

Hallelujah! (US; Vidor, King; 1929)
BFI/Monthly Film Bulletin. Sep 1974, v41, p209.
Film Daily. Aug 25, 1929, p8.
The Film Spectator. Nov 2, 1929, v8, p4-5.
The Film Spectator. Feb 15, 1930, v9, p20-22.
Films and Filming. May 1955, v8, p22.
The Hollywood Musical. p31.
The International Dictionary of Films and Filmmakers. v1, p192-93.
Literary Digest. Oct 5, 1929, p42-56.
Magill's Survey of Cinema. Series I. v2, p704-07.
The New York Times. Aug 21, 1929, p33.
Outlook. Oct 16, 1929, v153, p273.
Rob Wagner's Script. Jan 18, 1930, v2, p10.
Selected Film Criticism, 1921-1930. p127-28.
Time. Dec 16, 1929, v14, p58.
Toms, Coons, Mulattoes, Mammies, & Bucks. p36-45+.
Variety. Aug 28, 1929, p18.

Hallelujah, I'm a Bum (US; Milestone, Lewis; 1933)
Film Daily. Jan 27, 1933, p5.
Garbo and the Night Watchman. p228-31.
The Hollywood Musical. p72.
Hollywood Reporter. Dec 20, 1932, p3.
Love in the Film. p117-19.
Motion Picture Herald. Feb 18, 1933, p30.
Motion Picture Herald. Mar 4, 1933, p11-12.
The New York Times. Feb 9, 1933, p15.
The New Yorker. Feb 18, 1933, v9, p55.
Time. Feb 20, 1933, v21, p22.
Vanity Fair. Apr 1933, v40, p43.
Variety. Feb 14, 1933, p12.

Hamlet (US; 1911)
The Moving Picture World. Apr 22, 1911, p883.
Selected Film Criticism, 1896-1911. p43-44.

Handle With Care (US; Butler, David; 1932)
Film Daily. Dec 24, 1932, p4.
Hollywood Reporter. Dec 16, 1932, p3.
Motion Picture Herald. Dec 24, 1932, p24, 28.
The New York Times. Dec 24, 1932, p11.
Rob Wagner's Script. Dec 24, 1932, v8, p8-9.
Variety. Dec 27, 1932, p15.

Hands Across the Table (US; Leisen, Mitchell; 1935)
The Film Criticism of Otis Ferguson. p101-02.
Film Daily. Oct 25, 1935, p10.
The Films of Carole Lombard. p131-33.
Hollywood Director. p92-97.
Hollywood Reporter. Oct 4, 1935, p3.
Hollywood Spectator. Oct 26, 1935, v10, p10-11.
Literary Digest. Dec 7, 1935, v120, p24.
Lunatics and Lovers. p27-30.
Motion Picture Herald. Oct 19, 1935, p83.
The New Republic. Nov 13, 1935, v85, p18.
The New York Times. Nov 2, 1935, p13.
Rob Wagner's Script. Oct 26, 1935, v14, p10.
Talking Pictures. p64-67.
Time. Oct 28, 1935, v26, p54.
Variety. Nov 6, 1935, p20.

Hands Up! (US; Badger, Clarence; 1926)
Film Daily. Jan 24, 1926, p4.
Magill's Survey of Cinema. Silent Films. v2, p527-30.
The New York Times. Jan 18, 1926, p26.
Photoplay. Mar 1926, v24, p56.
Selected Film Criticism, 1921-1930. p128-29.
Variety. Jan 20, 1926, p40.

Hangmen Also Die (US; Lang, Fritz; 1943)
Commonweal. May 7, 1943, v38, p75.
Film Daily. Mar 23, 1943, p8.

The Films of Fritz Lang. p199-203.
The Films of World War II. p116-18.
Fritz Lang (Armour). p135-37.
Fritz Lang (Eisner). p221-38.
Hollywood Reporter. Mar 23, 1943, p3.
The Nation. May 1, 1943, v156, p643.
The New Republic. May 3, 1943, v108, p595.
The New York Times. Apr 16, 1943, p24.
The New Yorker. Apr 17, 1943, v19, p40.
Newsweek. Apr 26, 1943, v21, p88.
Time. Mar 29, 1943, v41, p40.
Variety. Mar 24, 1943, p20.

The Hangover Murders *See* Remember Last Night?

Happy Days (US; Stoloff, Benjamin; 1930)
Exhibitors Herald-World. Feb 22, 1930, p36.
Film Daily. Feb 16, 1930, p8.
The Film Spectator. Apr 12, 1930, v9, p25.
Judge. Mar 8, 1930, v98, p21.
Life. Mar 7, 1930, v95, p20.
The Nation. Mar 5, 1930, v130, p280.
New York Times. Feb 14, 1930, p20.
The New Yorker. Feb 22, 1930, v6, p80.
Outlook and Independent. Feb 26, 1930, v154, p355.
Time. Feb 24, 1930, v15, p54.
Variety. Feb 19, 1930, p33.

Hard to Get (US; Enright, Ray; 1938)
Film Daily. Nov 9, 1938, p5.
The Films of Olivia de Havilland. p121-26.
Hollywood Spectator. Nov 12, 1938, v13, p13-14.
Motion Picture Herald. Nov 12, 1938, p35.
The New Statesman and Nation. Mar 18, 1939, v17, p419.
The New York Times. Nov 14, 1938, p15.
Rob Wagner's Script. Nov 12, 1938, v19, p14-15.
Time. Nov 21, 1938, v32, p53.
Variety. Nov 9, 1938, p16.

Hard to Handle (US; LeRoy, Mervyn; 1933)
America in the Dark. p166-67.
Film Daily. Feb 3, 1933, p6.
The Films of James Cagney. p67-69.
The Gangster Film. p141-43.
The Hollywood Professionals. v5, p143-44.
Hollywood Reporter. Dec 28, 1932, p3.
Motion Picture Herald. Jan 7, 1933, p26-27.
The New York Times. Feb 2, 1933, p21.
The New Yorker. Feb 11, 1933, v9, p49.
Rob Wagner's Script. Jan 7, 1933, v8, p8.
Time. Feb 13, 1933, v21, p30.
Variety. Feb 7, 1933, p12.

The Hard Way (US; Sherman, Vincent; 1942)
Commonweal. Feb 26, 1943, v37, p471.
Film Daily. Sep 21, 1942, p6.
The Films of the Forties. p82-84.
Hollywood Reporter. Sep 21, 1942, p3.
Magill's Cinema Annual, 1985. p555-60.
Motion Picture Herald Product Digest. Sep 19, 1942, p923.
The Nation. Feb 20, 1943, p283.
The New Republic. Mar 29, 1943, v108, p414.
The New York Times. Mar 13, 1943, p9.
Time. Mar 1, 1943, p46+.
Variety. Sep 23, 1942, p8.

The Hardys Ride High (US; Seitz, George B.; 1939)
Film Daily. Apr 14, 1939, p13.
Hollywood Reporter. Apr 14, 1939, p3.
Motion Picture Herald. Apr 22, 1939, p38-39.
The New Statesman and Nation. Jul 29, 1939, v18, p177.
The New York Times. Apr 14, 1939, p28.
The New Yorker. Apr 22, 1939, v15, p66.
Rob Wagner's Script. May 13, 1939, v21, p16-17.
The Tatler. Aug 2, 1939, v153, p190.
Variety. Apr 19, 1939, p22.

Harlem on the Prairie (US; Newfield, Sam; 1937)
Film Daily. Feb 5, 1938, p4.
Hollywood Reporter. Nov 22, 1937, p2.
Motion Picture Herald. Nov 27, 1937, p54.
Time. Dec 13, 1937, v30, p24.
Variety. Feb 9, 1938, p14.

Harvest (Also titled: Regain) (FR; Pagnol, Marcel; 1939)
Commonweal. Oct 20, 1939, v30, p587.
The Film Criticism of Otis Ferguson. p267-68.
Film Daily. Jul 25, 1939, p9.
Films and Filming. Dec 1956, v3, p23-24.
French Film (Sadoul). p92.
The French Literary Filmmakers. p43-44, 59-60.
Hollywood Reporter. Dec 30, 1939, p3.
Kiss Kiss Bang Bang. p348.
Magill's Survey of Cinema. Foreign Language Films. v3, p1345-50.
Marcel Pagnol. p103-05.
Motion Picture Herald. Aug 5, 1939, p89.
The Nation. Aug 5, 1939, v149, p154.
The New Masses. Aug 22, 1939, v32, p30-31.
The New Masses. Oct 3, 1939, v33, p31.
The New Republic. Aug 23, 1939, v100, p75.
The New York Times. Oct 3, 1939, p19.
The New Yorker. Sep 30, 1939, v15, p57.
Rob Wagner's Script. Jan 13, 1939, v21, p16.
Saint Cinema: Selected Writings, 1929-1970. p83-86.
Time. Oct 23, 1939, v34, p52-53.
Variety. Oct 11, 1939, p13.

The Harvey Girls (US; Sidney, George; 1946)
Commonweal. Jan 18, 1946, v43, p358.
Film Daily. Jan 3, 1946, p11.
The Hollywood Musical. p266-67.
Hollywood Musicals. p200-02.
Hollywood Reporter. Dec 31, 1945, p3.
Judy: The Films and Career of Judy Garland. p127-30.
Life. Dec 3, 1945, v19, p82-86.
Magill's Survey of Cinema. Series II. v3, p992-94.
Motion Picture Herald Product Digest. Jan 5, 1946, p2785.
The New York Times. Jan 25, 1946, p26.
Newsweek. Feb 2, 1946, v29, p19.
Saturday Review. Feb 2, 1946, v29, p19.
Time. Jan 28, 1946, v47, p99.
Variety. Jan 2, 1946, p8.

The Hasty Heart (GB; Sherman, Vincent; 1949)
Christian Century. Feb 8, 1949, v67, p191.
Commonweal. Feb 3, 1950, v51, p464.
Film Daily. Dec 2, 1949, p7.
Films in Review. Mar 1950, v1, p32-34.
The Films of Ronald Reagan. p169-72.
Hollywood Reporter. Dec 1, 1949, p3.
Library Journal. Feb 1, 1950, v55, p181.
Motion Picture Herald Product Digest. Jul 9, 1949, p4675.
The New Republic. Feb 6, 1950, v122, p22.
The New Yorker. Jan 28, 1950, v25, p74.
Newsweek. Jan 30, 1949, v35, p72.
Rotarian. Dec 1950, v77, p37.
Senior Scholastic. Jan 11, 1949, v55, p25.
Time. Feb 13, 1949, v55, p88.
Variety. Sep 21, 1949, p8.

Hat, Coat, and Glove (US; Miner, Worthington; 1934)
BFI/Monthly Film Bulletin. Aug 1981, v48, p164.
Film Daily. Jul 27, 1934, p7.
Literary Digest. Aug 11, 1934, v118, p29.
Motion Picture Herald. Jul 21, 1934, p46-47.
The New York Times. Jul 27, 1934, p21.
Time. Aug 6, 1934, v24, p32.
Variety. Jul 31, 1934, p14.

The Hatchet Man (US; Wellman, William A.; 1932)
The Cinema of Edward G. Robinson. p86-87.
Film Daily. Feb 7, 1932, p10.

Judge. Mar 5, 1932, v102, p22.
Magill's Cinema Annual, 1983. p447-51.
Motion Picture Herald. Feb 13, 1932, p35.
The New York Times. Feb 4, 1932, p25.
The New Yorker. Feb 13, 1932, v7, p58.
Rob Wagner's Script. May 5, 1932, v7, p9.
Time. Feb 15, 1932, v19, p28.
Variety. Feb 9, 1932, p15.
William A. Wellman (Thompson). p121-23+.

Haunted Gold (US; Wright, Mack V.; 1932)
The Films of the Thirties. p92.
The Great Western Pictures. p128.
Hollywood Reporter. Nov 12, 1932, p2.
Variety. Jan 17, 1933, p15.

Hauptmann von Koepenick, Der (Also titled: The Captain of Koepenick) (GER; Oswald, Richard; 1932)
Film Daily. Jan 20, 1933, p6.
London Mercury. Nov 1932, v27, p73-74.
Motion Picture Herald. Feb 18, 1933, p31.
The New York Times. Feb 28, 1932, p6.
The New Yorker. Jan 28, 1933, v8, p47.
Time. Jan 30, 1933, v21, p26.
Variety. Jan 12, 1932, p28.
Variety. Jan 24, 1933, p19.

Having Wonderful Time (US; Santell, Alfred; 1938)
Canadian Magazine. Jul 1938, v90, p28.
Commonweal. Jul 22, 1938, v28, p351.
Film Daily. Jun 30, 1938, p7.
The Films of Ginger Rogers. p138-40.
Hollywood Reporter. Jun 11, 1938, p3.
Hollywood Spectator. Jun 18, 1938, v13, p8-9.
Life. Jun 27, 1938, v4, p56-57.
Lunatics and Lovers. p267.
Motion Picture Herald. Jun 18, 1938, p38.
The New York Times. Jul 8, 1938, p11.
The New Yorker. Jul 9, 1938, v14, p49.
Newsweek. Jun 27, 1938, v11, p23.
Rob Wagner's Script. Jul 23, 1938, v19, p8-9.
Variety. Jun 15, 1938, p14.
World Film News. Sep 1938, v3, p223.

Hawaiian Nights *See* Down to Their Last Yacht

Háxan *See* Witchcraft Through the Ages

He Fell in Love with His Wife (US; Taylor, William Desmond; 1916)
The Moving Picture World. Feb 26, 1916, p1310.
The Moving Picture World. Mar 4, 1916, p1547.
The New York Dramatic Mirror. Feb 26, 1916, p28.
The New York Times. Feb 28, 1916, p7.
Variety. Mar 10, 1916, p29.

He Knew Women (US; Herbert, Hugh; 1930)
Exhibitors Herald-World. Apr 26, 1930, p28.
Film Daily. Apr 20, 1930, p11.
The Film Spectator. Jun 7, 1930, v9, p18-19.
The New York Times. Apr 22, 1930, p33.
The New Yorker. Apr 26, 1930, v6, p83.
Outlook and Independent. Apr 30, 1930, v154, p712.
Variety. Apr 23, 1930, p36.

He Who Gets Slapped (US; Sjostrom, Victor; 1924)
Cinema, the Magic Vehicle. v1, p108-09.
Film Daily. Nov 2, 1924, p11.
The Films of Norma Shearer. p90-94.
Magill's Survey of Cinema. Silent Films. v2, p531-33.
The Moving Picture World. Nov 15, 1924, p266.
Photoplay. Jan 1925, v27, p61.
Selected Film Criticism, 1921-1930. p129.
Variety. Nov 12, 1924, p24.

Head Over Heels in Love (Also titled: Head Over Heels)
(GB; Hale, Sonnie; 1937)
Canadian Magazine. Mar 1937, v87, p25.
Film Daily. Feb 5, 1937, p9.
Garbo and the Night Watchman. p248.
Graham Greene on Film. p139.
Hollywood Reporter. Feb 27, 1937, p6.
Motion Picture Herald. Feb 13, 1937, p37.
The New York Times. Feb 13, 1937, p9.
Rob Wagner's Script. Mar 13, 1937, v17, p11.
Selected Film Criticism: Foreign Films, 1930-1950. p73-74.
The Spectator. Mar 19, 1937, v158, p516.
Time. Feb 22, 1937, v29, p25.
Variety. Feb 17, 1937, p14.

The Headless Horseman (US; Venturini, Edward; 1922)
Exceptional Photoplays. Nov 1922, v3, p4.
Film Daily. Oct 22, 1922, p5.
The New York Times. Dec 25, 1922, p21.
Selected Film Criticism, 1921-1930. p129-30.
Variety. Jan 5, 1923, p42.

The Heart Bandit (US; Apfel, Oscar C.; 1924)
Film Daily. Jan 13, 1924, p6.
The Moving Picture World. Jan 19, 1924, p216.
Variety. Jan 31, 1924, p23.

The Heart of a Race Tout (US; 1909)
The Moving Picture World. Aug 7, 1909, p195.
Selected Film Criticism, 1896-1911. p45.

The Heart of Humanity (US; Holubar, Allen; 1919)
Exhibitor's Trade Review. Jan 4, 1919, p419.
Fifty Great American Silent Films, 1912-1920. p102-03.
Magill's Survey of Cinema. Silent Films. v2, p534-36.
Motion Picture News. Jan 4, 1919, p116.
Motion Picture News. Jan 11, 1919, p275-79, 295.
Motion Picture News. Jan 25, 1919, p614.
The Moving Picture World. Jan 5, 1919, p113.
The New York Dramatic Mirror. Dec 28, 1918, p1000.
The New York Times. Dec 22, 1918, p17.
Selected Film Criticism, 1912-1920. p109-11.
Variety. Jan 3, 1919, p38.
Variety. Jan 24, 1919, p44.
Wid's Daily. Jan 5, 1919, p19.

Heart of Paris *See* Gribouille

The Heart of Texas Ryan (US; Martin, E.A.; 1917)
The Moving Picture World. Mar 3, 1917, p1369.
The Moving Picture World. Feb 24, 1917, p1253.
The New York Dramatic Mirror. Mar 17, 1917, p26.
Photoplay. Jun 1917, v11, p154.
Selected Film Criticism, 1912-1920. p111-13.
Variety. Feb 23, 1917, p24.
The War, the West, and the Wilderness. p307.
Wid's Daily. Feb 22, 1917, p122.

Heartbeat (French title: Angele) (FR; Pagnol, Marcel;
1934)
Commonweal. Sep 15, 1939, v30, p481.
Dictionary of Films. p11.
Film Daily. Sep 14, 1939, p11.
French Film (Sadoul). p68-69.
Marcel Pagnol. p102-03.
Motion Picture Herald. Sep 16, 1939, p42.
The New York Times. Sep 5, 1939, p21.
Variety. Sep 6, 1939, p19.

Hearts Adrift (US; Porter, Edwin S.; 1915)
The Moving Picture World. Feb 21, 1914, p927, 1024.
The New York Dramatic Mirror. Jan 28, 1914, p37.
The New York Dramatic Mirror. Feb 18, 1914, p36.
Variety. Feb 20, 1914, p36.

Hearts Divided (US; Borzage, Frank; 1936)
Canadian Magazine. Jul 1936, v86, p30-31.
Commonweal. Jul 10, 1936, v24, p19.
Film Daily. Jun 9, 1936, p10.
Hollywood Reporter. Jun 4, 1936, p3.
Literary Digest. Jun 20, 1936, v121, p19.
Motion Picture Herald. Jun 13, 1936, p68-69.
The New York Times. Jun 13, 1936, p13.
Rob Wagner's Script. Jun 13, 1936, v15, p8.
Time. Jun 22, 1936, v27, p37.
Variety. Jun 17, 1936, p23.

Hearts of the World (US; Griffith, D.W.; 1918)
BFI/Monthly Film Bulletin. Feb 1976, v43, p37-38.
Exhibitor's Trade Review. Mar 30, 1918, p1365.
The Films of D.W. Griffith. p90-96.
Magill's Survey of Cinema. Silent Films. v2, p537-40.
Motion Picture Classics. Jul 1918, p18-19.
Motion Picture News. Apr 20, 1918, p2337.
Motion Picture News. Jan 17, 1920, p890.
The Moving Picture World. Apr 20, 1918, p369.
The New York Dramatic Mirror. Mar 30, 1918, p9.
The New York Times. Apr 5, 1918, p13.
Photoplay. Jun 1914, v14, p48, 111.
Selected Film Criticism, 1912-1920. p113-18.
Sight and Sound. May 1950, v19, p130-32.
Variety. Mar 15, 1918, p47, 49.
Variety. Mar 29, 1918, p49.
Variety. Apr 12, 1918, p2-3, 43.
Variety. Jun 7, 1918, p37.
The War, the West, and the Wilderness. p145-55.
Wid's Daily. May 12, 1918, p31-32.

Heaven Can Wait (US; Lubitsch, Ernst; 1943)
The Cinema of Ernst Lubitsch. p121-34.
Commonweal. Aug 13, 1943, v38, p421.
Ernst Lubitsch: A Guide to References and Resources. p155-59.
Ernst Lubitsch's American Comedy. p259-328.
Film Daily. Jul 21, 1943, p21.
The Films of the Forties. p96-97.
Heaven Can Wait.
Hollywood Reporter. Jul 21, 1943, p3.
Magill's Survey of Cinema. Series I. v2, p727.
Motion Picture Herald Product Digest. Jul 24, 1943, p1441.
The New Republic. Aug 30, 1943, v109, p284.
The New York Times. Aug 12, 1943, p15.
Newsweek. Aug 1943, v22, p84.
Photoplay. Sep 1943, v23, p32.
Time. Jul 19, 1943, v42, p96.
Variety. Jul 21, 1943, p22.

Heidi (US; Dwan, Allan; 1937)
Child Life. Oct 1937, v16, p456-57.
Commonweal. Nov 5, 1937, v27, p48.
Film Daily. Oct 12, 1937, p6.
The Films of Shirley Temple. p186-89.
Hollywood Reporter. Oct 9, 1937, p3.
Life. Oct 25, 1937, v3, p104-05.
Motion Picture Herald. Oct 16, 1937, p43.
The New Statesman and Nation. Dec 18, 1937, v14, p1064.
The New York Times. Nov 6, 1937, p14.
Rob Wagner's Script. Nov 13, 1937, v18, p8.
Saint Nicholas Magazine. Aug 1937, v64, p39.
Time. Oct 25, 1937, v30, p25.
Variety. Nov 10, 1937, p18.

The Heir to Genghis Khan *See* Storm Over Asia

The Heiress (US; Wyler, William; 1949)
Catholic World. Nov 1949, v170, p149.
Christian Century. Mar 22, 1949, v77, p383.
Commonweal. Oct 14, 1949, v51, p15.
Film Daily. Sep 7, 1949, p7.
Films in Review. Feb 1950, v1, p25-27.
The Films of Montgomery Clift. p113-18.
The Films of Olivia de Havilland. p219-21.

The Films of the Forties. p274-76.
Hollywood Reporter. Sep 7, 1949, p3.
Life. Oct 17, 1949, v27, p113, 118.
Magill's Survey of Cinema. Series I. v2, p730-33.
Motion Picture Herald. Sep 10, 1949, p9.
The New Republic. Oct 31, 1949, v121, p22.
The New York Times. Oct 7, 1949, p35.
The New Yorker. Oct 8, 1949, v25, p89.
Newsweek. Oct 17, 1949, v34, p94.
The Novel and the Cinema. p296-303.
Rotarian. May 1950, v76, p41.
Selected Film Criticism, 1941-50. p76-79.
Senior Scholastic. Sep 21, 1949, v55, p30.
Sequence. Aut 1950, v12, p43-44.
Sight and Sound. Dec 1950, v19, p332-33.
Theatre Arts. Nov 1949, v33, p8.
Time. Oct 24, 1949, v54, p101-02.
Variety. Sep 7, 1949, p11.
William Wyler. p149-65.
William Wyler: A Guide to References and Resources. p121-24.

Hell Below (US; Conway, Jack; 1933)
Film Daily. Apr 27, 1933, p4.
Hollywood Reporter. Mar 15, 1933, p3.
Motion Picture Herald. Apr 15, 1933, p30.
New Outlook. Jun 1933, v161, p48.
The New York Times. Apr 26, 1933, p13.
The New Yorker. May 6, 1933, v9, p58.
Newsweek. May 6, 1933, v1, p29.
Rob Wagner's Script. May 6, 1933, v9, p10.
Time. May 8, 1933, v21, p39.
Variety. May 2, 1933, p12.

Hell Divers (US; Hill, George; 1931)
Commonweal. Jan 6, 1932, v15, p270-71.
Film Daily. Dec 27, 1931, p10.
Hollywood Reporter. Nov 10, 1931, p3.
Judge. Jan 23, 1932, v102, p22.
Motion Picture Herald. Dec 26, 1931, p30.
The New Statesman and Nation. Mar 26, 1932, v3, p393.
The New York Times. Dec 23, 1931, p27.
The New Yorker. Jan 2, 1932, v7, p47.
Outlook and Independent. Jan 6, 1932, v160, p23.
Rob Wagner's Script. Jan 2, 1932, v6, p8.
Time. Jan 4, 1932, v19, p19.
Variety. Dec 29, 1931, p166.

Hello, Frisco, Hello (US; Humberstone, Bruce; 1943)
Commonweal. Apr 16, 1943, v37, p644.
Film Daily. Mar 15, 1943, p7.
The Films of Alice Faye. p159-64.
Hollywood Musical. p216, 240+.
Motion Picture Herald Product Digest. Mar 13, 1943, p1202-03.
The New York Times. Mar 25, 1943, p25.
Newsweek. Mar 29, 1943, v21, p67.
Time. Mar 29, 1943, v41, p39.
Variety. Mar 10, 1943, p15.

Hell's Angels (US; Hughes, Howard; 1930)
Beyond Formula: American Film Genres. p267-70.
BFI/Monthly Film Bulletin. Sep 1980, v47, p181-82.
Commonweal. Sep 17, 1930, v12, p499.
Dictionary of Films. p147.
Esquire. Aug 1938, v10, p72, 90.
Exhibitors Herald-World. May 31, 1930, p123.
Film Daily. Aug 24, 1930, p10.
The Films of Jean Harlow. p32-37.
The Films of the Thirties. p35-36.
Hell's Angels Movie Program.
James Whale. p42-45, 56-58.
Judge. Sep 6, 1930, v99, p23.
Judge. Dec 20, 1930, v99, p21.
Life. Sep 5, 1930, v96, p16.

Lorentz on Film. p48-49.
Magill's Survey of Cinema. Series I. v2, p734-36.
The Nation. Sep 3, 1930, v131, p254.
The New Republic. Oct 1, 1930, v64, p180.
The New York Times. Aug 16, 1930, p8.
The New Yorker. Aug 23, 1930, v6, p57-58.
Outlook and Independent. Aug 27, 1930, v155, p672.
Photoplay. Aug 1930, v38, p55.
Rob Wagner's Script. May 31, 1930, v3, p10-12.
Selected Film Criticism, 1921-1930. p130.
The Spectator. Nov 8, 1930, v145, p665.
Theatre Magazine. 1930, v52, p47-48.
Time. Jun 9, 1930, v15, p50.
Time. Nov 10, 1930, v16, p8.
Variety. Jun 4, 1930, p25.
Variety. Jan 17, 1940, p14.

Hell's Highway (US; Brown, Rowland; 1932)
Film Daily. Sep 27, 1932, p6.
Hollywood Reporter. Aug 11, 1932, p3.
Motion Picture Herald. Aug 20, 1932, p35.
The New York Times. Sep 26, 1932, p18.
The New Yorker. Oct 1, 1932, v8, p55.
Rob Wagner's Script. Sep 13, 1932, v7, p8-9.
Vanity Fair. Dec 1932, v39, p64.
Variety. Sep 27, 1932, p21.

Hell's Hinges (US; Hart, William S; Swickard, Charles; 1916)
BFI/Monthly Film Bulletin. Oct 1975, v42, p228.
Classics of the Silent Screen. p23-24.
The Complete Films of William S. Hart. p39-41.
Fifty Great American Silent Films, 1912-1920. p45-47.
Magill's Survey of Cinema. Silent Films. v2, p541-45.
The Moving Picture World. Feb 19, 1916, p1146.
The Moving Picture World. Feb 26, 1916, p1366.
The New York Dramatic Mirror. Feb 26, 1916, p28.
The New York Times. Feb 7, 1916, p9.
The Rivals of D.W. Griffith. p20-23.
Selected Film Criticism, 1912-1920. p118-19.
Variety. Feb 7, 1916, p21.

Hell's House (US; Higgin, Howard; 1932)
Bette Davis: Her Films and Career. p22-23.
Film Daily. Feb 14, 1932, p10.
Motion Picture Herald. Feb 20, 1932, p34.
The New York Times. Feb 12, 1932, p24.
The New Yorker. Feb 20, 1932, v8, p62.
Variety. Feb 16, 1932, p24.

Hellzapoppin' (US; Potter, H.C.; 1941)
Commonweal. Jan 9, 1942, v35, p296.
Film Daily. Dec 19, 1941, p7.
Hollywood Reporter. Dec 18, 1941, p3.
Motion Picture Herald Product Digest. Dec 20, 1941, p431.
The New York Times. Dec 26, 1941, p21.
Selected Film Criticism, 1941-1950. p79.
Time. Feb 2, 1942, v39, p55.
Variety. Dec 24, 1941, p8.

Help Wanted (US; 1911)
Film Reports. Jan 21, 1911, v2, p7.
Selected Film Criticism, 1896-1911. p45.

Henry V (GB; Olivier, Laurence; 1944)
Agee on Film. v1, p207-12, 361-66.
The Atlantic. Feb 1975, v235, p39-48+.
Canadian Forum. Oct 1946, v26, p161.
Catholic World. Aug 1946, v163, p457.
Chestnuts in Her Lap. p134-35.
Christian Science Monitor Magazine. Mar 30, 1946, p7.
Commonweal. Jun 21, 1944, v44, p238-39.
Cue. Jul 15, 1946, p12-14.
Film and Literature. p136.
Film Daily. Apr 22, 1946, p6.
Film Guide to Henry V.

Film Quarterly. Oct 1946, v2, p82-96.
The Films of Laurence Olivier. p96-99.
Focus on Shakespearean Films. p53-62.
Forum. Jul 1948, v106, p77-79.
The Great Adventure Films. p120-27.
The Great British Films. p75-78.
The Great Films. p165-68.
The Great Movies. p237-41.
Halliwell's Hundred. p127-30.
Hollywood Reporter. Apr 22, 1946, p3.
Hollywood Review. Apr 23, 1946, v37, p1+.
The International Dictionary of Films and Filmmakers. v1, p195-96.
Laurence Olivier (Hirsch). p60-76.
Life. May 20, 1946, v20, p38-42.
Life. Mar 10, 1947, v22, p86+.
Literature/Film Quarterly. Fall 1977, v5, p316-21.
Literature/Film Quarterly. 1983, v11, n3, p179-84.
The London Times. Nov 23, 1944, p6.
Magic Moments from the Movies. p148.
Magill's Survey of Cinema. Series II. v3, p1019-22.
The Making of Henry V. .
Motion Picture Exhibitor. Jan 10, 1945, v33, n10, sec2, p1649.
Motion Picture Herald Product Digest. Dec 2, 1944, p2201.
The Moving Image. p282-85.
The Nation. Jul 20, 1946, v163, p80.
The Nation. Aug 3, 1946, v163, p136.
The New Republic. Jul 8, 1946, v115, p14.
The New York Times. Jun 16, 1946, p30.
The New York Times Magazine. May 12, 1946, p22-23+.
The New Yorker. Jun 22, 1946, v22, p40-42.
Newsweek. Jun 17, 1946, v27, p102.
Photoplay. Nov 1946, v29, p35.
Saturday Review. May 25, 1946, v29, p26+.
Scholastic. Sep 6, 1946, v49, p40.
Scholastic. Oct 14, 1946, v49, p6.
Scholastic. Oct 21, 1946, v49, p22-23.
Selected Film Criticism: Foreign Films, 1930-1950. p74-79.
Shakespeare and the Film. p37-40.
Sight and Sound. Jan 1945, v8, p85-86.
Sight and Sound. Jul-Sep 1952, v22, p10-15.
Theater and Film. p144-50.
Theatre Arts. Jun 1945, v29, p337-40+.
Theatre Arts. Apr 1946, v30, p217-18.
Time. Apr 8, 1946, v47, p56-60.
Variety. Apr 24, 1946, p8.

Her Bodyguard (US; Beaudine, William; 1933)
Film Daily. Aug 5, 1933, p3.
Motion Picture Herald. Jul 8, 1933, p40.
New Outlook. Sep 1933, v162, p45.
The New York Times. Aug 7, 1933, p18.
Variety. Aug 8, 1933, p19.

Her Code of Honor (US; Stahl, John M.; 1919)
Exhibitor's Trade Review. Mar 15, 1919, p1145.
Motion Picture News. Mar 1, 1919, p1330.
Motion Picture News. Mar 15, 1919, p1705.
The Moving Picture World. Mar 15, 1919, p1530.
Variety. Mar 7, 1919, p66.
Wid's Daily. Mar 4, 1919, p3.

Her Double Life (US; Edwards, J. Gordon; 1916)
Variety. Sep 29, 1916, p26.
Wid's Daily. Oct 5, 1916, p101.

Her Enlisted Man *See* Red Salute

Her First Mate (US; Wyler, William; 1933)
Film Daily. Sep 2, 1933, p3.
Hollywood Reporter. Jul 15, 1933, p3.
Motion Picture Herald. Jul 22, 1933, p56.
The New York Times. Sep 2, 1933, p14.
Rob Wagner's Script. Aug 19, 1933, v10, p8.
Variety. Sep 5, 1933, p19.

William Wyler: A Guide to References and Resources. p73-74.
William Wyler (Anderegg). p34-36.

Her Jungle Love (US; Archainbaud, George; 1938)
Chestnuts in Her Lap. p38-41.
Film Daily. Mar 22, 1938, p10.
Hollywood Reporter. Mar 19, 1938, p3.
Motion Picture Herald. Mar 26, 1938, p42.
The New York Times. Apr 14, 1938, p27.
Rob Wagner's Script. Apr 9, 1938, v19, p11.
The Tatler. Apr 20, 1938, v148, p106.
Time. Apr 18, 1938, v31, p51.
Variety. Mar 23, 1938, p16.

Her Private Affair (US; Stein, Paul; Lloyd, Rollo; 1930)
Exhibitors Herald-World. Nov 9, 1929, p62.
Exhibitors Herald-World. Jan 18, 1930, v41.
Film Daily. Jan 12, 1930, p13.
The Film Spectator. Jan 4, 1930, v9, p22.
Judge. Feb 1, 1930, v98, p25.
The New York Times. Jan 11, 1930, p21.
The New Yorker. Jan 18, 1930, v5, p75.
Time. Jan 27, 1930, v15, p44.
Variety. Jan 15, 1930, p22.

Her Sister from Paris (US; Franklin, Sidney; 1925)
Film Daily. Aug 30, 1925, p6.
The Films of the Twenties. p109.
Magill's Survey of Cinema. Silent Films. v2, p546-49.
The Moving Picture World. Sep 5, 1925, p63.
Variety. Aug 26, 1925, p25.

Her Wedding Night (US; Tuttle, Frank; 1930)
Exhibitors Herald-World. Oct 4, 1930, p32.
Exhibitors Herald-World. Oct 11, 1930, p39.
Film Daily. Sep 28, 1930, p10.
The New York Times. Sep 29, 1930, p19.
Time. Oct 6, 1930, v16, p34.
Variety. Oct 1, 1930, p19.

Here Comes Mr. Jordan (US; Hall, Alexander; 1941)
American Film Criticism. p124-26.
Commonweal. Aug 29, 1941, v34, p448.
Film Daily. Jul 30, 1941, p4.
Hollywood Reporter. Jul 22, 1941, p3.
Life. Aug 18, 1941, v11, p56-58.
The London Times. Dec 22, 1941, p8.
Magill's Survey of Cinema. Series I. v2, p737-40.
Motion Picture Exhibitor. Aug 6, 1941, p801.
Motion Picture Herald Product Digest. Jul 26, 1941, p194.
The New Republic. Aug 25, 1941, v105, p251.
The New York Times. Aug 8, 1941, p13.
The New York Times. Aug 17, 1941, sec9, p3.
The New Yorker. Aug 16, 1941, v17, p52.
Newsweek. Aug 11, 1941, v18, p60.
One Good Film Deserves Another. p41-44.
Photoplay. Oct 1941, v19, p6.
Scholastic. Sep 15, 1941, v39, p28.
Scribner's Commentator. Oct 1941, v10, p108.
Time. Aug 25, 1941, v38, p74.
Variety. Jul 30, 1941, p18.

Here Comes the Band (US; Sloane, Paul; 1935)
Esquire. Nov 1935, v4, p106.
Film Daily. Sep 21, 1935, p4.
Hollywood Reporter. Jul 26, 1935, p4.
Motion Picture Herald. Aug 17, 1935, p49.
The New Masses. Oct 22, 1935, v17, p29-30.
Variety. Sep 25, 1935, p12.

Here I Am a Stranger (US; Del Ruth, Roy; 1939)
Film Daily. Oct 3, 1939, p7.
Hollywood Reporter. Sep 21, 1939, p4.
Motion Picture Herald. Sep 30, 1939, p39.
The New York Times. Sep 30, 1939, p11.
Rob Wagner's Script. Sep 30, 1939, v22, p16.

The Tatler. Mar 20, 1940, v155, p372.
Time. Oct 9, 1939, v34, p40-41.
Variety. Sep 27, 1939, p12.

Here Is a Man *See* The Devil and Daniel Webster

Here Is My Heart (US; Tuttle, Frank; 1934)
Film Daily. Dec 22, 1934, p3.
The Films of Bing Crosby. p65-67.
The Hollywood Musical. p97.
Hollywood Reporter. Nov 28, 1934, p3.
Motion Picture Herald. Dec 8, 1934, p36.
The New York Times. Dec 22, 1934, p21.
Time. Dec 31, 1934, v24, p14.
Variety. Dec 25, 1934, p12.

Heroes for Sale (US; Wellman, William A.; 1933)
Film Daily. Jul 22, 1933, p3.
Hollywood Reporter. May 17, 1933, p3.
Motion Picture Herald. May 27, 1933, p32.
The New York Times. Jul 22, 1933, p14.
Rob Wagner's Script. Jun 17, 1933, v9, p8-9.
Variety. Jul 25, 1933, p14.
We're in the Money. p96-100.
William A. Wellman (Thompson). p136-38.

Herr Arnes Pengar *See* Sir Arne's Treasure

Herrin von Atlantis, Die *See* Atlantide, L'

Heure Pres de Loi, Une *See* One Hour With You

Hiawatha (US; 1909)
The Bioscope. Jul 21, 1910, p37.
The Moving Picture World. Oct 23, 1909, p563.
The New York Dramatic Mirror. Nov 6, 1909, p14.
Selected Film Criticism, 1896-1911. p46-47.

Hidden Pearls (US; Melford, George H.; 1918)
Motion Picture News. Feb 23, 1918, p1181.
The Moving Picture World. Feb 16, 1918, p1003.
The Moving Picture World. Feb 23, 1918, p1141.
The New York Dramatic Mirror. Feb 16, 1918, p18.
Wid's Daily. Feb 7, 1918, p930-31.

High Pressure (US; LeRoy, Mervyn; 1932)
Film Daily. Jan 31, 1932, p10.
Hollywood Reporter. Dec 24, 1931, p2.
Judge. Mar 26, 1932, v102, p22.
Motion Picture Herald. Jan 9, 1932, p40.
The Nation. Mar 2, 1932, v134, p268.
The New York Times. Feb 1, 1932, p22.
The New Yorker. Feb 6, 1932, v7, p55.
Outlook. Mar 1932, v160, p188.
Rob Wagner's Script. Feb 13, 1932, v7, p9.
Time. Feb 8, 1932, v19, p20.
Variety. Feb 2, 1932, p15.

High Sierra (US; Walsh, Raoul; 1941)
American Film Criticism. p100-03.
Commonweal. Jan 31, 1941, v33, p376.
The Complete Films of Humphrey Bogart. p89-91.
Dreams and Dead Ends. p59-82.
Film Comment. Jan/Feb 1983, v19, p58-68+.
The Film Criticism of Otis Ferguson. p338-39.
Film Culture. Fall 1964, v34, p35-37.
Film Daily. Jan 20, 1941, p5.
Film Noir. p125-26.
High Sierra.
Humphrey Bogart: The Man and His Films. p108-09.
Journal of Popular Film. 1976, v5, n3-4, p248-62.
Literature/Film Quarterly. Sum 1977, v5, p269-71.
The London Times. Aug 4, 1941, p8.
Magill's Survey of Cinema. Series I. v2, p748-50.
Make It Again, Sam. p69-74.
Motion Picture Exhibitor. Jan 22, 1941, p677.
Movietone News. Nov 1975, v45, p14-21, 34-37.

The New Republic. Feb 10, 1941, v104, p180.
The New York Times. Jan 25, 1941, p11.
Time. Feb 17, 1941, v37, p94.
Variety. Jan 22, 1941, p16.

High Society Blues (US; Butler, David; 1930)
Exhibitors Herald-World. Apr 26, 1930, p28, 30.
Film Daily. Apr 20, 1930, p11.
The Film Spectator. Apr 12, 1930, v9, p22-23.
Judge. Jun 7, 1930, v98, p23.
Life. May 9, 1930, v95, p18, 26.
The New York Times. Apr 19, 1930, p15.
The New York Times. Apr 27, 1930, p5.
The New Yorker. Apr 26, 1930, v6, p83.
Time. May 5, 1930, v15, p32.
Variety. Apr 23, 1930, p26.

High Stakes (US; Sherman, Lowell; 1931)
BFI/Monthly Film Bulletin. May 1981, v48, p99.
Film Daily. May 31, 1931, p10.
Hollywood Reporter. Apr 28, 1931, p3.
Motion Picture Herald. May 9, 1931, p35.
Rob Wagner's Script. Oct 17, 1931, v6, p10.

High Tension (US; Dwan, Allan; 1936)
Film Daily. Jun 16, 1936, p24.
Hollywood Reporter. Jun 13, 1936, p3.
Motion Picture Herald. Jun 20, 1936, p66-67.
The New York Times. Jul 11, 1936, p11.
Variety. Jul 15, 1936, p55.

High, Wide and Handsome (US; Mamoulian, Rouben; 1937)
Commonweal. Aug 6, 1937, v26, p368.
Film Daily. Jul 22, 1937, p12.
Graham Greene on Film. p163-64.
The Hollywood Musical. p104-05.
Hollywood Reporter. Jul 22, 1937, p3.
Hollywood Spectator. Jul 31, 1937, v12, p8-9.
Life. Sep 27, 1937, v3, p16-17.
Mamoulian (Milne). p106-15.
Motion Picture Herald. Jul 24, 1937, p51.
The New Masses. Aug 3, 1937, v24, p29.
The New York Times. Jul 22, 1937, p15.
The New Yorker. Jul 31, 1937, v13, p49.
Newsweek. Jul 31, 1937, v10, p22.
Rob Wagner's Script. Aug 14, 1937, v17, p14.
The Spectator. Aug 27, 1937, v159, p347.
Time. Aug 2, 1937, v30, p34.
Variety. Jul 28, 1938, p16.
World Film News. Oct 1937, v2, p24.

The High Window *See* The Brasher Doubloon

Hindle Wakes (GB; Saville, Victor; 1931)
The Age of the Dream Palace. p318-19.
Motion Picture Herald. Oct 10, 1931, p46.
Variety. Oct 13, 1931, p15.

Hintertreppe *See* Backstairs

Hips, Hips, Hooray (US; Sandrich, Mark; 1934)
Film Daily. Jan 24, 1934, p6.
The Hollywood Musical. p84.
Motion Picture Herald. Jan 27, 1934, p40.
The New York Times. Feb 24, 1934, p18.
Variety. Feb 27, 1934, p17.

His Affair *See* This Is My Affair

His Brother's Wife (US; Van Dyke, W.S.; 1936)
Esquire. Oct 1936, v6, p194.
Film Daily. Aug 1, 1936, p7.
The Films of Barbara Stanwyck. p107-08.
The Films of Robert Taylor. p50-51.
Hollywood Reporter. Jul 29, 1936, p3.
Hollywood Spectator. Aug 15, 1936, v11, p6.

Motion Picture Herald. Aug 22, 1936, p39.
The New York Times. Aug 15, 1936, p6.
Rob Wagner's Script. Aug 22, 1936, v15, p13.
Starring Miss Barbara Stanwyck. p80, 83.
Time. Aug 17, 1936, v28, p48.
Variety. Aug 19, 1936, p16.
World Film News. Oct 1936, v1, p23.

His Double Life (US; Hopkins, Arthur; 1933)
Film Daily. Dec 16, 1933, p4.
Hollywood Reporter. Dec 16, 1933, p6.
Motion Picture Herald. Dec 30, 1933, p32, 34.
The New York Times. Dec 16, 1933, p12.
The New Yorker. Dec 23, 1933, v9, p49-50.
Newsweek. Dec 23, 1933, v2, p30.
Rob Wagner's Script. Dec 30, 1933, v10, p12.
Variety. Dec 19, 1933, p19.

His Girl Friday (US; Hawks, Howard; 1940)
American Film. Jul-Aug 1983, v8, p66-67+.
Ben Hecht: Hollywood Screenwriter. p79-108.
Cinema, the Magic Vehicle. v1, p310-11.
Commonweal. Jan 19, 1940, v31, p287.
Dictionary of Films. p150.
Film Art. p234-39.
The Film Criticism of Otis Ferguson. p281.
Film Daily. Jan 5, 1940, p5.
Film Reader. 1982, n5, p227-46.
Films and Filming. Jul 1962, v8, p48.
The Films of Cary Grant. p136-38.
The Films of Howard Hawks (Willis). p10-15.
From Reverence to Rape. p133-35.
Halliwell's Hundred. p131-34.
Hollywood Reporter. Nov 30, 1939, p3.
Howard Hawks (Murphy). p109-23.
Howard Hawks, Storyteller (Mast). p208-42.
The International Dictionary of Films and Filmmakers. v1, p200-01.
Jump Cut. Apr 1978, n17, p25-27.
Kiss Kiss Bang Bang. p350.
Motion Picture Herald. Jan 13, 1940, p38.
Movie Comedy (Byron). p60-63.
Movietone News. Apr 1975, n40, p8-11.
The Nation. Jan 20, 1940, v150, p81.
The New Republic. Jan 22, 1940, v102, p116.
The New York Times. Jan 12, 1940, p13.
The New Yorker. Jan 13, 1940, v15, p51-52.
Newsweek. Jan 15, 1940, v15, p33.
Photoplay. Feb 1940, v54, p63.
Pursuits of Happiness. p161-88.
Selected Film Criticism, 1931-40. p107-08.
The Spectator. Jul 19, 1940, v165, p61.
Talking Pictures. p315-21.
Time. Jan 22, 1940, v35, p76.
Variety. Jan 10, 1940, p14.
Wide Angle. n2 1976, v1, p22.
Wide Angle. n3 1983, v5, p50-58.
Women's Films and Female Experience. p140-44.

His Lordship (Also titled: Man of Affairs) (GB; Mason, Herbert; 1936)
Classic Film Collector. Wint 1973, n41, p27-28.
Film Daily. Jan 16, 1937, p7.
Literary Digest. Jan 30, 1937, v123, p24.
Motion Picture Herald. Nov 28, 1936, p64, 66.
The New York Times. Feb 20, 1937, p9.
Newsweek. Jan 30, 1937, v9, p20.
Saturday Review (London). Nov 21, 1936, v162, p672.
Scholastic. Jan 30, 1937, v29, p23.
Variety. Nov 18, 1936, p13.
Variety. Feb 24, 1937, p15.

His Majesty, Bunker Bean (US; Taylor, William Desmond; 1918)
Exhibitor's Trade Review. Mar 30, 1918, p1385.

Motion Picture News. Jan 12, 1918, p251.
Motion Picture News. Apr 20, 1918, p2355, 2416.
The Moving Picture World. Apr 20, 1918, p432.
The New York Dramatic Mirror. Apr 13, 1918, p527, 529.
Variety. Apr 12, 1918, p42.
Wid's Daily. Apr 18, 1918, p1088-89.

His Majesty, the American (US; Henabery, Joseph; 1919)
Exhibitor's Trade Review. Sep 13, 1919, p1283.
His Majesty the American. p83-102.
Magill's Survey of Cinema. Silent Films. v2, p550-53.
Motion Picture Classic. Jan 1920, p57.
Motion Picture News. Sep 27, 1919, p2659.
The Moving Picture World. Nov 8, 1919, p245.
Photoplay. Dec 1919, v17, p117.
Selected Film Criticism, 1912-1920. p119-20.
Variety. Oct 31, 1919, p57.
Wid's Daily. Sep 28, 1919, p2.

His People (US; Sloman, Edward; 1925)
Motion Picture News. Nov 13, 1926, v34, p1842-43.
Photoplay. Dec 1925, v24, p46.
Selected Film Criticism, 1921-1930. p130-31.
Spellbound in Darkness. p422.

His Picture in the Papers (US; Emerson, John; 1916)
His Majesty the American. p75-76, 84-91+.
The Moving Picture World. Feb 12, 1916, p973.
The Moving Picture World. Feb 19, 1916, p1193.
The New York Dramatic Mirror. Feb 12, 1916, p28.
Variety. Feb 4, 1916, p24.

His Royal Slyness (US; Roach, Hal; 1920)
Photoplay. Apr 1920, v17, p109.
Selected Film Criticism, 1912-1920. p120.

His Trust (US; Griffith, D.W.; 1911)
D.W. Griffith, His Biograph Films in Perspective. p158-60, 164-65.
The First Twenty Years. p150-51.
The Moving Picture World. Jan 28, 1911, p195-96.
Selected Film Criticism, 1896-1911. p48.

His Trust Fulfilled (US; Griffith, D.W.; 1911)
D.W. Griffith, His Biograph Films in Perspective. p158-60, 164-65.
The First Twenty Years. p150-51.
The Moving Picture World. Feb 4, 1911, v7, p243.
Selected Film Criticism, 1896-1911. p48.

His Woman (US; Sloman, Edward; 1931)
Claudette Colbert (Quirk). p37-40.
Film Daily. Dec 6, 1931, p10.
The Films of Gary Cooper. p97-98.
Hollywood Reporter. Nov 4, 1931, p3.
Hollywood Spectator. Feb 1932, v12, p11.
Motion Picture Herald. Dec 12, 1931, p38.
The New York Times. Dec 5, 1931, p21.
Variety. Dec 8, 1931, p15.

Histoire d'Amour, Une *See* Liebelei

History Is Made at Night (US; Borzage, Frank; 1937)
Canadian Magazine. Jun 1937, v87, p46.
Film Daily. Mar 8, 1937, p8.
Hollywood Reporter. Mar 6, 1937, p4.
Hollywood Spectator. Mar 13, 1937, v11, p6.
Magill's Cinema Annual 1984. p542-46.
Motion Picture Herald. Mar 13, 1937, p47, 50.
The Nation. Apr 10, 1937, v144, p419.
The New Statesman and Nation. May 8, 1937, v13, p772.
The New York Times. Mar 29, 1937, p14.
Newsweek. Mar 27, 1937, v9, p48.
Rob Wagner's Script. Apr 10, 1937, v17, p10.
Scholastic. Apr 24, 1937, v30, p29.
Stage. Feb 1937, v14, p60.

Time. Mar 29, 1937, v29, p51.
Variety. Mar 31, 1937, p17.

The Hit Parade (US; Meins, Gus; 1937)
Film Daily. Apr 3, 1937, p3.
Hollywood Reporter. Mar 31, 1937, p3.
Motion Picture Herald. Apr 10, 1937, p66, 68.
The New York Times. May 31, 1937, p11.
Rob Wagner's Script. May 15, 1937, v17, p10.
Variety. Jun 2, 1937, p15.

Hit the Deck (US; Reed, Luther; 1930)
Commonweal. Feb 19, 1930, v11, p454.
Exhibitors Herald-World. Jan 23, 1930, p34.
Film Daily. Jan 19, 1930, p10.
The Film Spectator. Jan 18, 1930, v9, p23.
The New York Times. Jan 15, 1930, p28.
The New York Times. Jan 19, 1930, p6.
The New Yorker. Jan 25, 1930, v5, p68.
Outlook and Independent. Jan 29, 1930, v154, p192.
Time. Jan 27, 1930, v15, p44.
Variety. Jul 22, 1930, p17.

Hitler, the Beast of Berlin *See* Beasts of Berlin

Hitler's Children (US; Dmytryk, Edward; 1942)
Commonweal. Feb 5, 1943, v37, p398-99.
Film Daily. Jan 6, 1943, p5.
The Films of World War II. p103-05.
Life. Feb 1, 1943, v14, p37+.
Motion Picture Herald Product Digest. Jan 2, 1943, p1089.
The New York Times. Feb 25, 1943, p27.
The New Yorker. Mar 6, 1943, v19, p59.
Scholastic. Mar 8, 1943, v42, p27.
Variety. Dec 30, 1942, p16.

Hitler's Madman (US; Sirk, Douglas; 1943)
BFI/Monthly Film Bulletin. Sep 1978, v45, p185-86.
Douglas Sirk (Stern). p53-54.
Film Daily. Jun 10, 1943, p8.
The Films of World War II. p144-45.
Hollywood Reporter. Dec 3, 1942, p4.
Motion Picture Herald Product Digest. Jun 12, 1943, p1361.
The New York Times. Aug 28, 1943, p15.

Hit-the-Trail-Holliday (US; Neilan, Marshall; 1918)
Exhibitor's Trade Review. Jun 15, 1918, p111-13, 128.
Motion Picture News. Jun 22, 1918, p3688.
The Moving Picture World. Jun 22, 1918, p1756, 1760.
The New York Times. Jun 10, 1918, p9.
Variety. Jun 14, 1918, p29.
Wid's Daily. Jun 9, 1918, p31-32.

Hitting a New High (US; Walsh, Raoul; 1937)
Commonweal. Dec 31, 1937, v27, p272.
Film Daily. Dec 3, 1937, p7.
Hollywood Reporter. Nov 30, 1937, p3.
Motion Picture Herald. Dec 4, 1937, p39.
The New York Times. Dec 27, 1937, p11.
The New Yorker. Dec 25, 1937, v13, p45.
Rob Wagner's Script. Dec 18, 1937, v18, p11.
Time. Dec 20, 1937, v30, p51.
Variety. Dec 1, 1937, p14.

H. M. Pulham, Esq. (US; Vidor, King; 1941)
Commonweal. Jan 2, 1942, v35, p270.
Film Comment. Jul-Aug 1973, v9, p47-49.
Film Daily. Nov 13, 1941, p7.
The Films of Hedy Lamarr. p144-49.
Hollywood Reporter. Nov 13, 1941, p3.
The London Times. Mar 23, 1942, p8.
Magill's Cinema Annual, 1982. p439-42.
Motion Picture Exhibitor. Nov 26, 1941, v27, n3, sec2, p896.
Motion Picture Herald Product Digest. Nov 15, 1941, p368.
The New Republic. Dec 29, 1941, v105, p892.
The New York Times. Dec 19, 1941, p35.
The New Yorker. Dec 20, 1941, v17, p90.

Newsweek. Dec 12, 1941, v18, p60.
Time. Jan 5, 1942, v39, p66.
Variety. Nov 13, 1941, p3.

Hold Autumn in Your Hand *See* The Southerner

Hold Back the Dawn (US; Leisen, Mitchell; 1941)
Billy Wilder (Dick). p25-26, 30-31.
The Bright Side of Billy Wilder, Primarily. p241-42.
Commonweal. Oct 17, 1941, v34, p613.
The Film Career of Billy Wilder. p61-63.
Film Daily. Jul 31, 1941, p6.
The Films of Olivia de Havilland. p173-80.
Hollywood Reporter. Jul 30, 1941, p3.
Journey Down Sunset Boulevard. 115-24.
Life. Oct 6, 1941, v11, p89-92.
The London Times. Sep 20, 1941, p8.
Motion Picture Exhibitor. Aug 6, 1941, p803.
Motion Picture Herald Product Digest. Aug 9, 1941, p208.
The New York Times. Oct 2, 1941, p29.
The New York Times. Oct 5, 1941, sec9, p5.
The New Yorker. Oct 4, 1941, v17, p79.
Newsweek. Sep 29, 1941, v18, p55.
Scholastic. Oct 20, 1941, v39, p30.
Scribners Commentator. Dec 1941, v11, p107-08.
Time. Sep 29, 1941, v38, p86.
Variety. Jul 30, 1941, p8.

Hold 'Em Yale (US; Lanfield, Sidney; 1935)
Film Daily. Apr 27, 1935, p7.
Hollywood Reporter. Mar 13, 1935, p3.
Literary Digest. May 1, 1935, v119, p30.
Motion Picture Herald. Mar 30, 1935, p40-41.
The New York Times. Apr 27, 1935, p20.
Rob Wagner's Script. May 4, 1935, v13, p8.
Variety. May 1, 1935, p17.

Hold Everything (US; Del Ruth, Roy; 1930)
Exhibitors Herald-World. Mar 29, 1930, p32.
Exhibitors Herald-World. May 3, 1930, p32.
Film Daily. Mar 30, 1930, p8.
The Film Spectator. May 24, 1930, v9, p21-22.
Life. May 16, 1930, v95, p28.
The New York Times. Apr 23, 1930, p24.
The New Yorker. May 3, 1930, v6, p90.
Outlook and Independent. May 7, 1930, v155, p32.
Rob Wagner's Script. Apr 12, 1930, v3, p11.
Time. May 5, 1930, v15, p32.
Variety. Mar 26, 1930, p25.

Hold That Co-ed (US; Marshall, George; 1938)
Film Daily. Sep 16, 1938, p7.
Hollywood Reporter. Sep 9, 1938, p3.
Hollywood Spectator. Sep 17, 1938, v13, p8.
The New York Times. Sep 24, 1938, p13.
Newsweek. Sep 26, 1938, v12, p22.
Rob Wagner's Script. Sep 24, 1938, v19, p8.
Time. Sep 26, 1938, v32, p50.
Variety. Sep 28, 1938, p14.

Hold That Ghost (US; Lubin, Arthur; 1941)
The Abbott and Costello Book. p68-71.
Commonweal. Aug 22, 1941, v34, p426.
Film Daily. Jul 30, 1941, p6.
Hollywood Reporter. Jun 25, 1941, p3.
The London Times. Nov 3, 1941, p8.
Motion Picture Exhibitor. Aug 6, 1941, p805.
Motion Picture Herald Product Digest. Jun 28, 1941, p169.
The New York Times. Aug 8, 1941, p13.
Time. Aug 25, 1941, v38, p74.
Variety. Jul 30, 1941, p18.

Hold That Kiss (US; Marin, Edwin L.; 1938)
Film Daily. May 12, 1938, p6.
Hollywood Reporter. May 7, 1938, p3.
Motion Picture Herald. May 14, 1938, p52.

The New York Times. Jun 11, 1938, p9.
The New Yorker. May 21, 1938, v14, p56.
Rob Wagner's Script. May 14, 1938, v19, p9.
Variety. May 11, 1938, p16.

Hold Your Man (US; Wood, Sam; 1933)
Film Daily. Jul 1, 1933, p3.
The Films of Clark Gable. p144-45.
The Films of Jean Harlow. p80-87.
Hollywood Reporter. Jun 12, 1933, p3.
Motion Picture Herald. Jul 8, 1933, p43-44.
New Outlook. Aug 1933, v162, p45.
The New York Times. Jul 1, 1933, p16.
The New Yorker. Jul 8, 1933, v9, p38.
Rob Wagner's Script. Jul 22, 1933, v9, p8.
Time. Jul 3, 1933, v22, p30.
Variety. Jul 4, 1933, p16.

Holiday (US; Griffith, Edward H.; 1930)
Close-Up. Oct 1930, v7, p247-48.
Commonweal. July 23, 1930, v12, p326.
Exhibitors Herald-World. Jun 14,1930, p107.
Film Daily. Jun 15, 1930, p10.
Judge. Aug 2, 1930, v99, p23.
Life. Jul 25, 1930, v96, p19.
The Nation. Aug 6, 1930, v131, p160-61.
The New York Times. July 3, 1930, p25.
The New Yorker. Jul 12, 1930, v6, p52-53.
Outlook and Independent. Jul 16, 1930, v155, p431.
Time. Jul 14, 1930, v16, p50.
Variety. Jul 9, 1930, p19.

Holiday (Also called: Free to Live; Unconventional Linda) (US; Cukor, George; 1938)
Canadian Magazine. Jul 1938, v90, p26.
Dictionary of Films. p151.
Esquire. Aug 1938, v10, p82.
Film Daily. May 20, 1938, p8.
The Films of Cary Grant. p120-23.
The Films of Katharine Hepburn. p96-100.
The Films of the Thirties. p214-15.
From Reverence to Rape. p131.
George Cukor (Phillips). p71-72.
Hollywood Genres. p161-62.
Hollywood Reporter. May 16, 1934, p3.
Lunatics and Lovers. p105-09.
Magill's Survey of Cinema. Series I. v2, p758-61.
Motion Picture Herald. May 21, 1938, p30, 32.
National Board of Review Magazine. Oct 1938, v13, p19-20.
The New Masses. Jun 7, 1938, v27, p29-30.
The New Republic. Jun 22, 1938, v95, p188.
The New Statesman and Nation. Nov 26, 1938, v16, p872.
The New York Times. Jun 24, 1938, p15.
The New Yorker. Jul 2, 1938, v14, p41-42.
Newsweek. Jun 13, 1938, v11, p21.
On Cukor. p119-27.
Rob Wagner's Script. May 28, 1938, v19, p8.
Selected Film Criticism, 1931-1940. p108.
Stage. Jun 1938, v15, p33.
Time. Jun 13, 1938, v31, p23-24.
Variety. May 18, 1938, p12.

Holiday Affair (US; Hartman, Don; 1949)
Christian Century. Jan 4, 1950, v67, p31.
Commonweal. Dec 9, 1949, v51, p268.
Film Daily. Nov 18, 1949, p8.
Hollywood Reporter. Nov 15, 1949, p3.
Motion Picture Herald. Nov 19, 1949, p89.
The New York Times. Nov 24, 1949, p48.
Newsweek. Dec 19, 1949, v34, p77.
Robert Mitchum on the Screen. p110-11.
Time. Dec 19, 1949, v54, p92.
Variety. Nov 16, 1949, p16.

Holiday Inn (US; Sandrich, Mark; 1942)
Commonweal. Aug 14, 1942, v35, p400.
Film Daily. Jun 15, 1942, p6.
The Films of Bing Crosby. p124-29.
The Hollywood Musical. p200, 207+.
The Hollywood Musical Goes to War. p66-67.
Hollywood Musicals. p183, 208+.
Hollywood Reporter. Jun 15, 1942, p3.
The London Times. Aug 3, 1942, p8.
Magill's Cinema Annual, 1982. p443-46.
Motion Picture Exhibitor. Jun 17, 1942, v28, n6, sec2, p1030.
Motion Picture Herald Product Digest. Jun 13, 1942, p713.
The New York Times. Aug 5, 1942, p16.
Newsweek. Aug 3, 1942, v20, p58.
Starring Fred Astaire. p230-43.
Time. Aug 31, 1942, v40, p94.
Variety. Jun 15, 1942, p3.

Hollywood (US; Cruze, James; 1923)
The Best Moving Pictures of 1922-1923. p78-85.
Film Daily. Aug 5, 1923, p6.
Magill's Survey of Cinema. Silent Films. v2, p554-57.
The New York Times. Jul 30, 1923, p11.
Photoplay. Oct 1923, v24, p72.
Selected Film Criticism, 1921-1930. p131-136.
Variety. Jul 26, 1923, p27.

Hollywood Boulevard (US; Florey, Robert; 1936)
Film Daily. Aug 4, 1936, p7.
The Films of Gary Cooper. p142-43.
Hollywood Reporter. Jul 31, 1936, p3.
Hollywood Spectator. Aug 29, 1936, v11, p7.
Magill's Survey of Cinema. Series II. v3, p1041-44.
Motion Picture Herald. Aug 22, 1936, p51.
The New York Times. Sep 21, 1936, p26.
Newsweek. Sep 26, 1936, v8, p27.
Rob Wagner's Script. Sep 19, 1936, v16, p10.
Variety. Sep 23, 1936, p16.
World Film News. Nov 1936, v1, p20.

Hollywood Cavalcade (US; Cummings, Irving; 1939)
Commonweal. Oct 27, 1939, v30, p14.
Film Daily. Oct 4, 1939, p7.
Hollywood Reporter. Oct 3, 1939, p3.
Hollywood Spectator. Oct 14, 1939, v14, p7-8.
Life. Oct 9, 1939, v7, p63-64.
Motion Picture Herald. Oct 7, 1939, p35.
The New York Times. Oct 14, 1939, p13.
The New Yorker. Oct 21, 1939, v15, p74.
Newsweek. Oct 16, 1939, v14, p43.
Photoplay. Dec 1939, v53, p62.
Rob Wagner's Script. Oct 14, 1939, v22, p16.
Scholastic. Oct 30, 1939, v35, p35.
The Tatler. Feb 21, 1940, v155, p236.
Time. Oct 23, 1939, v34, p52.
Variety. Oct 4, 1939, p12.

Hollywood Hotel (US; Berkeley, Busby; 1937)
The Busby Berkeley Book. p112.
Canadian Magazine. Feb 1938, v89, p29.
Commonweal. Jan 7, 1938, v27, p300.
Film Daily. Dec 27, 1937, p8.
Hollywood Reporter. Dec 21, 1937, p3.
Motion Picture Herald. Dec 25, 1937, p38.
The New Republic. Jan 19, 1938, v93, p311.
The New York Times. Jan 13, 1938, p17.
Rob Wagner's Script. Jan 29, 1938, v18, p10.
Time. Jan 24, 1938, v31, p37-38.
Variety. Dec 22, 1937, p16.

Hollywood Party (US; Dwan, Allan; 1934)
Film Daily. May 25, 1934, p6.
The Films of Laurel and Hardy. p156.
The Hollywood Musical. p88.
Hollywood Reporter. Mar 29, 1934, p3.
Laurel and Hardy. p267-69.

Motion Picture Herald. Jun 2, 1934, p39.
The New York Times. May 26, 1934, p12.
Newsweek. Jun 2, 1934, v3, p36.
Time. Jun 4, 1934, v23, p28.
Variety. May 29, 1934, p12.

Holy Matrimony (US; Stahl, John M.; 1943)
Around Cinemas, Second Series. p236-37.
Commonweal. Oct 1, 1943, v38, p586.
Film Daily. Aug 24, 1943, p6.
The Films of the Forties. p90-92.
Hollywood Reporter. Aug 23, 1943, p3.
Motion Picture Herald Product Digest. Aug 28, 1943, p1505-06.
The New Republic. Oct 4, 1943, v109, p457.
The New York Times. Sep 16, 1943, p25.
The New Yorker. Sep 25, 1943, v19, p55.
Newsweek. Sep 6, 1943, v22, p96.
Time. Aug 30, 1943, v42, p93.
Variety. Aug 25, 1943, p10.

Home in Indiana (US; Hathaway, Henry; 1944)
Commonweal. Jul 21, 1944, v40, p329.
Film Daily. May 25, 1944, p8.
Hollywood Reporter. May 24, 1944, p3.
The Nation. Jul 21, 1944, v159, p24.
The New York Times. Jun 22, 1944, p23.
The New Yorker. Jun 24, 1944, v20, p59.
Newsweek. Jul 3, 1944, v24, p81.
Variety. May 24, 1944, p10.

Home of the Brave (US; Robson, Mark; 1949)
Commonweal. May 20, 1949, v50, p149.
Film Daily. Apr 29, 1949, p8.
Films in Reveiw. Feb 1950, v1, p14-16, 36.
Guts & Glory. p132+.
Hollywood Reporter. Apr 29, 1949, p3.
Life. May 23, 1949, v26, p143-44.
Magill's Survey of Cinema. Series II. v3, p1045-47.
Motion Picture Herald Product Digest. Apr 30, 1949, p4590.
The Nation. May 21, 1949, v168, p590-91.
The New Republic. May 16, 1949, v120, p22.
The New York Times. May 13, 1949, p29.
The New York Times Magazine. May 1, 1949, p56-57.
The New Yorker. May 21, 1949, v25, p68.
Newsweek. May 16, 1949, v33, p86.
Rotarian. Jul 1949, v75, p50.
Saturday Review of Literature. Jun 11, 1949, v33, p26-27.
Senior Scholastic. May 18, 1949, v54, p27.
Sequence. New Year 1950, v10, p179-83.
Sight and Sound. Dec 1949, v18, p21.
Stanley Kramer, Film Maker. p43-54.
Theatre Arts. Jul 1949, v33, p9.
Time. May 9, 1949, v53, p100.
Toms, Coons, Mulattoes, Mammies & Bucks. p202-05.
Variety. May 4, 1949, p11.

Home, Sweet Home (US; Griffith, D.W.; 1914)
The Films of D.W. Griffith. p27-41.
The Moving Picture World. May 30, 1914, p1234-35, 1312.
The New York Dramatic Mirror. Mar 18, 1914, p30.
The New York Dramatic Mirror. May 20, 1914, p32.
Selected Films Criticism, 1912-1920. p120-22.
Variety. May 22, 1914, p22.

Home Sweet Homicide (US; Bacon, Lloyd; 1946)
Commonweal. Oct 11, 1946, v44, p623.
Film Daily. Jul 22, 1946, p3.
Hollywood Reporter. Jul 17, 1946, p3.
Motion Picture Herald Product Digest. Jul 27, 1946, p3124.
The New York Times. Sep 12, 1946, p5.
Newsweek. Sep 9, 1946, v28, p106+.
Time. Sep 16, 1946, v48, p106.
Variety. Jul 17, 1946, p8.

The Home Towners (US; Foy, Bryan; 1928)
Exhibitor's Herald-World and Moving Picture World. Nov 3, 1928, p52.
Film Daily. Oct 28, 1928, p8.
Magill's Survey of Cinema. Series II. v3, p1048-50.
The New York Times. Oct 24, 1928, p26.

Homme du Jour, L' (Also titled: The Man of the Hour) (FR; Duvivier, Julien; 1936)
Chevalier. p136-38.
The Golden Age of French Cinema, 1929-1939. p86-88.
Graham Greene on Film. p196-97.
The New Statesman and Nation. Jul 2, 1938, v16, p16.
The New York Times. Nov 21, 1940, p43.
The Spectator. Jul 1, 1938, v161, p.
The Tatler. Jul 6, 1938, v149, p6.
Variety. Nov 27, 1940, p16.
World Film News. Aug 1938, v3, p175.

Honey (US; Ruggles, Wesley; 1930)
Exhibitors Herald-World. Apr 5, 1930, p37.
Film Daily. Mar 30, 1930, p11.
Judge. May 3, 1930, v98, p23.
The New York Times. Mar 29, 1930, p23.
The New York Times. Apr 6, 1930, p5.
The New Yorker. Apr 5, 1930, v6, p92.
Variety. Apr 2, 1930, p19.

Honeymoon in Bali (US; Griffith, Edward H.; 1939)
Commonweal. Oct 6, 1939, v30, p539.
Film Daily. Sep 19, 1939, p7.
Hollywood Reporter. Sep 9, 1939, p3.
Hollywood Spectator. Sep 16, 1939, v14, p6-7.
Motion Picture Herald. Sep 16, 1939, p42.
The New York Times. Sep 21, 1939, p21.
The New Yorker. Sep 23, 1939, v15, p58.
Newsweek. Oct 2, 1939, v14, p35.
Rob Wagner's Script. Oct 7, 1939, v22, p16.
Time. Oct 2, 1939, v34, p49.
Variety. Sep 13, 1939, p12.

Honky Tonk (US; Conway, Jack; 1941)
Commonweal. Oct 17, 1941, v34, p614.
Film Daily. Sep 15, 1941, p6.
The Films of Clark Gable. p204-05.
The Films of Lana Turner. p106-09.
Hollywood Reporter. Sep 15, 1941, p3.
Life. Oct 13, 1941, v11, p103-04+.
The London Times. Dec 8, 1941, p8.
Motion Picture Exhibitor. Oct 1, 1941, p862.
Motion Picture Herald Product Digest. Sep 20, 1941, p273.
The New York Times. Oct 3, 1941, p27.
The New Yorker. Oct 4, 1941, v17, p80.
Newsweek. Oct 6, 1941, v18, p60-61.
Photoplay. Dec 1941, v20, p40-41+.
Time. Oct 13, 1941, v38, p96.
Variety. Sep 17, 1941, p9.

Honolulu (US; Buzzell, Edward; 1939)
Commonweal. Feb 24, 1939, v29, p497.
Film Daily. Feb 3, 1939, p12.
Hollywood Reporter. Jan 27, 1939, p3.
Hollywood Spectator. Feb 4, 1939, v13, p12.
Motion Picture Herald. Feb 4, 1939, p56.
The New York Times. Feb 23, 1939, p19.
The New Yorker. Feb 25, 1939, v15, p58.
Rob Wagner's Script. Feb 18, 1939, v21, p16.
Scholastic. Feb 25, 1939, v34, p34.
Time. Feb 20, 1939, v33, p68.
Variety. Feb 1, 1939, p13.

The Honor System (US; Walsh, Raoul; 1917)
The Moving Picture World. Mar 3, 1917, p1370.
The New York Dramatic Mirror. Jan 27, 1917, p65.
The New York Dramatic Mirror. Feb 17, 1917, p32.
The New York Times. Feb 13, 1917, p8.

Selected Film Criticism, 1912-1920. p122-23.
Variety. Feb 16, 1917, p24.
Wid's Daily. May 3, 1917, p274.

Hoodoo Ann (US; Ingraham, Lloyd; 1916)
The Moving Picture World. Apr 1, 1916, p154.
The Moving Picture World. Apr 15, 1916, p458.
The New York Dramatic Mirror. Apr 8, 1916, p31.
Selected Film Criticism, 1912-1920. p123-24.
Variety. Apr 7, 1916, p22.
Wid's Daily. Apr 6, 1916, p486.

Hook and Ladder (US; Sedgwick, Edward; 1924)
Film Daily. Jan 6, 1924, p7.
The Moving Picture World. Jan 19, 1924, p216.
Variety. Dec 21, 1927, p25.

Hoopla (US; Lloyd, Frank; 1933)
Film Daily. Dec 2, 1933, p3.
Hollywood Reporter. Oct 26, 1933, p3.
Motion Picture Herald. Dec 9, 1933, p39.
The New York Times. Dec 1, 1933, p23.
Rob Wagner's Script. Dec 23, 1933, v10, p10.
Time. Dec 11, 1933, v22, p31.
Variety. Dec 5, 1933, p17.

Hoosier Schoolboy (US; Nigh, William; 1937)
Film Daily. Jun 29, 1937, p11.
Hollywood Reporter. Jul 2, 1937, p3.
Motion Picture Herald. Jul 3, 1937, p48.
Variety. Jun 30, 1937, p21.

The Hoosier Schoolmaster (US; Figman, Max; 1914)
The Moving Picture World. Sep 26, 1914, p1727.
The Moving Picture World. Oct 24, 1914, p550.
Variety. Nov 13, 1914, p25.

The Horse Ate the Hat *See* An Italian Straw Hat

Horse Feathers (US; McLeod, Norman Z.; 1932)
American Film Criticism. p267-68.
Cinema Quarterly. Wint 1932, v1, p117.
The Comic Mind. p283-84.
Dictionary of Films. p151.
Film Daily. Aug 12, 1932, p3.
Hollywood Reporter. Jul 30, 1932, p3.
Judge. Sep 1932, v103, p22-23.
Living Age. Dec 1932, v343, p371-72.
Lorentz on Film. p96, 100-01.
Magill's Survey of Cinema. Series II. v3, p1051-53.
Motion Picture Herald. Aug 6, 1932, p35.
The Nation. Aug 31, 1932, v135, p198-99.
The New Outlook. Oct 1932, v161, p38.
The New Statesman and Nation. Oct 1, 1932, v4, p374-75.
The New York Times. Aug 11, 1932, p12.
The New Yorker. Aug 20, 1932, v8, p37-38.
Review of Reviews (London). Oct 1932, v82, p77.
Rob Wagner's Script. Aug 20, 1932, v8, p8.
Stage. Sep 1932, v9, p27.
Time. Aug 15, 1932, v20, p24.
Variety. Aug 16, 1932, p15.
Why a Duck? p93-140.

Hortobagy (HUNG; Hoellering, George; 1935)
Graham Greene on Film. p124-25.
London Mercury. Feb 1937, v35, p414.
The New Statesman and Nation. Dec 19, 1936, v12, p1028.
Sight and Sound. Wint 1936-37, v5, p141.
The Spectator. Dec 18, 1936, v157, p1081.
World Film News. Dec 1936, v1, p23.

The Hostages *See* Otages, Les

Hot Saturday (US; Seiter, William A.; 1932)
Film Daily. Nov 5, 1932, p4.
The Films of Cary Grant. p45-47.
Hollywood Reporter. Oct 11, 1932, p9.

Love in the Film. p95-97.
The New York Times. Nov 5, 1932, p12.
Time. Nov 14, 1932, v20, p33.
Variety. Nov 8, 1932, p16.

Hot Spot *See* I Wake Up Screaming

Hot Water (US; Taylor, Sam; Newmeyer, Fred; 1924)
Film Daily. Nov 2, 1924, p6.
The Moving Picture World. Oct 18, 1924, p624.
The New York Times. Oct 27, 1924, p27.
Variety. Sep 10, 1924, p26.

Hotel du Nord (FR; Carné, Marcel; 1938)
Commonweal. Jan 10, 1941, v33, p304.
Films and Filming. Feb 1965, v11, p37.
French Film (Sadoul). p84.
Graham Greene on Film. p229-30.
The New Statesman and Nation. Jun 10, 1939, v17, p892-93.
The New York Times. Dec 30, 1940, p21.
Sight and Sound. Sum 1939, v8, p79.
The Spectator. Jun 23, 1939, v162, p1088.
Variety. Feb 1, 1939, p18.

Hotel for Women (Also titled: Elsa Maxwell's Hotel for Women) (US; Ratoff, Gregory; 1939)
Commonweal. Aug 18, 1939, v30, p400.
Film Daily. Aug 28, 1939, p8.
Hollywood Spectator. Aug 5, 1939, v14, p8-9.
Motion Picture Herald. Aug 5, 1939, p85.
The New York Times. Aug 26, 1939, p20.
The New Yorker. Sep 2, 1939, v15, p51-52.
Rob Wagner's Script. Aug 26, 1939, v22, p16.
The Spectator. Mar 1, 1940, v164, p284.
Time. Aug 14, 1939, v33, p33.
Variety. Aug 2, 1939, p18.

Hotel Imperial (US; Stiller, Mauritz; 1927)
Film Daily. Jan 9, 1927, p8.
Magill's Survey of Cinema. Silent Films. v2, p558-61.
The New York Times. Jan 3, 1927, p16.
Photoplay. Jan 1927, v31, p53.
Selected Film Criticism, 1921-1930. p137-38.
Variety. Jan 5, 1927, p16.

Hotel Imperial (US; Florey, Robert; 1939)
Film Daily. May 17, 1939, p5.
Graham Greene on Film. p213-14.
Hollywood Reporter. May 9, 1939, p3.
Motion Picture Herald. May 13, 1939, p37, 40.
The New York Times. May 11, 1939, p31.
Rob Wagner's Script. Jul 4, 1939, v21, p18.
The Spectator. Apr 14, 1939, v162, p632.
Time. May 22, 1939, v33, p57.
Variety. May 10, 1939, p14.

The Hound of the Baskervilles (US; Lanfield, Sidney; 1939)
Basil Rathbone: His Life and His Films. p210-15.
Commonweal. Apr 7, 1939, v29, p665.
The Film Criticism of Otis Ferguson. p259.
Film Daily. Mar 27, 1939, p6.
The Films of Sherlock Holmes. p63-74.
Graham Greene on Film. p231, 234.
Hollywood Reporter. Mar 23, 1939, p3.
Hollywood Spectator. Apr 1, 1939, v13, p8-9.
Life. Apr 10, 1939, v6, p50.
Magill's Survey of Cinema. Series I. v2, p770-71.
Motion Picture Herald. Apr 1, 1939, p28, 30.
The New Republic. Jul 5, 1939, v99, p252.
The New York Times. Mar 25, 1939, p19.
The New Yorker. Apr 1, 1939, v15, p67-68.
Photoplay. Jun 1939, v53, p89.
Rob Wagner's Script. May 6, 1939, v21, p14.
Sherlock Holmes on the Screen. p173-74.
The Spectator. Jul 14, 1939, v163, p52.

The Tatler. Jul 19, 1939, v153, p98.
Time. Apr 3, 1939, v33, p40.
Variety. Mar 29, 1939, p14.

A House Divided (US; Wyler, William; 1931)
Film Daily. Jan 10, 1932, p9.
Hollywood Reporter. Nov 13, 1931, p3.
Judge. Feb 6, 1932, v102, p22.
Motion Picture Herald. Nov 28, 1931, p44.
The New York Times. Jan 9, 1932, p21.
The New York Times. Jan 17, 1932, p4.
The New Yorker. Jan 16, 1932, v7, p53.
Rob Wagner's Script. Nov 21, 1931, v6, p7, 31.
Variety. Jan 12, 1932, p28.
William Wyler: A Guide to References and Resources. p68-70.
William Wyler (Anderegg). p31-34.

The House of Rothschild (US; Werker, Alfred L.; 1934)
Commonweal. Mar 30, 1934, v19, p609.
Film Daily. Mar 8, 1934, p8.
Films in Review. Nov 1935, v36, p522,24.
The Films of Boris Karloff. p93-94.
The Films of the Thirties. p122-23.
Hollywood Reporter. Feb 23, 1934, p2.
Literary Digest. Mar 31, 1934, v117, p33.
Motion Picture Herald. Mar 10, 1934, p49.
The Nation. Apr 4, 1934, v138, p398.
The New Republic. Apr 4, 1934, v78, p216-17.
The New York Times. Mar 15, 1934, p27.
Newsweek. Mar 24, 1934, p38.
Variety. Mar 20, 1934, p16.

House of Strangers (US; Mankiewicz, Joseph L.; 1949)
The Cinema of Edward G. Robinson. p175-78.
Commonweal. Jul 8, 1949, v50, p319.
Film Daily. Jun 16, 1949, p8.
The Films of Susan Hayward. p143-145.
Hollywood Reporter. Jun 15, 1949, p3.
Joseph L. Mankiewicz. p77-81.
Motion Picture Herald Product Digest. Jun 18, 1949, p4649.
The New Republic. Jul 25, 1949, v121, p22.
The New York Times. Jul 2, 1949, p8.
Newsweek. Aug 1, 1949, v34, p65.
Rotarian. Oct 1949, v75, p39.
Sequence. New Year 1950, v10, p155-56.
Theatre Arts. Sep 1949, v33, p6.
Time. Jul 18, 1949, v54, p78.
Variety. Jun 15, 1949, p13.

The House on 56th Street (US; Florey, Robert; 1933)
Canadian Magazine. Jan 1934, v81, p35.
Film Daily. Dec 2, 1933, p3.
The Great Romantic Films. p22-25.
Hollywood Reporter. Oct 17, 1933, p3.
Motion Picture Herald. Dec 9, 1933, p42.
The New York Times. Dec 2, 1933, p9.
The New Yorker. Dec 9, 1933, v9, p91.
Rob Wagner's Script. Dec 16, 1933, v10, p10.
Time. Dec 11, 1933, v22, p31.
Variety. Dec 5, 1933, p16.

The House on 92nd Street (US; Hathaway, Henry; 1945)
Commonweal. Sep 26, 1945, v42, p576.
Film Daily. Sep 13, 1945, p6.
Film Noir. p134-35.
Films and the Second World War. p196-97.
The Films of World War II. p229-31.
Hollywood Reporter. Sep 12, 1945, p3.
Life. Oct 8, 1945, v19, p91-92+.
The London Times. Dec 31, 1945, p8.
Magill's Survey of Cinema. Series II. v3, p1065-68.
Motion Picture Exhibitor. Sep 19, 1945, v34, n20, sec2, p1794.
Motion Picture Herald Product Digest. Sep 15, 1941, p2645.
The New York Times. Sep 27, 1945, sec2, p24.
The New Yorker. Sep 29, 1945, v21, p56.

Newsweeek. Sep 24, 1945, v26, p94.
Scholastic. Oct 8, 1945, v47, p38.
Time. Oct 8, 1945, v46, p96+.
Variety. Sep 12, 1945, p16.

The House with Closed Shutters (US; Griffith, D.W.; 1910)
The Moving Picture World. Aug 20, 1919, p402.
Selected Film Criticism, 1896-1911. p48-50.

The Housekeeper's Daughter (US; Roach, Hal; 1939)
Commonweal. Nov 10, 1939, v31, p79.
Film Daily. Sep 14, 1939, p11.
Hollywood Reporter. Sep 11, 1939, p3.
Motion Picture Herald. Sep 16, 1939, p42, 46.
The New York Times. Dec 2, 1939, p21.
The New Yorker. Dec 9, 1939, v15, p98.
Rob Wagner's Script. Dec 2, 1939, v22, p16-17.
Variety. Sep 13, 1939, p12.

How Green Was My Valley (US; Ford, John; 1941)
Cinema: Novel into Film. p240-42.
Commonweal. Nov 7, 1941, v35, p72.
The Emergence of Film Art. p263-74.
The Film Criticism of Otis Ferguson. p396-98.
Film Daily. Oct 29, 1941, p6.
Film News. Sum 1977, v34, p24-25.
The Films of the Forties. p50-53.
Hollywood Reporter. Oct 29, 1941, p3.
Life. Nov 10, 1941, v11, p64-66+.
The London Times. Apr 24, 1942, p6.
The London Times. May 19, 1947, p6.
Magic Moments from the Movies. p90-91.
Magill's Survey of Cinema Series I. v2, p776-78.
Motion Picture Exhibitor. Oct 29, 1941, v26, n25, sec2, p881.
Motion Picture Herald Product Digest. Nov 1, 1941, p341.
The Moving Image. p349-50.
The Nation. Nov 15, 1941, v153, p491.
The New Republic. Dec 1, 1941, v105, p733.
The New York Times. Oct 19, 1941, p27.
The New York Times. Nov 2, 1941, sec9, p5.
The New Yorker. Nov 1, 1941, v17, p72.
Newsweek. Nov 3, 1941, v18, p59-60.
The Non-Western Films of John Ford. p170-95.
Photoplay. Jan 1942, v20, p14.
PM. Oct 29, 1941, p23.
Rob Wagner's Script. Jan 17, 1942, v28, p16.
Saturday Review. Feb 28, 1942, v25, p21.
Scholastic. Nov 10, 1941, v39, p28.
Selected Film Criticism, 1941-1950. p80-83.
Theatre Arts. Dec 1941, v25, p884+.
Theatre Arts. Jan 1942, v26, p59.
Time. Nov 24, 1941, v38, p100+.
50 Classic Motion Pictures. p146-51.

How He Lied to Her Husband (US; Lewis, Cecil; 1931)
Film Daily. Jan 18, 1931, p10.
Motion Picture Herald. Jan 24, 1931, p50.
The Nation. Feb 4, 1931, v132, p135-36.
The New York Times. Jan 17, 1931, p23.
The New Yorker. Jan 24, 1931, v6, p55.
Variety. Jan 28, 1931, p15.

How Jones Lost His Roll (US; 1905)
The First Twenty Years. p90.

The Howards of Virginia (US; Lloyd, Frank; 1940)
Child Life. Feb 1941, v20, p61.
Commonweal. Sep 20, 1940, v32, p449.
Film Daily. Sep 3, 1940, p8.
The Films of Cary Grant. p142-44.
Hollywood Reporter. Aug 29, 1940, p3.
Motion Picture Exhibitor. Sep 4, 1940, p601.
The New York Times. Sep 27, 1940, p27.
Newsweek. Sep 16, 1940, v16, p60.
Photoplay. Nov 1940, v54, p68.

Scholastic. Sep 23, 1940, v37, p39.
Time. Sep 16, 1940, v36, p88.
Variety. Sep 4, 1940, p18.

Huckleberry Finn (US; Taylor, William Desmond; 1920)
The Moving Picture World. Jan 17, 1920, p323.
The Moving Picture World. Feb 21, 1920, p1290-91.
Variety. Feb 27, 1920, p46.
Wid's Daily. Feb 29, 1920, p3.

Huckleberry Finn (US; Taurog, Norman; 1931)
Commonweal. Aug 26, 1931, v14, p406.
Film Daily. Aug 9, 1931, p10.
Hollywood Reporter. Jul 23, 1931, p3.
Hollywood Spectator. Aug 29, 1931, p12-13.
Life. Sep 4, 1931, v98, p21.
Motion Picture Herald. Aug 1, 1931, p30.
The New York Times. Aug 2, 1931, p3.
The New York Times. Aug 8, 1931, p16.
The New York Times. Aug 16, 1931, p3.
The New Yorker. Aug 15, 1931, v7, p43.
Outlook and Independent. Aug 26, 1931, v158, p534.
Rob Wagner's Script. Sep 5, 1931, v6, p8.
Time. Aug 17, 1931, v18, p17.
Variety. Aug 11, 1931, p22.

Huckleberry Finn (Also titled: The Adventures of
Huckleberry Finn) (US; Thorpe, Richard; 1939)
The Film Criticism of Otis Ferguson. p252.
Film Daily. Feb 17, 1939, p6.
Hollywood Reporter. Feb 8, 1939, p2.
Hollywood Spectator. Feb 18, 1939, v13, p8.
Motion Picture Herald. Feb 11, 1939, p35, 38.
The New Republic. Apr 26, 1939, v98, p336.
The New Statesman and Nation. May 20, 1939, v17, p778.
The New York Times. Mar 3, 1939, p21.
The New Yorker. Mar 4, 1939, v15, p64-65.
Newsweek. Feb 27, 1939, v13, p24.
Rob Wagner's Script. Apr 8, 1939, v21, p12.
Saint Nicholas. Mar 1939, v66, p39.
Scholastic. Feb 4, 1939, v34, p30.
Variety. Feb 15, 1939, p12.

The Hucksters (US; Conway, Jack; 1947)
Commonweal. Aug 1, 1947, v46, p386.
Film Daily. Jun 27, 1947, p10.
The Films of Clark Gable. p211.
The Films of the Forties. p212-15.
Hollywood Reporter. Jun 27, 1947, p3.
Life. Jul 28, 1947, v23, p103-04.
Motion Picture Herald Product Digest. Jun 28, 1947, p3701.
The Nation. Aug 2, 1947, v165, p130.
New Republic. Aug 11, 1947, v117, p34.
The New York Times. Jul 18, 1947, p21.
The New Yorker. Jul 19, 1947, v23, p46.
Newsweek. Jul 21, 1947, v30, p76+.
Time. Jul 21, 1947, v50, p91.
Variety. Jul 2, 1947, p13.

Hudson's Bay (US; Pichel, Irving; 1941)
Child Life. Feb 1941, v20, p61.
Commonweal. Jan 10, 1941, v33, p304.
The Film Criticism of Otis Ferguson. p329-30.
Film Daily. Dec 24, 1940, p7.
Hollywood Reporter. Dec 20, 1940, p3.
The London Times. May 12, 1941, p8.
Motion Picture Exhibitor. Dec 25, 1940, p660-61.
The New Republic. Jan 6, 1941, v104, p20.
The New York Times. Jan 10, 1941, p23.
Newsweek. Jan 20, 1941, v17, p62.
Paul Muni: His Life and His Films. p185-89.
Scholastic. Jan 27, 1941, v38, p34.
Time. Feb 3, 1941, v37, p71.
Variety. Dec 25, 1940, p16.

Hulda from Holland (US; O'Brien, John B.; 1916)
The Moving Picture World. Aug 12, 1916, p1102.
The New York Dramatic Mirror. Aug 5, 1916, p22.
The New York Times. Jul 31, 1916, p6.
Variety. Aug 4, 1916, p29.
Wid's Daily. Jul 20, 1916, p726.

The Human Beast *See* Bête Humaine, La

Human Cargo (US; Dwan, Allan; 1936)
Film Daily. Apr 21, 1936, p5.
Hollywood Reporter. Apr 18, 1936, p3.
Motion Picture Herald. Apr 25, 1936, p36.
The New York Times. May 16, 1936, p11.
Rob Wagner's Script. Jul 11, 1936, v15, p13-14.
Variety. May 27, 1936, p15.

The Human Comedy (US; Brown, Clarence; 1943)
Agee on Film. v1, p30-33.
Around Cinemas, Second Series. p224-26.
Commonweal. Mar 19, 1943, v37, p543.
Film Daily. Mar 1, 1943, p8.
The Films of World War II. p106-07.
Hollywood Reporter. Feb 26, 1943, p3.
Magill's Survey of Cinema. Series II. v3, p1073.
Motion Picture Herald. Feb 27, 1943, p34.
Motion Picture Herald Product Digest. Mar 6, 1943, p1198.
The Nation. Mar 20, 1943, v156, p426.
The New Republic. Mar 15, 1943, v107, p346.
The New York Times. Mar 3, 1943, p19.
The New York Times. Mar 7, 1943, sec2, p3.
Newsweek. Mar 15, 1943, v21, p78.
Time. Mar 22, 1943, v41, p56.
Variety. Mar 3, 1943, p14.

Human Hearts (US; Baggot, King; 1922)
Film Daily. Jul 14, 1922, p2.
Film Daily. Jul 16, 1922, p6.
Variety. Aug 4, 1922, p34.

Human Wreckage (US; Wray, John Griffith; 1923)
Film Daily. Jul 1, 1923, p4.
The New York Times. Jun 28, 1923, p10.
The New York Times. Jan 28, 1923, p10.
Photoplay. Jan 1923, v24, p65.
Selected Film Criticism, 1921-1930. p138.
Variety. Jul 4, 1923, p22.

Humoresque (US; Borzage, Frank; 1920)
The Moving Picture World. May 15, 1920, p982, 1073.
The New York Times. May 3, 1920, p14.
Variety. Jun 4, 1920, p27.
Wid's Daily. May 9, 1920, p3.

Humoresque (US; Negulesco, Jean; 1946)
Commonweal. Jan 20, 1947, v45, p281.
Film Daily. Dec 26, 1946, p11.
The Films of Joan Crawford. p160-63.
The Films of John Garfield. p143-47.
Fortnight. Dec 30, 1946, v1, p42.
The Great Romantic Films. p132-35.
Hollywood Reporter. Dec 23, 1946, p3.
Magill's Survey of Cinema. Series I. v2, p782-85.
Motion Picture Herald Product Digest. Dec 28, 1946, p3385.
The New Republic. Jan 20, 1947, v116, p37.
The New York Times. Dec 26, 1946, p28.
The New Yorker. Dec 28, 1946, v22, p44.
Newsweek. Dec 23, 1946, v28, p93.
Rob Wagner's Script. Jan 4, 1947, v33, p12.
Selected Film Criticism, 1941-1950. p83-84.
Time. Jan 13, 1947, v49, p97-98.
Variety. Dec 25, 1946, p12.

Humorous Phases of Funny Faces (US; Blackton, J.
Stuart; 1906)
Magill's Survey of Cinema. Silent Films. v2, p562-64.

Selected Film Criticism, 1896-1911. p50-51.
Views and Films Index. Jun 30, 1906, v1, p10.

The Hunchback of Notre Dame (US; Worsley, Wallace; 1923)
American Cinematographer. Jun 1985, v66, p34-43.
Exceptional Photoplays. Oct-Nov 1923, v4, p4.
Film Daily. Sep 16, 1923, p4.
From Quasimodo to Scarlett O'Hara. p27-30.
The Horror People. p12-14.
An Illustrated History of the Horror Film. p47.
Magill's Survey of Cinema. Silent Films. v2, p565-69.
The New York Times. Sep 3, 1923, p9.
Selected Film Criticism, 1921-1930. p138-40.
Spellbound in Darkness. p293-95.
Variety. Sep 6, 1923, p22.

The Hunchback of Notre Dame (US; Dieterle, William; 1939)
Classic Movie Monsters. p218-21.
Commonweal. Jan 12, 1940, v31, p266.
The Film Criticism of Otis Ferguson. p282.
Film Daily. Dec 15, 1939, p4.
Graham Greene on Film. p271.
Hollywood Reporter. Dec 15, 1939, p3.
Hollywood Spectator. Dec 23, 1939, v14, p15.
Life. Jan 1, 1940, v8, p37-39.
Magill's Survey of Cinema. Series I. v2, p786-92.
Make It Again, Sam. p81-87.
Motion Picture Herald. Dec 23, 1939, p37, 40.
The New Republic. Jan 22, 1940, v102, p116.
The New York Times. Jan 1, 1940, p29.
The New Yorker. Dec 30, 1939, v15, p47.
Newsweek. Jan 8, 1940, v15, p37.
Photoplay. Nov 1939, v53, p66-67.
Rob Wagner's Script. Dec 23, 1939, v14, p15.
Selected Film Criticism, 1931-1940. p109-10.
The Spectator. Feb 16, 1940, v164, p213.
Studio. May 1940, v119, p179.
Theatre Arts. Nov 1939, v23, p804.
Time. Jan 8, 1940, v35, p37.
Variety. Dec 20, 1939, p14.

The Hurricane (US; Ford, John; 1937)
Commonweal. Nov 26, 1937, v27, p132.
Fifty Classic Motion Pictures. p110-15.
Film Daily. Nov 10, 1937, p9.
The Films of John Ford. p253-57.
Hollywood Reporter. Nov 5, 1937, p3.
Life. Oct 25, 1937, v3, p106-07.
Life. Nov 22, 1937, v3, p44-47.
Literary Digest. Nov 27, 1937, v124, p34.
London Mercury. Mar 1938, v37, p539.
Magill's Survey of Cinema. Series I. v2, p793-95.
Motion Picture Herald. Nov 13, 1937, p39.
Motion Picture Herald. Aug 7, 1937, p16-17.
The New Masses. Nov 23, 1937, v25, p28-30.
The New York Times. Nov 10, 1937, p31.
The New Yorker. Nov 20, 1937, v13, p87-88.
Rob Wagner's Script. Nov 13, 1937, v18, p8.
Saint Nicholas. Oct 1937, v64, p371.
Samuel Goldwyn Presents. p184-87.
Scholastic. Dec 4, 1937, v31, p10.
Scribner's Magazine. Jan 1938, v103, p68.
The Spectator. Feb 4, 1938, v160, p179.
Stage. Sep 1937, v14, p36-38.
Stage. Dec 1937, v15, p99.
Those Fabulous Movie Years: The 30s. p124-25.
Time. Nov 15, 1937, v30, p41.
Variety. Nov 10, 1937, p18.

Hush Money (US; Lanfield, Sidney; 1931)
Film Daily. July 12, 1931, p10.
The Films of Myrna Loy. p118.
The Great Gangster Pictures. p199-200.

Hollywood Spectator. Aug 29, 1931, v12, p23-24.
Hollywood Spectator. Sep 26, 1931, v12, p11-12.
Judge. Aug 1, 1931, v100, p22.
Motion Picture Herald. Jun 13, 1931, p34.
The New York Times. Jul 11, 1931, p7.
Variety. Jul 14, 1931, p17.
Variety. Jul 19, 1931, p3.

Hypnotized (US; Sennett, Mack; 1932)
Film Daily. Dec 17, 1932, p2.
Hollywood Reporter. Dec 10, 1932, p2.
Motion Picture Herald. Dec 24, 1932, p24.
The New York Times. Jan 16, 1933, p13.
Rob Wagner's Script. Dec 24, 1932, v8, p9, 18.
Variety. Jan 17, 1933, p15.

Hypocrites (US; Weber, Lois; 1914)
The Moving Picture World. Feb 6, 1914, p832.
Selected Film Criticism, 1912-1920. p125.
Variety. Nov 7, 1914, p23.

I Accuse *See* J'Accuse

I Am a Fugitive from a Chain Gang (US; LeRoy, Mervyn; 1932)
America in the Dark. p170-71.
American Film Criticism. p274-77.
Armchair Detective. 1978, n1, v11, p128.
BFI/Monthly Film Bulletin. Mar 1979, v46, p58-59.
Cinema Quarterly. Spr 1933, v1, p181.
Cinema, the Magic Vehicle. v1, p204-05.
Close-Up. Mar 1933, v10, p36-39.
Crime Movies (Clarens). p108-10.
Dark Cinema. p140.
Dictionary of Films. p154.
Eighty Years of Cinema. p93-94.
Film Daily. Oct 21, 1932, p7.
Film Noir. p138-39.
The Films of the Thirties. p87-89.
From Quasimodo to Scarlett O'Hara. p163-66.
Hollywood Reporter. Oct 15, 1932, p3.
I Am a Fugitive from a Chain Gang. p9-44.
The International Dictionary of Films and Filmmakers. v1, p204-05.
Judge. Dec 1932, v103, p19, 27.
Kiss Kiss Bang Bang. p352.
Lorentz on Film. p99.
Magill's Survey of Cinema. Series I. v2, p803-05.
Movie Classics. Mar 1933, v4, p34.
National Board of Review Magazine. Nov 1932, v7, p8.
The New York Times. Nov 11, 1932, p17.
The New Yorker. Nov 19, 1932, v8, p65-66.
Paul Muni: His Life and His Films. p112-19.
Photoplay. Dec 1932, v43, p58.
Photoplay. Feb 1933, v43, p6.
Review of Reviews (London). Feb 1933, v83, p74-75.
Rob Wagner's Script. Nov 12, 1932, v8, p8.
Selected Film Criticism, 1931-1940. p112-13.
Stage. Dec 1932, v10, p27.
Stage. Jul 1933, v10, p35.
Time. Nov 21, 1932, v20, p30.
Vanity Fair. Dec 1932, v39, p46.
Variety. Nov 15, 1932, p19.
The Velvet Light Trap. Jun 1971, n1, p17-20.
We're in the Money. p92-96.

I Am the Law (US; Hall, Alexander; 1938)
The Cinema of Edward G. Robinson. p117-18.
Film Daily. Aug 24, 1938, p13.
Hollywood Reporter. Aug 18, 1938, p3.
Hollywood Spectator. Sep 3, 1938, v13, p8-9.
Motion Picture Herald. Aug 27, 1938, p53.
The New Statesman and Nation. Jan 7, 1939, v17, p13.
The New York Times. Aug 26, 1938, p14.
The New Yorker. Sep 3, 1938, v14, p44.
Newsweek. Sep 5, 1938, v12, p23.

Rob Wagner's Script. Sep 17, 1938, v20, p13.
Time. Sep 5, 1938, v32, p33.
Variety. Aug 31, 1938, p18.

I Cover the War (US; Lubin, Arthur; 1937)
Film Daily. Jun 29, 1937, p10.
Hollywood Reporter. Jun 24, 1937, p3.
Motion Picture Herald. Jul 10, 1937, p54.
The New York Times. Aug 2, 1937, p10.
Variety. Jul 7, 1937, p12.

I Cover the Waterfront (US; Cruze, James; 1933)
Claudette Colbert (Quirk). p55-57.
Commonweal. Jun 2, 1933, v18, p133.
Film Daily. May 19, 1933, p6.
Graham Greene on Film. p198.
Hollywood Reporter. Apr 6, 1933, p2.
Magill's Survey of Cinema. Series II. v3, p1083-85.
Motion Picture Herald. Apr 29, 1933, p26.
The New Statesman and Nation. Feb 3, 1934, v7, p155.
The New York Times. May 18, 1933, p17.
The New Yorker. May 27, 1933, v9, p45.
Newsweek. May 27, 1933, v1, p30.
Rob Wagner's Script. Jul 8, 1933, v9, p8.
The Spectator. Aug 5, 1938, v161, p232.
Time. May 29, 1933, v21, p33.
Variety. May 23, 1933, p15.

I Dream Too Much (US; Cromwell, John; 1935)
Commonweal. Dec 20, 1935, v23, p219.
Film Daily. Nov 27, 1935, p7.
The Films of Henry Fonda. p42-44.
The Fondas (Springer). p57-58.
Graham Greene on Film. p53.
Hollywood Reporter. Nov 16, 1935, p3.
Hollywood Spectator. Dec 7, 1935, v10, p10.
Motion Picture Herald. Dec 7, 1935, p39.
The New York Times. Nov 29, 1935, p24.
The New Yorker. Dec 7, 1935, v11, p93-94.
Newsweek. Dec 7, 1935, v6, p41.
Rob Wagner's Script. Jan 4, 1936, v14, p10.
Scholastic. Jan 18, 1936, v27, p28.
The Spectator. Feb 21, 1936, v156, p300.
Time. Dec 9, 1935, v26, p45.
Variety. Dec 4, 1935, p15.

I Found Stella Parish (Also titled: Stella Parish) (US;
    LeRoy, Mervyn; 1935)
Canadian Forum. Jan 1936, v15, p15.
Film Daily. Nov 2, 1935, p4.
Garbo and the Night Watchman. p240.
Hollywood Reporter. Oct 22, 1935, p3.
Hollywood Spectator. Nov 9, 1935, v10, p10-11.
Motion Picture Herald. Nov 2, 1935, p60.
The New York Times. Nov 4, 1935, p24.
Rob Wagner's Script. Nov 23, 1935, v14, p10.
Variety. Nov 6, 1935, p20.

I Kiss Your Hand, Madame (GER; Land, Robert; 1932)
Commonweal. Sep 21, 1932, v16, p492.
Film Daily. Aug 30, 1932, p8.
Motion Picture Herald. Sep 10, 1932, p42.
The New York Times. Aug 29, 1932, p9.
Variety. Aug 30, 1932, p8.

I Know Where I'm Going (GB; Powell, Michael;
    Pressburger, Emeric; 1945)
Agee on Film. v1, p274.
BFI/Monthly Film Bulletin. Oct 1884, v51, p317-18.
Chestnuts in Her Lap. p159-60.
Film Daily. Aug 13, 1947, p6.
Hollywood Reporter. Sep 26, 1946, p3.
The Los Angeles Times. Sep 28, 1946, sec2, p5.
Magill's Cinema Annual, 1983. p456-59.
Motion Picture Exhibitor. Oct 16, 1941, v36, n24, sec2,
    p2035.

Motion Picture Herald Product Digest. Dec 15, 1945, p2758.
The New Republic. Sep 22, 1947, v117, p39.
The New York Times. Aug 20, 1947, p25.
The New Yorker. Aug 23, 1945, v23, p2.
Newsweek. Sep 1, 1947, v30, p78-79.
Theatre Arts. Nov 1946, v30, p648.
Time. Sep 15, 1947, v50, p102+.
Variety. Nov 14, 1945, p12.
Variety. Sep 26, 1946, p3.

I Live for Love (US; Berkeley, Busby; 1935)
The Busby Berkeley Book. p98.
Film Daily. Oct 18, 1935, p8.
The Hollywood Musical. p107.
Hollywood Reporter. Oct 7, 1935, p3.
Motion Picture Herald. Oct 12, 1935, p41.
The New York Times. Oct 19, 1935, p21.
Variety. Oct 23, 1935, p12.

I Live in Grosvenor Square *See* Yank in London

I Live My Life (US; Van Dyke, W.S.; 1935)
Film Daily. Oct 14, 1935, p7.
The Films of Joan Crawford. p118-19.
Hollywood Reporter. Sep 18, 1935, p3.
Motion Picture Herald. Oct 5, 1935, p39.
The New York Times. Oct 12, 1935, p12.
The New Yorker. Oct 19, 1935, v11, p68.
Time. Oct 14, 1935, v26, p60.
Variety. Oct 16, 1935, p22.

I Love That Man (US; Brown, Harry Joe; 1933)
Film Daily. Jul 8, 1933, p6.
The Films of Nancy Carroll. p180-83.
Hollywood Reporter. Apr 8, 1933, p3.
Motion Picture Herald. May 6, 1933, p30.
New Outlook. Aug 1933, v162, p45.
The New York Times. Jul 10, 1933, p11.
Rob Wagner's Script. Jun 10, 1933, v9, p8.
Vanity Fair. Jun 1933, v40, 38-39.
Variety. Jul 11, 1933, p15.

I Loved You Wednesday (US; King, Henry; Menzies,
    William Cameron; 1933)
Film Daily. Jun 16, 1933, p7.
Hollywood Reporter. Jun 16, 1933, p3.
Judge. Aug 1933, v105, p22.
Motion Picture Herald. Jun 24, 1933, p42.
The New York Times. Jun 16, 1933, p20.
The New Yorker. Jun 24, 1933, v9, p55.
Rob Wagner's Script. Jul 1, 1933, v9, p8-9.
Time. Jun 26, 1933, v21, p40.
Variety. Jun 20, 1933, p11.

I Married a Communist *See* The Woman on Pier 13

I Married a Doctor (US; Mayo, Archie; 1936)
Commonweal. May 1, 1936, v24, p20.
Film Daily. Mar 31, 1936, p7.
Hollywood Reporter. Mar 27, 1936, p3.
Motion Picture Herald. Apr 4, 1936, p37.
The New York Times. Apr 20, 1936, p17.
Time. May 4, 1936, v27, p28.
Variety. Apr 22, 1936, p14.

I Married a Witch (US; Clair, René; 1942)
Commonweal. Dec 4, 1942, v37, p176.
Film Daily. Oct 22, 1942, p8.
Film Quarterly. Wint 1970-71, v24, p34-40.
The Films of Fredric March. p178-80.
The Films of Susan Hayward. p76-79.
Halliwell's Hundred. p143-46.
Hollywood Reporter. Oct 19, 1942, p3.
Life. Nov 2, 1942, v40, p74+.
The London Times. Mar 19, 1945, p6.
Magic and Myth of the Movies. p85-86.
Magill's Survey of Cinema. Series I. v2, p806-08.

Motion Picture Exhibitor. Oct 21, 1942, v28, n24, sec2, p1138.
Motion Picture Herald Product Digest. Oct 24, 1942, p969.
The New Republic. v30, 1942, v107, p715.
The New York Times. Nov 20, 1942, p27.
Newsweek. Nov 16, 1942, v20, p82.
René Clair (McGerr). p142-47+.
Rob Wagner's Script. Dec 19, 1942, v27, p22.
Selected Film Criticism, 1941-1950. p84-85.
Time. Nov 9, 1942, v40, p94+.
Variety. Oct 21, 1942, p8.

I Met a Murderer (GB; Kellino, Roy; 1939)
Agee on Film. v1, p150-51.
Film Daily. Sep 28, 1939, p7.
The Films of James Mason. p50.
Motion Picture Herald. Oct 14, 1939, p44.
The New Masses. Oct 17, 1939, v33, p29-30.
The New Republic. Oct 18, 1939, v100, p301.
The New York Times. Oct 2, 1939, p15.
The Spectator. Mar 24, 1939, v162, p484.
Variety. Mar 15, 1939, p18.

I Met Him in Paris (US; Ruggles, Wesley; 1937)
The Film Criticism of Otis Ferguson. p181.
Film Daily. May 24, 1937, p9.
Hollywood Reporter. May 19, 1937, p3.
Hollywood Spectator. Jun 5, 1937, v12, p13-14.
Life. May 31, 1937, v2, p48-60.
Lunatics and Lovers. p31.
Motion Picture Herald. May 29, 1937, p46.
The New Republic. Jun 16, 1937, v91, p159.
The New York Times. Jun 3, 1937, p29.
The New Yorker. Jun 5, 1937, v13, p61-62.
Rob Wagner's Script. May 29, 1937, v17, p10.
Time. Jun 7, 1937, v29, p34+.
Variety. Jun 9, 1937, p15.

I Met My Love Again (US; Ripley, Arthur; Logan, Joshua; 1938)
Film Daily. Jan 8, 1938, p3.
The Films of Henry Fonda. p64-65.
The Fondas (Springer). p72-73.
Hollywood Reporter. Jan 17, 1938, p3.
Motion Picture Herald. Jan 15, 1938, p52.
The New Masses. Feb 8, 1938, v26, p28.
The New York Times. Jan 15, 1938, p19.
Rob Wagner's Script. Mar 26, 1938, v19, p11.
Time. Jan 24, 1938, v31, p37.
Variety. Jan 12, 1938, p14.

I See a Dark Stranger (Also titled: The Adventuress) (GB; Launder, Frank; 1946)
Film Daily. Mar 4, 1947, p8.
The Great British Films. p94-96.
Hollywood Reporter. Mar 7, 1947, p3.
Life. Apr 7, 1947, v22, p60+.
Magill's Survey of Cinema, Series II. v2, p809-11.
Motion Picture Herald Product Digest. Mar 8, 1947, p3513.
New Republic. Apr 28, 1947, v116, p42.
The New Yorker. Apr 12, 1947, v23, p98.
Newsweek. Apr 14, 1947, v29, 94+.
Variety. Jul 10, 1946, p8.

I Stand Condemned *See* Moscow Nights

I Stole a Million (US; Tuttle, Frank; 1939)
Film Daily. Aug 22, 1939, p17.
The Great Gangster Pictures. p204-05.
Hollywood Spectator. Jul 22, 1939, v14, p8.
Motion Picture Herald. Jul 22, 1939, p53.
The New York Times. Aug 7, 1939, p11.
The New Yorker. Aug 12, 1939, v15, p48.
Variety. Aug 19, 1939, p12.

I Surrender Dear (US; Sennett, Mack; 1931)
Film Daily. Sep 27, 1931, p10.
Hollywood Reporter. Jun 25, 1931, p3.
Variety. Nov 10, 1931, p14.

I Take This Woman (US; Van Dyke, W.S.; 1940)
Commonweal. Mar 1, 1940, v31, p413.
Film Daily. Jan 31, 1940, p8.
The Films of Hedy Lamarr. p113-18.
The Films of Spencer Tracy. p153-55.
Motion Picture Herald. Feb 3, 1940, p42.
The New York Times. Dec 17, 1939, p7.
The New York Times. Feb 16, 1940, p23.
Newsweek. Feb 12, 1940, v15, p40.
Time. Mar 4, 1940, v35, p69.
Variety. Jan 31, 1940, p14.

I Wake Up Screaming (Also titled: Hot Spot) (US; Humberstone, Bruce; 1941)
Commonweal. Dec 26, 1941, v35, p248.
Film Daily. Oct 17, 1941, p5.
Hollywood Reporter. Oct 17, 1941, p4.
Motion Picture Herald Product Digest. Oct 18, 1941, p317.
The Nation. Jan 24, 1942, v154, p101.
The New York Times. Jan 17, 1942, p13.
Time. Dec 15, 1941, v38, p102.
Variety. Oct 22, 1941, p8.

I Walked With a Zombie (US; Tourneur, Jacques; 1943)
Film Daily. Mar 17, 1943, p6.
Focus on the Horror Film. p132-34+.
Hollywood Reporter. Mar 16, 1943, p3.
An Illustrated History of the Horror Film. p111-13, 203-04.
Magill's Survey of Cinema. Series II. v3, p1093-95.
Motion Picture Herald Product Digest. Mar 20, 1943, p1214.
The New York Times. Apr 22, 1943, p31.
Variety. Mar 17, 1943, p23.

I Wanted Wings (US; Leisen, Mitchell; 1941)
Commonweal. Apr 11, 1941, v33, p622.
Film Daily. Mar 27, 1941, p8.
The Films of William Holden. p55-57.
The Films of World War II. p44-45.
Hollywood Reporter. Mar 24, 1941, p3.
The London Times. Jun 27, 1941, p6.
Motion Picture Exhibitor. Apr 2, 1941, p723.
Motion Picture Herald Product Digest. Apr 5, 1941, p986.
The New York Times. Mar 27, 1941, p29.
The New York Times. Mar 30, 1941, sec9, p5.
The New Yorker. Mar 29, 1941, v17, p67.
Newsweek. Mar 31, 1941 c v17, p66-67.
Photoplay. Jun 1941, v19, p8.
Scholastic. Apr 14, 1941, v38, p30.
Scribner's Commentator. Aug 1941, v10, p107-08.
Variety. Mar 26, 1941, p16.
When Hollywood Ruled the Skies. p19-24.

I Was a Male War Bride (US; Hawks, Howard; 1949)
Commonweal. Sep 2, 1949, p509.
Film Daily. Aug 11, 1949 , p7.
The Films of Cary Grant. p200-02.
The Films of Howard Hawks. p16-21.
Focus on Howard Hawks. p52-53+.
Hawks on Hawks. p70-72.
Hollywood Reporter. Aug 10, 1949, p3.
Howard Hawks (Poague). p43-54.
Howard Hawks, Storyteller. p354-55.
Howard Hawks (Wood). p84-88.
Life. Sep 19, 1949, v27, p70+.
Magill's Survey of Cinema. Series II. v3, p1098-1102.
Motion Picture Herald Product Digest. Aug 13, 1949, p4713.
The New York Times. Aug 27, 1949, p7.
The New Yorker. Sep 3, 1949, v34, p62.
Newsweek. Sep 5, 1949, p67.
Rotarian. Nov 1949, v75, p34.

Scholastic. Oct 12, 1949, p19.
Time. Sep 12, 1949, v54, p98.
Variety. Aug 10, 1949, p8.

I Was a Spy (GB; Saville, Victor; 1933)
Bookman (London). Nov 1933, v85, p109.
Canadian Magazine. Dec 1933, v80, p36-37.
Cinema Quarterly. Aut 1933, v2, p40-44.
Film Daily. Jan 13, 1934, p4.
The Great Spy Films. p226-27.
Hollywood Reporter. Jan 13, 1934, p3.
Motion Picture Herald. Sep 23, 1933, p35.
The New Masses. Jan 23, 1934, v10, p29.
New Outlook. Feb 1934, v163, p49.
The New Republic. Feb 14, 1934, v78, p18.
The New Statesman and Nation. Sep 9, 1933, v6, p297.
The New York Times. Jan 15, 1934, p12.
Photoplay. Apr 1934, v45, p104.
Review of Reviews. Oct 1933, v84, p62.
Rotha on the Film. p126-27.
Saturday Review (London). Sep 9, 1933, p283.
Selected Film Criticism: Foreign Films, 1930-1950. p81.
Variety. Sep 19, 1933, p13.
Variety. Jan 16, 1934, p15.

I Wonder Who's Kissing Her Now? (US; Bacon, Lloyd; 1947)
Film Daily. Jun 10, 1947, p10.
The Hollywood Musical. p280, 286.
Hollywood Reporter. Jun 10, 1947, p3.
Motion Picture Herald Product Digest. Jun 14, 1947, p3678.
The New York Times. Jul 24, 1947, p27.
Variety. Jun 11, 1947, p8.

The Ice Follies of 1939 (US; Schunzel, Reinhold; 1939)
Film Daily. Mar 7, 1939, p13.
The Films of James Stewart. p68-69.
The Films of Joan Crawford. p133.
Hollywood Reporter. Mar 3, 1939, p3.
Motion Picture Herald. Mar 11, 1939, p43-44.
The New York Times. Mar 17, 1939, p25.
The New Yorker. Mar 18, 1939, v15, p66.
Photoplay. May 1939, v53, p63.
Rob Wagner's Script. Mar 25, 1939, v21, p16.
Time. Mar 27, 1939, v33, p68.
Variety. Mar 8, 1939, p18.

I'd Give My Life (US; Marin, Edwin L.; 1936)
Film Daily. Jul 28, 1936, p17.
Hollywood Reporter. Jul 24, 1936, p3.
Motion Picture Herald. Aug 29, 1936, p43.
The New York Times. Aug 17, 1936, p9.
Rob Wagner's Script. Sep 12, 1936, v16, p10.
Variety. Aug 19, 1936, p16.

Idiot's Delight (US; Brown, Clarence; 1939)
Canadian Magazine. Mar 1939, v91, p40.
Commonweal. Feb 17, 1939, v29, p470.
The Film Criticism of Otis Ferguson. p247-48.
Film Daily. Jan 31, 1939, p8.
The Films of Clark Gable. p189.
The Films of Norma Shearer. p224-28.
Graham Greene on Film. p214-15.
Hollywood Reporter. Jan 24, 1939, p3.
Hollywood Spectator. Feb 4, 1939, v13, p8-10.
McCall's. Apr 1939, v66, p4, 33.
Motion Picture Herald. Jan 28, 1939, p32-33.
The Nation. Feb 18, 1939, v148, p213-14.
National Board of Review Magazine. Feb 1939, v14, p16.
The New Republic. Feb 28, 1939, v98, p74.
The New Statesman and Nation. Apr 15, 1939, v17, p573.
The New York Times. Feb 3, 1939, p13.
The New Yorker. Feb 11, 1939, v14, p70-71.
Newsweek. Feb 6, 1939, v13, p24-25.
North American Review. Mar 1939, v247, p174-75.
Photoplay. Mar 1939, v53, p34-35.

Rob Wagner's Script. Jan 28, 1939, v21, p16.
Sight and Sound. Spr 1939, v8, p32.
The Spectator. Apr 21, 1939, v162, p668.
Stage. Mar 15, 1939, v16, p7.
The Tatler. Apr 19, 1939, v152, p98.
Time. Feb 13, 1939, v33, p29.
Variety. Jan 25, 1939, p11.

Idle Wives (US; Weber, Lois; 1916)
The Moving Picture World. Oct 7, 1916, p65.
Photoplay. Dec 1916, v10, p84.
Variety. Sep 22, 1916, p36.
Wid's Daily. Sep 28, 1916, p996.

The Idol Dancer (US; Griffith, D.W.; 1920)
The Films of D.W. Griffith. p138-44.
The Moving Picture World. Apr 3, 1920, p137.
The New York Times. Mar 22, 1920, p12.
Photoplay. Jun 1920, v18, p67.
Selected Film Criticism, 1912-1920. p125-26.
Variety. Mar 26, 1920, p50.
Wid's Daily. Mar 28, 1920, p3.

If I Had a Million (US; Lubitsch, Ernst; 1932)
The American Films of Ernst Lubitsch. p152-54.
Bookman (London). Jun 1933, v84, p171.
Cinema Quarterly. Spr 1933, v1, p182-83.
Ernst Lubitsch: A Guide to References and Resources. p119-21.
Film Daily. Dec 3, 1932, p4.
Film Society Review. Jan 1969, n4, p23-25.
The Films of Gary Cooper. p104-05.
The Films of W.C. Fields. p72-75.
Hollywood Reporter. Nov 3, 1932, p3.
Motion Picture Herald. Nov 12, 1932, p35.
The Nation. Dec 21, 1932, v135, p624-25.
National Board of Review Magazine. Dec 1932, v7, p9.
The New Statesman and Nation. Jan 21, 1932, v5, p74.
The New York Times. Dec 3, 1932, p21.
The New Yorker. Dec 10, 1932, v8, p69.
Photoplay. Jan 1933, v43, p57.
Pictures Will Talk. p52-54.
Rob Wagner's Script. Dec 10, 1932, v8, p8.
Selected Film Criticism, 1931-1940. p113-14.
Time. Dec 12, 1932, v20, p36.
Variety. Dec 6, 1932, p14.
W.C. Fields: A Life on Film. p86-89.

If I Were Free (US; Nugent, Elliott; 1933)
Film Daily. Dec 8, 1933, p6.
Motion Picture Herald. Dec 23, 1933, p47.
The New York Times. Jan 5, 1934, p25.
The New Yorker. Jan 13, 1934, v9, p67-68.
Newsweek. Jan 13, 1934, v3, p34.
Time. Dec 18, 1933, v22, p34.
Variety. Jan 9, 1934, p16.

If I Were King (US; Lloyd, Frank; 1938)
Basil Rathbone: His Life and His Films. p199-201.
Commonweal. Oct 7, 1938, v28, p616.
Esquire. Feb 1939, v11, p81.
Film Daily. Sep 19, 1938, p8.
The Films of Ronald Colman. p197-202.
Hollywood Reporter. Sep 14, 1938, p3.
Hollywood Spectator. Oct 1, 1938, v13, p9-10.
Magill's Survey of Cinema. Series II. v3, p1107-12.
Motion Picture Herald. Sep 17, 1938, p37, 40.
The New York Times. Sep 29, 1938, p31.
The New Yorker. Oct 1, 1938, v14, p48-49.
Newsweek. Oct 10, 1938, v12, p28-29.
Rob Wagner's Script. Nov 19, 1938, v20, p13.
Saint Nicholas. Oct 1938, v65, p39+.
Stage. Nov 1938, v16, p57.
Time. Oct 3, 1938, v32, p36.
Variety. Sep 21, 1938, p12.

If You Could Only Cook (US; Seiter, William A.; 1935)
Canadian Magazine. Feb 1936, v85, p38.
Film Daily. Dec 27, 1935, p4.
Garbo and the Night Watchman. p175-77.
Graham Greene on Film. p65.
Hollywood Reporter. Dec 7, 1935, p3.
Hollywood Spectator. Dec 21, 1935, v10, p11.
Judge. Feb 1936, v110, p14.
Literary Digest. Dec 21, 1935, v120, p22.
The New York Times. Dec 26, 1935, p21.
Rob Wagner's Script. Jan 11, 1936, v14, p12.
Time. Jan 6, 1936, v27, p28.
Variety. Jan 1, 1936, p44.

I'll Be Seeing You (US; Dieterle, William; 1944)
Commonweal. Mar 23, 1944, v41, p566.
Film Daily. Dec 20, 1944, p9.
Hollywood Reporter. Dec 19, 1944, p3.
The New York Times. Apr 6, 1945, p20.
Newsweek. Jan 22, 1945, v25, p88.
Theatre Arts. Apr 1945, v29, p231.
Time. Jan 22, 1945, v45, p91-92.
Variety. Dec 20, 1944, p8.

I'll Give a Million (US; Lang, Walter; 1938)
Film Daily. Jul 18, 1938, p9.
Hollywood Reporter. Jul 8, 1938, p3.
The New York Times. Jul 16, 1938, p7.
Rob Wagner's Script. Aug 16, 1938, v19, p23.
Time. Jul 25, 1938, v32, p22.
Variety. Jul 13, 1938, p15.

I'll Take Romance (US; Griffith, Edward H.; 1937)
Chestnuts in Her Lap. p34.
Film Daily. Dec 17, 1937, p9.
Hollywood Reporter. Dec 20, 1937, p3.
Motion Picture Herald. Dec 25, 1937, p39.
The New Statesman and Nation. Apr 2, 1938, v15, p567-68.
The New York Times. Dec 17, 1937, p33.
The New Yorker. Dec 18, 1937, v13, p84.
Rob Wagner's Script. Feb 5, 1938, v18, p10.
Time. Dec 20, 1937, v30, p51.
Variety. Dec 22, 1937, p16.
World Film News. Apr 1938, v3, p37.

Illicit (US; Mayo, Archie; 1931)
Exhibitors Herald-World. Oct 25, 1930, p42.
Film Daily. Jan 18, 1931, p10.
The Films of Barbara Stanwyck. p64-66.
Judge. Feb 7, 1931, v100, p22.
Life. Feb 20, 1931, v97, p20.
The New York Times. Jan 19, 1931, p25.
The New York Times. Jan 25, 1931, p5.
Outlook and Independent. Feb 4, 1931, v157, p192.
Rob Wagner's Script. Apr 4, 1931, v5, p9-10.
Starring Miss Barbara Stanwyck. p27.
Variety. Jan 21, 1931, p17.

I'm No Angel (US; Ruggles, Wesley; 1933)
Film Daily. Oct 14, 1933, p6.
Films and Filming. Oct 1970, v17, p32.
The Films of Cary Grant. p65-67.
The Films of Mae West. p81-90.
Hollywood Reporter. Sep 29, 1933, p3.
Life. Dec 1933, v100, p44.
Motion Picture Herald. Oct 7, 1933, p38.
The Nation. Nov 8, 1933, v137, p548.
New Outlook. Nov 1933, v162, p43.
The New Republic. Nov 29, 1933, v77, p73-75.
The New York Times. Oct 14, 1933, p18.
The New Yorker. Oct 14, 1933, v9, p53-54.
Newsweek. Oct 21, 1933, v2, p30.
Rob Wagner's Script. Oct 7, 1933, v10, p10.
Selected Film Criticism, 1931-1940. p115-16.
The Spectator. Dec 8, 1933, v151, p848.
Time. Oct 16, 1933, v22, p34.

Vanity Fair. Dec 1933, v41, p49, 58.
Variety. Oct 17, 1933, p19.
Views and Reviews. Sum 1970, v2, p3-9.
Women and Their Sexuality in the New Film. p218-19.

Imitation of Life (US; Stahl, John M.; 1934)
BFI/Monthly Film Bulletin. Nov 1981, v48, p229.
Cinema Texas Program Notes. Sep 20, 1979, v17, p43-49.
Claudette Colbert (Quirk). p2-3, 70-72.
Film Daily. Nov 23, 1934, p10.
The Films of the Thirties. p136-37.
Hollywood Reporter. Sep 10, 1934, p3.
Life. Feb 1935, v102, p35.
Literary Digest. Dec 8, 1934, p31.
Magill's Survey of Cinema. Series II. v3, p1128-29.
Motion Picture Herald. Dec 1, 1934, p39-42.
The New York Times. Nov 24, 1934, p19.
Rob Wagner's Script. Dec 8, 1934, v12, p8.
Selected Film Criticism, 1931-1940. p117.
Time. Dec 3, 1934, v24, p47.
Variety. Nov 27, 1934, p15.

The Immigrant (US; Chaplin, Charles; 1917)
Charles Chaplin: A Guide to References and Resources. p65.
The Comic Mind. p78-81.
The Films of Charlie Chaplin. p146-48.
Magill's Survey of Cinema. Silent Films. v1, p29-30.
The Moving Picture World. Jun 30, 1917, p2115.
The Rivals of D.W. Griffith. p32.
Selected Film Criticism, 1912-1920. p126-27.
The Silent Clowns. p90-92.
Spellbound in Darkness. p200-01.
Variety. Jun 22, 1917, p27.

The Immortal Vagabond (German title: Unsterbliche Lump, Der) (GER; Ucicky, Gustav; 1930)
Commonweal. Jun 8, 1932, v16, p158.
Film Daily. Aug 2, 1931, p11.
Hollywood Reporter. Jan 15, 1932, p3.
Motion Picture Herald. Jun 4, 1932, p41.
The New York Times. Aug 3, 1931, p15.
Rob Wagner's Script. Jan 16, 1932, v6, p10.
Variety. Mar 26, 1930, p39.

The Impatient Maiden (US; Whale, James; 1932)
Film Daily. Mar 6, 1932, p10.
Hollywood Reporter. Jan 15, 1932, p3.
James Whale (Curtis). pxiii-xiv, 89-91.
Motion Picture Herald. Feb 6, 1932, p35.
The New York Times. Mar 4, 1932, p17.
The New Yorker. Mar 12, 1932, v8, p56.
Time. Mar 14, 1932, v19, p26.
Variety. Mar 8, 1932, p14.

The Imperfect Lady *See* The Perfect Gentleman

The Impossible Voyage (French title: Voyage a Travers l'Impossible, Le) (FR; Melies, Georges; 1904)
The Emergence of Film Art. p17-18.
Film Before Griffith. p275, 318.

In Caliente (US; Bacon, Lloyd; 1935)
The Busby Berkeley Book. p96-97.
Esquire. Jul 1935, v3, p152.
The Film Criticism of Otis Ferguson. p84-85.
Film Daily. Jun 27, 1935, p6.
The Genius of Busby Berkeley. p173.
Hollywood Reporter. Jul 5, 1935, p4.
Motion Picture Herald. Jul 6, 1935, p74.
The New York Times. Jun 27, 1935, p16.
The New Yorker. May 25, 1935, v11, p70.
Time. Jun 3, 1935, v25, p50.
Variety. Jul 3, 1935, p14.

In Name Only (US; Cromwell, John; 1939)
Commonweal. Aug 14, 1939, v30, p400.
The Film Criticism of Otis Ferguson. p269-70.
Film Daily. Aug 3, 1939, p6.
The Films of Carole Lombard. p162-65.
The Films of Cary Grant. p132-35.
Hollywood Reporter. Aug 2, 1939, p3.
Hollywood Spectator. Sep 2, 1939, v14, p8.
Magill's Survey of Cinema. Series I. v2, p822-24.
The New Republic. Sep 6, 1939, v100, p132.
The New York Times. Aug 4, 1939, p11.
The New York Times. Aug 18, 1939, p16.
The New Yorker. Aug 12, 1939, v15, p48.
Photoplay. Oct 1939, v53, p64.
Rob Wagner's Script. Aug 26, 1939, v22, p16-17.
The Spectator. Dec 8, 1939, v163, p816.
Time. Aug 14, 1939, v34, p33.
Variety. Aug 9, 1939, p14.

In Old Arizona (US; Walsh, Raoul; Cummings, Irving; 1929)
Film Daily. Jan 13, 1929, p8.
The Film Mercury. Jan 4, 1929, v9, p14.
Magill's Survey of Cinema. Series II. v3, p1142-44.
The New York Times. Jan 21, 1929, p18.
Selected Film Criticism, 1921-1930. p141-42.
Variety. Jan 23, 1929, p18.
The Western. p56, 175-76.

In Old Chicago (US; King, Henry; 1938)
Commonweal. Jan 21, 1938, v27, p358.
Esquire. Jun 1938, v9, p89.
Film Daily. Jan 4, 1938, p6.
The Films of Alice Faye. p97-100.
The Films of the Thirties. p202-03.
The Films of Tyrone Power. p69-72.
The Foremost Films of 1938. p79-96.
From Quasimodo to Scarlett O'Hara. p274-76.
Hollywood Reporter. Dec 31, 1937, p3.
Hollywood Spectator. Jan 22, 1938, v12, p7.
Life. Jan 17, 1938, v4, p46-49.
Literary Digest. Jan 29, 1938, v125, p22.
London Mercury. Apr 1938, v37, p641.
Magill's Survey of Cinema. Series I. v2, p825-28.
Motion Picture Herald. Jan 8, 1938, p48.
National Board of Review Magazine. Feb 1938, v13, p15.
The New Statesman and Nation. Mar 12, 1938, v15, p410.
The New York Times. Jan 7, 1938, p15.
The New Yorker. Jan 15, 1938, v13, p52-53.
Newsweek. Jan 17, 1938, v11, p23.
Rob Wagner's Script. Jan 22, 1938, v18, p16.
Saint Nicholas. Nov 1937, v65, p41.
Scholastic. Feb 5, 1938, v32, p32.
Selected Film Criticism, 1931-1940. p118-20.
The Spectator. Mar 18, 1938, v160, p467.
Stage. Mar 1938, v15, p40.
Those Fabulous Movie Years: The 30s. p142-43.
Time. Jan 17, 1938, v31, p44-45.
Variety. Jan 5, 1938, p16.
World Film News. Apr 1938, v3, p33, 38.

In Old Kentucky (US; Griffith, D.W.; 1909)
D.W. Griffith, His Biograph Films in Perspective. p106-09.
The Moving Picture World. Apr 10, 1909, v4, p406.
The Moving Picture World. Oct 2, 1909, p450.
The New York Dramatic Mirror. Oct 9, 1909, p16.
Selected Film Criticism, 1896-1911. p51-52.
Spellbound in Darkness. p63.

In Old Kentucky (US; Marshall, George; 1935)
Film Daily. Jul 5, 1935, p5.
Hollywood Reporter. Jul 1, 1935, p3.
Hollywood Spectator. Dec 7, 1935, v10, p12-13.
Literary Digest. Nov 30, 1935, v120, p24.
Motion Picture Herald. Jul 13, 1935, p6.

The New York Times. Nov 29, 1935, p24.
Time. Dec 9, 1935, v26, p46.
Variety. Dec 4, 1935, p15.
Will Rogers in Hollywood. p168-70.

In Person (US; Seiter, William A.; 1935)
Film Daily. Nov 2, 1935, p4.
The Films of Ginger Rogers. p122-24.
Hollywood Reporter. Oct 29, 1935, p3.
Hollywood Spectator. Nov 9, 1935, v10, p13.
Motion Picture Herald. Nov 9, 1935, p57, 60.
The New Statesman and Nation. Feb 8, 1936, v11, p188-89.
The New York Times. Dec 13, 1935, p31.
The New Yorker. Dec 21, 1935, v11, p73-74.
Time. Dec 16, 1935, v26, p41.
Variety. Dec 18, 1935, p12.

In the Bishop's Carriage (US; Dawley, J. Searle; Porter, Edwin S.; 1913)
The Moving Picture World. Sep 13, 1913, p1186.
The Moving Picture World. Sep 20, 1913, p1246, 1266.
The Moving Picture World. Oct 4, 1913, p72.
The New York Dramatic Mirror. Sep 10, 1913, p26.
The New York Dramatic Mirror. Sep 17, 1913, p28.
Selected Film Criticism, 1912-1920. p127-29.

In the Days of the Thundering Herd (US; Campbell, Colin; 1914)
The Moving Picture World. Dec 12, 1914, p1506.
Selected Film Criticism, 1912-1920. p129-31.
Variety. Nov 14, 1914, p25.

In the Diplomatic Service (US; Bushman, Francis X.; 1916)
The Moving Picture World. Oct 21, 1916, p447.
The Moving Picture World. Oct 28, 1916, p537.
The New York Dramatic Mirror. Oct 21, 1916, p27.
Variety. Oct 20, 1916, p25.
Wid's Daily. Oct 26, 1916, p1058.

In the Good Old Summertime (US; Leonard, Robert Z.; 1949)
Commonweal. Aug 19, 1949, v50, p465.
Film Daily. Jun 30, 1949, p7.
The Hollywood Musical. p300, 304-05.
Hollywood Reporter. Jun 23, 1949, p3.
Judy: The Films and Career of Judy Garland. p153-56.
Magill's Survey of Cinema. Series II. v3, p1145-47.
Motion Picture Herald Product Digest. Jun 25, 1949, p4657.
The New York Times. Aug 5, 1949, p23.
The New Yorker. Aug 13, 1949, v25, p66+.
Newsweek. Aug 22, 1949, v35, p70.
Rotarian. Oct 1949, v75, p39.
Time. Jul 18, 1949, v54, p76.
Variety. Jun 29, 1949, p14.

In the Next Room (US; Cline, Edward; 1930)
Exhibitors Herald-World. Apr 19, 1930, p49.
Film Daily. Apr 6, 1930, p40.
Judge. Apr 29, 1930, v98, p23.
The New York Times. Apr 7, 1930, p21.
The New Yorker. Apr 12, 1930, v6, p100.
Time. Apr 21, 1930, v15, p70.

In This Our Life (US; Huston, John; 1941)
Bette Davis: Her Films and Career. p115-16.
Bijou. Apr 1977, v1, p63+.
The Cinema of John Huston. p45-52.
Commonweal. May 22, 1942, v36, p112-13.
Film Daily. Apr 9, 1942, p4.
Hollywood Reporter. Apr 7, 1942, p3.
The London Times. Sep 18, 1942, p6.
The Modern American Novel and the Cinema. p143-55.
Motion Picture Exhibitor. Apr 22, 1942, p994.
Motion Picture Herald Product Digest. Apr 11, 1942, p597.
Musician. May 1942, v47, p76.

The New York Times. May 9, 1942, p10.
Newsweek. May 18, 1942, v19, p50.
Time. May 11, 1942, v39, p88.
Variety. Apr 8, 1942, p8.

In Which We Serve (GB; Coward, Noel; 1942)
Chestnuts in Her Lap. p79-80.
Collier's. Jan 2, 1943, v111, p20-22.
Commonweal. Jan 8, 1942, v37, p301.
Fifty Classic British Films. p43-45.
Film Daily. Oct 16, 1942, p7.
Films and the Second World War. p107-08.
The Films of World War II. p94-97.
The Great British Films. p63-65.
The Great Films. p159-64.
Hollywood Reporter. Oct 16, 1942, p3.
The International Dictionary of Films and Filmmakers. v1,
  p208-09.
Life. Mar 25, 1942, v12, p106-09.
Life. Dec 21, 1942, v13, p59+.
The London Times. Sep 24, 1942, p6.
The London Times. Sep 28, 1942, p8.
The London Times. Apr 5, 1948, p6.
Magill's Survey of Cinema. Series I. v2, p833-35.
Motion Picture Exhibitor. Nov 4, 1943, v28, n26, sec2, p1143-
  44.
Motion Picture Herald Product Digest. Oct 17, 1942, p84+.
The New Republic. Dec 28, 1932, v107, p858.
The New York Times. Oct 25, 1942, sec8, p3.
The New York Times. Dec 24, 1942, p18.
Newsweek. Dec 21, 1942, v20, p80-82.
Photoplay. Feb 1943, v22, p64.
Rob Wagner's Script. Jan 9, 1943, v29, p14.
Scholastic. Dec 14, 1942, v41, p27.
Selected Film Criticism: Foreign Films, 1930-1950. p81-83.
Theatre Arts. Jan 1943, v27, p5.
Time. Dec 28, 1942, v40, p84+.
Variety. Oct 7, 1942, p8.

Incendiary Blonde (US; Marshall, George; 1945)
Commonweal. Aug 17, 1945, v42, p431.
Film Daily. Jun 12, 1945, p7.
Hollywood Reporter. Jun 11, 1945, p3.
Life. Aug 27, 1945, v19, p67-68+.
The New York Times. Jul 26, 1945, p13.
The New Yorker. Aug 4, 1945, v21, p36.
Newsweek. Aug 6, 1945, v26, p85.
Time. Aug 6, 1945, v46, p98+.
Variety. Jun 13, 1945, p17.

Incidents in the Life of Napoleon and Josephine (US;
  1909)
The Moving Picture World. Apr 10, 1909, p406.
Selected Film Criticism, 1896-1911. p52-53.

Inconnus dans le Maison *See* Strangers in the House

Indianapolis Speedway (US; Bacon, Lloyd; 1939)
Commonweal. Jul 28, 1939, v30, p340.
Film Daily. Jul 26, 1939, p7.
Hollywood Reporter. Oct 19, 1939, p3.
Hollywood Spectator. Nov 11, 1939, v14, p12.
Motion Picture Herald. Jul 22, 1939, p52-53.
The New York Times. Jul 15, 1939, p8.
Variety. Jul 19, 1939, p12.

Indiscreet (US; McCarey, Leo; 1931)
Film Daily. May 10, 1931, p10.
The Films of Gloria Swanson. p221-23.
Judge. May 30, 1931, v100, p24.
Life. Jun 5, 1931, v97, p20.
The New York Times. May 7, 1931, p21.
The New York Times. May 17, 1931, p5.
The New Yorker. May 16, 1931, v7, p73.
Outlook and Independent. May 13, 1931, v158, p59.

Time. May 18, 1931, v17, p52.
Variety. May 13, 1931, p36.

The Informer (US; Ford, John; 1935)
American Film Criticism. p314-16.
Catholic World. Aug 1935, v141, p605-06.
Commonweal. Mar 6, 1935, v23, p525-26.
Commonweal. Apr 3, 1935, v23, p637-81.
Esquire. Jul 1935, v3, p152, 164.
The Film and the Public. p132-35.
The Film Criticism of Otis Ferguson. p79-80.
Film Daily. May 1, 1935, p8.
Films and Filming. Jul 1960, v6, p10-12, 35.
The Films of the Thirties. p140-41.
From Quasimodo to Scarlett O'Hara. p202-05.
Graham Greene on Film. p26.
Hollywood Reporter. Apr 24, 1935, p3.
International Dictionary of Films and Filmmakers. v1, p210-
  11.
John Ford (Bogdanovich). p59-64.
Judge. Jun 1935, v108, p14.
Literary Digest. May 25, 1935, v119, p26.
Lorentz on Film. p128-29.
Magill's Survey of Cinema. Series I. v2, p839-43.
Motion Picture Herald. May 4, 1935, p35, 38.
Motion Picture Herald. Feb 11, 1935, p17-18.
The Nation. May 22, 1935, v140, p610+.
National Board of Review Magazine. Jun 1935, v10, p8-9.
The New Masses. May 28, 1935, v15, p29.
The New Republic. May 29, 1935, v83, p76.
The New Statesman and Nation. Oct 12, 1935, v10, p484.
The New York Times. May 10, 1935, p25.
The New Yorker. May 18, 1935, v11, p67.
Newsweek. May 11, 1935, v5, p29.
The Non-Western Films of John Ford. p152-61.
Novels Into Films. p65-90.
Rob Wagner's Script. Jun 22, 1935, v13, p9-10.
Scribner's Magazine. Feb 1937, v101, p78-79.
Selected Film Criticism, 1931-1940. p121-24.
The Spectator. Oct 11, 1935, v155, p547.
Theatre Arts Monthly. Aug 1951, v35, p58-83.
Those Fabulous Movie Years: The 30s. p75.
Time. May 20, 1935, v25, p32.
Vanity Fair. Jul 1935, v44, p38.
Variety. May 15, 1935, p19.
50 Classic Motion Pictures. p286-91.

An Innocent Magdalene (US; Dwan, Allan; 1916)
The Moving Picture World. Jun 17, 1916, p2059.
The Moving Picture World. Jun 24, 1916, p2301.
The New York Dramatic Mirror. Jun 10, 1916, p31.
Variety. Jun 16, 1916, p24.
Wid's Daily. Jun 8, 1916, p638.

Innocents of Paris (US; Wallace, Richard; 1929)
Film Daily. Apr 28, 1929, p9.
The Films of Maurice Chevalier. p72-75.
The Hollywood Musical. p24.
Literary Digest. May 18, 1929, v101, p25-26.
The New York Times. Apr 27, 1929, p16.
The New York Times. Aug 25, 1929, sec8, p5.
Outlook. Jul 13, 1929, v152, p396.
Photoplay. Jul 1929, v36, p54.
Selected Film Criticism, 1921-1930. p142.
Variety. May 1, 1929, p17.

The Inside of the White Slave Traffic (US; Beal, Frank;
  1913)
Motion Picture News. Dec 20, 1913, p31.
The New York Dramatic Mirror. Sep 24, 1913, p31.
The New York Times. Dec 9, 1913, p8.
Variety. Dec 12, 1913, p12, 15.

The Insidious Dr. Fu Manchu *See* The Mysterious Dr. Fu
  Manchu

Inspector General (US; Koster, Henry; 1949)
Christian Century. Jan 18, 1950, v67, p95.
Commonweal. Dec 30, 1949, v51, p342.
Film Daily. Nov 18, 1949, p6.
Hollywood Reporter. Nov 17, 1949, p3.
Library Journal. Feb 15, 1950, v130, p332.
Motion Picture Herald. Nov 19, 1949, p89.
The New Republic. Jan 23, 1950, v122, p20.
The New York Times. Dec 31, 1949, p9.
The New Yorker. Jan 14, 1950, v25, p75.
Newsweek. Jan 16, 1950, v35, p79.
Rotarian. Mar 1950, v76, p36.
Time. Jan 23, 1950, v55, p75.
Variety. Nov 23, 1949, p8.

Inspector Hornleigh (GB; Ford, Eugene; 1939)
Film Daily. Jun 19, 1939, p11.
Graham Greene on Film. p211-12.
Motion Picture Herald. Apr 22, 1939, p42.
The New York Times. Jun 15, 1939, p27.
The Spectator. Apr 7, 1939, v162, p592.
Time. Jun 26, 1939, v33, p46.
Variety. Jun 21, 1939, p16.
Variety. Oct 25, 1939, p23.

Inspiration (US; Brown, Clarence; 1931)
Exhibitors Herald-World. Dec 20, 1930, p31-32.
Film Daily. Feb 8, 1931, p10.
The Films of Greta Garbo. p95-97.
Garbo: A Portrait (Walker). p119-20.
Judge. Mar 7, 1931, v100, p20.
Life. Mar 6, 1931, v97, p22.
The New York Times. Feb 9, 1931, p25.
The New Yorker. Feb 14, 1931, v6, p67, 69.
Outlook and Independent. Feb 25, 1931, v157, p312.
Rob Wagner's Script. Mar 14, 1931, v5, p9-10.
Time. Feb 16, 1931, v17, p21.
Variety. Feb 11, 1931, p14.

Intermezzo (SWED; Molander, Gustav; 1936)
Film Daily. Dec 30, 1937, p8.
The Films of Ingrid Bergman. p53-55.
Hollywood Reporter. Dec 23, 1936, p15.
The New York Times. Dec 25, 1937, p6.
Swedish Film Classics. p45.
Variety. Dec 29, 1937, p19.

Intermezzo, a Love Story (Also titled: Escape to Happiness) (US; Ratoff, Gregory; 1939)
Commonweal. Oct 20, 1939, v30, p587.
Film Daily. Oct 4, 1939, p7.
The Films of Ingrid Bergman. p71-74.
Graham Greene on Film. p265-66.
The Great Romantic Films. p78-81.
Hollywood Reporter. Sep 27, 1939, p3.
Hollywood Spectator. Oct 14, 1939, v14, p5-6.
Magill's Survey of Cinema. Series II. v3, p1159-61.
Motion Picture Herald. Sep 30, 1939, p38-39.
The Nation. Nov 11, 1939, v149, p534.
The New York Times. Oct 6, 1939, p31.
The New Yorker. Oct 7, 1939, v15, p63.
Newsweek. Oct 9, 1939, v14, p34.
Photoplay. Dec 1939, v53, p63.
Selected Film Criticism, 1931-1940. p124-25.
The Spectator. Jan 26, 1940, v164, p108.
Time. Oct 16, 1939, v34, p101.
Variety. Oct 4, 1939, p12.

International House (US; Sutherland, Edward; 1933)
Film Daily. May 27, 1933, p3.
The Films of W.C. Fields. p80-82.
Hollywood Reporter. May 8, 1933, p2.
Motion Picture Herald. May 20, 1933, p33.
The Nation. June 21, 1933, v136, p708.
The New York Times. May 27, 1933, p11.

The New Yorker. Jun 3, 1933, v9, p58.
Rob Wagner's Script. May 27, 1933, v9, p9.
Time. Jun 5, 1933, v21, p20.
Vanity Fair. July 1933, v40, p59.
Variety. May 30, 1933, p15.
W.C. Fields: A Life on Film. p109-15.

Internes Can't Take Money (US; Santell, Alfred; 1937)
Canadian Magazine. Jun 1937, v87, p51.
Film Daily. Apr 12, 1937, p11.
The Films of Barbara Stanwyck. p114-15.
Hollywood Reporter. Apr 8, 1937, p3.
Motion Picture Herald. Apr 17, 1937, p44.
The New York Times. May 6, 1937, p23.
Starring Miss Barbara Stanwyck. p90-93.
Time. Apr 19, 1937, v29, p66.
Variety. May 12, 1937, p12.

Intolerance (Also titled: The Mother and the Law; The Fall of Babylon) (US; Griffith, D.W.; 1916)
American Silent Film. p75-77, 87-100+.
BFI/Monthly Film Bulletin. May 1979, v46, p106-07.
Classic Movies. p8-9.
Classics of the Silent Screen. p20-22.
Fifty Great American Silent Films, 1912-1920. p51-55.
The Films of D.W. Griffith. p62-89.
Magill's Survey of Cinema. Silent Films. v2, p570-74.
The New York Dramatic Mirror. Sep 16, 1916, p22.
The New York Times. Sep 6, 1916, p7.
Photoplay. Dec 1916, v11, p77-81.
Selected Film Criticism, 1912-1920. p132-40.
Variety. Sep 8, 1916, p 20.
Wid's Daily. Sep 7, 1916, p835.

Intruder in the Dust (US; Brown, Clarence; 1949)
Christian Century. Mar 15, 1950, v67, p351.
Cinema, the Magic Vehicle. v1, p504.
Commonweal. Dec 2, 1949, v51, p240.
Film Daily. Oct 11, 1949, p5.
Films in Review. Feb 1950, v1, p33+.
The Films of the Forties. p260-61.
Hollywood Reporter. Oct 11, 1949, p3.
The Hollywood Social Problem Films. p174-75, 250-51.
Library Journal. Feb 15, 1950, v75, p332.
Life. Dec 12, 1949, v27, p149-50.
Magill's Survey of Cinema. Series II. v3, p1166-68.
Motion Picture Herald. Oct 15, 1949, p49.
The Nation. Jan 14, 1950, v170, p45.
The New Republic. Dec 12, 1949, v121, p30.
The New York Times. Nov 23, 1949, p19.
The New Yorker. Nov 26, 1949, v25, p84+.
Newsweek. Dec 5, 1949, v34, p81.
Rotarian. May 1950, v76, p40.
Sequence. Sum 1950, n11, p13-14.
Sight and Sound. Mar 1950, v19, p29.
Toms, Coons, Mulattoes, Mammies & Bucks. p217-21.
Variety. Oct 12, 1949, p6.
Vintage Films. p109-13.

The Invaders *See* 49th Parallel

The Invisible Man (US; Whale, James; 1933)
American Film Criticism. p293-94.
Classic Movie Monsters. p132-39.
Commonweal. Dec 29, 1933, v19, p246.
A Companion to the Movies. p35-36.
Dictionary of Films. p159-60.
Film Daily. Nov 18, 1933, p4.
Great Horror Movies. p45-46.
Hollywood Reporter. Oct 27, 1933, p3.
Horror Movies (Clarens). p86-87.
James Whale: Ace Director. p16-17.
James Whale (Curtis). pxv, 102-08.
Judge. Jan 1934, v106, p12.
Magill's Survey of Cinema. Series II. v3, p1169-74.
Monsters from the Movies. p83-85.

Motion Picture Herald. Nov 4, 1933, p37-38.
Movie Monsters and Their Masters: The Birth of the Horror Film. p40.
The Nation. Dec 13, 1933, v137, p688.
The New Statesman and Nation. Feb 10, 1934, v7, p191.
The New York Times. Nov 18, 1933, p18.
The New York Times. Nov 26, 1933, p5.
The New York Times. Dec 3, 1933, p8.
The New Yorker. Nov 25, 1933, v9, p57.
Newsweek. Nov 25, 1933, v2, p33.
Science Fiction Studies in Film. p68-72.
Selected Film Criticism, 1931-1940. p125-26.
The Spectator. Feb 2, 1934, v152, p159.
Time. Nov 20, 1933, v22, p37.
Variety. Nov 21, 1933, p14.

The Invisible Ray (US; Hillyer, Lambert; 1936)
Film Daily. Jan 11, 1936, p3.
Hollywood Reporter. Jan 11, 1936, p3.
Hollywood Spectator. Feb 1, 1936, v10, p10.
Motion Picture Herald. Jan 25, 1936, p39.
The New York Times. Jan 11, 1936, p9.
Rob Wagner's Script. Feb 15, 1936, v15, p12-13.
Variety. Jan 15, 1936, p18.

Invisible Stripes (US; Bacon, Lloyd; 1939)
The Complete Films of Humphrey Bogart. p76-77.
Film Daily. Jan 16, 1940, p8.
The Great Gangster Pictures. p211-12.
Hollywood Reporter. Dec 28, 1939, p3.
Humphrey Bogart: The Man and His Films. p99.
Motion Picture Herald. Jan 6, 1940, p42.
The New York Times. Jan 13, 1940, p11.
The New Yorker. Jan 20, 1940, v15, p51.
Rob Wagner's Script. Jan 6, 1940, v23, p17.
Variety. Jan 3, 1940, p40.

Invitation to Happiness (US; Ruggles, Wesley; 1939)
Commonweal. Jun 9, 1939, v30, p189.
Film Daily. May 9, 1939, p6.
Hollywood Reporter. May 5, 1939, p3.
Hollywood Spectator. May 13, 1939, v14, p18.
Motion Picture Herald. May 13, 1939, p37.
The New York Times. Jun 8, 1939, p31.
Newsweek. Jun 5, 1939, v13, p34.
Photoplay. Jul 1939, v53, p62.
Rob Wagner's Script. Jun 17, 1939, v21, p16.
Time. Jun 19, 1939, v33, p74.
Variety. May 10, 1939, p14.

Irene (US; Green, Alfred E.; 1926)
Film Daily. Mar 7, 1926, p8.
Life. Mar 25, 1926, v87, p26.
The New York Times. Mar 1, 1926, p17.
Photoplay. Apr 1926, v29, p55.
Selected Film Criticism, 1921-1930. p192-93.
Variety. Mar 3, 1926, p34.

Irene (US; Wilcox, Herbert; 1940)
Commonweal. May 10, 1940, v32, p63.
Film Daily. Apr 19, 1940, p6.
Hollywood Reporter. Apr 19, 1940, p3.
Life. Aug 8, 1940, v8, p59.
Motion Picture Herald. May 24, 1940, p23.
Motion Picture Herald. Feb 3, 1940, p30.
The New York Times. May 24, 1940, p23.
Time. May 6, 1940, v35, p82+.
Variety. Apr 24, 1940, p16.

The Irish in Us (US; Bacon, Lloyd; 1935)
Film Daily. Aug 1, 1935, p10.
The Films of James Cagney. p102-04.
The Films of Olivia De Havilland. p63-66.
The Gangster Film. p170-72.
Hollywood Reporter. Jul 10, 1935, p4.
Literary Digest. Aug 10, 1935, p29.

Motion Picture Herald. Jul 20, 1935, p88.
The New York Times. Aug 1, 1935, p15.
The Spectator. Nov 29, 1935, v155, p900.
Time. Aug 12, 1935, v26, p34.
Variety. Aug 7, 1935, p21.

The Iron Duke (GB; Saville, Victor; 1934)
Cinema Quarterly. Aut 1934, v3, p114.
Classic Film Collector. Wint 1973, n41, p28-29.
Esquire. Mar 1935, v3, p142.
Film Daily. Jan 25, 1935, p6.
Films in Review. Nov 1985, v36, p524.
Hollywood Reporter. Jan 9, 1935, p5.
Literary Digest. Feb 9, 1935, v119, p22.
Motion Picture Herald. Dec 22, 1934, p38-39.
The New York Times. Jan 25, 1935, p27.
The New Yorker. Feb 2, 1935, v10, p56-57.
Newsweek. Feb 2, 1935, v5, p32.
The Spectator. Dec 7, 1934, v153, p876.
Time. Feb 4, 1935, v25, p38.
Variety. Dec 18, 1934, p13.
Variety. Jan 29, 1935, p14.

The Iron Horse (US; Ford, John; 1924)
BFI/Monthly Film Bulletin. Jun 1980, v47, p116.
Cameras West. p73-74.
Cinema, the Magic Vehicle. v1, p106-07.
Film Daily. Sep 7, 1924, p5.
From Quasimodo to Scarlett O'Hara. p34-36.
A History of Films. p92.
The International Dictionary of Films and Filmmakers. v1, p214-16.
Magill's Survey of Cinema. Silent Films. v2, p575-83.
The Moving Picture World. Sep 13, 1924, p137.
The New Republic. Nov 26, 1924, v41, p19-20.
There Must Be a Lone Ranger. p42, 54.
Variety. Sep 3, 1924, p23.
The War, the West, and the Wilderness. p386-96.
The Western Films of John Ford. p10-29.

Iron Man (Also titled: The Iron Man) (US; Browning, Tod; 1931)
Film Daily. Apr 19, 1931, p10.
The Films of Jean Harlow. p42-45.
Life. May 15, 1931, v97, p20.
Motion Picture Herald. Mar 28, 1931, p37.
The New York Times. Apr 18, 1931, p17.
The New Yorker. Apr 25, 1931, v7, p81-82.
Time. Apr 27, 1931, v17, p38.
Variety. Apr 22, 1931, p18.

Island of Lost Men (US; Neumann, Kurt; 1939)
Film Daily. Sep 7, 1939, p7.
Hollywood Reporter. Aug 2, 1939, p3.
Motion Picture Herald. Aug 5, 1939, p88-89.
The New York Times. Aug 17, 1939, p16.
Photoplay. Sep 1939, v53, p63.
Variety. Aug 23, 1939, p14.

Island of Lost Souls (US; Kenton, Erle C.; 1933)
Classics of the Horror Film. p114-16.
Film Daily. Jan 12, 1933, p6.
The Films of Bela Lugosi. p82-84.
Hollywood Reporter. Dec 2, 1932, p3.
Horror Movies (Clarens). p109-10.
Magill's Survey of Cinema. Series II. v3, p1185-88.
Midnight Marquee. Sep 1977, n26, p4-12.
Monsters from the Movies. p79-81.
Motion Picture Herald. Dec 10, 1932, p48, 50.
The New York Times. Jan 13, 1933, p19.
The New York Times. Jan 22, 1933, p5.
The New York Times. Jan 8, 1933, p4.
The New Yorker. Jan 21, 1933, v8, p46-47.
Science Fiction Studies in Film. p73-74.
Time. Jan 23, 1933, v21, p34.

Vanity Fair. Mar 1933, v40, p63.
Variety. Jan 17, 1933, p15.

The Island of Regeneration (US; Davenport, Harry; 1915)
Motion Picture News. Feb 20, 1915, p48.
Motography. May 29, 1915, p875, 910.
The Moving Picture World. Feb 13, 1915, p993.
The Moving Picture World. May 22, 1915, p1340.
The New York Dramatic Mirror. Feb 10, 1915, p28.
Variety. Jun 4, 1915, p18.
Vitagraph Life Portrayals. Mar 1915, p28.

Isle of Fury (US; McDonald, Frank; 1936)
The Complete Films of Humphrey Bogart. p35-36.
Film Daily. Dec 2, 1936, p7.
Humphrey Bogart: The Man and His Films. p59.
Motion Picture Herald. Sep 5, 1936, p41-42.
Rob Wagner's Script. Oct 24, 1936, v16, p10-11.
Variety. Nov 18, 1936, p29.

Isn't Life a Bitch *See* Chienne, La

Isn't Life Wonderful? (US; Griffith, D.W.; 1924)
BFI/Monthly Film Bulletin. Jun 1979, v46, p158-59.
Exceptional Photoplays. Dec-Jan, 1925, v5, p5.
Film Daily. Dec 1, 1924, p4.
The Films of D.W. Griffith. p205-10.
The Films of the Twenties. p105-08.
Magill's Survey of Cinema. Silent Films. v2, p584-86.
The Moving Picture World. Dec 13, 1924, p624.
Photoplay. Feb 1925, v27, p55.
Selected Film Criticism, 1921-1930. p145-47.
Variety. Dec 3, 1924, p27.
The War, the West, and the Wilderness. p183-84.

It (US; Badger, Clarence; 1927)
Film Daily. Feb 13, 1927, p8.
The Films of Gary Cooper. p31-32.
The Films of the Twenties. p164-66.
The Moving Picture World. Feb 12, 1927, p513.
Photoplay. Mar 1927, v31, p54.
Selected Film Criticism, 1921-1930. p147.
Variety. Feb 9, 1927, p14.

It Had to Happen (US; Del Ruth, Roy; 1936)
Film Daily. Feb 15, 1936, p6.
Garbo and the Night Watchman. p68.
Hollywood Reporter. Jan 27, 1936, p3.
Motion Picture Herald. Feb 15, 1936, p44.
The New York Times. Feb 15, 1936, p18.
Rob Wagner's Script. Feb 29, 1936, v15, p9.
Time. Feb 24, 1936, v27, p58.
Variety. Feb 19, 1936, p12.

It Happened at the Inn *See* Goupi Mains Rouge

It Happened in Brooklyn (US; Whorf, Richard; 1947)
Film Daily. Mar 12, 1947, p19.
The Films of Frank Sinatra. p51-53.
Hollywood Reporter. Mar 3, 1947, p3.
Motion Picture Herald Product Digest. Mar 8, 1947, p3513.
The New York Times. Mar 14, 1947, p28.
Variety. Mar 5, 1947, p8.

It Happened on 5th Avenue (US; Del Ruth, Roy; 1947)
Commonweal. Jun 20, 1947, v46, p241.
Film Daily. Feb 4, 1947, p12.
Hollywood Reporter. Feb 3, 1947, p3.
Motion Picture Herald Product Digest. Feb 8, 1947, p3457.
New Republic. Jun 30, 1947, v116, p35.
The New York Times. Jun 11, 1947, p33.
Newsweek. Jun 9, 1947, v29, p94.
Time. Jun 16, 1947, v49, p64.
Variety. Feb 5, 1947, p20.

It Happened One Night (US; Capra, Frank; 1934)
BFI/Monthly Film Bulletin. Feb 1978, v45, p33.
The Cinema of Frank Capra. p153-68.
The Cinema of Frank Capra (Poague). p205-17.
Claudette Colbert (Quirk). p65-67+.
Film Daily. Feb 23, 1934, p6.
The Films of Clark Gable. p150-52.
The Films of Frank Capra (Scherle and Levy). p123-29.
The Films of Frank Capra (Willis). p145-50.
Great Movie Memories. p18-20.
Hollywood Reporter. Jan 20, 1934, p3.
The International Dictionary of Films and Filmmakers. v1, p215-16.
Landmark Films. p92-99.
Literary Digest. Mar 10, 1934, v117, p38.
Magill's Survey of Cinema. Series I. v2, p852-55.
Motion Picture Herald. Mar 3, 1934, p38.
The Name Above the Title. p159-72.
The Nation. Mar 14, 1934, v138, p426.
The New Republic. May 9, 1934, v78, p364.
The New York Times. Feb 23, 1934, p23.
Rob Wagner's Script. Mar 24, 1934, v11, p8.
Selected Film Criticism, 1931-1940. p127.
Talking Pictures. p219-21.
Variety. Feb 27, 1934, p17.

It Happened Tomorrow (US; Clair, René; 1944)
Commonweal. Mar 24, 1944, v39, p564.
Film Daily. Mar 24, 1944, p8.
Hollywood Reporter. Mar 20, 1944, p3.
Magill's Cinema Annual, 1984. p552-56.
The New Republic. Jun 12, 1944, v110, p788.
The New York Times. May 29, 1944, p18.
Newsweek. Mar 20, 1944, v23, p92.
René Clair (McGerr). p148-50+.
Time. Apr 24, 1944, v43, p96.
Variety. Mar 22, 1944, p18.

It Happens Every Spring (US; Bacon, Lloyd; 1949)
Christian Century. Jul 20, 1949, v66, p879.
Commonweal. Jun 24, 1949, v50, p272.
Film Daily. May 5, 1949, p7.
Hollywood Reporter. May 5, 1949, p3.
Motion Picture Herald Product Digest. May 7, 1949, p4597.
The New Republic. Jun 27, 1949, v120, p22.
The New York Times. Jun 11, 1949, p11.
The New Yorker. Jun 18, 1949, v25, p52.
Newsweek. Jun 13, 1949, v33, p82+.
Rotarian. Sep 1949, v75, p36-37.
Time. June 6, 1949, v53, p97+.
Variety. May 11, 1949, p6.

The Italian (Also titled: The Wop) (US; Barker, Reginald; 1915)
American Silent Film. p63-66.
Fifty Great American Silent Films, 1912-1920. p23-25.
Magill's Survey of Cinema. Silent Films. v2, p587-89.
Motion Picture News. Jan 1, 1915, p29.
Motography. Jan 9, 1915, p77.
The New York Dramatic News. Dec 30, 1914, p26-27.
The Rivals of D.W. Griffith. p17-19.
Selected Film Criticism, 1912-1920. p140-41.
Variety. Jan 1, 1915, p29.

An Italian Straw Hat (French title: Chapeau de Paille d'Italie, Un; Also titled: The Horse Ate the Hat) (FR; Clair, René; 1927)
Cinema, the Magic Vehicle. v1, p133-34.
A History of Films. p166-67.
Magill's Survey of Cinema. Silent Films. v2, p590-93.
René Clair. p53-59+.
Variety. Sep 8, 1931, p50.

It's a Gift (US; McLeod, Norman Z.; 1934)
Film Daily. Nov 17, 1934, p3.
The Films of W.C. Fields. p103-05.
Hollywood Reporter. Nov 8, 1934, p3.
Literary Digest. Jan 19, 1935, v119, p30.
Magill's Survey of Cinema. Series II. v3, p1195-97.
Motion Picture Herald. Nov 24, 1934, p39.
The New York Times. Jan 5, 1934, p20.
The New Yorker. Jan 12, 1935, v10, p57.
Variety. Jan 8, 1935, p18.
W.C. Fields: A Life on Film. p152-61.

It's a Wonderful Life (US; Capra, Frank; 1946)
American Film. Oct 1978, v4, p39-51.
American Film and Society Since 1945. p21-22.
The Cinema of Frank Capra (Poague). p205-17.
Commonweal. Jan 3, 1947, v45, p305.
Cult Movies. p239-43.
Film Daily. Dec 19, 1946, p5.
Films in Review. Apr 1951, v2, p32-38.
The Films of Frank Capra (Scherle and Levy). p223-32.
The Films of Frank Capra (Willis). p59-87.
The Films of James Stewart. p103-05.
Frank Capra (Maland). p131-54.
Hollywood Reporter. Dec 19, 1946, p3.
The International Dictionary of Films and Filmmakers. v1, p216-17.
Life. Dec 30, 1946, v21, p68-73.
Magill's Survey of Cinema. Series I. v2, p856-59.
Motion Picture Herald Product Digest. Dec 21, 1946, p3373.
The Name Above the Title. p376-82+.
The Nation. Feb 15, 1947, v164, p193.
The New Republic. Jan 6, 1947, v116, p44.
The New York Times. Dec 23, 1946, p19.
The New Yorker. Dec 21, 1946, v22, p87.
Newsweek. Dec 30, 1946, v28, p72-73.
Selected Film Criticism, 1941-1950. p87-90.
Theatre Arts. Feb 1947, v31, p36-37.
Time. Dec 23, 1946, v48, p54.
Variety. Dec 25, 1946, p12.

It's a Wonderful World (US; Van Dyke, W.S.; 1939)
Claudette Colbert (Quirk). p110-11.
Commonweal. Jun 2, 1939, v30, p161.
The Film Criticism of Otis Ferguson. p257.
Film Daily. May 4, 1939, p20.
The Films of James Stewart. p70-72.
Hollywood Reporter. May 12, 1939, p3.
Hollywood Spectator. May 27, 1939, v14, p9.
Motion Picture Herald. May 6, 1939, p38.
The New Republic. May 31, 1939, v99, p102.
The New Statesman and Nation. Aug 19, 1939, v18, p277.
The New York Times. May 19, 1939, p27.
The New Yorker. May 20, 1939, v15, p77.
Photoplay. Jul 1939, v53, p63.
Rob Wagner's Script. May 27, 1939, v21, p22.
The Tatler. Aug 23, 1939, v153, p328.
Time. May 22, 1939, v33, p56.

It's in the Air (US; Riesner, Charles F.; 1935)
Film Daily. Oct 10, 1935, p7.
Hollywood Reporter. Oct 4, 1935, p3.
Motion Picture Herald. Nov 16, 1935, p66.
The New York Times. Nov 8, 1935, p18.
Time. Oct 28, 1935, v26, p53.

It's in the Bag (US; Wallace, Richard; 1945)
Commonweal. May 4, 1945, v42, p72.
Film Daily. Feb 13, 1945, p5.
Hollywood Reporter. Feb 6, 1945, p3.
Magill's Survey of Cinema. Series II. v2, p1198-1201.
Motion Picture Exhibitor. Feb 21, 1945, v33, n16, sec2, p1667.
Motion Picture Herald Product Digest. Feb 17, 1945, p2317.
The Nation. May 21, 1945, v160, p469.

The New York Times. Jun 4, 1945, p12.
The New Yorker. Jun 16, 1945, v21, p40.
Newsweek. May 21, 1945, v25, p100+.
Photoplay. May 1945, v16, p18.
Scholastic. Mar 12, 1945, v46, p24.
Time. Apr 23, 1945, v45, p94+.
Variety. Feb 14, 1945, p14.

It's Love Again (GB; Saville, Victor; 1936)
The Age of the Dream Palace. p219.
Canadian Magazine. Jul 1936, v86, p32.
Film Daily. May 12, 1936, p12.
Graham Greene on Film. p101.
Hollywood Reporter. May 19, 1936, p14.
Hollywood Spectator. Jun 20, 1936, v11, p13.
Literary Digest. May 23, 1936, v121, p20.
Motion Picture Herald. May 16, 1936, p33.
The Nation. May 27, 1936, v142, p688.
The New York Times. May 23, 1936, p12.
The New Yorker. May 23, 1936, v12, p69.
Newsweek. May 23, 1936, v7, p27.
Rob Wagner's Script. Jul 11, 1936, v15, p12.
The Spectator. Sep 18, 1936, v157, p455.
Time. Jun 1, 1936, v27, p22.
Variety. May 20, 1936, p23.
Variety. May 27, 1936, p14.

It's Love I'm After (US; Mayo, Archie; 1937)
Bette Davis: Her Films and Career. p82-83.
Film Daily. Jul 30, 1937, p10.
The Films of Olivia De Havilland. p99-102.
Hollywood Reporter. Jul 24, 1937, p3.
Hollywood Spectator. Jul 31, 1937, v12, p8.
Kiss Kiss Bang Bang. p359.
Life. Nov 15, 1937, v3, p100-01.
Motion Picture Herald. Jul 31, 1937, p40.
The Nation. Nov 20, 1937, v145, p567.
The New York Times. Nov 11, 1937, p31.
The New Yorker. Nov 13, 1937, v13, p78.
Scholastic. Oct 30, 1937, v31, p35.
Stage. Sep 1937, v14, p45.
Time. Nov 22, 1937, v30, p52.
Variety. Jul 21, 1937, p13.
Warner Brothers Presents. p185, 190.

It's No Laughing Matter (US; Weber, Lois; 1915)
Motion Picture News. Jan 23, 1915, p49.
Motography. Jan 30, 1915, p162, 186.
The Moving Picture World. Jan 30, 1915, p679.
The Moving Picture World. Feb 20, 1915, p1200.
The New York Dramatic Mirror. Jan 13, 1915, p28.
Variety. Jan 22, 1915, p25.

It's Tough to Be Famous (US; Green, Alfred E.; 1932)
Film Daily. Apr 10, 1932, p10.
Hollywood Reporter. Feb 23, 1932, p3.
Motion Picture Herald. Apr 16, 1932, p38-39.
National Board of Review Magazine. Apr 1932, v7, p8-10.
The New York Times. Apr 9, 1932, p18.
The New Yorker. Apr 16, 1932, v8, p57.
Rob Wagner's Script. May 14, 1932, v7, p9.
Time. Apr 18, 1932, v19, p17.

Ivan (Also titled: Ivan Dovzhenko) (USSR; Dovzhenko, Alexander; 1932)
Dictionary of Films. p161.
Film Daily. Feb 23, 1933, p6.
Kino. p290-91.
The Nation. Mar 8, 1933, v136, p269.
National Board of Review Magazine. Feb 1933, v8, p12.
The New York Times. Feb 27, 1933, p11.
Variety. Nov 29, 1932, p18.
Variety. Mar 7, 1933, p54.

Ivan the Terrible *See* Wings of a Serf

Ivanhoe (US; Brenon, Herbert; 1913)
  The Moving Picture World. Sep 20, 1913, p1318.
  Universal Weekly. Sep 20, 1913, p13.

J'Accuse *See* That They May Live

J'Accuse (Also titled: I Accuse) (FR; Gance, Abel; 1919)
  Abel Gance (Kramer and Welsh). p61-76.
  French Cinema. p295-302.
  The New York Times. May 23, 1920, sec6, p2.
  The New York Times. Oct 10, 1921, p16.
  The Parade's Gone By. p532-35.
  Variety. Oct 14, 1921, p42.
  Variety. Apr 26, 1939, p12.
  Wid's Daily. May 15, 1921, p3.

Jack London (US; Santell, Alfred; 1943)
  Commonweal. Dec 31, 1943, v39, p281.
  Film Daily. Nov 24, 1943, p6.
  The Films of Susan Hayward. p89-90.
  Hollywood Reporter. Nov 24, 1943, p3.
  Motion Picture Herald Product Digest. Nov 27, 1943, p1645.
  The New York Times. Mar 3, 1944, p19.
  The New Yorker. Feb 26, 1944, v20, p42.
  Variety. Nov 24, 1943, p18.

Jalna (US; Cromwell, John; 1935)
  The Hollywood Professionals. v5, p75-76.
  Hollywood Reporter. Jul 23, 1935, p3.
  Motion Picture Herald. Aug 17, 1935, p49, 52.
  The New York Times. Sep 14, 1935, p8.
  The New Yorker. Aug 24, 1935, v11, p45-46.
  Stage. Sep 1935, v12, p3.
  Time. Aug 19, 1935, v26, p28.
  Variety. Sep 18, 1935, p15.

Jamaica Inn (GB; Hitchcock, Alfred; 1939)
  Around Cinemas. p163-65.
  The Art of Alfred Hitchcock. p81-88.
  Commonweal. Oct 20, 1939, v30, p587.
  The Film Criticism of Otis Ferguson. p270.
  Film Daily. Oct 12, 1939, p5.
  Films and Filming. Jul 1970, v16, p52-58.
  The Films of Alfred Hitchcock. p74-77.
  Graham Greene on Film. p222-23.
  Hitchcock: The First Forty-four Films. p55-56.
  Hitchcock's British Films. p248-55.
  Hollywood Reporter. May 22, 1939, p3.
  Hollywood Spectator. Oct 14, 1939, v14, p6-7.
  Motion Picture Herald. May 27, 1939, p30.
  National Board of Review Magazine. Oct 1939, v14, p12.
  The New Masses. Oct 17, 1939, v33, p29.
  The New Republic. Sep 6, 1939, v100, p132.
  The New Statesman and Nation. May 13, 1939, v17, p736.
  The New York Times. Oct 12, 1939, p33.
  The New Yorker. Oct 14, 1939, v15, p88-89.
  Rob Wagner's Script. Nov 11, 1939, v22, p18.
  Selected Film Criticism: Foreign Films, 1930-1950. p88-89.
  The Spectator. May 19, 1939, v162, p852.
  Theatre Arts. May 1939, v33, p39.
  Time. Oct 30, 1939, v34, p49.
  Variety. May 31, 1939, p14.

Jane Eyre (US; Cabanne, Christy; 1934)
  Film Daily. Jul 17, 1934, p6.
  Motion Picture Herald. Jul 14, 1934, p42-44.
  Variety. Feb 20, 1935, p15.

Jane Eyre (US; Stevenson, Robert; 1944)
  Agee on Film. v1, p76-77.
  Cinema: Novel into Film. p271-73.
  Commonweal. Oct 29, 1943, v39, p36-37.
  The English Novel and the Movies. p83-94.
  Film Daily. Feb 3, 1944, p14.
  The Films of Elizabeth Taylor. p42-44.
  The Films of the Forties. p106-08.

  Hollywood Motion Picture Review. Feb 7, 1944, v30, p6.
  Hollywood Reporter. Feb 2, 1944, p3.
  Journal of Popular Film. 1977, v6, n1, p13-31.
  Literature/Film Quarterly. Spr 1975, v3, p145-59.
  The London Times. Dec 24, 1943, p6.
  Magill's Survey of Cinema. Series I. v2, p860-62.
  Motion Picture Exhibitor. Feb 9, 1944, v31, n13, sec2, p1452.
  Motion Picture Herald Product Digest. Feb 5, 1944, p1741.
  The Nation. Feb 12, 1944, v158, p197.
  The New Republic. Mar 13, 1944, v110, p346.
  The New York Times. Feb 4, 1944, p12.
  The New York Times. Feb 13, 1944, sec2, p3.
  Newsweek. Feb 14, 1944, v23, p88.
  The Novel and the Cinema. p244-51.
  Orson Welles, Actor and Director. p39-42.
  Photoplay. Aug 1943, v23, p40-41+.
  Rob Wagner's Script. Feb 19, 1944, v30, p18.
  Saturday Review. Feb 19, 1944, v27, p14.
  Scholastic. Dec 13, 1943, v43, p27.
  Selected Film Criticism, 1941-1950. p91-92.
  Time. Feb 21, 1944, v43, p96.
  Variety. Feb 2, 1944, p18.

Janice Meredith (US; Hopper, E. Mason; 1924)
  Film Daily. Aug 10, 1924, p4.
  Magill's Survey of Cinema. Silent Films. v2, p597-600.
  Photoplay. Oct 1924, v26, p53.
  Selected Film Criticism, 1921-1930. p147-48.
  Variety. Oct 13, 1924, p19.
  W.C. Fields: A Life on Film. p20-22.

Janosik (CZECH; Fric, Marc; 1935)
  Cinema, the Magic Vehicle. v1, p240-41.
  Graham Greene on Film. p86-87.
  Motion Picture Herald. Dec 5, 1936, p46.
  National Board of Review Magazine. Feb 1937, v12, p15.
  The New Masses. Dec 29, 1936, v22, p29-30.
  The New York Times. Dec 25, 1936, p19.
  The Spectator. Jul 10, 1936, v157, p56.

The January Uprising in Kiev in 1918 *See* Arsenal

Jardinier, Le *See* Arroseur Arrose, L'

Jazz Comedya *See* A Russian Jazz Comedy

The Jazz Singer (US; Crosland, Alan; 1927)
  Close-Up. Feb 1929, v4, p37-38.
  Dictionary of Films. p164.
  Film Daily. Oct 23, 1927, p6.
  The Film Spectator. Feb 4, 1928, v4, p7-8.
  The Hollywood Musical. p21-22.
  Hollywood Musicals. p30-34.
  The International Dictionary of Films and Filmmakers. p221-22.
  The Jazz Singer. 1979.
  Landmark Films. p52-61.
  Magill's Survey of Cinema. Series I. v2, p866-69.
  The Moving Picture World. Oct 22, 1927, p514.
  The New York Times. Oct 7, 1927, p24.
  Selected Film Criticism, 1921-1930. p148-50.
  Spellbound in Darkness. p463-64.
  Variety. Oct 12, 1927, p16.
  Variety. Apr 1, 1931, p12.
  Variety. Dec 31, 1952, p6.

Jealous Husbands (US; Tourneur, Maurice; 1924)
  Film Daily. Feb 3, 1924, p9.

Jealousy (US; De Limur, Jean; 1929)
  Exhibitor's Herald-World. Oct 19, 1929, p45.
  Film Daily. Sep 15, 1929, p13.
  The New York Times. Sep 14, 1929, p17.
  Variety. Sep 18, 1929, p29.

Jealousy (US; Neill, Roy William; 1934)
Film Daily. Nov 23, 1934, p10.
Hollywood Reporter. Nov 24, 1934, p3.
Motion Picture Herald. Dec 15, 1934, p41.
Time. Dec 3, 1934, v24, p46.
Variety. Nov 27, 1934, p63.

Jeffries-Sharkey Fight (US; 1899)
Film Before Griffith. p50.
A Million and One Nights. p46.
Two Reels and a Crank. p27.

Jennie Gerhardt (US; Gering, Marion; 1933)
Film Daily. Jun 9, 1933, p4.
Hollywood Reporter. May 31, 1933, p3.
Motion Picture Herald. Jun 10, 1933, p36, 38.
New Outlook. July 1933, v162, p42.
The New York Times. Jun 9, 1933, p20.
The New Yorker. Jun 17, 1933, v9, p47-48.
Newsweek. Jun 17, 1933, v1, p30.
Rob Wagner's Script. Jun 24, 1933, v9, p8-9.
Time. Jun 19, 1933, v21, p32.
Variety. Jun 13, 1933, p15.

Jericho (Also titled: Dark Sands) (GB; Freeland,
   Thornton; 1937)
Black Images in American Films, 1896-1954. p130.
Film Daily. Jul 22, 1938, p7.
Motion Picture Herald. Sep 4, 1937, p40.
The New York Times. Aug 17, 1938, p23.
The New Yorker. Aug 6, 1938, v14, p41-42.
Variety. Sep 8, 1937, p18.

Jesse James (US; King, Henry; 1939)
American Classic Screen. 1981, n3, v5, p25.
Collier's. Nov 26, 1939, v102, p14+.
Commonweal. Jan 27, 1939, v29, p386.
Film Daily. Jan 13, 1939, p7.
Film Notes. p104-05.
The Filming of the West. p361-62.
The Films of Henry Fonda. p76-78.
The Films of Tyrone Power. p84-88.
The Fondas (Springer). p85-87.
The Great Western Pictures. p162-64.
Hollywood Reporter. Jan 10, 1939, p3.
Hollywood Spectator. Jan 21, 1939, v13, p8-9.
Life. Jan 30, 1939, v6, p40-43.
Magill's Survey of Cinema. Series II. v3, p1212-15.
Make It Again, Sam. p88-93.
The Making of the Great Westerns. p57-76.
Motion Picture Herald. Jan 14, 1939, p43.
The New York Times. Jan 14, 1939, p13.
The New Yorker. Jan 21, 1939, v14, p59.
Newsweek. Jan 23, 1939, v13, p25.
Scholastic. Jan 21, 1939, v33, p30-31.
Sight and Sound. Spr 1939, v8, p32.
Stage. Mar 15, 1939, v16, p7.
Talking Pictures. p180-83.
Those Fabulous Movie Years: The 30s. p176.
Time. Jan 23, 1939, v33, p26.
Variety. Jan 11, 1939, p12.

Jew Suss *See* Power

Jewel Robbery (US; Dieterle, William; 1932)
Film Daily. Jul 23, 1932, p8.
Motion Picture Herald. Jun 11, 1932, p30-31.
The New York Times. Jul 23, 1932, p6.
Rob Wagner's Script. Jul 30, 1932, v7, p8-9.
Time. Aug 1, 1932, v20, p23.
Variety. Jul 26, 1932, p17.

Jezebel (US; Wyler, William; 1938)
Bette Davis: Her Films and Career. p84-87.
Esquire. Jun 1938, v9, p89.
Film Comment. Fall 1970, v6, p18-24.

Film Daily. Mar 11, 1938, p6.
The Films of Henry Fonda. p66-69.
The Films of the Thirties. p204-07.
The Fondas (Springer). p76-78.
From Quasimodo to Scarlett O'Hara. p279-82.
Hollywood Reporter. Mar 8, 1938, p3.
Kiss Kiss Bang Bang. p361.
A Library of Film Criticism: American Film Directors. p510.
Life. Mar 28, 1938, v4, p44-46+.
Magill's Survey of Cinema. Series I. v2, p870-73.
Motion Picture Herald. Mar 12, 1938, p36.
The Nation. Mar 26, 1938, v146, p365.
National Board of Review Magazine. Apr 1938, v13, p13.
The New Statesman and Nation. Apr 23, 1938, v15, p688.
The New York Times. Mar 11, 1938, p15.
The New Yorker. Mar 19, 1938, v14, p57-58.
Newsweek. Mar 21, 1938, v11, p25.
Rob Wagner's Script. Mar 26, 1938, v19, p10.
The Tatler. Apr 27, 1938, v148, p152.
Those Fabulous Movie Years: The 30s. p138-39.
Time. Mar 28, 1938, v31, p33.
Variety. Mar 16, 1938, p15.
Warner Brothers Presents. p128, 133.
William Wyler: A Guide to References and Resources. p95-99.
William Wyler (Anderegg). p85-95.
World Film News. May-Jun 1938, v3, p89.
World Film News. Jul 1938, v3, p131.

Joan the Woman (US; DeMille, Cecil B.; 1917)
Fifty Great American Silent Films, 1912-1920. p66-68.
The Films of Cecil B. DeMille. p122-27.
Magill's Survey of Cinema. Silent Films. v2, p601-03.
The Moving Picture World. Jan 13, 1917, p239, 259, 859.
The New York Times. Dec 25, 1916, p7.
Photoplay. Mar 1917, v11, p113-16.
Selected Film Criticism, 1912-1920. p141-44.
Variety. Dec 29, 1916, p22.
Wid's Daily. Jan 4, 1917, p9.

Joe and Ethel Turp Call on the President (US; Sinclair,
   Robert B.; 1939)
Commonweal. Dec 22, 1939, v31, p206.
Film Daily. Dec 7, 1939, p7.
Hollywood Reporter. Nov 30, 1939, p3.
Hollywood Spectator. Dec 9, 1939, v14, p8.
Motion Picture Herald. Dec 9, 1939, p74.
The New York Times. Jan 4, 1940, p19.
The New Yorker. Jan 13, 1940, v15, p52.
Rob Wagner's Script. Jan 13, 1940, v23, p16-17.
Time. Jan 22, 1940, v35, p78.
Variety. Dec 6, 1939, p14.

Johanna Enlists (US; Taylor, William Desmond; 1918)
Exhibitor's Trade Review. Sep 14, 1918, p1261.
Motion Picture News. Sep 14, 1918, p1754, 1762.
The Moving Picture World. Sep 14, 1918, p1610.
The New York Times. Sep 16, 1918, p9.
Variety. Sep 13, 1918, p45.
Wid's Daily. Sep 8, 1918, p27-28.

John Barleycorn (US; Bosworth, Hobart; 1914)
The Moving Picture World. Jul 18, 1914, p406.
Selected Film Criticism, 1912-1920. p144-45.
Variety. Jul 17, 1914, p17.

John Meade's Woman (US; Wallace, Richard; 1937)
Canadian Magazine. Mar 1937, v87, p25.
Commonweal. Mar 19, 1937, v25, p584.
Film Daily. Feb 11, 1937, p11.
Garbo and the Night Watchman. p247.
Hollywood Reporter. Feb 9, 1937, p3.
Motion Picture Herald. Feb 20, 1937, p40.
The New York Times. Feb 18, 1937, p19.
The New Yorker. Feb 20, 1937, v13, p61.
Rob Wagner's Script. Mar 6, 1937, v17, p10-11.

Time. Feb 22, 1937, v29, p25.
Variety. Feb 24, 1937, p15.

Johnny Apollo (US; Hathaway, Henry; 1940)
Classics of the Gangster Film. p102-05.
Commonweal. Apr 26, 1940, v32, p20.
Film Daily. Apr 16, 1940, p5.
The Films of Tyrone Power. p102-05.
Hollywood Reporter. Apr 12, 1940, p3.
Motion Picture Herald. Feb 3, 1940, p37.
Motion Picture Herald. Apr 20, 1940, p34-35.
The New York Times. Apr 13, 1940, p21.
Variety. Apr 17, 1940, p13.

Johnny Eager (US; LeRoy, Mervyn; 1941)
Commonweal. Feb 27, 1942, v35, p463.
Film Daily. Dec 10, 1941, p6.
Film Noir. p147.
The Films of Lana Turner. p110-13.
The Films of Robert Taylor. p93-94.
Hollywood Reporter. Dec 10, 1941, p3.
The London Times. Apr 6, 1941, p8.
Magill's Survey of Cinema. Series II. v3, p1224-28.
Motion Picture Exhibitor. Dec 24, 1941, v27, n7, sec2, p912.
Motion Picture Herald Product Digest. Dec 13, 1941, p405.
The Nation. Mar 14, 1942, v154, p321.
The New York Times. Feb 20, 1942, p21.
The New York Times. Mar 1, 1942, sec8, p3.
Newsweek. Jan 26, 1942, v19, p66.
Photoplay. Mar 1942, v20, p6.
Time. Feb 23, 1942, v39, p86.
Variety. Dec 10, 1941, p8.

Jolly Fellows *See* A Russian Jazz Comedy

Jolson Sings Again (US; Levin, Henry; 1949)
Commonweal. Aug 26, 1949, v50, p490.
Film Daily. Aug 12, 1949, p6.
Hollywood Reporter. Aug 12, 1949, p3.
Motion Picture Herald Product Digest. May 7, 1949, p4597.
The New York Times. Aug 18, 1949, p16.
The New Yorker. Aug 27, 1949, v25, p37.
Newsweek. Aug 29, 1949, v34, p73.
Rotarian. Nov 1949, v75, p34.
Theatre Arts. Nov 1949, v33, p2+.
Time. Sep 5, 1949, v54, p62.
Variety. Aug 17, 1949, p8.

The Jolson Story (US; Green, Alfred E.; 1946)
Agee on Film. v1, p227.
Commonweal. Oct 25, 1946, v45, p46.
Film Daily. Sep 16, 1946, p6.
The Films of the Forties. p180-81.
Fortnight. Nov 4, 1946, v1, p42.
Halliwell's Hundred. p151-55.
The Hollywood Musical. p274.
Hollywood Musicals. p215.
Hollywood Reporter. Sep 16, 1946, p3.
Magill's Survey of Cinema. Series I. v2, p877-80.
Motion Picture Herald Product Digest. Sep 21, 1946, p3209.
The Nation. Nov 9, 1947, v163, p537.
The New York Times. Oct 11, 1946, p28.
The New York Times Magazine. Oct 13, 1946, p30-31.
The New Yorker. Oct 19, 1946, v22, p112+.
Newsweek. Oct 14, 1946, v28, p112.
One Good Film Deserves Another. p50-55.
Selected Film Criticism, 1941-1950. p97-99.
Theatre Arts. Nov 1946, v30, p669-70.
Time. Oct 7, 1946, v48, p101.
Variety. Sep 18, 1946, p16.

Josette (US; Dwan, Allan; 1938)
Commonweal. Jun 24, 1938, v28, p245.
Film Daily. Jun 11, 1938, p3.
Hollywood Reporter. May 27, 1938, p3.
Motion Picture Herald. Jun 4, 1938, p32.

The New York Times. Jun 11, 1938, p9.
Rob Wagner's Script. Jun 18, 1938, v19, p14.
Time. Jun 13, 1938, v31, p24.
Variety. Jun 1, 1938, p12.

Le Jour se Lève (Also titled: Daybreak) (FR; Carné, Marcel; 1938)
American Film Criticism. p391.
Commonweal. Aug 16, 1940, v32, p352.
Film. Sep-Oct 1959, v21, p12-15.
The Film and the Public. p136-39.
Film Daily. Aug 5, 1940, p8.
Films and Filming. Feb 1964, v10, p15-16.
Films in Review. Apr 1963, v14, p201.
The Great French Films. p88-92.
Hollywood Reporter. Jun 30, 1939, p6.
Magill's Survey of Cinema. Foreign Language Films. v4, p1589-94.
The New Masses. Aug 13, 1940, v36, p21-22.
The New York Times. Jul 30, 1940, p16.
Rob Wagner's Script. Sep 21, 1940, v24, p17.
Selected Film Criticism: Foreign Films, 1930-1950. p40-41.
Time. Aug 19, 1940, v36, p79.
Variety. Jul 26, 1939, p27.

Journey for Margaret (US; Van Dyke, W.S.; 1942)
Commonweal. Dec 25, 1942, v37, p256.
Film Daily. Oct 28, 1942, p5.
The Films of World War II. p89-91.
Hollywood Reporter. Oct 28, 1942, p3.
The London Times. Mar 8, 1943, p8.
Motion Picture Exhibitor. Nov 4, 1942, v28, n26, sec2, p1141.
Motion Picture Herald Product Digest. Mar 28, 1942, p573.
The New Republic. Jan 4, 1943, v108, p22.
The New York Times. Dec 18, 1942, p36.
Scholastic. Jan 11, 1943, v41, p37.
Time. Jan 11, 1943, v41, p89.
Variety. Oct 28, 1942, p8.

Journey Into Fear (US; Foster, Norman; 1942)
Commonweal. Oct 30, 1942, v37, p43.
Commonweal. Mar 12, 1943, v37, p520.
Film Daily. Aug 7, 1942, p8.
Hollywood Reporter. Aug 5, 1942, p4.
Motion Picture Herald Product Digest. Aug 8, 1940, p903.
The New York Times. Mar 19, 1943, p15.
Orson Welles (Leaming). p229-32+.
Scholastic. Apr 5, 1943, v42, p32.
Time. Feb 15, 1943, v41, p50+.
Variety. Aug 5, 1942, p27.

Journey's End (US; Whale, James; 1930)
Cinema. Jun 1930, v1, p38.
Commonweal. Apr 23, 1930, v11, p715.
A Critical History of the British Cinema. p81-82.
Exhibitors Herald-World. Apr 19, 1930, p48.
Film Daily. Apr 13, 1930, p10.
The Film Spectator. May 10, 1930, v9, p21-22.
Hollywood Spectator. Sep 26, 1931, v12, p8.
James Whale (Curtis). p36-39, 52-56.
Judge. May 3, 1930, v98, p23.
Life. May 2, 1930, v95, p20.
Literary Digest. May 3, 1930, v105, p18-19.
Magill's Survey of Cinema. Series II. v3, p1229-31.
The Nation. Apr 30, 1930, v130, p524-25.
National Board of Review Magazine. May-Jun 1930, v5, p11.
The New York Times. Mar 2, 1930, p6.
The New York Times. Mar 21, 1930, p30.
The New York Times. Mar 30, 1930, p6.
The New York Times. Apr 9, 1930, p25.
The New York Times. Apr 13, 1930, p4.
The New Yorker. Apr 19, 1930, v6, p52-53.
Outlook and Independent. Apr 23, 1930, v154, p670.
Saturday Review (London). Apr 26, 1930, v149, p520.
The Spectator. May 26, 1930, v144, p700.

Theatre Magazine. Apr 1930, v51, p31.
Theatre Magazine. Jul 1930, v52, p44.
Time. Apr 21, 1930, v15, p68.
Variety. Apr 16, 1930, p21.
Variety. Apr 30, 1930, p17.

The Joy of Living (US; Garnett, Tay; 1938)
Film Daily. Mar 22, 1938, p10.
Hollywood Reporter. Mar 18, 1938, p3.
Motion Picture Herald. Mar 26, 1938, p39.
The New York Times. May 6, 1938, p27.
The New Yorker. May 7, 1938, v14, p66.
Newsweek. Apr 4, 1938, v11, p24.
Rob Wagner's Script. Apr 16, 1938, v19, p8.
Stage. Mar 1938, v15, p29.
Stage. May 1938, v15, p26.
Time. Apr 11, 1938, v31, p24.
Variety. Mar 23, 1938, p16.
World Film News. Aug 1938, v3, p173-74.

The Joyless Street (German title: Freudlose Gasse, Die;
  Also titled: Streets of Sorrow) (GER; Pabst, G.W.;
  1925)
BFI/Monthly Film Bulletin. Jan 1975, v42, p19-20.
Cinema, the Magic Vehicle. v1, p116.
From Caligari to Hitler. p167-70, 172-73.
G.W. Pabst (Atwell). p29-36.
The Haunted Screen. p256-60.
Magill's Survey of Cinema. Silent Films. v2, p604-07.
The New York Times. Jul 6, 1927, p23.
Spellbound in Darkness. p383.
Variety. Jul 6, 1927, p22.

Juarez (US; Dieterle, William; 1939)
Bette Davis: Her Films and Career. p94-95.
Commonweal. May 12, 1939, v30, p77.
The Film Criticism of Otis Ferguson. p254.
Film Daily. Apr 26, 1939, p7.
The Films of John Garfield. p61-64.
From Quasimodo to Scarlett O'Hara. p305-08.
Graham Greene on Film. p254-55.
Hollywood Reporter. Apr 26, 1939, p3.
Hollywood Spectator. May 13, 1939, v14, p8-9.
Magill's Survey of Cinema. Series II. v3, p1232-35.
Motion Picture Herald. Apr 29, 1939, p51.
The Nation. May 6, 1939, v148, p539-40.
National Board of Review Magazine. May 1939, v14, p14.
The New Masses. May 9, 1939, v31, p27-28.
The New Masses. May 23, 1939, v31, p28-29.
The New Republic. May 10, 1939, v99, p20.
The New Statesman and Nation. Nov 25, 1939, v18, p756.
The New York Times. Apr 26, 1939, p27.
The New Yorker. Apr 29, 1939, v15, p94-95.
Newsweek. May 8, 1939, v13, p22-23.
North American Review. Jun 1939, v247, p379-81.
Paul Muni: His Life and His Films. p172-77.
Photoplay. May 1939, v53, p22-23+.
Photoplay. Jul 1939, v53, p62.
Rob Wagner's Script. May 20, 1939, v21, p16-17.
Scholastic. May 13, 1939, v34, p33.
Sight and Sound. Sum 1939, v8, p74-75.
The Spectator. Nov 24, 1939, v163, p744.
Time. May 8, 1939, v33, p66.
Variety. Apr 26, 1939, p12.

Judas Was a Woman *See* Bête Humaine, La

Judge Hardy and Son (US; Seitz, George B.; 1939)
Film Daily. Dec 15, 1939, p4.
Hollywood Reporter. Dec 12, 1939, p3.
Motion Picture Herald. Dec 16, 1939, p25.
The New York Times. Jan 18, 1940, p27.
Photoplay. Jan 1940, v54, p59.
Rob Wagner's Script. Dec 16, 1939, v22, p17.
Variety. Dec 13, 1939, p11.

Judge Priest (US; Ford, John; 1934)
Film Daily. Aug 13, 1934, p4.
Hollywood Reporter. Aug 4, 1934, p3.
Life. Dec 1934, v101, p53-54.
Literary Digest. Oct 27, 1934, v118, p34.
Magill's Survey of Cinema. Series II. v3, p1236-38.
Motion Picture Herald. Aug 11, 1934, p31.
The New York Times. Oct 12, 1934, p33.
The Non-Western Films of John Ford. p23-28.
Rob Wagner's Script. Sep 29, 1934, v12, p8.
Selected Film Criticism, 1931-1940. p131.
Time. Sep 24, 1934, v24, p34.
Variety. Oct 16, 1934, p12.
Will Rogers in Hollywood. p145-52+.

Judith of Bethulia (US; Griffith, D.W.; 1914)
BFI/Monthly Film Bulletin. Apr 1979, v46, p81-82.
The Films of D.W. Griffith. p26-30.
The First Twenty Years. p163.
Magill's Survey of Cinema. Silent Films. v2, p608-15.
The Moving Picture World. Mar 7, 1914, p1242.
The Moving Picture World. Jun 13, 1914, p1608.
The New York Dramatic Mirror. Mar 18, 1914, p34.
Selected Film Criticism, 1912-1920. p146-48.
Variety. Mar 27, 1914, p20.

The Juggernaut (US; Ince, Ralph; 1915)
Motion Picture News. Mar 27, 1915, p59.
Motography. Apr 17, 1915, p611.
Motography. May 8, 1915, p745-46, 766.
The Moving Picture World. Mar 20, 1915, p1771.
The Moving Picture World. May 1, 1915, p810.
The New York Dramatic Mirror. Mar 17, 1915, p28.
Selected Film Criticism, 1912-1920. p49-50.
Variety. Mar 12, 1915, p23.

Julius Caesar (US; Griffith, D.W.; 1908)
The Moving Picture World. Dec 5, 1908, p448.
Selected Film Criticism, 1896-1911. p53.

July 14th *See* Quatorze Juillet

June Moon (US; Sutherland, Edward; 1931)
Film Daily. Mar 15, 1931, p10.
Judge. Apr 4, 1931, v100, p18.
Life. Apr 3, 1931, v97, p21.
Motion Picture Herald. Feb 28, 1931, p49.
The New York Times. Mar 14, 1931, p23.
The New York Times. Mar 22, 1931, p5.
Pictures Will Talk. p38.
Time. Mar 23, 1931, v17, p46.
Variety. Mar 18, 1931, p24.

The Jungle (US; Thomas, Augustus; Irving, George
  Henry; Pratt, John H.; 1914)
The Moving Picture World. Jun 20, 1914, p1675.
The Moving Picture World. Jun 13, 1914, p1553.
The New York Dramatic World. Apr 15, 1914, p35.
The New York Dramatic World. Jun 10, 1914, p34.
Selected Film Criticism, 1912-1920. p150-51.
Variety. Jun 26, 1914, p19.

Jungle Book (GB; Korda, Zoltan; 1942)
Commonweal. Apr 17, 1942, v35, p649.
Film Daily. Mar 25, 1942, p6.
The Great Adventure Films. p116-19.
Hollywood Reporter. Mar 25, 1942, p3.
Life. Mar 16, 1942, v12, p76-78.
The London Times. Jun 4, 1942, p6.
Magic Moments from the Movies. p112-13.
Motion Picture Exhibitor. Apr 8, 1942, p985.
The Nation. May 9, 1943, v154, p553.
The New York Times. Apr 6, 1942, p19.
Newsweek. Apr 6, 1942, v19, p64.
Photoplay. Jun 1942, v21, p6.
Scholastic. Jan 5, 1942, v39, p17-19+.

Time. Apr 13, 1942, v39, p92.
Variety. Mar 25, 1942, p8.

The Jungle Princess (US; Thiele, William; 1936)
Chestnuts in Her Lap. p21-22.
Film Daily. Nov 20, 1936, p9.
Graham Greene on Film. p126-27.
Hollywood Reporter. Nov 17, 1936, p3.
Hollywood Spectator. Dec 5, 1936, v11, p11.
Motion Picture Herald. Nov 28, 1936, p66, 68.
The New York Times. Dec 24, 1936, p21.
Rob Wagner's Script. Dec 19, 1936, v16, p10.
The Spectator. Jan 1, 1937, v158, p15.
Variety. Dec 30, 1936, p11.

Juno and the Paycock (GB; Hitchcock, Alfred; 1930)
The Art of Alfred Hitchcock. p26.
Exhibitors Herald-World. Jul 25, 1930, p35.
Film Daily. Jun 29, 1930, p11.
Hitchcock (Truffaut). p69, 212+.
Hitchcock's British Films. p116-22.
Judge. Jul 26, 1930, v99, p23.
The New York Times. Jun 30, 1930, p22.
The New York Times. Jul 6, 1930, p3.
The Spectator. Mar 8, 1930, v144, p363.
Variety. Jan 22, 1930, p80.

Just Around the Corner (US; Cummings, Irving; 1938)
Film Daily. Nov 2, 1938, p4.
The Films of Shirley Temple. p198-201.
Hollywood Reporter. Oct 29, 1938, p3.
Hollywood Spectator. Nov 12, 1938, v13, p11-12.
Motion Picture Herald. Nov 5, 1938, p36, 38.
The New York Times. Dec 3, 1938, p11.
The New Yorker. Dec 10, 1938, v14, p96-97.
Rob Wagner's Script. Nov 5, 1938, v20, p14-15.
Time. Nov 21, 1938, v32, p53.
Variety. Nov 2, 1938, p15.

Just Imagine (US; Butler, David; 1930)
Exhibitors Herald-World. Oct 18, 1930, p44.
Exhibitors Herald-World. Nov 29, 1930, p33.
Film Daily. Oct 19, 1930, p10.
Life. Dec 12, 1930, v96, p20.
The New York Times. Nov 18, 1930, p6.
The New York Times. Nov 22, 1930, p21.
The New York Times. Nov 30, 1930, p5.
Outlook and Independent. Dec 3, 1930, v156, p552.
Science Fiction Studies in Film. p51-57.
Time. Dec 8, 1930, v16, p42.
Variety. Nov 26, 1930, p18.

Just Pals (US; Ford, John; 1920)
Motion Picture News. Nov 27, 1920, p4163.
The Moving Picture World. Nov 27, 1920, p571.
Selected Film Criticism, 1912-1920. p151-52.
Wid's Daily. Nov 21, 1920, p15.

Kabinett des Doktors Caligari, Das *See* The Cabinet of
Dr. Caligari

The Kaiser, the Beast of Berlin (Also titled: The Kaiser;
the Beast of Berlin) (US; Julian, Rupert; 1918)
Exhibitor's Trade Review. Mar 23, 1918, p1303, 1307.
Magill's Survey of Cinema. Silent Films. v2, p616-18.
Motion Picture News. Mar 23, 1918, p1721, 1767-68.
The Moving Picture World. Mar 23, 1918, p1704.
The Moving Picture World. Apr 20, 1918, p438.
The New York Dramatic Mirror. Mar 23, 1918, p23.
The New York Times. Mar 10, 1918, p33.
Photoplay. Jun 1918, v14, p94.
Selected Film Criticism, 1912-1920. p152-53.
Variety. Mar 15, 1918, p45.
Wid's Daily. Mar 14, 1918, p1004-05.

Kameradschaft (Also titled: Comradeship) (GER; Pabst,
G.W.; 1931)
BFI/Monthly Film Bulletin. Mar 1978, v45, p57.
Cinema, the Magic Vehicle. v1, p182-83.
Close-Up. Mar 1932, v9, p3-9.
Commonweal. Jul 7, 1939, v30, p278.
Dictionary of Films. p172-73.
The Film and the Public. p123-26.
Film Daily. Nov 10, 1932, p6.
Films and Filming. Apr 1967, v13, p21.
From Caligari to Hitler. p239-42.
The German Cinema. p60-62.
G.W. Pabst (Atwell). p96-103.
The Haunted Screen. p314.
The Hollywood Spectator. Jan 14, 1933, v7, p1-2.
Hound and Horn: Essays on Cinema. p301-03.
The International Dictionary of Films and Filmmakers. v1,
p234-35.
The International Photographer. Feb 1933, v5, p30-31.
Kiss Kiss Bang Bang. p362.
London Mercury. May 1932, v26, p78.
Motion Picture Herald. Dec 10, 1932, p50.
The Nation. Nov 23, 1932, v135, p513-14.
National Board of Review Magazine. Dec 1932, v7, p8.
The New Republic. Jul 19, 1939, v99, p307.
The New Statesman and Nation. Mar 5, 1932, v3, p295-96.
The New York Times. Dec 27, 1931, p7.
The New York Times. Nov 9, 1932, p28.
Scrutiny of Cinema. p38-41.
Selected Film Criticism: Foreign Films, 1930-1950. p35.
Sight and Sound. Nov 1950, v19, p298-99.
The Spectator. Mar 12, 1932, v148, p365.
Time. Nov 21, 1932, v20, p28, 30.
Variety. Nov 15, 1932, p19.

Kampf, Der (Also titled: The Struggle) (USSR;
Wangenheim, Gustav; 1936)
Film Daily. Sep 11, 1936, p15.
Motion Picture Herald. Sep 19, 1936, p50.
The New Masses. Sep 22, 1936, v20, p29.
New Theatre. Oct 1936, v3, p16-17, 25.
The New York Times. Sep 11, 1936, p29.
The New Yorker. Sep 19, 1936, v12, p78.
Variety. Sep 16, 1936, p16.

Karamazov (German title: Mörder Dimitri Karamasoff,
Der; Also titled: The Brothers Karamazov; The
Murder of Karamazov) (GER; Ozep, Fedor; 1931)
Film Daily. Sep 27, 1931, p9.
From Caligari to Hitler. p251-53.
Hollywood Reporter. Nov 25, 1931, p3.
Judge. Oct 17, 1931, v101, p18.
Motion Picture Herald. Oct 10, 1931, p46.
The New York Times. Sep 21, 1931, p20.
The New Yorker. Sep 26, 1931, v7, p57.
Outlook and Independent. Sep 30, 1931, v159, p153.
Rob Wagner's Script. May 2, 1931, v5, p13-14.
Time. Sep 28, 1931, v18, p32.
Variety. Sep 22, 1931, p26.

Katia (FR; Tourneur, Maurice; 1938)
Film Daily. Jan 2, 1940, p11.
Graham Greene on Film. p201, 203.
London Mercury. Dec 1938, v39, p203-04.
Motion Picture Herald. Dec 2, 1939, p44.
The New York Times. Dec 23, 1939, p9.
The New Yorker. Dec 23, 1939, v15, p53.
Photoplay. Dec 1939, v53, p90.
The Spectator. Nov 4, 1938, v161, p767.
Time. Jan 15, 1940, v35, p63.
Variety. Nov 16, 1938, p15.

Keeper of the Flame (US; Cukor, George; 1942)
Commonweal. Apr 2, 1943, v37, p590.
Film Daily. Dec 21, 1942, p7.

The Films of Katharine Hepburn. p110-13.
The Films of Spencer Tracy. p178-79.
George Cukor. p75-78.
George Cukor (Phillips). p75-78.
Hollywood Reporter. Dec 16, 1942, p3.
The London Times. Apr 15, 1943, p2.
Motion Picture Exhibitor. Dec 16, 1942, v29, n6, sec2, p1174.
Motion Picture Herald Product Digest. Dec 19, 1942, p1065.
The New York Times. Mar 19, 1943, p15.
Newsweek. Mar 22, 1943, v21, p80-81.
Saturday Review. Feb 27, 1943, v26, p19.
Time. Jan 25, 1943, v41, p86+.
Variety. Dec 16, 1942, p16.

The Kennel Murder Case (US; Curtiz, Michael; 1933)
The Detective in Film. p38.
Film Daily. Oct 28, 1933, p5.
Hollywood Reporter. Oct 2, 1933, p3.
Motion Picture Herald. Nov 4, 1933, p38-39.
The New York Times. Oct 30, 1933, p14.
The New Yorker. Nov 4, 1933, v9, p59.
Rob Wagner's Script. Oct 28, 1933, v10, p10-11.
The Spectator. Feb 23, 1934, v152, p271.
Variety. Oct 31, 1933, p17.

Kentucky (US; Butler, David; 1938)
Commonweal. Jan 27, 1939, v29, p86.
Film Daily. Dec 20, 1938, p8.
Graham Greene on Film. p210.
Hollywood Reporter. Dec 15, 1938, p3.
Hollywood Spectator. Dec 24, 1938, v13, p12-13.
Motion Picture Herald. Dec 24, 1938, p37, 40.
The New Statesman and Nation. Feb 25, 1939, v17, p281.
The New York Times. Dec 24, 1938, p12.
The New Yorker. Dec 31, 1938, v14, p49.
Newsweek. Jan 2, 1939, v13, p25.
Rob Wagner's Script. Jan 7, 1939, v20, p16.
Saint Nicholas. Jan 1939, v66, p35+.
Scholastic. Jan 7, 1939, v33, p32.
The Spectator. Mar 3, 1939, v162, p349.
Time. Jan 2, 1939, v33, p17.
Variety. Dec 21, 1938, p14.

Kentucky Kernals (US; Stevens, George; 1934)
Film Daily. Nov 22, 1934, p8.
Hollywood Reporter. Oct 8, 1934, p3.
Motion Picture Herald. Sep 1, 1934, p43.
Motion Picture Herald. Oct 27, 1934, p41.
The New York Times. Jan 1, 1935, p20.
Variety. Jan 8, 1935, p18.

Kermesse Héroïque, La *See* Carnival in Flanders

The Kerry Gow (US; Olcott, Sidney; 1912)
Magill's Survey of Cinema. Silent Films. v2, p619-21.
The New York Dramatic Mirror. Nov 27, 1912, p28.
Selected Film Criticism, 1912-1920. p154.

The Keyhole (US; Curtiz, Michael; 1933)
Film Daily. Mar 31, 1933, p6.
Hollywood Reporter. Feb 25, 1933, p3.
Motion Picture Herald. Apr 8, 1933, p23.
The New York Times. Mar 31, 1933, p23.
Newsweek. Apr 8, 1933, v1, p26.
Rob Wagner's Script. Apr 8, 1933, v9, p10.
Time. Apr 10, 1933, v21, p27.
Variety. Apr 4, 1933, p15.

The Keys of the Kingdom (US; Stahl, John M.; 1944)
Agee on Film. v1, p134-35.
Around Cinemas. p246-48.
Catholic World. Feb 1945, v160, p454.
Commonweal. Jan 5, 1945, v41, p303-04.
Film Daily. Dec 15, 1944, p11.
The Films of Gregory Peck. p35-40.
Hollywood Reporter. Dec 13, 1944, p3.

Life. Jan 15, 1945, v18, p60-62.
The London Times. Mar 1, 1945, p7.
Magill's Survey of Cinema. Series II. v3, p1251-53.
Motion Picture Exhibitor. Dec 27, 1944, v33, n8, sec2, p1640.
Motion Picture Herald Product Digest. Dec 16, 1944, p2226.
The Nation. Jan 6, 1945, v160, p24-25.
New Movies. Jan-Feb 1945, v20, p5-6.
The New Republic. Jan 15, 1945, v112, p86.
The New York Times. Dec 30, 1944, p15.
The New Yorker. Dec 30, 1944, v20, p39.
Newsweek. Jan 8, 1945, v25, p86.
Scholastic. Feb 5, 1945, v46, p36.
Selected Film Criticism, 1941-1950. p101-03.
Time. Jan 1, 1945, v45, p40.
Variety. Dec 13, 1944, p8.

Kick In (US; Wallace, Richard; 1931)
Film Daily. May 24, 1931, p10.
Hollywood Reporter. Apr 20, 1931, p3.
Hollywood Spectator. Jun 20, 1931, v12, p9.
Life. Jun 19, 1931, v97, p19.
Motion Picture Herald. Apr 25, 1931, p37.
The New York Times. May 25, 1931, p17.
Variety. May 27, 1931, p56.

The Kid (US; Chaplin, Charles; 1921)
BFI/Monthly Film Bulletin. Mar 1975, v42, p111-12.
Charles Chaplin: A Guide to References and Resources. p69.
Cinema, the Magic Vehicle. v1, p67-68.
The Comic Mind. p92-95.
Exceptional Photoplays. Jan-Feb 1921, v3, p2, 6, 7.
Fifty Great American Silent Films, 1912-1920. p139-40.
Film Daily. Jan 16, 1921, p5.
The Films of Charlie Chaplin. p163-67.
From Quasimodo to Scarlett O'Hara. p9-12.
The International Dictionary of Films and Filmmakers. v1,
    p237-38.
Magill's Survey of Cinema. Silent Films. v2, p622-24.
The New Republic. Aug 23, 1922, v31, p358-59.
The New York Times. Jan 22, 1921, p9.
Selected Film Criticism, 1921-1930. p152-54.
The Silent Films. p170-78, 184-85.
Spellbound in Darkness. p263-68.
Variety. Jan 21, 1921, p40.

Kid Boots (US; Tuttle, Frank; 1926)
The Moving Picture World. Oct 26, 1926, p500.
The New York Times. Oct 11, 1926, p18.
Variety. Oct 13, 1926, p16.

The Kid Brother (US; Wilde, Ted; 1927)
The Comic Mind. p153-54.
Film Daily. Jan 30, 1927, p6.
The Films of the Twenties. p160-63.
Harold Lloyd. p92-99.
Harold Lloyd: The Shape of Laughter. p190-91.
Magill's Survey of Cinema. Silent Films. v2, p625-27.
The Moving Picture World. Jan 29, 1927, p369.
The New York Times. Jan 24, 1927, p14.
Photoplay. Mar 1927, v31, p52.
Selected Film Criticism, 1921-1930. p155.
The Silent Clowns. p206-08.
Variety. Jan 26, 1927, p20.

The Kid from Brooklyn (US; McLeod, Norman Z.; 1946)
Agee on Film. v1, p202.
Commonweal. Apr 19, 1946, v44, p15.
Film Daily. Mar 21, 1946, p8.
The Hollywood Musical. p183.
Hollywood Musicals. p269.
Hollywood Reporter. Mar 20, 1946, p3.
Life. May 6, 1946, v20, p71-74.
Motion Picture Herald Product Digest. Mar 30, 1946, p2918.
The Nation. May 25, 1946, v162, p636.
The New York Times. Apr 19, 1946, p25.
The New Yorker. Apr 20, 1946, v22, p85.

Newsweek. Apr 22, 1946, v27, p96+.
Samuel Goldwyn Presents. p242-45.
Theatre Arts. May 1946, v30, p276.
Time. Apr 22, 1946, v47, p98+.
Variety. Mar 20, 1946, p8.

The Kid from Spain (US; McCarey, Leo; 1932)
Around Cinemas. p82.
The Busby Berkeley Book. p46-49.
Film Daily. Nov 19, 1932, p4.
Hollywood Reporter. Oct 20, 1932, p3.
Motion Picture Herald. Nov 5, 1932, p42.
Movie Classic. Dec 1932, v3, p38-39.
The Nation. Dec 7, 1932, v135, p576.
The New Statesman and Nation. Mar 25, 1933, v5, p387.
The New York Times. Nov 18, 1932, p23.
The New Yorker. Nov 26, 1932, v8, p51.
Rob Wagner's Script. Dec 3, 1932, v8, p8.
Samuel Goldwyn Presents. p121-24.
The Spectator. Mar 24, 1933, v150, p425.
Time. Nov 28, 1932, v20, p21.
Variety. Nov 22, 1932, p16.

Kid Galahad (US; Curtiz, Michael; 1937)
Bette Davis: Her Films and Career. p78-79.
Casablanca and Other Major Films of Michael Curtiz. p113-15.
The Cinema of Edward G. Robinson. p109-11.
Classics of the Gangster Film. p46-50.
The Complete Films of Humphrey Bogart. p44-45.
Dark Cinema. p139.
The Film Criticism of Otis Ferguson. p181-82.
Film Daily. May 4, 1937, p8.
The Gangster Film. p110-12.
The Great Gangster Pictures. p221-22.
Hollywood Reporter. Apr 29, 1937, p3.
Hollywood Spectator. May 8, 1937, v12, p7-8.
Humphrey Bogart: The Man and His Films. p68-70.
Life. May 24, 1937, v2, p45-47.
Literary Digest. May 15, 1937, v123, p20.
Motion Picture Herald. May 8, 1937, p42.
The New Masses. Jun 22, 1937, v23, p29.
The New Republic. Jun 16, 1937, v91, p159.
The New Statesman and Nation. Jul 3, 1937, v14, p15.
The New York Times. May 27, 1937, p21.
The New Yorker. May 29, 1937, v13, p57-58.
Newsweek. May 29, 1937, v9, p24.
Rob Wagner's Script. Jun 5, 1937, v17, p8-9.
The Spectator. Jul 9, 1937, v159, p60.
Time. May 31, 1937, v29, p29.
Variety. Jun 2, 1937, p15.
Warner Brothers Presents. p234.

Kid Millions (US; Del Ruth, Roy; 1934)
Film Daily. Oct 17, 1934, p3.
The Hollywood Musical. p96.
Hollywood Reporter. Oct 27, 1934, p40.
Motion Picture. Oct 27, 1934, p40.
The New York Times. Nov 12, 1934, p17.
Samuel Goldwyn Presents. p141-44.
Time. Nov 19, 1934, v24, p26.
Variety. Nov 13, 1934, p15.

Kid Nightingale (US; Amy, George; 1939)
Commonweal. Dec 1, 1939, v31, p137.
Film Daily. Dec 11, 1939, p8.
Hollywood Reporter. Sep 14, 1939, p4.
Hollywood Spectator. Sep 30, 1939, v14, p9.
Motion Picture Herald. Sep 23, 1939, p48.
The New York Times. Dec 8, 1939, p33.
Photoplay. Dec 1939, v53, p63.
Rob Wagner's Script. Oct 21, 1939, v22, p17.
Variety. Nov 22, 1939, p16.

Kidnapped (US; Werker, Alfred L.; 1938)
Child Life. Jul 1938, v17, p327+.
Commonweal. Jun 17, 1938, v28, p217.
Esquire. Aug 1938, v10, p82.
Film Daily. May 28, 1938, p3.
Graham Greene on Film. p197.
Hollywood Reporter. May 18, 1938, p3.
Motion Picture Herald. May 21, 1938, p30.
The New York Times. May 28, 1938, p9.
The New Yorker. Jun 4, 1938, v14, p49-50.
Newsweek. Jun 6, 1938, v11, p23.
Rob Wagner's Script. May 28, 1938, v19, p8-9.
Saint Nicholas. Jun 1938, v65, p46-47.
The Spectator. Aug 5, 1938, v161, p232.
Time. Jun 6, 1938, v31, p40.
Variety. May 25, 1938, p12.
World Film News. Sep 1938, v3, p220.

Kiki (US; Taylor, Sam; 1931)
Film Daily. Mar 8, 1931, p10.
Judge. Apr 18, 1931, v100, p20.
Motion Picture Herald. Feb 21, 1931, p46.
The New York Times. Mar 6, 1931, p16.
The New Yorker. Mar 14, 1931, v7, p77.
Outlook and Independent. Mar 18, 1931, v157, p412.
Time. Mar 16, 1931, v17, p63.
Variety. Mar 11, 1931, p14.

The Killers (US; Siodmak, Robert; 1946)
American Film Genres. p43-46.
BFI/Monthly Film Bulletin. Oct 1981, v48, p208.
Burt Lancaster: A Pictorial Treasury of His Films. p30-31.
Cinema, the Magic Vehicle. v1, p432-33.
Dictionary of Films. p176.
Dreams and Dead Ends. p83-114.
Film Daily. Aug 12, 1946, p6.
Hemingway and the Movies. p173-205.
Hemingway on Film. p66-88.
Hollywood Genres. p140-42.
Hollywood Reporter. Aug 7, 1946, p3.
The International Dictionary of Films and Filmmakers. v1, p238-39.
Life. Sep 2, 1946, v21, p59-61.
Magill's Survey of Cinema. Series I. v3, p1254-56.
Motion Picture Herald Product Digest. Aug 17, 1946, p3150.
The Nation. Sep 14, 1946, v163, p305.
The New Republic. Sep 30, 1946, v115, p415.
The New York Times. Aug 29, 1946, p24.
The New Yorker. Sep 7, 1946, v22, p49.
Newsweek. Sep 9, 1946, v28, p106.
Rob Wagner's Script. Sep 28, 1946, v32, p13.
Selected Film Criticism, 1941-1950. p103.
Take One. Nov 1974, v4, p17-19.
Theatre Arts. Oct 1946, v30, p603.
Time. Sep 9, 1946, v48, p100.
Variety. Aug 7, 1946, p15.

Kimiko (Japanese title: Tsuma Yo Bara no Yoni; Also titled: Wife, Be Like a Rose) (JAPAN; Naruse, Mikio; 1935)
Asia. Jun 1937, v37, p463.
Cinema, the Magic Vehicle. v1, p245-46.
Film Daily. Apr 16, 1937, p10.
Hollywood Reporter. Apr 21, 1937, p7.
Literary Digest. Apr 10, 1937, v123, p28.
Motion Picture Herald. Apr 24, 1937, p43.
The Nation. Apr 10, 1937, v144, p419.
National Board of Review Magazine. Apr 1937, v12, p16.
The New York Times. Apr 13, 1937, p31.
The New Yorker. Apr 10, 1937, v13, p69-70.
Time. Apr 26, 1937, v29, p42.
Variety. Apr 14, 1937, p12.
World Film News. Jun 1937, v2, p23.

Kind Hearts and Coronets (GB; Hamer, Robert; 1949)
Commonweal. Jun 30, 1950, v52, p296.
Fifty Classic British Films. p73-75.
Film Daily. May 4, 1950, p7.
Films and Filming. Apr 1964, v10, p17-21.
Films in Review. Sep 1950, v1, p32-34.
The Great British Films. p131-33.
Hollywood Reporter. May 1, 1950, p3.
Kind Hearts and Coronets.
Life. Jun 19, 1950, v28, p79-80+.
Magill's Survey of Cinema. Series I. v2, p889-93.
Motion Picture Herald Product Digest. May 6, 1950, p285.
The New Republic. Jun 26, 1949, v122, p22.
The New Yorker. Jun 17, 1950, v26, p55.
Newsweek. Jul 3, 1950, v36, p68.
Rotarian. Jan 1951, v78, p39.
Saturday Review. Jul 15, 1950, v33, p30-32.
Sequence. Aut 1949, n9, p130-31.
Seventy Years of Cinema. p169.
Time. Nov 20, 1950, v56, p106+.
Variety. Jun 29, 1949, p20.

The King and the Chorus Girl (US; LeRoy, Mervyn; 1937)
Film Daily. Feb 25, 1937, p10.
Hollywood Reporter. Feb 22, 1937, p3.
Hollywood Spectator. Feb 27, 1937, v11, p8-9.
Life. Mar 27, 1937, v2, p24-25.
Literary Digest. Mar 27, 1937, v123, p21.
Motion Picture Herald. Mar 6, 1937, p44.
The New York Times. Mar 29, 1937, p14.
The New Yorker. Apr 3, 1937, v13, p72.
Newsweek. Mar 20, 1937, v9, p21.
Rob Wagner's Script. Apr 3, 1937, v17, p8.
Time. Apr 5, 1937, v29, p54-55.
Variety. Mar 31, 1937, p17.

King Kong (US; Cooper, Merian C.; Schoedsack, Ernest B.; 1933)
American Cinematographer. Jan 1977, v58, p60-67.
American Cinematographer. Aug 1983, v69, p48-53.
American Film. Mar 1977, v2, p71-72.
American Film. Dec 1976-Jan 1977, v2, p14-23.
American Film Criticism. p279-82.
American Image. 1977, v34, p1-11.
Ape: The Kingdom of Kong.
Around Cinemas. p87-90.
Beyond Formula: American Film Genres. p129-32.
Cinema of the Fantastic. p49-74.
Classic Movie Monsters. p282-315.
Classic Movies. p78-79.
Classics of the Horror Film. p97-103.
Commonweal. Aug 18, 1933, v18, p388.
A Companion to the Movies. p34-35.
Esquire. Sep 1971, v76, p146-49.
Film Daily. Feb 25, 1933, p4.
Film Daily. Jun 14, 1933, p6.
Films and Filming. Jan 1975, v21, p44-50.
Films Illustrated. Feb 1977, v6, p222-25.
Films Illustrated. Jan 1974, v3, p278.
Films in Review. Jan 1975, v26, p61.
Films in Review. Jan 1966, v17, p26-27.
The Films of the Thirties. p102-03.
Frames of Reference. p94-99.
Garbo and the Night Watchman. p234-35.
The Great Films. p92-97.
Great Horror Movies. p27-30.
Hal in the Classroom: Science Fiction Films. p103-12.
Halliwell's Hundred. p160-63.
Hi Fidelity. Oct 1975, v25, p97-98.
Hi Fidelity. Jul 1977, v27, p124+.
Hollywood Reporter. Feb 16, 1933, p3.
Horror Movies (Clarens). p117-20.

The International Dictionary of Films and Filmmakers. v1, p240-41.
Jump Cut. Nov-Dec 1974, n4, p11-12.
Jump Cut. Mar-Apr 1975, n6, p8-10.
London Mercury. Jun 1933, v28, p166-67.
The Making of King Kong: The Story Behind a Film Classic.
Monsters from the Movies. p122-25.
Motion Picture Herald. Feb 18, 1933, p27.
Motion Picture Herald. Feb 25, 1933, p37, 40.
Motion Picture Herald. Jun 24, 1933, p43.
Movie Classic. May 1933, v4, p42-43+.
Movie Maker. Mar 1977, v11, p184-85.
The Nation. Mar 22, 1933, v136, p326.
New Outlook. Apr 1933, v161, p47.
New Outlook. Jul 1933, v162, p43.
The New York Times. Mar 3, 1933, p12.
The New York Times. Mar 5, 1933, p3.
The New York Times. Jan 22, 1933, p4.
The New York Times. Mar 12, 1933, p3.
The New York Times. Sep 21, 1969, p17.
The New York Times. Jun 14, 1933, p22.
The New Yorker. Jun 24, 1933, v9, p54.
Newsweek. Mar 11, 1933, v1, p27.
Newsweek. Jun 24, 1933, v1, p30.
Photoplay. Apr 1933, v43, p30.
Photoplay. May 1933, v43, p46.
Quarterly Review of Film Studies. Nov 1976, v1, p373-87.
Rolling Stone. Feb 24, 1977, n233, p38-44.
Science Fiction Studies in Film. p62-68.
Selected Film Criticism, 1931-1940. p132.
Surrealism and American Feature Films. p59-80.
Take One. 1977, v5, p23.
Those Fabulous Movie Years: The 30s. p30-31.
Time. July 14, 1952, v60, p92.
Time. Jun 26, 1933, v21, p40.
Time. Mar 13, 1933, v21, p32.
Variety. Mar 7, 1933, p14.
Variety. Jun 20, 1933, p11.
Variety. Jan 19, 1977, p57.
We're in the Money. p69-74.
50 Classic Motion Pictures. p170-75.

King of Alcatraz (US; Florey, Robert; 1938)
Film Daily. Oct 12, 1938, p7.
The Great Gangster Pictures. p226-27.
Hollywood Reporter. Sep 28, 1938, p3.
Motion Picture Herald. Oct 1, 1938, p39, 42.
The New York Times. Oct 7, 1938, p21.
Rob Wagner's Script. Oct 15, 1938, v20, p13.
Time. Oct 17, 1938, v32, p32.
Variety. Oct 5, 1938, p14.

King of Burlesque (US; Lanfield, Sidney; 1936)
The Film Criticism of Otis Ferguson. p122.
Film Daily. Dec 26, 1935, p7.
Hollywood Reporter. Dec 21, 1935, p3.
Hollywood Spectator. Jan 4, 1936, v10, p13-14.
Motion Picture Herald. Jan 4, 1936, p49.
The New Statesman and Nation. Apr 25, 1936, v11, p632.
The New York Times. Jan 16, 1936, p25.
The New Yorker. Jan 25, 1936, v11, p55-56.
Rob Wagner's Script. Jan 4, 1936, v14, p10, 12.
Time. Jan 6, 1936, v27, p28.
Variety. Jan 22, 1936, p14.

King of Gamblers (US; Florey, Robert; 1937)
Film Daily. Apr 16, 1937, p10.
The Great Gangster Pictures. p227-28.
Hollywood Reporter. Apr 13, 1937, p3.
Motion Picture Herald. Apr 24, 1937, p38, 43.
The New York Times. Jul 3, 1937, p18.
Variety. Jul 7, 1937, p12.

The King of Jazz (US; Anderson, John Murray; 1930)
Close-Up. Nov 1929, v5, p412-14.
Close-Up. Jul 1930, v7, p60-62.
Commonweal. May 21, 1930, v12, p80-81.
Film Comment. Spr 1971, v7, p73-74.
Film Daily. Mar 30, 1930, p11.
The Hollywood Musical. p31.
The Hollywood Musical. p42, 53+.
Life. May 30, 1930, v95, p20.
The Nation. May 28, 1930, v130, p632.
The New York Times. May 3, 1930, p23.
The New York Times. May 11, 1930, p5.
The New York Times. Aug 6, 1933, p3.
The New Yorker. May 10, 1930, v6, p101.
Outlook and Independent. May 14, 1930, v155, p72.
Photoplay. Jun 1930, v38, p56.
Selected Film Criticism, 1921-1930. p155-57.
Time. May 12, 1930, v15, p64.
Variety. May 7, 1930, p21.

The King of Kings (US; DeMille, Cecil B.; 1927)
Close-Up. Dec 1927, v1, p65-69.
Close-Up. Feb 1928, v2, p21-32.
Exhibitor's Herald-World and Moving Picture World. Mar 10, 1928, p52.
Film Daily. May 1, 1927, p6.
The Films of Cecil B. DeMille. p250-59.
The Films of the Twenties. p167-69.
Independent. May 28, 1927, v118, p565.
Literary Digest. May 21, 1927, v93, p31-32.
Magill's Survey of Cinema. Silent Films. v2, p628-30.
The Moving Picture World. Apr 23, 1927, p746.
The New Republic. May 4, 1927, v50, p298-99.
The New York Times. Apr 20, 1927, p29.
The New York Times. Jan 22, 1928, sec8, p7.
The New York Times. Apr 20, 1927, p29.
Outlook. May 18, 1927, v146, p72-73.
Photoplay. Jun 1927, v32, p54-55.
Selected Film Criticism, 1921-1930. p158-59.
Variety. Apr 20, 1927, p15.

King of the Damned (GB; Forde, Walter; 1936)
Canadian Magazine. Feb 1936, v85, p38.
Film Daily. Feb 1, 1936, p7.
Hollywood Reporter. Jan 20, 1936, p3.
Literary Digest. Jan 25, 1936, v121, p19.
Motion Picture Herald. Jan 25, 1936, p39.
The New York Times. Feb 1, 1936, p9.
The Spectator. Jan 10, 1936, v156, p50.
Variety. Feb 5, 1936, p12.

King of the Jungle (US; Humberstone, Bruce; Marcin, Max; 1933)
Film Daily. Feb 25, 1933, p4.
The Films of the Thirties. p97-99.
Hollywood Reporter. Feb 23, 1933, p3.
Motion Picture Herald. Mar 4, 1933, p48-49.
The New York Times. Feb 25, 1933, p20.
The New Yorker. Mar 4, 1933, v9, p52.
Newsweek. Mar 4, 1933, v1, p28.
Rob Wagner's Script. Mar 18, 1933, v9, p8.
Time. Mar 6, 1933, v21, p24.
Variety. Feb 28, 1933, p15.

King of the Turf (US; Green, Alfred E.; 1939)
Film Daily. Feb 9, 1939, p8.
Motion Picture Herald. Feb 11, 1939, p35.
The New Statesman and Nation. Mar 11, 1939, v17, p357.
The New York Times. May 8, 1939, p21.
Rob Wagner's Script. Jun 10, 1939, v21, p17.
The Spectator. Mar 17, 1939, v162, p444.
Variety. Feb 15, 1939, p12.

King of the Underworld (US; Seiler, Lewis; 1939)
Classics of the Gangster Film. p68-71.
The Complete Films of Humphrey Bogart. p64-65.
Film Daily. Jan 13, 1939, p7.
The Great Gangster Pictures. p229-30.
Hollywood Reporter. Jan 12, 1939, p3.
Hollywood Spectator. Jan 21, 1939, v13, p11-12.
Humphrey Bogart: The Man and His Films. p87.
Motion Picture Herald. Jan 14, 1939, p46.
The New York Times. Jan 7, 1939, p6.
Variety. Jan 11, 1939, p12.

The King on Main Street (US; Bell, Monta; 1925)
Film Daily. Nov 1, 1925, p5.
The Moving Picture World. Nov 7, 1925, p60.
The New York Times. Oct 26, 1925, p25.
Photoplay. Jan 1926, v24, p46.
Selected Film Criticism, 1921-1930. p159.
Variety. Oct 28, 1925, p36.

King Solomon's Mines (GB; Stevenson, Robert; 1937)
Black Images in American Films, 1896-1954. p130.
Commonweal. Jul 16, 1937, v26, p307.
Film Daily. Jul 2, 1937, p8.
Graham Greene on Film. p161.
Great Britain and the East. Jun 24, 1937, v48, p907.
Hollywood Reporter. Jul 6, 1937, p3.
Literary Digest. Jul 17, 1937, v124, p34.
Motion Picture Herald. Jul 3, 1937, p44.
Motion Picture Herald. May 22, 1937, p16-17.
The New Masses. Jul 13, 1937, v24, p28.
The New Statesman and Nation. Jul 24, 1937, v14, p148.
The New York Times. Jul 3, 1937, p18.
The Spectator. Jul 30, 1937, v159, p203.
Stage. Sep 1937, v14, p44.
The Tatler. Aug 4, 1937, v145, p194.
Time. Jul 12, 1937, v30, p32.
Variety. Jun 30, 1937, p21.
World Film News. Sep 1937, v2, p26.

The King Steps Out (US; Sternberg, Josef von; 1936)
Canadian Magazine. Jul 1936, v86, p32.
Commonweal. May 29, 1936, v24, p132.
Esquire. Aug 1936, v6, p99.
Film Daily. May 18, 1936, p10.
The Films of Josef von Sternberg. p45.
Graham Greene on Film. p108.
The Hollywood Musical. p103.
Hollywood Reporter. Apr 27, 1936, p4.
Hollywood Spectator. May 23, 1936, v11, p10.
Motion Picture Herald. May 23, 1936, p44.
Movie Classic. May 1936, v10, p40-41+.
The New York Times. May 29, 1936, p15.
The New Yorker. Jun 6, 1936, v12, p63.
Newsweek. May 30, 1936, v7, p27.
Rob Wagner's Script. Jun 6, 1936, v15, p11.
The Spectator. Oct 9, 1936, v157, p582.
Stage. Jun 1936, v13, p40.
Time. Jun 1, 1936, v27, p24.
Variety. Jun 3, 1936, p15.
World Film News. Nov 1936, v1, p19-20.

King's Row (US; Wood, Sam; 1941)
Commonweal. Feb 13, 1942, v35, p418.
The Film Criticism of Otis Ferguson. p415-16.
Film Daily. Dec 23, 1941, p6.
The Films of Ronald Reagan (Thomas). p128-32.
The Films of the Forties. p58-61.
Halliwell's Hundred. p164-66.
Hollywood Reporter. Dec 23, 1941, p3.
Life. Feb 9, 1942, v12, p59-62.
The London Times. Sep 27, 1943, p8.
Magic Moments from the Movies. p106-07.
Magill's Survey of Cinema. Series. v3, p1265-68.
Motion Picture Exhibitor. Dec 31, 1941, v27, n8, sec2, p920.

Motion Picture Herald Product Digest. Dec 27, 1941, p429.
The New Republic. Feb 16, 1942, v106, p237-38.
The New York Times. Feb 3, 1942, p23.
The New York Times. Feb 8, 1942, sec9, p5.
The New Yorker. Feb 7, 1942, v17, p56.
Newsweek. Feb 16, 1942, v19, p72-73.
Rob Wagner's Script. Apr 11, 1942, v27, p18.
Selected Film Criticism, 1941-1950. p103-04.
Time. Feb 2, 1942, v39, p54.
Variety. Dec 24, 1941, p8.

The King's Vacation (US; Adolfi, John; 1933)
Bookman (London). Aug 1933, v84, p246.
Canadian Magazine. Mar 1933, v79, p43.
Film Daily. Jan 20, 1933, p6.
Hollywood Reporter. Jan 19, 1933, p3.
Motion Picture Herald. Jan 28, 1933, p24-25.
The New Statesman and Nation. Apr 15, 1933, v5, p477.
The New York Times. Jan 20, 1933, p21.
The New Yorker. Jan 23, 1933, v8, p47.
Rob Wagner's Script. Feb 25, 1933, v9, p9.
Time. Jan 30, 1933, v21, p26.
Variety. Jan 24, 1933, p19.

Kino Eye (Russian title: Kino-Glaz) (USSR; Vertov, Dziga; 1924)
Dictionary of Films. p177-178.
Eisenstein. p88.
A History of Films. p184.
A History of Narrative Film. p131, 136, 137.
The History of World Cinema. p139, 290.
Kino. p178-79.
Magill's Survey of Cinema. Silent Films. v2, p631-33.
Masters of the Soviet Cinema. p69-70.

Kismet (US; Gasnier, Louis J.; 1920)
Motion Picture News. Nov 6, 1920, p3621.
The Moving Picture World. Nov 6, 1920, p112.
The New York Times. Nov 15, 1920, p12.
Selected Film Criticism, 1912-1920. p154-55.
Variety. Oct 29, 1920, p41.
Wid's Daily. Oct 31, 1920, p3.

Kismet (US; Dillon, John Francis; 1930)
Exhibitors Herald-World. Nov 8, 1930, p39.
Film Daily. Nov 2, 1930, p10.
Judge. Nov 29, 1930, v99, p19.
Life. Nov 21, 1930, v96, p16.
The Nation. Nov 26, 1930, v131, p590.
The New York Times. Oct 31, 1930, p20.
The New York Times. Nov 9, 1930, p5.
Outlook and Independent. Nov 12, 1930, v156, p431.
Theatre Magazine. Jan 1931, v53, p47.
Time. Nov 10, 1930, v16, p68.
Variety. Nov 5, 1930, p23.

Kismet (Also titled: Oriental Dream) (US; Dieterle, William; 1944)
Commonweal. Sep 1, 1944, v40, p470-71.
Film Daily. Aug 22, 1944, p7.
The Films of Marlene Dietrich. p170-73.
The Films of Ronald Colman. p225-30.
Hollywood Reporter. Aug 22, 1944, p3.
Life. Nov 29, 1943, v15, p119-22+.
The New York Times. Aug 23, 1944, p16.
The New Yorker. Aug 26, 1944, v20, p36.
Newsweek. Sep 4, 1944, v24, p102.
Scholastic. Sep 18, 1944, v45, p30.
Time. Sep 4, 1944, v44, p90.
Variety. Aug 23, 1944, p18.

The Kiss (US; 1896)
American Silent Film. p20.
Behind the Screen. p95.
A History of Films. p24.
The Illustrated American. Jul 11, 1896, v20, p76.

The New York World. Apr 20, 1896, p21.
Selected Film Criticism, 1896-1911. p54.

The Kiss (US; Feyder, Jacques; 1929)
BFI/Monthly Film Bulletin. Oct 1974, v41, p236.
Film Daily. Nov 17, 1929, p9.
The Films of Greta Garbo. p82-86.
The New York Times. Nov 16, 1929, p25.
Variety. Nov 20, 1929, p30.

A Kiss Before the Mirror (US; Whale, James; 1933)
Film Daily. May 13, 1933, p3.
The Films of Nancy Carroll. p176-80.
Hollywood Reporter. Mar 3, 1933, p3.
James Whale. pxv, 98-101.
Motion Picture Herald. Mar 11, 1933, p24.
New Outlook. Jun 1933, v161, p49.
The New York Times. May 15, 1933, p16.
The New York Times. May 21, 1933, p3.
Rob Wagner's Script. Jun 3, 1933, v9, p8.
Time. May 22, 1933, v21, p24.
Vanity Fair. Jun 1933, v40, p38.
Variety. May 16, 1933, p21.

A Kiss for Cinderella (US; Brenon, Herbert; 1925)
Classics of the Silent Screen. p72-75.
Film Daily. Jan 3, 1926, p5.
Magill's Survey of Cinema. Silent Films. v2, p634-36.
The New York Times. Dec 26, 1925, p11.
Photoplay. Feb 1926, v24, p49.
Selected Film Criticism, 1921-1930. p160.
Variety. Jan 6, 1926, p41.

Kiss Me Again (US; Lubitsch, Ernst; 1925)
Ernst Lubitsch: A Guide to References and Resources. p82-85.
Film Daily. Aug 9, 1925, p7.
The Lubitsch Touch. p94-96.
The Moving Picture World. Aug 15, 1925, p736.
The New York Times. Aug 3, 1925, p10.
Spellbound in Darkness. p316, 320.
Variety. Aug 5, 1925, p31.

Kiss of Death (US; Hathaway, Henry; 1947)
Classics of the Gangster Film. p156-63.
Commonweal. Sep 12, 1947, v46, p530.
Film Daily. Aug 19, 1947, p10.
The Films of the Forties. p216-18.
Hollywood Reporter. Aug 13, 1947, p3.
Life. Sep 22, 1947, v23, p143-44+.
Motion Picture Herald Product Digest. Aug 23, 1947, p3794.
The Nation. Sep 13, 1947, v165, p264.
New Republic. Sep 22, 1947, v117, p38.
The New York Times. Aug 28, 1947, p28.
The New Yorker. Sep 6, 1947, v23, p68.
Newsweek. Sep 1, 1947, v30, p78.
Time. Sep 15, 1947, v50, p101.
Variety. Aug 13, 1947, p15.

Kitty (US; Leisen, Mitchell; 1946)
Commonweal. Mar 8, 1946, v43, p526.
Film Daily. Oct 16, 1945, p6.
The Films of the Forties. p160-61.
Hollywood Reporter. Oct 8, 1945, p3.
Motion Picture Herald Product Digest. Oct 6, 1945, p2669.
The New York Times. Apr 1, 1946, p23.
The New Yorker. Mar 30, 1946, v22, p59.
Newsweek. Mar 11, 1946, v27, p90.
Time. Mar 25, 1946, v47, p101.
Variety. Oct 10, 1945, p8.

Kitty Foyle (US; Wood, Sam; 1940)
Commonweal. Jan 24, 1941, v33, p351.
The Film Criticism of Otis Ferguson. p334.
Film Daily. Dec 23, 1940, p6.
The Films of Ginger Rogers. p162-66.
The Films of the Forties. p26-27.

Hollywood Reporter. Dec 17, 1940, p4.
Life. Dec 9, 1940, v9, p87-90.
The London Times. May 5, 1941, p8.
Magill's Survey of Cinema. Series II. v3, p1276-78.
Motion Picture Exhibitor. Jan 8, 1941, p667.
The New Republic. Jan 20, 1941, v104, p85.
The New York Times. Jan 9, 1941, p27.
The New Yorker. Jan 11, 1941, v16, p61.
Newsweek. Jan 6, 1941, 17, p51.
Scholastic. Jan 13, 1941, v37, p32.
Scribner's Commentator. Mar 1941, v9, p109.
Selected Film Criticism, 1931-1940. p133-35.
Time. Jan 13, 1941, v37, p73.
Variety. Dec 18, 1940, p16.

The Kleptomaniac (US; Porter, Edwin S.; 1906)
American Silent Film. p40-41.
The Emergence of Film Art. p31-32.
The First Twenty Years. p85.

Klondike Annie (US; Walsh, Raoul; 1936)
Canadian Magazine. Apr 1936, v85, p58.
Commonweal. Mar 6, 1936, v23, p524.
Film Daily. Feb 10, 1936, p3.
Films and Filming. Jul 1973, v19, p35-36.
The Films of Mae West. p115-24.
Garbo and the Night Watchman. p64-65.
Graham Greene on Film. p75-76.
Hollywood Reporter. Feb 5, 1936, p3.
Hollywood Spectator. Feb 29, 1936, v10, p5.
Motion Picture Herald. Feb 15, 1936, p44.
The New Masses. Mar 24, 1936, v18, p27.
The New Statesman and Nation. May 23, 1936, v11, p803.
The New York Times. Mar 12, 1936, p18.
The New Yorker. Mar 21, 1936, v12, p64.
The Spectator. May 22, 1936, v156, p931.
Stage. Apr 1936, v13, p46-47.
Time. Mar 9, 1936, v27, p44+.
Variety. Mar 18, 1936, p17.
Views and Reviews. Sum 1971, v3, p5-10.

A Knight of the Range (US; Jaccard, Jacques; 1916)
The Moving Picture World. Feb 5, 1916, p797, 831.
Variety. Jan 28, 1916, p22.

Knight Without Armor (GB; Feyder, Jacques; 1937)
The Age of the Dream Palace. p229-30.
Canadian Magazine. Jun 1937, v87, p52.
Commonweal. Jul 23, 1937, v26, p324.
Esquire. Oct 1937, v8, p121.
Film Daily. Jul 9, 1937, p8.
The Films of Marlene Dietrich. p132-36.
Graham Greene on Film. p170-71.
Great Britain and the East. Sep 9, 1937, v49, p365.
The Great Spy Pictures. p252-53.
Hollywood Reporter. Jun 2, 1937, p11.
Life. Jul 5, 1937, v3, p64-65.
Literary Digest. Jul 17, 1937, v124, p34.
London Mercury. Nov 1937, v37, p61-62.
Motion Picture Herald. Jun 19, 1937, p58, 60.
The New Masses. Jul 13, 1937, v24, p28.
The New Statesman and Nation. Sep 25, 1937, v14, p445.
The New York Times. Jul 9, 1937, p18.
The New Yorker. Jul 10, 1937, v13, p50-51.
Newsweek. Jul 3, 1937, v10, p20.
Rob Wagner's Script. Aug 14, 1937, v17, p15.
The Spectator. Oct 8, 1937, v159, p583.
Stage. Feb 1937, v14, p56-57.
Time. Jul 19, 1937, v30, p45.
Variety. Jun 16, 1937, p13.
Variety. Jul 14, 1937, p20.
World Film News. Nov 1937, v2, p18, 25.

Knock on Any Door (US; Ray, Nicholas; 1949)
Commonweal. Mar 11, 1949, v49, p543.
The Complete Films of Humphrey Bogart. p146-48.

Film Daily. Feb 21, 1949, p7.
Hollywood Reporter. Feb 21, 1949, p4.
Humphrey Bogart: The Man and His Films. p147.
Look. Mar 1949, v15, p100-03.
Motion Picture Herald Product Digest. Feb 26, 1949, p4513.
The New Republic. Mar 7, 1949, v120, p30.
The New York Times. Feb 23, 1949, p31.
The New Yorker. Mar 5, 1949, v25, p60+.
Newsweek. Mar 7, 1949, v33, p91.
Nicholas Ray: A Guide to References and Resources. p44-49 .
Nicholas Ray (Kreidl). p31-32.
Rotarian. Jun 1949, v74, p34.
Scholastic. Mar 16, 1949, v44, p26.
Sequence. Sum 1949, n8, p86-88.
Theatre Arts. Apr 1949, v33, p87.
Time. Mar 14, 1949, v53, p102+.
Variety. Feb 23, 1949, p10.

Knute Rockne, All American (US; Bacon, Lloyd; 1940)
Commonweal. Oct 18, 1940, v32, p530.
Film Daily. Oct 7, 1940, p6.
The Films of Ronald Reagan. p101-04.
Hollywood Reporter. Oct 7, 1940, p3.
The New York Times. Oct 19, 1940, p21.
Newsweek. Oct 14, 1940, v16, p72.
Time. Oct 21, 1940, v86, p92-93.
Variety. Oct 9, 1940, p16.

Koenigsmark (FR; Tourneur, Maurice; 1935)
Garbo and the Night Watchman. p46.
Hollywood Reporter. Dec 26, 1935, p3.
Saturday Review (London). Feb 1, 1936, v161, p160.
The Spectator. Jan 24, 1936, v156, p129.
The Tatler. Jan 29, 1936, v139, p190.
Variety. Dec 18, 1935, p13.

Konyets Sankt-Peterburga *See* The End of St. Petersburg

Krestyaniye *See* Peasants

The Kreutzer Sonata (FR; Guichard, Charles; 1938)
Film Daily. Dec 23, 1938, p4.
Motion Picture Herald. Jan 7, 1939, p40.
The New York Times. Dec 20, 1938, p30.
Variety. Dec 28, 1938, p13.

Krylya Kholopa *See* Wings of a Serf

Kuhle Wampe (Also titled: Whither Germany?) (GER; Dudow, Slatan; 1932)
Cinema Quarterly. Spr 1933, v1, p186.
Close-Up. Sep 1932, v9, p196-98.
Dictionary of Films. p180-81.
Film Daily. Apr 26, 1933, p4.
The German Cinema. p62-63.
The Haunted Screen. p334-35.
The Nation. Apr 5, 1933, v136, p382-84.
The New York Times. Apr 24, 1933, p11.
The New Yorker. Apr 29, 1933, v9, p45.
Screen. 1974-75, n4, v15, p71-79.
Screen. 1975-76, n4, v16, p5-15.
Variety. Apr 25, 1933, p18.

Kvinnas Ansikte, En *See* A Woman's Face

LaBreccia di Porta Pia *See* Presa di Roma

Laburnum Grove (GB; Reed, Carol; 1936)
Film Daily. Dec 4, 1941, p5.
Graham Greene on Film. p90-91.
Hollywood Reporter. May 15, 1936, p17.
The New York Times. Dec 2, 1941, p29.
The Spectator. Jul 31, 1936, v157, p199.
Variety. May 12, 1936, p15.
World Film News. Sep 1936, v1, p23.

The Lad from Old Ireland (US; Olcott, Sidney; 1910)
The Moving Picture World. Dec 3, 1910, p1296.
Selected Film Criticism, 1896-1911. p54.

Laddie (US; Stevens, George; 1935)
Film Daily. Mar 19, 1935, p4.
Hollywood Reporter. Feb 25, 1935, p2.
Motion Picture Herald. Mar 9, 1935, p48-49.
The New York Times. May 6, 1935, p22.
Newsweek. Apr 6, 1935, v5, p36.
Time. Apr 1, 1935, v25, p34.
Variety. May 8, 1935, p16.

Ladies and Gentlemen *See* The Great Garrick

Ladies in Love (US; Griffith, Edward H.; 1936)
Canadian Magazine. Dec 1936, v86, p38.
Film Daily. Oct 29, 1936, p11.
The Films of Tyrone Power. p49-51.
Motion Picture Herald. Oct 10, 1936, p53.
The New York Times. Oct 29, 1936, p31.
Newsweek. Oct 17, 1936, v8, p29.
Rob Wagner's Script. Oct 24, 1936, v16, p10.
Time. Oct 19, 1936, v28, p65.
Variety. Nov 4, 1936, p18.
World Film News. Jan 1937, v1, p26.

Ladies in Retirement (US; Vidor, Charles; 1941)
Commonweal. Nov 14, 1941, v35, p94.
Film Daily. Sep 9, 1941, p5.
Hollywood Reporter. Sep 5, 1941, p3.
The London Times. Apr 20, 1942, p8.
Magill's Survey of Cinema. Series II. v3, p1282-84.
Motion Picture Exhibitor. Sep 17, 1941, v26, n19, sec2, p847.
Motion Picture Herald Product Digest. Sep 13, 1941, p258.
The Nation. Nov 15, 1941, v153, p492.
The New Republic. Nov 3, 1941, v105, p587.
The New Yorker. Nov 8, 1941, v17, p66.
Newsweek. Oct 6, 1941, v18, p59.
Scholastic. Oct 6, 1941, v39, p30.
Time. Oct 6, 1941, v38, p92+.
Variety. Sep 10, 1941, p8.

Ladies of Leisure (US; Capra, Frank; 1930)
Exhibitors Herald-World. Apr 19, 1930, p49.
Film Daily. Apr 13, 1930, p10.
The Film Spectator. Apr 26, 1930, v9, p20.
The Films of Barbara Stanwyck. p64.
The Films of Frank Capra (Scherle and Levy). p83-86.
Frank Capra (Maland). p52-53.
Life. Jun 13, 1930, v95, p20.
The New York Times. May, 24, 1930, p21.
The New Yorker. May 31, 1930, v6, p61.
Outlook and Independent. Jun 4, 1930, v155, p192.
Starring Miss Barbara Stanwyck. p14-24.
Variety. May 28, 1930, p35.

Ladies of the Big House (US; Gering, Marion; 1931)
Film Daily. Jan 3, 1932, p8.
Hollywood Reporter. Dec 4, 1931, p3.
Motion Picture Herald. Dec 19, 1931, p50.
The New York Times. Jan 1, 1932, p31.
Outlook and Independent. Jan 13, 1932, v160, p55.
Rob Wagner's Script. Dec 26, 1931, v6, p8-9.
Time. Jan 11, 1932, v19, p25.
Variety. Jan 5, 1932, p19.

Ladies of the Jury (US; Menzies, William Cameron; 1931)
Film Daily. Apr 3, 1932, p10.
Hollywood Reporter. Nov 28, 1931, p3.
Motion Picture Herald. Dec 19, 1931, p46, 50.
The New York Times. Apr 2, 1932, p13.
The New York Times. Apr 10, 1932, p4.
Time. Apr 11, 1932, v19, p29.
Variety. Apr 5, 1932, p14.

Ladies They Talk About (US; Bretherton, Howard; Keighley, William; 1933)
Film Daily. Feb 25, 1933, p4.
The Films of Barbara Stanwyck. p86-87.
Garbo and the Night Watchman. p231-33.
The Great Gangster Pictures. p232-33.
Hollywood Reporter. Dec 29, 1932, p3.
Motion Picture Herald. Jan 7, 1933, p26.
The New York Times. Feb 25, 1933, p20.
Starring Miss Barbara Stanwyck. p54.
Variety. Feb 28, 1933, p15.

Lady Be Good (US; McLeod, Norman Z.; 1941)
The Busby Berkeley Book. p139-41.
Commonweal. Sep 26, 1941, v34, p548.
Film Daily. Jul 15, 1941, p7.
The Hollywood Musical. p184, 195.
Hollywood Reporter. Jul 14, 1941, p3.
Motion Picture Exhibitor. Jul 23, 1941, p796.
Motion Picture Exhibitor. Sep 3, 1941, p830.
Motion Picture Herald Product Digest. May 31, 1941, p146.
The New York Times. Sep 19, 1941, p27.
The New York Times. Sep 21, 1941, sec9, p3.
Scribner's Commentator. Dec 1941, v11, p106.
Time. Sep 29, 1941, v38, p86.
Variety. Jul 16, 1941, p8.
The World of Entertainment. p42-44.

Lady by Choice (US; Burton, David; 1934)
Film Daily. Oct 6, 1934, p3.
Hollywood Reporter. Sep 28, 1934, p3.
Motion Picture Herald. Oct 6, 1934, p59.
The New York Times. Nov 17, 1934, p17.
Variety. Nov 20, 1934, p15.

The Lady Consents (US; Roberts, Stephen; 1936)
Commonweal. Feb 14, 1936, v23, p440.
Film Daily. Jan 14, 1936, p7.
The Films of the Thirties. p158-59.
Hollywood Reporter. Jan 11, 1936, p3.
Hollywood Spectator. Jan 18, 1936, v10, p10-11.
Motion Picture Herald. Jan 18, 1936, p44, 46.
The New York Times. Feb 6, 1936, p23.
Rob Wagner's Script. Feb 8, 1936, v14, p10.
Time. Feb 17, 1936, v27, p48.
Variety. Feb 12, 1936, p18.

The Lady Escapes (US; Forde, Eugene; 1937)
Film Daily. Jun 2, 1937, p7.
Hollywood Spectator. Jun 5, 1937, v12, p15.
Variety. Aug 25, 1937, p17.

The Lady Eve (US; Sturges, Preston; 1941)
Between Flops. p145-53+.
Commonweal. Mar 14, 1941, v33, p520.
The Film Criticism of Otis Ferguson. p347-48.
Film Daily. Feb 27, 1941, p7.
The Films of Barbara Stanwyck. p134-38.
The Films of Henry Fonda. p100-02.
The Films of the Forties. p34-45.
The Fondas (Springer). p108-110.
Hollywood Reporter. Feb 24, 1941, p3.
Hollywood Spectator. Mar 15, 1941, v15, p14-15.
The London Times. May 19, 1941, p8.
Magill's Survey of Cinema. Series I. v2, p929-32.
Motion Picture Exhibitor. Mar 5, 1941, p700.
Motion Picture Herald Product Digest. Feb 8, 1941, p53.
The Nation. Mar 15, 1941, v152, p305.
The New Republic. Mar 17, 1941, v104, p372.
The New York Times. Feb 26, 1941, p17.
The New York Times. Mar 2, 1941, sec9, p5.
Newsweek. Mar 10, 1941, v17, p64.
Post Script. Spr-Sum 1982, v1, p33-47.
Preston Sturges: A Guide to References and Resources. p53-56.
Pursuits of Happiness. p45-70.

Rob Wagner's Script. Mar 22, 1941, v25, p16.
Scribner's Commentator. May 1941, v10, p107.
Selected Film Criticism, 1941-1950. p108-10.
Starring Miss Barbara Stanwyck. p145-47.
Talking Pictures. p41-44.
Time. Mar 10, 1941, v37, p86+.
Variety. Feb 26, 1941, p16.
The Village Voice. Jun 18, 1964, v9, p10+.

Lady for a Day (US; Capra, Frank; 1933)
Dictionary of Films. p184.
Film Daily. Aug 9, 1933, p5.
The Films of Frank Capra (Scherle and Levy). p117-22.
The Films of Frank Capra (Willis). p136-44.
Frank Capra (Maland). p78-79.
The Great Gangster Pictures. p234-35.
Judge. Oct 1933, v104, p16.
A Library of Film Criticism: American Film Directors. p29.
Life. Oct 1933, v100, p43.
Literary Digest. Sep 23, 1933, v116, p30.
Magill's Survey of Cinema. Series II. v3, p1285-87.
Motion Picture Herald. Jul 15, 1933, p70.
Movie-Made America. p209.
National Board of Review Magazine. Sep-Oct 1933, v8, p8-10.
The New Masses. July 3, 1934, p44.
New Outlook. Oct 1933, v162, p48.
The New York Times. Sep 8, 1933, p22.
The New York Times. Sep 17, 1933, p3.
The New Yorker. Sep 16, 1933, v9, p56.
Newsweek. Sep 16, 1933, v2, p39.
Photoplay. Sep 1933, v44, p56.
Photoplay. Dec 1933, v45, p118.
Rob Wagner's Script. Sep 30, 1933, v10, p10.
Selected Film Criticism, 1931-1940. p135-36.
Time. Sep 18, 1933, v22, p32.
Vanity Fair. Oct 1933, v41, p40.
Variety. Sep 15, 1933, p17.

The Lady Hamilton *See* That Hamilton Woman

Lady in the Dark (US; Leisen, Mitchell; 1944)
Chestnuts in Her Lap. p119-20.
Commonweal. Mar 10, 1944, v39, p521.
Film Daily. Feb 10, 1941, p8.
The Films of Ginger Rogers. p184-87.
Hollywood Reporter. Feb 10, 1944, p3.
Life. Mar 20, 1944, v16, p119+.
The London Times. Jun 1, 1944, p8.
Magic and Myth of the Movies. p109-10.
Magill's Survey of Cinema. Series II. v3, p1293-96.
Motion Picture Exhibitor. Feb 23, 1944, v31, n15, sec2, p1459.
Motion Picture Herald Product Digest. Feb 12, 1944, p8.
The New Republic. Apr 10, 1944, v110, p501.
The New York Times. Jan 23, 1944, sec2, p3.
The New Yorker. Mar 4, 1944, v20, p49.
Newsweek. Mar 6, 1944, v23, p80.
Scholastic. Mar 13, 1944, v44, p31.
Time. Feb 21, 1944, v43, p94.
Variety. Feb 16, 1944, p10.
Women's Film and Female Experience. p152-57, 160-61.

Lady in the Lake (US; Montgomery, Robert; 1946)
Commonweal. Jan 31, 1947, v45, p398.
Film Daily. Nov 29, 1946, p6.
Hollywood Reporter. Nov 26, 1946, p3.
Life. Jan 13, 1947, v22, p65-66.
Magill's Survey of Cinema, Series II. v3, p1297-1300.
Motion Picture Herald Product Digest. Nov 30, 1946, p3333.
New Republic. Feb 3, 1947, v116, p42.
The New York Times. Jan 24, 1947, p18.
The New Yorker. Feb 1, 1947, v22, p56.
Newsweek. Feb 3, 1947, v29, p73.
Raymond Chandler and Film. p121-53.
Raymond Chandler in Hollywood. p85-94.

Raymond Chandler on Screen. p 63-85.
Time. Jan 27, 1947, v49, p97.
Variety. Nov 27, 1946, p14.

Lady Jane Grey *See* Nine Days a Queen

Lady Killer *See* Gueule d'Amour

Lady Killer (US; Del Ruth, Roy; 1933)
America in the Dark. p167.
Classics of the Gangster Film. p25-28.
Esquire. Feb 1933, v1, p131.
Film Daily. Dec 28, 1933, p18.
The Films of James Cagney. p80-82.
The Gangster Film. p143-46.
Hollywood Reporter. Nov 17, 1933, p2.
Literary Digest. Jan 20, 1934, v117, p32.
Motion Picture Herald. Dec 2, 1933, p53.
The New York Times. Jan 1, 1934, p28.
Time. Jan 8, 1934, v23, p24.
Variety. Jan 2, 1934, p13.

Lady of Burlesque (US; Wellman, William A.; 1943)
Commonweal. May 28, 1943, v38, p146.
Film Daily. Apr 29, 1943, p13.
The Films of Barbara Stanwyck. p151-54.
Hollywood Reporter. Apr 29, 1943, p3.
Motion Picture Herald Product Digest. May 1, 1943, p1289.
The New York Times. May 14, 1943, p17.
Starring Miss Barbara Stanwyck. p93, 169.
Time. May 10, 1943, v41, p96+.
Variety. May 5, 1943, p8.
William A. Wellman (Thompson). p206-07.

A Lady of Scandal (US; Franklin, Sidney; 1930)
Basil Rathbone: His Life and His Films. p126-28.
Exhibitors Herald-World. Jun 21, 1930, p69.
Film Daily. Jun 1, 1930, p10.
Judge. Jul 12, 1930, v99, p21.
The New York Times. Jun 14, 1930, p9.
The New York Times. Jun 22, 1930, p3.
The New Yorker. Jun 21, 1930, v6, p71.
Outlook and Independent. Jul 2, 1930, v155, p351.
Rob Wagner's Script. Jun 21, 1930, v3, p12.
Time. Jun 30, 1930, v15, p23.
Variety. Jun 18, 1930, p37.

Lady of the Pavements (US; Griffith, D.W.; 1929)
Film Daily. Mar 17, 1929, p4.
The Film Spectator. Mar 9, 1929, v7, p8.
The Films of D.W. Griffith. p235-40.
Magill's Survey of Cinema. Silent Films. v2, p637-40.
The New York Times. Mar 11, 1929, p22.
Selected Film Criticism, 1921-1930. p161-62.
Variety. Mar 13, 1929, p14.

Lady of the Tropics (US; Conway, Jack; 1939)
Commonweal. Sep 1, 1939, v30, p439.
Film Daily. Aug 15, 1939, p7.
Hedy Lamarr. p106-12.
Hollywood Reporter. Aug 4, 1939, p3.
Hollywood Spectator. Sep 2, 1939, v14, p8.
Motion Picture Herald. Aug 12, 1939, p47.
The Nation. Sep 16, 1939, v149, p301.
The New Masses. Oct 3, 1939, v33, p31.
The New York Times. Sep 8, 1939, p28.
The New Yorker. Sep 16, 1939, v15, p62.
Newsweek. Aug 28, 1939, v14, p23.
Rob Wagner's Script. Sep 16, 1939, v22, p14.
Time. Aug 28, 1939, v34, p46.
Variety. Aug 9, 1939, p14.

A Lady Surrenders (US; Stahl, John M.; 1930)
Exhibitors Herald-World. Sep 27, 1930, p40.
Film Daily. Sep 21, 1930, p31.
Judge. Oct 25, 1930, v99, p23.
The New York Times. Oct 4, 1930, p15.

The New York Times. Oct 12, 1930, p5.
Outlook and Independent. Oct 15, 1930, v156, p272.
Time. Oct 20, 1930, v16, p38.
Variety. Oct 8, 1930, p23.

A Lady to Love (US; Sjostrom, Victor; 1930)
The Cinema of Edward G. Robinson. p69-71.
Exhibitors Herald-World. Mar 8, 1930, p40.
Film Daily. Mar 2, 1930, p10.
Judge. Mar 22, 1930, v98, p25.
The New York Times. Mar 1, 1930, p23.
The New Yorker. Mar 8, 1930, v6, p91.
Outlook and Independent. Mar 12, 1930, v154, p430.
Time. Mar 10, 1930, v15, p10.
Variety. Mar 5, 1930, p21.

The Lady Vanishes (GB; Hitchcock, Alfred; 1938)
American Film Criticism. p364-65.
The Art of Alfred Hitchcock. p75-80.
Cinema Texas Program Notes. Oct 6, 1980, v19, p71-74.
Commonweal. Nov 4, 1938, v29, p49.
A Critical History of British Cinema. p111.
Fifty Classic British Films. p31-33.
The Film Criticism of Otis Ferguson. p237-38.
Film Daily. Oct 5, 1938, p6.
Films and Filming. Jul 1963, v9, p43-47.
From Quasimodo to Scarlett O'Hara. p289-92.
The Great British Films. p42-44.
The Great Spy Films. p256-58.
Hitchcock: The First Forty-Four Films. p53-54.
Hitchcock (Truffaut). p105-20.
Hitchcock's British Films. p231-48.
Hollywood Reporter. Jun 1, 1939, p3.
Kiss Kiss Bang Bang. p366.
Magill's Survey of Cinema. Series I. v2, p933-38.
Mastering the Film and Other Essays. p76-77.
Motion Picture Herald. Sep 3, 1938, p42-43.
The Nation. Jan 7, 1939, v148, p45.
National Board of Review Magazine. Nov 1938, v13, p16.
The New Masses. Oct 18, 1938, v29, p29-30.
The New Republic. Oct 19, 1939, v96, p307.
The New Statesman and Nation. Oct 15, 1938, v16, p570.
The New York Times. Dec 26, 1938, p29.
The New Yorker. Dec 24, 1938, v14, p45.
Newsweek. Oct 17, 1938, v12, p28-29.
North American Review. Mar 1939, v247, p176-77.
Rob Wagner's Script. Apr 1, 1939, v21, p16.
Scholastic. Feb 25, 1939, v34, p34.
Selected Film Criticism: Foreign Films, 1930-1950. p92-93.
The Spectator. Oct 14, 1938, v161, p603.
Stage. Oct 1938, v16, p49.
Stage. Nov 1938, v16, p57.
Time. Nov 21, 1938, v32, p53.
Variety. Aug 31, 1938, p18.
World Film News. Nov 1938, v3, p311, 314.

Lady Windermere's Fan *See* The Fan

Lady Windermere's Fan (US; Lubitsch, Ernst; 1925)
The Cinema of Ernst Lubitsch. p41-50+.
The Comic Mind. p216, 218.
Ernst Lubitsch: A Guide to References and Resources. p85-88.
Film Daily. Dec 6, 1925, p42.
The Films of Ronald Colman. p89-92.
The Lubitsch Touch. p86-93.
Magill's Survey of Cinema. Silent Films. v2, p641-43.
The Moving Picture World. Dec 12, 1925, p575.
National Board of Review Magazine. Mar-Apr 1926, v1, p11-12.
The New York Times. Dec 28, 1925, p19.
Selected Film Criticism, 1921-1930. p162.
Spellbound in Darkness. p321-23.
Variety. Jan 13, 1926, p49.

Lady With a Past (US; Griffith, Edward H.; 1932)
Film Daily. Feb 21, 1932, p10.
Hollywood Reporter. Feb 3, 1932, p11.
Motion Picture Herald. Feb 13, 1932, p34-35.
The Nation. Mar 16, 1932, v134, p320-21.
The New York Times. Feb 22, 1932, p23.
Rob Wagner's Script. Jun 4, 1932, v7, p10-11.
Time. Feb 29, 1932, v19, p28.
Variety. Feb 23, 1932, p13.

The Lamb (US; Cabanne, Christy; 1915)
His Majesty the American. p28-34.
Motion Picture News. Oct 9, 1915, p84.
Motography. Oct 9, 1915, p715.
Motography. Nov 20, 1915, p1106.
The Moving Picture World. Oct 9, 1915, p340.
The Moving Picture World. Oct 13, 1917, p298.
The New York Dramatic Mirror. Sep 29, 1915, p30-31.
Photoplay. Dec 1915, v8, p85-86.
Selected Film Criticism, 1912-1920. p155-56.
Variety. Oct 1, 1915, p18.

Lancer Spy (US; Ratoff, Gregory; 1937)
Film Daily. Oct 5, 1937, p6.
The Films of Peter Lorre. p103-05.
The Great Spy Pictures. p259-60.
Hollywood Reporter. Sep 30, 1937, p3.
Motion Picture Herald. Oct 9, 1937, p42, 44.
The New Masses. Nov 23, 1937, v25, p30.
The New York Times. Nov 4, 1937, p29.
The New Yorker. Nov 13, 1937, v13, p77.
Rob Wagner's Script. Dec 18, 1937, v18, p12.
Time. Oct 18, 1937, v30, p28.
Variety. Oct 6, 1937, p12.

The Land Beyond the Sunset (US; 1904)
American Silent Film. p34-36.

Land O' Lizzards (US; Borzage, Frank; 1916)
The Moving Picture World. Sep 30, 1916, p2165.
The Moving Picture World. Oct 7, 1916, p65.
Variety. Sep 29, 1916, p27.

Land of Liberty (US; De Mille, Cecil B.; 1939)
Commonweal. Feb 7, 1941, v33, p402.
Film Daily. Jun 14, 1939, p6.
Hollywood Reporter. Jun 14, 1939, p3.
Library Journal. Feb 1, 1941, v66, p135.
Motion Picture Herald. Jun 17, 1939, p50.
The New York Times. Jun 16, 1939, p27.
The New Yorker. Jul 22, 1939, v15, p63-64.
Newsweek. Jan 27, 1941, v17, p47.
Rob Wagner's Script. Jun 24, 1939, v21, p16.
Time. Jun 26, 1939, v33, p45.
Variety. Jun 21, 1939, p26.
Variety. Jan 15, 1941, p14.

Lanterne Magique, La *See* The Magic Lantern

Larceny, Inc. (US; Bacon, Lloyd; 1942)
Around Cinemas, Series II. p208-09.
The Cinema of Edward G. Robinson. p139-40.
Film Daily. Mar 5, 1942, p8.
The Films of Anthony Quinn. p86-87.
Hollywood Reporter. Mar 4, 1942, p3.
The London Times. Sep 7, 1942, p8.
Magill's Survey of Cinema. Series II. v3, p1304-06.
Motion Picture Exhibitor. Mar 11, 1942, v27, n18, sec2, p966.
Motion Picture Herald Product Digest. Mar 7, 1941, p538.
The New York Times. May 5, 1942, p9.
Variety. Mar 4, 1942, p8.

Lardi di Biciclette *See* Bicycle Theif

Lassie Come Home (US; Wilson, Fred McLeod; 1943)
Agee on Film. v1, p54, 67.
Commonweal. Oct 22, 1943, v29, p16.

Film Daily. Aug 20, 1943, p5.
The Films of Elizabeth Taylor. p39-41.
The Films of the Forties. p102-03.
Hollywood Reporter. Aug 18, 1943, p3.
Magill's Survey of Cinema. Series II. v3, p1307.
Motion Picture Herald Product Digest. Aug 21, 1943, p1494.
The New York Times. Oct 8, 1943, p15.
The New Yorker. Oct 16, 1943, v19, p19.
Time. Oct 25, 1943, v42, p94.
Variety. Aug 18, 1943, p10.

The Last Command (US; Sternberg, Josef von; 1928)
The Cinema of Josef von Sternberg. p44-52.
Exhibitor's Herald-World and Moving Picture World. Feb 4, 1928, p61.
Film Daily. Feb 5, 1928, p6.
The Film Spectator. Feb 4, 1928, v4, p10.
The Films of Josef von Sternberg. p16-19.
The Films of the Twenties. p185-88.
Magill's Survey of Cinema. Silent Films. v2, p644-46.
The New York Times. Jan 23, 1928, p18.
The Parade's Gone By. p196-98+.
Selected Film Criticism, 1921-1930. p163-64.
Variety. Jan 25, 1928, p12.

The Last Days of Dolwyn *See* The Woman of Dolwyn

The Last Days of Pompeii (Italian title: Ultimi Giorni dei Pompeii, Gli) (IT; Maggi, Luigi; 1908)
A History of Narrative Film. p55.
The Italian Cinema. p19-20.

The Last Days of Pompeii (Italian title: Ultimi Giorni di Pompeii, Gli) (IT; Caserini, Mario; 1913)
The George Kleine Collection Catalog. p142-43.
The Italian Cinema. p28-29.
The New York Dramatic Mirror. Oct 8, 1913, p33.
The New York Dramatic Mirror. Oct 22, 1913, p32.
Variety. Oct 3, 1913, p15.

The Last Days of Pompeii (US; Schoedsack, Ernest B.; 1935)
Basil Rathbone: His Life and His Films. p154-57.
Esquire. Dec 1935, v4, p118, 199.
Film Daily. Oct 3, 1935, p8.
Hollywood Reporter. Sep 20, 1935, p3.
Literary Digest. Nov 9, l935, v120, p38.
Motion Picture Herald. Oct 12, 1935, p40.
National Board of Review Magazine. Nov 1935, v10, p3.
The New York Times. Oct 17, 1935, p29.
The New Yorker. Oct 26, 1935, v11, p73.
Scholastic. Nov 2, 1935, v27, p28.
Those Fabulous Movie Years: The 30s. p64-65.
Time. Oct 28, 1935, v26, p52.
Variety. Oct 23, 1935, p12.

The Last Flight (US; Dieterle, William; 1931)
The American Film Heritage. p176-78.
Film Daily. Aug 23, 1931, p18.
The Films of the Thirties. p65-66.
Life. Sep 11, 1931, v98, p19.
Motion Picture Herald. Sep 12, 1931, p26-27.
The New York Times. Aug 20, 1931, p17.
The New York Times. Aug 30, 1931, p5.
The New Yorker. Aug 29, 1931, v7, p47.
Time. Aug 31, 1931, v18, p20.

The Last Gangster (US; Ludwig, Edward; 1937)
The Cinema of Edward G. Robinson. p111-13.
Film Daily. Nov 9, 1937, p11.
The Films of James Stewart. p48-49.
Hollywood Reporter. Nov 9, 1937, p3.
Motion Picture Herald. Nov 13, 1937, p43.
The New Statesman and Nation. Dec 11, 1937, v14, p1014.
The New York Times. Dec 10, 1937, p33.
The New Yorker. Dec 11, 1937, v13, p101-02.

Rob Wagner's Script. Jan 15, 1938, v18, p8.
The Tatler. Apr 27, 1938, v148, p152.
Variety. Nov 10, 1937, p18.

The Last Laugh (German title: Letzte Mann, Der) (GER; Murnau, F.W.; 1924)
Dictionary of Films. p190-91.
The Emergence of Film Art. p87.
Exceptional Photoplays. Dec-Jan 1925, v5, p1.
Film Daily. Jan 4, 1925, p7.
From Caligari to Hitler. p99-102.
The Haunted Screen. p207-21.
A History of Narrative Film. p121-125.
The International Dictionary of Films and Filmmakers. v1, p258-59.
Life. Mar 5, 1925, v85, p18.
Literary Digest. Feb 28, 1925, v84, p26.
Magill's Survey of Cinema. Silent Films. v2, p647-49.
Motion Picture Classic. Aug 1926, v23, p24-25.
The Moving Picture World. Feb 7, 1925, p555.
Murnau (Eisner). p154-66.
The New Republic. Feb 25, 1925, v42, p19-20.
The New York Times. Jan 28, 1925, p14.
The New York Times. Dec 21, 1924, sec7, p3.
The New Yorker. Feb 21, 1925, v1, p28.
Selected Film Criticism, 1921-1930. p164-66.
Spellbound in Darkness. p368-73.
Variety. Dec 10, 1924, p34.

The Last Mile (US; Bischoff, Sam; 1932)
Film Daily. Aug 26, 1932, p7.
The Great Gangster Pictures. p241-42.
Motion Picture Herald. Jul 30, 1932, p33.
The New York Times. Aug 26, 1932, p20.
Rob Wagner's Script. Aug 6, 1932, v7, p8-9.
Time. Aug 8, 1932, v20, p18.
Variety. Aug 30, 1932, p21.

The Last Multi-Millionaire *See* Dernier Milliardaire, Le

The Last Night (Russian title: Poslednaya Noch) (USSR; Raizsman, Yuli; 1937)
Dictionary of Films. p290.
The Film Criticism of Otis Ferguson. p177-78.
Film Daily. May 3, 1937, p6.
Motion Picture Herald. May 8, 1937, p43.
The Nation. May 22, 1937, v144, p602.
National Board of Review Magazine. Jul 1937, v12, p13.
The New Republic. May 19, 1937, v91, p48.
The New Statesman and Nation. Nov 20, 1937, v14, p836.
The New Statesman and Nation. Aug 20, 1938, v16, p284.
The New York Times. Apr 28, 1937, p18.
Variety. May 12, 1937, p13.

The Last of Mrs. Cheney (US; Boleslavski, Richard; 1937)
Film Daily. Feb 19, 1937, p4.
The Films of Joan Crawford. p124-25.
Garbo and the Night Watchman. p246-47.
Hollywood Reporter. Feb 15, 1937, p3.
Hollywood Spectator. Feb 27, 1937, v11, p12.
Life. Mar 1, 1937, v2, p47.
Motion Picture Herald. Feb 27, 1937, p57, 59.
The New York Times. Feb 19, 1937, p15.
The New Yorker. Feb 27, 1937, v13, p61.
Rob Wagner's Script. Feb 20, 1937, v17, p6-7.
Time. Mar 1, 1937, v29, p66.
Variety. Feb 24, 1937, p15.

The Last of Mrs. Cheyney (US; Franklin, Sidney; 1929)
Film Daily. Aug 18, 1929, p10.
Film Daily. Sep 29, 1929, p8.
The Films of Norma Shearer. p159-61.
Magill's Survey of Cinema. Series II. v3, p1310-13.
The New York Times. Aug 13, 1929, p23.
Variety. Aug 14, 1929, p18.

The Last of the Mohicans (US; Tourneur, Maurice; 1920)
Magill's Survey of Cinema. Silent Films. v2, p650-53.
Motion Picture News. Dec 4, 1920, p4343.
The Moving Picture World. Dec 4, 1920, p589.
The Moving Picture World. Dec 11, 1920, p771.
Selected Film Criticism, 1912-1920. p156-57.
Wid's Daily. Nov 28, 1920, p2.

The Last of the Mohicans (US; Tourneur, Maurice; 1921)
Classics of the Silent Screen. p42-43.
Film Daily. Nov 28, 1920, p6.
The New York Times. Jan 3, 1921, p20.
Photoplay. Apr 1921, v19, p78.
Spellbound in Darkness. p280-81.

The Last of the Mohicans (US; Seitz, George B.; 1936)
Commonweal. Sep 11, 1936, v24, p467.
Film Daily. Aug 12, 1936, p9.
The Great Adventure Films. p58-61.
The Great Western Pictures. p180-82.
Hollywood Reporter. Aug 8, 1936, p3.
Motion Picture Herald. Aug 15, 1936, p54.
Motion Picture Herald. Jul 18, 1936, p16-17.
The New Masses. Sep 15, 1936, v20, p27.
The New Statesman and Nation. Oct 3, 1936, v12, p470.
The New York Times. Sep 3, 1936, p17.
Saint Nicholas. Sep 1936, v63, p29.
Saturday Review (London). Oct 10, 1936, v162, p480.
Scholastic. Oct 3, 1936, v29, p32.
Time. Sep 7, 1936, v28, p19.
Variety. Sep 9, 1936, p16.
World Film News. Nov 1936, v1, p18.

The Last Outpost (US; Barton, Charles; 1935)
Esquire. Dec 1935, v4, p118.
Film Daily. Sep 27, 1935, p7.
The Films of Cary Grant. p85-87.
Graham Greene on Film. p37-38.
Hollywood Reporter. Sep 24, 1935, p3.
Motion Picture Herald. Oct 12, 1935, p44.
The New Statesman and Nation. Dec 14, 1935, v10, p937.
The New York Times. Oct 5, 1935, p18.
The New Yorker. Oct 12, 1935, v11, p67-68.
The Spectator. Nov 29, 1935, v155, p900.
Variety. Oct 9, 1935, p14.

The Last Stand of the Dalton Boys (US; Kenyon, Jack; 1912)
The War, the West, and the Wilderness. p287-88.

Last Train from Madrid (US; Hogan, James; 1937)
Film Daily. Jun 11, 1937, p30.
The Films of Anthony Quinn. p46-47.
Graham Greene on Film. p154.
The Great Spy Pictures. p262-63.
Hollywood Reporter. Jun 5, 1937, p3.
Hollywood Spectator. Jun 19, 1937, v12, p13-14.
Literary Digest. Jun 19, 1937, v123, p18.
Motion Picture Herald. Jun 12, 1937, p80.
The New Masses. Jun 22, 1937, v23, p29.
The New York Times. Jun 19, 1937, p20.
Rob Wagner's Script. Jul 3, 1937, v17, p11.
Variety. Jun 23, 1937, p12.

The Last Will of Dr. Mabuse, Das *See* Testament des Dr. Mabuse, Das

The Late George Apley (US; Mankiewicz, Joseph L.; 1947)
Film Daily. Jan 31, 1947, p10.
The Films of Ronald Colman. p231-36.
Hollywood Reporter. Jan 31, 1947, p3.
Joseph L. Mankiewicz. p43-49.
Life. Apr 21, 1947, v22, p65-66.
Motion Picture Herald Product Digest. Feb 8, 1947, p3457.

The New York Times. Mar 21, 1947, p29.
Variety. Feb 5, 1947, p12.

Laugh, Clown, Laugh (US; Brenon, Herbert; 1928)
Faces, Forms, Films: The Artistry of Lon Chaney. p136-39+.
Film Daily. Jun 3, 1928, p9.
The Film Spectator. Apr 28, 1928, v5, p19.
Lon of 1000 Faces! p144-52.
The New York Times. May 28, 1928, p23.
The New York Times. Jun 3, 1928, sec8, p5.
Photoplay. Jun 1928, v34, p52.
Selected Film Criticism, 1921-1930. p166.
Variety. May 30, 1928, p14.

Laughing Bill Hyde (US; Henley, Hobart; 1918)
Exhibitor's Trade Review. Sep 21, 1918, p1345.
Motion Picture News. Oct 5, 1918, p2245.
The Moving Picture World. Oct 5, 1918, p120, 127.
The New York Times. Sep 23, 1918, p7.
Variety. Sep 27, 1918, p45.
Wid's Daily. Sep 29, 1918, p32.

The Laughing Lady (US; Schertzinger, Victor; 1930)
Exhibitors Herald-World. Jan 11, 1930, p33.
Film Daily. Jan 5, 1930, p13.
The Film Spectator. Mar 15, 1930, v9, p21.
Judge. Jan 25, 1930, v98, p23.
Life. Feb 7, 1930, v95, p20.
The New York Times. Jan 4, 1930, p21.
The New York Times. Jan 12, 1930, p6.
The New Yorker. Jan 11, 1930, v5, p71-72.
Outlook and Independent. Jan 15, 1930, v154, p113.
Rob Wagner's Script. Feb 15, 1930, v3, p12-13.
Time. Jan 13, 1930, v15, p48.
Variety. Jan 8, 1930, p89.

Laughter (US; D'Arrast, Harry D'Abbadie; 1930)
Commonweal. Nov 26, 1930, v13, p104.
Exhibitors Herald-World. Oct 25, 1930, p45.
Exhibitors Herald-World. Nov 22, 1930, p37.
Film Daily. Sep 21, 1930, p31.
The Films of Fredric March. p65-67.
The Films of Nancy Carroll. p120-25.
Judge. Dec 6, 1930, v99, p19.
Judge. Dec 20, 1930, v99, p21.
Life. Dec 5, 1930, v96, p36.
Lorentz on Film. p62-64.
Magill's Survey of Cinema. Series II. v3, p1333-36.
The Nation. Dec 24, 1930, v131, p713-14.
National Board of Review Magazine. Dec 1930, v5, p7.
The New York Times. Nov 15, 1930, p15.
The New York Times. Nov 23, 1930, p5.
The New Yorker. Nov 22, 1930, v6, p87.
Outlook and Independent. Nov 26, 1930, v156, p512.
Sight and Sound. Wint 1970-71, v40, p45.
Time. Nov 24, 1930, v16, p64.
Variety. Oct 8, 1930, p23.

Launcelot and Elaine (US; 1909)
The Moving Picture World. Nov 27, 1909, p759.
Selected Film Criticism, 1896-1911. p58.

Laura (US; Preminger, Otto; 1944)
America's Favorite Movies. p177-99.
The Cinema of Otto Preminger. p55-62.
Classic Film/Video Image. Mar 1980, n68, p24.
Commonweal. Oct 27, 1944, v41, p38.
Cult Movies. p199-202.
Dark City. p21-26.
Film Daily. Oct 17, 1944, p6.
Film Reader. 1978, n3, p90-105.
The Films of the Forties. p128-29.
International Dictionary of Films and Filmmakers. v1, p256-57.
The London Times. Nov 27, 1944, p8.
Magill's Survey of Cinema. Series I. v2, p948-51.

Motion Picture Exhibitor. Oct 18, 1941, v32, n23, sec2, p1601.
Motion Picture Herald Product Digest. Oct 14, 1944, p2138.
Movie (London). Sep 1962, v1, n2, p11-13.
A Neglected Art. p58-68.
New Captain George's Whizzbang. 1974, v3, p20-26+.
The New Republic. Oct 30, 1944, v111, p568.
The New York Times. Oct 12, 1944, p24.
The New Yorker. Oct 21, 1944, v20, p50.
Newsweek. Oct 23, 1944, 24, p100.
Rob Wagner's Script. Dec 2, 1944, v30, p15.
Scholastic. Nov 27, 1944, v45, p48.
Selected Film Criticism, 1941-1950. p112-13.
Thousand Eyes Magazine. Nov 1976, v2, p4-5.
Time. Oct 30, 1944, v44, p54+.
Variety. Oct 11, 1944, p12.
Vincent Price Unmasked. p62-64.

Law and Order (US; Cahn, Edward L.; 1932)
Film Daily. Mar 6, 1932, p10.
The Filming of the West. p192-93.
The Great Western Pictures. p186-88.
Magill's Survey of Cinema. Series II. v3, p1337-39.
The New York Times. Feb 29, 1932, p21.
Variety. Mar 1, 1932, p21.

Lawyer Man (US; Dieterle, William; 1932)
Film Daily. Dec 23, 1932, p6.
Hollywood Reporter. Nov 25, 1932, p3.
Motion Picture Herald. Dec 3, 1932, p30.
The New York Times. Dec 27, 1932, p10.
Variety. Jan 13, 1933, p27.

Lazybones (US; Borzage, Frank; 1925)
Film Daily. Oct 18, 1925, p6.
Photoplay. Jan 1926, v24, p49.
Selected Film Criticism, 1921-1930. p167.
Variety. Dec 9, 1925, p42.

Leah Kleschna (US; Dawley, J. Searle; 1913)
Motography. Nov 29, 1913, p384.
Motography. Dec 13, 1913, p8.
The Moving Picture World. Dec 13, 1913, p1287, 1344, 1346.
The Moving Picture World. Dec 20, 1913, p1392.
The New York Dramatic Mirror. Dec 17, 1913, p32.

Leatherstocking (US; Griffith, D.W.; 1909)
The Moving Picture World. Oct 9, 1909, p489.
Selected Film Criticism, 1896-1911. p59.

Leave Her to Heaven (US; Stahl, John M.; 1945)
Agee on Film. v1, p360.
Chestnuts in Her Lap. p173-74.
Commonweal. Jan 25, 1946, v43, p382.
Film Daily. Dec 20, 1945, p9.
Film Noir. p169-70.
Hollywood Reporter. Dec 20, 1945, p3.
The London Times. Mar 4, 1946, p8.
Magill's Survey of Cinema. Series I. v2, p963-65.
Motion Picture Exhibitor. Jan 9, 1946, v35, n10, sec2, p1860.
Motion Picture Herald Product Digest. Dec 29, 1945, p2778.
The New York Times. Dec 26, 1945, p15.
The New Yorker. Dec 29, 1945, v21, p59.
Newsweek. Dec 31, 1945, v26, p95.
Time. Jan 7, 1946, v47, p54.
Variety. Jan 2, 1946, p8.

The Legend of Prague *See* The Golem

The Legion of Terror (US; Coleman, C.C., Jr.; 1936)
Film Daily. Nov 3, 1936, p6.
Hollywood Reporter. Nov 9, 1936, p4.
Motion Picture Herald. Nov 7, 1936, p54, 56.
The New Masses. Nov 10, 1936, v21, p29.
The New York Times. Nov 2, 1936, p24.
Variety. Nov 4, 1936, p19.

The Lemon Drop Kid (US; Neilan, Marshall; 1934)
Film Daily. Oct 27, 1934, p4.
Hollywood Reporter. Sep 20, 1934, p3.
Motion Picture Herald. Sep 29, 1934, p33.
The New York Times. Oct 30, 1934, p16.
Variety. Oct 30, 1934, p16.

Lenin in 1918 (Russian title: Lenin v 1918 godu) (USSR; Romm, Mikhail; 1939)
Dictionary of Films. p188.
Film Daily. Jul 13, 1939, p7.
The Nation. Jul 15, 1939, v149, p82.
The New Masses. Jul 11, 1939, v32, p28-29.
The New Republic. Jul 26, 1939, v99, p335.
The New York Times. Jun 27, 1939, p27.
The New Yorker. Jul 8, 1939, v15, p70.
North American Review. Sep 1939, v248, p196-97.
Variety. Jun 28, 1939, p20.

Lenin in October (Russian title: Lenin v Oktyabre) (USSR; Romm, Mikhail; 1937)
Cinema, the Magic Vehicle. v1, p281.
Dictionary of Films. p188.
Film Daily. Apr 9, 1938, p5.
Graham Greene on Film. p206-07.
The New Masses. Mar 29, 1938, v27, p29-31.
The New Statesman and Nation. Nov 26, 1938, v16, p871-72.
The New Yorker. Apr 9, 1938, v14, p69.
The Spectator. Nov 25, 1938, v161, p901.
Variety. Apr 6, 1938, p14.

Lest We Forget (US; Perret, Léonce; 1918)
Exhibitor's Trade Review. Feb 9, 1918, p837, 909.
Motion Picture News. Feb 9, 1918, p862.
Motion Picture News. Feb 16, 1918, p1032-33.
The Moving Picture World. Feb 9, 1918, p840.
The Moving Picture World. Feb 16, 1918, p1004-05, 1008-09.
The New York Times. Jan 28, 1918, p13.
Variety. Feb 1, 1918, p46.
Wid's Daily. Feb 21, 1918, p957-58.

Let Freedom Ring (US; Conway, Jack; 1939)
Commonweal. Mar 10, 1939, v29, p552.
Esquire. May 1939, v11, p129.
Film Daily. Feb 20, 1939, p9.
The Films of Jeanette MacDonald and Nelson Eddy. p253-59.
Hollywood Reporter. Feb 15, 1938, p3.
Hollywood Spectator. Mar 4, 1939, v13, p8.
Motion Picture Herald. Feb 18, 1939, p42.
The New Masses. Mar 28, 1939, v31, p30.
The New York Times. Mar 10, 1939, p19.
Newsweek. Mar 6, 1939, v13, p28.
Photoplay. Apr 1939, v53, p53.
Rob Wagner's Script. Apr 29, 1939, v21, p18.
Time. Mar 13, 1939, v33, p30.
Variety. Feb 22, 1939, p12.

Let George Do It (GB; Varnel, Marcel; 1940)
Fifty Classic British Films. p37-39.
Film Daily. Oct 25, 1940, p6.
Hollywood Reporter. Oct 28, 1940, p3.
The London Times. Jul 15, 1940, p6.
Magill's Survey of Cinema. Series II. v3, p1348-50.
Motion Picture Exhibitor. Oct 30, 1940, p630.
The New York Times. Oct 14, 1940, p25.
Variety. Oct 16, 1940, p31.

Let Katy Do It (US; Franklin, Sidney; Franklin, Carl; 1916)
The Moving Picture World. Dec 11, 1915, p2028.
The Moving Picture World. Jan 1, 1916, p142.
The New York Dramatic Mirror. Dec 11, 1915, p33.
Photoplay. Mar 1916, v9, p105.
Selected Film Criticism, 1912-1920. p162-63.
Variety. Dec 10, 1915, p21.

Let Us Be Gay (US; Leonard, Robert Z.; 1930)
Commonweal. Jul 23, 1930, v12, p325.
Exhibitors Herald-World. Jul 26, 1930, p29.
Film Daily. Jul 13, 1930, p11.
The Films of Norma Shearer. p168-70.
Judge. Aug 9, 1930, v99, p23.
Life. Aug 8, 1930, v96, p17.
The New York Times. Jul 12, 1930, p16.
The New York Times. Jul 20, 1930, p3.
The New Yorker. Jul 19, 1930, v6, p54.
Outlook and Independent. Jul 30, 1930, v155, p510.
Time. Jul 28, 1930, v16, p54.
Variety. Jul 16, 1930, p15.

Let Us Live (US; Brahm, John; 1939)
Commonweal. Mar 17, 1939, v29, p580.
Crime Movies (Clarens). p164-66.
Film Daily. Feb 20, 1939, p9.
The Films of Henry Fonda. p79-80.
The Fondas (Springer). p88-90.
Hollywood Reporter. Feb 15, 1939, p2.
Hollywood Spectator. Mar 4, 1939, v13, p10-11.
Motion Picture Herald. Feb 18, 1939, p42-43.
National Board of Review Magazine. Apr 1939, v14, p20.
The New York Times. Mar 30, 1939, p19.
Variety. Feb 22, 1939, p12.

Let's Face It (US; Lanfield, Sidney; 1943)
Commonweal. Aug 27, 1943, v38, p467.
Film Daily. Aug 5, 1943, p10.
The Hollywood Musical. p216, 240.
Hollywood Reporter. Aug 5, 1943, p3.
Motion Picture Herald Product Digest. Aug 7, 1943, p1559.
The New York Times. Aug 5, 1943, p18.
Newsweek. Aug 16, 1943, v22, p92.
Time. Aug 23, 1943, v42, p94.
Variety. Aug 11, 1943, p10.

Let's Fall in Love (US; Burton, David; 1934)
Film Daily. Jan 20, 1934, p3.
The Hollywood Musical. p85.
Motion Picture Herald. Jan 13, 1934, p39.
The New York Times. Jan 22, 1934, p12.
Variety. Jan 23, 1934, p13.

Let's Get Married (US; Green, Alfred E.; 1937)
Film Daily. Apr 14, 1937, p7.
Hollywood Reporter. Mar 12, 1937, p3.
Motion Picture Herald. May 29, 1937, p48.

Let's Go Native (US; McCarey, Leo; 1930)
Exhibitors Herald-World. Jun 14, 1930, p109.
Exhibitors Herald-World. Sep 6, 1930, p40.
Film Daily. Aug 31, 1930, p10.
The Films of Jeanette MacDonald and Nelson Eddy. p57-62.
Judge. Sep 27, 1930, v99, p21.
The New York Times. Aug 30, 1930, p7.
The New Yorker. Sep 6, 1930, v6, p63.
Outlook and Independent. Sep 24, 1930, v156, p150.
Time. Mar 17, 1930, v15, p54.
Time. Sep 15, 1930, v16, p40.
Variety. Sep 3, 1930, p41.

Let's Make a Million (US; McCarey, Ray; 1937)
Film Daily. Mar 11, 1937, p8.
Motion Picture Herald. Feb 27, 1937, p60.
Rob Wagner's Script. Jan 23, 1937, v16, p13.
Variety. Jan 27, 1937, p13.

The Letter (US; De Limur, Jean; 1929)
Film Daily. Mar 17, 1929, p4.
The Films of the Twenties. p230-32.
The New York Times. Mar 8, 1929, p30.
Variety. Mar 13, 1929, p14.

The Letter (US; Wyler, William; 1940)
Around Cinemas. p221-22.
Bette Davis: Her Films and Career. p104-05.
BFI/Monthly Film Bulletin. Mar 1941, v8, p32.
Commonweal. Dec 6, 1940, v33, p180.
Film Daily. Nov 14, 1940, p5.
Film Noir. p170-71.
Halliwell's Hundred. p176-79.
Hollywood Reporter. Nov 14, 1940, p3.
Life. Dec 2, 1940, v9, p51-53+.
Magill's Survey of Cinema. Series II. v3, p1351-54.
Motion Picture Exhibitor. Nov 27, 1940, p647.
The New Republic. Dec 16, 1940, v103, p836.
The New Statesman and Nation. Jun 7, 1941, v21, p578.
The New York Times. Nov 23, 1940, p12.
The New York Times. Dec 1, 1940, sec10, p5.
The New Yorker. Nov 23, 1940, v16, p49.
Newsweek. Dec 2, 1940, v16, p48.
The Spectator. Jun 6, 1941, v166, p607.
Stage. Nov 1940, v1, p32.
Time. Dec 2, 1940, v36, p77.
Variety. Nov 20, 1940, p16.
William Wyler: A Guide to References and Resources. p105-08.
William Wyler (Anderegg). p95-103.
50 Classic Motion Pictures. p20-25.

A Letter of Introduction (US; Stahl, John M.; 1938)
Commonweal. Aug 19, 1938, v28, p430.
Film Daily. Jul 30, 1938, p3.
Hollywood Reporter. Jul 29, 1938, p3.
Motion Picture Herald. Aug 6, 1938, p44.
The New York Times. Sep 1, 1938, p17.
The New Yorker. Sep 3, 1938, v14, p44.
Newsweek. Aug 15, 1938, v12, p26-27.
Rob Wagner's Script. Aug 20, 1938, v20, p14.
Time. Aug 8, 1938, v32, p38.
Variety. Aug 3, 1938, p15.

A Letter to Three Wives (US; Mankiewicz, Joseph L.; 1949)
Collier's. Jan 22, 1949, v123, p40.
Commonweal. Feb 11, 1949, v49, p448.
Film Daily. Dec 6, 1948, p7.
Films in Review. Feb 1950, v1, p36-37.
The Films of Kirk Douglas. p54-56.
The Films of the Forties. p250-51.
Hollywood Reporter. Dec 3, 1948, p3.
Joseph L. Mankiewicz (Dick). p59-76.
Magill's Survey of Cinema. Series II. v3, p1355-57.
Motion Picture Herald Product Digest. Dec 4, 1949, p4405.
The Nation. Feb 26, 1949, v168, p256+.
The New Republic. Feb 7, 1949, v120, p31.
The New York Times. Jan 21, 1949, p24.
The New Yorker. Jan 29, 1949, v24, p53.
Newsweek. Jan 24, 1949, v33, p72.
Rotarian. Apr 1949, v74, p36.
Theatre Arts. Apr 1949, v33, p6+.
Time. Jan 17, 1949, v53, p86.
Variety. Dec 8, 1948, p10.

Letty Lynton (US; Brown, Clarence; 1932)
Film Daily. May 1, 1932, p10.
The Films of Joan Crawford. p97-102.
Judge. Jun 4, 1932, v102, p22.
London Mercury. Jul 1932, v26, p262.
Motion Picture Herald. May 7, 1932, p28, 30.
The Nation. May 25, 1932, v134, p607.
The New York Times. Apr 30, 1932, p19.
The New Yorker. May 7, 1932, v8, p64.
Rob Wagner's Script. Jul 2, 1932, v7, p10.
Time. May 9, 1932, v19, p23.
Variety. May 3, 1932, p14.

Letzte Mann, Der *See* The Last Laugh

Libeled Lady (US; Conway, Jack; 1936)
Canadian Magazine. Dec 1936, v86, p38.
The Film Criticism of Otis Ferguson. p161.
Film Daily. Oct 7, 1936, p4.
The Films of Jean Harlow. p144-47.
The Films of Myrna Loy. p199-200.
Hollywood Reporter. Oct 5, 1936, p3.
Judge. Dec 1936, v111, p32.
Literary Digest. Nov 7, 1936, v122, p22.
Lunatics and Lovers. p98-100.
Magill's Survey of Cinema. Series II. v3, p1358-62.
Motion Picture Herald. Oct 17, 1936, p47.
The New Republic. Nov 25, 1936, v89, p113.
The New Statesman and Nation. Nov 21, 1936, v12, p811.
The New York Times. Oct 31, 1936, p24.
The New Yorker. Oct 24, 1936, v12, p58-59.
Newsweek. Oct 24, 1936, v8, p39.
Rob Wagner's Script. Oct 10, 1936, v16, p10.
The Tatler. Nov 25, 1936, v142, p340.
Time. Oct 19, 1936, v28, p67.
Variety. Nov 4, 1936, p18.
World Film News. Jan 1937, v1, p24.

The Lie of Nina Petrovna (Also titled: Nina Petrovna) (FR; Tourjansky, Victor; 1937)
Film Daily. Apr 9, 1938, p5.
Hollywood Reporter. Nov 20, 1937, p7.
Motion Picture Herald. Apr 9, 1938, p42.
The New Statesman and Nation. Mar 26, 1938, v15, p527.
The New York Times. Mar 30, 1938, p19.
The New Yorker. Apr 9, 1938, v14, p69.
Time. Apr 11, 1938, v31, p24.

Liebe der Jeanne Ney, Die *See* The Love of Jeanne Ney

Liebe im 3/4 Takt (Also titled: Love in 3/4 Time) (GER; Marischka, Hubert; 1938)
Motion Picture Herald. Oct 28, 1938, p40, 42.
The New York Times. Sep 24, 1938, p13.
Variety. Sep 28, 1938, p21.

Liebelei (Also titled: Histoire d'Amour, Une) (GER; Ophuls, Max; 1932)
Cinema, the Magic Vehicle. v1, p205-06.
Dictionary of Films. p191-92.
Film Comment. Mar-Apr 1973, v9, p46-50.
Film Daily. Feb 29, 1936, p9.
Film in the Third Reich. p38-39.
From Caligari to Hitler. p231.
Hollywood Reporter. May 7, 1936, p4.
Magill's Survey of Cinema. Foreign Language Films. v4, p1780-84.
Motion Picture Herald. Mar 14, 1936, p58, 60.
The New York Times. Jul 2, 1933, p2.
The New York Times. Feb 28, 1936, p18.
Ophuls (Willemen). p17-18, 51-54.
Sequence. 1950, n10, p152-53.
The Spectator. Jan 19, 1934, v152, p83.
Variety. Apr 11, 1933, p20.
Variety. May 30, 1933, p54.
Variety. Mar 4, 1936, p31.

Liebesmelodie (Also titled: Reunion) (AUSTRIA; Tourjansky, Victor; 1935)
Graham Greene on Film. p64-65.
Hollywood Reporter. Apr 13, 1936, p4.
The New Statesman and Nation. Apr 11, 1936, v11, p568.
Saturday Review (London). Apr 18, 1936, v161, p512.
The Spectator. Apr 10, 1936, v156, p664.
The Tatler. Apr 29, 1936, v140, p190.

Lieutenant Souriant, Le *See* The Smiling Lieutenant

The Life and Death of Colonel Blimp *See* Colonel Blimp

The Life and Loves of Beethoven *See* Grande Amour de Beethoven, Une

Life Begins (US; Flood, James; 1932)
Commonweal. Sep 28, 1932, v16, p512.
Film Daily. Aug 12, 1932, p3.
Hollywood Reporter. Jul 30, 1932, p2.
Motion Picture Herald. Aug 13, 1932, p31.
The Nation. Sep 14, 1932, v135, p240.
The New York Times. Aug 26, 1932, p20.
Rob Wagner's Script. Nov 5, 1932, v8, p8.
Time. Sep 5, 1932, v20, p40.
Variety. Aug 30, 1932, p14.

Life Begins at Forty (US; Marshall, George; 1935)
Film Daily. Apr 5, 1935, p6.
Hollywood Reporter. Feb 1, 1935, p3.
Literary Digest. Apr 20, 1935, v119, p34.
Motion Picture Herald. Mar 23, 1935, p39.
The New York Times. Apr 5, 1935, p21.
The New Yorker. Apr 13, 1935, v11, p63.
Time. Apr 1, 1935, v25, p36.
Variety. Apr 10, 1935, p17.
Will Rogers in Hollywood. p155-56.

Life Begins for Andy Hardy (US; Seitz, George B.; 1940)
Film Daily. Aug 13, 1941, p13.
Hollywood Reporter. Aug 6, 1941, p3.
The London Times. Nov 3, 1941, p8.
Motion Picture Exhibitor. Aug 20, 1941, p813.
Motion Picture Herald Product Digest. Jul 26, 1941, p193.
The New York Times. Aug 22, 1941, p19.
Newsweek. Sep 8, 1941, v18, p68-69.
Scribner's Commentator. Nov 1941, v11, p106.
Variety. Aug 13, 1941, p8.

Life Begins in College (US; Seiter, William A.; 1937)
Film Daily. Sep 28, 1937, p8.
Hollywood Reporter. Sep 22, 1937, p5.
Motion Picture Herald. Oct 2, 1937, p38.
The New York Times. Oct 9, 1937, p16.
Time. Oct 11, 1937, v30, p36.
Variety. Sep 29, 1937, p14.

Life Dances On *See* Carnet de Bal, Un

Life Is Ours *See* Vie Est a Nous, La

The Life Line (US; Tourneur, Maurice; 1919)
Exhibitor's Trade Review. Oct 11, 1919, p1653.
Motion Picture News. Oct 11, 1919, p2897.
The Moving Picture World. Dec 20, 1919, p1013.
The New York Times. Sep 29, 1919, p16.
Variety. Oct 3, 1919, p57.
Wid's Daily. Oct 12, 1919, p18.

The Life of an American Fireman (US; Porter, Edwin S.; 1902)
Behind the Screen. p113-14.
The Emergence of Film Art. p22-25.
Film Before Griffith. p218-20.
The First Twenty Years. p30.
A History of Narrative Film. p20-24.
A Million and One Nights. p415, 420.
Motion Pictures. p32-36.

Life of an American Policeman (US; Porter, Edwin S.; 1905)
American Silent Film. p37-40.
A History of Films. p46-48.

The Life of Emile Zola (US; Dieterle, William; 1937)
Around Cinemas. p144-47.
Christian Century. Dec 1, 1937, v54, p1484-85.
Cinema, the Magic Vehicle. v1, p282.
Commonweal. Jul 30, 1937, v26, p347.
Dictionary of Films. p193.

Esquire. Oct 1937, v8, p121, 218-19.
The Film Criticism of Otis Ferguson. p188-90.
Film Daily. Jul 2, 1937, p8.
Fortune. Dec 1937, v16, p111.
From Quasimodo to Scarlett O'Hara. p257-59.
Graham Greene on Film. p177.
The Great Spy Films. p264-65.
Hollywood Reporter. Jun 29, 1937, p3.
Hollywood Spectator. Jul 17, 1937, v12, p4.
A Library of Film Criticism: American Film Directors. p91-92.
Life. Aug 9, 1937, v3, p30-33.
Literary Digest. Aug 14, 1937, v124, p31.
London Mercury. Dec 1937, v37, p198-99.
Lorentz on Film. p146-47.
Magill's Survey of Cinema. Series I. v2, p970-73.
Motion Picture Herald. Jul 10, 1937, p50.
The Nation. Sep 4, 1937, v145, p246.
National Board of Review Magazine. Oct 1937, v12, p9.
The New Masses. Oct 5, 1937, v25, p29.
The New Masses. Aug 17, 1937, v24, p29.
New Republic. Aug 18, 1937, v92, p48-49.
The New Statesman and Nation. Oct 23, 1937, v14, p644.
The New York Times. Aug 12, 1937, p14.
The New Yorker. Aug 14, 1937, v13, p58-59.
Newsweek. Aug 14, 1937, v10, p19.
Paul Muni: His Life and His Films. p164-72.
Rob Wagner's Script. Sep 11, 1937, v18, p10.
Scholastic. Sep 1 .937, v31, p34-35.
Scribner's Magazine. Oct 1937, v102, p64.
Selected Film Criticism, 1931-1940. p136-37.
Sight and Sound. Wint 1937-38, v6, p187.
The Spectator. Oct 29, 1937, v159, p743.
Stage. Sep 1937, v14, p30-33.
The Tatler. Oct 27, 1937, v146, p148.
Theatre Arts. Jun 1938, v22, p416.
Time. Aug 16, 1937, v30, p34-35.
Variety. Jun 30, 1937, p21.
Warner Brothers Presents. p277-79.
World Film News. Nov 1937, v2, p16-18.
World Film News. Dec 1937, v2, p28.

The Life of Jimmy Dolan (US; Mayo, Archie; 1933)
Commonweal. Aug 18, 1933, v18, p388.
Film Daily. Jun 14, 1933, p6.
Hollywood Reporter. Feb 16, 1933, p3.
Motion Picture Herald. Jun 24, 1933, p43.
New Outlook. Jul 1933, v162, p43.
The New York Times. Jun 14, 1933, p22.
The New Yorker. Jun 24, 1933, v9, p54.
Newsweek. Jun 24, 1933, v1, p30.
Rob Wagner's Script. Mar 25, 1933, v9, p10.
Time. Jun 26, 1933, v21, p40.
Variety. Jun 20, 1933, p11.

The Life of Moses (US; Kent, Charles; 1909; 1910)
The Bioscope. Feb 10, 1910, p15, 17.
Magill's Survey of Cinema. Silent Films. v2, p654-56.
The Moving Picture World. Dec 18, 1909, p878.
Selected Film Criticism, 1896-1911. p59-62.

The Life of Riley (US; Brecher, Irving; 1949)
Film Daily. Jan 27, 1949, p5.
Hollywood Reporter. Jan 26, 1949, p3.
Motion Picture Herald Product Digest. Jan 29, 1949, p4477.
The New York Times. Apr 18, 1949, p18.
Time. Mar 14, 1949, v53, p106.
Variety. Jan 26, 1949, p11.

Life on the Waterfront *See* Port of Seven Seas

Life With Father (US; Curtiz, Michael; 1947)
Commonweal. Aug 22, 1947, v46, p454.
Film Daily. Aug 15, 1947, p10.
The Films of Elizabeth Taylor. p60-63.
The Films of the Forties. p204-06.
Fortnight. Sep 12, 1947, v3, p29-30.

Hollywood Reporter. Aug 15, 1947, p3.
Life. Aug 18, 1947, v23, p64-66+.
Magill's Survey of Cinema. Second Series. v3, p1367-69.
Motion Picture Herald Product Digest. Aug 16, 1947, p3781.
New Republic. Sep 29, 1947, v117, p37.
The New York Times. Aug 16, 1947, p6.
The New York Times Magazine. Jul 13, 1947, p18-19.
The New Yorker. Aug 23, 1947, v23, p42.
Newsweek. Aug 18, 1947, v30, p76-77.
Selected Film Criticism, 1941-1950. p116-119.
Time. Aug 25, 1947, v50, p88.
Variety. Aug 20, 1947, p16.

Lifeboat (US; Hitchcock, Alfred; 1944)
Agee on Film. v1, p71-72.
Alfred Hitchcock: The First Forty-Four Films. p74-78+.
The Art of Alfred Hitchcock. p145-50.
Commonweal. Jan 28, 1944, v39, p374.
Film Comment. Jan-Feb 1976, v12, p32-34.
Film Daily. Jan 12, 1944, p29.
Films and the Second World War. p200-02.
The Films of Alfred Hitchcock. p118-20.
The Films of World War II. p168-70.
Framework. Wint 1977, n6, p24-29.
Hitchcock (Truffaut). p155-59.
Hollywood Reporter. Jan 12, 1944, p3.
Life. Jan 31, 1944, v16, p76-81.
Literature/Film Quarterly. Fall 1976, v4, p325-38.
The London Times. Mar 16, 1944, p6.
Magill's Survey of Cinema. Series I. v2, p974-77.
Motion Picture Exhibitor. Jan 26, 1944, v31, n11, sec2, p1445.
The Nation. Jan 22, 1944, v158, p108.
The New Republic. Jan 24, 1944, v110, p116.
The New Republic. Feb 14, 1944, v110, p212.
The New York Times. Jan 13, 1944, p17.
The New York Times. Jan 23, 1944, p11.
The New Yorker. Jan 15, 1944, v19, p48+.
The New Yorker. Feb 5, 1944, v19, p65.
Newsweek. Jan 17, 1944, v23, p66+.
Rob Wagner's Script. Jan 22, 1944, v30, p14.
Selected Film Criticism, 1941-1950. p119-20.
Time. Jan 31, 1944, v43, p94.
Variety. Jan 12, 1944, p24.

Light of Asia (CHINA; 1926)
Asia. Sep 1926, v26, p753.
Literary Digest. Sep 11, 1926, v90, p28.
Variety. May 16, 1928, p73.

The Light of Victory (US; Wolbert, William; 1919)
Exhibitor's Trade Review. Mar 15, 1919, p1147.
Motion Picture News. Mar 15, 1919, p1655-57, 1711.
The Moving Picture World. Mar 8, 1919, p1387.
Variety. Feb 28, 1919, p56.
Wid's Daily. Mar 2, 1919, p3.

The Light That Failed (US; Wellman, William A.; 1939)
Commonweal. Jan 12, 1940, v31, p266.
Film Daily. Dec 26, 1939, p6.
The Films of Ronald Colman. p203-06.
Graham Greene on Film. p262-64.
Hollywood Reporter. Dec 20, 1939, p3.
Hollywood Spectator. Jan 6, 1940, v14, p3.
Life. Dec 18, 1939, v7, p53-56.
Motion Picture Herald. Dec 23, 1939, p37.
The New Statesman and Nation. Jan 13, 1940, v19, p41.
The New York Times. Dec 25, 1939, p19.
Newsweek. Jan 8, 1940, v15, p37.
Photoplay. Feb 1940, v54, p63.
Saturday Review. May 11, 1940, v22, p21.
The Spectator. Jan 19, 1940, v164, p76.
Time. Jan 8, 1940, v35, p56.
Variety. Dec 27, 1939, p12.
William A. Wellman (Thompson). p189-95.

Lightnin' (US; King, Henry; 1930)
Exhibitors Herald-World. Dec 6, 1930, p28.
Film Daily. Nov 2, 1930, p10.
Judge. Dec 20, 1930, v99, p21.
Life. Dec 19, 1930, v96, p20.
The New York Times. Nov 28, 1930, p21.
The New York Times. Dec 7, 1930, p5.
Outlook and Independent. Dec 17, 1930, v156, p630.
Theatre Magazine. Feb 1931, v53, p48.
Time. Dec 15, 1930, v16, p32.
Variety. Dec 3, 1930, p14.
Will Rogers in Hollywood. p109-10.

The Lights of New York (US; Foy, Bryan; 1928)
Exhibitor's Herald-World and Moving Picture World. Aug 18, 1928, p61.
Film Daily. Jul 15, 1928, p6.
The Films of the Twenties. p196-97.
The New York Times. Jul 9, 1928, p25.
Photoplay. Sep 1928, v34, p57.
Selected Film Criticism, 1921-1930. p169.
Variety. Jul 11, 1928, p13.

Lilac Time (US; Fitzmaurice, George; 1928)
Exhibitor's Herald-World and Moving Picture World. Aug 18, 1928, p61.
Film Daily. Aug 12, 1928, p6.
The Film Spectator. Jun 23, 1928, v5, p8, 18.
The Films of Gary Cooper. p54-56.
The Films of the Twenties. p198-201.
Magill's Survey of Cinema. Silent Films. v2, p657-61.
The New York Times. Aug 4, 1928, p4.
Photoplay. Aug 1928, v34, p56.
Selected Film Criticism, 1921-1930. p170-71.
Variety. Aug 8, 1928, p12.

Lilies of the Field (US; Korda, Alexander; 1930)
Film Daily. Feb 23, 1930, p8.
Life. Mar 21, 1930, v95, p22, 30.
The New York Times. Feb 22, 1930, p13.
Time. Mar 10, 1930, v15, p58.
Variety. Feb 26, 1930, p35.

Liliom (FR; Lang, Fritz; 1934)
Film Daily. Mar 19, 1935, p4.
The Films of Fritz Lang. p168-71.
Fritz Lang: A Guide to References and Resources. p67-69.
Fritz Lang (Eisner). p149-59.
Hollywood Reporter. Jul 10, 1934, p3.
The Nation. Mar 27, 1935, v140, p372.
The New York Times. Mar 18, 1935, p14.
Time. Mar 25, 1935, v25, p46.
Variety. May 15, 1934, p30.
Variety. Mar 20, 1935, p31.

Liliom (US; Borzage, Frank; 1930)
Cinema. Dec 1930, v1, p37-38.
Exhibitors Herald-World. Sep 30, 1930, p37.
Exhibitors Herald-World. Aug 30, 1930, p28.
Film Daily. Sep 14, 1930, p12.
Life. Oct 31, 1930, v96, p22.
The New York Times. Oct 4, 1930, p15.
The New York Times. Oct 12, 1930, p5.
Outlook and Independent. Oct 22, 1930, v156, p315.
Selected Film Criticism, 1921-1930. p171-73.
Time. Oct 20, 1930, v16, p38.
Variety. Oct 8, 1930, p22.

Lillian Russell (US; Cummings, Irving; 1940)
Commonweal. May 31, 1940, v32, p130.
Film Daily. May 16, 1940, p12.
The Films of Alice Faye. p131-36.
Life. May 20, 1940, v8, p55-56+.
Motion Picture Herald. May 18, 1940, p48.
The Nation. Jun 8, 1940, v150, p716.
The New York Times. May 18, 1940, p11.

Newsweek. May 27, 1940, v15, p48+.
Photoplay. May 1940, v54, p15.
Photoplay. Jun 1940, v54, p27-40.
Time. Jun 3, 1940, v35, p73.
Variety. May 22, 1940, p14.

Lily Turner (US; Wellman, William A.; 1933)
Film Daily. Jun 15, 1933, p4.
Hollywood Reporter. Apr 20, 1933, p3.
Motion Picture Herald. Apr 29, 1933, p26, 28.
New Outlook. Jun 1933, v161, p42.
The New York Times. Jun 15, 1933, p21.
The New Yorker. Jun 24, 1933, v9, p54-55.
Rob Wagner's Script. Jun 3, 1933, v9, p8.
Time. Jun 26, 1933, v21, p40.
Variety. Jun 20, 1933, p11.
William A. Wellman (Thompson). p132-33.

Lines of White on a Sullen Sea (US; Griffith, D.W.; 1909)
American Silent Film. p48.
The Moving Picture World. Nov 6, 1909, p644-45.
Selected Film Criticism, 1896-1911. p62.

The Lion Has Wings (GB; Powell, Michael; 1939)
Canadian Forum. Jan 1940, v19, p327.
Commonweal. Dec 22, 1939, v31, p206.
Film Daily. Jan 24, 1940, p4.
Graham Greene on Film. p249-50.
Motion Picture Herald. Nov 18, 1939, p49.
The New Statesman and Nation. Nov 4, 1939, v18, p644.
The New York Times. Jan 22, 1940, p11.
Sight and Sound. Spr 1940, v9, p8.
The Tatler. Nov 8, 1939, v154, p176.
Time. Nov 20, 1939, v34, p80.
Variety. Jan 24, 1940, p14.

Listen, Darling (US; Marin, Edwin L.; 1938)
Commonweal. Nov 4, 1938, v29, p49.
Film Daily. Oct 18, 1938, p9.
Hollywood Reporter. Oct 14, 1938, p3.
Hollywood Spectator. Oct 29, 1938, v13, p10.
Judy: The Films and Career of Judy Garland. p59-61.
Motion Picture Herald. Oct 22, 1938, p27, 32.
The New York Times. Nov 24, 1938, p37.
Rob Wagner's Script. Nov 19, 1938, v20, p14.
Time. Oct 31, 1938, v32, p28.
Variety. Oct 19, 1938, p12.

The Little American (US; DeMille, Cecil B.; 1917)
The Films of Cecil B. DeMille. p132-35.
The Moving Picture World. Jul 21, 1917, p24.
Photoplay. Sep 1917, v12, p101.
Variety. Jul 6, 1917, p24.
Wid's Daily. Jul 12, 1917, p440-41.

Little Annie Rooney (US; Beaudine, William; 1925)
BFI/Monthly Film Bulletin. Jun 1974, v41, p137-38.
Film Daily. Oct 25, 1925, p6.
The Moving Picture World. Oct 31, 1925, p717.
Photoplay. Oct 1925, v28, p50.
Selected Film Criticism, 1921-1930. p173.
Variety. Oct 21, 1925, p34.

Little Caesar (US; LeRoy, Mervyn; 1930)
American Film Criticism. p247-49.
American Film Genres. p21-40.
BFI/Monthly Film Bulletin. Nov 1975, v43, p38-39.
The Cinema of Edward G. Robinson. p78-81.
Cinema, the Magic Vehicle. v1, p179.
The Classic American Novel and the Movies. p286-96.
Classics of the Gangster Film. p9-12.
Crime Movies. p54-57.
Dictionary of Films. p194.
Dreams and Dead Ends. p25-42.
Eighty Years of Cinema. p84.

Exhibitors Herald-World. Jan 17, 1931, p60.
Film Daily. Nov 16, 1930, p11.
Films and Filming. Jan 1964, v10, p7-12.
The Films of the Thirties. p45-46.
The Great Gangster Pictures. p245-48.
Halliwell's Hundred. p310-13.
Hollywood Genres. p86-90.
Journal of Popular Film. Sum 1972, v1, p209-27.
Judge. Jan 31, 1931, v100, p22.
Judge. Feb 7, 1931, v100, p22.
Landmark Films: The Cinema and Our Century. p64-71.
Life. Jan 30, 1931, v97, p21.
Little Caesar. p9-28.
Magill's Survey of Cinema. Series II. v3, p1390-92.
The New York Times. Jan 10, 1931, p19.
The New York Times. Jan 18, 1931, p5.
The New Yorker. Jan 17, 1931, v6, p65, 67.
Outlook and Independent. Jan 21, 1931, v157, p113.
Photoplay. Dec 1930, v39, p112.
Selected Film Criticism, 1931-1940. p138.
Theatre Magazine. Apr 1931, v53, p60.
Those Fabulous Movie Years: The 30s. p20.
Time. Jan 19, 1931, v17, p24.
Variety. Jan 14, 1931, p12.
The Velvet Light Trap. Jun 1971, v1, p5-11.
Vintage Films. p16-18.
Warner Brothers Presents. p60-61.

The Little Colonel (US; Butler, David; 1935)
Film Daily. Mar 22, 1935, p7.
Film Notes. p96.
The Films of Shirley Temple. p146-53.
Hollywood Reporter. Feb 6, 1935, p3.
Motion Picture Herald. Feb 16, 1935, p46.
The New York Times. Mar 22, 1935, p26.
The New Yorker. Mar 23, 1935, v11, p62.
Saturday Review (London). Aug 31, 1935, v160, p128.
Theatre Arts Monthly. Jun 1935, v19, p407.
Time. Mar 11, 1935, v25, p52.
Variety. Mar 27, 1935, p15.

The Little Foxes (US; Wyler, William; 1941)
Bette Davis: Her Films and Career. p110-12.
BFI/Monthly Film Bulletin. Nov 1941, v8, p151.
Commonweal. Sep 5, 1941, v34, p473.
The Film Criticism of Otis Ferguson. p383-85.
Film Daily. Aug 12, 1941, p7.
Hollywood Reporter. Aug 12, 1941, p3.
Life. Sep 1, 1941, v11, p47-50.
The London Times. Jan 19, 1941, p8.
Magill's Survey of Cinema. Series I. v2, p984-87.
Motion Picture Herald. Aug 16, 1941, p34.
Motion Picture Herald Product Digest. Aug 23, 1941, p217.
The New Republic. Sep 1, 1941, v105, p2781.
New Statesman and Nation. Jan 24, 1941, v23, p57.
The New York Times. Aug 22, 1941, p19.
The New York Times. Aug 24, 1941, sec9, p3.
The New Yorker. Aug 23, 1941, v17, p35.
Newsweek. Aug 25, 1941, v18, p53-54.
One Good Film Deserves Another. p36-40.
Samuel Goldwyn (Epstein). p92-97.
Samuel Goldwyn Presents. p216-19.
Scribner's Commentator. Nov 1941, v11, p105.
Spectator. Jan 23, 1941, v168, p82.
Theatre Arts. Oct 1941, v25, p730.
Theatre World. Oct 1941, v36, p30.
Time. Sep 1, 1941, v38, p86-87.
Today's Cinema. Apr 12, 1941, p217.
Variety. Aug 13, 1941, p8.
William Wyler: A Guide to References and Resources. p108-11.
William Wyler (Anderegg). p104-12.

The Little Giant (US; Del Ruth, Roy; 1933)
The Cinema of Edward G. Robinson. p93-96.
Commonweal. Jun 16, 1933, v18, p190.
Film Daily. Apr 14, 1933, p11.
The Gangster Film. p113-15.
Hollywood Reporter. Apr 6, 1933, p3.
Judge. Jul 1933, v104, p20.
Motion Picture Herald. Apr 15, 1933, p28.
The Nation. Jun 14, 1933, v136, p678+.
The New York Times. May 27, 1933, p11.
The New Yorker. Jun 3, 1933, v9, p58.
Rob Wagner's Script. May 27, 1933, v9, p8.
Time. Jun 5, 1933, v21, p19.
Variety. May 30, 1933, p15.

Little Lord Fauntleroy (US; Green, Alfred E.; 1921)
BFI/Monthly Film Bulletin. Jun 1974, v41, p138.
Film Daily. Sep 18, 1921, p3.
The New York Times. Sep 16, 1921, p17.
Photoplay. Dec 1921, v21, p60.
Selected Film Criticism, 1921-1930. p174.
Variety. Sep 23, 1921, p42.

Little Lord Fauntleroy (US; Cromwell, John; 1936)
Canadian Magazine. Apr 1936, v85, p58.
Children's Novels and the Movies. p69-80.
Commonweal. Mar 13, 1936, v23, p552.
Film Daily. Feb 25, 1936, p9.
The Hollywood Professionals. v5, p76-78.
Hollywood Reporter. Feb 21, 1936, p3.
Hollywood Spectator. Feb 29, 1936, v10, p5-6.
Literary Digest. Mar 21, 1936, v121, p20.
Motion Picture Herald. Feb 29, 1936, p40.
The New York Times. Apr 3, 1936, p27.
The New Yorker. Apr 11, 1936, v12, p69.
Newsweek. Mar 21, 1936, v7, p24.
Rob Wagner's Script. Apr 11, 1936, v15, p10.
Time. Mar 23, 1936, v27, p48.
Variety. Apr 8, 1936, p16.

Little Man, What Now? (US; Borzage, Frank; 1934)
BFI/Monthly Film Bulletin. Aug 1978, v45, p164.
Commonweal. Jun 15, 1934, v20, p188.
Film Daily. Jun 1, 1934, p7.
Hollywood Reporter. May 19, 1934, p4.
The Hollywood Social Problem Films. p75-76, 97-98, 209-10.
Literary Digest. Jun 16, 1934, v117, p30.
Motion Picture Herald. May 26, 1934, p38-39.
The Nation. Jun 20, 1934, v138, p714.
The New York Times. Jun 1, 1934, p29.
Newsweek. Jun 9, 1934, p36.
Time. Jun 11, 1934, v23, p48.
Variety. Jun 5, 1934, p12.

The Little Minister (US; Wallace, Richard; 1934)
Film Daily. Dec 22, 1934, p3.
The Films of Katharine Hepburn. p58-62.
Hollywood Reporter. Dec 10, 1934, p3.
Literary Digest. Jan 12, 1935, v119, p31.
Magill's Survey of Cinema. Series II. v3, p1393-95.
The New York Times. Dec 28, 1934, p25.
Variety. Jan 1, 1935, p18.

Little Miss Broadway (US; Cummings, Irving; 1938)
Film Daily. Jul 9, 1938, p3.
The Films of Shirley Temple. p194-97.
Hollywood Reporter. Jul 2, 1938, p3.
Motion Picture Herald. Jul 9, 1938, p28.
The New York Times. Jul 23, 1938, p10.
The New Yorker. Jul 23, 1938, v14, p53.
Rob Wagner's Script. Aug 16, 1938, v19, p22.
Saint Nicholas. Jul 1938, v65, p40.
Time. Aug 1, 1938, v32, p28.
Variety. Jul 6, 1938, p15.

Little Miss Marker (US; Hall, Alexander; 1934)
Film Daily. May 19, 1934, p3.
The Films of Shirley Temple. p130-33.
The Films of the Thirties. p124-26.
The Great Gangster Films. p250-51.
The Hollywood Musical. p88.
Hollywood Reporter. Apr 27, 1934, p3.
Motion Picture Herald. Dec 22, 1934, p35.
Motion Picture Herald. May 5, 1934, p44.
The New York Times. May 19, 1934, p18.
Newsweek. May 26, 1934, v3, p35.
Time. May 28, 1934, v23, p36.
Variety. May 22, 1934, p15.

Little Miss Nobody (US; Blystone, John G.; 1936)
Film Daily. Mar 24, 1936, p8.
Hollywood Reporter. Mar 21, 1936, p3.
Motion Picture Herald. Mar 28, 1936, p40.
The New York Times. Jun 6, 1936, p21.
Rob Wagner's Script. May 30, 1936, v15, p10.
Time. Jun 22, 1936, v27, p37.
Variety. Jun 10, 1936, p18.

Little Old New York (US; Olcott, Sidney; 1923)
Exceptional Photoplays. Oct-Nov 1923, v4, p3.
Film Daily. Aug 5, 1923, p6.
Photoplay. Oct 1923, v24, p72.
Selected Film Criticism, 1921-1930. p174-75.
Variety. Aug 9, 1923, p26.

Little Orphan Annie (US; Campbell, Colin; 1918)
Exhibitor's Trade Review. Dec 14, 1918, p145.
Motion Picture News. Dec 21, 1918, p3770.
The Moving Picture World. Dec 14, 1918, p1246.
The Moving Picture World. Jan 11, 1919, p249.
Selected Film Criticism, 1912-1920. p163-64.
Variety. Dec 6, 1918, p39.

Little Orphan Annie (US; Robertson, John S.; 1932)
Film Daily. Dec 24, 1932, p4.
Hollywood Reporter. Oct 8, 1932, p2.
Motion Picture Herald. Oct 29, 1932, p31, 34.
The New York Times. Dec 26, 1932, p26.
Rob Wagner's Script. Oct 29, 1932, v8, p9.

The Little Princess (US; Lang, Walter; 1939)
Commonweal. Mar 17, 1939, v29, p580.
Film Daily. Feb 24, 1939, p3.
The Films of Shirley Temple. p202-05.
Hollywood Reporter. Feb 18, 1939, p3.
Hollywood Spectator. Mar 4, 1939, v13, p7-8.
Motion Picture Herald. Feb 25, 1939, p42.
The New Statesman and Nation. May 13, 1939, v17, p736.
The New York Times. Mar 11, 1939, p21.
The New Yorker. Mar 11, 1939, v15, p74-75.
Newsweek. Mar 20, 1939, v13, p32-33.
Photoplay. May 1939, v53, p62.
Rob Wagner's Script. Mar 4, 1939, v21, p16.
Saint Nicholas. Mar 1939, v66, p25.
Scholastic. Mar 25, 1939, v34, p30.
Time. Mar 20, 1939, v33, p47.
Variety. Feb 22, 1939, p12.

The Little Shepherd of Kingdom Come (US; Worsley, Wallace; 1920)
The Moving Picture World. Jan 24, 1920, p510-11.
The Moving Picture World. Feb 28, 1920, p1522.
Variety. Feb 20, 1920, p40.
Wid's Daily. Feb 22, 1920, p17.

Little Tough Guy (US; Young, Harold; 1938)
Film Daily. Jul 11, 1938, p7.
Graham Greene on Film. p198-99.
Hollywood Reporter. Jul 7, 1938, p3.
Motion Picture Herald. Jul 16, 1938, p58.
The New York Times. Aug 18, 1938, p23.

The Spectator. Aug 12, 1938, v161, p264.
Time. Jul 25, 1938, v32, p22.
Variety. Aug 24, 1938, p12.
World Film News. Sep 1938, v3, p220, 222.

Little Women (US; Cukor, George; 1933)
American Review. May 1934, v3, p151-53.
Around Cinemas. p102-04.
Children's Novels and the Movies. p28-38.
The Classic American Novel and the Movies. p62-72.
Commonweal. Dec 22, 1933, v19, p217.
Film Daily. Nov 16, 1933, p6.
The Films of Katharine Hepburn. p50-54.
From Quasimodo to Scarlett O'Hara. p177-79.
George Cukor (Phillips). p65-67.
Hollywood Reporter. Oct 31, 1933, p7.
Judge. Jan 1934, v106, p12.
A Library of Film Criticism: American Film Directors. p65-66.
Life. Jan 1934, v101, p44.
Literary Digest. Dec 2, 1933, v116, p38.
Magill's Survey of Cinema. Series I. v2, p988-91.
Motion Picture Herald. Nov 11, 1933, p27, 30.
The Nation. Nov 29, 1933, v137, p630-31.
National Board of Review Magazine. Dec 1933, v8, p9.
The New York Times. Nov 17, 1933, p22.
The New York Times. Mar 17, 1934, p10.
The New Yorker. Nov 18, 1933, v9, p61-62.
Newsweek. Nov 25, 1933, v2, p32.
On Cukor. p75-81.
Photoplay. Nov 1934, v46, p32-33+.
Pictorial Review. Feb 1934, v35, p86.
Rob Wagner's Script. Dec 23, 1933, v10, p10.
Selected Film Criticism, 1931-1940. p138-40.
The Spectator. Feb 2, 1934, v152, p159.
Those Fabulous Movie Years: The 30s. p47.
Time. Nov 27, 1933, v22, p30.
Vanity Fair. Jan 1934, v41, p46.
Variety. Nov 21, 1933, p14.

Little Women (US; LeRoy, Mervyn; 1949)
Children's Novels and the Movies. p28-38.
The Classic American Novel and the Movies. p62-72.
Commonweal. Apr 1, 1949, v49, p612.
Film Daily. Feb 25, 1949, p7.
The Films of Elizabeth Taylor. p72-75.
Hollywood Reporter. Feb 23, 1949, p3.
Motion Picture Herald Product Digest. Feb 26, 1949, p4514.
The New York Times. Mar 11, 1949, p33.
The New Yorker. Mar 19, 1949, v25, p82.
Newsweek. Mar 28, 1949, v33, p84.
Rotarian. Jul 1949, v75, p50.
Time. Mar 14, 1949, v53, p102.
Variety. Feb 23, 1949, p10.

The Littlest Rebel (US; Butler, David; 1935)
Child Life. Mar 1936, v15, p119.
Commonweal. Dec 27, 1935, v23, p244.
Esquire. Feb 1936, v4, p99.
Film Daily. Nov 22, 1935, p8.
The Films of Shirley Temple. p160-63.
Graham Greene on Film. p78.
Hollywood Reporter. Nov 19, 1935, p3.
Hollywood Spectator. Dec 7, 1935, v10, p8.
Magill's Survey of Cinema. Series I. v2, p992-95.
Motion Picture Herald. Nov 30, 1935, p58.
The New York Times. Dec 20, 1935, p30.
The New Yorker. Dec 28, 1935, v11, p50.
Newsweek. Dec 28, 1935, v6, p24.
Scholastic. Jan 18, 1936, v27, p31.
The Spectator. May 29, 1935, v156, p978.
Time. Dec 30, 1935, v26, p16.
Variety. Dec 25, 1935, p15.

Live, Love and Learn (US; Fitzmaurice, George; 1937)
Film Daily. Oct 20, 1937, p6.
Hollywood Reporter. Oct 15, 1937, p3.
Motion Picture Herald. Oct 23, 1937, p54, 56.
The New Statesman and Nation. Nov 27, 1937, v14, p875.
The New York Times. Nov 19, 1937, p27.
The New Yorker. Nov 27, 1937, v13, p73.
Rob Wagner's Script. Dec 18, 1937, v18, p10.
Time. Nov 1, 1937, v30, p45.
Variety. Oct 20, 1937, p12.

Lives of a Bengal Lancer (US; Hathaway, Henry; 1935)
A Companion to the Movies. p207.
Esquire. Mar 1935, v3, p142.
The Film Criticism of Otis Ferguson. p65-66.
Film Daily. Jan 12, 1935, p3.
Film Daily. Dec 26, 1934, p3.
Film Notes. p94.
The Films of Gary Cooper. p129-31.
The Great Adventure Films. p44-47.
Great Britain and the East. Mar 14, 1935, v44, p320.
Hollywood Reporter. Jan 16, 1935, p2.
Hollywood Reporter. Dec 26, 1934, p3.
Judge. Mar 1935, v108, p30.
Literary Digest. Jan 26, 1935, v119, p35.
Magill's Survey of Cinema. Series II. v3, p1404-08.
Motion Picture. Mar 1935, v49, p40-41.
Motion Picture Herald. Jan 5, 1935, p35.
The Nation. Jan 30, 1935, v140, p139-40.
The New Masses. Jan 22, 1935, v14, p30.
The New Republic. Jan 23, 1935, v81, p305.
The New York Times. Jan 12, 1935, p12.
The New Yorker. Jan 19, 1935, v10, p58-59.
Newsweek. Jan 19, 1935, v5, p26.
Saturday Review (London). Feb 23, 1935, v159, p247.
Scholastic. Feb 9, 1935, v26, p29.
The Spectator. Feb 8, 1935, v154, p206.
The Spectator. Feb 22, 1935, v154, p289.
Time. Jan 21, 1935, v25, p33.
Vanity Fair. Mar 1935, v44, p53.
Variety. Jan 15, 1935, p13.

Living Dangerously (GB; Brenon, Herbert; 1936)
Film Daily. Dec 5, 1936, p7.
Graham Greene on Film. p88-89.
Hollywood Reporter. Dec 8, 1936, p3.
Motion Picture Herald. Mar 21, 1936, p41, 44.
The Spectator. Jul 17, 1936, v157, p97.
Variety. Apr 1, 1936, p17.

The Living Dead (German title: Unheimliche Geschichten) (GER; Oswald, Richard; 1932)
BFI/Monthly Film Bulletin. Aug 1974, v41, p188.
Variety. Sep 27, 1932, p21.

Living on Velvet (US; Borzage, Frank; 1935)
Film Daily. Mar 8, 1935, p6.
Hollywood Reporter. Mar 2, 1935, p3.
Motion Picture Herald. Mar 16, 1935, p39, 42.
The New York Times. Mar 8, 1935, p25.
The New Yorker. Mar 16, 1935, v11, p71.
The Spectator. Jul 26, 1935, v155, p150.
Variety. Mar 19, 1935, p15.

Lloyds of London (US; King, Henry; 1936)
Canadian Magazine. Jan 1937, v87, p44.
Commonweal. Dec 11, 1936, v25, p194.
Film Daily. Nov 27, 1936, p17.
The Films of Tyrone Power. p52-56.
Graham Greene on Film. p149.
Hollywood Reporter. Nov 23, 1936, p3, 13.
Hollywood Spectator. Dec 19, 1936, v11, p7.
Life. Dec 7, 1936, v1, p46-49.
Literary Digest. Dec 5, 1936, v122, p20.
Motion Picture Herald. Nov 28, 1936, p64.

The New Masses. Dec 22, 1936, v21, p29.
New Theatre. Mar 1937, v3, p46.
The New York Times. Nov 26, 1936, p39.
Newsweek. Dec 5, 1936, v8, p19-20.
Rob Wagner's Script. Dec 5, 1936, v16, p10.
Scholastic. Jan 9, 1937, v219, p28.
The Spectator. May 7, 1937, v158, p860.
Time. Dec 7, 1936, v28, p24+.
Variety. Dec 2, 1936, p18.
World Film News. Jun 1937, v2, p22.

The Locket (US; Granet, Bert; 1946)
Commonweal. Feb 21, 1946, v45, p469.
Film Daily. Dec 20, 1946, p22.
Hollywood Reporter. Dec 17, 1946, p3.
Motion Picture Herald Product Digest. Dec 21, 1946, p3373.
The New Republic. Apr 7, 1947, v116, p39.
The New York Times. Mar 20, 1947, p38.
Newsweek. Mar 31, 1947, v29, p94.
Robert Mitchum on the Screen. p91-92.
Time. Feb 3, 1946, v49, p95.
Variety. Dec 18, 1946, p14.

The Lodger (GB; Hitchcock, Alfred; 1926)
The Art of Alfred Hitchcock. p6-10.
BFI/Monthly Film Bulletin. Jul 1976, v43, p156.
Cinema, the Magic Vehicle. v1, p121-22.
The Films of Alfred Hitchcock. p24-25.
Hitch. p51-68, 85-92.
Hitchcock: The First Forty-Four Films. p8-10.
Hitchcock's British Films. p31-41+.
Magill's Survey of Cinema. Silent Films. v2, p662-64.
Variety. Sep 20, 1942, p15.

The Lodger (US; Brahm, John; 1944)
Chestnuts in Her Lap. p109.
Commonweal. Feb 4, 1944, v39, p399.
The Films of the Forties. p104-05.
Focus on Film. Sum 1975, n21, p47-56.
Hollywood Reporter. Jan 5, 1944, p3.
The London Times. Feb 14, 1944, p8.
Magill's Survey of Cinema. Series II. v3, p1409-12.
Motion Picture Exhibitor. Jan 12, 1944, v31, n9, sec2, p1437-38.
Motion Picture Herald Product Digest. Jan 8, 1944, p1705.
The Nation. Feb 12, 1944, v158, p197.
The New York Times. Jan 20, 1944, p15.
The New Yorker. Jan 22, 1944, v19, p46-47.
Newsweek. Jan 24, 1944, v13, p78.
Time. Jan 17, 1944, v43, p52+.
Variety. Jan 5, 1944, p16.

The Lodger (GB; Elvey, Maurice; 1932)
London Mercury. Oct 1932, v26, p502.
Motion Picture Herald. Oct 15, 1932, p66-67.
Variety. Sep 20, 1932, p15.

Lombardi, Ltd. (US; Conway, Jack; 1919)
Exhibitor's Trade Review. Oct 4, 1919, p1589.
Magill's Survey of Cinema. Silent Films. v2, p665-67.
Motion Picture News. Oct 4, 1919, p2871.
Motion Picture News. Nov 8, 1919, p3462.
The Moving Picture World. Oct 4, 1919, p60-61.
Variety. Oct 31, 1919, p57.
Wid's Daily. Sep 28, 1919, p7.

London After Midnight (US; Browning, Tod; 1927)
Classics of the Horror Film. p125-29.
Faces, Forms, Films: The Artistry of Lon Chaney. p143-44+.
Film Daily. Dec 17, 1927, p7.
The Horror People. p63-66+.
An Illustrated History of the Horror Film. p51, 61+.
London After Midnight.
Moving Picture World. Dec 17, 1927, p25.
The New York Times. Dec 31, 1927, p31.
Variety. Dec 14, 1927, p18.

London Belongs to Me *See* Dulcimer Street

London by Night (US; Thiele, William; 1937)
Film Daily. Jul 20, 1937, p10.
Hollywood Reporter. Jul 17, 1937, p3.
Hollywood Spectator. Jul 31, 1937, v12, p14-15.
Motion Picture Herald. Jul 24, 1937, p47.
The New York Times. Aug 13, 1937, p13.
Rob Wagner's Script. Aug 14, 1937, v17, p18.
Variety. Aug 4, 1937, p19.

The Lone White Sail (Russian title: Byeleyet Parus Odinoky) (USSR; Legoshin, Vladimir; 1937)
Dictionary of Films. p47.
Film Daily. May 13, 1938, p5.
The New Statesman and Nation. Jan 14, 1939, v17, p49.
The New York Times. May 7, 1938, p18.
The Spectator. Jan 13, 1939, v162, p52.
Time. May 23, 1938, v31, p40.
Variety. May 11, 1938, p16.

The Lonedale Operator (US; Griffith, D.W.; 1911)
American Silent Film. p44.
D.W. Griffith, His Biograph Films in Perspective. p174-77.
The Emergence of Film Art. p52.
Motion Pictures. p57-68.
The Moving Picture World. Apr 8, 1911, p780.
The New York Dramatic Mirror. Mar 29, 1911, p31.
Selected Film Criticism, 1896-1911. p63-64.

The Lonely Villa (US; Griffith, D.W.; 1909)
American Silent Film. p44.
D.W. Griffith, His Biograph Films in Perspective. p89-91+.
The Emergence of Film Art. p45-46.
A Million and One Nights. p503-05.
Motion Pictures. p56-68.
The Moving Picture World. Jun 19, 1909, p834.
The New York Dramatic Mirror. Jun 19, 1909, p16.
Selected Film Criticism, 1896-1911. p64-65.

Lonesome (US; Fejos, Paul; 1928)
Cinema, the Magic Vehicle. v1, p145-46.
Film Daily. Jun 24, 1928, p5.
The Film Spectator. Jun 23, 1928, v5, p7, 16-17.
Magill's Survey of Cinema. Silent Films. v2, p668-70.
The New York Times. Oct 2, 1928, p23.
Photoplay. Jul 1928, v34, p56.
Selected Film Criticism, 1921-1930. p176.
Variety. Nov 10, 1928, p15.

Lonesome Luke's Wild Women (US; Roach, Hal; 1917)
The Films of Hal Roach. p7-10.
Harold Lloyd. p13-29.
Harold Lloyd: The Shape of Laughter. p144-46.
The New York Dramatic Mirror. Aug 25, 1917, p21.

Long Pants (US; Capra, Frank; 1927)
The Comic Mind. p166-68, 173-74.
Film Daily. Apr 3, 1927, p8.
The Moving Picture World. Apr 9, 1927, p585.
The New York Times. Mar 29, 1927, p23.
Photoplay. Jun 1927, v32, p56.
Selected Film Criticism, 1921-1930. p176-77.
The Silent Clowns. p280-81.
Variety. Mar 20, 1927, p14.

The Long Voyage Home (US; Ford, John; 1940)
American Cinematographer. Dec 1940, v21, p542.
Art Digest. Jun 1940, v14, p17.
Art Digest. Aug 1940, v14, p10.
Art Digest. Sep 1940, v14, p34.
Art News. Aug 1940, v38, p13+.
Baltimore Museum of Art News. Nov 1940, v2, p66.
Commonweal. Oct 24, 1940, v33, p24.
The Complete Films of John Wayne. p103-04.
The Film Criticism of Otis Ferguson. p313-14.

Film Daily. Oct 9, 1940, p8.
Filmograph. 1975, v4, p2-15, 27-32+.
Life. Nov 11, 1940, v9, p83-84+.
The London Times. Feb 24, 1941, p6.
Lorentz on Film. p197-201.
Magill's Survey of Cinema. Series I. v3, p1003-05.
Motion Picture Exhibitor. Oct 16, 1940, p624-25.
The New Republic. Oct 21, 1940, v103, p558.
The New York Times. Oct 9, 1940, p30+.
The New York Times. Oct 13, 1944, sec9, p5.
The Non-Western Films of John Ford. p258-62.
On Film: Unpopular Essays on a Popular Art. p88-94.
O'Neill on Film. p89-102.
Parnassus. Oct 1940, v12, p38.
Quarterly of Film, Radio & Television. Sum 1953, v7, p370-84.
Reruns. p51-54.
Saturday Review. Oct 26, 1940, v23, p22.
Scholastic. Oct 28, 1940, p39.
Scribner's Commentator. Dec 1940, v9, p105-06.
Theatre Arts. Dec 1940, v24, p867-69.
Time. Oct 28, 1940, 36, p82+.
Variety. Oct 9, 1940, p16.

Look for the Silver Lining (US; Butler, David; 1949)
Commonweal. Jul 8, 1948, v50, p319.
Film Daily. Jul 1, 1949, p5.
The Hollywood Musical. p300-01.
Hollywood Reporter. Jun 23, 1949, p3.
Motion Picture Herald Product Digest. Jun 25, 1949, p4658.
The New York Times. Jun 24, 1949, p29.
The New Yorker. Jul 2, 1949, v25, p200.
Rotarian. Nov 1949, v75, p34.
Time. Jul 4, 1949, v54, p65.
Variety. Jun 29, 1949, p14.

Look Out, Mr. Moto (US; Foster, Norman; 1937)
The Films of Peter Lorre. p108-10.
Hollywood Reporter. Oct 23, 1937, p2.
Motion Picture Herald. Oct 30, 1937, p50.
The New York Times. Aug 22, 1937, p3.

Looking for Trouble (US; Wellman, William A.; 1934)
Film Daily. Feb 21, 1934, p7.
The Films of Spencer Tracy. p104-05.
Hollywood Reporter. Jan 22, 1934, p3.
The New York Times. Apr 12, 1934, p27.
Newsweek. Apr 21, 1934, p35.
Time. Apr 23, 1934, v23, p34.
Variety. Apr 17, 1934, p18.
William A. Wellman (Thompson). p145-46.

Lord Jeff (Also titled: The Boy from Barnardos) (US; Wood, Sam; 1938)
Commonweal. Jul 15, 1938, v28, p329.
Film Daily. Jun 23, 1938, p5.
Hollywood Reporter. Jun 18, 1938, p3.
Hollywood Spectator. Jun 25, 1938, v13, p6-7.
Motion Picture Herald. Jun 25, 1938, p47.
The New Statesman and Nation. Aug 13, 1938, v16, p251.
The New York Times. Jul 1, 1938, p22.
The New Yorker. Jul 2, 1938, v14, p42.
Rob Wagner's Script. Jul 23, 1938, v19, p9-10.
Time. Jul 4, 1938, v32, p18.
Variety. Jun 22, 1938, p14.
World Film News. Sep 1938, v3, p220, 225.

Lorna Doone (US; Tourneur, Maurice; 1922)
Film Daily. Dec 10, 1922, p2.
The New York Times. Dec 4, 1922, p20.
Variety. Dec 8, 1922, p33.

Lost Boundaries (US; Werker, Alfred L.; 1949)
Catholic World. Aug 1949, v169, p388.
Commonweal. Jul 15, 1942, v50, p341.
Film Daily. Jun 28, 1949, p8.

Hollywood Reporter. Jul 20, 1949, p3.
Life. Jul 4, 1949, v27, p64-66.
Motion Picture Herald Product Digest. Jul 2, 1949, p4665.
The Nation. Jul 30, 1949, v169, p114-15.
The New Republic. Jul 4, 1949, v121, p37.
The New York Times. Jul 1, 1949, p14.
The New Yorker. Jul 9, 1949, v25, p37.
Newsweek. Jul 4, 1949, v34, p72.
Rotarian. Nov 1949, v85, p34.
Saturday Review. Sep 10, 1949, v32, p32.
Theatre Arts. Oct 1949, v33, p95.
Time. Jul 4, 1949, v54, p65.
Variety. Jun 19, 1949, p14.

Lost Horizon (US; Capra, Frank; 1937)
America's Favorite Movies. p22-39.
Canadian Magazine. May 1937, v87, p31.
Commonweal. Mar 26, 1937, v25, p612.
Esquire. May 1937, v7, p112, 182.
Fifty Classic Motion Pictures. p92-97.
The Film Criticism of Otis Ferguson. p169.
Film Daily. Mar 4, 1937, p5.
The Films of Frank Capra (Scherle and Levy). p143-56.
The Films of Frank Capra (Willis). p99-106.
The Films of Ronald Colman. p183-90.
Frank Capra (Maland). p98-101.
From Quasimodo to Scarlett O'Hara. p239-40.
Graham Greene on Film. p145-48.
The Great Romantic Films. p52-55.
Halliwell's Hundred. p180-83.
Hollywood Reporter. Feb 20, 1937, p3.
Hollywood Spectator. Feb 27, 1937, v11, p8.
A Library of Film Criticism: American Film Directors. p31-33.
Literary Digest. Mar 6, 1937, v123, p20.
London Mercury. Jun 1937, v36, p187.
Love in the Film. p133-36.
Magill's Survey of Cinema. Series I. v3, p1006-008.
Motion Picture Herald. May 30, 1936, p16-17.
National Board of Review Magazine. Mar 1937, v12, p11, 14.
The New Masses. Mar 16, 1937, v22, p27-28.
The New Republic. Mar 17, 1937, v90, p168.
The New Statesman and Nation. Apr 17, 1937, v13, p636.
New Theatre. Apr 1937, v4, p27-28.
The New York Times. Mar 4, 1937, p27.
The New Yorker. Mar 6, 1937, v13, p62.
Newsweek. Mar 6, 1937, v9, p30-31.
Reruns. p36-40.
Rob Wagner's Script. Mar 13, 1937, v17, p10.
Scholastic. Mar 20, 1937, v30, p22-23.
Selected Film Criticism, 1931-1940. p141-42.
Sight and Sound. Sum 1937, v6, p79.
Sociology and Social Research. May 1937, v21, p497.
Souvenir Programs of Twelve Classic Movies, 1927-1941. p161-80.
The Spectator. Apr 30, 1937, v158, p805.
Stage. Apr 1937, v14, p53-54.
The Tatler. Apr 28, 1937, v144, p152.
Those Fabulous Movie Years: The 30s. p122-23.
Time. Mar 8, 1937, v29, p54+.
Variety. Mar 10, 1937, p14.
We're in the Money. p144.
World Film News. Jun 1937, v2, p20.

The Lost Lady *See* Safe in Hell

The Lost Moment (US; Gable, Martin; 1947)
BFI/Monthly Film Bulletin. Jun 1985, v50, p170-71.
Commonweal. Dec 19, 1947, v47, p256.
Film Daily. Oct 17, 1947, p6.
The Films of Susan Hayward. p119-22.
Hollywood Reporter. Oct 13, 1947, p3.
Magill's Cinema Annual, 1983. p465-68.
Motion Picture Herald Product Digest. Oct 25, 1947, p3894.
The New Republic. Dec 1, 1947, v117, p34.
Newsweek. Jan 5, 1948, v31, p69.

Time. Dec 8, 1947, v50, p103-04.
Variety. Oct 15, 1947, p10.

The Lost Patrol (US; Ford, John; 1934)
BFI/Monthly Film Bulletin. Jun 1977, v44, p134.
Film Daily. Feb 9, 1934, p15.
The Films of Boris Karloff. p90-92.
Hollywood Reporter. Jan 24, 1934, p3.
John Ford (Bogdanovich). p102-05.
Literary Digest. Apr 14, 1934, v117, p36.
Magill's Survey of Cinema. Series II. v3, p1443-45.
Motion Picture Herald. Feb 3, 1934, p33.
The New Republic. Apr 18, 1934, v78, p272.
The New York Times. Apr 2, 1934, p13.
The Non-Western Films of John Ford. p57-59.
Variety. Apr 3, 1934, p17.

The Lost Squadron (US; Archainbaud, George; 1932)
Film Daily. Mar 6, 1932, p10.
Film Notes. p82.
Grierson on Documentary. p40-42.
Hollywood Reporter. Feb 2, 1932, p3.
Judge. Apr 2, 1932, v102, p22.
Motion Picture Herald. Mar 5, 1932, p62-63.
The New York Times. Mar 11, 1932, p15.
The New Yorker. Mar 19, 1932, v8, p77.
Rob Wagner's Script. Jun 11, 1932, v7, p11, 29.
Time. Mar 21, 1932, v19, p37.
Variety. Mar 15, 1932, p14.

The Lost Weekend (US; Wilder, Billy; 1945)
Agee on Film. v1, p182-84.
The Atlantic. Jun 1946, v178, p140-41.
Billy Wilder (Dick). p52-57.
Billy Wilder (Madsen). p66-71.
The Bright Side of Billy Wilder, Primarily. p86-93.
Canadian Forum. Apr 1946, v26, p18.
Cinema: Novel Into Film. p293-95.
Commonweal. Dec 7, 1945, v153, p205-06.
The Film Career of Billy Wilder. p71-73.
Film Daily. Aug 14, 1945, p11.
The Films of the Forties. p155-59.
Hollywood Reporter. Aug 14, 1945, p3.
Journey Down Sunset Boulevard. p325-32.
Life. Oct 15, 1945, v19, p133-36+.
The London Times. Oct 5, 1945, p6.
Magill's Survey of Cinema. Series I. v3, p1009-11.
Motion Picture Exhibitor. Aug 22, 1945, v34, n16, sec2, p1767.
Motion Picture Herald Product Digest. Aug 18, 1945, p2639.
The Nation. Dec 22, 1945, v161, p697.
New Movies. Oct 1945, v20, p4-5.
The New Republic. Jan 7, 1945, v114, p23.
The New York Sun. Dec 2, 1945, p3.
The New York Times. Dec 3, 1945, p17.
The New Yorker. Dec 1, 1945, v21, p112.
Newsweek. Dec 10, 1945, v26, p112+.
Photoplay. Dec 1945, v28, p24.
Rob Wagner's Script. Dec 15, 1945, v31, p14.
Running Away from Myself. p53-59.
Saturday Review. Dec 29, 1945, v28, p20.
Saturday Review. Feb 2, 1946, v29, p18.
Selected Film Criticism, 1941-1950. p125-27.
Theatre Arts. Nov 1945, v29, p638-39.
Time. Dec 3, 1945, v46, p98.
Variety. Aug 15, 1945, p14.
Vintage Films. p81-84.

The Lost World (US; O'Hoyt, Henry; 1925)
Film Daily. Feb 15, 1925, p6.
Life. Mar 5, 1925, v85, p24.
Magill's Survey of Cinema. Silent Films. v2, p671-78.
The New York Times. Feb 9, 1925, p15.
Spellbound in Darkness. p393-94.
Variety. Feb 11, 1925, p31.

The Lost Zeppelin (US; Sloman, Edward; 1930)
Exhibitors Herald-World. Feb 15, 1930, p29-30.
Film Daily. Feb 9, 1930, p13.
The New York Times. Feb 3, 1930, p17.
The New Yorker. Feb 8, 1930, v5, p71.
Outlook and Independent. Feb 12, 1930, v154, p272.

The Lottery Man (US; Reid, Wallace; 1919)
Exhibitor's Trade Review. Oct 18, 1919, p1727.
Motion Picture News. Oct 25, 1919, p3203.
The Moving Picture World. Dec 20, 1919, p1013.
Variety. Oct 10, 1919, p61.
Wid's Daily. Oct 19, 1919, p2.

Louise (FR; Gance, Abel; 1939)
Abel Gance (Kramer and Welsh). p156.
Commonweal. Mar 8, 1940, v31, p435.
Graham Greene on Film. p228.
Hollywood Reporter. Jun 17, 1939, p3.
Motion Picture Herald. Feb 10, 1940, p40.
The New Statesman and Nation. Jun 10, 1939, v17, p893.
The New York Times. Feb 3, 1940, p9.
The New Yorker. Feb 10, 1940, v15, p64.
Newsweek. Feb 5, 1940, v15, p33.
Sight and Sound. Sum 1939, v8, p78-79.
The Spectator. Jun 16, 1939, v162, p1036.
Variety. Jun 21, 1939, p26.

Louisiana Purchase (US; Cummings, Irving; 1941)
Commonweal. Jan 16, 1942, v35, p320.
The Film Criticism of Otis Ferguson. p407-08.
Film Daily. Dec 1, 1941, p12.
Hollywood Reporter. Nov 28, 1941, p3.
Life. Jan 19, 1942, v12, p59-60+.
The London Times. Feb 23, 1942, p8.
Motion Picture Exhibitor. Dec 10, 1941, p904.
Motion Picture Herald Product Digest. Nov 29, 1941, p385.
The New Republic. Jan 12, 1942, v106, p43.
The New York Times. Jan 1, 1942, p37.
The New York Times. Jan 4, 1942, sec9, p5.
Newsweek. Jan 12, 1942, v19, p46-47.
Time. Jan 26, 1942, v39, p46.
Variety. Nov 26, 1941, p9.

Louisiana Story (US; Flaherty, Robert; 1948)
Film Daily. Sep 23, 1948, p6.
Hollywood Reporter. Dec 15, 1948, p3.
Magill's Survey of Cinema. Series I. v3, p1012-14.
The New York Times. Sep 29, 1948, p36.
Robert Flaherty: A Guide to References and Resources. p107-09.
Variety. Sep 22, 1948, p8.

Loulou *See* Pandora's Box

Love Affair (US; Freeland, Thornton; 1932)
The Complete Films of Humphrey Bogart. p21.
Film Daily. Apr 17, 1932, p11.
Humphrey Bogart: The Man and His Films. p43.
Motion Picture Herald. May 7, 1932, p32.
Variety. Apr 19, 1932, p15.

Love Affair (US; McCarey, Leo; 1939)
Canadian Magazine. Apr 1939, v91, p46.
Commonweal. Mar 31, 1939, v29, p640.
Film Comment. Fall 1971, v11, p58-59.
The Film Criticism of Otis Ferguson. p255.
Film Daily. Mar 13, 1939, p10.
From Quasimodo to Scarlett O'Hara. p301-02.
Hollywood Reporter. Mar 10, 1939, p3.
Hollywood Spectator. Mar 18, 1939, v13, p5-6.
Life. Mar 20, 1939, v6, p43-46.
Lorentz on Film. p162-64.
Love in the Film. p151-54.
Magill's Survey of Cinema. Series II. v3, p1446-48.
Motion Picture Herald. Mar 18, 1939, p49, 52.

National Board of Review Magazine. Apr 1939, v14, p17.
The New Statesman and Nation. Apr 22, 1939, v17, p607.
The New York Times. Mar 17, 1939, p25.
The New Yorker. Mar 18, 1939, v15, p66.
Newsweek. Mar 20, 1939, v13, p33.
Photoplay. Jun 1939, v53, p89.
Rob Wagner's Script. Mar 18, 1939, v21, p16.
Selected Film Criticism, 1931-1940. p142-44.
Sight and Sound. Sum 1939, v8, p76.
Stage. Mar 15, 1939, v16, p22-23.
Talking Pictures. p308-13.
Time. Mar 20, 1939, v33, p45.
Variety. Mar 15, 1939, p16.

Love Among the Millionaires (US; Tuttle, Frank; 1930)
Film Daily. Jul 13, 1930, p10.
Life. Jul 25, 1930, v96, p19.
The New York Times. Jul 5, 1930, p17.
The New Yorker. Jul 12, 1930, v6, p53.
Outlook and Independent. Jul 16, 1930, v155, p431.
Rob Wagner's Script. Jul 5, 1930, v3, p12.
Variety. Jul 9, 1930, p19.

Love and War (US; 1899)
The First Twenty Years. p11-12.

Love Before Breakfast (US; Lang, Walter; 1936)
Canadian Magazine. Apr 1936, v85, p58.
Film Daily. Mar 14, 1936, p7.
The Films of Carole Lombard. p134-35.
Hollywood Reporter. Feb 15, 1936, p3.
Hollywood Spectator. Feb 29, 1936, v10, p11-12.
Motion Picture Herald. Feb 29, 1936, p41.
The New York Times. Mar 14, 1936, p10.
Rob Wagner's Script. Apr 4, 1936, v15, p12.
Time. Mar 16, 1936, v27, p58.
Variety. Mar 18, 1936, p17.

Love Crazy (US; Conway, Jack; 1941)
Commonweal. Jun 6, 1941, v34, p161.
Film Daily. May 16, 1941, p7.
The Films of Myrna Loy. p221-22.
Hollywood Reporter. May 13, 1941, p3.
Motion Picture Herald Product Digest. May 17, 1941, p121.
The New York Times. Jun 6, 1941, p25.
The New Yorker. May 31, 1941, v17, p59.
Newsweek. May 26, 1941, v17, p68.
Scribner's Commentator. Aug 1941, v10, p106.
Variety. May 14, 1941, p16.

Love Finds Andy Hardy (US; Seitz, George B.; 1938)
Commonweal. Jul 29, 1938, v28, p370.
Film Daily. Jul 13, 1938, p5.
The Films of Lana Turner. p67-69.
The Foremost Films of 1938. p114-28.
Hollywood Reporter. Jul 11, 1938, p3.
Judy: The Films and Career of Judy Garland. p62-65.
Life. Aug 8, 1938, v5, p32-33.
Magill's Survey of Cinema. Series I. v3, p1015-17.
Motion Picture Herald. Jul 16, 1938, p61.
The New Masses. Aug 9, 1938, v28, p29.
The New York Times. Jul 22, 1938, p10.
Time. Aug 8, 1938, v32, p38.
Variety. Jul 13, 1938, p15.
World Film News. Oct 1938, v3, p266.

The Love Flower (US; Griffith, D.W.; 1920)
The Films of D.W. Griffith. p145-49.
The Moving Picture World. Sep 4, 1920, p110.
The New York Times. Aug 23, 1920, p9.
Variety. Aug 20, 1920, p37.
Wid's Daily. Aug 29, 1920, p3.

Love from a Stranger (US; Lee, Rowland V.; 1937)
Film Daily. Apr 21, 1937, p8.
Garbo and the Night Watchman. p250-51.

Hollywood Reporter. Jan 6, 1937, p3.
Motion Picture Herald. Feb 13, 1937, p60.
The Nation. May 8, 1937, v144, p545.
The New York Times. Apr 19, 1937, p27.
The New Yorker. Apr 24, 1937, v13, p64.
Rob Wagner's Script. Aug 14, 1937, v17, p17.
The Spectator. Jan 29, 1937, v158, p168.
The Tatler. Jan 20, 1937, v143, p98.
Time. Apr 26, 1937, v29, p44.
Variety. Jan 27, 1937, p13.
Variety. Apr 21, 1937, p14.
World Film News. Feb 1937, v1, p27.

Love in 3/4 Time *See* Liebe im 3/4 Takt

Love in Bloom (US; Nugent, Elliott; 1935)
Film Daily. Apr 20, 1935, p4.
Hollywood Reporter. Feb 26, 1935, p3.
Motion Picture Herald. Mar 9, 1935, p48.
The New York Times. Apr 20, 1935, p16.
Variety. Apr 24, 1935, p13.

Love in Exile (GB; Werker, Alfred L.; 1936)
Hollywood Reporter. Jan 1, 1936, p8.
Motion Picture Herald. May 30, 1936, p41.
The New York Times. Dec 10, 1936, p35.
Time. Dec 21, 1936, v28, p22.
Variety. May 27, 1936, p15.
Variety. Dec 16, 1936, p14.

Love Is a Racket (US; Wellman, William A.; 1932)
Film Daily. May 29, 1932, p10.
Motion Picture Herald. Jun 18, 1932, p38.
The New York Times. Jun 11, 1932, p9.
Time. Jun 20, 1932, v19, p24.
Variety. Jun 14, 1932, p16.
William A. Wellman (Thompson). p121, 127.

Love Is News (US; Garnett, Tay; 1937)
Film Daily. Mar 9, 1937, p10.
The Films of Tyrone Power. p57-59.
Hollywood Reporter. Feb 15, 1937, p4.
Hollywood Spectator. Feb 27, 1937, v11, p10-11.
Life. Mar 15, 1937, v2, p26-29.
Motion Picture Herald. Feb 27, 1937, p60, 62.
The New York Times. Mar 6, 1937, p10.
Rob Wagner's Script. Feb 27, 1937, v17, p8.
Saint Nicholas. Mar 1937, v64, p31.
The Spectator. Jun 25, 1937, v158, p1188.
Time. Mar 8, 1937, v29, p56.
Variety. Mar 10, 1937, p15.
World Film News. Aug 1937, v2, p10.

Love Is on the Air (US; Grinde, Nick; 1937)
Film Daily. Nov 16, 1937, p15.
The Films of Ronald Reagan. p31-34.
Hollywood Reporter. Aug 19, 1937, p3.
Motion Picture Herald. Oct 16, 1937, p46.
The New York Times. Nov 12, 1937, p27.
Variety. Sep 15, 1937, p13.

Love Letters (US; Dieterle, William; 1945)
Commonweal. Aug 24, 1945, v42, p453.
Film Daily. Aug 20, 1945, p5.
The Films of Jennifer Jones. p53-58.
Hollywood Reporter. Aug 20, 1945, p3.
Life. Sep 24, 1945, v19, p73-74+.
The Nation. Sep 29, 1945, v161, p321.
The New Republic. Oct 8, 1945, v113, p470.
The New Yorker. Sep 8, 1945, v21, p42.
Newsweek. Sep 3, 1945, v26, p86.
Time. Sep 10, 1945, v46, p98.
Variety. Aug 22, 1945, p20.

Love Me Forever (US; Schertzinger, Victor; 1935)
Commonweal. Jul 19, 1935, v22, p307.
Esquire. Sep 1935, v4, p144.

The Film Criticism of Otis Ferguson. p83-84.
Film Daily. Jun 28, 1935, p6.
The Hollywood Musical. p98, 102.
Hollywood Reporter. Jun 3, 1935, p3.
Literary Digest. Jul 6, 1935, v120, p29.
London Mercury. Oct 1935, v32, p581.
Movie Classic. Sep 1935, v9, p18.
The New Republic. Jul 24, 1935, v83, p308.
The New York Times. Jun 28, 1935, p24.
The New Yorker. Jul 6, 1935, v11, p45.
Newsweek. Jul 6, 1935, v6, p18.
Time. Jul 8, 1935, v26, p33.
Vanity Fair. Aug 1935, v44, p45.
Variety. Jul 3, 1935, p14.

Love Me Tonight (US; Mamoulian, Rouben; 1932)
Chevalier. p108-13.
Cinema Quarterly. Wint 1932, v1, p115.
Eighty Years of Cinema. p92-93.
Film Daily. Aug 13, 1932, p10.
The Films of Jeanette MacDonald and Nelson Eddy. p95-106.
The Films of Myrna Loy. p137-38.
The Hollywood Musical. p41-43.
Hollywood Reporter. Aug 5, 1932, p3.
Judge. Sep 1932, v103, p22.
Lorentz on Film. p94-98.
Magill's Survey of Cinema. Series I. v3, p1022-25.
Mamoulian (Milne). p51-62.
Motion Picture Herald. Aug 20, 1932, p34.
Movie. Spr 1977, n24, p53-54.
The Nation. Sep 14, 1932, v135, p239-40.
The New York Times. Aug 19, 1932, p20.
The New Yorker. Aug 20, 1932, v8, p38.
Photoplay. Oct 1932, v42, p52.
Rob Wagner's Script. Aug 27, 1932, v8, p8-9.
Selected Film Criticism, 1931-1940. p144-45.
Time. Aug 29, 1932, v20, p26.
Vanity Fair. Oct 1932, v39, p44.
Variety. Aug 23, 1932, p15.

The Love of Jeanne Ney (German title: Liebe der Jeanne Ney, Die; Also titled: The Loves of Jeanne Ney) (GER; Pabst, G.W.; 1927)
BFI/Monthly Film Bulletin. Aug 1979, v46, p187.
Close-Up. Jan 1928, v2, p4.
Film Daily. Jul 15, 1928, p6.
From Caligari to Hitler. p172-78.
G.W. Pabst (Atwell). p43-48.
The Haunted Screen. p211-13+.
The New York Times. Jan 15, 1928, sec8, p7.
Variety. Feb 8, 1928, p6.

Love on the Dole (GB; Baxter, John; 1941)
Film Daily. Oct 19, 1945, p8.
Hollywood Reporter. Nov 13, 1945, p3.
Motion Picture Herald. Apr 19, 1941, p48.
The New Yorker. Oct 20, 1945, v21, p79.
Theatre Arts. Dec 1945, v29, p704, 710.
Variety. Apr 30, 1941, p16.

Love on the Run (US; Van Dyke, W.S.; 1936)
Canadian Magazine. Dec 1936, v86, p39.
Film Daily. Nov 17, 1936, p9.
The Films of Clark Gable. p178-80.
The Films of Joan Crawford. p122-23.
Hollywood Reporter. Nov 13, 1936, p3.
Hollywood Spectator. Nov 21, 1936, v11, p11.
Motion Picture Herald. Nov 21, 1936, p46, 51.
The New York Times. Nov 28, 1936, p13.
The New Yorker. Nov 28, 1936, v12, p65.
Newsweek. Nov 28, 1936, v8, p20.
Rob Wagner's Script. Jan 23, 1937, v16, p12.
Time. Dec 7, 1936, v28, p23.
Variety. Dec 2, 1936, p18.

The Love Parade (US; Lubitsch, Ernst; 1929)
Cinema. Jan 1930, v1, p38.
Ernst Lubitsch: A Guide to References and Resources. p98-100.
Film Daily. Nov 24, 1929, p8.
The Films of Maurice Chevalier. p76-81.
The Hollywood Musical. p32.
The International Dictionary of Films and Filmmakers. v1, p268-69.
Life. Dec 13, 1929, v94, p22.
Magill's Survey of Cinema. Series I. v3, p1026-28.
The New York Times. Nov 20, 1929, p32.
Photoplay. Dec 1929, v37, p52.
Selected Film Criticism, 1921-1930. p178-80.
Time. Dec 2, 1929, v14, p39-40.
Variety. Nov 27, 1929, p21.

Lovers Courageous (US; Leonard, Robert Z.; 1932)
Film Daily. Feb 21, 1932, p10.
Motion Picture Herald. Feb 27, 1932, p36.
The Nation. Mar 16, 1932, v134, p321.
The New York Times. Feb 20, 1932, p11.
Time. Feb 29, 1932, v19, p28.
Variety. Feb 23, 1932, p19.

Love's Lariat (US; Marshall, George; Carey, Harry; 1916)
The Moving Picture World. Aug 5, 1916, p942.
The Moving Picture World. Aug 1916, p1306.
The New York Dramatic Mirror. Jul 29, 1916, p23.
Variety. Jul 28, 1916, p24.
Wid's Daily. Jul 27, 1916, p751.

Loves of a Dictator (GB; Saville, Victor; 1935)
Hollywood Reporter. Jun 17, 1935, p8.
Literary Digest. Jun 15, 1935, v119, p26.
The New York Times. Jun 1, 1935, p18.
The New Yorker. Jun 8, 1935, v11, p61.
Newsweek. Jun 8, 1935, v5, p23.
Variety. Jun 5, 1935, p15.

The Loves of Toni *See* Toni

The Lower Depths (French title: Bas-Fonds, Les; Also titled: Underworld) (FR; Renoir, Jean; 1936)
Dictionary of Films. p26.
Esquire. Jan 1938, v9, p107.
Film Comment. Jul-Aug 1974, v10, p23-25.
The Film Criticism of Otis Ferguson. p193-95.
Film Daily. Sep 10, 1937, p9.
Films and Filming. Feb 1964, v10, p14.
From Quasimodo to Scarlett O'Hara. p260-62.
Graham Greene on Film. p184.
Jean Renoir: A Guide to References and Resources. p99-101.
Jean Renoir: My Life and My Films. p128-34.
Jean Renoir: The French Films, 1924-1939. p257-81.
Kiss Kiss Bang Bang. p377.
Magill's Survey of Cinema. Foreign Language Films. v4, p1853-58.
Motion Picture Herald. Sep 25, 1937, p55.
The Nation. Sep 25, 1937, v145, p330.
National Board of Review Magazine. Oct 1937, v12, p13.
The New Masses. Sep 21, 1937, v24, p29.
The New Republic. Sep 15, 1937, v92, p159.
The New Statesman and Nation. Dec 4, 1937, v14, p919-20.
The New York Times. Sep 11, 1937, p20.
The New Yorker. Sep 11, 1937, v13, p63.
Selected Film Criticism: Foreign Films, 1930-1950. p101.
Time. Sep 20, 1937, v30, p30+.
Variety. Sep 15, 1937, p15.

Lucky Devils (US; Ince, Ralph; 1933)
BFI/Monthly Film Bulletin. Apr 1981, v48, p80-81.
Film Daily. Jan 28, 1933, p15.
Hollywood Reporter. Dec 27, 1932, p3.
Motion Picture Herald. Dec 31, 1932, p38, 40.
The New York Times. Feb 20, 1933, p11.
Variety. Feb 21, 1933, p14.

Lucky Jordan (US; Tuttle, Frank; 1942)
Commonweal. Feb 5, 1943, v37, p399.
Film Daily. Nov 16, 1942, p5.
The Films of Alan Ladd. p76-82.
The Films of World War II. p98.
Hollywood Reporter. Nov 16, 1942, p3.
The London Times. Apr 28, 1943, p6.
Motion Picture Exhibitor. Dec 2, 1942, v29, n4, sec2, p1162.
Motion Picture Herald Product Digest. Nov 21, 1942, p1017.
The New York Times. Jan 25, 1943, p10.
Time. Feb 15, 1943, v41, p52.
Variety. Nov 18, 1942, p8.

Lucky Night (US; Taurog, Norman; 1939)
Film Daily. May 1, 1939, p10.
The Films of Myrna Loy. p211.
Hollywood Reporter. Apr 29, 1939, p3.
Hollywood Spectator. May 13, 1939, v14, p10.
Motion Picture Herald. Apr 29, 1939, p54.
The New York Times. May 5, 1939, p29.
Rob Wagner's Script. Jun 3, 1939, v21, p18.
Time. May 22, 1939, v33, p57.
Variety. May 3, 1939, p16.

The Lucky Number (GB; Asquith, Anthony; 1933)
Cinema Quarterly. Sum 1933, v1, p242-43.
Motion Picture Herald. Sep 9, 1933, p35.
The New Statesman and Nation. Jun 3, 1933, v5, p733-34.
Variety. Jun 6, 1933, p15.

Lucrezia Borgia (FR; Gance, Abel; 1937)
Abel Gance (Kramer and Welsh). p21, 156.
Hollywood Spectator. Apr 30, 1938, v13, p9.
Motion Picture Herald. Oct 23, 1937, p56.
The New York Times. Oct 13, 1937, p27.
Variety. Oct 20, 1937, p12.

Luise, Konigin von Preussen (Also titled: Louise, Queen of Prussia) (GER; Froelich, Carl; 1931)
Film Daily. Oct 6, 1932, p4.
From Caligari to Hitler. p263-64.
Motion Picture Herald. Oct 15, 1932, p65-66.
The New York Times. Oct 5, 1932, p26.
The New Yorker. Oct 15, 1932, v8, p64.
Variety. Dec 22, 1931, p21.
Variety. Oc 11, 1932, p20.

Lulaby *See* The Sin of Madelon Claudet

Lulu *See* Pandora's Box

Lumiere First Program (FR; Lumiere, Louis; 1896)
Dictionary of Films. p200-01.
The Illustrated American. Jul 11, 1896, v20, p76.
The New York Dramatic Mirror. Jul 4, 1896, p17.
The New York Dramatic Mirror. Jul 11, 1896, p17.
Selected Film Criticism, 1896-1911. p65-67.

Lummox (US; Brenon, Herbert; 1930)
Exhibitors Herald-World. Feb 22, 1930, p37.
Film Daily. Feb 16, 1930, p8.
The Film Spectator. Mar 15, 1930, v9, p20.
Judge. Apr 19, 1930, v98, p25.
Life. Apr 28, 1930, v95, p18.
The New York Times. Jul 21, 1929, p4.
The New York Times. Mar 24, 1930, p25.
The New York Times. Mar 30, 1930, p5.
The New Yorker. Mar 29, 1930, v6, p52-53.
Outlook and Independent. Apr 2, 1930, v154, p551.
Rob Wagner's Script. Apr 12, 1930, v3, p10.
Time. Mar 31, 1930, v15, p34.
Variety. Feb 26, 1930, p7.
Variety. Mar 26, 1930, p39.

M (German title: M, Mörder unter uns) (GER; Lang, Fritz; 1931)
American Film Criticism. p282-87.

Cinema, the Magic Vehicle. v1, p183-84.
The Classic Cinema. p129-48.
Classics of the Foreign Film. p70-73.
Close-Up. p58-66.
Dictionary of Films. p202.
Eighty Years of Cinema. p87.
The Films of Fritz Lang. p154-63.
The Films of Peter Lorre. p63-66.
Fritz Lang: A Guide to References and Resources. p58-63.
Fritz Lang (Armour). p98-103.
Fritz Lang (Eisner). p111-28.
From Caligari to Hitler. p218-22.
From Quasimodo to Scarlett O'Hara. p169-72.
The German Cinema. p54-55.
The Great Movies. p48-50.
The Haunted Screen. p320-23.
Hollywood Reporter. Apr 15, 1933, p3.
The International Dictionary of Films and Filmmakers. v1, p270-71.
Judge. May 1933, v104, p24.
Judge. Jun 1933, v104, p16.
Kiss Kiss Bang Bang. p377-78.
Literature/Film Quarterly. 1979, n4, v7, p300-08.
Lorentz on Film. p110-12.
Magill's Survey of Cinema. Foreign Language Films. v4, p1873-79.
Motion Picture Herald. Apr 8, 1933, p28.
The Nation. Apr 19, 1933, v136, p454-55.
The New Outlook. May 1933, v161, p47.
The New Republic. Apr 1933, v74, p282.
The New Statesman and Nation. Jun 11, 1932, v3, p766.
The New York Times. Apr 3, 1933, p13.
The New Yorker. Apr 8, 1933, v9, p57.
Newsweek. Apr 8, 1933, v1, p26.
Photoplay. Jun 1933, v44, p97.
Rob Wagner's Script. May 2, 1936, v15, p10.
Saturday Review (London). Jun 6, 1931, v151, p829.
Selected Film Criticism: Foreign Films, 1930-1950. p101-03.
The Sociology of Film Art. p66-68.
The Spectator. Oct 20, 1933, v151, p522.
The Spectator. Jun 11, 1932, v148, p829.
Time. Apr 10, 1933, v21, p27.
Tower of Babel. p97-101.
Variety. Apr 4, 1933, p15.
Variety. Apr 18, 1933, p4.
Variety. Jun 2, 1931, p15.

Ma and Pa Kettle (US; Lamont, Charles; 1949)
Film Daily. Mar 28, 1949, p8.
Hollywood Reporter. Mar 23, 1949, p3.
Motion Picture Herald Product Digest. Apr 2, 1949, p4557.
The New York Times. Aug 12, 1949, p13.
Rotarian. Aug 1949, v75, p42.
Variety. Mar 23, 1949, p8.

Mabel at the Wheel (US; Sennett, Mack; Normand, Mabel; 1914)
Charles Chaplin: A Guide to References and Resources. p41-42.
The Films of Charlie Chaplin. p41-42.
Magill's Survey of Cinema. Silent Films. v2, p679-81.
The New York Dramatic Mirror. Apr 22, 1914, p40.

Macbeth (US; Emerson, John; 1916)
The Moving Picture World. Jun 24, 1916, p2258.
The New York Times. Jun 5, 1916, p9.
Selected Film Criticism, 1912-1920. p165-67.
Variety. Jun 9, 1916, p23.

Macht der Finsternis, Der *See* Power of Darkness

The Macomber Affair (US; Korda, Zoltan; 1947)
Commonweal. Apr 25, 1947, v46, p39.
Film Daily. Jan 23, 1947, p8.
The Films of Gregory Peck. p56-62.
Hemingway and Film. p89-105.

Hollywood Reporter. Jan 17, 1947, p3.
Magill's Survey of Cinema, Series II. v4, p1481-83.
Motion Picture Herald Product Digest. Feb 1, 1947, p3445.
New Republic. May 5, 1947, v116, p39.
The New York Times. Apr 21, 1947, p21.
The New Yorker. Apr 26, 1947, v23, p80.
Newsweek. Apr 28, 1947, v29, p95.
Time. Apr 7, 1947, v49, p99.
Variety. Jan 22, 1947, p17.

Mad About Music (US; Taurog, Norman; 1938)
Commonweal. Mar 11,1938, v27, p554.
Film Daily. Feb 28, 1938, p6.
Hollywood Reporter. Feb 25, 1938, p3.
Motion Picture Herald. Mar 5, 1938, p37.
The New Masses. Mar 15, 1938, v26, p27.
The New Statesman and Nation. Mar 26, 1938, v15, p527.
The New York Times. Mar 12, 1938, p13.
Rob Wagner's Script. Mar 5, 1938, v19, p6.
Saint Nicholas. Mar 1938, v65, p44.
Scholastic. Mar 19, 1938, v32, p35.
Scribner's Magazine. May 1938, v103, p64.
The Spectator. Apr 1, 1938, v160, p583.
Time. Mar 7, 1938, v31, p38.
Variety. Mar 2, 1938, p15.

The Mad Game (US; Cummings, Irving; 1933)
Film Daily. Nov 11, 1933, p3.
Hollywood Reporter. Oct 6, 1933, p5.
Motion Picture Herald. Oct 28, 1933, p55.
The New York Times. Nov 13, 1933, p21.
Newsweek. Nov 18, 1933, v2, p35.
Rob Wagner's Script. Nov 4, 1933, v10, p9.
Time. Nov 13, 1933, v22, p22.
Variety. Nov 14, 1933, p30.

The Mad Genius (US; Curtiz, Michael; 1931)
Film Daily. Oct 25, 1931, p10.
The Films of Boris Karloff. p54-55.
Hollywood Reporter. Apr 29, 1931, p3.
Horror Movies (Clarens). p103-04.
Judge. Nov 14, 1931, v101, p18.
Motion Picture Herald. Oct 31, 1931, p36, 38.
The New York Times. Oct 24, 1931, p20.
The New Yorker. Oct 31, 1931, v7, p65-66.
Outlook and Independent. Nov 11, 1931, v159, p342.
Rob Wagner's Script. Mar 5, 1932, v7, p10.
Time. Nov 2, 1931, v18, p21.
Variety. Oct 27, 1931, p19.

Mad Love (US; Freund, Karl; 1935)
Cinema of the Fantastic. p107-24.
Classics of the Horror Film. p130-33.
Commonweal. Aug 16, 1935, v22, p387.
Esquire. Oct 1935, v4, p97.
Film Daily. Jul 1, 1935, p11.
Film Heritage. Wint 1969-70, v5, p24-29.
The Films of Peter Lorre. p88-90.
Hollywood Reporter. Jun 27, 1935, p3.
Masters of Menace: Greenstreet and Lorre. p26-30.
Motion Picture Herald. Jul 6, 1935, p74-75.
The New Masses. Aug 13, 1935, v16, p30.
The New York Times. Aug 5, 1935, p20.
Time. Jul 22, 1935, v26, p30.
Variety. Aug 7, 1935, p21.

The Mad Miss Manton (US; Jason, Leigh; 1938)
Commonweal. Nov 4, 1938, v29, p49.
Film Daily. Oct 27, 1938, p5.
The Films of Barbara Stanwyck. p124-25.
The Films of Henry Fonda. p74-75.
The Fondas (Springer). p83-85.
Hollywood Reporter. Oct 6, 1938, p3.
Hollywood Spectator. Oct 15, 1938, v13, p9-10.
Lunatics and Lovers. p182.
The Mad Miss Manton. 1985.

Motion Picture Herald. Oct 15, 1938, p36-37.
The New Republic. Nov 2, 1938, v96, p362.
The New York Times. Oct 21, 1938, p27.
The New Yorker. Oct 29, 1938, v14, p58.
Rob Wagner's Script. Dec 10, 1938, v20, p10.
Starring Miss Barbara Stanwyck. p115-16, 120.
Variety. Oct 12, 1938, p15.

Mad Wednesday *See* The Sin of Harold Diddlebock

Madam Satan (US; DeMille, Cecil B.; 1930)
Exhibitors Herald-World. Oct 4, 1930, p30.
Film Daily. Oct 5, 1930, p10.
The Films of Cecil B. DeMille. p266-71.
Judge. Nov 1, 1930, v99, p20.
Life. Oct 24, 1930, v96, p20.
The New York Times. Oct 6, 1930, p21.
The New York Times. Mar 30, 1930, p5.
Outlook and Independent. Oct 22, 1930, v156, p315.
Time. Oct 20, 1930, v16, p38.

Madame Bovary (FR; Renoir, Jean; 1934)
Film Daily. Nov 20, 1934, p7.
From Quasimodo to Scarlett O'Hara. p187-89.
Jean Renoir: A Guide to References and Resources. p86-87.
Jean Renoir (Durgnat). p94-97.
Jean Renoir: The French Films, 1924-1939. p142-64.
Motion Picture Herald. Dec 8, 1934, p51.
The Nation. Dec 5, 1934, v139, p657-58.
The New York Times. Nov 19, 1934, p19.
Sight ι& Sound. Spr 1965, v34, p71-75.

Madame Bovary (US; Minnelli, Vincente; 1949)
Agee on Film. v1, p119.
Commonweal. Sep 2, 1949, v50, p509.
Film Daily. Aug 1, 1949, p7.
The Films of James Mason. p90-91.
The Films of Jennifer Jones. p85-92.
Hollywood Reporter. Aug 1, 1949, p3.
Life. Oct 7, 1949, v27, p112+.
Motion Picture Herald Product Digest. Aug 6, 1949, p4705.
The New York Times. Aug 26, 1949, p15.
The New Yorker. Sep 3, 1949, v25, p61.
Newsweek. Aug 29, 1949, v34, p72.
The Novel and the Cinema. p252-61.
Novels Into Film. p197-214.
Rotarian. Nov 1949, v75, p34.
Theatre Arts. Nov 1949, v33, p2.
Time. Aug 15, 1949, v54, p78.
Variety. Aug 3, 1949, p16.

Madame Butterfly (US; Gering, Marion; 1932)
Film Daily. Dec 24, 1932, p4.
Films in Review. Apr 1962, v13, p242-43.
The Films of Cary Grant. p48-50.
Hollywood Reporter. Dec 10, 1932, p3.
Motion Picture Herald. Dec 31, 1932, p38.
Motion Picture Herald. Jan 21, 1933, p19.
The New York Times. Dec 26, 1932, p26.
Time. Jan 2, 1933, v21, p18.
Variety. Dec 27, 1932, p14.

Madame Curie (US; LeRoy, Mervyn; 1943)
Agee on Film. v1, p64, 68.
Around Cinemas. p255-57.
Cinema, the Magic Vehicle. v1, p378.
Commonweal. Dec 31, 1943, v39, p281.
Film Daily. Nov 22, 1943, p7.
Hollywood Reporter. Nov 19, 1943, p3.
Life. Dec 13, 1943, v15, p118-22+.
Magill's Survey of Cinema. Series I. v3, p1033-35.
Motion Picture Herald Product Digest. Nov 20, 1943, p1633.
The New York Times. Dec 17, 1943, p23.
The New York Times Magazine. Sep 26, 1943, p18.
The New Yorker. Dec 18, 1943, v19, p53.
Newsweek. Dec 27, 1943, v22, p82.

Time. Dec 20, 1943, v42, p54.
Variety. Nov 24, 1943, p18.

Madame Du Barry *See* Du Barry

Madame Du Barry (US; Dieterle, William; 1934)
Film Daily. Aug 8, 1934, p7.
Motion Picture Herald. Aug 18, 1934, p35.
The New York Times. Oct 25, 1934, p26.
Time. Oct 22, 1934, v24, p43.
Variety. Oct 30, 1934, p16.

Madame Dubarry (Also titled: Passion) (GER; Lubitsch,
   Ernst; 1919)
The Chicago Daily News. May 10, 1921, p22.
Ernst Lubitsch: A Guide to References and Resources. p53-56.
Exceptional Photoplays. Nov 1920, n1, p3.
From Caligari to Hitler. p48-49.
The German Cinema. p20-21.
The Haunted Screen. p80-86.
The London Times. Nov 28, 1922, p10.
The Lubitsch Touch. p27-33.
The Moving Picture World. Nov 27, 1920, p469, 513.
The New York Times. Dec 13, 1920, p19.
The New York Times. Dec 23, 1920, p28.
The New York Times. Jan 30, 1921, sec6, p2.
The New York Times. Jan 26, 1923, p14.
The New York Times. Jul 1, 1923, sec6, p2.
Variety. Dec 17, 1920, p40.
Wid's Daily. Oct 10, 1920, p4.

Madame Racketeer (US; Hall, Alexander; Gribble, Harry
   Wagstaff; 1932)
Dark Cinema. p137.
Film Daily. Jul 23, 1932, p6.
The Great Gangster Pictures. p261-62.
Motion Picture Herald. Jul 30, 1932, p32.
The New York Times. Jul 23, 1932, p6.
The New Yorker. Jul 30, 1932, v8, p36.
Rob Wagner's Script. Sep 24, 1932, v8, p8.
Time. Aug 1, 1932, v20, p23.

Madame Sans Gene (US; Perret, Léonce; 1925)
Film Daily. Apr 26, 1925, p6.
The Films of Gloria Swanson. p176-82.
Magill's Survey of Cinema. Silent Films. v2, p682-85.
The Moving Picture World. May 2, 1985, p47.
The New York Times. Apr 18, 1925, p19.
Spellbound in Darkness. p116.
Variety. Apr 22, 1925, p34.

Madame Spy (US; Freund, Karl; 1933)
Film Daily. Feb 10, 1934, p4.
Hollywood Reporter. Dec 23, 1933, p2.
Motion Picture Herald. Jan 6, 1934, p31.
The New York Times. Feb 10, 1934, p20.
Variety. Feb 13, 1934, p14.

Madame X (US; Lloyd, Frank; 1920)
Magill's Survey of Cinema. Silent Films. v2, p686-88.
The Moving Picture World. Sep 25, 1920, p529.
The New York Dramatic Mirror. Oct 2, 1920, p609.
Photoplay. Sep 1920, v18, p67.
Selected Film Criticism, 1912-1920. p167-68.
Variety. Oct 1, 1920, p34.
Wid's Daily. Oct 3, 1920, p3.

Madame X (US; Barrymore, Lionel; 1929)
Exhibitor's Herald-World. Aug 17, 1929, p80.
Film Daily. Apr 28, 1929, p32.
The Films of the Twenties. p239-40.
The New York Times. Apr 25, 1929, p32.
Outlook. May 8, 1929, v152, p73.
Variety. May 1, 1929, p17.

Madame X (US; Wood, Sam; 1937)
Film Daily. Sep 27, 1937, p12.
Hollywood Reporter. Sep 22, 1937, p3.
Motion Picture Herald. Oct 2, 1937, p36.
The New York Times. Oct 25, 1937, p23.
The New Yorker. Oct 30, 1937, v13, p90.
Rob Wagner's Script. Oct 16, 1937, v18, p13.
Time. Oct 11, 1937, v30, p36.
Variety. Sep 29, 1937, p14.

Made for Each Other (US; Cromwell, John; 1939)
Commonweal. Feb 24, 1939, v29, p497.
Film Daily. Feb 6, 1939, p7.
The Films of Carole Lombard. p158-61.
The Films of James Stewart. p65-67.
Hollywood Reporter. Feb 1, 1939, p3.
Hollywood Spectator. Feb 18, 1939, v13, p7-8.
Life. Feb 20, 1939, v6, p54-55.
Motion Picture Herald. Feb 4, 1939, p56.
The New Statesman and Nation. Apr 1, 1939, v17, p493.
The New York Times. Feb 17, 1939, p17.
The New Yorker. Feb 18, 1939, v15, p66-67.
Newsweek. Feb 13, 1939, v13, p29.
Photoplay. Apr 1939, v53, p98.
Time. Feb 27, 1939, v33, p30.
Variety. Feb 1, 1939, p13.

Madelon *See* Port of Seven Seas

Mademoiselle Docteur (Also titled: Salonique) (FR; Pabst, G.W.; 1937)
Graham Greene on Film. p186.
G.W. Pabst (Atwell). p117-19.
Hollywood Reporter. Apr 28, 1937, p15.
Motion Picture Herald. May 1, 1937, p34.
Motion Picture Herald. Dec 18, 1937, p51.
Variety. Apr 21, 1937, p15.

Madmen of Europe *See* An Englishman's Home

Maedchen in Uniform (Also titled: Girls in Uniform) (GER; Sagan, Leontine; 1931)
BFI/Monthly Film Bulletin. Jan 1982, v49, p14-15.
Cinema, the Magic Vehicle. v1, p187-88.
Classics of the Foreign Film. p64-65.
Close-Up. Mar 1932, v9, p39-42.
Commonweal. Dec 21, 1932, v17, p216.
Dictionary of Films. p204.
Film Daily. Sep 23, 1932, p6.
Film Society Review. Feb 1968, p10-12.
From Caligari to Hitler. p226-29.
From Quasimodo to Scarlett O'Hara. p161-63.
The German Cinema. p57-58.
The Haunted Screen. p325-26.
The International Dictionary of Films and Filmmakers. v1, p273-74.
Judge. Nov 1932, v103, p20.
Kiss Kiss Bang Bang. p378-79.
Life. Nov 1932, v99, p38-39.
Literary Digest. Nov 26, 1932, v114, p13.
Motion Picture Herald. Oct 1, 1932, p54.
The Nation. Oct 12, 1932, v135, p338.
National Board of Review Magazine. Sep-Oct 1932, v7, p9.
New Outlook. Nov 1932, v161, p46.
The New Republic. Oct 5, 1932, v72, p207-08.
The New Statesman and Nation. Mar 5, 1932, v3, p296.
The New York Times. Sep 21, 1932, p25.
Rob Wagner's Script. Dec 10, 1932, v8, p10-11.
Saturday Review. May 19, 1956, v39, p50.
Scrutiny of Cinema. p56-57, 59-60.
Selected Film Criticism: Foreign Films, 1930-1950. p103-06.
The Spectator. May 7, 1932, v148, p660.
Theatre Arts. Nov 1932, v16, p881.
Time. Oct 3, 1932, v20, p38.

Vanity Fair. Nov 1932, v39, p46.
Variety. Sep 27, 1932, p17.

The Magic Cloak of Oz (US; Baum, L. Frank; 1914)
The Moving Picture World. Sep 19, 1914, p1598.

The Magic Lantern (French title: Lanterne Magique, La) (FR; Melies, Georges; 1902)
Film Before Griffith. p352, 358.
The First Twenty Years. p53.

Magic Night (Also titled: Goodnight, Vienna) (GB; Wilcox, Herbert; 1932)
Film Daily. Nov 3, 1932, p6.
Motion Picture Herald. May 7, 1932, p32.
Motion Picture Herald. Nov 12, 1932, p36.
The New Outlook. Dec 1932, v161, p46.
The New Statesman and Nation. Apr 9, 1932, v3, p452.
The New York Times. Nov 3, 1932, p25.
The New Yorker. Nov 12, 1932, v8, p60.
Variety. Nov 8, 1932, p16.

Magic Town (US; Lang, Walter; 1947)
Commonweal. Oct 17, 1947, v47, p17.
Film Daily. Aug 27, 1947, p6.
The Films of James Stewart. p106-08.
Hollywood Reporter. Aug 20, 1947, p3.
Motion Picture Herald Product Digest. Aug 23, 1947, p3793.
The New York Times. Oct 8, 1947, p29.
Newsweek. Oct 26, 1947, v30, p98.
Scholastic. Nov 10, 1947, v51, p30.
Time. Oct 20, 1947, p102.

The Magnificent Ambersons (US; Welles, Orson; 1942)
American Cinematographer. Nov 1976, v57, p1238-39+.
American Film. Mar 1976, v1, p22-26.
Chestnuts in Her Lap. p89-90.
The Cinema of Orson Welles. p6-7, 65-82.
Commonweal. Aug 21, 1942, v36, p423.
Film Comment. Sum 1971, v7, p48-50.
Film Daily. Jul 3, 1942, p5.
The Films of Orson Welles. p48-71.
Focus on Orson Welles. p123-28.
The Great Movies. p244-46.
Hollywood Reporter. Jul 1, 1942, p3.
The International Dictionary of Films and Filmmakers. v1, p274-75.
Literature/Film Quarterly. Sum 1974, v2, p196-206.
The London Times. Mar 5, 1943, p6.
Magic Moments from the Movies. p115-16.
The Magic World of Orson Welles. p103-33.
Magill's Survey of Cinema. Series I. v3, 1036-38.
Motion Picture Exhibitor. Jul 1, 1942, v28, n8, sec2, p1044.
Motion Picture Herald Product Digest. Jul 4, 1942, p749.
The New Republic. Aug 10, 1942, v107, p173.
The New York Times. Aug 8, 1942, p13.
The New York Times. Aug 16, 1942, sec8, p3.
The New Yorker. Aug 15, 1942, v18, p53.
Newsweek. Jul 20, 1942, v20, p56.
Orson Welles: A Critical View. p59-63.
Orson Welles, Actor and Director. p35-36.
Orson Welles (McBride). p52-85.
A Ribbon of Dreams. p63-83.
Rob Wagner's Script. Jul 4, 1942, v27, p24.
Selected Film Criticism, 1941-1950. p132-33.
Time. Jul 20, 1942, v40, p42+.
Variety. Jul 1, 1942, p8.

The Magnificent Brute (US; Blystone, John G.; 1936)
Film Daily. Oct 24, 1936, p7.
Motion Picture Herald. Oct 3, 1936, p47.
The New York Times. Oct 24, 1936, p23.
Rob Wagner's Script. Oct 31, 1936, v16, p10.
Time. Oct 26, 1936, v28, p70.
Variety. Oct 28, 1936, p14.

Magnificent Doll (US; Borzage, Frank; 1946)
Commonweal. Dec 27, 1946, v45, p281.
Film Daily. Nov 29, 1946, p6.
The Films of David Niven. p80-81.
The Films of Ginger Rogers. p220-22.
Hollywood Reporter. Nov 15, 1946, p3.
Motion Picture Herald Product Digest. Nov 23, 1946, p3321.
The New York Times. Dec 9, 1946, p34.
The New Yorker. Dec 21, 1946, v22, p88.
Newsweek. Dec 16, 1946, v28, p102+.
Time. Dec 16, 1946, v48, p101.
Variety. Nov 20, 1946, p22.

The Magnificent Fraud (US; Florey, Robert; 1939)
Commonweal. Aug 4, 1939, v30, p359.
Film Daily. Jul 20, 1939, p11.
Hollywood Spectator. Jul 22, 1939, v14, p6-7.
Motion Picture Herald. Jul 22, 1939, p48, 50.
The New York Times. Jul 20, 1939, p16.
Photoplay. Sep 1939, v53, p63.
Variety. Jul 19, 1939, p12.

The Magnificent Lie (US; Viertel, Berthold; 1931)
Film Daily. Jul 26, 1931, p10.
Hollywood Reporter. Jul 20, 1931, p3.
Hollywood Spectator. Aug 15, 1931, v12, p22-23.
Hollywood Spectator. Aug 29, 1931, v12, p11-12.
Life. Aug 14, 1931, v98, p18.
Motion Picture Herald. Jul 25, 1931, p28, 34.
The New York Times. Jul 25, 1931, p11.
The New York Times. Aug 2, 1931, p3.
The New Yorker. Aug 1, 1931, v7, p45.
Outlook and Independent. Aug 12, 1931, v158, p470.
Rob Wagner's Script. Aug 29, 1931, v6, p10.
Time. Aug 3, 1931, v18, p26.
Variety. Jul 28, 1931, p14.

Magnificent Obsession (US; Stahl, John M.; 1935)
Canadian Magazine. Feb 1936, v85, p37.
Commonweal. Jan 17, 1936, v23, p330.
Esquire. Mar 1936, v5, p105.
Film Daily. Dec 31, 1935, p6.
The Films of Robert Taylor. p43-45.
Hollywood Reporter. Dec 31, 1935, p3.
Hollywood Spectator. Jan 18, 1936, v10, p12.
Magill's Survey of Cinema. Series II. v4, p1488-90.
Motion Picture Herald. Jan 11, 1936, p52.
The New York Times. Dec 31, 1935, p11.
The New Yorker. Jan 11, 1936, v11, p64.
Scholastic. Feb 8, 1936, v28, p30.
Variety. Jan 8, 1936, p12.

Maid of Salem (US; Lloyd, Frank; 1937)
Canadian Magazine. Mar 1937, v87, p23.
Christian Science Monitor Magazine. Jan 27, 1937, p4+.
Claudette Colbert (Quirk). p92-95.
Commonweal. Mar 12, 1937, v25, p556.
Film Daily. Jan 26, 1937, p8.
Graham Greene on Film. p136-37.
Hollywood Reporter. Jan 21, 1937, p3.
Hollywood Spectator. Jan 30, 1937, v11, p10-11.
Life. Feb 1, 1937, v2, p61.
Life. Feb 8, 1937, v2, p24-27.
Literary Digest. Feb 6, 1937, v123, p24.
Motion Picture Herald. Jan 30, 1937, p47.
Movie Classic. Jan 1937, v11, p52+.
The New York Times. Mar 4, 1937, p27.
The New Yorker. Mar 6, 1937, v13, p61-62.
Newsweek. Feb 20, 1937, v9, p21.
Photoplay. Mar 1937, v51, p15.
Rob Wagner's Script. Feb 20, 1937, v17, p6.
Saint Nicholas. Oct 1936, v63, p15.
Scholastic. Feb 27, 1937, v30, p28.
Sight and Sound. Spr 1937, v6, p21.
The Spectator. Mar 5, 1937, v158, p403.

Stage. Jan 1937, v14, p67.
Time. Mar 8, 1937, v29, p57-58.
Variety. Mar 10, 1937, p14.

Main du Diable, La *See* Carnival of Sinners

Maisie (US; Marin, Edwin L.; 1939)
Film Daily. Jun 7, 1939, p6.
Hollywood Reporter. Jun 2, 1939, p3.
Hollywood Spectator. Jun 10, 1939, v14, p7.
Motion Picture Herald. Jul 1, 1939, p44-45.
The New York Times. Jun 23, 1939, p23.
The New Yorker. Jun 24, 1939, v15, p65.
Newsweek. Jul 3, 1939, v14, p29.
Photoplay. Aug 1939, v53, p54.
Rob Wagner's Script. Jun 17, 1939, v21, p16.
The Tatler. Sep 6, 1939, v153, p420.
Time. Jul 3, 1939, v34, p35.
Variety. Jun 7, 1939, p12.

The Major and the Minor (US; Wilder, Billy; 1942)
Billy Wilder (Dick). p33-37.
The Bright Side of Billy Wilder, Primarily. p71-73.
Commonweal. Sep 18, 1932, v36, p519.
The Film Career of Billy Wilder. p65-67.
Film Daily. Sep 3, 1942, p18.
The Films of Ginger Rogers. p177-78.
Hollywood Reporter. Aug 28, 1942, p3.
Journey Down Sunset Boulevard. p196-213.
Life. Aug 17, 1942, v13, p37-38.
The London Times. Dec 17, 1942, p6.
Magill's Survey of Cinema. Series I. v3, p1043-45.
Motion Picture Exhibitor. Sep 9, 1942, v28, n18, sec2, p1096.
Motion Picture Herald Product Digest. Aug 29, 1942, p869.
The New York Times. Sep 17, 1942, p21.
The New Yorker. Sep 19, 1942, v18, p52.
Newsweek. Sep 7, 1942, v20, p79-80.
Time. Sep 28, 1942, v40, p82+.
Variety. Sep 2, 1942, p18.

Major Barbara (GB; Pascal, Gabriel; 1941)
The Collected Screenplays of Bernard Shaw. p91-119.
Commonweal. May 30, 1941, v34, p136.
The Film Criticism of Otis Ferguson. p365-66.
Film Daily. May 5, 1941, p13.
The Great British Films. p59-62.
Hollywood Reporter. Apr 30, 1941, p3.
Hollywood Spectator. Jun 1, 1941, v16, p18-19.
The London Times. Apr 2, 1941, p6.
The London Times. Feb 14, 1949, p6.
Magill's Survey of Cinema. Series II. v4, p1495-97.
Motion Picture Exhibitor. May 14, 1941, p747.
Motion Picture Exhibitor. Sep 17, 1941, v26, n19, p851.
Motion Picture Herald Product Digest. Mar 22, 1941, p85.
The New Republic. Jun 9, 1941, v104, p793.
The New York Times. May 15, 1941, p15.
The New York Times. May 18, 1941, sec9, p3.
The New Yorker. May 24, 1941, v17, p82+.
Newsweek. May 19, 1941, v17, p75.
On Film: Unpopular Essays on a Popular Art. p83-112.
Scholastic. Sep 22, 1941, v39, p30.
Scribner's Commentator. Aug 1941, v10, p105-06.
Selected Film Criticism: Foreign Films, 1930-1950. p106-07.
Theatre Arts. Feb 1941, v25, p88-89.
Time. Jun 2, 1941, 37, p80+.
Variety. May 7, 1941, p12.

Make a Wish (US; Neumann, Kurt; 1937)
Film Daily. Aug 27, 1937, p16.
Motion Picture Herald. Sep 4, 1937, p43-44.
The New York Times. Sep 23, 1937, p33.
The New Yorker. Oct 2, 1937, v13, p60.
Rob Wagner's Script. Sep 4, 1937, v18, p12.
Saint Nicholas. Aug 1937, v64, p44.
Time. Sep 6, 1937, v30, p64.
Variety. Aug 25, 1937, p17.

Make Me a Star (US; Beaudine, William; 1932)
Film Daily. Jul 2, 1932, p6.
The Films of Fredric March. p87-88.
The Films of Gary Cooper. p99-100.
Judge. Aug 1932, v103, p22.
Motion Picture Herald. Jun 18, 1932, p31, 34.
The Nation. Jul 20, 1932, v135, p63.
The New York Times. Jul 1, 1932, p19.
Rob Wagner's Script. Jul 9, 1932, v7, p11, 22.
Time. Jul 11, 1932, v20, p22.
Variety. Jul 5, 1932, p14.

Make Way for Tomorrow (US; McCarey, Leo; 1937)
Cinema Arts. Jul 1937, v1, p32.
Esquire. Aug 1937, v8, p101, 160.
Film Comment. Sep-Oct 1973, v9, p10.
Film Daily. Apr 27, 1937, p10.
Film Notes. p102-03.
The Films of the Thirties. p190-91.
From Quasimodo to Scarlett O'Hara. p248-51.
Graham Greene on Film. p150-51.
Hollywood Reporter. Apr 22, 1937, p3.
Hollywood Spectator. May 8, 1937, v12, p5-6.
Literary Digest. May 8, 1937, v123, p29.
Motion Picture Herald. May 1, 1937, p32.
National Board of Review Magazine. Jul 1937, v12, p9.
The New Masses. Jul 6, 1937, v24, p27.
The New York Times. May 10, 1937, p23.
Newsweek. May 22, 1937, v9, p26.
Rob Wagner's Script. Jul 3, 1937, v17, p10.
Selected Film Criticism, 1931-1940. p145-46.
Sociology and Social Research. Sep 1937, v22, p97.
Time. May 17, 1937, v29, p56+.
Variety. May 12, 1937, p12.
World Film News. Aug 1937, v2, p10, 24.

Male and Female (US; DeMille, Cecil B.; 1919)
The Autobiography of Cecil B. DeMille. p224-26.
Cecil B. DeMille. p71-74.
DeMille: The Man and His Pictures. p71-75.
Exhibitor's Trade Review. Nov 22, 1919, p2135.
Fifty Great American Silent Films, 1912-1920. p114-17.
The Films of Cecil B. DeMille. p174-79.
The Films of Gloria Swanson. p79-86.
Magill's Survey of Cinema. Silent Films. v2, p689-92.
Motion Picture News. Dec 6, 1919, p4142.
The Moving Picture World. Dec 6, 1919, p681, 690.
The New York Times. Nov 24, 1919, p13.
Photoplay. Dec 1919, v17, p72-73.
Selected Film Criticism, 1912-1920. p168-70.
Variety. Nov 28, 1919, p58.
Wid's Daily. Nov 30, 1919, p3.

The Male Animal (US; Nugent, Elliott; 1942)
Commonweal. Apr 10, 1942, v35, p622.
Film Daily. Mar 3, 1942, p6.
The Films of Henry Fonda. p107-09.
The Films of Olivia De Havilland. p189-92.
The Fondas (Springer). p115-17.
Hollywood Reporter. Mar 3, 1942, p3.
The London Times. Jul 27, 1942, p8.
Magill's Survey of Cinema. Series I. v3, p1046-48.
Motion Picture Exhibitor. Mar 11, 1942, v27, n18, sec2, p966.
Motion Picture Herald Product Digest. Mar 7, 1942, p537.
The New York Times. Mar 28, 1942, p11.
Time. Mar 23, 1942, v39, p74.
Variety. Mar 4, 1942, p8.

The Maltese Falcon (US; Huston, John; 1941)
American Imago. v35, n3, p275-96.
America's Favorite Movies. p135-53.
Armchair Detective. 1981, v14, n1, p86-87.
Cinema: The Novel into Films. p299-302.
Classic Movies. p158-59.
Commonweal. Oct 17, 1941, v34, p614.

Dark City. p7-12.
Differentiating the Media. p46-55.
Film and Literature. p129-36.
Film Art. p166-70.
Film Comment. May-Jun 1980, v16, p27-32.
Film Criticism. Wint 1982, v6, p45-50.
The Film Criticism of Otis Ferguson. p390.
Film Culture. 1959, v19, p66-101.
Film Daily. Sep 30, 1941, p8.
Film News. Oct 1973, v30, p18.
Film Noir. p181-82.
Film Society Review (New York). Feb 1966, p21-22.
Films and Filming. Nov 1964, v11, p45-50.
Films and Filming. Mar 1974, v20, p56-58.
Films in Review. Mar 1980, v31, p160-62.
The Films of Peter Lorre. p140-44.
Focus on Film. Jun 1978, n30, p4-6.
The Great Films. p153-56.
Hollywood Reporter. Sep 30, 1941, p3.
Humphrey Bogart (Barbour). p80-84.
Humphrey Bogart: The Man and His Films. p112-13.
The International Dictionary of Films and Filmmakers. v1, p275-76.
Journal of Popular Film and TV. 1978, v7, n1, p42-55.
Library Quarterly. 1975, v45, p46-55.
The London Times. Jun 22, 1942, p8.
Magic Moments from the Movies. p100-01.
Magill's Survey of Cinema. Series I. v3, p1049-52.
Make It Again, Sam. p114-19.
Malliwell's Hundred. p187-91.
Motion Picture Exhibitor. Oct 15, 1941, v26, n23, sec2, p871-72.
Motion Picture Herald Product Digest. Oct 4, 1941, p298.
The Movies on Your Mind. p53-78.
The New Republic. Oct 20, 1941, v105, p508.
The New York Times. Oct 4, 1941, p18.
The New York Times. Oct 12, 1941, sec9, p5.
The New Yorker. Oct 4, 1941, v17, p79.
Newsweek. Oct 13, 1941, v18, p66.
Running Away from Myself. p144-54.
Scribner's Commentator. Dec 1941, v11, p108.
Selected Film Criticism, 1941-1950. p135-36.
Time. Oct 20, 1941, v38, p100.
University Film Association Journal. 1975, v27, p39+.
Variety. Oct 1, 1941, p9.
Velvet Light Trap. Sum 1983, n20, p2-9.
50 Classic Motion Pictures. p32-37.

The Maltese Falcon (US; Del Ruth, Roy; 1931)
The Detective in Film. p39-41.
Dictionary of Films. p206.
Film Daily. May 31, 1931, p10.
The Great Gangster Pictures. p265-67.
Hollywood Reporter. Apr 8, 1931, p3.
Judge. June 20, 1931, v100, p20.
Life. Jun 26, 1931, v97, p18.
Make It Again, Sam: A Survey of Movie Remakes. p114-19.
Motion Picture Herald. Apr 18, 1931, p40.
The New Masses. Jan 12, 1937, v22, p27.
The New York Times. May 29, 1931, p26.
The New Yorker. Jun 6, 1931, v7, p70.
Outlook and Independent. Jun 24, 1931, v158, p247.
Time. Jun 8, 1931, v17, p30.
Variety. Jun 2, 1931, p15.

Mamba (US; Rogell, Albert S.; 1930)
Commonweal. Apr 16, 1930, v11, p688.
Exhibitors Herald-World. Mar 22, 1930, p38.
Film Daily. Mar 16, 1930, p8.
Forgotten Horrors. p29-31.
Life. Apr 18, 1930, v95, p20, 27.
The New York Times. Mar 11, 1930, p25.
The New Yorker. Mar 22, 1930, v6, p53.
Time. Apr 7, 1930, v15, p69.
Variety. Mar 19, 1930, p20.

Mammy (US; Curtiz, Michael; 1930)
Commonweal. Apr 23, 1930, v11, p715.
Exhibitors Herald-World. Apr 5, 1930, p37.
Film Daily. Mar 30, 1930, p8.
The Film Spectator. May 24, 1930, v9, p22-23.
Judge. Apr 12, 1930, v98, p21.
Life. Apr 28, 1930, v95, p18.
The Nation. Apr 16, 1930, v130, p465.
The New York Times. Mar 27, 1930, p24.
The New York Times. Mar 30, 1930, p5.
The New Yorker. Apr 5, 1930, v6, p91.
Outlook and Independent. Apr 9, 1930, v154, p594.
Time. Apr 7, 1930, v15, p69.
Variety. Apr 2, 1930, p19.

Man About Town (US; Sandrich, Mark; 1939)
Commonweal. Jul 14, 1939, v30, p300.
Film Daily. Jun 13, 1939, p14.
Hollywood Reporter. Jun 8, 1939, p3.
Hollywood Spectator. Jun 24, 1939, v14, p6.
Motion Picture Herald. Jun 17, 1939, p50.
The New Statesman and Nation. Jul 15, 1939, v17, p84-85.
The New York Times. Jun 29, 1939, p19.
The New Yorker. Jun 24, 1939, v15, p65.
Newsweek. Jun 26, 1939, v13, p26.
Rob Wagner's Script. Jun 24, 1939, v21, p17.
Time. Jul 10, 1939, v33, p27.
Variety. Jun 14, 1939, p14.

The Man from Blankley's (US; Green, Alfred E.; 1930)
Exhibitors Herald-World. Apr 26, 1930, p30.
Film Daily. Apr 6, 1930, p40.
Judge. Apr 19, 1930, v98, p25.
Life. Apr 18, 1930, v95, p20.
The Nation. Apr 16, 1930, v130, p465.
National Board of Review Magazine. Apr 1930, v5, p6.
The New York Times. Mar 29, 1930, p23.
The New York Times. Apr 6, 1930, p5.
The New York Times. Apr 13, 1930, p6.
The New Yorker. Apr 5, 1930, v6, p91-92.
Outlook and Independent. Apr 16, 1930, v154, p632.
Rob Wagner's Script. May 17, 1930, v3, p10.
Time. Apr 7, 1930, v15, p68.
Variety. Apr 2, 1930, p19.

The Man from Home (US; DeMille, Cecil B.; Apfel, Oscar C.; 1914)
The Films of Cecil B. DeMille. p41-46.
The Moving Picture World. Nov 21, 1914, p1088.
The Moving Picture World. Nov 28, 1914, p1294.
The New York Dramatic World. Nov 18, 1914, p32.
Variety. Nov 6, 1914, p23.

The Man from Monterey (US; Wright, Mack V.; 1933)
Film Daily. Aug 16, 1933, p7.
Hollywood Reporter. Apr 8, 1933, p2.
Motion Picture Herald. Aug 26, 1933, p79.
Variety. Aug 22, 1933, p22.

The Man from Music Mountain (US; Kane, Joseph; 1938)
Film Daily. Aug 13, 1938, p8.
Hollywood Reporter. Aug 4, 1938, p3.
Hollywood Spectator. Aug 20, 1938, v13, p12-13.
Magill's Survey of Cinema. Series II. v4, p1501-04.
Motion Picture Herald. Aug 13, 1938, p62.
Variety. Aug 17, 1938, p23.

The Man from Painted Post (US; Henabery, Joseph; 1917)
His Majesty the American. p63-68.
The Moving Picture World. Oct 20, 1927, p400.
The New York Times. Oct 1, 1917, p14.
Variety. Oct 5, 1917, p.
Wid's Daily. Oct 4, 1917, p629.

Man Hunt (Also titled: Manhunt) (US; Lang, Fritz; 1941)
Action. Nov-Dec 1973, v8, n6, p27-28.
BFI/Monthly Film Bulletin. Sep 30, 1941, n93, p118.
Commonweal. Jun 27, 1941, v34, p233.
Dialogue on Film. Apr 1974, v3, n5, p2-13.
The Film Criticism of Otis Ferguson. p371-73.
Film Daily. Jun 13, 1941, p6.
The Films of Fritz Lang. p194-98.
The Films of World War II. p48-49.
Fritz Lang: A Guide to References and Resources. p81-83.
Fritz Lang (Armour). p133-35+.
Fritz Lang (Eisner). p209-20.
Hollywood Picture. May 25, 1943, p22.
Hollywood Reporter. Jun 9, 1941, p3.
Life. Jun 30, 1941, v10, p67-68+.
The London Times. Sep 22, 1941, p8.
Magic and Myth of the Movies. p141-42.
Magic Moments from the Movies. p87-89.
Motion Picture Exhibitor. Jun 25, 1941, p773.
Motion Picture Herald Product Digest. May 3, 1941, p128.
The Nation. Jun 21, 1941, v152, p732.
The New Republic. Jun 23, 1941, v104, p858.
The New Republic. Jun 30, 1941, v104, p887.
The New Republic. Jul 7, 1941, v105, p21.
The New York Times. Jun 14, 1941, p20.
The New York Times. Jun 22, 1941, sec9, p3.
The New Yorker. Jun 21, 1941, v17, p70.
Newsweek. Jun 23, 1941, v17, p52.
Sight and Sound. Sum 1941, p25.
Sight and Sound. Aut 1955, v25, p92-97.
Time. Jun 30, 1941, v37, p65.
Variety. Jun 11, 1941, p14.

Man Hunt (US; Clemens, William; 1936)
Film Daily. Jan 29, 1936, p8.
Hollywood Reporter. Jan 3, 1936, p3.
Hollywood Spectator. Jan 18, 1936, v10, p13-14.
The New York Times. Jan 30, 1936, p14.
Variety. Feb 12, 1936, p18.

The Man I Killed (Also titled: Broken Lullaby) (US; Lubitsch, Ernst; 1932)
The American Films of Ernst Lubitsch. p126-36.
Ernst Lubitsch: A Guide to References and Resources. p110-12.
Film Daily. Jan 24, 1932, p10.
Film Notes. p81-82.
Film Society Review. Jan 1969, n4, p22-23.
Grierson on Documentary. p47-48.
Hollywood Reporter. Jan 7, 1932, p3.
London Mercury. Oct 1932, v26, p562.
The Lubitsch Touch. p118-22.
Motion Picture Herald. Jan 16, 1932, p38, 40.
The Nation. Feb 17, 1932, v134, p212.
National Board of Review Magazine. Feb 1932, v7, p16.
The New York Times. Jan 20, 1932, p17.
The New Yorker. Jan 30, 1932, v7, p51-52.
Outlook and Independent. Feb 3, 1932, v160, p150.
Rob Wagner's Script. Feb 6, 1932, v6, p10.
Time. Feb 1, 1932, v19, p48.
Variety. Jan 26, 1932, p21.

The Man I Married (US; Pichel, Irving; 1940)
Commonweal. Aug 16, 1940, v32, p352.
Film Daily. Jul 16, 1940, p6.
Hollywood Reporter. Jul 15, 1940, p3.
Motion Picture Herald. Jul 20, 1940, p26.
The New York Times. Aug 3, 1940, p9.
The New Yorker. Aug 17, 1940, v16, p44.
Scholastic. Sep 23, 1940, v37, p39.
Time. Aug 12, 1940, v36, p32.
Variety. Jul 17, 1940, p16.

The Man in Grey (US; Arliss, Leslie; 1943)
BFI/Monthly Film Bulletin. Aug 1985, v52, p258-59.
Commonweal. Dec 21, 1945, v43, p265.

Film Daily. Dec 3, 1945, p7.
The Films of James Mason. p65-66.
The Great British Films. p69-71.
Hollywood Reporter. Nov 28, 1945, p8.
Magill's Survey of Cinema. Series II. v4, p1505-07.
Motion Picture Herald Product Digest. Dec 8, 1945, p2746.
The New York Times. Jan 30, 1945, p16.
Time. Dec 18, 1944, v46, p101.
Variety. Aug 18, 1943, p26.

The Man in Possession (US; Wood, Sam; 1931)
Film Daily. Jul 19, 1931, p10.
Hollywood Spectator. Aug 1, 1931, v12, p18-19.
Hollywood Spectator. Aug 15, 1931, v12, p10.
Judge. Aug 8, 1931, v101, p22.
Life. Aug 7, 1931, v98, p16.
Motion Picture Herald. Jan 3, 1931, p74.
Motion Picture Herald. Jun 13, 1931, p31.
The New York Times. Jul 18, 1931, p16.
The New Yorker. Jul 25, 1931, v7, p54.
Outlook and Independent. Jul 29, 1931, v158, p406.
Rob Wagner's Script. Aug 8, 1931, v5, p10.
Theatre Magazine. Mar 1931, v53, p47.
Time. Jul 27, 1931, v18, p31.
Variety. Jul 21, 1931, p34.

The Man in the Iron Mask (US; Whale, James; 1939)
Commonweal. Jul 21, 1939, v30, p320.
Film Daily. Jun 30, 1939, p10.
Hollywood Reporter. Jun 27, 1939, p3.
James Whale (Curtis). p170-71, 173-74.
Magill's Survey of Cinema. Series II. v4, p1508-12.
Motion Picture Herald. Jul 1, 1939, p42.
The New York Times. Jul 14, 1939, p11.
The New Yorker. Jul 15, 1939, v15, p57-58.
Newsweek. Jul 17, 1939, v14, p31.
Photoplay. Sep 1939, v53, p62.
Rob Wagner's Script. Aug 12, 1939, v22, p18.
Time. Jul 24, 1939, v34, p43.
Variety. Jun 28, 1939, p14.

Man Killer *See* Private Detective 62

Man of Affairs *See* His Lordship

Man of Aran (GB; Flaherty, Robert; 1934)
Commonweal. Nov 9, 1934, v21, p66.
Film Daily. Oct 20, 1934, p3.
From Quasimodo to Scarlett O'Hara. p184-87.
Hollywood Reporter. Oct 23, 1934, p3.
The International Dictionary of Films and Filmmakers. p277-78.
Literary Digest. Nov 3, 1934, v118, p32.
Magill's Survey of Cinema. Series II. v4, p1516-18.
Man of Aran.
Motion Picture Herald. Oct 27, 1934, p41.
The Nation. Oct 31, 1934, v139, p518.
The New Republic. Nov 7, 1934, v80, p366.
The New York Times. Oct 19, 1934, p27.
Newsweek. Oct 20, 1934, v4, p39.
Rob Wagner's Script. Feb 9, 1935, v12, p9.
Robert Flaherty: A Guide to References and Resources. p102-04.
Robert J. Flaherty. p91-92, 163-64, 178-80.
Selected Film Criticism: Foreign Films, 1930-1950. p107-08.
Time. Oct 29, 1934, v24, p56.
Variety. May 29, 1934, p13.
Variety. Oct 23, 1934, p18.

Man of Conquest (US; Nicholls, George, Jr.; 1939)
Commonweal. Apr 21, 1939, v29, p722.
Film Daily. Apr 10, 1939, p6.
Hollywood Reporter. Apr 7, 1939, p3.
Motion Picture Herald. Apr 15, 1939, p57.
National Board of Review Magazine. May 1939, v14, p18.
The New York Times. Apr 28, 1939, p31.

The New Yorker. Apr 29, 1939, v15, p95.
Newsweek. Apr 17, 1939, v13, p26.
Photoplay. Jul 1939, v53, p63.
Rob Wagner's Script. Jun 3, 1939, v21, p17-18.
Scholastic. Apr 29, 1939, v34, p33.
Spectator. Jul 14, 1939, v163, p52.
Time. Apr 17, 1939, v33, p49.
Variety. Apr 21, 1939, p25.

Man of Iron (US; McGann, William; 1935)
Film Daily. Dec 7, 1935, p7.
Hollywood Reporter. Nov 2, 1935, p3.
Hollywood Spectator. Nov 23, 1935, v10, p10-11.
Motion Picture Herald. Nov 16, 1935, p64.
The New York Times. Dec 7, 1935, p22.
Rob Wagner's Script. Nov 9, 1935, v14, p11-12.
Variety. Dec 11, 1935, p19.

The Man of the Hour *See* Homme du Jour, L'

The Man of the Hour (US; Tourneur, Maurice; 1914)
The Moving Picture World. Oct 24, 1914, p496.
The New York Dramatic Mirror. Oct 7, 1914, p30.
Variety. Oct 10, 1914, p25.

Man of the Waterfront *See* Port of Seven Seas

The Man on the Flying Trapeze (US; Bruckman, Clyde; 1935)
American Film Criticism. p317-18.
The Film Criticism of Otis Ferguson. p88-89.
Film Daily. Aug 3, 1935, p3.
The Films of W. C. Fields. p117-20.
Hollywood Reporter. Jun 26, 1935, p4.
Literary Digest. Aug 10, 1935, v120, p29.
Motion Picture Herald. Aug 10, 1935, p52.
The New York Times. Aug 3, 1935, p52.
The New Yorker. Aug 3, 1935, v11, p41.
Rob Wagner's Script. Aug 24, 1935, v13, p8.
Stage. Sep 1935, v12, p3.
Time. Aug 12, 1935, v26, p33.
Variety. Aug 7, 1935, p21.
W. C. Fields: A Life on Film. p173-80.

A Man There Was (Swedish title: Terje Vigen) (SWED; Sjostrom, Victor; 1916)
Cinema, the Magic Vehicle. v1, p46-47.
Film Daily. Feb 29, 1920, p8.

A Man to Remember (US; Kanin, Garson; 1938)
Commonweal. Nov 11, 1938, v29, p77.
Film Daily. Oct 3, 1938, p8.
Hollywood Reporter. Sep 27, 1938, p3.
Motion Picture Herald. Oct 1, 1938, p39.
The New Masses. Nov 22, 1938, v29, p28.
The New Statesman and Nation. Apr 1, 1939, v17, p493.
The New York Times. Nov 7, 1938, p23.
The New Yorker. Nov 12, 1938, v14, p95.
Newsweek. Apr 17, 1939, v13, p26.
Rob Wagner's Script. Dec 24, 1938, v20, p11.
Time. Oct 24, 1938, v32, p24.
Variety. Oct 5, 1938, p14.
Variety. Nov 9, 1938, p16.

The Man Who Broke the Bank at Monte Carlo (US; Roberts, Stephen; 1935)
Film Daily. Oct 28, 1935, p4.
The Films of Ronald Colman. p169-72.
Graham Greene on Film. p50.
Hollywood Reporter. Oct 23, 1935, p3.
Hollywood Spectator. Nov 9, 1935, v10, p9-10.
Motion Picture Herald. Nov 16, 1935, p65.
The New York Times. Nov 15, 1935, p20.
Rob Wagner's Script. Dec 14, 1935, v14, p10.
The Spectator. Feb 7, 1936, v156, p211.

Time. Nov 25, 1935, v26, p47.
Variety. Nov 20, 1935, p16.

The Man Who Came Back (US; Walsh, Raoul; 1931)
Around Cinemas. p44-46.
Exhibitors Herald-World. Dec 27, 1930, p21-22.
Film Daily. Jan 4, 1931, p10.
Life. Jan 23, 1931, v97, p20.
Motion Picture Herald. Jan 3, 1931, p74.
The New York Times. Jan 3, 1931, p21.
The New Yorker. Jan 10, 1931, v6, p57, 59.
Outlook and Independent. Jan 21, 1931, v157, p113.
Theatre Magazine. Mar 1931, v53, p47.
Time. Jan 12, 1931, v17, p22.
Variety. Jan 7, 1931, p22.

The Man Who Came to Dinner (US; Keighley, William; 1941)
Bette Davis: Her Films and Career. p113-14.
Commonweal. Jan 16, 1942, v35, p320-21.
The Film Criticism of Otis Ferguson. p408-09.
Film Daily. Dec 24, 1941, p8.
Hollywood Reporter. Dec 23, 1941, p3.
The London Times. May 13, 1942, p6.
Motion Picture Exhibitor. Dec 31, 1941, p919-20.
Motion Picture Herald Product Digest. Dec 27, 1941, p429.
The New Republic. Jan 12, 1942, v106, p53.
The New York Times. Jan 2, 1942, p25.
The New Yorker. Jan 3, 1942, v17, p50.
Newsweek. Jan 12, 1942, v19, p45.
Scholastic. Jan 5, 1942, 39, p32.
Time. Jan 26, 1942, v39, p44.
Variety. Jul 7, 1942, p44.

The Man Who Changed His Name (GB; Edwards, Henry; 1934)
Film Daily. Oct 16, 1934, p9.
Hollywood Reporter. Oct 20, 1934, p3.
Motion Picture Herald. Oct 27, 1934, p45.
The New York Times. Oct 17, 1934, p26.
Variety. Oct 23, 1934, p25.

The Man Who Could Work Miracles (GB; Mendes, Lothar; 1936)
Film Daily. Feb 24, 1937, p6.
Garbo and the Night Watchman. p71-72.
Graham Greene on Film. p97-98.
London Mercury. Oct 1936, v34, p538.
Motion Picture Herald. Aug 22, 1936, p40.
National Board of Review Magazine. May 1937, v12, p9.
The New Statesman and Nation. Aug 29, 1936, v12, p289.
The New York Times. Feb 22, 1937, p13.
The New Yorker. Feb 20, 1937, v13, p60.
Rob Wagner's Script. Mar 6, 1937, v17, p10.
Scholastic. Mar 13, 1937, v30, p20.
Science Fiction Studies in Film. p87.
The Spectator. Sep 4, 1936, v157, p379.
Time. Mar 1, 1937, v29, p66.
Variety. Aug 12, 1936, p18.
Variety. Feb 24, 1937, p15.
World Film News. Oct 1936, v1, p24.

The Man Who Knew Too Much (GB; Hitchcock, Alfred; 1934)
The Art of Alfred Hitchcock. p34-35.
Cinema Quarterly. Aut 1934, v3, p114, 119.
Cinema, the Magic Vehicle. v1, p229-30.
A Critical History of the British Cinema. p108-09.
Dictionary of Films. p209-10.
Esquire. Jul 1935, v3, p152.
The Film Criticism of Otis Ferguson. p74-75.
Film Daily. Mar 22, 1935, p7.
The Films of Peter Lorre. p85-87.
From Quasimodo to Scarlett O'Hara. p200-02.
Hitchcock: The First Forty-Four Films. p38-40.

Hitchcock (Truffaut). p86-91+.
Hitchcock's British Films. p167-81.
Hollywood Reporter. Mar 29, 1935, p7.
Judge. May 1935, v108, p19.
Life. Jun 1935 f, v102, p28.
Literary Digest. Apr 6, 1935, v119, p29.
Magill's Survey of Cinema. Series II. v4, p1519-22.
Masters of Menace: Greenstreet and Lorre. p22-26.
National Board of Review Magazine. May 1935, v10, p12.
The New Republic. May 1, 1935, v82, p341.
The New York Times. Mar 23, 1935, p11.
The New Yorker. Mar 30, 1935, v11, p64.
Rob Wagner's Script. Jun 1, 1935, v13, p10.
Selected Film Criticism: Foreign Films, 1930-1950. p109-10.
The Spectator. Dec 14, 1934, v153, p924.
Time. Apr 8, 1935, v25, p25.
Vanity Fair. May 1935, v44, p45.
Variety. Jan 8, 1935, p39.
Variety. Mar 4, 1935, p17.

The Man Who Laughs (US; Leni, Paul; 1928)
Exhibitor's Herald-World and Moving Picture World. Oct 13, 1928, p46.
Film Daily. May 6, 1928, p4.
Photoplay. May 1928, v33, p55.
Selected Film Criticism, 1921-1930. p181.
Variety. May 2, 1928, p14.

The Man Who Lived Twice (US; Lachman, Harry; 1936)
Film Daily. Oct 13, 1936, p13.
Hollywood Reporter. Oct 19, 1936, p3.
Motion Picture Herald. Oct 24, 1936, p56, 58.
The New York Times. Oct 12, 1936, p23.
The Tatler. Jan 27, 1937, v143, p144.
Variety. Oct 14, 1936, p15.

The Man Who Played God (US; Adolfi, John; 1932)
Bette Davis: Her Films and Career. p24-25.
Commonweal. Feb 24, 1932, v15, p469-70.
Film Daily. Feb 14, 1932, p10.
Hollywood Reporter. Jan 14, 1932, p3.
The Nation. Mar 2, 1932, v134, p268.
National Board of Review Magazine. Mar 1932, v7, p9-13.
The New York Times. Feb 11, 1932, p16.
The New Yorker. Feb 20, 1932, v8, p61-62.
Time. Feb 22, 1932, v19, p44.
Variety. Feb 16, 1932, p24.

The Man Who Reclaimed His Head (US; Ludwig, Edward; 1934)
Film Daily. Jan 8, 1935, p8.
Hollywood Reporter. Dec 1, 1934, p3.
Motion Picture Herald. Dec 8, 1934, p51.
Time. Dec 24, 1934, v24, p22.
Variety. Jan 15, 1935, p13.

Man, Woman, and Sin (US; Bell, Monta; 1927)
Film Daily. Dec 18, 1927, p18.
Magill's Survey of Cinema. Silent Films. v2, p696-98.
The Moving Picture World. Dec 17, 1927, p23.
The New York Times. Dec 5, 1927, p26.
Variety. Dec 7, 1927, p18.

Manhandled (US; Dwan, Allan; 1924)
Allan Dwan: The Last Pioneer. p70-76.
Film Daily. Aug 3, 1924, p6.
The Films of Gloria Swanson. p160-64.
Magill's Survey of Cinema. Silent Films. v2, p699-701.
A Million and One Nights. p830.
The New York Times. Jul 29, 1924, p9.
Variety. Jul 30, 1924, p24.

Manhandled (US; Foster, Lewis R.; 1949)
Film Daily. Jun 10, 1949, p6.
Hollywood Reporter. Apr 12, 1949, p3.
Motion Picture Herald Product Digest. Apr 16, 1949, p4573.

The New York Times. May 26, 1949, p34.
Newsweek. Jun 6, 1949, v33, p80+.
Variety. Apr 13, 1949, p11.

Manhattan Melodrama (US; Van Dyke, W.S.; 1934)
Crime Movies. p122-24.
Film Daily. May 2, 1934, p7.
The Films of Clark Gable. p167-68.
The Films of Myrna Loy. p154-56.
Hollywood Reporter. Apr 16, 1934, p3.
Magill's Survey of Cinema. Series II. v4, p1527-29.
Motion Picture Herald. Apr 28, 1934, p31.
The New York Times. May 5, 1934, p5.
Time. May 14, 1934, v23, p24.
Variety. May 8, 1934, p14.

Manhattan Parade (US; Bacon, Lloyd; 1931)
Film Daily. Jan 3, 1932, p8.
Hollywood Reporter. Dec 11, 1931, p3.
Motion Picture Herald. Jan 2, 1932, p30-31.
The New York Times. Dec 25, 1931, p29.
Time. Jan 4, 1932, v19, p19.
Variety. Dec 29, 1931, p167.

Mannequin (US; Borzage, Frank; 1937)
Commonweal. Dec 31, 1937, v27, p272.
Film Daily. Dec 29, 1937, p7.
The Films of Joan Crawford. p128-29.
The Films of Spencer Tracy. p142-43.
Hollywood Reporter. Dec 15, 1937, p3.
Motion Picture Herald. Dec 18, 1937, p54.
The New Statesman and Nation. Feb 12, 1938, v15, p248.
The New York Times. Jan 21, 1938, p15.
The New Yorker. Jan 22, 1938, v13, p55.
Rob Wagner's Script. Feb 12, 1938, v19, p8.
The Tatler. Feb 16, 1938, v147, p282.
Time. Jan 24, 1938, v31, p36.
Variety. Dec 22, 1937, p16.

Man-Proof (US; Thorpe, Richard; 1937)
Commonweal. Jan 14, 1938, v27, p327.
Film Daily. Jan 11, 1938, p10.
The Films of Myrna Loy. p206.
Hollywood Reporter. Dec 10, 1937, p3.
Motion Picture Herald. Dec 18, 1937, p50-51.
The New Yorker. Jan 22, 1938, v13, p55-56.
Rob Wagner's Script. Jan 15, 1938, v18, p9.
The Spectator. Jan 21, 1938, v160, p87.
Variety. Dec 15, 1937, p17.

Man's Castle (US; Borzage, Frank; 1933)
America in the Dark. p216-17.
Film Daily. Dec 12, 28, 1933, p18.
The Films of Spencer Tracy. p101-03.
The Films of the Thirties. p114-15.
Hollywood Reporter. Oct 11, 1933, p3.
Motion Picture Herald. Jan 6, 1934, p30.
The New York Times. Dec 30, 1933, p9.
The New York Times. Jan 14, 1934, p5.
Rob Wagner's Script. Dec 2, 1933, v10, p9.
Rob Wagner's Script. Jun 11, 1938, v19, p11.
Selected Film Criticism, 1931-1940. p146.
Time. Nov 13, 1933, v22, p22.
Vanity Fair. Feb 1934, v41, p45.
Variety. Jan 2, 1934, p13.

Manslaughter (US; DeMille, Cecil B.; 1922)
Film Daily. Sep 24, 1921, p2.
The Films of Cecil B. DeMille. p209-14.
The New York Times. Sep 18, 1922, p14.
Photoplay. Nov 1922, v22, p65.
Selected Film Criticism, 1921-1930. p182.
Variety. Sep 22, 1922, p41.

Manslaughter (US; Abbott, George; 1930)
Claudette Colbert (Quirk). p31-34.
Exhibitors Herald-World. Jul 26, 1930, p29.
Exhibitors Herald-World. Aug 2, 1930, p26.
Film Daily. Jul 27, 1930, p10.
The Films of Fredric March. p63-64.
Judge. Aug 16, 1930, v99, p23.
Life. Aug 22, 1930, v96, p19.
The Nation. Aug 20, 1930, v131, p209.
The New York Times. Jul 24, 1930, p26.
The New York Times. Aug 3, 1930, p5.
The New Yorker. Aug 2, 1930, v6, p54-55.
Outlook and Independent. Aug 6, 1930, v155, p551.
Time. Aug 4, 1930, v16, p25.
Variety. Jul 30, 1930, p17.

Mantrap (US; Fleming, Victor; 1926)
Film Daily. Jul 25, 1926, p5.
Magill's Survey of Cinema. Silent Films. v2, p706-08.
Variety. Jul 14, 1926, p16.

The Manxman (GB; Hitchcock, Alfred; 1929)
The Art of Alfred Hitchcock. p15-18.
Film Daily. Dec 22, 1929, p10.
The Films of Alfred Hitchcock. p28-29.
Hitchcock: The First Forty-Four Films. p16-20.
Hitchcock's British Films. p85-94.
The New York Times. Dec 17, 1929, p28.
Variety. Feb 20, 1929, p17.
Variety. Dec 18, 1929, p31.

The March of Time (US; Rochemont, Louis de; 1935-51)
The American Newsreel, 1911-1967. p230-33.
Catholic World. Aug 1936, v143, p602.
Christian Science Monitor Magazine. Oct 30, 1935, p3+.
Documentary: History of the Non-Fiction Film. p121-22.
The Documentary Tradition. p104-11.
Film Library Quarterly. 1973, n2, v6, p48.
Films Beget Films. p43-44.
Graham Greene on Film. p34-35.
Hollywood Reporter. Feb 1, 1935, p3.
The International Dictionary of Films and Filmmakers. v1, p281-82.
Journal of Popular Film. Fall 1973, v2, p378-87.
Journal of Popular Film. 1976, n2, v5, p126-45.
The March of Time, 1935-1951.
Motion Picture Herald. Aug 24, 1935, p58.
The Nation. Feb 20, 1935, v140, p232.
National Board of Review Magazine. Dec 1935, v10, p4.
The New Masses. Jul 9, 1935, v16, p29-30.
The New Masses. Sep 3, 1935, v17, p29-30.
The New Masses. Oct 8, 1935, v17, p29-30.
The New Masses. Aug 18, 1936, v20, p29.
The New Republic. Aug 19, 1936, v8, p43-45.
The New Statesman and Nation. Sep 4, 1937, v14, p339.
The New York Times. Feb 2, 1935, p10.
The New Yorker. Feb 9, 1935, v10, p59.
Newsweek. Feb 9, 1935, v5, p38-39.
Non-Fiction Film. p109-11.
Penguin Film Review. May 1949, n9, p17-21.
Quarterly of Film, Radio, and Television. Sum 1957, p354-61.
Rob Wagner's Script. Feb 9, 1935, v12, p8.
Sight and Sound. Aut 1935, v4, p123.
The Spectator. Nov 8, 1935, v155, p774.
Time. Jun 1, 1936, v27, p40-42.
World Film News. Oct 1936, v1, p6-7.

Mare Nostrum (Also titled: Our Sea) (US; Ingram, Rex; 1926)
Film Daily. Feb 28, 1926, p6.
From Quasimodo to Scarlett O'Hara. p53-54.
Magill's Survey of Cinema. Silent Films. v2, p709-11.
The Moving Picture World. Feb 27, 1926, p785-86.
National Board of Review Magazine. Mar-Apr 1926, v1, p15-16.

The New York Times. Feb 16, 1926, p22.
Rex Ingram: Master of the Silent Cinema. p153-79.
Selected Film Criticism, 1921-1930. p182-85.
Spellbound in Darkness. p411-12.
Variety. Feb 17, 1926, p40.

Margie (US; King, Henry; 1946)
Commonweal. Nov 8, 1946, v45, p96.
Film Daily. Oct 16, 1946, p11.
Hollywood Reporter. Oct 16, 1946, p3.
Life. Nov 4, 1946, v21, p137-38+.
Magill's Survey of Cinema. Series II. v4, p1533-37.
Motion Picture Herald Product Digest. Oct 19, 1946, p3261.
The New Republic. Nov 11, 1946, v115, p629.
The New York Times. Oct 17, 1946, p28.
The New Yorker. Oct 26, 1946, v22, p108.
Newsweek. Oct 28, 1946, v28, p94.
Time. Oct 28, 1946, v48, p104+.
Variety. Oct 16, 1946, p8.

Maria Rosa (US; DeMille, Cecil B.; 1916)
The Films of Cecil B. DeMille. p114-17.
The Moving Picture World. May 13, 1916, p1180.
The New York Dramatic Mirror. May 6, 1916, p28.
The New York Dramatic Mirror. May 13, 1916, p27.
The New York Times. May 8, 1916, p7.
Photoplay. Mar 1916, v10, p167.
Photoplay. Jul 1916, v10, p120.
Variety. Apr 28, 1916, p29.
Wid's Daily. May 4, 1916, p551.

Marie Antoinette (US; Van Dyke, W.S.; 1938)
Catholic World. Oct 1938, v148, p89-90.
Commonweal. Aug 26, 1938, v28, p451.
Esquire. Dec 1938, v10, p139-40.
The Film Criticism of Otis Ferguson. p231.
Film Daily. Jul 13, 1938, p5.
The Films of Norma Shearer. p212-23.
The Films of Tyrone Power. p76-79.
The Great Romantic Films. p64-67.
Hollywood Reporter. Jul 9, 1938, p3.
Life. Jul 11, 1938, v5, p41-43.
Life. Jul 25, 1938, v5, p43-45.
London Mercury. Dec 1938, v39, p203.
McCall's. Oct 1938, v65, p4, 80.
Motion Picture Herald. Jul 16, 1938, p52.
Motion Picture Herald. Mar 26, 1938, p16-17.
National Board of Review Magazine. Oct 1938, v13, p19.
The New Masses. Aug 30, 1938, v28, p30.
The New Statesman and Nation. Oct 29, 1938, v16, p689.
The New York Times. Aug 17, 1938, p23.
The New Yorker. Aug 20, 1938, v14, p40-41.
Newsweek. Aug 22, 1938, v12, p21.
Rob Wagner's Script. Jul 23, 1938, v19, p8.
Sight and Sound. Wint 1938-39, v7, p161.
The Tatler. Nov 16, 1938, v150, p286.
Those Fabulous Movie Years: The 30s. p132-33.
Time. Aug 22, 1938, v32, p41.
Variety. Jul 13, 1938, p15.
World Film News. Nov 1938, v3, p314.

Marie Walewska *See* Conquest

Marius (FR; Korda, Alexander; 1931)
Cinema, the Magic Vehicle. v1, p193-94.
Classics of the Foreign Film. p84-87.
Dictionary of Films. p210-11.
The Great French Films. p34-37.
Magill's Survey of Cinema. Foreign Language Films. v4, p1954-60.
The Nation. May 3, 1933, v136, p511.
The New York Times. Apr 14, 1933, p22.
The New Yorker. May 15, 1948, v24, p78.
Variety. Apr 25, 1933, p15.
Variety. Jun 2, 1933, p14.

The Mark of Cain (US; De Grasse, Joseph; 1916)
The Moving Picture World. Aug 12, 1916, p1147.
Wid's Daily. Aug 24, 1916, p810.

Mark of the Vampire (US; Browning, Tod; 1935)
BFI/Monthly Film Bulletin. Mar 1979, v46, p59.
Classics of the Horror Film. p125-29.
Film Daily. Mar 28, 1935, p4.
The Films of Bela Lugosi. p113-17.
Hollywood Reporter. Mar 23, 1935, p3.
Hollywood Reporter. May 10, 1935, p4.
Motion Picture Herald. Apr 6, 1935, p48.
The New York Times. May 3, 1935, p23.
Time. May 6, 1935, v25, p40.
Variety. May 8, 1935, p45.

The Mark of Zorro (US; Niblo, Fred; 1920)
Fifty Great American Silent Films, 1912-1920. p136-38.
The Films of the Twenties. p45-48.
His Majesty the American. p119-31.
Magill's Survey of Cinema. Silent Films. v2, p712-15.
The Moving Picture World. Dec 11, 1920, p719.
The New York Times. Nov 29, 1920, p20.
Photoplay. Mar 1921, v19, p62.
Selected Film Criticism, 1912-1920. p170.
Variety. Dec 3, 1920, p32.
Wid's Daily. Dec 5, 1920, p3.

The Mark of Zorro (US; Mamoulian, Rouben; 1940)
Film Daily. Nov 6, 1940, p5.
The Films of Tyrone Power. p110-13.
The London Times. Feb 3, 1941, p6.
Magic Moments from the Movies. p82.
Magill's Survey of Cinema. Series I. v3, p1070-75.
Mamoulian (Milne). p121-27.
Motion Picture Exhibitor. Nov 13, 1940, p636.
The New York Times. Nov 4, 1940, p33.
The New York Times. Nov 10, 1940, sec9, p5.
Rob Wagner's Script. Nov 9, 1940, v24, p16.
Selected Film Criticism, 1931-1940. p147-49.
Swordsmen of the Screen. p176-77.
Variety. Nov 6, 1940, p16.

A Marked Man (US; Ford, John; 1917)
The Moving Picture World. Nov 3, 1917, p752.
The Moving Picture World. Nov 10, 1917, p875.

Marked Men (US; Ford, John; 1919)
Exhibitor's Trade Review. Dec 27, 1919, p432.
The Moving Picture World. Jan 24, 1920, p559.
Wid's Daily. Dec 21, 1919, p3.

Marked Woman (US; Bacon, Lloyd; 1937)
Bette Davis: Her Films and Career. p76-77.
The Complete Films of Humphrey Bogart. p42-43.
Crime Movies (Clarens). p157-59.
Film Daily. Feb 26, 1937, p10.
Fortune. Dec 1937, v16, p112.
Graham Greene on Film. p166.
The Great Gangster Pictures. p270.
Hollywood Reporter. Feb 23, 1937, p3.
Hollywood Spectator. Mar 13, 1937, v11, p8-9.
Humphrey Bogart: The Man and His Films. p67.
Kiss Kiss Bang Bang. p384-85.
Life. Apr 19, 1937, v2, p49-51.
Magill's Survey of Cinema. Series II. v4, p1541-43.
Motion Picture Herald. Mar 6, 1937, p39.
The Nation. May 8, 1937, v144, p545.
National Board of Review Magazine. May 1937, v12, p10.
The New Statesman and Nation. Sep 11, 1937, v14, p375.
The New York Times. Apr 12, 1937, p15.
The New Yorker. Apr 17, 1937, v13, p63, 65.
Newsweek. Apr 10, 1937, v9, p25.
Rob Wagner's Script. Apr 17, 1937, v17, p10.
Time. Apr 19, 1937, v29, p66.

Variety. Apr 14, 1937, p12.
The Velvet Light Trap. Fall 1972, v6, p20-25.

The Marriage Circle (US; Lubitsch, Ernst; 1924)
The American Films of Ernst Lubitsch. p46-93.
Ernst Lubitsch: A Guide to References and Resources. p75-77.
Ernst Lubitsch's American Comedy. p5-18.
Film Daily. Feb 10, 1924, p5.
The Films of the Twenties. p90-92.
The Lubitsch Touch. p60-69.
Magill's Survey of Cinema. Silent Films. v2, p716-19.
Motion Picture Magazine. May 1925, v19, p52-53.
The Moving Picture World. Feb 16, 1924, p581.
The New York Times. Feb 4, 1924, p23.
The New York Times. Oct 12, 1924, sec8, p5.
Photoplay. Apr 1924, v25, p61.
Selected Film Criticism, 1921-1930. p185-86.
The Spectator. May 17, 1924, v132, p788.
Spellbound in Darkness. p316-20.
Variety. Feb 7, 1924, p22.

The Marriage of Corbal (GB; Grune, Karl; Brunn, F.;
1936)
Graham Greene on Film. p78-80.
Hollywood Reporter. Jun 13, 1936, p6.
Motion Picture Herald. Jun 13, 1936, p69.
The Spectator. Jun 5, 1936, v156, p1036.
Variety. Jun 10, 1936, p35.

Married Before Breakfast (US; Marin, Edwin L.; 1937)
Film Daily. Jul 26, 1937, p7.
Hollywood Reporter. Jun 14, 1937, p3.
Motion Picture Herald. Jun 26, 1937, p88-89.
The New York Times. Jul 23, 1937, p16.
Rob Wagner's Script. Jun 26, 1937, v17, p12.
Variety. Jul 28, 1937, p27.

Marseillaise, La *See* Captain of the Guard

Marseillaise, La (FR; Renoir, Jean; 1937)
Cinema, the Magic Vehicle. v1, p297.
Dictionary of Films. p211-12.
Film Daily. Nov 10, 1939, p9.
Film Society Review. Dec 1968, p34-39.
Hollywood Quarterly. Jul 1946, v1, p416-19.
Jean Renoir: A Guide to References and Resources. p106-12.
Jean Renoir (Durgnat). p158-71.
Jean Renoir: My Life and My Films. p126-27.
Jean Renoir: The French Films, 1924-1939. p323-50.
Motion Picture Herald. Nov 18, 1939, p49.
National Board of Review Magazine. Dec 1939, v14, p15.
The New Masses. Nov 21, 1939, v33, p28-29.
The New York Times. Nov 6, 1939, p20.
Saint Cinema: Selected Writings, 1929-1970. p87-90.
Sight and Sound. Wint 1937-38, v6, p180-81.
Sight and Sound. Sum 1938, v7, p51-52.
Sight and Sound. Wint 1967-68, v37, p41-42.
Sight and Sound. Wint 1979-80, v49, p36-41.
Studio. Jul 1940, v120, p14-15.
Theatre Arts. Jan 1940, v24, p68.
Variety. Mar 16, 1938, p17.
Variety. Nov 15, 1939, p20.

The Martin Mystery *See* The Master Cracksman

The Martyrs of the Alamo (US; Cabanne, Christy; 1915)
Motion Picture News. Jun 12, 1915, p53.
Motion Picture News. Oct 9, 1915, p48.
Motion Picture News. Nov 6, 1915, p86.
Motography. Oct 30, 1915, p914.
Motography. Nov 27, 1915, p1164.
The Moving Picture World. Nov 6, 1915, p1155.
Variety. Oct 29, 1915, p22.

Marusia (USSR; Bulgakov, Leo; 1938)
Film Daily. Dec 16, 1938, p10.
Motion Picture Herald. Dec 31, 1938, p54.

The New York Times. Dec 12, 1938, p26.
Variety. Dec 21, 1938, p15.

The Marx Brothers at the Circus *See* At the Circus

Mary Burns, Fugitive (US; Howard, William K.; 1935)
Film Daily. Nov 9, 1935, p7.
Garbo and the Night Watchman. p102.
Hollywood Reporter. Nov 7, 1935, p4.
Hollywood Spectator. Nov 23, 1935, p7-8.
Motion Picture Herald. Nov 16, 1935, p63.
The New Masses. Nov 19, 1935, v17, p30.
The New York Times. Nov 16, 1935, p19.
Rob Wagner's Script. Dec 28, 1935, v14, p10.
Time. Nov 25, 1935, v26, p50.
Variety. Nov 20, 1935, p16.

Mary Jane's Mishap (GB; Smith, G.A.; 1901)
Behind the Screen. p105.

Mary of Scotland (US; Ford, John; 1936)
Canadian Magazine. Sep 1936, v86, p28.
Catholic World. Sep 1936, v143, p725-26.
Commonweal. Aug 21, 1936, v24, p407.
Esquire. Oct 1936, v6, p109, 193.
The Film Criticism of Otis Ferguson. p146-48.
Film Daily. Jul 24, 1936, p7.
Films and Filming. Apr 1969, v15, p86-87.
The Films of Fredric March. p137-39.
The Films of Katharine Hepburn. p75-79.
Hollywood Reporter. Jul 24, 1936, p3.
Hollywood Spectator. Aug 1, 1936, v11, p8-9.
Judge. Sep 1936, v111, p29.
Literary Digest. Aug 8, 1936, v122, p18.
Magill's Survey of Cinema. Series II. v4, p1547-49.
Motion Picture Herald. Jul 25, 1936, p62.
The Nation. Aug 8, 1936, v143, p165.
The New Masses. Aug 18, 1936, v20, p29-30.
The New Republic. Aug 19, 1936, v88, p47-48.
The New Statesman and Nation. Aug 29, 1936, v12, p289.
The New York Times. Jul 31, 1936, p22.
The New York Times. Jul 26, 1936, p3.
The New York Times. Aug 9, 1936, p3.
The New Yorker. Aug 8, 1936, v12, p48-49.
Newsweek. Aug 1, 1936, v8, p22-23.
The Non-Western Films of John Ford. p247-49.
Rob Wagner's Script. Aug 8, 1936, v15, p10.
Scholastic. Sep 19, 1936, v29, p17.
Time. Aug 10, 1936, v28, p27.
Variety. Aug 5, 1936, p16.
World Film News. Sep 1936, v1, p25.

Mary Stevens, M.D. (US; Bacon, Lloyd; 1933)
Canadian Magazine. Sep 1933, v80, p34.
Film Daily. Jul 28, 1933, p8.
Hollywood Reporter. Jun 16, 1933, p3.
Motion Picture Herald. Aug 12, 1933, p44.
New Outlook. Sep 1933, v162, p44.
The New York Times. Aug 5, 1933, p9.
Time. Aug 14, 1933, v22, p21.
Variety. Aug 8, 1933, p19.

The Mask of Fu Manchu (US; Brabin, Charles; 1932)
Boris Karloff and His Films. p55-59.
Film Daily. Dec 3, 1932, p4.
The Films of Boris Karloff. p79-82.
The Films of Myrna Loy. p141-44.
The Films of the Thirties. p90-91.
The New York Times. Dec 3, 1932, p21.
Variety. Dec 6, 1932, p15.

The Masked Rider (US; Balshofer, Fred J.; 1916)
Magill's Survey of Cinema. Silent Films. v2, p720-22.
The Moving Picture World. Jun 17, 1916, p1987, 2114.
Wid's Daily. Jun 22, 1916, p664.

The Masquerader (US; Wallace, Richard; 1933)
Canadian Magazine. Sep 1933, v80, p33-34.
Film Daily. Mar 8, 1933, p2.
The Films of Ronald Colman. p153-58.
Hollywood Reporter. Feb 14, 1933, p5.
Motion Picture Herald. Feb 25, 1933, p37.
New Outlook. Oct 1933, v162, p49.
The New York Times. Sep 4, 1933, p9.
The New York Times. Sep 10, 1933, p3.
Newsweek. Sep 9, 1933, v2, p31.
Rob Wagner's Script. Sep 2, 1933, v10, p8-9.
Samuel Goldwyn Presents. p128-30.
Time. Sep 11, 1933, v22, p47.
Variety. Sep 5, 1933, p19.

The Massacre (US; Griffith, D.W.; 1912)
The Emergence of Film Art. p53-54.

The Master Cracksman (Also titled: The Martin Mystery)
(US; Carey, Harry; 1914)
The New York Dramatic Mirror. Apr 15, 1914, p38.
The New York Dramatic Mirror. Jun 10, 1914, p52.
The New York Dramatic Mirror. Jan 27, 1915, p26.
Variety. Jun 19, 1914, p21.

Mat *See* Mother

Mata Hari (US; Fitzmaurice, George; 1931)
BFI/Monthly Film Bulletin. Sep 1978, v45, p186-87.
Film Daily. Jan 3, 1932, p8.
The Films of Greta Garbo. p105-07.
Garbo: A Portrait (Walker). p120-24.
The Great Spy Pictures. p296, 298.
Hollywood Reporter. Nov 27, 1931, p3.
Hollywood Spectator. Mar 1932, v12, p7.
Motion Picture Herald. Jan 9, 1932, p37.
The Nation. Jan 20, 1932, v134, p82.
The New York Times. Jan 1, 1932, p31.
The New Yorker. Jan 9, 1932, v7, p71.
Outlook and Independent. Jan 13, 1932, v160, p55.
Rob Wagner's Script. Feb 6, 1932, v6, p8-9.
Time. Jan 11, 1932, v19, p25.
Variety. Jan 5, 1932, p19.

Maternelle, La (FR; Benoit-Levy, Jean; Epstein, Marie;
1933)
Canadian Magazine. Jan 1936, v85, p32.
Canadian Magazine. May 1936, v85, p60.
Cinema Quarterly. Wint 1933-34, v2, p118-21.
Classics of the Foreign Films. p94-95.
The Film Criticism of Otis Ferguson. p99-100.
Film Daily. Oct 17, 1935, p4.
The Golden Age of French Cinema, 1929-1939. p108-11.
The Great French Films. p240-41.
Hollywood Reporter. Aug 22, 1935, p7.
Literary Digest. Oct 26, 1935, v120, p22.
Motion Picture Herald. Nov 16, 1935, p64.
The Nation. Nov 6, 1935, v141, p548.
National Board of Review Magazine. Sep-Oct 1935, v10, p11.
The New Masses. Nov 26, 1935, v17, p30.
The New Republic. Oct 30, 1935, v84, p335.
The New York Times. Oct 15, 1935, p19.
The New Yorker. Oct 19, 1935, v11, p68.
Newsweek. Oct 26, 1935, v6, p29.
Rotha on the Film. p130-31.
The Spectator. Nov 17, 1933, v151, p695.
Time. Oct 28, 1935, v26, p51.
Variety. Sep 26, 1933, p56.
Variety. Oct 23, 1935, p12.

A Matter of Life and Death *See* Stairway to Heaven

Mayerling (FR; Litvak, Anatole; 1936)
Fifty Classic Motion Pictures. p158-63.
The Film Criticism of Otis Ferguson. p195.
Film Daily. Sep 9, 1937, p11.

From Quasimodo to Scarlett O'Hara. p265-66.
The Golden Age of French Cinema, 1929-1939. p88-90.
Graham Greene on Film. p113, 115.
The Great French Films. p242-43.
Hollywood Reporter. Mar 4, 1936, p3.
Literary Digest. Sep 18, 1937, v124, p32.
London Mercury. Dec 1936, v35, p192.
Magill's Survey of Cinema. Foreign Language Films. v4,
p1987-90.
Motion Picture Herald. Sep 25, 1937, p52.
The Nation. Sep 25, 1937, v145, p330.
National Board of Review Magazine. Nov 1937, v12, p15.
The New Masses. Sep 21, 1937, v24, p29.
The New Republic. Sep 15, 1937, v92, p160.
The New Statesman and Nation. Oct 31, 1936, v12, p672.
The New York Times. Sep 14, 1937, p27.
The New Yorker. Sep 18, 1937, v13, p69.
Rob Wagner's Script. Jan 22, 1936, v18, p16-17.
Saturday Review (London). Nov 7, 1936, v162, p608.
Selected Film Criticism: Foreign Films, 1930-1950. p113.
The Spectator. Nov 6, 1936, v157, p808.
Stage. Sep 1937, v14, p47.
Stage. Nov 1937, v15, p81.
Time. Sep 20, 1937, v30, 29.
Time. Sep 20, 1937, v30, p29.
Variety. Feb 19, 1936, p32.
Variety. Sep 15, 1937, p13.
World Film News. Dec 1936, v1, p23.

The Mayor of Hell (US; Mayo, Archie; 1933)
Cinema Quarterly. Wint 1933-34, v2, p123-24.
Film Daily. Jun 23, 1933, p6.
Hollywood Reporter. May 9, 1933, p2.
Judge. Aug 1933, v104, p23.
Motion Picture Herald. May 20, 1933, p32-33.
New Outlook. Aug 1933, v162, p44.
The New York Times. July 1, 1933, p16.
The New Yorker. Jul 8, 1933, v9, p38.
Newsweek. July 8, 1933, v1, p32.
Rob Wagner's Script. Jul 1, 1933, v9, p8.
Time. Jul 10, 1933, v22, p41.
Variety. July 4, 1933, p16.
We're in the Money. p153-54.

Maytime (US; Leonard, Robert Z.; 1937)
Commonweal. Apr 9, 1937, v25, p670.
Fifty Classic Motion Pictures. p268-73.
Film Daily. Mar 8, 1937, p8.
The Films of Jeanette MacDonald and Nelson Eddy. p190-204.
The Great Romantic Films. p56-59.
The Hollywood Musical. p130-31.
Hollywood Reporter. Mar 4, 1937, p3.
Hollywood Spectator. Mar 13, 1937, v11, p5-6.
Motion Picture Herald. Mar 13, 1937, p43.
Motion Picture Herald. Mar 27, 1937, p15.
The New York Times. Mar 19, 1937, p27.
The New Yorker. Mar 27, 1937, v13, p54.
Newsweek. Mar 27, 1937, v9, p47.
Rob Wagner's Script. Mar 13, 1937, v17, p10.
Saint Nicholas. May 1937, v64, p41.
Sight and Sound. Sum 1937, v6, p79.
Time. Mar 29, 1937, v29, p49.
Time. Mar 29, 1937, v29, p49.
Variety. Mar 24, 1937, p16.
World Film News. Jul 1937, v2, p24.

Mazurka (GER; Forst, Willi; 1936)
Graham Greene on Film. p130-31.
Hollywood Reporter. Jan 27, 1936, p9.
The New Statesman and Nation. Feb 20, 1937, v13, p287.
The Spectator. Feb 5, 1937, v158, p219.
Variety. Jan 1, 1936, p58.
World Film News. Mar 1937, v1, p27.

Me and My Gal (US; Walsh, Raoul; 1932)
Film Daily. Dec 10, 1932, p18.
Motion Picture Herald. Dec 17, 1932, p34-35.
The New York Times. Dec 12, 1932, p18.
Rob Wagner's Script. Dec 24, 1932, v8, p8.
Variety. Dec 13, 1932, p15.

Meet Dr. Christian (US; Vorhaus, Bernard; 1939)
Commonweal. Dec 8, 1939, v31, p164.
Film Daily. Oct 19, 1939, p8.
Hollywood Reporter. Oct 14, 1939, p3.
Hollywood Spectator. Oct 28, 1939, v14, p11.
Motion Picture Herald. Oct 21, 1939, p36.
The New York Times. Dec 1, 1939, p27.
Photoplay. Jan 1940, v54, p59.
Variety. Oct 18, 1939, p14.

Meet John Doe (US; Capra, Frank; 1941)
Commonweal. Mar 29, 1941, v33, p575-76.
Enclitic. Fall 81-Spr 82, v5-6, p111-19.
Family Circle. Apr 11, 1941, p15-16+.
Film Criticism. Wint 1981, v5, p49-57.
The Film Criticism of Otis Ferguson. p349-51.
Film Daily. Mar 13, 1941, p7.
The Films of Barbara Stanwyck. p138-41.
The Films of Frank Capra (Scherle and Levy). p175-86.
The Films of Frank Capra (Willis). p38-57.
The Films of Gary Cooper. p178-80.
The Films of the Forties. p28-30.
Great Film Directors: A Critical Anthology. p160-72.
Hollywood Reporter. Mar 13, 1941, p3.
Hollywood Spectator. Mar 15, 1941, v15, p13.
Life. Mar 10, 1941, v10, p43-46.
The London Times. Oct 3, 1941, p6.
Magic Moments from the Movies. p92-93.
Magill's Survey of Cinema. Series I. v3, p1087-90.
Motion Picture Exhibitor. Mar 19, 1941, p715.
Motion Picture Herald Product Digest. Mar 8, 1941, p73.
The Nation. Mar 29, 1941, v152, p390.
The New Republic. Mar 24, 1941, v104, p405.
The New York Times. Mar 12, 1941, p25.
The New York Times. Mar 16, 1941, sec9, p5.
The New Yorker. Mar 22, 1941, v17, p80.
Newsweek. Mar 24, 1941, v17, p68.
Rob Wagner's Script. Mar 22, 1941, v25, p16.
Scholastic. Mar 17, 1941, v38, p38.
Scribner's Commentator. May 1941, v10, p105-06.
Selected Film Criticism, 1941-1950. p137-44.
Starring Miss Barbara Stanwyck. p134-38.
Talking Pictures. p223-24.
Time. Mar 3, 1941, v38, p78.
Variety. Mar 19, 1941, p16.
50 Classic Motion Pictures. p224-29.

Meet Me in St. Louis (US; Minnelli, Vincente; 1944)
Agee on Film. v1, p126-28, 356-57.
Australian Journal of Screen Theory. 1977, n3, p7-25.
Commonweal. Dec 8, 1941, v41, p206.
Film Art. p268-74.
Film Daily. Nov 1, 1944, p6.
The Films of the Forties. p124-27.
Hollywood Reporter. Jan 1, 1944, p3.
The International Dictionary of Films and Filmmakers. v1, p290-91.
Judy: The Films and Career of Judy Garland. p117-22.
Life. Dec 11, 1944, v17, p68-70+.
The London Times. Feb 26, 1945, p8.
Magill's Survey of Cinema. Series I. v3, p1091-94.
The MGM Years. p58-59.
Motion Picture Exhibitor. Nov 1, 1945, v32, n25, sec2, p1611.
Motion Picture Herald Product Digest. Nov 4, 1944, p2165.
The Nation. Nov 25, 1944, v159, p670.
The New Republic. Dec 18, 1944, v111, p837.
The New York Times. Nov 29, 1944, p20.
The New Yorker. Dec 9, 1941, v20, p50.

Newsweek. Dec 11, 1944, v24, p104.
Rob Wagner's Script. Jan 6, 1945, v31, p2.
Selected Film Criticism, 1941-1950. p144-45.
Time. Nov 27, 1944, v44, p104.
Variety. Nov 1, 1944, p10.
Vincente Minnelli and the Film Musical. p40-45+.
Vintage Films. p72-75.
The World of Entertainment. p90-118.

Meet Nero Wolfe (US; Biberman, Herbert; 1936)
Film Daily. Jul 16, 1936, p8.
Motion Picture Herald. Jul 25, 1936, p66.
The New Masses. Jul 28, 1936, v20, p30.
The New York Times. Jul 16, 1936, p20.
The New Yorker. Jul 25, 1936, v12, p56-57.
Newsweek. Jul 25, 1936, v8, p29.
Time. Jul 27, 1936, v28, p40-41.
Variety. Jul 22, 1936, p17.

Meet the Missus (US; Santley, Joseph; 1937)
Film Daily. May 25, 1937, p6.
Hollywood Reporter. May 22, 1937, p3.
Motion Picture Herald. May 29, 1937, p46, 48.
The New York Times. Jul 2, 1937, p25.
Rob Wagner's Script. Jun 26, 1937, v17, p12.
Variety. Jul 7, 1937, p12.

Memory Lane (US; Stahl, John M.; 1926)
Film Daily. Jan 31, 1926, p5.
Magill's Survey of Cinema. Silent Films. v2, p723-25.
Variety. Feb 3, 1926, p42.

Memphis Belle (US; Wyler, William; 1944)
Commonweal. Apr 14, 1944, v39, p652.
Film Daily. Mar 24, 1944, p7.
The Nation. Apr 15, 1944, v158, p456.
The New Republic. Apr 10, 1944, v110, p510.
The New York Times. Apr 14, 1944, p1.
Newsweek. Apr 3, 1944, v23, p94.
Scholastic. May 8, 1944, v44, p27.
Time. Apr 17, 1944, v43, p94+.
Variety. Mar 22, 1944, p18.
William Wyler. p122-26.
William Wyler: A Guide to References and Resources. p114-15.

Men Are Not Gods (GB; Reisch, Walter; 1937)
Canadian Magazine. Mar 1937, v87, p24.
Film Daily. Jan 20, 1937, p12.
Hollywood Reporter. Dec 29, 1936, p7.
Motion Picture Herald. Jan 2, 1937, p68.
The New Masses. Dec 29, 1936, v23, p27.
The New York Times. Jan 19, 1937, p28.
The New Yorker. Jan 23, 1937, v12, p63.
Rob Wagner's Script. Feb 13, 1937, v17, p8.
Selected Film Criticism: Foreign Films, 1930-1950. p113-14.
Time. Jan 25, 1937, v29, p46.
Variety. Dec 9, 1936, p13.
Variety. Jan 20, 1937, p14.

Men Are Such Fools (US; Berkeley, Busby; 1938)
The Busby Berkeley Book. p115.
Commonweal. Jul 1, 1938, v28, p273.
The Complete Films of Humphrey Bogart. p56-57.
Film Daily. Jun 17, 1938, p5.
Humphrey Bogart: The Man and His Films. p76-78.
Motion Picture Herald. Apr 23, 1938, p44.
The New York Times. Jun 17, 1938, p25.
Time. Jun 27, 1938, v31, p26.
Variety. Jun 22, 1938, p14.

Men in White (US; Boleslavski, Richard; 1934)
Commonweal. Jun 29, 1934, v20, p244.
Film Daily. Mar 28, 1934, p9.
The Films of Clark Gable. p153.
The Films of Myrna Loy. p165-66.

Hollywood Reporter. Feb 3, 1934, p3.
Literary Digest. Jun 23, 1934, v117, p28.
Motion Picture Herald. Feb 17, 1934, p34.
The New York Times. Jun 9, 1934, p18.
Time. Apr 30, 1934, v23, p20.
Variety. May 1, 1934, p14.
Variety. Jun 12, 1934, p19.

Men Make Steel (US; Reed, Roland; 1938)
Lorentz on Film. p154-57.
Variety. Apr 20, 1938, p15.

Men Who Have Made Love to Me (US; Berthelet, Arthur; 1918)
Exhibitor's Trade Review. Jan 26, 1918, p680.
Exhibitor's Trade Review. Feb 16, 1918, p903.
Motion Picture News. Feb 2, 1918, p734.
Motography. Feb 2, 1918, p226.
The Moving Picture World. Feb 2, 1918, p525, 722.
Selected Film Criticism, 1912-1920. p170-72.
Variety. Feb 1, 1918, p45.
Wid's Daily. Jan 17, 1918, p873.

Men With Wings (US; Wellman, William A.; 1938)
Commonweal. Nov 1, 1938, v29, p105.
Esquire. Feb 1939, v11, p81, 141.
Film Daily. Oct 24, 1938, p7.
Graham Greene on Film. p205.
Hollywood Reporter. Oct 20, 1938, p3.
Hollywood Spectator. Oct 29, 1938, v13, p11.
Life. Oct 10, 1938, v5, p30-32.
Motion Picture Herald. Oct 29, 1938, p40.
The New Masses. Nov 8, 1938, v29, p29.
The New York Times. Oct 27, 1938, p27.
Rob Wagner's Script. Oct 29, 1938, v20, p13-14.
Saint Nicholas. Oct 1938, v65, p41.
The Spectator. Nov 18, 1938, v161, p858.
Time. Nov 7, 1938, v32, p41.
Variety. Oct 26, 1938, p13.
William A. Wellman (Thompson). p174-81+.

Men Without Women (US; Ford, John; 1930)
Commonweal. Feb 12, 1930, v11, p425.
Exhibitors Herald-World. Feb 8, 1930, p34.
Film Daily. Feb 2, 1930, p11.
John Ford (Bogdanovitch). p51-52.
Judge. Mar 8, 1930, v98, p21.
Life. Mar 21, 1930, v95, p20.
The Nation. Mar 19, 1930, v130, p337.
National Board of Review Magazine. Mar 1930, v5, p8.
The New York Times. Feb 1, 1930, p15.
The New York Times. Feb 9, 1930, p5.
The New Yorker. Feb 8, 1930, v5, p69.
Outlook and Independent. Feb 12, 1930, v154, p272.
Rob Wagner's Script. May 10, 1930, v3, p10.
Variety. Feb 5, 1930, p24.

Mercy Killer *See* The Crime of Dr. Forbes

Merely Mary Ann (US; King, Henry; 1931)
Film Daily. Sep 13, 1931, p10.
Hollywood Reporter. Jul 8, 1931, p3.
Hollywood Spectator. Sep 12, 1931, v12, p7-8.
Motion Picture Herald. Aug 1, 1931, p30.
The New York Times. Sep 12, 1931, p15.
The New Yorker. Sep 19, 1931, v7, p67.
Rob Wagner's Script. Oct 31, 1931, v6, p8.
Time. Sep 21, 1931, v18, p42.
Variety. Sep 15, 1931, p24.

Merlusse (Also titled: The Codfish) (FR; Pagnol, Marcel; 1936)
The Film Criticism of Otis Ferguson. p218-19.
Film Daily. Dec 16, 1937, p5.
Graham Greene on Film. p62, 64.
Hollywood Reporter. Jan 7, 1937, p10.

Motion Picture Herald. Dec 25, 1937, p42.
The Nation. Mar 26, 1938, v146, p366.
National Board of Review Magazine. Feb 1938, v13, p18.
The New Republic. Apr 6, 1938, v94, p275.
The New Statesman and Nation. Mar 28, 1936, v11, p494-95.
The New York Times. Mar 17, 1938, p17.
Saturday Review (London). Apr 11, 1936, v161, p480.
Scholastic. Feb 1, 1936, v28, p26.
The Spectator. Apr 3, 1936, v156, p616.
Variety. Jan 1, 1936, p58.
Variety. Mar 23, 1938, p16.

The Mermaid (FR; 1904)
The First Twenty Years. p53.

Merrily We Go to Hell (US; Arzner, Dorothy; 1932)
Film Daily. Jun 11, 1932, p18.
The Films of Cary Grant. p36-37.
The Films of Fredric March. p84-86.
Motion Picture Herald. Jun 18, 1932, p34.
The New York Times. Jun 11, 1932, p9.
The New Yorker. Jun 18, 1932, v8, p53.
Rob Wagner's Script. Jul 16, 1932, v7, p8.
Time. Jun 20, 1932, v19, p24.
Variety. Jun 14, 1932, p17.
The Work of Dorothy Arzner. p12-18.

Merrily We Live (US; McLeod, Norman Z.; 1938)
Film Daily. Mar 1, 1938, p5.
Hollywood Reporter. Feb 23, 1938, p3.
Lunatics and Lovers. p158.
Motion Picture Herald. Feb 26, 1938, p38.
The New Statesman and Nation. Mar 26, 1938, v15, p527.
The New York Times. Mar 18, 1938, p23.
The New Yorker. Mar 26, 1938, v14, p60-61.
Rob Wagner's Script. Mar 5, 1938, v19, p6-7.
Stage. May 1938, v15, p27.
Time. Mar 14, 1938, v31, p52.
Variety. Mar 2, 1938, p15.

Merry-Go-Round of 1938 (US; Cummings, Irving; 1937)
Film Daily. Oct 26, 1937, p6.
Hollywood Reporter. Sep 27, 1937, p3.
Motion Picture Herald. Oct 23, 1937, p56, 58.
The New York Times. Nov 26, 1937, p27.
Rob Wagner's Script. Nov 13, 1937, v18, p9.
Time. Nov 29, 1937, v30, p41.
Variety. Oct 27, 1937, p18.

The Merry Widow (US; 1908)
Selected Film Criticism, 1896-1911. p69.
Views and Film Index. Feb 1, 1908, p5.

The Merry Widow (US; Stroheim, Erich von; 1925)
Close-Up. Jun 1931, p137.
Close-Up. Mar 1931, p22, 26.
The Comic Mind. p8, 12.
Dictionary of Films. p216-17.
Film Daily. Aug 30, 1925, p4.
The Films of the Twenties. p114-17.
Life. Oct 1, 1925, v86, p24.
Magill's Survey of Cinema. Silent Films. v2, p726-29.
A Million and One Nights. p493.
The Moving Picture World. Sep 12, 1925, p168.
The New York Times. Aug 27, 1925, p14.
Spellbound in Darkness. p337.
Stroheim: A Pictorial Record of His Nine Films. p135-76.
Stroheim (Finler). p83-93.
Variety. Sep 2, 1925, p36.

The Merry Widow (French title: La Veuve Joyeuse) (US; Lubitsch, Ernst; 1934)
The Cinema of Ernst Lubitsch. p57-69.
Ernst Lubitsch: A Guide to References and Resources. p124-29.
Ernst Lubitsch's American Comedies. p89-115.
Film Daily. Oct 13, 1934, p4.

The Films of Jeanette MacDonald. p111-16.
The Films of Jeanette MacDonald and Nelson Eddy. p115-28.
Great Hollywood Movies. p21-22+.
The Hollywood Musical. p93.
Hollywood Musicals. p135-38.
Hollywood Reporter. Sep 1, 1934, p3.
Life. Dec 1934, p34.
Literary Digest. Oct 27, 1934, v118, p34.
Magill's Survey of Cinema. Series II. v4, p1568-70.
Motion Picture Herald. Sep 8, 1934, p34.
The Nation. Nov 14, 1934, v139, p574.
The New Republic. Nov 21, 1934, v81, p46.
The New York Times. Oct 12, 1934, p12.
Rob Wagner's Script. Dec 1, 1934, v12, p10.
Selected Film Criticism, 1931-1940. p151.
Time. Oct 22, 1934, v24, p42.
Variety. Oct 16, 1934, p12.

The Merry Wives of Windsor (US; 1909)
The New York Dramatic Mirror. Nov 30, 1910, p30.
Selected Film Criticism, 1896-1911. p69.

Merry-Go-Round (US; Stroheim, Erich von; 1923)
The Best Moving Pictures of 1922-23. p85-92.
Film Daily. Jul 8, 1923, p10.
The Films of the Twenties. p73-74.
A History of Narrative Film. p223.
Magill's Survey of Cinema. Silent Films. v2, p730-32.
The New York Times. Jul 2, 1923, p16.
Selected Film Criticism, 1921-1930. p186-90.
Spellbound in Darkness. p328, 337.
Stroheim: A Pictorial Record of His Nine Films. p73-94.
Stroheim (Finler). p17-22.
Variety. Jul 4, 1923, p22.

Merry-Go-Round (US; Cahn, Edward L.; 1932)
Close-Up. Jun 1931, v8, p137.
Hollywood Reporter. Sep 8, 1932, p2.
Motion Picture Herald. Sep 17, 1932, p36, 38.
The New York Times. Dec 19, 1932, p19.
Rob Wagner's Script. Oct 8, 1932, v8, p8.

A Message to Garcia (US; Marshall, George; 1936)
Commonweal. Apr 17, 1936, v23, p698.
Esquire. Jun 1936, v5, p110.
Film Daily. Apr 9, 1936, p10.
The Films of Barbara Stanwyck. p104-05.
Hollywood Reporter. Mar 2, 1936, p3.
Hollywood Spectator. Mar 14, 1936, v10, p7.
Motion Picture Herald. Mar 14, 1936, p56.
The New York Times. Apr 10, 1936, p27.
Newsweek. Apr 11, 1936, v7, p42.
Scholastic. Apr 4, 1936, v28, p27.
Starring Miss Barbara Stanwyck. p77.
Time. Apr 20, 1936, v27, p48.
Variety. Apr 15, 1936, p16.

Metropolis (German title: Schicksal Einer Menschheit Im Jahre 2000, Das) (GER; Lang, Fritz; 1927)
Authors on Film. p59-67.
BFI/Monthly Film Bulletin. Apr 1976, v43, p91.
Cinema of the Fantastic. p15-32.
Cinema, the Magic Vehicle. v1, p122-23.
Dictionary of Films. p217-18.
Film Daily. Mar 13, 1927, p8.
Film Notes of the Wisconsin Film Society 1960. p36-38.
The Film Spectator. Sep 3, 1927, v4, p4-5.
The Films of Fritz Lang. p123-41.
Fritz Lang (Armour). p31-35+.
Fritz Lang (Eisner). p83-94.
From Caligari to Hitler. p149-50, 162-64.
From Quasimodo to Scarlett O'Hara. p86-88.
The Haunted Screen. p224-25, 235-36.
A History of Films. p137-39.
A History of Narrative Film. p118, 235.
The History of World Cinema. p96-97.

Life. Mar 24, 1927, v89, p24.
Magill's Survey of Cinema. Silent Films. v2, p733-44.
The Moving Picture World. Mar 12, 1927, p135.
The Nation. Mar 23, 1927, v124, p323-24.
The New York Times. Mar 7, 1927, p16.
The New York Times. Mar 6, 1927, sec8, p7.
Photoplay. May 1927, v31, p52.
Scientific American. Apr 1927, v136, p244-45.
Selected Film Criticism, 1921-1930. p192-93.
Spellbound in Darkness. p386-89.
This Film Business. p146-53.
Variety. Feb 23, 1927, p16.
Variety. Mar 16, 1927, p16.

Metropolitan (US; Boleslavski, Richard; 1935)
Canadian Magazine. Dec 1935, v84, p42.
Film Daily. Oct 18, 1935, p8.
Hollywood Reporter. Oct 16, 1935, p3.
Hollywood Spectator. Oct 26, 1935, v10, p12.
Motion Picture Herald. Oct 26, 1935, p72.
Motion Picture Herald. Nov 2, 1935, p15.
The New York Times. Oct 18, 1935, p27.
Newsweek. Oct 26, 1935, v6, p29.
Rob Wagner's Script. Nov 2, 1935, v14, p11.
Scholastic. Nov 23, 1935, v27, p28.
Time. Oct 28, 1935, v26, p54.
Variety. Oct 23, 1935, p12.

Mexican Spitfire (US; Goodwins, Leslie; 1939)
Film Daily. Dec 14, 1939, p8.
Hollywood Reporter. Dec 7, 1939, p3.
Hollywood Spectator. Dec 23, 1939, v14, p17.
Motion Picture Herald. Dec 16, 1939, p25.
The New York Times. Jan 10, 1940, p16.
Photoplay. Mar 1940, v54, p62.
Time. Jan 22, 1940, v35, p79.
Variety. Dec 13, 1939, p11.

Michael and Mary (GB; Saville, Victor; 1931)
Film Daily. Jan 10, 1932, p8.
Motion Picture Herald. Nov 21, 1931, p49-50.
The New York Times. Mar 5, 1932, p11.
Variety. Mar 8, 1932, p23.

Michael Strogoff (Also titled: The Soldier and the Lady) (US; Nicholls, George, Jr.; 1937)
Canadian Magazine. May 1937, v87, p31.
Graham Greene on Film. p155.
Hollywood Reporter. Feb 16, 1937, p3.
Hollywood Spectator. Feb 27, 1937, v11, p13.
Life. Mar 22, 1937, v2, p40-43.
Motion Picture Herald. Feb 27, 1937, p55.
The New Masses. Apr 27, 1937, v23, p29.
The New York Times. Apr 10, 1937, p11.
Newsweek. Mar 13, 1937, v9, p31.
Scholastic. Apr 3, 1937, v30, p20.
Stage. Jan 1937, v14, p67.
The Tatler. Jul 21, 1937, v145, p102.
Time. Mar 15, 1937, v29, p33.
Variety. Apr 14, 1937, p12.
World Film News. Sep 1937, v2, p28-29.

Mickey (US; Jones, F. Richard; Young, James; 1918)
Exhibitor's Trade Review. Aug 3, 1918, p750.
Fifty Great American Silent Films, 1912-1920. p99-101.
Magill's Survey of Cinema. Silent Films. v2, p745-47.
Motion Picture News. Jan 19, 1918, p365.
Motion Picture News. Aug 3, 1918, p719.
The Moving Picture World. Aug 10, 1918, p880.
The Moving Picture World. Jan 18, 1919, p389.
The New York Dramatic Mirror. Aug 17, 1918, p240.
Selected Film Criticism, 1912-1920. p172-74.
Variety. Dec 6, 1918, p39.
Wid's Daily. Aug 11, 1918, p4.

The Middleman (GB; Tucker, George Loane; 1915)
Motion Picture News. May 15, 1915, p65.
Motography. May 15, 1915, p808.
Motography. May 22, 1915, p815.
The Moving Picture World. May 15, 1915, p1094.
The Moving Picture World. May 22, 1915, p1342.
Variety. Mar 5, 1915, p22.

Midnight (US; Leisen, Mitchell; 1939)
Canadian Magazine. Apr 1939, v91, p46.
Claudette Colbert (Quirk). p107-11.
Commonweal. Apr 7, 1939, v29, p665.
The Film Career of Billy Wilder. p54-56.
Film Daily. Mar 15, 1939, p12.
Hollywood Director. p125-33.
Hollywood Reporter. Mar 9, 1939, p3.
Hollywood Spectator. Mar 18, 1939, v13, p9.
Magill's Survey of Cinema. Series II. v4, p1574-77.
Motion Picture Herald. Mar 18, 1939, p48.
The New Statesman and Nation. May 13, 1939, v17, p736.
The New York Times. Apr 6, 1939, p31.
The New Yorker. Apr 8, 1939, v15, p70.
Newsweek. Mar 27, 1939, v13, p28.
Photoplay. May 1939, v53, p63.
Rob Wagner's Script. Mar 18, 1939, v21, p16.
Time. Apr 17, 1939, v33, p50.
Variety. Mar 15, 1939, p16.

Midnight Madness (US; Flood, James; 1937)
Film Daily. Jun 8, 1937, p7.
Hollywood Reporter. Jun 4, 1937, p3.
Motion Picture Herald. Jun 12, 1937, p78, 80.
The New York Times. Jul 17, 1937, p18.
Variety. Jul 21, 1937, p19.

A Midnight Romance (US; Weber, Lois; 1919)
Exhibitor's Trade Review. Mar 22, 1919, p1213.
Motion Picture News. Mar 22, 1919, p1855.
The Moving Picture World. Mar 22, 1919, p1696.
Variety. Mar 14, 1919, p46, 48.
Wid's Daily. Mar 16, 1919, p3.

A Midsummer Night's Dream (US; 1909)
The Moving Picture World. Jan 8, 1910, p10-11.
The New York Dramatic Mirror. Jan 1, 1910, p17.
Selected Film Criticism, 1896-1911. p70-72.

A Midsummer Night's Dream (US; Reinhardt, Max; Dieterle, William; 1935)
Around Cinemas. p151-64.
Christian Science Monitor Magazine. Oct 2, 1935, p5.
Commonweal. Nov 1, 1935, v23, p19.
Esquire. Feb 1936, v5, p99, 172.
The Film Criticism of Otis Ferguson. p97-98.
Film Daily. Oct 10, 1935, p7.
The Films of James Cagney. p105-10.
The Films of Olivia de Havilland. p53-58.
Focus on Shakespeare. p43-53.
Focus on Shakespearean Film. p43-52.
From Quasimodo to Scarlett O'Hara. p207-10.
Garbo and the Night Watchman. p79-80, 157-61.
Graham Greene on Film. p28-29.
Hollywood Reporter. Oct 9, 1935, p3.
Hollywood Spectator. Nov 9, 1935, v10, p6-7.
Judge. Nov 1935, v109, p18.
Life. Oct 19, 1935, v14, p10.
Literary Digest. Sep 14, 1935, v120, p29-30.
London Mercury. Nov 1935, v33, p62.
Magill's Survey of Cinema. Series II. v4, p1587-89.
Motion Picture. Dec 1935, v50, p35+.
Motion Picture Herald. Oct 12, 1935, p38.
Movie Classic. May 1935, v8, p43.
The Nation. Oct 23, 1935, v141, p491-92.
National Board of Review Magazine. Nov 1935, v10, p12.
The New Masses. Oct 15, 1935, v17, p29-30.

The New Republic. Oct 16, 1935, v84, p272.
The New Statesman and Nation. Oct 19, 1935, v10, p557.
The New Yorker. Oct 19, 1935, v11, p67.
Newsweek. Oct 12, 1935, v6, p28.
Rob Wagner's Script. Oct 19, 1935, v14, p10.
Rob Wagner's Script. Sep 28, 1935, v14, p10.
Saturday Review (London). Oct 19, 1935, v160, p352.
Scholastic. Oct 26, 1935, v27, p10-12.
Selected Film Criticism, 1931-1940. p152-54.
Shakespeare and the Film. p25-36.
Shakespeare on Film. p51-65.
The Spectator. Oct 18, 1935, v155, p606.
Time. Oct 21, 1935, v26, p44-45.
Variety. Oct 16, 1935, p22.
Yale Review. Dec 1935, v25, p311-20.

The Mighty (US; Cromwell, John; 1930)
Exhibitors Herald-World. Nov 23, 1929, p54.
Exhibitors Herald-World. Jan 11, 1930, p32.
Film Daily. Jan 5, 1930, p12.
Judge. Jan 18, 1930, v98, p23.
Life. Jan 24, 1930, v95, p23.
The New York Times. Dec 30, 1929, p16.
The New York Times. Jan 12, 1930, p6.
The New Yorker. Jan 11, 1930, v5, p71.
Outlook and Independent. Jan 15, 1930, v154, p113.
Rob Wagner's Script. Jan 11, 1930, v2, p8.
Time. Jan 13, 1930, v15, p48.
Variety. Jan 1, 1930, p24.

The Mighty Barnum (US; Lang, Walter; 1934)
Film Daily. Nov 23, 1934, p10.
Hollywood Reporter. Nov 22, 1934, p2.
Literary Digest. Jan 15, 1935, v119, p31.
The Mighty Barnum.
Motion Picture Herald. Dec 1, 1934, p38.
The Nation. Jan 23, 1935, v140, p112.
The New York Times. Dec 24, 1934, p17.
Newsweek. Dec 22, 1934, p24.
Time. Dec 31, 1934, v24, p15.

Mighty Joe Young (US; Schoedsack, Ernest B.; 1949)
Commonweal. Jul 22, 1949, v50, p368.
Film Daily. May 31, 1949, p6.
Holiday. Nov 1949, v6, p26.
Hollywood Reporter. May 24, 1949, p3.
Life. Jul 25, 1949, v27, p94-95.
Motion Picture Herald Product Digest. May 28, 1949, p4625.
The New York Times. Jul 28, 1949, p19.
The New Yorker. Aug 6, 1949, v25, p39.
Newsweek. Aug 8, 1949, v34, p68.
Sequence. New Year, 1950, n10, p156.
Time. Aug 8, 1949, v54, p70.
Variety. May 25, 1949, p8.

Mighty Like a Moose (US; McCarey, Leo; 1926)
The Films of Hal Roach. p33-34.
Magill's Survey of Cinema. Silent Films. v2, p748-50.
Variety. Jun 23 1926, p19.

The Mikado (GB; Schertzinger, Victor; 1939)
Film Daily. May 16, 1939, p6.
Hollywood Reporter. Jun 9, 1939, p3.
London Mercury. Feb 1939, v39, p438-39.
Motion Picture Herald. May 20, 1939, p27, 43.
The Nation. Jun 17, 1939, v148, p708.
National Board of Review Magazine. May 1939, v14, p18.
The New Statesman and Nation. Jan 21, 1939, v17, p84-85.
The New York Times. Jun 2, 1939, p27.
The New Yorker. Jun 3, 1939, v15, p72.
Newsweek. Feb 20, 1939, v13, p24+.
North American Review. Sep 1939, v248, p191-92.
Rob Wagner's Script. Jun 24, 1939, v21, p16.
Scholastic. Mar 25, 1939, v34, p30.
Selected Film Criticism: Foreign Films, 1930-1950. p115.
Stage. Mar 15, 1939, v16, p28-29.

The Tatler. Jan 25, 1939, v151, p144.
Time. Jun 5, 1939, v33, p66.
Variety. Jan 25, 1939, p15.

Mildred Pierce (US; Curtiz, Michael; 1945)
America in the Dark. p217-20.
American Film. Jul-Aug 1982, v7, p72-73+.
American Quarterly. Spr 1978, v30, p3-20.
Canadian Forum. Mar 1946, v25, p288.
Casablanca and Other Major Films of Michael Curtiz. p121-43.
Commonweal. Oct 5, 1945, v42, p598.
Film Daily. Oct 1, 1945, p6.
Film Noir. p187-88.
Film Reader. Jan 1977, n2, p65-70.
Film Reader. 1982, n5, p164-72.
The Films of Joan Crawford. p156-59.
The Films of the Forties. p149-50.
Historical Journal of Film, Radio, and Television. 1983, v3, n1, p88-89.
Hollywood Reporter. Sep 28, 1945, p3.
Hollywood Review. Oct 1, 1945, v36, p1+.
Literature/Film Quarterly. 1983, v11, n1, p66-68.
The London Times. Apr 29, 1946, p6.
Magic and Myth of the Movies. p211-29, 271-74.
Magill's Survey of Cinema. Series I. v3, p1098-1100.
Mildred Pierce. p9-53.
Motion Picture Exhibitor. Oct 3, 1945, v34, n22, sec2, p1804-05.
Motion Picture Herald Product Digest. Oct 6, 1945, p2670.
The New Republic. Oct 22, 1945, v113, p528.
The New York Times. Sep 29, 1945, p12.
The New Yorker. Oct 6, 1945, v21, p95.
Newsweek. Oct 15, 1945, v26, p102.
Screen. 1982, v23, n1, p31-44.
Seeing Is Believing. p296-304.
Selected Film Criticism, 1941-1950. p147-49.
Time. Oct 22, 1944, v46, p100.
Variety. Oct 3, 1945, p20.
Velvet Light Trap. Fall 1972, n6, p29.
Velvet Light Trap. 1982, n19, p35-39.
Women in Film Noir. p68-82.
Women's Film and Female Experience. p123-31.
Women's Pictures. p29-31, 34-35.

The Militant Suffragette (SWED; 1914)
The Moving Picture World. Apr 25, 1914, p494.
The Moving Picture World. May 2, 1914, p718.
The New York Dramatic Mirror. Apr 22, 1914, p34.

The Milky Way (US; McCarey, Leo; 1936)
Commonweal. Feb 7, 1936, v23, p414.
Esquire. Apr 1936, v5, p104.
The Film Criticism of Otis Ferguson. p119-20.
Film Daily. Jan 28, 1936, p8.
Graham Greene on Film. p58-59.
Harold Lloyd: The King of Daredevil Comedy. p132-40.
Harold Lloyd: The Shape of Laughter. p210-11.
Hollywood Reporter. Jan 25, 1936, p2.
Hollywood Spectator. Feb 1, 1936, v10, p14.
Literary Digest. Feb 8, 1936, v121, p19-20.
Lunatics and Lovers. p125.
Motion Picture Herald. Feb 1, 1936, p46, 48.
The Nation. Apr 15, 1936, v142, p492.
National Board of Review Magazine. May 1936, v11, p13.
The New Republic. Feb 26, 1936, v86, p75.
The New Statesman and Nation. Mar 14, 1936, v11, p385.
The New York Times. Mar 26, 1936, p27.
The New Yorker. Apr 4, 1936, v12, p71.
Newsweek. Feb 8, 1936, v7, p25.
Rob Wagner's Script. Feb 8, 1936, v14, p10-11.
The Spectator. Mar 20, 1936, v156, p512.
Time. Feb 24, 1936, v27, p58.
Variety. Apr 1, 1936, p16.

The Mill on the Floss (GB; Whelan, Tim; 1937)
Commonweal. Dec 1, 1939, v31, p137.
Film Daily. Nov 16, 1939, p6.
Hollywood Reporter. Jan 20, 1937, p7.
Motion Picture Herald. Feb 13, 1937, p63.
The New York Times. Nov 15, 1939, p19.
Rob Wagner's Script. Jun 1, 1940, v23, p17.
Selected Film Criticism: Foreign Films, 1930-1950. p115-16.
Variety. Nov 22, 1939, p16.
World Film News. Aug 1937, v2, p25.

Million Dollar Legs (US; Cline, Edward; 1932)
Canadian Forum. Sep 1932, v12, p478.
The Comic Mind. p289-90.
Dictionary of Films. p220-21.
Film Daily. Jul 9, 1932, p6.
Film Notes. p83-84.
The Films of W.C. Fields. p69-71.
Hollywood Reporter. Jun 23, 1932, p7.
Judge. Sep 1932, v103, p22.
Lorentz on Film. p95-96.
Magill's Survey of Cinema. Series I. v3, p1101-03.
Motion Picture Herald. Jul 2, 1932, p40-41.
The Nation. Aug 3, 1932, v135, p111.
The New York Times. Jul 9, 1932, p7.
Pictures Will Talk. p44-50.
Reruns. p26-30.
Time. Jul 18, 1932, v20, p19.
Variety. Jun 12, 1932, p17.
W.C. Fields: A Life on Film. p82-85.

Million Dollar Legs (US; Grinde, Nick; 1939)
Film Daily. Sep 14, 1939, p11.
Hollywood Spectator. Jul 22, 1939, v14, p8-9.
Motion Picture Herald. Jul 8, 1939, p38.
The New York Times. Apr 16, 1939, p5.
Variety. Jul 12, 1939, p12.

Million, Le (Also titled: The Million) (FR; Clair, René; 1931)
American Film Criticism. p254-56.
BFI/Monthly Film Bulletin. Nov 1977, v44, p246-47.
The Bookman. Aug 1931, v73, p634.
Celluloid: The Film To-Day. p181-95.
Cinema Journal. Spr 1977, v16, p34-50.
Cinema, the Magic Vehicle. v1, p187.
The Comic Mind. p226-31.
Dictionary of Films. p220.
Eighty Years of Cinema. p87.
Film Daily. May 24, 1931, p10.
From Quasimodo to Scarlett O'Hara. p150-51.
Gotta Sing Gotta Dance. p89-91.
The Great French Films. p30-33.
Hollywood Spectator. Aug 29, 1931, v12, p15.
The International Dictionary of Films and Filmmakers. v1, p299.
Judge. Jun 13, 1931, v100, p22.
Magill's Survey of Cinema. Foreign Language Films. v5, p2054-57.
The Nation. Jun 10, 1931, v132, p645-46.
National Board of Review Magazine. Jul 1931, v6, p13.
The New Statesman and Nation. May 2, 1931, v1, p360.
New Theatre. Feb 1936, v3, p13.
The New York Times. May 21, 1931, p33.
The New Yorker. May 30, 1931, v7, p59-60.
Outlook and Independent. Jun 3, 1931, v158, p154.
Photoplay. Aug 1931, v40, p58.
René Clair (McGerr). p89-99.
Rob Wagner's Script. Jul 25, 1931, v5, p10.
Scrutiny of Cinema. p35-36.
Selected Film Criticism: Foreign Films, 1930-1950. p116-17.
The Spectator. May 2, 1931, v146, p698.
Time. Jun 1, 1931, v17, p51.
Variety. Apr 29, 1931, p50.
Variety. May 27, 1931, p57.

The Millionaire (US; Adolfi, John; 1931)
Film Daily. Apr 12, 1931, p32.
Films in Review. Nov 1985, v36, p519, 521.
Hollywood Spectator. Jun 20, 1931, v12, p9-10.
Life. May 8, 1931, v97, p20.
Motion Picture Herald. Mar 14, 1931, p43.
The Nation. May 27, 1931, v132, p590.
The New York Times. Apr 9, 1931, p30.
The New Yorker. Apr 18, 1931, v7, p77-78.
Outlook and Independent. Apr 22, 1931, v157, p570.
Rob Wagner's Script. May 23, 1931, v5, p8-9.
Time. Apr 20, 1931, v17, p28.
Variety. Apr 15, 1931, p20.

Mimi (GB; Stein, Paul L.; 1935)
Film Daily. Jun 5, 1935, p10.
Graham Greene on Film. p10-11.
Hollywood Reporter. Jun 7, 1935, p3.
Motion Picture Herald. Jun 8, 1935, p77.
The New York Times. Jan 10, 1936, p16.
The Spectator. Aug 2, 1935, v155, p186.
Variety. Apr 17, 1935, p15.
Variety. Jun 5, 1935, p15.

Min and Bill (US; Hill, George; 1930)
Exhibitors Herald-World. Oct 18, 1930, p46.
Film Daily. Nov 23, 1930, p11.
Judge. Dec 13, 1930, v99, p19.
Life. Dec 12, 1930, v96, p20.
Magill's Survey of Cinema. Series I. v3, p1107-10.
The New York Times. Nov 24, 1930, p26.
The New York Times. Nov 30, 1930, p5.
The New Yorker. Nov 29, 1930, v6, p67.
Outlook and Independent. Dec 3, 1930, v156, p552.
Time. Dec 8, 1930, v16, p42.
Variety. Nov 26, 1930, p18.

The Mind Reader (US; Del Ruth, Roy; 1933)
Film Daily. Apr 7, 1933, p7.
Hollywood Reporter. Feb 14, 1933, p4.
Motion Picture Herald. Feb 25, 1933, p37.
New Outlook. May 1933, v161, p47.
The New York Times. Apr 7, 1933, p22.
The New Yorker. Apr 15, 1933, v9, p55.
Newsweek. Apr 15, 1933, v1, p27.
Time. Apr 17, 1933, v21, p28.
Variety. Apr 11, 1933, p17.

Ministry of Fear (US; Lang, Fritz; 1944)
Commonweal. Feb 23, 1945, v41, p475.
Film Daily. Oct 19, 1944, p11.
Film Noir. p188.
The Films of Fritz Lang. p209-12.
Fritz Lang: A Guide to References and Resources. p87-90.
Fritz Lang (Eisner). p239-46.
Graham Greene on Film. p27-32.
The Great Spy Pictures. p171-96.
Hollywood Reporter. Oct 8, 1944, p3.
Literature/Film Quarterly. Fall 1974, v2, p310-23.
The London Times. May 22, 1944, p8.
Magill's Survey of Cinema. Series II. v4, p1590-93.
Motion Picture Exhibitor. Nov 1, 1945, v32, n25, sec2, p1607-08.
Motion Picture Herald Product Digest. Oct 21, 1944, p2149.
The New Republic. Feb 26, 1945, v112, p296.
The New York Times. Feb 8, 1945, p15.
The New Yorker. Feb 10, 1945, v20, p36+.
Newsweek. Jan 29, 1945, v25, p94.
Sight and Sound. Spr 1977, v46, n2, p114-18.
Time. Feb 5, 1945, v45, p92.
Variety. Oct 18, 1944, p10.

Mioche, Le (Also titled: Forty Little Mothers) (FR; Moguy, Leonide; 1938)
Film Daily. Dec 23, 1938, p4.

Motion Picture Herald. Dec 31, 1938, p54.
The Nation. Dec 24, 1938, v147, p702.
The New York Times. Dec 23, 1938, p16.
The New Yorker. Dec 31, 1938, v14, p49.
Newsweek. Apr 29, 1940, v15, p44.
Photoplay. Jun 1940, v54, p68.
Time. Jan 9, 1939, v33, p37.
Variety. Apr 17, 1940, p13.

The Miracle Man (US; Tucker, George Loane; 1919)
Exhibitor's Trade Review. Jul 26, 1919, p621.
Fifty Great American Silent Films, 1912-1920. p107-09.
Magill's Survey of Cinema. Silent Films. v2, p751-53.
Motion Picture News. Sep 6, 1919, p2057.
The Moving Picture World. Sep 13, 1919, p1637-38, 1706.
The New York Times. Aug 27, 1919, p9.
Photoplay. Oct 1919, v17, p76-78.
Selected Film Criticism, 1912-1920. p174-76.
Variety. Aug 29, 1919, p66.
Wid's Daily. Aug 31, 1919, p3.

The Miracle Man (US; McLeod, Norman Z.; 1932)
Film Daily. Apr 24, 1932, p10.
Hollywood Reporter. Mar 11, 1932, p3.
Motion Picture Herald. Apr 30, 1932, p40.
The New York Times. Apr 21, 1932, p25.
The New Yorker. Apr 30, 1932, v8, p53.
Rob Wagner's Script. Apr 9, 1932, v7, p10.
Time. May 2, 1932, v19, p24.
Variety. Apr 26, 1932, p13.

The Miracle of Morgan's Creek (US; Sturges, Preston; 1944)
Agee on Film. v1, p73-76, 342-43.
The Atlantic. Dec 1944, v174, p110+.
Best Film Plays, 1943-44. p223-98.
Between Flops. p177-92+.
Film Daily. Jan 5, 1944, p6.
The International Dictionary of Films and Filmmakers. v1, p300.
Life. Feb 14, 1944, v16, p45-46+.
The London Times. Dec 24, 1943, p6.
Magic Moments from the Movies. p131.
Magill's Survey of Cinema. Series I. v3, p1111-13.
Motion Picture Exhibitor. Jan 12, 1944, v31, n9, sec2, p1435-36.
Motion Picture Herald Product Digest. Jan 8, 1944, p1705.
Musician. May 1944, v49, p96.
The Nation. Feb 5, 1944, v158, p167-69.
The National Society of Film Critics on Movie Comedy. p87-88.
New Captain George's Whizzbang. 1974, v3, p20-26+.
The New Republic. Feb 7, 1944, v110, p180.
The New York Times. Jan 20, 1944, p15.
The New York Times. Jan 30, 1944, sec2, p3.
The New Yorker. Jan 29, 1944, v19, p46.
Newsweek. Jan 31, 1944, v23, p78.
Preston Sturges: A Guide to References and Resources. p63-67.
Rob Wagner's Script. Feb 19, 1944, v30, p18.
Selected Film Criticism, 1941-1950. p150-51.
Talking Pictures. p47-50.
Time. Feb 14, 1944, v43, p93.
Variety. Jan 5, 1944, p16.

Miracle of the Wolves (French title: Fille de l'Eau, La) (FR; Bernard, Raymond; 1925)
Exceptional Photoplays. Feb-Mar 1925, v5, p2.
Film Daily. May 10, 1925, p9.
French Cinema. p367-76.
Magill's Survey of Cinema. Silent Films. v2, p754-56.
The Moving Picture World. Mar 7, 1925, p38.
Outlook. Apr 8, 1925, v139, p522-23.
Selected Film Criticism, 1921-1930. p195-96.
Variety. Feb 25, 1925, p30.
Variety. Jul 30, 1930, p28.

Miracle on 34th Street (US; Seaton, George; 1947)
Commonweal. Jun 6, 1947, v46, p189.
Film Daily. May 2, 1947, p10.
The Films of the Forties. p201-03.
Fortnight. Jun 2, 1947, v2, p28.
Hollywood Reporter. May 2, 1947, p3.
Life. Jun 16, 1947, v22, p65-66+.
Magill's Survey of Cinema, Series II. v4, p1597-99.
Motion Picture Herald Product Digest. May 10, 1947, p3621.
New Movies. Sum 1947, v22, p25.
New Republic. Jun 2, 1947, v113, p36.
The New York Times. Jun 5, 1947, p32.
The New Yorker. Jun 14, 1947, v23, p88.
Newsweek. Jun 2, 1947, v29, p85-86.
Saturday Review. Jul 12, 1947, v30, p22-24.
Selected Film Criticism, 1941-1950. p151-52.
Time. Jun 9, 1947, v49, p99.
Variety. May 7, 1947, p18.

The Miracle Woman (US; Capra, Frank; 1931)
Cinema and Sentiment. p116-17.
Dictionary of Films. p221.
Film Daily. Aug 2, 1931, p10.
The Films of Barbara Stanwyck. p72-73.
Frank Capra (Maland). p54-57.
Frank Capra: The Man and His Films. p55.
Hollywood Reporter. Jun 4, 1931, p3.
Hollywood Spectator. Aug 15, 1931, v12, p22.
Hollywood Spectator. Sep 12, 1931, v12, p10.
Journal of Popular Film and Television. Aug-Sep 1979, p293-309.
Life. Sep 11, 1931, v98, p19.
Magill's Cinema Annual, 1983. p473-75.
The Nation. Sep 2, 1931, v133, p237.
The New York Times. Aug 17, 1931, p18.
Outlook and Independent. Aug 26, 1931, v158, p534.
Photoplay. Aug 1931, v40, p56.
Rob Wagner's Script. Sep 5, 1931, v6, p10.
Starring Miss Barbara Stanwyck. p32-34.
Variety. Jul 28, 1931, p14.

Miracles for Sale (US; Browning, Tod; 1939)
Film Daily. Aug 11, 1939, p6.
The Hollywood Professionals. v4, p49-50.
Motion Picture Herald. Aug 5, 1939, p88.
The New York Times. Aug 10, 1939, p15.
Variety. Aug 16, 1939, p14.

Misérables, Les (FR; 1913)
The New York Dramatic Mirror. Apr 16, 1914, p28.

Misérables, Les (US; Lloyd, Frank; 1917)
The Moving Picture World. Dec 22, 1917, p1800.
The New York Dramatic Mirror. Dec 15, 1917, p18.
The New York Dramatic Mirror. Dec 22, 1917, p36.
The New York Times. Dec 5, 1917, p13.
Photoplay. Mar 1918, v13, p70-71.
Selected Film Criticism, 1912-1920. p158-61.
Variety. Dec 7, 1917, p48.
Wid's Daily. Jan 10, 1918, p855-56.

Misérables, Les (US; Boleslavski, Richard; 1935)
Canadian Magazine. Jun 1935, v83, p33.
Catholic World. May 1935, v141, p218.
Cinema Quarterly. Sum 1935, v3, p241.
Commonweal. May 10, 1935, v22, p47.
Esquire. Jun 1935, v3, p144, 182-83.
The Film Criticism of Otis Ferguson. p77-78.
Film Daily. Apr 3, 1935, p10.
The Films of Fredric March. p126-29.
From Quasimodo to Scarlett O'Hara. p195-97.
Hollywood Reporter. Mar 30, 1935, p3.
Judge. Jul 1935, v109, p16.
Literary Digest. May 4, 1935, v119, p24.
Magill's Survey of Cinema. Series I. v3, p1114-16.
Motion Picture Herald. Apr 6, 1935, p46.

The Nation. May 8, 1935, v140, p556.
National Board of Review Magazine. May 1935, v10, p10.
The New Masses. Nov 10, 1936, v21, p29-30.
The New Republic. May 15, 1935, v83, p19.
The New Statesman and Nation. May 4, 1935, v9, p622.
The New York Times. Apr 22, 1935, p14.
The New Yorker. Apr 27, 1935, v11, p69-70.
Newsweek. Apr 27, 1935, v5, p21-22.
Rob Wagner's Script. May 11, 1935, v13, p10.
Saturday Review (London). May 11, 1935, v159, p599.
Saturday Review (London). Dec 15, 1934, v158, p538.
Scholastic. May 4, 1935, v26, p28-29+.
The Spectator. May 3, 1935, v154, p731.
Stage. Jun 1935, v12, p60.
The Tatler. May 1, 1935, p210.
Theatre Arts Monthly. Jun 1935, v19, p409-10.
Time. Apr 29, 1935, v25, p52.
Variety. Apr 24, 1935, p12.

Misérables, Les (FR; Bernard, Raymond; 1934)
Cinema Quarterly. Wint 1935, v3, p111.
Dictionary of Films. p221-22.
The Great French Films. p241.
Motion Picture Herald. Jul 25, 1936, p66.
The New Masses. Nov 10, 1936, v21, p29-30.
The New Republic. Nov 11, 1936, v89, p47.
The New York Times. Oct 28, 1936, p31.
The New Yorker. Oct 31, 1936, v12, p60-61.
Variety. Nov 4, 1936, p18.

Misere au Borinage *See* Borinage

Miss Lulu Bett (US; Mille, William C. de; 1921)
Film Daily. Dec 25, 1921, p49.
The Films of the Twenties. p52-53.
Magill's Survey of Cinema. Silent Films. v2, p757-60.
The New York Times. Dec 25, 1921, sec6, p2.

Miss Susie Slagle's (US; Berry, John; 1946)
Film Daily. Dec 13, 1945, p6.
Hollywood Reporter. Dec 6, 1945, p3.
Hygeia. Mar 1946, v24, p180-82.
The New York Times. Feb 7, 1946, p29.
The New Yorker. Feb 16, 1946, v22, p87.
Newsweek. Feb 4, 1946, v27, p93.
Scholastic. Jan 7, 1946, v47, p31.
Time. Feb 25, 1946, v47, p96.
Variety. Dec 12, 1945, p12.

Mrs. Leffingwell's Boots (US; Edwards, Walter; 1918)
The Moving Picture World. Oct 12, 1918, p275.
The Moving Picture World. Oct 19, 1918, p452, 454.
The New York Dramatic Mirror. Oct 12, 1918, p552.
Variety. Oct 4, 1918, p47.
Wid's Daily. Sep 29, 1918, p9-10.

Mrs. Mike (US; King, Louis; 1949)
Christian Century. Feb 1, 1950, v67, p159.
Commonweal. Feb 24, 1950, v51, p537.
Film Daily. Dec 22, 1949, p5.
Hollywood Reporter. Dec 19, 1949, p3.
Library Journal. Feb 1, 1950, v75, p180.
Motion Picture Herald. Dec 23, 1949, p29.
Newsweek. Jan 9, 1950, v35, p69.
Rotarian. Apr 1950, v76, p39.
Variety. Dec 21, 1949, p8.

Mrs. Miniver (US; Wyler, William; 1942)
BFI/Monthly Film Bulletin. Jul 1942, v9, p89.
Catholic World. Sep 1942, v155, p725-26.
Commonweal. Jun 26, 1942, v36, p230.
Documentary Newsletter. 1942, v3, p112.
Film Daily. May 13, 1942, p6.
Films and the Second World War. p116-19.
The Films of World War II. p71-73.
Hollywood Reporter. May 13, 1942, p3.

Hollywood Spectator. Sep 1, 1942, v17, p12-13.
Life. Jun 8, 1942, v12, p68-70+.
The London Times. Jun 6, 1942, p3.
The London Times. Jun 8, 1942, p3.
The London Times. Jul 8, 1942, p6.
The London Times. Feb 2, 1948, p7.
Look. Aug 11, 1942, v6, p50-54.
Magill's Survey of Cinema. Series I. v3, p1131.
Motion Picture Exhibitor. May 20, 1941, v28, n2, sec2, p1010.
Motion Picture Herald Product Digest. May 16, 1942, p661-62.
The New Republic. Jun 15, 1942, v106, p830-31.
The New York Times. Jun 5, 1942, p23.
The New York Times. Jun 14, 1942, sec8, p3.
The New Yorker. Jun 6, 1942, v41, p76.
Newsweek. Jun 15, 1942, v19, p63-64.
One Good Film Deserves Another. p45-49.
Politics and Film. p124-26.
Rob Wagner's Script. Aug 1, 1942, v27, p23.
Scholastic. Sep 14, 1942, v41, p35.
Selected Film Criticism, 1941-1950. p156-59.
Sight and Sound. Sum 1942, v11, p39.
The Spectator. Jul 17, 1942, v169, p59.
Time. Jun 29, 1942, v39, p72.
Variety. May 13, 1942, p8.
William Wyler: A Guide to References and Resources. p111-13.
William Wyler (Anderegg). p114-22.
Women's Film and Female Experience. p93-95.

Mrs. Wiggs of the Cabbage Patch (US; Taurog, Norman; 1934)
Film Daily. Oct 27, 1934, p4.
Hollywood Reporter. Aug 17, 1934, p7.
Motion Picture Herald. Jul 14, 1934, p48.
Motion Picture Herald. Aug 25, 1934, p31.
The New York Times. Oct 29, 1934, p14.
Time. Oct 29, 1934, v24, p56.
Variety. Oct 30, 1934, p16.
W.C. Fields: A Life on Film. p148-51.

Mission to Moscow (US; Curtiz, Michael; 1943)
Agee on Film. v1, p37-39, 53.
Commonweal. May 21, 1943, v38, p124-25.
Commonweal. Jun 4, 1943, v38, p167-68.
Film Daily. Apr 29, 1943, p13.
The Films of World War II. p122-23.
Hollywood Reporter. Apr 29, 1943, p3.
Life. May 10, 1943, v14, p39-40+.
Mission to Moscow. 1984.
Motion Picture Herald. May 1, 1943, p34.
Motion Picture Herald Product Digest. May 8, 1943, p1304.
The Nation. May 8, 1943, v156, p651.
The Nation. May 22, 1943, v156, p749.
The New Republic. May 10, 1943, v108, p636.
The New York Times. Apr 30, 1943, p25.
The New Yorker. May 8, 1943, v19, p58-59.
Newsweek. May 10, 1943, v21, p74+.
Saturday Review of Literature. May 15, 1943, v26, p17, 38.
Saturday Review of Literature. Jun 5, 1943, v26, p12-15.
Time. May 10, 1943, v41, p23-24.
Variety. May 5, 1943, p8.

Mississippi (US; Sutherland, Edward; 1935)
Film Daily. Apr 2, 1935, p11.
The Films of Bing Crosby. p68-71.
The Films of W. C. Fields. p112-16.
The Hollywood Musical. p100.
Motion Picture Herald. Mar 2, 1935, p54-55.
The New York Times. Apr 18, 1935, p27.
The New Yorker. Apr 27, 1935, v11, p70.
Photoplay. Apr 1935, v47, p54-55+.
Rob Wagner's Script. Mar 30, 1935, v13, p6.
Time. Apr 1, 1935, v25, p34.
Variety. Apr 24, 1935, p12.
W.C. Fields: A Life on Film. p168-72.

Mr. and Mrs. Smith (US; Hitchcock, Alfred; 1941)
The Art of Alfred Hitchcock. p109-14.
BFI/Monthly Film Bulletin. Aug 1985, v52, p258-61.
Commonweal. Feb 7, 1941, v33, p401.
The Film Criticism of Otis Ferguson. p343.
Film Daily. Jan 20, 1941, p5.
Films and Filming. Aug 1977, v23, p37.
The Films of Alfred Hitchcock. p99-102.
The Films of Carole Lombard. p173-77.
Hitchcock: The First Forty-Four Films. p62-67.
Hollywood Reporter. May 13, 1942, p2.
Life. Jan 27, 1941, v10, p53-54+.
The London Times. Mar 31, 1941, p6.
Magill's Survey of Cinema. Series II. v5, p1604-08.
Motion Picture Exhibitor. Jan 22, 1941, p681.
The New Republic. Mar 3, 1941, v104, p306.
The New York Times. Feb 21, 1941, p16.
The New York Times. Feb 23, 1941, sec9, p5.
The New Yorker. Mar 1, 1941, v17, p53.
Newsweek. Feb 3, 1941, v17, p58.
Spectator. Apr 4, 1941, p371.
Time. Feb 17, 1941, v37, p94.
Variety. Jan 22, 1941, p16.

Mr. Barnes of New York (US; Costello, Maurice; Gaillord, Robert; 1914)
The Moving Picture World. Oct 3, 1914, p106.
The New York Dramatic Mirror. Sep 23, 1914, p28.
Variety. Sep 18, 1914, p19.

Mr. Belvedere Goes to College (US; Nugent, Elliott; 1949)
Commonweal. Apr 22, 1949, v50, p48.
Film Daily. Apr 5, 1949, p5.
The Films of Shirley Temple. p246-47.
Hollywood Reporter. Apr 1, 1949, p3.
Motion Picture Herald Product Digest. Apr 9, 1949, p4566.
The New York Times. Apr 16, 1949, p11.
The New Yorker. Apr 23, 1949, v25, p48.
Newsweek. Apr 18, 1949, v33, p91.
Rotarian. Aug 1949, v75, p42.
Saturday Review. May 7, 1949, v32, p34-35.
Scholastic. Apr 27, 1949, v54, p21.
Theatre Arts. Jun 1949, v33, p8.
Time. May 2, 1949, v53, p90+.
Variety. Apr 6, 1949, p8.

Mr. Deeds Goes to Town (US; Capra, Frank; 1936)
American Film Criticism. p334-37.
Around Cinemas. p31-35.
Canadian Magazine. Jul 1936, v86, p30.
Cinema, the Magic Vehicle. v1, p254-55.
Commonweal. Apr 24, 1936, v23, p724.
Dictionary of Films. p223.
Esquire. Jun 1936, v5, p111.
An Examination of Narrative Structure in Four Films of Frank Capra. p22-92.
The Film Criticism of Otis Ferguson. p127-28.
Film Daily. Mar 27, 1936, p9.
The Films of Frank Capra (Scherle and Levy). p135-42.
The Films of Frank Capra (Willis). p17-22.
The Films of Gary Cooper. p139-41.
Frank Capra (Maland). p93-98+.
Frank Capra: The Man and His Films. p75-78, 110-12, 117-20.
From Quasimodo to Scarlett O'Hara. p220-22.
Garbo and the Night Watchman. p135-37, 182-84.
Graham Greene on Film. p96-97.
Hollywood Genres. p158-59.
Hollywood Reporter. Mar 25, 1936, p3.
Hollywood Spectator. Apr 11, 1936, v11, p9, 21.
Literary Digest. Apr 11, 1936, v121, p19.
Lunatics and Lovers. p116-19.
Magill's Survey of Cinema. Series II. v4, p1613-15.
Motion Picture Herald. Apr 25, 1936, p37.
The Nation. May 13, 1936, v142, p623-24.

National Board of Review Magazine. May 1936, v11, p11.
The New Masses. Apr 28, 1936, v19, p29.
The New Republic. Apr 22, 1936, v86, p315-16.
The New Statesman and Nation. Aug 29, 1936, v12, p289.
New Theatre. May 1936, p17-18.
New Theatre. Apr 1936, v3, p17-18.
The New York Times. Apr 17, 1936, p17.
The New York Times. Nov 9, 1937, p19.
The New Yorker. Apr 25, 1936, v12, p47.
Newsweek. Apr 18, 1936, v7, p32.
Rob Wagner's Script. Apr 25, 1936, v15, p12.
Saturday Review. Dec 31, 1938, v19, p13.
Saturday Review (London). Sep 5, 1936, v162, p320.
Scholastic. May 16, 1936, v28, p23.
Selected Film Criticism, 1931-1940. p155-57.
The Spectator. Aug 28, 1936, v157, p343.
Talking Pictures. p221-23.
The Tatler. Sep 2, 1936, v141, p424.
Theatre Arts. Sep 1941, v25, p668.
Time. Apr 27, 1936, v27, p36.
Variety. Apr 22, 1936, p14.
We're in the Money. p140-44.
World Film News. Oct 1936, v1, p23.
50 Classic Motion Pictures. p45-49.

Mr. Flow (Also titled: Compliments of Mr. Flow) (FR; Siodmak, Robert; 1937)
The New Statesman and Nation. Jun 12, 1937, v13, p964.
Sight and Sound. Sum 1937, v6, p83.
The Spectator. Jun 18, 1937, v158, p1144.
Variety. Jan 13, 1937, p30.
World Film News. Aug 1937, v2, p27.

Mr. Jones at the Ball (US; 1911)
Film Reports. Mar 4, 1911, v2, p7.
Selected Film Criticism, 1896-1911. p72.

Mr. Lucky (US; Potter, H.C.; 1943)
Commonweal. Jul 16, 1943, v38, p323.
Film Daily. May 11, 1943, p6.
The Films of Cary Grant. p164-66.
Hollywood Reporter. May 4, 1943, p4.
Magill's Survey of Cinema. Series II. v4, p1616-18.
Motion Picture Herald Product Digest. May 8, 1943, p1301-02.
The New Republic. Aug 9, 1943, v109, p196.
The New York Times. Jul 23, 1943, p21.
Newsweek. Jul 26, 1943, v22, p68.
Time. Sep 20, 1943, v42, p94.
Variety. May 5, 1943, p16.

Mr. Moto Takes a Vacation (US; Foster, Norman; 1939)
Film Daily. Jul 25, 1939, p8.
The Films of Peter Lorre. p121-22.
Hollywood Reporter. Nov 11, 1938, p3.
The New York Times. Jun 19, 1939, p12.
Time. Jul 3, 1939, v34, p36.
Variety. Nov 16, 1938, p15.

Mr. Robinson Crusoe (US; Sutherland, Edward; 1932)
Film Daily. Sep 23, 1932, p6.
Film Notes. p84.
Hollywood Reporter. Aug 17, 1932, p3.
Motion Picture Herald. Oct 1, 1932, p53.
The New Outlook. Nov 1932, v161, p47.
The New York Times. Sep 22, 1932, p25.
Rob Wagner's Script. Aug 27, 1932, v8, p8.
Time. Oct 3, 1932, v20, p36.
Variety. Sep 27, 1932, p17.

Mr. Skeffington (US; Sherman, Vincent; 1944)
Agee on Film. v1, p95-96.
Bette Davis: Her Films and Career. p126-28.
Commonweal. Jun 9, 1944, v40, p184-85.
Film Daily. May 31, 1944, p10.
Hollywood Reporter. May 26, 1944, p3.
The London Times. Aug 9, 1945, p6.

Magill's Survey of Cinema. Series I. v3, p1125-27.
Motion Picture Exhibitor. May 17, 1944, v32, n1, sec2, p1518.
Motion Picture Herald Product Digest. May 27, 1944, p1909.
The Nation. Jun 3, 1944, v158, p661.
The New Republic. Jun 31, 1944, v111, p133.
The New York Times. May 26, 1944, p23.
The New Yorker. May 27, 1944, v20, p61.
Newsweek. Jun 5, 1944, v23, p90.
Time. Jun 5, 1944, v43, p94+.
Variety. May 31, 1944, p20.

Mr. Skitch (US; Cruze, James; 1933)
Film Daily. Dec 23, 1933, p3.
Hollywood Reporter. Dec 6, 1933, p3.
Motion Picture Herald. Dec 16, 1933, p30.
The New York Times. Dec 23, 1933, p19.
Variety. Dec 26, 1933, p11.
Will Rogers in Hollywood. p134.

Mr. Smith Goes to Washington (US; Capra, Frank; 1939)
American Film Criticism. p377-83.
American Visions. p253-68.
Audience. Jul 1977, v9, p2-4.
Cinema and Sentiment. p118-31.
The Cinema of Frank Capra. p180-89.
Commonweal. Oct 27, 1939, v31, p14.
Commonweal. Nov 1, 1940, v33, p58.
Dictionary of Films. p223-24.
Examination of Narrative Structure in Four Films of Frank Capra. p93-136.
Film Comment. Nov-Dec 1972, v8, p10-14.
Film Criticism. Wint 1981, v5, p12-22.
The Film Criticism of Otis Ferguson. p273-74.
Film Daily. Oct 6, 1939, p8.
Film News. Sep 1973, v30, p22-23.
The Films of Frank Capra (Scherle and Levy). p165-74.
The Films of Frank Capra (Willis). p23-37.
The Films of James Stewart. p73-75.
The Films of the Thirties. p242-43.
Frank Capra (Maland). p160-64+.
Frank Capra: The Man and His Films. p79-81, 105-06, p115-16.
From Quasimodo to Scarlett O'Hara. p319-22.
Hollywood Reporter. Sep 8, 1939, p3.
Hollywood Spectator. Oct 14, 1939, v14, p7.
The International Dictionary of Films and Filmmakers. v1, p301-02.
Journal of American Studies. Dec 1979, v13, p377-92.
Journal of Popular Film. Sum 1974, v3, p245-55.
Life. Oct 16, 1939, v7, p67-74.
Literature/Film Quarterly. 1983, n1, v11, p28-35.
Magill's Survey of Cinema. Series I. v3, p1128-30.
Motion Picture Herald. Oct 7, 1939, p35, 38.
The Name Above the Title. p254-66, 273-93.
The Nation. Oct 28, 1939, v149, p476-77.
National Board of Review Magazine. Nov 1939, v14, p13-15.
The New Masses. Oct 31, 1939, v33, p29.
The New Masses. Jul 8, 1941, v40, p26-27.
The New Republic. Nov 1, 1939, v100, p369-70.
The New York Times. Oct 20, 1939, p27.
The New Yorker. Oct 21, 1939, v15, p73-74.
Newsweek. Oct 23, 1939, v14, p30+.
Photoplay. Nov 1939, v53, p65.
Photoplay. Apr 1940, v54, p12.
Rob Wagner's Script. Oct 28, 1939, v22, p16.
Rob Wagner's Script. Nov 4, 1939, v22, p10-11.
Scholastic. Oct 30, 1939, v35, p30.
Selected Film Criticism, 1931-1940. p157-61.
The Spectator. Jan 5, 1940, v164, p16.
Talking Pictures. p278-83.
Theatre Arts. Feb 1940, v24, p119-24.
Theatre Arts. Mar 1940, v24, p156.
Those Fabulous Movie Years: The 30s. p156.
Time. Oct 23, 1939, v34, p51.
Time. Oct 30, 1939, v34, p39.

Variety. Oct 11, 1939, p13.
We're in the Money. p145-48.
Wide Angle. 1980, v3, n3, p4-11.
World Horizons. Oct 1939, v4, p22-23.

Mister V (Also titled: Pimpernel Smith) (GB; Howard, Leslie; 1941)
Commonweal. Feb 27, 1942, v35, p463.
Hollywood Reporter. Feb 12, 1942, p3.
Motion Picture Herald Product Digest. Jul 5, 1941, p450.
The Nation. Mar 14, 1942, v154, p320.
Newsweek. Feb 23, 1942, v19, p55.
Scholastic. Mar 2, 1942, v40, p29.
Time. Mar 16, 1942, v39, p92.
Variety. Jul 9, 1941, p14.

Moana (Also titled: Moana: A Romance of the Golden Age) (US; Flaherty, Robert; 1926)
Asia. Aug-Dec 1925, v25, p638-51.
BFI/Monthly Film Bulletin. Dec 1975, v42, p272-73.
Exceptional Photoplay. Nov-Dec 1925, p1.
Film Daily. Feb 21, 1926, p6.
The New Republic. Mar 3, 1926, v46, p46-47.
The New York Times. Feb 8, 1926, p24.
Robert Flaherty: A Guide to References and Resources. p97-98.
Selected Film Criticism, 1921-1930. p197-99.
Variety. Feb 10, 1926, p40.

Moby Dick (US; Bacon, Lloyd; 1930)
Exhibitors Herald-World. Aug 23, 1930, p36.
Film Daily. Aug 17, 1930, p14.
Judge. Sep 13, 1930, v99, p21.
Life. Sep 5, 1930, v96, p16.
Literary Digest. Aug 30, 1930, v106, p15-16.
The Nation. Sep 3, 1930, v131, p254.
The New York Times. Aug 15, 1930, p20.
The New York Times. Aug 24, 1930, p5.
The New Yorker. Aug 23, 1930, v6, p58.
Outlook and Independent. Aug 27, 1930, v155, p672.
Theatre Magazine. Oct 1930, v52, p47.
Time. Aug 25, 1930, v16, p48.
Variety. Aug 20, 1930, p14.

A Modern Hero (US; Pabst, G.W.; 1934)
Film Daily. Apr 3, 1934, p7.
G.W. Pabst (Atwell). p115-17.
Magill's Survey of Cinema. Series II. v4, p1626-29.
Motion Picture Herald. Apr 28, 1934, p38-40.
The New York Times. Apr 20, 1934, p17.
Variety. Apr 24, 1934, p14.

A Modern Muskateer (US; Dwan, Allan; 1917)
Allan Dwan: The Last Pioneer. p45-48.
His Majesty the American. p83-102.
The Moving Picture World. Dec 29, 1917, p1996.
The New York Dramatic Mirror. Jan 5, 1918, p16.
The New York Dramatic Mirror. Jan 19, 1918, p23.
The New York Times. Dec 31, 1917, p5.
Photoplay. Mar 1918, v13, p104.
Selected Film Criticism, 1912-1920. p176-77.
Variety. Jan 4, 1918, p40.
Wid's Daily. Jan 3, 1918, p840.

Modern Times (US; Chaplin, Charles; 1936)
American Film Criticism. p329-34.
Canadian Magazine. Nov 1935, v84, p40.
Canadian Magazine. Jan 1936, v85, p31.
Canadian Magazine. Apr 1936, v85, p57.
Charles Chaplin: A Guide to References and Resources. p74-75.
Cinema, the Magic Vehicle. v1, p250-51.
Commonweal. Feb 21, 1936, v23, p468.
Dictionary of Films. p224-25.
Eighty Years of Cinema. p108.
Esquire. May 1936, v5, p195-96.
The Film Criticism of Otis Ferguson. p117-19.

Film Daily. Feb 7, 1936, p10.
Films and Filming. Oct 1954, v1, p18.
The Films of Charles Chaplin. p197-203.
The Films of the Thirties. p159-61.
From Quasimodo to Scarlett O'Hara. p217-20.
Garbo and the Night Watchman. p255-76.
Graham Greene on Film. p51-53.
Hollywood as Historian. p57-61.
Hollywood Reporter. Feb 6, 1936, p2.
Hollywood Spectator. Feb 15, 1936, v10, p3.
The International Dictionary of Films and Filmmakers. v1, p303-05.
Judge. Apr 1936, v110, p22.
Landmark Films. p110-19.
A Library of Film Criticism: American Film Directors. p49-50.
Life. Apr 1936, v103, p20.
Literary Digest. Nov 2, 1935, v120, p26-27.
London Mercury. Mar 1936, v33, p532-33.
Lorentz on Film. p134-35.
Magill's Survey of Cinema. Series I. v3, p1134-37.
Motion Picture Herald. Feb 8, 1936, p9.
The Nation. Feb 19, 1936, v142, p232.
The Nation. Apr 1, 1936, v142, p430.
National Board of Review Magazine. May 1936, v11, p11.
The New Masses. Feb 18, 1936, v18, p29-30.
The New Masses. Sep 24, 1935, v16, p29-30.
The New Republic. Feb 19, 1936, v86, p48.
The New Statesman and Nation. Feb 15, 1936, v11, p226.
New Theatre. Mar 1936, v3, p6-8, 35-37.
New Theatre. Nov 1935, v2, p12-13, p31.
The New York Times. Feb 6, 1936, p23.
The New Yorker. Feb 15, 1936, v11, p57-58.
Newsweek. Feb 8, 1936, v7, p19.
Newsweek. Feb 15, 1936, v7, p26.
Rob Wagner's Script. Feb 15, 1936, v15, p10.
Saturday Review. Mar 14, 1936, v13, p13.
Saturday Review (London). Feb 22, 1936, v161, p256.
Scholastic. Feb 15, 1936, v28, p24-25.
Selected Film Criticism, 1931-1940. p161-64.
Sight and Sound. Jan-Mar 1955, v24, p140-41.
The Spectator. Feb 14, 1936, v156, p254.
Stage. Mar 1936, v13, p24-27.
Theatre Arts. May 1936, v20, p346-47.
Time. Feb 17, 1936, v27, p44-46.
Time. Apr 21, 1947, v49, p32.
Variety. Feb 12, 1936, p16.
The Village Voice. May 21, 1964, v9, p15.
World Film News. Aug 1936, v1, p18.

Mon Couer T'Appelle *See* My Heart is Calling You

Monastery (FR; Alexandre, Robert; 1937)
Commonweal. Feb 11, 1938, v27, p440.
Film Daily. Feb 2, 1938, p6.
Hollywood Reporter. Feb 21, 1938, p3.
Motion Picture Herald. Feb 5, 1938, p52.
The New York Times. Mar 10, 1938, p16.
Time. Dec 20, 1937, v30, p35.
Variety. Feb 2, 1938, p17.

Monkey Business (US; McLeod, Norman Z.; 1931)
American Film Criticism. p256-57.
Dictionary of Films. p226.
Film Comment. Fall 1971, v7, p55-57.
Film Daily. Sep 27, 1931, p8.
Hollywood Reporter. Jul 24, 1931, p3.
Hollywood Spectator. Sep 12, 1931, v12, p14.
Judge. Oct 31, 1931, v101, p20.
Magill's Survey of Cinema. Series I. v3, p1141-43.
The Marx Brothers. p54-58.
Motion Picture Herald. Aug 1, 1931, p30.
The Nation. Oct 28, 1931, v133, p466-67.
The New Statesman and Nation. Oct 3, 1931, v2, p405.
The New York Times. Oct 8, 1931, p22.
The New Yorker. Oct 17, 1931, v7, p65, 67.

Outlook and Independent. Sep 23, 1931, v159, p118.
Photoplay. Oct 1931, v40, p51.
Rob Wagner's Script. Nov 14, 1931, v6, p8.
Selected Film Criticism, 1931-1940. p164.
Time. Oct 19, 1931, v18, p46.
Variety. Apr 8, 1931, p18.
Why a Duck? p52-94.

The Monkey's Paw (US; Ruggles, Wesley; 1932)
Film Daily. Jun 1, 1933, p10.
Hollywood Reporter. Sep 20, 1932, p3.
Motion Picture Herald. Oct 1, 1932, p53-54.
Rob Wagner's Script. Oct 1, 1932, v8, p8-9.
Variety. Jun 6, 1933, p14.

Monsieur Beaucaire (US; Olcott, Sidney; 1924)
Film Daily. Aug 17, 1924, p5.
Magill's Survey of Cinema. Silent Films. v2, p768-71.
The New York Times. Aug 12, 1924, p12.
Rudolph Valentino. p85-89.
Variety. Aug 13, 1924, p19.

Monsieur Beaucaire (US; Marshall, George; 1946)
Film Daily. May 15, 1946, p10.
Hollywood Reporter. May 13, 1946, p3.
Motion Picture Herald Product Digest. May 18, 1946, p2997.
The New York Times. Sep 5, 1946, p23.
The New Yorker. Sep 14, 1946, v22, p105.
Newsweek. Sep 2, 1946, v28, p78.
Theatre Arts. Aug 1946, v30, p440.
Time. Sep 2, 1946, v48, p91.
Variety. May 15, 1946, p8.

Monsieur Verdoux (US; Chaplin, Charles; 1947)
Charles Chaplin: A Guide to References and Resources. p76-77.
Cinema. Jun 1947, v1, p11-12+.
Film Daily. Apr 15, 1947, p8.
The Films of Charles Chaplin. p211-15.
Fortnight. Nov 7, 1947, v3, p30.
The Great Films. p185-88.
Hollywood Reporter. Apr 14, 1947, p3.
Magill's Survey of Cinema, Series II. v4, p1630-32.
Motion Picture Herald Product Digest. Apr 19, 1947, p3585.
New Movies. Sum 1947, v22, p5-6.
The New York Times. Jul 4, 1964, p8.
Selected Film Criticism, 1941-1950. p160-166.

Montana Moon (US; St. Clair, Malcolm; 1930)
Exhibitors Herald-World. Apr 19, 1930, p49.
Film Daily. Apr 13, 1930, p11.
The Films of Joan Crawford. p76-77.
The New York Times. Apr 14, 1930, p24.
Outlook and Independent. Apr 30, 1930, v154, p712.
Rob Wagner's Script. May 10, 1930, v3, p10-12.
Time. Apr 28, 1930, v15, p42.
Variety. Apr 16, 1930, p46.

Monte Carlo (US; Lubitsch, Ernst; 1930)
American Film Criticism. p236-38.
The American Films of Ernst Lubitsch. p118-23.
Cinema. Dec 1930, v1, p38, 41.
The Cinema of Ernst Lubitsch. p85-86+.
The Comic Mind. p221-22.
Commonweal. Sep 7, 1930, v12, p499.
Ernst Lubitsch: A Guide to Reference and Resources. p104-07.
Exhibitors Herald-World. Sep 6, 1930, p38.
Exhibitors Herald-World. Aug 2, 1930, p26-27.
Film Daily. Aug 31, 1930, p10.
Film Society Review. Jan 1969, v4, p20-21.
The Films of Jeanette MacDonald and Nelson Eddy. p48-57.
Gotta Sing Gotta Dance. p56-59.
The Hollywood Musical. p38-39.
Judge. Sep 20, 1930, v99, p21.
Life. Sep 19, 1930, v96, p18.
The Lubitsch Touch. p111-14.

The Nation. Oct 1, 1930, v131, p356-57.
The New York Times. Jun 8, 1930, p6.
The New York Times. Aug 28, 1930, p22.
The New York Times. Sep 7, 1930, p5.
The New Yorker. Sep 6, 1930, v6, p63.
Outlook and Independent. Sep 17, 1930, v156, p112.
Selected Film Criticism, 1921-1930. p199-201.
Theatre Magazine. Nov 1930, v52, p48.
Time. Sep 8, 1930, v16, p25.
Variety. Sep 3, 1930, p19.

The Moon and Sixpence (US; Lewin, Albert; 1942)
Around Cinemas, Second Series. p220-22.
Commonweal. Oct 2, 1942, v36, p566-67.
Film Daily. Sep 9, 1942, p6.
Hollywood Reporter. Sep 8, 1942, p3.
Life. Sep 14, 1942, v13, p50-52+.
The London Times. Feb 8, 1943,, p8.
Magill's Survey of Cinema. Series II. v4, p1638-41.
Motion Picture Exhibitor. Sep 23, 1942, v28, n20, sec2, p1117.
Motion Picture Herald Product Digest. Sep 19, 1942, p912.
The New Republic. Oct 19, 1942, v106, p498.
The New York Times. Oct 28, 1942, p26.
Newsweek. Oct 19, 1942, v20, p78.
Selected Film Criticism, 1941-1950. p166-68.
Time. Oct 19, 1942, v40, p96+.
Variety. Sep 9, 1942, p14.

The Moon Is Down (US; Pichel, Irving; 1943)
Agee on Film. v1, p35-36, 67.
Commonweal. Apr 9, 1943, v37, p617.
Film Daily. Mar 10, 1943, p7.
The Films of World War II. p111-14.
Hollywood Reporter. Mar 10, 1943, p3.
Motion Picture Herald Product Digest. Mar 13, 1943, p1201.
The Nation. May 1, 1943, v156, p643.
The New York Times. Mar 27, 1943, p8.
Newsweek. Apr 5, 1943, v21, p86.
Theatre Arts. May 1943, v27, p289.
Variety. Mar 10, 1943, p15.

Moon Over Morocco *See* Sous la Lune du Maroc

Moonlight Sonata (GB; Mendes, Lothar; 1937)
Commonweal. May 20, 1938, v28, p106.
Film Daily. Apr 25, 1938, p6.
Hollywood Reporter. Mar 11, 1937, p11.
Hollywood Spectator. Aug 20, 1937, v13, p10-11.
Motion Picture Herald. Mar 13, 1937, p50.
Motion Picture Herald. May 14, 1938, p36.
The New York Times. Jun 6, 1937, p4.
The New Yorker. May 14, 1938, v14, p73.
Newsweek. May 23, 1938, v11, p21.
Rob Wagner's Script. Jul 9, 1938, v19, p18.
Selected Film Criticism: Foreign Films, 1930-1950. p120.
Sociology and Social Research. Nov 1938, v23, p197.
The Tatler. May 26, 1937, v144, p372.
Time. May 16, 1938, v31, p57.
Variety. Feb 24, 1937, p17.
World Film News. Jul 1937, v2, p25.

The Moon's Our Home (US; Seiter, William A.; 1936)
Commonweal. Apr 24, 1936, v23, p724.
Film Daily. Apr 6, 1936, p13.
The Films of Henry Fonda. p48-49.
Graham Greene on Film. p83-84.
Hollywood Reporter. Apr 2, 1936, p3.
Hollywood Spectator. Apr 11, 1936, v11, p27.
Literary Digest. Apr 25, 1936, v121, p34.
Lunatics and Lovers. p104-05.
Motion Picture Herald. Apr 11, 1936, p56.
The New York Times. May 13, 1936, p29.
The New Yorker. May 16, 1936, v12, p63.
Rob Wagner's Script. May 30, 1936, v15, p10.
The Spectator. Jun 26, 1936, v156, p1171.

Time. Apr 20, 1936, v27, p47.
Variety. May 20, 1936, p12.
World Film News. Aug 1936, v1, p17.

Moontide (US; Mayo, Archie; 1942)
Commonweal. May 8, 1942, v36, p62.
Film Daily. Apr 17, 1942, p8.
Hollywood Reporter. Apr 17, 1942, p3.
The London Times. Oct 19, 1942, p8.
Motion Picture Exhibitor. Apr 22, 1942, p993.
Motion Picture Herald Product Digest. Apr 18, 1942, p609.
The New Republic. May 11, 1942, v106, p639-40.
The New York Times. Apr 30, 1942, p14.
The New York Times. May 3, 1942, sec8, p3.
The New Yorker. May 2, 1942, v18, p51.
Newsweek. May 4, 1942, v19, p54.
Scholastic. May 18, 1942, v40, p36.
Time. May 18, 1942, v39, p84-85.
Variety. Apr 22, 1942, p8.

Mörder Dimitri Karamazov, Der *See* Karamazov

Mörder Unter Uns *See* M

More Than a Secretary (US; Green, Alfred E.; 1936)
Film Daily. Dec 11, 1936, p18.
Hollywood Reporter. Dec 1, 1936, p3.
Motion Picture Herald. Dec 26, 1936, p56.
The New York Times. Dec 11, 1936, p35.
The New Yorker. Dec 19, 1936, v12, p88-89.
Time. Dec 21, 1936, v28, p23.
Variety. Dec 16, 1936, p14.

The More the Merrier (US; Stevens, George; 1943)
Best Film Plays, 1943-44. p451-510.
Cinema, the Magic Vehicle. v1, p379.
Commonweal. May 28, 1943, v38, p146.
Film Daily. Apr 7, 1943, p6.
The Films of World War II. p124-26.
Hollywood Reporter. Apr 1, 1943, p3.
Magill's Survey of Cinema. Series I. v3, p1147-50.
Motion Picture Herald Product Digest. Apr 10, 1943, p1249.
The Nation. Jun 12, 1943, v156, p844.
The New Republic. Jun 28, 1943, v108, p863.
The New York Times. May 14, 1943, p17.
The New York Times. May 16, 1943, sec2, p3.
The New Yorker. May 15, 1943, v19, p52.
Rob Wagner's Script. May 29, 1943, v29, p14.
Selected Film Criticism, 1941-1950. p163-64.
Time. May 17, 1943, v41, p98.
Variety. Apr 7, 1943, p8.

Morgenrot (Also titled: Dawn) (GER; Ucicky, Gustav; 1933)
Contemporary Review. May 1933, v143, p617.
Film Daily. May 18, 1933, p7.
Film in the Third Reich. p16-17.
From Caligari to Hitler. p269-70.
Motion Picture Herald. May 27, 1933, p32.
The Nation. May 31, 1933, v136, p622.
Nazi Cinema. p20-21.
The New Republic. Jun 14, 1933, v75, p128.
The New York Times. Mar 19, 1933, p4.
Newsweek. Apr 15, 1933, v1, p27.
Variety. Feb 28, 1933, p39.
Variety. May 23, 1933, p19.

A Mormon Maid (US; Leonard, Robert Z.; 1917)
The Moving Picture World. Mar 3, 1917, p1372, 1409.
The New York Dramatic Mirror. Feb 24, 1917, p26.
The New York Times. Apr 23, 1917, p11.
Photoplay. Apr 1917, v11, p81-82.
Selected Film Criticism, 1912-1920. p177.
Variety. Feb 16, 1917, p23.
Wid's Daily. Feb 22, 1917, p118.

Morning Glory (US; Sherman, Lowell; 1933)
BFI/Monthly Film Bulletin. Jul 1977, v44, p156.
Film Daily. Aug 16, 1933, p7.
The Films of Katharine Hepburn. p46-49.
Hollywood Reporter. Jul 12, 1933, p3.
Magill's Survey of Cinema. Series I. v3, p1150-53.
Motion Picture Herald. Jul 29, 1933, p28.
National Board of Review Magazine. Sep-Oct 1933, v8, p8-10.
The New York Times. Aug 18, 1933, p18.
The New York Times. Aug 27, 1933, p3.
The New York Times. Mar 17, 1934, p10.
The New Yorker. Aug 26, 1933, v9, p41.
Newsweek. Aug 26, 1933, v2, p30.
Photoplay. Oct 1933, v44, p56.
Rob Wagner's Script. Sep 2, 1933, v10, p9-10.
Selected Film Criticism, 1931-1940. p165-66.
The Spectator. Nov 3, 1933, v151, p620.
Time. Aug 28, 1933, v22, p18.
Variety. Aug 22, 1933, p22.

Morocco (US; Sternberg, Josef von; 1930)
American Film Criticism. p240-43.
BFI/Monthly Film Bulletin. May 1978, v45, p101.
The Cinema of Josef von Sternberg. p79-81.
Classic Film Scripts: Morocco and Shanghai Express. p60-136.
Exhibitors Herald-World. Oct 25, 1930, p42.
Film Daily. Nov 16, 1930, p10.
Film Notes. p79-80.
Films in Review. Jul-Aug 1950, v1, p7-10, 46-47.
The Films of Gary Cooper. p85-86.
The Films of Josef von Sternberg. p28-30.
The Films of Marlene Dietrich. p92-95.
From Quasimodo to Scarlett O'Hara. p123-25.
Great Film Directors. p700-02.
Judge. Dec 6, 1930, v99, p19, 31.
Life. Dec 5, 1930, v96, p36, 44.
London Mercury. Jun 1931, v24, p172.
Magill's Survey of Cinema. Series II. v4, p1650-53.
Movie. Sum 1965, v13, p27-28.
Movies and Methods. p265-66.
National Board of Review Magazine. Nov 1930, v5, p4.
The New Statesman and Nation. Apr 4, 1931, v1, p221.
The New York Times. Nov 17, 1930, p29.
The New York Times. Nov 23, 1930, p5.
The New Yorker. Nov 22, 1930, v6, p85-86.
Outlook and Independent. Nov 26, 1930, v156, p512.
Saturday Review (London). Apr 11, 1931, v151, p528.
Sublime Marlene. p38-41.
Talking Pictures. p270-72.
Theatre Magazine. Feb 1931, v53, p47.
Those Fabulous Movie Years: The 30s. p14-15.
Time. Nov 24, 1930, v16, p64.
Variety. Nov 19, 1930, p21.

Mort du Cygne, La (Also titled: The Dying Swan) (FR; Benoit-Levy, Jean; 1938)
The New Statesman and Nation. Feb 19, 1938, v15, p288.
The Spectator. Feb 25, 1938, v160, p311.
Variety. Mar 9, 1938, p14.
World Film News. Apr 1938, v3, p39.

The Mortal Storm (US; Borzage, Frank; 1940)
Commonweal. Jul 5, 1940, v32, p233.
Film and the Second World War. p33-34.
Film Daily. Jun 11, 1940, p6.
The Films of James Stewart. p84-86.
The Films of World War II. p34-36.
Life. Jun 17, 1940, v8, p41.
The London Times. Sep 27, 1940, p6.
Magill's Survey of Cinema. Series II. v4, p1654-57.
The New Republic. Jul 8, 1940, v103, p54.
The New York Times. Jun 21, 1940, p25.
The New York Times. Jun 23, 1940, sec9, p3.
Newsweek. Jun 24, 1940, v15, p50.
Scholastic. Sep 23, 1940, v37, p39.

Time. Jul 1, 1940, v36, p34.
Variety. Jun 12, 1940, v14.

Mortmain (US; Marston, Theodore; 1915)
Motion Picture News. May 8, 1915, p45.
Motion Picture News. Sep 4, 1915, p65.
Motography. Aug 28, 1915, p408.
Motography. Sep 11, 1915, p504, 531, 549-50.
The Moving Picture World. Sep 4, 1915, p1665-66.
The New York Dramatic Mirror. Sep 1, 1915, p34.
Variety. Sep 3, 1915, p21.
Vitagraph Life Portrayals. Sep 1915, p32.

Moscow Laughs *See* A Russian Jazz Comedy

Moscow Nights (Also titled: I Stand Condemned) (GB;
   Asquith, Anthony; 1935)
Commonweal. Jul 17, 1936, v24, p307.
Film Daily. Jun 9, 1936, p10.
The Films of Laurence Olivier. p68-69.
Graham Greene on Film. p35-36.
Laurence Olivier: Theater and Cinema. p47-49.
Motion Picture Herald. Nov 30, 1935, p63-64.
The New Masses. Jul 14, 1936, v20, p30.
The New Statesman and Nation. Nov 16, 1935, v10, p737.
The New York Times. Jul 2, 1936, p27.
Newsweek. Jul 11, 1936, v8, p27.
Saturday Review (London). Nov 16, 1935, v160, p480.
The Spectator. Nov 15, 1935, v155, p814.
Time. Jul 13, 1936, v28, p53.
Variety. Nov 20, 1935, p39.

The Most Dangerous Game (US; Schoedsack, Ernest B.;
   1932)
Film Daily. Sep 10, 1932, p6.
Hollywood Reporter. Aug 16, 1932, p7.
Horror Movies (Clarens). p122-24.
Motion Picture Herald. Jul 30, 1932, p32.
The New York Times. Nov 21, 1932, p21.
The New Yorker. Nov 26, 1932, v8, p51.
Variety. Nov 22, 1932, p16.

The Mother (US; Tourneur, Maurice; 1914)
The Moving Picture World. Oct 3, 1914, p106.
The New York Dramatic Mirror. Sep 23, 1914, p28.
Variety. Sep 18, 1914, p19.

Mother (Russian Tittle: Mat) (USSR; Pudovkin,
   Vsevolod; 1926)
American Silent Film. p157-58.
Cinema, the Magic Vehicle. v1, p118-19.
Close-Up. Oct 1928, v3, p33-34.
Close-Up. Nov 1928, v3, p12-14.
Close-Up. Jan 1929, v4, p27-32.
Close-Up. May 1930, v5, p437.
Dictionary of Films. p212-13.
Film Daily. Mar 13, 1927, p8.
A History of Narrative Film. p184-85.
The International Dictionary of Films and Filmmakers. v1,
   p285-86.
Kino. p208-12.
Magill's Survey of Cinema. Silent Films. v2, p772-74.
The New Republic. July 3, 1929, v59, p179-80.
The New York Times. Jan 8, 1928, sec8, p3.
Spellbound in Darkness. p518-20.
Variety. May 4, 1927, p24.
Variety. Jun 12, 1934, p19.

The Mother and the Law *See* Intolerance

Mother Carey's Chickens (US; Lee, Rowland V.; 1938)
Commonweal. Aug 5, 1938, v28, p390.
Film Daily. Jul 25, 1938, p5.
Hollywood Reporter. Jul 22, 1938, p4.
Hollywood Spectator. Aug 6, 1938, v13, p12-13.
The New York Times. Aug 5, 1938, p11.

The New Yorker. Aug 6, 1938, v14, p41.
Time. Aug 1, 1938, v32, p28.
Variety. Jul 27, 1938, p17.

Mother Is a Freshman (US; Bacon, Lloyd; 1949)
Commonweal. Mar 25, 1949, v49, p592.
Film Daily. Feb 28, 1949, p7.
Hollywood Reporter. Feb 25, 1949, p3.
Motion Picture Herald Product Digest. Mar 5, 1949, p4521.
The New York Times. Mar 12, 1949, p10.
Newsweek. Mar 14, 1949, v33, p82.
Rotarian. Jun 1949, v74, p34.
Time. Mar 7, 1949, v53, p98.
Variety. Mar 2, 1949, p8.

Mother Wore Tights (US; Lang, Walter; 1947)
Commonweal. Sep 19, 1947, v46, p554.
Film Daily. Aug 19, 1947, p8.
The Hollywood Musical. p280, 286.
Hollywood Reporter. Aug 20, 1947, p3.
Magill's Survey of Cinema, Series II. v4, p1658-60.
Motion Picture Herald Product Digest. Aug 23, 1947, p3793.
The New York Times. Aug 21, 1947, p33.
Newsweek. Sep 1, 1947, v30, p77.
Time. Sep 8, 1947, v50, p100.
Variety. Aug 20, 1947, p16.

The Mothering Heart (US; Griffith, D.W.; 1913)
The New York Dramatic Mirror. Jul 9, 1913, p28.
Selected Film Criticism, 1912-1920. p178.

Moulin Rouge (US; Lanfield, Sidney; 1933)
Canadian Magazine. Mar 1934, v81, p29.
The Hollywood Musical. p84.
Hollywood Reporter. Dec 15, 1933, p3.
Judge. Mar 1934, v106, p16.
Motion Picture Herald. Feb 10, 1934, p38.
Motion Picture Herald. Dec 23, 1933, p43.
The New York Times. Feb 8, 1934, p14.
The New Yorker. Feb 17, 1934, v10, p68.
Rob Wagner's Script. Feb 17, 1934, v11, p14.
Time. Jan 22, 1934, v23, p41.
Variety. Feb 13, 1934, p14.

Mourning Becomes Electra (US; Nichols, Dudley; 1947)
Commonweal. Nov 28, 1947, v47, p175.
Film Daily. Nov 19, 1947, p8.
The Films of Kirk Douglas. p40-43.
Hollywood Reporter. Nov 21, 1947, p3.
Life. Dec 8, 1947, v23, p63-66.
Motion Picture Herald Product Digest. Nov 22, 1947, p3941.
New Republic. Dec 8, 1947, v117, p36-37.
The New York Times. Nov 20, 1947, p38.
The New York Times Magazine. Nov 16, 1947, p36-37.
The New Yorker. Nov 22, 1947, v23, p127-28.
Newsweek. Nov 24, 1947, v30, p92.
Rosalind Russell (Yanni). p92-98.
Saturday Review. Nov 29, 1947, v30, p41.
Saturday Review. Dec 13, 1947, v30, p22-24.
Time. Nov 24, 1947, v50, p103.
Variety. Nov 19, 1947, p8.

The Mouthpiece (US; Flood, James; Nugent, Elliott;
   1932)
Film Daily. Apr 24, 1932, p10.
The Great Gangster Pictures. p280-81.
Hollywood Reporter. Mar 17, 1932, p3.
Motion Picture Herald. Mar 26, 1932, p35.
The New York Times. Apr 21, 1932, p25.
The New Yorker. Apr 30, 1932, v8, p53.
Rob Wagner's Script. May 28, 1932, v7, p10.
Time. May 2, 1932, v19, p24.
Variety. Apr 26, 1932, p13.
We're in the Money. p23-27.

Movie Crazy (US; Bruckman, Clyde; 1932)
Film Daily. Aug 12, 1932, p3.
Harold Lloyd: The King of Daredevil Comedy. p120-25.
Harold Lloyd: The Shape of Laughter. p204-07.
Motion Picture Herald. Sep 24, 1932, p31, 34.
The New Outlook. Oct 1932, v161, p38.
The New York Times. Sep 15, 1932, p19.
Rob Wagner's Script. Dec 3, 1932, v8, p9.
Stage. Sep 1932, v9, p27.
Time. Sep 26, 1932, v20, p26.
Vanity Fair. Oct 1932, v39, p69.
Variety. Sep 20, 1932, p14.

Mude Tod, Der *See* Destiny

The Mummy (US; Freund, Karl; 1932)
Boris Karloff and His Films. p59-68.
Classic Movie Monsters. p162-69.
Classics of the Horror Film. p88-93.
The Film Journal. Jan-Mar 1973, v2, p45-50.
The Films of Boris Karloff. p83-86.
Great Horror Movies. p47-48.
Hollywood Reporter. Nov 15, 1932, p3.
Horror! p165-66.
Horror Movies (Clarens). p95.
Horrors. p185-93.
Magill's Survey of Cinema. Series II. v4, p1664-67.
Make It Again, Sam. p125-26.
Monsters from the Movies. p106-08.
Motion Picture Herald. Dec 3, 1932, p27.
The New York Times. Jan 7, 1933, p11.
Time. Jan 16, 1933, v21, p19.
Variety. Jan 3, 1933, p15.

Murder! (GB; Hitchcock, Alfred; 1930)
The Art of Alfred Hitchcock. p26-30.
BFI/Monthly Film Bulletin. Jul 1975, v42, p165.
Cinema, the Magic Vehicle. v1, p181.
Exhibitors Herald-World. Nov 1, 1930, p41.
Film Daily. Oct 26, 1930, p10.
Hitchcock (Truffaut). p73-75+.
Hitchcock's British Films. p123-38.
The Nation. Nov 12, 1930, v131, p536.
The New York Times. Oct 25, 1930, p20.
The New York Times. Nov 2, 1930, p5.
The New York Times. Jul 19, 1931, p2.
Outlook and Independent. Nov 5, 1930, v156, p393.
The Spectator. Oct 11, 1930, v145, p489.
Variety. Aug 13, 1930, p15.
Variety. Oct 29, 1930, p27.

Murder by the Clock (US; Sloman, Edward; 1931)
Classics of the Horror Film. p70-72.
Film Daily. Jul 19, 1931, p10.
Hollywood Reporter. Jun 29, 1931, p26.
Hollywood Spectator. Aug 15, 1931, v12, p9-10.
Hollywood Spectator. Aug 29, 1931, v12, p24.
Life. Aug 7, 1931, v98, p16.
The New York Times. Jul 18, 1931, p16.
The New York Times. Jul 26, 1931, p3.
The New Yorker. Jul 25, 1931, v7, p53-54.
Outlook and Independent. Jul 29, 1931, v158, p406.
Time. Jul 27, 1931, v18, p31.
Variety. Jul 21, 1931, p12.

Murder Goes to College (US; Riesner, Charles; 1937)
Film Daily. Feb 24, 1937, p6.
Hollywood Reporter. Feb 19, 1937, p3.
Motion Picture Herald. Mar 6, 1937, p39.
Rob Wagner's Script. Mar 13, 1937, v17, p11.
Variety. Mar 31, 1937, p19.

The Murder Man (US; Whelan, Tim; 1935)
Film Daily. Jul 9, 1935, p7.
The Films of Spencer Tracy. p116-17.
Graham Greene on Film. p16.

Hollywood Reporter. Jul 6, 1935, p4.
Motion Picture Herald. Jul 20, 1935, p85.
The New York Times. Jul 27, 1935, p16.
The New Yorker. Jul 27, 1935, v11, p41.
Rob Wagner's Script. Aug 10, 1935, v13, p11.
The Spectator. Aug 23, 1935, v155, p290.
Time. Aug 5, 1935, v26, p19.
Variety. Jul 31, 1935, p19.

Murder, My Sweet (Also titled: Farewell, My Lovely)
(US; Dmytryk, Edward; 1944)
Commonweal. Feb 23, 1945, v41, p476.
Film Daily. Dec 8, 1944, p11.
The Films of the Forties. p140-41.
Hollywood Reporter. Dec 6, 1944, p3.
The London Times. Apr 16, 1945, p6.
Magill's Survey of Cinema. Series I. v3, p1164-66.
Motion Picture Exhibitor. Dec 13, 1944, v33, n6, sec2, p1633-34.
Motion Picture Herald Product Digest. Dec 9, 1944, p2214.
The Nation. Dec 16, 1944, v159, p753.
The New Republic. Mar 26, 1945, v112, p422.
The New York Times. Mar 9, 1945, p16.
The New Yorker. Mar 17, 1945, v21, p46.
Newsweek. Feb 26, 1945, v25, p100.
Raymond Chandler in Hollywood. p48-55.
Raymond Chandler on Film. p109-20.
Raymond Chandler on Screen. p11-36.
Running Away from Myself. p154-59.
Scholastic. Apr 3, 1945, v46, p28.
Storytelling and Mythmaking. p280-83.
Time. Dec 18, 1944, v44, p94.
Variety. Mar 14, 1945, p16.

The Murder of Karamazov *See* Karamazov

Murder on a Honeymoon (US; Corrigan, Lloyd; 1935)
Film Daily. Feb 14, 1935, p4.
Hollywood Reporter. Jan 21, 1935, p3.
Literary Digest. Mar 16, 1935, v119, p22.
Motion Picture Herald. Feb 2, 1935, p55, 58.
The New York Times. Mar 4, 1935, p12.
The New Yorker. Feb 23, 1935, v11, p61-62.
Rob Wagner's Script. Mar 2, 1935, v13, p10-11.
Variety. Mar 6, 1935, p20.

Murders in the Rue Morgue (US; Florey, Robert; 1932)
Film Daily. Feb 14, 1932, p10.
The Films of Bela Lugosi. p68-73.
Hollywood Reporter. Jan 6, 1932, p3.
Hollywood Spectator. Mar 1932, v12, p7.
Horror Movies (Clarens). p94.
Motion Picture Herald. Feb 20, 1932, p34, 38.
The New York Times. Feb 11, 1932, p16.
The New Yorker. Feb 20, v8, p62.
Variety. Feb 16, 1932, p24.

Murders in the Zoo (US; Sutherland, Edward; 1933)
Classics of the Horror Film. p112-13.
Film Daily. Apr 1, 1933, p3.
Hollywood Reporter. Mar 1, 1933, p3.
Motion Picture Herald. Mar 11, 1933, p19.
The New York Times. Jan 13, 1933, p19.
The New York Times. Apr 3, 1933, p13.
Newsweek. Apr 8, 1933, v1, p26.
Rob Wagner's Script. Apr 8, 1933, v9, p10.

Music for Madame (US; Blystone, John G.; 1937)
Film Daily. Sep 15, 1937, p8.
Hollywood Reporter. Sep 10, 1937, p3.
Motion Picture Herald. Sep 18, 1937, p42, 44.
The New York Times. Oct 23, 1937, p14.
Scholastic. Oct 9, 1937, v31, p36.
Variety. Sep 15, 1937, p13.

Music Is Magic (US; Marshall, George; 1935)
Film Daily. Sep 24, 1935, p12.
The Films of Alice Faye. p35-36.
Hollywood Reporter. Sep 21, 1935, p4.
Motion Picture Herald. Oct 12, 1935, p41.
Rob Wagner's Script. Nov 9, 1935, v14, p10.
Variety. Nov 20, 1935, p16.

The Muskateers of Pig Alley (US; Griffith, D.W.; 1912)
D.W. Griffith, His Biograph Films in Perspective. p33.
The New York Dramatic Mirror. Nov 13, 1912, p30.
Selected Film Criticism, 1912-1920. p178-79.

Mutiny at Odessa *See* Revolution in Russia

Mutiny on the Bounty (US; Lloyd, Frank; 1935)
Around Cinemas. p124-26.
Canadian Magazine. Jan 1936, v85, p30.
Esquire. Jan 1936, v5, p156.
The Film Criticism of Otis Ferguson. p103-05.
Film Daily. Nov 1, 1935, p7.
The Films of Clark Gable. p167-69.
From Quasimodo to Scarlett O'Hara. p211-16.
The Great Adventure Films. p62-67.
Hollywood Reporter. Oct 28, 1935, p1, 3.
Hollywood Spectator. Nov 9, 1935, v10, p7-8.
Judge. Jan 1936, v110, p14, 27.
Literary Digest. Nov 30, 1936, v120, p24.
London Mercury. Feb 1936, v33, p433-34.
Magill's Survey of Cinema. Series I. v3, p1167-69.
Motion Picture Herald. Sep 9, 1935, p57.
Movie Classic. Jan 1936, v9, p10.
The Nation. Dec 4, 1935, v141, p658.
National Board of Review Magazine. Dec 1935, v10, p7.
The New Republic. Nov 27, 1935, v85, p74-75.
The New Statesman and Nation. Jan 11, 1936, v11, p49.
The New York Times. Nov 3, 1935, p4.
The New York Times. Nov 9, 1935, p19.
The New York Times. Nov 17, 1935, p5.
The New York Times. Jul 26, 1936, p4.
The New Yorker. Nov 16, 1935, v11, p79-80.
Newsweek. Nov 16, 1935, v6, p19.
Rob Wagner's Script. Nov 23, 1935, v16, p10.
Saturday Review (London). Jan 4, 1936, v161, p32.
Scholastic. Nov 23, 1935, v27, p28.
Selected Film Criticism, 1931-1940. p166-69.
Stage. May 1936, v13, p44-45.
The Tatler. Jan 8, 1936, v139, p52.
The Tatler. Jan 15, 1936, v139, p98.
Theatre Arts Monthly. Feb 1936, v20, p136-38.
Those Fabulous Movie Years: The 30s. p78.
Time. Nov 18, 1935, v26, p32.
Variety. Nov 13, 1935, p16.
Vintage Films. p23-26.
World Film News. Sep 1936, v1, p22.
50 Classic Motion Pictures. p74-79.

My American Wife (US; Young, Harold; 1936)
Film Daily. Jul 21, 1936, p11.
Hollywood Reporter. Jul 18, 1936, p3.
Motion Picture Herald. Jul 25, 1936, p66.
The New York Times. Aug 21, 1936, p12.
Rob Wagner's Script. Aug 22, 1936, v15, p10.
Scholastic. Oct 3, 1936, v29, p32.
Time. Aug 17, 1936, v28, p48.
Variety. Aug 26, 1936, p20.

My Best Girl (US; Taylor, Sam; 1927)
BFI/Monthly Film Bulletin. Sep 1974, v41, p209-10.
Film Daily. Nov 13, 1927, p6.
Magill's Survey of Cinema. Silent Films. v2, p775-77.
The Moving Picture World. Nov 9, 1927, p20.
The New York Times. Nov 7, 1927, p26.
Variety. Nov 9, 1927, p20.

My Bill (US; Farrow, John; 1938)
Commonweal. Jul 22, 1938, v28, p351.
Film Daily. Jul 8, 1938, p6.
Motion Picture Herald. Jun 18, 1938, p38-39.
The New York Times. Jul 7, 1938, p22.
The New Yorker. Jul 16, 1938, v14, p45.
Rob Wagner's Script. Jul 23, 1938, v19, p8.
Time. Jul 18, 1938, v32, p21.
Variety. Jun 15, 1938, p14.

My Cousin (US; José, Edward; 1918)
Exhibitor's Trade Review. Nov 23, 1918, p1987-89.
Motion Picture News. Dec 7, 1918, p3423.
The Moving Picture World. Oct 19, 1918, p450.
The Moving Picture World. Dec 7, 1918, p1119.
The New York Times. Nov 25, 1918, p11.
The Photo-Play World. Feb 1919, p33.
Selected Film Criticism, 1912-1920. p179-80.
Variety. Nov 29, 1918, p41.
Wid's Daily. Dec 1, 1918, p18.

My Darling Clementine (US; Ford, John; 1946)
About John Ford. p12-14, 50-51, 109-110+.
Cineaste. Fall 1968, v2, p2-6.
The Cinema of John Ford. p99-111.
Cinema, the Magic Vehicle. v1, p428-29.
Commonweal. Dec 6, 1946, v45, p202.
Dictionary of Films. p231-32.
Film Comment. Fall 1971, v7, p8-17.
Film Daily. Oct 9, 1946, p8.
The Filming of the West. p491-96+.
Films and Filming. Jun 1962, v8, p15-17+.
The Films of Henry Fonda. p127-29.
The Films of the Forties. p182-85.
The Fondas (Springer). p133-35.
Hollywood Genres. p67-70.
Hollywood Reporter. Oct 9, 1946, p3.
The International Dictionary of Films and Filmmakers. v1, p307-09.
Magill's Survey of Cinema. Series I. v3, p1685-88.
Motion Picture Herald Product Digest. Oct 12, 1946, p3249.
My Darling Clementine.
New Movies. Jan 1947, v22, p6-8.
The New Republic. Dec 16, 1946, v115, p836+.
The New York Times. Dec 4, 1946, p44.
The New Yorker. Dec 14, 1946, v22, p89.
Newsweek. Nov 11, 1946, v28, p102+.
Quarterly Journal of Film, Radio and Television. Wint 1952, v7, p116-28.
Rob Wagner's Script. Nov 9, 1946, v32, p10.
Selected Film Criticism, 1941-1950. p169-72.
Seventy Years of Cinema. p158.
Theatre Arts. Dec 1946, v30, p715.
Variety. Oct 9, 1946, p14.
The Western Films of John Ford. p58-73.
Wide Angle. 1978, v2, p14-20.

My Favorite Blonde (US; Lanfield, Sidney; 1941)
Commonweal. Apr 10, 1942, v35, p621.
Film Daily. Mar 18, 1942, p8.
The Films of the Forties. p65-67.
Hollywood Reporter. Aug 18, 1942, p3.
Life. Apr 20, 1942, v12, p55-56+.
The London Times. Jun 29, 1942, p8.
Motion Picture Exhibitor. Mar 25, 1942, p973.
Motion Picture Herald Product Digest. Mar 21, 1942, p561.
Musician. May 1942, v47, p75.
The New York Times. Apr 2, 1942, p27.
Newsweek. Apr 13, 1942, v19, p67-68.
Time. Apr 20, 1942, v39, p88.
Variety. Mar 18, 1942, p8.

My Favorite Brunette (US; Nugent, Elliott; 1947)
Commonweal. Apr 4, 1947, v45, p614.
Film Daily. Feb 21, 1947, p8.

Hollywood Reporter. Feb 18, 1947, p3.
Motion Picture Herald Product Digest. Feb 22, 1947, p3485.
New Republic. Apr 7, 1947, v116, p39.
The New York Times. Mar 20, 1947, p38.
Newsweek. Mar 31, 1947, v29, p92+.
Scholastic. Mar 31, 1947, v50, p30.
Time. Mar 31, 1947, v49, p99.
Variety. Feb 19, 1947, p8.

My Favorite Wife (US; Kanin, Garson; 1940)
Commonweal. May 17, 1940, v32, p83.
The Film Criticism of Otis Ferguson. p302.
Film Daily. May 3, 1940, p8.
The Films of Cary Grant. p139-41.
Life. May 13, 9140, v8, p55-57.
Magill's Survey of Cinema. Series I. v3, p1175-77.
The New Republic. Jun 17, 1940, v102, p824.
The New York Times. May 31, 1940, p5.
The New York Times. Jun 2, 1940, sec9, p3.
Time. May 20, 1940, v35, p86.
Variety. May 1, 1940, p18.

My Foolish Heart (US; Robson, Mark; 1949)
Christian Century. Feb 15, 1950, v67, p223.
Commonweal. Jan 20, 1950, v51, p415.
Film Daily. Oct 17, 1949 , p7.
The Films of Susan Hayward. p146-51.
Hollywood Reporter. Oct 17, 1949, p3.
Library Journal. Mar 1, 1950, v75, p411.
Motion Picture Herald. Oct 22, 1949, p58.
The New Yorker. Jan 28, 1950, v25, p75.
Newsweek. Jan 23, 1950, v35, p80.
Rotarian. Apr 1950, v76, p39.
Samuel Goldwyn Presents. p269-71.
Time. Feb 6, 1950, v55, p83.
Variety. Oct 19, 1949, p8.

My Four Years in Germany (US; Nigh, William; 1918)
Exhibitor's Trade Review. Jan 26, 1918, p629.
Exhibitor's Trade Review. Mar 9, 1918, p1119.
Exhibitor's Trade Review. Mar 30, 1918, p1389.
Exhibitor's Trade Review. Apr 6, 1918, p1461.
Exhibitor's Trade Review. May 11, 1918, p1838.
Motion Picture News. Mar 16, 1918, p1602.
Motion Picture News. Mar 23, 1918, p1768.
The Moving Picture World. Mar 30, 1918, p1863.
The New York Times. Mar 11, 1918, p9.
Photoplay. Jun 1918, v14, p94.
Selected Film Criticism, 1912-1920. p180-82.
Variety. Mar 15, 1918, p45, 48.
The War, the West, and the Wilderness. p135-39.
Wid's Daily. Mar 21, 1918, p1020.

My Gal Sal (US; Cummings, Irving; 1941)
Commonweal. May 15, 1941, v36, p88.
Film Daily. Apr 27, 1942, p8.
The Films of Rita Hayworth. p130-36.
The Films of the Forties. p68-70.
The Hollywood Musical. p200, 206.
Hollywood Reporter. Apr 16, 1942, p3.
Life. May 18, 1942, v12, p45-48.
The London Times. Sep 11, 1942, p6.
Motion Picture Exhibitor. Apr 22, 1942, p998.
Motion Picture Herald Product Digest. Apr 18, 1942, p609.
Musician. May 1942, v47, p76.
The New York Times. May 1, 1942, p23.
The New York Times. May 3, 1942, sec8, p3.
Newsweek. May 11, 1942, v19, p76.
Time. May 4, 1942, v39, p86.
Variety. Apr 22, 1942, p8.

My Heart Is Calling You (French title: Mon Couer
     T'Appelle) (GB; Gallone, Carmine; 1934)
Film Daily. Jan 26, 1935, p3.
Hollywood Reporter. Oct 16, 1934, p3.

The New York Times. Apr 15, 1934, p16.
Variety. Apr 17, 1934, p14.

My iz Kronshtadta *See* We From Kronstadt

My Little Chickadee (US; Cline, Edward; 1940)
Film Daily. Feb 13, 1940, p4.
The Films of Mae West. p143-50.
The Films of W.C. Fields. p140-47.
Hollywood Reporter. Feb 7, 1940, p3.
Life. Feb 19, 1940, v8, p83-85.
The London Times. May 20, 1940, p4.
The New York Times. Mar 16, 1940, p8.
Newsweek. Feb 26, 1940, v15, p30.
Rob Wagner's Script. Mar 9, 1940, v23, p7.
Selected Film Criticism, 1931-1940. p169-71.
Time. Feb 26, 1940, v35, p66.
Variety. Feb 14, 1940, p18.
W.C. Fields: A Life on Film. p206-16.
Women and Their Sexuality in the New Film. p235-38.

My Lucky Star (US; Del Ruth, Roy; 1938)
Film Daily. Sep 12, 1938, p8.
Hollywood Reporter. Aug 27, 1938, p3.
Hollywood Spectator. Sep 3, 1938, v13, p12-13.
Motion Picture Herald. Sep 3, 1938, p38-39.
The New York Times. Sep 10, 1938, p20.
The New Yorker. Sep 3, 1938, v14, p62.
Rob Wagner's Script. Sep 3, 1938, v20, p11.
Saint Nicholas. Sep 1938, v65, p41+.
Time. Sep 19, 1938, v32, p26.
Variety. Sep 14, 1938, p15.

My Man (US; Mayo, Archie; 1929)
Film Daily. Dec 20, 1928, p8.
Film Daily. May 19, 1929, p8.
The Hollywood Musical. p21.
Hollywood Musicals. p34.
The New York Times. Dec 22, 1928, p14.
Variety. Dec 26, 1928, p11.

My Man Godfrey (US; La Cava, Gregory; 1936)
American Film Criticism. p343-44.
Canadian Magazine. Oct 1936, v86, p46.
Commonweal. Jul 24, 1936, v24, p328.
Esquire. Oct 1936, v6, p193.
Film Daily. Jun 16, 1936, p24.
The Films of Carole Lombard. p138-41.
The Films of the Thirties. p171-72.
Graham Greene on Film. p105-06.
Hollywood Genres. p157-58.
Hollywood Reporter. Jun 12, 1936, p3.
The Hollywood Social Problem Films. p98-101.
Hollywood Spectator. Aug 15, 1936, v11, p6.
Judge. Oct 1936, v111, p12.
A Library of Film Criticism: American Film Directors. p242.
Lunatics and Lovers. p152-56.
Magill's Survey of Cinema. Series I. v3, p1178-80.
Motion Picture Herald. Jun 20, 1936, p67.
The New Masses. Sep 29, 1936, v21, p29.
The New Statesman and Nation. Sep 26, 1936, v12, p428.
The New York Times. Sep 18, 1936, p18.
The New Yorker. Sep 26, 1936, v12, p67.
Newsweek. Sep 12, 1936, v8, p42.
Rob Wagner's Script. Aug 29, 1936, v16, p10-11.
Sight and Sound. Aut 1936, v5, p81-82.
The Spectator. Oct 2, 1936, v157, p543.
Stage. Oct 1936, v14, p26.
Talking Pictures. p292-94.
Time. Sep 14, 1936, v28, p30.
World Film News. Nov 1936, v1, p19.

My Official Wife (US; Young, James; 1914)
The Moving Picture World. Jun 6, 1914, p1390.
The Moving Picture World. Aug 29, 1914, p1288.
The New York Dramatic Mirror. Apr 1, 1914, p34.

The New York Dramatic Mirror. Jul 22, 1914, p26.
The New York Times. Jul 14, 1914, p9.
Selected Film Criticism, 1912-1920. p182-83.
Variety. Jul 17, 1914, p17.

My Reputation (US; Bernhardt, Curtis; 1946)
Commonweal. Feb 8, 1946, v43, p430.
Film Daily. Jan 10, 1946, p6.
The Films of Barbara Stanwyck. p164-65.
The Great Romantic Films. p120-23.
Hollywood Reporter. Jan 8, 1946, p3.
Magill's Cinema Annual, 1985. p586-91.
Motion Picture Herald Product Digest. Jan 12, 1946, p2793.
The New York Times. Jan 26, 1946, p19.
The New Yorker. Jan 26, 1946, v21, p76.
Newsweek. Jan 28, 1946, v27, p93.
Starring Miss Barbara Stanwyck. p47, 181.
Variety. Jan 9, 1946, p79.

My Sister Eileen (US; Hall, Alexander; 1942)
Commonweal. Oct 16, 1942, v36, p616.
Film Daily. Sep 14, 1942, p6.
Life. Oct 12, 1942, v13, p127-30.
The London Times. Jan 11, 1943, p8.
Magill's Survey of Cinema. Series II. v4, p1693-95.
Motion Picture Exhibitor. Sep 23, 1942, v28, n20, sec2, p1113.
Motion Picture Herald Product Digest. Sep 19, 1942, p909.
The New York Times. Oct 23, 1942, p25.
Newsweek. Sep 28, 1942, v20, p64.
Scholastic. Nov 9, 1942, v41, p35.
Time. Sep 28, 1942, v40, p82.
Variety. Sep 16, 1942, p8.

My Son, My Son (US; Vidor, Charles; 1940)
Film Daily. Feb 6, 1940, p6.
Hollywood Reporter. Mar 6, 1940, p3.
Motion Picture Herald. Feb 3, 1940, p37.
Motion Picture Herald. Mar 9, 1940, p48.
The Nation. Jun 8, 1940, v150, p716.
The New Republic. May 20, 1940, v102, p672.
The New York Times. May 10, 1940, p26.
Scholastic. Apr 1, 1940, v36, p34+.
Variety. Mar 13, 1940, p16.

Mystere de la Chambre Jaune, Le (Also titled: The Mystery of the Yellow Room) (FR; Herbier, Marcel L'; 1931)
Film Daily. May 31, 1931, p11.
The New York Times. May 26, 1931, p33.
Variety. Feb 18, 1931, p35.

The Mysterious Dr. Fu Manchu (Also titled: Dr. Fu Manchu; The Insidious Dr. Fu Manchu) (US; Lee, Rowland V.; 1929)
Film Daily. Jul 28, 1929, p9.
The New York Times. Jul 22, 1929, p17.
Outlook. Aug 7, 1929, v152, p596.
Variety. Jul 24, 1929, p29.
Variety. May 7, 1930, p38.

Mysterious Island (US; Hubbard, Lucien; 1929)
Film Daily. Dec 22, 1929, p11.
The Film Spectator. Mar 15, 1930, v9, p21.
The New York Times. Dec 21, 1929, p17.
Outlook. Jan 1, 1930, v154, p33.
Time. Jan 6, 1930, v15, p38.
Variety. Dec 25, 1929, p30.

The Mysterious Lady (US; Niblo, Fred; 1928)
Film Daily. Aug 12, 1928, p6.
The Film Spectator. Sep 29, 1928, v6, p15.
The Films of Greta Garbo. p65-70.
Magill's Survey of Cinema. Silent Films. v2, p778-80.
The New York Times. Aug 6, 1928, p15.
Variety. Aug 8, 1928, p20.

The Mystery of Edwin Drood (US; Walker, Stuart; 1935)
Esquire. Apr 1935, v3, p144.
Film Daily. Mar 20, 1935, p11.
Hollywood Reporter. Jan 17, 1935, p3.
Hollywood Reporter. Mar 27, 1935, p2.
Magill's Survey of Cinema. Series II. v4, p1696-99.
Motion Picture Herald. Mar 30, 1935, p40.
Movie Classic. Feb 1935, v7, p42.
The New York Times. Mar 21, 1935, p27.
Rob Wagner's Script. Feb 16, 1935, v13, p8.
Time. Feb 11, 1935, v25, p49.
Variety. Mar 27, 1935, p31.

The Mystery of Mr. X (US; Selwyn, Edgar; 1934)
Film Daily. Feb 24, 1934, p3.
Hollywood Reporter. Feb 20, 1934, p3.
Literary Digest. Mar 10, 1934, v117, p38.
Motion Picture Herald. Mar 3, 1934, p35.
The New York Times. Feb 26, 1934, p21.
Variety. Feb 27, 1934, p17.

Mystery of the Wax Museum (Also titled: The Wax Museum) (US; Curtiz, Michael; 1933)
The American Film Heritage. p28-31.
Classics of the Horror Film. p105-11.
Film Comment. Spr 1971, v7, p71-72.
Film Daily. Feb 18, 1933, p3.
Hollywood Reporter. Dec 23, 1932, p3.
Motion Picture Herald. Jan 7, 1933, p23.
Mystery of the Wax Museum. p9-36.
The New York Times. Feb 18, 1933, p13.
The New Yorker. Feb 25, 1933, v9, p56.
Rob Wagner's Script. Feb 4, 1933, v8, p7.
Selected Film Criticism, 1931-1940. p171.
Time. Feb 27, 1933, v21, p35.
Vanity Fair. Mar 1933, v40, p63.
Variety. Feb 21, 1933, p14.

The Naked City (US; Dassin, Jules; 1948)
Agee on Film. v1, p301.
Commonweal. Mar 12, 1948, v47, p546.
Film Daily. Jan 22, 1948, p5.
Fortnight. Feb 13, 1948, v4, p49.
Hollywood Reporter. Jan 21, 1948, p3.
The International Dictionary of Films and Filmmakers. v1, p309-10.
Life. Mar 22, 1948, v24, p127-28.
Magill's Survey of Cinema. Series II. v4, p1700-03.
Motion Picture Herald Product Digest. Jan 31, 1948, p4038.
New Movies. Apr 1948, v23, p5-7.
The New York Times. Mar 5, 1948, p17.
New Yorker. Mar 13, 1948, v24, p80.
Newsweek. Mar 1, 1948, v31, p72.
Selected Film Criticism, 1941-1950. p175.
Sequence. Aut 1948, n5, p38-40.
Time. Mar 22, 1948, v51, p96+.
Variety. Jan 21, 1948, p8.

Nana (FR; Renoir, Jean; 1926)
Film Daily. Aug 4, 1929, p8.
Jean Renoir: A Guide to References and Resources. p63-65.
Jean Renoir: The French Films, 1924-1939. p19-37.
Magill's Survey of Cinema. Silent Films. v2, p781-83.
The New York Times. Jan 22, 1928, sec8, p7.
Variety. May 19, 1926, p20.

Nana (US; Arzner, Dorothy; 1934)
Film Daily. Feb 2, 1934, p8.
The Films of the Thirties. p116-17.
Hollywood Reporter. Jan 4, 1934, p3.
Literary Digest. Feb 17, 1934, v117, p47.
Motion Picture Herald. Jan 13, 1934, p38.
The Nation. Feb 21, 1934, v138, p228.
The New York Times. Feb 2, 1934, p20.
Newsweek. Feb 10, 1934, v3, p37-38.

Samuel Goldwyn. p68-73.
Samuel Goldwyn Presents. p134-36.
Variety. Feb 6, 1934, p14.

Nancy Drew, Reporter (US; Clemens, William; 1939)
Hollywood Reporter. Jan 21, 1939, p4.
Hollywood Spectator. Feb 4, 1939, v13, p18-19.
Motion Picture Herald. Feb 4, 1939, p61.
Variety. Mar 1, 1939, p15.

Nancy Steele Is Missing (US; Marshall, George; 1937)
Commonweal. Apr 9, 1937, v25, p670.
Film Daily. Mar 10, 1937, p8.
The Films of Peter Lorre. p98-99.
Hollywood Reporter. Mar 3, 1937, p3.
Motion Picture Herald. Mar 20, 1937, p55.
The New York Times. Mar 8, 1937, p22.
The New Yorker. Mar 13, 1937, v13, p77-78.
Time. Mar 15, 1937, v29, p34.
Variety. Mar 10, 1937, p14.

Nanook of the North (US; Flaherty, Robert; 1922)
American Silent Film. p235.
Cinema. p13-15.
Classics of the Silent Screen. p41.
The Emergence of Film Art. p215-21.
Film Daily. Jun 18, 1922, p6.
Filmmakers on Filmmaking. p57.
The Great Films. p24-26.
A History of Narrative Film. p219-20.
Motion Picture Classic. Oct 1927, p72.
My Eskimo Friends. p123.
National Board of Review Magazine. Apr 1927, v2, p4-5.
The New Republic. Aug 9, 1922, v26, p306-07.
The New York Times. Jun 26, 1927, sec8, p2.
Photoplay. Mar 1928, p125.
Robert Flaherty: A Guide to References and Resources. p95-96.
Spellbound in Darkness. p342-48.
Variety. Jun 16, 1922, p40.
Variety. Sep 1, 1948, p14.
The War, the West, and the Wilderness. p473-81.
The World of Robert Flaherty. p36.

Napoleon (French title: Napoleon vu par Abel Gance;
    Bonaparte et la Revolution; Napoleon Bonaparte)
    (FR; Gance, Abel; 1927)
Abel Gance (Kramer and Welsh). p11-14, 20-21, 93-114.
Classic Film Collector. Aug 23, 1977, p12-13.
Classic Movies. p132-33.
Dictionary of Films. p236-38.
Film 71-72. p276-80.
The Films of My Life. p29-32.
French Cinema. p428-45.
French Film. p27-31.
The Great French Films. p19-25.
A History of Films. p161-64.
A History of Narrative Film. p324-26.
The History of World Cinema. p143-44.
The Los Angeles Times. Jul 16, 1981, sec6, p1.
Magill's Survey of Cinema. Silent Films. v2, p787-92.
Napoleon vu par Abel Gance. p1-76.
The New Republic. Feb 14, 1981, v184, p24-26.
The New York Times. Jun 5, 1927, sec7, p5.
The New York Times. Mar 4, 1928, sec9, p6.
The New York Times. Feb 12, 1929, p23.
The New York Times. Sep 25, 1967, p56.
The New York Times. Oct 2, 1967, p58.
The New Yorker. Feb 16, 1981, v66, p114.
Newsweek. Feb 2, 1981, p78.
Persistence of Vision. p25-28.
Sight and Sound. Wint 1971-72, v41, p18-19.
Time. Feb 2, 1981, v117, p70.
Variety. Apr 27, 1927, p20.
Variety. Jan 23, 1929, p34.
Variety. May 29, 1935, p14.

Variety. Mar 30, 1955, p9.
Variety. Sep 22, 1971, p6.

The Narrow Corner (US; Green, Alfred E.; 1933)
Film Daily. Jun 20, 1933, p4.
Hollywood Reporter. May 11, 1933, p3.
Motion Picture Herald. Jul 22, 1933, p56.
New Outlook. Aug 1933, v162, p45.
The New York Times. Jul 14, 1933, p15.
Rob Wagner's Script. Sep 16, 1933, v10, p12.
Time. Jul 24, 1933, v22, p43.
Variety. Jul 18, 1933, p37.

The Narrow Trail (US; Hillyer, Lambert; 1917)
The Complete Films of William S. Hart. p74-76.
Magill's Survey of Cinema. Silent Films. v2, p793-95.
The Moving Picture World. Dec 29, 1917, p1959.
The Moving Picture World. Jan 5, 1917, p137.
The New York Dramatic Mirror. Sep 1, 1917, p24.
The New York Dramatic Mirror. Jan 5, 1918, p24.
Variety. Jan 11, 1918, p41.
The Western. p93-96.
Wid's Daily. Jan 10, 1918, p854-55.

National Velvet (US; Brown, Clarence; 1944)
Agee on Film. v1, p132-34.
Commonweal. Dec 29, 1944, v41, p276.
Film Daily. Dec 6, 1944, p7.
The Films of Elizabeth Taylor. p48-52.
The Films of the Forties. p130-33.
Focus on Film. Wint 1973, n23, p34-35+.
Hollywood Reporter. Dec 6, 1944, p3.
Life. Jan 1, 1945, v18, p48-50.
The London Times. Jun 20, 1945, p6.
Magill's Survey of Cinema. Series II. v4, p1710-12.
Motion Picture Herald Product Digest. Dec 9, 1944, p2213.
The Nation. Dec 23, 1944, v159, p781-82.
The New Republic. Feb 5, 1945, v112, p175.
The New York Times. Dec 15, 1944, p25.
The New Yorker. Dec 23, 1944, v20, p48.
Newsweek. Dec 18, 1944, v24, p80.
Rob Wagner's Script. Feb 17, 1945, p14.
Scholastic. Feb 5, 1945, v46, p36.
Selected Film Criticism, 1941-1950. p175-76.
Time. Dec 25, 1944, v44, p44.
Variety. Dec 6, 1944, p14.

Naughty Marietta (US; Van Dyke, W.S.; 1935)
Film Daily. Feb 20, 1935, p9.
The Films of Jeanette MacDonald and Nelson Eddy. p144-54.
The Hollywood Musical. p98-102.
Hollywood Musicals. p135-37+.
Hollywood Reporter. Feb 18, 1935, p3.
Hollywood Reporter. Mar 26, 1935, p2.
Judge. May 1935, v108, p18.
Literary Digest. Apr 6, 1935, v119, p28.
Magill's Survey of Cinema. Series I. v3, p1186-89.
Motion Picture Herald. Mar 2, 1935, p54.
The New York Times. Mar 23, 1935, p11.
The New Yorker. Mar 30, 1935, v11, p64.
Newsweek. Mar 30, 1935, v5, p29.
Photoplay. May 1936, v49, p45.
Rob Wagner's Script. May 11, 1935, v13, p10.
Saturday Review (London). Apr 27, 1935, v159, p544.
Selected Film Criticism, 1931-1940. p172-73.
Time. Apr 1, 1935, v25, p34.
Variety. Mar 27, 1935, p15.

The Navigator (US; Keaton, Buster; Crisp, Donald; 1924)
Buster Keaton (Robinson). p107-18.
Cinema, the Magic Vehicle. v1, p102-03.
The Comic Mind. p134.
The Film Career of Buster Keaton. p55-58.
Film Daily. May 11, 1924, p47.
The Films of the Twenties. p100-02.
Life. Nov 6, 1924, v84, p26.

Magill's Survey of Cinema. Silent Films. v2, p796-99.
Motion Picture Classic. Dec 1924, v20, p49.
The Moving Picture World. Sep 13, 1924, p138.
The New York Times. Oct 13, 1924, p21.
Photoplay. Dec 1924, v27, p50.
The Silent Clowns. p237-40.
Variety. Oct 15, 1924, p27.

Navy Blue and Gold (US; Wood, Sam; 1937)
Film Daily. Nov 17, 1937, p8.
The Films of James Stewart. p50-52.
Hollywood Reporter. Nov 12, 1937, p3.
Motion Picture Herald. Nov 20, 1937, p34.
The New York Times. Dec 24, 1937, p21.
The New Yorker. Dec 25, 1937, v13, p45.
Time. Nov 29, 1937, v30, p42.
Variety. Nov 17, 1937, p16.

Nearly a King (US; Thomson, Frederick; 1916)
The Moving Picture World. Feb 26, 1916, p1315.
The New York Dramatic Mirror. Feb 26, 1916, p27.
The New York Times. Feb 14, 1916, p11.
Variety. Feb 18, 1916, p22.

Nell Gwyn (GB; Wilcox, Herbert; 1934)
Cinema Quarterly. Aut 1934, v3, p46.
Commonweal. Jul 5, 1935, v22, p267.
Fifty Classic British Films. p13-15.
The Great British Films. p21-23.
Literary Digest. Jun 29, 1935, v119, p28.
Magill's Cinema Annual, 1984. p557-60.
The New York Times. Jun 20, 1935, p16.
The New Yorker. Jun 29, 1935, v11, p54.
The New Yorker. Jun 29, 1935, v11, p54.
Newsweek. Jun 29, 1935, v5, p23.
Photoplay. Oct 1934, v46, p95.
Saturday Review (London). Oct 6, 1934, v158, p224.
Selected Film Criticism: Foreign Films, 1930-1950. p123.
The Spectator. Sep 28, 1934, v153, p434.
Time. Jul 1, 1935, v26, p34.
Vanity Fair. Sep 1934, v43, p50.
Variety. Jun 26, 1935, p23.
Wilson Library Bulletin. Oct 1935, v10, p136-37.

Neptune's Daughter (US; Brenon, Herbert; 1914)
The Green Book Magazine. Sep 1914, v12, p496.
The Moving Picture World. May 9, 1914, p796-97.
The Moving Picture World. Jun 6, 1914, p1452-53.
The New York Dramatic Mirror. Apr 29, 1914, p36.
Selected Film Criticism, 1912-1920. p183-84.
Variety. Apr 19, 1914, p22.

Neptune's Daughter (US; Buzzell, Edward; 1949)
Christian Century. Jul 20, 1949, v66, p879.
Commonweal. Jun 24, 1949, v50, p272.
Film Daily. Jun 1, 1949, p6.
Hollywood Reporter. May 18, 1949, p3.
Motion Picture Herald Product Digest. May 21, 1949, p4617.
The New York Times. Jun 10, 1949, p32.
Newsweek. Jun 13, 1949, v33, p82.
Rotarian. Sep 1949, v75, p37.
Time. Jun 27, 1949, v53, p90.
Variety. May 18, 1949, p8.

Nero (IT; 1909)
The Moving Picture World. Nov 6, 1909, p645.
Selected Film Criticism, 1896-1911. p73.

Nets *See* The Wave

Never Give a Sucker a Break (US; Conway, Jack; 1933)
Hollywood Reporter. Apr 21, 1933, p3.
Motion Picture Herald. May 6, 1933, p27.

Never Give a Sucker an Even Break (US; Cline, Edward; 1941)
The Film Criticism of Otis Ferguson. p395-96.

Film Daily. Oct 8, 1941, p6.
The Films of W. C. Fields. p154-61.
Halliwell's Hundred. p231-34.
Hollywood Reporter. Oct 6, 1941, p3.
Magill's Survey of Cinema. Series I. v3, p1193-95.
Motion Picture Exhibitor. Oct 15, 1941, v26, n23, sec2, p871.
Motion Picture Herald Product Digest. Oct 11, 1941, p305.
The New Republic. Nov 10, 1941, v105, p622.
The New York Times. Oct 27, 1941, p21.
Time. Nov 24, 1941, v30, p104.
Variety. Oct 8, 1941, p9.
W.C. Fields: A Life on Film. p230-38.

Never Say Die (US; Nugent, Elliott; 1939)
Film Daily. Mar 7, 1939, p13.
Graham Greene on Film. p210.
Hollywood Reporter. Mar 2, 1939, p3.
Hollywood Spectator. Mar 18, 1939, v13, p10.
Motion Picture Herald. Mar 11, 1939, p40.
The New York Times. Mar 9, 1939, p18.
Photoplay. May 1939, v53, p63.
The Spectator. Mar 3, 1939, v162, p349.
Variety. Mar 8, 1939, p18.

Never the Twain Shall Meet (US; Tourneur, Maurice; 1925)
Film Daily. Aug 2, 1925, p6.
Magill's Survey of Cinema. Silent Films. v2, p800-02.
The New York Times. Jul 29, 1925, p4.
Variety. Jul 29, 1925, p34.

Never the Twain Shall Meet (US; Van Dyke, W.S.; 1931)
Film Daily. Jun 7, 1931, p10.
Hollywood Reporter. Apr 16, 1931, p3.
Hollywood Spectator. Aug 1, 1931, v12, p9-10.
Life. Jul 3, 1931, v98, p18.
Motion Picture Herald. May 30, 1931, p55.
The New York Times. Jun 6, 1931, p15.
The New York Times. Jun 14, 1931, p5.
The New Yorker. Jun 13, 1931, v7, p65.
Outlook and Independent. Jun 10, 1931, v158, p181.
Rob Wagner's Script. Jul 25, 1931, v5, p8.
Variety. Jun 9, 1931, p19.

The New Adventures of Dr. Fu Manchu (US; Lee, Rowland V.; 1930)
Exhibitors Herald-World. May 10, 1930, p32.
Film Daily. May 4, 1930, p11.
Life. May 23, 1930, v95, p18.
The New York Times. May 3, 1930, p23.
Outlook and Independent. May 14, 1930, v155, p73.

The New Adventures of Get-Rich-Quick Wallingford (Also titled: The New Adventures of J. Rufus Wallingford; The New Wallingford) (US; Wood, Sam; 1931)
Film Daily. Oct 11, 1931, p11.
Hollywood Reporter. Sep 10, 1931, p3.
Motion Picture Herald. Sep 19, 1931, p34.
The New York Times. Oct 10, 1931, p20.
The New York Times. Oct 18, 1931, p5.
The New Yorker. Oct 17, 1931, v7, p67.
Outlook and Independent. Oct 28, 1931, v159, p281.
Rob Wagner's Script. Nov 7, 1931, v6, p11.
Variety. Oct 15, 1931, p21.
Variety. Oct 22, 1931, p23.

The New Babylon (Russian title: Novyi Vavilon) (USSR; Kozintsev, Grigori; 1929)
Film Daily. Dec 8, 1929, p8.
Magill's Cinema Annual, 1984. p566-69.
The New York Times. Dec 2, 1929, p28.
Variety. Dec 4, 1929, p15.

The New Earth (Dutch titles: Nieuwe Gronden; ZuiderZee) (NETHER; Ivens, Joris; 1934)
China Weekly Review. Apr 17, 1937, v80, p240-41.

Current History. Jul 1937, v46, p107.
Dictionary of Films. p243-44.
The Documentary Tradition. p162-63.
The Film Criticism of Otis Ferguson. p124-26.
Film on the Left. p116-22.
Joris Ivens, Film-Maker. p76-77.
The New Masses. Mar 31, 1936, v19, p29-30.
The New Republic. Apr 15, 1936, v86, p278.
Non-Fiction Film. p91.
Variety. Mar 3, 1937, p14.

A New Gulliver (Russian title: Novyi Gulliver) (USSR; Ptushko, Alexander; 1935)
Dictionary of Films. p251.
Esquire. Mar 1936, v5, p105, 185.
The Film Criticism of Otis Ferguson. p102.
Film Daily. Oct 29, 1935, p6.
Garbo and the Night Watchman. p164-66.
Hollywood Reporter. Oct 12, 1935, p6.
Kino. p309, 440.
Literary Digest. Nov 2, 1935, v120, p24-25.
The Nation. Nov 20, 1935, v141, p604.
National Board of Review Magazine. Dec 1935, v10, p12.
The New Masses. Nov 12, 1935, v17, p29-30.
The New Masses. Oct 22, 1935, v17, p29-30.
The New Statesman and Nation. Nov 13, 1937, v14, p836.
The New York Times. Nov 4, 1935, p24.
The New Yorker. Nov 9, 1935, v11, p77-78.
Newsweek. Nov 9, 1935, v6, p27.
Rob Wagner's Script. Jan 4, 1936, v14, p12.
Sight and Sound. Sum 1935, v4, p60-62.
Sight and Sound. Wint 1936-37, v5, p141.
Time. Nov 4, 1935, v26, p53.
Variety. May 1, 1935, p17.
Variety. Nov 6, 1935, p21.

The New Moon (US; Conway, Jack; 1930)
Film Daily. Dec 28, 1930, p11.
Judge. Jan 17, 1931, v100, p24.
The New York Times. Dec 24, 1930, p18.
The New York Times. Dec 28, 1930, p5.
The New Yorker. Jan 3, 1931, v6, p68.
Outlook and Independent. Jan 7, 1931, v157, p32.
Rob Wagner's Script. Apr 11, 1931, v5, p12-13.
Time. Jan 5, 1931, v17, p25.
Variety. Dec 31, 1930, p19.

New Year's Eve (German title: Sylvester—Tragodie einer Nacht) (GER; Pick, Lupu; 1923)
Cinema, the Magic Vehicle. v1, p95-96.

The New York Hat (US; 1912)
American Silent Film. p49.
A Million and One Nights. p513-14.
Motion Pictures. p68-71.

New York Nights (US; Milestone, Lewis; 1930)
Exhibitors Herald-World. Feb 8, 1930, p33.
Film Daily. Feb 2, 1930, p11.
Judge. Mar 1, 1930, v98, p32.
The New York Times. Feb 1, 1930, p15.
Rob Wagner's Script. Mar 22, 1930, v3, p10.
Variety. Feb 5, 1930, p24.

News Is Made at Night (US; Werker, Alfred L.; 1939)
Film Daily. Jul 17, 1939, p12.
Hollywood Spectator. Jul 22, 1939, v14, p9.
Motion Picture Herald. Jul 15, 1939, p54.
The New York Times. Jul 13, 1939, p17.
Variety. Jul 19, 1939, p12.

Next of Kin (GB; Dickinson, Thorold; 1942)
Commonweal. Apr 30, 1943, v38, p44.
Film Daily. Apr 8, 1943, p8.
Films and the Second World War. p103-04.
Hollywood Reporter. Apr 7, 1943, p3.

The London Times. May 14, 1942, p6.
Motion Picture Exhibitor. May 24, 1943, v108, p701.
Motion Picture Herald Product Digest. Jun 6, 1942, p698.
Motion Picture Herald Product Digest. Apr 17, 1943, p1262.
The New York Times. May 6, 1943, p25.
Newsweek. May 17, 1943, v21, p79-80.
Saturday Review. Aug 8, 1942, v25, p18.
Time. Apr 19, 1943, v40, p94+.
Variety. Jun 17, 1942, p20.

Next Time I Marry (US; Kanin, Garson; 1938)
Film Daily. Dec 9, 1938, p7.
Hollywood Reporter. Dec 14, 1938, p2.
Hollywood Spectator. Dec 24, 1938, v13, p24-25.
Motion Picture Herald. Dec 10, 1938, p48.
The New York Times. Dec 2, 1938, p27.
Variety. Dec 7, 1938, p12.

Next Time We Love (US; Griffith, Edward H.; 1936)
Esquire. Apr 1936, v5, p104.
Film Daily. Jan 31, 1936, p5.
The Films of James Stewart. p28-30.
Hollywood Reporter. Jan 28, 1936, p3.
Motion Picture Herald. Feb 8, 1936, p55.
The New York Times. Jan 31, 1936, p16.
The New Yorker. Feb 8, 1936, v11, p61.
Rob Wagner's Script. Feb 15, 1936, v15, p11-12.
Time. Feb 10, 1936, v27, p28.
Variety. Feb 5, 1936, p12.

Nicholas Nickelby (GB; Cavalcanti, Alberto; 1947)
Dickens and Film. p310-14.
Film Daily. Nov 12, 1947, p6.
Hollywood Reporter. Apr 2, 1947, p3.
Life. Dec 22, 1947, v23, p2-3.
Motion Picture Herald Product Digest. Nov 15, 1947, p3930.
New Republic. Dec 15, 1947, v117, p31.
The New York Times. Dec 1, 1947, p38.
The New Yorker. Dec 6, 1947, v23, p92.
Newsweek. Dec 22, 1947, v30, p82.
Variety. Mar 26, 1947, p12.

Nick Carter, Master Detective (US; Tourneur, Jacques; 1939)
Film Daily. Dec 14, 1939, p8.
Hollywood Reporter. Dec 6, 1939, p3.
Hollywood Spectator. Dec 23, 1939, v14, p15-16.
Motion Picture Herald. Dec 9, 1939, p72.
The New York Times. Dec 14, 1939, p35.
Rob Wagner's Script. Dec 16, 1939, v22, p16-17.
Variety. Dec 13, 1939, p11.

Niebelungen (Nibelungen, Die, Part 2) (GER; Lang, Fritz; 1924)
Cinema, the Magic Vehicle. v1, p103-05.
Film Daily. Aug 30, 1925, p6.
The Films of Fritz Lang. p106-22.
Fritz Lang (Armour). p65-76+.
Fritz Lang (Eisner). p69-82.
From Caligari to Hitler. p91-95, 97.
The Haunted Screen. p151-70.
Life. Oct 1, 1925, v86, p24.
Magill's Survey of Cinema. Silent Films. v2, p803-05.
The New York Times. Aug 24, 1925, p17.
Spellbound in Darkness. p374.
Variety. Apr 16, 1924, p26.

Niebelungen, Die, Part One *See* Siegfried

Nieuwe Gronden *See* The New Earth

Night After Night (US; Mayo, Archie; 1932)
Film Daily. Oct 29, 1932, p6.
The Great Gangster Pictures. p290-91.
Hollywood Reporter. Sep 27, 1932, p3.
Motion Picture Herald. Oct 8, 1932, p92.

The New York Times. Oct 31, 1932, p18.
The New Yorker. Nov 5, 1932, v8, p66.
Photoplay. Feb 1933, v43, p14.
Rob Wagner's Script. Oct 15, 1932, v8, p8-9.
Time. Nov 7, 1932, v20, p38.
Variety. Nov 1, 1932, p12.

Night and Day (US; Curtiz, Michael; 1946)
Commonweal. Aug 2, 1946, v44, p383.
Film Daily. Jul 9, 1946, p8.
The Films of Cary Grant. p180-82.
The Hollywood Musical. p271.
Hollywood Musicals. p211-12.
Hollywood Reporter. Jul 9, 1946, p3.
Life. Aug 5, 1946, v21, p101-02+.
Magill's Survey of Cinema. Series II. v4, p1713-16.
Motion Picture Herald Product Digest. Jul 13, 1946, p3089.
The New York Times. Jul 26, 1946, p16.
The New Yorker. Jul 1, 1946, v22, p48.
Newsweek. Jul 1, 1946, v28, p78.
Theatre Arts. Aug 1946, v30, p494.
Time. Jul 8, 1946, v48, p98.
Variety. Jul 10, 1946, p8.

A Night at the Opera (US; Wood, Sam; 1935)
American Film Criticism. p322-28.
Canadian Magazine. Feb 1936, v85, p38.
Classic Movies. p36-37.
Eighty Years of Cinema. p105.
Esquire. Jan 1936, v5, p156.
The Film Criticism of Otis Ferguson. p105-07.
Film Daily. Oct 17, 1935, p4.
Films and Filming. Feb 1965, v11, p16-20.
The Films of the Thirties. p150-51.
Garbo and the Night Watchman. p203-05.
The Great Films. p108-13.
Halliwell's Hundred. p235-38.
The Hollywood Musical. p110-11.
Hollywood Reporter. Oct 14, 1935, p3.
Hollywood Spectator. Oct 26, 1935, v10, p9.
Judge. Dec 1935, v109, p16.
Kiss Kiss Bang Bang. p396-97.
Literary Digest. Nov 16, 1935, v120, p26.
Magill's Survey of Cinema. Series I. v3, p1196-99.
The Marx Brothers. p78-85.
Motion Picture Herald. Oct 26, 1935, p72.
The Nation. Jan 1, 1936, v142, p28.
New Republic. Dec 11, 1935, v85, p130.
The New Statesman and Nation. Mar 7, 1936, v11, p345.
The New York Times. Dec 7, 1935, p22.
The New Yorker. Dec 14, 1935, v11, p92-93.
Newsweek. Nov 23, 1935, v6, p29.
Rob Wagner's Script. Nov 9, 1935, v14, p10.
Selected Film Criticism, 1931-1940. p173.
Stage. Jan 1936, v13, p36-38.
Time. Nov 18, 1935, v26, p34-35.
Variety. Dec 11, 1935, p19.
Why a Duck? p185-234.
World Film News. Sep 1936, v1, p25.
50 Classic Motion Pictures. p122-27.

Night Flight (US; Brown, Clarence; 1933)
Canadian Magazine. Dec 1933, v80, p36.
Film Daily. Oct 4, 1933, p6.
The Films of Myrna Loy. p159-60.
Garbo and the Night Watchman. p235.
Garbo and the Night Watchman. p25.
Hollywood Reporter. Aug 9, 1933, p2.
A Library of Film Criticism: American Film Directors. p20.
Lorentz on Film. p126-27.
Motion Picture Herald. Aug 19, 1933, p40, 42.
The Nation. Oct 25, 1933, v137, p492-93.
National Board of Review Magazine. Nov 1933, v8, p12.
New Outlook. Nov 1933, v162, p43.
The New York Times. Oct 7, 1933, p18.

The New Yorker. Oct 14, 1933, v9, p54.
Rob Wagner's Script. Oct 7, 1933, v10, p12.
Time. Oct 16, 1933, v22, p33.
Vanity Fair. Oct 1933, v41, p58.
Variety. Oct 10, 1933, p23.

A Night in Casablanca (US; Mayo, Archie; 1946)
Agee on Film. v1, p201-02.
Commonweal. Jun 14, 1946, v44, p217.
Hollywood Quarterly. Apr 1947, v2, p264-69.
Hollywood Reporter. Apr 15, 1946, p3.
Life. Apr 1, 1946, p65-66+.
Motion Picture Herald Product Digest. Apr 20, 1946, p2949.
The Nation. May 25, 1946, p636.
The New York Times. Aug 12, 1946, p17.
The New Yorker. Aug 10, 1946, v22, p44.
Newsweek. Jul 8, 1946, p86.
Take One. May-Jun 1968, v1, p14-15.
Theatre Arts. May 1946, v30, p274-75.
Time. May 20, 1946, p89.
Variety. Apr 17, 1946, p10.

Night Key (US; Corrigan, Lloyd; 1937)
Film Daily. Apr 21, 1937, p8.
The Films of Boris Karloff. p125-26.
Hollywood Reporter. Apr 16, 1937, p3.
Motion Picture Herald. Apr 24, 1937, p46, 49.
The New York Times. Apr 19, 1937, p27.
Time. Apr 26, 1937, v29, p41.
Variety. Apr 21, 1937, p15.

Night Life of the Gods (US; Sherman, Lowell; 1935)
Esquire. Apr 1935, v3, p144.
Film Daily. Feb 23, 1935, p3.
Hollywood Reporter. Dec 7, 1934, p3.
Motion Picture Herald. Jan 12, 1935, p26.
The New Republic. Mar 20, 1935, v82, p160.
The New York Times. Feb 23, 1935, p14.
Time. Mar 4, 1935, v25, p16.
Variety. Feb 27, 1935, p12.

Night Mail (GB; Wright, Basil; Watt, Harry; 1936)
A Critical History of the British Cinema. p137-38.
Dictionary of Films. p244.
Documentary and Educational Films of the 1930s. p107-09.
Don't Look at the Camera. p79-97.
The Film Criticism of Otis Ferguson. p208.
Graham Greene on Film. p60.
The International Dictionary of Films and Filmmakers. v1, p319-20.
London Mercury. May 1936, v34, p59-60.
Non-Fiction Film: A Critical History. p50-53.
The Rise and Fall of British Documentary. p65-78.
Sight and Sound. Spr 1936, v5, p28-29.
The Spectator. Mar 20, 1936, v156, p512.

Night Must Fall (US; Thorpe, Richard; 1937)
Esquire. Jul 1937, v8, p97.
The Film Criticism of Otis Ferguson. p178-80.
Film Daily. Apr 22, 1937, p14.
Graham Greene on Film. p154.
Hollywood Reporter. Apr 17, 1937, p3.
Hollywood Spectator. Apr 24, 1937, v12, p9.
London Mercury. Aug 1937, v36, p381.
Magill's Survey of Cinema. Series II. v4, p1717-20.
Motion Picture Herald. Apr 10, 1937, p66.
The Nation. May 22, 1937, v144, p602.
National Board of Review Magazine. Jun 1937, v12, p7.
The New Republic. Jun 2, 1937, v91, p102-03.
The New York Times. Apr 30, 1937, p17.
The New Yorker. May 8, 1937, v13, p63-64.
Rob Wagner's Script. May 8, 1937, v17, p8.
Sight and Sound. Sum 1937, v6, p81.
Stage. Apr 1937, v14, p75.
The Tatler. Jul 14, 1937, v145, p52.
Theatre Arts. Jun 1938, v22, p421.

Time. May 10, 1937, v29, p67-68.
Variety. May 5, 1937, p16.
World Film News. Aug 1937, v2, p5.

Night Nurse (US; Wellman, William A.; 1931)
Film Daily. Jul 19, 1931, p11.
The Films of Barbara Stanwyck. p70-71.
The Films of Clark Gable. p123-24.
Hollywood Reporter. Jun 9, 1931, p3.
Hollywood Spectator. Aug 29, 1931, v12, p23.
Judge. Aug 22, 1931, v101, p24.
Life. Aug 7, 1931, v98, p16.
Motion Picture Herald. Jul 25, 1931, p34.
The New York Times. Jul 17, 1931, p23.
The New Yorker. Jul 25, 1931, v7, p54.
Outlook and Independent. Aug 12, 1931, v158, p470.
Starring Miss Barbara Stanwyck. p29.
Time. Jul 27, 1931, v18, p30.
Variety. Jul 21, 1931, p12.
William A. Wellman (Thompson). p115-16.

The Night of Nights (US; Milestone, Lewis; 1939)
Film Daily. Jan 2, 1940, p8.
Hollywood Reporter. Nov 22, 1939, p3.
Hollywood Spectator. Dec 9, 1939, v14, p7-8.
Motion Picture Herald. Nov 25, 1939, p40.
The New York Times. Dec 28, 1939, p17.
Rob Wagner's Script. Dec 9, 1939, v22, p15.
Variety. Nov 29, 1939, p14.

A Night to Remember (US; Wallace, Richard; 1942)
Film Daily. Jan 15, 1943, p6.
Hollywood Reporter. Dec 7, 1942, p3.
The London Times. May 3, 1943, p6.
Magill's Survey of Cinema, Series II. v4, p1728-31.
Motion Picture Exhibitor. Dec 16, 1943, v29, n6, sec2, p1169.
Motion Picture Herald Product Digest. Dec 19, 1942, p1066.
The New York Times. Jan 1, 1943, p27.
Variety. Jan 6, 1943, p50.

Night Train (Also titled: Night Train to Munich; Gestapo) (GB; Reed, Carol; 1940)
The Film Criticism of Otis Ferguson. p331-33.
Film Daily. Oct 25, 1940, p6.
Hollywood Reporter. Jan 16, 1941, p3.
The London Times. Jul 29, 1940, p6.
Lorentz on Film. p208-09.
Magic Moments from the Movies. p75.
Motion Picture Exhibitor. Oct 2, 1940, p613.
Motion Picture Herald Product Digest. Apr 19, 1941, p112.
The New Republic. Jan 13, 1941, v104, p54.
Scholastic. Jan 13, 1941, v37, p32.
Scribner's Commentator. Apr 1941, v9, p106-07.
Time. Jan 13, 1941, v37, p73.
Variety. Oct 30, 1940, p14.

Nightingale (Russian title: Grunya Kornakova) (USSR; Ekk, Nikolai; 1936)
Film Daily. Nov 6, 1936, p13.
Hollywood Reporter. Nov 9, 1936, p4.
Kino. p338.
Motion Picture Herald. Nov 14, 1936, p60, 64.
The New Masses. Nov 10, 1936, v21, p29.
The New York Times. Nov 4, 1936, p41.
Variety. Nov 11, 1936, p15.
World Film News. Jan 1937, v1, p27.

Nightmare Alley (US; Goulding, Edmund; 1947)
Commonweal. Nov 7, 1947, v47, p95.
Film Daily. Oct 9, 1947, p8.
The Films of Tyrone Power. p144-46.
Hollywood Reporter. Oct 9, 1947, p3.
Magill's Survey of Cinema, Series I. v3, p1207-09.
Motion Picture Herald Product Digest. Oct 11, 1947, p3873.
The Nation. Nov 8, 1947, v165, p510.
The New York Times. Oct 31, 1947, p31.

The New Yorker. Oct 18, 1947, v23, p112.
Newsweek. Oct 20, 1947, v30, p94.
Time. Nov 3, 1947, v50, p99.
Variety. Oct 15, 1947, p10.

Nina Petrovna *See* The Lie of Nina Petrovna

Nine Days a Queen (Also titled: Tudor Rose; Lady Jane Grey) (GB; Stevenson, Robert; 1936)
Canadian Magazine. Sep 1936, v86, p29.
Cinema, the Magic Vehicle. v1, p267-68.
Film Daily. Jun 26, 1936, p21.
Graham Greene on Film. p73-74.
Hollywood Reporter. May 12, 1936, p10.
Hollywood Spectator. Jul 4, 1936, v11, p11-12.
Judge. Nov 1936, v111, p12.
Literary Digest. Aug 8, 1936, v122, p18.
Motion Picture Herald. May 16, 1936, p36-37.
Motion Picture Herald. Jun 20, 1936, p10-11.
The Nation. Oct 24, 1936, v143, p502.
The New York Times. Oct 3, 1936, p21.
The New Yorker. Sep 26, 1936, v12, p66-67.
Newsweek. Aug 29, 1936, v8, p25.
Rob Wagner's Script. Aug 8, 1936, v15, p10-11.
Saturday Review (London). May 9, 1936, v161, p608.
Selected Film Criticism: Foreign Films, 1930-1950. p123-24.
The Spectator. May 8, 1936, v156, p835.
The Tatler. May 13, 1936, v140, p286.
Time. Sep 7, 1936, v28, p20.
Variety. Oct 7, 1936, p15.
World Film News. Aug 1936, v1, p19.

Ninotchka (US; Lubitsch, Ernst; 1939)
The American Films of Ernst Lubitsch. p172-78.
The Cinema of Ernst Lubitsch. p113-20.
Cinema, the Magic Vehicle. v1, p320.
The Comic Mind. p223-24.
Commonweal. Nov 3, 1939, v31, p47.
Dictionary of Films. p246.
Ernst Lubitsch: A Guide to References and Resources. p141-44.
Ernst Lubitsch's American Comedy. p190-224.
The Film Career of Billy Wilder. p57-59.
The Film Criticism of Otis Ferguson. p274-75.
Film Daily. Oct 10, 1939, p6.
Film Society Review. Jan 1969, v4, p30-31.
Films and Filming. Mar 1962, v8, p21-23, 45.
The Films of Greta Garbo. p144-50.
From Quasimodo to Scarlett O'Hara. p316-19.
Garbo: A Portrait. p155-56.
Graham Greene on Film. p271-72.
The Great Films. p125-29.
Hollywood Reporter. Oct 7, 1939, p3.
Hollywood Spectator. Oct 14, 1939, v14, p5.
Kiss Kiss Bang Bang. p398.
Life. Nov 20, 1939, v7, p44-45.
Lorentz on Film. p179-80.
The Lubitsch Touch. p139-40, 149-51.
Magill's Survey of Cinema. Series I. v3, p1210-13.
Motion Picture Herald. Oct 14, 1939, p38.
The Nation. Nov 25, 1939, v149, p587.
National Board of Review Magazine. Nov 1939, v14, p11-13.
The New Masses. Sep 12, 1939, v32, p27-29.
The New Republic. Nov 1, 1939, v100, p370.
The New York Times. Nov 10, 1939, p27.
The New Yorker. Nov 18, 1939, v15, p85-86.
Newsweek. Oct 30, 1939, v14, p37.
Photoplay. Nov 1939, v53, p64.
Rob Wagner's Script. Dec 9, 1939, v22, p14.
Selected Film Criticism, 1931-1940. p174-76.
The Spectator. Feb 23, 1940, v164, p248.
Talking Pictures. p324-27.
Theatre Arts. Oct 30, 1939, v24, p37.
Time. Nov 6, 1939, v34, p76.
Variety. Oct 11, 1939, p13.

No Answer from F.P.1. *See* F.P.1. Antwortet Nicht

No Limit (US; Tuttle, Frank; 1931)
Exhibitors Herald-World. Dec 27, 1930, p21.
Film Daily. Jan 18, 1931, p10.
Life. Feb 6, 1931, v97, p20.
The New York Times. Jan 17, 1931, p23.
The New Yorker. Jan 24, 1931, v6, p55.
Outlook and Independent. Jan 28, 1931, v157, p151.
Time. Jan 26, 1931, v17, p26.
Variety. Jan 21, 1931, p30.

No Man of Her Own (US; Ruggles, Wesley; 1932)
Film Daily. Dec 31, 1932, p4.
The Films of Carole Lombard. p100-03.
The Films of Clark Gable. p140.
Hollywood Reporter. Dec 17, 1932, p3.
Motion Picture Herald. Dec 24, 1932, p28.
The New York Times. Dec 31, 1932, p10.
Time. Jan 9, 1933, v21, p37.
Variety. Jan 3, 1933, p27.

No Marriage Ties (US; Ruben, J. Walter; 1933)
BFI/Monthly Film Bulletin. May 1981, v48, p100.
Film Daily. Aug 4, 1933, p4.
Hollywood Reporter. Jun 6, 1933, p11.
Motion Picture Herald. Aug 12, 1933, p46.
New Outlook. Sep 1933, v162, p45.
The New York Times. Aug 4, 1933, p18.
The New Yorker. Aug 12, 1933, v9, p43.
Rob Wagner's Script. Aug 19, 1933, v10, p10.
Time. Aug 14, 1933, v22, p21.
Variety. Aug 8, 1933, p19.

No More Ladies (US; Griffith, Edward H.; 1935)
Commonweal. Jul 5, 1935, v22, p267.
Film Daily. Jun 12, 1935, p4.
The Films of Joan Crawford. p116-17.
Literary Digest. Jul 6, 1935, v120, p29.
Motion Picture Herald. Jun 8, 1935, p73.
Movie Classic. Sep 1935, v9, p88.
The New Statesman and Nation. Jul 6, 1935, v10, p16.
The New York Times. Jun 22, 1935, p18.
The New Yorker. Jan 22, 1935, v11, p53.
Rob Wagner's Script. Jun 15, 1935, v13, p8.
Time. Jun 24, 1935, v25, p50.
Variety. Jun 26, 1935, p23.

No More Orchids (US; Lang, Walter; 1932)
Film Daily. Dec 31, 1932, p4.
The Films of Carole Lombard. p98-99.
Hollywood Reporter. Nov 12, 1932, p3.
The New York Times. Jan 2, 1933, p29.
Variety. Jan 3, 1933, p19.

No, No, Nanette (US; Badger, Clarence; 1930)
Exhibitors Herald-World. Jan 11, 1930, p32.
Film Daily. Jan 12, 1930, p12.
The Film Spectator. Mar 15, 1930, v9, p19.
Judge. Feb 1, 1930, v98, p25.
Life. Jan 31, 1930, v95, p22.
The New York Times. Dec 20, 1930, p33.
The New York Times. Dec 22, 1930, p5.
The New Yorker. Jan 11, 1930, v5, p72.
Outlook and Independent. Jan 15, 1930, v154, p113.
Rob Wagner's Script. Mar 8, 1930, v3, p12.
Variety. Jan 8, 1930, p89.

No One Man (US; Corrigan, Lloyd; 1932)
Film Daily. Jan 24, 1932, p11.
Hollywood Reporter. Jan 5, 1932, p2.
Motion Picture Herald. Jan 30, 1932, p45, 48.
The New York Times. Jan 23, 1932, p18.
Rob Wagner's Script. Jan 23, 1932, v6, p9-10.
Time. Feb 1, 1932, v19, p48.
Variety. Jan 26, 1932, p21.

No Other Woman (US; Ruben, J. Walter; 1933)
BFI/Monthly Film Bulletin. Sep 1981, v48, p183-84.
Film Daily. Jan 13, 1933, p5.
Hollywood Reporter. Dec 9, 1932, p3.
Motion Picture Herald. Jan 21, 1933, p29.
The New York Times. Jan 30, 1933, p9.
Time. Jan 23, 1933, v21, p34.
Variety. Jan 31, 1933, p29.

No Relations *See* Sans Famille

Noah's Ark (US; Curtiz, Michael; 1929)
Film Daily. Mar 17, 1929, p4.
The Film Spectator. Nov 17, 1928, v6, p10.
The Films of the Twenties. p211-13.
The New York Times. Mar 13, 1929, p28.
Variety. Nov 7, 1929, p15.

Nobody Lives Forever (US; Negulesco, Jean; 1946)
Film Daily. Sep 27, 1946, p16.
The Films of John Garfield. p138-42.
Hollywood Reporter. Sep 24, 1946, p3.
The New York Times. Nov 2, 1946, p12.
The New Yorker. Nov 2, 1946, v22, p101.
Newsweek. Nov 18, 1946, v28, p106+.
Time. Nov 18, 1946, v48, p104.
Variety. Sep 25, 1946, p10.

None But the Lonely Heart (US; Odets, Clifford; 1944)
Commonweal. Dec 1, 1944, v41, p176.
Film Daily. Oct 3, 1944, p6.
Film Quarterly. Jan 1947, v2, p153-60.
Films in Review. Apr 1951, v2, p32-38.
The Films of Cary Grant. p173-76.
Hollywood Reporter. Oct 2, 1944, p3.
The London Times. Feb 22, 1945, p6.
Magill's Survey of Cinema. Series I. v3, p1217-19.
Motion Picture Exhibitor. Oct 18, 1944, v32, n23, sec2, p1600.
The Nation. Dec 2, 1944, v159, p698.
The New Republic. Dec 11, 1944, v111, p800.
The New York Times. Nov 18, 1944, p16.
The New Yorker. Nov 25, 1944, v20, p78.
Newsweek. Nov 27, 1944, v24, p110-11.
Running Away from Myself. p109-12.
Theatre Arts. Dec 1944, v28, p719-20.
Time. Nov 20, 1944, v44, p92+.
Variety. Oct 4, 1944, p8.

Nora Prentiss (US; Sherman, Vincent; 1947)
Commonweal. Feb 21, 1947, v45, p470.
Film Daily. Feb 7, 1947, p6.
Hollywood Reporter. Feb 4, 1947, p3.
Motion Picture Herald Product Digest. Feb 8, 1947, p3457.
New Republic. Mar 17, 1947, v116, p43.
The New York Times. Feb 22, 1947, p16.
Newsweek. Mar 10, 1947, v29, p89.
Time. Mar 31, 1947, v49, p102.
Variety. Feb 5, 1947, p12.

The North Star (US; Milestone, Lewis; 1943)
Agee on Film. v1, p81-82+.
Commonweal. Nov 19, 1943, v34, p117-18.
Film Daily. Oct 13, 1943, p11.
The Films of World War II. p153-55.
Hollywood Reporter. Oct 12, 1943, p3.
Life. Nov 1, 1943, v15, p118-22.
Magill's Annual Survey of Cinema, 1983. p476-80.
Motion Picture Herald Product Digest. Oct 16, 1943, p1585.
The Nation. Oct 30, 1943, v157, p509.
New Movies 18. Oct 1943, p23.
The New Republic. Nov 8, 1943, v109, p653.
The New York Times. Nov 5, 1943, p23.
The New York Times Magazine. Oct 10, 1943, p16.

Time. Nov 8, 1943, v42, p54.
Variety. Oct 13, 1943, p10.

Northwest Mounted Police (US; DeMille, Cecil B.; 1940)
Commonweal. Nov 15, 1940, v33, p128.
The Fifty Worst Films of All Time. p164-69.
Film Daily. Oct 22, 1940, p6.
The Films of Cecil B. DeMille. p320-25.
The Films of Gary Cooper. p174-77.
The London Times. Nov 25, 1940, p6.
Motion Picture Exhibitor. Oct 30, 1940, p628.
Motion Picture Herald Product Digest. Jun 9, 1945, p2486.
Nature Magazine. May 1940, v33, p302.
The New Republic. Jan 6, 1941, v104, p21.
The New York Times. Nov 7, 1940, p33.
The New York Times. Nov 10, 1940, sec9, p5.
Newsweek. Nov 18, 1940, v16, p60+.
Scribner's Commentator. Jan 1941, v9, p108-09.
Time. Nov 11, 1940, v36, p74.
Variety. Oct 23, 1940, p14.

Northwest Passage (US; Vidor, King; 1940)
Commonweal. Mar 15, 1940, v31, p456.
Film Comment. Jul-Aug 1973, v9, p10-49.
The Film Criticism of Otis Ferguson. p287-89.
Film Daily. Feb 12, 1940, p5.
The Films of Spencer Tracy. p155-77.
The Great Adventure Films. p100-05.
King Vidor (Baxter). p63-75.
Life. Mar 18, 1940, v8, p50-51.
The London Times. Aug 19, 1940, p6.
Magill's Survey of Cinema. Series II. v4, p1745-48.
Nature Magazine. May 1940, v33, p302.
The New Republic. Mar 4, 1940, v102, p308.
The New York Times. Mar 8, 1940, p25.
The New York Times. Mar 17, 1940, sec9, p5.
Newsweek. Feb 26, 1940, v15, p15.
Scholastic. Feb 16, 1940, v36, p36.
Time. Mar 4, 1940, v35, p67.
A Tree Is a Tree. p235-38.
Variety. Feb 14, 1940, p18.

Nosferatu (German title: Nosferatu—Eine Symphonie des Grauens) (GER; Murnau, F.W.; 1922)
BFI/Monthly Film Bulletin. Feb 1974, v41, p37-38.
Cinema, the Magic Vehicle. v1, p79-80.
Classic Movies. p74-76.
From Caligari to Hitler. p77-81.
The Haunted Screen. p97-106.
A History of Films. p142, 144.
A History of Narrative Film. p120-21.
The History of World Cinema. p95.
An Illustrated History of the Horror Film. p21-25.
International Dictionary of Films and Filmmakers. p326-27.
Magill's Survey of Cinema. Silent Films. v2, p806-09.
Murnau (Eisner). p108-19.
The New York Times. Jun 4, 1929, p29.
Variety. Dec 25, 1925, p62.

Not Against the Flesh *See* Vampyr, ou L'Étrange Adventure de David Gray

Not So Dumb (US; Vidor, King; 1930)
Exhibitors Herald-World. Feb 15, 1930, p29.
Film Daily. Feb 19, 1930, p13.
Judge. Mar 1, 1930, v98, p25.
Life. Feb 14, 1930, v95, p22.
The Nation. Mar 5, 1930, v130, p280.
The New York Times. Feb 8, 1930, p12.
The New Yorker. Feb 15, 1930, v5, p75.
Outlook and Independent. Feb 19, 1930, v154, p313.
Rob Wagner's Script. Mar 1, 1930, v3, p10-11.
Variety. Feb 12, 1930, p18.

Nothing Sacred (US; Wellman, William A.; 1937)
Ben Hecht: Hollywood Screenwriter. p79-108.
The Comic Mind. p252-53.
Film Daily. Nov 24, 1937, p11.
The Films of Carole Lombard. p147-50.
The Films of Fredric March. p150-53.
Hollywood Reporter. Nov 19, 1937, p3.
Kiss Kiss Bang Bang. p400-01.
Life. Dec 6, 1937, v3, p36-39.
Life. Dec 13, 1937, v3, p70-71.
Literary Digest. Dec 18, 1937, v124, p33-34.
Lunatics and Lovers. p125-27.
Magill's Survey of Cinema. Series I. v3, p1224-26.
Motion Picture Herald. Nov 27, 1937, p52.
Motion Picture Herald. Aug 21, 1937, p16-17.
The Nation. Dec 18, 1937, v145, p696-97.
The New Masses. Jan 4, 1938, v26, p26-27.
The New Statesman and Nation. Feb 12, 1938, v15, p248.
The New York Times. Nov 26, 1937, p27.
The New Yorker. Dec 4, 1937, v13, p100-01.
Newsweek. Dec 6, 1937, v10, p33.
Rob Wagner's Script. Dec 4, 1937, v18, p10.
Scribner's Magazine. Feb 1938, v103, p65.
The Spectator. Feb 18, 1938, v160, p271.
Stage. Oct 1937, v15, p95.
Stage. Nov 1937, v15, p63-66.
Stage. Jan 1938, v15, p63-64.
Time. Dec 6, 1937, v30, p49.
Variety. Dec 1, 1937, p14.
William A. Wellman (Thompson). p169-73.

Notorious (US; Hitchcock, Alfred; 1946)
The Art of Alfred Hitchcock. p161-74.
Ben Hecht: Hollywood Screenwriter. p163-67.
BFI/Monthly Film Bulletin. Apr 1947, v14, p51.
Cinema, the Magic Vehicle. v1, p418-19.
Commonweal. Sep 6, 1946, v44, p504.
Film Daily. Jul 25, 1946, p7.
Film Heritage. Spr 1969, v4, p6-10.
The Films of Alfred Hitchcock. p125-29.
The Films of Cary Grant. p183-86.
The Films of Ingrid Bergman. p114-16.
Hitchcock (Taylor). p200-03+.
Hitchcock: The First Forty-Four Films. p80-90+.
Hitchcock (Truffaut). p163-72+.
Hollywood Reporter. Jul 24, 1946, p6.
Life. Aug 26, 1946, v21, p76-78.
Magill's Survey of Cinema. Series II. v4, p1752-55.
Motion Picture Herald Product Digest. Jul 27, 1946, p3113.
The Nation. Aug 17, 1946, v163, p194.
The New York Times. Aug 16, 1946, p19.
The New Yorker. Aug 24, 1946, v22, p42.
Newsweek. Aug 26, 1946, v28, p78.
Rob Wagner's Script. Sep 28, 1946, v32, p12.
Selected Film Criticism, 1941-1950. p176.
The Strange Case of Alfred Hitchcock. p195-98.
Theatre Arts. Sep 1946, v30, p520.
Time. Aug 19, 1946, v48, p98+.
Variety. Jul 24, 1946, p14.

The Notorious Gentleman (GB; Launder, Frank; Gilliat, Sidney; 1945)
Agee on Film. v1, p219-22.
Commonweal. Nov 15, 1946, v45, p116.
Film Daily. Oct 28, 1946, p7.
Hollywood Reporter. Oct 18, 1946, p3.
Motion Picture Herald Product Digest. Oct 26, 1946, p3273.
The Nation. Sep 28, 1946, p361-62.
The New York Times. Nov 14, 1946, p39.
The New Yorker. Nov 23, 1946, v22, p75.
Newsweek. Nov 25, 1946, v28, p106+.
Theatre Arts. Dec 1946, v30, p716.
Time. Sep 30, 1946, v48, p101.

The Notorious Lady (US; Baggot, King; 1927)
Film Daily. Apr 17, 1927, p6.
The New York Times. Apr 11, 1927, p18.
Variety. Apr 13, 1927, p18.

Nous la Liberté, À (FR; Clair, René; 1931)
À Nous la Liberte/Entre' Acte. p9-107.
American Film Criticism. p265-67.
BFI/Monthly Film Bulletin. Oct 1977, v44, p218.
Cinema, the Magic Vehicle. v1, p206-07.
The Comic Mind. p224-31.
Dictionary of Films. p13.
Film Daily. May 22, 1932, p10.
Films in Review. Nov 1954, v5, p486-87.
From Quasimodo to Scarlett O'Hara. p158-61.
The Golden Age of French Cinema. p94-95.
Gotta Sing Gotta Dance. p91-94.
The Great Films. p88-91.
The Great French Films. p38-41.
The International Dictionary of Films and Filmmakers. v 1, p8-9.
Judge. Jun 18, 1932, v102, p24.
Kiss Kiss Bang Bang. p401.
London Mercury. May 1932, v26, p77.
Lorentz on Film. p88-90.
Magill's Survey of Cinema. Foreign Language Films. v1, p1-4.
The Nation. Jun 8, 1932, v134, p659-60.
National Board of Review Magazine. Jun 1932, v7, p6.
The New Republic. Jun 1, 1932, v71, p74-75.
The New Statesman and Nation. Feb 20, 1932, v3, p230.
New Theatre. Feb 1936, v3, p13.
The New York Times. Jun 10, 1932, p5.
The New York Times. Feb 14, 1932, p6.
The New York Times. May 18, 1932, p25.
The New York Times. May 29, 1932, p3.
The New York Times. Feb 10, 1935, p5.
The New Yorker. May 28, 1932, v8, p52.
René Clair (McGerr). p101-10.
Rob Wagner's Script. Jul 9, 1932, v7, p10, 178.
Saturday Review. Oct 16, 1954, v37, p31-32.
Saturday Review. May 19, 1956, v39, p50.
Saturday Review (London). Feb 20, 1932, v153, p200.
Scrutiny of Cinema. p36-38.
Selected Film Criticism: Foreign Films, 1930-1950. p3-4.
The Spectator. Feb 20, 1932, v148, p249.
Time. May 30, 1932, v19, p36.
Variety. Jan 5, 1932, p23.
The Village Voice. Nov 16, 1955, v1, p6.

Novyi Vavilon *See* New Babylon

Now, Voyager (US; Rapper, Irving; 1942)
Around Cinemas, Second Series. p238-39.
Bette Davis: Her Films and Career. p117-20.
Camera Obscura. Spr 1981, n7, p88-109.
Chestnuts in Her Lap. p101-02.
Commonweal. Oct 23, 1942, v37, p17.
Film Daily. Aug 17, 1942, p6.
The Films of the Forties. p71-73.
The Great Romantic Films. p101-04.
Hollywood Reporter. Aug 17, 1942, p3.
The International Dictionary of Films and Filmmakers. v1, p329-30.
The London Times. Nov 4, 1943, p6.
Magill's Survey of Cinema. Series II. v4, p1756-58.
Motion Picture Exhibitor. Aug 26, 1942, v28, n16, sec2, p1081.
Motion Picture Herald Product Digest. Aug 22, 1942, p853.
The New Republic. Nov 2, 1942, v107, p577.
The New York Times. Oct 23, 1942, p25.
Newsweek. Nov 2, 1942, v20, p78.
Now, Voyager. p9-52.
Rob Wagner's Script. Dec 19, 1942, v27, p22.
Selected Film Criticism, 1941-1950. p176-77.
Talking Pictures. p288-90.

Time. Nov 2, 1942, v40, p96.
Variety. Aug 19, 1942, p8.
Women's Film and Female Experience. p112-18.

Nuit du Carrefour, La (FR; Renoir, Jean; 1932)
Jean Renoir: A Guide to References and Resources. p79-81.
Jean Renoir (Durgnat). p76-84.
Jean Renoir: My Life and My Films. p117-18.
Jean Renoir: The French Films, 1924-1939. p102-11.
Jean Renoir: The World of His Films. p201-02, 252-55.
The New York Times. Jun 5, 1932, p10.
Sight and Sound. Sum 1939, v8, p79.
Variety. May 10, 1932, p19.

Number Seventeen (GB; Hitchcock, Alfred; 1932)
Grierson on Documentary. p75-76.
Hitchcock: The First Forty-Four Films. p36-37.
Hitchcock's British Films. p154-60.
Variety. Aug 2, 1932, p17.

Nurse Edith Cavell (US; Wilcox, Herbert; 1939)
Commonweal. Sep 29, 1939, v30, p519.
Commonweal. Nov 17, 1939, v31, p95.
Esquire. Dec 1939, v12, p152.
Film Daily. Aug 22, 1939, p17.
Graham Greene on Film. p247-48.
The Great Spy Pictures. p339-40.
Hollywood Reporter. Aug 18, 1939, p3.
Hollywood Spectator. Sep 2, 1939, v14, p12.
Life. Sep 11, 1939, v7, p74-77.
Motion Picture Herald. Aug 26, 1939, p50.
The Nation. Oct 14, 1939, v149, p422.
The New York Times. Sep 22, 1939, p27.
The New Yorker. Sep 23, 1939, v15, p57-58.
Newsweek. Sep 18, 1939, v14, p37.
Photoplay. Nov 1939, v53, p64.
Rob Wagner's Script. Oct 7, 1939, v22, p17.
Scholastic. Oct 9, 1939, v35, p10.
Sociology and Social Research. Jan 1940, v24, p295.
The Spectator. Oct 27, 1939, v163, p584.
Time. Sep 11, 1939, v34, p58-59.
Variety. Aug 23, 1939, p14.

October (Russian title: Okytabr; Also titled: Ten Days That Shook the World) (USSR; Eisenstein, Sergei; 1927)
Cinema, the Magic Vehicle. v1, p129-30.
Close-Up. Aug 1928, v2, p6-7.
Close-Up. Feb 1929, v4, p95-96.
Close-Up. Dec 1928, v3, p90-96.
Dictionary of Film. p257-58.
Eisenstein. p21-22, 117-26.
Film Daily. Nov 18, 1928, p4.
Film Notes of the Wisconsin Film Society 1960. p48-53.
A History of Films. p190-91.
A History of Narrative Film. p176-81.
The History of World Cinema. p133-34.
The International Dictionary of Films and Filmmakers. v1, p336-37.
Kino. p231-39.
Magill's Survey of Cinema. Silent Films. v2, p810-14.
Masters of the Soviet Cinema. p199-200.
The Nation. Dec 26, 1928, v127, p720-21.
The New Republic. Nov 21, 1928, v57, p17-18.
The New Republic. Jul 3, 1929, v59, p179-80.
The New York Times. Nov 3, 1928, p24.
Sergei Eisenstein, a Biography. p96-116.
Spellbound in Darkness. p518-19.
Variety. Nov 7, 1928, p24.

Odd Man Out (GB; Reed, Carol; 1947)
Commonweal. May 9, 1947, v46, p94.
Fifty Classic British Films. p67-69.
Film Daily. Feb 28, 1947, p8.
The Films of James Mason. p82-83.

The Great British Films. p106-09.
Hollywood Reporter. Feb 26, 1947, p3.
Life. May 12, 1947, v22, p131-32+.
Magill's Survey of Cinema. Series II. v4, p1763-65.
Motion Picture Herald Product Digest. Feb 15, 1947, p3473.
The New Republic. May 12, 1947, v116, p39.
The New York Times. Apr 24, 1947, p30.
The New Yorker. May 3, 1947, v23, p94.
Newsweek. May 5, 1947, v29, p92.
Saturday Review. May 24, 1947, v30, p22-25.
Seventy Years of Cinema. p163-64.
Variety. Feb 12, 1947, p14.

Of Human Bondage (US; Cromwell, John; 1934)
Bette Davis: Her Films and Career. p54-57.
Commonweal. Jul 20, 1934, v20, p309.
The English Novel and the Movies. p228-37.
Film Daily. Jun 27, 1934, p6.
The Films of the Thirties. p127-28.
Hollywood Reporter. Jun 28, 1934, p3.
Magill's Survey of Cinema. Series I. v3, p1237-39.
Motion Picture Herald. Jul 7, 1934, p48.
The New Republic. Jul 18, 1934, v79, p268.
The New York Times. Jun 29, 1934, p17.
Newsweek. Jul 7, 1934, p33.
Rob Wagner's Script. Jul 14, 1934, v11, p8.
Selected Film Criticism, 1931-1940. p177.
Time. Jul 9, 1934, v24, p44.
Variety. Jul 3, 1934, p26.

Of Human Bondage (US; Cromwell, John; 1946)
Commonweal. Aug 9, 1946, v44, p408.
Film Daily. Jul 10, 1946, p10.
Hollywood Reporter. Jul 10, 1946, p3.
Motion Picture Herald Product Digest. Jul 6, 1946, p3077.
The New York Times. Jul 6, 1946, p11.
The New Yorker. Jul 13, 1946, v22, p77.
Newsweek. Jul 22, 1946, v28, p90.
Time. Jul 15, 1946, v48, p98.
Variety. Jul 3, 1946, p10.

Of Human Hearts (US; Brown, Clarence; 1938)
Film Daily. Feb 8, 1938, p9.
The Films of James Stewart. p53-55.
Hollywood Reporter. Feb 4, 1938, p3.
Life. Feb 28, 1938, v4, p30-31.
The Nation. Feb 26, 1938, v146, p254.
National Board of Review Magazine. Feb 1938, v13, p13.
The New Statesman and Nation. Mar 12, 1938, v15, p412.
The New Yorker. Feb 12, 1938, v13, p59.
Rob Wagner's Script. Apr 2, 1938, v19, p10.
Scholastic. Feb 26, 1938, v32, p30+.
Stage. Mar 1938, v15, p31.
Time. Feb 21, 1938, v31, p56-57.
World Film News. Apr 1938, v3, p36-37.

Of Mice and Men (US; Milestone, Lewis; 1939)
Cinema, the Magic Vehicle. v1, p314-15.
Collier's. Jan 6, 1940, v105, p14-15.
Commonweal. Jan 19, 1940, v31, p287.
Esquire. Dec 1939, v12, p152, 154, 156.
The Film Criticism of Otis Ferguson. p285-86.
Film Daily. Dec 27, 1939, p8.
The Films of Hal Roach. p75-78.
From Quasimodo to Scarlett O'Hara. p339-41.
Hollywood Reporter. Nov 22, 1939, p3.
Hollywood Spectator. Jan 6, 1940, v14, p7-8.
Lewis Milestone (Millichap). p92-104+.
Life. Jan 8, 1940, v8, p42-43.
Lorentz on Film. p186-87.
Magill's Survey of Cinema. Series I. v3, p1240-45.
Motion Picture Herald. Dec 30, 1939, p48.
The Nation. Jan 20, 1940, v150, p80-81.
National Board of Review Magazine. Feb 1940, v15, p18.
The New Masses. Mar 5, 1940, v34, p29-30.

The New Republic. Feb 19, 1940, v102, p247.
The New York Times. Feb 17, 1940, p9.
The New Yorker. Feb 17, 1940, v16, p77.
Newsweek. Jan 15, 1940, v16, p32.
Photoplay. Feb 1940, v54, p62.
Scrutiny. Apr 1942, v10, p350-51.
The Spectator. Apr 19, 1940, v164, p556.
Theatre Arts. Mar 1940, v24, p213.
Those Fabulous Movie Years: The 30s. p179.
Time. Jan 15, 1940, v35, p60.
Variety. Jan 3, 1940, p40.

Off the Record (US; Flood, James; 1939)
Film Daily. Feb 23, 1939, p8.
Hollywood Reporter. Jan 19, 1939, p4.
Hollywood Spectator. Feb 4, 1939, v13, p16-17.
Motion Picture Herald. Jan 28, 1939, p37.
The New York Times. Feb 18, 1939, p12.
Rob Wagner's Script. Jan 28, 1939, v20, p18.
Variety. Feb 22, 1939, p12.

The Office Wife (US; Bacon, Lloyd; 1930)
Film Daily. Sep 28, 1930, p10.
Life. Oct 24, 1930, v96, p20.
The New York Times. Sep 27, 1930, p21.
The New York Times. Oct 5, 1930, p5.
Outlook and Independent. Oct 8, 1930, v156, p234.
Time. Oct 6, 1930, v16, p34.
Variety. Oct 1, 1930, p19.

O.H.M.S. (Also titled: You're in the Army Now) (GB; Walsh, Raoul; 1937)
Hollywood Reporter. Feb 11, 1937, p19.
Motion Picture Herald. Feb 20, 1937, p46.
The New York Times. Apr 16, 1937, p27.
The Tatler. Feb 3, 1937, v143, p190.
Variety. Feb 3, 1937, p15.

Oil for the Lamps of China (US; LeRoy, Mervyn; 1935)
Esquire. Aug 1935, v4, p153.
Film Daily. Apr 30, 1935, p8.
Graham Greene on Film. p36.
The Hollywood Professionals. v5, p149-50.
Hollywood Reporter. Apr 27, 1935, p4.
Judge. Jul 1935, v109, p17, 28.
Literary Digest. Jun 22, 1935, v119, p28.
Mervyn LeRoy: Take One. p124-25.
Motion Picture Herald. May 18, 1935, p46.
The Nation. Jul 10, 1935, v141, p56.
The New York Times. Jun 6, 1935, p25.
The New Yorker. Jun 15, 1935, v11, p62.
Rob Wagner's Script. Jun 1, 1935, v13, p9.
The Spectator. Nov 15, 1935, v155, p814.
Time. Jun 10, 1935, v25, p24+.
Variety. Jun 12, 1935, p12.

Okay America (Also titled: O.K. America) (US; Garnett, Tay; 1932)
Hollywood Reporter. Aug 12, 1932, p3.
The New Outlook. Oct 1932, v161, p38.
The New York Times. Sep 10, 1932, p18.
Rob Wagner's Script. Aug 20, 1932, v8, p9.
Time. Sep 5, 1932, v20, p40.
Variety. Sep 13, 1932, p19.

The Oklahoma Kid (US; Bacon, Lloyd; 1939)
Commonweal. Mar 17, 1939, v29, p580.
The Complete Films of Humphrey Bogart. p66-68.
Film Daily. Mar 15, 1939, p12.
The Films of James Cagney. p134-37.
Graham Greene on Film. p221.
The Great Western Pictures. p239-40.
Hollywood Reporter. Mar 14, 1939, p3.
Humphrey Bogart: The Man and His Films. p92-94.
Motion Picture Herald. Mar 18, 1939, p48.
The New Masses. Mar 28, 1939, v31, p29-30.

The New Statesman and Nation. May 6, 1939, v17, p680.
The New York Times. Mar 11, 1939, p21.
Newsweek. Mar 6, 1939, v13, p27.
Rob Wagner's Script. Mar 25, 1939, v21, p16.
Scholastic. Mar 18, 1939, v34, p30.
The Spectator. May 12, 1939, v162, p804.
Stage. Mar 15, 1939, v16, p30-31.
Time. Mar 20, 1939, v33, p46.
Variety. Mar 15, 1939, p16.

Old Acquaintance (US; Sherman, Vincent; 1943)
Agee on Film. v1, p60.
Bette Davis: Her Films and Career. p124-25.
Commonweal. Nov 26, 1943, v39, p145.
Film Daily. Nov 5, 1943, p11.
Hollywood Reporter. Nov 3, 1943, p3.
Magill's Survey of Cinema. Series I. v3, p1249-51.
Motion Picture Herald Product Digest. Nov 6, 1943, p1613.
The Nation. Nov 13, 1943, v157, p565.
The New York Times. Nov 15, 1943, p20.
Newsweek. Nov 15, 1943, v22, p104.
Time. Nov 22, 1943, v42, p94.
Variety. Nov 3, 1943, p16.

The Old and the New (Russian title: Staroye I Novoye;
    Also titled: The General Line) (USSR; Eisenstein,
    Sergei; 1929)
Close-Up. Feb 1929, v4, p48-52.
Close-Up. Jan 1930, v6, p34-39.
Close-Up. Apr 1930, v6, p314-16.
The Complete Films of Eisenstein. p69-77.
Dictionary of Films. p354-55.
Eisenstein at Work. p38-41.
Exhibitors Herald-World. May 10, 1930, p32.
Film Daily. May 4, 1930, p10.
Judge. Jun 21, 1930, v98, p23.
Kino. p262-69.
The Nation. May 14, 1930, v130, p577-78.
National Board of Review Magazine. May-Jun 1930, v5, p7.
The New Republic. Jun 4, 1930, v63, p73.
The New York Times. May 3, 1930, p23.
The New Yorker. May 10, 1930, v6, p99-101.
Outlook and Independent. May 21, 1930, v155, p110.
Rob Wagner's Script. Jun 21, 1930, v3, p10-12.
Scrutiny of Cinema. p25-27.
Time. May 19, 1930, v15, p62.
Variety. May 14, 1930, p43.

The Old Dark House (US; Whale, James; 1932)
BFI/Monthly Film Bulletin. Jul 1979, v46, p159.
Boris Karloff and His Films. p50-55.
Classics of the Horror Film. p80-83.
Horror Movies (Clarens). p84-85.
The International Dictionary of Films and Filmmakers. v1,
    p337-38.
James Whale (Curtis). p92-97.
Journey Into Darkness. p132-62.
Motion Picture Herald. Jul 16, 1932, p52.
The New York Times. Oct 28, 1932, p22.
The New Yorker. Nov 5, 1932, v8, p65.
Review of Reviews (London). Nov 1932, v82, p76-77.
Sight and Sound. Sum 1973, v42, p167.
Time. Nov 7, 1932, v20, p39.
Variety. Nov 1, 1932, p12.

Old English (US; Green, Alfred E.; 1930)
Commonweal. Sep 3, 1930, v12, p445-46.
Exhibitors Herald-World. Aug 30, 1930, p29.
Film Daily. Aug 24, 1930, p10.
Films in Review. Nov 1985, v36, p518-19.
Judge. Sep 13, 1930, v99, p21.
Life. Sep 19, 1930, v96, p18.
National Board of Review Magazine. Oct 1930, v5, p10.
The New York Times. Jun 20, 1930, p21.
The New York Times. Aug 22, 1930, p19.

The New York Times. Aug 31, 1930, p5.
The New Yorker. Aug 30, 1930, v6, p49.
Outlook and Independent. Sep 3, 1930, v156, p32.
Theatre Magazine. Nov 1930, v52, p47.
Time. Sep 1, 1930, v16, p44.
Variety. Aug 27, 1930, p21.

Old Ironsides (US; Cruze, James; 1926)
Film Daily. Dec 19, 1926, p6.
The Films of the Twenties. p152-54.
From Quasimodo to Scarlett O'Hara. p78-82.
Literary Digest. Jan 1, 1927, v92, p31-36.
Magill's Survey of Cinema. Silent Films. v2, p815-17.
The Moving Picture World. Dec 11, 1926, p441.
The New York Times. Dec 7, 1926, p21.
Outlook. Feb 23, 1927, v145, p234-35.
Photoplay. Feb 1927, v31, p52.
Selected Film Criticism, 1921-1930. p210.
Variety. Dec 8, 1926, p16.

The Old Maid (US; Goulding, Edmund; 1939)
Bette Davis: Her Films and Career. p96-97.
Commonweal. Aug 25, 1939, v30, p421.
The Film Criticism of Otis Ferguson. p269.
Film Daily. Aug 1, 1939, p7.
The Great Romantic Films. p72-77.
Hollywood Reporter. Jul 29, 1939, p3.
Hollywood Spectator. Aug 5, 1939, v14, p6.
Life. Aug 21, 1939, v7, p58-59.
Magill's Survey of Cinema. Series II. v4, p1771-74.
Motion Picture Herald. Aug 5, 1939, p84.
The Nation. Aug 19, 1939, v149, p204.
The New Masses. Sep 5, 1939, v32, p30.
The New Republic. Sep 6, 1939, v100, p132.
The New Yorker. Aug 19, 1939, v15, p52-53.
Newsweek. Aug 21, 1939, v14, p25.
North American Review. Sum 1939, v248, p192-94.
Photoplay. Jun 1939, v53, p60-61.
Photoplay. Oct 1939, v53, p64.
The Spectator. Jan 19, 1940, v164, p76.
Time. Aug 21, 1939, v34, p41.
Variety. Aug 2, 1939, p18.

Old Mother Riley, Detective (US; Comfort, Lance; 1943)
Magill's Survey of Cinema. Series II. v4, p1778-80.
Motion Picture Herald Product Digest. Feb 13, 1943, p1159.
Variety. Aug 18, 1943, p10.

The Old Swimmin' Hole (US; De Grasse, Joseph; 1921)
Film Daily. Feb 20, 1921, p2.
Magill's Survey of Cinema. Silent Films. v2, p818-20.
The New York Times. Feb 28, 1921, p16.
Photoplay. May 1921, v19, p51.
Spellbound in Darkness. p281-82.

Old Wives for New (US; DeMille, Cecil B.; 1918)
Exhibitor's Trade Review. Jun 1, 1918, p2078-81, 2083-84.
The Films of Cecil B. DeMille. p148-51.
Motion Picture News. Jun 8, 1918, p3453.
Motion Picture News. Jun 15, 1918, p3579.
The Moving Picture World. May 25, 1918, p1191.
The Moving Picture World. Jun 8, 1918, p1470.
The New York Times. May 20, 1918, p9.
Photoplay. Aug 1918, v14, p95, 102.
Selected Film Criticism, 1912-1920. p184.
Variety. May 24, 1918, p40.
Wid's Daily. May 26, 1918, p27-28.

Oliver Twist (US; 1912)
Motion Picture News. May 25, 1912, p20.
The Moving Picture World. May 18, 1912, p648-49.
The Moving Picture World. Jun 1, 1912, p813, 842-43.
The New York Dramatic Mirror. Jun 5, 1912, p27.

Oliver Twist (US; Young, James; 1916)
Fifty Great American Silent Films, 1912-1920. p63-65.
The Moving Picture World. Dec 23, 1916, p1817, 4037.
The Moving Picture World. Dec 30, 1916, p2015.
The New York Dramatic Mirror. Dec 16, 1916, p28.
The New York Times. Dec 11, 1916, p7.
Selected Film Criticism, 1912-1920. p184-85.
Variety. Dec 15, 1916, p37.
Wid's Daily. Dec 21, 1916, p1191.

Oliver Twist (US; Lloyd, Frank; 1922)
Film Daily. Nov 12, 1922, p3.
The Films of the Twenties. p67-68.
The New York Times. Oct 30, 1922, p11.
Variety. Nov 10, 1922, p42.
Variety. Mar 26, 1975, p26.

Oliver Twist (US; Cowen, William; 1933)
Film Daily. Feb 25, 1933, p4.
Hollywood Reporter. Feb 22, 1933, p3.
Motion Picture Herald. Mar 4, 1933, p48.
New Outlook. May 1933, v161, p46.
The New York Times. Apr 13, 1933, p15.
The New Yorker. Apr 22, 1933, v9, p50.
Variety. Apr 18, 1933, p21.

Oliver Twist (GB; Lean, David; 1948)
The Cinema of David Lean. p73-82.
David Lean and His Films. p53-84.
David Lean (Anderegg). p46-60+.
Dickens and Film. p298-309.
Film Daily. May 3, 1951, p7.
Hollywood Reporter. Jul 16, 1951, p3.
Life. Mar 7, 1949, v26, p38-39.
Motion Picture Herald Product Digest. Jun 26, 1950, p4219.
The New York Times. Jul 31, 1951, p17.
The New York Times Magazine. Nov 23, 1947, p24-25.
Time. Oct 4, 1948, v52, p96.
Variety. Jun 30, 1948, p10.

Olympiad (German title: Olympische Spiele; Also titled: Olympia) (GER; Riefenstahl, Leni; 1938)
Classics of the Foreign Film. p112-13.
Dictionary of Films. p258-59.
Documentary: History of the Non-Fiction Film. p105, 107-10.
The Documentary Tradition. p136-37.
Eighty Years of Cinema. p116.
Film Comment. Nov-Dec 1973, v9, p32-37.
Film Culture. Spr 1973, n56/57, p122-61, 170-92.
Film in the Third Reich. p132-37.
Film Quarterly. Fall 1960, v14, p14-17.
Film Quarterly. Fall 1974, v28, p8-12.
The Films of Leni Riefenstahl. p61-82.
The German Cinema. p96-98.
The International Dictionary of Films and Filmmakers. v1, p339-40.
Leni Riefenstahl (Berg-Pan). p137-61.
The New York Times. Mar 9, 1940, p19.
The New York Times. Mar 30, 1940, p11.
Non-Fiction Film. p87.
Nonfiction Film Theory and Criticism. p250-62, 323-41.
Notes on the Making of Olympia.
Propaganda and the German Cinema, 1933-1945. p112-21.
Swastika: Cinema of Oppression. p55.
Village Voice. Sep 15, 1960, v5, p11-12.
Village Voice. May 4, 1967, v12, p27.
World Film News. Oct 1938, v3, p248-49, 268.

On an Island With You (US; Thorpe, Richard; 1948)
Film Daily. May 3, 1948, p6.
Hollywood Reporter. Apr 27, 1948, p3.
Motion Picture Herald Product Digest. May 1, 1948, p4145.
The New York Times. Jul 30, 1948, p13.
Newsweek. Jun 21, 1948, v31, p94.

Time. Aug 30, 1948, v52, p72.
Variety. Apr 28, 1948, p8.

On Approval (GB; Brook, Clive; 1944)
AFFS Newsletter. Apr 1964, v2, p4.
Fifty Classic British Films. p49-51.
Film Daily. Jan 29, 1945, p8.
Hollywood Reporter. Feb 22, 1945, p3.
The London Times. Apr 10, 1944, p8.
Magill's Survey of Cinema. Series II. v4, p1781-83.
Motion Picture Exhibitor. Feb 7, 1945, v33, n14, sec2, p1660.
Motion Picture Herald Product Digest. May 27, 1944, p1910.
The New Republic. Feb 12, 1945, v112, p227.
The New York Times. Jan 29, 1945, p17.
Selected Film Criticism: Foreign Films, 1930-1950. p125-26.
Time. Mar 5, 1945, v45, p91.
Variety. Mar 22, 1944, p18.

On Borrowed Time (US; Bucquet, Harold S.; 1939)
Commonweal. Jul 14, 1939, v30, p300.
Film Daily. Jun 28, 1939, p9.
Hollywood Reporter. Jun 30, 1939, p3.
Hollywood Spectator. Jul 8, 1939, v14, p9.
Life. Jul 10, 1939, v7, p56-57.
Motion Picture Herald. Jul 1, 1939, p45.
The Nation. Jul 15, 1939, v149, p82.
National Board of Review Magazine. Oct 1939, v14, p12.
The New Masses. Jul 18, 1939, v32, p29.
The New Republic. Jul 26, 1939, v99, p335.
The New York Times. Jul 7, 1939, p13.
The New Yorker. Jul 8, 1939, v15, p69.
Newsweek. Jul 10, 1939, v14, p31.
Photoplay. Sep 1939, v53, p62.
Rob Wagner's Script. Jul 29, 1939, v21, p16.
Time. Jul 17, 1939, v34, p54.
Variety. Jul 5, 1939, p14.

On the Avenue (US; Del Ruth, Roy; 1937)
Film Daily. Feb 3, 1937, p9.
Film Notes. p100.
The Films of Alice Faye. p77-80.
Graham Greene on Film. p157-60.
The Hollywood Musical. p144-45.
Hollywood Reporter. Feb 1, 1937, p3.
Hollywood Spectator. Feb 13, 1937, v11, p7-8.
Motion Picture Herald. Feb 13, 1937, p56.
The New York Times. Feb 5, 1937, p17.
The New Yorker. Feb 13, 1937, v12, p60.
Rob Wagner's Script. Feb 13, 1937, v17, p8.
Time. Feb 15, 1937, v29, p56-58.
Variety. Feb 10, 1937, p14.
World Film News. Sep 1937, v2, p28.

On the Night of the Fire *See* The Fugitive

On the Subject of Nice *See* A Propos de Nice

On the Town (US; Kelly, Gene; Donen, Stanley; 1949)
Christian Century. Jan 25, 1950, v67, p127.
Commonweal. Dec 23, 1949, v51, p319.
Film Daily. Dec 13, 1949, p7.
The Films of Frank Sinatra. p63-66.
The Films of Gene Kelly. p99-111.
Holiday. May 1950, v7, p22+.
The Hollywood Musical. p300-08+.
Hollywood Reporter. Dec 6, 1949, p3.
Magill's Survey of Cinema. Series I. v3, p1259-61.
Motion Picture Herald Product Digest. Sep 10, 1949, p10.
The New Republic. Dec 26, 1949, v121, p23.
The New York Times. Dec 9, 1949, p37.
Newsweek. Dec 19, 1949, v34, p76.
Rotarian. Mar 1950, v76, p37.
Scholastic. Jan 11, 1950, v55, p25.
Sequence. Sum 1950, n11, p36-38.
Seventy Years of Cinema. p171.
Sight and Sound. Apr 1950, v19, p74-75.

Stanley Donen (Casper). p25-34.
Time. Jan 2, 1950, v55, p62+.
Variety. Dec 7, 1949, p6.

On Trial (US; Mayo, Archie; 1928)
Exhibitor's Herald-World and Moving Picture World. Dec 1,
    1928, p59.
Film Daily. Nov 18, 1928, p4.
The Film Spectator. Nov 24, 1928, v6, p6-7, 10-11.
Magill's Survey of Cinema. Series II. v4, p1792-95.
The New York Times. Nov 15, 1928, p26.
Variety. Nov 21, 1928, p30.

On with the Show (US; Crosland, Alan; 1929)
Film Daily. Jun 2, 1929, p9.
The Hollywood Musical. p34.
Hollywood Musicals. p46-47.
The New York Times. May 29, 1928, p28.
Photoplay. Aug 1929, v36, p54.
Selected Film Criticism, 1921-1930. p212-13.
Variety. Jun 5, 1929, p15.

On Your Toes (US; Enright, Ray; 1939)
Film Daily. Oct 14, 1939, p10.
Graham Greene on Film. p273.
Hollywood Reporter. Oct 23, 1939, p3.
Hollywood Spectator. Nov 11, 1939, v14, p9.
Motion Picture Herald. Oct 28, 1939, p43.
The Nation. Oct 28, 1939, v149, p477.
The New York Times. Oct 21, 1939, p12.
The New Yorker. Oct 28, 1939, v15, p64.
The Spectator. Feb 23, 1940, v164, p248.
Time. Oct 30, 1939, v34, p49.
Variety. Oct 25, 1939, p11.

Once a Gentleman (US; Cruze, James; 1930)
Exhibitors Herald-World. Jul 19, 1930, p32.
Film Daily. Jul 13, 1930, p10.
The New York Times. Oct 4, 1930, p15.
Variety. Oct 8, 1930, p22.

Once More My Darling (US; Donen, Stanley; 1949)
Christian Century. Feb 1, 1950, v67, p159.
Commonweal. Aug 19, 1949, v50, p465.
Film Daily. Jul 28, 1949, p6.
Filmfacts. 1950, v3, p25.
Films and Filming. Apr 1950, v6, p24-25.
Films in Review. Mar 1960, v11, p168-69.
Hollywood Reporter. Jul 25, 1949, p3.
Motion Picture Herald Product Digest. Jul 30, 1949, p4698.
The New York Times. Sep 26, 1949, p17.
Newsweek. Aug 15, 1949, v34, p78.
Sight and Sound. Spr 1950, v29, p93.
Time. Sep 12, 1949, v54, p101.
Variety. Jul 27, 1949, p12.

Once Upon a Honeymoon (US; McCarey, Leo; 1942)
Commonweal. Dec 4, 1942, v35, p16+.
Film Daily. Nov 4, 1942, p6.
The Films of Cary Grant. p161-63.
The Films of Ginger Rogers. p210-11.
Hollywood Reporter. Nov 7, 1942, p4.
Motion Picture Herald Product Digest. Nov 7, 1942, p1006.
The New York Times. Nov 13, 1942, p28.
Newsweek. Nov 23, 1942, v20, p66.
Time. Nov 30, 1942, v40, p96.
Variety. Nov 4, 1942, p8.

One A.M. (US; Chaplin, Charles; 1916)
Charles Chaplin: A Guide to References and Resources. p61.
The Films of Charlie Chaplin. p126-28.
Magill's Survey of Cinema. Silent Films. v1, p28-29.
Variety. Aug 4, 1916, p26.
Wid's Daily. Aug 3, 1916, p759.

One Exciting Night (US; Griffith, D.W.; 1922)
Film Daily. Oct 29, 1922, p2.
The Films of D.W. Griffith. p185-90.
The New York Times. Oct 24, 1922, p17.
Variety. Oct 13, 1922, p42.

One Foot in Heaven (US; Rapper, Irving; 1941)
Chestnuts in Her Lap. p74-75.
Commonweal. Oct 24, 1941, v35, p16+.
Film Daily. Sep 30, 1941, p8.
The Films of Fredric March. p172-74.
Hollywood Reporter. Sep 30, 1941, p3.
The London Times. May 4, 1942, p8.
Magill's Survey of Cinema. Series II. v4, p1798-1801.
Motion Picture Exhibitor. Oct 15, 1941, v26, n23, sec2, p872.
Motion Picture Herald Product Digest. Aug 9, 1941, p206.
The New York Times. Nov 14, 1941, p28.
The New York Times. Nov 16, 1941, sec9, p5.
The New York Times. Nov 23, 1941, sec9, p5.
The New Yorker. Nov 22, 1941, v17, p98.
Newsweek. Oct 13, 1941, v18, p69.
Scholastic. Nov 10, 1941, v39, p28.
Time. Oct 27, 1941, v38, p97.
Variety. Oct 1, 1941, p9.

One Heavenly Night (US; Fitzmaurice, George; 1930)
Exhibitors Herald-World. Nov 8, 1930, p40.
Film Daily. Dec 7, 1930, p10.
Life. Feb 6, 1931, v97, p20.
The New York Times. Jan 10, 1931, p19.
The New York Times. Jan 18, 1931, p5.
Samuel Goldwyn Presents. p101-03.
Time. Jan 12, 1931, v17, p24.
Variety. Jan 14, 1931, p12.

One Hour Before Dawn (US; King, Henry; 1920)
The Moving Picture World. Jul 24, 1920, p507.
The Moving Picture World. Aug 28, 1920, p1154-55.
Variety. Jul 16, 1920, p32.
Wid's Daily. Jul 18, 1920, p5.

One Hour With You (French titled: Heure Pres de Loi,
    Une) (US; Lubitsch, Ernst; 1932)
The American Films of Ernst Lubitsch. p136-39.
Canadian Forum. May 1932, v12, p318.
Chevalier. p101-05.
The Cinema of Ernst Lubitsch. p70-77.
Ernst Lubitsch: A Guide to References and Resources. p113-16.
Film Daily. Mar 6, 1932, p10.
The Films of Jeanette MacDonald and Nelson Eddy. p86-94.
The Hollywood Musical. p39-40.
Hollywood Reporter. Feb 10, 1932, p3.
Judge. Apr 23, 1932, v102, p26.
The Lubitsch Touch. p122-24.
Magill's Survey of Cinema. Series I. v3, p1268-71.
Motion Picture Herald. Apr 2, 1932, p35, 38.
The Nation. Apr 13, 1932, v134, p445.
The New York Times. Mar 24, 1932, p17.
The New Yorker. Apr 2, 1932, v8, p56.
Photoplay. Apr 1932, v41, p50.
Rob Wagner's Script. Apr 2, 1932, v7, p10.
Selected Film Criticism, 1931-1940. p179-81.
Time. Apr 4, 1932, v19, p22.
Variety. Mar 29, 1932, p24.

One Hundred Men and a Girl (US; Koster, Henry; 1937)
Esquire. Dec 1937, v8, p166.
Film Daily. Sep 3, 1937, p9.
Hollywood Reporter. Sep 3, 1937, p3.
Hollywood Spectator. Sep 11, 1937, v12, p13-14.
Independent Woman. Dec 1937, v16, p398.
Life. Sep 6, 1937, v3, p81-83.
Literary Digest. Oct 2, 1937, v124, p34.
Magill's Survey of Cinema. Series I. v3, p1272-74.
Motion Picture Herald. Sep 11, 1937, p40.

Motion Picture Herald. Sep 18, 1937, p29.
The New Masses. Oct 5, 1937, v25, p29.
The New Statesman and Nation. Dec 11, 1937, v14, p1014.
The New York Times. Sep 8, 1937, p15.
The New Yorker. Sep 18, 1937, v13, p69.
Newsweek. Sep 20, 1937, v10, p24.
Rob Wagner's Script. Sep 11, 1937, v18, p10-11.
Scholastic. Oct 9, 1937, v31, p36.
Selected Film Criticism, 1931-1940. p181-82.
The Tatler. Dec 15, 1937, v146, p482, xviii.
Time. Sep 20, 1937, v30, p29.
Variety. Sep 8, 1937, p18.
World Film News. Dec 1937, v2, p30.

One in a Million (US; Lanfield, Sidney; 1936)
Canadian Magazine. Mar 1937, v87, p25.
Film Daily. Dec 22, 1936, p10.
Hollywood Reporter. Dec 19, 1936, p3.
Literary Digest. Jan 9, 1937, v123, p23-24.
Motion Picture Herald. Dec 26, 1936, p52.
The New York Times. Jan 1, 1937, p19.
The New Yorker. Jan 9, 1937, v12, p65.
Rob Wagner's Script. Jan 9, 1937, v16, p12.
Saint Nicholas. Feb 1937, v64, p34.
Scholastic. Jan 30, 1937, v29, p23.
The Spectator. Jun 25, 1937, v158, p1188.
Time. Jan 11, 1937, v29, p56.
Variety. Jan 6, 1937, p40.

One Million B.C. (US; Roach, Hal; Roach Jr., Hal; 1940)
Commonweal. May 17, 1940, v32, p83.
Film Daily. Apr 16, 1940, p9.
Hollywood Reporter. Apr 10, 1940, p3.
Motion Picture Herald. Apr 13, 1940, p40.
The New York Times. Apr 27, 1940, p9.
Time. May 13, 1940, v35, p104.
Variety. May 1, 1940, p18.

One More River (US; Whale, James; 1934)
Film Daily. Aug 10, 1934, p9.
Hollywood Reporter. Aug 1, 1934, p3.
James Whale (Curtis). p112-17.
Literary Digest. Aug 25, 1934, v118, p28.
Magill's Survey of Cinema. Series II. v4, p1805-08.
Motion Picture Herald. Aug 11, 1934, p31.
The New York Times. Aug 10, 1934, p21.
Time. Aug 20, 1934, v24, p38.
Variety. Aug 14, 1934, p15.

One More Spring (US; King, Henry; 1935)
Esquire. Apr 1935, v3, p144, p150.
Film Daily. Feb 12, 1935, p8.
Hollywood Reporter. Jan 31, 1935, p2.
Literary Digest. Mar 9, 1935, v119, p34.
Motion Picture Herald. Feb 9, 1935, p58.
The New York Times. Feb 22, 1935, p27.
The New Yorker. Mar 2, 1935, v11, p56.
Time. Mar 4, 1935, v25, p16.
Variety. Feb 27, 1935, p12.

One Night of Love (US; Schertzinger, Victor; 1934)
Film Daily. Jul 6, 1934, p4.
The Hollywood Musical. p93.
Hollywood Musicals. p141, 146.
Hollywood Reporter. May 28, 1934, p3.
Literary Digest. Sep 22, 1934, p28.
Magill's Survey of Cinema. Series I. v3, p1275-78.
Motion Picture Herald. Jun 30, 1934, p52.
The New Republic. Sep 26, 1934, v80, p184-85.
The New York Times. Sep 7, 1934, p25.
Newsweek. Sep 15, 1934, v4, p30.
Rob Wagner's Script. Sep 1, 1934, v12, p10.
Selected Film Criticism, 1931-1940. p183-84.
Time. Sep 17, 1934, v24, p38.
Variety. Sep 11, 1934, p11.

One of Our Aircraft Is Missing (GB; Powell, Michael; Pressburger, Emeric; 1942)
Commonweal. Oct 9, 1942, v36, p594.
Film Daily. Sep 3, 1942, p19.
The Films of the Second World War. p105-06.
Hollywood Reporter. Sep 2, 1942, p3.
The London Times. Apr 21, 1942, p2.
The London Times. Apr 22, 1942, p6.
The London Times. Apr 25, 1942, p6.
Motion Picture Exhibitor. Sep 9, 1942, v28, n18, sec2, p1112.
Motion Picture Herald Product Digest. Apr 11, 1943, p598.
The New Republic. Nov 16, 1942, v107, p641.
The New York Times. Nov 2, 1942, p17.
Newsweek. Sep 21, 1942, v20, p80+.
Time. Sep 28, 1942, v40, p85.
Variety. Apr 29, 1942, p8.

One Rainy Afternoon (US; Lee, Rowland V.; 1936)
Commonweal. May 15, 1936, v24, p76.
Film Daily. Apr 27, 1936, p8.
Garbo and the Night Watchman. p62-64.
Graham Greene on Film. p86-87.
Hollywood Reporter. Apr 23, 1936, p3.
Hollywood Spectator. May 9, 1936, v11, p7.
Motion Picture Herald. May 2, 1936, p47.
The New Masses. May 26, 1936, v19, p29-30.
The New Statesman and Nation. Jul 11, 1936, v12, p53.
The New York Times. May 14, 1936, p29.
The New Yorker. May 16, 1936, v12, p62-63.
Newsweek. May 16, 1936, v7, p42.
Rob Wagner's Script. May 23, 1936, v15, p10.
Scholastic. May 16, 1936, v28, p23.
The Spectator. Jul 10, 1936, v157, p56.
Time. May 4, 1936, v27, p26.
Variety. May 20, 1936, p12.
World Film News. Aug 1936, v1, p17-18.

One Romantic Night (US; Stein, Paul; 1930)
Around Cinemas. p41-43.
Commonweal. Jun 11, 1930, v12, p165-66.
Exhibitors Herald-World. Apr 5, 1930, p37.
Film Daily. Mar 30, 1930, p8.
Judge. Jun 28, 1930, v98, p23.
Life. Jun 27, 1930, v95, p17.
The New York Times. May 31, 1930, p19.
The New York Times. Jun 8, 1930, p5.
The New Yorker. Jun 7, 1930, v6, p71.
Outlook and Independent. Jun 11, 1930, v155, p229.
Rob Wagner's Script. Jul 5, 1930, v3, p10.
Time. Jun 16, 1930, v15, p23.
Variety. Jun 4, 1930, p36.

One Sunday Afternoon (US; Roberts, Stephen; 1933)
Film Daily. Sep 2, 1933, p3.
The Films of Gary Cooper. p113-14.
Hollywood Reporter. Aug 15, 1933, p3.
Make It Again, Sam. p134-38.
Motion Picture Herald. Aug 26, 1933, p78.
New Outlook. Oct 1933, v162, p49.
The New York Times. Sep 2, 1933, p14.
The New Yorker. Sep 9, 1933, v9, p54.
Rob Wagner's Script. Sep 2, 1933, v10, p11.
The Spectator. Oct 20, 1933, v151, p522.
Time. Sep 11, 1933, v22, p47.
Variety. Sep 5, 1933, p19.

One Sunday Afternoon (US; Walsh, Raoul; 1948)
Film Daily. Dec 14, 1948, p7.
Hollywood Reporter. Dec 6, 1948, p3.
Motion Picture Herald Product Digest. Dec 11, 1948, p4418.
The New York Times. Dec 27, 1948, p16.
Time. Jan 17, 1949, v53, p88.
Variety. Dec 8, 1948, p11.

"...one-third of a nation" (Also titled: One-Third of a
Nation) (US; Murphy, Dudley; 1939)
Commonweal. Feb 17, 1939, v29, p470.
Film Daily. Feb 15, 1939, p7.
Hollywood Reporter. Jan 11, 1939, p8.
Hollywood Spectator. Feb 18, 1939, v13, p9.
Magic and Myth of the Movies. p115-16.
Motion Picture Herald. Feb 18, 1939, p43, 48.
The Nation. Feb 18, 1939, v148, p214.
National Board of Review Magazine. Feb 1939, v14, p18.
The New York Times. Feb 11, 1939, p13.
The New Yorker. Feb 18, 1939, v15, p67.
North American Review. Mar 1939, v247, p176.
Scholastic. Mar 4, 1939, v34, p30.
Time. Feb 20, 1939, v33, p68.
Variety. Feb 15, 1939, p12.

One Touch of Venus (US; Seiter, William A.; 1948)
Film Daily. Aug 23, 1948, p6.
Motion Picture Herald Product Digest. Aug 28, 1948, p4275 .
The New York Times. Oct 29, 1948, p29.
Newsweek. Sep 20, 1948, v32, p102.
Time. Sep 27, 1948, v52, p96.
Variety. Aug 25, 1948, p8.

One Way Passage (US; Garnett, Tay; 1932)
Film Daily. Aug 23, 1932, p9.
Hollywood Spectator. Nov 21, 1936, v11, p17.
Love in the Film. p89-91.
Magill's Survey of Cinema. Series II. v4, p1812-14.
Motion Picture Herald. Jul 30, 1932, p31.
The New York Times. Oct 14, 1932, p23.
The New Yorker. Oct 22, 1932, v8, p57.
Rob Wagner's Script. Jan 7, 1933, v8, p9.
Time. Oct 24, 1932, v20, p54.
Variety. Oct 18, 1932, p15.

One Week (US; Keaton, Buster; Cline, Edward; 1920)
Buster Keaton (Robinson). p39-45.
The Comic Mind. p138-39.
The Film Career of Buster Keaton. p17-18.
Magill's Survey of Cinema. Silent Films. v2, p828-30.
The Silent Clowns. p128-31.

Only Angels Have Wings (US; Hawks, Howard; 1939)
Commonweal. May 26, 1939, v30, p132.
Eighty Years of Cinema. p119-21.
The Film Criticism of Otis Ferguson. p256.
Film Daily. May 15, 1939, p7.
Films and Filming. Jul 1962, v8, p48.
The Films of Cary Grant. p129-31.
The Films of Howard Hawks. p75-88.
Graham Greene on Film. p247.
Hollywood Reporter. May 11, 1939, p3.
Hollywood Spectator. May 27, 1939, v14, p6-7.
Howard Hawks (Murphy). p187-214.
Howard Hawks (Poague). p27-43.
Howard Hawks, Storyteller. p105-31.
Howard Hawks (Wood). p17-24.
Literature/Film Quarterly. 1976, n3, v4, p286-88.
Magill's Survey of Cinema. Series I. v3, p1279-83.
Motion Picture Herald. May 20, 1939, p42.
Movietone News. Apr 1975, n40, p1-4+.
The New Republic. May 31, 1939, v99, p102.
The New Statesman and Nation. Oct 21, 1939, v18, p549.
The New York Times. May 12, 1939, p25.
The New Yorker. May 20, 1939, v15, p77.
Newsweek. May 22, 1939, v13, p35.
Post Script. 1981, n1, v1, p36-40.
Quarterly Review of Film Studies. 1976, n3, v4, p286-88.
Rob Wagner's Script. May 20, 1939, v21, p16.
Selected Film Criticism, 1931-1940. p186-89.
The Spectator. Oct 20, 1939, v163, p544.
Stage. Jun 1939, v16, p5.
Talking Pictures. p272-74.

Time. May 22, 1939, v33, p57.
Variety. May 17, 1939, p12.

Only Yesterday (US; Stahl, John M.; 1933)
BFI/Monthly Film Bulletin. Nov 1981, v48, p231.
Film Daily. Nov 10, 1933, p12.
The Great Romantic Films. p18-21.
Hollywood Reporter. Oct 28, 1933, p3.
Literary Digest. Nov 25, 1933, v116, p31.
Motion Picture Herald. Nov 25, 1933, p38.
The New York Times. Nov 10, 1933, p25.
Newsweek. Nov 18, 1933, v2, p35.
Rob Wagner's Script. Nov 4, 1933, v10, p8.
Time. Nov 20, 1933, v22, p39.
Variety. Nov 14, 1933, p17.

Open City (Italian title: Roma, Città Aperta; Also titled:
Rome, Open City) (IT; Rossellini, Roberto; 1945)
Agee on Films. v1, p194-98, 236-37+.
Cinema, The Magic Vehicle. v1, p401-02.
Classic Movies. p104-06.
Classics of the Foreign Film. p148-53.
Commonweal. Mar 22, 1946, v43, p573-74.
Cue. Mar 2, 1946, p14-15.
Dictionary of Films. p316-17.
Film Daily. Mar 7, 1946, p6.
Hollywood Quarterly. Oct 1946, v2, p91-96.
The International Dictionary of Films and Filmmakers. v1,
p398-400.
Italian Cinema (Bondanella). p37-42+.
The Italian Cinema (Leprohon). p91-94.
Life. Mar 4, 1946, v20, p111-12+.
Motion Picture Herald Product Digest. Mar 2, 1946, p2870.
The Nation. Apr 13, 1946, v162, p443.
The New Republic. Jul 15, 1946, v115, p46.
The New York Times. Feb 26, 1946, p21.
The New Yorker. Mar 2, 1946, p81.
Newsweek. Mar 4, 1946, v27, p86.
Passion and Defiance. p62-65+.
Patterns of Realism. p67-74.
PM. Feb 10, 1946, p10.
Roberto Rossellini (Guarner). p13-18.
Rossellini: The War Trilogy. p1-160.
Saturday Review. Apr 6, 1946, v29, p16-18.
Selected Film Criticism: Foreign Films, 1930-1950. p126-28.
Seventy Years of Cinema. p53-54.
Theatre Arts. Apr 1946, v30, p213-15+.
Time. Mar 4, 1946, v47, p94+.
Variety. Dec 24, 1945, p12.
Variety. Feb 27, 1946, p8.
Vintage Films. p76-80.

Orage (Also titled: The Storm; The Tempest) (FR;
Allégret, Marc; 1937)
Film Daily. Dec 13, 1938, p9.
Graham Greene on Film. p190-92.
London Mercury. Jul 1938, v38, p256.
Motion Picture Herald. Feb 12, 1938, p50, 52.
The New Statesman and Nation. Jun 11, 1938, v15, p991.
The New York Times. Dec 12, 1938, p26.
The New Yorker. Dec 17, 1938, v14, p88.
Rob Wagner's Script. Jun 10, 1939, v21, p17.
The Spectator. Jun 10, 1938, v160, p1056.
Variety. Mar 23, 1938, p17.
World Film News. Aug 1938, v3, p175.

Orchids to You (US; Seiter, William A.; 1935)
Film Daily. Aug 10, 1935, p4.
Hollywood Reporter. Jun 10, 1935, p4.
Literary Digest. Aug 17, 1935, v120, p28.
Motion Picture Herald. Jun 22, 1935, p70.
Movie Classic. Sep 1935, v9, p88.
The New York Times. Aug 10, 1935, p16.
Time. Jul 15, 1935, v26, p38.
Variety. Aug 14, 1935, p15.

Oriental Dream *See* Kismet

Orphans of the Storm (US; Griffith, D.W.; 1922)
American Silent Film. p178-86.
BFI/Monthly Film Bulletin. Jan 1975, v42, p20.
Film Daily. Jan 8, 1922, p3.
The Films of D.W. Griffith. p169.
The Films of the Twenties. p54-60.
Magill's Survey of Cinema. Silent Films. v2, p831-34.
The Moving Picture World. Dec 31, 1921, p1125.
The New York Times. Jan 29, 1922, sec6, p2.
Photoplay. Jul 1922, p93.
Selected Film Criticism, 1921-1930. p213-14.
Spellbound in Darkness. p255-57.
Variety. Jan 6, 1922, p42.
The Village Voice. Oct 7, 1971, p71.

O.S.S. (US; Pichel, Irving; 1946)
Commonweal. Jul 12, 1946, v44, p309.
Film Daily. May 15, 1946, p10.
The Films of Alan Ladd. p103-08.
Hollywood Reporter. May 13, 1946, p3.
Motion Picture Herald Product Digest. May 18, 1946, p2997.
The New York Times. May 27, 1946, p15.
The New Yorker. Jun 1, 1946, v27, p75.
Newsweek. Jun 3, 1946, p89.
Time. Jun 10, 1946, v47, p101.
Variety. May 15, 1946, p8.

Ossessione (Also titled: Amants Diaboliques, Les) (IT; Visconti, Luchino; 1942)
Film Quarterly. Spr 1960, v8, p11-22.
A History of Narrative Film. p381-82.
The International Dictionary of Films and Filmmakers. v1, p347-48.
The Italian Cinema (Leprohon). p86-89.
Magill's Survey of Cinema. Foreign Language Films. v5, p2328-34.
The New York Times. Oct 2, 1976, p15.
The New Yorker. Jun 13, 1977, v53, p70.
Patterns of Realism. p53-60.
Sight and Sound. Spr 1948, v17, p25-26.
Variety. Nov 10, 1976, p6.
Variety. Sep 8, 1976, p7.

Otages, Les (Also titled: The Hostages) (FR; Bernard, Raymond; 1939)
Graham Greene on Film. p234-35.
Motion Picture Herald. Apr 22, 1939, p39, 42.
The New Statesman and Nation. Jul 15, 1939, v18, p84.
The Spectator. Jul 21, 1939, v163, p92.
The Tatler. Jul 26, 1939, v153, p144.
Variety. May 3, 1939, p20.

Othello (US; 1910)
The Moving Picture World. Apr 30, 1910, p690.
Selected Film Criticism, 1896-1911. p74-75.

Other Men's Women (US; Wellman, William A.; 1931)
Film Daily. Apr 26, 1931, p10.
The Films of James Cagney. p45-46.
The New York Times. Apr 20, 1931, p16.
Variety. Apr 22, 1931, p19.
William A. Wellman (Thompson). p108-10.

Our Betters (US; Cukor, George; 1933)
BFI/Monthly Film Bulletin. Nov 1977, v44, p247.
Collier's. Apr 1933, v91, p18.
Film Daily. Feb 24, 1933, p7.
Garbo and the Night Watchman. p233-34.
George Cukor (Phillips). p37-39.
Hollywood Reporter. Feb 18, 1933, p3.
Judge. Apr 1933, v104, p21.
Motion Picture Herald. Mar 4, 1933, p48.
The Nation. Mar 15, 1933, v136, p299.
The New York Times. Feb 24, 1933, p13.

The New Yorker. Mar 4, 1933, v9, p52.
Newsweek. Mar 4, 1933, v1, p28.
Time. Mar 6, 1933, v21, p24.
Variety. Feb 28, 1933, p15.

Our Blushing Brides (Also titled: Blushing Brides) (US; Beaumont, Harry; 1930)
Exhibitors Herald-World. Aug 9, 1930, p33.
Film Daily. Aug 3, 1930, p10.
The Films of Joan Crawford. p78-79.
Life. Aug 22, 1930, v96, p19.
The New York Times. Aug 2, 1930, p16.
The New York Times. Aug 17, 1930, p3.
The New Yorker. Aug 9, 1930, v6, p56.
Outlook and Independent. Aug 13, 1930, v155, p591.
Variety. Aug 6, 1930, p21.

Our Daily Bread (US; Vidor, King; 1934)
Film Daily. Aug 8, 1934, p7.
Hollywood Reporter. Jun 30, 1934, p3.
The Hollywood Social Problem Films. p58-63+.
Literary Digest. Oct 20, 1934, v118, p31.
Magill's Survey of Cinema. Series I. v3, p1284-86.
Motion Picture Herald. Aug 18, 1934, p38.
The New Republic. Aug 29, 1934, v80, p75.
The New York Times. Oct 3, 1934, p25.
Newsweek. Aug 11, 1934, v4, p20.
Time. Oct 8, 1934, v24, p36.
Variety. Oct 9, 1934, p18.

Our Dancing Daughters (US; Beaumont, Harry; 1928)
American Silent Film. p312-13+.
Classics of the Silent Screen. p110-11.
Exhibitor's Herald-World and Moving Picture World. Sep 22, 1928, p50.
Film Daily. Oct 14, 1928, p4.
The Film Spectator. Jun 9, 1928, v5, p19.
The Film Spectator. Jun 23, 1928, v5, p9-10.
The Films of Joan Crawford. p64-66.
Magill's Survey of Cinema. Silent Films. v2, p835-38.
The New York Times. Oct 8, 1928, p14.
Photoplay. Aug 1928, v34, p56.
Selected Film Criticism, 1921-1920. p214.
Variety. Oct 10, 1928, p22.

Our Hospitality (US; Keaton, Buster; 1923)
Buster Keaton (Robinson). p50-52.
Cinema, the Magic Vehicle. v1, p88-89.
The Comic Mind. p141-42.
Exceptional Photoplays. Oct 1923, v4, p5.
The Film Career of Buster Keaton. p50-52.
Film Daily. Nov 18, 1923, p11.
Magill's Survey of Cinema. Silent Films. v2, p839-41.
The Moving Picture World. Nov 24, 1923, p405.
The New York Times. Dec 10, 1923, p20.
The Silent Clowns. p213-17.
Variety. Dec 13, 1923, p22.

Our Little Girl (US; Robertson, John S.; 1935)
Film Daily. Jun 7, 1935, p10.
The Films of Shirley Temple. p152-55.
Hollywood Reporter. May 17, 1935, p3.
Motion Picture Herald. Jun 15, 1935, p78.
The New York Times. Jun 7, 1935, p24.
Time. Jun 17, 1935, v25, p40.
Variety. Jun 12, 1935, p12.

Our Mrs. McChesney (US; Ince, Ralph; 1918)
Exhibitor's Trade Review. Aug 31, 1918, p1078-79, 1089.
Motion Picture News. Aug 31, 1918, p1367.
The Moving Picture World. Aug 31, 1918, p1302.
The Moving Picture World. Sep 14, 1918, p1613.
The New York Times. Aug 19, 1918, p7.
Variety. Aug 23, 1918, p40.
Wid's Daily. Aug 25, 1918, p27-28.

Our Neighbors, the Carters (US; Murphy, Ralph; 1939)
Film Daily. Nov 3, 1939, p6.
Graham Greene on Film. p258.
Motion Picture Herald. Nov 4, 1939, p47.
The New Statesman and Nation. Dec 16, 1939, v18, p893.
The New York Times. Feb 15, 1940, p15.
Rob Wagner's Script. Nov 18, 1939, v22, p17-18.
The Spectator. Dec 22, 1939, v163, p900.
Variety. Nov 8, 1939, p18.

Our Relations (US; Lachman, Harry; 1936)
Film Daily. Jul 14, 1936, p11.
Hollywood Reporter. Jul 10, 1936, p3.
Laurel & Hardy. p329-42.
Motion Picture Herald. Nov 21, 1936, p54-55.
The New York Times. Nov 11, 1936, p55.
Rob Wagner's Script. Nov 28, 1936, v16, p11.
Variety. Nov 18, 1936, p13.

Our Sea *See* Mare Nostrum

Our Town (US; Wood, Sam; 1940)
Commonweal. Jun 7, 1940, v32, p149.
The Film Criticism of Otis Ferguson. p300-02.
Film Daily. May 13, 1940, p8.
The Films of William Holden. p45-47.
Hollywood Spectator. Jun 1, 1940, v15, p5-6.
Life. May 27, 1940, v8, p53-55.
The London Times. Nov 25, 1940, p6.
Lorentz on Film. p196-97.
Magic and Myth of the Movies. p92-93.
Magill's Survey of Cinema. Series II. v4, p1834-37.
The Nation. Jun 22, 1940, v150, p763.
The New Republic. Jun 17, 1940, v102, p824.
The New York Times. Jun 14, 1940, p25.
The New York Times. Jun 16, 1940, sec9, p3.
Newsweek. Jun 3, 1940, v15, p44+.
Rob Wagner's Script. Jun 15, 1940, v24, p16.
Selected Film Criticism, 1931-1940. p189-90.
Sight and Sound. Mar 1951, v19, p433-48.
Theatre Arts. Nov 1940, v24, p815-24.
Time. Jun 3, 1940, v35, p72.
Variety. May 15, 1940, p16.

Out of the Fog (US; Capellani, Albert; 1919)
Exhibitor's Trade Review. Feb 15, 1919, p855.
Motion Picture News. Feb 15, 1919, p1063.
The Moving Picture World. Jan 18, 1919, p368.
The Moving Picture World. Feb 22, 1919, p1015, 1080.
The New York Times. Feb 10, 1919, p11.
Variety. Feb 21, 1919, p68.
Wid's Daily. Feb 9, 1919, p10.

Out of the Fog (US; Litvak, Anatole; 1941)
Commonweal. Jul 4, 1941, v34, p258.
Film Daily. Jun 11, 1941, p9.
The Films of John Garfield. p96-99.
Hollywood Reporter. Jun 6, 1941, p20.
Motion Picture Herald Product Digest. Jun 14, 1941, p147.
The Nation. Jun 21, 1941, v152, p732.
The New York Times. Jun 21, 1941, p20.
The New Yorker. Jun 21, 1941, v17, p70.
Newsweek. Jun 23, 1941, v17, p53.
Variety. Jun 11, 1941, p14.

Out of the Past (US; Tourneur, Jacques; 1947)
Classics of the Gangster Film. p149-55.
Film Daily. Nov 20, 1947, p8.
The Films of Kirk Douglas. p37-39.
Hollywood Reporter. Nov 14, 1947, p3.
Magill's Survey of Cinema, Series I. v3, p1287-89.
Motion Picture Herald Product Digest. Nov 22, 1947, p3942.
The New York Times. Nov 26, 1947, p18.
Newsweek. Dec 8, 1947, v30, p84.
Robert Mitchum on the Screen. p100-01.

Time. Dec 15, 1947, v50, p104.
Variety. Nov 19, 1947, p8.

Out West With the Hardys (US; Seitz, George B.; 1938)
Commonweal. Dec 23, 1938, v29, p245.
Film Daily. Dec 12, 1938, p10.
Hollywood Reporter. Nov 19, 1938, p3.
Hollywood Spectator. Nov 26, 1938, v13, p13-14.
Motion Picture Herald. Nov 26, 1938, p24, 27.
The New Masses. Dec 20, 1938, v29, p30.
The New Statesman and Nation. Feb 18, 1939, v17, p246.
The New York Times. Dec 9, 1938, p31.
The New Yorker. Dec 17, 1938, v14, p87-88.
Rob Wagner's Script. Dec 24, 1938, v20, p11.
Variety. Nov 23, 1938, p14.

The Outcasts of Poker Flat (US; Ford, John; 1919)
Exhibitor's Trade Review. Jun 28, 1919, p326.
Motion Picture News. Jun 28, 1919, p227.
Motion Picture News. Jul 12, 1919, p531-32.
The Moving Picture World. Jun 28, 1919, p2007.
Variety. Jul 11, 1919, p61.
Wid's Daily. Jun 29, 1919, p17.

The Outcasts of Poker Flats (US; Cabanne, Christy; 1937)
Film Daily. Mar 16, 1937, p12.
Hollywood Reporter. Mar 12, 1937, p3.
Literary Digest. Mar 27, 1937, v123, p21.
Motion Picture Herald. Mar 20, 1937, p49.
The New York Times. Apr 27, 1937, p18.
Time. Apr 26, 1937, v29, p41.
Variety. May 5, 1937, p27.

The Outlaw (US; Hughes, Howard; Hawks, Howard; 1943)
Commonweal. Jul 26, 1946, v44, p360.
Film Daily. Feb 15, 1943, p7.
Hollywood Reporter. Feb 8, 1943, p3.
Life. Jan 20, 1941, v10, p42+.
Motion Picture Herald Product Digest. Feb 13, 1943, p1157.
The New York Times. Sep 12, 1947, p18.
Rob Wagner's Script. Apr 27, 1946, v32, p14.
Selected Film Criticism, 1941-1950. p177-80.
Time. Mar 25, 1946, v47, p98.
Time. Jun 10, 1946, v47, p98.
Time. Feb 17, 1947, v49, p102.
Variety. Feb 10, 1943, p8.
Variety. Mar 20, 1946, p8.

The Outsider (GB; Lachman, Harry; 1931)
Around Cinemas. p161-63.
Film Daily. Mar 29, 1933, p8.
Motion Picture Herald. May 2, 1931, p42.
The New York Times. Jun 7, 1931, p6.
Variety. Apr 29, 1931, p50.
Variety. Apr 4, 1933, p15.

Outward Bound (US; Milton, Robert; 1930)
Commonweal. Oct 1, 1930, v12, p555-56.
Exhibitors Herald-World. Sep 27, 1930, p39.
Film Daily. Sep 21, 1930, p31.
The Films of the Thirties. p41-42.
Life. Oct 3, 1930, v96, p20.
Literary Digest. Oct 4, 1930, v107, p19-20.
The Nation. Oct 15, 1930, v131, p424.
National Board of Review Magazine. Oct 1930, v5, p8.
The New York Times. Sep 18, 1930, p28.
The New York Times. Oct 16, 1930, p29.
The New Yorker. Sep 27, 1930, v6, p63.
Outlook and Independent. Oct 1, 1930, v156, p192.
Time. Sep 29, 1930, v16, p38.
Variety. Sep 24, 1930, p23.

Over the Hill to the Poorhouse (US; Millarde, Harry; 1920)
Exceptional Photoplays. Jan-Feb 1921, p5.

Motion Picture News. Oct 2, 1920, p2703.
The Moving Picture World. Oct 2, 1920, p623, 683.
The New York Times. Sep 18, 1920, p16.
Selected Film Criticism, 1912-1920. p185-87.
Variety. Sep 24, 1920, p44.
Wid's Daily. Sep 26, 1920, p4.

The Ox-Bow Incident (Also titled: Strange Incident) (US; Wellman, William A.; 1942)
Best Film Plays, 1943-44. p511-60.
Cinema: The Novel into Films. p361-63.
Commonweal. Jun 4, 1943, v38, p169.
The Film and the Public. p146-49.
Film Daily. May 10, 1943, p6.
The Filming of the West. p527-29.
The Films of Anthony Quinn. p92-93.
The Films of Henry Fonda. p124-26.
The Films of the Forties. p85-87.
The Fondas (Springer). p129-32.
Hollywood Reporter. May 6, 1943, p3.
Life. May 24, 1943, v14, p41-42+.
Literature/Film Quarterly. Sum 1976, v4, p240-48.
Magic Moments from the Movies. p122.
Magill's Survey of Cinema. Series I. v3, p1290-92.
The Making of the Great Westerns. p122-36.
Motion Picture Exhibitor. May 19, 1943, v30, n2, sec2, p1269.
Motion Picture Herald Product Digest. May 8, 1943, p1302.
The New Republic. May 17, 1943, v108, p669-70.
The New York Times. May 10, 1943, p15.
The New York Times. May 16, 1943, sec2, p3.
The New Yorker. May 15, 1943, v19, p51.
Novels into Film. p170-96.
Our Modern Art. p1-8.
Scholastic. Apr 19, 1943, v42, p35.
Time. May 3, 1943, v41, p94.
Variety. May 15, 1943, p8.
Vintage Films. p68-71.
William A. Wellman (Thompson). p207-11+.
50 Classic Motion Pictures. p194-99.

Pacific Express *See* Union Pacific

Pacific Liner (US; Landers, Lew; 1938)
Canadian Magazine. Feb 1939, v91, p44.
Commonweal. Jan 20, 1939, v29, p358.
Film Daily. Jan 6, 1939, p6.
Hollywood Reporter. Dec 22, 1938, p3.
Motion Picture Herald. Dec 31, 1938, p52, 54.
The New York Times. Jan 18, 1939, p17.
The New Yorker. Jan 21, 1939, v14, p59.
Rob Wagner's Script. Jan 14, 1939, v20, p18.
Time. Jan 9, 1939, v33, p37.
Variety. Dec 28, 1938, p13.

Page Miss Glory (US; LeRoy, Mervyn; 1935)
Film Daily. Jul 8, 1935, p17.
Hollywood Reporter. Jul 3, 1935, p9.
Literary Digest. Sep 7, 1935, v120, p30.
Mervyn LeRoy: Take One. p125, 226.
Motion Picture Herald. Jul 13, 1935, p57.
The New York Times. Aug 29, 1935, p25.
Rob Wagner's Script. Aug 31, 1935, v14, p10-11.
The Spectator. Dec 13, 1935, v155, p984.
Time. Sep 9, 1935, v26, p47.
Variety. Sep 4, 1935, p14.

Pagliacci (Also titled: A Clown Must Laugh) (GB; Grune, Karl; 1937)
Film Daily. Oct 17, 1938, p7.
Motion Picture Herald. Feb 6, 1937, p52.
Motion Picture Herald. Jan 9, 1937, p16-17.
The New York Times. Oct 12, 1938, p35.
Variety. Dec 30, 1936, p27.
World Film News. May 1937, v2, p23-24.

Pagliacci (US; Coffman, Joe W.; 1931)
Film Daily. Mar 1, 1931, p11.
Judge. Mar 14, 1931, v100, p22.
Motion Picture Herald. Mar 7, 1931, p61.
The New York Times. Feb 21, 1931, p15.
The New Yorker. Mar 7, 1931, v7, p72.
Time. Mar 2, 1931, v17, p26.
Variety. Feb 25, 1931, p22.

The Painted Lady (US; 1912)
The New York Dramatic Mirror. Oct 30, 1912, p31.
Selected Film Criticism, 1912-1920. p188.

The Painted Lady (US; Bennett, Chester; 1924)
Film Daily. Sep 28, 1924, p6.
The Moving Picture World. Oct 4, 1924, p628.

The Painted Veil (US; Boleslavski, Richard; 1934)
Film Daily. Nov 24, 1934, p3.
The Films of Greta Garbo. p125-28.
Life. Feb 1935, v102, p32.
Literary Digest. Dec 22, 1934, v118, p27.
Motion Picture Herald. Nov 10, 1934, p39.
The Nation. Dec 19, 1934, v139, p722.
The New York Times. Dec 7, 1934, p29.
Newsweek. Apr 15, 1934, v4, p22.
Rob Wagner's Script. Jan 12, 1935, v12, p10.
Selected Film Criticism, 1931-1940. p192-93.
Time. Dec 3, 1934, v24, p45.
Variety. Dec 11, 1934, p19.

A Pair of Silk Stockings (US; Edwards, Walter; 1918)
Exhibitor's Trade Review. Jul 20, 1918, p588.
Motion Picture News. Jul 20, 1918, p361.
Motion Picture News. Jul 27, 1918, p642.
The Moving Picture World. Jul 27, 1918, p587.
The Moving Picture World. Aug 3, 1918, p723.
Photoplay. Oct 1918, v14, p102.
Photoplay. Nov 1918, v14, p125.
Variety. Jul 19, 1918, p38.
Wid's Daily. Jul 14, 1918, p9-10.

Paisan (Also titled: Paisà) (IT; Rossellini, Roberto; 1946)
BFI/Monthly Film Bulletin. Nov 1980, v47, p226-27.
Cinema, the Magic Vehicle. v1, p417-18.
Commonweal. Apr 23, 1948, v48, p654.
Film Comment. Fall 1964, v2, p17-21.
Film Culture. Wint 1963-64, v31, p61-67.
Film Daily. Feb 26, 1948, p6.
Films and Filming. Feb 1966, v12, p36-42.
The Great Films. p181-84.
Hollywood Reporter. Jan 23, 1948, p3.
The International Dictionary of Films and Filmmakers. v1, p353-54.
Italian Cinema (Bondanella). p42-50+.
The Italian Cinema (Leprohon). p94-95.
Life. Jul 19, 1948, v25, p41-44.
The New Republic. Mar 29, 1948, v118, p31.
The New York Times. Mar 30, 1948, p26.
The New Yorker. Nov 9, 1946, v22, p75.
The New Yorker. Mar 27, 1948, v24, p71.
Newsweek. Apr 12, 1948, v31, p87.
Passion and Defiance. p67-70+.
Patterns of Realism. p75-80.
Roberto Rossellini (Guarner). p19-24.
Rossellini: The War Trilogy. p161-348.
Selected Film Criticism: Foreign Films, 1930-1950. p129-30.
Sight and Sound. Aut 1946, v15, p83-84.
Springtime in Italy. p89-113.
Time. Apr 19, 1948, v51, p92+.
Variety. Feb 11, 1948, p14.

The Paleface (US; McLeod, Norman Z.; 1948)
Collier's. Nov 27, 1948, v122, p76.
Film Daily. Oct 21, 1948, p8.
Hollywood Reporter. Dec 20, 1948, p3.

Life. Jan 3, 1949, v26, p61.
Magill's Survey of Cinema. Series II. v4, p1850-52.
Motion Picture Herald Product Digest. Oct 30, 1948, p4366.
The Nation. Jan 15, 1949, v168, p81.
The New Republic. Dec 27, 1948, v119, p30.
The New York Times. Dec 16, 1948, p41.
The New Yorker. Dec 25, 1948, v24, p37.
Newsweek. Dec 27, 1948, v32, p69.
Time. Dec 27, 1948, v52, p58.
Variety. Oct 20, 1948, p11.

The Palm Beach Story (US; Sturges, Preston; 1942)
Between Flops. p159-77+.
Claudette Colbert (Quirk). p126-27.
Commonweal. Jan 1, 1943, v37, p280.
Film Daily. Nov 2, 1942, p11.
The Films of the Forties. p77-79.
Halliwell's Hundred. p262-66.
Hollywood Reporter. Nov 3, 1942, p3.
Life. Dec 7, 1942, v13, p61+.
The London Times. Aug 26, 1943, p6.
Magill's Survey of Cinema. Series II. v4, p1853-55.
Motion Picture Exhibitor. Nov 4, 1942, v28, n26, sec2, p1147.
Motion Picture Herald Product Digest. Nov 7, 1942, v993.
The New York Times. Dec 11, 1942, p33.
The New York Times. Dec 13, 1942, sec8, p3.
Newsweek. Dec 14, 1942, v20, p94.
Postscript. Spr-Summ 1982, v1, p33-47.
Preston Sturges: A Guide to References and Resources. p60-63.
Script. May 1948, p41.
Selected Film Criticism, 1941-1950. p180-82.
Time. Jan 4, 1943, v151, p87.
Variety. Nov 4, 1942, p8.
The Village Voice. Jun 18, 1964, v9, p10+.

Palmy Days (US; Sutherland, Edward; 1931)
The Busby Berkeley Book. p40-41.
Film Daily. Sep 27, 1931, p18.
Hollywood Reporter. Aug 3, 1931, p3.
Judge. Oct 24, 1931, v101, p18.
Life. Oct 23, 1931, v98, p18.
Motion Picture Herald. Sep 5, 1931, p44.
The New York Times. May 10, 1931, p4.
The New York Times. Sep 24, 1931, p21.
The New York Times. Oct 4, 1931, p5.
The New Yorker. Oct 3, 1931, v7, p70.
Outlook and Independent. Oct 7, 1931, v159, p183.
Samuel Goldwyn Presents. p107-09.
Time. Oct 5, 1931, v18, p21.
Variety. Sep 29, 1931, p14.

Pandora's Box (German title: Büchse der Pandora, Die;
    Also titled: Lulu; Loulou) (GER; Pabst, G.W.; 1928)
BFI/Monthly Film Bulletin. May 1974, v41, p111-12.
Close-Up. Oct 1928, p57-58.
Close-Up. Apr 1929, p24-30.
Close-Up. May 1930, p423-24.
Film Daily. Dec 8, 1929, p8.
From Caligari to Hitler. p178-79.
G.W. Pabst. p51-63.
The Haunted Screen. p27-29, 278-80, 295-303+.
The International Dictionary of Films and Filmmakers. v1,
    p71-72.
Magill's Survey of Cinema. Silent Films. v2, p842-46.
The New York Times. Dec 2, 1929, p28.
Pandora's Box.
Sight and Sound. Sum 1965, v34, p123-27.
Variety. Dec 11, 1929, p39.

Panthea (US; Dwan, Allan; 1917)
Allan Dwan: The Last Pioneer. p42-44.
Fifty Great American Silent Films, 1912-1920. p71-73.
Magill's Survey of Cinema. Silent Films. v2, p847-89.
The Moving Picture World. Jan 27, 1917, p540.
The Moving Picture World. Jan 6, 1917, p139.

The New York Dramatic Mirror. Jan 20, 1917, p26.
The New York Times. Jan 8, 1917, p9.
Photoplay. Apr 1917, v11, p77-79.
Selected Film Criticism, 1912-1920. p188-89.
Variety. Jan 12, 1917, p26.
Wid's Daily. Jan 11, 1917, p248.

Parachute Jumper (US; Green, Alfred E.; 1932)
Bette Davis: Her Films and Career. p38-39.
Film Daily. Jan 27, 1933, p5.
Garbo and the Night Watchman. p228.
Hollywood Reporter. Dec 20, 1932, p3.
Motion Picture Herald. Dec 31, 1932, p38.
The New York Times. Jan 26, 1933, p12.
Rob Wagner's Script. Dec 31, 1932, v8, p8.
Time. Feb 6, 1933, v21, p24.
Variety. Jan 31, 1933, p12.

The Paradine Case (US; Hitchcock, Alfred; 1948)
Alfred Hitchcock: The First Forty-Four Films. p86-90.
The Art of Alfred Hitchcock. p175-84.
Commonweal. Jan 23, 1948, v47, p373.
David O'Selznick's Hollywood. p374-80.
The Films of Alfred Hitchcock. p130-33.
The Films of Gregory Peck. p78-82.
Fortnight. Jan 16, 1948, v4, p25-26.
Hitchcock (Truffaut). p167-73+.
Hollywood Reporter. Dec 30, 1947, p3.
Life. Jan 19, 1948, v24, p65-66.
Motion Picture Herald Product Digest. Jan 3, 1948, p4001.
New Movies. Jan 1, 1948, v23, p4-5.
New Republic. Jan 19, 1948, v118, p36.
The New York Times. Jan 9, 1948, p26.
The New Yorker. Jan 10, 1948, v23, p77.
Newsweek. Jan 19, 1948, v31, p89.
Selected Film Criticism, 1941-1950. p182-184.
Theatre Arts. Nov 1947, v31, p50.
Time. Jan 12, 1948, v51, p54+.
Variety. Dec 31, 1947, p10.

Paradise for Three (US; Buzzell, Edward; 1938)
Film Daily. Jan 20, 1938, p6.
Hollywood Reporter. Jan 15, 1938, p3.
Motion Picture Herald. Jan 22, 1938, p38.
The New York Times. Feb 16, 1938, p17.
The New Yorker. Feb 19, 1938, v14, p58-59.
Rob Wagner's Script. Mar 5, 1938, v19, p7.
Variety. Jan 19, 1938, p19.

Paramount on Parade (US; Arzner, Dorothy; Brower,
    Otto; Goulding, Edmund; Heerman, Victor; Knopf,
    Edwin H.; Lee, Rowland V.; Lubitsch, Ernst;
    Mendes, Lothar; Schertzinger, Victor; Sutherland,
    Edward; Tuttle, Frank; 1930)
The American Films of Ernst Lubitsch. p117-18.
Chevalier. p82-86.
Exhibitors Herald-World. Apr 26, 1930, p28.
Exhibitors Herald-World. May 10, 1930, p32.
Film Daily. Apr 20, 1930, p10.
Film Society Review. Jan 1969, v4, p20.
The Film Spectator. May 10, 1930, v9, p9-10.
The Film Spectator. Apr 12, 1930, v9, p23-24.
The Films of Fredric March. p58-59.
The Films of Gary Cooper. p74-74.
The Films of Nancy Carroll. p106-09.
The Hollywood Musical. p48.
Judge. May 24, 1930, v98, p23.
Life. May 16, 1930, v95, p18.
The Nation. May 14, 1930, v130, p578.
The New York Times. Apr 21, 1930, p20.
The New York Times. Apr 27, 1930, p5.
The New Yorker. Apr 26, 1930, v6, p81.
Outlook and Independent. Apr 30, 1930, v154, p712.
Rob Wagner's Script. Jun 14, 1930, v3, p10.
Selected Film Criticism, 1921-1930. p215-16.

Time. May 5, 1930, v15, p32.
Variety. Apr 23, 1930, p26.

Paris Commune (Also titled: People of the Eleventh
  Legion; Down in Paris) (USSR; Roshal, Gregori;
  1937)
Film Daily. Jun 14, 1937, p13.
The New Masses. Jun 15, 1937, v23, p29.
The New York Times. Jun 2, 1937, p20.
Partisan Review. Aug-Sep 1938, v5, p52-53.
Variety. May 9, 1937, p15.

Paris Honeymoon (US; Tuttle, Frank; 1938)
Film Daily. Jan 26, 1939, p12.
The Films of Bing Crosby. p94-98.
Hollywood Reporter. Dec 14, 1938, p3.
Motion Picture Herald. Dec 17, 1938, p52.
The New York Times. Jan 26, 1939, p17.
Time. Feb 6, 1939, v33, p36.
Variety. Dec 21, 1938, p14.

Paris in Spring (Also titled: Paris Love Song) (US;
  Milestone, Lewis; 1935)
Film Daily. May 28, 1935, p10.
Graham Greene on Film. p7.
Hollywood Reporter. May 25, 1935, p3.
Lewis Milestone (Millichap). p81-82.
Motion Picture Herald. Jun 1, 1935, p47.
The New York Times. Jul 13, 1935, p16.
The New Yorker. Jul 20, 1935, v11, p48.
Rob Wagner's Script. Aug 10, 1935, v13, p8.
The Spectator. Jul 12, 1935, v155, p54.
Time. Jul 15, 1935, v26, p41.
Variety. Jul 17, 1935, p27.

Paris-Mediterranée (FR; May, Joe; 1932)
The New Statesman and Nation. Oct 14, 1933, v6, p446.
The New York Times. Mar 27, 1932, p6.
The Spectator. Oct 6, 1933, v151, p441.
Variety. Mar 8, 1932, p23.

Parlor, Bedroom and Bath (US; Sedgwick, Edward; 1931)
Film Daily. Apr 5, 1931, p10.
Judge. May 2, 1931, v100, p20.
Life. Apr 24, 1931, v97, p22.
Motion Picture Herald. Jan 31, 1931, p53-54.
The New York Times. Apr 4, 1931, p23.
The New York Times. Feb 14, 1932, p6.
Time. Apr 13, 1931, v17, p72.
Variety. Apr 8, 1931, p19.

Parnell (US; Stahl, John M.; 1937)
Canadian Magazine. Apr 1937, v87, p37.
Canadian Magazine. Jun 1937, v87, p44.
Commonweal. Jun 18, 1937, v26, p216.
Film Daily. Jun 7, 1937, p9.
The Films of Clark Gable. p181.
The Films of Myrna Loy. p203.
Graham Greene on Film. p155-56.
Hollywood Reporter. Jun 3, 1937, p3.
Hollywood Spectator. Jun 19, 1937, v12, p8.
Life. Jun 14, 1937, v2, p43-46.
Literary Digest. Jun 5, 1937, v123, p36-39.
Motion Picture Herald. Jun 12, 1937, p78.
Motion Picture Herald. Feb 13, 1937, p16-17.
The New Statesman and Nation. Jul 17, 1937, v14, p113.
The New York Times. Jun 4, 1937, p27.
The New Yorker. Jun 12, 1937, v13, p62-63.
Newsweek. Jun 12, 1937, v9, p28.
Rob Wagner's Script. Jun 12, 1937, v17, p8.
The Spectator. Jul 23, 1937, v159, p143.
Stage. Feb 1937, v14, p62-63.
The Tatler. Jul 28, 1937, v145, p148.
Time. Jun 14, 1937, v29, p25.
Variety. Jun 9, 1937, p15.
World Film News. Aug 1937, v2, p26.

Part I of the Maxim Trilogy *See* The Youth of Maxim

Partie de Campagne, Une (Also titled: A Day in the
  Country; Ways of Love) (FR; Renoir, Jean; 1936;
  1950)
Cinema, the Magic Vehicle. v1, p251-53.
The Comic Mind: Comedy and the Movies. p237.
Commonweal. Jan 12, 1951, v53, p351.
Dictionary of Films. p393-94.
Eighty Years of Cinema. p109-10.
Film Daily. Jan 4, 1951, p.
The Great French Films. p63-66.
The International Dictionary of Films and Filmmakers. v1,
  p355-56.
Jean Renoir: A Guide to References and Resources. p96-99.
Jean Renoir: My Life and My Films. p128-30.
Jean Renoir: The French Films, 1924-1939. p234-56.
Jean Renoir: The World of His Films. p34-36.
Kiss Kiss Bang Bang. p314-15.
Library Journal. Mar 1, 1951, v76, p418.
Life. Jan 15, 1951, v30, p59-60+.
Love in the Film. p124-26.
Magill's Survey of Cinema. Foreign Language Films. v2, p733-
  38.
The Nation. Jan 13, 1951, v172, p45.
The New Republic. Jan 1, 1951, v124, p23.
The New York Times. Dec 13, 1950, p50.
The New Yorker. Dec 16, 1950, v26, p143.
Newsweek. Dec 18, 1950, v36, p93.
Saturday Review. Jan 27, 1951, v34, p28.
Time. Dec 18, 1950, v56, p94+.
Variety. Dec 20, 1950, p18.

The Party Ticket *See* Anna

A Pass to Life *See* The Road to Life

Passage to Marseilles (US; Curtiz, Michael; 1944)
Commonweal. Apr 7, 1944, v39, p624.
The Films of Humphrey Bogart. p115-16.
The Films of Peter Lorre. p162-64.
Hollywood Reporter. Feb 16, 1944, p3.
Humphrey Bogart: The Man and his Films. p128-30.
The New York Times. Feb 17, 1944, p12.
The New Yorker. Feb 19, 1944, v20, p44+.
Newsweek. Feb 28, 1944, v23, p84.
Time. Feb 28, 1944, v43, p96.
Variety. Feb 16, 1944, p10.

The Passing of the Third Floor Back (GB; Brenon,
  Herbert; 1918)
Exhibitor's Trade Review. May 4, 1918, p1770.
Motion Picture News. Apr 6, 1918, p2056.
Motion Picture News. Apr 27, 1918, p2526.
The Moving Picture World. May 11, 1918, p895, 900.
The Moving Picture World. May 18, 1918, p951.
Selected Film Criticism, 1912-1920. p190-91.
Wid's Daily. May 2, 1918, p1121.

The Passing of the Third Floor Back (GB; Viertel,
  Berthold; 1935)
Commonweal. May 15, 1936, v24, p76.
Film Daily. Apr 30, 1936, p6.
Garbo and the Night Watchman. p42.
Graham Greene on Film. p33-34.
The Great British Films. p27-29.
Hollywood Reporter. Jan 28, 1936, p2.
Hollywood Spectator. Feb 15, 1936, v10, p8.
Motion Picture Herald. Oct 19, 1935, p87.
The Nation. May 13, 1936, v142, p623-24.
The New York Times. Apr 29, 1936, p19.
Rob Wagner's Script. Feb 22, 1936, v15, p10.
The Spectator. Nov 1, 1935, v155, p718.
Variety. Sep 25, 1935, p42.
Variety. May 6, 1936, p19.

Passion *See* Madame Dubarry

The Passion Flower (US; Mille, William C. de; 1930)
Exhibitors Herald-World. Oct 25, 1930, p42.
Film Daily. Dec 21, 1930, p10.
Life. Jan 9, 1931, v97, p22.
The New York Times. Dec 22, 1930, p16.
Variety. Dec 24, 1930, p20.

The Passion of Joan of Arc (French title: Passion de
Jeanne d'Arc, La) (FR; Dreyer, Carl-Theodor; 1928)
American Film Criticism. p214-20.
Carl-Theodor Dreyer's La Passion de Jeanne d'Arc.
Classics of the Foreign Film. p42-45.
Close-Up. Jul 1928, v3, p15-23.
Dictionary of Films. p275-76.
Film Culture. Sum 1963, v29, p22-27.
Film Daily. Sep 9, 1933, p6.
Film Daily. Apr 14, 1929, p12.
Filmguide to La Passion de Jeanne d'Arc.
Films and Filming. Jun 1961, v7, p11-13, 40.
Films in Review. Aug 1964, v15, p481-82.
The Films of Carl-Theodor Dreyer. p66-92, 212-16.
Four Screenplays by Carl-Theodor Dreyer. p5-71.
French Cinema. p486-99.
French Film (Sadoul). p55-57.
From Quasimodo to Scarlett O'Hara. p107-10.
The Great French Films. p26-29.
Hollywood Quarterly. Fall 1950, v5, p53-60.
The International Dictionary of Films and Filmmakers. v1,
p356-58.
Literary Digest. Jun 8, 1929, v101, p2-3.
Magill's Survey of Cinema. Silent Films. v2, p 854-57.
Motion Picture Herald. Sep 16, 1933, p39.
The Nation. Sep 27, 1933, v137, p364.
The New Republic. Apr 10, 1929, v58, p228.
The New York Times. Jan 20, 1929, sec8, p7.
Sight and Sound. Dec 1950, v19, p337-39.
Theatre Arts. May 13, 1929, v13, p373-74.
Variety. Apr 10, 1929, p25.

The Passionate Plumber (US; Sedgwick, Edward; 1932)
Film Daily. Mar 13, 1932, p10.
Hollywood Reporter. Jan 13, 1932, p3.
Judge. Apr 9, 1932, v102, p22.
Motion Picture Herald. Mar 19, 1932, p42.
The Nation. Mar 30, 1932, v134, p380.
The New Statesman and Nation. Apr 23, 1932, v3, p526.
The New York Times. Mar 12, 1932, p19.
The New Yorker. Mar 19, 1932, v8, p77.
Rob Wagner's Script. Mar 12, 1932, v7, p12.
Time. Mar 21, 1932, v19, p38.
Variety. Mar 15, 1932, p14.

A Passport to Hell (US; Lloyd, Frank; 1932)
Film Daily. Aug 25, 1932, p8.
Hollywood Reporter. Aug 12, 1932, p3.
Motion Picture Herald. Sep 3, 1932, p43.
The New York Times. Aug 27, 1932, p13.
Time. Sep 5, 1932, v20, p40.
Variety. Aug 30, 1932, p21.

Passport to Pimlico (GB; Cornelius, Henry; 1949)
Christian Century. Apr 19, 1950, v67, p511.
Commonweal. Nov 25, 1949, v51, p213.
Film Daily. Oct 10, 1949, p8.
Hollywood Reporter. Nov 1, 1949, p3.
Magill's Survey of Cinema. Series I. v3, p1299-1301.
Motion Picture Herald Product Digest. Oct 8, 1949, p41.
The New Republic. Nov 14, 1949, v121, p37.
The New York Times. Oct 27, 1949, p35.
The New York Times Magazine. Aug 28, 1949, p42-43.
The New Yorker. Nov 5, 1949, v25, p110.
Newsweek. Nov 14, 1949, v34, p91.
Rotarian. Jun 1950, v76, p37.

Scholastic. Oct 26, 1949, v55, p29.
Selected Film Criticism: Foreign Films, 1930-1950. p130-31.
Sight and Sound. Sum 1949, v18, p90.
Time. Oct 31, 1949, v54, p78.
Variety. May 18, 1949, p8.

The Patchwork Girl of Oz (Also titled: The Ragged Girl
of Oz) (US; MacDonald, J. Farrell; Baum, L. Frank;
1914)
The Moving Picture World. Sep 26, 1914, p1737.
The Moving Picture World. Oct 3, 1914, p15, 48.
The New York Dramatic Mirror. Sep 23, 1914, p32.
Variety. Sep 26, 1914, p22.

Patria (US; Hughes, Rupert; 1917)
Photoplay. Apr 1917, v11, p172.
Selected Film Criticism, 1912-1920. p193.
Variety. Nov 24, 1916, p30.
The War, the West, and the Wilderness. p90-91.

The Patriot (US; Lubitsch, Ernst; 1928)
Ernst Lubitsch: A Guide to References and Resources. p92-95.
Exhibitor's Herald-World and Moving Picture World. Sep 22,
1928, p50.
Exhibitor's Herald-World and Moving Picture World. Sep 29,
1928, p49.
Film Daily. Aug 26, 1928, p4.
The Film Mercury. August 31, 1929, v8, p6.
The Film Spectator. Apr 28, 1928, v5, p7-8.
Lorentz on Films. p28-29.
The Lubitsch Touch. p107-14.
The New York Times. Aug 18, 1928, p7.
The New York Times. Aug 26, 1928, sec8, p5.
Photoplay. Jun 1928, v34, p53.
Selected Film Criticism, 1921-1930. p218-21.
Variety. Aug 22, 1928, p14.

Payment Deferred (US; Mendes, Lothar; 1932)
Film Daily. Nov 10, 1932, p6.
Hollywood Reporter. Sep 12, 1932, p3.
Motion Picture Herald. Sep 24, 1932, p31.
National Board of Review Magazine. Nov 1932, v7, p10.
The New York Times. Nov 8, 1932, p26.
The New Yorker. Nov 12, 1932, v8, p60.
Variety. Nov 15, 1932, p23.

The Pearl (MEX; Fernandez, Emilio; 1948)
Commonweal. Mar 5, 1948, v47, p522.
Cue. Feb 21, 1948, p18.
Film Daily. Feb 16, 1948, p4.
Fortnight. Mar 12, 1948, v4, p30.
Hollywood Reporter. Feb 11, 1948, p3.
Motion Picture Herald Product Digest. Feb 14, 1948, p4057.
The New Republic. Mar 1, 1948, v118, p26.
The New York Times. Feb 18, 1948, p36.
The New York Times Magazine. Feb 15, 1948, p34-35.
The New Yorker. Feb 28, 1948, v24, p62.
Newsweek. Mar 8, 1948, v31, p83.
Selected Film Criticism, 1930-1950. p131-33.
Time. Mar 1, 1948, v51, p84+.
Variety. Feb 11, 1948, p14.

Pearls of the Crown (French title: Perles de la Couronne,
Les; Sept Perles de la Couronne) (FR; Guitry, Sacha;
Jacque, Christian; 1937)
The Film Criticism of Otis Ferguson. p221.
Film Daily. Apr 13, 1938, p7.
Graham Greene on Film. p175.
Hollywood Reporter. Jun 15, 1937, p3.
London Mercury. Nov 1937, v37, p61.
The Nation. Apr 23, 1938, v146, p485.
National Board of Review Magazine. May 1938, v13, p14.
The New Republic. May 25, 1938, v95, p76.
The New Statesman and Nation. Oct 15, 1937, v14, p604.
The New York Times. Apr 12, 1938, p26.
The New Yorker. Apr 23, 1938, v14, p52.

Newsweek. May 2, 1938, v11, p23.
Rob Wagner's Script. Jun 11, 1938, v19, p10.
Selected Film Criticism: Foreign Films, 1930-1950. p133-35.
Sight and Sound. Aut 1937, v6, p144.
The Spectator. Oct 22, 1937, v159, p682.
Time. Apr 25, 1938, v31, p46.
Variety. Apr 13, 1938, p15.
Variety. May 26, 1937, p14.
World Film News. Dec 1937, v2, p31.

Peasants (Russian title: Krestyaniye) (USSR; Ermler, Friedrich; 1935)
Cinema, the Magic Vehicle. v1, p247-48.
Dictionary of Films. p180.
The Film Criticism of Otis Ferguson. p92-93.
Film Daily. Sep 5, 1935, p14.
Garbo and the Night Watchman. p161-64.
Kino. p325-27.
Motion Picture Herald. Sep 14, 1935, p38.
National Board of Review Magazine. Nov 1935, v10, p11.
The New Masses. Sep 10, 1935, v16, p29-30.
The New Republic. Sep 18, 1935, v84, p159-60.
The New York Times. Aug 29, 1935, p25.
Soviet Film. 1975, n215, p39.
Time. Sep 16, 1935, v26, p61.
Variety. May 29, 1935, p34.
Variety. Sep 4, 1935, p31.

Peg O' My Heart (US; Vidor, King; 1922)
Film Daily. Dec 17, 1922, p2.
The New York Times. Jan 22, 1923, p10.
Variety. Jan 25, 1923, p41.

Peggy (US; Ince, Thomas H.; 1916)
Fifty Great American Silent Films, 1912-1920. p42-44.
The Moving Picture World. Jan 22, 1916, p620.
The Moving Picture World. Mar 18, 1916, p1895.
The New York Dramatic Mirror. Jan 1, 1916, p24.
The New York Dramatic Mirror. Jan 22, 1916, p29.
Photoplay. Apr 1916, v9, p101-02.
Selected Film Criticism, 1912-1920. p194-95.
Variety. Jan 21, 1916, p27.

The Penalty (US; Worsley, Wallace; 1920)
Fifty Great American Silent Films, 1912-1920. p133-35.
Magill's Survey of Cinema. Silent Films. v2, p858-61.
Motion Picture News. Nov 27, 1920, p12.
The Moving Picture World. Aug 21, 1920, p1069.
Photoplay. Feb 1921, v19, p66.
Selected Films Criticism, 1912-1920. p195-97.
Variety. Nov 19, 1920, p34.
Wid's Daily. Nov 21, 1920, p3.

Penitentiary (US; Brahm, John; 1938)
Film Daily. Feb 5, 1938, p4.
Hollywood Reporter. Feb 2, 1938, p3.
Motion Picture Herald. Feb 5, 1938, p53.
The New York Times. Mar 7, 1938, p13.
Rob Wagner's Script. Feb 12, 1938, v19, p8-9.
Variety. Jan 26, 1938, p15.

Pennies from Heaven (US; McLeod, Norman Z.; 1936)
Film Daily. Nov 16, 1936, p7.
The Films of Bing Crosby. p80-82.
Hollywood Reporter. Nov 12, 1936, p3.
Hollywood Spectator. Nov 7, 1936, v11, p10-11.
Literary Digest. Dec 26, 1936, v122, p23.
Motion Picture Herald. Dec 19, 1936, p56, 58.
The New York Times. Dec 10, 1936, p35.
The New Yorker. Dec 19, 1936, v12, p88.
Rob Wagner's Script. Dec 19, 1936, v16, p10.
Time. Nov 23, 1936, v28, p28.
Variety. Dec 16, 1936, p14.
World Film News. May 1937, v2, p24.

Penny Serenade (US; Stevens, George; 1941)
Commonweal. May 30, 1941, v36, p136.
The Film Criticism of Otis Ferguson. p360-61.
Film Daily. Apr 16,1941, p7.
The Films of Cary Grant. p149-52.
Hollywood Reporter. Apr 16, 1941, p3.
The London Times. Jul 14, 1941, p8.
Magill's Survey of Cinema. Series II. v3, p1883-87.
Motion Picture Exhibitor. Apr 30, 1941, p737.
The New Republic. May 19, 1942, v104, p697.
The New York Times. May 23, 1941, p25.
The New Yorker. May 31, 1941, 17, p59.
Newsweek. Apr 28, 1941, v17, p63+.
Scribner's Commentator. Aug 1941, v10, p107.
Talking Pictures. p294-97.
Time. May 5, 1941, v37, p94.
Variety. Apr 16, 1941, p16.

Penrod and Sam (US; McGann, William; 1937)
Film Daily. Mar 17, 1937, p14.
Hollywood Reporter. Jan 7, 1937, p3.
Motion Picture Herald. Jan 16, 1937, p28.
The New York Times. Mar 29, 1937, p14.
Rob Wagner's Script. Apr 24, 1937, v17, p11.
Scholastic. Feb 27, 1937, v30, p28.
Time. Mar 8, 1937, v29, p53.
Variety. Mar 17, 1937, p14.

Penrod and Sam (US; Beaudine, William; 1931)
Film Daily. Sep 27, 1931, p8.
Hollywood Reporter. Aug 18, 1931, p3.
The New York Times. Sep 26, 1931, p25.
The New York Times. Jul 19, 1931, p4.
The New York Times. Oct 4, 1931, p5.
The New Yorker. Oct 3, 1931, v7, p71.
Variety. Sep 29, 1931, p22.

Pension Mimosas (FR; Feyder, Jacques; 1935)
Cinema, the Magic Vehicle. v1, p228-29.
Dictionary of Films. p279-80.
The Golden Age of French Cinema. p125-27+.
Motion Picture Herald. May 16, 1936, p36.
The New York Times. May 6, 1936, p27.

Penthouse (US; Van Dyke, W.S.; 1933)
Film Daily. Sep 9, 1933, p4.
The Films of Myrna Loy. p157-58.
Hollywood Reporter. Aug 22, 1933, p2.
Motion Picture Herald. Sep 9, 1933, p35.
New Outlook. Oct 1933, v162, p48.
The New York Times. Sep 9, 1933, p9.
The New Yorker. Sep 16, 1933, v9, p56.
Rob Wagner's Script. Oct 21, 1933, v10, p8.
Time. Sep 18, 1933, v22, p34.
Variety. Sep 12, 1933, p17.

People of the Eleventh Legion *See* Paris Commune

Pépé le Moko (FR; Duvivier, Julien; 1937)
Cinema, the Magic Vehicle. v1, p262-63.
Commonweal. Mar 21, 1941, v33, p543.
Dictionary of Films. p280.
The Golden Age of French Cinema, 1929-1939. p56-60.
Graham Greene on Film. p144-45.
The Great French Films. p71-74.
The Great Gangster Pictures. p308-09.
Hollywood Reporter. Jun 8, 1937, p10.
The International Dictionary of Films and Filmmakers. v1, p360-61.
Magill's Survey of Cinema. Foreign Language Films. v5, p2400-03.
Motion Picture Herald. Mar 20, 1937, p52.
The New Republic. Feb 17, 1941, v104, p210.
The New York Times. Mar 4, 1941, p20.
Rob Wagner's Script. Apr 19, 1941, v25, p17.
Saint Cinema: Selected Writings, 1929-1970. p100-01.

Selected Film Criticism: Foreign Films, 1930-1950. p135-37.
Sight and Sound. Spr 1937, v6, p27.
The Spectator. Apr 23, 1937, v158, p759.
The Tatler. Apr 14, 1937, v144, p52.
Time. Mar 10, 1941, v37, p89.
Variety. Mar 24, 1937, p17.
World Film News. Jun 1937, v2, p20.

Pepper (US; Tinling, James; 1936)
Canadian Magazine. Oct 1936, v86, p46.
Film Daily. Aug 8, 1936, p3.
Hollywood Reporter. Jul 9, 1936, p3.
Literary Digest. Jul 25, 1936, v122, p18.
Motion Picture Herald. Jul 18, 1936, p52.
The New York Times. Aug 24, 1936, p11.
Variety. Aug 12, 1936, p18.

Peppy Polly (US; Clifton, Elmer; 1919)
Exhibitor's Trade Review. Apr 19, 1919, p1529.
Motion Picture News. Apr 19, 1919, p2527.
The Moving Picture World. Apr 19, 1919, p432.
The New York Times. Apr 7, 1919, p11.
Variety. Apr 11, 1919, p56.
Wid's Daily. Apr 13, 1919, p13.

The Perfect Gentleman (Also titled: The Imperfect Lady)
   (US; Whelan, Tim; 1935)
Film Daily. Dec 19, 1935, p4.
Graham Greene on Film. p50.
Hollywood Reporter. Nov 30, 1935, p3.
Hollywood Spectator. Dec 21, 1935, v10, p11-12.
Motion Picture Herald. Dec 28, 1935, p65.
The New York Times. Dec 19, 1935, p33.
The Spectator. Feb 7, 1936, v156, p211.
The Tatler. Feb 5, 1936, v139, p246.
Variety. Dec 25, 1935, p15.

Perfect Sap (US; Higgin, Howard; 1927)
Film Daily. Jan 16, 1927, p8.
The New York Times. Jan 11, 1927, p18.
Variety. Jan 12, 1927, p16.

The Perfect Specimen (US; Curtiz, Michael; 1937)
Film Daily. Sep 28, 1937, p8.
Hollywood Reporter. Sep 24, 1937, p3.
Hollywood Spectator. Mar 27, 1937, v11, p9-10.
Motion Picture Herald. Oct 2, 1937, p38, 41.
The New York Times. Oct 28, 1937, p29.
Rob Wagner's Script. Nov 6, 1937, v18, p8.
Time. Nov 1, 1937, v30, p44.
Variety. Sep 29, 1937, p15.

Perfect Strangers *See* Vacation from Marriage

Perfect Understanding (US; Gardner, Cyril; 1933)
Film Daily. Feb 24, 1933, p7.
Hollywood Reporter. Feb 24, 1933, p3.
Motion Picture Herald. Mar 4, 1933, p49.
New York Times. Feb 23, 1933, p20.
Variety. Feb 28, 1933, p14.

The Perils of Pauline (US; 1914)
Magill's Survey of Cinema. Silent Films. v1, p95-100.
The Moving Picture World. Apr 4, 1914, p38.
The New York Dramatic Mirror. Apr 1, 1914, p42.
The New York Dramatic Mirror. May 13, 1914, p49.
The New York Dramatic Mirror. Oct 7, 1914, p36.
Selected Film Criticism, 1912-1920. p197-98.
Variety. Apr 10, 1914, p21.

The Perils of Pauline (US; Marshall, George; 1947)
Commonweal. Jul 25, 1947, v46, p358.
Life. Jul 7, 1947, v23, p81.
Motion Picture Herald Product Digest. May 31, 1947, p3653.
New Republic. Jul 14, 1947, v117, p34.
The New York Times. Jul 10, 1947, p17.
The New Yorker. Jul 12, 1947, v23, p58.

Newsweek. Jul 7, 1947, v30, p92.
Time. Jul 7, 1947, v50, p66.
Variety. May 28, 1947, p8.

Pershing's Crusaders (US; Hoagland, Herbert C.; 1918)
Exhibitor's Trade Review. Jun 22, 1918, p157.
Motion Picture News. May 25, 1918, p3143.
The New York Dramatic Mirror. May 25, 1918, p742.
The New York Times. May 20, 1918, p9.
Variety. May 10, 1918, p44.
Variety. May 31, 1918, p29.

Personal (US; Porter, Edwin S.; 1904)
Film Before Griffith. p207-09, 212-16.
The First Twenty Years. p58-60.

Personal Property (US; Van Dyke, W.S.; 1937)
Film Daily. Mar 16, 1937, p12.
The Films of Jean Harlow. p148-53.
The Films of Robert Taylor. p57-58.
Garbo and the Night Watchman. p248, 250.
Hollywood Reporter. Mar 11, 1937, p3.
Hollywood Spectator. Mar 27, 1937, v11, p9-10.
Literary Digest. Mar 27, 1937, v123, p21.
Motion Picture Herald. Mar 20, 1937, p44, 49.
The New York Times. Apr 11, 1937, p27.
Rob Wagner's Script. Apr 17, 1937, v17, p10-11.
Time. Mar 29, 1937, v29, p50.
Variety. Apr 21, 1937, p14.

Persons in Hiding (US; King, Louis; 1939)
Commonweal. Feb 3, 1939, v29, p413.
Film Daily. Jan 24, 1939, p6.
Graham Greene on Film. p210.
Hollywood Reporter. Jan 21, 1939, p3.
The New Statesman and Nation. Feb 25, 1939, v17, p281.
The New York Times. Mar 2, 1939, p19.
The Spectator. Mar 3, 1939, v162, p349.
The Tatler. Mar 8, 1939, v151, p420.
Variety. Jan 25, 1939, p11.

Pescados *See* The Wave

Pesn o Geroyakh *See* Song of the Heroes

Peter Ibbetson (US; Hathaway, Henry; 1935)
Canadian Magazine. Oct 1935, v84, p41.
Cinema, the Magic Vehicle. v1, p244.
Esquire. Jan 1936, v5, p156, 178.
Film Daily. Oct 31, 1935, p14.
The Films of Gary Cooper. p132-35.
Hollywood Reporter. Oct 25, 1935, p3.
Hollywood Spectator. Dec 7, 1935, v10, p11.
Motion Picture Herald. Nov 9, 1935, p60.
The New York Times. Nov 8, 1935, p18.
The New Yorker. Nov 16, 1935, v11, p80.
Rob Wagner's Script. Nov 30, 1935, v14, p8-9.
Saturday Review (London). Jan 25, 1936, v161, p128.
Surrealism and American Feature Films. p81-100.
Time. Nov 18, 1935, v26, p32+.
Variety. Nov 13, 1935, p16.

Peter Pan (US; Brenon, Herbert; 1924)
Exceptional Photoplays. Dec-Jan 1925, v5, p2.
Film Daily. Jan 11, 1925, p6.
Literary Digest. Jan 17, 1925, v84, p26-27.
A Million and One Nights. p704.
The Moving Picture World. Jan 10, 1925, p136.
The New York Times. Dec 29, 1924, p11.
Photoplay. Mar 1925, v27, p44.
Selected Film Criticism, 1921-1930. p222-26.
Variety. Dec 31, 1924, p26.

Peter the First (Russian title: Pyotr I) (USSR; Petrov,
   Vladimir M.; 1937)
Film Daily. Dec 31, 1937, p8.
Hollywood Reporter. Dec 28, 1937, p3.

National Board of Review Magazine. Feb 1938, v13, p16.
The New Masses. Jan 4, 1938, v26, p26.
The New Republic. Jan 19, 1938, v93, p311.
The New Statesman and Nation. Jun 24, 1939, v17, p975.
The New York Times. Dec 25, 1937, p10.
The New Yorker. Jan 1, 1938, v13, p43.
Partisan Review. Aug-Sep 1938, v5, p54-55.
The Spectator. Jun 30, 1939, v162, p1128.
Variety. Dec 22, 1937, p24.

Petit Cafe, Le *See* Playboy of Paris

The Petrified Forest (US; Mayo, Archie; 1936)
Bette Davis: Her Films and Career. p66-67.
Canadian Magazine. Mar 1936, v85, p40-41.
Classics of the Gangster Film. p36-41.
Commonweal. Feb 7, 1936, v23, p414.
The Complete Films of Humphrey Bogart. p26-28.
Film Daily. Jan 21, 1936, p8.
The Gangster Film. p94-101.
Garbo and the Night Watchman. p177-79.
Graham Greene on Film. p89-90.
Hollywood Reporter. Jan 7, 1936, p3.
Hollywood Spectator. Jan 18, 1936, v10, p9.
Humphrey Bogart: The Man and His Films. p51-52.
Literary Digest. Feb 8, 1936, v121, p19.
Magill's Survey of Cinema. Series II. v4, p1888-91.
National Board of Review Magazine. Feb 1936, v11, p17.
The New Statesman and Nation. Jul 25, 1936, v12, p125.
The New York Times. Feb 7, 1936, p14.
Newsweek. Feb 1, 1936, v7, p33.
Rob Wagner's Script. Feb 15, 1936, v15, p10-11.
Selected Film Criticism, 1931-1940. p193-96.
The Spectator. Jul 24, 1936, v157, p139.
Stage. Jan 1936, v13, p54.
Stage. Feb 1936, v13, p9.
The Tatler. Jul 29, 1936, v141, p190.
Those Fabulous Movie Years: The 30s. p108-09.
Time. Feb 17, 1936, v27, p48.
Variety. Feb 12, 1936, p16.
Warner Brothers Presents. p128.
World Film News. Sep 1936, v1, p22.

Petticoat Fever (US; Fitzmaurice, George; 1936)
Canadian Magazine. May 1936, v85, p60.
Film Daily. Mar 14, 1936, p7.
The Films of Myrna Loy. p191-93.
Hollywood Reporter. Mar 11, 1936, p3.
Motion Picture Herald. Mar 21, 1936, p41.
The New York Times. Mar 21, 1936, p13.
Rob Wagner's Script. Apr 4, 1936, v15, p12.
Time. Mar 30, 1936, v27, p34.
Variety. Mar 25, 1936, p15.

Pettigrew's Girl (US; Melford, George; 1919)
Exhibitor's Trade Review. Apr 19, 1919, p1523.
Magill's Survey of Cinema. Silent Films. v2, p865-67.
Motion Picture News. Apr 19, 1919, p2526.
The Moving Picture World. Apr 12, 1919, p275.
The New York Times. Apr 14, 1919, p11.
Variety. Apr 18, 1919, p53.
Wid's Daily. Mar 16, 1919, p17.

The Phantom of the Opera (US; Julian, Rupert; 1925)
BFI/Monthly Film Bulletin. May 1975, v42, p120-21.
Classics of the Horror Film. p12-35.
Classics of the Silent Screen. p68-69.
Faces, Forms, Films: The Artistry of Lon Chaney. p107-10.
Film Daily. Feb 16, 1930, p8.
Films in Review. Oct 1962, v13, p505-08.
The Films of the Twenties. p121-25.
The Horror People. p8, 14.
An Illustrated History of the Horror Film. p47-50, 221.
The International Dictionary of Films and Filmmakers. v1, p362-63.
Magill's Survey of Cinema. Silent Films. v2, p868-69.

The Moving Picture World. Feb 7, 1925, p605.
The Moving Picture World. Sep 19, 1925, p256.
The New York Times. Sep 7, 1925, p15.
Variety. Sep 9, 1925, p35.
Variety. Feb 12, 1930, p14.

The Phantom of the Opera (US; Lubin, Arthur; 1943)
Around Cinemas. p252-54.
Film Daily. Aug 17, 1943, p9.
The Films of Jeanette MacDonald and Nelson Eddy. p339-46.
The Films of the Forties. p93-95.
Hollywood Reporter. Aug 13, 1943, p3.
Magill's Survey of Cinema. Series II. v3, p1326-29.
Make It Again, Sam. p139-44.
Motion Picture Herald Product Digest. Aug 21, 1943, p1493-94.
The New York Times. Oct 15, 1943, p15.
Rob Wagner's Script. Oct 23, 1943, v39, p14-15.
Selected Film Criticism, 1941-1950. p184-85.
Time. Aug 30, 1943, v42, p93.
Variety. Aug 18, 1943, p10.

The Phantom President (US; Taurog, Norman; 1932)
Before My Eyes. p343-49.
Claudette Colbert (Quirk). p49-51.
Film Daily. Sep 23, 1932, p6.
Hollywood Reporter. Sep 17, 1932, p3.
Judge. Nov 1932, v103, p20.
Motion Picture Herald. Sep 24, 1932, p30.
The New Outlook. Nov 1932, v161, p47.
The New York Times. Oct 1, 1932, p10.
The New Yorker. Oct 8, 1932, v8, p58.
Overland Monthly. Nov 1932, v90, p281.
Review of Reviews (London). Dec 1932, v82, p77-78.
Rob Wagner's Script. Oct 1, 1932, v8, p8.
Time. Oct 10, 1932, v20, p32.
Vanity Fair. Nov 1932, v39, p47+.
Variety. Oct 4, 1932, p15.

The Philadelphia Story (US; Cukor, George; 1940)
American Film Criticism. p404-05.
Around Cinema, Second Series. p145-48.
Commonweal. Jan 17, 1941, v33, p328.
The Film Criticism of Otis Ferguson. p324-25.
Film Daily. Nov 26, 1940, p7.
Films and Filming. Jul 1962, v8, p24-25.
The Films of Cary Grant. p145-48.
The Films of James Stewart. p190-93.
The Films of Katharine Hepburn. p101-04.
The Films of the Forties. p20-22.
George Cukor (Phillips). p72-75.
Halliwell's Hundred. p267-29.
Hollywood Reporter. Dec 4, 1940, p3.
The International Dictionary of Films and Filmmakers. v1, p363-64.
Life. Jan 6, 1941, v10, p31-32.
The London Times. Mar 3, 1941, p6.
Magill's Survey of Cinema. Series I. v3, p1330-34.
Make It Again, Sam. p145-50.
Motion Picture Exhibitor. Dec 11, 1940, p651.
Motion Picture Herald Product Digest. Mar 8, 1941, p76.
Movies and Methods. p79-80.
The National Society of Film Critics on Movie Comedy. p79-80.
The New Republic. Dec 13, 1940, v103, p809.
The New York Times. Dec 27, 1940, p22.
Newsweek. Dec 16, 1940, v16, p64.
Pursuits of Happiness. p133-60.
Rob Wagner's Script. Dec 21, 1940, v24, p17-18.
Scribner's Commentator. Mar 1941, v9, p107-08.
Selected Film Criticism, 1931-1940. p196-97.
Time. Jan 20, 1041, v38, p77-78.
Unholy Fools. p72-73.
Variety. Nov 27, 1940, p16.

Piccadilly Incident (Also titled: They Met at Midnight) (GB; Wilcox, Herbert; 1946)
Film Daily. Jan 30, 1948, p6.
Hollywood Reporter. Jan 28, 1948, p3.
Hollywood Review. Feb 9, 1948, v40, p137-38.
Motion Picture Herald Product Digest. Sep 7, 1946, p3185.
The New York Times. Aug 5, 1948, p16.
Twenty-five Thousand Sunsets. p144-51.
Variety. Aug 28, 1948, p14.

Piccadilly Jim (US; Leonard, Robert Z.; 1936)
Canadian Magazine. Nov 1936, v86, p38.
Film Daily. Aug 6, 1936, p14.
Hollywood Reporter. Aug 3, 1936, p3.
Literary Digest. Aug 15, 1936, v122, p20.
Motion Picture Herald. Aug 15, 1936, p59.
The New York Times. Aug 31, 1936, p19.
Rob Wagner's Script. Oct 3, 1936, v16, p10.
Time. Aug 31, 1936, v28, p23.
Variety. Sep 2, 1936, p18.

Pick a Star (US; Sedgwick, Edward; 1937)
Film Daily. Apr 20, 1937, p8.
Hollywood Reporter. Apr 15, 1937, p6.
Laurel & Hardy. p353-54.
Motion Picture Herald. Apr 24, 1937, p38.
The New York Times. May 28, 1937, p17.
Rob Wagner's Script. Jun 5, 1937, v17, p8.
Time. Jun 7, 1937, v29, p35.
Variety. Jun 2, 1937, p15.

Pick Up (US; Gering, Marion; 1933)
Film Daily. Mar 25, 1933, p3.
Hollywood Reporter. Mar 13, 1933, p3.
Motion Picture Herald. Mar 25, 1933, p19.
The New York Times. Mar 25, 1933, p13.
Rob Wagner's Script. Apr 1, 1933, v9, p9.
Time. Apr 3, 1933, v21, p34.
Variety. Mar 28, 1933, p27.

The Picture of Dorian Gray (US; Lewin, Albert; 1945)
Agee on Film. v1, p147-49.
BFI/Monthly Film Bulletin. Nov 1985, v52, p355-56.
Chestnuts in Her Lap. p148-50.
Cinema: The Novel into Films. p365-71.
Commonweal. Mar 16, 1945, v41, p543-44.
Film Daily. Feb 26, 1945, p6.
The Films of the Forties. p142-45.
Hollywood Reporter. Feb 26, 1945, p3.
Life. Mar 19, 1945, v18, p99-102+.
The London Times. May 2, 1945, p6.
Magic Moments from the Movies. p55-71, 252-55.
Magill's Survey of Cinema. Series I. v3, p1335-38.
Motion Picture Exhibitor. Mar 7, 1945, v33, n18, sec2, p1673.
Motion Picture Herald Product Digest. Mar 3, 1945, p2337.
The Nation. Mar 10, 1945, v160, p285.
The New Republic. Mar 19, 1945, v112, p389.
The New York Times. Mar 2, 1945, p15.
The New Yorker. Mar 10, 1945, v21, p48.
Rob Wagner's Script. Mar 31, 1945, v31, p14.
Saturday Review. Mar 10, 1945, v28, p24-25.
Scholastic. Mar 16, 1945, v46, p23.
Selected Film Criticism, 1941-1950. p185-86.
Theatre Arts. Apr 1945, v39, p230-31.
Time. Mar 12, 1945, v45, p94.
Variety. Mar 7, 1945, p20.

The Picture Snatcher (US; Bacon, Lloyd; 1933)
America in the Dark. p167.
Film Daily. May 19, 1933, p6.
The Films of James Cagney. p70-72.
The Gangster Film. p146-48.
Motion Picture Herald. Apr 1, 1933, p22.
The Nation. Jun 7, 1933, v136, p652.
The New York Times. May 19, 1933, p20.

The New Yorker. May 27, 1933, v9, p44-45.
Newsweek. May 27, 1933, v1, p30.
Rob Wagner's Script. May 13, 1933, v9, p8-9.
Time. May 15, 1933, v21, p36.
Vanity Fair. Jun 1933, v40, p37.
Variety. May 23, 1933, p15.

The Pied Piper (US; Pichel, Irving; 1942)
Around Cinemas, Second Series. p219.
Commonweal. Aug 21, 1942, v36, p424.
Film Daily. Jul 8, 1942, p7.
Life. Aug 10, 1942, v13, p47-50.
The London Times. Nov 28, 1942, p6.
Magic Moments from the Movies. p114.
Motion Picture Exhibitor. Jul 15, 1942, p1049.
Motion Picture Herald Product Digest. Jul 11, 1942, p965.
The New York Times. Aug 13, 1942, p15.
The New Yorker. Aug 15, 1942, v18, p53.
Newsweek. Jul 27, 1942, v20, p69.
Scholastic. Sep 14, 1942, v41, p35.
Time. Aug 10, 1942, v40, p86+.
Variety. Jul 8, 1942, p8.

Pigskin Parade (US; Butler, David; 1936)
Film Daily. Oct 20, 1936, p8.
The Hollywood Musical. p93-94.
Hollywood Reporter. Oct 17, 1936, p3.
Hollywood Spectator. Oct 24, 1936, v11, p10-11.
Motion Picture Herald. Oct 24, 1936, p54.
The New York Times. Nov 14, 1936, p23.
Rob Wagner's Script. Nov 14, 1936, v16, p14.
Time. Nov 2, 1936, v28, p22.
Variety. Nov 18, 1936, p12.

The Pilgrim (US; Chaplin, Charles; 1923)
Charles Chaplin: A Guide to References and Resources. p70-71.
Cinema, the Magic Vehicle. v1, p77-78.
The Comic Mind. p64-65.
Film Daily. Nov 19, 1922, p3.
The Films of Charlie Chaplin. p174-76.
The New York Times. Feb 26, 1923, p15.
The Silent Clowns. p178-80.
Spellbound in Darkness. p263, 268, 273.
Variety. Mar 1, 1923, p32.

Pilgrimage (US; Ford, John; 1933)
Film Daily. Jul 17, 1933, p7.
The Films of John Ford. p25-27.
Motion Picture Herald. Jul 22, 1933, p53.
The Nation. Aug 2, 1933, v137, p139.
New Outlook. Aug 1933, v162, p44.
The New York Times. Jul 13, 1933, p17.
Newsweek. Jul 22, 1933, v1, p31.
Rob Wagner's Script. Aug 19, 1933, v10, p11, 27.
Time. Jul 24, 1933, v22, p43.
Vanity Fair. Jul 1933, v40, p45.
Variety. Jul 18, 1933, p36.

Pimpernel Smith *See* Mister V

Pinky (US; Kazan, Elia; 1949)
Commonweal. Oct 14, 1949, v51, p15.
Film Daily. Sep 30, 1949, p7.
Hollywood Reporter. Sep 30, 1949, p3.
Library Journal. Feb 1, 1950, v75, p180.
Life. Oct 17, 1949, v27, p112-15.
Magill's Survey of Cinema. Series I. v3, p1346-48.
Motion Picture Herald. Oct 1, 1949, p33.
The New Republic. Oct 3, 1949, v121, p23.
The New York Times. Sep 30, 1949, p28.
The New Yorker. Oct 1, 1949, v26, p50.
Newsweek. Oct 10, 1949, v34, p89.
Rotarian. Feb 1950, v76, p39.
Selected Film Criticism, 1941-1950. p187-89.
Sequence. New Year 1950, p179-83.

Time. Oct 10, 1949, v54, p96+.
Variety. Oct 5, 1949, p8.

Pinocchio (US; Sharpstein, Ben; Luske, Hamilton; 1940)
Around Cinemas. p204-06.
The Art of Walt Disney. p199-226.
Big Screen, Little Screen. np.
Chestnuts in Her Lap. p172-73.
Commonweal. Feb 23, 1940, v31, p387.
Current History. Mar 1940, 51, p50-51.
The Disney Films. p32-37.
The Disney Version. p231-35.
The Film Criticism of Otis Ferguson. p289-91.
Film Daily. Jan 30, 1940, p6.
Hollywood Reporter. Jan 30, 1940, p3.
Life. Mar 11, 1940, v13, p65-68.
The London Times. Mar 14, 1940, p6.
The London Times. Mar 18, 1946, p8.
Magill's Survey of Cinema. Series II. v4, p1902-05.
Motion Picture Herald. Feb 3, 1940, p42.
Movie. Spr 1977, v24, p44-52.
The Nation. Feb 17, 1940, v150, p261-62.
National Board of Review Magazine. Mar 1940, v15, p10-11.
The New Republic. Mar 11, 1940, v102, p346.
The New York Times. Feb 8, 1940, p18.
The New York Times. Feb 11, 1940, sec9, p5.
The New York Times. Mar 24, 1940, sec9, p5.
Newsweek. Feb 19, 1940, v15, p32-33.
Popular Mechanics. Jan 1940, v123, p17-24+.
Rob Wagner's Script. Feb 10, 1940, v23, p17.
Saturday Review. Feb 17, 1940, v21, p17.
Scholastic. Dec 18, 1939, v35, p20E-21E.
Selected Film Criticism, 1931-1940. p198-99.
Theatre Arts. Jan 1940, v24, p6-7.
Time. Feb 26, 1940, v35, p64+.
Variety. Jan 31, 1940, p14.
Variety. Jan 13, 1971, p24.
Walt Disney: A Guide to References and Resources. p17-18.

Pinto (US; Schertzinger, Victor; 1920)
The Moving Picture World. Feb 7, 1920, p940.
Wid's Daily. Feb 1, 1920, p2.

Pippa Passes (US; Griffith, D.W.; 1909)
American Silent Film. p51.
D.W. Griffith, His Biograph Films in Perspective. p111-16.
The Emergence of Film Art. p47-48.
A History of Narrative Film. p68.
The Moving Picture World. Oct 16, 1909, p529-30.
Selected Film Criticism, 1896-1911. p74-75.
Spellbound in Darkness. p 60, 63, 83.

The Pirate (US; Minnelli, Vincente; 1948)
Commonweal. Jun 4, 1948, v48, p186.
Film Daily. Mar 31, 1948, p7.
The Films of Gene Kelly. p74-82.
The Hollywood Musical. p293.
Hollywood Reporter. Mar 29, 1948, p3.
Judy: The Films and Career of Judy Garland. p139-42.
Life. Jun 21, 1948, v24, p75.
Motion Picture Herald Product Digest. Apr 3, 1948, p4110.
The New Republic. Jun 7, 1948, v118, p29.
The New York Times. May 21, 1948, p19.
The New Yorker. May 29, 1948, v24, p66.
Newsweek. Jun 7, 1948, v31, p83.
Sequence. Wint 1948-49, n6, p44-46.
Time. Jun 21, 1948, v51, p96+.
Variety. Mar 31, 1948, p15.
Vincente Minnelli and the Film Musical. p127-32.

The Pit (US; Tourneur, Maurice; 1914)
The Moving Picture World. Jan 2, 1915, p86, 135.
The New York Dramatic Mirror. Dec 30, 1914, p32.

Pitfall (US; Toth, Andre de; 1948)
Commonweal. Sep 3, 1948, v48, p499.
Film Daily. Aug 2, 1948, p6.
Motion Picture Herald Product Digest. Aug 7, 1948, p4267.
The New Republic. Sep 6, 1948, v119, p30.
The New York Times. Aug 25, 1948, p31.
Newsweek. Aug 23, 1948, v32, p80+.
Time. Sep 6, 1948, v52, p86.
Variety. Aug 4, 1948, p11.

The Plainsman (US; DeMille, Cecil B.; 1937)
Esquire. Feb 1937, v7, p101.
Film Daily. Nov 24, 1936, p7.
The Films of Cecil B. DeMille. p304-07.
The Films of Gary Cooper. p147-49.
The Films of the Thirties. p180-81.
Garbo and the Night Watchman. p193-94.
Graham Greene on Film. p131-32.
Hollywood Reporter. Nov 21, 1936, p3.
Hollywood Spectator. Dec 5, 1936, v11, p9-10.
Judge. Feb 1937, v112, p24.
A Library of Film Criticism: American Film Directors. p86.
Life. Dec 14, 1936, v1, p8.
Life. Jan 4, 1937, v2, p62-68.
Literary Digest. Jan 23, 1937, v123, p21.
London Mercury. Mar 1937, v35, p504.
Magill's Survey of Cinema. Series I. v3, p1352-54.
Motion Picture Herald. Nov 28, 1936, p66.
Movie Classic. Dec 1936, v11, p50+.
The Nation. Jan 30, 1937, v144, p137.
The New Masses. Jan 26, 1937, v22, p39.
The New Statesman and Nation. Feb 13, 1937, v13, p245.
The New York Times. Jan 14, 1937, p16.
The New Yorker. Jan 23, 1937, v12, p61, 63.
Newsweek. Jan 16, 1937, v9, p30.
Saint Nicholas. Oct 1936, v63, p15.
Scholastic. Jan 9, 1937, v29, p28.
Sight and Sound. Spr 1937, v6, p21-22.
The Spectator. Feb 12, 1937, v158, p267.
Stage. Jan 1937, v14, p58-59+.
Stage. Apr 1937, v14, p56-57.
Those Fabulous Movie Years: The 30s. p102-03.
Time. Dec 28, 1936, v28, p19-20.
Variety. Jan 20, 1937, p14.
World Film News. Mar 1937, v1, p24.

Platinum Blonde (US; Capra, Frank; 1931)
The American Film Heritage. p120.
BFI/Monthly Film Bulletin. Jan 1974, v41, p58-59.
Film Daily. Nov 1, 1931, p10.
The Films of Frank Capra (Scherle and Levy). p99-102.
The Films of Frank Capra (Willis). p127-30.
The Films of Jean Harlow. p54-59.
Frank Capra (Maland). p65-69.
Frank Capra: The Man and His Films. p55-56.
Hollywood Reporter. Sep 21, 1931, p3.
A Library of Film Criticism: American Film Directors. p37.
Life. Nov 20, 1931, v98, p21.
Motion Picture Herald. Oct 3, 1931, p33.
The New York Times. Oct 31, 1931, p22.
Rob Wagner's Script. Dec 5, 1931, v6, p10.
Variety. Nov 3, 1931, p27.

Play Girl (US; Enright, Ray; 1932)
Film Daily. Mar 20, 1932, p10.
Motion Picture Herald. Feb 27, 1932, p40.
The New York Times. Mar 19, 1932, p11.
Rob Wagner's Script. Apr 16, 1932, v7, p10-11.
Variety. Mar 22, 1932, p13.

Playboy of Paris (French title: Petit Cafe, Le) (US;
    Berger, Ludwig; 1930)
Chevalier. p91-95.
Film Daily. Nov 2, 1930, p10.
Life. Nov 21, 1930, v96, p16.

The New York Times. Nov 1, 1930, p23.
Theatre Magazine. Mar 1931, v53, p48.
Variety. Nov 15, 1930, p30.

The Plough and the Stars (US; Ford, John; 1937)
BFI/Monthly Film Bulletin. May 1980, v47, p99.
Commonweal. Jan 8, 1937, v25, p304.
Esquire. Mar 1937, v7, p111, 188-89.
The Film Criticism of Otis Ferguson. p169-70.
Film Daily. Dec 26, 1936, p4.
The Films of Barbara Stanwyck. p112-13.
From Quasimodo to Scarlett O'Hara. p231-34.
Hollywood Reporter. Dec 22, 1936, p3.
Hollywood Spectator. Jan 2, 1937, v11, p17-18.
Literary Digest. Sep 19, 1936, v122, p21-22.
Literary Digest. Jan 16, 1937, v123, p23.
Motion Picture Herald. Jan 2, 1937, p65.
Motion Picture Herald. Aug 22, 1936, p16-17.
The Nation. Feb 13, 1937, v144, p194.
National Board of Review Magazine. Jan 1937, v12, p8.
The New Masses. Feb 9, 1937, v22, p29-30.
The New York Times. Jan 29, 1937, p15.
The New Yorker. Feb 6, 1937, v12, p60.
Newsweek. Jan 23, 1937, v9, p30.
Rob Wagner's Script. Jan 23, 1937, v16, p12-13.
Scholastic. Jan 23, 1937, v29, p14+.
Scribner's Magazine. Apr 1937, v101, p61.
Stage. Feb 1937, v14, p54.
Starring Miss Barbara Stanwyck. p83, 90.
The Tatler. Feb 17, 1937, v143, p282.
Time. Feb 1, 1937, v29, p45.
Variety. Feb 3, 1937, p14.
We're in the Money. p165-66.
The Western Films of John Ford. p162-69.
World Film News. Mar 1937, v1, p25.

The Plow That Broke the Plains (US; Lorentz, Pare; 1936)
Christian Century. Jun 3, 1936, v53, p788-89.
Documentary: History of the Non-Fiction Film. p115-18.
Esquire. Aug 1936, v6, p99, 108.
Film on the Left. p93-109.
From Quasimodo to Scarlett O'Hara. p222-24.
Literary Digest. May 16, 1936, v121, p22.
Lorentz on Film. p135-36.
The Nation. Jun 10, 1936, v142, p753.
National Board of Review Magazine. Jun 1936, v11, p9.
The New Republic. Aug 5, 1936, v87, p382.
New Theatre. Jul 1936, v3, p18-19.
The New York Times. Jun 10, 1936, p18.
The New York Times. Aug 4, 1936, p11.
Non-Fiction Film: A Critical History. p100-02.
Pare Lorentz and the Documentary Film. p21-49.
Scribner's Magazine. Jan 1939, v105, p8-10.
Survey Graphic. Jun 1936, v25, p357.
Time. May 25, 1936, v27, p47-48.
Variety. Jun 3, 1936, p15.
We're in the Money. p165-66.

Pluck of the Irish *See* Great Guy

Pocomania (US; Leonard, Arthur; 1939)
Film Daily. Dec 14, 1939, p6.
Motion Picture Herald. Dec 9, 1939, p74.

Poet and Tsar (USSR; Levin, Moissei; 1938)
Film Daily. Sep 1, 1938, p7.
The New Masses. Sep 6, 1938, v28, p29-30.
The New York Times. Aug 25, 1938, p15.
Variety. Sep 7, 1938, p13.

Poil de Carotte (Also titled: The Red Head) (FR; Duvivier, Julien; 1933)
Cinema Quarterly. Wint 1933-34, v2, p121.
Cinema, the Magic Vehicle. v1, p203-04.
Classics of the Foreign Film. p92-93.

Commonweal. Jun 30, 1933, v18, p246.
Film Daily. May 31, 1933, p7.
From Quasimodo to Scarlett O'Hara. p172-74.
The Golden Age of French Cinema, 1929-1939. p107-08.
The Great French Films. p47-49.
Kiss Kiss Bang Bang. p301.
Motion Picture Herald. Jun 17, 1933, p37.
The Nation. Jun 7, 1933, v136, p650+.
National Board of Review Magazine. Jun 1933, v8, p9.
The New Statesman and Nation. Nov 4, 1933, v6, p551.
The New York Times. May 26, 1933, p24.
The New Yorker. May 27, 1933, v9, p44.
Newsweek. Jun 10, 1933, v1, p29.
Photoplay. Sep 1933, v44, p102.
Rob Wagner's Script. Sep 16, 1933, v10, p11-12.
Selected Film Criticism: Foreign Films, 1930-1950. p148.
The Spectator. Nov 3, 1933, v151, p620.
Time. Jun 12, 1933, v21, p30.
Vanity Fair. Aug 1933, v40, p37.
Variety. Dec 20, 1932, p55.
Variety. May 30, 1933, p15.

The Poisoned Flume (US; Dwan, Allan; 1911)
Allan Dwan: The Last Pioneer. p20.
The Bioscope. Aug 24, 1911, p401.
Selected Film Criticism, 1896-1911. p75-76.

Polly of the Circus (US; Horan, Charles; 1917)
Fifty Great American Silent Films, 1912-1920. p82-83.
Magill's Survey of Cinema. Silent Films. v2, p872-75.
Motion Picture News. Sep 22, 1917, p2035.
The Moving Picture World. Sep 22, 1917, p1857.
The New York Dramatic Mirror. Sep 8, 1917, p25.
The New York Times. Sep 10, 1917, p8.
Photoplay. Sep 1917, v12, p55.
Selected Film Criticism, 1912-1920. p199-200.
Variety. Sep 14, 1917, p37.
Wid's Daily. Sep 20, 1917, p598.

Polly of the Circus (US; Santell, Alfred; 1932)
Film Daily. Mar 20, 1932, p10.
The Films of Clark Gable. p132.
Hollywood Reporter. Jan 20, 1932, p3.
Motion Picture Herald. Mar 26, 1932, p35.
The New York Times. Mar 19, 1932, p11.
The New Yorker. Mar 26, 1932, v8, p52.
Rob Wagner's Script. Apr 23, 1932, v7, p10-11.
Time. Mar 7, 1932, v19, p30.
Variety. Mar 22, 1932, p13.

Pollyanna (US; Powell, Paul; 1920)
The Films of the Twenties. p36-38.
The Moving Picture World. Jan 24, 1920, p636.
The Moving Picture World. Feb 14, 1920, p975.
The New York Times. Jan 19, 1920, p16.
Variety. Jan 24, 1920, p60.
Wid's Daily. Jan 25, 1920, p17.

The Pony Express (US; Cruze, James; 1925)
Film Daily. Sep 20, 1925, p4.
The Moving Picture World. Sep 26, 1925, p332.
The New York Times. Sep 14, 1925, p16.
Photoplay. Nov 1925, v28, p48.
Selected Film Criticism, 1921-1930. p227-28.
Sunset. Nov 1925, v55, p37-39.
Variety. Sep 16, 1925, p40.

The Pool Sharks (US; Middleton, Edwin; 1915)
Motion Picture News. Oct 2, 1915, p85.
Selected Film Criticism, 1912-1920. p201-02.
W.C. Fields. p12-13.

A Poor Little Rich Girl (US; Tourneur, Maurice; 1917)
Fifty Great American Silent Films, 1912-1920. p74-76.
Magill's Survey of Cinema. Silent Films. v2, p876-79.
The Moving Picture World. Mar 17, 1917, p1760-61, 1823.

The New York Dramatic Mirror. Feb 10, 1917, p31.
The New York Dramatic Mirror. Mar 10, 1917, p26.
The New York Times. Mar 5, 1917, p5.
The Rivals of D.W. Griffith. p34-35.
Selected Film Criticism, 1912-1920. p202-03.
Variety. Mar 9, 1917, p22.
Wid's Daily. Mar 8, 1917, p150.

The Poor Little Rich Girl (US; Cummings, Irving; 1936)
Commonweal. Jul 24, 1936, v24, p328.
Film Daily. Jun 6, 1936, p7.
The Films of Alice Faye. p61-64.
The Films of Shirley Temple. p170-73.
Hollywood Reporter. May 28, 1936, p3.
Hollywood Spectator. Jun 6, 1936, v11, p11-12.
Motion Picture Herald. Jun 6, 1936, p56, 60.
The New York Times. Jun 26, 1936, p16.
The New Yorker. Jul 4, 1936, v12, p45.
Newsweek. Jun 27, 1936, v7, p20.
Rob Wagner's Script. Jul 25, 1936, v15, p10.
Time. Jul 6, 1936, v28, p48.
Variety. Jul 1, 1936, p12.

A Poor Relation (US; Badger, Clarence; 1921)
Film Daily. Apr 9, 1922, p3.
The Moving Picture World. Apr 15, 1922, p762.
Variety. Apr 14, 1922, p39.
Will Rogers in Hollywood. p39.

Poppy (US; José, Edward; 1917)
The Moving Picture World. Jun 9, 1917, p1624.
The New York Dramatic Mirror. Jun 13, 1917, p26.
The New York Dramatic Mirror. Jun 2, 1917, p30.
Photoplay. Aug 1917, v12, p84.
Selected Film Criticism, 1912-1920. p203-04.
Variety. Jun 8, 1917, p24.
Wid's Daily. Jun 14, 1917, p375.

Poppy (US; Sutherland, Edward; 1936)
Commonweal. Jul 10, 1936, v24, p287.
Film Daily. Jun 9, 1936, p10.
The Films of W. C. Fields. p121-27.
Graham Greene on Film. p87-88.
Hollywood Reporter. Jun 5, 1936, p3.
Hollywood Spectator. Jun 20, 1936, v11, p3.
Judge. Aug 1936, v111, p20, 29.
Literary Digest. Jun 20, 1936, v121, p19.
The New Masses. Jun 30, 1936, v19, p30.
The New Statesman and Nation. Jul 18, 1936, v12, p87.
The New York Times. Jun 18, 1936, p19.
The New Yorker. Jun 27, 1936, v12, p61.
Newsweek. Jun 20, 1936, v7, p24.
Rob Wagner's Script. Jul 11, 1936, v15, p12.
The Spectator. Jul 17, 1936, v157, p97.
Stage. Jun 1936, v13, p41.
Stage. Jul 1936, v13, p6.
Time. Jun 22, 1936, v27, p37.
Variety. Jun 24, 1936, p29.
W. C. Fields: A Life on Film. p181-86.
World Film News. Aug 1936, v1, p20.
World Film News. Dec 1936, v1, p20.

The Poppy Girl's Husband (US; Hart, William S.; Hillyer, Lambert; 1919)
The Complete Films of William S. Hart. p105-07.
Exhibitor's Trade Review. Apr 5, 1919, p1373.
Motion Picture News. Apr 5, 1919, p2185.
The Moving Picture World. Apr 5, 1919, p124-25.
The New York Times. Mar 24, 1919, p11.
Variety. Mar 28, 1919, p93.
Wid's Daily. Mar 30, 1919, p27.

Port of Seven Seas (Also titled: Fanny; Madelon; Man of the Waterfront; Life on the Waterfront) (US; Whale, James; 1938)
Film Daily. Jun 28, 1938, p6.

Hollywood Reporter. Mar 24, 1938, p3.
James Whale (Curtis). p161-63.
Motion Picture Herald. Apr 9, 1938, p42.
The New York Times. Jul 15, 1938, p13.
Time. Jul 11, 1938, v32, p42.
Variety. Jun 29, 1938, p12.
World Film News. Aug 1938, v3, p173.

Port of Shadows *See* Quai des Brumes

Portia on Trial (US; Nicholls, George, Jr.; 1937)
Film Daily. Nov 5, 1937, p8.
Hollywood Reporter. Oct 28, 1937, p3.
Motion Picture Herald. Nov 6, 1937, p36.
The New York Times. Dec 3, 1937, p29.
The New Yorker. Dec 11, 1937, v13, p102.
Variety. Nov 10, 1937, p19.

Portrait of Jennie (US; Dieterle, William; 1949)
Collier's. Feb 5, 1949, v123, p46.
Commonweal. Apr 1, 1949, v49, p611.
David O'Selznick's Hollywood. p380-86.
Film Daily. Dec 30, 1948, p6.
The Films of Jennifer Jones. p73-80.
Hollywood Reporter. Dec 24, 1948, p3.
Magill's Survey of Cinema. Series I. v3, p1358-60.
Motion Picture Herald Product Digest. Jan 1, 1949, p4441.
The New York Times. Mar 30, 1949, p31.
The New Yorker. Apr 29, 1949, v25, p95.
Newsweek. Apr 4, 1949, v33, p82.
Time. Apr 4, 1949, v53, p100+.
Variety. Dec 29, 1948, p6.

Poslednaya Noch *See* The Last Night

Possessed (US; Brown, Clarence; 1931)
Decency in Motion Pictures. p36-37.
Film Daily. Nov 29, 1931, p23.
The Films of Clark Gable. p129-30.
The Films of Joan Crawford. p89-91.
Hollywood Reporter. Oct 20, 1931, p3.
A Library of Film Criticism: American Film Directors. p21-22.
Motion Picture Herald. Oct 31, 1931, p36.
The New York Times. Nov 28, 1931, p20.
The New Yorker. Dec 5, 1931, v7, p91-92.
Outlook and Independent. Dec 2, 1931, v159, p439.
Time. Dec 7, 1931, v18, p30.
Variety. Dec 1, 1931, p15.

Possessed (US; Bernhardt, Curtis; 1947)
Commonweal. Jun 13, 1947, v46, p216.
Film Daily. Jun 3, 1947, p8.
The Films of Joan Crawford. p164-67.
Hollywood Reporter. May 20, 1947, p3.
Motion Picture Herald Product Digest. May 31, 1947, p3653.
The New York Times. May 30, 1947, p25.
The New Yorker. Jun 7, 1947, v23, p111.
Newsweek. Jun 16, 1947, v29, p96.
Time. Jun 16, 1947, v49, p63.
Variety. Jun 4, 1947, p16.

The Postman Always Rings Twice (US; Garnett, Tay; 1946)
Agee on Film. v1, p199.
Commonweal. Apr 5, 1946, v43, p623.
Film Daily. Mar 15, 1946, p16.
The Films of John Garfield. p130-37.
The Films of Lana Turner. p222-26.
The Films of the Forties. p163-67.
Hollywood Reporter. Jan 30, 1946, p3.
Life. Apr 29, 1946, v20, p129-30+.
Magill's Survey of Cinema. Series I. v3, p1365-67.
Motion Picture Herald Product Digest. Mar 16, 1946, p2893.
The Nation. May 11, 1946, v162, p580.
The New Republic. May 20, 1946, v114, p732.
The New York Times. May 3, 1946, p15.

The New Yorker. May 11, 1946, v22, p64.
Newsweek. May 13, 1946, v27, p94+.
Rob Wagner's Script. May 11, 1946, v32, p23.
Screening the Novel. p46-64.
Selected Film Criticism, 1941-1950. p192-95.
Theatre Arts. May 1946, v30, p284.
Time. May 6, 1946, v47, p96+.
Variety. Mar 3, 1946, p8.

Potemkin *See* Battleship Potemkin

Potomok Chingis-Khan *See* Storm Over Asia

Power (Also titled: Jew Suss) (GB; Mendes, Lothar; 1934)
Film Daily. Oct 5, 1934, p8.
Hollywood Reporter. Oct 4, 1934, p4.
Motion Picture Herald. Oct 13, 1934, p64.
The New York Times. Oct 5, 1934, p29.
Rob Wagner's Script. Dec 29, 1934, v12, p8.
Selected Film Criticism: Foreign Films, 1930-1950. p139-40.
Time. Oct 15, 1934, v24, p19.
Variety. Oct 9, 1934, p18.

The Power and the Glory (US; Howard, William K.;
    1933)
Film Daily. Aug 18, 1933, p13.
The Films of Spencer Tracy. p94-99.
Hollywood Reporter. Jun 19, 1933, p3.
Magill's Survey of Cinema. Series I. v3, p1368-70.
Motion Picture Herald. Aug 26, 1933, p78.
The Nation. Sep 13, 1933, v137, p308.
National Board of Review Magazine. Sep-Oct 1933, v8, p8-10.
New Outlook. Oct 1933, v162, p49.
The New York Times. Aug 17, 1933, p13.
The New York Times. Aug 27, 1933, p3.
The New York Times. Jul 30, 1933, p3.
Newsweek. Aug 26, 1933, v2, p30.
Preston Sturges: A Guide to References and Resources. p37-40.
Rob Wagner's Script. Sep 16, 1933, v10, p10.
Selected Film Criticism, 1931-1940. p200-01.
The Spectator. Nov 10, 1933, v151, p660.
Talking Pictures. p28-34.
Time. Aug 28, 1933, v22, p18.
Variety. Aug 22, 1933, p22.

Power of Darkness (German title: Macht der Finsternis,
    Der) (USSR; Weine, Robert; 1922)
Film Daily. Nov 28, 1928, p7.
The New York Times. Jul 27, 1927, p27.
Variety. Oct 31, 1928, p31.

Presa di Roma (Also titled: Breccia di Porta Pia, La) (IT;
    Alberini, Filoteo; 1905)
A History of Narrative Film. p55.
The Italian Cinema. p7-12.

Presenting Lily Mars (US; Taurog, Norman; 1943)
Commonweal. May 28, 1943, v38, p147.
Film Daily. Apr 28, 1943, p8.
Hollywood Reporter. Apr 28, 1943, p3.
Judy: The Films and Career of Judy Garland. p105-08.
Motion Picture Herald Product Digest. May 1, 1943, p1289.
The New York Times. Apr 30, 1943, p25.
Variety. Apr 28, 1943, p8.

President Roosevelt's Inauguration (US; 1905)
The George Kleine Collection Catalog. p105-06.

The President Vanishes (US; Wellman, William A.; 1934)
Commonweal. Dec 21, 1934, v21, p236.
Film Daily. Nov 17, 1934, p3.
Hollywood Reporter. Nov 12, 1934, p3.
Literary Digest. Dec 22, 1934, v118, p27.
Motion Picture Herald. Nov 24, 1934, p36.
The Nation. Dec 26, 1934, v139, p750.
The New York Times. Dec 8, 1934, p18.
Newsweek. Dec 15, 1934, v4, p18-19.

Time. Dec 17, 1934, v27, p33.
Variety. Dec 11, 1934, p19.
William A. Wellman (Thompson). p158-60.

The President's Mystery (US; Rosen, Phil; 1936)
Film Daily. Sep 28, 1936, p14.
Hollywood Spectator. Oct 10, 1936, v11, p23.
Motion Picture Herald. Oct 3, 1936, p42.
The Nation. Nov 7, 1936, v143, p558.
The New Masses. Oct 27, 1936, v21, p27.
The New York Times. Oct 19, 1936, p22.
Rob Wagner's Script. Oct 31, 1936, v16, p10.
Time. Oct 12, 1936, v28, p34+.
Variety. Oct 21, 1936, p15.
World Film News. Jan 1937, v1, p24.

Prestige (US; Garnett, Tay; 1932)
Film Daily. Feb 7, 1932, p10.
Hollywood Reporter. Jan 9, 1932, p3.
Motion Picture Herald. Jan 16, 1932, p38.
The New York Times. Feb 5, 1932, p25.
Rob Wagner's Script. Jan 16, 1932, v6, p8-9.
Time. Feb 15, 1932, v19, p28.
Variety. Feb 9, 1932, p19.

The Pretty Sister of Jose (US; Dwan, Allan; 1915)
Motion Picture News. Jan 2, 1915, p34.
Motion Picture News. Jun 12, 1915, p68.
Motography. Jun 5, 1915, p953.
The Moving Picture World. Jun 12, 1915, p1787.
The New York Dramatic Mirror. Jun 2, 1915, p28.
Variety. Jun 4, 1915, p18.

Pride and Prejudice (US; Leonard, Robert Z.; 1940)
Commonweal. Aug 2, 1940, v32, p311.
The English Novel and the Movies. p44-51.
Film Daily. Jul 9, 1940, p6.
The Films of Laurence Olivier. p85-88.
The Films of the Forties. p12-15.
Halliwell's Hundred. p278-81.
Hollywood Reporter. Jul 17, 1940, p3.
Laurence Olivier (Hirsch). p51-54.
Laurence Olivier: Theater and Cinema. p82-84.
The London Times. Nov 1, 1940, p6.
Magill's Survey of Cinema. Series II. v4, p1919-23.
The Nation. Aug 19, 1940, v103, p246.
The New York Times. Mar 14, 1940, sec9, p5.
The New York Times. Aug 9, 1940, p19.
The New Yorker. Aug 17, 1940, v16, p43.
Newsweek. Jul 22, 1940, v16, p35.
Novels into Film. p115-46.
Rob Wagner's Script. Aug 17, 1940, v24, p16.
Scholastic. Sep 16, 1940, v36, p38.
Selected Film Criticism, 1931-1940. p202-03.
Time. Jul 29, 1940, v36, p44-45.
Variety. Jul 10, 1940, p12.

The Pride of the Clan (US; Tourneur, Maurice; 1917)
The Moving Picture World. Jan 20, 1917, p354, 423.
The New York Dramatic Mirror. Jan 13, 1917, p26.
The New York Times. Jan 8, 1917, p9.
Selected Film Criticism, 1912-1920. p204-06.
Variety. Jan 5, 1917, p27.
Wid's Daily. Jan 11, 1917, p27-28.

Pride of the Marines (US; Daves, Delmer; 1945)
Commonweal. Aug 17, 1945, v42, p431.
Film Daily. Aug 7, 1945, p5.
The Films of John Garfield. p124-29.
The Films of World War II. p226-28.
Hollywood Reporter. Aug 7, 1945, p3.
The Hollywood Social Problem Films. p227-30.
Life. Aug 6, 1945, v19, p79-81.
Magill's Survey of Cinema. Series II. v4, p1924-26.
Motion Picture Exhibitor. Aug 22, 1945, v34, n16, sec2,
    p1768.

Motion Picture Herald Product Digest. Aug 11, 1945, p2639.
The New Republic. Sep 24, 1945, v113, p374.
The New York Times. Aug 27, 1945, p7.
The New Yorker. Sep 8, 1945, v21, p42.
Newsweek. Aug 27, 1945, v26, p88.
Running Away from Myself. p43-45.
Scholastic. Oct 1, 1945, v47, p35.
Theatre Arts. Oct 1945, v29, p579.
Time. Sep 3, 1945, v46, p92+.
Variety. Aug 8, 1945, p22.
Velvet Light Trap. Sum 1983, n20, p27-33.

The Pride of the Yankees (US; Wood, Sam; 1942)
Commonweal. Jul 31, 1942, v36, p352.
Film Daily. Jul 16, 1942, p5.
The Films of Gary Cooper. p187-89.
Hollywood Reporter. Jul 16, 1942, p3.
The London Times. Nov 23, 1942, p8.
Magill's Survey of Cinema. Series II. v4, p1927-29.
Motion Picture Exhibitor. Jul 29, 1942, v28, n12, sec2, p1058.
Motion Picture Herald Product Digest. Jul 18, 1942, p781.
The New Republic. Jul 27, 1942, v107, p118.
The New York Times. Jul 16, 1942, p23.
The New Yorker. Jul 18, 1942, v18, p42.
Newsweek. Jul 20, 1942, 20, p56+.
Samuel Goldwyn (Epstein). p145-50.
Samuel Goldwyn Presents. p223-25.
Time. Aug 3, 1942, v40, p74.
Variety. Jul 15, 1942, p9.

The Primal Lure (US; Hart, William S.; 1916)
The Complete Films of William S. Hart. p44-45.
The Moving Picture World. May 20, 1916, p1350.
The Moving Picture World. Jun 3, 1916, p1714.
The Moving Picture World. Jun 17, 1916, p2110.
The New York Dramatic Mirror. May 13, 1916, p31.
The New York Times. May 8, 1916, p7.
Variety. May 12, 1916, p19.
Wid's Daily. May 11, 1916, p568.

The Primrose Path (US; La Cava, Gregory; 1940)
Commonweal. Apr 5, 1940, v31, p514.
The Film Criticism of Otis Ferguson. p294.
Film Daily. Mar 18, 1940, p4.
The Films of Ginger Rogers. p156-58.
Focus on Film. 1977, n27, p47-49.
Life. Mar 25, 1940, v8, p48+.
The London Times. Jun 17, 1940, p4.
The New Republic. Apr 8, 1940, v102, p474.
The New York Times. Mar 23, 1940, p16.
The New York Times. Mar 24, 1940, sec9, p5.
The New York Times. Mar 31, 1940, sec9, p5.
The New Yorker. Mar 30, 1940, v16, p71.
Saturday Review. May 11, 1940, v22, p21.
Time. Apr 1, 1940, v35, p70-71.
Variety. Mar 20, 1940, p16.

The Prince and the Pauper (US; 1909)
The Moving Picture World. Aug 14, 1909, p225.
Selected Film Criticism, 1896-1911. p76-77.

The Prince and the Pauper (US; Keighley, William; 1937)
The Classic American Novel and the Movies. p105-13.
Commonweal. May 7, 1937, v26, p48.
Esquire. Jul 1937, v8, p97.
Film Daily. Apr 8, 1937, p11.
The Films of Errol Flynn. p53.
Hollywood Reporter. Apr 6, 1937, p3.
Hollywood Spectator. Apr 24, 1937, v12, p7.
Life. May 10, 1937, v2, p34-36.
Motion Picture Herald. Apr 17, 1937, p42.
The New Masses. May 18, 1937, v23, p31.
The New York Times. May 6, 1937, p23.
The New Yorker. May 15, 1937, v13, p85-86.
Newsweek. May 8, 1937, v9, p20.
Rob Wagner's Script. May 15, 1937, v17, p8.

Variety. May 12, 1937, p12.
Warner Brothers Presents. p156-57.

The Prince of Foxes (US; King, Henry; 1949)
Christian Century. Jan 18, 1950, v67, p95.
Commonweal. Dec 30, 1949, v51, p341.
Film Daily. Aug 22, 1949, p8.
The Films of Tyrone Power. p158-60.
Hollywood Reporter. Aug 24, 1949, p3.
Motion Picture Herald Product Digest. Aug 27, 1949, p4729.
The New York Times. Dec 24, 1949, p11.
Newsweek. Jan 2, 1950, v35, p52.
Orson Welles (Leaming). p252.
Rotarian. Mar 1950, v81, p37.
Scholastic. Dec 7, 1949, v55, p30.
Sight and Sound. Dec 1949, v18, p21.
Time. Jan 9, 1950, v55, p84-85.
Variety. Aug 24, 1949, p18.

The Princess Comes Across (US; Howard, William R.; 1936)
Canadian Magazine. Jul 1936, v86, p32.
Film Daily. May 12, 1936, p12.
The Films of Carole Lombard. p136-37.
Hollywood Reporter. May 7, 1936, p3.
Hollywood Spectator. May 23, 1936, v11, p11.
Lunatics and Lovers. p178-80.
Motion Picture Herald. May 16, 1936, p29, 30.
The New York Times. Jun 4, 1936, p27.
Newsweek. May 23, 1936, v7, p27.
Rob Wagner's Script. Jun 27, 1936, v15, p11.
Time. Jun 1, 1936, v27, p26.
Variety. Jun 10, 1936, p18.
World Film News. Sep 1936, v1, p24.

Princess Nicotine (US; 1909)
The New York Dramatic Mirror. Aug 21, 1909, p20.
Selected Film Criticism, 1896-1911. p77.

Princess O'Rourke (US; Krasna, Norman; 1943)
Agee on Film. v1, p53, 61.
Commonweal. Oct 22, 1943, v39, p15.
Film Daily. Sep 21, 1943, p5.
The Films of Olivia De Havilland. p199-201.
Hollywood Reporter. Sep 21, 1943, p3.
Magill's Survey of Cinema. Series II. v4, p1930-33.
Motion Picture Herald Product Digest. Sep 25, 1943, p1553.
The Nation. Nov 20, 1943, v157, p593.
The New York Times. Nov 6, 1943, p16.
Time. Nov 22, 1943, v42, p94.
Variety. Sep 22, 1943, p12.

Princess Virtue (US; Myton, Fred; Leonard, Robert Z.; 1917)
The Moving Picture World. Nov 17, 1917, p1033.
Selected Film Criticism, 1912-1920. p206-07.
Variety. Nov 2, 1917, p49.
Wid's Daily. Nov 15, 1917, p728.

Prison Nurse (US; Cruze, James; 1938)
Film Daily. Mar 4, 1938, p7.
Hollywood Reporter. May 3, 1938, p3.
Motion Picture Herald. Mar 12, 1938, p42.
The New York Times. Mar 4, 1938, p17.
Variety. Mar 9, 1938, p14.

Prison Without Bars (GB; Hurst, Brian Desmond; 1938)
Commonweal. Mar 24, 1939, v29, p609.
Film Daily. Feb 16, 1939, p6.
Hollywood Reporter. Mar 4, 1939, p4.
Life. Mar 13, 1939, v6, p57-59.
London Mercury. Oct 1938, v38, p557.
Motion Picture Herald. Apr 15, 1939, p60.
The New Masses. Apr 18, 1939, v31, p31.
The New Statesman and Nation. Sep 17, 1938, v16, p416.
The New Statesman and Nation. Oct 1, 1938, v16, p492.

The New York Times. Apr 10, 1939, p13.
The New Yorker. Mar 25, 1939, v15, p66-67.
Rob Wagner's Script. Apr 15, 1939, v21, p19.
Scholastic. Mar 4, 1939, v34, p30.
The Spectator. Oct 7, 1938, v161, p559.
Time. Mar 27, 1939, v33, p66.
Variety. Oct 5, 1938, p21.

The Prisoner of Shark Island (US; Ford, John; 1936)
BFI/Monthly Film Bulletin. May 1980, v47, p99.
Canadian Magazine. Apr 1936, v85, p57.
The Film Criticism of Otis Ferguson. p120-22.
Film Daily. Feb 13, 1936, p7.
Hollywood Reporter. Feb 12, 1936, p2.
Hollywood Spectator. Feb 29, 1936, v10, p7-8.
Literary Digest. Feb 22, 1936, v121, p22.
Motion Picture Herald. Feb 22, 1936, p59.
The Nation. Mar 4, 1936, v142, p293.
National Board of Review Magazine. Mar 1936, v11, p12.
The New Republic. Mar 4, 1936, v86, p110.
The New York Times. Feb 13, 1936, p25.
The New Yorker. Feb 22, 1936, v12, p65-66.
Newsweek. Feb 22, 1936, v7, p31.
The Non-Western Films of John Ford. p48-50.
Rob Wagner's Script. Mar 28, 1936, v15, p10.
Stage. Feb 1936, v13, back cover.
Talking Pictures. p177-80.
Time. Feb 24, 1936, v27, p57.
Variety. Feb 19, 1936, p12.

The Prisoner of Zenda (US; Porter, Edwin S.; 1913)
Motion Picture News. Feb 22, 1913, p16.
Motography. Mar 15, 1913, p213.
Motography. Apr 19, 1913, p274.
The Moving Picture World. Feb 1, 1913, p477.
The Moving Picture World. Mar 1, 1913, p871-72.
Selected Film Criticism, 1912-1920. p207-09.

The Prisoner of Zenda (GB; Tucker, George Loane; 1915)
Variety. Mar 26, 1915, p24.

The Prisoner of Zenda (US; Ingram, Rex; 1922)
Exceptional Photoplays. Mar-May 1922, p5, 6.
Film Daily. Apr 30, 1922, p3.
The New York Times. Aug 1, 1922, p14.
Photoplay. Jul 1922, v22, p52.
Selected Film Criticism, 1921-1930. p230-32.
Variety. Aug 4, 1922, p34.

The Prisoner of Zenda (US; Cromwell, John; 1937)
Cinema. Spr 1968, v4, p19-21.
Classic Movies. p86-88.
A Companion to the Movies. p195.
The Film Criticism of Otis Ferguson. p195-96.
Film Daily. Sep 2, 1937, p9.
Films and Filming. Mar 1971, v17, p40-42.
The Films of David Niven. p44-45.
The Films of Ronald Colman. p191-96.
The Great Adventure Films. p68-73.
Halliwell's Hundred. p282-85.
Hollywood Reporter. Aug 28, 1937, p3.
Hollywood Spectator. Sep 11, 1937, v12, p12-13.
Life. Sep 13, 1937, v3, p94-95.
London Mercury. Dec 1937, v37, p199.
Love in the Film. p129-32.
Magill's Survey of Cinema. Series I. v3, p1375-78.
Make It Again, Sam. p151-56.
Motion Picture Herald. Sep 4, 1937, p39.
The New Republic. Sep 15, 1937, v92, p160.
The New Statesman and Nation. Nov 6, 1937, v14, p720+.
The New York Times. Sep 3, 1937, p12.
The New Yorker. Sep 11, 1937, v13, p62.
Newsweek. Sep 13, 1937, v10, p26.
Rob Wagner's Script. Oct 9, 1937, v18, p8.
Saint Nicholas. Jul 1937, v64, p37+.
Scholastic. Sep 25, 1937, v31, p36.

Selected Film Criticism, 1931-1940. p203-04.
The Spectator. Nov 19, 1937, v159, p900.
Those Fabulous Movie Years: The 30s. p127.
Time. Sep 13, 1937, v30, p32.
Variety. Sep 1, 1937, p22.
World Film News. Nov 1937, v2, p25.
World Film News. Dec 1937, v2, p22.

Prisoners (USSR; Cherviakov, Evgeny; 1937)
Film Daily. Mar 5, 1937, p21.
Motion Picture Herald. Feb 27, 1937, p58.
The New York Times. Feb 20, 1937, p9.
Variety. Feb 24, 1937, p19.

Private Detective 62 (Also titled: Man Killer) (US; Curtiz, Michael; 1933)
Commonweal. Jul 21, 1933, v18, p309.
Film Daily. Jul 8, 1933, p6.
Hollywood Reporter. Apr 19, 1933, p3.
Motion Picture Herald. Jul 15, 1933, p20.
New Outlook. Aug 1933, v162, p44.
The New York Times. Jul 7, 1933, p20.
Newsweek. Jul 15, 1933, v1, p31.
Variety. Jul 11, 1933, p15.

The Private Life of Don Juan (GB; Korda, Alexander; 1934)
Film Daily. Nov 15, 1934, p11.
His Majesty the American. p198-205.
Hollywood Reporter. Oct 27, 1934, p3.
Life. Feb 1935, v102, p32.
Magill's Survey of Cinema. Series II. v4, p1933-35.
Motion Picture Herald. Sep 22, 1934, p43.
The New Republic. Jan 9, 1935, v81, p246.
The New York Times. Dec 10, 1934, p16.
Rob Wagner's Script. Feb 2, 1935, v12, p8.
Selected Film Criticism: Foreign Films, 1930-1950. p140-41.
Time. Dec 17, 1934, v24, p33.
Variety. Dec 18, 1934, p12.

The Private Life of Helen of Troy (US; Korda, Alexander; 1927)
Film Daily. Dec 18, 1927, p6.
Magill's Survey of Cinema. Silent Films. v3, p883-85.
The Moving Picture World. Dec 17, 1927, p23.
The New York Times. Dec 10, 1927, p14.
Variety. Dec 14, 1927, p18.
Variety. Jan 4, 1928, p38.

The Private Life of Henry VIII (GB; Korda, Alexander; 1933)
American Film Criticism. p290-92.
Around Cinemas. p98-100.
Bookman (London). Feb 1934, v85, p439.
Canadian Magazine. Dec 1933, v80, p37.
Cinema Quarterly. Aut 1933, v2, p39-40.
A Critical History of the British Cinema. p116-17.
Eighty Years of Cinema. p96-97.
Fifty Classic British Films. p10-12.
Film Daily. Sep 21, 1933, p6.
From Quasimodo to Scarlett O'Hara. p174-76.
The Great British Films. p15-18.
Hollywood Reporter. Sep 20, 1933, p3.
The International Dictionary of Films and Filmmakers. v1, p372-73.
Literary Digest. Oct 28, 1933, v116, p36.
Lorentz on Film. p127-28.
Magill's Survey of Cinema. Series I. v3, p1379-82.
Motion Picture Herald. Sep 23, 1933, p34.
The Nation. Oct 25, 1933, v137, p493.
National Board of Review Magazine. Nov 1933, v8, p9.
New Outlook. Nov 1933, v162, p43.
The New Statesman and Nation. Oct 28, 1933, v6, p516.
The New York Times. Oct 13, 1933, p25.
The New York Times. Jul 30, 1933, p2.

The New York Times. Nov 12, 1933, p5.
The New York Times. Nov 26, 1933, p4.
The New York Times. Oct 22, 1933, p3.
The New Yorker. Oct 21, 1933, v9, p56-57.
Newsweek. Oct 21, 1933, v2, p30.
Rob Wagner's Script. Dec 2, 1933, v10, p8.
Rotha on the Film. p123-25.
Selected Film Criticism: Foreign Films, 1930-1950. p142.
Sight and Sound. Wint 1933-34, v2, p124-25.
The Spectator. Oct 27, 1933, v151, p574.
Time. Oct 16, 1933, v22, p33.
Vanity Fair. Dec 1933, v41, p58.
Variety. Oct 17, 1933, p19.
World Film News. Aug 1938, v3, p175.

Private Lives (US; Franklin, Sidney; 1931)
Film Daily. Dec 20, 1931, p10.
The Films of Norma Shearer. p178-80.
Hollywood Reporter. Nov 17, 1931, p3.
Judge. Feb 20, 1931, v101, p20.
Motion Picture Herald. Dec 26, 1931, p30.
The Nation. Jan 6, 1932, v134, p28.
The New York Times. Dec 19, 1931, p16.
The New York Times. Dec 27, 1931, p5.
The New Yorker. Dec 26, 1931, v7, p49.
Outlook and Independent. Dec 23, 1931, v159, p534.
Outlook and Independent. May 20, 1931, v158, p90.
Rob Wagner's Script. Jan 23, 1932, v6, p8.
Time. Dec 28, 1931, v18, p22.
Variety. Dec 22, 1931, p15.

The Private Lives of Elizabeth and Essex (Also titled: Elizabeth the Queen) (US; Curtiz, Michael; 1939)
Bette Davis: Her Films and Career. p98-101.
Canadian Forum. Jan 1940, v19, p327.
Casablanca and Other Major Films of Michael Curtiz. p73-75.
Commonweal. Nov 17, 1939, v31, p97.
Cosmopolitan. Jan 1940, v31, p97.
Film Daily. Sep 28, 1939, p6.
The Films of Errol Flynn. p82-86.
The Films of Olivia De Havilland. p147-52.
Hollywood Reporter. Sep 28, 1939, p3.
Hollywood Spectator. Oct 14, 1939, v14, p6.
Life. Oct 23, 1939, v7, p35-36+.
Magill's Survey of Cinema. Series I. v3, p1383-87.
Motion Picture Herald. Sep 30, 1939, p38.
The Nation. Dec 9, 1939, v149, p662.
National Board of Review Magazine. Dec 1939, v14, p14.
The New Masses. Dec 19, 1939, v33, p29.
The New York Times. Dec 2, 1939, p21.
The New Yorker. Dec 9, 1939, v15, p97-98.
Newsweek. Nov 6, 1939, v14, p34.
Photoplay. Dec 1939, v53, p62.
Rob Wagner's Script. Nov 18, 1939, v22, p16.
Scholastic. Dec 4, 1939, v35, p21E-23E.
The Spectator. Mar 29, 1940, v164, p448.
Studio. Jun 1940, v119, p210-11.
Theatre Arts. Nov 1939, v23, p803.
Those Fabulous Movie Years: The 30s. p180-81.
Time. Nov 13, 1939, v34, p80+.
Variety. Oct 4, 1939, p12.

Private Number (US; Del Ruth, Roy; 1936)
Film Daily. Jun 12, 1936, p13.
Hollywood Reporter. May 16, 1936, p3.
Motion Picture Herald. May 30, 1936, p36.
Time. Jun 15, 1936, v27, p57.
Variety. Jun 17, 1936, p23.

Private Worlds (US; La Cava, Gregory; 1935)
Claudette Colbert (Quirk). p80-83.
Esquire. Jun 1935, v3, p144.
The Film Criticism of Otis Ferguson. p71-72.
Film Daily. Mar 9, 1935, p3.
The Films of the Thirties. p152-53.

Hollywood Reporter. Mar 5, 1935, p3.
Literary Digest. Apr 13, 1935, v119, p36.
Motion Picture Herald. Mar 16, 1935, p38.
National Board of Review Magazine. Apr 1935, v10, p10.
The New Republic. Apr 17, 1935, v82, p285-86.
The New York Times. Mar 28, 1935, p25.
The New Yorker. Apr 6, 1935, v11, p77-78.
Newsweek. Apr 6, 1935, v5, p36.
Rob Wagner's Script. Mar 23, 1935, v13, p8.
The Spectator. Jul 26, 1935, v155, p150.
Theatre Arts Monthly. Jun 1935, v19, p406.
Time. Apr 8, 1935, v25, p26.
Vanity Fair. May 1935, v44, p46.
Variety. Apr 3, 1935, p17.

The Prize Fighter and the Lady (US; Van Dyke, W.S.; 1933)
Film Daily. Nov 4, 1933, p4.
The Films of Myrna Loy. p161-64.
Hollywood Reporter. Oct 20, 1933, p3.
Judge. Jan 1934, v106, p12.
Literary Digest. Nov 25, 1933, v116, p31.
Motion Picture Herald. Oct 28, 1933, p55.
The Nation. Nov 22, 1933, v137, p605.
New Outlook. Dec 1933, v162, p46.
The New York Times. Nov 11, 1933, p11.
The New Yorker. Nov 18, 1933, v9, p62.
Newsweek. Nov 18, 1933, v2, p34.
Rob Wagner's Script. Dec 23, 1933, v10, p10-11.
Time. Nov 13, 1933, v22, p20.
Vanity Fair. Jan 1934, v41, p46.
Variety. Nov 14, 1933, p17.

Professional Soldier (US; Garnett, Tay; 1936)
Film Daily. Dec 27, 1935, p4.
Hollywood Spectator. Jan 4, 1936, v10, p16-17.
Motion Picture Herald. Jan 4, 1936, p48.
The New York Times. Jan 30, 1936, p14.
Rob Wagner's Script. Feb 22, 1936, v15, p10.
Scholastic. Jan 25, 1936, v27, p29.
The Spectator. May 22, 1936, v156, p931.
Time. Feb 10, 1936, v27, p26.
Variety. Feb 5, 1936, p12.

Professional Sweetheart (US; Seiter, William A.; 1933)
Film Daily. May 27, 1933, p3.
The Films of Ginger Rogers. p78-79.
Hollywood Reporter. May 23, 1933, p3.
Judge. Sep 1933, v104, p20-21.
Motion Picture Herald. Jun 3, 1933, p37.
New Outlook. Aug 1933, v162, p45.
The New York Times. Jul 14, 1933, p15.
Newsweek. Jul 22, 1933, v1, p30.
Vanity Fair. Oct 1933, v41, p40.
Variety. Jul 18, 1933, p36.

Professor Beware (US; Nugent, Elliott; 1938)
Commonweal. Jul 29, 1938, v28, p370.
Film Daily. Jul 14, 1938, p5.
Harold Lloyd: The King of Daredevil Comedy. p141-47.
Harold Lloyd: The Shape of Laughter. p212-13.
Hollywood Reporter. Jul 12, 1938, p3.
Motion Picture Herald. Jul 16, 1938, p52, 55.
The New Masses. Jul 26, 1938, v28, p30.
The New Statesman and Nation. Jul 23, 1938, v16, p153.
The New York Times. Jul 14, 1938, p17.
The New Yorker. Jul 16, 1938, v14, p44-45.
Newsweek. Jul 18, 1938, v12, p24-25.
Rob Wagner's Script. Jul 1938, v19, p9.
Saint Nicholas. Jun 1938, v65, p46.
The Spectator. Jul 22, 1938, v161, p143.
Time. Jul 18, 1938, v32, p21.
Variety. Jul 13, 1938, p15.
World Film News. Aug 1938, v3, p171.

Professor Mamlock (USSR; Minkin, Adolph; Rappoport, Herbert; 1938)
Dictionary of Films. p294-95.
The Film Criticism of Otis Ferguson. p242-43.
Film Daily. Nov 11, 1938, p4.
Graham Greene on Film. p240-41.
Life and Letters To-day. May 1939, v21, p124-26.
The Nation. Nov 26, 1938, v147, p574.
National Board of Review Magazine. Dec 1938, v13, p20.
The New Masses. Nov 22, 1938, v29, p27-28.
The New Republic. Dec 14, 1938, v97, p174.
The New Statesman and Nation. Apr 1, 1939, v17, p492.
The New Statesman and Nation. Sep 2, 1939, v18, p342.
The New York Times. Nov 8, 1938, p26.
The New Yorker. Nov 19, 1938, v14, p87.
Selected Film Criticism: Foreign Films, 1930-1950. p143.
The Spectator. Mar 31, 1939, v162, p532.
The Spectator. Sep 1, 1939, v163, p325.
The Tatler. Apr 1939, v152, p6.
Time. Nov 21, 1938, v32, p53.
Variety. Nov 9, 1938, p19.

Promenade en Bicyclette *See* Excursion

A Propos de Nice (Also titled: On the Subject of Nice) (FR; Vigo, Jean; 1932)
Documentary: A History of Non-Fiction Film. p75-77.
The Documentary Tradition. p77-79.
The Essential Cinema. p134-40.
Film. Dec 1955, n6, p22.
The Films of Jean Vigo. p11-42.
French Film (Sadoul). p43.
The International Dictionary of Films and Filmmakers. v1, p9-10.
Jean Vigo (Sales Gomes). p52-79.
Literature/Film Quarterly. n3, 1976, v4, p251-63.
Travelling. Sum 1979, n55, p50.

Prosperity (US; Wood, Sam; 1932)
Film Daily. Nov 26, 1932, p4.
Hollywood Reporter. Nov 1, 1932, p3.
Motion Picture Herald. Nov 12, 1932, p35.
The New York Times. Nov 26, 1932, p11.
The New Yorker. Dec 3, 1932, v8, p72-73.
Rob Wagner's Script. Nov 19, 1932, v8, p8.
Time. Dec 5, 1932, v20, p34.
Variety. Nov 29, 1932, p18.

Prudence on Broadway (US; Borzage, Frank; 1919)
Exhibitor's Trade Review. Jul 12, 1919, p473.
Motion Picture News. Jul 12, 1919, p599.
The Moving Picture World. Jul 12, 1919, p281.
Variety. Jul 18, 1919, p42.
Wid's Daily. Sep 14, 1919, p14.

Prunella (US; Tourneur, Maurice; 1918)
Exhibitor's Trade Review. May 25, 1918, p1995-97.
Exhibitor's Trade Review. Jun 15, 1918, p116.
Fifty Great American Silent Films, 1912-1920. p96-98.
Magill's Survey of Cinema. Silent Films. v3, p886-88.
Marguerite Clark. p53-54, 102-06.
Motion Picture Classic. Aug 1918, p60, 62.
Motion Picture News. Jun 8, 1918, p3400.
Motion Picture News. Jun 15, 1918, p3600.
The Moving Picture World. Mar 23, 1918, p1707.
The Moving Picture World. Jun 8, 1918, p1472.
The New York Times. Jun 3, 1918, p9.
Photoplay. Aug 1918, v14, p80.
Selected Film Criticism, 1912-1920. 209-10.
Variety. Jun 7, 1918, p33.
Wid's Daily. May 26, 1918, p15-16.

The Public Enemy (US; Wellman, William A.; 1931)
America in the Dark. p160-61.
American Film Criticism. p251-53.
American History/American Film. p57-75.

Around Cinemas. p21.
Beyond Formula: American Film Genres. p174-77.
BFI/Monthly Film Bulletin. Feb 1976, v43, p39.
Cinema, the Magic Vehicle. v1, p191-92.
Classics of the Gangster Film. p13-16.
Dictionary of Films. p296.
Dreams and Dead Ends. p43-58.
Film Daily. Apr 26, 1931, p10.
Films and Filming. Jan 1964, v10, p7-12.
Films in America, 1929-1969. p36.
Films in Review. Aug-Sep 1958, v9, p365-66.
The Films of James Cagney. p49-53.
From Quasimodo to Scarlett O'Hara. p144-46.
The Great Films. p83-87.
The Great Gangster Pictures. p319-20.
Hollywood Genres. p86-90.
The International Dictionary of Films and Filmmakers. v1, p377-78.
Judge. May 16, 1931, v100, p20.
Judge. Aug 8, 1931, v101, p22.
A Library of Film Criticism: American Film Directors. p498.
Life. May 22, 1931, v97, p18.
Lorentz on Film. p73-74.
Magill's Survey of Cinema. Series I. v3, p1395-98.
National Board of Review Magazine. May 1931, v6, p7-12.
The New York Times. Apr 24, 1931, p27.
The New Yorker. May 2, 1931, v7, p63-64.
Outlook and Independent. May 20, 1931, v158, p90.
The Public Enemy. 1981.
The Public Enemy. p11-35.
Rob Wagner's Script. Jun 13, 1931, v5, p8-9.
Sight and Sound. May 1951, v20, p12.
Those Fabulous Movie Years: The 30s. p21.
Time. May 4, 1931, v17, p44.
Variety. Apr 29, 1931, p12.
The Velvet Light Trap. Jun 1971, n1, p5-11.
Warner Brothers Presents. p61-62.
William A. Wellman (Thompson). p110-14+.
50 Classic Motion Pictures. p62-67.

Pugachev (USSR; Petrov-Bytov, P.P.; 1938)
Film Daily. Jul 11, 1938, p7.
The New Masses. Jul 19, 1938, v28, p31.
The New York Times. Jul 4, 1938, p10.
Variety. Jul 13, 1938, p17.

The Purchase Price (US; Wellman, William A.; 1932)
Film Daily. Jul 16, 1932, p4.
The Films of Barbara Stanwyck. p80-81.
Motion Picture Herald. Jul 16, 1932, p52.
The New York Times. Jul 16, 1932, p5.
The New Yorker. Jul 23, 1932, v8, p45.
Starring Miss Barbara Stanwyck. p47.
Time. Jul 25, 1932, v20, p22.
Variety. Jul 19, 1932, p25.
William A. Wellman (Thompson). p123-27.

Puritan, Le (FR; Musso, Jeff; 1938)
Film Daily. Mar 20, 1939, p10.
Motion Picture Herald. Mar 25, 1939, p41, 44.
The Nation. Mar 25, 1939, v148, p357-58.
The New Masses. Feb 28, 1939, v30, p28-29.
The New Statesman and Nation. Mar 26, 1938, v15, p526-27.
Rob Wagner's Script. Jun 10, 1939, v21, p16.
Time. May 15, 1939, v33, p59.
Variety. Mar 23, 1938, p17.

Pursued (US; Walsh, Raoul; 1947)
Commonweal. Mar 14, 1947, v45, p540.
Each Man in His Own Time. p336-37.
Film Daily. Feb 21, 1947, p7.
Magill's Survey of Cinema, Series II. v4, p1950-52.
Motion Picture Herald Product Digest. Feb 22, 1947, p3485.
New Republic. Mar 3, 1947, v116, p39.
The New York Times. Mar 8, 1947, p10.

The New Yorker. Mar 15, 1947, v23, p66+.
Newsweek. Mar 17, 1947, v29, p100.
Robert Mitchum on the Screen. p95-96.
Time. Mar 31, 1947, v49, p100.

Puttin' on the Ritz (US; Sloman, Edward; 1930)
Exhibitors Herald-World. Feb 22, 1930, p36.
Film Daily. Feb 16, 1930, p9.
The Film Spectator. Apr 26, 1930, v9, p18-19.
Judge. Mar 8, 1930, v98, p21.
The Nation. Mar 5, 1930, v130, p280.
The New York Times. Feb 15, 1930, p15.
The New York Times. Feb 23, 1930, p5.
The New Yorker. Feb 22, 1930, v6, p80.
Outlook and Independent. Feb 26, 1930, v154, p355.
Time. Mar 3, 1930, v15, p28.
Variety. Feb 19, 1930, p21.

Putyovka v Zhizn *See* The Road to Life

Pygmalion (GB; Asquith, Anthony; Howard, Leslie; 1938)
The Age of the Dream Palace. p237-38.
American Film Criticism. p362-64.
Canadian Magazine. Mar 1939, v91, p41.
Cinema, the Magic Vehicle. v1, p288-89.
Classics of the Foreign Film. p128-29.
Commonweal. Dec 9, 1938, v29, p190.
A Critical History of the British Cinema. p103.
Dictionary of Films. p297.
Eighty Years of Cinema. p114-16.
Fifty Classic British Films. p34-36.
Film and Literature. p228-42.
The Film Criticism of Otis Ferguson. p243-44.
Film Daily. Nov 25, 1938, p6.
The Films of Anthony Asquith. p89-96.
The Great British Films. p45-48.
Hollywood Spectator. Jan 21, 1939, v13, p16.
Life. Dec 12, 1938, v5, p30-32.
Living Age. May 1939, v356, p245-46.
London Mercury. Nov 1938, v39, p63-64.
Lorentz on Film. p161-62.
Magill's Survey of Cinema. Series I. v3, p1399-1403.
Motion Picture Herald. Sep 10, 1938, p55, 58.
The Nation. Dec 24, 1938, v147, p701-02.
National Board of Review Magazine. Jan 1939, v14, p14.
The New Masses. Dec 13, 1938, v29, p29-30.
The New Republic. Dec 28, 1938, v97, p231.
The New Statesman and Nation. Oct 8, 1938, v16, p529.
The New Statesman and Nation. Jul 1, 1939, v18, p12-13.
The New York Times. Dec 8, 1938, p34.
The New York Times. Dec 11, 1938, p7-8.
The New Yorker. Dec 3, 1938, v14, p100-01.
Newsweek. Dec 5, 1938, v12, p24.
Newsweek. Feb 13, 1939, v13, p29.
North American Review. Mar 1939, v247, p178-79.
Photoplay. Feb 1939, v53, p48.
Photoplay. May 1939, v53, p68+.
Rob Wagner's Script. Jan 7, 1939, v20, p16.
Saturday Review. Dec 24, 1938, v19, p8.
Scholastic. Dec 17, 1938, v33, p29.
Selected Film Criticism: Foreign Films, 1930-1950. p143-45.
Sight and Sound. Aut 1938, v7, p126.
Sociology and Social Research. May 1939, v23, p497.
The Spectator. Oct 14, 1938, v161, p603.
Stage. Dec 1938, v16, p20-21.
The Tatler. Oct 19, 1938, v150, p102.
Theater and Film. p61-75.
Theatre Arts. Nov 1938, v22, p813.
Time. Dec 5, 1938, v32, p26+.
Variety. Sep 7, 1938, p13.
World Film News. Oct 1938, v3, p236-37.
World Film News. Nov 1938, v3, p313.

Quai des Brumes (Also titled: Port of Shadows; The Foggy Quay) (FR; Carné, Marcel; 1938)
Cinema, the Magic Vehicle. v1, p287-88.
Dictionary of Films. p299.
Eighty Years of Cinema. p114.
The Film Criticism of Otis Ferguson. p275-77.
Film Daily. Nov 1, 1939, p7.
Films and Filming. Feb 1964, v10, p14-15.
Films in Review. Apr 1963, v14, p199-200.
From Quasimodo to Scarlett O'hara. p322-25.
The Great French Films. p80-83.
The International Dictionary of Films and Filmmakers. v1, p379-80.
Kiss Kiss Bang Bang. p417.
Magill's Survey of Cinema. Foreign Language Films. v5, p2473-79.
Motion Picture Herald. Sep 3, 1938, p43.
National Board of Review Magazine. Nov 1939, v14, p15.
The New Masses. Nov 4, 1939, v33, p30-31.
The New Republic. Nov 22, 1939, v101, p142.
The New Statesman and Nation. Jan 14, 1939, v17, p48-49.
The New York Times. Oct 30, 1939, p13.
The New York Times. Dec 25, 1939, p28.
The New Yorker. Nov 4, 1939, v15, p66-67.
The Spectator. Jan 27, 1939, v162, p128.
Variety. Jun 15, 1938, p15.

Quality Street (US; Franklin, Sidney; 1927)
Film Daily. Nov 13, 1927, p8.
The Moving Picture World. Nov 12, 1927, p26.
The New York Times. Nov 2, 1927, p24.
Variety. Nov 9, 1927, p20.

Quality Street (US; Stevens, George; 1937)
Canadian Magazine. May 1937, v87, p31.
Film Daily. Mar 10, 1937, p8.
The Films of Katharine Hepburn. p83-86.
Hollywood Reporter. Mar 6, 1937, p3.
Hollywood Spectator. Mar 27, 1937, v11, p6-7.
Kiss Kiss Bang Bang. p422.
Motion Picture Herald. Mar 20, 1937, p49, 52.
The New York Times. Apr 9, 1937, p19.
The New Yorker. Apr 10, 1937, v13, p70.
Rob Wagner's Script. Mar 27, 1937, v17, p8.
Scholastic. Apr 3, 1937, v30, p21.
Time. Apr 5, 1937, v29, p55.
Variety. Apr 14, 1937, p12.
World Film News. Jun 1937, v2, p21-22.

Quatorze Juillet (Also titled: Fourteenth of July; July 14th) (FR; Clair, René; 1933)
Cinema Quarterly. Spr 1933, v1, p179-80.
Cinema, the Magic Vehicle. v1, p214-15.
Film Daily. Oct 21, 1933, p4.
Hollywood Spectator. Feb 10, 1932, v8, p7.
Judge. Jul 1933, v104, p20.
Literary Digest. Nov 11, 1933, v116, p31.
Motion Picture Herald. Jan 28, 1933, p24.
The Nation. Nov 1, 1933, v137, p520.
The New Statesman and Nation. Feb 18, 1933, v5, p189-90.
The New York Times. Oct 20, 1933, p14.
The New Yorker. Oct 21, 1933, v9, p57.
Newsweek. Oct 28, 1933, v2, p28.
Photoplay. Jan 1934, v45, p110.
René Clair (McGerr). p110-17.
Review of Reviews. Mar 1933, v83, p72.
Selected Film Criticism: Foreign Films, 1930-1950. p89-91.
Time. Oct 30, 1933, v22, p22.
Vanity Fair. Jul 1933, v40, p45+.
Variety. Feb 7, 1933, p12.
Variety. Oct 24, 1933, p17.

Que Viva Mexico *See* Thunder Over Mexico

Queen Christina (US; Mamoulian, Rouben; 1933)
Commonweal. Jul 20, 1934, v20, p299-300.
Film Daily. Dec 28, 1933, p18.
The Films of Greta Garbo. p119-24.
Hollywood Reporter. Dec 11, 1933, p3.
Literary Digest. Jan 13, 1934, v117, p34.
Love in the Film. p103-07.
Magill's Survey of Cinema. Series I. v3, p1404-06.
Mamoulian (Milne). p72-80.
Motion Picture Herald. Dec 30, 1933, p29.
The Nation. Jan 24, 1934, v138, p112.
The New Republic. Jan 31, 1934, v77, p336.
The New York Times. Dec 27, 1933, p23.
Newsweek. Jan 6, 1934, v3, p36.
Variety. Jan 2, 1934, p13.

Queen Elizabeth (French title: Amours de la Reine
  Elisabeth) (FR; Mercanton, Louis; Desfontaines,
  Henri; 1912)
Dictionary of Films. p10-11.
A History of Films. p67.
A History of Narrative Film. p37-38.
Magill's Survey of Cinema. Silent Films. v3, p889-91.
Motion Picture Herald. Jan 2, 1937, p58.
Motion Pictures. p45-52.

Queen Kelly (US; Stroheim, Erich von; 1928)
BFI/Monthly Film Bulletin. Sep 1985, v52, p294-95.
Cinema, the Magic Vehicle. v1, p150-51.
Dictionary of Films. p301-02.
Film Culture. Jan 1955, v1, p33-35.
Film Heritage. Fall 1966, v2, p24-29.
The Films of Gloria Swanson. p211-13.
Saint Cinema: Selected Writings, 1929-1970. p168-72.
The Silent Voice. p182-88.
Stroheim: A Pictorial Record of His Nine Films. p209-28.
Stroheim (Finler). p107-14.
Variety. Sep 5, 1984, p6.

Queen of Destiny *See* Sixty Glorious Years

The Queen of Sheba (US; Edwards, J. Gordon; 1921)
Film Daily. Apr 17, 1921, p2.
Magill's Survey of Cinema. Silent Films. v2, p892-94.
Motion Picture Classic. Jul 1921, v12, p88.
The New York Times. Apr 11, 1921, p9.
Selected Film Criticism, 1921-1930. p232.

Quick Millions (US; Brown, Rowland; 1931)
Film Daily. Apr 19, 1931, p10.
The Films of Spencer Tracy. p71-72.
From Quasimodo to Scarlett O'Hara. p148-49.
The Great Gangster Pictures. p323-24.
Judge. May 9, 1931, v100, p22.
Life. May 8, 1931, v97, p20.
National Board of Review Magazine. May 1931, v6, p7-12.
The New Statesman and Nation. Jul 18, 1931, v2, p80.
The New York Times. Apr 18, 1931, p17.
The New York Times. Apr 26, 1931, p5.
The New Yorker. Apr 25, 1931, v7, p82.
Outlook and Independent. May 6, 1931, v158, p27.
The Spectator. Aug 1, 1931, v147, p153.
Variety. Apr 22, 1931, p18.

Quick Millions (US; St. Clair, Malcolm; 1939)
Film Daily. Sep 22, 1939, p6.
Hollywood Reporter. Aug 8, 1939, p3.
Hollywood Spectator. Sep 2, 1939, v14, p14-15.
Motion Picture Herald. Aug 12, 1939, p50.
The New York Times. Sep 22, 1939, p27.
Variety. Aug 16, 1939, p14.

Quo Vadis? (IT; Guazzoni, Enrico; 1913)
Film Daily. Aug 28, 1921, p4.
The Italian Cinema. p27-28.
The Moving Picture World. May 17, 1913, p681-82.

The New York Dramatic Mirror. Apr 30, 1914, p28.
Selected Film Criticism, 1912-1920. p212-15.
Variety. Apr 25, 1913, p8.

Rachel and the Stranger (US; Foster, Norman; 1948)
Commonweal. Oct 8, 1948, v48, p618.
Film Daily. Aug 4, 1948, p6.
The Films of William Holden. p81-84.
Hollywood Reporter. Aug 3, 1948, p3.
Motion Picture Herald Product Digest. Aug 7, 1948, p4265.
The New York Times. Sep 20, 1948, p21.
Robert Mitchum on the Screen. p102-03.
Time. Sep 27, 1948, v52, p94+.
Variety. Aug 8, 1948, p11.

Racket Busters (US; Bacon, Lloyd; 1938)
Classics of the Gangster Film. p63-67.
Commonweal. Aug 5, 1938, v28, p390.
The Complete Films of Humphrey Bogart. p60-61.
Film Daily. Oct 6, 1938, p7.
The Gangster Film. p187-89.
The Great Gangster Pictures. p327-28.
Hollywood Reporter. Aug 19, 1938, p3.
Motion Picture Herald. Aug 20, 1938, p47.
The New Masses. Aug 23, 1938, v28, p30-31.
The New York Times. Aug 11, 1938, p13.
Time. Aug 22, 1938, v32, p41.
Variety. Aug 17, 1938, p23.

Raffles (US; D'Arrast, Harry D'Abbadie; 1930)
Exhibitors Herald-World. Aug 2, 1930, p26.
Film Daily. Jul 27, 1930, p10.
The Films of Ronald Colman. p131-34.
Judge. Aug 16, 1930, v99, p23.
Life. Aug 15, 1930, v96, p17.
The Nation. Aug 6, 1930, v131, p161.
The New York Times. Jul 25, 1930, p20.
The New York Times. Aug 3, 1930, p5.
The New Yorker. Aug 2, 1930, v6, p54.
Outlook and Independent. Aug 13, 1930, v155, p591.
Samuel Goldwyn Presents. p91-93.
Variety. Jul 30, 1930, p17.

Raffles (US; Wood, Sam; 1939)
Commonweal. Jan 12, 1940, v31, p266-67.
Film Daily. Jan 16, 1940, p5.
The Films of David Niven. p67-69.
The Films of Olivia De Havilland. p153-56.
Hollywood Reporter. Dec 19, 1939, p3.
Hollywood Spectator. Jan 6, 1940, v14, p8.
Motion Picture Herald. Dec 23, 1939, p40.
The New York Times. Jan 13, 1940, p11.
The New Yorker. Jan 6, 1939, v15, p51.
Rob Wagner's Script. Jan 20, 1940, v23, p18.
Samuel Goldwyn Presents. p114-16, 208-11.
Time. Jan 29, 1940, v35, p68.
Variety. Dec 20, 1939, p47.

Rage in Heaven (US; Van Dyke, W.S.; 1941)
Commonweal. Apr 4, 1941, v33, p602.
Film Daily. Mar 13, 1941, p8.
The Films of Ingrid Bergman. p78-81.
Hollywood Reporter. Mar 5, 1941, p3.
Motion Picture Herald Product Digest. Feb 8, 1941, p55.
The New Republic. Mar 31, 1941, v104, p435.
The New York Times. Mar 21, 1941, p19.
Time. Sep 18, 1939, v34, p59.
Variety. Mar 5, 1941, p16.

The Rage of Paris (US; Koster, Henry; 1938)
Commonweal. Jul 8, 1938, v28, p301.
Film Daily. Jun 14, 1938, p5.
Hollywood Reporter. Jun 9, 1938, p3.
Motion Picture Herald. Jun 18, 1938, p39.
The New York Times. Jul 2, 1938, p10.
The New Yorker. Jun 25, 1938, v14, p52-53.

Newsweek. Jun 27, 1938, v11, p23.
Rob Wagner's Script. Jun 18, 1938, v19, p14.
The Spectator. Sep 9, 1938, v161, p403.
Time. Jul 4, 1938, v32, p18.
Variety. Jun 15, 1938, p14.
World Film News. Sep 1938, v3, p222.
World Film News. Oct 1938, v3, p266.

The Ragged Girl of Oz *See* The Patchwork Girl of Oz

Rain (US; Milestone, Lewis; 1932)
Film Daily. Oct 14, 1932, p6.
The Films of Joan Crawford. p101-02.
Hollywood Reporter. Sep 9, 1932, p3.
Judge. Nov 1932, v103, p20.
Lewis Milestone (Millichap). p60-68+.
Magill's Survey of Cinema. Series I. v3, p1415-18.
Make It Again, Sam. p157-62.
Motion Picture Herald. Sep 17, 1932, p36.
The New Outlook. Nov 1932, v161, p47.
The New York Times. Oct 13, 1932, p22.
The New Yorker. Oct 22, 1932, v8, p56-57.
Rob Wagner's Script. Sep 17, 1932, v8, p8.
Time. Oct 3, 1932, v20, p37.
Vanity Fair. Nov 1932, v39, p58.
Variety. Oct 18, 1932, p14.

Rain or Shine (US; Capra, Frank; 1930)
Exhibitors Herald-World. Aug 16, 1930, p30.
Film Daily. Aug 10, 1930, p10.
The Films of Frank Capra (Scherle and Levy). p87-90.
Frank Capra (Maland). p54.
Judge. Aug 30, 1930, v99, p23.
Life. Aug 29, 1930, v95, p18.
The New Yorker. Aug 16, 1930, v6, p55-56.
Time. Aug 18, 1930, v16, p46.
Variety. Jul 23, 1930, p19.

The Rains Came (US; Brown, Clarence; 1939)
Commonweal. Sep 22, 1939, v30, p500.
Film Daily. Sep 11, 1939, p5.
The Films of Myrna Loy. p212-14.
The Films of Tyrone Power. p95-98.
Hollywood Reporter. Sep 7, 1939, p3.
Hollywood Spectator. Sep 30, 1939, v14, p6.
Motion Picture Herald. Sep 9, 1939, p46.
The New Statesman and Nation. Dec 30, 1939, v18, p956.
The New York Times. Sep 9, 1939, p11.
The New Yorker. Sep 16, 1939, v15, p61-62.
Newsweek. Sep 18, 1939, v14, p37.
Photplay. Nov 1939, v53, p64.
Rob Wagner's Script. Sep 16, 1939, v22, p14-15.
Sociology and Social Research. Jan 1940, v24, p296.
The Spectator. Dec 29, 1939, v163, p932.
Those Fabulous Movie Years: The 30s. p166-67.
Time. Sep 18, 1939, v34, p50.
Variety. Sep 13, 1939, p12.

Ramona (US; Griffith, D.W.; 1910)
D.W. Griffith, His Biograph Films in Perspective. p130-33+.
The Emergence of Film Art. p51.
The Film Index. May 28, 1910, v5, p18.
The Moving Picture World. Jun 4, 1910, p933, 942.
Selected Film Criticism, 1896-1911. p77-81.

Ramona (US; King, Henry; 1936)
Commonweal. Oct 30, 1936, v25, p20.
Esquire. Dec 1936, v6, p133.
Film Daily. Sep 16, 1936, p25.
Garbo and the Night Watchman. p138-41.
Hollywood Reporter. Sep 12, 1936, p3.
Hollywood Spectator. Sep 26, 1936, v11, p6-7.
Judge. Nov 1936, v111, p22.
Motion Picture Herald. Nov 19, 1936, p45.
The New York Times. Oct 7, 1936, p32.
Rob Wagner's Script. Sep 26, 1936, v16, p10-11.

Saint Nicholas. Sep 1936, v63, p29.
The Spectator. Jan 15, 1937, v158, p83.
Stage. Oct 1936, v14, p26.
Time. Oct 5, 1936, v28, p28.
Variety. Oct 14, 1936, p15.
World Film News. Jan 1937, v1, p26.

Rasputin (FR; Herbier, Marcel L'; 1939)
Commonweal. Nov 3, 1939, v31, p47.
Film Daily. Oct 27, 1939, p7.
Motion Picture Herald. Oct 21, 1939, p38.
National Board of Review Magazine. Dec 1939, v14, p16.
The New Masses. Oct 31, 1939, v33, p29-30.
The New York Times. Oct 17, 1939, p31.
The New Yorker. Oct 21, 1939, v15, p74.
Variety. Oct 18, 1939, p14.

Rasputin and the Empress (Also titled: Rasputin) (US; Boleslavski, Richard; 1932)
Cinefantastique. Fall 1970, v1, p11-13.
Commonweal. Feb 22, 1933, v17, p469.
Film Daily. Dec 28, 1932, p10.
Hollywood Reporter. Dec 24, 1932, p3.
Magill's Survey of Cinema. Series I. v3, p1425-28.
Motion Picture Herald. Dec 31, 1932, p36.
The Nation. Jan 18, 1933, v136, p76.
The New Outlook. Feb 1933, v161, p49.
The New Republic. Apr 19, 1933, v74, p282.
The New York Times. Dec 24, 1932, p11.
Photoplay. Feb 1933, v43, p68.
Rob Wagner's Script. Apr 1, 1933, v9, p8-9.
Time. Jan 2, 1933, v21, p18.
Vanity Fair. Feb 1933, v39, p48.
Variety. Dec 27, 1932, p14.

The Rat (US; Cutts, Graham; 1926)
Film Daily. Jan 6, 1926, p6.
Magill's Survey of Cinema. Silent Films. v3, p899-901.
Variety. Sep 23, 1925, p40.

The Rat (GB; Raymond, Jack; 1937)
Film Daily. Jan 31, 1938, p8.
Hollywood Reporter. Dec 1, 1937, p14.
Motion Picture Herald. Nov 27, 1937, p55.
The New York Times. Feb 28, 1938, p19.
Variety. Nov 24, 1937, p16.
World Film News. Apr 1938, v3, p39.

Raub der Mona Lisa, Der (Also titled: The Theft of the Mona Lisa) (GER; Bolvary, Geza von; 1931)
Film Daily. Apr 3, 1932, p10.
Motion Picture Herald. Apr 9, 1932, p24.
National Board of Review Magazine. May 1932, v7, p10.
The New York Times. Mar 30, 1932, p15.
The New Yorker. Apr 9, 1932, v8, p66-67.
Variety. Sep 15, 1931, p28.
Variety. Apr 5, 1932, p22.

The Raven (US; Friedlander, Louis; 1935)
Film Daily. Jun 4, 1935, p6.
The Films of Bela Lugosi. p110-12.
The Films of Boris Karloff. p109-11.
Hollywood Reporter. Jun 1, 1935, p3.
Motion Picture Herald. Jun 15, 1935, p78.
The New York Times. Jul 5, 1935, p9.
The New Yorker. Jul 13, 1935, v11, p52.
Rob Wagner's Script. Jul 13, 1935, v13, p10-11.
Time. Jan 17, 1935, v25, p40.
Variety. Jul 10, 1935, p19.

The Razor's Edge (US; Goulding, Edmund; 1946)
Commonweal. Dec 13, 1946, v45, p230-31.
Film Daily. Nov 20, 1946, p12.
The Films of the Forties. p186-87.
The Films of Tyrone Power. p139-43.
Fortnight. Dec 30, 1946, v1, p41-42.

Hollywood Reporter. Nov 20, 1946, p3.
Life. Aug 12, 1946, v21, p75-83.
Life. Nov 18, 1946, v21, p97-100.
Magill's Survey of Cinema. Series I. v3, p1429-33.
Motion Picture Herald Product Digest. Nov 30, 1946, p3334.
The New Republic. Dec 9, 1946, v115, p76.
The New York Times. Nov 20, 1946, p42.
The New Yorker. Nov 30, 1946, v22, p86+.
Newsweek. Dec 2, 1946, v28, p109.
Rob Wagner's Script. Jan 4, 1947, v33, p13-14.
Selected Film Criticism, 1941-1950. p196-98.
Theatre Arts. Jan 1947, v31, p41.
Time. Dec 9, 1946, v48, p101.
Variety. Nov 20, 1946, p22.

Razumov (FR; Allégret, Marc; 1937)
Motion Picture Herald. Mar 27, 1937, p46.
The Nation. Mar 27, 1937, v144, p362-63.
National Board of Review Magazine. Apr 1937, v12, p14.
The New York Times. Mar 9, 1937, p27.
Time. Mar 22, 1937, v29, p41.
Variety. Mar 17, 1937, p15.

Re Burlone, Il (IT; Guazzoni, Enrico; 1936)
Motion Picture Herald. Apr 4, 1936, p37.
The New York Times. Mar 28, 1936, p11.
Variety. Apr 8, 1936, p17.

Reaching for the Moon (US; Goulding, Edmund; 1931)
Exhibitors Herald-World. Dec 20, 1930, p31.
Film Daily. Jan 4, 1931, p10.
Life. Jan 16, 1931, v97, p20.
The New York Times. Dec 30, 1930, p24.
The New Yorker. Jan 10, 1931, v6, p57.
Outlook and Independent. Jan 14, 1931, v157, p71.
Time. Jan 5, 1931, v17, p25.
Variety. Jan 7, 1931, p22.

Ready Money (US; Apfel, Oscar C.; 1914)
The Moving Picture World. Nov 14, 1914, p996.
The Moving Picture World. Nov 21, 1914, p1083.
The New York Dramatic Mirror. Nov 11, 1914, p30.
Variety. Nov 14, 1914, p25.

Ready, Willing and Able (US; Enright, Ray; 1937)
Film Daily. Mar 16, 1937, p12.
Hollywood Reporter. Jan 23, 1937, p3.
Hollywood Spectator. Feb 13, 1937, v11, p8-9.
Motion Picture Herald. Feb 6, 1937, p47.
The New York Times. Mar 15, 1937, p27.
Rob Wagner's Script. Mar 27, 1937, v17, p10.
Time. Mar 22, 1937, v29, p41.
Variety. Mar 17, 1937, p14.

The Real Glory (US; Hathaway, Henry; 1939)
Commonweal. Sep 29, 1939, v30, p519.
Film Daily. Sep 15, 1939, p5.
The Films of Gary Cooper. p166-68.
Graham Greene on Film. p261-62.
Hollywood Reporter. Sep 12, 1939, p3.
Hollywood Spectator. Sep 30, 1939, v14, p7.
Life. Oct 2, 1939, v7, p381.
Motion Picture Herald. Sep 16, 1939, p39.
The New Masses. Oct 10, 1939, v33, p30-31.
The New Republic. Oct 4, 1939, v100, p243.
The New Statesman and Nation. Dec 23, 1939, v18, p927-28.
The New York Times. Sep 15, 1939, p26.
The New Yorker. Sep 23, 1939, v15, p58.
Newsweek. Sep 25, 1939, v14, p42-43.
Photoplay. Oct 1939, v53, p26-27+.
Photoplay. Nov 1939, v53, p64.
Rob Wagner's Script. Oct 14, 1939, v22, p16.
Samuel Goldwyn Presents. p205-07.
Scholastic. Oct 9, 1939, v35, p10.
The Spectator. Jan 12, 1940, v164, p44.

Time. Sep 25, 1939, v34, p33.
Variety. Sep 13, 1939, p12.

Reap the Wild Wind (US; DeMille, Cecil B.; 1942)
Commonweal. Apr 3, 1942, v35, p592.
The Complete Films of John Wayne. p117-18.
Film Daily. Mar 19, 1942, p7.
The Films of Cecil B. DeMille. p326-29.
The Films of Susan Hayward. p69-72.
Hollywood Reporter. Mar 19, 1942, p3.
Motion Picture Herald Product Digest. Mar 21, 1942, p574.
The New York Times. Mar 27, 1942, p27.
Newsweek. Apr 6, 1942, v30, p37.
Scholastic. Mar 30, 1942, v40, p37.
Time. Apr 20, 1942, v39, p86+.
Variety. Mar 25, 1942, p8.

Rebecca (US; Hitchcock, Alfred; 1940)
The Art of Alfred Hitchcock. p89-96.
Cinema: The Novel into Films. p396-99.
Commonweal. Apr 12, 1940, v31, p534.
The Film Criticism of Otis Ferguson. p295.
Film Daily. Mar 26, 1940, p6.
The Films of Alfred Hitchcock. p88-93.
The Films of Laurence Olivier. p82-83.
Framework. Aut 1980, n13, p19-24.
Halliwell's Hundred. p294-97.
Hitchcock: The First Forty-Four Films. p57-60.
Hitchcock (Truffaut). p127-40+.
Hollywood Reporter. Mar 21, 1940, p3.
Hollywood Reporter. Mar 21, 1940, p3.
Hollywood Spectator. Apr 1, 1940, v14, p6.
Laurence Olivier (Hirsch). p47-51.
Laurence Olivier: Theater and Cinema. p77-81.
Life. Jan 15, 1940, v7, p31-32+.
The London Times. Jun 27, 1940, p4.
Magill's Survey of Cinema. Series I. v3, p1434-37.
Motion Picture Herald. Mar 30, 1940,, p59.
The New Republic. Apr 8, 1940, v102, p474.
The New York Times. Mar 29, 1940, p25.
The New York Times. Mar 31, 1940, sec9, p5.
The New Yorker. Mar 30, 1940, v16, p71.
Newsweek. Apr 8, 1940, v15, p34.
Saturday Review. Jun 8, 1940, v22, p21.
Scholastic. Apr 3, 1940, v36, p35.
Selected Film Criticism, 1931-1940. p206-07.
Theatre Arts. May 1940, v24, p320.
Thousand Eyes Magazine. May 1976, n10, p6-7.
Time. Apr 15, 1940, v35, p96+.
Variety. Mar 27, 1940, p17.

Rebecca of Sunnybrook Farm (US; Neilan, Marshall; 1917)
Magill's Survey of Cinema. Silent Films. v3, p902-04.
Motion Picture News. Sep 22, 1917, p2035.
The Moving Picture World. Sep 22, 1917, p1855, 1896.
The New York Dramatic Mirror. Sep 15, 1917, p18.
Selected Film Criticism, 1912-1920. p215-17.
Variety. Sep 7, 1917, p34.
Wid's Daily. Sep 13, 1917, p852.

Rebecca of Sunnybrook Farm (US; Dwan, Allan; 1938)
Commonweal. Mar 25, 1938, v27, p608.
Film Daily. Mar 10, 1938, p7.
The Films of Shirley Temple. p190-93.
Hollywood Reporter. Mar 5, 1938, p3.
Motion Picture Herald. Mar 12, 1938, p36, 39.
The New York Times. Mar 26, 1938, p12.
Rob Wagner's Script. Apr 9, 1938, v19, p10.
Saint Nicholas. Mar 1938, v65, p39+.
Scholastic. Apr 2, 1938, v32, p35.
Time. Mar 21, 1938, v31, p38+.
Variety. Mar 9, 1938, p14.

Rebell, Der (Also titled: The Rebel) (GER; Trenker, Luis; 1933)
Cinema Quarterly. Aut 1933, v2, p46.
Film Daily. Jul 27, 1933, p9.
Film in the Third Reich. p14-16.
From Caligari to Hitler. p261-62.
Nazi Cinema. p23-24.
The New Outlook. Sep 1933, v162, p44.
The New York Times. Jul 27, 1933, p20.
Rob Wagner's Script. Aug 5, 1933, v9, p9.
Selected Film Criticism: Foreign Films, 1930-1950. p147.
Variety. Aug 1, 1933, p14.

Rebellion *See* Revolution in Russia

Rebound (US; Griffith, Edward H.; 1931)
Film Daily. Aug 30, 1931, p10.
Motion Picture Herald. Jun 13, 1931, p34.
The New York Times. Aug 29, 1931, p16.
The New Yorker. Sep 5, 1931, v7, p54-55.
Outlook and Independent. Jul 15, 1931, v158, p342.
Rob Wagner's Script. Oct 24, 1931, v6, p9-10.
Rob Wagner's Script. Jun 27, 1931, v5, p8.
Time. Jul 20, 1931, v18, p32.
Variety. Sep 1, 1931, p21.

Reckless (US; Fleming, Victor; 1935)
Film Daily. Apr 17, 1935, p6.
The Films of Jean Harlow. p112-17.
Hollywood Reporter. Apr 1, 1935, p3.
Hollywood Reporter. Apr 26, 1935, p6.
Motion Picture Herald. Apr 13, 1935, p48.
The New York Times. Apr 20, 1935, p16.
The New Yorker. Apr 27, 1935, v11, p70.
Time. Apr 29, 1935, v25, p53.
Variety. Apr 24, 1935, p12.

The Reckless Hour (US; Dillon, John Francis; 1931)
Film Daily. Aug 2, 1931, p10.
Hollywood Reporter. Jun 1, 1931, p3.
Hollywood Spectator. Aug 29, 1931, v12, p22.
Life. Aug 28, 1931, v98, p18.
Motion Picture Herald. May 4, 1931, p44.
The New York Times. Aug 1, 1931, p16.
The New Yorker. Aug 8, 1931, v7, p49.
Rob Wagner's Script. Aug 29, 1931, v10, p8-10.
Variety. Aug 4, 1931, p21.

The Reckless Moment (US; Ophuls, Max; 1949)
Christian Century. Dec 21, 1949, v66, p1527.
Commonweal. Jan 20, 1950, v51, p416.
Film Comment. Sum 1971, v7, p65-66.
Film Daily. Oct 17, 1949, p7.
The Films of James Mason. p90-91.
Hollywood Reporter. Oct 12, 1949, p3.
Magill's Survey of Cinema. Series II. v5, p1990-93.
Motion Picture Herald Product Digest. Oct 22, 1949, p58.
The New York Times. Dec 30, 1949, p13.
Newsweek. Dec 19, 1949, v34, p76.
Rotarian. Feb 1950, v76, p39.
Sequence. New Year 1950, n10, p156.
Sight and Sound. Jan 1950, v18, p31.
Variety. Oct 19, 1949, p8.

The Red Danube (US; Sidney, George; 1949)
Catholic World. Nov 1949, v170, p148-49.
Commonweal. Dec 16, 1949, v51, p294.
Film Daily. Sep 26, 1949, p6.
Hollywood Reporter. Sep 20, 1949, p3.
Motion Picture Herald. Sep 4, 1949, p25.
The New Republic. Dec 26, 1949, v121, p22-23.
The New York Times. Dec 9, 1949, p37.
The New Yorker. Dec 17, 1949, v25, p116.
Newsweek. Dec 19, 1949, v34, p76.
Rotarian. Feb 1950, v76, p39.
Scholastic. Oct 19, 1949, v55, p25.

Sequence. Sum 1950, n11, p10-11.
Variety. Sep 21, 1949, p8.

Red Dust (US; Fleming, Victor; 1932)
Film Daily. Nov 5, 1932, p4.
The Films of Clark Gable. p134-37.
The Films of Jean Harlow. p74-79.
Hollywood Reporter. Oct 11, 1932, p3.
Life. Jan 1933, v100, p37.
Magill's Survey of Cinema. Series I. v3, p1438-40.
Make It Again, Sam: A Survey of Movie Remakes. p163-67.
The New York Times. Nov 5, 1932, p12.
The New Yorker. Nov 12, 1932, v8, p60.
Overland Monthly. Nov 1932, v90, p281.
Photoplay. Dec 1932, v43, p57.
Selected Film Criticism, 1931-1940. p208.
Time. Oct 17, 1932, v20, p36.
Vanity Fair. Dec 1932, v39, p64.
Variety. Nov 8, 1932, p16.

The Red Head *See* Poil de Carotte

Red Headed Woman (US; Conway, Jack; 1932)
Film Daily. Jul 1, 1932, p6.
The Films of Jean Harlow. p68-73.
Judge. Aug 1932, v103, p22.
Motion Picture Herald. Jun 25, 1932, p25.
The New York Times. Jul 1, 1932, p19.
The New Yorker. Jul 9, 1932, v8, p44.
Rob Wagner's Script. Jul 9, 1932, v7, p10.
Time. Jun 13, 1932, v19, p29.
Variety. Jul 5, 1932, p14.

Red, Hot and Blue (US; Farrow, John; 1949)
Commonweal. Oct 28, 1949, v51, p70.
Film Daily. Jul 8, 1949, p5.
The Hollywood Musical. p303.
Hollywood Reporter. Jul 1, 1949, p3.
Motion Picture Herald Product Digest. Jul 2, 1949, p4666.
The New York Times. Oct 20, 1949, p39.
Newsweek. Nov 14, 1949, v34, p88.
Rotarian. Mar 1950, v76, p37.
Time. Nov 7, 1949, v54, p94+.
Variety. Jul 6, 1949, p9.

The Red Kimono (US; Lang, Walter; 1925)
Film Daily. Feb 14, 1926, p9.
Magill's Survey of Cinema. Silent Films. v3, p905-07.
Photoplay. Mar 1926, v24, p123.
Selected Film Criticism, 1921-1930. p233.
Variety. Feb 3, 1926, p37.

The Red Lantern (US; Capellani, Albert; 1919)
Exhibitor's Trade Review. May 10, 1919, p1769.
Magill's Survey of Cinema. Silent Films. v3, p908-10.
Motion Picture News. Mar 22, 1919, p1804.
Motion Picture News. May 19, 1919, p3059-62, 3093.
The Moving Picture World. Mar 22, 1919, p1643.
The Moving Picture World. May 10, 1919, p920-22, 933.
The Moving Picture World. Jun 14, 1919, p1625.
The New York Times. May 5, 1919, p11.
Selected Film Criticism, 1912-1920. p217-18.
Variety. May 9, 1919, p53.
Wid's Daily. May 4, 1919, p23.

The Red Menace (US; Springsteen, R.G.; 1949)
Christian Century. Jul 20, 1949, v66, p879.
Film Daily. May 26, 1949, p7.
Hollywood Reporter. May 25, 1949, p3.
Motion Picture Herald Product Digest. Jun 4, 1949, p4634.
The New Republic. Jul 11, 1949, v121, p26.
The New York Times. Jun 27, 1949, p18.
Newsweek. Jul 11, 1949, v34, p69.
Rotarian. Sep 1949, v75, p37.
Time. Jul 18, 1949, v54, p78.
Variety. May 25, 1949, p8.

The Red Pony (US; Milestone, Lewis; 1949)
Commonweal. Apr 1, 1949, v49, p611.
Film Daily. Feb 3, 1949, p7.
The Films of Myrna Loy. p237.
Hollywood Reporter. Feb 3, 1949, p3.
Lewis Milestone (Millichap). p157-68.
Magill's Survey of Cinema. Series II. v5, p1997-99.
Motion Picture Herald Product Digest. Feb 12, 1949, p4494.
The New Republic. Mar 21, 1949, v120, p30.
The New York Times. Mar 9, 1949, p33.
The New Yorker. Mar 19, 1949, v25, p83.
Newsweek. Mar 21, 1949, v33, p89-90.
Robert Mitchum on the Screen. p106-07.
Rotarian. Apr 1949, v74, p37.
Scholastic. Apr 6, 1949, v54, p30.
Time. Mar 28, 1949, v53, p96+.
Variety. Feb 9, 1949, p13.

Red River (US; Hawks, Howard; 1948)
Commonweal. Sep 10, 1948, v48, p524.
The Complete Films of John Wayne. p160-62.
Film Daily. Jul 14, 1948, p4.
The Films of Howard Hawks (Willis). p43-53.
The Films of Montgomery Clift. p105-12.
The Films of the Forties. p238-41.
Hollywood Reporter. Jul 12, 1948, p3.
Howard Hawks (Poague). p141-45+.
Howard Hawks, Storyteller. p58-61+.
The International Dictionary of Films and Filmmakers. v1, p387-88.
Life. Aug 16, 1948, v25, p73-76.
Magill's Survey of Cinema. Series II. v5, p2000-02.
Motion Picture Herald Product Digest. Jul 17, 1948, p4241.
The New Republic. Oct 18, 1948, v119, p29.
The New York Times. Oct 1, 1948, p31.
The New Yorker. Oct 9, 1948, v24, p111.
Newsweek. Aug 30, 1948, v32, p78.
Rotarian. Mar 1949, v74, p39.
Time. Oct 11, 1948, v52, p100+.
Variety. Jul 14, 1948, p12.
Vintage Films. p93-96.

Red Salute (Also titled: Arms and the Girl; Her Enlisted Man) (US; Lanfield, Sidney; 1935)
Esquire. Nov 1935, v4, p106.
The Film Criticism of Otis Ferguson. p96-97.
Film Daily. Sep 12, 1935, p4.
The Films of Barbara Stanwyck. p100-01.
Graham Greene on Film. p36-37.
Hollywood Reporter. Sep 7, 1935, p3.
Literary Digest. Oct 19, 1935, v120, p24.
Motion Picture Herald. Sep 21, 1935, p44.
The New Masses. Oct 22, 1935, v17, p30.
The New Republic. Oct 2, 1935, v84, p199.
The New York Times. Sep 30, 1935, p13.
Rob Wagner's Script. Dec 21, 1935, v14, p10.
The Spectator. Nov 22, 1935, v155, p863.
Starring Miss Barbara Stanwyck. p75.
Time. Oct 7, 1935, v26, p31.
Variety. Oct 2, 1935, p16.

The Red Shoes (GB; Powell, Michael; Pressburger, Emeric; 1948)
Canadian Forum. Mar 1949, v28, p282.
Commonweal. Oct 29, 1948, v49, p70.
Film Daily. Oct 22, 1948, p4.
Fortnight. Dec 31, 1948, v5, p29.
The Great British Films. p121-24.
Halliwell's Hundred. p298-301.
Hollywood Reporter. Oct 22, 1948, p3.
Life. Mar 8, 1948, v24, p110-11.
Magill's Survey of Cinema. Series I. v3, p1441-43.
Motion Picture Herald Product Digest. Oct 23, 1948, p4357.
The Nation. Nov 6, 1948, v167, p529.
The New Republic. Oct 25, 1948, v119, p28.

The New York Times. Oct 23, 1948, p9.
The New York Times Magazine. Oct 10, 1948, p60-61.
The New Yorker. Oct 23, 1948, v24, p107.
Newsweek. Oct 25, 1948, v32, p101.
Rotarian. Jan 1949, v74, p52.
School and Society. Dec 4, 1948, v68, p386.
Sight and Sound. Aut 1948, v17, p143-44.
Theatre Arts. Jan 1949, v33, p52.
Time. Oct 25, 1948, v52, p102.
Variety. Aug 4, 1948, p11.
Vintage Films. p97-100.

The Red Window (US; Durkin, James; 1916)
The Moving Picture World. May 6, 1916, p982.
The New York Dramatic Mirror. May 6, 1916, p28.
The New York Times. Apr 24, 1916, p11.
Variety. Apr 28, 1916, p28.
Wid's Daily. May 4, 1916, p548.

Redemption (US; Niblo, Fred; 1930)
Exhibitors Herald-World. Apr 12, 1930, p56.
Film Daily. May 4, 1930, p11.
The New York Times. May 3, 1930, p23.
The New Yorker. May 10, 1930, v6, p101.
Outlook and Independent. May 21, 1930, v155, p110.
Time. May 19, 1930, v15, p62.
Variety. May 7, 1930, p38.

Redes *See* The Wave

The Redman and the Child (US; 1908)
The New York Dramatic Mirror. Aug 8, 1908, p7.

The Redman's View (US; Griffith, D.W.; 1909)
The New York Dramatic Mirror. Dec 18, 1909, p15-16.
The New York Dramatic Mirror. Dec 25, 1909, p15.
Spellbound in Darkness. p64-67.

Redskin (US; Schertzinger, Victor; 1929)
Film Daily. Feb 3, 1929, p8.
Magill's Survey of Cinema. Silent Films. v3, p911-14.
The New York Times. Jan 28, 1929, p21.
Photoplay. Feb 1929, v35, p54.
Variety. Jan 30, 1929, p34.

Reform School (US; Popkin, Leo C.; 1939)
Film Daily. May 12, 1939, p12.
Motion Picture Herald. May 6, 1939, p38.
Variety. May 3, 1939, p16.

Regain *See* Harvest

The Regeneration (US; Walsh, Raoul; 1915)
Motion Picture News. Oct 2, 1915, p83.
Motography. Oct 9, 1915, p767.
The Moving Picture World. Oct 2, 1915, p94.
The Moving Picture World. Jan 18, 1919, p390.
Photoplay. Nov 1915, v8, p177.
Photoplay. Dec 1915, v8, p164.
Selected Film Criticism, 1912-1920. p219.
Variety. Sep 24, 1915, p21.

Regle du Jeu, Le (Also titled: The Rules of the Game) (FR; Renoir, Jean; 1939)
Cinema Journal. Fall 1973, v13, p25-44.
Cinema, the Magic Vehicle. v1, p305-07.
The Classic Cinema. p149-70.
Classics of the Foreign Film. p130-35.
Close-Up: Critical Perspective on Film. p67-73.
The Comic Mind. p232-43.
Dictionary of Films. p309-10.
Eighty Years of Cinema. p118.
Film and the Critical Eye. p170-202.
Film Quarterly. Wint 1967-68, v21, p2-8.
Filmguide to The Rules of the Game.
Films and Filming. Nov 1961, v8, p27.
Films and Filming. Nov 1962, v9, p21-25.

Films in Review. Jan 1961, v12, p40-41.
The Films of My Life. p42-43.
French Film (Sadoul). p87-88.
The Golden Age of French Cinema, 1929-1939. p119-21.
The Great French Films. p92-96.
The International Dictionary of Films and Filmmakers. v1, p389-91.
Jean Renoir: A Guide to References and Resources. p114-27.
Jean Renoir (Durgnat). p185-212.
Jean Renoir: My Life and My Films. p169-73.
Jean Renoir: The French Films, 1924-1939. p378-40.
Jean Renoir: The World of His Films. p89-94, 132-38.
Jump Cut. Dec 30, 1976, n12-13, p45-51.
Kiss Kiss Bang Bang. p429-32.
Literature/Film Quarterly. Wint 1977, v5, p50-56.
Literature/Film Quarterly. 1982, v10, n3, p162-79.
Mastering the Film and Other Essays. p57-65.
Movie Comedy (Byron). p220-22.
Movie Man. p145-48.
New Left Review. May-Jun 1964, n25, p58-60.
New York Film Bulletin. 1961, v2, n1, p3-5.
The New York Times. Apr 10, 1950, p15.
The New York Times. Jan 19, 1961, p26.
The New Yorker. Apr 22, 1950, v26, p105.
The New Yorker. Sep 20, 1969, v55, p150-52.
Private Screenings. p30-31.
Quarterly Review of Film Studies. 1982, v7, n3, p199-280.
The Rules of the Game: A Film by Jean Renoir. p5-21.
Screen. Feb 1970, v11, p3-13.
Screen. Wint 1972-73, v13, p41-43.
Selected Film Criticism: Foreign Films, 1930-1950. p154.
Take One. Jul-Aug 1968, v1, p10-12.
Theory of Film Practice. p141-42.
Unholy Fools, Wits, Comics, Disturbers of the Peace. p326-30.
Variety. Aug 30, 1939, p19.
The Village Voice. Jan 26, 1961, v6, p11-12.

Reign of Terror (Also titled: The Black Book) (US; Mann, Anthony; 1949)
Commonweal. Sep 16, 1949, v50, p561.
Film Daily. May 23, 1949, p8.
Hollywood Reporter. Jul 14, 1949, p3.
Motion Picture Herald Product Digest. May 21, 1949, p4617.
The New Yorker. Oct 15, 1949, v25, p126.
Newsweek. Dec 5, 1949, v34, p82.
Variety. May 18,1949, p8.

The Remarkable Andrew (US; Heisler, Stuart; 1942)
Commonweal. Mar 20, 1942, v35, p536.
Film Daily. Jan 19, 1942, p6.
The Films of William Holden. p62-64.
Hollywood Reporter. Jan 16, 1942, p3.
The London Times. May 4, 1942, p8.
Motion Picture Exhibitor. Jan 28, 1942, p937.
Motion Picture Herald Product Digest. Jan 25, 1941, p473-74.
The New York Times. Mar 6, 1942, p17.
The New York Times. Mar 8, 1942, sec8, p3.
Newsweek. Mar 16, 1942, v19, p72.
Scholastic. Apr 13, 1942, v40, p32.
Time. Mar 30, 1942, v39, p74.
Variety. Jan 21, 1942, p18.

Rembrandt (GB; Korda, Alexander; 1936)
Around Cinemas. p134-36.
Canadian Magazine. Jan 1937, v87, p43-44.
Chestnuts in Her Lap. p15-17.
Cinema, the Magic Vehicle. v1, p259-60.
Classics of the Foreign Film. p100-01.
Commonweal. Dec 18, 1936, v25, p220.
A Critical History of the British Cinema. p117.
Esquire. Feb 1937, v7, p101.
The Film Criticism of Otis Ferguson. p162-64.
Film Daily. Nov 21, 1936, p7.
Garbo and the Night Watchman. p71.
Graham Greene on Film. p117-20.

The Great British Films. p32-35.
Hollywood Reporter. Nov 5, 1936, p3.
Judge. Jan 1937, v112, p46.
Life. Nov 30, 1936, v1, p26-28.
Literary Digest. Dec 12, 1936, v122, p21+.
London Mercury. Dec 1936, v35, p191.
Lorentz on Film. p136-38.
Magill's Survey of Cinema. Series II. v5, p2007-10.
Motion Picture Herald. Oct 31, 1936, p16-17.
Motion Picture Herald. Nov 21, 1936, p51, 54.
Motion Picture Herald. Nov 30, 1936, p16-17.
The Nation. Dec 19, 1936, v143, p742.
National Board of Review Magazine. Jan 1937, v12, p7.
The New Masses. Dec 15, 1936, v21, p57.
The New Republic. Dec 16, 1936, v89, p218.
The New Statesman and Nation. Nov 14, 1936, v12, p772.
The New York Times. Dec 3, 1936, p31.
The New Yorker. Dec 5, 1936, v12, p102.
Newsweek. Dec 12, 1936, v8, p32.
Rob Wagner's Script. Jan 2, 1937, v16, p12.
Saturday Review (London). Nov 14, 1936, v162, p640.
Scholastic. Nov 21, 1936, v29, p18-22.
Selected Film Criticism: Foreign Films, 1930-1950. p149.
Sociology and Social Research. May 1937, v1, p498.
The Spectator. Nov 20, 1936, v157, p905.
Stage. Nov 1936, v14, p52-53.
Stage. Dec 1936, v14, p16.
The Tatler. Nov 18, 1936, v142, p294.
Time. Dec 14, 1936, v28, p26+.
Variety. Nov 18, 1936, p12.
Variety. Dec 9, 1936, p12.
World Film News. Dec 1936, v1, p21.

Remember? (US; McLeod, Norman Z.; 1939)
Film Daily. Dec 20, 1939, p7.
The Films of Robert Taylor. p78-79.
Hollywood Reporter. Nov 2, 1939, p3.
Motion Picture Herald. Nov 11, 1939, p42-43.
The New York Times. Dec 15, 1939, p33.
The New Yorker. Dec 23, 1939, v15, p53.
Photoplay. Jan 1940, v54, p58.
Rob Wagner's Script. Nov 11, 1939, v22, p18.
Variety. Nov 8, 1939, p14.

Remember Last Night? (Also titled: The Hangover Murders) (US; Whale, James; 1935)
Film Daily. Nov 21, 1935, p9.
Hollywood Reporter. Oct 11, 1935, p3.
James Whale (Curtis). pxvii-xviii, 129-30.
Motion Picture Herald. Oct 12, 1935, p41, 44.
The New York Times. Nov 21, 1935, p27.
Variety. Nov 27, 1935, p14.

Remember the Night (US; Leisen, Mitchell; 1940)
Commonweal. Feb 2, 1940, v31, p328.
Film Daily. Jan 9, 1940, p5.
The Films of Barbara Stanwyck. p132-33.
Hollywood Reporter. Jan 6, 1940, p3.
Motion Picture Herald. Jan 13, 1940, p3.
The New York Times. Jan 18, 1940, p27.
Preston Sturges: A Guide to References and Resources. p45-47.
Starring Miss Barbara Stanwyck. p133-34.
Time. Jan 29, 1940, v35, p69.
Variety. Jan 10, 1940, p14.

Remodeling Her Husband (US; Gish, Lillian; 1920)
Fifty Great American Silent Films, 1912-1920. p125-26.
Lillian Gish: The Movies, Mr. Griffith, and Me. p223-26.
Magill's Survey of Cinema. Silent Films. v3, p918-20.
Motion Picture News. Jun 19, 1920, p501.
The Moving Picture World. Jun 19, 1920, p1630.
The New York Times. Jun 7, 1920, p20.
Photoplay. Sep 1920, v18, p106.
Selected Film Criticism, 1912-1920. p219-20.

Variety. Jun 11, 1920, p33-34.
Wid's Daily. Jun 13, 1920, p12.

Remontons Les Champs-Elysees *See* Champs Elysees

Rendezvous (US; Howard, William K.; 1935)
Canadian Magazine. Jan 1936, v85, p33.
Film Daily. Oct 23, 1935, p4.
Hollywood Reporter. Oct 23, 1935, p3.
Motion Picture Herald. Nov 9, 1935, p64.
The Nation. Nov 20, 1935, v141, p604.
The New York Times. Oct 26, 1935, p12.
The New Yorker. Nov 2, 1935, v11, p75-76.
Newsweek. Nov 2, 1935, v6, p47.
Scholastic. Dec 7, 1935, v27, p12.
Time. Nov 4, 1935, v26, p53-54.
Variety. Oct 30, 1935, p14.

Reno (US; Farrow, John; 1939)
Commonweal. Dec 22, 1939, v31, p206.
Film Daily. Nov 16, 1939, p6.
Hollywood Reporter. Nov 10, 1939, p3.
Motion Picture Herald. Nov 18, 1939, p44.
The New York Times. Dec 21, 1939, p29.
Photoplay. Jan 1940, v54, p58.
Variety. Dec 13, 1939, p11.

Repeat Performance (US; Werker, Alfred L.; 1947)
Commonweal. Jul 11, 1947, v46, p311.
Film Daily May 23, 1947. p6.
Hollywood Reporter.
Motion Picture Herald Product Digest. May 15, 1947, p3475.
The New Republic. Jul 21, 1947, v117, p34.
The New York Times. Jul 2, 1947, p19.
The New Yorker. Jul 5, 1947, v23, p42.
Newsweek. Jul 14, 1947, v30, p89.
Time. Jul 14, 1947, v50, p90.
Variety. May 28, 1947, p15.

Rescued by Rover (GB; Hepworth, Cecil M.; 1905)
The First Twenty Years. p93-94.
A History of Films. p50-51.
A Million and One Nights. p414.

Rescued from an Eagle's Nest (US; Porter, Edwin S.; 1907)
The Moving Picture World. Feb 1, 1908, p71.
Selected Film Criticism, 1896-1911. p81-82.

Reserved for Ladies (Also titled: Service for Ladies) (GB; Korda, Alexander; 1932)
Film Daily. May 22, 1932, p10.
Hollywood Reporter. Mar 4, 1932, p3.
Motion Picture Herald. Feb 6, 1932, p38, 40.
Motion Picture Herald. May 28, 1932, p88.
The New York Times. May 21, 1932, p9.
The New Yorker. May 29, 1932, v8, p52.
Photoplay. Aug 1932, v42, p52.
Rob Wagner's Script. Aug 20, 1932, v7, p8-9.
Selected Film Criticism: Foreign Films, 1930-1950. p150.
Time. May 30, 1932, v19, p34.
Variety. May 24, 1932, p37.

The Restless Sex (US; Leonard, Robert Z.; 1920)
The Moving Picture World. Jun 26, 1920, p1789.
The New York Times. Sep 13, 1920, p12.
Variety. Jun 18, 1920, p29.
Wid's Daily. Jun 13, 1920, p6.

Restless Youth (US; Cabanne, Christy; 1929)
Variety. Jan 9, 1929, p34.

Resurrection (US; 1909)
The Moving Picture World. May 29, 1909, p712.
The New York Dramatic Mirror. May 29, 1909, p15.
Selected Film Criticism, 1896-1911. p82-83.

Resurrection (US; José, Edward; 1918)
Exhibitor's Trade Review. Apr 27, 1918, p1689.
Exhibitor's Trade Review. Jun 1, 1918, p2083.
Motion Picture News. May 18, 1918, p2957, 3002.
The Moving Picture World. May 11, 1918, p898.
The Moving Picture World. May 18, 1918, p1035.
The New York Times. May 20, 1918, p9.
Variety. May 24, 1918, p35.
Wid's Daily. May 12, 1918, p21-22.

Resurrection (US; Carewe, Edwin; 1927)
Film Daily. Apr 10, 1927, p6.
The Moving Picture World. Apr 16, 1927, p667.
The New York Times. May 17, 1927, p29.
Outlook. Oct 12, 1927, v147, p165-66.
Variety. May 18, 1927, p20.

Resurrection (US; Carewe, Edwin; 1931)
Film Daily. Jan 25, 1931, p10.
Judge. Feb 14, 1931, v100, p22.
Motion Picture Herald. Jan 10, 1931, p51-52.
The New York Times. Jan 24, 1931, p15.
The New York Times. Dec 6, 1931, p5.
The New Yorker. Jan 31, 1931, v6, p51.
Time. Feb 2, 1931, v17, p40.
Variety. Jan 28, 1931, p15.

The Return of Doctor X (Also titled: The Return of Dr. X) (US; Sherman, Vincent; 1939)
The Complete Films of Humphrey Bogart. p75.
Film Daily. Nov 28, 1939, p12.
Humphrey Bogart: The Man and His Films. p95.
Motion Picture Herald. Dec 2, 1939, p44.
The New York Times. Nov 23, 1939, p38.
The New Yorker. Dec 2, 1939, v15, p93.
The Seal of Dracula. p22.
Variety. Nov 29, 1939, p14.

The Return of Frank James (US; Lang, Fritz; 1940)
Commonweal. Aug 23, 1940, v32, p371.
The Film Criticism of Otis Ferguson. p307.
Film Daily. Aug 12, 1940, p7.
The Filming of the West. p361-63.
The Films of Fritz Lang. p186-89.
The Films of Henry Fonda. p96-97.
The Fondas (Springer). p104-05.
Fritz Lang: A Guide to References and Resources. p76-78.
Fritz Lang (Armour). p118-22.
The London Times. Dec 23, 1940, p6.
Magic Moments from the Movies. p84.
Motion Picture Herald Product Digest. Apr 5, 1941, p100.
The New Republic. Sep 2, 1940, v103, p303.
The New York Herald Tribune. Aug 10, 1940, p6.
The New York Herald Tribune. Aug 11, 1940, p3.
The New York Times. Aug 10, 1940, p16.
The New York Times. Aug 18, 1940, sec9, p3.
The New York Times. Oct 8, 1940, p16.
Photoplay. Oct 1940, v54, p66.
Take One. Mar-Apr 1972, n10, p14-17.
Variety. Aug 14, 1940, p14.

The Return of Maxim (Russian title: Vozvrashcheniye Maksima) (USSR; Kozintsev, Gregori; Trauberg, Leonid; 1937)
Cinema, the Magic Vehicle. v1, p271.
Dictionary of Films. p427-28.
Film Daily. Nov 3, 1937, p10.
Kino. p322-23.
The Nation. Nov 20, 1937, v145, p566.
National Board of Review Magazine. Dec 1937, v12, p12.
The New Masses. Nov 16, 1937, v25, p28-30.
The New York Times. Nov 2, 1937, p33.

The Return of October (US; Lewis, Joseph H.; 1948)
Commonweal. Dec 31, 1948, v49, p306.
Film Daily. Oct 21, 1948, p7.

Hollywood Reporter. Oct 19, 1948, p3.
Motion Picture Herald Product Digest. Oct 23, 1948, p4357.
The New Republic. Mar 14, 1949, v120, p30.
The New York Times. Feb 23, 1949, p31.
Rotarian. Jan 1949, v74, p52.
Variety. Oct 20, 1948, p16.

Return to Life (US; Cartier, Henri; 1938)
Film Daily. Aug 10, 1938, p7.
Magazine of Art. Feb 1942, v35, p61.
The New Masses. Aug 16, 1938, v28, p29-30.
The New York Times. Aug 4, 1938, p15.
Variety. Aug 10, 1938, p27.

Reunion *See* Liebesmelodie

Reunion (US; Taurog, Norman; 1936)
Canadian Magazine. Dec 1936, v86, p38.
Film Daily. Nov 13, 1936, p9.
Hollywood Reporter. Nov 10, 1936, p3.
Motion Picture Herald. Nov 21, 1936, p46.
The New York Times. Nov 27, 1936, p27.
The New Yorker. Dec 5, 1936, v12, p103.
Rob Wagner's Script. Nov 21, 1936, v16, p10.
Time. Dec 7, 1936, v28, p23.
Variety. Dec 2, 1936, p18.

Reunion in France (Also titled: Reunion) (US; Dassin, Jules; 1942)
Commonweal. Jan 22, 1943, v37, p350.
The Complete Films of John Wayne. p127-28.
Film Daily. Dec 2, 1942, p6.
The Films of Joan Crawford. p150-51.
The Films of World War II. p108-10.
Hollywood Reporter. Dec 2, 1942, p3.
Motion Picture Herald Product Digest. Dec 5, 1942, p1041.
The New York Times. Mar 5, 1942, p20.
The New Yorker. Feb 6, 1943, v18, p52.
Time. Jan 4, 1943, v41, p86.
Variety. Dec 2, 1942, p8.

Reunion in Vienna (US; Franklin, Sidney; 1933)
Canadian Magazine. Aug 1933, v80, p34-35.
Film Daily. May 2, 1933, p4.
Hollywood Reporter. Apr 17, 1933, p3.
Judge. Jun 1933, v104, p16.
Motion Picture Herald. May 6, 1933, p26.
The Nation. May 17, 1933, v136, p567.
New Outlook. Jun 1933, v161, p48.
The New York Times. Apr 29, 1933, p14.
The New Yorker. May 6, 1933, v9, p57-58.
Newsweek. May 6, 1933, v1, p30.
Rob Wagner's Script. Jun 24, 1933, v9, p8.
Time. May 8, 1933, v21, p40.
Variety. May 2, 1933, p12.

Revelation (US; Baker, George D.; 1918)
Exhibitor's Trade Review. Feb 23, 1918, p989, 994.
Motion Picture Classic. May 1918, p52-53.
Motion Picture News. Feb 16, 1918, p933.
Motion Picture News. Mar 9, 1918, p1466.
Motion Picture News. Jul 24, 1920, p777.
The Moving Picture World. Feb 2, 1918, p723.
The Moving Picture World. Mar 9, 1918, p1408.
The New York Times. Feb 18, 1918, p9.
Variety. Mar 1, 1918, p41.
Wid's Daily. Mar 21, 1918, p1021.

Revolution in Russia (Also titled: Rebellion; Mutiny at Odessa) (FR; 1905)
The George Kleine Collection Catalog. p112.

Revolutionists (Also titled: A Generation of Conquerors) (USSR; Stroyeva, Vera; 1936)
Film Daily. Dec 29, 1936, p15.
Graham Greene on Film. p149.

Motion Picture Herald. Feb 6, 1937, p50.
The Nation. Jan 16, 1937, v144, p81.
National Board of Review Magazine. Feb 1937, v12, p16.
The New Masses. Jan 5, 1937, v22, p27-29.
New Theatre. Mar 1937, v4, p46, 57.
The New York Times. Dec 26, 1936, p15.
The Spectator. May 7, 1939, v162, p860.
Variety. Dec 30, 1936, p11.

The Reward of the Faithless (British title: The Ruling Passion) (US; Ingram, Rex; 1917)
The Moving Picture World. Feb 10, 1917, p868.
The Moving Picture World. Feb 17, 1917, p1079.
The New York Dramatic Mirror. Feb 3, 1917, p28.
Rex Ingram. p46-47, 50.
Selected Film Criticism, 1912-1920. p222-23.
Variety. Feb 2, 1917, p22.
Wid's Daily. Feb 1, 1917, p71.

Rhapsody in Blue (US; Rapper, Irving; 1945)
Commonweal. Jul 6, 1945, v42, p286-87.
Film Daily. Jun 27, 1945, p7.
Hollywood Reporter. Jun 27, 1945, p3.
Life. Jul 16, 1945, v19, p89-92.
The New Republic. Jul 23, 1945, v113, p103.
The New York Times. Jun 28, 1945, p22.
The New York Times Magazine. Jun 3, 1945, p24-25.
The New Yorker. Jul 7, 1945, v21, p36.
Newsweek. Jul 9, 1945, v26, p102.
Theatre Arts. Nov 1945, v29, p645.
Time. Jul 2, 1945, v46, p85.
Variety. Jun 27, 1945, p16.

Rhodes (Also titled: Rhodes of Africa; Rhodes, the Empire Builder) (GB; Viertel, Berthold; 1936)
Around Cinemas. p127-29.
Canadian Magazine. Feb 1936, v85, p37.
Esquire. May 1936, v5, p115.
The Film Criticism of Otis Ferguson. p123-24.
Film Daily. Feb 21, 1936, p13.
Graham Greene on Film. p61.
Hollywood Reporter. Feb 25, 1936, p3.
Hollywood Spectator. Mar 28, 1936, v10, p6-7.
Literary Digest. Mar 7, 1936, v121, p21.
Motion Picture Herald. Mar 7, 1936, p50.
The Nation. Mar 18, 1936, v142, p360.
National Board of Review Magazine. Mar 1936, v11, p13.
The New Republic. Mar 18, 1936, v86, p166.
The New Statesman and Nation. Mar 21, 1936, v11, p457.
The New York Times. Feb 23, 1936, p4.
The New York Times. Feb 29, 1936, p11.
The New Yorker. Feb 29, 1936, v12, p51.
Rob Wagner's Script. Mar 28, 1936, v15, p10.
Saturday Review (London). Mar 27, 1936, v161, p416.
Selected Film Criticism: Foreign Films, 1930-1950. p150-51.
The Spectator. Mar 27, 1936, v156, p575.
Stage. Feb 1936, v13, p61.
The Tatler. Mar 25, 1936, v139, p562.
Time. Mar 9, 1936, v27, p44.
Variety. Mar 4, 1936, p26.

Rhodes, the Empire Builder *See* Rhodes

Rhythm on the Range (US; Taurog, Norman; 1936)
Film Daily. Jul 18, 1936, p7.
The Films of Bing Crosby. p77-79.
Garbo and the Night Watchman. p181-82.
Graham Greene on Film. p93-94.
Hollywood Reporter. Jul 15, 1936, p3.
Hollywood Spectator. Aug 1, 1936, v11, p9.
Motion Picture Herald. Jul 25, 1936, p64, 66.
The New Statesman and Nation. Aug 15, 1936, v12, p224.
The New York Times. Jul 30, 1936, p22.
The New Yorker. Aug 8, 1936, v12, p49.
Newsweek. Aug 1, 1936, v8, p23.

Rob Wagner's Script. Aug 22, 1936, v15, p12-13.
The Spectator. Mar 27, 1936, v156, p575.
Time. Aug 10, 1936, v28, p26-27.
Variety. Aug 5, 1936, p16.

Rich and Strange (Also titled: East of Shanghai) (GB; Hitchcock, Alfred; 1931)
The Age of the Dream Palace. p310-11.
The Art of Alfred Hitchcock. p30-34.
BFI/Monthly Film Bulletin. Aug 1975, p187.
A Critical History of the British Cinema. p108.
Film Daily. Mar 27, 1932, p22.
Grierson on Documentary. p50-52.
Hitchcock: The First Forty-Four Films. p32-36.
Hitchcock's British Films. p145-54.
Motion Picture Herald. Apr 9, 1932, p25.
Variety. Dec 29, 1931, p167.

The Rich Are Always With Us (US; Green, Alfred E.; 1932)
Bette Davis: Her Films and Career. p28-29.
Film Daily. May 15, 1932, p10.
Judge. Jun 11, 1932, v102, p24.
Motion Picture Herald. May 21, 1932, p103.
The New York Times. May 16, 1932, p19.
Rob Wagner's Script. Jun 18, 1932, v7, p10.
Time. May 23, 1932, v19, p30.
Variety. May 17, 1932, p14.

The Rich Bride *See* The Country Bride

Rich Man, Poor Girl (US; Schunzel, Reinhold; 1938)
Commonweal. Sep 2, 1938, v28, p477.
Film Daily. Aug 9, 1938, p7.
The Films of Lana Turner. p72-74.
Hollywood Reporter. Aug 6, 1938, p3.
Motion Picture Herald. Aug 13, 1938, p62.
The New York Times. Aug 19, 1938, p13.
The New Yorker. Aug 27, 1938, v14, p52-53.
Scholastic. Sep 17, 1938, v33, p12.
Time. Aug 29, 1938, v32, p23.
Variety. Aug 17, 1938, p22.

Rich Man's Folly (US; Cromwell, John; 1931)
Film Daily. Nov 22, 1931, p10.
The Hollywood Professionals: King Vidor, John Cromwell. p63.
Hollywood Reporter. Oct 16, 1931, p3.
Judge. Dec 19, 1931, v101, p24.
Motion Picture Herald. Dec 5, 1931, p54-55.
The New York Times. Nov 27, 1931, p29.
The New York Times. Dec 6, 1931, p5.
The New Yorker. Dec 5, 1931, v7, p92.
Outlook and Independent. Dec 9, 1931, v159, p471.
Rob Wagner's Script. Dec 26, 1931, v6, p10.
Variety. Dec 1, 1931, p21.

Richard III (US; 1908)
The Moving Picture World. Oct 3, 1908, p253.
Selected Film Criticism, 1896-1911. p83-84.

Richard III (US; Keene, James; 1912)
The Moving Picture World. Apr 12, 1913, p188.
The Moving Picture World. Sep 2, 1913, p1411.
The New York Dramatic Mirror. Sep 11, 1912, p27.
The New York Dramatic Mirror. Oct 9, 1912, p27.
The New York Dramatic Mirror. May 14, 1913, p28.

Richelieu *See* Cardinal Richelieu

The Richest Girl in the World (US; Seiter, William A.; 1934)
Film Daily. Sep 8, 1934, p3.
Hollywood Reporter. Aug 25, 1934, p3.
Motion Picture Herald. Sep 15, 1934, p25.
The New York Times. Sep 21, 1934, p21.
Time. Oct 1, 1934, v24, p20.
Variety. Sep 25, 1934, p13.

Ride a Crooked Mile (US; Green, Alfred E.; 1938)
Film Daily. Dec 7, 1938, p5.
Hollywood Reporter. Nov 30, 1938, p3.
Hollywood Spectator. Dec 10, 1938, v13, p14-15.
Motion Picture Herald. Dec 3, 1938, p36.
The New Masses. Dec 27, 1938, v30, p27-28.
The New York Times. Dec 29, 1938, p15.
Variety. Dec 7, 1938, p12.

Ride the Pink Horse (US; Montgomery, Robert; 1947)
Commonweal. Oct 10, 1947, v46, p623.
Film Daily. Sep 12, 1947, p10.
Motion Picture Herald Product Digest. Sep 20, 1947, p3841.
The Nation. Nov 8, 1947, v165, p511.
New Republic. Nov 3, 1947, v117, p30.
The New York Times. Oct 9, 1947, p32.
The New Yorker. Oct 18, 1947, v23, p113.
Newsweek. Oct 20, 1947, v30, p97.
Time. Oct 13, 1947, v50, p106.
Variety. Sep 17, 1947, p16.

Riffraff (US; Ruben, J. Walter; 1936)
Esquire. Apr 1936, v5, p104.
Film Daily. Dec 24, 1935, p7.
The Films of Jean Harlow. p124-29.
The Films of Spencer Tracy. p123-25.
Garbo and the Night Watchman. p103-05.
Hollywood Reporter. Dec 19, 1935, p3.
Hollywood Spectator. Jan 4, 1936, v10, p17-19.
Motion Picture Herald. Dec 28, 1935, p64.
The New Masses. Jan 21, 1936, v18, p29-30.
New Theatre. Oct 1935, v2 p6-7, 33.
The New York Times. Jan 13, 1936, p14.
The New Yorker. Jan 18, 1936, v11, p52-53.
Rob Wagner's Script. Feb 8, 1936, v14, p10.
Time. Jan 20, 1936, v27, p58.
Variety. Jan 15, 1936, p18.

The Right to Live (US; Keighley, William; 1935)
Esquire. Apr 1935, v3, p144, 150.
Film Daily. Feb 16, 1935, p7.
Hollywood Reporter. Feb 8, 1935, p3.
Literary Digest. Mar 2, 1935, v119, p24.
Motion Picture Herald. Feb 23, 1935, p59.
The New York Times. Feb 16, 1935, p9.
The New Yorker. Feb 23, 1935, v11, p62.
Time. Feb 25, 1935, v25, p54.
Variety. Feb 20, 1935, p15.

The Ring (GB; Hitchcock, Alfred; 1927)
The Art of Alfred Hitchcock. p12-14.
BFI/Monthly Film Bulletin. Jul 1979, v46, p156.
Hitchcock: The First Forty-Four Films. p12-15.
Hitchcock's British Films. p58-64+.
Variety. Oct 19, 1927, p28.

The Rink (Also titled: At the Rink) (US; Chaplin, Charles; 1916)
Charles Chaplin: A Guide to References and Resources. p63.
The Films of Charlie Chaplin. p135-36.
Magill's Survey of Cinema. Silent Films. v1, p28-29.
The Rivals of D.W. Griffith. p30-31.
The Silent Clowns. p95-96+.
Variety. Dec 15, 1916, p35.
Wid's Daily. Dec 14, 1916, p1166.

Rio (US; Brahm, John; 1939)
Basil Rathbone: His Life and His Films. p226-28.
Film Daily. Sep 26, 1939, p7.
Hollywood Reporter. Sep 21, 1939, p4.
Hollywood Spectator. Sep 30, 1939, v14, p8.
Motion Picture Herald. Oct 14, 1939, p42, 44.
The New York Times. Oct 27, 1939, p27.
Newsweek. Oct 9, 1939, v14, p36.
Rob Wagner's Script. Oct 21, 1939, v22, p16.

Time. Oct 9, 1939, v34, p40.
Variety. Oct 4, 1939, p12.

Rio Rita (US; Reed, Luther; 1929)
Cinema. Jan 1930, v1, p42.
Exhibitor's Herald-World. Nov 2, 1929, p54.
Exhibitor's Herald-World. Nov 30, 1929, p47.
Film Daily. Oct 13, 1929, p8.
The Hollywood Musical. p33.
Magill's Survey of Cinema. Series II. v5, p2022-24.
The New York Times. Oct 7, 1929, p22.
Selected Film Criticism, 1921-1930. p233-34.
Variety. Oct 9, 1929, p23.

Riptide (Also titled: Rip Tide) (US; Goulding, Edmund; 1934)
Film Daily. Mar 31, 1934, p4.
Hollywood Reporter. Mar 21, 1934, p3.
Motion Picture Herald. Mar 31, 1934, p50.
The New York Times. Mar 31, 1934, p8.
Newsweek. Apr 7, 1934, v3, p23.
Time. Apr 9, 1934, v23, p37.
Variety. Apr 3, 1934, p17.

Riso Amaro *See* Bitter Rice

The River (US; Borzage, Frank; 1928)
Film Daily. Dec 30, 1928, p8.
The Film Spectator. Feb 9, 1929, v7, p9-10.
Journal of Popular Film. Sum 1976, v5, p132-38.
The New York Times. Dec 24, 1928, p11.
Selected Film Criticism, 1921-1930. p234-35.
Variety. Dec 26, 1928, p11.

The River (US; Lorentz, Pare; 1937)
Around Cinemas. p36-39.
Business Week. Feb 19, 1938, p35-36.
Current History. Apr 1938, v48, p55.
Current History. May 1938, v48, p46-47.
Dictionary of Films. p314.
Documentary: History of the Non-Fiction Film. p118, 120-21.
The Documentary Tradition. p123-25.
Esquire. Jan 1938, v9, p107, 177-78.
Film Comment. Spr 1965, v3, p38-60.
The Film Criticism of Otis Ferguson. p203-05.
Film on the Left. p137-44.
From Quasimodo to Scarlett O'Hara. p263-65.
Hollywood as Historian. p37-43.
Literary Digest. Nov 20, 1937, v124, p34.
London Mercury. Aug 1938, v38, p358-59.
Magazine of Art. Dec 1937, v30, p723-25.
Motion Picture Herald. Dec 11, 1937, p38, 40.
The Nation. Oct 30, 1937, v145, p485.
National Board of Review Magazine. Nov 1937, v12, p11.
The New Masses. Jan 18, 1938, v26, p29-30.
The New Republic. Nov 10, 1937, v93, p17.
The New York Times. Feb 5, 1938, p19.
The New Yorker. Feb 5, 1938, v13, p53-54.
Non-Fiction Film: A Critical History. p102-06.
Pare Lorentz and the Documentary Film. p50-78.
Rob Wagner's Script. Jan 8, 1938, v18, p14-15.
Saturday Review. Apr 9, 1938, v17, p8.
Scribner's Magazine. Jan 1939, v105, p10-11+.
Scribner's Magazine. Jan 1938, v103, p67-68.
Scribner's Magazine. Apr 1938, v103, p65-66.
Sight and Sound. Sum 1938, v7, p89-90.
The Tatler. Jul 6, 1938, v149, p6.
Theatre Arts. Apr 1938, v22, p303.
Time. Nov 8, 1937, v30, p49.
Variety. Feb 9, 1938, p15.
World Film News. Jul 1938, v3, p121.
World Film News. Aug 1938, v3, p177.

The Road Back (US; Whale, James; 1937)
Commonweal. Jul 9, 1937, v26, p288.
The Film Criticism of Otis Ferguson. p184-85.

Film Daily. Jun 18, 1937, p12.
Graham Greene on Film. p172-73.
Hollywood Reporter. Jun 18, 1937, p3.
Hollywood Spectator. Jul 3, 1937, v12, p5-6.
James Whale: Ace Director. p6-7.
Life. Jun 28, 1937, v2, p30-31.
Life. Jul 19, 1937, v3, p93.
Literary Digest. Jul 3, 1937, v123, p22-23.
Motion Picture. Jun 1937, v53, p18.
Motion Picture. Aug 1937, v54, p48-49.
Motion Picture Herald. Jun 26, 1937, p88.
Motion Picture Herald. Apr 24, 1937, p16-17.
The New Masses. Jun 29, 1937, v24, p28.
The New Republic. Jun 30, 1937, v91, p222-23.
The New Yorker. Jun 26, 1937, v13, p63-64.
Newsweek. Jun 26, 1937, v9, p22-23.
Rob Wagner's Script. Jul 31, 1937, v17, p12.
Stage. Apr 1937, v14, p75.
Stage. Jun 1937, v14, p61.
The Tatler. Oct 13, 1937, v146, p52.
Time. Jun 28, 1937, v29, p51.
Variety. Jun 23, 1937, p12.
World Film News. Oct 1937, v2, p24.

The Road to Glory (US; Hawks, Howard; 1936)
Esquire. Oct 1936, v6, p194.
Esquire. Nov 1936, v6, p211.
Film Daily. Jun 2, 1936, p29.
The Films of Fredric March. p140-42.
The Films of Howard Hawks. p172.
Hollywood Reporter. May 29, 1936, p3.
Hollywood Spectator. Jun 6, 1936, v11, p10.
Howard Hawks. p102-09.
Literary Digest. Jul 11, 1936, v122, p22.
Movie Classic. Jun 1936, v10, p30-31+.
The Nation. Sep 26, 1936, v143, p374.
The New Masses. Aug 18, 1936, v20, p30.
The New York Times. Aug 6, 1936, p22.
The New Yorker. Aug 15, 1936, v12, p44.
Rob Wagner's Script. Aug 29, 1936, v16, p10.
The Tatler. Nov 11, 1936, v142, p244.
Time. Aug 17, 1936, v28, p46+.
Variety. Aug 12, 1936, p18.
World Film News. Oct 1930, v1, p25.
World Film News. Dec 1936, v1, p20.

The Road to Life (Russian title: Putyovka v Zhizn; Also titled: A Pass to Life) (USSR; Ekk, Nikolai; 1931)
Cinema, the Magic Vehicle. v1, p189-90.
Commonweal. Mar 9, 1932, v15, p508.
Dictionary of Films. p296-97.
Film Daily. Jan 31, 1932, p11.
Hollywood Reporter. Jan 26, 1932, p3.
Kino. p284-85.
Literary Digest. Mar 19, 1932, v112, p18.
Motion Picture Herald. Feb 6, 1932, p42.
The New Republic. Feb 10, 1932, v69, p351.
The New York Times. Jan 28, 1932, p24.
The New York Times. Feb 7, 1932, p4.
Outlook. Mar 1932, v160, p188.
Partisan Review. Jul 1938, v5, p47.
Theatre Arts. Apr 1932, v16, p274.
Time. Feb 8, 1932, v19, p20.
Variety. Feb 2, 1932, p19.

Road to Morocco (US; Butler, David; 1942)
Around Cinemas, Second Series. p216-17.
Film Daily. Oct 5, 1942, p6.
The Films of Bing Crosby. p131-35.
Hollywood Reporter. Oct 2, 1942, p3.
The London Times. Nov 16, 1942.
Magill's Survey of Cinema. Series I. v3, p1454-57.
Motion Picture Exhibitor. Oct 7, 1942, v28, n22, sec2, p1126.
Motion Picture Herald Product Digest. Oct 3, 1942, p933.
The New York Times. Nov 12, 1942, p30.

The New York Times. Nov 15, 1942, sec8, p3.
Rob Wagner's Script. Nov 21, 1942, v27, p18.
Selected Film Criticism, 1941-1950. p200.
Variety. Oct 7, 1942, p8.

The Road to Reno (US; Simon, S. Sylvan; 1938)
Film Daily. Aug 31, 1938, p8.
The Films of the Thirties. p220-21.
Hollywood Reporter. Aug 26, 1938, p3.
Hollywood Spectator. Sep 3, 1938, v13, p14.
The New York Times. Oct 3, 1938, p11.
Rob Wagner's Script. Oct 22, 1938, v20, p14.
Variety. Oct 5, 1938, p14.

The Road to Reno (US; Wallace, Richard; 1931)
Film Daily. Oct 11, 1931, p10.
Hollywood Reporter. Aug 20, 1931, p3.
Judge. Oct 31, 1931, v101, p20.
Motion Picture Herald. Sep 5, 1931, p44.
The New York Times. Oct 10, 1931, p20.
The New York Times. Oct 18, 1931, p5.
The New Yorker. Oct 17, 1931, v7, p68.
Variety. Oct 13, 1931, p15.

The Road to Singapore (US; Schertzinger, Victor; 1940)
Commonweal. Mar 29, 1940, v31, p494.
Film Daily. Feb 26, 1940, p8.
The Films of Bing Crosby. p105-08.
Motion Picture Herald. Feb 24, 1940, p36.
The New York Times. Mar 14, 1940, p29.
Newsweek. Mar 25, 1940, v15, p37.
Photoplay. Apr 1940, v54, p19.
Photoplay. May 1940, v54, p50-51, 72.
Time. Mar 25, 1940, v35, p94.
Variety. Feb 28, 1940, p16.

Road to Utopia (US; Walker, Hal; 1946)
Commonweal. Mar 29, 1946, v43, p599.
Film Daily. Dec 5, 1945, p10.
The Films of Bing Crosby. p157-62.
The Hollywood Musical. p267.
Hollywood Reporter. Dec 5, 1945, p3.
Life. Feb 4, 1946, v20, p80-82.
Motion Picture Herald Product Digest. Dec 8, 1945.
The New York Times. Feb 28, 1946, p20.
The New Yorker. Mar 2, 1946, v22, p81.
Newsweek. Mar 11, 1946, v27, p90.
Theatre Arts. Feb 1946, v30, p103.
Time. Mar 4, 1946, v47, p96.
Variety. Dec 5, 1945, p16.

The Road to Yesterday (US; DeMille, Cecil B.; 1925)
Film Daily. Nov 15, 1925, p4.
The Films of Cecil B. DeMille. p242-45.
The Moving Picture World. Dec 12, 1925, p574.
Photoplay. Jan 1926, v24, p48.
Selected Film Criticism, 1921-1930.
Variety. Dec 2, 1925, p40.

Road to Zanzibar (US; Schertzinger, Victor; 1940)
Commonweal. Apr 25, 1941, v36, p17.
The Film Criticism of Otis Ferguson. p355-57.
Film Daily. Apr 10, 1941, p7.
The Films of Bing Crosby. p114-19.
Hollywood Reporter. Mar 10, 1941, p3.
The London Times. Jun 2, 1941, p8.
Motion Picture Exhibitor. Mar 19, 1941, p710.
Motion Picture Herald Product Digest. Mar 8, 1941, p73.
The New Republic. May 5, 1941, v104, p633.
The New York Times. Apr 10, 1941, p29.
The New York Times. Apr 13, 1941, sec9, p5.
Newsweek. Apr 7, 1941, v17, p64.
Scribner's Commentator. Jul 1941, v10, p106-07.
Variety. May 21, 1941, p14.

Roadhouse Nights (US; Henley, Hobart; 1930)
Exhibitors Herald-World. Feb 15, 1930, p29.
Exhibitors Herald-World. Mar 1, 1930, p35.
Film Daily. Feb 23, 1930, p8.
The Great Gangster Pictures. p332-33.
Judge. Mar 15, 1930, v98, p25.
Life. Apr 4, 1930, v95, p34.
London Mercury. Aug 1930, v22, p363.
The New York Times. Mar 2, 1930, p5.
The New York Times. Feb 22, 1930, p13.
The New Yorker. Mar 1, 1930, v6, p67.
Outlook and Independent. Mar 5, 1930, v154, p393.
Variety. Feb 26, 1930, p24.

The Roaring Twenties (US; Walsh, Raoul; 1939)
Classics of the Gangster Film. p72-76.
Commonweal. Nov 10, 1939, v31, p79.
The Complete Films of Humphrey Bogart. p71-72.
Crime Movies (Clarens). p155-56.
The Film Criticism of Otis Ferguson. p277-78.
Film Daily. Oct 16, 1939, p6.
The Films of James Cagney. p143-46.
The Films of the Thirties. p244-46.
From Quasimodo to Scarlett O'Hara. p326-29.
The Great Gangster Pictures. p333-35.
Hollywood Reporter. Oct 12, 1939, p3.
Hollywood Spectator. Oct 28, 1939, v14, p10-11.
Humphrey Bogart: The Man and His Films. p96-98.
The International Dictionary of Films and Filmmakers. v1, p394-95.
Magill's Survey of Cinema. Series I. v3, p1458-61.
Motion Picture Herald. Oct 21, 1939, p38.
Movietone News. Nov 1975, n45, p14-21.
National Board of Review Magazine. Dec 1939, v14, p11-12.
The New Masses. Nov 21, 1939, v33, p29-30.
The New Republic. Dec 6, 1939, v101, p194.
The New York Times. Nov 11, 1939, p12.
The New Yorker. Nov 11, 1939, v15, p69.
Newsweek. Oct 30, 1939, v14, p39.
On Film. Spr 1984, n12, p28-36.
Photoplay. Dec 1939, v53, p63.
Rob Wagner's Script. Nov 4, 1939, v22, p16-17.
Selected Film Criticism, 1931-1940. p209-11.
The Spectator. Mar 1, 1940, v164, p284.
Time. Nov 13, 1939, v34, p86.
Variety. Oct 25, 1939, p11.

The Robber Symphony (GB; Feher, Friedrich; 1936)
Dictionary of Films. p315.
Film Daily. Feb 6, 1937, p3.
Graham Greene on Film. p76, 78.
Hollywood Reporter. May 16, 1936, p4.
Motion Picture Herald. May 9, 1936, p43.
National Board of Review Magazine. Feb 1937, v12, p17.
The New York Times. Jan 27, 1937, p17.
Sight and Sound. Sum 1936, v5, p27.
The Spectator. May 29, 1936, v156, p978.
Time. Feb 8, 1937, v29, p58.
Variety. Jan 27, 1937, p12.

Roberta (US; Seiter, William A.; 1935)
Around Cinemas. p180-82.
Film Daily. Feb 12, 1935, p8.
The Films of Ginger Rogers. p112-15.
The Fred Astaire & Ginger Rogers Book. p45-53.
The Hollywood Musical. p105+.
Hollywood Musicals. p90-91.
Hollywood Reporter. Feb 9, 1935, p3.
Hollywood Reporter. Mar 15, 1935, p2.
Literary Digest. Mar 23, 1935, v119, p28.
Magill's Survey of Cinema. Series II. v5, p2029-33.
Motion Picture Herald. Feb 23, 1935, p54.
The Nation. Mar 27, 1935, v140, p372.
The New Statesman and Nation. Jun 8, 1935, v9, p863.
The New York Times. Mar 8, 1935, p25.

The New Yorker. Mar 16, 1935, v11, p70-71.
Rob Wagner's Script. Mar 9, 1935, v13, p8.
Selected Film Criticism, 1931-1940. p211-12.
The Spectator. May 31, 1935, v154, p918.
Starring Fred Astaire. p83-95.
Time. Mar 18, 1935, v25, p28.
Variety. Mar 31, 1935, p15.

Robin Hood (US; Dwan, Allan; 1922)
Allan Dwan: The Last Pioneer. p53-65.
The Best Moving Picture of 1922-1923. p37-44.
Film Daily. Nov 5, 1922, p2.
From Quasimodo to Scarlett O'Hara. p19-21.
His Majesty the American. p132-38.
Magill's Survey of Cinema. Silent Films. v3, p921-24.
The New York Times. Oct 31, 1922, Addenda p15.
Photoplay. Jan 1923, p64.
Variety. Oct 20, 1922, p40.

Rockabye (Also titled: Rock-a-bye) (US; Cukor, George; 1932)
Film Daily. Dec 3, 1932, p4.
George Cukor (Phillips). p36-37.
Hollywood Reporter. Nov 1, 1932, p2.
Motion Picture Herald. Nov 26, 1932, p30.
The New York Times. Dec 5, 1932, p21.
Rob Wagner's Script. Nov 26, 1932, v8, p8.
Time. Nov 14, 1932, v20, p33.
Variety. Dec 6, 1932, p15.

The Rogue Song (US; Barrymore, Lionel; 1930)
Commonweal. Feb 12, 1930, v11, p425.
Exhibitors Herald-World. Feb 8, 1930, p32.
Film Daily. Feb 2, 1930, p8.
The Film Spectator. Feb 15, 1930, v9, p18.
The Hollywood Musical. p42.
Judge. Mar 1, 1930, v98, p25.
Laurel & Hardy. p181-85.
Life. Mar 28, 1930, v95, p18, 28.
Literary Digest. Feb 22, 1930, v104, p32.
The Nation. Feb 19, 1930, v130, p226.
The New York Times. Jan 29, 1930, p26.
The New Yorker. Feb 8, 1930, v5, p71.
Outlook and Independent. Feb 12, 1930, v154, p272.
Rob Wagner's Script. Feb 15, 1930, v3, p10.
Rob Wagner's Script. Jul 26, 1930, v3, p13.
Sociology and Social Research. Mar 1930, v14, p398.
Time. Jan 27, 1930, v15, p42.
Variety. Feb 5, 1930, p19.

Roi S'Amuse, Le (FR; Colombier, Pierre; 1938)
The New Statesman and Nation. Apr 9, 1938, v15, p614.
The Spectator. Apr 22, 1938, v160, p706.
World Film News. May-Jun 1938, v3, p89.

Rojo no Reikon *See* Souls on the Road

Roma, Cittè Aperta *See* Open City

Roman d'un Tricheur, Le (Also titled: The Story of a Cheat; The Cheat; Confessions of a Cheat) (FR; Guitry, Sacha; 1936)
Dictionary of Films. p317-18.
The Film Criticism of Otis Ferguson. p238.
Film Daily. Oct 12, 1938, p9.
The Golden Age of French Cinema, 1929-1939. p51-53.
The Great French Films. p243-44.
Motion Picture Herald. Oct 15, 1938, p40.
The Nation. Oct 15, 1938, v147, p390.
The New Masses. Oct 11, 1938, v29, p29-30.
The New York Times. Jan 31, 1942, p13.
The New York Times. Sep 27, 1938, p25.
The New Yorker. Oct 1, 1938, v14, p48.
Rob Wagner's Script. Jan 7, 1939, v20, p16-17.
Sight and Sound. Spr 1937, v6, p25-26.
The Spectator. Oct 22, 1937, v159, p682.

The Tatler. Oct 6, 1937, v146, p6.
Time. Oct 10, 1938, v32, p37.
Variety. Oct 14, 1936, p54.
World Film News. Nov 1937, v2, p25.

Roman Scandals (US; Tuttle, Frank; 1933)
The Busby Berkeley Book. p72-73.
Esquire. Feb 1933, v1, p131.
Film Daily. Dec 14, 1933, p6.
The Films of the Thirties. p110-11.
The Genius of Busby Berkeley. p167-68.
Hollywood Reporter. Jul 17, 1933, p3, 65.
Hollywood Reporter. Nov 17, 1933, p3.
Judge. Feb 1934, v106, p14.
Motion Picture. Jan 1934, v46, p22-23.
Motion Picture Herald. Dec 9, 1933, p35.
The New Masses. Jan 2, 1934, v10, p28-29.
New Outlook. Jan 1934, v163, p43.
The New York Times. Dec 25, 1933, p28.
Rob Wagner's Script. Dec 2, 1933, v10, p10-11.
Samuel Goldwyn Presents. p128-30.
Time. Dec 25, 1933, v22, p22.
Vanity Fair. Feb 1934, v41, p45.
Variety. Dec 26, 1933, p11.

Romance (US; Withey, Chet; 1920)
Motion Picture News. May 29, 1920, p4545.
The Moving Picture World. Feb 28, 1920, p1329.
The Moving Picture World. May 29, 1920, p1195, 1239.
The New York Times. May 17, 1920, p19.
Selected Film Criticism, 1912-1920. p223-24.
Variety. Mar 12, 1920, p55.
Variety. Mar 19, 1920, p56.
Variety. Apr 9, 1920, p62.
Wid's Daily. May 23, 1920, p3.

Romance (US; Brown, Clarence; 1930)
Commonweal. Sep 3, 1930, v12, p446.
Film Daily. Aug 24, 1930, p10.
The Films of Greta Garbo. p91-94.
Judge. Oct 11, 1930, v99, p21.
Life. Sep 26, 1930, v96, p20.
National Board of Review Magazine. Nov 1931, v6, p9.
The New Republic. Sep 17, 1930, v64, p127-28.
The New York Times. Aug 23, 1930, p7.
The New Yorker. Aug 30, 1930, v6, p49-50.
Outlook and Independent. Sep 3, 1930, v156, p32.
Saturday Review (London). Sep 13, 1930, v150, p313-14.
Time. Sep 1, 1930, v16, p44.
Variety. Aug 27, 1930, p21.

Romance in Manhattan (US; Roberts, Stephen; 1934)
Film Daily. Nov 21, 1934, p11.
Hollywood Reporter. Nov 5, 1934, p3.
The New York Times. Jan 18, 1935, p29.
Variety. Jan 22, 1935, p14.

Romance in the Dark (US; Potter, H.C.; 1938)
Film Daily. Feb 14, 1938, p6.
Hollywood Reporter. Feb 16, 1938, p3.
Motion Picture Herald. Feb 19, 1938, p47.
The New York Times. Mar 21, 1938, p18.
Rob Wagner's Script. Mar 12, 1938, v19, p8.
Time. Feb 21, 1938, v31, p57.
Variety. Feb 16, 1938, p15.

The Romance of Happy Valley (US; Griffith, D.W.; 1919)
D.W. Griffith: An American Life. p381-83.
D.W. Griffith: His Life and Work. p193-95.
Exhibitor's Trade Review. Feb 1, 1919, p715.
The Films of D.W. Griffith. p102-06.
Motion Picture News. Feb 8, 1919, p918.
The Moving Picture World. Jan 25, 1919, p542.
The Moving Picture World. Feb 8, 1919, p804.
The New York Times. Jan 27, 1919, p11.
Selected Film Criticism, 1912-1920. p224-25.

Variety. Jan 31, 1919, p52.
Wid's Daily. Feb 2, 1919, p23.

The Romance of Rosy Ridge (US; Rowland, Roy; 1947)
Commonweal. Oct 3, 1947, v46, p598.
Film Daily. Jul 2, 1947, p10.
Hollywood Reporter. Jul 2, 1947, p3.
Motion Picture Herald Product Digest. Jul 5, 1947, p3713.
The New York Times. Sep 12, 1947, p18.
Newsweek. Sep 22, 1947, v30, p89.
Time. Sep 29, 1947, v50, p101.

Romance on the High Seas (US; Curtiz, Michael; 1948)
Commonweal. July 23, 1948, v48, p356.
Film Daily. Jun 9, 1948, p6.
Hollywood Reporter. Jun 8, 1948, p3.
Motion Picture Herald Product Digest. Jun 12, 1948, p4197.
The New York Times. Jun 26, 1948, p10.
Newsweek. July 5, 1948, v32, p70.
Variety. Jun 9, 1948, p12.

Romance Sentimentale (Also titled: The Silver Lining)
 (USSR; Eisenstein, Sergei; 1931)
Close-Up. Dec 1930, v7, p447-48.
The Spectator. Oct 3, 1931, v147, p414.
Variety. Oct 27, 1931, p19.

Rome Express (GB; Forde, Walter; 1932)
Cinema Quarterly. Wint 1932, v1, p113.
Film Daily. Feb 25, 1933, p4.
Hollywood Reporter. Feb 7, 1933, p5.
Motion Picture Herald. Jan 21, 1933, p29.
The Nation. Mar 15, 1933, v136, p298-99.
The New York Times. Dec 18, 1932, p6.
The New York Times. Feb 27, 1933, p11.
The New Yorker. Mar 4, 1933, v9, p51-52.
Rob Wagner's Script. Mar 18, 1933, v9, p8.
Selected Film Criticism: Foreign Films, 1930-1950. p152-53.
The Spectator. Jul 26, 1935, v155, p151.
Time. Mar 6, 1933, v21, p24.
Variety. Dec 6, 1932, p15.
Variety. Feb 28, 1933, p15.

Rome, Open City *See* Open City

Romeo and Juliet (US; 1908)
The New York Dramatic Mirror. Jun 13, 1908, p10.
Selected Film Criticism, 1896-1911. p84.

Romeo and Juliet (US; 1911)
The Moving Picture World. Aug 19, 1911, p446.
Selected Film Criticism, 1896-1911. p84-85.

Romeo and Juliet (US; Edwards, J. Gordon; 1916)
Fifty Great American Silent Films, 1912-1920. p58-60.
Magill's Survey of Cinema. Silent Films. v3, p925-27.
The Moving Picture World. Nov 11, 1916, p837, 840.
Photoplay. Jan 1917, v11, p96-100.
Selected Film Criticism, 1912-1920. p225-29.
Variety. Oct 27, 1916, p28.
Wid's Daily. Oct 26, 1916, p1053.

Romeo and Juliet (US; Noble, John W.; 1916)
The Moving Picture World. Oct 21, 1916, p448.
The Moving Picture World. Nov 4, 1916, p685.
The New York Times. Oct 27, 1916, p28.
Photoplay. Jan 1917, v11, p96-100.
Selected Film Criticism, 1912-1920. p225-29.
Variety. Oct 27, 1916, p28.
Wid's Daily. Oct 26, 1916, p1052.

Romeo and Juliet (US; Cukor, George; 1936)
Canadian Magazine. Sep 1936, v86, p28.
Catholic World. Oct 1936, v144, p85-88.
Commonweal. Sep 4, 1936, v24, p446.
Delineator. Oct 1936, v129, p1.
Esquire. Oct 1936, v6, p109.

The Film Criticism of Otis Ferguson. p148-50.
Film Daily. Jul 16, 1936, p2.
Films. Nov 1939, p35.
Films and Filming. Nov 1954, v1, p15.
The Films of Norma Shearer. p202-11.
From Quasimodo to Scarlett O'Hara. p224-27.
Garbo and the Night Watchman. p186-88.
George Cukor (Phillips). p41-44.
Graham Greene on Film. p109-11.
Hollywood Reporter. Jul 16, 1936, p4-5.
Hollywood Spectator. Aug 1, 1936, v11, p7.
Judge. Sep 1936, v111, p12.
Library Journal. Aug 1936, v61, p589-90.
A Library of Film Criticism: American Film Directors. p68-69.
Literary Digest. Apr 18, 1936, v121, p23.
Literary Digest. Aug 15, 1936, v122, p20.
London Mercury. Nov 1936, v35, p57.
Magill's Survey of Cinema. Series II. v5, p2053-58.
Motion Picture. May 1936, v51, p34-35+.
Motion Picture Herald. Mar 28, 1936, p16-17.
Movie Classic. Jun 1936, v10, p38-39₁+.
Movie Classic. Oct 1936, v11, p50.
Movie Classic. Nov 1936, v11, p37-39.
The Nation. Oct 10, 1936, v143, p429.
National Board of Review Magazine. Sep-Oct 1936, v11, p6.
The New Masses. Sep 1, 1936, v20, p29.
The New Republic. Sep 2, 1936, v88, p104.
The New Statesman and Nation. Oct 17, 1936, v12, p588.
New Theatre. Sep 1936, v3, p21-22.
The New York Times. Aug 21, 1936, p12.
The New York Times. May 15, 1936, p24.
The New Yorker. Aug 22, 1936, v12, p36-38.
Photoplay. Sep 1936, v50, p46-48+.
Rob Wagner's Script. Sep 26, 1936, v16, p10.
Saturday Review (London). Oct 24, 1936, v162, p544.
Scholastic. Sep 19, 1936, v29, p17.
Selected Film Criticism, 1931-1940. p212-15.
Shakespeare and the Film. p27-36.
Sight and Sound. Aut 1936, v5, p79-81.
The Spectator. Oct 23, 1936, v157, p679.
Stage. Sep 1936, v13, p57.
The Tatler. Oct 21, 1936, v142, p102.
Those Fabulous Movie Years: The 30s. p106-07.
Time. Aug 24, 1936, v28, p30-32.
Variety. Aug 26, 1936, p20.
World Film News. Oct 1936, v1, p23.
World Film News. Dec 1936, v1, p15.

Romola (US; King, Henry; 1925)
Film Daily. Dec 7, 1924, p7.
The New York Times. Dec 2, 1924, p13.
The New Yorker. Apr 25, 1925, v1, p31.

Room Service (US; Seiter, William A.; 1938)
Commonweal. Oct 7, 1938, v28, p616.
Esquire. Jan 1939, v11, p110.
Film Daily. Sep 14, 1938, p7.
Hollywood Reporter. Sep 7, 1938, p3.
Hollywood Spectator. Sep 17, 1938, v13, p8-9.
Motion Picture Herald. Sep 10, 1938, p58.
The New Masses. Sep 27, 1938, v29, p30.
The New York Times. Sep 22, 1938, p27.
The New Yorker. Sep 24, 1938, v14, p65.
Rob Wagner's Script. Oct 29, 1938, v20, p12-13.
Sight and Sound. Wint 1938-39, v7, p161.
The Spectator. Dec 9, 1938, v161, p1000.
Time. Oct 3, 1938, v32, p36.
Variety. Sep 14, 1938, p15.
World Film News. Nov 1938, v3, p312-13.

Rope (US; Hitchcock, Alfred; 1948)
The Art of Alfred Hitchcock. p185-92.
Canadian Forum. Dec 1948, v28, p207.
Commonweal. Aug 27, 1948, v48, p475.
Film Daily. Aug 26, 1948, p5.

Films and Filming. Mar 1963, v9, p41-42.
The Films of Alfred Hitchcock. p142-45.
The Films of James Stewart. p115-117.
Hitchcock: The First Forty-Four Films. p90-96.
Hitchcock (Truffaut). p179+.
Hollywood Reporter. Aug 26, 1948, p3.
Life. July 26, 1948, v25, p57-58+.
Motion Picture Herald Product Digest. Aug 28, 1948, p4197.
The New Republic. Sep 13, 1948, v119, p29-30.
The New York Times. Aug 27, 1948, p12.
Newsweek. Aug 9, 1948, v32, p68.
Time. Sep 13, 1948, v52, p102+.
Variety. Sep 1, 1948, p14.

Rory O'More (US; Olcott, Sidney; 1911)
The Moving Picture World. Aug 19, 1911, p445-46.
Selected Film Criticism, 1896-1911. p85-86.

Rosalie (US; Van Dyke, W.S.; 1937)
Canadian Magazine. Mar 1938, v89, p33.
Commonweal. Jan 7, 1938, v27, p300.
Film Daily. Dec 22, 1937, p5.
The Films of Jeanette MacDonald and Nelson Eddy. p213-20.
Hollywood Reporter. Dec 17, 1937, p3.
Judge. Feb 1938, v114, p26.
Motion Picture Herald. Dec 25, 1937, p38-39.
Motion Picture Herald. Nov 6, 1937, p34-35.
The New York Times. Dec 31, 1937, p9.
The New Yorker. Jan 8, 1938, v13, p61-62.
Newsweek. Jan 10, 1938, v11, p27-28.
Photoplay. Feb 1938, v52, p46-47.
Rob Wagner's Script. Dec 25, 1937, v18, p4.
Time. Jan 3, 1938, v31, p30.
Variety. Dec 22, 1937, p16.

The Rosary (US; Campbell, Colin; 1915)
Motion Picture News. Apr 17, 1915, p97.
Motion Picture News. Jun 26, 1915, p12, 68.
Motion Picture News. Jul 3, 1915, p69.
Motography. Jul 3, 1915, p26-27, 47.
The Moving Picture World. Jun 19, 1915, p2014.
The Moving Picture World. Jun 26, 1915, p2105.
The New York Dramatic Mirror. Jun 30, 1915, p28.
Selected Film Criticism, 1912-1920. p229-31.

Rose Marie (US; Van Dyke, W.S.; 1936)
Canadian Magazine. Mar 1936, v85, p40.
Commonweal. Jan 31, 1936, v23, p386.
Film Daily. Jan 13, 1936, p10.
The Films of David Niven. p33.
The Films of Jeanette MacDonald and Nelson Eddy. p165-76.
The Hollywood Musical. p128-29.
Hollywood Reporter. Jan 9, 1936, p3.
Hollywood Spectator. Jan 18, 1936, v10, p9-10.
Movie Classic. Jan 1936, v9, p25+.
The New York Times. Feb 1, 1936, p9.
The New Yorker. Feb 8, 1936, v11, p60-61.
Rob Wagner's Script. Feb 11, 1936, v14, p10.
Scholastic. Feb 8, 1936, v28, p30.
Stage. Jan 1936, v13, p8.
Time. Feb 10, 1936, v27, p26.
Variety. Feb 5, 1936, p9.

Rose of the Rancho (US; DeMille, Cecil B.; Buckland, Wilfred; 1914)
The Films of Cecil B. DeMille. p47-51.
The Moving Picture World. Nov 21, 1914, p1078.
The Moving Picture World. Nov 28, 1914, p1294.
The Moving Picture World. Dec 12, 1914, p1531.
The New York Dramatic Mirror. Nov 25, 1914, p32.
Variety. Nov 20, 1914, p27.

Rose of the Rancho (US; Gering, Marion; 1936)
Canadian Magazine. Nov 1935, v84, p40.
Commonweal. Jan 17, 1936, v23, p330.
Film Daily. Jan 4, 1936, p3.

Garbo and the Night Watchman. p174-75.
Graham Greene on Film. p56.
Hollywood Reporter. Jan 7, 1936, p4.
Motion Picture Herald. Jan 11, 1936, p45, 52.
Newsweek. Jan 11, 1936, v7, p25.
Scholastic. Feb 8, 1936, v28, p30.
The Spectator. Mar 6, 1936, v156, p396.
Time. Jan 13, 1936, v27, p42.
Variety. Jan 15, 1936, p18.

Rose of Washington Square (US; Ratoff, Gregory; 1939)
Commonweal. May 19, 1939, v30, p106.
Film Daily. May 8, 1939, p8.
The Films of Alice Faye. p109-14.
The Films of Tyrone Power. p89-91.
Hollywood Reporter. May 4, 1939, p3.
Hollywood Spectator. May 13, 1939, v14, p11-12.
Motion Picture Herald. May 13, 1939, p37.
The New York Times. May 6, 1939, p21.
The New Yorker. May 13, 1939, v15, p77.
Newsweek. May 15, 1939, v13, p33.
Photoplay. Jul 1939, v53, p62.
Rob Wagner's Script. May 20, 1939, v21, p17-18.
Saint Nicholas. Apr 1939, v66, p37.
Time. May 15, 1939, v33, p58.
Variety. May 10, 1939, p14.

Rosita (US; Lubitsch, Ernst; 1923)
Ernst Lubitsch: A Guide to References and Resources. p72-74.
Exceptional Photoplays. Oct-Nov 1923, v4, p5.
Film Daily. Sep 9, 1923, p3.
Magill's Survey of Cinema. Silent Films. v3, p928-30.
The Moving Picture World. Sep 15, 1923, p262, 265.
The New York Times. Sep 4, 1923, p4.
Photoplay. Nov 1923, v24, p74.
Selected Film Criticism, 1921-1930. p243-44.

Roue, La (FR; Gance, Abel; 1923)
Abel Gance (Kramer and Welsh). p12-14, 79-91.
Cinema, the Magic Vehicle. v1, p92-94.
French Cinema. p326-40.
Variety. Jan 19, 1923, p47.

Rough Riders (US; Fleming, Victor; 1927)
Film Daily. Mar 20, 1927, p6.
The Moving Picture World. Mar 19, 1927, p213.
The New York Times. Mar 16, 1927, p28.
Outlook. Mar 30, 1927, v145, p393-94.
Variety. Mar 30, 1927, p14.

Roughly Speaking (US; Curtiz, Michael; 1945)
Film Daily. Jan 1, 1945, p6.
The Films of the Forties. p151-52.
Hollywood Reporter. Jan 31, 1945, p4.
The London Times. Sep 6, 1945, p6.
Magill's Cinema Annual, 1983. p490-93.
Motion Picture Exhibitor. Feb 7, 1945, v33, n14, sec2, p1662.
Motion Picture Herald Product Digest. Feb 3, 1945, p2297.
The New Republic. Feb 19, 1945, v112, p264.
The New York Times. Feb 1, 1945, p18.
Newsweek. Feb 12, 1945, v25, p98.
Time. Feb 26, 1945, v45, p94.
Variety. Jan 31, 1945, p3.

Roxie Hart (US; Wellman, William A.; 1942)
Agee on Film. v1, p336.
Commonweal. Feb 27, 1942, 35, p463.
Film Daily. Feb 3, 1942, p7.
The Films of Ginger Rogers. p171-74.
Hollywood Reporter. Feb 3, 1942, p3.
The London Times. Jun 17, 1942, p6.
Magill's Survey of Cinema. Series II. v5, p2063-65.
Motion Picture Exhibitor. Feb 11, 1942, v27, n14, sec2, p947.
Motion Picture Herald Product Digest. Feb 7, 1942, p493.
The New York Times. Feb 20, 1942, p21.
Newsweek. Mar 2, 1942, v19, p50.

Rob Wagner's Script. Feb 28, 1942, p10.
Selected Film Criticism, 1941-1950. p201-02.
Time. Mar 2, 1942, v39, p74.
Variety. Feb 4, 1942, p8.
William A. Wellman (Thompson). p203-06+.

The Royal Bed (US; Sherman, Lowell; 1931)
Exhibitors Herald-World. Dec 13, 1930, p28.
Film Daily. Feb 1, 1931, p11.
Judge. Feb 21, 1931, v100, p23.
The New York Times. Jan 31, 1931, p15.
Time. Jan 12, 1931, v17, p22.
Variety. Aug 4, 1931, p21.

A Royal Divorce (GB; Raymond, Jack; 1938)
Hollywood Reporter. Aug 30, 1939, p3.
Motion Picture Herald. Oct 15, 1938, p40.
The New Statesman and Nation. Sep 24, 1938, v16, p456.
Variety. May 12, 1938, p19.
World Film News. Nov 1938, v3, p314.

The Royal Family of Broadway (Also titled: The Royal
   Family) (US; Cukor, George; Gardner, Cyril; 1930)
Around Cinemas. p52-54.
Exhibitors Herald-World. Dec 27, 1930, p22.
Film Daily. Dec 28, 1930, p10.
The Films of Fredric March. p68-70.
George Cukor (Phillips). p28-29.
Judge. Jan 17, 1931, v100, p24.
Life. Jan 9, 1931, v97, p22.
Motion Picture Herald. Jan 3, 1931, p74.
The New York Times. Dec 23, 1930, p25.
The New York Times. Dec 28, 1930, p5.
The New Yorker. Jan 3, 1931, v6, p67-68.
On Cukor. p34-36.
Outlook and Independent. Jan 7, 1931, v157, p32.
Rob Wagner's Script. Mar 7, 1931, v5, p8.
Saturday Review (London). May 16, 1931, v151, p716.
The Spectator. May 16, 1931, v146, p768.
Theatre Magazine. Feb 1931, v53, p47.
Time. Jan 5, 1931, v17, p25.
Variety. Dec 24, 1930, p20.

Ruggles of Red Gap (US; McCarey, Leo; 1935)
Cinema Quarterly. Spr 1935, v3, p181.
Commonweal. Mar 29, 1935, v21, p628.
Esquire. Apr 1935, v3, p144, 150.
Film Comment. Sep-Oct 1973, v9, p9-10.
Film Daily. Feb 19, 1935, p6.
Film Notes. p94-95.
The Films of the Thirties. p138-39.
Garbo and the Night Watchman. p55.
Hollywood Reporter. Feb 2, 1935, p3.
Hollywood Reporter. Mar 14, 1935, p2.
Life. May 1935, v102, p34.
Literary Digest. Mar 23, 1935, v119, p28.
Lunatics and Lovers. p122-24.
Magill's Survey of Cinema. Series II. v5, p2066-69.
Motion Picture. Apr 1935, v49, p26.
Motion Picture Herald. Feb 16, 1935, p47.
The Nation. Mar 20, 1935, v140, p341.
The New Masses. Mar 26, 1935, v14, p29.
The New Republic. Mar 20, 1935, v82, p160.
The New Statesman and Nation. Mar 23, 1935, v9, p418.
The New York Times. Mar 7, 1935, p26.
The New Yorker. Mar 16, 1935, v11, p70.
Newsweek. Mar 16, 1935, v5, p29.
Rob Wagner's Script. Mar 16, 1935, v13, p9-10.
Saturday Review (London). Mar 23, 1935, v159, p376.
Selected Film Criticism, 1931-1940. p215-17.
The Spectator. Mar 22, 1935, v154, p476.
Theatre Arts Monthly. Jun 1935, v19, p409.
Time. Mar 18, 1935, v25, p28.
Vanity Fair. Apr 1935, v44, p46.

Variety. Mar 13, 1935, p15.
Variety. Mar 20, 1935, p15.

Rulers of the Sea (US; Lloyd, Frank; 1939)
Commonweal. Nov 24, 1939, v31, p119.
Film Daily. Sep 15, 1939, p5.
Hollywood Reporter. Sep 13, 1939, p3.
Motion Picture Herald. Sep 16, 1939, p39.
The New Statesman and Nation. Nov 18, 1939, v18, p710.
The New York Times. Nov 9, 1939, p27.
The New Yorker. Nov 11, 1939, v15, p69.
Newsweek. Nov 13, 1939, v14, p31.
Photoplay. Dec 1939, v53, p62.
Rob Wagner's Script. Sep 23, 1939, v22, p16.
The Spectator. Nov 24, 1939, v163, p744.
The Tatler. Nov 29, 1939, v154, p278.
Time. Dec 11, 1939, v34, p80.
Variety. Sep 20, 1939, p15.

The Ruling Passion *See* The Reward of the Faithless

Rumba (US; Gering, Marion; 1935)
Film Daily. Feb 23, 1935, p3.
The Films of Carole Lombard. p129-30.
Hollywood Reporter. Jan 23, 1935, p3.
Motion Picture Herald. Feb 2, 1935, p55.
The New York Times. Feb 25, 1935, p13.
Time. Feb 18, 1935, v25, p71.
Variety. Feb 27, 1935, p12.

Rumpelstiltskin (US; West, Raymond B.; 1915)
Motion Picture News. May 15, 1915, p65.
Motography. May 22, 1915, p830-31, 856.
The Moving Picture World. May 15, 1915, p1073, 1089, 1162.
The New York Dramatic Mirror. May 12, 1915, p36.
The Rivals of D.W. Griffith. p36-39.

A Russian Jazz Comedy (Russian title: Vesyolye Rebatat;
   Jazz Comedya; Also titled: Moscow Laughs; Jolly
   Fellows) (USSR; Alexandrov, Grigori; 1934)
Cinema, the Magic Vehicle. v1, p231-32.
Dictionary of Films. p402.
Film Daily. Mar 23, 1935, p4.
Graham Greene on Film. p23-24.
Motion Picture Herald. Apr 27, 1935, p54.
The New Statesman and Nation. Sep 28, 1935, v10, p412.
The New Statesman and Nation. Jan 4, 1936, v11, p16.
The New York Times. Mar 25, 1935, p12.
The Spectator. Sep 27, 1935, v155, p462.
Variety. Mar 27, 1935, p15.

Rythm Romance *See* Some Like It Hot

Sable Cicada (CHINA; Poh, Richard; 1939)
Film Daily. Jan 19, 1939, p10.
The New York Times. Jan 14, 1939, p13.
Time. Jan 30, 1939, v33, p50.
Variety. Jan 18, 1939, p19.
Variety. Feb 25, 1942, p8.

Sabotage (Also titled: A Woman Alone) (GB; Hitchcock,
   Alfred; 1936)
American Film Criticism. p356.
The Art of Alfred Hitchcock. p55-66.
A Critical History of the British Cinema. p110-11.
The English Novel and the Movies. p218-27.
Esquire. Apr 1937, v7, p117.
Film Daily. Jan 9, 1937, p4.
Film Society Review. Jan 1966, p12.
Graham Greene on Film. p122-23.
Hitchcock: The First Forty-Four Films. p46-50.
Hitchcock (Truffaut). p107-11.
Hitchcock's British Films. p205-16.
Hollywood Reporter. Jan 7, 1937, p35.
London Mercury. Jan 1937, v35, p322.
Motion Picture Herald. Jan 2, 1937, p67, 69.

The Nation. Mar 13, 1937, v144, p306.
The New Statesman and Nation. Dec 12, 1936, v12, p982.
New Theatre. Mar 1937, v4, p57-58.
The New York Times. Feb 27, 1937, p9.
Scholastic. Jan 30, 1937, v29, p23.
Selected Film Criticism: Foreign Films, 1930-1950. p198.
The Spectator. Dec 11, 1936, v157, p1037.
The Tatler. Dec 23, 1936, v142, p532.
Theatre Arts. May 1949, v33, p37.
Time. Jan 18, 1937, v29, p26.
Variety. Dec 16, 1936, p15.
Variety. Mar 3, 1937, p14.
World Film News. Jan 1937, v1, p27.
World Film News. Feb 1937, v1, p27.

Saboteur (US; Hitchcock, Alfred; 1942)
AFFS Newsletter. Feb 1965, p12-13.
The Art of Alfred Hitchcock. p125-32.
Commonweal. May 15, 1942, v36, p87.
Film Daily. Apr 23, 1942, p7.
The Films of Alfred Hitchcock. p109-13.
The Films of World War II. p67-68.
Hitchcock: The First Forty-four Films. p68-70.
Hitchcock (Truffaut). p145-51+.
Hollywood Reporter. Apr 23, 1942, p3.
Life. May 11, 1942, v12, p67-71.
Literature/Film Quarterly. 1984, v12, n1, p58-64.
The London Times. May 28, 1942, p6.
Magic Moments from the Movies. p110-11.
Magill's Survey of Cinema. Series II. v5, p2076-79.
Motion Picture Exhibitor. May 6, 1942, v27, n26, sec2, p1002-03.
Motion Picture Herald Product Digest. May 2, 1942, p634.
The Nation. May 23, 1942, v154, p609.
The New Republic. May 18, 1942, v106, p669.
The New York Times. May 8, 1942, p27.
The New Yorker. May 9, 1942, v18, p67.
Newsweek. May 4, 1942, v19, p54.
Theatre Arts. May 1942, v26, p318-19.
Time. May 11, 1942, v39, p87.
Variety. Apr 19, 1942, p8.

Sadie Thompson (US; Walsh, Raoul; 1928)
Each Man in His Own Time. p204-12.
Film Daily. Feb 12, 1928, p8.
The Film Spectator. Feb 18, 1928, v5, p5.
The Films of Gloria Swanson. p206-10.
Magill's Survey of Cinema. Silent Films. v2, p931-34.
The New York Times. Feb 6, 1928, p12.
Variety. Feb 8, 1928, p16.

Safe in Hell (Also titled: The Lost Lady) (US; Wellman, William A.; 1931)
Film Daily. Dec 20, 1931, p10.
The Films of the Thirties. p69-70.
Hollywood Reporter. Nov 12, 1931, p3.
Judge. Jan 9, 1932, v102, p20, 29.
Motion Picture Herald. Dec 26, 1931, p30.
The New York Times. Dec 19, 1931, p16.
The New Yorker. Dec 26, 1931, v7, p50.
Variety. Dec 22, 1931, p15.
We're in the Money. p54-55.
William A. Wellman (Thompson). p119-20.

Safety in Numbers (US; Schertzinger, Victor; 1930)
Exhibitors Herald-World. May 3, 1930, p32.
Exhibitors Herald-World. Jun 7, 1930, p90.
Film Daily. Jun 8, 1930, p10.
The Films of Carole Lombard. p75-77.
Judge. Jun 28, 1930, v98, p23.
Life. Jun 20, 1930, v95, p20.
The New York Times. May 31, 1930, p19.
Variety. Jun 4, 1930, p25.

Safety in Numbers (US; St. Clair, Malcolm; 1938)
Film Daily. Sep 9, 1938, p15.
Hollywood Reporter. Aug 5, 1938, p3.
Hollywood Spectator. Aug 20, 1938, v13, p12.
Motion Picture Herald. Aug 13, 1938, p62.
The New York Times. Sep 6, 1938, p17.
Time. Sep 12, 1938, v32, p46.
Variety. Sep 7, 1938, p12.

Safety Last (US; Roach, Hal; 1923)
The Best Moving Pictures of 1922-1923. p107.
The Comic Mind. p159-60.
Film Daily. April 8, 1923, p2.
The Films of Hal Roach. p21.
Harold Lloyd. p55-60.
Harold Lloyd: The Shape of Laughter. p156-60.
The International Dictionary of Films and Filmmakers. v1, p403.
Magill's Survey of Cinema. Silent Films. v3, p935-42.
The New York Times. Apr 2, 1923, p22.
Photoplay. Jun 1923, v24, p65.
Selected Film Criticism, 1921-1930. p244.
The Silent Clowns. p197-98.
Variety. Apr 5, 1923, p36.

Sahara (US; Korda, Zoltan; 1943)
Agee on Film. v1, p53, 67, 160.
Commonweal. Nov 12, 1943, v39, p96.
The Complete Films of Humphrey Bogart. p113-14.
Film Daily. Sep 29, 1943, p6.
The Films of World War II. p155-56.
Guts & Glory . p47-51+.
Hollywood Reporter. Sep 27, 1943, p3.
Humphrey Bogart: The Man and His Films. p127.
Motion Picture Herald Product Digest. Oct 2, 1943, p1565.
The New York Times. Nov 12, 1943, p25.
Newsweek. Oct 25, 1943, v22, p110.
Time. Oct 18, 1943, v42, p94.
Variety. Sep 29, 1943, p8.

Saigon (US; Fenton, Leslie; 1948)
Film Daily. Feb 9, 1948, p6.
The Films of Alan Ladd. p124-27.
Hollywood Reporter. Feb 3, 1948, p3.
Motion Picture Herald Product Digest.
The New York Times. Apr 1, 1948, p30.
The New Yorker. Apr 10, 1948, v24, p104.
Newsweek. Mar 29, 1948, v31, p80.
Variety. Feb 4, 1948, p13.

Sailing Along (GB; Hale, Sonnie; 1938)
The Age of the Dream Palace. p221-22.
Film Daily. Mar 23, 1938, p9.
Hollywood Reporter. Mar 30, 1938, p3.
Hollywood Spectator. Apr 9, 1938, v12, p9-10.
Motion Picture Herald. Feb 12, 1938, p50.
The New York Times. Apr 16, 1938, p17.
Rob Wagner's Script. May 21, 1938, v19, p9.
Selected Film Criticism: Foreign Films, 1930-1950. p154-56.
The Tatler. Apr 27, 1938, v148, p152.
Time. Apr 11, 1938, v31, p23.
Variety. Feb 9, 1938, p15.
World Film News. Jul 1938, v3, p130-31.

Sailor Be Good (US; Cruze, James; 1933)
Film Daily. Mar 1, 1933, p6.
Hollywood Reporter. Dec 29, 1932, p7.
The New York Times. Feb 27, 1933, p11.
Variety. Feb 28, 1933, p39.

Saint Louis Blues (Also titled: St. Louis Blues) (US; Walsh, Raoul; 1939)
Commonweal. Feb 24, 1939, v29, p497.
Film Daily. Jan 27, 1939, p11.
Hollywood Reporter. Jan 19, 1939, p3.
Hollywood Spectator. Feb 4, 1939, v13, p13-14.

Motion Picture Herald. Jan 28, 1939, p33.
The New York Times. Feb 9, 1939, p17.
Time. Feb 13, 1939, v33, p29.
Variety. Feb 8, 1939, p17.

A Sainted Devil (US; Henabery, Joseph; 1924)
Film Daily. Nov 30, 1924, p5.
The Moving Picture World. Nov 29, 1924, p548.
The New York Times. Nov 24, 1924, p15.
Rudolph Valentino. p99.
Variety. Nov 26, 1924, p24.

Saints and Sinners (GB; Arliss, Leslie; 1949)
Catholic World. Oct 1949, v170, p68.
Christian Century. May 17, 1950, v67, p631.
Commonweal. Sep 23, 1949, v50, p586.
The New Republic. Sep 26, 1949, v121, p28.
The New York Times. Sep 12, 1949, p17.
The New York Times. Sep 18, 1949, Sec 2, p1.
The New Yorker. Sep 17, 1949, v25, p66+.
Newsweek. Sep 26, 1949, v34, p89.
Rotarian. Jul 1950, v77, p37.
Time. Sep 19, 1949, v54, p106.
Variety. Jul 6, 1949, p9.

Sakkjatek Orultje, A *See* A Chess Maniac

Sally (US; Dillon, John Francis; 1929)
Film Daily. Dec 29, 1929, p8.
The Hollywood Musical. p35.
The New York Times. Dec 24, 1929, p14.
Variety. Dec 25, 1929, p20.

Sally in Our Alley (GB; Elvey, Maurice; 1931)
Motion Picture Herald. Jul 25, 1931, p28.
Variety. Jul 21, 1931, p34.

Sally, Irene and Mary (US; Seiter, William A.; 1938)
Film Daily. Feb 28, 1938, p6.
The Films of Alice Faye. p93-96.
The Hollywood Musical. p147.
Hollywood Reporter. Feb 26, 1938, p3.
Motion Picture Herald. Mar 5, 1938, p40.
The New York Times. Feb 26, 1938, p9.
Rob Wagner's Script. Mar 12, 1938, v19, p8.
Time. Mar 7, 1938, v31, p38.
Variety. Mar 2, 1938, p15.

Sally of the Sawdust (US; Griffith, D.W.; 1925)
BFI/Monthly Film Bulletin. Dec 1974, p289.
Film Daily. Aug 9, 1925, p6.
The Films of D.W. Griffith. p211-15.
Life. Aug 27, 1925, v86, p26.
Photoplay. Aug 1925, v28, p50.
Selected Film Criticism, 1921-1930. p245-46.
Variety. Aug 5, 1925, p30.
W.C. Fields: A Life on Film. p27-30.

Salome (US; Bryant, Charles; 1922)
The Best Moving Pictures of 1922-1923. p103.
Film Daily. Jan 7, 1923, p2.
The New Republic. Jan 24, 1923, v33, p225-26.
The New York Times. Jan 1, 1923, p18.
Selected Film Criticism, 1921-1930. p246-47.
Spellbound in Darkness. p495-97.
Variety. Jan 5, 1923, p42.

Salomy Jane (US; Beyfuss, Alexander E.; 1914)
The Moving Picture World. Nov 7, 1914, p768, 836, 1183.
The New York Dramatic Mirror. Nov 4, 1914, p30.
Variety. Oct 30, 1914, p27.

Salonique *See* Mademoiselle Docteur

The Salvation Hunters (US; Sternberg, Josef von; 1925)
The Cinema of Josef von Sternberg. p27-32.
Exceptional Photoplays. Dec-Jan 1925, v5, p3-4.
Film Daily. Feb 8, 1925, p6.

The Films of Josef von Sternberg. p10-12.
From Quasimodo to Scarlett O'Hara. p39-41.
Life. Jan 29, 1925, v85, p32.
The Moving Picture World. Feb 14, 1925, p701.
The New Republic. Nov 18, 1925, v44, p332-33.
The New York Times. Feb 2, 1925, p14.
Selected Film Criticism, 1921-1930. p247-49.
Spellbound in Darkness. p270, 273, 407.
Variety. Feb 4, 1925, p33.

Salvation Nell (US; Beyfuss, Alexander E.; 1915)
Motion Picture News. Jun 25, 1915, p67.
Motion Picture News. Aug 28, 1915, p85.
Motion Picture News. Oct 16, 1915, p70.
Motography. Jun 19, 1915, p995.
Motography. Jul 17, 1915, p103.
Motography. Aug 21, 1915, p352.
Motography. Sep 4, 1915, p475, 500.
The Moving Picture World. Aug 7, 1915, p1023.
The Moving Picture World. Aug 28, 1915, p1493.
The Moving Picture World. Oct 23, 1915, p692.
The New York Dramatic Mirror. Aug 25, 1915, p28.
Variety. Aug 25, 1915, p19.

Samarang (US; Wing, Ward; 1933)
Film Daily. May 18, 1933, p7.
Hollywood Reporter. Apr 12, 1933, p3.
Motion Picture Herald. May 20, 1933, p32.
The Nation. Jul 26, 1933, v137, p112.
New Outlook. Aug 1933, v162, p45.
The New York Times. Jun 29, 1933, p22.
The New Yorker. Jul 8, 1933, v9, p38.
Photoplay. Sep 1933, v44, p50-51+.
Rob Wagner's Script. Apr 29, 1933, v9, p8.
Time. Jul 10, 1933, v22, p41.
Variety. Jul 4, 1933, p16.

Samson and Delilah (French title: Samson et Delilah)
  (FR; 1908)
The Moving Picture World. Oct 3, 1908, p253.
Selected Film Criticism, 1896-1911. p87-88.

Samson and Delilah (US; DeMille, Cecil B.; 1949)
Christian Century. Apr 5, 1950, v67, p447.
Commonweal. Dec 30, 1949, v51, p341.
Film Daily. Oct 21, 1949 , p4.
The Films of Cecil B. DeMille. p340-49.
The Films of Hedy Lamarr. p202-10.
The Films of the Forties. p266-70.
Hollywood Reporter. Oct 21, 1949, p3.
Life. Dec 5, 1949, v27, p138-41+.
Motion Picture Herald. Oct 22, 1949, p57.
Motion Picture Herald. Oct 22, 1949, p57.
The Nation. Feb 18, 1950, v170, p161.
The New Republic. Dec 26, 1949, 121, p23.
The New York Times. Dec 22, 1949, p29.
The New York Times Magazine. Dec 11, 1949, p62-63.
The New Yorker. Dec 31, 1949, v25, p48.
Newsweek. Nov 28, 1949, v34, p70-72.
Rotarian. Jun 1950, v76, p38.
Selected Film Criticism, 1941-1950. p202-03.
Time. Dec 26, 1949, v54, p52-53.
Variety. Oct 26, 1949, p18.

San Antonio (US; Butler, David; 1945)
Commonweal. Jan 4, 1946, v43, p309.
Film Daily. Nov 26, 1945, p6.
The Films of Errol Flynn. p141-43.
Hollywood Reporter. Nov 23, 1945, p12.
Motion Picture Herald Product Digest. .
The New York Times. Dec 29, 1945, p19.
Newsweek. Jan 7, 1946, v27, p90.
Scholastic. Nov 19, 1945, v47, p25.
Time. Jan 14, 1946, v47, p90+.
Variety. Nov 12, 1945, p10.

San Francisco (US; Van Dyke, W.S.; 1936)
Canadian Magazine. Jul 1936, v86, p31.
Canadian Magazine. Sep 1936, v86, p30.
Esquire. Sep 1936, v6, p98.
Film Daily. Jun 26, 1936, p21.
The Films of Clark Gable. p173-76.
The Films of Jeanette MacDonald and Nelson Eddy. p177-89.
The Films of Spencer Tracy. p129-31.
Hollywood Reporter. Jun 23, 1936, p3.
Hollywood Spectator. Jul 4, 1936, v11, p12.
Judge. Aug 1936, v111, p20.
Literary Digest. Jul 11, 1936, v122, p18.
Magill's Survey of Cinema. Series I. v3, p1487-89.
Motion Picture Herald. Jul 4, 1936, p45.
The New Masses. Jul 14, 1936, v20, p29-30.
The New Statesman and Nation. Aug 1, 1936, v12, p160.
The New York Times. Jun 27, 1936, p21.
The New Yorker. Jul 4, 1936, v12, p45.
Newsweek. Jul 4, 1936, v8, p21.
Rob Wagner's Script. Jun 27, 1936, v15, p9-10.
Selected Film Criticism, 1931-1940. p217-19.
The Tatler. Aug 5, 1936, v141, p236.
Those Fabulous Movie Years: The 30s. p100-01.
Time. Jul 6, 1936, v28, p48-49.
Variety. Jul 1, 1936, p12.
World Film News. Aug 1936, v1, p18.
50 Classic Motion Pictures. p38-43.

San Quentin (US; Bacon, Lloyd; 1937)
The Complete Films of Humphrey Bogart. p46-47.
Film Daily. Aug 6, 1937, p13.
The Gangster Film. p186-87.
Hollywood Reporter. Mar 23, 1937, p3.
Hollywood Spectator. Apr 10, 1937, v12, p15.
Humphrey Bogart: The Man and His Films. p64-66.
Motion Picture Herald. Apr 3, 1937, p40.
The New York Times. Aug 4, 1937, p15.
The New Yorker. Aug 7, 1937, v13, p33.
Rob Wagner's Script. Jul 31, 1937, v17, p12.
Time. Aug 16, 1937, v30, p37.
Variety. Jul 28, 1937, p16.

Sanders of the River (GB; Korda, Zoltan; 1935)
Black Images in American Film, 1896-1954. p129-30.
Cinema Quarterly. Spr 1935, v3, p175-76.
Esquire. Sep 1935, v4, p144.
Film Daily. Jun 26, 1935, p7.
Hollywood Reporter. Apr 3, 1935, p3.
Literary Digest. Jul 6, 1935, v120, p29.
Motion Picture Herald. Apr 20, 1935, p36.
The New Masses. Jul 1935, v16, p29-30.
The New Republic. Jul 10, 1935, v83, p250.
The New Statesman and Nation. Apr 13, 1935, v9, p521.
The New York Times. Jun 27, 1935, p16.
The New York Times. Jan 2, 1936, p21.
The New York Times. Apr 3, 1935, p20.
The New Yorker. Jul 6, 1935, v11, p45.
Rob Wagner's Script. Aug 31, 1935, v14, p12.
Rotha on the Film. p139-40.
Selected Film Criticism, 1931-1940. p156.
The Spectator. Apr 5, 1935, v154, p566.
Time. Jul 8, 1935, v26, p32.
Vanity Fair. Aug 1935, v44, p45.
Variety. Jul 3, 1935, p14.

Sands of Iwo Jima (US; Dwan, Allan; 1949)
Christian Century. Jan 25, 1950, v67, p127.
Commonweal. Jan 27, 1950, v51, p438.
The Complete Films of John Wayne. p174-76.
Film Daily. Dec 14, 1949, p7.
Films in Review. Mar 1950, v1, p34-35.
Guts & Glory. p94-101.
Hollywood Reporter. Dec 14, 1949, p3.
Magill's Survey of Cinema. Series II. v5, p2080-82.
Motion Picture Herald Product Digest. Dec 17, 1949, p121.

The New York Times. Dec 31, 1949, p9.
The New Yorker. Jan 14, 1950, v25, p76.
Newsweek. Jan 16, 1950, v35, p78.
Rotarian. Mar 1950, v76, p37.
Selected Film Criticism, 1941-1950. p203-05.
Time. Jan 16, 1950, v55, p86+.
Variety. Dec 14, 1949, p8.

Sang d'un Poète, Le *See* The Blood of a Poet

Sans Famille (Also titled: No Relations) (FR; Mouizy, Andre; 1935)
Film Daily. Jun 7, 1935, p10.
Graham Greene on Film. p47.
The New Statesman and Nation. Jan 18, 1936, v11, p83.
The New York Times. Jun 4, 1935, p26.
Saturday Review (London). Jan 11, 1936, v161, p64.
The Spectator. Jan 17, 1936, v156, p91.

Santa Fe Trail (US; Curtiz, Michael; 1940)
BFI/Monthly Film Bulletin. Aug 1980, v47, p164.
Christian Century. Mar 19, 1941, v58, p382.
Commonweal. Dec 27, 1940, v33, p257.
Film Daily. Dec 16, 1940, p7.
The Films of Errol Flynn. p97-100.
The Films of Olivia de Havilland. p161-66.
The Films of Ronald Reagan. p109-14.
Hollywood Reporter. Dec 16, 1940, p3.
The New Republic. Jan 6, 1941, v104, p20.
The New York Times. Dec 21, 1940, p21.
Saturday Review. Mar 1, 1941, v23, p9.
Scholastic. Dec 16, 1940, v37, p38.
Time. Dec 23, 1940, v36, p45.
Variety. Dec 18, 1940, p16.

Sarah and Son (US; Arzner, Dorothy; 1930)
Exhibitors Herald-World. Mar 22, 1930, p38.
Film Daily. Mar 16, 1930, p8.
The Film Spectator. Apr 26, 1930, v9, p19-20.
The Films of Fredric March. p53-55.
Judge. Apr 5, 1930, v98, p23, 26.
Life. Apr 11, 1930, v95, p22, 34.
National Board of Review Magazine. Mar 1930, v5, p9.
The New York Times. Mar 13, 1930, p22.
The New Yorker. Mar 22, 1930, v6, p53.
Outlook and Independent. Mar 26, 1930, v154, p513.
Rob Wagner's Script. Apr 26, 1930, v3, p10.
Saturday Review (London). Jun 7, 1930, v149, p723.
Time. Mar 31, 1930, v15, p34.
Variety. Mar 19, 1930, p34.

Saratoga (US; Conway, Jack; 1937)
Esquire. Oct 1937, v8, p121.
Film Daily. Jul 19, 1937, p10.
The Films of Clark Gable. p182-84.
The Films of Jean Harlow. p154.
Graham Greene on Film. p163.
Hollywood Reporter. Jul 14, 1937, p3.
Hollywood Spectator. Jul 31, 1937, v12, p13-14.
Literary Digest. Aug 7, 1937, v124, p31.
Motion Picture Herald. Jul 24, 1937, p46.
The New York Times. Jul 23, 1937, p16.
The New Yorker. Jul 24, 1937, v13, p64.
Rob Wagner's Script. Jul 31, 1937, v17, p12-13.
Time. Aug 2, 1937, v30, p33-34.
Variety. Jul 14, 1937, p20.
World Film News. Sep 1937, v2, p27.

Saratoga Trunk (US; Wood, Sam; 1945)
Commonweal. Oct 26, 1945, v43, p46.
Film Daily. Nov 23, 1945, p6.
The Films of Gary Cooper. p201-03.
The Films of Ingrid Bergman. p110-14.
Hollywood Reporter. Nov 21, 1945, p3.
Ingrid Bergman. p56-61.
The London Times. Jan 24, 1945, p6.

Magill's Survey of Cinema. Series II. v4, p1083-85.
Motion Picture Exhibitor. Nov 18, 1945, v35, n4, sec2, p1838.
Motion Picture Herald Product Digest. Nov 24, 1945, p2725.
The New York Times. Nov 22, 1945, p39.
The New Yorker. Nov 24, 1945, v21, p67.
Newsweek. Dec 3, 1945, v26, p97.
Theatre Arts. Dec 1945, v29, p706-07.
Time. Nov 26, 1945, v46, p98.
Variety. Nov 21, 1945, p10.

Satan Met a Lady (US; Dieterle, William; 1936)
Bette Davis: Her Films and Career. p70-71.
The Detective in Film. p41.
Film Daily. Jul 23, 1936, p7.
Hollywood Reporter. Jul 30, 1936, p3.
Make It Again, Sam. p114-19.
Masters of Menace: Greenstreet and Lorre. p62-63.
The New York Times. Jul 23, 1936, p24.
The New Yorker. Aug 1, 1936, v12, p39.
Variety. Jul 29, 1936, p14.
World Film News. Sep 1936, v1, p24.

Saturday Night (US; DeMille, Cecil B.; 1922)
Film Daily. Jan 29, 1922, p2.
The Films of Cecil B. DeMille. p204-07.
Variety. Jan 27, 1922, p39.

Saturday's Children (US; Sherman, Vincent; 1940)
Commonweal. May 10, 1940, v32, p63.
Film Daily. Apr 17, 1940, p6.
The Films of John Garfield. p75-79.
Hollywood Reporter. Apr 9, 1940, p3.
Motion Picture Herald. Feb 24, 1940, p33.
Motion Picture Herald. Apr 13, 1940, p38.
The New York Times. May 4, 1940, p13.
Scholastic. Apr 22, 1940, v36, p36.
Time. Apr 29, 1940, v35, p84+.
Variety. Apr 10, 1940, p14.

Saturday's Heroes (US; Killy, Edward; 1937)
Film Daily. Oct 18, 1937, p14.
Hollywood Reporter. Sep 11, 1937, p3.
Motion Picture Herald. Sep 18, 1937, p44.
The New York Times. Oct 16, 1937, p22.
Variety. Sep 29, 1937, p14.

Saturday's Millions (US; Sedgwick, Edward; 1933)
Film Daily. Oct 14, 1933, p6.
Hollywood Reporter. Sep 23, 1933, p2.
Motion Picture Herald. Sep 23, 1933, p34-35.
The New York Times. Oct 14, 1933, p18.
Variety. Oct 17, 1933, p19.

Savage Gold (US; Dyott, G.M.; 1933)
Commonweal. Aug 18, 1933, v18, p388.
Film Daily. May 23, 1933, p4.
Motion Picture Herald. Jul 29, 1933, p32.
New Outlook. Sep 1933, v162, p45.
The New York Times. Jul 25, 1933, p17.
Variety. Aug 1, 1933, p14.

Savoy Hotel 217 (GER; Ucicky, Gustav; 1936)
Graham Greene on Film. p107-08.
The New Statesman and Nation. Oct 10, 1936, v12, p510.
Sight and Sound. Aut 1936, v5, p85.
The Spectator. Oct 9, 1936, v157, p582.
World Film News. Nov 1936, v1, p21.

The Saxon Charm (US; Binyon, Claude; 1948)
Commonweal. Oct 15, 1948, v49, p13.
Film Daily. Sep 8, 1948, p7.
The Films of Susan Hayward. p127-28.
Hollywood Reporter. Sep 2, 1948, p3.
Motion Picture Herald Product Digest. Sep 11, 1948, p4310.
The New Republic. Oct 25, 1948, v119, p28.
The New York Times. Sep 30, 1948, p32.
The New Yorker. Oct 9, 1948, v24, p112.

Newsweek. Sep 27, 1948, v32, p88.
Rotarian. Jan 1949, v74, p53.
Time. Oct 18, 1948, v52, p102+.
Variety. Sep 8, 1948, p10.

Say It in French (US; Stone, Andrew L.; 1938)
Film Daily. Nov 25, 1938, p6.
Hollywood Reporter. Nov 17, 1938, p3.
Motion Picture Herald. Nov 26, 1938, p27.
The New York Times. Dec 1, 1938, p29.
Time. Dec 12, 1938, v32, p40.
Variety. Nov 30, 1938, p12.

A Scandal in Paris *See* Thieves Holiday

A Scandal in Paris (US; Wiene, Robert; 1929)
The New York Times. Jun 10, 1929, p23.
Variety. Jun 10, 1929, p23.
Variety. Aug 14, 1929, p31.

Scandal Street (US; Hogan, James; 1938)
Film Daily. Feb 5, 1938, p4.
Hollywood Reporter. Feb 4, 1938, p3.
Motion Picture Herald. Feb 12, 1938, p48.
The New York Times. Feb 5, 1938, p19.
Variety. Feb 9, 1938, p14.

Scaramouche (US; Ingram, Rex; 1923)
Film Daily. Oct 14, 1923, p5.
From Quasimodo to Scarlett O'Hara. p23-25.
The New York Times. Oct 12, 1923, p7.
Photoplay. Dec 1923, v25, p72.
Selected Film Criticism, 1921-1930. p72.
Variety. Sep 20, 1923, p23.
Variety. Oct 4, 1923, p22.

Scarface: Shame of a Nation (Also titled: Scarface: The Shame of the Nation) (US; Hawks, Howard; 1932)
American Film Criticism. p260-62.
BFI/Monthly Film Bulletin. Aug 1980, v47, p164-65.
Cinema, the Magic Vehicle. v1, p207-08.
Classics of the Gangster Film. p21-24.
Crime Movies (Clarens). p83-100.
Dark Cinema. p136.
Dictionary of Films. p327-28.
Film Comment. Jan-Feb 1983, v19, p58-68+.
Film Daily. Apr 17, 1932, p10.
Films and Filming. Jul 1962, v8, p21-22.
The Films of Howard Hawks. p131-39.
The Films of My Life. p70.
From Quasimodo to Scarlett O'Hara. p154-56.
The Gangster Film. p87-93.
Great Film Directors: A Critical Anthology. p439-40, 452-58.
The Great Gangster Pictures. p347-48.
Hollywood Genres. p90-95.
Hollywood Reporter. Mar 3, 1932, p3.
Howard Hawks (Poague). p94-102.
Howard Hawks, Storyteller. p71-104.
Howard Hawks (Wood). p58-68.
The International Dictionary of Films and Filmmakers. v1, p412-14.
Journal of Popular Film. 1984, n1, v18, p30-42.
Judge. Jun 4, 1932, v102, p22.
Literary Digest. Jul 30, 1932, v114, p14.
London Mercury. Oct 1932, v26, p562-63.
Magill's Survey of Cinema. Series I. v3, p1490-92.
Motion Picture Herald. May 28, 1932, p87.
Movie Classic. May 1932, v2, p42-43+.
Movietone News. Apr 1975, n40, p8-11.
National Board of Review Magazine. Mar 1932, v7, p9-13.
The New Statesman and Nation. Jul 2, 1932, v4, p13.
The New York Times. May 20, 1932, p22.
The New Yorker. May 28, 1932, v8, p51-52.
Outlook. Apr 1932, v160, p229.
Paul Muni: His Life and His Films. p105-11.
Photoplay. May 1932, v41, p48.

Rob Wagner's Script. Mar 12, 1932, v7, p10.
Selected Film Criticism, 1931-1940. p220-21.
Talking Pictures. p6-10.
Time. Apr 18, 1932, v19, p17.
Variety. May 24, 1932, p29.
The Velvet Light Trap. Jun 1971, n1, p12-17.
The Village Voice. Oct 15, 1979, v24, p45-57.
World Film News. Apr 1938, v3, p38.

Scarlet Dawn (US; Dieterle, William; 1932)
Film Daily. Nov 5, 1932, p4.
Hollywood Reporter. Oct 11, 1932, p9.
Motion Picture Herald. Nov 12, 1932, p36-37.
The New York Times. Nov 4, 1932, p25.
Rob Wagner's Script. Oct 29, 1932, v8, p8.
Time. Nov 14, 1932, v20, p33.
Variety. Nov 8, 1932, p16.

Scarlet Days (US; Griffith, D.W.; 1919)
D.W. Griffith: An American Life. p409-12.
D.W. Griffith: His Life and Work. p208.
Exhibitor's Trade Review. Nov 22, 1919, p2143.
The Films of D.W. Griffith. p121-25.
Motion Picture Classic. Jan 1920, p56-57.
Motion Picture News. Nov 22, 1919, p3792.
The Moving Picture World. Nov 22, 1919, p453.
The New York Times. Nov 10, 1919, p18.
Selected Film Criticism, 1912-1920. p231.
Variety. Nov 14, 1919, p58.
Wid's Daily. Nov 23, 1919, p3.

The Scarlet Empress (US; Sternberg, Josef von; 1934)
BFI/Monthly Film Bulletin. Jun 1978, v45, p123-24.
The Cinema of Josef von Sternberg. p113-21.
Film Daily. Sep 15, 1934, p4.
The Films of Josef von Sternberg. p37-40.
The Films of Marlene Dietrich. p112-15.
Hollywood Reporter. Apr 17, 1934, p3.
The International Dictionary of Films and Filmmakers. v1, p414-15.
Life. Nov 1934, v101, p42-43.
Literary Digest. Sep 29, 1934, v118, p29.
Magill's Survey of Cinema. Series II. v5, p2106-09.
Motion Picture Herald. Feb 10, 1934, p39.
Motion Picture Herald. Apr 28, 1934, p31-34.
The Nation. Oct 3, 1934, p392.
The New York Times. Sep 15, 1934, p15.
Rob Wagner's Script. Aug 11, 1934, v11, p7-8.
Selected Film Criticism, 1931-1940. p222-23.
Time. Sep 3, 1934, v34, p66.
Variety. Sep 18, 1934, p11.

The Scarlet Letter (US; 1911)
The Moving Picture World. Apr 22, 1911, p881-82.
Selected Film Criticism, 1896-1911. p87-88.

The Scarlet Letter (US; Sjostrom, Victor; 1926)
BFI/Monthly Film Bulletin. Nov 1974, v41, p260-61.
Cinema, the Magic Vehicle. v1, p123.
Classics of the Silent Screen. p78-79.
Film Daily. Aug 15, 1926, p5.
From Quasimodo to Scarlett O'Hara. p62-64.
Magill's Cinema Annual, 1985. p602-06.
The New York Times. Aug 10, 1926, p19.
Photoplay. Oct 1926, v30, p53.
Selected Film Criticism, 1921-1930. p250.
Variety. Aug 11, 1926, p11.

The Scarlet Letter (US; Vignola, Robert G.; 1934)
Film Daily. Sep 18, 1934, p7.
Hollywood Reporter. Jul 6, 1934, p3.
Motion Picture Herald. Jul 14, 1934, p40-42.
Variety. Sep 25, 1934, p14.

The Scarlet Pimpernel (GB; Young, Harold; 1935)
The Age of the Dream Palace. p235-37.
Cinema Quarterly. Aut 1934, v3, p114.
Esquire. Apr 1935, v3, p144.
Fifty Classic British Films. p19-21.
The Film Criticism of Otis Ferguson. p67.
Film Daily. Jan 25, 1935, p6.
Filmfront. Mar 15, 1935, v1, p5.
The Great Adventure Films. p23-33.
The Great Spy Films. p404-05.
Hollywood Reporter. Jan 9, 1935, p3.
Hollywood Reporter. Feb 15, 1935, p2.
Hollywood Reporter. Jan 4, 1934, p3.
Judge. Apr 1935, v108, p17.
Life. Apr 1935, v102, p34.
Literary Digest. Feb 23, 1935, v119, p33.
Magill's Survey of Cinema. Series I. v4, p1493-96.
Motion Picture Herald. Jan 26, 1935, p47.
The Nation. Feb 20, 1935, v140, p232.
The New Masses. Feb 26, 1935, v14, p29-30.
The New York Times. Feb 8, 1935, p27.
The New Yorker. Feb 9, 1935, v10, p58-59.
Newsweek. Feb 16, 1935, v5, p38.
Rob Wagner's Script. Apr 6, 1935, v13, p8.
Saturday Review (London). Jan 5, 1935, v159, p22.
Selected Film Criticism: Foreign Films, 1930-1950. p156-60.
The Spectator. Dec 28, 1934, v153, p992.
Time. Feb 18, 1935, v25, p70-71.
Vanity Fair. Mar 1935, v44, p53.
Variety. Feb 12, 1935, p19.

Scarlet Street (US; Lang, Fritz; 1945)
The Cinema of Edward G. Robinson. p157-62.
Commonweal. Feb 22, 1946, v43, p481.
Film Daily. Dec 28, 1945, p17.
Film Noir. p247-48.
The Films of Fritz Lang. p213-17.
Fritz Lang: A Guide to References and Resources. p92-95.
Fritz Lang (Armour). p152-55+.
Fritz Lang (Eisner).
Hollywood Reporter. Dec 21, 1945, p3.
Life. Jan 21, 1946, v20, p72-74.
The London Times. Feb 25, 1946, p8.
Magill's Survey of Cinema. Series II. v5, p2110-12.
Motion Picture Exhibitor. Jan 9, 1946, v35, n10, sec2, p1860.
Motion Picture Herald Product Digest. Dec 29, 1945, p2777.
The New York Times. Feb 15, 1946, p29.
The New Yorker. Feb 23, 1946, v22, p76.
Newsweek. Feb 25, 1946, v27, p90.
Running Away from Myself. p116-19.
Sight and Sound. Spr 1955, v24, p198.
Sight and Sound. Sum 1955, v25, p15-21.
Sight and Sound. Aut 1955, v25, p92-97.
Time. Jan 21, 1946, v47, p97.
Variety. Jan 2, 1946, p8.

Scenes and Incidents, Russo-Japanese Peace Conference (US; 1905)
The George Kleine Collection Catalog. p115-16.

Schatten eine Nachtliche Halluzination *See* Warning Shadows

Scherben *See* Shattered

Schicksal Einer Menschheit Im Jahre 2000, Das *See* Metropolis

School for Husbands (GB; Marton, Andrew; 1939)
Commonweal. Feb 10, 1939, v29, p441.
Film Daily. Jan 23, 1939, p10.
Hollywood Reporter. Dec 19, 1939, p3.
Motion Picture Herald. Feb 18, 1939, p50.
The New York Times. Feb 7, 1939, p16.
Variety. Feb 1, 1939, p13.

Scipio Africanus (Also titled: Scipione L'Africano; Scipio the African) (IT; Gallone, Carmine; 1939)
Film Daily. Sep 29, 1939, p9.
The New York Times. Sep 23, 1939, p22.
Time. Nov 27, 1939, v34, p83.
Variety. Sep 8, 1937, p19.

Sciuscia, La *See* Shoe Shine

Scotland Yard Commands (US; Flood, James; 1937)
Film Daily. Feb 16, 1937, p7.
Hollywood Reporter. Feb 9, 1937, p3.
Motion Picture Herald. Feb 20, 1937, p46.
Variety. Mar 31, 1937, p19.

The Scoundrel (US; Hecht, Ben; MacArthur, Charles; 1935)
Ben Hecht: Hollywood Screenwriter. p109-40.
Catholic World. Aug 1935, v141, p605-06.
Cinema Quarterly. Sum 1935, v3, p233-34.
Commonweal. May 17, 1935, v22, p77.
Esquire. Jul 1935, v3, p164.
The Film Criticism of Otis Ferguson. p78.
Film Daily. Apr 30, 1935, p8.
The Five Lives of Ben Hecht. p151-55.
Garbo and the Night Watchman. p60, 80-81.
Hollywood Reporter. Apr 12, 1935, p3.
Hollywood Reporter. May 9, 1935, p6.
Judge. Jun 1935, v108, p14, 23.
Life. Jul 1935, v102, p23.
Literary Digest. May 18, 1935, v119, p30.
Magill's Survey of Cinema. Series II. v5, p2113-15.
Motion Picture Herald. May 4, 1935, p35.
The Nation. May 22, 1935, v140, p612.
National Board of Review Magazine. Jun 1935, v10, p10.
The New Masses. May 14, 1935, v15, p28.
The New Republic. May 15, 1935, v83, p19.
The New York Times. May 3, 1935, p23.
The New Yorker. May 11, 1935, v11, p66-67.
Newsweek. May 11, 1935, v5, p28.
Rob Wagner's Script. Jul 27, 1935, v13, p8.
Saturday Review (London). Jun 1, 1935, v159, p703.
Selected Film Criticism, 1931-1940. p223-24.
The Spectator. May 31, 1935, v154, p918.
Stage. Jun 1935, v12, p60.
The Tatler. Jun 3, 1936, v140, p432.
Time. May 13, 1935, v25, p36.
Vanity Fair. Jun 1935, v44, p48.
Variety. May 8, 1935, p16.

The Sea Beast (US; Webb, Millard; 1926)
Film Daily. Jan 24, 1926, p6.
From Quasimodo to Scarlett O'Hara. p56-59.
The New York Times. Jan 16, 1926, p8.
Photoplay. Mar 1926, v24, p55.
Selected Film Criticism, 1921-1930. p251.
Variety. Jan 6, 1926, p39.
Variety. Jan 20, 1926, p37.

Sea Devils (US; Stoloff, Benjamin; 1937)
Film Daily. Feb 11, 1937, p11.
Hollywood Reporter. Feb 8, 1937, p3.
Motion Picture Herald. Feb 20, 1937, p42.
The New York Times. Mar 16, 1937, p26.
Rob Wagner's Script. Feb 13, 1937, v17, p10.
Scholastic. Mar 13, 1937, v30, p20.
Variety. Mar 17, 1937, p14.

The Sea God (US; Abbott, George; 1930)
Exhibitors Herald-World. Aug 23, 1930, p38.
Film Daily. Sep 7, 1930, p10.
The Films of the Thirties. p39-40.
The New York Times. Sep 6, 1930, p9.
The New Yorker. Sep 13, 1930, v6, p78.
Time. Sep 22, 1930, v16, p30.
Variety. Sep 10, 1930, p29.

The Sea Hawk (US; Curtiz, Michael; 1940)
Casablanca and Other Major Films of Michael Curtiz. p43-59.
Film Daily. Jul 23, 1940, p6.
Films and Filming. May 1977, v23, p10-16.
The Films of Errol Flynn. p91-96.
The Great Adventure Films. p106-11.
The London Times. Aug 5, 1940, p8.
Magill's Survey of Cinema. Series I. v4, p1497-98.
Make It Again, Sam. p173-75.
Moviemaker. May 1973, n7, p328.
The New York Times. Aug 10, 1940, p16.
Newsweek. Aug 19, 1940, v16, p46.
The Sea Hawk. p11-43.
Swordsmen of the Screen. p237-40.
Time. Aug 19, 1940, v36, p78.
Variety. Jul 24, 1940, p14.

The Sea of Grass (US; Kazan, Elia; 1947)
Commonweal. Mar 14, 1947, v45, p540.
Film Daily. Feb 13, 1947, p6.
The Films of Katharine Hepburn. p130-33.
The Films of Spencer Tracy. p191-92.
Hollywood Reporter. Feb 12, 1947, p3.
Motion Picture Herald Product Digest. Feb 15, 1947, p3473.
New Republic. Mar 17, 1947, v116, p42.
The New York Times. Feb 28, 1947, p27.
The New Yorker. Mar 1, 1947, v23, p56+.
Newsweek. Mar 10, 1947, v29, p94-95.
Time. Mar 17, 1947, v49, p100+.
Variety. Feb 12, 1947, p14.

The Sea Wolf (US; Bosworth, Hobart; 1913)
Motion Picture News. Nov 8, 1913, p17, 48.
Motography. Nov 15, 1913, p359-60.
The Moving Picture World. Nov 1, 1913, p480.
The Moving Picture World. Dec 6, 1913, p1214, 1216.
The New York Dramatic Mirror. Oct 29, 1913, p32.
Selected Film Criticism, 1912-1920. p231-33.
Variety. May 8, 1914, p20.

The Sea Wolf (US; Melford, George; 1920)
The Moving Picture World. May 29, 1920, p1229, 1236.
Variety. May 14, 1920, p36.
Wid's Daily. May 23, 1920, p6.

The Sea Wolf (US; Curtiz, Michael; 1941)
The Cinema of Edward G. Robinson. p131-34.
The Classic American Novel and the Movies. p192-205.
Commonweal. Apr 4, 1941, v33, p602.
The Film Criticism of Otis Ferguson. p353-54.
Film Daily. Mar 24, 1941, p6.
The Films of John Garfield. p93-95.
The Films of the Forties. p31-33.
The London Times. Jan 26, 1942, p8.
Magill's Survey of Cinema. Series II. v5, p2116-19.
Make It Again, Sam. p176-84.
Motion Picture Exhibitor. Apr 2, 1941, p721.
Motion Picture Herald Product Digest. Mar 8, 1941, p74.
The New Republic. Apr 28, 1941, v104, p601.
The New York Times. Mar 22, 1941, p20.
The New York Times. Mar 30, 1941, sec9, p5.
The New Yorker. Mar 29, 1941, v17, p66.
Newsweek. Mar 31, 1941, v17, p66.
Scribner's Commentator. Jun 1941, v10, p106-07.
Time. Apr 14, 1941, v37, p93.
Variety. Mar 26, 1941, p16.

The Search (US; Zinnemann, Fred; 1948)
Agee on Film. v1, p302.
Commonweal. Apr 23, 1948, v48, p654.
Film Daily. Mar 22, 1948, p6.
The Films of Montgomery Clift. p99-104.
Fortnight. Jul 16, 1948, v5, p29-30.
Hollywood Reporter. Mar 22, 1948, p3.
Life. Apr 5, 1948, v24, p75-78.
Magill's Survey of Cinema. Series I. v4, p1499-1501.

Motion Picture Herald Product Digest. Apr 3, 1948, p4111.
The New Republic. Apr 12, 1948, v118, p21.
The New York Times. Mar 24, 1948, p30.
The New York Times Magazine. Mar 14, 1948, p22-23.
The New Yorker. Apr 3, 1948, v24, p58.
Newsweek. Apr 5, 1948, v31, p88.
Saturday Review. Apr 10, 1948, v31, p24-26.
Sequence. New Year 1950, n10, p152.
Sight and Sound. Dec 1949, v18, p21.
Time. Mar 29, 1948, v51, p98+.
Variety. Mar 24, 1948, p8.
Vintage Films. p101-04.

Seas Beneath (US; Ford, John; 1931)
Film Daily. Feb 1, 1931, p10.
John Ford (Bogdanovich). p53-54.
Motion Picture Herald. Feb 7, 1931, p52.
The New York Times. Jan 31, 1931, p15.
Time. Feb 9, 1931, v17, p28.
Variety. Feb 4, 1931, p16.

Second Bureau (French title: Deuxieme Bureau) (FR; Billon, Pierre; 1935)
Canadian Forum. Jan 1936, v15, p15.
Graham Greene on Film. p46-47.
The New Statesman and Nation. Jan 18, 1936, v11, p83.
The New Statesman and Nation. Mar 20, 1937, v13, p480.
The New York Times. Feb 17, 1936, p21.
Saturday Review (London). Jun 1, 1935, v159, p703.
The Spectator. Jan 17, 1936, v156, p91.
The Spectator. May 31, 1935, v154, p918.
Variety. Feb 19, 1936, p12.
Variety. Dec 23, 1936, p18.

Second Fiddle (US; Lanfield, Sidney; 1939)
Commonweal. Jul 14, 1939, v30, p300.
Film Daily. Jul 3, 1939, p8.
The Films of Tyrone Power. p92-94.
Hollywood Reporter. Jun 29, 1939, p3.
Hollywood Spectator. Jul 8, 1939, v14, p8-9.
Motion Picture Herald. Jul 8, 1939, p35.
The New York Times. Jul 1, 1939, p11.
Photoplay. Sep 1939, v53, p62.
Rob Wagner's Script. Jul 4, 1939, v21, p17-18.
The Tatler. Feb 14, 1940, v155, p202.
Time. Jul 17, 1939, v33, p42.
Variety. Jul 5, 1939, p14.

Second Honeymoon (US; Lang, Walter; 1937)
Film Daily. Nov 11, 1937, p12.
The Films of Tyrone Power. p66-68.
Hollywood Reporter. Nov 8, 1937, p3.
Motion Picture Herald. Nov 13, 1937, p39, 42.
The New Statesman and Nation. Feb 12, 1938, v15, p248.
The New York Times. Nov 13, 1937, p11.
Rob Wagner's Script. Dec 18, 1937, v18, p10.
Variety. Nov 10, 1937, p19.
World Film News. Apr 1938, v3, p39.

The Secret Agent (GB; Hitchcock, Alfred; 1936)
American Film Criticism. p341-43.
The Art of Alfred Hitchcock. p45-54.
Canadian Magazine. Sep 1936, v86, p30.
Cinema, the Magic Vehicle. v1, p260-61.
The English Novel and the Movies. p218-27.
The Film Criticism of Otis Ferguson. p138-40.
Film Daily. Jun 13, 1936, p4.
The Films of Peter Lorre. p94-95.
Garbo and the Night Watchman. p209-12.
Graham Greene on Film. p74-75.
The Great Spy Pictures. p412.
Hitchcock: The First Forty-Four Films. p44-46.
Hitchcock's British Films. p193-205.
Hollywood Reporter. May 18, 1936, p6.
Life. Aug 1936, v103, p26-27.
Masters of Menace: Greenstreet and Lorre. p32-36.

Motion Picture Herald. May 23, 1936, p44-45.
The New Masses. Jun 30, 1936, v20, p30.
The New Republic. Jun 24, 1936, v87, p205.
The New Statesman and Nation. May 16, 1936, v11, p764.
The New York Times. Jun 13, 1936, p13.
The New Yorker. Jun 13, 1936, v12, p67.
Newsweek. Jun 13, 1936, v7, p40-41.
Rob Wagner's Script. Jul 25, 1936, v15, p11-12.
Selected Film Criticism: Foreign Films, 1930-1950. p163-64.
The Spectator. May 15, 1936, v156, p879.
Stage. Feb 1936, v13, p8.
The Tatler. May 20, 1936, v140, p332.
Time. Jun 15, 1936, v27, p56.
Variety. Jun 17, 1936, p23.

The Secret Life of Walter Mitty (US; McLeod, Norman Z.; 1947)
Canadian Forum. Oct 1947, v27, p160-61.
Canadian Forum. Feb 1948, v27, p255.
Collier's. Jul 5, 1947, v120, p14-15.
Commonweal. Aug 29, 1947, v46, p476.
Cue. Aug 9, 1947, p9.
Film Daily. Jul 15, 1947, p8.
The Films of Boris Karloff. p198-99.
The Films of the Forties. p207-09.
Fortnight. Sep 26, 1947, v3, p30.
Harpers. Oct 1947, v195, p384.
Life. Aug 4, 1947, v23, p89.
Life. Aug 18, 1947, v23, p18-19+.
Motion Picture Herald Product Digest. Jul 19, 1947, p3733.
The Nation. Aug 30, 1947, v165, p209.
New Republic. Sep 15, 1947, v117, p36.
The New York Times. Aug 15, 1947, p12.
The New York Times Magazine. Jun 29, 1947, p20-21.
The New Yorker. Aug 16, 1947, v23, p58.
Newsweek. Aug 18, 1947, v30, p76.
Samuel Goldwyn (Epstein). p122-26.
Samuel Goldwyn Presents. p251-54.
Scholastic. Oct 6, 1947, v51, p33.
Selected Film Criticism, 1941-1950. p205-07.
Theatre Arts. Oct 1947, v31, p50.
Time. Aug 18, 1947, v50, p95.
Variety. Jul 16, 1947, p14.

The Secret of Dr. Kildare (US; Bucquet, Harold S.; 1939)
Commonweal. Dec 15, 1939, v30, p187.
Film Daily. Nov 28, 1939, p10.
Hollywood Reporter. Nov 18, 1939, p3.
Hollywood Spectator. Nov 25, 1939, v14, p7.
Motion Picture Herald. Nov 25, 1939, p43.
The New York Times. Dec 8, 1939, p33.
The New Yorker. Dec 16, 1939, v15, p58.
Rob Wagner's Script. Jan 13, 1939, v21, p17.
Variety. Nov 22, 1939, p14.

Secret Service of the Air (US; Smith, Noel; 1939)
Film Daily. Mar 6, 1939, p14.
The Films of Ronald Reagan. p67-72.
Hollywood Reporter. Feb 3, 1939, p3.
Hollywood Spectator. Feb 18, 1939, v13, p12-13.
Motion Picture Herald. Mar 11, 1939, p42.
The New York Times. Mar 2, 1939, p19.
Variety. Mar 8, 1939, p18.

The Secret Six (US; Hill, George; 1931)
Film Daily. May 3, 1931, p30.
The Films of Clark Gable. p116.
The Great Gangster Pictures. p348-50.
Life. May 29, 1931, v97, p20.
Motion Picture Herald. Apr 25, 1931, p40.
The New York Times. May 2, 1931, p23.
Outlook and Independent. Apr 29, 1931, v157, p603.
The Spectator. Sep 5, 1931, v147, p292.
Variety. May 6, 1931, p22.

Secrets (US; Borzage, Frank; 1924)
Film Daily. Mar 30, 1924, p6.
The New York Times. Mar 16, 1933, p21.
Photoplay. Apr 1924, v25, p60.
Selected Film Criticism, 1921-1930. p251-52.
Variety. Mar 26, 1924, p26.

Secrets (US; Borzage, Frank; 1933)
Film Daily. Mar 16, 1933, p4.
Hollywood Reporter. Feb 11, 1933, p3.
Motion Picture Herald. Feb 18, 1933, p27, 30.
The New York Times. Mar 16, 1933, p21.
The New Yorker. Mar 25, 1933, v9, p49.
Rob Wagner's Script. Apr 8, 1933, v9, p10-11.
Time. Mar 27, 1933, v21, p22.
Variety. Mar 21, 1933, p16.

Secrets of a Soul (German title: Geheimnisse Einer Seele)
(GER; Pabst, G.W.; 1926)
BFI/Monthly Film Bulletin. Jun 1979, v46, p134.
From Caligari to Hitler. p170-72.
G.W. Pabst (Atwell). p37-42.
The Haunted Screen. p350.
Magill's Survey of Cinema. Silent Films. v3, p947-49.
National Board of Review Magazine. Sep-Oct 1926, v1, p7-8.
The New York Times. Apr 25, 1927, p20.
Spellbound in Darkness. p383-86.
Variety. Jan 18, 1928, p23.

Secrets of an Actress (US; Keighley, William; 1938)
Film Daily. Oct 11, 1938, p6.
Hollywood Reporter. Oct 7, 1938, p3.
Motion Picture Herald. Oct 15, 1938, p37, 40.
The New York Times. Oct 8, 1938, p10.
Variety. Oct 12, 1938, p15.

See Here, Private Hargrove (US; Ruggles, Wesley; 1944)
Commonweal. Mar 17, 1944, v34, p544.
Film Daily. Feb 18, 1944, p6.
The Films of World War II. p180-81.
Hollywood Reporter. Feb 14, 1944, p3.
The New York Times. Mar 22, 1944, p17.
Newsweek. Mar 6, 1944, v 23, p80.
Photoplay. Mar 1944, v24, p48.
Time. Mar 20, 1944, v43, p94.
Variety. Feb 23, 1944, p10.

Seed (US; Stahl, John M.; 1931)
Bette Davis: Her Films and Career. p16.
Film Daily. May 17, 1931, p10.
Hollywood Reporter. Apr 2, 1931, p3.
Life. Jun 5, 1931, v97, p20.
Motion Picture Herald. Apr 25, 1931, p36.
The New York Times. May 15, 1931, p20.
The New Yorker. May 23, 1931, v7, p70.
Outlook and Independent. May 13, 1931, v158, p59.
Time. May 25, 1931, v17, p58.
Variety. May 20, 1931, p16.

The Senator Was Indiscreet (US; Kaufmann, George S.;
     1947)
Commonweal. Jan 30, 1948, v47, p399.
Film Daily. Dec 11, 1947, p10.
The Films of Myrna Loy. p234.
Hollywood Reporter. Dec 10, 1947, p3.
Life. Jan 5, 1948, v24, p53-55.
Motion Picture Herald Product Digest. Dec 13, 1947, p3973.
New Republic. Jan 5, 1948, v118, p32.
The New York Times. Dec 27, 1947, p9.
The New Yorker. Jan 10, 1948, v23, p78.
Newsweek. Jan 5, 1948, v31, p68-69.
Scholastic. Jan 19, 1948, v51, p31.
Time. Jan 5, 1948, v51, p71.
Variety. Dec 10, 1947, p12.

Sentimental Journey (US; Lang, Walter; 1946)
Commonweal. Mar 29, 1946, v43, p599.
Film Daily. Feb 13, 1946, p7.
Hollywood Reporter. Feb 6, 1946, p3.
Motion Picture Herald Product Digest. Feb 9, 1946, p2837.
The New York Times. Mar 7, 1946, p33.
The New Yorker. Mar 9, 1946, v22, p89.
Newsweek. Mar 18, 1946, v27, p98.
Time. Mar 11, 1946, v47, p97.
Variety. Feb 6, 1946, p12.

Sentimental Tommy (US; Robertson, John S.; 1921)
Film Daily. Apr 3, 1921, p4.
Magill's Survey of Cinema. Silent Films. v3, p950-52.
Motion Picture Classic. Jun 1921, v12, p54-55.
The New York Times. May 9, 1921, p16.
Photoplay. Jul 1921, v20, p58.
Selected Film Criticism, 1921-1930. p252.

Sept Perles de la Couronne *See* Pearls of the Crown

Sequoia (US; Franklin, Chester M.; 1935)
Film Daily. Dec 22, 1934, p3.
Hollywood Reporter. Feb 28, 1935, p2.
Hollywood Reporter. Nov 8, 1935, p2.
Literary Digest. Mar 9, 1935, v119, p34.
The Nation. Mar 6, 1935, v140, p288.
National Board of Review Magazine. Feb 1935, v10, p10.
The New York Times. Feb 23, 1935, p14.
Newsweek. Feb 2, 1935, v5, p32.
Rob Wagner's Script. Mar 2, 1935, v13, p11.
Scholastic. Dec 15, 1935, v25, p29.
Time. Feb 4, 1935, v25, p38.
Vanity Fair. Feb 1935, v43, p42-43.
Variety. Feb 27, 1935, p12.

Sergeant Madden (US; Sternberg, Josef von; 1939)
Commonweal. Apr 7, 1939, v29, p665.
Film Daily. Mar 22, 1939, p10.
The Films of Josef von Sternberg. p46-47.
Hollywood Reporter. Mar 15, 1939, p3.
Hollywood Spectator. Apr 1, 1939, v13, p9.
Motion Picture Herald. Mar 18, 1939, p52.
The New York Times. Mar 24, 1939, p27.
Photoplay. May 1939, v53, p63.
Rob Wagner's Script. Apr 29, 1939, v21, p18.
Time. Apr 3, 1939, v33, p41.
Variety. Mar 22, 1939, p20.

Sergeant York (US; Hawks, Howard; 1941)
Catholic World. Oct 1941, v154, p86.
Commonweal. Jul 1941, 34, p306.
The Film Criticism of Otis Ferguson. p385-86.
Film Daily. Jul 3, 1941, p4.
The Films of Gary Cooper. p181-83.
The Films of Howard Hawks (Willis). p168-71.
The Films of World War II. p51-52.
Hawks on Hawks. p93-94, 169-70.
Hollywood Reporter. Jul 2, 1941, p3.
Life. Jul 14, 1941, v11, p63-65.
The London Times. Dec 1, 1941, p8.
Lorentz on Film. p214-15.
Magill's Survey of Cinema. Series I. v4, p1509-11.
Motion Picture Exhibitor. Jul 9, 1941, p786.
Motion Picture Exhibitor. Sep 3, 1941, v26, n17, sec2, p839.
Motion Picture Herald Product Digest. Apr 19, 1941, p111.
The New Republic. Sep 29, 1941, v105, p404-05.
The New York Times. Jul 3, 1941, p15.
The New York Times. Jul 6, 1941, sec9, p3.
The New Yorker. Jul 5, 1941, v17, p47.
Newsweek. Jul 14, 1941, v18, p61-62.
Rob Wagner's Script. Aug 30, 1941, v27, p14.
Scholastic. Sep 15, 1941, v39, p28.
Selected Film Criticism, 1941-1950. p207-08.
Time. Aug 4, 1941, v38, p70.
Variety. Jul 2, 1941, p12.

Service DeLuxe (US; Lee, Rowland V.; 1938)
Commonweal. Nov 4, 1938, v29, p49.
Film Daily. Oct 18, 1938, p9.
Hollywood Reporter. Oct 13, 1938, p3.
Hollywood Spectator. Oct 29, 1938, v13, p11-12.
Motion Picture Herald. Oct 29, 1938, p44.
The New York Times. Oct 24, 1938, p13.
Rob Wagner's Script. Nov 19, 1938, v20, p14.
The Spectator. Feb 10, 1939, v162, p216.
Time. Oct 31, 1938, v32, p28.
Variety. Oct 19, 1938, p12.

Service for Ladies *See* Reserved for Ladies

Service for Ladies (US; D'Arrast, Harry D'Abbadie; 1927)
Film Daily. Aug 21, 1927, p6.
The New York Times. Aug 15, 1927, p22.
Variety. Aug 17, 1927, p24.

The Set-Up (US; Wise, Robert; 1949)
Cinema, the Magic Vehicle. v1, p509-10.
Film Daily. Mar 22, 1949, p6.
Hollywood Reporter. Mar 21, 1949, p3.
Magill's Survey of Cinema. Series II. v5, p2142-43.
Motion Picture Herald Product Digest. Mar 26, 1949, p4550.
The Nation. May 7, 1949, v168, p538-39.
The New Republic. Apr 25, 1949, v120, p29.
The New York Times. Mar 30, 1949, p31.
Newsweek. Apr 11, 1949, v33, p89.
Rotarian. Jun 1949, v74, p34+.
Sequence. Aut 1949, n9, p132-34.
Time. Apr 18, 1949, v53, p102.
Variety. Mar 23, 1949, p8.

The Seven Ages (US; 1905)
The First Twenty Years. p87.

Seven Chances (US; Keaton, Buster; 1925)
American Silent Film. p272-73.
Buster Keaton (Robinson). p119-27.
Cinema, the Magic Vehicle. v1, p115-16.
The Comic Mind. p134-35.
The Film Career of Buster Keaton. p58-60.
Film Daily. Mar 22, 1925, p8.
A History of Narrative Film. p206.
Magill's Survey of Cinema. Silent Films. v3, p953-56.
The Moving Picture World. Mar 28, 1925, p353.
The Silent Clowns. p225, 234.
The Silent Clowns. p234, 236.
Variety. Mar 18, 1925, p40.

Seven Days Leave (US; Wallace, Richard; 1930)
Exhibitors Herald-World. Feb 1, 1930, p32.
Film Daily. Jan 26, 1930, p9.
The Film Spectator. Feb 15, 1930, v9, p17-18.
The Films of Gary Cooper. p78-79.
Judge. Feb 15, 1930, v98, p25.
The New York Times. Jan 25, 1930, p13.
The New Yorker. Feb 1, 1930, v5, p58, 60.
Outlook and Independent. Feb 5, 1930, v154, p230.
Rob Wagner's Script. Mar 1, 1930, v3, p12-13.
Time. Feb 10, 1930, v15, p30.
Variety. Jan 29, 1930, p21.

Seven Keys to Baldpate (US; Ford, Hugh; 1917)
Motion Picture News. Sep 15, 1917, p1856.
Selected Film Criticism, 1912-1920. p233-34.
Variety. Aug 3, 1917, p29.
Wid's Daily. Sep 13, 1917, p592.

Seven Keys to Baldpate (US; Hamilton, William; Killy, Edward; 1935)
Film Daily. Nov 30, 1935, p4.
Hollywood Reporter. Nov 26, 1935, p3.
Hollywood Spectator. Dec 7, 1935, v10, p12.
Motion Picture Herald. Dec 7, 1935, p68, 70.

The New York Times. Dec 14, 1935, p11.
Rob Wagner's Script. Jan 18, 1936, v14, p8-9.
Scholastic. Jan 25, 1936, v27, p28.
Time. Dec 16, 1935, v26, p44.
Variety. Dec 18, 1935, p12.

Seven Sinners (GB; Courville, Albert de; 1936)
Film Daily. Jul 31, 1936, p5.
Hollywood Reporter. Jul 11, 1936, p6.
The New Statesman and Nation. Aug 8, 1936, v12, p192.
The New York Times. Aug 22, 1936, p6.
Rob Wagner's Script. Sep 12, 1936, v16, p10.
Time. Aug 31, 1936, v28, p23.
Variety. Aug 26, 1936, p20.

Seven Years Bad Luck (US; Linder, Max; 1921)
Cinema, the Magic Vehicle. v1, p73-74.
Film Daily. May 1, 1921, p14.

1776 (US; Griffith, D.W.; 1910)
The Moving Picture World. Sep 18, 1909, p379.
Selected Film Criticism, 1896-1911. p88-89.

Seventh Heaven (US; Borzage, Frank; 1927)
BFI/Monthly Film Bulletin. Jul 1980, v47, p142.
Cinema, the Magic Vehicle. v1, p140-41.
Film Daily. May 29, 1927, p6.
The Film Spectator. May 28, 1927, v3, p5-7.
From Quasimodo to Scarlett O'Hara. p88-91.
Magill's Survey of Cinema. Silent Films. v3, p957-60.
The Moving Picture World. May 28, 1927, p288.
The New York Times. May 26, 1927, p22.
Photoplay. Jul 1927, v32, p54.
Selected Film Criticism, 1921-1930. p253-58.
Variety. May 11, 1927, p14.

Seventh Heaven (US; King, Henry; 1937)
Canadian Magazine. Mar 1937, v87, p25.
Commonweal. Apr 16, 1937, v25, p698.
Esquire. Jun 1937, v7, p121.
Film Daily. Mar 18, 1937, p12.
Hollywood Reporter. Mar 16, 1937, p2.
Hollywood Spectator. Mar 27, 1937, v11, p7.
Literary Digest. Apr 3, 1937, v123, p20.
Motion Picture Herald. Mar 27, 1937, p42.
The New York Times. Mar 26, 1937, p25.
The New Yorker. Mar 27, 1937, v13, p55.
Newsweek. Apr 3, 1937, v9, p27.
Rob Wagner's Script. Mar 27, 1937, v17, p9.
The Tatler. Jun 2, 1937, v144, p422.
Time. Apr 5, 1937, v29, p53.
Variety. Mar 31, 1937, p17.
World Film News. Jul 1937, v2, p24.

The Seventh Veil (GB; Bennett, Compton; 1945)
Around Cinemas, Second Series. p267-69.
Commonweal. Dec 21, 1945, v43, p265.
Cue. Jan 5, 1946, p11.
Film Daily. Jan 16, 1946, p10.
The Films of James Mason. p78-79.
The Great British Films. p88-90.
Hollywood Reporter. Dec 31, 1945, p3.
Life. Jan 28, 1946, v20, p65-66+.
Magill's Survey of Cinema. Series I. v4, p1523-25.
Motion Picture Herald Product Digest. Nov 10, 1945, p2786.
The New York Times. Dec 26, 1945, p15.
The New Yorker. Jan 5, 1946, v21, p61.
Newsweek. Dec 24, 1945, v26, p90.
Selected Film Criticism: Foreign Films, 1930-1950. p165-66.
Time. Dec 31, 1945, v46, p90.
Variety. Oct 31, 1945, p17.

Sex (US; Niblo, Fred; 1920)
Magill's Survey of Cinema. Silent Films. v3, p957-60.
The Moving Picture World. Mar 13, 1920, p1825.
The Moving Picture World. Mar 20, 1920, p2011.

Variety. Apr 2, 1920, p94.
Wid's Daily. Mar 21, 1920, p3.

Shadow of a Doubt (US; Hitchcock, Alfred; 1943)
Agee on Film. v1, p66-67+.
The Art of Alfred Hitchcock. p133-44.
Cinema, the Magic Vehicle. v1, p372-73.
Commonweal. Jan 29, 1943, v36, p373.
Film Daily. Jan 8, 1943, p5.
The Films of Alfred Hitchcock. p114-17.
The Films of the Forties. p80-81.
The Great Horror Movies. p91-92.
Hitchcock: The First Forty-four Films. p70-78.
Hitchcock (Truffaut). p151-58+.
Hollywood Reporter. Jan 8, 1943, p5.
Life. Jan 25, 1943, v14, p70-73.
Magill's Survey of Cinema. Series I. v4, p1526-28.
The New Republic. Feb 8, 1943, v108, p182.
The New York Times. Jan 13, 1943, p18.
The New Yorker. Jan 16, 1943, v18, p44.
Newsweek. Jan 25, 1943, v21, p77-78.
Rob Wagner's Script. Mar 20, 1943, v29, p14-15.
Selected Film Criticism, 1941-1950. p209.
Time. Jan 18, 1943, v41, p98.
Variety. Jan 13, 1943, p8.

Shadows (US; Forman, Tom; 1922)
The Best Moving Pictures of 1922-1923. p27-30.
Film Daily. Nov 5, 1922, p5-6,.
Selected Film Criticism, 1921-1930. p258-261.
Variety. Nov 3, 1922, p42.

Shadows of the Orient (US; Lynwood, Burt; 1936)
Film Daily. Oct 13, 1937, p8.
Motion Picture Herald. Feb 15, 1936, p44, 48.
The New York Times. Oct 11, 1937, p26.
Variety. Oct 13, 1937, p16.

Shall We Dance (US; Sandrich, Mark; 1937)
Canadian Magazine. Jun 1937, v87, p52.
Commonweal. May 21, 1937, v26, p104.
Film Daily. Apr 20, 1937, p9.
Film Notes. p101-02.
The Films of Ginger Rogers. p132-34.
The Fred Astaire & Ginger Rogers Book. p116-28.
The Hollywood Musical. p133, 138.
Hollywood Musicals. p101-03.
Hollywood Reporter. Apr 27, 1937, p3.
Hollywood Spectator. May 8, 1937, v12, p8-9.
Journal of Popular Film and Television. Fall 1980, v8, p15-24.
Literary Digest. May 15, 1937, v123, p20.
Magill's Survey of Cinema. Series I. v4, p1529-33.
Motion Picture Herald. May 8, 1937, p42.
The New York Times. May 14, 1937, p21.
The New Yorker. May 15, 1937, v13, p86-87.
Newsweek. May 15, 1937, v9, p26.
Rob Wagner's Script. May 8, 1937, v17, p8.
Scholastic. May 15, 1937, v30, p26.
The Spectator. Jun 4, 1937, v158, p1051.
Starring Fred Astaire. p151-61.
The Tatler. May 26, 1937, v144, p372.
Time. May 10, 1937, v29, p67.
Variety. May 12, 1937, p12.
World Film News. Jul 1937, v2, p23.

Shame of a Nation *See* Westfront 1918

Shanghai (US; Flood, James; 1935)
Esquire. Sep 1935, v4, p144.
Film Daily. Jul 20, 1935, p7.
Hollywood Reporter. Jul 12, 1935, p3.
Hollywood Reporter. Jul 27, 1935, p5.
Literary Digest. Aug 3, 1935, v120, p25.
Motion Picture Herald. Jul 20, 1935, p88.
The New Masses. Jul 30, 1935, v16, p30.
The New York Times. Jul 20, 1935, p16.

The New Yorker. Jul 27, 1935, v11, p42.
Rob Wagner's Script. Jul 27, 1935, v13, p8.
Time. Jul 29, 1935, v26, p42.
Variety. Jul 24, 1935, p21.

Shanghai Drama *See* Drame de Shanghai, Le

Shanghai Express (US; Sternberg, Josef von; 1932)
The Cinema of Josef von Sternberg. p90-100.
Dictionary of Films. p337-38.
Film Daily. Feb 21, 1932, p10.
The Films of Josef von Sternberg. p34-35.
The Films of Marlene Dietrich. p100-03.
Grierson on Documentary. p38-40.
Hollywood Reporter. Jan 27, 1932, p3.
Judge. Mar 12, 1932, v102, p22.
Magill's Survey of Cinema. Series II. v5, p2167-70.
Motion Picture Herald. Feb 27, 1932, p35-36.
The Nation. Mar 2, 1932, v134, p267-68.
National Board of Review Magazine. Mar 1932, v7, p9-13.
The New Statesman and Nation. Mar 26, 1932, v3, p393.
The New York Times. Feb 18, 1932, p25.
The New Yorker. Feb 27, 1932, v8, p48-49.
Outlook. Mar 1932, v160, p188.
Photoplay. Apr 1932, v41, p51.
Rob Wagner's Script. Feb 13, 1932, v7, p8.
Selected Film Criticism, 1931-1940. p225-27.
The Spectator. Mar 26, 1932, v148, p444.
Sublime Marlene. p49-53.
Time. Feb 29, 1932, v19, p28.
Variety. Feb 23, 1932, p13.

The Shanghai Gesture (US; Sternberg, Josef von; 1941)
Commonweal. Jan 30, 1942, v35, p370.
Film Daily. Dec 26, 1941, p8.
Hollywood Reporter. Dec 24, 1941, p3.
Motion Picture Herald Product Digest. Dec 27, 1941, p442.
The New York Times. Dec 26, 1941, p21.
The New Yorker. Jan 3, 1942, v17, p50.
Newsweek. Jan 5, 1942, v19, p54.
Time. Jan 26, 1942, v39, p45.
Variety. Dec 24, 1941, p8.

The Shape of Things to Come *See* Things to Come

Sharpshooters (US; Tinling, James; 1938)
Film Daily. Dec 7, 1938, p6.
Hollywood Reporter. Sep 17, 1938, p3.
Hollywood Spectator. Oct 1, 1938, v13, p11-12.
Motion Picture Herald. Sep 24, 1938, p42.
The New York Times. Dec 5, 1938, p19.
Variety. Sep 21, 1938, p13.

Shattered (German title: Scherben) (GER; Pick, Lupu; 1921)
Cinema, the Magic Vehicle. v1, p72-73.
Film Daily. Nov 20, 1921, p15.
From Caligari to Hitler. p104-05.
The Haunted Screen. p179-84.
The New York Times. Dec 11, 1921, sec6, p3.
Spellbound in Darkness. p363-64.
Variety. Jul 13, 1920, p20.
Variety. Aug 5, 1921, p25.

Shchors (Also titled: Shors) (USSR; Dovzhenko, Alexander; 1939)
Dictionary of Films. p338.
Film Daily. Nov 22, 1939, p7.
The International Dictionary of Films and Filmmakers. v1, p423-24.
Kino. p353-55.
The New Masses. Dec 5, 1939, v33, p28-29.
The New York Times. Nov 21, 1939, p19.
Sight and Sound. Sum 1957, v27, p48.
Variety. Dec 13, 1939, p52.

She (US; 1911)
The Moving Picture World. Dec 23, 1911, p976.
Selected Film Criticism, 1896-1911. p89-91.

She (US; Pichel, Irving; Holden, Lansing C.; 1935)
Esquire. Sep 1935, v4, p144.
Film Daily. Jul 8, 1935, p17.
Hollywood Reporter. Jul 2, 1935, p4.
Hollywood Reporter. Jul 31, 1935, p4.
Literary Digest. Jul 27, 1935, v120, p27.
Motion Picture Herald. Jul 13, 1935, p61.
The Nation. Aug 7, 1935, v141, p168.
The New York Times. Jul 26, 1935, p18.
The New Yorker. Aug 3, 1935, v11, p41.
Rob Wagner's Script. Jul 27, 1935, v13, p8-9.
The Spectator. Oct 25, 1935, v155, p663.
Time. Jul 22, 1935, v26, p30.
Variety. Jul 31, 1935, p19.

She Done Him Wrong (US; Sherman, Lowell; 1933)
American Film Criticism. p279.
Dictionary of Films. p338-39.
Film Daily. Feb 10, 1933, p7.
Film Notes. p88-89.
Films and Filming. Oct 1970, v17, p32.
The Films of Cary Grant. p51-54.
The Films of Mae West. p67-80.
The Films of the Thirties. p95-96.
Hollywood Reporter. Jan 10, 1933, p3.
The International Dictionary of Films and Filmmakers. v1,
   p424-25.
Judge. May 1933, v104, p24.
Lorentz on Film. p108.
Magill's Survey of Cinema. Series I. v4, p1539-41.
Motion Picture Herald. Feb 18, 1933, p31.
Movie-Made America. p184-87.
The Nation. Mar 1, 1933, v136, p242.
National Board of Review Magazine. Mar 1933, v8, p12-13.
New Outlook. Mar 1933, v161, p49.
The New York Times. Feb 10, 1933, p12.
The New York Times. Feb 19, 1933, p5.
The New Yorker. Feb 18, 1933, v8, p54.
Photoplay. Mar 1933, v43, p59.
Popcorn Venus. p162.
Rob Wagner's Script. Jan 28, 1933, v8, p8.
Selected Film Criticism, 1931-1940. p227-28.
Time. Feb 6, 1933, v21, p25.
Vanity Fair. Mar 1933, v40, p63.
Variety. Feb 14, 1933, p12.
Views and Reviews. Fall 1970, v2, p4-10.
Vintage Films. p19-22.
We're in the Money. p55-57.
Women and Their Sexuality in the New Film. p217.
50 Classic Motion Pictures. p2-7.

She Had to Say Yes (US; Amy, George; Berkeley, Busby;
   1933)
The Busby Berkeley Book. p64.
Film Daily. Jul 28, 1933, p8.
Hollywood Reporter. May 29, 1933, p5.
Motion Picture Herald. Jun 17, 1933, p36.
The New York Times. Jul 29, 1933, p14.
Newsweek. Aug 5, 1933, v2, p30.
Rob Wagner's Script. Jul 8, 1933, v9, p8.

She Married Her Boss (US; La Cava, Gregory; 1935)
Canadian Magazine. Dec 1935, v84, p44.
Claudette Colbert (Quirk). p83-86.
Esquire. Nov 1935, v4, p106.
Film Daily. Sep 27, 1935, p7.
Hollywood Reporter. Aug 6, 1935, p3.
Hollywood Reporter. Oct 2, 1935, p7.
Literary Digest. Oct 5, 1935, v120, p26.
The New York Times. Sep 27, 1935, p25.
The New Yorker. Oct 5, 1935, v11, p69-70.

Newsweek. Sep 14, 1935, v6, p28.
Rob Wagner's Script. Oct 12, 1935, v14, p11.
Time. Sep 30, 1935, v26, p29.
Vanity Fair. Nov 1935, v45, p49.
Variety. Oct 2, 1935, p16.

She Wanted a Millionaire (US; Blystone, John G.; 1932)
Film Daily. Feb 14, 1932, p10.
Motion Picture Herald. Feb 27, 1932, p36.
The New York Times. Feb 20, 1932, p11.
Time. Feb 29, 1932, v19, p28.
Variety. Feb 23, 1932, p13.

She Wore a Yellow Ribbon (US; Ford, John; 1949)
About John Ford. p245-47.
Cinema, the Magic Vehicle. v1, p516-17.
Commonweal. Dec 6, 1949, v51, p294.
The Complete Films of John Wayne. p170-72.
Fifty Memorable American Films. p68-71.
Film Daily. Jul 28, 1949, p7.
The Films of the Forties. p262-65.
Hollywood Reporter. Jul 27, 1949, p3.
The International Dictionary of Films and Filmmakers. v1,
   p425-26.
John Ford (Bogdanovich). p87+.
Magill's Survey of Cinema. Series II. v5, p2171-74.
Motion Picture Herald Product Digest. Jul 30, 1949, p4697.
The New York Times. Nov 18, 1949, p35.
The New Yorker. Dec 3, 1949, v25, p74.
Newsweek. Dec 12, 1949, v34, p88+.
Rotarian. Jan 1950, p41.
Seventy Years of Cinema. p169-70.
Time. Oct 24, 1949, v54, p103.
Variety. Jul 27, 1949, p12.
The Western Films of John Ford. p108-27.

The Sheik (US; Melford, George; 1921)
Film Daily. Nov 13, 1921, p5.
Magill's Survey of Cinema. Silent Films. v3, p964-68.
Motion Picture Classic. Jan 1922, v13, p66.
The Moving Picture World. Nov 19, 1921, v53, p336.
The New Republic. Oct 13, 1926, v48, p217-18.
The New York Times. Nov 7, 1921, p20.
Selected Film Criticism, 1921-1930. p261-62.
Spellbound in Darkness. p275.
World Film News. Sep 1938, v3, p224.

The Sheik Steps Out (US; Pichel, Irving; 1937)
Film Daily. Jul 29, 1937, p6.
Hollywood Reporter. Jul 26, 1937, p3.
Motion Picture Herald. Jul 31, 1937, p37.
Rob Wagner's Script. Sep 4, 1937, v18, p12.
The Tatler. Mar 16, 1938, v147, p466.
Variety. Jul 28, 1937, p27.

The Sheriff's Son (US; Schertzinger, Victor; 1919)
Exhibitor's Trade Review. Apr 12, 1919, p1449.
Motion Picture News. Feb 1, 1919, p778.
Motion Picture News. Apr 12, 1919, p2356.
The Moving Picture World. Apr 12, 1919, p272-73.
The New York Times. Mar 31, 1919, p11.
Variety. Apr 4, 1919, p68.
Wid's Daily. Apr 6, 1919, p21.

Sherlock Holmes (US; 1908)
The New York Dramatic Mirror. Dec 19, 1908, p7.
Selected Film Criticism, 1896-1911. p92.

Sherlock Holmes (US; Barthelet, Arthur; 1916)
The Moving Picture World. May 13, 1916, p1228.
The Moving Picture World. May 27, 1916, p1530.
The New York Dramatic Mirror. May 20, 1916, p25.
Selected Film Criticism, 1912-1920. p234-37.
Variety. May 12, 1916, p18.
Wid's Daily. May 18, 1916, p583.

Sherlock Holmes (US; Parker, Albert; 1922)
Film Daily. May 14, 1922, p2.
The Films of Sherlock Holmes. p11.
Magill's Cinema Annual, 1984. p494-97.
The New York Times. May 8, 1922, p14.
Photoplay. Jul 1922, p52.
Selected Film Criticism, 1921-1930. p262.
Variety. Jan 27, 1922, p40.
Variety. May 12, 1922, p33.

Sherlock Holmes (US; Howard, William K.; 1932)
Film Daily. Nov 12, 1932, p6.
The Films of Sherlock Holmes. p37-42.
The Great Gangster Pictures. p354-56.
Hollywood Reporter. Oct 18, 1932, p3.
Motion Picture Herald. Nov 26, 1932, p31.
The New York Times. Nov 12, 1932, p20.
Sherlock Holmes on the Screen. p107-20.
Variety. Nov 15, 1932, p19.

Sherlock Holmes and the Terror by Night *See* Terror by Night

Sherlock Holmes Jr. (US; Porter, Edwin S.; 1911)
The Moving Picture World. Aug 5, 1911, p291.
Selected Film Criticism, 1896-1911. p92-93.

Sherlock Jr. (US; Keaton, Buster; 1924)
Buster Keaton (Robinson). p96-106.
Cinema, the Magic Vehicle. v1, p101-02.
Classics of the Silent Screen. p59.
The Comic Mind. p132-33.
Exceptional Photoplays. May 1924, v4, p1-2.
The Film Career of Buster Keaton. p53-55.
From Quasimodo to Scarlett O'Hara. p33-34.
The International Dictionary of Films and Filmmakers. v1, p427-28.
Life. Jun 19, 1924, v83, p28.
Magill's Survey of Cinema. Silent Films. v3, p969-71.
The Moving Picture World. May 17, 1924, p319.
The New York Times. May 26, 1924, p21.
Photoplay. Jul 1924, v26, p46.
The Silent Clowns. p227-35.
Variety. May 28, 1924, p27.

She's a Sheik (US; Badger, Clarence; 1927)
Magill's Survey of Cinema. Silent Films. v3, p972-74.
The Moving Picture World. Nov 26, 1927, p27.
The New York Times. Nov 21, 1927, p20.
Variety. Nov 23, 1927, p22.

The Shining Hour (US; Borzage, Frank; 1938)
Canadian Magazine. Feb 1939, v91, p44.
Commonweal. Dec 16, 1938, v29, p216.
Film Daily. Nov 28, 1938, p4.
The Films of Joan Crawford. p130-32.
Hollywood Reporter. Nov 11, 1938, p3.
Hollywood Spectator. Nov 26, 1938, v13, p12.
Motion Picture Herald. Nov 19, 1938, p40.
The New Masses. Jan 31, 1939, v30, p27.
The New York Times. Jan 20, 1939, p15.
The New Yorker. Jan 28, 1938, v14, p51.
Rob Wagner's Script. Dec 10, 1938, v20, p8-9.
The Tatler. Dec 14, 1938, v150, p470.
Time. Dec 5, 1938, v32, p30.
Variety. Nov 16, 1938, p15.

Shipmates Forever (US; Borzage, Frank; 1935)
Canadian Magazine. Nov 1935, v84, p40.
Film Daily. Oct 17, 1935, p4.
The Hollywood Musical. p106.
Hollywood Reporter. Sep 17, 1935, p6.
Motion Picture Herald. Sep 28, 1935, p246.
The New York Times. Oct 17, 1935, p29.
Rob Wagner's Script. Oct 12, 1935, v14, p10.

Time. Oct 21, 1935, v26, p45.
Variety. Oct 23, 1935, p12.

The Shocking Miss Pilgrim (US; Seaton, George; 1947)
Commonweal. Feb 7, 1947, v45, p424.
Film Daily. Jan 2, 1947, p16.
The Hollywood Musical. p280.
Motion Picture Herald Product Digest. Jan 4, 1947, p3397.
New Republic. Feb 17, 1947, v116, p40.
The New York Times. Feb 12, 1947, p34.
Newsweek. Feb 10, 1947, v29, p94.
Variety. Jan 1, 1947, p14.

Shoe Shine (Italian title: Sciuscia, La) (IT; De Sica, Vittorio; 1946)
Agee on Film. v1, p278-80+.
Canadian Forum. Apr 1948, v28, p16.
Cinema, the Magic Vehicle. v1, p423-24.
Classics of the Foreign Film. p166-68.
Commonweal. Sep 12, 1947, v46, p529-30.
Dictionary of Films. p330.
Film Daily. Aug 27, 1947, p6.
Films and Filming. Oct-Nov 1964, v11, p12-16.
Hollywood Quarterly. Fall 1949, v4, p14-27.
The International Dictionary of Films and Filmmakers. v1, p415-16.
Life. Aug 25, 1947, v23, p52-54.
The Nation. Oct 11, 1946, v165, p390-91.
The New Republic. Sep 8, 1947, v117, p38-39.
The New York Times. Aug 27, 1947, p19.
The New Yorker. Aug 30, 1947, v23, p38.
Newsweek. Aug 11, 1947, v30, p89.
Passion and Defiance. p74-75+.
Patterns of Realism. p146-49.
Selected Film Criticism: Foreign Films, 1930-1950. p166-67.
Seventy Years of Cinema. p158-59.
Theatre Arts. Oct 1947, v31, p53-55.
Time. Sep 8, 1947, v50, p99-100.
Variety. May 22, 1946, p10.
Variety. Aug 13, 1947, p22.
Vintage Films. p85-88.

Shoes (US; Weber, Lois; 1916)
Magill's Survey of Cinema. Silent Films. v3, p975-77.
The Moving Picture World. Jun 24, 1916, p2257.
The Moving Picture World. Jul 1, 1916, p152.
Variety. Jun 16, 1916, p24.
Wid's Daily. Jun 15, 1916, p647.

Shooting of Dan McGrew (US; Badger, Clarence; 1924)
Film Daily. Mar 30, 1924, p7.
The Moving Picture World. Apr 12, 1924, p585.
The New York Times. Jun 9, 1924, p14.
Variety. Jun 11, 1924, p28.

Shooting Stars (US; Asquith, Anthony; 1928)
BFI/Monthly Films Bulletin. Jan 1976, v43, p15.
Film Daily. May 6, 1928, p5.
The Films of Anthony Asquith. p49-50.
Literary Digest. Mar 24, 1928, v96, p28.
The New York Times. Mar 4, 1928, sec9, p9.
Variety. Feb 29, 1928, p23.
Variety. Jun 13, 1928, p12.

The Shop Around the Corner (US; Lubitsch, Ernst; 1940)
BFI/Monthly Film Bulletin. Mar 31, 1940, p42-43.
The Cinema of Ernst Lubitsch. p27-40.
Commonweal. Feb 2, 1940, v31, p328.
Ernst Lubitsch. p146-49.
Ernst Lubitsch: A Guide to References and Resources. p146-49.
Ernst Lubitsch's American Comedy. p159-89.
Film Daily. Jan 8, 1940, p4.
The Films of James Stewart. p80-83.
Hollywood Reporter. Jan 3, 1940, p3.
The Illustrated London News. Jun 8, 1940, p790.
The London Times. May 27, 1940, p4.

Magill's Survey of Cinema. Series II. v5, p2183-85.
Motion Picture Herald. Jan 6, 1940, p42.
National Board of Review Magazine. Feb 1940, p21-22.
The New Republic. Feb 19, 1940, v102, p247.
New Statesman and Nation. Jun 1, 1940, p700.
The New York Times. Jan 26, 1940, p13.
Newsweek. Jan 29, 1940, p4.
Photoplay. Mar 1940, p63.
Sight and Sound. Spr 1940, p14.
Spectator. May 31, 1940, p749.
Talking Pictures. p171-73.
Time. Feb 5, 1940, v35, p62-63.
Variety. Jan 10, 1940, p14.

Shopworn (US; Grinde, Nick; 1932)
Film Daily. Apr 3, 1932, p10.
Judge. Apr 23, 1932, v102, p26, 29.
Motion Picture Herald. Apr 9, 1932, p23-24.
The New York Times. Apr 4, 1932, p13.
Rob Wagner's Script. Jun 4, 1932, v7, p10.
Starring Miss Barbara Stanwyck. p39, 41.
Time. Mar 28, 1932, v19, p52.
Variety. Apr 5, 1932, p14.

The Shopworn Angel (US; Wallace, Richard; 1929)
Film Daily. Jan 6, 1929, p6.
The Films of Gary Cooper. p59-61.
The New York Times. Jan 1, 1929, p60.
Variety. Jan 9, 1929, p11.

The Shopworn Angel (US; Potter, H.C.; 1938)
Commonweal. Jul 15, 1938, v28, p329.
The Film Criticism of Otis Ferguson. p223-24.
Film Daily. Jun 29, 1938, p8.
The Films of James Stewart. p59-60.
Hollywood Reporter. Jul 6, 1938, p3.
Motion Picture Herald. Jul 9, 1938, p28, 31.
The New Republic. Jul 20, 1938, v95, p308.
The New York Times. Jul 8, 1938, p11.
The New Yorker. Jul 9, 1938, v14, p49.
Rob Wagner's Script. Sep 3, 1938, v20, p11.
The Tatler. Aug 10, 1938, v148, p240.
Time. Jul 11, 1938, v32, p43.
Variety. Jul 13, 1938, p15.
World Film News. Sep 1938, v3, p222-23.

Shore Acres (US; Ingram, Rex; 1920)
The Moving Picture World. Jan 20, 1920, p144.
The Moving Picture World. Apr 3, 1920, p135.
The New York Times. May 17, 1920, p19.
Photoplay. Jun 1920, p99.
Rex Ingram: Master of the Silent Cinema. p65-68.
Selected Film Criticism, 1912-1920. p237.
Variety. May 21, 1920, p34.
Wid's Daily. Mar 28, 1920, p22.

Should Ladies Behave? (US; Beaumont, Harry; 1933)
Esquire. Feb 1934, v1, p131.
Film Daily. Dec 6, 1933, p7.
The New York Times. Dec 18, 1933, p24.
The New Yorker. Dec 23, 1933, v9, p49.
Rob Wagner's Script. Dec 16, 1933, v10, p10-11.
Time. Dec 18, 1933, v22, p35.
Variety. Dec 19, 1933, p19.

Shoulder Arms (US; Chaplin, Charles; 1918)
Motion Picture Classic. Jan 1919, p48.
The Moving Picture World. Nov 2, 1918, p621, 623-24.
The New York Times. Oct 21, 1918, p15.
Selected Film Criticism, 1912-1920. p237-38.
Variety. Oct 25, 1918, p36.
Wid's Daily. Oct 30, 1918, p4.

Show Boat (US; Pollard, Harry; 1929)
Film Daily. May 5, 1929, p8.
The Film Spectator. Apr 20, 1929, v7, p6.

The Hollywood Musical. p26.
The New York Times. Apr 18, 1929, p32.
Outlook. May 22, 1929, v152, p155.
Photoplay. Jun 1929, v36, p55.
Selected Film Criticism, 1921-1930. p263-64.
Variety. Apr 24, 1929, p13.

Show Boat (US; Whale, James; 1936)
Commonweal. May 8, 1936, v24, p48.
Film Daily. Apr 30, 1936, p6.
The Films of the Thirties. p166-68.
Graham Greene on Film. p82-83.
The Hollywood Musical. p27, 120+.
Hollywood Reporter. Apr 27, 1936, p3.
Hollywood Spectator. May 9, 1936, v11, p7-8.
James Whale: Ace Director. p5-6.
James Whale (Curtis). pxviii, 132-39.
Literary Digest. May 9, 1936, v121, p20.
Magill's Survey of Cinema. Series I. v4, p1545-48.
Make It Again, Sam. p185-91.
Motion Picture. May 1936, v51, p32.
Motion Picture Herald. May 9, 1936, p39.
Motion Picture Herald. Apr 18, 1936, p16-17.
Movie Classic. May 1936, v10, p36-37.
The Nation. Jun 10, 1936, v142, p754.
The New York Times. May 15, 1936, p29.
The New Yorker. May 23, 1936, v12, p67, 69.
Newsweek. May 16, 1936, v7, p41.
Rob Wagner's Script. May 16, 1936, v15, p10.
Selected Film Criticism, 1931-1940. p228-31.
The Spectator. Jun 26, 1936, v156, p1171.
The Tatler. Jun 17, 1936, v140, p524.
Time. May 18, 1936, v27, p61.
Variety. May 20, 1936, p12.

The Show of Shows (Also titled: Show of Shows) (US; Adolfi, John; 1929)
BFI/Monthly Film Bulletin. Dec 1977, v44, p268.
Film Daily. Nov 24, 1929, p8.
The Film Mercury. Nov 29, 1929, v10, p6.
The Films of Myrna Loy. p89-91.
The Hollywood Musical. p34.
Hollywood Musicals. p37-38.
The New York Times. Nov 21, 1929, p24.
Outlook. Dec 11, 1929, v153, p593.
Selected Film Criticism, 1921-1930. p264-66.
Variety. Nov 27, 1929, p21.

Show People (US; Vidor, King; 1928)
Exhibitor's Herald-World and Moving Picture World. Oct 27, 1928, p52.
Film Comment. Jul-Aug 1973, v9, p17-18.
Film Daily. Nov 18, 1928, p4.
The Film Spectator. Jan 5, 1929, v7, p8.
King Vidor (Baxter). p35-39.
Magill's Survey of Cinema. Silent Films. v3, p981-86.
The New York Times. Nov 12, 1928, p18.
Photoplay. Aug 1928, v34, p57.
Selected Film Criticism, 1921-1930. p267.
The Silent Clowns. p290-92.
Variety. Nov 14, 1928, p22.

The Showoff (Also titled: The Show-Off) (US; Reisner, Charles F; 1934)
Film Daily. Mar 17, 1934, p4.
The Films of Spencer Tracy. p107.
Hollywood Reporter. Feb 22, 1934, p3.
Motion Picture Herald. Mar 3, 1934, p35-38.
The New York Times. Mar 17, 1934, p11.
Newsweek. Mar 24, 1934, v3, p39.
Variety. Mar 20, 1934, p16.

A Shriek in the Night (US; Ray, Albert; 1933)
Film Daily. Jul 22, 1933, p3.
The Films of Ginger Rogers. p80-81.

Forgotten Horrors: Early Talkie Chillers from Poverty Row.
   p87-88.
Hollywood Reporter. Mar 17, 1933, p3.
Motion Picture Herald. Mar 25, 1933, p22.
The New York Times. Jul 24, 1933, p11.
Rob Wagner's Script. Apr 1, 1933, v9, p8.
Variety. Jul 25, 1933, p34.

Sick Abed (US; Wood, Sam; 1920)
   The Moving Picture World. Jun 26, 1920, p1793.
   Photoplay. Sep 1920, v18, p106.
   Selected Film Criticism, 1912-1920. p238.
   Variety. Jun 26, 1920, p1793.
   Wid's Daily. Jun 27, 1920, p13.

Sidewalks of London (Also titled: St. Martin's Lane) (GB;
      Whelan, Tim; 1938)
   Fifty Classic British Films. p28-30.
   Film Daily. Jan 31, 1940, p8.
   Hollywood Spectator. Feb 15, 1940, v14, p12.
   Motion Picture Herald. Feb 10, 1940, p38.
   Motion Picture Herald. Jul 9, 1938, p31.
   The New York Times. Feb 15, 1940, p15.
   The New Yorker. Feb 17, 1940, v16, p77.
   Photoplay. Mar 1940, v54, p63.
   Rob Wagner's Script. Feb 10, 1940, v23, p16-17.
   Selected Film Criticism: Foreign Films, 1930-1950. p167-69.
   Time. Mar 4, 1940, v35, p69.
   Variety. Jan 24, 1940, p14.

Sidewalks of New York (US; White, Jules; Meyers, Zion;
      1931)
   BFI/Monthly Film Bulletin. Oct 1975, v42, p248.
   Film Daily. Nov 15, 1931, p10.
   Hollywood Reporter. Jul 31, 1931, p7.
   Motion Picture Herald. Aug 15, 1931, p34.
   Variety. Nov 17, 1931, p15.

Siegfried (German title: Niebelungen, Die, Part One)
      (GER; Lang, Fritz; 1922)
   The Emergence of Film Art. p99.
   Film Daily. Aug 30, 1925, p6.
   Films and Filming. Oct 1966, v13, p56-57.
   Films & Filming. Oct 1969, v16, p50-51.
   The Films of Fritz Lang. p106-22.
   Fritz Lang: A Guide to References and Resources. p42-47.
   Fritz Lang (Armour). p65-76+.
   Fritz Lang (Eisner). p66-82.
   From Caligari to Hitler. p91-95.
   The Haunted Screen. p166-70.
   A History of Narrative Film. p118.
   Magill's Survey of Cinema. Silent Films. v2, p803-05.
   The New York Times. Aug 24, 1925, p17.
   Sight and Sound. Apr 1950, v19, p83-85.
   Variety. Apr 12, 1967, p6.
   Variety. Apr 16, 1924, p26.

The Sign of the Cross (US; DeMille, Cecil B.; 1932)
   Around Cinemas. p75-78.
   Cinema. Jul 1964, v2, p50.
   Claudette Colbert (Quirk). p51-54.
   Commonweal. Dec 21, 1932, v17, p215-16.
   Film Daily. Dec 2, 1932, p11.
   Film Notes. p86-87.
   The Films of Cecil B. De Mille, p278-83.
   The Films of Fredric March. p93-95.
   Hollywood Reporter. Nov 23, 1932, p3.
   Magill's Cinema Annual, 1985. p607-14.
   Motion Picture. Nov 1932, v44, p34-35+.
   Motion Picture Herald. Dec 10, 1932, p8, 44.
   Motion Picture Herald. Dec 3, 1932, p22.
   Motion Picture Herald. Dec 17, 1932, p17.
   Movie Classic. Sep 1932, v3, p42-43+.
   The Nation. Dec 21, 1932, v135, p625.
   The New York Times. Nov 20, 1932, p4.

The New York Times. Dec 21, 1932, p25.
The New York Times. Dec 11, 1932, p7.
The New Yorker. Dec 10, 1932, v8, p69.
Rob Wagner's Script. Jan 21, 1933, v8, p8-9.
Selected Film Criticism, 1931-1940. p231-32.
Time. Dec 5, 1932, v20, p32.
Variety. Dec 6, 1932, p14.

The Sign of the Four (Also titled: The Sign of Four) (GB;
      Cutts, Graham; 1932)
   Film Daily. Jul 22, 1932, p8.
   Hollywood Reporter. Aug 17, 1932, p3.
   Motion Picture Herald. Jun 4, 1932, p36.
   Motion Picture Herald. Jul 30, 1932, p32.
   The New York Times. Aug 20, 1932, p7.
   Sherlock Holmes on the Screen. p152-56.
   Variety. Aug 30, 1932, p21.

The Silent Enemy (US; Carver, H.P.; 1930)
   Close-Up. Aug 1930, v7, p117-18.
   Commonweal. Jun 11, 1930, v12, p165.
   Exhibitors Herald-World. Aug 9, 1930, p33.
   Exhibitors Herald-World. May 24, 1930, p36.
   Film Daily. May 18, 1930, p12.
   Judge. Jun 28, 1930, v98, p23.
   Life. Jul 4, 1930, v96, p17.
   The Nation. May 28, 1930, v130, p632.
   National Board of Review Magazine. May-Jun 1930, v5, p9.
   The New Republic. Jun 4, 1930, v63, p73.
   The New York Times. May 20, 1930, p32.
   The New York Times. May 25, 1930, p5.
   The New Yorker. May 24, 1930, v6, p88.
   Outlook and Independent. May 28, 1930, v155, p151.
   Time. May 26, 1930, v15, p58.
   Variety. May 21, 1930, p19.
   The War, the West, and the Wilderness. p545-60.

The Silent Witness (GB; Varnel, Marcel; 1932)
   Film Daily. Feb 7, 1932, p10.
   Hollywood Reporter. Jan 8, 1932, p3.
   Judge. Mar 5, 1932, v102, p22.
   Motion Picture Herald. Feb 13, 1932, p34.
   The New York Times. Feb 9, 1932, p15.
   Rob Wagner's Script. Apr 2, 1932, v7, p10-11.
   Time. Feb 15, 1932, v19, p28.
   Variety. Feb 8, 1932, p21.

The Silk Express (US; Enright, Ray; 1933)
   Film Daily. Jun 23, 1933, p6.
   Hollywood Reporter. May 10, 1933, p3.
   Motion Picture Herald. Jun 10, 1933, p36.
   The New York Times. Jun 28, 1933, p24.
   Variety. Jun 27, 1933, p15.

The Silver Cord (US; Cromwell, John; 1933)
   Commonweal. May 26, 1933, v18, p108.
   Film Daily. May 5, 1933, p7.
   The Hollywood Professionals. v5, p65, 68.
   Hollywood Reporter. Apr 21, 1933, p3.
   Motion Picture Herald. May 13, 1933, p22.
   The Nation. May 24, 1933, v136, p595.
   New Outlook. Jun 1933, v161, p49.
   The New York Times. May 5, 1933, p18.
   The New Yorker. May 13, 1933, v9, p52.
   Rob Wagner's Script. Jun 10, 1933, v9, p8.
   Time. May 15, 1933, v21, p36.
   Variety. May 9, 1933, p14.

Silver Dollar (US; Green, Alfred E.; 1932)
   Film Daily. Nov 5, 1932, p4.
   The Films of the Thirties. p93-94.
   Hollywood Reporter. Oct 25, 1932, p3.
   Judge. Dec 1932, v103, p27.
   Magill's Survey of Cinema. Series II. v5, p2186-88.
   The New York Times. Dec 23, 1932, p20.
   The New Yorker. Dec 31, 1932, v8, p40.

Rob Wagner's Script. Jan 28, 1933, v8, p8-9.
Stage. Dec 1932, v10, p27.
Time. Jan 2, 1933, v21, p18.
Variety. Dec 27, 1932, p14.

The Silver Horde (US; Archainbaud, George; 1930)
Film Daily. Oct 26, 1930, p10.
The Films of the Thirties. p43-44.
The New York Times. Oct 25, 1930, p20.
Time. Nov 10, 1930, v16, p68.
Variety. Oct 29, 1930, p27.

The Silver Lining *See* Romance Sentimentale

Simple Charity (US; Griffith, D.W.; 1910)
The Moving Picture World. Nov 26, 1910, p1236.
The New York Dramatic Mirror. Nov 16, 1910, p30.
Selected Film Criticism, 1896-1911. p93-94.

The Sin Flood (US; Lloyd, Frank; 1921)
Film Daily. Sep 4, 1921, p5.
Magill's Survey of Cinema. Silent Films. v3, p987-90.
The New York Times. Oct 30, 1922, p11.
Variety. Nov 3, 1922, p42.

The Sin of Harold Diddlebock (Also titled: Mad
  Wednesday; The Sin of Hilda Diddlebock) (US;
  Sturges, Preston; 1947)
Between Flops. p202-20+.
Film Daily. Apr 4, 1947, p8.
Harold Lloyd: The King of Daredevil Comedy. p148-56.
Harold Lloyd: The Shape of Laughter. p214-15.
Hollywood Reporter. Feb 18, 1947, p3.
Motion Picture Herald Product Digest. Mar 1, 1947, p3503.
The New York Times. Jan 25, 1951, p21.
Newsweek. Dec 1, 1947, v30, p90.
Scholastic. May 5, 1947, v50, p38.
Variety. Feb 19, 1947, p8.

The Sin of Madelon Claudet (Also titled: Lullaby) (US;
  Selwyn, Edgar; 1931)
Commonweal. Nov 18, 1931, v15, p77.
Film Daily. Nov 1, 1931, p10.
Hollywood Reporter. Jul 14, 1931, p3.
Judge. Nov 28, 1931, v101, p18.
Life. Nov 20, 1931, v98, p20.
Magill's Survey of Cinema. Series II. v5, p2189-92.
Motion Picture Herald. Oct 3, 1931, p29, 32.
The Nation. Nov 25, 1931, v133, p582+.
The New York Times. Oct 31, 1931, p22.
The New Yorker. Nov 7, 1931, v7, p79, 81.
Rob Wagner's Script. Nov 7, 1931, v6, p10.
Time. Nov 9, 1931, v18, p49.
Variety. Nov 3, 1931, p17.

Sin Takes a Holiday (US; Stein, Paul; 1930)
Basil Rathbone: His Life and His Films. p135-37.
Exhibitors Herald-World. Nov 29, 1930, p31.
Exhibitors Herald-World. Dec 6, 1930, p29-30.
Film Daily. Nov 23, 1930, p10.
Life. Dec 19, 1930, v96, p20.
The New York Times. Nov 28, 1930, p23.
The New York Times. Dec 7, 1930, p5.
Outlook and Independent. Dec 10, 1930, v156, p591.
Variety. Dec 3, 1930, p14.

Since You Went Away (US; Cromwell, John; 1944)
Agee on Film. v1, p106-08, 349-51.
Claudette Colbert (Quirk). p487.
Commonweal. Aug 4, 1944, v40, p374-75.
David O. Selznick's Hollywood. p334-45+.
Film Daily. Jul 19, 1944, p8.
Films and Filming. Oct 1981, n325, p46-47.
Films and the Second World War. p195-96.
The Films of Jennifer Jones. p42-51.
The Films of Shirley Temple. p220-23.

The Films of World War II. p198-99.
Hollywood Reporter. Jul 19, 1944, p3.
Life. Jul 24, 1944, v17, p53-55.
The London Times. Jan 11, 1945, p6.
Magic Moments of the Movies. p130.
Magill's Survey of Cinema. Series II. v5, p2193-95.
Motion Picture Exhibitor. Jul 26, 1944, v32, n11, sec2, p1549.
Motion Picture Herald Product Digest. Jul 22, 1944, p2095.
The Nation. Jul 29, 1944, v159, p137.
The New Republic. Jul 17, 1944, v111, p77.
The New York Times. Jul 21, 1944, p16.
The New Yorker. Jul 29, 1944, v20, p42-43.
Newsweek. Jul 10, 1944, v225, p85-86.
Rob Wagner's Script. Jul 29, 1944, v30, p14.
Saturday Review. Jul 29, 1944, v27, p16.
Scholastic. Sep 11, 1944, v45, p32.
Selected Film Criticism, 1941-1950. p210-12.
Theatre Arts. Sep 1944, v28, p543.
Time. Jul 17, 1944, v44, p94+.
Variety. Jul 19, 1944, p13.
Women's Film and Female Experience. p98-102.

Sing As We Go (GB; Dean, Basil; 1934)
Fifty Classic British Films. p16-17.
Hollywood Reporter. Jul 2, 1934, p3.
Magill's Survey of Cinema. Series I. v4, p1557-59.

Sing, Baby, Sing (US; Lanfield, Sidney; 1936)
Film Daily. Aug 4, 1936, p7.
The Films of Alice Faye. p69-72.
Hollywood Reporter. Aug 1, 1936, p3.
Judge. Oct 1936, v111, p12, 20.
Literary Digest. Aug 22, 1936, v122, p24.
Motion Picture Herald. Aug 15, 1936, p54, 59.
The New York Times. Sep 12, 1936, p20.
The New Yorker. Sep 26, 1936, v12, p67.
Rob Wagner's Script. Aug 22, 1936, v15, p11-12.
Sight and Sound. Wint 1936-37, v5, p137.
Time. Aug 31, 1936, v28, p23.
Variety. Sep 16, 1936, p16.
World Film News. Nov 1936, v1, p20.

Sing, Sinner, Sing (US; Christy, Howard; 1933)
Film Daily. Aug 12, 1933, p4.
Hollywood Reporter. Jul 29, 1933, p3.
Motion Picture Herald. Aug 19, 1933, p42.
The New York Times. Aug 15, 1933, p20.
Newsweek. Aug 19, 1933, v2, p28.
Variety. Aug 15, 1933, p14.

Sing, You Sinners (US; Ruggles, Wesley; 1938)
Commonweal. Sep 2, 1938, v28, p477.
Film Daily. Aug 9, 1938, p7.
The Films of Bing Crosby. p91-93.
Hollywood Reporter. Aug 6, 1938, p3.
Motion Picture Herald. Aug 13, 1938, p59.
National Board of Review Magazine. Oct 1938, v13, p13.
The New York Times. Aug 18, 1938, p23.
The New Yorker. Aug 27, 1938, v14, p53.
Rob Wagner's Script. Oct 1, 1938, v20, p10.
Time. Aug 29, 1938, v32, p23.
Variety. Aug 17, 1938, p22.

Singapore (US; Brahm, John; 1947)
Film Daily. Aug 13, 1947, p8.
Hollywood Reporter. Aug 6, 1947, p3.
Motion Picture Herald Product Digest. Aug 16, 1947, p3782.
The New York Times. Sep 17, 1947, p31.
Newsweek. Sep 29, 1947, v30, p94.
Time. Oct 6, 1947, v50, p101-02.
Variety. Aug 6, 1947, p12.

The Singing Fool (US; Bacon, Lloyd; 1929)
Film Daily. Sep 23, 1928, p6.
Film Daily. Jul 7, 1929, p8.
The Films of the Twenties. p202-05.

The Hollywood Musical. p21.
The New York Times. Sep 20, 1928, p33.
Variety. Sep 26, 1928, p14.

The Singing Kid (US; Keighley, William; 1936)
Canadian Magazine. May 1936, v85, p60.
Esquire. Jun 1936, v5, p110, 200.
Film Daily. Mar 13, 1936, p6.
Hollywood Reporter. Mar 10, 1936, p3.
Hollywood Spectator. Mar 28, 1936, v10, p8.
Literary Digest. Mar 28, 1936, v121, p19.
Motion Picture Herald. Mar 21, 1936, p38.
The New York Times. Apr 4, 1936, p11.
Rob Wagner's Script. Apr 11, 1936, v15, p10-11.
Time. Apr 13, 1936, v27, p32+.
Variety. Apr 8, 1936, p16.
World Film News. Sep 1936, v1, p25.

The Single Standard *See* The Battle of the Sexes

The Single Standard (US; Robertson, John S.; 1929)
Exhibitor's Herald-World. Aug 17, 1929, p80.
Film Daily. Aug 4, 1929, p8.
The Films of Greta Garbo. p79-81.
The New York Times. Jul 29, 1929, p23.
Variety. Jul 31, 1929, p17.

The Sinking of the Lusitania (US; McCay, Winsor Z.; 1918)
Magill's Survey of Cinema. Silent Films. v3, p995-98.
The Moving Picture World. May 18, 1918, p1034.
Selected Film Criticism, 1912-1920. p238-39.

Sinners' Holiday (US; Adolfi, John; 1930)
Exhibitors Herald-World. Oct 25, 1930, p43-44.
Film Daily. Oct 12, 1930, p14.
Life. Oct 31, 1930, v96, p22.
The New York Times. Oct 11, 1930, p21.
Time. Oct 27, 1930, v16, p26.
Variety. Oct 15, 1930, p25.

Sinners in Paradise (US; Whale, James; 1938)
Film Daily. May 9, 1938, p23.
Hollywood Reporter. Apr 28, 1938, p2.
James Whale (Curtis). p165, 167.
The New York Times. May 20, 1938, p17.
Rob Wagner's Script. May 7, 1938, v19, p9.
Variety. May 4, 1938, p15.

Sinners in the Sun (US; Hall, Alexander; 1932)
Film Daily. May 15, 1932, p10.
The New York Times. May 14, 1932, p11.
Time. May 23, 1932, v19, p30.
Variety. May 17, 1932, p15.

Sioux Indian Dance (US; 1894)
East Orange Gazette. Sep 27, 1894, p10.
Film Before Griffith. p48.
Newark Evening News. Sep 24, 1924, p16.
Orange Chronicle. Sep 27, 1894, p6.

Sir Arne's Treasure (German title: Herr Arnes Pengar) (SWED; Stiller, Mauritz; 1919)
The New York Times. Dec 25, 1921, sec6, p2.
Swedish Cinema. p35-39.
Variety. Dec 2, 1925, p43.
Wid's Daily. Dec 11, 1921, p13.

Sir Arne's Treasure (SWED; Sjostrom, Victor; 1921)
Film Daily. Dec 11, 1921, p13.
The New York Times. Dec 25, 1921, sec6, p2.
Spellbound in Darkness. p364-65.
Swedish Film Classics. p17-21.
Variety. Dec 2, 1925, p43.

Sister Kenny (US; Nichols, Dudley; 1946)
Commonweal. Oct 25, 1946, v45, p47.
Film Daily. Jul 17, 1946, p4.
Hollywood Reporter. Jul 16, 1946, p3.
Life. Sep 16, 1946, v21, p76-78.
Motion Picture Herald Product Digest. Jul 20, 1946, p3101.
The New York Times. Sep 30, 1946, p21.
The New Yorker. Sep 28, 1946, v22, p91.
Newsweek. Sep 23, 1946, v28, p92+.
Rosalind Russell (Yanni). p88-91.
Theatre Arts. Oct 1946, v30, p602-03.
Time. Sep 30, 1946, v48, p101.
Variety. Jul 17, 1946, p8.

The Sisters (US; Litvak, Anatole; 1938)
Bette Davis: Her Films and Career. p88-89.
Commonweal. Oct 21, 1938, v28, p677.
Esquire. Feb 1939, v11, p141.
Film Daily. Oct 10, 1938, p9.
The Films of Errol Flynn. p70-72.
Graham Greene on Film. p218.
Hollywood Reporter. Oct 4, 1938, p3.
Hollywood Spectator. Oct 15, 1938, v13, p7-8.
Life. Oct 31, 1938, v5, p39-41.
Motion Picture Herald. Oct 8, 1938, p40.
The New Statesman and Nation. Apr 15, 1939, v17, p573.
The New York Times. Oct 15, 1938, p21.
The New Yorker. Oct 15, 1938, v14, p62-63.
Rob Wagner's Script. Oct 15, 1938, v20, p13.
The Spectator. Apr 28, 1939, v162, p708.
Time. Oct 17, 1938, v32, p23.
Variety. Oct 5, 1938, p14.

Sitting Pretty (US; Brown, Harry Joe; 1933)
Film Daily. Nov 22, 1933, p10.
The Films of Ginger Rogers. p85-87.
Hollywood Reporter. Nov 13, 1933, p3.
Literary Digest. Dec 16, 1933, v116, p47.
Motion Picture Herald. Dec 2, 1933, p53, 56.
The New York Times. Dec 2, 1933, p9.
Rob Wagner's Script. Nov 25, 1933, v10, p10.
Time. Dec 11, 1933, v22, p31.
Variety. Dec 5, 1933, p16.

Sitting Pretty (US; Lang, Walter; 1948)
Commonweal. Mar 26, 1948, v47, p597.
Film Daily. Feb 24, 1948, p4.
Hollywood Reporter. Feb 24, 1948, p3.
Magill's Survey of Cinema. Series I. v4, p1564-66.
Motion Picture Herald Product Digest. Feb 28, 1948, p4077.
The New Republic. Apr 5, 1948, v118, p20.
The New York Times. Mar 11, 1948, p35.
The New Yorker. Mar 20, 1948, v24, p46+.
Newsweek. Mar 22, 1948, v31, p93.
Saturday Review. May 8, 1948, v31, p22.
Time. Mar 29, 1948, v51, p102.
Variety. Feb 25, 1948, p8.

Six Hours to Live (US; Dieterle, William; 1932)
Film Daily. Oct 18, 1932, p7.
Hollywood Reporter. Oct 5, 1932, p3.
Love in the Film. p98-99.
The New York Times. Oct 22, 1932, p18.
The New Yorker. Oct 29, 1932, v8, p52.
Time. Oct 31, 1932, v20, p21.
Variety. Oct 25, 1932, p15.

Six Thousand Enemies (US; Seitz, George B.; 1939)
Film Daily. Jun 12, 1939, p11.
Hollywood Reporter. May 24, 1939, p3.
Motion Picture Herald. May 27, 1939, p32.
The New York Times. Jun 9, 1939, p26.
The New Yorker. Jun 17, 1939, v15, p76.
The Tatler. Dec 27, 1939, v154, p424.
Time. Jun 19, 1939, v39, p74.
Variety. May 31, 1939, p14.

Sixty Glorious Years (Also titled: Queen of Destiny) (GB;
   Wilcox, Herbert; 1938)
   Canadian Magazine. Dec 1938, v90, p41.
   Commonweal. Dec 2, 1938, v29, p161.
   Film Daily. Nov 17, 1938, p5.
   Graham Greene on Film. p203.
   Motion Picture Herald. Oct 29, 1938, p40, 42.
   The New Masses. Nov 29, 1938, v29, p31.
   The New Statesman and Nation. Oct 22, 1938, v16, p608.
   The New York Times. Nov 18, 1938, p25.
   The New Yorker. Nov 26, 1938, v14, p73-72.
   Rob Wagner's Script. Nov 9, 1940, v24, p16-17.
   Scholastic. Dec 3, 1938, v33, p33.
   Selected Film Criticism: Foreign Films, 1930-1950. p146.
   The Spectator. Nov 4, 1938, v161, p767.
   The Tatler. Oct 26, 1938, v150, p148.
   Time. Nov 28, 1938, v32, p51.
   Variety. Oct 26, 1938, p15.

The Skin Game (GB; Hitchcock, Alfred; 1931)
   Film Daily. Jun 21, 1931, p10.
   Films and Filming. Jul 1970, v16, p52-58.
   Hitchcock's British Films. p139-45.
   Motion Picture Herald. Jun 27, 1931, p35.
   The Nation. Jul 8, 1931, v133, p48.
   The New York Times. Jun 20, 1931, p20.
   The New Yorker. Jun 27, 1931, v7, p57.
   Variety. Jun 30, 1931, p20.
   Variety. Mar 18, 1931, p38.

Skippy (US; Taurog, Norman; 1931)
   Film Daily. Apr 5, 1931, p10.
   Life. Apr 24, 1931, v97, p22.
   Magill's Survey of Cinema. Series II. v5, p2196-98.
   Motion Picture Herald. Mar 21, 1931, p42.
   The Nation. Apr 29, 1931, v132, p485.
   National Board of Review Magazine. May 1931, v6, p12.
   The New York Times. Apr 4, 1931, p23.
   The New Yorker. Apr 11, 1931, v7, p91.
   Outlook and Independent. Apr 8, 1931, v157, p508.
   Photoplay. Jun 1931, v40, p28-29+.
   Pictures Will Talk. p38-41.
   Rob Wagner's Script. May 9, 1931, v5, p8-9.
   Time. Apr 13, 1931, v17, p72.
   Variety. Apr 15, 1931, p33.

Sky Devils (US; Sutherland, Edward; 1932)
   Film Daily. Jan 24, 1932, p10.
   The Films of Spencer Tracy. p77-78.
   Hollywood Reporter. Dec 19, 1931, p3.
   Motion Picture Herald. Jan 2, 1932, p30.
   The Nation. Mar 30, 1932, v134, p380.
   The New Statesman and Nation. Jul 2, 1932, v4, p13.
   The New York Times. Mar 4, 1932, p17.
   The New Yorker. Mar 12, 1932, v8, p55-56.
   Time. Mar 14, 1932, v19, p26.
   Variety. Mar 8, 1932, p14.

Skyscraper Souls (US; Selwyn, Edgar; 1932)
   Commonweal. Aug 24, 1932, v16, p411.
   Film Daily. Aug 5, 1932, p4.
   Motion Picture Herald. Jul 16, 1932, p51.
   New Outlook. Oct 1932, v161, p38.
   The New York Times. Aug 5, 1932, p11.
   The New Yorker. Aug 13, 1932, v8, p37.
   Time. Aug 15, 1932, v20, p26.
   Variety. Aug 9, 1932, p17.

Slattery's Hurricane (US; Toth, Andre de; 1949)
   Film Daily. Aug 4, 1949, p6.
   Hollywood Reporter. Aug 3, 1949, p3.
   Motion Picture Herald Product Digest. Aug 6, 1949, p4705.
   The New Republic. Aug 29, 1949, v121, p31.
   The New York Times. Aug 13, 1949, p6.
   Newsweek. Aug 22, 1949, v34, p70.

Rotarian. Nov 1949, v80, p35.
   Time. Sep 5, 1949, v54, p62.
   Variety. Aug 3, 1949, p16.

Slave Ship (US; Garnett, Tay; 1937)
   Film Daily. Jun 17, 1937, p7.
   Graham Greene on Film. p162.
   Hollywood Reporter. Jun 12, 1937, p3.
   Literary Digest. Jun 26, 1937, v123, p23.
   Motion Picture Herald. Mar 13, 1937, p16-17.
   The New York Times. Jun 17, 1937, p19.
   The New Yorker. Jun 26, 1937, v13, p64.
   Rob Wagner's Script. Jun 26, 1937, v17, p12.
   Time. Jun 28, 1937, v29, p51.
   Variety. Jun 23, 1937, p12.
   World Film News. Sep 1937, v2, p25.

Sleep My Love (US; Sirk, Douglas; 1948)
   Claudette Colbert (Quirk). p155.
   Commonweal. Feb 27, 1948, v47, p496.
   Douglas Sirk (Stern). p56-60.
   Film Daily. Jan 13, 1948, p6.
   Hollywood Reporter. Jan 12, 1948, p3.
   The New York Times. Feb 19, 1948, p29.
   Newsweek. Mar 1, 1948, v31, p72.
   Time. Feb 16, 1948, v51, p100.
   Variety. Jan 14, 1948, p10.

A Slight Case of Murder (US; Bacon, Lloyd; 1938)
   The Cinema of Edward G. Robinson. p113-15.
   The Film Criticism of Otis Ferguson. p216.
   Film Daily. Feb 8, 1938, p9.
   The Gangster Film. p115-16.
   Graham Greene on Film. p192-93.
   The Great Gangster Pictures. p365.
   Hollywood Reporter. Feb 3, 1938, p3.
   Motion Picture Herald. Feb 12, 1938, p48.
   The New Masses. Mar 1, 1938, v26, p30-31.
   The New Statesman and Nation. Jun 18, 1938, v15, p1028.
   The New York Times. Feb 28, 1938, p19.
   The New Yorker. Mar 5, 1938, v14, p47.
   Rob Wagner's Script. Mar 5, 1938, v19, p7.
   The Spectator. Jun 17, 1938, v160, p1096.
   The Tatler. Jun 22, 1938, v148, p532.
   Time. Mar 7, 1938, v31, p38.
   Variety. Feb 9, 1938, p14.
   World Film News. Jul 1938, v3, p126.
   World Film News. Aug 1938, v3, p172-73.

Slightly French (US; Sirk, Douglas; 1949)
   Douglas Sirk (Stern). p59.
   Film Daily. Feb 16, 1949, p8.
   Hollywood Reporter. Feb 3, 1949, p3.
   Motion Picture Herald Product Digest. Feb 19, 1949, p4505.
   The New York Times. May 27, 1949, p25.
   Newsweek. Jun 6, 1949, v33, p80.
   Variety. Feb 9, 1949, p13.

Slightly Scarlet (US; Gasnier, Louis; Knopf, Edwin H.;
   1930)
   Exhibitors Herald-World. Mar 8, 1930, p39-40.
   Film Daily. Mar 2, 1930, p10.
   The Film Spectator. Mar 1, 1930, v9, p19.
   Judge. Mar 29, 1930, v98, p21.
   The New York Times. Mar 1, 1930, p23.
   The New York Times. Mar 9, 1930, p5.
   The New Yorker. Mar 8, 1930, v6, p89.
   Pictures Will Talk. p32-33.
   Rob Wagner's Script. Apr 19, 1930, v3, p11.
   Time. Mar 10, 1930, v15, p60.
   Variety. Mar 5, 1930, p33.

The Slim Princess (US; Schertzinger, Victor; 1920)
   The Moving Picture World. Feb 14, 1920, p1085.
   The Moving Picture World. Jul 10, 1920, p254.

Variety. Jul 2, 1920, p27-28.
Wid's Daily. Jul 4, 1920, p9.

The Slipper Episode (FR; Limur, Jean de; 1938)
Film Daily. May 26, 1938, p6.
The New Masses. Jun 7, 1938, v27, p30.
The New York Times. May 19, 1938, p25.
Variety. Jun 1, 1938, p13.

Small Town Girl (US; Wellman, William A.; 1936)
Film Daily. Apr 2, 1936, p12.
The Films of James Stewart. p33.
The Films of Robert Taylor. p46-47.
Hollywood Reporter. Mar 31, 1936, p3.
Hollywood Spectator. Apr 11, 1936, v11, p23, 25.
Motion Picture Herald. Apr 11, 1936, p54.
The New York Times. Apr 11, 1936, p19.
Newsweek. Apr 18, 1936, v7, p32.
Rob Wagner's Script. Apr 25, 1936, v15, p13.
Time. Apr 20, 1936, v27, p49-50.
Variety. Apr 15, 1936, p16.
William A. Wellman (Thompson). p159-60+.

Smart Money (US; Green, Alfred E.; 1931)
America in the Dark. p166.
The Cinema of Edward G. Robinson. p81-83.
Classics of the Gangster Film. p17-20.
Film Daily. Jun 21, 1931, p10.
The Films of James Cagney. p54-55.
The Great Gangster Pictures. p366.
Hollywood Reporter. May 6, 1931, p3.
Life. Jul 10, 1931, v98, p22.
Motion Picture Herald. May 16, 1931, p34.
The New York Times. Jun 19, 1931, p21.
Outlook and Independent. Jul 8, 1931, v158, p311.
Time. Jun 29, 1931, v17, p20.
Variety. Jun 23, 1931, p18.

Smart Woman (US; La Cava, Gregory; 1931)
Film Daily. Oct 11, 1931, p11.
Hollywood Reporter. Jul 16, 1931, p3.
Motion Picture Herald. Aug 1, 1931, p34.
The New York Times. Oct 12, 1931, p28.
The New York Times. Oct 18, 1931, p5.
Rob Wagner's Script. Dec 5, 1931, v6, p9-10.
Variety. Oct 13, 1931, p14.

Smash Up—The Story of a Woman (US; Heisler, Stuart; 1947)
Commonweal. Apr 25, 1947, v46, p38.
Film Daily. Feb 6, 1947, p7.
The Films of Susan Hayward. p113-16.
Hollywood Reporter. Feb 5, 1947, p3.
Life. Apr 14, 1947, v22, p79-80+.
Motion Picture Herald Product Digest. Feb 15, 1947, p3475.
The New York Times. Apr 11, 1947, p31.
The New Yorker. Apr 19, 1947, v23, p44.
Newsweek. Apr 28, 1947, v29, p95.
Variety. Feb 5, 1947, p12.

Smashing the Spy Ring (US; Cabanne, Christy; 1939)
Film Daily. Jan 19, 1939, p10.
The Great Spy Pictures. p435-36.
Variety. Jan 18, 1939, p12.

Smilin' Through (US; Borzage, Frank; 1941)
Commonweal. Oct 24, 1941, v35, p18.
Film Daily. Sep 12, 1941, p6.
The Films of Jeanette MacDonald and Nelson Eddy. p174-78.
The Films of the Forties. p42-43.
Motion Picture Exhibitor. Sep 17, 1941, p847-48.
Motion Picture Herald Product Digest. Jul 26, 1941, p196.
Motion Picture Herald Product Digest. Sep 13, 1941, p257.
The New York Times. Dec 5, 1941, p29.
Newsweek. Oct 20, 1941, v18, p75.

Time. Oct 20, 1941, v38, p101.
Variety. Sep 17, 1941, p9.

Smilin' Through (US; Franklin, Sidney; 1932)
Film Daily. Oct 15, 1932, p4.
The Films of Fredric March. p89-92.
The Films of Norma Shearer. p186-91.
The Great Romantic Films. p14.
Hollywood Reporter. Sep 8, 1932, p3.
The New York Times. Oct 15, 1932, p13.
Photoplay. Sep 1933, v44, p38-39.
Rob Wagner's Script. Nov 26, 1932, v8, p8.
Time. Oct 24, 1932, v20, p52.
Variety. Oct 18, 1932, p15.

Smiling Along (GB; Banks, Monty; 1938)
Film Daily. Mar 1, 1939, p11.
The New York Times. Feb 20, 1939, p13.
Photoplay. Mar 1939, v53, p53.
Variety. Dec 14, 1938, p14.

The Smiling Lieutenant (French title: Lieutenant Souriant, Le) (US; Lubitsch, Ernst; 1931)
The American Films of Ernst Lubitsch. p124-26.
Chevalier. p96-100.
Claudette Colbert (Quirk). p36-37.
Ernst Lubitsch: A Guide to References and Resources. p107-10.
Film Daily. May 24, 1931, p10.
Film Society Review. Jan 1969, v4, p22.
The Films of the Thirties. p57-59.
Judge. Jun 13, 1931, v100, p22.
Life. Jun 12, 1931, v97, p20.
The Lubitsch Touch. p114-18.
Motion Picture Herald. Jul 11, 1931, p26.
The Nation. Jun 10, 1931, v132, p646.
The New Statesman and Nation. Aug 1, 1931, v2, p141.
The New York Times. Apr 12, 1931, p6.
The New York Times. May 23, 1931, p13.
The New York Times. May 31, 1931, p5.
The New Yorker. May 30, 1931, v7, p60.
Outlook and Independent. Jun 3, 1931, v158, p154.
Photoplay. Jul 1931, v40, p50.
Rob Wagner's Script. Jul 8, 1931, v5, p8.
Selected Film Criticism, 1931-1940. p234-36.
The Spectator. Aug 1, 1931, v147, p153.
Time. Jun 1, 1931, v17, p51.
Variety. May 27, 1931, p56.

Smoky (US; King, Louis; 1946)
Commonweal. Jul 26, 1946, v44, p360.
Film Daily. Jun 14, 1946, p8.
Hollywood Reporter. Jun 13, 1946, p3.
Motion Picture Herald Product Digest. Jun 15, 1946, p3041.
The New York Times. Jun 27, 1946, p29.
The New Yorker. Jul 6, 1946, v22, p43.
Newsweek. Jul 8, 1946, v28, p85.
Time. Jul 8, 1946, v48, p98.
Variety. Jun 19, 1946, p8.

Smouldering Fires (US; Brown, Clarence; 1925)
BFI/Monthly Film Bulletin. Jun 1979, v46, p157.
Film Daily. Dec 7, 1924, .
Life. Jun 4, 1925, v85, p35.
Magill's Survey of Cinema. Silent Films. v3, p999-1001.
The New York Times. Mar 31, 1925, p17.
Photoplay. Feb 1925, v27, p57.
Selected Film Criticism, 1921-1930. p268.
Variety. Apr 1, 1925, p38.

The Snake Pit (US; Litvak, Anatole; 1948)
Canadian Forum. Feb 1949, v28, p255.
Commonweal. Nov 12, 1948, v49, p118.
Film Daily. Nov 3, 1948, p9.
The Films of Olivia de Havilland. p214-18.
Hollywood as Historian. p134-58.
Hollywood Reporter. Nov 4, 1948, p3.

The Hollywood Social Problem Films. p260-61.
Life. Nov 29, 1948, v25, p71-72.
Magill's Survey of Cinema. Series II. v5, p2202-04.
Motion Picture Herald Product Digest. Nov 13, 1948, p4383.
The New Republic. Nov 8, 1948, v119, p28-29.
The New York Times. Nov 5, 1948, p29.
The New Yorker. Nov 13, 1948, v24, p129.
Newsweek. Nov 8, 1948, v32, p92.
Rotarian. Jan 1949, v74, p53.
Saturday Review. Nov 27, 1948, v31, p28-30.
Scholastic. Dec 1, 1948, v53, p28.
Sequence. Aut 1949, n9, p134-35.
Theatre Arts. Mar 1949, v33, p7.
Time. Dec 20, 1948, v52, p44-46.
Variety. Nov 3, 1948, p11.

The Snob (US; Bell, Monta; 1924)
Film Daily. Nov 2, 1924, p10.
Magill's Survey of Cinema. Silent Films. v3, p1002-04.
The Moving Picture World. Nov 8, 1924, p172.
The New York Times. Dec 15, 1924, p14.
Variety. Dec 17, 1924, p36.

Snow White (US; Dawley, J. Searle; Ames, Winthrop; 1916)
Fifty Great American Silent Films, 1912-1920. p69-70.
Magill's Survey of Cinema. Silent Films. v3, p1005-07.
The Moving Picture World. Jan 6, 1916, p97, 139.
The New York Dramatic Mirror. Nov 25, 1916, p25.
The New York Dramatic Mirror. Dec 30, 1916, p26.
Photoplay. Jul 1917, v13, p89.
Selected Film Criticism, 1912-1920. p239-40.
Variety. Dec 29, 1916, p21.
Wid's Daily. Nov 23, 1916, p11.

Snow White and the Seven Dwarfs (US; Hand, David; 1937)
America's Favorite Movies. p40-60.
The Art of Walt Disney. p165-99.
Chestnuts in Her Lap, 1936-1946. p31-33.
Child Life. May 1938, v17, p216-17.
Christian Century. Jul 20, 1938, v55, p886-87.
Christian Science Monitor Magazine. Feb 2, 1938, p8-9.
Cinema, the Magic Vehicle. v1, p275-76.
Commonweal. Jan 28, 1938, v27, p386.
Current History. Jun 1938, v48, p46-47.
Dictionary of Films. p345.
The Disney Films. p25-32.
The Disney Version. p195-97, 213-27.
Esquire. Jun 1938, v9, p150.
The Film Criticism of Otis Ferguson. p209-11.
Film Daily. Dec 27, 1937, p8.
Films and Filming. May 1965, v11, p36.
The Foremost Films of 1938. p49-62.
From Quasimodo to Scarlett O'Hara. p272-74.
Hollywood Reporter. Dec 22, 1937, p3.
The International Dictionary of Films and Filmmakers. v1, p436-38.
Judge. Mar 1938, v114, p29.
Life. Dec 13, 1937, v3, p6+.
Life. Apr 4, 1938, v4, p18-19.
Literary Digest. Jan 22, 1938, v125, p22-23.
London Mercury. Apr 1938, v37, p640.
Lorentz on Film. p148-51.
Magill's Survey of Cinema. Series I. v4, p1575-77.
Motion Picture Herald. Dec 25, 1937, p36.
The Nation. Jan 22, 1938, v146, p108-09.
National Board of Review Magazine. Jan 1938, v13, p10-11.
The New Masses. Jan 25, 1938, v26, p25.
New Republic. Jan 26, 1938, v93, p339.
The New Statesman and Nation. Feb 26, 1938, v15, p327.
The New York Times. Jan 14, 1938, p21.
The New York Times. May 2, 1938, p16.
The New York Times. Jan 3, 1939, p18.
The New Yorker. Jan 15, 1938, v13, p52.

Newsweek. Dec 6, 1937, v10, p33-34.
Newsweek. Jan 17, 1938, v11, p24.
Photoplay. Apr 1938, v52, p22-23.
Popular Science. Jan 1938, v132, p50-52+.
Reader's Digest. Jun 1938, v32, p25-26.
Rob Wagner's Script. Jan 8, 1938, v18, p14.
Saint Nicholas. Dec 1937, v65, p47.
Scholastic. Jan 22, 1938, v31, p8.
Scribner's Magazine. Mar 1938, v103, p65-66.
Selected Film Criticism, 1931-1940. p237-38.
The Spectator. Mar 4, 1938, v160, p359.
Stage. Feb 1938, v15, p26-29.
Studio. May 1939, v17, p198.
The Tatler. Mar 2, 1938, v147, p374.
Time. Dec 27, 1937, v30, p19-20.
Time. Apr 24, 1939, v33, p66.
Variety. Dec 29, 1937, p17.
Village Voice. Aug 2, 1973, v18, p71+.
Walt Disney: A Guide to References and Resources. p15-17.
Walt Disney: An American Original. p130-45.
World Film News. Apr 1938, v3, p36.

So Big (US; Wellman, William A.; 1932)
Bette Davis: Her Films and Career. p26-27.
Canadian Forum. Oct 1932, v13, p37.
Film Daily. May 1, 1932, p11.
The Films of Barbara Stanwyck. p78-79.
Hollywood Reporter. Mar 3, 1932, p2.
Motion Picture Herald. Mar 19, 1932, p42.
The New York Times. Apr 30, 1932, p19.
The New Yorker. May 7, 1932, v8, p63.
Starring Miss Barbara Stanwyck. p41-42.
Time. Apr 25, 1932, v19, p29.
Variety. May 3, 1932, p14.
William A. Wellman (Thompson). p121-25.

So Dear to My Heart (US; Schuster, Harold; 1948)
Collier's. Feb 19, 1949, v123, p62+.
Commonweal. Feb 11, 1949, v49, p448.
The Disney Films. p85-88.
Film Daily. Dec 13, 1948, p6.
Hollywood Reporter. Dec 8, 1948, p4.
Motion Picture Herald Product Digest. Dec 11, 1948, p4418.
The New York Times. Jan 31, 1949, p14.
The New Yorker. Feb 5, 1949, v24, p76.
Newsweek. Feb 7, 1949, v33, p85.
Time. Jan 24, 1949, v53, p84+.
Variety. Dec 8, 1948, p11.
Walt Disney: A Guide to References and Resources. p37-38.

So Ends Our Night (US; Cromwell, John; 1941)
Commonweal. Feb 28, 1941, v33, p476.
Film Daily. Jan 27, 1941, p7.
The Films of Fredric March. p169-71.
Hollywood Reporter.
The London Times. Apr 18, 1941, p6.
Magill's Survey of Cinema. Series II. v5, p2208-10.
Motion Picture Exhibitor. Jan 22, 1941, p681.
The New York Times. Feb 28, 1941, p17.
The New York Times. Mar 2, 1941, sec9, p5.
Newsweek. Feb 24, 1941, 17, p58.
Scholastic. Feb 3, 1941, v38, p32.
Scribner's Commentator. May 1941, v10, p108.
Time. Feb 10, 1941, v37, p70-71.
Variety. Jan 29, 1941, p18.

So Proudly We Hail! (US; Sandrich, Mark; 1943)
Agee on Film. v1, p52-53.
Claudette Colbert (Quirk). p127-30.
Commonweal. Sep 17, 1943, v38, p538.
Film Daily. Jun 22, 1943, p6.
The Films of World War II. p149-50.
Guts & Glory. p218.
Hollywood Reporter. Jun 23, 1943, p3.
Life. Oct 4, 1943, v15, p69-72+.

Motion Picture Herald Product Digest. Jun 26, 1943, p1385.
The New Republic. Sep 27, 1943, v109, p426.
The New York Times. Sep 10, 1943, p29.
Newsweek. Sep 20, 1943, v22, p104.
Time. Sep 27, 1943, v42, p94+.
Variety. Jun 23, 1943, p24.

So Red the Rose (US; Vidor, King; 1935)
Canadian Magazine. Dec 1935, v84, p42.
Canadian Magazine. Jan 1936, v85, p31.
Esquire. Jan 1936, v5, p156.
Film Daily. Nov 9, 1935, p7.
Hollywood Reporter. Nov 4, 1935, p3.
Judge. Dec 1935, v109, p16, 31.
Literary Digest. Nov 23, 1935, v120, p26.
Motion Picture Herald. Nov 16, 1935, p63.
The Nation. Dec 18, 1935, v141, p724.
The New Masses. Dec 10, 1935, v17, p29-30.
The New York Times. Nov 28, 1935, p39.
The New Yorker. Nov 30, 1935, v11, p73-74.
Newsweek. Nov 30, 1935, v6, p27-28.
Scholastic. Jan 18, 1936, v27, p28.
Time. Dec 2, 1935, v26, p40.
Variety. Dec 4, 1935, p15.

So This Is Africa (US; Cline, Edward; 1933)
Film Daily. Apr 22, 1933, p4.
Hollywood Reporter. Jan 19, 1933, p2.
Motion Picture Herald. Jan 28, 1933, p24.
The New York Times. Apr 24, 1933, p11.

So This Is London (US; Blystone, John G.; 1930)
Exhibitors Herald-World. May 31, 1930, p123-24.
Film Daily. May 25, 1930, p17.
Judge. Jul 12, 1930, v99, p21.
The New York Times. May 24, 1930, p21.
The New York Times. Jun 1, 1930, p5.
The New Yorker. May 31, 1930, v6, p61.
Rob Wagner's Script. Jun 28, 1930, v3, p10.
Time. Jun 16, 1930, v15, p23.
Variety. May 28, 1930, p21.
Will Rogers in Hollywood. p108.

So This is New York (US; Fleischer, Rich; 1948)
Commonweal. Jun 25, 1948, v48, p260.
Film Daily. May 10, 1948, p10.
Motion Picture Herald Product Digest. May 15, 1948, p4161.
Stanley Kramer, Film Maker. p27-34.
Time. May 10, 1948, v51, p100.
Variety. May 12, 1948, p8.

So This Is Paris (US; Lubitsch, Ernst; 1926)
The Cinema of Ernst Lubitsch. p93-104.
Ernst Lubitsch: A Guide to References and Resources. p88-89.
Film Daily. Aug 15, 1926, p6.
The Films of Myrna Loy. p46.
Magill's Survey of Cinema. Silent Films. v3, p1008-12.
The Moving Picture World. Sep 4, 1926, p41.
The New York Times. Aug 22, 1926, sec7, p2.
The New York Times. Aug 16, 1926, p10.
Photoplay. Sep 1926, v30, p55.
Selected Film Criticism, 1921-1930. p268.
Spellbound in Darkness. p323-24.
Variety. Aug 18, 1926, p58.

Soak the Rich (US; Hecht, Ben; MacArthur, Charles; 1936)
Esquire. Apr 1936, v5, p104.
Film Daily. Feb 6, 1936, p9.
Hollywood Spectator. Feb 15, 1936, v10, p8.
Motion Picture Herald. Feb 15, 1936, p48.
New Theatre. Mar 1936, v3, p33.
The New York Times. Feb 5, 1936, p14.
The New York Times. Aug 25, 1935, p2.
The New York Times. Oct 27, 1935, p5.
The New Yorker. Feb 15, 1936, v11, p58.

Rob Wagner's Script. Feb 15, 1936, v15, p10.
The Tatler. Mar 18, 1936, v139, p512.
Variety. Feb 12, 1936, p18.

The Social Lion (US; Sutherland, Edward; 1930)
Exhibitors Herald-World. Jun 21, 1930, p70.
Film Daily. Jun 15, 1930, p10.
Judge. Jul 12, 1930, v99, p21, 29.
Life. Jul 4, 1930, v95, p17.
The New York Times. Jun 14, 1930, p9.
The New Yorker. Jun 21, 1930, v6, p71-72.
Pictures Will Talk. p33-34.
Rob Wagner's Script. Jul 12, 1930, v3, p11.
Time. Jun 30, 1930, v15, p23.
Variety. Jun 18, 1930, p37.

The Social Secretary (US; Emerson, John; 1916)
The Moving Picture World. Sep 16, 1916, p1821, 1889.
The New York Dramatic Mirror. Sep 9, 1916, p27.
Variety. Sep 15, 1916, p26.
Wid's Daily. Sep 1916, p843.

Soil (USSR; Dovzhenko, Alexander; 1930)
Film Daily. Oct 19, 1930, p11.
From Quasimodo to Scarlett O'Hara. p126.
Judge. Nov 15, 1930, v99, p19.
The Nation. Oct 29, 1930, v131, p480, 482.
National Board of Review Magazine. Dec 1930, v5, p9.
The New York Times. Oct 21, 1930, p34.
The New York Times. Oct 26, 1930, p5.
The New York Times. Oct 21, 1930, p34.
The New York Times. Oct 26, 1930, p5.
Outlook and Independent. Oct 29, 1930, v156, p353.
Variety. Oct 22, 1930, p35.

The Soil Is Thirsty (Russian title: Zemlya Zhazhdyat; Also titled: The Earth Thirsts) (USSR; Raizman, Yuli; 1930)
Film Daily. May 8, 1932, p10.
Kino. p282-83.
The New York Times. May 6, 1932, p15.
The New Yorker. May 14, 1932, v8, p50.

The Soldier and the Lady *See* Michael Strogoff

Soldiers of Fortune (US; Dwan, Allan; 1919)
Exhibitor's Trade Review. Nov 15, 1919, p2057.
Motion Picture News. Nov 22, 1919, p3790.
The Moving Picture World. Nov 22, 1919, p453-54.
The New York Times. Nov 24, 1919, p13.
Variety. Nov 14, 1919, p59.
Wid's Daily. Nov 16, 1919, p9.

Some Like It Hot (Also titled: Rhythm Romance) (US; Archainbaud, George; 1939)
Commonweal. Jun 2, 1939, v30, p161.
Film Daily. May 9, 1939, p6.
Hollywood Reporter. May 6, 1939, p3.
Motion Picture Herald. May 13, 1939, p40.
The New York Times. May 25, 1939, p31.
Rob Wagner's Script. May 27, 1939, v21, p22.
Variety. May 10, 1939, p14.

Something to Sing About (US; Schertzinger, Victor; 1937)
Film Daily. Aug 31, 1937, p7.
The Films of James Cagney. p121-24.
Hollywood Reporter. Aug 27, 1937, p3.
Hollywood Spectator. Sep 11, 1937, v12, p23-25.
Motion Picture Herald. Sep 4, 1937, p39.
The New Masses. Oct 5, 1937, v25, p29.
The New York Times. Sep 21, 1937, p29.
The New Yorker. Sep 25, 1937, v13, p65.
Rob Wagner's Script. Sep 25, 1937, v18, p6.
Scribner's Magazine. Dec 1937, v102, p51.
The Spectator. Feb 8, 1938, v160, p271.

Time. Sep 25, 1937, v30, p36.
Variety. Sep 1, 1937, p22.

Somewhere I'll Find You (US; Ruggles, Wesley; 1941)
Chestnuts in Her Lap. p84-85.
Commonweal. Sep 11, 1942, v36, p497.
Film Daily. Aug 6, 1942, p12.
The Films of Clark Gable. p206-07.
The Films of Lana Turner. p114-17.
Hollywood Reporter.
The London Times. Dec 21, 1942, p8.
Motion Picture Exhibitor. Aug 12, 1942, p1065-66.
Motion Picture Herald Product Digest. Aug 8, 1941, p825-26.
Musician. Sep 1942, v47, p154.
The New York Times. Aug 28, 1942, p22.
The New Yorker. Aug 19, 1942, v18, p37.
Time. Sep 14, 1942, v40, p94-95.
Variety. Aug 5, 1942, p8.

Somewhere in the Night (US; Mankiewicz, Joseph L.; 1946)
Commonweal. Jun 28, 1946, v44, p261.
Film Daily. May 7, 1946, p8.
Hollywood Reporter. May 5, 1946, p3.
Joseph L. Mankiewicz. p36-40.
Motion Picture Herald Product Digest. May 11, 1946, p2986.
The New York Times. Jun 13, 1946, p24.
The New Yorker. Jun 29, 1946, v22, p64+.
Newsweek. Jun 24, 1946, v27, p94+.
Time. Jun 24, 1946, v47, p101.
Variety. May 8, 1946, p8.

Son of Frankenstein (US; Lee, Rowland V.; 1939)
Boris Karloff and His Films. p115-18.
Classics of the Horror Film. p48-49.
Film Daily. Jan 31, 1939, p8.
Hollywood Reporter. Jan 13, 1939, p3.
Hollywood Spectator. Jan 21, 1939, v13, p10-11.
Horrors! p147-51.
Monsters from the Movies. p36-37.
Motion Picture Herald. Jan 21, 1939, p40-41.
The New York Times. Jan 30, 1939, p9.
The Spectator. Mar 10, 1939, v162, p404.
Time. Jan 23, 1939, v33, p27.
Variety. Jan 18, 1939, p12.

Son of Fury (US; Cromwell, John; 1942)
Commonweal. Feb 6, 1942, v35, p394.
Film Daily. Jan 6, 1942, p7.
The Films of Tyrone Power. p122-25.
Hollywood Reporter. Jan 5, 1942, p3.
Motion Picture Herald Product Digest. Jan 10, 1942, p449.
The New York Times. Jan 30, 1942, p23.
Newsweek. Feb 2, 1942, v19, p61.
Time. Feb 2, 1942, v39, p55.
Variety. Jul 7, 1942, p44.

The Son of Mongolia (Russian title: Syn Mongolii)
   (USSR; Trauberg, Ilya; 1936)
Dictionary of Films. p364.
Film Daily. Nov 24, 1936, p7.
Kino. p325.
Motion Picture Herald. Dec 19, 1936, p58.
The Nation. Dec 5, 1936, v143, p677-78.
The New Masses. Nov 8, 1936, v21, p29.
The New York Times. Nov 21, 1936, p21.

Son of the Gods (US; Lloyd, Frank; 1930)
Exhibitors Herald-World. Feb 8, 1930, p34.
Film Daily. Feb 2, 1930, p8.
The Film Spectator. Feb 15, 1930, v9, p22.
Judge. Feb 22, 1930, v98, p21.
Life. Mar 14, 1930, v95, p20.
The Nation. Feb 19, 1930, v130, p226.
The New York Times. Jan 31, 1930, p24.

The New Yorker. Feb 8, 1930, v5, p71.
Outlook and Independent. Feb 19, 1930, v154, p313.

The Son of the Sheik (US; Fitzmaurice, George; 1926)
Classics of the Silent Screen. p74-75.
Film Daily. Aug 1, 1926, p5.
Life. Aug 19, 1926, v88, p24.
Magill's Survey of Cinema. Silent Films. v3, p1013-16.
The New York Times. Jul 26, 1926, p13.
Photoplay. Oct 1926, v30, p53.
Rob Wagner's Script. Jun 11, 1938, v19, p11.
Selected Film Criticism, 1921-1930. p269.
Variety. Jul 14, 1926, p16.

The Son-Daughter (US; Brown, Clarence; 1932)
Film Daily. Dec 31, 1932, p4.
Hollywood Reporter. Dec 8, 1932, p3.
Judge. Feb 1933, v104, p18-19.
The New York Times. Jan 2, 1933, p29.
Rob Wagner's Script. Dec 17, 1932, v8, p10-11.
Time. Jan 9, 1933, v21, p37.
Variety. Jan 3, 1933, p27.

A Song is Born (US; Hawks, Howard; 1948)
Film Daily. Aug 25, 1948, p5.
Hollywood Reporter. Aug 25, 1948, p3.
Motion Picture Herald Product Digest. Sep 4, 1948, p4302.
The New Republic. Nov 8, 1948, v119, p29.
The New York Times. Oct 20, 1948, p37.
The New Yorker. Oct 30, 1948, v24, p73.
Newsweek. Nov 1, 1948, v32, p80.
Samuel Goldwyn Presents. p258-69.
Time. Nov 1, 1948, v52, p92.
Variety. Aug 25, 1948, p8.

Song O' My Heart (US; Borzage, Frank; 1930)
Commonweal. Apr 2, 1930, v11, p621-22.
Exhibitors Herald-World. Mar 15, 1930, p35.
Film Daily. Mar 16, 1930, p8.
Life. Mar 28, 1930, v95, p18.
Literary Digest. Apr 26, 1930, v105, p17-18.
The Nation. Apr 16, 1930, v130, p465.
The New York Times. Mar 12, 1930, p32.
The New Yorker. Mar 22, 1930, v6, p53.
Outlook and Independent. Mar 26, 1930, v154, p513.
Time. Mar 24, 1930, v15, p60.
Variety. Mar 19, 1930, p20.

The Song of Bernadette (US; King, Henry; 1943)
Agee on Film. v1, p72-73, 341-42.
Around Cinemas. p257-60.
Commonweal. Feb 11, 1944, v39, p421-22.
Film Daily. Dec 27, 1943, p3.
The Films of Jennifer Jones. p37-42.
Hollywood Reporter. Dec 22, 1943, p3.
Magill's Survey of Cinema. Series I. v4, p1581-83.
Motion Picture Herald Product Digest. Dec 25, 1943, p1685-86.
The Nation. Jan 29, 1944, v158, p137.
The New Republic. Mar 6, 1944, v110.
The New York Times. Jan 27, 1944, p15.
The New Yorker. Jan 29, 1944, v19, p44.
Newsweek. Feb 7, 1944, v23, p75.
Saturday Review. Feb 19, 1944, p14.
Time. Feb 7, 1944, v43, p54.
Variety. Dec 22, 1943, p12.
Vincent Price Unmasked. p159-61.

Song of Ceylon (GB; Wright, Basil; 1935)
Cinema Quarterly. Sum 1934, v2, p231-32.
Cinema Quarterly. Wint 1935, v3, p109-10.
A Critical History of the British Cinema. p137.
Dictionary of Films. p348.
The Documentary Tradition. p101-03.
International Dictionary of Films and Filmmakers. v1, p440-41.

The New York Times. Aug 16, 1937, p15.
Quarterly Review of Film Studies. Fall 1980, v5, p459-77.
The Spectator. Oct 4, 1935, v155, p506.
Variety. Aug 18, 1937, p39.

The Song of Freedom (GB; Wills, J. Elder; 1936)
Film Daily. Jul 15, 1938, p10.
Graham Greene on Film. p103.
Motion Picture Herald. Sep 5, 1936, p43.
The New Statesman and Nation. Sep 26, 1936, v12, p428.
The Spectator. Sep 25, 1936, v157, p495.
Variety. Sep 9, 1936, p17.

Song of Love (US; Brown, Clarence; 1947)
Commonweal. Oct 24, 1947, v47, p42.
Film Daily. Jul 21, 1947, p10.
The Films of Katharine Hepburn. p134-38.
Hollywood Reporter. Jul 21, 1947, p3.
Motion Picture Herald Product Digest. Jul 26, 1947, p3745.
The Nation. Nov 8, 1947, v165, p511.
The New York Times. Oct 10, 1947, p31.
The New York Times Magazine. Aug 17, 1947, p24-25.
The New Yorker. Oct 11, 1947, v23, p102.
Scholastic. Oct 13, 1947, v51, p44.
Theatre Arts. Nov 1947, v31, p52.
Time. Oct 13, 1947, v50, p105.
Variety. Jul 23, 1947, p10.

The Song of Songs (US; Mamoulian, Rouben; 1933)
Around Cinemas. p95-97.
Cinema Quarterly. Aut 1933, v2, p44.
Commonweal. Aug 4, 1933, v18, p349.
Film Daily. Jul 22, 1933, p3.
The Films of Marlene Dietrich. p 108-11.
Hollywood Reporter. Jun 12, 1933, p4.
Literary Digest. Aug 5, 1933, v116, p22.
Mamoulian (Milne). p63-71.
Motion Picture Herald. Jul 1, 1933, p28-29.
The Nation. Aug 30, 1933, v137, p250+.
National Board of Review Magazine. Sep-Oct 1933, v8, p8-10.
New Outlook. Sep 1933, v162, p45.
The New Republic. Sep 6, 1933, v76, p102.
The New York Times. Jul 20, 1933, p22.
The New Yorker. Jul 29, 1933, v9, p40.
Newsweek. Jul 29, 1933, v1, p30.
Pictorial Review. Oct 1933, v35, p70.
Rob Wagner's Script. Aug 5, 1933, v9, p8.
The Spectator. Sep 29, 1933, v151, p401.
Time. Jul 31, 1933, v22, p19.
Vanity Fair. Sep 1933, v41, p45.
Variety. Jul 25, 1933, p14.

The Song of the Eagle (US; Murphy, Ralph; 1933)
Film Daily. Apr 27, 1933, p4.
Hollywood Reporter. Apr 13, 1933, p7.
Motion Picture Herald. Apr 29, 1933, p26.
The New York Times. Apr 29, 1933, p14.
Rob Wagner's Script. Apr 29, 1933, v9, p8.
Time. May 8, 1933, v21, p40.
Variety. May 2, 1933, p13.

Song of the Flame (US; Crosland, Alan; 1930)
Commonweal. May 28, 1930, v12, p109-10.
Exhibitors Herald-World. May 17, 1930, p41.
Film Daily. Apr 27, 1930, p13.
The Film Spectator. Jun 7, 1930, v9, p18.
Judge. Jun 7, 1930, v98, p23.
The Nation. May 28, 1930, v130, p632.
The New York Times. May 7, 1930, p24.
The New Yorker. May 17, 1930, v6, p87.
Outlook and Independent. May 21, 1930, v155, p110.
Time. May 19, 1930, v15, p62.
Variety. May 14, 1930, p19.

Song of the Heroes (Russian title: Pesn o Geroyakh; Also titled: A Song About Heroes) (USSR; Ivens, Joris; 1932)
Joris Ivens, Film-Maker. p77-78.
The New Masses. Mar 31, 1936, v19, p29.

Song of the Shirt (US; 1908)
The Moving Picture World. Nov 28, 1908, p423.
Selected Film Criticism, 1896-1911. p94.

Song of the South (US; Disney, Walt; 1946)
The Disney Films. p73-78.
Film Daily. Nov 1, 1946, p7.
The Hollywood Musical. p276.
Hollywood Reporter. Oct 29, 1946, p3.
Motion Picture Herald Product Digest. Nov 2, 1946, p3285.
The New York Times. Nov 28, 1946, p40.
The New Yorker. Nov 30, 1946, v22, p88.
Toms, Coons, Mulattoes, Mammies, & Bucks. p191-92.
Variety. Nov 6, 1946, p18.
Walt Disney: A Guide to References and Resources. p31-33.

Song of the Streets (FR; Trivas, Victor; 1939)
Commonweal. Sep 8, 1939, v30, p459.
Film Daily. Sep 14, 1939, p11.
Motion Picture Herald. Aug 26, 1939, p56.
The New Masses. Sep 5, 1939, v32, p30-31.
The New York Times. Sep 5, 1939, p21.

The Song of the Wildwood Flute (US; Griffith, D.W.; 1910)
A History of Narrative Film. p10-11.
The New York Dramatic Mirror. Nov 30, 1910, p30.
Selected Film Criticism, 1896-1911. p94-95.

A Song to Remember (US; Vidor, Charles; 1945)
Commonweal. Feb 16, 1945, v41, p449.
Etude. Dec 1944, v67, p680-82.
Film Daily. Jan 18, 1945, p8.
Hollywood Reporter. Jan 18, 1945, p3.
Life. Feb 5, 1945, v18, p71.
The New York Times Magazine. Dec 31, 1944, p20-21.
The New Yorker. Feb 3, 1945, v25, p94-95.
Paul Muni: His Life and His Films. p199-204.
Scholastic. Nov 27, 1944, v45, p48.
Theatre Arts. Dec 1944, v28, p725-27.
Time. Feb 12, 1945, v45, p52+.
Variety. Jan 24, 1945, p10.

Sons of the Desert (Also titled: Fraternally Yours) (US; Seiter, William A; 1934)
Cinema Texas Program Notes. Dec 4, 1976, v11, p67-73.
Film Daily. Jan 6, 1934, p6.
The Films of Hal Roach. p64-66.
The Films of Laurel and Hardy. p151-54.
Hollywood Reporter. Nov 10, 1933, p3.
Laurel and Hardy. p253-61.
Motion Picture Herald. Jan 20, 1934, p58.
The New York Times. Jan 12, 1934, p29.
Variety. Jan 9, 1934, p16.

Sorority House (US; Farrow, John; 1939)
Commonweal. May 26, 1939, v30, p132.
Film Daily. Apr 24, 1939, p5.
Hollywood Reporter. Apr 19, 1939, p3.
Hollywood Spectator. Apr 29, 1939, v14, p11.
Motion Picture Herald. Apr 22, 1939, p39.
The New York Times. May 18, 1939, p31.
Scholastic. May 27, 1939, v34, p31.
Variety. May 10, 1939, p14.

Sorrowful Jones (US; Lanfield, Sidney; 1949)
Commonweal. Jun 24, 1949, v50, p272.
Film Daily. Apr 19, 1949, p5.
Hollywood Reporter. Apr 12, 1949, p3.
Life. Jun 6, 1949, v26, p129-32.

Motion Picture Herald Product Digest. Aug 16, 1949, p4573.
The New Republic. Jun 20, 1949, v120, p30.
The New York Times. Jun 6, 1949, p15.
The New Yorker. Jun 11, 1949, v25, p84.
Newsweek. Jun 20, 1949, v33, p87.
Rotarian. Oct 1949, v75, p38.
Time. June 27, 1949, v53, p89.
Variety. Apr 13, 1949, p11.

The Sorrows of Satan (US; Griffith, D.W.; 1926)
Film Daily. Nov 14, 1926, p6.
Film Spectator. Apr 30, 1927, v3, p9.
The Films of D.W. Griffith. p220-26.
Magill's Survey of Cinema. Silent Films. v3, p1017-20.
The Moving Picture World. Oct 23, 1926, p502.
The New York Times. Oct 13, 1926, p21.
Selected Film Criticism, 1921-1930. p270-71.
Variety. Oct 20, 1926, p60.

Sorry, Wrong Number (US; Litvak, Anatole; 1948)
Commonweal. Sep 10, 1948, v48, p524.
Film Daily. Jul 27, 1948, p7.
The Films of Barbara Stanwyck. p190-93.
The Films of Burt Lancaster. p39-40.
The Films of the Forties. p242-43.
Hollywood Reporter. Jul 26, 1948, p3.
Life. Aug 23, 1948, v25, p70-72.
Magill's Survey of Cinema. Series II. v5, p2225-27.
Motion Picture Herald Product Digest. Jul 31, 1948, p4257.
The New Republic. Sep 13, 1948, v119, p30.
The New York Times. Sep 2, 1948, p18.
The New Yorker. Sep 11, 1948, v24, p59.
Newsweek. Sep 6, 1948, v32, p75.
Starring Miss Barbara Stanwyck. p211-15.
Time. Sep 20, 1948, v52, p96+.
Variety. Jul 28, 1948, p15.

Sortie des Ouvriers de l'Usine Lumiere (FR; Lumiere, Louis; 1895)
Dictionary of Films. p200-01.
A History of Narrative Film. p10-11.

S.O.S Iceberg (US; Garnett, Tay; 1933)
Cinema Quarterly. Wint 1933-34, v2, p124.
Film Daily. Nov 28, 1933, p4.
Hollywood Reporter. Sep 5, 1933, p4.
Motion Picture Herald. Sep 23, 1933, p33.
The New York Times. Sep 25, 1933, p18.
The New Yorker. Sep 30, 1933, v9, p47.
Newsweek. Sep 30, 1933, v2, p46.
Time. Oct 2, 1933, v 22, p40.
Variety. Sep 26, 1933, p15.

S.O.S.—Tidal Wave (Also titled: SOS—Tidal Wave) (US; Auer, John H.; 1939)
Film Daily. Jun 2, 1939, p6.
Hollywood Reporter. May 25, 1939, p3.
Motion Picture Herald. Jun 3, 1939, p36.
The New York Times. Jun 22, 1939, p19.
The New Yorker. Jul 1, 1939, v15, p57.
Time. Jul 3, 1939, v33, p36.
Variety. Jun 21, 1939, p26.

So's Your Old Man (US; La Cava, Gregory; 1926)
Film Daily. Nov 7, 1926, p8.
The Moving Picture World. Nov 20, 1926, p365.
The New York Times. Nov 1, 1926, p28.
Variety. Nov 3, 1926, p16.
W.C. Fields: A Life on Film. p42-47.

The Soul of Kura-San (US; Le Saint, E.J.; 1916)
The Moving Picture World. Nov 11, 1916, p838, 846.
The New York Dramatic Mirror. Nov 4, 1916, p27.
Photoplay. Dec 1916, v11, p20.
Variety. Nov 3, 1916, p29.
Wid's Daily. Nov 9, 1916, p1085.

Souls at Sea (US; Hathaway, Henry; 1937)
Film Daily. Aug 10, 1937, p6.
The Films of Gary Cooper. p150-52.
Hollywood Reporter. Aug 6, 1937, p3.
Literary Digest. Aug 28, 1937, v124, p29.
Motion Picture Herald. Aug 14, 1937, p58.
Motion Picture Herald. Jan 30, 1937, p16-17.
The New Masses. Aug 31, 1937, v24, p27.
The New Statesman and Nation. Sep 11, 1937, v14, p375.
The New York Times. Aug 10, 1937, p23.
The New Yorker. Aug 21, 1937, v13, p52.
Newsweek. Aug 21, 1937, v10, p24+.
Rob Wagner's Script. Aug 28, 1937, v17, p11.
Scribner's Magazine. Nov 1937, v102, p64.
Sight and Sound. Aut 1937, v6, p139-40.
Time. Aug 23, 1937, v30, p49.
Variety. Aug 11, 1937, p19.
World Film News. Oct 1937, v2, p23.

Souls for Sale (US; Hughes, Rupert; 1923)
Film Daily. Apr 1, 1923, p2.
The New York Times. Apr 9, 1923, p14.
Photoplay. Jun 1923, v24, p65.
Selected Film Criticism, 1921-1930. p271.
Variety. Mar 29, 1923, p33.

Souls on the Road (Japanese title: Rojo no Reikon) (JAPAN; Murata, Minoru; 1921)
Cinema, the Magic Vehicle. v1, p69-71.

Sous la Lune du Maroc (Also titled: Moon Over Morocco) (FR; Duvivier, Julien; 1933)
Motion Picture Herald. Feb 25, 1933, p41.
The Nation. Feb 8, 1933, v136, p158.
The New York Times. Jan 23, 1933, p9.
Variety. Jan 24, 1933, p21.

Sous les Toits de Paris (Also titled: Under the Roofs of Paris) (FR; Clair, René; 1930)
American Film Criticism. p246-47.
BFI/Monthly Film Bulletin. Nov 1977, v44, p247-48.
Cinema, the Magic Vehicle. v1, p175-76.
Close-Up. Jun 1930, v6, p495-98, 509-10.
Close-Up. Oct 1930, v7, p276-78.
Dictionary of Films. p350-51.
Eighty Years of Cinema. p83.
Film Daily. Dec 28, 1930, p11.
From Quasimodo to Scarlett O'Hara. p130-32.
Gotta Sing Gotta Dance. p81-89.
The Great French Films. p239-40.
The International Photographer. Apr 1931, v3, p8, 27.
Lorentz on Film. p64.
Magill's Survey of Cinema. Foreign Language Films. v7, p3223-28.
Motion Picture Herald. Jan 10, 1931, p52.
The Nation. Jan 7, 1931, v132, p25-26.
The Nation (London). Dec 20, 1930, v48, p406-07.
National Board of Review Magazine. Feb 1931, v6, p13.
The New York Times. Dec 16, 1930, p34.
The New Yorker. Dec 27, 1930, v6, p29.
Outlook and Independent. Dec 31, 1930, v156, p712.
René Clair (McGerr). p77-86.
Rob Wagner's Script. Feb 28, 1931, v5, p10.
Saturday Review (London). Dec 20, 1930, v150, p821.
Selected Film Criticism, 1930-1950. p182-85.
The Spectator. Dec 20, 1930, v145, p975.
Time. Dec 29, 1930, v16, p17.
Variety. May 14, 1930, p39.
Variety. Dec 24, 1930, p21.

South Riding (GB; Saville, Victor; 1938)
Commonweal. Aug 19, 1938, v28, p430.
A Critical History of the British Cinema. p89-91.
The Film Criticism of Otis Ferguson. p232.
Film Daily. Jun 29, 1938, p8.

Hollywood Reporter. Jan 22, 1938, p7.
Love in the Film. p141-43.
Motion Picture Herald. Jan 22, 1938, p40.
The New Masses. Jul 12, 1938, v28, p31.
The New Statesman and Nation. Jan 8, 1938, v15, p47.
The New York Times. Aug 2, 1938, p15.
The New Yorker. Jul 30, 1938, v14, p39.
Rob Wagner's Script. Dec 17, 1938, v20, p18-19.
Selected Film Criticism: Foreign Films, 1930-1950. p169-70.
Stage. Oct 1938, v16, p49.
The Tatler. Jan 19, 1938, v147, p98.
Time. Jul 11, 1938, v32, p42.
Variety. Jan 19, 1938, p19.
Variety. Jul 27, 1938, p17.

Southern Mail *See* Courrier-Sud

A Southern Yankee (US; Sedgwick, Edward; 1948)
Film Daily. Aug 9, 1948, p5.
Hollywood Reporter. Aug 6, 1948, p3.
Motion Picture Herald Product Digest. Aug 7, 1948, p4265.
The New York Times. Nov 25, 1948, p47.
Variety. Aug 11, 1948, p8.

The Southerner (Also titled: Hold Autumn in Your Hand)
(US; Renoir, Jean; 1945)
Agee on Film. v1, p166-68.
Commonweal. Jun 1, 1945, v42, p167-68.
Film Daily. May 8, 1945, p10.
Films in Review. Nov 1954, v5, p449-56.
Hollywood Reporter. May 2, 1945, p3.
The International Dictionary of Films and Filmmakers. v1, p442.
Jean Renoir: A Guide to References and Resources. p136-37.
The London Times. Sep 3, 1945, p6.
Magill's Survey of Cinema. Series I. v4, p1594-96.
Motion Picture Exhibitor. May 16, 1945, v24, n2, sec2, p1714.
Motion Picture Herald Product Digest. May 5, 1945, p2433.
The Nation. Jun 9, 1945, v160, p657.
New Movies. May 1945, v20, p3-4.
The New Republic. Sep 10, 1945, v113, p317.
The New York Times. Aug 27, 1945, p22.
The New Yorker. Aug 18, 1945, v21, p57.
Newsweek. Aug 6, 1945, v26, p85.
PM. Aug 27, 1945, p16.
Scholastic. Sep 17, 1945, v42, p32.
Screen Writer. Oct 1945, v1, p1-7.
Selected Film Criticism, 1941-1950. p218-22.
Theatre Arts. May 1945, v29, p277-78.
Theatre Arts. Oct 1945, v29, p580.
Time. May 21, 1945, v45, p96+.
Variety. May 2, 1945, p27.

Spain in Flames (USSR; Amkino; Film Historians, Inc.; 1937)
Commonweal. Mar 5, 1937, v25, p528.
Film Daily. Feb 11, 1937, p11.
Motion Picture Herald. Feb 13, 1937, p36-37.
The Nation. Mar 27, 1937, v144, p340-41.
The New Masses. Feb 9, 1937, v23, p29.
The New York Times. Jan 30, 1937, p21.
Rob Wagner's Script. Mar 13, 1937, v17, p11.
Variety. Feb 3, 1937, p15.

The Spanish Dancer (US; Brenon, Herbert; 1923)
Film Daily. Oct 14, 1923, p5.
The New York Times. Oct 8, 1923, p20.
Photoplay. Dec 1923, v25, p72.
Selected Film Criticism, 1921-1930. p271-72.
Variety. Oct 11, 1923, p26.

The Spanish Earth (US; Ivens, Joris; 1937)
Dictionary of Films. p351-52.
Documentary: History of the Non-Fiction Film. p135-36.
The Documentary Tradition. p146-47, 165-66.
Esquire. Jan 1938, v9, p178.

The Film Criticism of Otis Ferguson. p190-92.
Film Daily. Aug 27, 1937, p16.
Film on the Left. p149-58.
From Quasimodo to Scarlett O'Hara. p262-63.
Hemingway on Film. p33-47.
International Dictionary of Films and Filmmakers. v1, p442-43.
Joris Ivens: Fifty Years of Film-Making. p73-75.
Joris Ivens, Film-Maker. p49-51.
Literary Digest. Sep 11, 1937, v124, p33.
London Mercury. Dec 1937, v37, p198.
Motion Picture Herald. Sep 4, 1937, p39-40.
National Board of Review Magazine. Oct 1937, v12, p16.
The New Masses. Aug 24, 1937, v24, p28.
The New Republic. Sep 1, 1937, v92, p103.
The New Statesman and Nation. Nov 13, 1937, v14, p795.
The New York Times. Aug 21, 1937, p7.
The New Yorker. Aug 21, 1937, v13, p51-52.
Non-Fiction Film: A Critical History. p92-94.
Nonfiction Film Theory and Criticism. p349-75.
The Spectator. Nov 12, 1937, v159, p844.
Time. Aug 23, 1937, v30, p48-49.
Variety. Jul 21, 1937, p5.
World Film News. Dec 1937, v2, p23.

Sparrows (US; Beaudine, William; 1926)
Classics of the Silent Screen. p76-77.
Film Daily. Sep 26, 1926, p6.
Magill's Survey of Cinema. Silent Films. v3, p1020-24.
The Moving Picture World. Oct 9, 1926, p370.
The New York Times. Sep 20, 1926, p21.
Photoplay. Aug 1926, v30, p55.
Selected Film Criticism, 1921-1930. p272.
Variety. Sep 22, 1926, p14.

Spawn of the North (US; Hathaway, Henry; 1938)
Canadian Magazine. Sep 1938, v90, p58.
Commonweal. Sep 9, 1938, v28, p505.
Film Daily. Sep 9, 1938, p15.
The Films of Henry Fonda. p72-73.
The Fondas (Springer). p81-82.
Hollywood Reporter. Aug 16, 1938, p3.
Hollywood Spectator. Sep 3, 1938, v13, p9.
Motion Picture Herald. Aug 20, 1938, p46.
The New York Times. Sep 8, 1938, p27.
Newsweek. Sep 5, 1938, v12, p23.
Rob Wagner's Script. Sep 3, 1938, v20, p10.
Saint Nicholas. Aug 1938, v65, p41+.
The Spectator. Sep 23, 1938, v161, p479.
Time. Sep 5, 1938, v32, p33.
Variety. Aug 24, 1938, p12.
World Film News. Oct 1938, v3, p264-65.

Speak Easily (US; Sedgwick, Edward; 1932)
Film Daily. Aug 20, 1932, p5.
Motion Picture Herald. Aug 27, 1932, p38-39.
The New Outlook. Oct 1932, v161, p38.
The New York Times. Aug 19, 1932, p20.
The New Yorker. Aug 27, 1932, v8, p38.
Rob Wagner's Script. Oct 22, 1932, v8, p8.
Time. Aug 29, 1932, v20, p26.
Variety. Aug 23, 1932, p15.

Special Agent (US; Keighley, William; 1935)
Bette Davis: Her Films and Career. p63.
Canadian Magazine. Nov 1935, v84, p39.
Film Daily. Sep 19, 1935, p6.
Hollywood Reporter. Aug 15, 1935, p4.
Motion Picture Herald. Aug 24, 1935, p55.
The New York Times. Sep 19, 1935, p28.
The New Yorker. Sep 28, 1935, v11, p64.
Time. Sep 30, 1935, v25, p29.
Variety. Sep 25, 1935, p12.

Specter of the Rose (US; Hecht, Ben; 1946)
Ben Hecht: Hollywood Screenwriter. p166-67+.
Commonweal. Jun 28, 1946, v44, p261.
Film Daily. May 20, 1946, p10.
Hollywood Reporter. May 17, 1946, p3.
Magill's Cinema Annual, 1983. p504-07.
Motion Picture Herald Product Digest. May 25, 1946, p3006.
The New York Times. Sep 2, 1946, p12.
The New Yorker. Sep 14, 1946, v22, p102+.
Newsweek. Jul 29, 1946, v28, p77.
Theatre Arts. May 1946, v30, p277-78+.
Time. Jun 24, 1946, v47, p98+.
Variety. May 22, 1946, p10.

Speedy (US; Wilde, Ted; 1928)
Film Daily. Apr 15, 1928, p4.
The Film Spectator. Apr 28, 1928, v5, p10-11.
Harold Lloyd: The King of Daredevil Comedy. p100-07.
Harold Lloyd: The Shape of Laughter. p192-93.
The New York Times. 4Apr 7, 1928, p20.
Selected Film Criticism, 1921-1930. p271-73.
The Silent Clowns. p192-96+.
Variety. Apr 11, 1928, p12.

Spellbound (US; Hitchcock, Alfred; 1945)
Agee on Film. v1, p179-80.
The Art of Alfred Hitchcock. p151-60.
Commonweal. Nov 9, 1945, v43, p95.
Film and the Dream Scene. p104-12.
Film Daily. Oct 31, 1945, p7.
Film Quarterly. Jan 1946, v1, p154-58.
The Films of Alfred Hitchcock. p121-24.
The Films of Gregory Peck. p45-50.
The Films of Ingrid Bergman. p105-09.
High Fidelity and Musical America. Jul 1975, v25, p97-98.
Hitchcock: The First Forty-Four Films. p79-84.
Hitchcock (Truffaut). p163-69+.
Hollywood Reporter. Oct 31, 1945, p3.
Ingrid Bergman. p67-72.
The London Times. May 17, 1946, p6.
Magic and Myth of the Movies. p106-07, 110-15.
Magill's Survey of Cinema. Series I. v4, p1597-1600.
Motion Picture Exhibitor. Nov 14, 1945, v35, n2, sec2, p1827.
Motion Picture Herald Product Digest. Nov 3, 1945, p2701.
The Nation. Nov 10, 1945, v161, p506.
A Neglected Art. p69-70.
New Movies. Nov 1945, v20, p5-6.
The New Republic. Dec 3, 1945, v113, p747.
The New York Times. Nov 2, 1945, p22.
The New Yorker. Nov 3, 1945, v21, p69.
Newsweek. Nov 5, 1945, v26, p104.
Rob Wagner's Script. Nov 17, 1945, v31, p14.
Running Away from Myself. p59-64.
Scholastic. Nov 12, 1945, n47, p29.
Selected Film Criticism, 1941-1950. p222-25.
Surrealism and the Cinema. p55-58.
Theatre Arts. Dec 1945, v29, p707-08.
Time. Nov 5, 1945, v46, p98.
Variety. Oct 15, 1945, p17.

Spendthrift (US; Walsh, Raoul; 1936)
Film Daily. Jul 23, 1936, p7.
The Films of Henry Fonda. p50-51.
Hollywood Reporter. Jun 12, 1936, p3.
Hollywood Spectator. Jun 20, 1936, v11, p11.
Literary Digest. Aug 1, 1936, v122, p19-20.
Motion Picture Herald. Jun 20, 1936, p66.
The New York Times. Jul 23, 1936, p24.
The New Yorker. Aug 1, 1936, v12, p39.
Rob Wagner's Script. Jul 25, 1936, v15, p11.
Variety. Jul 29, 1936, p14.

The Spider (US; Menzies, William Cameron; MacKenna,
   Kenneth; 1931)
Film Daily. Aug 16, 1932, p6.

Hollywood Spectator. Sep 12, 1931, v12, p9-10.
Judge. Oct 17, 1931, v101, p18.
The New York Times. Sep 5, 1931, p7.
Variety. Sep 8, 1931, p15.

The Spiders (Germen titles: Spinnen, Die; Golden See,
   Der; Brillantenschiff, Das; Also titled: The Golden
   Lake; Diamond Ship) (GER; Lang, Fritz; 1919;
   1920)
The Cinema of Fritz Lang. p21.
The Films of Fritz Lang. p18, 76-81.
Fritz Lang: A Guide to References and Resources. p24-26, 27-
30.
Fritz Lang (Eisner). p32-42.
The Haunted Screen. p237-40.

Spies (German title: Spione) (GER; Lang, Fritz; 1928)
BFI/Monthly Film Bulletin. May 1976, v43, p112.
Cinema and Society. p137-38, 143+.
The Cinema of Fritz Lang. p70-76.
Cinema, the Magic Vehicle. v1, p153-54.
Film Daily. Mar 10, 1929, p8.
The Films of Fritz Lang. p142-46.
Fritz Lang: A Guide to References and Resources. p52-55.
Fritz Lang (Armour). p130-33, 145-46.
Fritz Lang (Eisner). p95-105.
Fritz Lang: The Image and the Look. p71-77+.
From Caligari to Hitler. p150-51.
The Haunted Screen. p246-47, 353.
Magill's Survey of Cinema. Silent Films. v3, p1025-27.
The New York Times. May 5, 1929, p29.
Variety. Mar 6, 1929, p26.
Variety. Sep 27, 1978, p5.

Spinnen, Die *See* The Spiders

The Spiral Staircase (US; Siodmak, Robert; 1946)
Agee on Film. v1, p192-93.
Commonweal. Feb 22, 1946, v43, p480.
Film Daily. Jan 10, 1946, p6.
The Films of the Forties. p162-63.
Hollywood Reporter. Jan 4, 1946, p3.
Hollywood Review. Jan 7, 1946, v36, p1-2.
Life. Feb 18, 1946, v20, p69-71.
Magill's Survey of Cinema. Series I. v4, p1601-03.
Motion Picture Herald Product Digest. Jan 5, 1946, p2785.
The Nation. Mar 23, 1946, v162, p354.
The New York Times. Feb 7, 1946, p29.
The New Yorker. Feb 9, 1946, v21, p80.
Newsweek. Jan 28, 1946, v27, p94-95.
Selected Film Criticism, 1941-1950. p225-28.
Time. Feb 4, 1946, v47, p90.
Variety. Jan 9, 1946, p79.

The Spirit of Culver (US; Santley, Joseph; 1939)
Film Daily. Mar 1, 1939, p10.
Hollywood Reporter. Feb 25, 1939, p3.
Hollywood Spectator. Mar 4, 1939, v13, p9-10.
Motion Picture Herald. Mar 4, 1939, p39, 42.
The New York Times. Mar 9, 1939, p18.
Photoplay. May 1939, v53, p62.
Rob Wagner's Script. Apr 1, 1939, v21, p16.
Scholastic. Mar 18, 1939, v34, p30.
Variety. Mar 1, 1939, p15.

Spirit of '76 (US; Siegmann, George; 1917)
Fifty Great American Silent Films, 1912-1920. p80-81.
The Moving Picture World. Aug 6, 1921, p634.
The New York Dramatic Mirror. Jul 7, 1917, p16.
Photoplay. Aug 1918, v14, p75.
Photoplay. Oct 1921, v20, p94.
Selected Film Criticism, 1912-1920. p241-42.

Spite Marriage (US; Sedgwick, Edward; 1929)
BFI/Monthly Film Bulletin. Mar 1977, v44, p56.
Buster Keaton (Robinson). p169-75.

The Film Career of Buster Keaton. p75-78.
Film Daily. Mar 31, 1929, p8.
Life. Apr 19, 1929, v93, p29, 40.
The New York Times. Mar 25, 1929, p32.
Photoplay. Apr 1929, v35, p54.
Variety. Mar 27, 1929, p12.

Spitfire (US; Cromwell, John; 1934)
Film Daily. Feb 23, 1934, p6.
The Films of Katharine Hepburn. p55-57.
Hollywood Reporter. Feb 7, 1934, p3.
Motion Picture Herald. Feb 24, 1934, p39.
The Nation. Mar 24, 1934, v138, p342.
The New York Times. Mar 9, 1934, p22.
Newsweek. Mar 17, 1934, v3, p38.
Variety. Mar 13, 1934, p16.

Spitfire (Also titled: First of the Few) (GB; Howard,
   Leslie; 1942)
Commonweal. Jun 25, 1943, v38, p252.
Film Daily. Apr 22, 1943, p9.
The Films of David Niven. p70-71.
Hollywood Reporter. Apr 12, 1943, p3.
The London Times. Aug 20, 1942, p2.
Magill's Survey of Cinema. Series II. v4, p2235-37.
Motion Picture Exhibitor. May 5, 1943, v29, n26, sec2, p1258.
Motion Picture Herald Product Digest. Sep 5, 1942, p889.
Motion Picture Herald Product Digest. Apr 5, 1943, p1275.
The New York Times. Jun 14, 1943, p13.
The New York Times. Jun 20, 1943, sec2, p3.
The New Yorker. Jun 19, 1943, v19, p50.
Time. Jun 28, 1943, v41, p54+.
Variety. Sep 2, 1942, p18.

Splendor (US; Nugent, Elliott; 1935)
Film Daily. Nov 19, 1935, p8.
The Films of David Niven. p32.
Hollywood Reporter. Nov 20, 1935, p10.
Hollywood Spectator. Dec 7, 1935, v10, p13.
The New York Times. Nov 23, 1935, p23.
The New Yorker. Nov 30, 1935, v11, p74.
Newsweek. Nov 30, 1935, v6, p28.
Rob Wagner's Script. Dec 7, 1935, v14, p10-11.
Samuel Goldwyn Presents. p155-57.
The Tatler. Jan 22, 1936, v139, p144.
Variety. Nov 27, 1935, p14.

The Spoilers (US; Campbell, Colin; 1914)
Aspects of American Film History Prior to 1920. p37-39.
Classics of the Silent Screen. p16-19.
Magill's Survey of Cinema. Silent Films. v3, p1028-30.
The Moving Picture World. Apr 11, 1914, p186.
The Moving Picture World. Jul 25, 1914, p624.
The New York Dramatic Mirror. Mar 25, 1914, p30.
The New York Dramatic Mirror. Apr 15, 1914, p31.
The New York Dramatic World. Apr 1, 1914, p32.
Selected Film Criticism, 1912-1920. p242-43.
Variety. Apr 17, 1914, p22.

The Spoilers (US; Carewe, Edwin; 1930)
Exhibitors Herald-World. Sep 13, 1930, p39.
Film Daily. Sep 21, 1930, p31.
The Films of Gary Cooper. p80-82.
Judge. Oct 25, 1930, v99, p23.
The New York Times. Sep 20, 1930, p15.
Photoplay. Nov 1930, v38, p53.
Selected Film Criticism, 1920-1931. p273-74.
Those Fabulous Movie Years: The 30s. p16-17.
Time. Oct 6, 1930, v16, p34.
Variety. Sep 24, 1930, p23.

The Spoilers (US; Enright, Ray; 1942)
Commonweal. Jun 12, 1942, v36, p183.
The Complete Films of John Wayne. p119-21.
Film Daily. Apr 13, 1942, p5.
The Films of Marlene Dietrich. p160-63.

Hollywood Reporter. Apr 10, 1942, p3.
Motion Picture Herald Product Digest. Apr 18, 1942, p609.
The New York Times. May 22, 1942, p27.
Time. Apr 27, 1942, v39, p86+.
Variety. Apr 15, 1942, p8.

Sporting Blood (US; Brabin, Charles; 1931)
Film Daily. Aug 16, 1931, p10.
The Films of Clark Gable. p125.
Hollywood Reporter. Jul 9, 1931, p3.
Hollywood Spectator. Sep 12, 1931, v12, p23.
Hollywood Spectator. Sep 26, 1931, v12, p10-11.
Life. Sep 4, 1931, v98, p21.
Motion Picture Herald. Jul 18, 1931, p38.
The New York Times. Aug 15, 1931, p18.
The New York Times. Aug 23, 1931, p5.
Outlook and Independent. Aug 26, 1931, v158, p534.
Rob Wagner's Script. Oct 3, 1931, v6, p10.
Time. Aug 24, 1931, v18, p21.
Variety. Aug 18, 1931, p17.

Spring Madness (US; Simon, S. Sylvan; 1938)
Commonweal. Dec 16, 1938, v29, p216.
The Film Criticism of Otis Ferguson. p241-42.
Film Daily. Nov 15, 1938, p8.
Hollywood Reporter. Nov 9, 1938, p3.
Hollywood Spectator. Nov 26, 1938, v13, p10-11.
Motion Picture Herald. Nov 12, 1938, p40.
The New Masses. Dec 20, 1938, v29, p30.
The New Republic. Dec 14, 1938, v97, p174.
The New York Times. Dec 1, 1938, p29.
The New Yorker. Dec 3, 1938, v14, p101.
Rob Wagner's Script. Dec 10, 1938, v20, p11.
Time. Nov 28, 1938, v32, p51.
Variety. Nov 16, 1938, p15.

Springtime in the Rockies (US; Kane, Joseph; 1937)
Film Daily. Nov 23, 1937, p22.
Motion Picture Herald. Nov 27, 1937, p54.
Variety. Nov 24, 1937, p16.

The Spy in Black *See* U-Boat 29

Squadrone Bianco, Lo (Also titled: The White Squadron)
   (IT; Genina, Augusto; 1936)
Film Daily. Dec 15, 1939, p8.
Graham Greene on Film. p181, 184.
Motion Picture Herald. Dec 26, 1936, p56.
The New Statesman and Nation. Nov 27, 1937, v14, p875.
The New York Times. Dec 1, 1939, p27.
The Spectator. Dec 3, 1937, v159, p992.
Variety. Nov 11, 1936, p15.

The Squaw Man (US; DeMille, Cecil B.; Apfel, Oscar C.;
   1914)
Behind the Screen. p164.
The Films of Cecil B. DeMille. p20-26.
Magill's Survey of Cinema. Silent Films. v3, p1031-34.
The Moving Picture World. Feb 28, 1914, p1068-69.
The Moving Picture World. Feb 7, 1914, p730.
The New York Dramatic Mirror. Feb 25, 1914, p36.
Selected Film Criticism, 1912-1920. p243-46.
Variety. Feb 20, 1914, p23.

The Squaw Man (US; DeMille, Cecil B.; 1918)
The Films of Cecil B. DeMille. p160-63.
The Moving Picture World. Nov 16, 1918, p759.
The Moving Picture World. Dec 21, 1918, p1390.
The New York Dramatic Mirror. Dec 21, 1917, p918.
The New York Times. Dec 30, 1918, p7.
Variety. Nov 8, 1918, p41.
Wid's Daily. Jan 12, 1919, p15-16.

St. Martin's Lane *See* Sidewalks of London

Stablemates (US; Wood, Sam; 1938)
Commonweal. Oct 28, 1938, v29, p21.
Film Daily. Oct 3, 1938, p8.
Hollywood Reporter. Oct 1, 1938, p3.
Hollywood Spectator. Oct 15, 1938, v13, p9.
Motion Picture Herald. Oct 8, 1938, p38.
The New York Times. Oct 21, 1938, p27.
Rob Wagner's Script. Oct 22, 1938, v20, p12-14.
Time. Oct 17, 1938, v32, p32.
Variety. Oct 5, 1938, p14.

Stachka *See* Strike

Stage Door (US; La Cava, Gregory; 1937)
Around Cinemas. p149-51.
Esquire. Jan 1938, v9, p107.
The Film Criticism of Otis Ferguson. p201-03.
Film Daily. Sep 13, 1937, p8.
The Films of Ginger Rogers. p135-37.
The Films of Katharine Hepburn. p87-90.
The Films of the Thirties. p182-83.
From Quasimodo to Scarlett O'Hara. p267-69.
Hollywood Reporter. Sep 8, 1937, p3.
A Library of Film Criticism: American Film Directors. p243.
Life. Jan 11, 1937, v2, p39.
Life. Sep 27, 1937, v3, p102-05.
Literary Digest. Oct 9, 1937, v124, p34.
Magill's Survey of Cinema. Series II. v5, p2242-45.
Motion Picture Herald. Sep 18, 1937, p42.
The Nation. Oct 30, 1937, v145, p486.
National Board of Review Magazine. Nov 1937, v12, p12.
The New Masses. Oct 19, 1937, v25, p28.
The New Republic. Oct 27, 1937, v92, p343.
The New Statesman and Nation. Jan 1, 1938, v15, p7.
The New York Times. Oct 8, 1937, p27.
The New Yorker. Oct 9, 1937, v13, p67.
Newsweek. Sep 27, 1937, v10, p24.
Photoplay. Nov 1937, v51, p40-41.
Rob Wagner's Script. Oct 16, 1937, v18, p8-9.
Scholastic. Oct 9, 1937, v31, p36.
Sight and Sound. Wint 1937-38, v6, p187.
The Spectator. Jan 7, 1938, v160, p15.
Time. Oct 18, 1937, v30, p28-29.
Variety. Sep 15, 1937, p13.
World Film News. Feb 1938, v3, p30.

Stage Struck (US; Berkeley, Busby; 1936)
The Busby Berkeley Book. p100-01.
Film Daily. Aug 11, 1936, p10.
Hollywood Reporter. Aug 6, 1936, p4.
Hollywood Spectator. Aug 15, 1936, v11, p7-8.
Judge. Oct 1936, v111, p20.
Motion Picture Herald. Aug 15, 1936, p59.
The New York Times. Sep 28, 1936, p14.
Rob Wagner's Script. Sep 5, 1936, v16, p10.
Stage. Oct 1936, v14, p26.
Time. Sep 21, 1936, v28, p25-26.
Variety. Sep 30, 1936, p17.

Stagecoach (US; Ford, John; 1939)
Action. Sep-Oct 1971, v6, p6-40.
American Film Criticism. p365-68.
American Visions. p116-26.
America's Favorite Movies. p104-18.
Beyond Formula. p30-33.
Cinema, the Magic Vehicle. v1, p303-05.
Classic Film Collector. Wint 1975, n49, p22-23.
Commonweal. Mar 10, 1939, v29, p552.
The Complete Films of John Wayne. p88-90.
Dictionary of Films. p353-54.
Discourse. Spr 1981, n3, p26-44.
Eighty Years of Cinema. p118-19.
Esquire. Mar 1980, v93, p128.
Film Daily. Feb 15, 1939, p7.
Film News. Sep-Oct 1979, v36, p27.

Film Quarterly. Wint 1975-76, v29, p26-38.
Film Reader. 1982, n5, p95-108.
The Filming of the West. p375-80.
Films and Filming. Jun 1962, v8, p15.
From Quasimodo to Scarlett O'Hara. p293-95.
The Great Western Pictures. p341-44.
Hollywood Reporter. Feb 3, 1939, p3.
Hollywood Spectator. Feb 18, 1939, v13, p6-7.
The International Dictionary of Films and Filmmakers. v1,
  p444-46.
John Ford (Bogdanovich). p69-72.
John Ford's Stagecoach.
Journal of Aesthetic Education. Apr 1975, v9, p18-31.
Journal of Popular Film. 1978, n2, v8, p34-41.
Journal of Popular Film and Television. Spr 1980, v8, p35-36.
Landmark Films. p130-39.
Life. Feb 27, 1939, v6, p31-32+.
Literature/Film Quarterly. Spr 1977, v5, p174-80.
Magill's Survey of Cinema. Series I. v4, p1612-15.
Make It Again, Sam. p200-04.
The Making of the Great Westerns. p39-56.
Motion Picture Herald. Feb 11, 1939, p35.
The Nation. Mar 11, 1939, v148, p302.
National Board of Review Magazine. May 1939, v14, p20.
The New Masses. Mar 28, 1939, v31, p29.
The New Statesman and Nation. Jun 17, 1939, v17, p934.
The New York Times. Mar 3, 1939, p21.
The New Yorker. Mar 4, 1939, v15, p64.
Newsweek. Mar 6, 1939, v13, p27.
Photoplay. Apr 1939, v53, p52.
Photoplay. Apr 1940, v54, p11.
Rob Wagner's Script. Mar 11, 1939, v21, p16.
Scholastic. Feb 25, 1939, v34, p34.
Selected Film Criticism, 1931-1940. p240-43.
The Six-Gun Mystique. p70-71.
Stage. Mar 15, 1939, v16, p30-31.
Stories Into Film. p92-109.
The Structure of John Ford's Stagecoach.
Studio. Sep 1940, v120, p84.
Talking Pictures. p227-30.
The Tatler. Jun 21, 1939, v152, p524.
Theatre Arts. Jun 1939, v23, p425.
Those Fabulous Movie Years: The 30s. p177.
Time. Mar 13, 1939, v33, p30.
Variety. Feb 8, 1939, p17.
The Western Films of John Ford. p30-41.

Stairway to Heaven (Also titled: A Matter of Life and
  Death) (GB; Pressburger, Emeric; Powell, Michael;
  1945)
Classics of the Foreign Film. p154-57.
Commonweal. Jan 3, 1947, v45, p305.
Film Daily. Dec 18, 1946, p8.
The Films of David Niven. p76-78.
Hollywood Reporter. Dec 16, 1946, p3.
Life. Dec 9, 1946, v21, p123-24+.
The London Times. Sep 26, 1946, p6.
Magill's Survey of Cinema. Series II. v5, p2249-55.
Motion Picture Exhibitor. Dec 25, 1946, v37, n8, sec2, p2079.
Motion Picture Herald Product Digest. Nov 16, 1946, p3310.
The Moving Image. p394-95.
The New Republic. Jan 13, 1947, v116, p37.
The New York Times. Dec 26, 1946, p28.
The New Yorker. Jan 11, 1947, v22, p64.
Newsweek. Jan 6, 1947, v29, p69.
Selected Film Criticism: Foreign Films, 1930-1950. p170-71.
Sight and Sound. 1946-47, v15, p155-56.
Theatre Arts. Feb 17, 1947, v31, p37-38.
Time. Dec 30, 1946, v48, p66.
Variety. Nov 13, 1946, p16.

Stand Up and Fight (US; LeRoy, Mervyn; 1939)
Commonweal. Jan 27, 1939, v29, p386.
Esquire. Apr 1939, v11, p164-65.

Film Daily. Jan 4, 1939, p7.
The Films of Robert Taylor. p71-72.
Hollywood Reporter. Dec 30, 1938, p3.
Hollywood Spectator. Jan 7, 1939, v13, p11-12.
Motion Picture Herald. Jan 7, 1939, p36, 38.
The New Masses. Feb 7, 1939, v30, p28.
The New Statesman and Nation. Oct 21, 1939, v18, p549.
The New York Times. Jan 27, 1939, p17.
Newsweek. Jan 16, 1939, v13, p27.
Rob Wagner's Script. Feb 11, 1939, v21, p18.
Saint Nicholas. Jan 1939, v66, p41.
Scholastic. Feb 4, 1939, v34, p31.
Time. Jan 16, 1939, v33, p26.
Variety. Jan 11, 1939, p12.

Stand-In (US; Garnett, Tay; 1937)
Commonweal. Oct 22, 1937, v26, p606.
The Complete Films of Humphrey Bogart. p51-52.
Film Daily. Oct 5, 1937, p6.
Hollywood Reporter. Oct 1, 1937, p3.
Humphrey Bogart: The Man and His Films. p72-74.
Life. Nov 1, 1937, v3, p96-99.
Literary Digest. Nov 6, 1937, v124, p34.
Motion Picture Herald. Oct 9, 1937, p39.
The New Masses. Nov 30, 1937, v25, p27.
The New Statesman and Nation. Nov 27, 1937, v14, p875.
The New York Times. Nov 19, 1937, p27.
The New Yorker. Nov 20, 1937, v13, p88.
Newsweek. Nov 1, 1937, v10, p29.
Scholastic. Oct 30, 1937, v31, p35.
The Spectator. Dec 10, 1937, v159, p1049.
Stage. Oct 1937, v15, p94.
Time. Nov 8, 1937, v30, p49.
Variety. Nov 6, 1937, p12.
World Film News. Apr 1938, v3, p34.

Stanley and Livingstone (US; King, Henry; 1939)
Africa on Film. p55-63.
Commonweal. Aug 11, 1939, v30, p380.
Esquire. Nov 1939, v12, p102-03.
The Film Criticism of Otis Ferguson. p266-67, 272.
Film Daily. Aug 7, 1939, p10.
The Films of Spencer Tracy. p150-52.
Graham Greene on Film. p246-47.
Hollywood Reporter. Aug 1, 1939, p3.
Hollywood Spectator. Sep 2, 1939, v14, p9.
Life. Aug 14, 1939, v7, p60.
Motion Picture Herald. Aug 5, 1939, p84-85.
National Board of Review Magazine. Oct 1939, v14, p12.
The New Masses. Aug 29, 1939, v32, p30-31.
The New Republic. Aug 23, 1939, v100, p75.
The New York Times. Aug 5, 1939, p18.
The New Yorker. Aug 12, 1939, v15, p47-48.
Newsweek. Aug 14, 1939, v14, p23.
Photoplay. Oct 1939, v53, p64.
Rob Wagner's Script. Aug 12, 1939, v22, p16-18.
Scholastic. Sep 18, 1939, v35, p32.
The Spectator. Oct 20, 1939, v163, p544.
The Tatler. Oct 25, 1939, v154, p104.
Time. Aug 14, 1939, v34, p32.
Variety. Aug 2, 1939, p18.
World Horizon. Jan 1939, v4, p28-29.

Star for a Night (US; Seiler, Lewis; 1936)
Film Daily. Aug 14, 1936, p6.
Hollywood Reporter. Aug 6, 1936, p3.
Motion Picture Herald. Aug 15, 1936, p62.
The New York Times. Sep 5, 1936, p7.
Variety. Aug 26, 1936, p20.

A Star Is Born (US; Wellman, William A.; 1937)
Canadian Magazine. Jun 1937, v87, p45.
Commonweal. May 14, 1937, v26, p78.
David O'Selznick's Hollywood. p191-205.
Esquire. Jul 1937, v8, p165-66.

The Film Criticism of Otis Ferguson. p176-77.
Film Daily. Apr 23, 1937, p7.
The Films of Fredric March. p147-49.
The Films of Lana Turner. p52-53.
From Quasimodo to Scarlett O'Hara. p243-46.
Hollywood Reporter. Apr 19, 1937, p3.
Hollywood Spectator. May 8, 1937, v12, p6-7.
A Library of Film Criticism: American Film Directors. p495.
Life. May 3, 1937, v2, p38+.
Literary Digest. May 1, 1937, v123, p20.
Magill's Survey of Cinema, Series I. v4, p1616-18.
Motion Picture Herald. May 1, 1937, p30.
Motion Picture Herald. Feb 27, 1937, p16-17.
Movie-Made America. p192.
National Board of Review Magazine. May 1937, v12, p8-10.
The New Masses. May 4, 1937, v23, p36.
New Republic. May 19, 1937, v91, p47-48.
The New Statesman and Nation. Sep 18, 1937, v14, p407.
The New York Times. Apr 23, 1937, p25.
The New Yorker. May 1, 1937, v13, p63.
The New Yorker. Feb 19, 1938, v14, p58.
Newsweek. May 1, 1937, v9, p29.
Rob Wagner's Script. May 1, 1937, v17, p8.
Saint Nicholas. Mar 1937, v64, p31.
Scholastic. May 8, 1937, v30, p28.
Selected Film Criticism, 1931-1940. p243-45.
Sight and Sound. Aut 1937, v6, p139.
The Spectator. Sep 24, 1937, v159, p499.
Stage. Mar 1937, v14, p60.
Stage. May 1937, v14, p69.
Time. May 3, 1937, v29, p28+.
Variety. Apr 28, 1937, p15.
William A. Wellman (Thompson). p162-68+.
World Film News. Oct 1937, v2, p20.
World Film News. Jul 1937, v2, p23.
World Film News. Nov 1937, v2, p23.

The Star Maker (US; Del Ruth, Roy; 1939)
Commonweal. Sep 15, 1939, v30, p481.
Film Daily. Aug 23, 1939, p9.
The Films of Bing Crosby. p101-04.
Hollywood Reporter. Aug 22, 1939, p3.
Hollywood Spectator. Sep 2, 1939, v14, p11-12.
Motion Picture Herald. Aug 26, 1939, p50, 55.
The New Statesman and Nation. Sep 23, 1939, v18, p426.
The New York Times. Aug 31, 1939, p14.
The New Yorker. Sep 2, 1939, v15, p51.
Newsweek. Sep 4, 1939, v14, p29.
Photoplay. Aug 1939, v53, p56.
Rob Wagner's Script. Sep 9, 1939, v22, p21.
Time. Sep 4, 1939, v34, p50.
Variety. Aug 23, 1939, p14.

Star of Midnight (US; Roberts, Stephen; 1935)
Film Daily. Apr 11, 1935, p9.
The Films of Ginger Rogers. p116-17.
Graham Greene on Film. p14.
Hollywood Reporter. Mar 25, 1935, p3.
Hollywood Reporter. Apr 18, 1935, p6.
Literary Digest. Apr 20, 1935, v119, p34.
Motion Picture Herald. Apr 6, 1935, p48.
The New York Times. Apr 12, 1935, p26.
The New Yorker. Apr 20, 1935, v11, p71-72.
Rob Wagner's Script. May 11, 1935, v13, p10.
The Spectator. Aug 16, 1935, v155, p257.
Time. Apr 22, 1935, v25, p60.
Variety. Apr 17, 1935, p14.

Star Spangled Rhythm (US; Marshall, George; 1942)
Commonweal. Jan 15, 1943, v37, p328.
Film Daily. Dec 31, 1942, p8.
The Films of Bing Crosby. p136-37.
The Films of Clark Gable. p80-81.
Halliwell's Hundred. p334-38.
The Hollywood Musical. p214-16.

The Hollywood Musical Goes to War. p100-01.
Hollywood Musicals. p175-76.
Motion Picture Exhibitor. Jan 13, 1943, v29, n10, sec2, p1186.
The New Republic. Mar 1, 1943, v108, p283.
The New York Times. Dec 31, 1942, p20.
Time. Jan 18, 1943, v41, p98-99.
Variety. Dec 30, 1942, p16.

The Star Witness (US; Wellman, William A.; 1931)
Film Daily. Aug 2, 1931, p10.
The Great Gangster Pictures. p370.
Hollywood Spectator. Sep 26, 1931, v12, p9.
Life. Aug 28, 1931, v98, p18.
Motion Picture Herald. Jul 25, 1931, p28.
The New York Times. Aug 4, 1931, p19.
Outlook and Independent. Aug 19, 1931, v158, p502.
Rob Wagner's Script. Sep 9, 1931, v6, p9-10.
Time. Aug 10, 1931, v18, p32.
Variety. Aug 4, 1931, p21.
William A. Wellman (Thompson). p116-18.

Stark Love (US; Brown, Karl; 1927)
Film Daily. Mar 6, 1927, p8.
The New York Times. Feb 28, 1927, p22.
Photoplay. May 1927, v31, p52.
Selected Film Criticism, 1921-1930. p274.
Variety. Mar 2, 1927, p16.

Staroye I Novoye *See* The Old and the New

The Stars Look Down (GB; Reed, Carol; 1939)
The Age of the Dream Palace. p307-09.
Cinema, the Magic Vehicle. v1, p311-12.
Commonweal. Aug 8, 1941, v34, p376.
Dictionary of Films. p355-56.
Film Daily. Jul 9, 1941, p5.
Films and Filming. Jan 1962, v8, p22-23, 45-46.
The Great British Films. p49-51.
Kiss Kiss Bang Bang. p439-40.
Magill's Survey of Cinema. Series II. v5, p2263-66.
Mastering the Film and Other Essays. p15-19.
Motion Picture Herald. Jan 27, 1940, p53.
The New Republic. Aug 11, 1941, v105, p189.
The New York Times. Jul 24, 1941, p15.
Newsweek. Jul 28, 1941, v18, p53.
Rob Wagner's Script. Aug 30, 1941, v26, p15.
Selected Film Criticism: Foreign Films, 1930-1950. p171.
The Spectator. Jan 26, 1940, v164, p265.
The Tatler. Jan 31, 1940, v155, p134.
Theatre Arts. Oct 1941, v25, p731.
Time. Jul 28, 1941, v38, p75.
Variety. Jan 3, 1940, p40.

Start Cheering (US; Rogell, Albert S.; 1938)
The Hollywood Musical. p146.
Hollywood Reporter. Jan 28, 1938, p3.
Motion Picture Herald. Feb 5, 1938, p48, 52.
The New York Times. Mar 17, 1938, p17.
Rob Wagner's Script. Apr 2, 1938, v19, p10-11.

State Fair (US; King, Henry; 1933)
Film Daily. Jan 27, 1933, p5.
Judge. Mar 1933, v104, p20.
Lorentz on Film. p108-09.
Motion Picture Herald. Feb 4, 1933, p38.
The Nation. Feb 15, 1933, v136, p186-87.
National Board of Review Magazine. Mar 1933, v8, p12-13.
The New York Times. Jan 27, 1933, p13.
The New York Times. Feb 5, 1933, p5.
The New Yorker. Feb 4, 1933, v8, p49.
Rob Wagner's Script. Feb 4, 1933, v8, p6.
Selected Film Criticism, 1931-1940. p245-46.
Time. Feb 6, 1933, v21, p24.
Vanity Fair. Mar 1933, v40, p63.
Variety. Jan 31, 1933, p12.
Will Rogers in Hollywood. p125-29.

State of the Union (US; Capra, Frank; 1948)
Commonweal. May 7, 1948, v48, p80.
Film Daily. Mar 29, 1948, p7.
The Films of Frank Capra (Scherle and Levy). p233-38.
The Films of Katharine Hepburn. p139-42 .
The Films of Spencer Tracy. p195-96.
Hollywood Reporter. Mar 24, 1948, p3.
Life. May 10, 1948, v24, p81-82+.
Magill's Survey of Cinema. Series I. v4, p1627-30.
Motion Picture Herald Product Digest. Apr 3, 1948, p4110.
The New Republic. May 10, 1948, v118, p30.
The New York Times. Apr 23, 1948, p28.
The New Yorker. May 1, 1948, v24, p82.
Newsweek. May 3, 1948, v31, p80.
Time. May 3, 1948, v51, p90+.
Variety. Mar 24, 1948, p8.

State's Attorney (US; Archainbaud, George; 1932)
Film Daily. May 8, 1932, p10.
Motion Picture Herald. May 14, 1932, p43, 46.
The New York Times. May 5, 1932, p23.
The New Yorker. May 14, 1932, v8, p51.
Rob Wagner's Script. Jun 25, 1932, v7, p10.
Time. May 2, 1932, v19, p24.
Variety. May 10, 1932, p18.

Steamboat Bill, Jr. (US; Reisner, Charles F.; 1928)
Buster Keaton (Robinson). p169-75.
Cinema, the Magic Vehicle. v1, p149-56.
The Comic Mind. p134-35.
Exhibitor's Herald-World and Moving Picture World. Jul 7, 1928, p52.
The Film Career of Buster Keaton. p70-73.
Film Daily. May 20, 1928, p5.
The Film Spectator. Jun 23, 1928, v5, p14-15.
Life. Oct 5, 1928, v92, p28.
Magill's Survey of Cinema. Silent Films. v3, p1042-48.
Motion Picture Classic. Aug 27, 1928, v27, p53.
National Board of Review Magazine. Sep 1928, v3, p9.
The New York Times. May 15, 1928, p17.
Selected Film Criticism, 1921-1930. p274-75.
The Silent Clowns. p213-17+.
Variety. May 16, 1928, p13.

Steamboat 'Round the Bend (US; Ford, John; 1935)
American History/American Film. p77-96.
Canadian Magazine. Oct 1935, v84, p42.
Esquire. Oct 1935, v4, p97.
Film Daily. Jul 25, 1935, p3.
Hollywood Reporter. Jul 22, 1935, p3.
Literary Digest. Sep 28, 1935, v120, p26.
Motion Picture Herald. Aug 3, 1935, p59, 62.
The New York Times. Sep 20, 1935, p17.
The New Yorker. Sep 28, 1935, v11, p63.
Newsweek. Sep 14, 1935, v6, p28.
The Non-Western Films of John Ford. p28.
Rob Wagner's Script. Aug 31, 1935, v14, p10.
Time. Sep 2, 1935, v26, p40.
Variety. Sep 25, 1935, p12.
Will Rogers in Hollywood. p162-67.

Steamboat Willie (US; Disney, Walt; Iwerks, Ub; 1928)
The Art of Walt Disney. p51-52, 57-58, 63-64.
Disney Animation. p34-35.
Exhibitor's Herald-World. Jul 27, 1929, p57.
Exhibitor's Herald-World and Moving Picture World. Dec 1, 1928, p59.
The Great Cartoon Directors. p16.
The International Dictionary of Films and Filmmakers. v1, p450-51.
Of Mice and Magic. p34-35, 38.
Variety. Nov 21, 1928, p13.

Stella Dallas (US; King, Henry; 1925)
Film Daily. Nov 22, 1925, p6.
Life. Dec 10, 1925, v86, p24.

Magill's Survey of Cinema. Silent Films. v3, p1049-52.
The Moving Picture World. Nov 28, 1925, p342.
Photoplay. Dec 1925, v24, p46.
Selected Film Criticism, 1921-1930. p275-77.
Spellbound in Darkness. p399-400.
Variety. Nov 18, 1925, p42.

Stella Dallas (US; Vidor, King; 1937)
Commonweal. Aug 13, 1937, v26, p388.
Dictionary of Films. p356-57.
Esquire. Oct 1937, v8, p121.
Film Daily. Jul 27, 1937, p4.
The Films of Barbara Stanwyck. p119-20.
The Films of the Thirties. p194-95.
The Great Romantic Films. p60-63.
Hollywood Reporter. Jul 23, 1937, p3.
Hollywood Spectator. Jul 31, 1937, v9, p7-8.
King Vidor (Baxter). p55.
Literary Digest. Aug 21, 1937, v124, p26.
Magill's Survey of Cinema. Series I. v4, p1631-33.
Motion Picture Herald. Jul 31, 1937, p36.
The New York Times. Aug 6, 1937, p21.
The New Yorker. Jul 31, 1937, v13, p49.
Newsweek. Aug 7, 1937, v10, p22.
Popcorn Venus. p184.
Rob Wagner's Script. Aug 28, 1937, v18, p10.
Samuel Goldwyn Presents. p178-80.
Selected Film Criticism, 1931-1940. p248-50.
Starring Miss Barbara Stanwyck. p99-100, 103-04, 109-10.
Time. Aug 9, 1937, v30, p36.
A Tree Is a Tree. p210, 261.
Variety. Jul 28, 1937, p16.
World Film News. Dec 1937, v2, p23.

Stella Maris (US; Neilan, Marshall; 1918)
Exhibitor's Trade Review. Feb 2, 1918, p755, 764.
Fifty Great American Silent Films, 1912-1920. p89-92.
Magill's Survey of Cinema. Silent Films. v3, p1053-56.
Motion Picture Classic. Apr 1918, p36-37.
Motion Picture News. Feb 2, 1918, p733.
The Moving Picture World. Jan 5, 1918, p109.
The Moving Picture World. Feb 2, 1918, p723.
The Moving Picture World. Feb 9, 1918, p864.
The New York Dramatic Mirror. Feb 2, 1918, p22.
Photoplay. Apr 1918, v13, p69-70.
The Rivals of D.W. Griffith. p12-13.
Selected Film Criticism, 1912-1920. 246-49.
Variety. Jan 25, 1918, p41.
Wid's Daily. Jan 31, 1918, p903-04.

Stella Parish *See* I Found Stella Parish

Stepping Out (US; Niblo, Fred; 1919)
Exhibitor's Trade Review. Oct 4, 1919, p1585.
Motion Picture News. Oct 4, 1919, p2875.
The Moving Picture World. Oct 4, 1919, p158.
The New York Times. Sep 22, 1919, p8.
Variety. Sep 26, 1919, p60.
Wid's Daily. Oct 5, 1919, p3.

Stolen Heaven (US; Stone, Andrew L.; 1938)
Film Daily. Apr 25, 1938, p6.
Hollywood Reporter. Apr 9, 1938, p3.
Motion Picture Herald. Apr 23, 1938, p40, 44.
The New York Times. May 12, 1938, p27.
The New Yorker. May 21, 1938, v14, p56.
Newsweek. May 23, 1938, v11, p20.
Rob Wagner's Script. May 21, 1938, v19, p9.
Time. May 23, 1938, v31, p40.
Variety. Apr 27, 1938, p22.

Stolen Holiday (US; Curtiz, Michael; 1936)
Film Daily. Dec 22, 1936, p10.
Hollywood Reporter. Dec 16, 1936, p4.
Motion Picture Herald. Dec 26, 1936, p54.
The New Statesman and Nation. Mar 27, 1937, v13, p523.

The New York Times. Feb 1, 1937, p15.
Newsweek. Feb 6, 1937, v9, p36.
Rob Wagner's Script. Feb 27, 1937, v17, p8.
Time. Feb 8, 1937, v29, p57.
Variety. Feb 3, 1937, p14.

The Stolen Kiss (US; Webb, Kenneth; 1920)
The Moving Picture World. Mar 20, 1920, p1878-79, 2011.
Variety. Apr 9, 1920, p60-61.
Wid's Daily. Mar 14, 1920, p16.

A Stolen Life (US; Bernhardt, Curtis; 1946)
Bette Davis: Her Films and Career. p134-35.
Commonweal. May 17, 1946, v44, p119.
Film Daily. May 2, 1946, p7.
The Great Romantic Films. p124-27.
Hollywood Reporter. May 1, 1946, p8.
Life. Jun 17, 1946, v20, p119-22.
Motion Picture Herald Product Digest. May 4, 1946, p2973.
The New York Times. May 2, 1946, p27.
The New Yorker. May 4, 1946, v22, p46+.
Newsweek. May 13, 1946, v27, p92.
Theatre Arts. Jun 1946, v30, p346-47.
Time. May 13, 1946, v47, p98.
Variety. May 1, 1946, p8.

A Stolen Life (GB; Czinner, Paul; 1939)
Commonweal. Jun 2, 1939, v30, p161.
Film Daily. Apr 25, 1939, p7.
Hollywood Reporter. Apr 22, 1939, p3.
Motion Picture Herald. Feb 18, 1939, p48, 50.
The Nation. Jul 1, 1939, v149, p24-25.
The New Statesman and Nation. Jan 28, 1939, v17, p127-28.
The New York Times. Jun 15, 1939, p27.
The New Yorker. Jun 17, 1939, v15, p75.
Newsweek. May 22, 1939, v13, p35.
Photoplay. Jul 1939, v53, p63.
Rob Wagner's Script. Apr 29, 1939, v21, p18-19.
Time. Jun 5, 1939, v33, p66.
Variety. Feb 1, 1939, p13.

The Storm *See* Orage

Storm at Daybreak (US; Boleslavski, Richard; 1933)
Film Daily. Jul 22, 1933, p3.
Hollywood Reporter. Jun 22, 1933, p3.
Motion Picture Herald. Jul 1, 1933, p25.
New Outlook. Sep 1933, v162, p44.
The New York Times. Jul 22, 1933, p14.
The New Yorker. Jul 29, 1933, v9, p40.
Newsweek. Jul 29, 1933, v1, p31.
Time. Jul 17, 1933, v22, p34.
Vanity Fair. Sep 1933, v41, p45-46.
Variety. Jul 25, 1933, p14.

Storm in a Teacup (GB; Saville, Victor; Dalrymple, Ian; 1937)
Film Daily. Nov 18, 1937, p7.
Hollywood Reporter. Jun 21, 1937, p3.
Literary Digest. Feb 8, 1938, v125, p22.
Motion Picture Herald. Jun 12, 1937, p82.
The New York Times. Mar 22, 1938, p18.
The New Yorker. Mar 19, 1938, v14, p57.
Rob Wagner's Script. May 7, 1938, v19, p9.
The Spectator. Jun 1937, v158, p1144.
Time. Apr 11, 1938, v31, p23.
Variety. Jun 9, 1937, p15.
World Film News. Jul 1937, v2, p22-23.

Storm Over Asia (Russian title: Potomok Chingis-Khan; Also titled: The Heir to Genghis Khan; The Descendant of Genghis Khan) (USSR; Pudovkin, Vsevolod; 1928)
American Film Criticism. p238-40.
Cinema, the Magic Vehicle. v1, p141-42.
Classics of the Foreign Film. p48-51.

Close-Up. Jan 1929, v4, p37-46.
Close-Up. Feb 1929, v4, p33-36.
Dictionary of Films. p291.
Exhibitors Herald-World. Sep 13, 1930, p40.
Film Daily. Sep 7, 1930, p10.
Judge. Sep 27, 1930, v99, p21.
Kino. p248-50.
The New Statesman and Nation. Mar 22, 1930, v34, p773-74.
The New York Times. Nov 17, 1929, p5.
The New York Times. Sep 8, 1930, p17.
The New Yorker. Sep 13, 1930, v6, p77-78.
Outlook and Independent. Sep 17, 1930, v156, p112.
Rob Wagner's Script. Feb 28, 1931, v5, p8-10.
Scrutiny of Cinema. p46-49.
Time. Sep 22, 1930, v16, p30.
Variety. Mar 6, 1929, p15.
Variety. Sep 10, 1930, p29.

Storm Over Bengal (US; Salkow, Sidney; 1938)
Chestnuts in Her Lap. p46-47.
Film Daily. Nov 17, 1938, p5.
Hollywood Reporter. Nov 4, 1938, p4.
Motion Picture Herald. Nov 12, 1938, p35.
The New Masses. Dec 27, 1938, v30, p28.
The New York Times. Dec 8, 1938, p34.
Variety. Dec 14, 1938, p14.

Storm Over the Andes (US; Cabanne, Christy; 1935)
Canadian Magazine. Oct 1935, v84, p42.
Film Daily. Sep 25, 1935, p4.
Hollywood Reporter. Aug 31, 1935, p3.
Motion Picture Herald. Oct 19, 1935, p86.
Rob Wagner's Script. Sep 28, 1935, v14, p10.
Time. Sep 23, 1935, v26, p46.
Variety. Oct 2, 1935, p16.

Storms Over Mont Blanc *See* Avalanche

The Story of a Cheat *See* Roman d'un Tricheur, Le

The Story of Alexander Graham Bell (US; Cummings, Irving; 1939)
Commonweal. Apr 14, 1939, v29, p693.
Film Daily. Apr 3, 1939, p7.
The Films of Henry Fonda. p81-82.
The Fondas (Springer). p90-91.
Hollywood Reporter. Mar 30, 1939, p3.
Magill's Survey of Cinema. Series II. v5, p2281-83.
Motion Picture Herald. Apr 8, 1939, p60-61.
The Nation. Apr 22, 1939, v148, p478.
The New York Times. Apr 1, 1939, p17.
Newsweek. Apr 10, 1939, v13, p29.
Photoplay. Jun 1939, v53, p58.
Saint Nicholas. May 1939, v66, p31+.
Scholastic. Apr 22, 1939, v34, p30.
Time. Apr 10, 1939, v33, p53.
Variety. Apr 5, 1939, p15.

The Story of Dr. Wassell (US; DeMille, Cecil B.; 1943)
Commonweal. Jun 16, 1944, v40, p233.
Film Daily. Apr 26, 1944, p11.
The Films of Cecil B. DeMille. p330-35.
The Films of Gary Cooper. p194-96.
The Films of World War II. p192-94.
Hollywood Reporter. Apr 24, 1944, p3.
The Nation. Jun 10, 1944, v158, p688.
The New Republic. Jun 26, 1944, v110, p850.
The New York Times. Apr 25, 1943, sec2, p3.
The New York Times. Oct 10, 1943, p3.
New Yorker. Jun 17, 1944, v20, p68.
Newsweek. Jun 12, 1944, v23, p72.
Variety. Apr 26, 1944, p12.

The Story of Dr. Ehrlich's Magic Bullet *See* Dr. Ehrlich's Magic Bullet

The Story of G.I. Joe (Also titled: G.I. Joe) (US; Wellman, William A.; 1945)
Agee on Film. v1, p171-75.
Chestnuts in Her Lap. p158-59.
Commonweal. Jul 27, 1945, v42, p358.
Film Daily. Jun 18, 1945, p56.
Film Quarterly. Oct 1945, v1, p34-39.
The Films of World War II. p232-33.
Guts & Glory. p62-69.
Hollywood Reporter. Jun 18, 1945, p3.
Life. Jul 9, 1945, v19, p61-62+.
The London Times. Sep 27, 1945, p8.
Magill's Survey of Cinema. Series I. v4, p1638-40.
Motion Picture Exhibitor. Jun 27, 1945, v34, n8, sec2, p1738.
Motion Picture Herald Product Digest. Jun 23, 1945, p2509.
Musician. Jul 1945, v50, p137.
The Nation. Sep 15, 1945, v161, p264-66.
The New Republic. Aug 13, 1945, v113, p190.
The New York Times. Oct 6, 1945, p9.
The New Yorker. Oct 6, 1945, v21, p85.
Newsweek. Jul 6, 1945, v26, p98+.
Robert Mitchum on the Screen. p86-87.
Scholastic. Sep 24, 1945, v47, p32.
Theatre Arts. Oct 1945, v29, p581-82.
Time. Jul 23, 1945, v46, p96.
Variety. Jun 20, 1945, p11.
Visions of War. p92-100.
William A. Wellman (Thompson). p212-15+.

The Story of Louis Pasteur (US; Dieterle, William; 1936)
American Journal of Public Health. Mar 1936, v26, p292-93.
Canadian Magazine. Mar 1936, v85, p40.
Cinema, the Magic Vehicle. v1, p265-66.
Commonweal. Jan 24, 1936, v23, p356.
Esquire. Mar 1936, v5, p105, 183-84.
Film Daily. Nov 23, 1935, p8.
Graham Greene on Film. p85-86.
Hollywood Reporter. Nov 20, 1935, p3.
Hollywood Spectator. Dec 7, 1935, p6-7.
Hygeia. Mar 1936, v14, p200-01.
Literary Digest. Feb 1, 1936, v121, p20.
London Mercury. Aug 1936, v34, p350.
Magill's Survey of Cinema. Series II. v5, p2284-86.
Motion Picture Herald. Nov 30, 1935, p58.
The Nation. Mar 4, 1936, v142, p293.
National Board of Review Magazine. Feb 1936, v11, p15.
The New Masses. Feb 25, 1936, v18, p30.
The New Republic. Feb 5, 1936, v85, p369.
The New Statesman and Nation. Jun 27, 1936, v11, p1029.
The New York Times. Feb 10, 1936, p15.
The New York Times. Jan 30, 1936, p14.
Newsweek. Feb 15, 1936, v7, p27.
Paul Muni: His Life and His Films. p146-51.
Photoplay. Mar 1936, v49, p8-9.
Rob Wagner's Script. Feb 29, 1936, v15, p8.
Scholastic. Jan 18, 1936, v27, p28.
The Spectator. Jul 3, 1936, v157, p15.
The Tatler. Jul 1, 1936, v141, p6.
Time. Feb 17, 1936, v27, p46+.
Variety. Feb 12, 1936, p16.
Warner Brothers Presents. p272, 277.
World Film News. Aug 1936, v1, p17.

The Story of Temple Drake (US; Roberts, Stephen; 1933)
Film Daily. May 6, 1933, p4.
The Films of the Thirties. p104-05.
The Great Gangster Pictures. p376-78.
Hollywood Reporter. May 11, 1933, p4.
Judge. Aug 1933, v104, p23.
Motion Picture Herald. May 13, 1933, p22.
The Nation. May 24, 1933, v136, p594.
The New Republic. Jun 14, 1933, v75, p128.
The New York Times. May 6, 1933, p11.
The New Yorker. May 13, 1933, v9, p51-52.

Time. May 15, 1933, v21, p36.
Variety. May 9, 1933, p14.

The Story of the Kelly Gang (AUST; 1904)
Australian Cinema. p29-31.
Film Before Griffith. p88-90.
A Million and One Nights. p680.

The Story of Vernon and Irene Castle (US; Potter, H.C.; 1939)
Commonweal. Apr 14, 1939, v29, p693.
Film Daily. Mar 31, 1939, p6.
The Fred Astaire & Ginger Rogers Book. p153-67.
Graham Greene on Film. p225-27.
Hollywood Reporter. Mar 28, 1939, p3.
Hollywood Spectator. Apr 15, 1939, v14, p31.
Magill's Survey of Cinema. Series II. v5, p2287-89.
Motion Picture Herald. Apr 1, 1939, p26.
The New York Times. Mar 31, 1939, p19.
The New Yorker. Apr 8, 1939, v15, p69-70.
Newsweek. Apr 3, 1939, v13, p31.
North American Review. Jun 1939, v247, p383.
Photoplay. Jun 1939, v53, p58.
Rob Wagner's Script. Apr 8, 1939, v21, p12.
Scholastic. Apr 22, 1939, v34, p30.
Sight and Sound. Sum 1939, v8, p76.
The Spectator. Jun 9, 1939, v162, p997.
Stage. Apr 1, 1939, v16, p34-36.
Starring Fred Astaire. p187-99.
The Tatler. Jun 14, 1939, v152, p478.
Time. Apr 10, 1939, v33, p49-52.
Variety. Apr 5, 1939, p15.

Stowaway (US; Seiter, William A.; 1936)
Film Daily. Dec 16, 1936, p8.
The Films of Alice Faye. p73-76.
The Films of Shirley Temple. p178-81.
Hollywood Reporter. Dec 21, 1936, p3.
Hollywood Spectator. Jan 2, 1936, v11, p14-15.
Motion Picture Herald. Dec 26, 1936, p54, 56.
The New York Times. Dec 19, 1936, p16.
The New Yorker. Dec 26, 1936, v12, p49.
Rob Wagner's Script. Dec 26, 1936, v16, p11.
Saint Nicholas. Jan 1937, v64, p40.
Time. Dec 28, 1936, v28, p19.
Variety. Dec 23, 1936, p18.
World Film News. Jun 1937, v2, p21.

Straight, Place and Show (US; Butler, David; 1938)
Film Daily. Sep 29, 1938, p6.
Motion Picture Herald. Oct 1, 1938, p38.
The New York Times. Oct 1, 1938, p10.
The New Yorker. Oct 8, 1938, v14, p55-56.
Rob Wagner's Script. Oct 8, 1938, v20, p13.
Time. Oct 3, 1938, v32, p36.
Variety. Sep 28, 1938, p14.

Straight Shooting (US; Ford, John; 1917)
John Ford. p116+.
Magill's Survey of Cinema. Silent Films. v3, p1063-65.
Motion Picture News. Sep 8, 1917, p1668.
The Moving Picture World. Sep 1, 1917, p1432.
The Moving Picture World. Sep 8, 1917, p1519.
The Rivals of D.W. Griffith. p23-25.
Selected Film Criticism, 1912-1920. p249-50.
The Western Films of John Ford. p10-29.

Stranded (US; Borzage, Frank; 1935)
Film Daily. Jun 21, 1935, p22.
Hollywood Reporter. Jun 28, 1935, p3.
Motion Picture Herald. Jun 29, 1935, p66.
Movie Classic. Sep 1935, v9, p88.
The New York Times. Jun 22, 1935, p18.
The New Yorker. Jun 29, 1935, v11, p54-55.
Time. Jul 1, 1935, v26, p35.
Variety. Jun 26, 1935, p23.

Strange Incident *See* The Ox-Bow Incident

Strange Interlude (US; Leonard, Robert Z.; 1932)
Commonweal. Oct 5, 1932, v16, p539.
Film Daily. Jul 8, 1932, p22.
The Films of Clark Gable. p139.
The Films of Norma Shearer. p180-85.
Literary Digest. Sep 24, 1932, v114, p18-19.
Lorentz on Film. p91-94.
The Nation. Sep 28, 1932, v135, p292.
The New Republic. Sep 14, 1932, v72, p124-25.
The New York Times. Sep 1, 1932, p24.
The New Yorker. Sep 3, 1932, v8, p43-44.
Rob Wagner's Script. Jul 23, 1932, v7, p8.
Time. Jul 25, 1932, v20, p22.
Vanity Fair. Sep 1932, v39, p45.
Variety. Sep 6, 1932, p15.

The Strange Love of Martha Ivers (US; Milestone, Lewis; 1946)
Around Cinemas, Second Series. p270-71.
Commonweal. Aug 9, 1946, v44, p408.
Film Daily. Mar 14, 1946, p10.
Films in Review. Mar 1951, v2, p32-36.
The Films of Barbara Stanwyck. p168-71.
The Films of Kirk Douglas. p33-36.
Hollywood Reporter. Mar 13, 1946, p3.
Lewis Milestone (Millichap). p142-54.
Life. Aug 19, 1946, v21, p103-04+.
Motion Picture Herald Product Digest. Mar 23, 1946, p2907.
The New Republic. Sep 9, 1946, v115, p293.
The New York Times. Aug 3, 1946, p18.
The New Yorker. Aug 3, 1946, v22, p38.
Newsweek. Aug 5, 1946, v28, p93.
Starring Miss Barbara Stanwyck. p195-98.
Time. Jul 29, 1946, v48, p88.
Variety. Mar 13, 1946, p10.

The Stranger (US; Welles, Orson; 1946)
Agee on Film. v1, p204-05.
The Cinema of Orson Welles. p84-85.
Commonweal. Jul 12, 1946, v44, p309.
Film Daily. May 23, 1946, p7.
The Films of World War II. p238-39.
Hollywood Reporter. May 21, 1946, p3.
Life. Jun 3, 1946, v20, p75-78.
Magill's Survey of Cinema. Series II. v5, p2294-97.
Motion Picture Herald Product Digest. May 25, 1946, p3005.
The Nation. Jun 22, 1946, v162, p765.
The New Republic. Sep 16, 1946, v115, p326-27.
The New York Times. Jul 11, 1946, p18.
The New Yorker. Jun 29, 1946, v22, p64.
Newsweek. Jul 15, 1946, v28, p97.
Selected Film Criticism, 1941-1950. p228-29.
Theatre Arts. Aug 1946, v30, p441.
Time. Jun 17, 1946, v47, p98.
Variety. May 22, 1946, p10.

Strangers in Love (US; Mendes, Lothar; 1932)
Film Daily. Mar 6, 1932, p10.
The Films of Fredric March. p82-83.
Motion Picture Herald. Feb 20, 1932, p33.
The New York Times. Mar 5, 1932, p11.
Rob Wagner's Script. Feb 27, 1932, v7, p8.
Saturday Review (London). Apr 16, 1932, v153, p394.
Time. Mar 14, 1932, v19, p26.
Variety. Mar 8, 1932, p23.

Strangers in the House (French title: Inconnus dans la Maison, Les) (FR; Decoin, Henri; 1942)
Film Daily. Oct 19, 1949, p6.
Hollywood Reporter. Jul 24, 1950, p3.
The New Republic. Oct 31, 1949, v121, p22.
The New York Times. Oct 13, 1949, p33.

The New Yorker. Oct 15, 1949, v25, p126.
Variety. Oct 19, 1949, p18.

Strangers May Kiss (US; Fitzmaurice, George; 1931)
Film Daily. Apr 12, 1931, p32.
The Films of Norma Shearer. p168-73.
Life. May 1, 1931, v97, p22.
Motion Picture Herald. Feb 28, 1931, p51.
The New York Times. Apr 11, 1931, p17.
The New York Times. Apr 19, 1931, p5.
Outlook and Independent. Jan 7, 1931, v157, p442.
Rob Wagner's Script. Mar 21, 1931, v5, p8-9.
Time. Apr 20, 1931, v17, p28.
Variety. Apr 15, 1931, p33.

The Strangers Return (US; Vidor, King; 1933)
Cinema Quarterly. Aut 1933, v2, p48.
Film Daily. Jul 29, 1933, p4.
Hollywood Reporter. Jul 1, 1933, p3.
Judge. Sep 1933, v105, p20.
Literary Digest. Aug 12, 1933, v116, p15.
Motion Picture Herald. Jul 15, 1933, p20.
The Nation. Aug 16, 1933, v137, p196.
New Outlook. Sep 1933, v162, p45.
The New York Times. Jul 28, 1933, p18.
Newsweek. Aug 5, 1933, v2, p30.
Rob Wagner's Script. Oct 21, 1933, v10, p8-9.
Time. Jul 31, 1933, v22, p19.
Variety. Aug 1, 1933, p14.

The Stratton Story (US; Wood, Sam; 1949)
Collier's. Sep 17, 1949, v124, p22-23.
Collier's. Sep 24, 1949, v124, p28-29.
Commonweal. May 20, 1949, v50, p149.
Film Daily. Apr 20, 1949, p7.
The Films of James Stewart. p122-24.
Hollywood Reporter. Apr 20, 1949, p3.
Life. May 9, 1949, v26, p83-84.
Magill's Survey of Cinema. Series II. v5, p2303-05.
Motion Picture Herald Product Digest. Apr 23, 1949, p4581.
The New Republic. May 30, 1949, v120, p23.
The New York Times. May 13, 1949, p29.
The New Yorker. May 21, 1949, v25, p68+.
Newsweek. May 23, 1949, v33, p84.
Rotarian. Jul 1949, v75, p51.
Theatre Arts. Jun 1949, v33, p8.
Time. May 9, 1949, v53, p100+.
Variety. Apr 20, 1949, p11.

Strauss' Great Waltz *See* Waltzes From Vienna

The Strawberry Blonde (US; Walsh, Raoul; 1941)
Commonweal. Mar 7, 1941, v33, p498.
Each Man in His Own Time. p314-16.
The Film Criticism of Otis Ferguson. p345-46.
Film Daily. Feb 13, 1941, p7.
The Films of James Cagney. p158-61.
The Films of Rita Hayworth. p117-19.
Hollywood Reporter. Feb 13, 1941, p3.
The London Times. Aug 25, 1941, p2.
Magill's Survey of Cinema. Series II. v5, p2310-13.
Motion Picture Exhibitor. Feb 19, 1941, p692-93.
Movietone News. Nov 1975, n45, p24-30.
The New Republic. Mar 10, 1941, v104, p341.
The New York Times. Feb 2, 1941, p11.
Newsweek. Feb 24, 1941, p17, p54+.
Scholastic. Feb 24, 1941, v38, p37.
Time. Mar 3, 1941, v37, p82.
Variety. Feb 19, 1941, p16.

Street Angel (US; Borzage, Frank; 1928)
BFI/Monthly Film Bulletin. Jul 1980, v47, p143.
Exhibitor's Herald-World and Moving Picture World. Jul 7, 1928, p52.
Film Daily. Apr 15, 1928, p4.
The Film Spectator. Apr 28, 1928, v5, p9-10.

The New York Times. Apr 10, 1928, p33.
Variety. Apr 11, 1928, p13.

Street Girl (US; Ruggles, Wesley; 1929)
Exhibitor's Herald-World. Sep 21, 1929, p56.
Film Daily. Jul 21, 1929, p13.
The Hollywood Musical. p27.
Magill's Survey of Cinema. Series II. v5, p2314-16.
The New York Times. Jul 31, 1929, p17.
Variety. Aug 7, 1929, p21.

Street of Chance (US; Cromwell, John; 1930)
Exhibitors Herald-World. Feb 8, 1930, p33.
Film Daily. Feb 2, 1930, p11.
The Film Spectator. Mar 15, 1930, v9, p18-19.
Life. Feb 21, 1930, v95, p20.
National Board of Review Magazine. Feb 1930, v5, p13.
The New York Times. Feb 3, 1930, p17.
The New York Times. Feb 9, 1930, p5.
The New Yorker. Feb 8, 1930, v5, p69, 71.
Outlook and Independent. Feb 19, 1930, v154, p313.
Rob Wagner's Script. Mar 22, 1930, v3, p10-12.
Time. Feb 17, 1930, v15, p40.
Variety. Feb 5, 1930, p24.

Street of Women (US; Mayo, Archie; 1932)
Film Daily. May 29, 1932, p10.
Motion Picture Herald. Jun 4, 1932, p41.
The New York Times. May 30, 1932, p16.
Time. Jun 6, 1932, v19, p23.
Variety. May 31, 1932, p15.

Street Scene (US; Vidor, King; 1931)
Close-Up. Dec 1931, v8, p330-31.
Commonweal. Sep 16, 1931, v14, p470.
Film Daily. Aug 30, 1931, p10.
Hollywood Reporter. Aug 3, 1931, p3.
Hollywood Spectator. Aug 29, 1931, v12, p17.
Hollywood Spectator. Sep 12, 1931, v12, p6-7.
Hollywood Spectator. Sep 26, 1931, v12, p22.
The International Photographer. Oct 1931, v3, p29.
Life. Sep 18, 1931, v98, p19.
Magill's Survey of Cinema. Series II. v5, p2317-20.
Motion Picture Herald. Aug 22, 1931, p32.
The Nation. Sep 16, 1931, v133, p290.
National Board of Review Magazine. Sep 1931, v6, p9.
The New Republic. Sep 9, 1931, v68, p100-01.
The New York Times. Aug 27, 1931, p22.
The New Yorker. Sep 5, 1931, v7, p53-54.
Outlook and Independent. Sep 9, 1931, v159, p54.
Photoplay. Oct 1931, v40, p49.
Rob Wagner's Script. Oct 10, 1931, v6, p8.
Samuel Goldwyn Presents. p104-06.
Selected Film Criticism, 1931-1940. p250-52.
The Spectator. Jan 16, 1932, v148, p78.
Time. Sep 7, 1931, v18, p29.
A Tree Is a Tree. p202-05.
Variety. Sep 1, 1931, p21.

The Street With No Name (US; Newman, Lionel; 1948)
Commonweal. Jul 30, 1948, v48, p379.
Film Daily. Jun 25, 1948, p3.
Motion Picture Herald Product Digest. Jun 26, 1948, p4213.
The New Republic. Jul 26, 1948, v119, p29.
The New York Times. Jul 15, 1948, p26.
The New Yorker. Jul 24, 1948, v24, p38.
Newsweek. Jul 5, 1948, v32, p71.
Time. Aug 9, 1948, v52, p74+.
Variety. Jun 23, 1948, p6.

The Streets of New York (US; Nigh, William; 1939)
Commonweal. May 5, 1939, v30, p49.
Film Daily. Apr 10, 1939, p6.
Hollywood Reporter. Apr 5, 1939, p3.
Hollywood Spectator. Apr 15, 1939, v14, p33.
Motion Picture Herald. Apr 8, 1939, p64.

The New York Times. May 1, 1939, p21.
Scholastic. Apr 29, 1939, v34, p33.
Time. Apr 24, 1939, v33, p68.
Variety. Apr 19, 1939, p22.

Streets of Sorrow *See* The Joyless Street

Strictly Dishonorable (US; Stahl, John M.; 1931)
Film Daily. Nov 15, 1931, p10.
Hollywood Reporter. Oct 9, 1931, p3.
Motion Picture Herald. Nov 7, 1931, p51.
The New Statesman and Nation. Mar 21, 1931, v1, p150.
The New York Times. Nov 11, 1931, p27.
The New York Times. Nov 15, 1931, p5.
The New Yorker. Nov 21, 1931, v7, p70.
Outlook and Independent. Nov 25, 1931, v159, p407.
Rob Wagner's Script. Nov 14, 1931, v6, p8.
Time. Nov 16, 1931, v18, p23.
Variety. Nov 17, 1931, p14.

Strike (Russian title: Stachka) (USSR; Eisenstein, Sergei; 1924)
Cinema, the Magic Vehicle. v1, p100-01.
Eisenstein. p78-88.
Film Notes of the Wisconsin Film Society. p43-47.
A History of Narrative Film. p146-48.
Kino. p180-84.
Masters of the Soviet Cinema. p207.
The New York Times. Mar 15, 1968, p30.

Strike Me Pink (US; Taurog, Norman; 1936)
Commonweal. Jan 31, 1936, v23, p386.
Film Daily. Jan 14, 1936, p7.
Graham Greene on Film. p59-60.
Hollywood Reporter. Jan 10, 1936, p3.
Hollywood Spectator. Jan 18, 1936, v10, p13.
Literary Digest. Jan 25, 1936, v121, p19.
Motion Picture Herald. Jan 25, 1936, p35.
The New Statesman and Nation. Mar 21, 1936, v11, p457-58.
The New York Times. Jan 17, 1936, p15.
The New Yorker. Jan 25, 1936, v11, p55.
Newsweek. Jan 25, 1936, v7, p30.
Rob Wagner's Script. Jan 18, 1936, v14, p12.
Samuel Goldwyn Presents. p158-60.
Sight and Sound. Spr 1936, v5, p22.
The Spectator. Mar 20, 1936, v156, p513.
Time. Jan 27, 1936, v27, p47.
Variety. Jan 22, 1936, p14.

Strike Up the Band (US; Berkeley, Busby; 1940)
The Busby Berkeley Book. p128-31.
Commonweal. Oct 11, 1940, v32, p512.
Film Daily. Sep 17, 1940, p5.
The Films of the Forties. p16-17.
The Hollywood Musical. p170-71.
The Hollywood Musical Goes to War. p63-64, 156-59.
Hollywood Musicals. p162-64.
Hollywood Reporter. Sep 13, 1940, p3.
Judy: The Films and Career of Judy Garland. p81-84.
The London Times. Dec 23, 1940, p6.
Motion Picture Exhibitor. Oct 2, 1940, p611.
Newsweek. Sep 30, 1940, v16, p57.
Scholastic. Oct 21, 1940, v37, p42.
Variety. Sep 18, 1940, p14.
The World of Entertainment. p30-39.

Strong Boy (US; Ford, John; 1929)
Film Daily. Apr 7, 1929, p5.
The New York Times. Apr 1, 1929, p22.
Variety. Apr 3, 1929, p20.

The Strong Man (US; Capra, Frank; 1926)
BFI/Monthly Film Bulletin. Aug 1976, v43, p179.
The Comic Mind. p171-73.
Film Daily. Sep 12, 1926, p5.
Life. Oct 14, 1926, v88, p28.

Magill's Survey of Cinema. Silent Films. v3, p1066-69.
The Moving Picture World. Sep 18, 1926, p166.
The New York Times. Sep 7, 1926, p44.
The New Yorker. Sep 18, 1926, v2, p50-51.
Photoplay. Nov 1926, v30, p52.
Selected Film Criticism, 1921-1930. p277-78.
The Silent Clowns. p276-78.
Variety. Sep 8, 1926, p16.

The Struggle *See* Kampf, Der

The Struggle (US; Griffith, D.W.; 1931)
BFI/Monthly Film Bulletin. May 1979, v46, p108.
Film Daily. Dec 13, 1931, p10.
The Films of D.W. Griffith. p253-58.
Hollywood Spectator. Feb 1932, v12, p10-11.
Magill's Survey of Cinema. Series I. v4, p1645-47.
Movie. Aut 1965, n14, p43-44.
The New York Times. Dec 11, 1931, p35.
The New Yorker. Dec 19, 1931, v7, p62.
Outlook and Independent. Dec 23, 1931, v159, p534.
Photoplay. Feb 1932, v41, p98.
Selected Film Criticism, 1931-1940. p253-54.
Time. Dec 21, 1931, v18, p25.
Variety. Dec 15, 1931, p21.

The Student of Prague (German title: Student von Prag, Der) (GER; Rye, Stellan; 1913)
Cinema, the Magic Vehicle. v1, p39-40.
The Haunted Screen. p39-44.
Magill's Survey of Cinema. Silent Films. v3, p1070-74.

The Student of Prague (German title: Student von Prag, Der) (GER; Robison, Arthur; 1935)
Graham Greene on Film. p72.
The New Statesman and Nation. May 9, 1936, v11, p705.
The Spectator. May 1, 1936, v156, p791.
The Tatler. Jun 3, 1936, v140, p432.

The Student Prince (Also titled: A Student Prince in Old Heidelberg) (US; Lubitsch, Ernst; 1927)
The Cinema of Ernst Lubitsch. p49-60.
Ernst Lubitsch: A Guide to References and Resources. p90-92.
Film Daily. Oct 2, 1927, p6.
The Films of Norma Shearer. p140-43.
The Lubitsch Touch. p102-06.
The Moving Picture World. Sep 24, 1927, p250.
The New York Times. Sep 22, 1927, p33.
Variety. Sep 28, 1927, p24.

Student von Prag, Der *See* The Student of Prague

A Study in Scarlet (US; Marin, Edwin L.; 1933)
Commonweal. Jun 23, 1933, v18, p214.
Film Daily. May 26, 1933, p6.
The Films of Sherlock Holmes. p42-44.
Forgotten Horrors: Early Talkie Chillers from Poverty Row. p88-90.
Motion Picture Herald. Jun 10, 1933, p40.
New Outlook. Jul 1933, v162, p42.
The New York Times. Jun 1, 1933, p15.
The New Yorker. Jun 10, 1933, v9, p48.
Newsweek. Jun 10, 1933, v1, p30.
Sherlock Holmes on the Screen. p121-24.
Time. Jun 12, 1933, v21, p30.
Variety. Jun 6, 1933, p14.

Sturme der Leidenschaft *See* Tempest

Sturme Uber Dem Montblanc *See* Avalanche

Submarine D-1 (US; Bacon, Lloyd; 1937)
Film Daily. Nov 18, 1937, p7.
Motion Picture Herald. Nov 13, 1937, p47.
The New York Times. Dec 30, 1937, p15.
Rob Wagner's Script. Dec 4, 1937, v18, p10.
Time. Nov 29, 1937, v30, p41.

Variety. Nov 17, 1937, p16.
World Film News. May-Jun 1938, v3, p74-75.

Submarine Patrol (US; Ford, John; 1938)
Commonweal. Nov 25, 1938, v28, p132.
Film Daily. Nov 1, 1938, p6.
Hollywood Reporter. Oct 28, 1938, p3.
Hollywood Spectator. Nov 12, 1938, v13, p10-11.
Motion Picture Herald. Nov 5, 1938, p38, 40.
National Board of Review Magazine. Dec 1938, v13, p17.
The New Masses. Dec 6, 1938, v29, p30-31.
The New Republic. Nov 30, 1938, v97, p101.
The New York Times. Nov 19, 1938, p9.
The Non-Western Films of John Ford. p106-08.
Rob Wagner's Script. Nov 26, 1938, v20, p12.
Time. Nov 28, 1938, v32, p51.
Variety. Nov 2, 1938, p15.

A Submarine Pirate (US; Chaplin, Sydney; Avery, Charles; 1915)
Motion Picture News. Nov 27, 1915, p73.
Motion Picture News. Dec 25, 1915, p119.
Motography. Nov 27, 1915, p1111, 1143-44.
The Moving Picture World. Nov 27, 1915, p1681.
The New York Dramatic Mirror. Nov 20, 1915, p36.
The New York Dramatic Mirror. Dec 18, 1915, p29.
The New York Times. Nov 15, 1915, p11.
The New York Times. Jun 9, 1919, p16.
Variety. Nov 19, 1915, p23.

A Successful Calamity (US; Adolfi, John; 1932)
Film Daily. Aug 24, 1932, p10.
Motion Picture Herald. Oct 1, 1932, p52.
The New York Times. Sep 23, 1932, p22.
Rob Wagner's Script. Nov 19, 1932, v8, p8.
Sociology and Social Research. Nov 1932, v17, p198.
Time. Oct 3, 1932, v20, p38.
Variety. Sep 27, 1932, p17.

Such a Little Queen (US; Porter, Edwin S.; Ford, Hugh; 1914)
The Moving Picture World. Oct 3, 1914, p45.
The Moving Picture World. Oct 10, 1914, p253.
The New York Dramatic Mirror. Sep 23, 1914, p28.
Variety. Sep 26, 1914, p22.

Such Men Are Dangerous (US; Hawks, Kenneth; 1930)
Exhibitors Herald-World. Mar 15, 1930, p36.
Film Daily. Mar 9, 1930, p4.
The Film Spectator. Feb 15, 1930, v9, p21.
The New York Times. Mar 8, 1930, p21.
The New Yorker. Mar 15, 1930, v6, p87.
Outlook and Independent. Mar 19, 1930, v154, p471.
Rob Wagner's Script. Apr 19, 1930, v3, p10.
Time. Mar 24, 1930, v15, p60.
Variety. Mar 12, 1930, p33.

Suds (US; Dillon, John Francis; 1920)
Fifty Great American Silent Films, 1912-1920. p127-29.
Magill's Survey of Cinema. Silent Films. v3, p1078-80.
Photoplay. Sep 1920, v18, p67.
Selected Film Criticism, 1912-1920. p250.
Variety. Jul 2, 1920, p27-28.
Wid's Daily. Jul 4, 1920, p5.

Suez (US; Dwan, Allan; 1938)
Commonweal. Oct 29, 1938, v29, p21.
Film Daily. Oct 17, 1938, p7.
The Films of Tyrone Power. p80-83.
Hollywood Reporter. Oct 15, 1938, p3.
Hollywood Spectator. Oct 29, 1938, v13, p9-10.
Life. Oct 24, 1938, v5, p37-40.
Motion Picture Herald. Oct 22, 1938, p27.
The New York Times. Oct 15, 1938, p21.
The New Yorker. Oct 22, 1938, v14, p56-57.
Newsweek. Oct 24, 1938, v12, p33.

Photoplay. Nov 1938, v52, p38-39.
Photoplay. Jan 1939, v53, p81.
Rob Wagner's Script. Oct 29, 1938, v20, p12.
Saint Nicholas. Nov 1938, v66, p29+.
Scholastic. Oct 29, 1938, v33, p30-31.
Those Fabulous Movie Years: The 30s. p134-35.
Time. Oct 24, 1938, v32, p24+.
Time. Dec 12, 1938, v32, p39.
Variety. Oct 19, 1938, p12.

The Suicide Club *See* Trouble for Two

The Sullivans (Also titled: The Fighting Sullivans) (US; Bacon, Lloyd; 1944)
Commonweal. Feb 25, 1944, v39, p470-71.
Film Daily. Feb 3, 1944, p9.
The Films of World War II. p171-74.
Musician. May 1944, v49, p96.
Newsweek. Feb 21, 1944, v23, p91.
Scholastic. Apr 10, 1944, v44, p31.
Variety. Feb 9, 1944, p12.

Sullivan's Travels (US; Sturges, Preston; 1941)
America in the Dark. p61-62.
Between Flops. p151-63+.
Commonweal. Feb 13, 1942, v35, p419.
The Film Criticism of Otis Ferguson. p410-11.
Film Daily. Dec 5, 1941, p5.
Halliwell's Hundred. p338-41.
Hollywood Reporter. Dec 5, 1941, p3.
The International Dictionary of Films and Filmmakers. v1, p457-58.
Life. Jan 26, 1942, v12, p51-54.
The London Times. Jan 1, 1942, p6.
Magic Moments from the Movies. p61-63.
Magill's Survey of Cinema. Series I. v4, p1648-51.
Motion Picture Exhibitor. Dec 10, 1941, p908.
Motion Picture Herald Product Digest. Dec 13, 1941, p405.
Movie Maker. Dec 1973, v7, p830-31+.
The New Republic. Jan 26, 1941, v106, p117.
The New York Times. Jan 29, 1942, p25.
Newsweek. Feb 9, 1942, v19, p64.
PM. Jan 18, 1942, p46.
Preston Sturges: A Guide to References and Resources. p56-60.
Rob Wagner's Script. Feb 14, 1942, v28, p14-15.
Selected Film Criticism, 1941-1950. p228-30.
Sight and Sound. Wint 1977-78, v48, p50-52.
Talking Pictures. p44-47.
Time. Feb 9, 1942, v39, p36.
Variety. Dec 10, 1941, p8.

A Summer Idyl (US; Griffith, D.W.; 1910)
The Moving Picture World. Sep 17, 1910, p631.
Selected Film Criticism, 1896-1911. p95-96.

The Sun Never Sets (US; Lee, Rowland V.; 1939)
Basil Rathbone: His Life and His Films. p216-19.
Chestnuts in Her Lap. p47-50.
Commonweal. Jun 16, 1939, v30, p218.
Film Daily. Jun 12, 1939, p11.
Hollywood Reporter. Jun 1, 1939, p3.
Hollywood Spectator. Jun 10, 1939, v14, p5-6.
The New Masses. Jun 27, 1939, v32, p31.
The New York Times. Jun 9, 1939, p26.
The New Yorker. Jun 10, 1939, v15, p74-75.
Newsweek. Jun 12, 1939, v13, p35.
Photoplay. Aug 1939, v53, p55.
Rob Wagner's Script. Jun 10, 1939, v21, p16-17.
The Tatler. Jul 12, 1939, v153, p52.
Time. Jun 19, 1939, v33, p74.
Variety. Jun 7, 1939, p12.

Sun Valley Serenade (US; Humberstone, Bruce; 1941)
Commonweal. Sep 26, 1941, 34, p547.
Film Daily. Jul 24, 1941, p6.
The Hollywood Musical Goes to War. p98-99.

Hollywood Reporter. Jul 24, 1941, p3.
The London Times. Jan 6, 1942, p6.
Magill's Survey of Cinema. Series II. v5, p2359-62.
Motion Picture Exhibitor. Aug 6, 1941, p804-05.
Motion Picture Exhibitor. Sep 3, 1941, v26, n17, sec2, p836.
Motion Picture Herald Product Digest. May 17, 1941, p137.
The New Republic. Oct 20, 1941, v105, p508.
The New York Times. Sep 6, 1941, p20.
Newsweek. Sep 1, 1941, v18, p49-50.
Scribner's Commentator. Nov 1941, v11, p108.
Time. Sep 22, 1941, v38, p83.
Variety. Jul 23, 1941, p8.

Sunny (US; Seiter, William A.; 1930)
Exhibitors Herald-World. Oct 11, 1930, p38.
Film Daily. Dec 28, 1930, p10.
The Hollywood Musical. p63, 191.
Life. Jan 16, 1931, v97, p20.
The New York Times. Dec 27, 1930, p16.
Time. Jan 5, 1931, v17, p25.
Variety. Dec 31, 1930, p19.

Sunny Side Up (US; Butler, David; 1929)
Cinema. Jan 1930, v1, p38.
Film Daily. Oct 6, 1929, p9.
The Hollywood Musical. p32.
The New York Times. Oct 4, 1929, p24.
Selected Film Criticism, 1921-1930. p280-81.
Variety. Oct 9, 1929, p31.

Sunrise (US; Murnau, F.W.; 1927)
American Cinematographer. Apr 1984, v65, p28-34.
American Silent Film. 323-28.
Cinema, the Magic Vehicle. v1, p128-29.
Classics of the Film. p56-60.
Close-Up. Mar 1928, v2, p38-45.
Dictionary of Film. p361-62.
Exhibitor's Herald-World and Moving Picture World. Jul 21, 1928, p53.
Film Daily. Oct 2, 1927, p6.
The Film Spectator. Dec 24, 1927, v4, p4-5.
The Films of the Twenties. p177-81.
From Quasimodo to Scarlett O'Hara. p99-101.
A History of Film. p148.
The International Dictionary of Films and Filmmakers. v1, p459-61.
Literary Digest. Dec 23, 1927, v95, p28-29.
Magill's Survey of Cinema. Silent Films. v3, p1081-83.
The Moving Picture World. Oct 1, 1927, p312.
Murnau (Eisner). p167-86.
The New Republic. Oct 26, 1927, v52, p263-64.
The New York Times. Sept 24, 1927, Addenda p15.
Photoplay. Dec 1927, v33, p52.
Selected Film Criticism, 1921-1930. p282-85.
Spellbound in Darkness. p461-63.
Variety. Sep 28, 1927, p21.

Supernatural (US; Halperin, Victor; 1933)
Film Daily. Apr 22, 1933, p4.
The Films of Carole Lombard. p106-08.
Motion Picture Herald. Apr 29, 1933, p30.
The New York Times. Apr 22, 1933, p16.
The New Yorker. Apr 29, 1933, v9, p45.
Newsweek. Apr 29, 1933, v1, p27.
Time. May 1, 1933, v21, p38.
Variety. Apr 25, 1933, p18.

Super-Sleuth (US; Stoloff, Benjamin; 1937)
Film Daily. Jul 13, 1937, p4.
Hollywood Reporter. Jul 10, 1937, p3.
Motion Picture Herald. Jul 17, 1937, p46.
The New Masses. Jul 27, 1937, v24, p29.
The New York Times. Jul 17, 1937, p18.
The New Yorker. Jul 24, 1937, v13, p64.
Rob Wagner's Script. Jul 17, 1937, v17, p15-16.
Variety. Jul 14, 1937, p20.

Surrender (US; Sloman, Edward; 1927)
Film Daily. Oct 16, 1927, p6.
The Moving Picture World. Nov 12, 1927, p26.
The New York Times. Oct 11, 1927, p1.
Photoplay. Aug 1927, v32, p55.
Selected Film Criticism, 1921-1930. p286.
Variety. Nov 9, 1927, p25.

Susan and God (US; Cukor, George; 1940)
Commonweal. Jun 21, 1940, v32, p192.
Film Daily. Jun 6, 1940, p7.
The Films of Fredric March. p163-65.
The Films of Joan Crawford. p139-41.
The Films of Rita Hayworth. p109-10.
George Cukor (Phillips). p104-05.
Hollywood Reporter. Jun 1, 1940, p3.
Motion Picture Herald Product Digest. May 4, 1940, p46.
The New York Times. Jul 12, 1940, p11.
Newsweek. Jun 17, 1940, v15, p52+.
Time. Jul 1, 1940, v36, p34.
Variety. Jun 5, 1940, p14.

Susan Lenox: Her Fall and Rise (US; Leonard, Robert Z.; 1931)
Film Daily. Oct 18, 1931, p10.
The Films of Clark Gable. p126-28.
The Films of Greta Garbo. p98-104.
Fortune. Dec 1932, v6, p57.
Hollywood Reporter. Jul 13, 1931, p3.
Life. Nov 13, 1931, v98, p18.
Motion Picture Herald. Jul 18, 1931, p41.
Motion Picture Herald. Oct 24, 1931, p27.
The Nation. Nov 11, 1931, v133, p526+.
The New York Times. Oct 17, 1931, p20.
The New Yorker. Oct 24, 1931, v7, p68-69.
Outlook and Independent. Oct 28, 1931, v159, p281.
Screening the Novel. p18-45.
Time. Oct 26, 1931, v18, p34.
Variety. Oct 20, 1931, p21.

Susannah of the Mounties (US; Seiter, William A.; 1939)
Commonweal. Jul 7, 1939, v30, p278.
Film Daily. Jun 27, 1939, p8.
The Films of Shirley Temple. p206-07.
Hollywood Reporter. Jun 17, 1939, p3.
Hollywood Spectator. Jun 24, 1939, v14, p5.
Motion Picture Herald. Jun 24, 1939, p39, 42.
The New York Times. Jun 24, 1939, p13.
Rob Wagner's Script. Jul 4, 1939, v21, p16.
Saint Nicholas. Jul 1939, v66, p41+.
Time. Jul 3, 1939, v34, p35.
Variety. Jun 21, 1939, p16.

Suspicion (US; Hitchcock, Alfred; 1941)
Around Cinemas. p194-95.
The Art of Alfred Hitchcock. p115-24.
Commonweal. Dec 5, 1941, v35, p179.
The Film Criticism of Otis Ferguson. p394-95.
Film Daily. Sep 18, 1941, p10.
The Films of Alfred Hitchcock. p103-08.
The Films of Cary Grant. p153-56.
The Films of the Forties. p48-49.
Hitchcock: The First Forty-Four Films. p65-68.
Hitchcock (Truffaut). p140-43+.
Hollywood Reporter. Sep 18, 1941, p3.
Life. Dec 1941, v11, p59-60+.
The London Times. Dec 4, 1941, p6.
Magill's Survey of Cinema. Series I. v4, p1663-66.
Motion Picture Exhibitor. Oct 1, 1941, v26, n21, sec2, p863-64.
Motion Picture Herald Product Digest. Sep 4, 1941, p273.
The New Republic. Nov 10, 1941, v105, p622.
The New York Times. Nov 21, 1941, p23.
The New York Times. Nov 23, 1941, sec9, p5.
The New Yorker. Nov 22, 1941, v17, p98.

Newsweek. Nov 17, 1941, v18, p55.
Rob Wagner's Script. Jan 31, 1942, v27, p14.
Scholastic. Dec 8, 1941, v39, p30.
Screen. 1976, v17, n3, p68-112.
Selected Film Criticism, 1941-1950. p233-35.
Time. Nov 17, 1941, v38, p92.
Variety. Sep 24, 1941, p8.
Women's Film and Female Experience. p176-85.

Sutter's Gold (US; Cruze, James; 1936)
Canadian Magazine. May 1936, v85, p59.
Film Daily. Mar 28, 1936, p7.
Hollywood Reporter. Mar 26, 1936, p3.
Motion Picture Herald. Feb 15, 1936, p14-15.
Motion Picture Herald. Mar 28, 1936, p41.
The New York Times. Mar 27, 1936, p25.
The New Yorker. Apr 4, 1936, v12, p72.
Time. Apr 6, 1936, v27, p46.
Variety. Apr 1, 1936, p16.

Suzy (US; Fitzmaurice, George; 1936)
Canadian Magazine. Nov 1936, v86, p38.
Film Daily. Jul 14, 1936, p11.
The Films of Cary Grant. p94-97.
The Films of Jean Harlow. p136-43.
Hollywood Reporter. Jul 9, 1936, p3.
Hollywood Spectator. Jul 18, 1936, v11, p3.
Judge. Sep 1936, v111, p12, 28.
Literary Digest. Jul 25, 1936, v122, p18.
Motion Picture Herald. Jul 18, 1936, p52, 54.
The New York Times. Jul 25, 1936, p16.
The New Yorker. Aug 1, 1936, v12, p39.
Rob Wagner's Script. Jul 25, 1936, v15, p10.
Time. Aug 3, 1936, v28, p29.
Variety. Jul 29, 1936, p14.
World Film News. Sep 1936, v1, p22-23.

Svengali (US; Mayo, Archie; 1931)
Film Daily. May 3, 1931, p30.
Hollywood Spectator. Jun 20, 1931, v12, p16-17.
Horror Movies (Clarens). p102-03.
Judge. May 23, 1931, v100, p22.
Kiss Kiss Bang Bang. p447.
Life. May 22, 1931, v97, p18.
Magill's Survey of Cinema. Series II. v5, p2384-86.
Motion Picture Herald. May 9, 1931, p35.
Motion Picture Herald. Jul 11, 1931, p25.
The Nation. May 27, 1931, v132, p590.
The New York Times. May 1, 1931, p30.
The New Yorker. May 9, 1931, v7, p69-70.
Outlook and Independent. May 13, 1931, v158, p59.
Time. May 11, 1931, v17, p46, 48.
Variety. May 6, 1931, p22.

Swamp Water (US; Renoir, Jean; 1941)
Commonweal. Nov 28, 1941, v35, p144.
Film Daily. Oct 20, 1941, p8.
Hollywood Reporter. Oct 20, 1941, p3.
Jean Renoir: A Guide to References and Resources. p129-31.
Jean Renoir (Durgnat).
Motion Picture Herald Product Digest. Oct 18, 1941, p318.
The New York Times. Nov 17, 1941, p15.
Newsweek. Nov 24, 1941, v18, p72.
Scholastic. Dec 8, 1941, v39, p30.
Variety. Oct 22, 1941, p8.

Swanee River (US; Lanfield, Sidney; 1939)
Étude. Feb 1940, v58, p85.
Film Daily. Dec 26, 1939, p6.
Hollywood Reporter. Dec 20, 1939, p3.
Hollywood Spectator. Jan 6, 1940, v14, p5-6.
Motion Picture Herald. Dec 23, 1939, p40.
The New York Times. Dec 30, 1939, p9.
The New Yorker. Jan 6, 1940, v15, p51.
Rob Wagner's Script. Jan 6, 1940, v23, p17-18.

Time. Jan 15, 1940, v35, p62.
Variety. Dec 27, 1939, p12.

Sweepings (US; Cromwell, John; 1933)
BFI/Monthly Film Bulletin. Nov 1979, v46, p240.
Film Daily. Mar 22, 1933, p6.
Hollywood Reporter. Mar 10, 1933, p3.
Judge. May 1933, v104, p23-24.
Motion Picture Herald. Mar 18, 1933, p32.
The Nation. Apr 12, 1933, v136, p422.
The New York Times. Mar 24, 1933, p22.
The New Yorker. Apr 1, 1933, v8, p50.
Rob Wagner's Script. Apr 15, 1933, v9, p8.
Time. Apr 3, 1933, v21, p34.
Variety. Mar 28, 1933, p15.

Sweet Adeline (US; LeRoy, Mervyn; 1935)
Film Daily. Jan 5, 1935, p4.
The Hollywood Musical. p99.
Hollywood Reporter. Dec 4, 1934, p3.
Motion Picture. Feb 1935, v49, p54-55.
Motion Picture Herald. Dec 15, 1934, p41, 44.
The New Masses. Jan 15, 1935, v14, p29-30.
The New York Times. Jan 7, 1935, p13.
Time. Dec 31, 1934, v24, p15.
Variety. Jan 8, 1935, p18.

Sweet Music (US; Green, Alfred E.; 1935)
Film Daily. Feb 20, 1935, p9.
The Hollywood Musical. p98.
Hollywood Reporter. Feb 20, 1935, p3.
Hollywood Reporter. Mar 1, 1935, p2.
Motion Picture Herald. Mar 2, 1935, p55, 58.
Movie Classic. Mar 1935, v8, p23.
The New York Times. Feb 21, 1935, p23.
The New Yorker. Mar 2, 1935, v11, p55-56.
Time. Mar 4, 1935, v25, p16.
Time. Dec 31, 1934, v24, p15.
Variety. Feb 27, 1935, p12.

The Sweetheart of Sigma Chi (US; Marin, Edwin L.; 1933)
Film Daily. Oct 26, 1933, p7.
Hollywood Reporter. Oct 6, 1933, p5.
Motion Picture Herald. Oct 14, 1933, p34.
The New York Times. Nov 9, 1933, p27.
Variety. Nov 14, 1933, p30.

Sweethearts (US; Van Dyke, W.S.; 1938)
Canadian Magazine. Feb 1939, v91, p44.
Commonweal. Jan 6, 1939, v29, p302.
Film Daily. Dec 19, 1938, p6.
The Films of Jeanette MacDonald and Nelson Eddy. p231-46.
Hollywood Reporter. Dec 16, 1938, p3.
Hollywood Spectator. Dec 24, 1938, v13, p16.
Life. Oct 24, 1938, v5, p28-29.
Motion Picture Herald. Dec 24, 1938, p37.
The New Statesman and Nation. Mar 11, 1939, v17, p357.
The New York Times. Dec 23, 1938, p16.
Newsweek. Jan 2, 1939, v13, p25.
Photoplay. Jan 1939, v53, p54.
Photoplay. Jun 1939, v53, p10.
Rob Wagner's Script. Dec 24, 1938, v20, p9-10.
The Tatler. Mar 15, 1939, v151, p466.
Variety. Dec 21, 1938, p14.

Swing High, Swing Low (US; Leisen, Mitchell; 1937)
The Film Criticism of Otis Ferguson. p174-75.
Film Daily. Mar 15, 1937, p18.
The Films of Carole Lombard. p142-46.
Hollywood Director. p104-15.
Hollywood Reporter. Mar 10, 1937, p3.
Hollywood Spectator. Mar 27, 1937, v11, p9.
Motion Picture Herald. Mar 20, 1937, p44.
The New Republic. May 5, 1937, v90, p386.
The New Statesman and Nation. Apr 3, 1937, v13, p555.

The New York Times. Apr 15, 1937, p19.
Rob Wagner's Script. Mar 27, 1937, v17, p8.
Time. Mar 22, 1937, v29, p41.
Variety. Apr 21, 1937, p14.
World Film News. May 1937, v2, p25.

Swing Time (US; Stevens, George; 1936)
American Film Criticism. p344-45.
Beyond Formula: American Film Genres. p87-90.
Commonweal. Sep 11, 1936, v24, p467.
Esquire. Nov 1936, v6, p125.
Film Daily. Aug 26, 1936, p6.
The Films of Ginger Rogers. p129-31.
The Fred Astaire & Ginger Rogers Book. p98-116.
The Hollywood Musical. p117-19.
Hollywood Reporter. Aug 24, 1936, p3.
Hollywood Spectator. Aug 29, 1936, v11, p5.
Literary Digest. Sep 12, 1936, v122, p17.
Magill's Survey of Cinema. Series II. v5, p2398-2404.
Motion Picture Herald. Aug 29, 1936, p43.
Movie Classic. Nov 1936, v11, p34-35+.
The New Masses. Sep 8, 1936, v20, p29.
The New Statesman and Nation. Oct 24, 1936, v12, p628.
The New York Times. Aug 28, 1936, p21.
The New Yorker. Sep 5, 1936, v12, p59.
Newsweek. Sep 5, 1936, v8, p27.
Rob Wagner's Script. Sep 19, 1936, v16, p10.
Stage. Oct 1936, v14, p26.
Starring Fred Astaire. p133-49.
Time. Sep 7, 1936, v28, p19.
Variety. Sep 2, 1936, p18.
World Film News. Oct 1936, v1, p25.

Swing Your Lady (US; Enright, Ray; 1938)
The Complete Films of Humphrey Bogart. p53.
Film Daily. Jan 10, 1938, p6.
The Films of Ronald Reagan. p37-38.
Hollywood Reporter. Jan 5, 1938, p3.
Humphrey Bogart: The Man and His Films. p75.
The New York Times. Jan 27, 1938, p17.
The New Yorker. Jan 29, 1938, v13, p48.
Rob Wagner's Script. Feb 2, 1938, v19, p8.
Time. Jan 17, 1938, v31, p44.
Variety. Jan 26, 1938, p14.

Swiss Family Robinson (US; Ludwig, Edward; 1940)
Film Daily. Feb 1, 1940, p 7.
Hollywood Reporter. Jan 13, 1940, p3.
Life. Feb 5, 1940, v8, p33-34+.
Motion Picture Herald. Nov 18, 1939, p41.
Motion Picture Herald. Feb 3, 1940, p42-44.
The New York Times. Feb 9, 1940, p15.
Scholastic. Feb 19, 1940, v36, p38.
Time. Feb 19, 1940, v35, p83-85.
Variety. Feb 7, 1940, p14.

Swiss Miss (US; Blystone, John G.; 1938)
Film Daily. May 10, 1938, p6.
Hollywood Reporter. May 4, 1938, p2.
Hollywood Spectator. May 14, 1938, v13, p10.
Laurel & Hardy. p365-72.
Motion Picture Herald. May 7, 1938, p39.
Motion Picture Herald. Feb 26, 1938, p16-17.
The New York Times. Jun 4, 1938, p18.
Newsweek. Jun 20, 1938, v11, p23.
Variety. May 11, 1938, p16.
World Film News. Aug 1938, v3, p171.

The Sworn Enemy (US; Marin, Edwin L.; 1936)
Film Daily. Jul 7, 1936, p6.
Hollywood Reporter. Jul 1, 1936, p3.
Motion Picture Herald. Jul 11, 1936, p109.
The New York Times. Sep 12, 1936, p20.
Rob Wagner's Script. Sep 12, 1936, v16, p10.
Time. Sep 21, 1936, v28, p25.
Variety. Sep 16, 1936, p16.

Sylvester—Tragodie einer Nacht *See* New Year's Eve

Sylvia Scarlett (US; Cukor, George; 1935)
BFI/Monthly Film Bulletin. Dec 1979, v41, p260.
Canadian Magazine. Feb 1936, v85, p37.
Esquire. Mar 1936, v5, p105.
Film Daily. Dec 12, 1935, p4.
The Films of Cary Grant. p88-90.
The Films of Katharine Hepburn. p71-74.
George Cukor (Phillips). p67-71.
Hollywood Spectator. Dec 21, 1935, v10, p9.
Judge. Mar 1936, v110, p28.
Literary Digest. Jan 18, 1936, v121, p20.
Magill's Survey of Cinema. Series II. v5, p2404-07.
Motion Picture Herald. Jan 18, 1936, p46.
The New York Times. Jan 10, 1936, p16.
The New Yorker. Jan 18, 1936, v11, p53.
Newsweek. Jan 4, 1936, v7, p25.
On Cukor. p91-97.
Rob Wagner's Script. Dec 28, 1935, v14, p10.
Saturday Review (London). May 2, 1936, v161, p568.
Time. Jan 13, 1936, v27, p42.
Variety. Jan 15, 1936, p18.
The Velvet Light Trap. Wint 1971-72, n3, p19-23.

Symphony of Six Million (US; Tuttle, Frank; 1932)
Film Daily. Apr 10, 1932, p10.
Motion Picture Herald. Apr 2, 1932, p35.
Motion Picture Herald. May 28, 1932, p87.
The New York Times. Apr 15, 1932, p23.
The New Yorker. Apr 23, 1932, v8, p57.
Time. Apr 11, 1932, v19, p29.
Variety. Apr 19, 1932, p14.

Syn Mongolii *See* The Son of Mongolia

Tabu (US; Murnau, F.W.; Flaherty, Robert; 1931)
The Bookman. Aug 1931, v73, p634.
Cinema, the Magic Vehicle. v1, p185-86.
Classics of the Silent Screen. p116-17.
Close-Up. Jun 1931, v8, p118-19.
Commonweal. Jul 1, 1931, v14, p246.
Creative Art. Jun 1931, v8, p462-63.
Dictionary of Films. p365.
Film Comment. Sum 1971, v7, p23-27.
Film Culture. 1959, n20, p13-16.
Film Daily. Mar 22, 1931, p10.
Film Heritage. Spr 1966, v1, p35-37.
Film Society Review. Sep 1967, p15-16.
From Quasimodo to Scarlett O'Hara. p135-37.
Hollywood Spectator. Aug 1, 1931, v12, p19.
Judge. Apr 18, 1931, v100, p20.
Judge. May 2, 1931, v100, p20.
Kiss Kiss Bang Bang. p449.
Life. May 22, 1931, v97, p18.
Literary Digest. Apr 4, 1931, v109, p37-38.
Lorentz on Film. p72-73.
Magill's Survey of Cinema. Series II. v5, p2408-11.
Motion Picture Herald. Mar 21, 1931, p39.
Murnau (Eisner). p202-20.
National Board of Review Magazine. Apr 1931, v6, p9.
The New Republic. Apr 1, 1931, v66, p183.
The New Statesman and Nation. Jan 20, 1934, v7, p86.
The New York Times. Mar 19, 1931, p21.
The New Yorker. Mar 28, 1931, v7, p75.
Outlook and Independent. Mar 25, 1931, v157, p442.
Rob Wagner's Script. Mar 28, 1931, v5, p11.
Robert Flaherty: A Guide to References and Resources. p99-101.
The Spectator. Sep 26, 1931, v147, p383.
Time. Mar 30, 1931, v17, p33.
Variety. Mar 25, 1931, p17.
The World of Robert Flaherty. p76-79.

Tagebuch einer Verlorenen, Das *See* The Diary of a Lost Dutch Girl

Tail Spin (US; Del Ruth, Roy; 1939)
Film Daily. Feb 15, 1939, p7.
The Films of Alice Fay. p105-08.
Hollywood Reporter. Jan 28, 1939, p3.
Hollywood Spectator. Feb 4, 1939, v13, p12-13.
Motion Picture Herald. Feb 4, 1939, p56, 61.
The New Statesman and Nation. May 6, 1939, v17, p680.
The New York Times. Feb 11, 1939, p13.
Newsweek. Feb 20, 1939, v13, p29.
Photoplay. Apr 1939, v53, p52.
Rob Wagner's Script. Mar 25, 1939, v21, p16.
The Spectator. May 12, 1939, v162, p804.
Time. Feb 20, 1939, v33, p68.
Variety. Feb 1, 1939, p13.

Take a Letter Darling (US; Leisen, Mitchell; 1942)
Commonweal. Jul 3, 1942, p256.
Film Daily. May 6, 1942, p6.
Hollywood Reeporter. May 5, 1942, p3.
Magill's Cinema Annual, 1985. p632-37.
Motion Picture Herald Product Digest. May 9, 1942, p645.
The New York Times. May 28, 1942, p13.
Newsweek. May 25, 1942, v19, p62.
Time. Jun 8, 1942, v39, p50.
Variety. May 6, 1942, p8.

Take Me Out to the Ball Game (US; Berkeley, Busby; 1949)
The Busby Berkeley Book. p158-61.
Commonweal. Mar 25, 1949, v44, p592.
Film Daily. Mar 9, 1949, p7.
The Films of Frank Sinatra. p60-62.
The Films of Gene Kelly. p95-98.
The Hollywood Musical. p300.
Hollywood Reporter. Mar 8, 1949, p3.
Motion Picture Herald Product Digest. Mar 12, 1949, p4529.
The New York Times. Mar 10, 1949, p35.
Newsweek. Mar 21, 1949, v33, p89.
Rotarian. Jun 1949, v74, p51.
Stanley Donen (Casper). p22-24.
Time. Mar 28, 1949, v53, p98+.
Variety. Mar 9, 1949, p6.

A Tale of Two Cities, Part I (US; 1911)
Film Reports. Mar 4, 1911, v2, p6.
A Million and One Nights. p549.
The Moving Picture World. Mar 4, 1911, p483.
Selected Film Criticism, 1896-1911. p96-97.

A Tale of Two Cities, Part II (US; 1911)
A Million and One Nights. p549.
The Moving Picture World. Mar 11, 1911, p540.
Selected Film Criticism, 1896-1911. p97.

A Tale of Two Cities, Part III (US; 1911)
A Million and One Nights. p549.
The Moving Picture World. Mar 11, 1911, p540.
Selected Film Criticism, 1896-1911. p97-98.

A Tale of Two Cities (US; Lloyd, Frank; 1917)
Fifty Great American Silent Films, 1912-1920. p77-79.
Magill's Survey of Cinema. Silent Films. v3, p1088-90.
The Moving Picture World. Mar 31, 1917, p2118, 2162.
The Moving Picture World. Feb 14, 1920, p1010-11.
The New York Dramatic Mirror. Mar 24, 1917, p26.
The New York Times. Mar 12, 1917, p9.
Photoplay. Jun 1917, v12, p91-92.
Selected Film Criticism, 1912-1920. p250-52.
Variety. Mar 16, 1917, p34.
Wid's Daily. Mar 15, 1917, p164.

A Tale of Two Cities (US; Conway, Jack; 1935)
Canadian Magazine. Dec 1935, v84, p44.
Canadian Magazine. Jan 1936, v85, p31.
Commonweal. Dec 20, 1935, v23, p219.
Dickens and Film. p269-78.
Esquire. Mar 1936, v5, p105.
The Film Criticism of Otis Ferguson. p110-12.
Film Daily. Nov 30, 1935, p4.
The Films of Ronald Colman. p173-78.
The Films of the Thirties. p156-57.
Garbo and the Night Watchman. p130-32.
Hollywood Reporter. Nov 27, 1935, p3, 5.
Hollywood Spectator. Dec 7, 1935, v10, p7-8.
Judge. Feb 1936, v110, p14.
Literary Digest. Dec 14, 1935, v120, p21.
London Mercury. May 1936, v34, p59-60.
Magill's Survey of Cinema. Series I. v4, p1667-70.
Motion Picture Herald. Dec 7, 1935, p66.
Movie Classic. Nov 1935, v9, p40+.
The New Masses. Jan 14, 1936, v18, p29-30.
The New Republic. Jan 8, 1936, v85, p254.
The New York Times. Dec 26, 1935, p21.
The New Yorker. Dec 28, 1935, v11, p49-50.
Newsweek. Dec 28, 1935, v6, p24.
Photoplay. Nov 1935, v48, p34.
Rob Wagner's Script. Jan 11, 1936, v14, p12.
Saturday Review (London). Apr 25, 1936, v161, p544.
Scholastic. Jan 4, 1936, v27, p8-9.
Selected Film Criticism, 1931-1940. p254-56.
Sociology and Social Research. Mar 1937, v21, p398.
Stage. Dec 1935, v13, p40-41.
Time. Dec 30, 1935, v26, p16.
Variety. Jan 1, 1936, p44.
World Film News. Sep 1936, v1, p24.

Tales from the Vienna Woods (AUSTRIA; Jacoby, Georg; 1937)
Graham Greene on Film. p174.
Hollywood Reporter. Apr 16, 1937, p6.
Hollywood Spectator. Apr 24, 1937, v12, p13.
The New York Times. Nov 2, 1935, p13.
Rob Wagner's Script. Apr 24, 1937, v17, p10.
Sight and Sound. Aut 1937, v6, p144.
The Spectator. Oct 15, 1937, v159, p631.
World Film News. Dec 1937, v2, p31.

Tales of Manhattan (US; Duvivier, Julien; 1942)
The Cinema of Edward G. Robinson. p140-43.
Commonweal. Sep 18, 1942, v36, p518-19.
Film Daily. Aug 5, 1942, p7.
The Films of Ginger Rogers. p175-76.
The Films of Henry Fonda. p116-17.
The Films of Rita Hayworth. p137-40.
The Films of W.C. Fields. p164-69.
The Fondas. p122-24.
Hollywood Reporter. Aug 4, 1942, p3.
Life. Jul 27, 1942, v13, p44+.
The London Times. Apr 1, 1943, p6.
Motion Picture Exhibitor. Aug 12, 1942, p1068.
Motion Picture Herald Product Digest. Aug 8, 1942, p825.
Musician. Aug 1942, v47, p116.
The New Republic. Oct 12, 1942, v107, p466.
The New York Times. Sept 25, 1942, p25.
The New York Times. Oct 4, 1942, sec8, p3.
The New Yorker. Sep 26, 1942, v18, p73.
Newsweek. Sep 28, 1942, v20, p62+.
Time. Sep 21, 1942, v40, p69.
Variety. Aug 5, 1942, p8.
W.C. Fields: A Life on Film. p240-42.

Talk of the Devil (GB; Reed, Carol; 1937)
Film Daily. May 18, 1937, p8.
Hollywood Reporter. Jan 13, 1937, p7.
The New York Times. May 15, 1937, p23.

Variety. Dec 23, 1936, p18.
Variety. May 19, 1937, p22.

Talk of the Town (US; Stevens, George; 1942)
Commonweal. Sep 11, 1942, v36, p496.
Film Comment. Jul/Aug 1975, v11, p52-56.
Film Daily. Jul 27, 1942, p8.
Films and Filming. May 1973, v19, p67-68.
The Films of Cary Grant. p157-60.
The Films of Ronald Colman. p215-18.
Hollywood Reporter. Jul 27, 1942, p3.
Life. Sep 7, 1942, v13, p68-70+.
The London Times. Nov 30, 1942, p8.
Magill's Survey of Cinema. Series I. v4, p1671-74.
Motion Picture Exhibitor. Jul 29, 1942, v28, n12, sec2, p1061.
Motion Picture Herald Product Digest. Aug 1, 1942, p809.
The New Republic. Sep 21, 1942, 107, p349.
The New York Times. Aug 28, 1942, p22.
The New Yorker. Aug 29, 1942, v18, p37.
Newsweek. Aug 24, 1942, v20, p60.
Rob Wagner's Script. Aug 29, 1942, v27, p21.
Selected Film Criticism, 1941-1950. p235.
Time. Aug 17, 1942, v40, p42+.
Variety. Jul 29, 1942, p8.

The Taming of the Shrew (US; 1908)
The Moving Picture World. Nov 28, 1908, p423.
Selected Film Criticism, 1896-1911. p98-99.

The Taming of the Shrew (US; Taylor, Sam; 1929)
BFI/Monthly Film Bulletin. Sep 1974, v41, p210.
Film Daily. Oct 8, 1929, p8.
The Films of the Twenties. p254-56.
His Majesty the American. p175-84.
Literary Digest. Dec 21, 1929, v103, p18-19.
The New York Times. Nov 30, 1929, p23.
Variety. Dec 4, 1929, p15.

Tangier (US; Waggner, George; 1946)
Commonweal. May 17, 1946, v44, p120.
Film Daily. Mar 1, 1946, p8.
Hollywood Reporter. Mar 6, 1946, p3.
Motion Picture Herald Product Digest. Mar 16, 1946, p2895.
The New York Times. Jun 7, 1946, sec2, p16.
Variety. Mar 6, 1946, p12.

Tarnished Angel (US; Goodwins, Leslie; 1938)
Film Daily. Oct 26, 1938, p7.
Hollywood Reporter. Oct 22, 1938, p3.
Hollywood Spectator. Oct 29, 1938, v13, p18.
Motion Picture Herald. Oct 29, 1938, p44.
The New York Times. Nov 15, 1938, p27.
Variety. Nov 16, 1938, p15.

Tarnished Lady (US; Cukor, George; 1931)
Film Daily. Apr 19, 1931, p10.
The Films of the Thirties. p55-56.
George Cukor (Phillips). p31-32.
Judge. May 23, 1931, v100, p22.
Life. May 15, 1931, v97, p20.
Motion Picture Herald. May 9, 1931, p40.
The New Statesman and Nation. Jun 6, 1931, v1, p545.
The New York Times. Apr 30, 1931, p29.
The New Yorker. May 9, 1931, v7, p67, 69.
Outlook and Independent. May 13, 1931, v158, p59.
Rob Wagner's Script. Jul 11, 1931, v5, p9-10.
Time. May 11, 1931, v17, p48.
Variety. May 6, 1931, p22.

Tarzan and His Mate (US; Gibbons, Cedric; 1934)
Commonweal. May 4, 1934, v20, p21.
Film Daily. Apr 16, 1934, p8.
Hollywood Reporter. Apr 7, 1934, p3.
Literary Digest. May 5, 1934, v117, p44.
Motion Picture Herald. Apr 28, 1934, p35.
The Nation. May 16, 1934, v138, p573-74.

The New York Times. Apr 21, 1934, p12.
Newsweek. Apr 28, 1934, v3, p38.
Time. Apr 30, 1934, v23, p20.
Variety. Apr 24, 1934, p14.

Tarzan Finds a Son (US; Thorpe, Richard; 1939)
Film Daily. Jun 7, 1939, p6.
Hollywood Reporter. May 27, 1939, p3.
Life. Jun 26, 1939, v6, p64-67.
Motion Picture Herald. Jun 3, 1939, p38.
The New York Times. Jun 15, 1939, p27.
The New Yorker. Jun 17, 1939, v15, p75-76.
Newsweek. Jun 19, 1939, v13, p33.
Photoplay. Aug 1939, v53, p54.
Time. Jun 26, 1939, v33, p45.
Variety. May 31, 1939, p14.

Tarzan of the Apes (US; Sidney, Scott; 1918)
Exhibitor's Trade Review. Feb 2, 1918, p716-17.
Exhibitor's Trade Review. Feb 9, 1918, p815, 837.
Magill's Survey of Cinema. Silent Films. v3, p1091-94.
Motion Picture News. Jan 26, 1918, p582.
Motion Picture News. Feb 16, 1918, p1030.
The Moving Picture World. Feb 16, 1918, p1002.
The Moving Picture World. Apr 27, 1918, p594.
The New York Times. Jan 28, 1918, p13.
Selected Film Criticism, 1912-1920. 252-53.
Variety. Feb 1, 1918, p47.
Wid's Daily. Feb 14, 1918, p935-36.

Tarzan, the Ape Man (US; Van Dyke, W.S.; 1932)
Africa on Film. p36-38.
Film Daily. Mar 27, 1932, p22.
Films in Review. Oct 1960, v11, p452-63.
Fortune. Dec 1932, v6, p56.
Hollywood Reporter. Feb 9, 1932, p3.
Literary Digest. Apr 16, 1932, v113, p18.
Magill's Survey of Cinema. Series I. v4, p1675-77.
Motion Picture Herald. Feb 20, 1932, p33.
National Board of Review Magazine. Apr 1932, v7, p8-10.
The New Statesman and Nation. May 21, 1932, v3, p661-62.
The New York Times. Mar 28, 1932, p11.
The New Yorker. Apr 2, 1932, v8, p56.
Outlook. Apr 1932, v160, p228-29.
Rob Wagner's Script. Jun 11, 1932, v7, p10.
Time. Apr 4, 1932, v19, p22.
Variety. Mar 29, 1932, p25.

Taxi! (US; Del Ruth, Roy; 1932)
Film Daily. Jan 10, 1932, p8.
The Films of James Cagney. p58-60.
The Great Gangster Pictures. p380-81.
Hollywood Reporter. Nov 14, 1931, p3.
Judge. Feb 6, 1932, v102, p22.
Lorentz on Film. p83-84.
Motion Picture Herald. Jan 16, 1932, p40.
The Nation. Feb 3, 1932, v134, p150.
The New York Times. Jan 8, 1932, p27.
The New Yorker. May 30, 1936, v12, p59.
Outlook and Independent. Jan 20, 1932, v160, p87.
The Spectator. Feb 3, 1932, v154, p150.
Time. Jan 18, 1932, v19, p22.
Variety. Jan 12, 1932, p15.

Television Spy (US; Dmytryk, Edward; 1939)
Film Daily. Oct 13, 1939, p6.
Hollywood Reporter. Oct 6, 1939, p4.
Motion Picture Herald. Oct 14, 1939, p42.
Variety. Nov 22, 1939, p16.

Tell England (Also titled: The Battle of Gallipoli) (GB; Asquith, Anthony; Barkas, Geoffrey; 1931)
Celluloid: The Film To-Day. p169-80.
Cinema, the Magic Vehicle. v1, p198-99.
A Critical History of the British Cinema. p100-01.
Film Daily. Dec 6, 1931, p10.

The Films of Anthony Asquith. p57-61.
Motion Picture Herald. Dec 12, 1931, p38.
The New York Times. Dec 7, 1931, p16.
The New Yorker. Dec 12, 1931, v7, p79.
Outlook and Independent. Dec 16, 1931, v159, p503.
Saturday Review (London). Apr 4, 1931, v151, p497.
The Spectator. Apr 11, 1931, v146, p581.
Variety. Dec 8, 1931, p15.

Tell It to the Marines (US; Hill, George; 1927)
Film Daily. Jan 23, 1927, p6.
The Moving Picture World. Jan 1, 1927, p54.
The New York Times. Dec 24, 1926, p18.

Tell No Tales (US; Fenton, Leslie; 1939)
Commonweal. Jun 9, 1939, v30, p189.
Film Daily. May 15, 1939, p7.
Film Daily. May 24, 1939, p6.
Hollywood Reporter. May 10, 1939, p3.
Motion Picture Herald. May 13, 1939, p40.
The New York Times. Jun 2, 1939, p27.
The New Yorker. Jun 10, 1939, v15, p75.
Rob Wagner's Script. Jun 3, 1939, v21, p16-17.
Time. Jun 5, 1939, v33, p67.
Variety. May 17, 1939, p12.

The Tempest *See* Orage

Tempest (US; Taylor, Sam; 1928)
BFI/Monthly Film Bulletin. Jan 1975, v42, p20-21.
Close-Up. Apr 1929, p16.
Exhibitor's Herald-World and Moving Picture World. Sep 1, 1928, p52.
Film Daily. May 27, 1928, p6.
The Film Spectator. Apr 28, 1928, v5, p8.
The Films of the Twenties. p193-95.
The New York Times. May 18, 1928, p27.
Photoplay. Jun 1928, v34, p52.
Selected Film Criticism, 1921-1930. p286.
Variety. May 23, 1928, p21.

Tempest (German title: Sturme der Leidenschaft) (GER; Siodmak, Robert; 1932)
Commonweal. Mar 30, 1932, v15, p609.
Film Daily. Mar 20, 1932, p11.
Motion Picture Herald. Mar 26, 1932, p34-35.
The Nation. Mar 30, 1932, v134, p380.
The New York Times. Mar 16, 1932, p17.
The New Yorker. Mar 26, 1932, v8, p52.
Rob Wagner's Script. Jun 18, 1932, v7, p11.
Variety. Mar 22, 1932, p61.

The Temptress (US; Niblo, Fred; Stiller, Mauritz; 1926)
Film Daily. Oct 17, 1926, p5.
The Films of Greta Garbo. p48-51.
The Films of the Twenties. p144-46.
From Quasimodo to Scarlett O'Hara. p64-67.
The Moving Picture World. Oct 23, 1926, p503.
The New York Times. Oct 11, 1926, p18.
Photoplay. Dec 1926, v31, p52.
Spellbound in Darkness. p452.
Variety. Oct 13, 1926, p17.

Ten Cents a Dance (US; Barrymore, Lionel; 1931)
Film Daily. Mar 8, 1931, p10.
The Films of Barbara Stanwyck. p67-69.
Motion Picture Herald. Mar 14, 1931, p43.
National Board of Review Magazine. Mar 1931, v6, p9.
The New York Times. Mar 7, 1931, p17.
Rob Wagner's Script. May 16, 1931, v5, p8-9.
Starring Miss Barbara Stanwyck. p27-29.
Time. Mar 16, 1931, v17, p62.
Variety. Mar 11, 1931, p15.

The Ten Commandments (US; DeMille, Cecil B.; 1923)
The Films of Cecil B. DeMille. p220-29.
Magill's Survey of Cinema. Silent Films. v3, p1099-1101.

The New York Times. Dec 22, 1923, p8.
Photoplay. Feb 1924, v25, p62.
Selected Film Criticism, 1921-1930. p287-88.
Variety. Dec 27, 1923, p26.

Ten Days That Shook the World *See* October

Ten Gentlemen from West Point (US; Hathaway, Henry; 1942)
Film Daily. May 28, 1942, p6.
Hollywood Reporter. May 28, 1942, p3.
The London Times. Sep 28, 1942, p8.
Motion Picture Exhibitor. Jun 3, 1942, p1021.
Motion Picture Herald Product Digest. May 30, 1942, p685.
The New York Times. Jun 5, 1942, p23.
The New Yorker. May 30, 1942, v18, p49.
Time. Jun 15, 1942, v39, p48.
Variety. Jun 3, 1942, p8.

Tendre Ennemie, Le (Also titled: The Tender Enemy) (FR; Ophuls, Max; 1938)
Film Daily. Apr 9, 1938, p5.
London Mercury. Feb 1937, v35, p414.
Motion Picture Herald. May 7, 1938, p39.
The New Statesman and Nation. Apr 9, 1938, v15, p614.
The New York Times. Mar 31, 1938, p15.
The New Yorker. Apr 9, 1938, v14, p69.
The Spectator. Apr 22, 1938, v160, p706.
Time. Apr 11, 1938, v31, p24.
Variety. Apr 6, 1938, p14.
World Film News. May-Jun 1938, v3, p89.

Tennessee Johnson (US; Dieterle, William; 1942)
Agee on Film. v1, p25-26.
Commonweal. Jan 29, 1943, v37, p374.
Film Daily. Dec 16, 1942, p6.
Hollywood Reporter. Dec 16, 1942, p3.
Motion Picture Herald Product Digest. Dec 19, 1942, p1065.
The Nation. Jan 23, 1943, v156, p139.
The New Republic. Jan 25, 1943, v108, p119.
The New York Times. Jan 13, 1943, p18.
The New Yorker. Jan 16, 1943, v18, p45.
Newsweek. Jan 25, 1943, v21, p78-79.
Time. Jan 11, 1943, v41, p88.
Variety. Dec 16, 1942, p16.

Terje Vigen *See* A Man There Was

Terror by Night (Also titled: Sherlock Holmes and the Terror by Night) (US; Neill, Roy William; 1946)
Basil Rathbone: His Life and His Films. p309-11.
Film Daily. Feb 4, 1946, p7.
The Films of Sherlock Holmes. p174-80.
Hollywood Reporter. Jan 24, 1946, p3.
Motion Picture Herald Product Digest. Feb 2, 1946, p2830.
The New York Times. Feb 9, 1946, p9.
Sherlock Holmes on the Screen. p186-87.
Variety. Jan 30, 1946, p12.

The Terror of Tiny Town (US; Newfield, Sam; 1938)
The Fifty Worst Films of All Time. p239-44.
Film Daily. Jul 19, 1938, p7.
Hollywood Reporter. Jul 11, 1938, p4.
Motion Picture Herald. Jul 23, 1938, p42.
The New York Times. May 1, 1938, p3.
The New York Times. Jun 19, 1938, p3.
Time. Aug 1, 1938, v32, p28.

Tess of the D'Urbervilles (US; Dawley, J. Searle; 1913)
Motion Picture News. Aug 2, 1913, p12-13.
Motography. Sep 20, 1913, p212.
The Moving Picture World. Aug 23, 1913, p854-55.
The Moving Picture World. Sep 13, 1913, p1155, 1221.
The Moving Picture World. Oct 4, 1913, p36.
The New York Dramatic Mirror. Sep 10, 1913, p28.
Selected Film Criticism, 1912-1920. p253-55.

Tess of the Storm Country (US; Porter, Edwin S.; 1914)
Magill's Survey of Cinema. Silent Films. v3, p1102-04.
The Moving Picture World. Apr 4, 1914, p40, 124.
The New York Dramatic Mirror. Mar 25, 1914, p34, 39.
Selected Film Criticism, 1912-1920. p255-56.
Variety. Apr 3, 1914, p21.

Tess of the Storm Country (US; Robertson, John S.; 1922)
Film Daily. Nov 19, 1922, p2.
The New York Times. Nov 13, 1922, p12.
Variety. Nov 17, 1922, p41.

Tess of the Storm Country (US; Santell, Alfred; 1932)
Film Daily. Nov 19, 1932, p4.
Motion Picture Herald. Nov 26, 1932, p31.
The New York Times. Nov 19, 1932, p20.
Photoplay. Dec 1932, v43, p32-33.
Time. Nov 28, 1932, v20, p22.
Variety. Nov 22, 1932, p17.

The Test of Honor (US; Robertson, John S.; 1919)
Exhibitor's Trade Review. Apr 19, 1919, p1531.
Motion Picture News. Apr 12, 1919, p2309-11.
Motion Picture News. Apr 19, 1919, p2530.
The Moving Picture World. Apr 19, 1919, p365-66, 428.
The New York Times. Apr 7, 1919, p11.
Variety. Apr 11, 1919, p57.
Wid's Daily. Apr 13, 1919, p27.

Test Pilot (US; Fleming, Victor; 1938)
Commonweal. Apr 29, 1938, v28, p21.
Esquire. Jul 1938, v10, p89.
Film Daily. Apr 15, 1938, p7.
The Films of Clark Gable. p185.
The Films of Myrna Loy. p207-08.
The Films of Spencer Tracy. p144-46.
Hollywood Reporter. Apr 15, 1938, p3.
Hollywood Spectator. Apr 23, 1938, v13, p5.
Judge. Jun 1938, v114, p28.
A Library of Film Criticism: American Film Directors. p113-14.
Life. Apr 25, 1938, v4, p47-49.
Magill's Survey of Cinema. Series II. v5, p2439-42.
Motion Picture Herald. Apr 23, 1938, p40.
The Nation. May 7, 1938, v146, p540-41.
National Board of Review Magazine. May 1938, v13, p10.
The New Republic. May 11, 1938, v95, p19.
The New Statesman and Nation. May 28, 1938, v15, p912.
The New York Times. Apr 16, 1938, p17.
The New Yorker. Apr 23, 1938, v14, p52.
Newsweek. Apr 25, 1938, v11, p27.
Rob Wagner's Script. Apr 23, 1938, v19, p15.
Saint Nicholas. May 1938, v65, p39+.
Scholastic. May 21, 1938, v32, p32.
The Spectator. May 27, 1938, v160, p960.
The Tatler. Jun 1, 1938, v148, p390.
Time. Apr 25, 1938, v31, p46.
Variety. Apr 20, 1938, p15.
World Film News. Jul 1938, v3, p128-29.

Testament des Dr. Mabuse, Das (Also titled: The Testament of Dr. Mabuse; The Last Will of Dr. Mabuse) (GER; Lang, Fritz; 1933)
Cinema Quarterly. Aut 1934, v3, p49-50.
Cinema, the Magic Vehicle. v1, p218-19.
Classics of the Horror Film. p32-34.
Dictionary of Films. p89.
Film in the Third Reich. p39-40.
Films and Filming. Jan 1965, v11, p39.
The Films of Fritz Lang. p164-67.
Fritz Lang: A Guide to References and Resources. p63-67.
Fritz Lang (Armour). p79-94+.
Fritz Lang (Eisner). p57-68.
From Caligari to Hitler. p248-50.
The German Cinema. p63-64.

The Haunted Screen. p323-25.
The International Dictionary of Films and Filmmakers. v1, p128-29.
Magill's Survey of Cinema. Foreign Language Films. v7, p3030-33.
Movietone News. Sep 10, 1974, n35, p10.
The New York Times. Mar 20, 1943, p11.
The New Yorker. Apr 3, 1943, v19, p70.
Tower of Babel. p101-05.
Variety. May 9, 1933, p15.
Variety. Apr 25, 1933, p15.
The Village Voice. Sep 12, 1974, v19, p78-79.
Wide Angle. Wint 1980, v3, p18-26.
Wide Angle. 1979, n3, v3, p18-26.

The Texan (US; Cromwell, John; 1930)
Exhibitors Herald-World. May 24, 1930, p36.
Film Daily. Apr 27, 1930, p13.
The Film Spectator. Apr 26, 1930, v9, p20-21.
The Films of Gary Cooper. p75-77.
Judge. Jun 7, 1930, v98, p23.
Life. Jun 13, 1930, v95, p20.
The New York Times. May 17, 1930, p21.
The New Yorker. May 24, 1930, v6, p89, 91.
Outlook and Independent. Jun 4, 1930, v155, p192.
Rob Wagner's Script. Jun 14, 1930, v3, p10-12.
Time. Jun 2, 1930, v15, p64.
Variety. May 21, 1930, p27.

The Texans (US; Hogan, James; 1938)
Canadian Magazine. Aug 15, 1938, v90, p58.
Commonweal. Aug 12, 1938, v28, p411.
Film Daily. Jul 29, 1938, p11.
The Great Western Pictures. p352-53.
Hollywood Reporter. Jul 14, 1938, p3.
The New York Times. Jul 28, 1938, p23.
The New Yorker. Aug 6, 1938, v14, p41.
Newsweek. Aug 8, 1938, v12, p22+.
Rob Wagner's Script. Aug 20, 1938, v20, p14-15.
The Tatler. Sep 7, 1938, v149, p424.
Time. Aug 15, 1938, v32, p36.
Variety. Aug 3, 1938, p15.
World Film News. Sep 1938, v3, p221.

The Texas Rangers (US; Vidor, King; 1936)
Film Daily. Aug 22, 1936, p4.
Film Notes. p99.
Graham Greene on Film. p106-07.
Hollywood Reporter. Aug 19, 1936, p3.
Hollywood Spectator. Aug 29, 1936, v11, p5-6.
Judge. Oct 1936, v111, p20.
Literary Digest. Sep 5, 1936, v122, p23.
Motion Picture Herald. Aug 29, 1936, p44.
The New York Times. Sep 24, 1936, p29.
The New Yorker. Oct 3, 1936, v12, p61.
Rob Wagner's Script. Sep 5, 1936, v16, p11.
Scholastic. Oct 3, 1936, v29, p32.
The Spectator. Oct 9, 1936, v157, p582.
Time. Sep 7, 1936, v28, p20+.
Variety. Sep 30, 1936, p17.
We're in the Money. p89-90.
World Film News. Nov 1936, v1, p18.

Thais (FR; 1911)
The New York Dramatic Mirror. Apr 12, 1911, p99.
Selected Film Criticism, 1896-1911. p99.

Thaïs (US; Crane, Frank; 1917)
Magill's Survey of Cinema. Silent Films. v3, p1105-07.
Motion Picture Classic. Feb 1918, p21-25.
Motion Picture Magazine. Mar 1918, v15, p98.
The New York Dramatic Mirror. Dec 22, 1917, p23.
The New York Dramatic Mirror. Jan 5, 1918, p24.
Photoplay. Apr 1918, v13, p70.
Selected Film Criticism, 1912-1920. p256-57.
Variety. Jan 4, 1918, p42.

Thank You, Mr. Moto (US; Foster, Norman; 1937)
Film Daily. Nov 26, 1937, p7.
The Films of Peter Lorre. p106-07.
Hollywood Reporter. Nov 22, 1937, p3.
Masters of Menace: Greenstreet and Lorre. p38-40.
Motion Picture Herald. Nov 27, 1937, p55.
The New York Times. Jan 3, 1938, p16.
Rob Wagner's Script. Jan 8, 1938, v18, p15.
Variety. Jan 12, 1938, p15.

Thank Your Lucky Stars (US; Butler, David; 1943)
Commonweal. Oct 8, 1943, v38, p612.
The Complete Films of Humphrey Bogart. p112.
Film Daily. Aug 18, 1943, p6.
The Films of Errol Flynn. p130-31.
The Films of John Garfield. p116.
The Films of Olivia De Havilland. p197-98.
The Films of World War II. p151-52.
Hollywood Reporter. Aug 17, 1943, p3.
Humphrey Bogart: The Man and His Films. p127.
Motion Picture Herald Product Digest. Aug 21, 1943, p1493.
The New York Times. Oct 2, 1943, p19.
Newsweek. Oct 4, 1943, v42, p92.
Variety. Aug 18, 1943, p10.

Thanks a Million (US; Del Ruth, Roy; 1935)
Canadian Magazine. Jan 1936, v85, p32.
Film Daily. Oct 25, 1935, p10.
The Hollywood Musical. p98, 107+.
Hollywood Musicals. p109, 112.
Hollywood Reporter. Oct 21, 1935, p3.
Hollywood Spectator. Nov 9, 1935, v10, p9.
Motion Picture Herald. Nov 2, 1935, p56.
The New York Times. Nov 14, 1935, p17.
Rob Wagner's Script. Nov 16, 1935, v14, p8.
Saturday Review (London). Dec 21, 1935, v160, p640.
Scholastic. Dec 7, 1935, v27, p12.
The Spectator. Dec 20, 1935, v155, p1028.
Time. Nov 25, 1935, v26, p48.
Variety. Nov 20, 1935, p16.

Thanks for Everything (US; Seiter, William A.; 1938)
Commonweal. Dec 23, 1938, v29, p245.
Film Daily. Dec 9, 1938, p7.
Graham Greene on Film. p218-19.
Hollywood Reporter. Dec 3, 1938, p3.
Motion Picture Herald. Dec 10, 1938, p46.
The New Statesman and Nation. Apr 15, 1939, v17, p573.
The New York Times. Dec 10, 1938, p13.
The New Yorker. Dec 17, 1938, v14, p87.
Rob Wagner's Script. Jan 14, 1939, v20, p18.
The Spectator. Apr 28, 1939, v162, p708.
Time. Dec 19, 1938, v32, p21-22.
Variety. Dec 7, 1938, p12.

Thanks for the Memory (US; Archainbaud, George; 1938)
Commonweal. Dec 16, 1938, v29, p216.
Film Daily. Nov 8, 1938, p4.
Hollywood Reporter. Nov 4, 1938, p3.
Hollywood Spectator. Nov 12, 1938, v13, p12.
Motion Picture Herald. Nov 12, 1938, p38.
The New York Times. Dec 8, 1938, p34.
Rob Wagner's Script. Dec 10, 1938, v20, p10.
Time. Dec 19, 1938, v32, p22.
Variety. Nov 9, 1938, p16.

That Certain Age (US; Ludwig, Edward; 1938)
Canadian Magazine. Oct 1938, v90, p55.
Commonweal. Oct 21, 1938, v28, p677.
Film Daily. Oct 4, 1938, p8.
The Films of Nancy Carroll. p220-24.
The Foremost Films of 1938. p182-98.
Hollywood Reporter. Sep 29, 1938, p3.
Life. Oct 3, 1938, v5, p32-33.
Motion Picture Herald. Oct 8, 1938, p38, 40.
The New York Times. Nov 5, 1938, p15.

The New Yorker. Nov 5, 1938, v14, p58.
Rob Wagner's Script. Nov 26, 1938, v20, p12.
Scholastic. Oct 29, 1938, v33, p29.
Stage. Nov 1938, v16, p60.
Time. Oct 10, 1938, v32, p38.
Variety. Oct 5, 1938, p14.

That Certain Woman (US; Goulding, Edmund; 1937)
Bette Davis: Her Films and Career. p80-81.
Bette Davis: Her Films and Career. p78-81.
Esquire. Nov 1937, v8, p122.
Film Daily. Aug 20, 1937, p6.
The Films of Henry Fonda. p60-63.
The Fondas (Springer). p70-71.
Hollywood Reporter. Jul 28, 1937, p3.
Hollywood Spectator. Aug 14, 1937, v12, p6-7.
Motion Picture Herald. Aug 7, 1937, p48, 52.
The New Masses. Sep 28, 1937, v25, p29.
The New York Times. Sep 16, 1937, p29.
Rob Wagner's Script. Oct 16, 1937, v18, p8.
Time. Sep 27, 1937, v30, p36.
Variety. Aug 4, 1937, p19.

That Chink at Golden Gulch (US; Griffith, D.W.; 1910)
Film Reports. Oct 22, 1910, v1, p6.
Selected Film Criticism, 1896-1911. p99.

That Forsyte Woman (US; Bennett, Compton; 1949)
Christian Century. Jan 18, 1950, v67, p95.
Commonweal. Nov 25, 1949, v51, p213.
Film Daily. Oct 28, 1949, p6.
The Films of Errol Flynn. p161-64.
Hollywood Reporter. Oct 24, 1949, p3.
Library Journal. Feb 1, 1950, v75, p181.
Motion Picture Herald. Oct 22, 1949, p57.
The New York Times. Nov 11, 1949, p31.
Newsweek. Dec 12, 1949, v34, p87.
Rotarian. Mar 1950, v86, p37.
Time. Nov 14, 1949, v54, p108.
Variety. Oct 26, 1949, p18.

That Girl from Paris (US; Jason, Leigh; 1936)
Film Daily. Dec 22, 1936, p10.
Hollywood Reporter. Dec 12, 1936, p3.
Literary Digest. Dec 26, 1936, v122, p23.
Motion Picture Herald. Dec 19, 1936, p56.
The New York Times. Jan 1, 1937, p19.
Time. Jan 11, 1937, v29, p57.
Variety. Jan 6, 1937, p40.

That Hagen Girl (US; Godfrey, Peter; 1947)
Commonweal. Nov 7, 1947, v47, p95.
Film Daily. Oct 22, 1947, p9.
The Films of Ronald Reagan. p148-52.
The Films of Shirley Temple. p238-39.
Hollywood Reporter. Oct 22, 1947, p3.
Motion Picture Herald Product Digest. Oct 25, 1947, p3893.
New Republic. Nov 10, 1947, v117, p34.
The New York Times. Oct 25, 1947, p13.
The New Yorker. Nov 1, 1947, v23, p73.
Time. Nov 10, 1947, v50, p104.
Variety. Oct 22, 1947, p12.

That Hamilton Woman (Also titled: The Lady Hamilton)
   (US; Korda, Alexander; 1941)
Commonweal. Apr 25, 1941, v34, p16.
Film Daily. Mar 20, 1941, p8.
Films and Filming. Aut 1941, v10, p54.
The Films of Laurence Olivier. p89-91.
The Films of World War II. p46-47.
The Great Romantic Films. p86-89.
Laurence Olivier. p54-58.
Laurence Olivier: Theater and Cinema. p84-89.
Life. Apr 7, 1941, v10, p41-44.
The London Times. Jul 31, 1941, p6.
Magill's Survey of Cinema. Series I. v4, p1685-88.

Motion Picture Exhibitor. Apr 2, 1941, p720.
The Nation. Mar 29, 1941, v152, p390.
The New Republic. Apr 21, 1941, v104, p533-34.
The New York Times. Apr 4, 1941, p25.
Newsweek. Apr 14, 1941, v17, p68.
Scholastic. Apr 14, 1941, v38, p43.
Scribner's Commentator. Jun 1941, v10, p105.
Time. Mar 31, 1941, v37, p71.
Variety. Mar 26, 1941, p16.
The Village Voice. Oct 22, 1970, v15, p59.
Vivien Leigh (Edwards). p128-29.

That I May Live (US; Dwan, Allan; 1937)
Film Daily. May 11, 1937, p9.
Hollywood Reporter. Feb 27, 1937, p3.
Motion Picture Herald. Mar 6, 1937, p45.
The New York Times. May 10, 1937, p23.
Rob Wagner's Script. Apr 17, 1937, v17, p10.
Variety. May 12, 1937, p13.

That Lady in Ermine (US; Lubitsch, Ernst; Preminger,
   Otto; 1948)
The Cinema of Ernst Lubitsch. p113+.
The Cinema of Otto Preminger. p88-89+.
Commonweal. Sep 3, 1948, v48, p499.
Ernst Lubitsch: A Guide to References and Resources. p171-75.
Film Daily. Jul 15, 1948, p5.
Hollywood Reporter. Jul 14, 1948, p3.
Motion Picture Herald Product Digest. Jul 17, 1948, p4241.
The New York Times. Aug 25, 1948, p31.
Newsweek. Sep 6, 1948, p3.
Variety. Jul 14, 1948, p12.

That Royle Girl (US; Griffith, D.W.; 1925)
Film Daily. Jan 17, 1926, p6.
Films of D.W. Griffith. p216-19.
The Films of W.C. Fields. p41-43.
The Moving Picture World. Jan 23, 1926, p342.
The New York Times. Jan 4, 1926, p33.
Photoplay. Mar 1926, v24, p55.
Selected Film Criticism, 1921-1930. p288-90.
Variety. Jan 13, 1926, p40.
W.C. Fields: A Life on Film. p31-33.

That They May Live (French title: J'Accuse) (FR; Gance,
   Abel; 1937)
Abel Gance (Kramer and Welsh). p61-76+.
Dictionary of Films. p163.
Film Daily. Nov 10, 1939, p9.
The Nation. Nov 11, 1939, v149, p533.
National Board of Review Magazine. Dec 1939, v14, p15.
The New Masses. Nov 7, 1939, v33, p29-30.
The New Republic. Nov 8, 1939, v101, p16.
The New Statesman and Nation. May 7, 1938, v15, p770.
The New York Times. Nov 7, 1939, p31.
Rob Wagner's Script. Jan 27, 1940, v23, p18.
Selected Film Criticism: Foreign Films, 1930-1950. p174.
The Tatler. May 25, 1938, v148, p344.
Theatre Arts. Jan 1940, v24, p70.
Variety. Apr 26, 1939, p12.
World Film News. Jul 1938, v3, p131.

That Uncertain Feeling (US; Lubitsch, Ernst; 1941)
Commonweal. May 2, 1941, v34, p39.
Ernst Lubitsch: A Guide to References and Resources. p149-52.
Film Daily. Mar 14, 1941, p7.
Hollywood Reporter. Mar 27, 1941, p3.
Motion Picture Herald Product Digest. Mar 22, 1941, p46.
The New York Times. May 2, 1941, p25.
Scholastic. Mar 10, 1941, v38, p40.
Time. Mar 31, 1941, v37, p70.
Variety. Mar 19, 1941, p16.

That's Right, You're Wrong (US; Butler, David; 1939)
Commonweal. Dec 8, 1939, v31, p164.
Film Daily. Nov 20, 1939, p6.

Hollywood Spectator. Nov 25, 1939, v14, p5.
Motion Picture Herald. Nov 18, 1939, p44, 48.
The New York Times. Nov 30, 1939, p25.
Rob Wagner's Script. Dec 2, 1939, v22, p17.
Scholastic. Dec 4, 1939, v35, p32.
Variety. Nov 22, 1939, p14.

The Theft of the Mona Lisa *See* Raub der Mona Lisa,
   Der

Theodora Goes Wild (US; Boleslavski, Richard; 1936)
Film Daily. Nov 5, 1936, p6.
Film Society Review. Oct 1965, p29.
Graham Greene on Film. p137.
Hollywood Reporter. Nov 2, 1936, p3.
Hollywood Spectator. Nov 7, 1936, v11, p7.
Lunatics and Lovers. p206-09.
Magill's Survey of Cinema. Series II. v5, p2454-56.
Motion Picture Herald. Nov 14, 1936, p58.
The New Masses. Nov 24, 1936, v21, p29.
The New Statesman and Nation. Feb 13, 1937, v13, p245.
The New York Times. Nov 13, 1936, p27.
The New Yorker. Nov 21, 1936, v12, p81.
Newsweek. Nov 14, 1936, v8, p60.
Rob Wagner's Script. Nov 21, 1936, v16, p10.
The Spectator. Mar 5, 1937, v158, p403.
Talking Pictures. p276-78.
Time. Nov 23, 1936, v28, p26.
Variety. Nov 18, 1936, p12.

There Goes My Heart (US; McLeod, Norman Z.; 1938)
Commonweal. Oct 28, 1938, v29, p21.
Film Daily. Sep 27, 1938, p6.
The Films of Fredric March. p157-59.
The Films of Nancy Carroll. p214-19.
Hollywood Reporter. Sep 23, 1938, p2.
Hollywood Spectator. Oct 1, 1938, v13, p12-13.
Motion Picture Herald. Oct 1, 1938, p38.
The New Masses. Oct 18, 1938, v29, p30-31.
The New York Times. Oct 14, 1938, p24.
The New Yorker. Oct 15, 1938, v14, p63.
Newsweek. Oct 17, 1938, v12, p29.
Rob Wagner's Script. Dec 17, 1938, v20, p18.
The Spectator. Nov 11, 1938, v160, p807.
Time. Oct 10, 1938, v32, p39.
Variety. Sep 28, 1938, p14.

There Goes the Bride (GB; de Courville, Albert; 1932)
Film Daily. Mar 1, 1933, p6.
Hollywood Reporter. Nov 9, 1932, p3.
Motion Picture Herald. Mar 11, 1933, p24.
The New York Times. Mar 4, 1933, p11.
Variety. Nov 15, 1932, p52.
Variety. Mar 7, 1933, p54.

There Goes the Groom (US; Santley, Joseph; 1937)
Film Daily. Oct 12, 1937, p6.
Hollywood Reporter. Sep 25, 1937, p5.
Motion Picture Herald. Oct 2, 1937, p32.
The New York Times. Dec 25, 1937, p10.
Rob Wagner's Script. Nov 6, 1937, v18, p8.
Variety. Oct 13, 1937, p16.

There's Always a Woman (US; Hall, Alexander; 1938)
Commonweal. May 13, 1938, v28, p77.
Film Daily. Mar 19, 1938, p3.
Hollywood Reporter. Mar 16, 1938, p3.
Motion Picture Herald. Mar 19, 1938, p41, 46.
The New York Times. Apr 29, 1938, p17.
Rob Wagner's Script. Apr 30, 1938, v19, p8-9.
Stage. May 1938, v15, p27.
Time. Apr 18, 1938, v31, p51.
Variety. May 4, 1938, p15.

There's Always Tomorrow (US; Sloman, Edward; 1934)
Film Daily. Nov 10, 1934, p4.
The Films of Robert Taylor. p28-29.
Hollywood Reporter. Aug 22, 1934, p3.
Motion Picture Herald. Nov 17, 1934, p53-54.
The New York Times. Nov 10, 1934, p19.
Time. Sep 17, 1934, v24, p40.

There's That Woman Again (US; Hall, Alexander; 1938)
Film Daily. Dec 13, 1938, p8.
Hollywood Reporter. Dec 10, 1938, p3.
Motion Picture Herald. Dec 17, 1938, p49, 52.
The New York Times. Jan 6, 1939, p25.
The New Yorker. Jan 14, 1939, v14, p61.
Photoplay. Feb 1939, v53, p49.
Rob Wagner's Script. Dec 24, 1938, v20, p10-11.
Time. Jan 16, 1939, v33, p26.
Variety. Jan 11, 1939, p12.

These Glamour Girls (US; Simon, S. Sylvan; 1939)
Film Daily. Aug 22, 1939, p17.
Hollywood Reporter. Aug 15, 1939, p3.
Motion Picture Herald. Aug 19, 1939, p51.
The New York Times. Aug 31, 1939, p14.
Photoplay. Oct 1939, v53, p64.
Variety. Sep 6, 1939, p14.

These Three (US; Wyler, William; 1936)
Canadian Magazine. Apr 1936, v85, p58.
Canadian Magazine. Jul 1936, v86, p30.
Commonweal. Apr 3, 1936, v23, p636.
Esquire. May 1936, v5, p115, 194-95.
Film Daily. Feb 25, 1936, p9.
The Films of the Thirties. p164-65.
Graham Greene on Film. p69, 72.
The Great Romantic Films. p42-45.
Hollywood Reporter. Feb 22, 1936, p3.
Hollywood Spectator. Feb 29, 1936, v10, p5-6.
A Library of Film Criticism: American Film Directors. p508-09.
Literary Digest. Mar 14, 1936, v121, p22.
Magill's Survey of Cinema. Series I. v4, p1693-97.
Motion Picture Herald. Feb 29, 1936, p41, 44.
The Nation. Apr 15, 1936, v142, p222.
The New Republic. Apr 1, 1936, v86, p222.
The New Statesman and Nation. May 2, 1936, v11, p668.
The New York Times. Mar 19, 1936, p22.
The New Yorker. Mar 28, 1936, v12, p55-56.
Newsweek. Mar 21, 1936, v7, p24.
Photoplay. Mar 1936, v49, p76.
Rob Wagner's Script. Mar 7, 1936, v15, p10.
Samuel Goldwyn (Anderegg). p44-46.
Samuel Goldwyn Presents. p161-63.
Sight and Sound. Sum 1936, v5, p24.
The Spectator. May 1, 1936, v156, p791.
Time. Mar 30, 1936, v27, p33.
Variety. Mar 25, 1936, p15.
William Wyler (Anderegg). p46-50.

They Died with Their Boots On (US; Walsh, Raoul; 1941)
Commonweal. Dec 5, 1941, v35, p180.
Each Man in His Own Time. p324-27.
Film Daily. Nov 21, 1941, p6.
The Filming of the West. p364-65.
The Films of Anthony Quinn. p83.
The Films of Errol Flynn. p106-11.
The Films of the Forties. p44-47.
Hollywood Reporter. Nov 19, 1941, p3.
Life. Dec 8, 1941, v11, p75-78.
The London Times. Apr 20, 1942, p8.
Magill's Survey of Cinema. Series II. v4, p2461-66.
The Making of the Great Westerns. p108-21.
Motion Picture Exhibitor. Nov 26, 1941, v17, n3, sec2, p898.
Motion Picture Herald Product Digest. Nov 22, 1941, p373.
The New York Times. Nov 21, 1941, p23.

The New York Times. Nov 30, 1941, sec9, p5.
Newsweek. Dec 1, 1941, v18, p70.
Time. Dec 22, 1941, v38, p47.
Variety. Nov 19, 1941, p9.

They Drive by Night (US; Walsh, Raoul; 1940)
Commonweal. Aug 9, 1940, v32, p330.
The Complete Films of Humphrey Bogart. p86-88.
Each Man in His Own Time. p302-03.
The Film Criticism of Otis Ferguson. p311.
Film Daily. Jul 12, 1940, p6.
Hollywood Reporter. Jul 9, 1940, p3.
Humphrey Bogart (Michael). p106-07.
Magill's Cinema Annual, 1983. p508-14.
Movietone News. Nov 1975, n45, p21-24.
The New Republic. Sep 30, 1940, v103, p448.
The New York Times. Jul 27, 1940, p17.
Newsweek. Jul 29, 1940, v16, p36.
Time. Aug 5, 1940, v36, p56.
Variety. Jul 10, 1940, p12.

They Gave Him a Gun (US; Van Dyke, W.S.; 1937)
Esquire. Aug 1937, v8, p101.
Film Daily. May 17, 1937, p21.
The Films of Spencer Tracy. p134-35.
Hollywood Reporter. May 4, 1937, p3.
Hollywood Spectator. May 22, 1937, v12, p14.
Literary Digest. May 22, 1937, v123, p28.
Motion Picture Herald. May 15, 1937, p50.
The New York Times. May 14, 1937, p21.
The New Yorker. May 22, 1937, v13, p70-71.
Rob Wagner's Script. Jul 17, 1937, v17, p14.
Time. May 24, 1937, v29, p55.
Variety. May 19, 1937, p22.
World Film News. Aug 1937, v2, p26.

They Had to See Paris (US; Borzage, Frank; 1929)
Exhibitor's Herald-World. Dec 7, 1929, p54.
Film Daily. Oct 13, 1929, p9.
The New York Times. Oct 12, 1929, p11.
Selected Film Criticism, 1929-1930. p290.
Variety. Oct 16, 1929, p17.

They Knew What They Wanted (US; Kanin, Garson; 1940)
Commonweal. Oct 25, 1940, v33, p24.
The Film Criticism of Otis Ferguson. p312-13.
Film Daily. Oct 9, 1940, p8.
The Films of Carole Lombard. p169-72.
Life. Sep 30, 1940, v9, p47-50.
The London Times. Jan 6, 1941, p6.
Motion Picture Exhibitor. Oct 16, 1940, p620.
Motion Picture Herald Product Digest. Apr 5, 1941, p100.
The Nation. Dec 2, 1944, p699.
The New Republic. Oct 21, 1940, v103, p558.
The New York Times. Oct 11, 1940, p25.
Newsweek. Oct 21, 1940, v16, p59.
Spectator. Jan 10, 1941, p35.
Theatre Arts. Dec 1940, v24, p869-70.
Time. Nov 4, 1940, v36, p79.
Variety. Oct 9, 1940, p16.

They Live by Night (Also titled: The Twisted Road) (US; Ray, Nicholas; 1949)
Cinema Texas Program Notes. Mar 6, 1985, v28, p39-42.
Cinema Texas Program Notes. Nov 5, 1979, v17, p69-75.
Cinema Texas Program Notes. Apr 2, 1975, v8, p1-5.
Film Daily. Jun 28, 1948, p8.
Hollywood Reporter. Jun 24, 1948, p3.
The Hollywood Social Problem Films. p153-54+.
Magill's Survey of Cinema. Series II. v6, p2467-69.
Motion Picture Herald. Sep 24, 1949, p25.
The New York Times. Nov 4, 1949, p33.
The New Yorker. Nov 12, 1949, v25, p102.
Newsweek. Oct 24, 1949, v34, p87.

Nicholas Ray: A Guide to References and Resources. p49-53.
Nicholas Ray (Kreidl). p25-28.
Rotarian. Jan 1950, v76, p41.
Time. Nov 28, 1949, v54, p82+.

They Made Me a Criminal (US; Berkeley, Busby; 1939)
The Busby Berkeley Book. p120-21.
Commonweal. Feb 3, 1939, v29, p413.
The Film Criticism of Otis Ferguson. p247.
Film Daily. Jan 18, 1939, p5.
The Films of John Garfield. p54-57.
Hollywood Reporter. Dec 31, 1938, p3.
Hollywood Spectator. Jan 7, 1939, v13, p13-14.
Motion Picture Herald. Jan 7, 1939, p38, 40.
The New Masses. Jan 31, 1939, v30, p27.
The New Republic. Feb 22, 1939, v98, p73-74.
The New York Times. Jan 21, 1939, p19.
The New Yorker. Jan 28, 1939, v14, p50-51.
Newsweek. Jan 30, 1939, v13, p24.
Photoplay. Mar 1939, v53, p53.
Rob Wagner's Script. Jan 28, 1939, v20, p16-17.
Rob Wagner's Script. Sep 16, 1939, v22, p15.
Time. Jan 30, 1939, v33, p50.
Variety. Jan 25, 1939, p11.

They Met at Midnight *See* Piccadilly Incident

They Met in Bombay (US; Brown, Clarence; 1941)
Commonweal. Jul 11, 1941, v34, p278.
Film Daily. Jun 24, 1941, p8.
The Films of Clark Gable. p203.
Hollywood Reporter. Jun 23, 1941, p3.
Motion Picture Herald Product Digest. Jun 28, 1941, p145.
The New York Times. Jul 4, 1941, p17.
Newsweek. Jul 7, 1941, v18, p51-52.
Time. Jul 21, 1941, v38, p74.
Variety. Jun 25, 1941, p16.

They Shall Have Music (US; Mayo, Archie; 1939)
Commonweal. Jul 28, 1939, v30, p340.
ιEt1ude. Oct 1939, v57, p626.
Film Daily. Jul 14, 1939, p8.
Hollywood Spectator. Jul 22, 1939, v14, p5-6.
Motion Picture Herald. Jul 15, 1939, p53.
Motion Picture Herald. Jul 22, 1939, p54.
The New Masses. Jul 25, 1939, v32, p29-30.
The New Statesman and Nation. Dec 23, 1939, v18, p298.
The New York Times. Jul 26, 1939, p17.
The New Yorker. Jul 29, 1939, v15, p57.
Newsweek. Jul 31, 1939, v14, p29.
North American Review. Sep 1939, v248, p191.
Photoplay. Sep 1939, v53, p62.
Rob Wagner's Script. Aug 12, 1939, v22, p16.
Samuel Goldwyn Presents. p201-04.
Time. Aug 7, 1939, v34, p24.
Variety. Jul 12, 1939, p12.

They Were Expendable (US; Ford, John; 1945)
Commonweal. Dec 28, 1945, v43, p288.
The Complete Films of John Wayne. p146-48.
Film Daily. Nov 23, 1943, p6.
Films and the Second World War. p189-91.
The Films of World War II. p234-35.
Hollywood Reporter. Nov 19, 1945, p3.
John Wayne and the Movies. p93-94.
Life. Dec 31, 1945, v19, p61-62.
The London Times. Dec 10, 1945, p8.
Magill's Survey of Cinema. Series I. v4, p1698-1702.
Motion Picture Exhibitor. Nov 28, 1945, v35, n4, sec2, p1836.
Motion Picture Herald Product Digest. Nov 24, 1945, p2725.
The New York Times. Dec 21, 1945, p25.
The New Yorker. Dec 22, 1945, v21, p50.
Newsweek. Dec 31, 1945, v26, p94.
The Non-Western Films of John Ford. p109-20.
Scholastic. Jan 14, 1946, v47, p31.
Sequences. Sum 1950, n11, p19-24.

Theatre Arts. Jan 1946, v30, p44.
Theatre Arts. Feb 1946, v30, p101-02.
Time. Dec 24, 1945, v46, p98+.
Variety. Nov 21, 1941, p10.
Visions of War. p135-44.

They Were Five *See* Belle Équippe, La

They Won't Forget (US; LeRoy, Mervyn; 1937)
Black Images in American Films, 1896-1954. p192.
Cinema, the Magic Vehicle. v1, p274-75.
Esquire. Oct 1937, v8, p121.
The Film Criticism of Otis Ferguson. p185-87.
Film Daily. Jun 14, 1937, p12.
The Films of Lana Turner. p54-60.
Fortune. Dec 1937, v16, p113.
From Quasimodo to Scarlett O'Hara. p254-56.
Graham Greene on Film. p178.
Hollywood Reporter. Jun 9, 1937, p3.
Hollywood Spectator. Jun 19, 1937, v12, p8-9.
Life. Jul 19, 1937, v3, p32-35.
Literary Digest. Jun 26, 1937, v123, p23.
Literary Digest. Jul 24, 1937, v124, p29.
Lorentz on Film. p147-48.
Magill's Survey of Cinema. Series II. v6, p2474-77.
Motion Picture Herald. Jun 19, 1937, p58.
National Board of Review Magazine. Oct 1937, v12, p10.
The New Masses. Jul 20, 1937, v24, p28.
The New Republic. Jul 28, 1937, v91, p335.
The New Statesman and Nation. Oct 30, 1937, v14, p684.
The New York Times. Jul 15, 1937, p16.
The New Yorker. Jul 17, 1937, v13, p56.
Newsweek. Jul 10, 1937, v10, p23.
Rob Wagner's Script. Jul 31, 1937, v17, p12.
Scribner's Magazine. Oct 1937, v102, p64.
Sight and Sound. Wint 1937-38, v6, p186.
Sociology and Social Research. Jan 1938, v22, p298.
Time. Jul 26, 1937, v30, p22.
Variety. Jun 30, 1937, p20.
Warner Brothers Presents. p79-80.
We're in the Money. p120-22.
World Film News. Oct 1937, v2, p22.
World Film News. Dec 1937, v2, p22-23.

The Thief of Bagdad (US; Walsh, Raoul; 1924)
BFI/Monthly Film Bulletin. Feb 1975, v42, p43-44.
Film Daily. Mar 23, 1924, p3.
The Films of the Twenties. p93-97.
The Great Films. p35-38.
His Majesty the American. p139-44.
Life. Dec 4, 1924, v84, p50.
Magill's Survey of Cinema. Silent Films. v3, p1108-11.
The Moving Picture World. Mar 29, 1924, p397.
The New York Times. Mar 19, 1924, p19.
Photoplay. May 1924, v25, p54.
Selected Film Criticism, 1921-1930. p290-91.

The Thief of Bagdad (GB; Berger, Ludwig; Whelan, Tim; Powell, Michael; 1940)
Audience. Nov 1976, v9, p2-9.
Cinema of the Fantastic. p177-98.
Commonweal. Oct 25, 1940, v33, p24.
Film Daily. Oct 15, 1940, p7.
The Great British Films. p55-58.
Halliwell's Hundred. p346-49.
High Fidelity and Musical America. Sep 1977, v27, p116.
Life. Oct 14, 1940, v9, p39-40+.
The London Times. Dec 23, 1940, p6.
Magic Moments from the Movies. p76-78.
Magill's Survey of Cinema. Series I. v4, p1703-08.
Motion Picture Exhibitor. Oct 16, 1940, p621.
Motion Picture Herald Product Digest. Mar 22, 1941, p88.
The New Republic. Oct 21, 1940, v103, p24.
The New York Times. Mar 31, 1940, sec9, p5.
The New York Times. May 14, 1940, sec9, p5.

The New York Times. Dec 6, 1940, p28.
The New York Times. Dec 12, 1940, sec10, p9.
Newsweek. Oct 28, 1940, p16.
Scholastic. Sep 23, 1940, v37, p32.
Scribner's Commentator. Feb 1941, v9, p108.
Time. Nov 4, 1940, v36, p76+.
Variety. Oct 16, 1940, p16.

Thieves Highway (US; Dassin, Jules; 1949)
Commonweal. Sep 16, 1949, v50, p560.
Film Daily. Sep 8, 1949, p8.
Hollywood Reporter. Sep 2, 1949, p3.
Motion Picture Herald. Sep 3, 1949, p1.
The New York Times. Sep 24, 1949, p8.
Newsweek. Oct 3, 1949, v34, p80.
Rotarian. Dec 1949, v75, p39.
Time. Oct 10, 1949, v54, p98+.
Variety. Sep 7, 1949, p11.

Thieves Holiday (Also titled: A Scandal in Paris) (US;
    Sirk, Douglas; 1946)
Commonweal. Aug 9, 1946, v44, p408.
Film Daily. Jul 10, 1946, p3.
Hollywood Reporter. Jul 10, 1946, p3.
Motion Picture Herald Product Digest. Jul 20, 1946, p3112.
The New York Times. Sep 16, 1946, p9.
Newsweek. Jul 22, 1946, v28, p92.
Time. Aug 26, 1946, v48, p95-96.

Thin Ice (US; Lanfield, Sidney; 1937)
Film Daily. Aug 24, 1937, p4.
The Films of Tyrone Power. p63-65.
Hollywood Reporter. Aug 21, 1937, p3.
Hollywood Spectator. Aug 28, 1937, v12, p11.
Motion Picture Herald. Aug 28, 1937, p49.
The New York Times. Sep 4, 1937, p8.
The New Yorker. Sep 4, 1937, v13, p60.
Newsweek. Sep 6, 1937, v10, p27.
Rob Wagner's Script. Sep 4, 1937, v18, p12.
Stage. Sep 1937, v14, p46.
Variety. Aug 25, 1937, p17.

The Thin Man (US; Van Dyke, W.S.; 1934)
The Detective in Film. p93-96, 225.
Film Daily. May 23, 1934, p7.
The Films of Myrna Loy. p169-71.
The Films of the Thirties. p129-30.
Hollywood Reporter. May 10, 1934, p3.
The International Dictionary of Films and Filmmakers. v1,
    p469-70.
Literary Digest. Jul 14, 1934, v118, p29.
Magill's Survey of Cinema. Series I. v4, p1709-11.
Motion Picture Herald. May 19, 1934, p69.
The New Republic. Nov 25, 1936, v89, p112.
The New York Times. Jun 30, 1934, p18.
Time. Jul 9, 1934, v24, p44.
Variety. Jul 3, 1934, p26.

Things to Come (Also titled: The Shape of Things to
    Come) (GB; Menzies, William Cameron; 1936)
Canadian Magazine. May 1936, v85, p58.
Cinema of the Fantastic. p151-76.
Classics of the Foreign Film. p104-07.
Commonweal. Apr 10, 1936, v23, p664.
The Film Criticism of Otis Ferguson. p129-30.
Film Daily. Apr 20, 1936, p8.
Focus on the Science Fiction Film. p41-45.
Garbo and the Night Watchman. p60, 62, 126-30.
Graham Greene on Film. p54-55.
The Great British Films. p30-31.
Great Horror Movies. p151-52.
Hollywood Reporter. Apr 18, 1936, p2.
Hollywood Spectator. Apr 25, 1936, v11, p9-10.
The International Dictionary of Films and Filmmakers. v1,
    p470-71.

Life. Jun 1936, v103, p22.
Literary Digest. Mar 28, 1936, v121, p19.
London Mercury. Apr 1936, v33, p630.
Magill's Survey of Cinema. Series I. v4, p1716-18.
Motion Picture Herald. Mar 7, 1936, p46.
The Nation. Apr 29, 1936, v142, p560.
National Board of Review Magazine. May 1936, v11, p12.
The New Masses. May 5, 1936, v19, p27.
The New Republic. Apr 29, 1936, v86, p345-46.
The New Statesman and Nation. Feb 29, 1936, v11, p298.
New Theatre. Apr 1936, v3, p18.
The New York Times. Apr 18, 1936, p33.
The New York Times. Feb 21, 1936, p21.
The New Yorker. Apr 25, 1936, v12, p45-47.
Newsweek. Apr 4, 1936, v7, p33.
Rob Wagner's Script. Apr 25, 1936, v15, p12-13.
Saturday Review. Nov 2, 1935, v13, p11-12.
Saturday Review (London). Feb 29, 1936, v161, p288.
Saturday Review (London). Aug 29, 1936, v162, p288.
Scholastic. May 16, 1936, v28, p22.
Science Fiction Studies in Film. p78-90.
Selected Film Criticism: Foreign Films, 1930-1950. p174-76.
The Spectator. Feb 28, 1936, v156, p343.
Stage. Dec 1935, v13, p57-59.
The Tatler. Mar 4, 1936, v139, p512.
Theatre Arts Monthly. May 1936, v20, p347-48.
Time. Apr 6, 1936, v27, p43-46.
Variety. Mar 4, 1936, p26.
Variety. Apr 22, 1936, p14.

Think Fast, Mr. Moto (US; Foster, Norman; 1937)
Film Daily. Apr 6, 1937, p8.
The Films of Peter Lorre. p100-02.
Hollywood Reporter. Apr 2, 1937, p3.
Hollywood Spectator. Apr 10, 1937, v12, p17.
Masters of Menace: Greenstreet and Lorre. p38-39.
Motion Picture Herald. Apr 17, 1937, p42, 44.
The New York Times. Aug 16, 1937, p15.
Rob Wagner's Script. Aug 28, 1937, v17, p10.
The Tatler. Sep 22, 1937, v145, p516.
Variety. Aug 18, 1937, p27.

The Third Degree (US; Curtiz, Michael; 1927)
Film Daily. Jan 6, 1927, p6.
Magill's Survey of Cinema. Silent Films. v3, p1112-15.
The Moving Picture World. Jan 8, 1927, p142.
The New York Times. Feb 15, 1927, p23.
Variety. Jan 5, 1927, p17.
Variety. Feb 16, 1927, p19.

The Third Man (GB; Reed, Carol; 1949)
Christian Century. Mar 8, 1950, v67, p319.
Cinema Texas Program Notes. Nov 1981, v21, p13-17.
Cinema, the Magic Vehicle. v1, p507-08.
Commonweal. Jan 13, 1950, v51, p391.
Fifty Classic British Films. p76-87.
Film and Literature. p174-80.
Film Daily. Feb 1, 1950, p7.
Films and Filming. Mar 1969, v15, p87-88.
Films in Review. Mar 1950, v1, p25-27.
Fortnight. Mar 17, 1950, v8, p31.
The Great British Films. p134-36.
Hollywood Reporter. Jan 31, 1950, p3.
The International Dictionary of Films and Filmmakers. p471-
    72.
Library Journal. Apr 1, 1950, v75, p571.
Life. Mar 13, 1950, v28, p85-86.
Literature/Film Quarterly. Fall 1974, v2, p332-47.
Magill's Survey of Cinema. Series I. v4, p1719-22.
Motion Picture Herald. Dec 3, 1949, p106.
The Nation. Apr 1950, v170, p306-07.
The New Republic. Feb 6, 1950, v122, p4.
The New Yorker. Feb 4, 1950, p79.
Newsweek. Feb 13, 1950, v35, p88-89.
Orson Welles (Leaming). p362-63.

Rotarian. May 1950, v76, p41.
Scholastic. Feb 22, 1950, v57, p21.
Selected Film Criticism: Foreign Films, 1930-1950. p176.
Sequence. New Year 1950, n10, p176-177.
Seventy Years of Cinema. p169.
Time. Feb 6, 1950, v55, p82-83.
Variety. Sep 7, 1949, p11.
Vintage Films. p119-22.

The Thirteen (Russian title: Trinadtsat) (USSR; Romm, Mikhail; 1936)
Cinema, the Magic Vehicle. v1, p263-64.
Film Daily. Jun 24, 1937, p7.
Motion Picture Herald. Jul 17, 1937, p50-51.
National Board of Review Magazine. Oct 1937, v12, p16.
The New Masses. Jun 29, 1937, v24, p28.
The New York Times. Jun 19, 1937, p20.
The New Yorker. Jul 3, 1937, v13, p49.
Variety. May 26, 1937, p15.
Variety. Jun 23, 1937, p33.
World Film News. Sep 1937, v2, p29.
World Film News. Aug 1938, v3, p175.

Thirteen Hours by Air (US; Leisen, Mitchell; 1936)
Film Daily. Apr 30, 1936, p6.
Hollywood Director. p99-100.
Hollywood Reporter. Mar 14, 1936, p3.
Hollywood Spectator. Apr 11, 1936, v11, p21, 23.
Motion Picture Herald. Mar 21, 1936, p40.
The New York Times. Apr 30, 1936, p17.
The New Yorker. May 9, 1936, v12, p71.
Rob Wagner's Script. Apr 11, 1936, v15, p10.
The Spectator. Jun 12, 1936, v156, p1080.
Time. Apr 6, 1936, v27, p43.
Variety. May 6, 1936, p18.

13 Rue Madeleine (US; Hathaway, Henry; 1946)
Agee on Films. v1, p242-43.
Commonweal. Jan 17, 1947, v45, p352.
Film Daily. Dec 19, 1946, p8.
The Films of James Cagney. p182-84.
Hollywood Reporter. Dec 17, 1946, p3.
Life. Jan 20, 1946, v22, p16+.
Motion Picture Herald Product Digest. Dec 21, 1946, p3374.
The Nation. Mar 1, 1947, v164, p257.
The New Republic. Jan 27, 1947, v116, p42.
The New York Times. Jan 16, 1947, p30.
The New Yorker. Jan 25, 1947, v22, p70.
Newsweek. Jan 20, 1947, v29, p92+.
Time. Jan 6, 1947, v49, p89.
Variety. Dec 18, 1946, p14.

The Thirteenth Chair (US; Seitz, George B.; 1937)
Film Daily. May 4, 1937, p8.
Hollywood Reporter. Apr 29, 1937, p3.
Motion Picture Herald. May 8, 1937, p43, 46.
The New York Times. Jun 18, 1937, p25.
Time. May 17, 1937, v29, p56.
Variety. Jun 2, 1937, p15.

The Thirteenth Man (US; Nigh, William; 1937)
Film Daily. Aug 3, 1937, p7.
Hollywood Reporter. Jul 22, 1937, p3.
The New York Times. Jan 1, 1938, p11.
Variety. Aug 4, 1937, p25.

39 East (US; Robertson, John S.; 1920)
Motion Picture News. Sep 25, 1920, p2497.
The Moving Picture World. Sep 25, 1920, p1841.
The New York Dramatic Mirror. Sep 1920, p516.
Selected Film Criticism, 1912-1920. p257-58.
Variety. Sep 17, 1920, p35.
Wid's Daily. Sep 19, 1920, p3.

Thirty Seconds Over Tokyo (Also titled: 30 Seconds Over Tokyo) (US; LeRoy, Mervyn; 1944)
Commonweal. Dec 22, 1944, v41, p254-56.
Film Daily. Nov 15, 1944, p7.
The Films of Spencer Tracy. p187-88.
The Films of World War II. p207-08.
Hollywood Reporter. Nov 14, 1944, p3.
Life. Nov 17, 1944, v17, p49-50.
The Nation. Dec 2, 1944, v159, p699.
The New York Times. Nov 16, 1944, p19.
The New Yorker. Dec 2, 1944, v20, p85.
Newsweek. Nov 20, 1944, v24, p98.
Scholastic. Dec 11, 1944, v45, p32.
Time. Dec 4, 1944, v44, p93.
Variety. Nov 15, 1944, p8.

The Thirty-Nine Steps (GB; Hitchcock, Alfred; 1935)
The Age of the Dream Palace. p228-29.
American Film Criticism. p318-19.
The Art of Alfred Hitchcock. p37-44.
Canadian Magazine. Oct 1935, v84, p40.
Cinema Quarterly. Sum 1935, v3, p241.
Cinema, the Magic Vehicle. v1, p249.
Classic Film Collector. Spr 1976, n50, p14+.
Classics of the Foreign Film. p98-99.
A Critical History of the British Cinema. p109-10.
Dictionary of Films. p373-74.
Esquire. Oct 1935, v4, p97.
Film Daily. Sep 14, 1935, p7.
Film News. Jan-Feb 1979, v36, p26.
The Great British Films. p24-26.
The Great Spy Pictures. p469-72.
Hitchcock: The First Forty-Four Films. p40-44.
Hitchcock (Truffaut). p94-98+.
Hitchcock's British Films. p181-92.
Hollywood Reporter. Jun 29, 1935, p7.
The International Dictionary of Films and Filmmakers. v1, p472-73.
Judge. Sep 1935, v109, p14.
Kiss Kiss Bang Bang. p452.
Landmark Films: The Cinema and Our Century. p100-09.
Literature/Film Quarterly. Sum 1975, v3, p232-39.
Lorentz on Film. p129-30.
Magill's Survey of Cinema. Series I. v4, p1723-25.
Mastering the Film and Other Essays. p74-76.
Motion Picture Herald. Jul 6, 1935, p75.
The Nation. Apr 1, 1936, v142, p430.
The New Masses. Oct 1, 1935, v17, p45.
The New Statesman and Nation. Jun 22, 1935, v9, p928.
The New York Times. Sep 14, 1935, p8.
The New York Times. Jul 14, 1935, p2.
The New York Times. Sep 22, 1935, p5.
The New Yorker. Sep 14, 1935, v11, p63-64.
Saturday Review (London). Jun 22, 1935, v159, p797.
The Spectator. Jun 14, 1935, v154, p1014.
Theatre Arts Monthly. Feb 1936, v20, p139-40.
Time. Sep 23, 1935, v26, p44.
Variety. Jun 19, 1935, p21.
Variety. Sep 18, 1935, p15.
Vintage Films. p27-30.
50 Classic Motion Pictures. p218-23.

This Above All (US; Litvak, Anatole; 1941)
Commonweal. Jun 5, 1942, v36, p160.
Film Daily. May 13, 1942, p6.
The Films of Tyrone Power. p126-29.
Hollywood Reporter. May 13, 1942, p3.
The London Times. Sep 16, 1942, p6.
Motion Picture Exhibitor. May 20, 1942, p1014.
Motion Picture Herald Product Digest. May 16, 1942, p661.
The New Republic. Jun 1, 1942, v106, p766.
The New York Times. May 13, 1942, p14.
Newsweek. May 18, 1942, v19, p51.

Time. Jun 1, 1942, v39, p78.
Variety. May 13, 1942, p8.

This Day and Age (US; DeMille, Cecil B.; 1933)
Film Daily. Aug 16, 1933, p7.
The Films of Cecil B. De Mille. p284-87.
The Great Gangster Pictures. p386-87.
Hollywood Reporter. Jul 18, 1933, p3.
Motion Picture Herald. Jul 29, 1933, p28-29.
National Board of Review Magazine. Sep-Oct 1933, v8, p8-10.
The New York Times. Sep 1, 1933, p15.
Rob Wagner's Script. Aug 19, 1933, v10, p10-11.
The Spectator. Oct 6, 1933, v151, p441.
Time. Sep 4, 1933, v22, p22.
Variety. Aug 29, 1933, p14.
We're in the Money. p112-15.

This Gun for Hire (US; Tuttle, Frank; 1942)
Commonweal. May 29, 1942, v36, p136.
Film Daily. Mar 23, 1942, p8.
Film Noir. p289-90.
The Films of Alan Ladd. p63-69.
The Films of the Forties. p62-64.
Graham Greene on Film. p24-27.
Hollywood Reporter. Mar 17, 1942, p3.
Life. Jun 22, 1942, v12, p48+.
The London Times. Jun 1, 1942, p8.
Magill's Survey of Cinema. Series II. v4, p2481-82.
Motion Picture Exhibitor. Mar 25, 1942, v27, n20, sec2, p973-74.
Motion Picture Herald Product Digest. Mar 21, 1942, p563.
The New York Times. May 14, 1942, p14.
The New Yorker. May 23, 1942, v18, p62.
Time. Jun 8, 1942, v39, p50.
Variety. Mar 18, 1942, p8.

This Is My Affair (Also titled: His Affair) (US; Seiter, William A.; 1937)
Commonweal. Jun 11, 1937, v26, p188.
Film Daily. May 18, 1937, p8.
The Films of Barbara Stanwyck. p116-18.
The Films of Robert Taylor. p59-60.
Graham Greene on Film. p164.
Hollywood Reporter. May 14, 1937, p3.
Hollywood Spectator. May 22, 1937, v12, p14-15.
Literary Digest. Jun 12, 1937, v123, p21-22.
Motion Picture Herald. May 22, 1937, p57.
The New York Times. May 28, 1937, p17.
The New Yorker. May 29, 1937, v13, p58.
Rob Wagner's Script. Jun 5, 1937, v17, p8.
The Spectator. Aug 20, 1937, v159, p312.
Starring Miss Barbara Stanwyck. p93.
Time. Jun 7, 1937, v29, p35.
Variety. Jun 2, 1937, p15.
World Film News. Oct 1937, v2, p24-25.

This Is the Army (US; Curtiz, Michael; 1943)
Commonweal. Aug 27, 1943, v38, p466.
Film Daily. Jul 29, 1943, p8.
The Films of Ronald Reagan. p141-44.
The Films of World War II. p141-43.
Hollywood Reporter. Jul 29, 1943, p3.
Motion Picture Herald Product Digest. Jul 31, 1943, p1453.
The New York Times. Jul 29, 1943, p11.
The New York Times Magazine. Jun 27, 1943, p12.
Newsweek. Aug 9, 1943, v22, p84.
Rob Wagner's Script. Aug 28, 1943, p14.
Selected Film Criticism, 1941-1950. p235-36.
Time. Aug 16, 1943, v42, p93.
Variety. Aug 4, 1943, p8.

This Is the Night (US; Tuttle, Frank; 1932)
Canadian Forum. Jun 1932, v12, p358.
Film Daily. Apr 17, 1932, p10.
The Films of Cary Grant. p32-33.
Motion Picture Herald. Apr 23, 1932, p31, 34.

The Nation. May 11, 1932, v134, p553.
The New York Times. Apr 16, 1932, p11.
Rob Wagner's Script. Apr 16, 1932, v7, p10.
Time. Apr 25, 1932, v19, p32.
Variety. Apr 19, 1932, p15.

This Land Is Mine (US; Renoir, Jean; 1943)
Agee on Film. v1, p35-36+.
Commonweal. Jun 4, 1943, v38, p170.
Film Daily. Mar 17, 1943, p6.
Hollywood Reporter. Mar 17, 1943, p3.
Jean Renoir: A Guide to References and Resources. p131-33.
Motion Picture Herald Product Digest. Mar 20, 1943, p1213.
The New Republic. Apr 26, 1943, v108, p566.
The New York Times. May 28, 1943, p19.
The New Yorker. Jun 5, 1943, v19, p46+.
Newsweek. May 3, 1943, v21, p86.
Time. Apr 26, 1943, v39, p97.
Variety. Mar 17, 1943, p8.

This Man in Paris (GB; MacDonald, David; 1939)
Graham Greene on Film. p231.
Motion Picture Herald. Jul 8, 1939, p35, 38.
The New Statesman and Nation. Jul 8, 1939, v18, p49.
The Spectator. Jun 30, 1939, v162, p1128.
Variety. Jul 5, 1939, p16.

This Man Is News (GB; MacDonald, David; 1938)
Film Daily. Jul 26, 1939, p7.
Motion Picture Herald. Oct 1, 1938, p42, 44.
The New York Times. Jul 20, 1939, p16.
The Spectator. Sep 9, 1938, v161, p403.
World Film News. Oct 1938, v3, p267.

This Modern Age (US; Grinde, Nick; 1931)
Film Daily. Sep 6, 1931, p23.
The Films of Joan Crawford. p86-88.
Hollywood Spectator. Sep 26, 1931, v12, p24-25.
Life. Oct 9, 1931, v98, p18.
Motion Picture Herald. Jun 13, 1931, p28.
The New York Times. Sep 7, 1931, p19.
Rob Wagner's Script. Aug 8, 1931, v5, p8-9.
Time. Sep 14, 1931, v18, p50.
Variety. Sep 8, 1931, p15.

This Reckless Age (US; Tuttle, Frank; 1932)
Film Daily. Jan 10, 1932, p8.
Hollywood Reporter. Dec 19, 1931, p3.
Judge. Jan 30, 1932, v102, p22.
Motion Picture Herald. Jan 16, 1932, p38.
The New York Times. Jan 9, 1932, p21.
Outlook and Independent. Jan 20, 1932, v160, p87.
Rob Wagner's Script. Jan 9, 1932, v6, p10-11.
Time. Jan 18, 1932, v19, p22.
Variety. Jan 12, 1932, p15.

This Thing Called Love (US; Hall, Alexander; 1940)
Film Daily. Feb 17, 1941, p8.
Motion Picture Exhibitor. Jan 8, 1941, p667.
The New Republic. Mar 3, 1941, v104, p307.
The New York Times. Feb 14, 1940, p15.
The New York Times. Feb 16, 1940, sec9, p5.
Scribner's Commentator. Apr 1941, v9, p107-08.
Variety. Dec 25, 1940, p16.

This Time for Keeps (US; Thorpe, Richard; 1947)
Commonweal. Jan 2, 1948, v47, p304.
Film Daily. Oct 17, 1947, p10.
Motion Picture Herald Product Digest. Oct 11, 1947, p3873.
New Republic. Dec 22, 1947, v117, p33.
The New York Times. Dec 5, 1947 p33.
Stanley Donen (Casper). p19.
Variety. Oct 8, 1947, p8.

Thoroughbreds Don't Cry (US; Green, Alfred E.; 1937)
Chestnuts in Her Lap. p28-29.
Film Daily. Nov 24, 1937, p11.

Hollywood Reporter. Nov 13, 1937, p3.
Judy: The Films and Career of Judy Garland. p51-54.
Motion Picture Herald. Nov 20, 1937, p34.
The New Statesman and Nation. Dec 18, 1937, v14, p1065.
The New York Times. Nov 26, 1937, p27.
The New Yorker. Dec 4, 1937, v13, p101.
The Tatler. Dec 22, 1937, v146, p528.
Variety. Nov 17, 1937, p16.

The Thread of Destiny (US; Griffith, D.W.; 1910)
The Emergence of Film Art. p49-50.

Threads of Destiny (US; Smiley, Joseph W.; 1914)
The Moving Picture World. Nov 7, 1914, p846.
The New York Dramatic Mirror. Aug 19, 1914, p25.
The New York Dramatic Mirror. Oct 28, 1914, p33.
Variety. Oct 24, 1914, p22.

Three Bad Men (US; Ford, John; 1926)
Film Daily. Oct 17, 1926, p6.
Magill's Survey of Cinema. Silent Films. v3, p1116-19.
Variety. Aug 18, 1926, p61.
The Western Films of John Ford. p12, 20, 23-29.
The Western: From Silents to the Seventies. p145.

Three Blind Mice (US; Seiter, William A.; 1938)
Commonweal. Jul 8, 1938, v28, p301.
Film Daily. Jun 18, 1938, p4.
The Films of David Niven. p52-53.
Hollywood Reporter. Jun 3, 1938, p3.
Hollywood Spectator. Jun 11, 1938, v13, p6.
Motion Picture Herald. Jun 11, 1938, p35.
The New York Times. Jun 18, 1938, p18.
Rob Wagner's Script. Jun 25, 1938, v19, p13.
Time. Jun 27, 1938, v31, p26.
Variety. Jun 8, 1938, p17.

Three Broadway Girls *See* The Greeks Had a Word for Them

The Three Caballeros (US; Ferguson, Norman; 1944)
The Art of Walt Disney. p273-76.
The Disney Films. p64-67.
Film Daily. Dec 15, 1944, p6.
Hollywood Reporter. Dec 12, 1944, p3.
The New York Times. Feb 5, 1945, p20.
Of Mice and Magic. p66-68+.
Variety. Dec 13, 1944, p8.
Walt Disney: A Guide to References and Resources. p28-29.

Three Comrades (US; Borzage, Frank; 1938)
America in the Dark. p213-144.
Commonweal. Jun 10, 1938, v28, p188.
Esquire. Aug 1938, v10, p82, 90.
Film Daily. May 24, 1938, p6.
The Films of Robert Taylor. p67-68.
F.S. Fitzgerald's Three Comrades. 1978.
Hollywood Reporter. May 21, 1938, p3.
Judge. Jul 1938, v114, p26.
A Library of Film Criticism: American Film Directors. p6.
Magill's Survey of Cinema. Series I. v4, p1731-33.
Motion Picture Herald. May 28, 1938, p54, 57.
National Board of Review Magazine. Jun 1938, v13, p10-11.
The New Masses. Jun 21, 1938, v27, p31.
The New Republic. Jun 22, 1938, v95, p188.
The New York Times. Jun 3, 1938, p17.
The New Yorker. Jun 4, 1938, v14, p49.
Newsweek. Jun 6, 1938, v11, p22-23.
Rob Wagner's Script. Jun 4, 1938, v19, p11.
Stage. Jul 1938, v15, p49.
Time. Jun 6, 1938, v31, p41.
Variety. May 25, 1938, p12.
World Film News. Aug 1938, v3, p173.

Three Faces East (US; Julian, Rupert; 1926)
Film Daily. Feb 21, 1926, p6.
The New York Times. Feb 16, 1926, p22.

Photoplay. Mar 1926, v24, p54.
Selected Film Criticism, 1921-1930. p291.
Variety. Feb 10, 1926, p40.

Three Faces East (US; Del Ruth, Roy; 1930)
Film Daily. Sep 7, 1930, p10.
The Great Spy Films. p476-78.
Judge. Oct 4, 1930, v99, p23.
The New York Times. Sep 6, 1930, p9.
The New York Times. Sep 14, 1930, p5.
The New Yorker. Sep 13, 1930, v6, p78-79.
Time. Sep 15, 1930, v16, p38.
Variety. Sep 10, 1930, p17.

Three Godfathers (Also titled: 3 Godfathers) (US; Ford, John; 1949)
The Complete Films of John Wayne. p163-66.
Film Daily. Dec 1, 1948, p7.
Hollywood Reporter. Dec 1, 1948, p3.
Motion Picture Herald Product Digest. Dec 4, 1948, p4405.
The New York Times. Mar 4, 1949, p25.
The New Yorker. Mar 12, 1949, v25, p87.
Newsweek. Jan 31, 1949, v33, p75.
Rotarian. Apr 1, 1949, v74, p37.
Time. Feb 7, 1949, v53, p84+.
Variety. Dec 1, 1948, p11.
The Western Films of John Ford. p92-107.

Three Little Girls in Blue (US; Humberstone, Bruce; 1946)
Commonweal. Oct 4, 1946, v44, p598.
Film Daily. Sep 5, 1946, p7.
The Hollywood Musical. p275.
Hollywood Musicals. p205-07.
Hollywood Reporter. Sep 4, 1946, p3.
Motion Picture Herald Product Digest. Sep 14, 1946, p3198.
The New York Times. Sep 26, 1946, p32.
The New Yorker. Oct 5, 1946, v22, p82.
Newsweek. Oct 7, 1946, v28, p96.
Time. Oct 7, 1946, v48, p102+.
Variety. Sep 4, 1946, p10.

Three Loves Has Nancy (US; Thorpe, Richard; 1938)
Film Daily. Sep 6, 1938, p11.
Hollywood Reporter. Aug 26, 1938, p4.
Hollywood Spectator. Sep 3, 1938, v13, p11-12.
The New York Times. Sep 2, 1938, p21.
Rob Wagner's Script. Sep 10, 1938, v20, p8.
Time. Sep 12, 1938, v32, p46.
Variety. Sep 7, 1938, p12.

The Three Maxims (GB; Wilcox, Herbert; 1936)
Hollywood Reporter. Jul 14, 1936, p4.
Motion Picture Herald. Aug 1, 1936, p56-57.
Variety. Jul 15, 1936, p31.

Three Men and Lillian *See* Drei von der Tankstelle, Die

The Three Men from the Gas Station *See* Drei von der Tankstelle, Die

Three Men on a Horse (US; LeRoy, Mervyn; 1936)
Commonweal. Dec 25, 1936, v25, p249.
Film Daily. Nov 13, 1936, p9.
Motion Picture Herald. Dec 5, 1936, p42.
The New Statesman and Nation. Feb 6, 1937, v13, p203.
The New York Times. Nov 26, 1936, p39.
The New Yorker. Dec 5, 1936, v12, p103.
Rob Wagner's Script. Dec 26, 1936, v16, p10.
Time. Nov 30, 1936, v28, p42.
Variety. Dec 2, 1936, p18.

The Three Musketeers (US; Niblo, Fred; 1921)
Film Daily. Sep 4, 1921, p2.
Magill's Survey of Cinema. Silent Films. v3, p1120-24.
The New York Times. Aug 29, 1921, p14.
The New York Times. Oct 2, 1921, sec7, p3.

Photoplay. Nov 1921, v20, p60.
Selected Film Criticism, 1921-1930. p292.
Variety. Sep 2, 1921, p61.

The Three Musketeers (US; Lee, Rowland V.; 1935)
Film Daily. Oct 7, 1935, p7.
Hollywood Reporter. Oct 2, 1935, p7.
Motion Picture Herald. Oct 12, 1935, p40.
The New York Times. Nov 1, 1935, p25.
Newsweek. Nov 2, 1935, v6, p46.
Rob Wagner's Script. Nov 16, 1935, v14, p8.
The Spectator. Jan 24, 1936, v156, p129.
Time. Nov 11, 1935, v26, p26.
Variety. Nov 6, 1935, p20.

The Three Musketeers (US; Dwan, Allan; 1939)
Esquire. May 1939, v11, p128.
Film Daily. Feb 20, 1939, p9.
Hollywood Reporter. Feb 4, 1939, p3.
Hollywood Spectator. Feb 18, 1939, v13, p12.
Motion Picture Herald. Feb 11, 1939, p38.
The New York Times. Feb 18, 1939, p12.
Newsweek. Feb 27, 1939, v13, p25.
Rob Wagner's Script. Mar 25, 1939, v21, p16.
The Spectator. Apr 14, 1939, v162, p632.
Time. Feb 27, 1939, v33, p30.
Variety. Feb 8, 1939, p17.

The Three Musketeers (US; Lewis, Joseph H.; 1948)
Commonweal. Nov 5, 1948, v49, p95.
Film Daily. Oct 13, 1948, p8.
The Films of Gene Kelly. p83-90.
The Films of Lana Turner. p160-65.
Halliwell's Hundred. p366-69.
Hollywood Reporter. Oct 19, 1948, p3.
Magill's Survey of Cinema. Series II. v6, p2505-10.
Motion Picture Herald Product Digest. Oct 16, 1948, p4349 .
The New York Times. Oct 21, 1948, p33.
The New Yorker. Oct 30, 1948, v24, p72.
Newsweek. Nov 1, 1948, v32, p81.
Rotarian Jan 1949. v64, p53.
Time. Nov 1, 1948, v52, p90+.
Variety. Oct 20, 1948, p11.
Vincent Price Unmasked. p177-79.

The Three Must-Get-Theirs (US; Linder, Max; 1921)
Film Daily. Sep 10, 1922, p4.
Motion Picture Classic. Nov 1922, v15, p102.
The New York Times. Aug 28, 1922, p14.
Photoplay. Nov 6, 1922, v22, p90-91.
Selected Film Criticism, 1921-1930. p292-93.
Spellbound in Darkness. p288-89.

Three on a Match (US; LeRoy, Mervyn; 1932)
Bette Davis: Her Films and Career. p34-35.
The Complete Films of Humphrey Bogart. p24.
Film Daily. Oct 29, 1932, p6.
The Great Gangster Pictures. p389-90.
Hollywood Reporter. Sep 16, 1932, p3.
Humphrey Bogart: The Man and His Films. p47.
Motion Picture Herald. Oct 1, 1932, p52-53.
The New York Times. Oct 29, 1932, p18.
Time. Nov 7, 1932, v20, p39.
Variety. Nov 1, 1932, p12.

Three on a Weekend *See* Bank Holiday

The Three Penny Opera (German title: Dreigroschenoper, Die; Also titled: The Beggar's Opera) (GER; Pabst, G.W.; 1931)
BFI/Monthly Film Bulletin. Jul 1974, v41, p161-62.
Celluloid: The Film To-Day. p105-19.
Cinema, the Magic Vehicle. v1, p184-85.
Classics of the Foreign Film. p66-69.
Close-Up. Jun 1931, v8, p128-29.
Dictionary of Films. p92-93.

Eighty Years of Cinema. p88-89.
Film Daily. May 24, 1931, p11.
Film Quarterly. Fall 1960, v14, p43-45.
Films and Filming. Apr 1961, v7, p15-17, 38.
Films and Filming. Apr 1967, v13, p20.
From Caligari to Hitler. p236-39.
From Quasimodo to Scarlett O'Hara. p152-54.
The German Cinema. p55-56.
G.W. Pabst (Atwell). p83-96.
The Haunted Screen. p316-18.
Hound and Horn. Jan-Mar 1933, v6, p284-98.
The International Dictionary of Films and Filmmakers. v1, p133-34.
Jump Cut. 1977, n15, p17-21.
National Board of Review Magazine. Jun 1931, v6, p11.
The New York Times. May 18, 1931, p21.
The New Yorker. May 23, 1931, v7, p69.
Outlook and Independent. May 27, 1931, v158, p123.
Variety. May 20, 1931, p16.
A World on Film. p348.

Three Smart Girls (US; Koster, Henry; 1936)
Canadian Magazine. Mar 1937, v87, p24.
Film Daily. Jan 20, 1937, p12.
Garbo and the Night Watchman. p244-46.
Graham Greene on Film. p139-40.
Hollywood Reporter. Dec 1, 1936, p2.
Hollywood Spectator. Dec 19, 1936, v11, p5-6.
Motion Picture Herald. Jan 30, 1937, p47, 50.
The New Statesman and Nation. Mar 20, 1937, v13, p480.
The New York Times. Jan 25, 1937, p22.
Rob Wagner's Script. Dec 12, 1936, v16, p13-14.
Scholastic. Jan 30, 1937, v29, p23.
Selected Film Criticism, 1931-1940. p256-57.
Sight and Sound. Spr 1937, v6, p22.
The Spectator. Mar 26, 1937, v158, p580.
The Tatler. Mar 31, 1936, v143, p562.
Time. Dec 21, 1936, v28, p22.
Variety. Jan 27, 1937, p12.
World Film News. May 1937, v2, p22-23.

Three Smart Girls Grow Up (US; Koster, Henry; 1939)
Canadian Magazine. Apr 1939, v91, p46.
Commonweal. Mar 31, 1939, v29, p641.
Film Daily. Mar 20, 1939, p10.
Graham Greene on Film. p211.
Hollywood Reporter. Mar 17, 1939, p3.
Motion Picture Herald. Mar 25, 1939, p40.
The New Statesman and Nation. Apr 1, 1939, v17, p493.
The New York Times. Mar 18, 1939, p9.
The New Yorker. Mar 25, 1939, v15, p66.
Newsweek. Mar 27, 1939, v13, p29.
Photoplay. Jun 1939, v53, p89.
Rob Wagner's Script. Apr 22, 1939, v21, p16.
Saint Nicholas. Apr 1939, v66, p37.
Scholastic. Apr 15, 1939, v34, p34.
The Spectator. Apr 7, 1939, v162, p592.
Time. Mar 27, 1939, v33, p68.
Variety. Mar 22, 1939, p20.

Three Songs of Lenin (Russian title: Tri Pensi o Leninye; Also titled: Three Songs About Lenin) (USSR; Vertov, Dzega; 1934)
Dictionary of Films. p383.
The Documentary Tradition. p100.
The Film Criticism of Otis Ferguson. p56-58.
Film Daily. Nov 3, 1934, p4.
Film Propaganda. p103-15.
Garbo and the Night Watchman. p82, 197-99.
Kino. p311-13.
London Mercury. Dec 1935, v33, p195.
Motion Picture Herald. Nov 17, 1934, p52.
The Nation. Nov 21, 1934, v139, p602.
The New Statesman and Nation. Nov 2, 1935, v10, p638.
The New York Times. Nov 7, 1934, p32.

Three Waltzes *See* Trois Valses

Three Weeks (US; Crosland, Alan; 1924)
Film Daily. Apr 6, 1924, p9.
Magill's Survey of Cinema. Silent Films. v3, p1129-31.
The Moving Picture World. Apr 12, 1924, p585.
Photoplay. Apr 1924, v25, p61.
Selected Film Criticism, 1921-1930. p294.

Three Wise Girls (US; Beaudine, William; 1932)
Film Daily. Feb 7, 1932, p10.
Motion Picture Herald. Feb 13, 1932, p35.
The New York Times. Feb 6, 1932, p14.
Variety. Feb 9, 1932, p19.

The Three Wise Guys (US; Seitz, George B.; 1936)
Film Daily. May 23, 1936, p7.
Hollywood Reporter. May 6, 1936, p3.
Motion Picture Herald. May 16, 1936, p29.
The New York Times. May 23, 1936, p12.
Rob Wagner's Script. Jun 20, 1936, v15, p12.
Time. Jun 1, 1936, v27, p22.
Variety. May 27, 1936, p14.

Three Women (US; Lubitsch, Ernst; 1924)
Ernst Lubitsch: A Guide to References and Resources. p77-80.
Film Daily. Oct 19, 1924, p25.
The Moving Picture World. Sep 27, 1924, p334.
The New York Times. Oct 6, 1924, p25.
Variety. Oct 8, 1924, p27.

Three Women (USSR; Arnshtam, L.; 1936)
Film Daily. Feb 12, 1936, p6.
National Board of Review Magazine. Apr 1936, v11, p13.
The New Masses. Mar 17, 1936, v18, p27-28.
The New York Times. Feb 12, 1936, p25.
The New Yorker. Feb 22, 1936, v12, p66.

Three-Cornered Moon (US; Nugent, Elliott; 1933)
Claudette Colbert (Quirk). p58-59.
Film Daily. Aug 8, 1933, p2.
Hollywood Reporter. Jul 15, 1933, p3.
Motion Picture Herald. Aug 12, 1933, p44.
The Nation. Aug 30, 1933, v137, p252.
New Outlook. Sep 1933, v162, p45.
The New York Times. Aug 12, 1933, p14.
Newsweek. Aug 19, 1933, v2, p28.
Rob Wagner's Script. Aug 19, 1933, v10, p9.
Variety. Aug 15, 1933, p14.

Through the Dark (US; Hill, George; 1924)
Film Daily. Jan 20, 1924, p7.
The Moving Picture World. Jan 19, 1924, p216.
The New York Times. Jan 8, 1927, p27.
Variety. Jan 20, 1924, p27.

Thunder Afloat (US; Seitz, George B.; 1939)
Commonweal. Oct 13, 1939, v30, p564.
Film Daily. Sep 19, 1939, p7.
Hollywood Reporter. Sep 14, 1939, p3.
Motion Picture Herald. Sep 23, 1939, p48.
The New York Times. Oct 13, 1939, p27.
The New Yorker. Oct 21, 1939, v15, p74.
Rob Wagner's Script. Sep 23, 1939, v22, p16.
Time. Sep 25, 1939, v34, p33.
Variety. Sep 20, 1939, p15.

Thunder Below (US; Wallace, Richard; 1932)
Film Daily. Jun 18, 1932, p4.
Motion Picture Herald. Jun 25, 1932, p28-29.
The New York Times. Jun 20, 1932, p11.
Rob Wagner's Script. Jun 18, 1932, v7, p10.
Time. May 16, 1932, v19, p40.
Variety. Jun 21, 1932, p14.

Thunder in the City (GB; Gering, Marion; 1937)
The Cinema of Edward G. Robinson. p74-79.
Film Daily. Apr 27, 1937, p10.
Graham Greene on Film. p138-39.
Hollywood Reporter. Feb 2, 1937, p3.
Motion Picture Herald. Feb 13, 1937, p62.
The New York Times. Apr 23, 1937, p25.
The New Yorker. May 21, 1937, v13, p63.
The Spectator. Mar 19, 1937, v158, p516.
Time. May 3, 1937, v29, p30.
Variety. Jan 27, 1937, p12.
Variety. Apr 28, 1937, p15.
World Film News. May 1937, v2, p24.

Thunder Over Mexico (Spanish title: Que Viva Mexico)
(US; Eisenstein, Sergei; 1931)
Adelphi. Aug 1933, v6, p372-74.
Around Cinemas. p100-02.
Cinema Quarterly. Spr 1934, v2, p182-83.
Cinema Quarterly. Wint 1932, v1, p73-80.
Classics of the Foreign Film. p74-79.
Close-Up. Jun 1933, v10, p210-12.
Close-Up. Dec 1933, v10, p361-63.
Close-Up. Sep 1933, v10, p248-57.
The Complete Films of Eisenstein. p79-87.
CQ. Wint 1932, v1, p73-80.
Dictionary of Films. p302-03.
The Documentary Tradition. p80-90.
Eisenstein At Work. p61-74.
Film Culture. Wint-Spr 1970, v48-49, p72.
Film Daily. Sep 20, 1933, p8.
Hollywood Reporter. May 11, 1933, p4.
Hound and Horn. Oct-Dec 1933, v7, p144.
Kino. p275-76.
Literary Digest. Oct 7, 1933, v116, p31.
Little Theatres. Oct 1934, v2, p16-17.
Lorentz on Film. p118-19.
Motion Picture Herald. May 20, 1933, p29.
The Nation. Jul 19, 1933, v137, p83-84.
The Nation. Oct 4, 1933, v137, p391-92.
The New Masses. Sep 1933, v9, p28.
New Outlook. Oct 1933, v162, p48.
The New Republic. Jul 5, 1933, v75, p210.
The New Republic. Oct 4, 1933, v76, p213-14.
The New Statesman and Nation. Jan 20, 1934, v7, p85-86.
The New Statesman and Nation. Mar 10, 1934, v7, p339.
The New Statesman and Nation. May 5, 1934, v7, p673.
The New York Times. Sep 25, 1933, p18.
The New Yorker. Sep 30, 1933, v9, p46-47.
Newsweek. Sep 9, 1933, v2, p30.
Rob Wagner's Script. May 13, 1933, v9, p8.
Sergei Eisenstein and Upton Sinclair: The Making and Unmaking of Que Viva Mexico! 1970.
Sight and Sound. Aut 1958, v27, p305-08.
Sight and Sound. Aut 1938, v8, p89-92.
Sociology and Social Research. Mar 1934, v18, p398.
The Spectator. Jan 12, 1934, v152, p46.
Survey Graphic. Nov 1933, v22, p558-59.
Theatre Arts Monthly. Nov 1932, v16, p926-33.
Time. Oct 2, 1933, v22, p39-40.
Vanity Fair. Oct 1933, v41, p39-40.
Variety. Sep 26, 1933, p15.
Vogue. Jul 1, 1933, v82, p49.

Thunderbolt (US; Sternberg, Josef von; 1929)
BFI/Monthly Film Bulletin. Aug 1974, v41, p187-88.
Exhibitor's Herald-World. Aug 3, 1929, p59.
Film Daily. Jun 30, 1929, p12.
The New York Times. Aug 21, 1929, p17.
Selected Film Criticism, 1921-1930. p294.
Variety. Jun 26, 1929, p22.

Tiger Shark (US; Hawks, Howard; 1932)
Film Daily. Aug 23, 1932, p9.
Films and Filming. Jul 1962, v8, p22-23.

The Films of Howard Hawks. p105-07.
Hollywood Reporter. Aug 12, 1932, p2.
Howard Hawks (Poague). p87-88.
Motion Picture Herald. Aug 27, 1932, p38.
New Outlook. Nov 1932, v161, p46.
The New Statesman and Nation. Dec 10, 1932, v4, p728.
The New York Times. Sep 23, 1932, p22.
The New Yorker. Oct 1, 1932, v8, p55.
Rob Wagner's Script. Oct 1, 1932, v8, p9.
Time. Oct 3, 1932, v20, p37.
Variety. Sep 27, 1932, p17.
The Velvet Light Trap. Jun 1971, n1, p12-17.

Tight Little Island (Also titled: Whiskey Galore) (GB;
    MacKendrick, Alexander; 1949)
Christian Century. Feb 1, 1950, v67, p159.
Commonweal. Jan 13, 1950, v51, p391.
Film Daily. Nov 23, 1949, p7.
Films in Review. Feb 1950, v1, p29-30.
The Great British Films. p128-30.
Hollywood Reporter. Nov 18, 1949, p3.
Magill's Survey of Cinema. Series I. v4, p1738-42.
Motion Picture Herald. Nov 19, 1949, p90.
The New Republic. Jan 9, 1950, v120, p23.
The New York Times. Dec 26, 1949, p33.
The New Yorker. Dec 24, 1949, v25, p55.
Newsweek. Jan 2, 1950, v35, p52.
Rotarian. Apr 1950, v76, p39.
Time. Jan 23, 1950, v55, p75-76.
Variety. Jun 22, 1949, p20.

Till the Clouds Roll By *See* When the Clouds Roll By

Till the Clouds Roll By (US; Whorf, Richard; 1946)
Agee on Films. v1, p234-35.
American Film and Society Since 1945. p18-19.
Commonweal. Dec 20, 1946, v45, p255.
Film Daily. Nov 12, 1946, p7.
The Films of Frank Sinatra. p48-50.
The Hollywood Musical. p278-79.
Hollywood Musicals. p211-13.
Hollywood Reporter. Nov 12, 1946, p3.
Judy: The Films and Career of Judy Garland. p127-30.
Motion Picture Herald Product Digest. Nov 16, 1946, p3309.
The Nation. Dec 28, 1946, v163, p766.
The New Republic. Dec 30, 1946, v115, p932.
The New York Times. Dec 6, 1946, p27.
The New Yorker. Dec 14, 1946, v22, p88.
Newsweek. Dec 16, 1946, v28, p104+.
Theatre Arts. Feb 1947, v31, p35.
Time. Jan 6, 1947, v49, p90.
Variety. Nov 13, 1946, p16.

Till the End of Time (US; Dmytryk, Edward; 1946)
Commonweal. Aug 9, 1946, v44, p408.
Film Daily. Jun 14, 1946, p8.
Hollywood Reporter. Jun 12, 1946, p3.
Motion Picture Herald Product Digest. Jun 15, 1946, p3041.
The New York Times. Jul 24, 1946, p24.
The New Yorker. Aug 3, 1946, v22, p38.
Newsweek. Aul 22, 1946, v28, p30+.
Robert Mitchum on the Screen. p88-89.
Time. Jul 15, 1946, p97.
Variety. Jun 12, 1946, p6.

Tillie and Gus (US; Martin, Francis; 1933)
Film Daily. Nov 11, 1933, p3.
The Films of W.C. Fields. p83-85.
Hollywood Reporter. Sep 29, 1933, p3.
Motion Picture Herald. Nov 18, 1933, p42.
The New York Times. Nov 13, 1933, p21.
Rob Wagner's Script. Oct 21, 1933, v10, p10.
Time. Oct 23, 1933, v22, p43.
Variety. Nov 14, 1933, p17.
W.C. Fields: A Life on Film. p119-24.

Tillie's Punctured Romance (US; Sennett, Mack; 1914)
Charles Chaplin: A Guide to References and Resources. p51-
    52.
The Comic Mind. p54-56+.
The Films of Charlie Chaplin. p75-77.
Magill's Survey of Cinema. Silent Films. v3, p1136-39.
The Moving Picture World. Nov 14, 1914, p914, 992.
The New York Dramatic Mirror. Nov 4, 1914, p36.
Selected Film Criticism, 1912-1920. p258-59.
Variety. Jan 1, 1915, p29.

Time in the Sun (US; Seton, Marie; 1939)
Dictionary of Films. p303.
The Film Criticism of Otis Ferguson. p312.
Film Daily. Oct 19, 1939, p8.
Hollywood Reporter. Oct 11, 1939, p3.
The New Masses. Oct 15, 1940, v37, p23.
The New Republic. Sep 30, 1940, v103, p448.
The New York Times. Oct 1, 1940, p29.
Saint Cinema: Selected Writings, 1929-1970. p93-94.
Sight and Sound. Aut 1939, v8, p89-92.
Sight and Sound. Jul-Sep 1953, v23, p8-13.
Theatre Arts. Dec 1939, v23, p848-49.
Time. Jul 22, 1940, v36, p78.
Variety. Oct 9, 1940, p18.

The Time of Your Life (US; Potter, H.C.; 1948)
Agee on Film. v1, p307, 387.
Commonweal. Jun 4, 1948, v48, p186.
Film Daily. May 26, 1948, p6.
The Films of James Cagney. p185-87.
Life. Jun 14, 1948, v24, p51-52.
Motion Picture Herald Product Digest. May 29, 1948, p4182.
The New Republic. Jun 14, 1948, v118, p29.
The New York Times. May 27, 1948, p29.
The New Yorker. Jun 5, 1948, v24, p60.
Newsweek. Jun 7, 1948, v31, p82.
Time. Jun 14, 1948, v51, p98.
Variety. May 26, 1948, p8.

Time Out for Romance (US; St. Clair, Malcolm; 1937)
Film Daily. Feb 10, 1937, p6.
Hollywood Reporter. Feb 6, 1937, p3.
Literary Digest. Feb 20, 1937, v123, p24.
Motion Picture Herald. Feb 20, 1937, p42.
The New York Times. Mar 13, 1937, p23.
Variety. Mar 17, 1937, p15.

The Time, the Place and the Girl (US; Butler, David;
    1946)
Commonweal. Dec 20, 1946, v45, p256.
Film Daily. Dec 13, 1946, p6.
The Hollywood Musical. p279.
Hollywood Reporter. Dec 10, 1946, p3.
Motion Picture Herald Product Digest. Dec 14, 1946, p3361.
The New York Times. Dec 27, 1946, p14.
Newsweek. Jan 13, 1947, v29, p84.
Time. Jan 13, 1947, v49, p100.
Variety. Dec 11, 1946, p8.

Tin Pan Alley (US; Lang, Walter; 1940)
Film Daily. Nov 25, 1940, p9.
The Films of Alice Faye. p137-42.
The Hollywood Musical. p179, 190+.
Life. Nov 25, 1940, v9, p41-42.
The London Times. Feb 3, 1941, p6.
Motion Picture Exhibitor. Nov 27, 1940, p646.
The New York Times. Nov 22, 1940, p27.
Time. Dec 9, 1940, v36, p85.
Variety. Nov 27, 1940, p16.

To Be or Not to Be (US; Lubitsch, Ernst; 1942)
American Film. Nov 1979, v5, p80-81+.
Beyond Formula. p274-77.
BFI/Monthly Film Bulletin. May 31, 1942, p63.
The Cinema of Ernst Lubitsch. p85-92.

Commonweal. Mar 13, 1942, v35, p513.
Ernst Lubitsch: A Guide to References and Resources. p152-55.
Ernst Lubitsch's American Comedy. p225-56.
Film Comment. May-Jun 1974, v10, p38-43.
Film Comment. Mar-Apr 1976, v12, p20-25.
Film Daily. Feb 19, 1942, p8.
Films and the Second World War. p120-21.
The Films of Carole Lombard. p178-85.
The Films of World War II. p64.
Framework. Wint 1977, n5, p12-14, 24-29.
Halliwell's Hundred. p374-76.
The Hollywood Hallucination. p208-21.
Hollywood Reporter. Feb 18, 1942, p3.
The International Dictionary of Films and Filmmakers. v1, p477-78.
Life. Mar 9, 1942, v12, p63-66.
Literature/Film Quarterly. Aut 1975, v3, p299-308.
The London Times. Apr 30, 1942, p6.
Magill's Survey of Cinema. Series I. v4, p1743-46.
Motion Picture Exhibitor. Feb 25, 1942, v27, n16, sec2, p959.
Motion Picture Herald. Feb 21, 1942, p36.
Motion Picture Herald Product Digest. Feb 28, 1942, p526.
Movie-Radio Guide. Feb 14-20, 1942, p2-3.
Movies and Methods. p297-305.
National Board of Review Magazine. Mar 1942, p5-6.
The New Republic. Mar 23, 1942, v106, p309.
New Statesman and Nation. May 2, 1942, p288.
The New York Times. Mar 7, 1942, p13.
The New York Times. May 22, 1942, sec8, p3.
Newsweek. Mar 2, 1942, v19, p50.
PM. Mar 8, 1942, p23.
Rob Wagner's Script. Feb 28, 1942, v27, p10.
Scholastic. Mar 23, 1942, v40, p32.
Selected Film Criticism, 1941-1950. p236-38.
Sight and Sound. Sum 1942, p15-16.
Spectator. May 8, 1942, p442.
Talking Pictures. p303-06.
Time. Mar 16, 1942, v39, p90.
Variety. Feb 18, 1942, p8.

To Each His Own (US; Leisen, Mitchell; 1946)
Commonweal. Jun 7, 1946, v44, p193.
Film Daily. Mar 12, 1946, p12.
The Films of Olivia De Havilland. p209-11.
The Films of the Forties. p168-69.
The Great Romantic Films. p128-31.
Hollywood Reporter. Mar 12, 1946, p3.
Magill's Survey of Cinema. Series II. v6, p2526-29.
Motion Picture Herald Product Digest. Mar 16, 1946, p2894.
The Nation. Jul 6, 1946, v163, p25.
The Nation. Oct 26, 1946, v163, p482.
The New York Times. May 24, 1946, p15.
The New Yorker. May 25, 1946, v22, p76.
Newsweek. May 27, 1946, v27, p90.
Rob Wagner's Script. Aug 3, 1946, v32, p12-13.
Selected Film Criticism, 1941-1950. p238-40.
Theatre Arts. Jun 1946, v30, p346+.
Time. Jun 17, 1946, v47, p98.
Variety. Mar 13, 1946, p10.

To Have and Have Not (US; Hawks, Howard; 1944)
Agee on Film. v1, p121-22.
Commonweal. Nov 3, 1944, v41, p72+.
Faulkner and Film. p109-13.
Film Comment. May-Jun 1973, v9, p30-35.
Film Culture. Fall 1964, v34, p35-37.
Film Daily. Oct 18, 1944, p11.
Film Quarterly. 1977, v30, n3, p19-28.
The Films of Howard Hawks (Willis). p157-61.
Hemingway and Film. p48-65.
Hemingway and the Cinema. p82-113.
Hollywood Reporter. Oct 11, 1944, p3.
Howard Hawks (Wood). p25-32.
Humphrey Bogart (Michael). p132-33.

International Dictionary of Films and Filmmakers. v1, p478-79.
Journal of Popular Film. Sum 1981, v9, p95-97.
Life. Oct 16, 1944, v17, p77-80.
The London Times. Jun 15, 1945, p6.
Magic and Myth of the Movies. p21-26.
Magill's Survey of Cinema. Series I. v4, p1752-55.
The Modern American Novel and the Cinema. p70-79.
Motion Picture Exhibitor. Oct 18, 1944, v32, n23, sec2, p1601.
Motion Picture Herald Product Digest. Oct 14, 1944, p2137.
Movies and Methods. p34-37.
Movietone News. Apr 1975, n40, p11-14.
The Nation. Nov 4, 1944, c159, p569.
New Captain George's Whizzbang. 1974, v3, p20-26+.
The New Republic. Oct 23, 1944, 111, p521-22.
The New York Times. Oct 12, 1944, p24.
The New Yorker. Oct 14, 1944, v20, p60-61.
Newsweek. Oct 16, 1944, v24, p100+.
Quarterly Review of Film Studies. 1982, v7, n2, p185-89.
Rob Wagner's Script. Feb 17, 1945, v31, p14.
Theatre Arts. Dec 1944, v28, p720-21+.
Time. Oct 23, 1944, v44, p92.
To Have and Have Not. p9-53.
Variety. Oct 11, 1944, p12.

To Live in Peace (Italian title: Vivere Pace) (IT; Zampa, Luigi; 1947)
Commonweal. Dec 12, 1947, v47, p226.
Film Daily. Dec 8, 1947, p9.
Hollywood Reporter. Nov 13, 1947, p3.
The Nation. Dec 13, 1947, v165, p655-56.
New Republic. Dec 8, 1947, v117, p37.
The New York Times. Nov 25, 1947, p37.
The New Yorker. Nov 22, 1947, v23, p127.
Newsweek. Dec 1, 1947, v30, p90.
Saturday Review. Jan 31, 1948, v31, p22-24.
Time. Dec 1, 1947, v50, p106.
Variety. Nov 26, 1947, p11.

To Mary—With Love (US; Cromwell, John; 1936)
Film Daily. Jul 21, 1936, p11.
The Films of Myrna Loy. p197-98.
Hollywood Reporter. Jul 17, 1936, p3.
Hollywood Spectator. Aug 1, 1936, v11, p7-8.
Judge. Sep 1936, v111, p12.
Motion Picture Herald. Jul 25, 1936, p62, 64.
The New Masses. Sep 8, 1936, v20, p29.
The New York Times. Aug 27, 1936, p16.
The New Yorker. Sep 5, 1936, v12, p59.
Rob Wagner's Script. Aug 8, 1936, v15, p11-12.
Time. Aug 10, 1936, v28, p26.
Variety. Sep 2, 1936, p21.

To the Shores of Tripoli (US; Humberstone, Bruce; 1942)
Commonweal. Apr 3, 1942, v35, p592.
Film Daily. May 11, 1941, p7.
Hollywood Reporter. Aug 10, 1942, p3.
The London Times. Aug 3, 1942, p8.
Motion Picture Exhibitor. Mar 25, 1942, p976.
Motion Picture Herald Product Digest. Mar 14, 1942, p549.
Musician. May 1942, v47, p75.
The New York Times. Mar 26, 1942, p27.
Scholastic. Apr 13, 1942, v40, p32.
Time. Apr 6, 1942, v39, p82.
Variety. Mar 11, 1942, p8.

To the Victor (GB; Stevenson, Robert; 1938)
Film Daily. Feb 10, 1938, p6.
Hollywood Reporter. Apr 9, 1938, p3.
Motion Picture Herald. Feb 19, 1938, p46.
The Nation. Apr 23, 1938, v146, p484-85.
National Board of Review Magazine. Apr 1938, v13, p16.
The New Masses. May 3, 1938, v27, p29-31.
The New Republic. Apr 20, 1938, v94, p333.

The New York Times. Apr 13, 1938, p21.
Rob Wagner's Script. May 7, 1938, v19, p9.
Scholastic. May 21, 1938, v32, p32.
Time. Apr 11, 1938, v31, p23.

The Toast of New York (US; Lee, Rowland V.; 1937)
Film Daily. Jul 13, 1937, p4.
The Films of Cary Grant. p110-12.
Hollywood Reporter. Jul 9, 1937, p3.
Hollywood Spectator. Jul 17, 1937, v12, p7-8.
Life. Aug 2, 1937, v3, p42-44.
Literary Digest. Aug 7, 1937, v124, p31.
Motion Picture Herald. Jul 17, 1937, p48.
The New Masses. Aug 3, 1937, v24, p29.
The New York Times. Jul 23, 1937, p16.
The New Yorker. Jul 31, 1937, v13, p49.
Rob Wagner's Script. Jul 31, 1937, v17, p14.
Time. Aug 2, 1937, v30, p34.
Variety. Jul 14, 1937, p20.

Tobacco Road (US; Ford, John; 1941)
Commonweal. Mar 7, 1941, v33, p497-98.
Film Daily. Feb 21, 1941, p5.
Hollywood Reporter. Feb 21, 1941, p3.
Life. Mar 24, 1941, v10, p98-99.
Motion Picture Herald Product Digest. Mar 8, 1941, p73.
The New Republic. Mar 10, 1941, v104, p341.
The New York Times. Feb 21, 1941, p16.
The New Yorker. Mar 1, 1941, v17, p53.
Newsweek. Mar 3, 1941, v17, p58.
The Non-Western Films of John Ford. p71-75.
Scholastic. Mar 10, 1941, v38, p40.
Scribner's Commentary. Apr 1941, v9, p104.
Time. Mar 10, 1941, v37, p88.
Variety. Feb 26, 1941, p16.

Today We Live (US; Hawks, Howard; 1933)
Film Daily. Apr 15, 1933, p3.
The Films of Gary Cooper. p109-12.
The Films of Joan Crawford. p103-04.
Hollywood Reporter. Mar 17, 1933, p3.
Motion Picture Herald. Apr 22, 1933, p35.
The New York Times. Apr 15, 1933, p16.
The New Yorker. Apr 22, 1933, v8, p50-51.
Newsweek. Apr 22, 1933, v1, p30.
Pictorial Review. Jul 1933, v34, p68.
Rob Wagner's Script. Jun 3, 1933, v9, p9.
Time. Apr 24, 1933, v21, p44.
Vanity Fair. Jun 1933, v40, p37.
Variety. Apr 18, 1933, p21.

Tol'able David (US; King, Henry; 1921)
American Silent Film. p163-65.
BFI/Monthly Film Bulletin. Mar 1975, v42, p67-68.
Classics of the Silent Screen. p36-38.
Film Daily. Nov 20, 1921, p2.
Films in Review. Oct 1958, p16.
A History of Narrative Film. p218.
The International Dictionary of Films and Filmmakers. v1, p480-81.
Magill's Survey of Cinema. Silent Films. v3, p1140-42.
Motion Picture Classic. Mar 1921, v2, p43.
The Moving Picture World. Dec 5, 1921, v52, p589.
The New York Times. Jan 2, 1922, p20.
Selected Film Criticism, 1921-1930. p294-95.
Variety. Jan 6, 1922, p42.

Tol'able David (US; Blystone, John G.; 1930)
Exhibitors Herald-World. Nov 22, 1930, p35-36.
Film Daily. Nov 16, 1930, p10.
Judge. Dec 13, 1930, v99, p19.
National Board of Review Magazine. Dec 1930, v5, p6.
The New York Times. Nov 17, 1930, p29.
The New Yorker. Nov 22, 1930, v6, p87-88.
Outlook and Independent. Dec 10, 1930, v156, p591.
Those Fabulous Movie Years: The 30s. p12.

Time. Dec 1, 1930, v16, p27.
Variety. Nov 19, 1930, p21.

The Toll Gate (US; Hillyer, Lambert; 1920)
The Complete Films of William S. Hart. p121-23.
The Moving Picture World. May 1, 1920, p727.
The New York Times. Apr 19, 1920, p13.
Photoplay. Jul 1920, v18, p72.
Selected Film Criticism, 1912-1920. p259-60.
Variety. Apr 23, 1920, p43.
Wid's Daily. Apr 25, 1920, p20.

The Toll of the Sea (US; Franklin, Chester M.; 1922)
The Best Moving Pictures of 1922-1923. p101.
Film Daily. Dec 3, 1922, p7.
Magill's Survey of Cinema. Silent Films. v3, p1143-46.
The New York Times. Nov 27, 1922, p18.
Selected Film Criticism, 1921-1930. p295.
Variety. Dec 1, 1922, p35.

Tom Brown of Culver (US; Wyler, William; 1932)
Commonweal. Aug 10, 1932, v16, p371.
Motion Picture Herald. Jul 16, 1932, p52.
The New York Times. Jul 30, 1932, p16.
The New Yorker. Aug 6, 1932, v8, p41-42.
Time. Aug 8, 1932, v20, p18.
Variety. Aug 2, 1932, p15.

Tom Brown's School Days (Also titled: Tom Brown's Schooldays) (US; Stevenson, Robert; 1940)
Catholic World. Sep 1940, v151, p729-30.
Children's Novels and the Movies. p1-14.
Commonweal. Jul 12, 1940, v32, p252-53.
Film Daily. Jun 24, 1940, p8.
Hollywood Reporter. Jun 19, 1940, p3.
Motion Picture Herald. May 4, 1940, p46.
Motion Picture Herald. Jun 22, 1940, p44.
The New York Times. Jun 28, 1940, p22.
Newsweek. Jul 8, 1940, v16, p43.
Time. Jul 8, 1940, v36, p67.
Variety. Jun 26, 1940, p16.

Tom, Dick, and Harry (US; Kanin, Garson; 1941)
Commonweal. Aug 1, 1941, v34, p351.
The Film Criticism of Otis Ferguson. p378-80.
Film Daily. Jul 14, 1941, p7.
The Films of Ginger Rogers. p167-70.
Hollywood Reporter. Jul 11, 1941, p3.
Life. Jul 28, 1941, v11, p59-62.
The London Times. Nov 24, 1941, p8.
Motion Picture Exhibitor. Jul 23, 1941, p793.
Motion Picture Herald Product Digest. May 3, 1941, p121.
The New Republic. Jul 28, 1941, v105, p117.
The New York Times. Jul 18, 1941, p22.
The New York Times. Jul 20, 1941, sec9, p3.
Newsweek. Jul 28, 1941, v18, p52.
Scribner's Commentator. Oct 1941, v10, p105.
Time. Jul 28, 1941, v38, p74.
Variety. Jul 16, 1941, p8.

Tom Sawyer (US; Taylor, William Desmond; 1917)
The Moving Picture World. Dec 22, 1917, p1803, 1848.
The Moving Picture World. Dec 29, 1917, p1995.
The New York Dramatic Mirror. Dec 8, 1917, p16.
The New York Dramatic Mirror. Dec 15, 1917, p18.
Photoplay. Mar 1918, v13, p72.
Selected Film Criticism, 1912-1920. p260-62.
Variety. Dec 7, 1917, p50.
Wid's Daily. Dec 13, 1917, p800.

Tom Sawyer (US; Cromwell, John; 1930)
Commonweal. Jan 7, 1931, v13, p273.
Exhibitors Herald-World. Oct 18, 1930, p45.
Film Daily. Nov 23, 1930, p10.
Life. Jan 9, 1931, v97, p22.
Motion Picture. Nov 1930, v40, p51.

The New York Times. Dec 20, 1930, p20.
The New York Times. Dec 14, 1930, p6.
The New York Times. Dec 28, 1930, p5.
The New Yorker. Dec 27, 1930, v6, p29.
Outlook and Independent. Dec 31, 1930, v156, p712.
The Spectator. Apr 25, 1931, v146, p662.
Time. Dec 29, 1930, v16, p17.
Variety. Dec 24, 1930, p20.

Tom Sawyer, Detective (US; King, Louis; 1938)
Hollywood Reporter. Dec 17, 1938, p2.
Hollywood Spectator. Dec 24, 1938, v13, p25, 35.
Motion Picture Herald. Dec 24, 1938, p40.
Saint Nicholas. Dec 1938, v66, p38+.
Variety. Feb 15, 1939, p13.

Tomorrow and Tomorrow (US; Wallace, Richard; 1932)
Film Daily. Jan 31, 1932, p10.
Hollywood Reporter. Jan 9, 1932, p3.
Motion Picture Herald. Feb 6, 1932, p38.
The New York Times. Jan 30, 1932, p13.
The New Yorker. Feb 6, 1932, v7, p55.
Outlook and Independent. Feb 3, 1932, v160, p150.
Rob Wagner's Script. Mar 12, 1932, v7, p11.
Time. Feb 8, 1932, v19, p20.
Variety. Feb 2, 1932, p15.

Tomorrow Is Forever (US; Pichel, Irving; 1946)
Claudette Colbert (Quirk). p143-48.
Commonweal. Feb 8, 1946, v43, p430.
Film Daily. Jan 16, 1946, p10.
Hollywood Reporter. Jan 15, 1946, p3.
Motion Picture Herald Product Digest. Jan 19, 1946, p2805.
The New York Times. Feb 22, 1946, p21.
The New Yorker. Feb 23, 1946, v22, p77.
Newsweek. Feb 25, 1946, v27, p89.
Orson Welles (Leaming). p299, 303, 309.
Time. Feb 25, 1946, v47, p94+.
Variety. Jan 16, 1946, p18.

Toni (Also titled: The Loves of Toni) (FR; Renoir, Jean; 1934)
BFI/Monthly Film Bulletin. Oct 1974, v41, p236-37.
Cinema, the Magic Vehicle. v1, p227-28.
The Comic Mind: Comedy and the Movies. p236-37.
Dictionary of Films. p379-80.
Film Society Review. Oct 1968, v4, p23-26.
Hollywood Reporter. Apr 3, 1935, p2.
Jean Renoir: A Guide to References and Resources. p87-89.
Jean Renoir (Durgnat). p137-44.
Jean Renoir: My Life and My Films. p154-57.
Jean Renoir: The French Films, 1924-1939. p165-84.
Jean Renoir: The World of His Films. p55-57, 203.
Motion Picture Herald. Nov 14, 1936, p64.
The New Masses. Nov 17, 1936, v21, p28-29.
The New York Times. Sep 19, 1968, p62.
Variety. Mar 19, 1935, p27.

Tonight Is Ours (US; Walker, Stuart; 1933)
Film Daily. Jan 21, 1933, p3.
The Films of Fredric March. p96-98.
Hollywood Reporter. Dec 30, 1932, p3.
Motion Picture Herald. Jan 7, 1933, p23.
The New York Times. Jan 21, 1933, p10.
The New Yorker. Jan 28, 1933, v8, p47-48.
Rob Wagner's Script. Jan 7, 1933, v8, p8.
Time. Jan 30, 1933, v21, p26.
Variety. Jan 24, 1933, p12.

Tonight or Never (US; LeRoy, Mervyn; 1931)
Film Daily. Dec 20, 1931, p10.
Hollywood Reporter. Nov 5, 1931, p3.
Judge. Jan 16, 1932, v102, p22.
Motion Picture Herald. Nov 14, 1931, p40.
The Nation. Jan 6, 1932, v134, p28.
The New York Times. Dec 18, 1931, p29.

The New Yorker. Dec 26, 1931, v7, p50.
Rob Wagner's Script. Jan 9, 1932, v6, p8.
Samuel Goldwyn Presents. p116-17.
Time. Dec 28, 1931, v18, p22.
Variety. Dec 22, 1931, p15.

Too Busy to Work (US; Blystone, John G.; 1932)
Film Daily. Dec 3, 1932, p4.
Motion Picture Herald. Nov 12, 1932, p36.
The New York Times. Dec 3, 1932, p21.
Rob Wagner's Script. Dec 3, 1932, v8, p8.
Time. Dec 12, 1932, v20, p36.
Variety. Dec 6, 1932, p14.
Will Rogers in Hollywood. p122.

Too Hot to Handle (US; Conway, Jack; 1938)
Commonweal. Oct 14, 1938, v28, p645.
Esquire. Jan 1939, v11, p110.
Film Daily. Sep 14, 1938, p7.
Films in Review. Mar 1975, v26, p163-66+.
The Films of Clark Gable. p186-88.
The Films of Myrna Loy. p209-10.
Hollywood Reporter. Sep 10, 1938, p3.
Hollywood Spectator. Sep 17, 1938, v13, p8-9.
Life. Sep 26, 1938, v5, p31.
Magill's Cinema Annual, 1984. p596-99.
Motion Picture Herald. Sep 17, 1938, p37.
The New Masses. Oct 11, 1938, v29, p30.
The New York Times. Sep 30, 1938, p24.
The New Yorker. Sep 24, 1938, v14, p65-66.
Newsweek. Sep 26, 1938, v12, p22.
Rob Wagner's Script. Sep 24, 1938, v20, p8.
Time. Sep 26, 1938, v32, p50.
Variety. Sep 21, 1938, p12.
World Film News. Nov 1938, v3, p288-89.

Too Many Parents (US; McGowan, Robert F.; 1936)
Film Daily. Mar 10, 1936, p8.
Hollywood Reporter. Mar 7, 1936, p3.
Motion Picture Herald. Mar 14, 1936, p56.
Rob Wagner's Script. Apr 18, 1936, v15, p11.
Variety. Apr 22, 1936, p29.

Too Much Harmony (US; Sutherland, Edward; 1933)
Film Daily. Sep 23, 1933, p10.
The Films of Bing Crosby. p53-54.
Hollywood Reporter. Sep 2, 1933, p3.
The New York Times. Sep 23, 1933, p11.
Newsweek. Sep 30, 1933, v2, p47.
Pictures Will Talk. p58.
Rob Wagner's Script. Sep 30, 1933, v10, p12.
Variety. Sep 26, 1933, p20.

Top Hat (US; Sandrich, Mark; 1935)
Commonweal. Sep 13, 1935, v22, p472.
A Companion to the Movies. p110-11.
Eighty Years of Cinema. p105-06.
Esquire. Nov 1935, v4, p106.
Film Daily. Aug 16, 1935, p7.
Films and Filming. Oct 1962, v9, p45-48.
The Films of Ginger Rogers. p118-21.
The Fred Astaire & Ginger Rogers Book. p55-79.
Garbo and the Night Watchman. p119-20.
Graham Greene on Film. p30.
The Great Movies. p87-88.
The Hollywood Musical. p98, 105+.
Hollywood Musicals. p92-95.
Hollywood Reporter. Aug 13, 1935, p3.
Howard Hawks, Storyteller. p21-24.
The International Dictionary of Films and Filmmakers. v1, p481-82.
Life. Nov 1935, v102, p50.
Literary Digest. Sep 7, 1935, v120, p30.
Magill's Survey of Cinema. Series I. v4, p1765-69.
Motion Picture Herald. Aug 24, 1935, p55.
The New York Times. Aug 30, 1935, p12.

The New York Times. Sep 8, 1935, p3.
The New Yorker. Sep 7, 1935, v11, p62.
Newsweek. Sep 7, 1935, v6, p22.
Publisher's Weekly. Jul 16, 1949, v156, p221.
Reruns. p31-35.
Rob Wagner's Script. Aug 31, 1935, v14, p11-12.
Selected Film Criticism, 1931-1940. p257-60.
The Spectator. Oct 25, 1935, v155, p663.
Stage. Sep 9, 1935, v26, p47-48.
Starring Fred Astaire. p97-117.
The Thousand Eyes. Sep 1976, n2, p6-7+.
Time. Sep 9, 1935, v26, p47-48.
Vanity Fair. Oct 1935, v45, p46.
Variety. Sep 4, 1935, p14.
50 Classic Motion Pictures. p68-73.

Top of the Town (US; Murphy, Ralph; 1937)
Film Daily. Mar 27, 1937, p8.
Motion Picture Herald. Apr 3, 1937, p37, 40.
Motion Picture Herald. Jan 23, 1937, p16-17.
The New York Times. Mar 27, 1937, p19.
Rob Wagner's Script. Apr 10, 1937, v17, p10.
Stage. Jan 1937, v14, p66.
Time. Apr 12, 1937, v29, p50.
Variety. Mar 31, 1937, p17.

Topaze (US; D'Arrast, Harry; 1933)
Film Daily. Feb 10, 1933, p7.
The Films of Myrna Loy. p148-49.
Hollywood Reporter. Feb 2, 1933, p3.
Magill's Survey of Cinema. Series II. v6, p2537-39.
Motion Picture Herald. Feb 11, 1933, p30.
The Nation. Mar 1, 1933, v136, p242.
National Board of Review Magazine. Mar 1933, v8, p7.
New Outlook. Mar 1933, v161, p49.
The New York Times. Feb 10, 1933, p10.
The New York Times. Feb 19, 1933, p5.
The New York Times. Dec 30, 1933, p9.
The New York Times. Feb 16, 1935, p9.
The New Yorker. Feb 18, 1933, v8, p54-55.
Newsweek. Feb 17, 1933, v1, p26.
Rob Wagner's Script. Feb 18, 1933, v8, p8.
Time. Feb 20, 1933, v21, p22.
Vanity Fair. Apr 1933, v40, p43.
Variety. Feb 14, 1933, p21.

Topper (US; McLeod, Norman Z.; 1937)
Film Daily. Jul 12, 1937, p10.
The Films of Cary Grant. p106-09.
Hollywood Reporter. Jul 8, 1937, p3.
Hollywood Spectator. Jul 17, 1937, v12, p5-6.
Life. Jul 26, 1937, v3, p38-40.
Literary Digest. Aug 14, 1937, v124, p31.
Lunatics and Lovers. p187-89.
Magill's Survey of Cinema. Series I. v4, p1770-72.
Motion Picture Herald. Jul 17, 1937, p50.
The New Masses. Sep 7, 1937, v24, p28.
The New Statesman and Nation. Sep 25, 1937, v14, p445.
The New York Times. Aug 20, 1937, p21.
The New Yorker. Aug 28, 1937, v13, p46.
Rob Wagner's Script. Aug 14, 1937, v17, p14.
Sight and Sound. Aut 1937, v6, p142.
The Spectator. Oct 1, 1937, v159, p547.
Time. Jul 26, 1937, v30, p24+.
Variety. Jul 14, 1937, p20.

Topper Takes a Trip (US; McLeod, Norman Z.; 1939)
Film Daily. Jan 5, 1939, p6.
Hollywood Reporter. Dec 28, 1938, p3.
Hollywood Spectator. Jan 7, 1939, v13, p12-13.
Life. Jan 2, 1939, v6, p22-25.
The New Statesman and Nation. Mar 18, 1939, v17, p419.
The New York Times. Dec 30, 1938, p11.
The New Yorker. Jan 7, 1939, v14, p43-44.
Newsweek. Jan 9, 1939, v13, p33.

Photoplay. Mar 1939, v53, p52.
Rob Wagner's Script. Mar 11, 1939, v21, p16-17.
Time. Jan 9, 1939, v33, p37.
Variety. Jan 4, 1939, p14.

Tops Is the Limit *See* Anything Goes

The Torch Singer (US; Hall, Alexander; Somnes, George; 1933)
Film Daily. Oct 7, 1933, p4.
Hollywood Reporter. Aug 24, 1933, p3.
Motion Picture Herald. Sep 2, 1933, p37.
The New York Times. Oct 7, 1933, p18.
Rob Wagner's Script. Sep 9, 1933, v10, p10.
Variety. Oct 10, 1933, p17.

The Torrent (US; Bell, Monta; 1926)
Life. Mar 25, 1926, v87, p26.
Photoplay. May 1926, v24, p50.
Selected Film Criticism, 1921-1930. p295-96.
Spellbound in Darkness. p450, 452.
Variety. Feb 24, 1926, p42.

Tortilla Flat (US; Fleming, Victor; 1942)
Commonweal. Jun 12, 1942, v36, p182-83.
Film Daily. Apr 22, 1942, p6.
The Films of Hedy Lamarr. p150-55.
The Films of John Garfield. p104-07.
The Films of Spencer Tracy. p175-77.
Hollywood Reporter. Apr 22, 1942, p3.
Life. Jun 1, 1942, v12, p39-41.
The London Times. Oct 12, 1942, p8.
Motion Picture Exhibitor. May 6, 1942, p1002.
Motion Picture Herald Product Digest. Apr 25, 1942, p621-22.
The New Republic. Jun 1, 1942, v106, p766.
The New York Times. May 22, 1942, p27.
The New Yorker. May 23, 1942, v18, p63.
Newsweek. Jun 1, 1942, v19, p66.
Time. May 18, 1942, v39, p84.
Variety. Apr 22, 1942, p8.

Tosca, La (FR; 1909)
The New York Dramatic Mirror. Jun 19, 1909, p16.
Selected Film Criticism, 1896-1911. p100.

Tösen från Stormytorpet *See* The Girl from the Marsh Croft

Touchdown (US; McLeod, Norman Z.; 1931)
Film Daily. Nov 15, 1931, p10.
Hollywood Reporter. Oct 19, 1931, p3.
Hollywood Spectator. Feb 1932, v12, p11-12.
Life. Dec 1931, v98, p49.
Motion Picture Herald. Oct 31, 1931, p36.
The New York Times. Nov 16, 1931, p23.
The New York Times. Nov 22, 1931, p5.
The New Yorker. Nov 21, 1931, v7, p71.
Outlook and Independent. Dec 2, 1931, v159, p439.
Variety. Nov 17, 1931, p15.

Tovarich (US; Litvak, Anatole; 1937)
Basil Rathbone: His Life and His Films. p188-90.
Canadian Magazine. Feb 1938, v89, p29.
Claudette Colbert (Quirk). p98-101.
Commonweal. Dec 17, 1937, v27, p220.
Film Daily. Dec 4, 1937, p7.
Hollywood Reporter. Dec 1, 1937, p3.
Life. Dec 20, 1937, v3, p22-23.
Literary Digest. Oct 31, 1936, v122, p22.
Motion Picture Herald. Dec 4, 1937, p39.
The New Masses. Jan 4, 1938, v26, p26.
The New Republic. Nov 4, 1936, v89, p21.
The New York Times. Dec 31, 1937, p9.
The New Yorker. Jan 1, 1938, v14, p43.
Newsweek. Oct 24, 1936, v8, p40.
Newsweek. Dec 20, 1937, v10, p30.

Photoplay. Jan 1938, v52, p38-39.
Rob Wagner's Script. Dec 25, 1937, v18, p4.
Scholastic. Jan 22, 1938, v31, p8.
Stage. Nov 1936, v14, p48-49.
Stage. Oct 1937, v15, p95.
Theatre Arts. Dec 1936, v20, p920-21.
Time. Jan 3, 1938, v31, p29.
Variety. Dec 8, 1937, p16.

Tower of London (US; Lee, Rowland V.; 1939)
Boris Karloff and His Films. p118-20.
Commonweal. Dec 8, 1939, v31, p164.
Film Daily. Nov 21, 1939, p6.
The Films of Boris Karloff. p145-48.
Hollywood Reporter. Nov 17, 1939, p3.
Motion Picture Herald. Nov 25, 1939, p43.
The New York Times. Dec 12, 1939, p37.
The New Yorker. Dec 9, 1939, v15, p98.
Rob Wagner's Script. Dec 9, 1939, v22, p15.
Scholastic. Dec 4, 1939, v35, p32.
Time. Dec 11, 1939, v34, p80.
Variety. Nov 22, 1939, p14.

The Toy Wife (US; Thorpe, Richard; 1938)
Commonweal. Jul 8, 1938, v28, p301.
Film Daily. Jun 6, 1938, p6.
Hollywood Reporter. Jun 1, 1938, p3.
Hollywood Spectator. Jun 11, 1938, v13, p7.
Motion Picture Herald. Jun 4, 1938, p32.
The New York Times. Jun 24, 1938, p15.
The New Yorker. Jun 18, 1938, v14, p53-54.
Time. Jun 20, 1938, v31, p38-39.

Tracked by the Police (US; Enright, Ray; 1927)
Film Daily. May 22, 1927, p7.
Magill's Survey of Cinema. Silent Films. v3, p1147-49.
The Moving Picture World. May 21, 1927, p212.
The New York Times. Apr 27, 1927, p22.

Trade Winds (US; Garnett, Tay; 1938)
Canadian Magazine. Feb 1939, v91, p44.
Commonweal. Jan 6, 1939, v29, p302.
Film Daily. Dec 28, 1938, p4.
The Films of Fredric March. p160-62.
Hollywood Reporter. Dec 20, 1938, p3.
Hollywood Spectator. Jan 7, 1939, v13, p9.
Motion Picture Herald. Dec 24, 1938, p40.
The Nation. Jan 21, 1939, v148, p102.
The New Masses. Dec 27, 1938, v30, p28.
The New York Times. Jan 13, 1939, p17.
The New Yorker. Jan 14, 1939, v14, p60-61.
Newsweek. Jan 2, 1939, v13, p25.
Photoplay. Feb 1939, v53, p48.
Rob Wagner's Script. Jan 14, 1939, v20, p17-18.
Time. Dec 26, 1938, v32, p30.
Variety. Dec 21, 1938, p14.

Trader Horn (US; Van Dyke, W.S.; 1931)
Africa on Film: Myth and Reality. p49-54.
American Heritage. Jun 1968, v19, p38-45+.
Celluloid: The Film To-Day. p196-211.
Commonweal. Feb 18, 1931, v13, p440.
Film Daily. Jan 25, 1931, p10.
Focus on Film. Sum 1972, n10, p57-58.
From Quasimodo to Scarlett O'Hara. p138-40.
Judge. Mar 14, 1931, v100, p22, 29.
Life. Feb 20, 1931, v97, p20.
Literary Digest. Mar 7, 1931, v108, p32.
Magill's Survey of Cinema. Series II. v6, p2554-57.
Motion Picture Herald. Jan 24, 1931, p52.
National Board of Review Magazine. Apr 1931, v6, p11.
The New Statesman and Nation. Mar 28, 1931, v1, p186.
The New York Times. Feb 4, 1931, p21.
The New Yorker. Feb 14, 1931, v6, p67.
Outlook and Independent. Feb 25, 1931, v157, p312.
Photoplay. Apr 1931, v39, p30+.

Rob Wagner's Script. Jan 1931, v4, p6.
Selected Film Criticism, 1931-1940. p261-63.
The Spectator. Mar 28, 1931, v146, p499.
Theatre Arts Magazine. Apr 1931, v53, p48.
Time. Feb 2, 1931, v17, p40.
Variety. Feb 11, 1931, p14.
Views and Reviews. Sum 1971, v3, p35-45, 51-58.
The War, the West and the Wilderness. p560-66.

Traffic in Souls (US; Tucker, George Loane; 1913)
The Moving Picture World. Nov 22, 1913, p849.
The New York Dramatic Mirror. Nov 19, 1913, p33.
Selected Film Criticism, 1912-1920. p262-64.
Variety. Nov 28, 1913, p12.

Trail of the Lonesome Pine (US; Hathaway, Henry; 1936)
Canadian Magazine. Apr 1936, v85, p57.
Commonweal. Mar 6, 1936, v23, p524.
Esquire. May 1936, v5, p115.
Film Daily. Feb 20, 1936, p3.
The Films of Henry Fonda. p45-47.
The Fondas (Springer). p59-60.
Graham Greene on Film. p74.
Hollywood Reporter. Feb 19, 1936, p3.
Hollywood Spectator. Feb 29, 1936, v10, p6-7.
Literary Digest. Feb 29, 1936, v121, p20.
Motion Picture. Apr 1936, v51, p38-39+.
Motion Picture Herald. Feb 29, 1936, p45.
The New York Times. Feb 20, 1936, p23.
The New Yorker. Feb 29, 1936, v12, p51.
Newsweek. Feb 29, 1936, v7, p32.
Photoplay. Mar 1936, v49, p37.
Rob Wagner's Script. Mar 21, 1936, v15, p12.
Scholastic. Mar 28, 1936, v28, p26.
The Spectator. May 15, 1936, v156, p879.
The Tatler. May 20, 1936, v140, p332.
Time. Mar 2, 1936, v27, p25.
Variety. Feb 26, 1936, p15.

The Tramp (US; Chaplin, Charles; 1915)
Chaplin's Films. p70-71.
Charles Chaplin: A Guide to References and Resources. p55.
Charlie Chaplin. p72-74.
The Comic Mind. p73-82+.
Essanay News. Apr 24, 1915, p1.
The Films of Charlie Chaplin. p75-76.
Motion Picture News. Apr 24, 1915, p72.
The Moving Picture World. Apr 24, 1915, p619.
Photoplay. Apr 1916, v9, p68-70, 175.
The Silent Clowns. p80-82.

Tramp, Tramp, Tramp (US; Edwards, Harry; 1926)
BFI/Monthly Film Bulletin. Feb 1978, v45, p33-34.
The Comic Mind. p167-71.
Film Daily. Jan 6, 1926, p6.
The Films of Joan Crawford. p39.
Magill's Survey of Cinema. Silent Films. v3, p1153-61.
The New York Times. May 24, 1926, p24.
Photoplay. May 1926, v24, p49.
Selected Film Criticism, 1921-1930. p296.
The Silent Clowns. p274-76+.
Variety. May 26, 1926, p17.

Transatlantic (US; Howard, William K.; 1931)
Film Daily. Jul 26, 1931, p10.
Hollywood Reporter. Jun 29, 1931, p26.
Hollywood Spectator. Sep 12, 1931, v12, p10-12, 22.
Life. Aug 28, 1931, v98, p18.
Motion Picture Herald. Jul 18, 1931, p40.
The New York Times. Jul 31, 1931, p15.
The New Yorker. Aug 8, 1931, v7, p48-49.
Outlook and Independent. Aug 12, 1931, v158, p470.
Rob Wagner's Script. Jul 18, 1931, v5, p10.
Time. Aug 10, 1931, v18, p30.
Variety. Aug 4, 1931, p18.

Transatlantic Tunnel (Also titled: The Tunnel) (GB; Elvey, Maurice; 1935)
Canadian Magazine. Dec 1935, v84, p45.
Canadian Magazine. Jan 1936, v85, p32.
Film Daily. Oct 22, 1935, p8.
Motion Picture Herald. Nov 2, 1935, p60.
The New York Times. Oct 28, 1935, p16.
The New Yorker. Nov 2, 1935, v11, p76.
Rob Wagner's Script. Nov 2, 1935, v14, p10.
Science Fiction Studies in Film. p74-77.
Selected Film Criticism: Foreign Films, 1930-1950. p178-79.
The Spectator. Nov 22, 1935, p863.
Time. Nov 4, 1935, v26, p56.
Vanity Fair. Dec 1935, v45, p51.
Variety. Oct 30, 1935, p14.

The Trap (US; Thornby, Robert; 1922)
Film Daily. May 7, 1922, p5.
Variety. May 5, 1922, p33.

Trapeze (GER; Dupont, E.A.; 1932)
Film Daily. May 10,1932, p11.
Judge. Jun 4, 1932, v19, p23.
Motion Picture Herald. May 14, 1932, p48.
The Nation. May 25, 1932, v134, p607.
The New York Times. May 3, 1932, p25.
Time. May 9, 1932, v19, p23.
Variety. May 10, 1932, p19.
Variety. Feb 20, 1934, p25.

Trapped by Television (US; Lord, Del; 1936)
Film Daily. Jun 16, 1936, p24.
Motion Picture Herald. Aug 8, 1936, p42.
The New York Times. Jun 15, 1936, p24.
Variety. Jun 17, 1936, p23.

Traumende Mund, Der (Also titled: The Dreaming Mouth) (GER; Czinner, Paul; 1932)
Cinema Quarterly. Spr 1933, v1, p183.
Close-Up. Dec 1932, v9, p254-56.
From Caligari to Hitler. p255-56.
The New Statesman and Nation. Jan 28, 1933, v5, p102.
The New Statesman and Nation. Apr 15, 1933, v5, p477.
Variety. Nov 8, 1932, p17.
Variety. Feb 6, 1934, p14.

Treasure Island (US; Tourneur, Maurice; 1920)
Fifty Great American Silent Films, 1912-1920. p123-24.
The Moving Picture World. Apr 24, 1920, p560, 600.
The New York Times. Apr 12, 1920, p13.
Variety. Apr 16, 1920, p36.
Wid's Daily. Apr 18, 1920, p12.

Treasure Island (US; Fleming, Victor; 1934)
BFI/Monthly Film Bulletin. Oct 1977, v44, p219-20.
Children's Novels and the Movies. p58-61.
Film Daily. Aug 8, 1934, p7.
Hollywood Reporter. Jun 23, 1934, p3.
Motion Picture Herald. Jul 14, 1934, p44.
The New York Times. Aug 18, 1934, p5.
Newsweek. Aug 25, 1934, v4, p24.
Time. Aug 27, 1934, v24, p42.
Variety. Aug 21, 1934, p17.

The Treasure of the Sierra Madre (US; Huston, John; 1948)
The Cinema of John Huston. p58-72.
Commonweal. Feb 6, 1948, v47, p424.
Film and Literature. p168-73.
Film Daily. Jan 7, 1948, p7.
The Films of Humphrey Bogart. p136-41.
The Great Films. p189-92.
Hollywood Reporter. Jan 6, 1948, p3.
Humphrey Bogart: The Man and His Films. p143-44.
The International Dictionary of Films and Filmmakers. v1, p485-86.

Life. Feb 2, 1948, v24, p63-66.
Magill's Survey of Cinema. Series I. v4, p1773-76.
Motion Picture Herald Product Digest. Jan 10, 1949, p4009.
The Nation. Jan 31, 1948, v166, p136-38.
The New Republic. Jan 26, 1948, v118, p35.
The New York Times. Jan 24, 1948, p11.
The New Yorker. Jan 24, 1948, v23, p50.
Newsweek. Jan 26, 1948, v31, p88.
Screening the Novel. p84-115.
Sequence. Spr 1949, n7, p34-36.
Seventy Years of Cinema. p165-67.
Time. Feb 2, 1948, v51, p80+.
Variety. Jan 7, 1948, p56.

A Tree Grows in Brooklyn (US; Kazan, Elia; 1945)
Agee on Film. v1, p141-43.
Commonweal. Mar 9, 1945, v41, p517-18.
Film Daily. Jan 24, 1945, p11.
Hollywood Reporter. Jan 24, 1945, p3.
Life. Feb 26, 1945, v18, p43-45.
The London Times. Apr 9, 1945, p8.
Magill's Survey of Cinema, Series II. v6, p2561-63.
Motion Picture Herald Product Digest. Jan 27, 1945, p2289.
Movie. Win 1971-1972, v19, p14-16.
The Nation. Feb 17, 1945, v155, p192-93.
The New Republic. Mar 12, 1945, v112, p360.
The New York Times. Mar 1, 1945, p25.
The New York Times. Mar 4, 1945, sec2, p1.
The New York Times Magazine. Aug 6, 1944, p14-15.
The New Yorker. Mar 3, 1945, v21, p48.
Newsweek. Feb 19, 1945, v25, p100+.
Rob Wagner's Script. Mar 17, 1945, v31, p14-15.
Scholastic. Feb 26, 1945, v46, p42.
Selected Film Criticism, 1941-1950. p245.
Theatre Arts. Mar 1945, v29, p172-75.
Time. Feb 19, 1945, v45, p91.
Variety. Jan 24, 1945, p10.
Women's Film and Female Experience. p103-12.

Trent's Last Case (US; Hawks, Howard; 1929)
Film Daily. Jun 2, 1929, p8.

The Trespasser (US; Goulding, Edmund; 1929)
Exhibitor's Herald-World. Nov 16, 1929, p68.
Film Daily. Nov 17, 1929, p8.
Magill's Survey of Cinema. Series II. v6, p2564-66.
The New York Times. Nov 2, 1929, p14.
Variety. Sep 18, 1929, p15.
Variety. Oct 2, 1929, p34.

Tri Pense o Leninye *See* Three Songs of Lenin

Trifling Women (US; Ingram, Rex; 1922)
The Best Moving Pictures of 1922-1923. p97-98.
Film Daily. Oct 8, 1922, p3.
The New York Times. Oct 4, 1922, p23.
Selected Film Criticism, 1921-1930. p296-97.
Variety. Oct 6, 1922, p40.

Trilby (US; Tourneur, Maurice; 1915)
Motion Picture News. Sep 4, 1915, p55.
Motion Picture News. Sep 25, 1915, p85-86.
Motion Picture News. Oct 9, 1915, p53.
Motography. Sep 18, 1915, p581.
Motography. Sep 25, 1915, p639.
The Moving Picture World. Sep 4, 1915, p1603.
The Moving Picture World. Sep 18, 1915, p2010-11.
The New York Dramatic Mirror. Sep 15, 1915, p32.
Variety. Sep 10, 1915, p21.

Trinadtsat *See* The Thirteen

Triumph des Willens (Also titled: Triumph of the Will) (GER; Riefenstahl, Leni; 1935)
Cinema Journal. Fall 1975, v15, p48-57.
Dictionary of Films. p383-84.
Documentary: A History of the Non-Fiction Film. p103-05.

The Documentary Tradition. p138-40.
Eighty Years of Cinema. p102-03.
Film Comment. Nov 1973, v9, p32-37.
Film Comment. Wint 1965, v3, p16-23.
Film Culture. Spr 1973, n56/57, p162-69.
Film in the Third Reich. p73-76.
Film Propaganda. p177-89.
Filmguide to Triumph of the Will.
The Films of Leni Riefenstahl. p27-59.
The German Cinema. p78-82.
The Haunted Screen. p335-36.
The International Dictionary of Films and Filmmakers. v1, p486-88.
Leni Riefenstahl (Berg-Pan). p97-134.
Leni Riefenstahl: The Fallen Film Goddess. p84-112.
Nazi Cinema. p25-29.
Nonfiction Film Theory and Criticism. p250-62.
Propaganda and the German Cinema, 1933-1945. p147-59.
Screen. 1979, n1, v20, p63-86.
Swastika: Cinema of Oppression. p48-55.

The Triumph of Sherlock Holmes (GB; Hiscott, Leslie; 1935)
Film Daily. May 28, 1935, p10.
Hollywood Reporter. Jun 1, 1935, p7.
Motion Picture Herald. Mar 9, 1935, p52.
The New York Times. May 27, 1935, p20.
Sherlock Holmes on the Screen. p156-58.
Variety. May 29, 1935, p14.

Trois Valses (Also titled: Three Waltzes) (FR; Berger, Ludwig; 1939)
Film Daily. May 11, 1939, p6.
London Mercury. Apr 1939, v39, p633.
Motion Picture Herald. May 13, 1939, p40, 42.
The New Statesman and Nation. Mar 11, 1939, v17, p357.
The New York Times. Apr 25, 1939, p19.
The Tatler. Mar 29, 1939, v151, p562.
Variety. Jan 25, 1939, p15.

Troopship (GB; Whelan, Tim; 1938)
Film Daily. Apr 27, 1938, p24.
National Board of Review Magazine. May 1938, v13, p12.
The New York Times. Apr 26, 1938, p18.
The New Yorker. Apr 30, 1938, v14, p53.
Variety. Apr 27, 1938, p23.

Tropic Holiday (US; Reed, Theodore; 1938)
Canadian Magazine. Jul 1938, v90, p26.
Commonweal. Jul 15, 1938, v28, p329.
Motion Picture Herald. Jun 25, 1938, p47.
The New York Times. Jun 30, 1938, p21.
Rob Wagner's Script. Jul 9, 1938, v19, p16.
Time. Jul 11, 1938, v32, p43.
Variety. Jul 6, 1938, p15.

Trouble for Two (Also titled: The Suicide Club) (US; Ruben, J. Walter; 1936)
Film Daily. Jun 1, 1936, p8.
Hollywood Reporter. May 18, 1936, p3.
Motion Picture Herald. May 30, 1936, p40-41.
The New Statesman and Nation. Jul 18, 1936, v12, p87.
The New York Times. May 30, 1936, p7.
The New Yorker. Jun 6, 1936, v12, p63.
Rob Wagner's Script. May 30, 1936, v15, p10.
The Tatler. Jul 22, 1936, v141, p144.
Time. Jun 8, 1936, v27, p42.
Variety. Jun 3, 1936, p15.

Trouble in Paradise (US; Lubitsch, Ernst; 1932)
American Film Criticism. p272-74.
The American Films of Ernst Lubitsch. p147-52.
The Cinema of Ernst Lubitsch. p77-85.
The Comic Mind. p218-20.
Dictionary of Films. p384.
Ernst Lubitsch: A Guide to References and Resources. p116-19.

Ernst Lubitsch's American Comedy. p34-86.
Film Comment. Fall 1970, v6, p47-48.
Film Daily. Nov 10, 1932, p6.
Film Notes. p85-86.
Film Society Review. Jan 1969, n4, p23.
The Films of the Thirties. p81-83.
Halliwell's Hundred. p381-84.
Hollywood Reporter. Oct 8, 1932, p3.
The Lubitsch Touch. p125-32.
Magill's Survey of Cinema. Series II. v6, p2567-71.
Motion Picture Herald. Oct 29, 1932, p31.
Movie Comedy (Byron). p72-75.
The Nation. Dec 7, 1932, v135, p576.
New Outlook. Dec 1932, v161, p47.
The New Statesman and Nation. Dec 24, 1932, v4, p833.
The New York Times. Nov 9, 1932, p28.
The New Yorker. Nov 19, 1932, v8, p66.
Photoplay. Dec 1932, v43, p57.
Rob Wagner's Script. Oct 29, 1932, v8, p8.
Selected Film Criticism, 1931-1940. p263-64.
Talking Pictures. p164-69.
Time. Nov 21, 1932, v20, p28.
Vanity Fair. Dec 1932, v39, p64.
Variety. Nov 15, 1932, p19.

True Confession (US; Ruggles, Wesley; 1937)
Film Daily. Nov 22, 1937, p4.
The Films of Carole Lombard. p151-55.
Graham Greene on Film. p190.
Hollywood Reporter. Nov 17, 1937, p3.
Motion Picture Herald. Nov 20, 1937, p39.
The New Masses. Jan 18, 1938, v26, p30-31.
The New York Times. Dec 16, 1937, p35.
The New Yorker. Dec 25, 1937, v13, p45.
Rob Wagner's Script. Dec 18, 1937, v18, p10-11.
The Spectator. Dec 31, 1937, v159, p1177.
Stage. Jan 1938, v15, p65-66.
Time. Dec 27, 1937, v30, p21.
Variety. Nov 24, 1937, p16.

True Heart Susie (US; Griffith, D.W.; 1919)
BFI/Monthly Film Bulletin. Sep 1975, v42, p2091.
D.W. Griffith: An American Life. p406-08.
D.W. Griffith: First Artist of the Movies. p105-08.
D.W. Griffith: His Life and Work. p199-200.
Exhibitor's Trade Review. Jun 14, 1919, p133.
The Films of D.W. Griffith. p115-20.
Lillian Gish: The Movies, Mr. Griffith, and Me. p209-10.
Magill's Survey of Cinema. Silent Films. v3, p1162-65.
Motion Picture Classic. Aug 1919, p60.
Motion Picture News. Jun 7, 1919, p3813.
Motion Picture News. Jun 14, 1919, p4029.
The Moving Picture World. Jun 14, 1919, p1677.
The New York Times. Jun 2, 1919, p20.
Photoplay. Sep 1919, v16, p117.
Selected Film Criticism, 1912-1920. p266.
Variety. Jun 6, 1919, p49.
Wid's Daily. Jun 8, 1919, p25.

Tsar to Lenin (US; Eastman, Max; 1937)
Commonweal. Apr 16, 1937, v25, p698.
Film Daily. Mar 15, 1937, p18.
Motion Picture Herald. Mar 27, 1937, p46.
National Board of Review Magazine. Apr 1937, v12, p16.
The New Republic. Apr 7, 1937, v90, p264.
The New York Times. Mar 9, 1937, p27.
Time. Mar 22, 1937, v29, p42.
Variety. Mar 10, 1937, p14.

Tsuma Yo Bara no Yoni *See* Kimiko

Tudor Rose *See* Nine Days a Queen

Tugboat Annie (US; LeRoy, Mervyn; 1933)
Canadian Magazine. Sep 1933, v80, p32-33.
Cinema Quarterly. Aut 1933, v2, p47-48.

Film Daily. Aug 12, 1933, p4.
Hollywood Reporter. Jul 8, 1933, p3.
Motion Picture Herald. Aug 12, 1933, p44.
National Board of Review Magazine. Sep-Oct 1933, v8, p8-10.
New Outlook. Sep 1933, v162, p44.
The New York Times. Aug 12, 1933, p14.
The New Yorker. Aug 19, 1933, v9, p41.
Newsweek. Aug 19, 1933, v2, p28.
Rob Wagner's Script. Aug 19, 1933, v10, p8.
Time. Aug 7, 1933, v22, p23-24.
Time. Aug 21, 1933, v22, p29.
Variety. Aug 15, 1933, p14.

Tulsa (US; Heisler, Stuart; 1949)
Film Daily. Mar 21, 1949, p8.
The Films of Susan Hayward. p129-31.
Hollywood Reporter. Mar 21, 1949, p4.
Motion Picture Herald Product Digest. Mar 19, 1949, p4537.
The New York Times. May 27, 1949, p25.
Newsweek. Apr 25, 1949, v33, p91.
Rotarian. Jul 1949, v75, p51.
Time. Jun 20, 1949, v53, p86+.
Variety. Mar 23, 1949, p8.

Tumbleweeds (US; Baggot, King; 1925)
The Complete Films of William S. Hart. p148-51.
Film Daily. Dec 27, 1925.
Film Daily. May 9, 1939, p6.
The Films of the Twenties. p129-30.
Magill's Survey of Cinema. Silent Films. v3, 1166-68.
Motion Picture Herald. May 13, 1930, p42.
The Moving Picture World. Jan 2, 1926, p60.
Selected Film Criticism, 1921-1930.
Variety. Dec 23, 1925, p36.

The Tunnel *See* Transatlantic Tunnel

Turbine 50,000 *See* Counterplan

The Turn in the Road (US; Vidor, King; 1919)
Exhibitor's Trade Review. Mar 29, 1919, p1289.
Motion Picture Classic. Jun 1919, p46.
Motion Picture News. Mar 29, 1919, p2020.
The Moving Picture World. Mar 15, 1919, p1658-65.
The Moving Picture World. Mar 29, 1919, p1841.
The Moving Picture World. Apr 12, 1919, p209-10.
The New York Times. Mar 30, 1919, sec4, p6.
Selected Film Criticism, 1912-1920. p266-67.
A Tree Is a Tree. p78-81.
Variety. Mar 21, 1919, p53.

Turn to the Right (US; Ingram, Rex; 1922)
Film Daily. Jan 29, 1922, p3.
Motion Picture Classic. Apr 1922, v14, p87.
The New York Times. Jan 24, 1922, p11.
Selected Film Criticism, 1921-1930. p298-99.
Variety. Jan 27, 1922, p39.

Twelve Crowded Hours (US; Landers, Lew; 1939)
Film Daily. Mar 1, 1939, p10.
Hollywood Reporter. Feb 15, 1939, p2.
Hollywood Spectator. Mar 4, 1939, v13, p14.
Motion Picture Herald. Feb 18, 1939, p43.
The New York Times. Feb 24, 1939, p15.
Variety. Mar 1, 1939, p15.

Twelve O'Clock High (US; King, Henry; 1949)
Christian Century. Mar 22, 1950, v73, p383.
Commonweal. Feb 3, 1950, v51, p464.
Film Daily. Dec 21, 1949, p8.
Films in Review. Mar 1950, v2, p29-31.
The Films of Gregory Peck. p90-96.
Hollywood Reporter. Dec 21, 1949, p3.
Life. Feb 20, 1950, v28, p55-58.
Magill's Survey of Cinema. Series I. v4, p1786-80.
Motion Picture Herald Product Digest. Dec 24, 1949, p129.
The New Republic. Jan 30, 1950, v122, p30.

The New Yorker. Feb 4, 1950, v25, p78.
Newsweek. Jan 23, 1950, v35, p79.
Rotarian. May 1950, v76, p41.
Scholastic. Feb 8,1950, v56, p41.
Sequence. Sum 1950, n11, p10-11.
Sight and Sound. May 1950, v19, p125-126.
Time. Jan 30, 1950, v55, p84+.
Variety. Dec 21, 1949, p8.

12:10 (GB; Brenon, Herbert; 1919)
Exhibitor's Trade Review. Jan 3, 1920, p521.
Motion Picture News. Jan 3, 1920, p486.
The Moving Picture World. Jan 3, 1920, p146-47.
The New York Times. Dec 22, 1919, p18.
Wid's Daily. Dec 28, 1919, p11.

Twentieth Century (Also titled: The Twentieth Century;
   20th Century) (US; Hawks, Howard; 1934)
BFI/Monthly Film Bulletin. Apr 1979, v46, p83.
Commonweal. May 18, 1934, v20, p76.
Film Daily. May 4, 1934, p9.
Hawks on Hawks. p63-65.
Hollywood Reporter. Apr 13, 1934, p3.
Howard Hawks (Poague). p133-34.
Howard Hawks: Storyteller. p42-50, 189-212.
Literary Digest. May 19, 1934, v117, p36.
Magill's Survey of Cinema. Series I. v4, p1791-94.
Motion Picture Herald. Apr 7, 1934, p68.
Motion Picture Herald. Apr 21, 1934, p35.
New Outlook. Jun, 1934, v163, p45.
The New York Times. May 4, 1934, p24.
The New York Times. May 13, 1934, p2.
Rob Wagner's Script. May 19, 1934, v11, p9.
Selected Film Criticism, 1931-1940. p264-67.
Time. May 14, 1934, v23, p24.
Variety. May 8, 1934, p14.

Twenty Thousand Years in Sing Sing (US; Curtiz,
   Michael; 1933)
Bette Davis: Her Films and Career. p36-37.
Film Daily. Jan 11, 1933, p11.
The Films of Spencer Tracy. p89-90.
The Great Gangster Pictures. p398-99.
Hollywood Reporter. Oct 27, 1932, p3.
Judge. Feb 1933, v104, p18.
Motion Picture Herald. Nov 5, 1932, p44.
The New York Times. Jan 10, 1933, p26.
The New Yorker. Jan 21, 1933, v8, p47.
Time. Jan 23, 1933, v21, p35.
Variety. Jan 17, 1933, p14.

Twenty-Three and a Half Hours' Leave (US; King, Henry;
   1919)
Exhibitor's Trade Review. Nov 8, 1919, p1977.
Motion Picture News. Nov 8, 1919, p3502.
Motion Picture News. Dec 13, 1919, p4265.
The Moving Picture World. Nov 8, 1919, p246.
The New York Times. Oct 27, 1919, p9.
Selected Film Criticism, 1912-1920. p267-68.
Variety. Oct 31, 1919, p61.
Wid's Daily. Nov 2, 1919, p4.

The Twisted Road *See* They Live by Night

The Twisted Trail (US; Griffith, D.W.; 1910)
The Moving Picture World. Apr 9, 1910, p553.
Selected Film Criticism, 1896-1911. p100-01.

Two Against the World (US; McGann, William; 1936)
The Complete Films of Humphrey Bogart. p31-32.
Film Daily. Jul 11, 1936, p3.
Hollywood Reporter. May 12, 1936, p3.
Humphrey Bogart: The Man and His Films. p52-54.
Motion Picture Herald. May 23, 1936, p41.
Time. Jul 13, 1936, v28, p54.
Variety. Jul 15, 1936, p31.

Two Against the World (US; Mayo, Archie; 1932)
Commonweal. Sep 21, 1932, v16, p492.
Film Daily. Aug 20, 1932, p5.
Motion Picture Herald. Jul 30, 1932, p32-33.
The New York Times. Aug 19, 1932, p20.
Variety. Aug 23, 1932, p19.

Two Hearts in Waltz Time *See* Zwei Herzen im 3/4 Takt

Two in a Crowd (US; Green, Alfred E.; 1936)
Film Daily. Aug 8, 1936, p3.
Hollywood Reporter. Aug 5, 1936, p3.
Motion Picture Herald. Oct 10, 1936, p53.
The New York Times. Oct 5, 1936, p25.
Newsweek. Sep 26, 1936, v8, p27.
Rob Wagner's Script. Oct 17, 1936, v16, p10.
Variety. Oct 7, 1936, p15.

Two Kinds of Women (US; Mille, William C. de; 1932)
Film Daily. Jan 17, 1932, p8.
Hollywood Reporter. Dec 24, 1931, p3.
Judge. Feb 6, 1932, v102, p22.
Motion Picture Herald. Jan 23, 1932, p46.
The New York Times. Jan 16, 1932, p13.
Rob Wagner's Script. Jan 16, 1932, v6, p8.
Time. Jan 25, 1932, v19, p25.

The Two Mrs. Carrolls (US; Godfrey, Peter; 1947)
Commonweal. Apr 18, 1947, v46, p16.
Film Daily. Apr 1, 1947, p8.
The Films of Barbara Stanwyck. p175-77.
The Films of Humphrey Bogart. p131-33.
Hollywood Reporter. Apr 1, 1947, p3.
Humphrey Bogart: The Man and His Films. p136-38.
Motion Picture Herald Product Digest. Apr 5, 1947, p3561.
The New York Times. Apr 7, 1947, p20.
The New Yorker. Apr 5, 1947, v23, p82.
Newsweek. Apr 14, 1947, v29, p94.
Time. May 12, 1947, v49, p101.
Variety. Apr 2, 1947, p16.

The Two Orphans (US; 1911)
The Moving Picture World. Sep 23, 1911, p869-70.
Selected Film Criticism, 1896-1911. p101-02.

Two Seconds (US; LeRoy, Mervyn; 1932)
Film Daily. May 22, 1932, p10.
Motion Picture Herald. May 28, 1932, p88.
The Nation. Jun 22, 1932, v134, p708.
National Board of Review Magazine. May 1932, v7, p11.
The New York Times. May 19, 1932, p25.
The New Yorker. May 28, 1932, v8, p52.
Rob Wagner's Script. Jul 2, 1932, v7, p10.
Time. May 30, 1932, v19, p35.
Variety. May 24, 1932, p37.

Two Smart People (US; Dassin, Jules; 1946)
Film Daily. Jun 6, 1946, p8.
Hollywood Reporter. Jun 5, 1946, p3.
Motion Picture Herald Product Digest. Jun 8, 1946, p3029.
The New York Times. Feb 15, 1946, p20.
Variety. Jun 5, 1946, p13.

Two Souls *See* Zwei Menschen

Two Weeks (US; Franklin, Sidney; 1920)
The Moving Picture World. Jan 10, 1920, p212.
The Moving Picture World. Feb 7, 1920, p939.
The New York Times. Jan 26, 1920, p16.
Variety. Feb 6, 1920, p53.
Wid's Daily. Feb 1, 1920, p19.

Two Years Before the Mast (US; Farrow, John; 1946)
Agee on Film. v1, p215-16.
Commonweal. Oct 18, 1946, v45, p17.
Film Daily. Aug 23, 1946, p10.
The Films of Alan Ladd. p109-14.

Hollywood Reporter. Sep 3, 1946, p3.
Motion Picture Herald Product Digest. Aug 31, 1946, p3173.
The Nation. Aug 31, 1946, v163, p250.
The New York Times. Sep 25, 1946, p39.
The New Yorker. Sep 28, 1946, v22, p92.
Newsweek. Oct 7, 1946, v28, p93.
Time. Sep 2, 1946, v48, p91.
Variety. Aug 28, 1946, p14.

Two-Faced Woman (Also titled: The Twins) (US; Cukor, George; 1941)
Commonweal. Dec 12, 1941, v35, p198.
Film Daily. Oct 23, 1941, p7.
The Films of Greta Garbo. p151-55.
George Cukor (Phillips). p99-100.
Hollywood Reporter. Oct 22, 1941, p3.
Motion Picture Herald Product Digest. Oct 25, 1941, p329.
The New Republic. Dec 15, 1941, v105. p829-30.
The New York Times. Jan 1, 1942, p37.
Newsweek. Dec 8, 1941, v18, p69-70.
Time. Dec 8, 1941, v38, p60.
Time. Dec 22, 1941, v38, p46.
Variety. Oct 22, 1941, p8.

Tycoon (US; Wallace, Richard; 1947)
The Complete Films of John Wayne. p154-56.
Film Daily. Dec 3, 1947, p8.
Hollywood Reporter. Dec 3, 1947, p3.
Motion Picture Herald Product Digest. Dec 6, 1947, p3965.
New Republic. Dec 29, 1947, v117, p34.
The New York Times. Dec 26, 1947, p22.
The New Yorker. Dec 27, 1947, v23, p38.
Newsweek. Jan 12, 1948, v31, p81.
Time. Jan 19, 1948, v51, p102.
Variety. Dec 17, 1947, p8.

The Typhoon (US; Barker, Reginald; 1914)
The Moving Picture World. Oct 10, 1914, p253.
Variety. Nov 27, 1914, p24.

U-Boat 29 (Also titled: The Spy in Black) (GB; Powell, Michael; 1939)
Film Daily. Oct 11, 1939, p6.
The Great Spy Pictures. p443.
Hollywood Reporter. Oct 18, 1939, p3.
Motion Picture Herald. Apr 15, 1939, p60-61.
The New Republic. Dec 20, 1939, v101, p260.
The New Statesman and Nation. Aug 12, 1939, v18, p244.
The New York Times. Oct 6, 1939, p31.
Newsweek. Oct 16, 1939, v14, p44.
Rob Wagner's Script. Oct 28, 1939, v22, p17.
Selected Film Criticism: Foreign Films, 1930-1950. p180.
Variety. Oct 11, 1939, p13.

Ultima Giorni dei Pompeii, Gli *See* The Last Days of Pompeii

The Unafraid (US; DeMille, Cecil B.; Apfel, Oscar C.; 1915)
The Films of Cecil B. DeMille. p63-66.
The Moving Picture World. Apr 10, 1915, p245.
The Moving Picture World. Apr 24, 1915, p646.
The New York Dramatic Mirror. Apr 7, 1914, p28.

Uncle Tom's Cabin (US; 1903)
The Emergence of Film Art. p26-27.
Film Before Griffith. p281.
A Million and One Nights. p517.
Spellbound in Darkness. p34.

Uncle Tom's Cabin (US; 1910)
The Moving Picture World. Aug 6, 1910, p298.
Selected Film Criticism, 1896-1911. p102-03.

Uncle Tom's Cabin (US; Daly, William Robert; 1914)
The Moving Picture World. Aug 22, 1914, p1077, 1152.
The New York Dramatic Mirror. Aug 12, 1914, p29.
Variety. Sep 4, 1914, p13.

Uncle Tom's Cabin (US; Dawley, J. Searle; 1918)
Exhibitor's Trade Review. Jun 29, 1918, p320.
Exhibitor's Trade Review. Jul 13, 1918, p474.
Marguerite Clark. p104, 135.
Motion Picture News. Jul 13, 1918, p256.
The Moving Picture World. May 25, 1918, p1168.
The Moving Picture World. Jul 20, 1918, p453, 458.
Selected Film Criticism, 1912-1920. p268-69.
Variety. Aug 9, 1918, p33.
Wid's Daily. Jul 7, 1918, p29-30.

Unconquered (US; DeMille, Cecil B.; 1947)
Commonweal. Oct 24, 1947, v47, p42.
Film Daily. Sep 24, 1947, p8.
The Films of Boris Karloff. p202-03.
The Films of Cecil B. De Mille. p336-39.
The Films of Gary Cooper. p206-08.
Hollywood Reporter. Sep 24, 1947, p3.
Life. Nov 24, 1947, v23, p116-17.
Motion Picture Herald Product Digest. Sep 27, 1947, p3849.
The New York Times. Oct 11, 1947, p11.
The New Yorker. Oct 11, 1947, v23, p102.
Newsweek. Oct 13, 1947, v30, p88-90.
Scholastic. Nov 17, 1947, v51, p35.
Time. Oct 27, 1947, v50, p99.
Variety. Sep 24, 1947, p11.

Unconventional Linda *See* Holiday

Under a Texas Moon (US; Curtiz, Michael; 1930)
Exhibitors Herald-World. Apr 26, 1930, p30.
Film Daily. Apr 6, 1930, p40.
The Film Spectator. Apr 26, 1930, v9, p21.
Life. May 2, 1930, v95, p20.
The New York Times. Apr 4, 1930, p22.
The New York Times. Apr 20, 1930, p5.
The New Yorker. Apr 12, 1930, v6, p99-100.
Outlook and Independent. Apr 16, 1930, v154, p632.
Time. Apr 14, 1930, v15, p38.
Variety. Apr 9, 1930, p22.

Under Capricorn (US; Hitchcock, Alfred; 1949)
The Art of Alfred Hitchcock. p193-200.
Christian Century. Oct 19, 1949, v66, p1246.
Cinema, the Magic Vehicle. v1, p517-18.
Commonweal. Sep 16, 1949, v50, p561.
Film Daily. Sep 8, 1949, p8.
The Films of Alfred Hitchcock. p146-48.
Fortnight. Sep 30, 1949, v7, p31.
Hitchcock: the First Forty-four Films. p97-102.
Hitchcock (Truffaut). p184+.
Hollywood Reporter. Sep 8, 1949, p3.
Motion Picture Herald. Sep 10, 1949, p9.
The New Republic. Sep 26, 1949, v121, p27.
The New York Times. Sep 9, 1949, p28.
The New Yorker. Sep 10, 1949, v25, p62.
Newsweek. Sep 19, 1949, v34, p80.
Rotarian. Dec 1949, v80, p39.
Scholastic. Oct 12, 1949, v55, p19.
Selected Film Criticism, 1941-1950. p181.
Sequence. New Year 1950, n10, p154-55.
Sight and Sound. Dec 1949, v18, p21.
Theatre Arts. Oct 1949, v33, p7.
Time. Sep 26, 1949, v54, p99.
Variety. Sep 14, 1949, p8.

Under Eighteen (US; Mayo, Archie; 1931)
Film Daily. Jan 3, 1932, p8.
Hollywood Reporter. Nov 17, 1931, p3.
Motion Picture Herald. Jan 2, 1932, p31.
The New York Times. Dec 26, 1931, p15.

Rob Wagner's Script. Jan 9, 1932, v6, p9-10.
Variety. Dec 29, 1931, p167.

Under Four Flags (US; 1918)
Exhibitor's Trade Review. Dec 14, 1918, p153.
Exhibitor's Trade Review. Dec 21, 1918, p194.
Motion Picture News. Nov 30, 1918, p3269.
The Moving Picture World. Nov 30, 1918, p988.
The New York Times. Nov 18, 1918, p13.
Variety. Nov 22, 1918, p45.

Under the Pampas Moon (US; Tinling, James; 1935)
Film Daily. Jun 1, 1935, p4.
Hollywood Reporter. May 18, 1935, p3.
Motion Picture Herald. May 25, 1935, p52.
The New York Times. May 31, 1935, p11.
Variety. Jun 5, 1935, p15.

Under the Red Robe (GB; Sjostrom, Victor; 1937)
Film Daily. Jun 1, 1937, p9.
Great Britain and the East. Aug 12, 1937, v49, p241.
Hollywood Reporter. Jul 19, 1937, p3.
Motion Picture Herald. Jun 12, 1937, p80.
The New Statesman and Nation. Aug 14, 1937, v14, p252.
The New York Times. Jun 1, 1937, p27.
Rob Wagner's Script. Jul 31, 1937, v17, p14.
Selected Film Criticism: Foreign Films, 1930-1950. p181.
The Spectator. Aug 20, 1937, v159, p312.
Time. May 31, 1937, v29, p32+.
Variety. Jun 2, 1937, p15.
World Film News. Aug 1937, v2, p24.

Under the Roofs of Paris *See* Sous les Toits de Paris

Under Two Flags (US; Browning, Tod; 1922)
Film Daily. Oct 1, 1922, p4.
Magill's Survey of Cinema. Silent Films. v3, p1169-71.
The New York Times. Sep 25, 1922, p10.
Variety. Sep 29, 1922, p41.

Under Two Flags (US; Lloyd, Frank; 1936)
Canadian Magazine. May 1936, v85, p59.
Canadian Magazine. Jun 1936, v85, p41.
Film Daily. Apr 28, 1936, p4.
The Films of Ronald Colman. p179-82.
Graham Greene on Film. p91-92.
Hollywood Reporter. Apr 24, 1936, p2.
Hollywood Spectator. May 9, 1936, v11, p8-9.
Motion Picture. May 1936, v51, p27.
Motion Picture Herald. May 9, 1936, p39.
The New Statesman and Nation. Aug 8, 1936, v12, p192.
The New York Times. May 1, 1936, p19.
Newsweek. May 2, 1936, v7, p26.
Rob Wagner's Script. May 16, 1936, v15, p10.
The Spectator. Aug 7, 1936, v157, p235.
The Tatler. Aug 12, 1936, v141, p282.
Time. May 11, 1936, v27, p56.
Variety. May 6, 1936, p18.
World Film News. Sep 1936, v1, p23.

Under Western Stars (US; Kane, Joseph; 1938)
Film Daily. Apr 14, 1938, p8.
Hollywood Reporter. Apr 11, 1938, p3.
Hollywood Spectator. Apr 16, 1938, v13, p27-28.
Motion Picture Herald. Apr 16, 1938, p33.
The New Masses. Jul 12, 1938, v28, p30-31.
The New Yorker. Jul 2, 1938, v14, p42.
Time. May 9, 1938, v31, p44-45.
Variety. Apr 20, 1938, p15.

Undercurrent (US; Minnelli, Vincente; 1946)
Commonweal. Nov 29, 1946, v45, p168.
Film Daily. Oct 1, 1946, p6.
The Films of Katharine Hepburn. p126-29.
The Films of Robert Taylor. p106-07.
Hollywood Reporter. Oct 1, 1946, p3.
Motion Picture Herald Product Digest. Oct 5, 1946, p3237.

The New Republic. Dec 23, 1946, v115, p879.
The New York Times. Nov 29, 1946, p36.
The New Yorker. Dec 7, 1946, v22, p98.
Newsweek. Dec 2, 1946, v28, p109.
Robert Mitchum on the Screen. p90.
Theatre Arts. Jan 1947, v31, p41-43.
Time. Nov 11, 1946, v48, p102+.
Variety. Oct 2, 1946, p8.

Underground (GB; Asquith, Anthony; 1929)
Film Daily. Mar 10, 1929, p8.
The Films of Anthony Asquith. p51-53.
The New York Times. Feb 26, 1929, p31.
Variety. Aug 22, 1928, p34.
Variety. Feb 27, 1929, p95.

The Under-Pup (US; Wallace, Richard; 1939)
Commonweal. Sep 8, 1939, v30, p459.
Film Daily. Aug 25, 1939, p7.
Hollywood Reporter. Aug 24, 1939, p3.
Life. Sep 18, 1939, v7, p55.
Motion Picture Herald. Aug 26, 1939, p50.
The New Statesman and Nation. Dec 2, 1939, v18, p788.
The New York Times. Sep 5, 1939, p21.
The New Yorker. Sep 16, 1939, v15, p62.
Newsweek. Sep 4, 1939, v14, p29.
Rob Wagner's Script. Sep 23, 1939, v22, p16-17.
Time. Aug 28, 1939, v33, p47.
Variety. Aug 30, 1939, p14.

Underworld *See* The Lower Depths

Underworld (US; Sternberg, Josef von; 1927)
The Cinema of Josef von Sternberg. p37-43.
Film Daily. Aug 28, 1927, p6.
The Films of Josef von Sternberg. p13-16.
From Quasimodo to Scarlett O'Hara. p91-95.
The Moving Picture World. Sep 3, 1927, p48.
National Board of Review Magazine. Aug 1927, v2, p10-11.
The New York Times. Aug 22, 1927, p21.
Photoplay. Sep 1927, v32, p52.
Selected Film Criticism, 1921-1930. p299-300.
Spellbound in Darkness. p458-60.
Variety. Aug 24, 1927, p22.

Unfaithful (US; Cromwell, John; 1931)
Film Daily. Mar 1, 1931, p10.
Motion Picture Herald. Feb 28, 1931, p51.
The New York Times. Mar 7, 1931, p17.
Outlook and Independent. Mar 18, 1931, v157, p413.
Rob Wagner's Script. Mar 14, 1931, v5, p8.
Time. Mar 16, 1931, v17, p64.
Variety. Mar 11, 1931, p14.

Unfaithfully Yours (US; Sturges, Preston; 1948)
Between Flops. p227-33+.
Commonweal. Nov 26, 1948, v49, p176.
Film Daily. Oct 1, 1948, p12.
Hollywood Reporter. Sep 29, 1948, p3.
Magill's Survey of Cinema. Series II. v6, p2590-92.
Motion Picture Herald Product Digest. Oct 9, 1948, p4341.
The New Republic. Nov 22, 1948, v119, p28.
The New York Times. Nov 6, 1948, p9.
The New Yorker. Nov 13, 1948, v24, p130.
Newsweek. Nov 14, 1948, v32, p92.
Preston Sturges: A Guide to References and Resources. p77-79.
Time. Dec 6, 1948, v52, p104+.
Variety. Sep 28, 1948, p18.

The Unguarded Hour (US; Wood, Sam; 1936)
Canadian Magazine. May 1936, v85, p61.
Commonweal. Apr 24, 1936, v23, p724.
Film Daily. Apr 1, 1936, p4.
Hollywood Reporter. Apr 1, 1936, p2.
Hollywood Spectator. Apr 11, 1936, v11, p25, 27.
Motion Picture Herald. Apr 4, 1936, p40.

The New York Times. Apr 4, 1936, p11.
The New Yorker. Apr 11, 1936, v12, p69-70.
Newsweek. Apr 11, 1936, v7, p42.
Rob Wagner's Script. Jun 6, 1936, v15, p10-11.
Time. Apr 13, 1936, v27, p32.
Variety. Apr 8, 1936, p16.

Unheimliche Geschichten *See* The Living Dead

The Unholy Garden (US; Fitzmaurice, George; 1931)
Film Daily. Sep 20, 1931, p10.
The Films of Ronald Colman. p139-42.
Hollywood Reporter. Jul 29, 1931, p3.
Judge. Nov 21, 1931, v101, p18.
Motion Picture Herald. Aug 8, 1931, p149.
The New York Times. Oct 29, 1931, p27.
The New York Times. May 17, 1931, p5.
The New York Times. Nov 8, 1931, p5.
Variety. Nov 3, 1931, p27.

The Unholy Three (US; Conway, Jack; 1925)
Film Daily. Aug 9, 1925.
Life. Aug 27, 1925, v86, p26.
Photoplay. Jul 1925, v28, p51.
Selected Film Criticism, 1921-1930. p300-01.
Spellbound in Darkness. p394.
Variety. Aug 8, 1925, p30.

The Unholy Three (US; Conway, Jack; 1930)
BFI/Monthly Film Bulletin. Mar 1979, v46, p59-60.
Exhibitors Herald-World. Jul 19, 1930, p33.
Faces, Forms, Film: The Artistry of Lon Chaney. p94-99+.
Film Daily. Jul 6, 1930, p10.
The Films of the Thirties. p31-33.
The Great Gangster Pictures. p403-05.
Judge. Aug 2, 1930, v99, p23.
Lon of 1000 Faces! p190-202.
Magill's Survey of Cinema. Series II. v6, p2597-99.
The New York Times. Jul 5, 1930, p17.
The New York Times. Jul 6, 1930, p2.
The New York Times. Jul 13, 1930, p3.
The New Yorker. Jul 12, 1930, v6, p53.
Outlook and Independent. Jul 16, 1930, v155, p431.
Photoplay. Aug 1930, v38, p55.
Selected Film Criticism, 1921-1930. p301-02.
Time. Jul 14, 1930, v16, p50.
Variety. Jul 9, 1930, p19.

The Uninvited (US; Allen, Lewis; 1944)
Classics of the Horror Film. p162-64.
Commonweal. Feb 4, 1944, v39, p400.
Film Daily. Jan 6, 1944, p5.
Hollywood Reporter. Jan 4, 1944, p3.
The London Times. Apr 3, 1944, p8.
Magic and Myth of the Movies. p91-92.
Magill's Survey of Cinema. Series I. v4, p1801-04.
Motion Picture Exhibitor. Jan 12, 1944, v31, n9, sec2, p1436.
Motion Picture Herald Product Digest. Jan 8, 1944, p1705.
The New Captain George's Whizzbang. 1974, v3, p20-26+.
The New York Times. Feb 21, 1944, p19.
The New York Times. Feb 27, 1944, p3.
Newsweek. Feb 28, 1944, v23, p83.
Scholastic. Mar 13, 1944, v44, p31.
Time. Feb 21, 1944, v43, p94+.
Variety. Jan 5, 1944, p16.

Union Depot (US; Green, Alfred E.; 1932)
Film Daily. Jan 17, 1932, p8.
Judge. Feb 27, 1932, v102, p29.
Motion Picture Herald. Dec 26, 1931, p31.
The New York Times. Jan 15, 1932, p24.
The New Yorker. Jan 23, 1932, v7, p55-56.
Outlook and Independent. Jan 27, 1932, v160, p119.
Rob Wagner's Script. Feb 27, 1932, v7, p8.
Time. Jan 25, 1932, v19, p25.
Variety. Jan 19, 1932, p25.

Union Pacific (Also titled: Pacific Express) (US; DeMille,
Cecil B.; 1939)
Commonweal. May 5, 1939, v30, p48.
Dictionary of Films. p395.
Film Daily. Apr 28, 1939, p6.
The Filming of the West. p358-60.
The Films of Cecil B. De Mille. p314-19.
Graham Greene on Film. p224-25.
The Great Western Pictures. p373-75.
Hollywood Reporter. Apr 27, 1939, p3.
Hollywood Spectator. May 13, 1939, v14, p9-10.
Life. May 1, 1939, v6, p35-36.
Magill's Survey of Cinema. Series II. v6, p2600-02.
Motion Picture Herald. Apr 29, 1939, p51.
The Nation. Jun 3, 1939, v148, p654.
The New York Times. May 11, 1939, p31.
The New Yorker. May 13, 1939, v15, p76-77.
Newsweek. May 1, 1939, v13, p43-45.
Oregon History Quarterly. Jun 1940, v41, p128-31.
Photoplay. Jul 1939, v53, p90.
Rob Wagner's Script. May 6, 1939, v21, p12.
Saint Nicholas. May 1939, v66, p31.
The Spectator. Jun 2, 1939, v162, p957.
Stage. May 15, 1939, v16, p6.
Starring Miss Barbara Stanwyck. p125-28.
Those Fabulous Movie Years: The 30s. p172.
Time. May 8, 1939, v33, p66-67.
Variety. May 3, 1939, p16.
World Horizons. Mar 1939, v3, p34-35.

The Unknown (US; Browning, Tod; 1927)
Film Daily. Jun 26, 1927, p8.
The Film Spectator. Aug 20, 1927, v3, p7.
The Films of Joan Crawford. p48-49.
The Moving Picture World. Jun 18, 1927, p524.
The New York Times. Jun 13, 1927, p17.
Selected Film Criticism, 1921-1930. p302-03.
Variety. Jun 15, 1927, p20.

The Unpardonable Sin (US; Neilan, Marshall; 1919)
Exhibitor's Trade Review. May 17, 1919, p1825.
Motion Picture News. May 17, 1919, p3270.
The Moving Picture World. May 17, 1919, p1017-18.
The New York Times. May 3, 1919, p11.
Selected Film Criticism, 1912-1920. p269.
Variety. May 9, 1919, p52.
Wid's Daily. Mar 23, 1919, p23.

An Unseen Enemy (US; Griffith, D.W.; 1912)
The New York Dramatic Mirror. Sep 18, 1912, p28.
Selected Film Criticism, 1912-1920. p269-70.

Unsterbliche Lump, Die *See* The Immortal Vagabond

The Unsuspected (US; Curtiz, Michael; 1947)
Commonweal. Oct 17, 1947, v47, p17.
Film Daily. Sep 17, 1947, p10.
Hollywood Reporter. Sep 17, 1947, p3.
Magill's Survey of Cinema, Series II. v6, p2603-05.
Motion Picture Herald Product Digest. Sep 20, 1947, p3841.
New Republic. Oct 20, 1947, v117, p39.
The New York Times. Oct 4, 1947, p9.
Newsweek. Oct 13, 1947, v30, p89.
Variety. Sep 17, 1947, p16.

Untamed (US; Conway, Jack; 1929)
Exhibitor's Herald-World. Dec 14, 1929, p44.
The New York Times. Nov 30, 1929, p23.
Variety. Dec 4, 1929, p15.

Up the River (US; Werker, Alfred L.; 1938)
Film Daily. Nov 11, 1938, p4.
The Great Gangster Pictures. p405-06.
Hollywood Reporter. Nov 5, 1938, p3.
Hollywood Spectator. Nov 12, 1938, v13, p15-16.
Motion Picture Herald. Nov 12, 1938, p35, 38.

The New Masses. Dec 20, 1938, v29, p29-30.
The New York Times. Dec 3, 1938, p11.
The New Yorker. Dec 10, 1938, v14, p96.
Time. Dec 12, 1938, v32, p40.
Variety. Nov 9, 1938, p16.

Vacation from Marriage (Also titled: Perfect Strangers)
(GB; Korda, Alexander; 1945)
Agee on Film. v1, p193.
Commonweal. Dec 21, 1945, v43, p265.
Film Daily. Dec 3, 1945, p6.
The Great British Films. p82-84.
Hollywood Reporter. Nov 28, 1945, p3.
Life. Apr 8, 1946, v20, p65-67.
The London Times. Aug 31, 1945, p8.
Magill's Survey of Cinema. Series II. v6, p2608-11.
Motion Picture Exhibitor. Nov 28, 1945, v35, n4, sec2, p1840.
Motion Picture Herald Product Digest. Dec 1, 1945, p2733.
The Nation. Mar 23, 1940, v162, p355.
The New York Times. Mar 15, 1945, p27.
The New Yorker. Mar 23, 1946, v22, p77.
Newsweek. Jan 14, 1946, v27, p93.
Time. Feb 18, 1946, v47, p98.
Variety. Nov 28, 1945, p10.

Vagabond Bien-Aimé, Le *See* The Beloved Vagabond

The Vagabond King (Also titled: The Vagabond) (US;
Berger, Ludwig; 1930)
Commonweal. Mar 12, 1930, v11, p536.
Exhibitors Herald-World. Mar 1, 1930, p35.
Film Daily. Feb 23, 1930, p10.
The Film Spectator. Apr 12, 1930, v9, p21-22.
The Films of Jeanette MacDonald and Nelson Eddy. p39-47.
The Hollywood Musical. p42-43.
Life. Mar 28, 1930, v95, p20.
The Nation. Mar 19, 1930, v130, p337.
National Board of Review Magazine. Mar 1930, v5, p10.
The New York Times. Mar 2, 1930, p5.
The New Yorker. Mar 1, 1930, v6, p67-68.
Outlook and Independent. Mar 5, 1930, v154, p393.
Rob Wagner's Script. Apr 26, 1930, v3, p11-12.
Time. Mar 17, 1930, v15, p56.
Variety. Feb 26, 1930, p24.

The Vagabond Lover (US; Neilan, Marshall; 1929)
Film Daily. Dec 1, 1929, p10.
The Hollywood Musical. p37.
The New York Times. Nov 27, 1929, p30.
Variety. Dec 4, 1929, p15.

Valiant Is the World for Carrie (US; Ruggles, Wesley;
1936)
Canadian Magazine. Nov 1936, v86, p37.
Film Daily. Sep 22, 1936, p8.
Literary Digest. Oct 3, 1936, v122, p20.
Motion Picture Herald. Sep 26, 1936, p42.
The New Masses. Oct 20, 1936, v21, p28-29.
The New York Times. Oct 8, 1936, p27.
The New Yorker. Oct 17, 1936, v12, p77.
Newsweek. Oct 3, 1936, v8, p34.
Rob Wagner's Script. Oct 17, 1936, v16, p10-11.
Time. Oct 19, 1936, v28, p64-65.
Variety. Oct 14, 1936, p15.

Valley of the Giants (US; Keighley, William; 1938)
Commonweal. Sep 16, 1938, v28, p534.
Film Daily. Sep 12, 1938, p8.
Hollywood Reporter. Sep 23, 1938, p3.
Hollywood Spectator. Oct 1, 1938, v13, p13.
Motion Picture Herald. Sep 17, 1938, p41.
The New Masses. Sep 20, 1938, v28, p30.
The New York Times. Sep 10, 1938, p20.
The New Yorker. Sep 17, 1938, v14, p62.
Rob Wagner's Script. Oct 1, 1938, v20, p11.
The Spectator. Jan 20, 1939, v162, p88.

Time. Sep 19, 1938, v32, p24.
Variety. Aug 17, 1938, p22.

The Vampire (US; 1910)
The New York Dramatic Mirror. Nov 16, 1910, p30.
Selected Film Criticism, 1896-1911. p103.

Vampyr, ou L'Étrange Adventure de David Gray (Also
titled: Not Against the Flesh; Castle of Doom;
Vampire) (GER; FR; Dreyer, Carl-Theodor; 1931)
The Celluloid Vampire. p26-33.
The Cinema of Carl Dreyer. p107-23.
Cinema, the Magic Vehicle. v1, p194-95.
Classics of the Horror Film. p63-69.
Close-Up. Mar 1931, v8, p50.
Dictionary of Films. p398.
Dreyer (Nash). p55-57.
Eighty Years of Cinema. p88.
Film Culture. Wint 1964-65.
Film Culture. Spr 1964, v32, p56-59.
Film Daily. Aug 14, 1934, p10.
Film Quarterly. Fall 1965, v19, p34-35.
Films and Filming. Dec 1960, v7, p17-19, 43.
The Films of Carl-Theodor Dreyer. p93-116.
Great Film Directors. p225-27.
Horror in the Cinema. p43-46.
Horror Movies (Clarens). p131-36.
The International Dictionary of Films and Filmmakers. v1,
p501-02.
Monsters from the Movies. p102-03.
The New York Times. Jul 31, 1932, p3.
Quarterly of Film, Radio and Television. Wint 1952, v7, p191-
202.
Screen. Aut 1976, v17, p29-267.
Sight and Sound. Apr-Jun 1951, v21, p157-61.
Transcendental Style in Film. p117-18.
The Vampire Cinema. p44, 46-47.

Vanessa: Her Love Story (Also titled: Vanessa) (US;
Howard, William K.; 1935)
Canadian Magazine. Jun 1935, v83, p32.
Film Daily. Feb 19, 1935, p6.
Hollywood Reporter. Feb 14, 1935, p3.
Motion Picture Herald. Feb 23, 1935, p55, 58.
The New York Times. Apr 13, 1935, p11.
The New Yorker. Apr 20, 1935, v11, p72.
Rob Wagner's Script. Apr 27, 1935, v13, p10.
Time. Mar 11, 1935, v25, p52.
Variety. Apr 17, 1935, p14.

Vanina (German title: Vanina Oder die Galgenhochzeit)
(GER; von Gerlach, Arthur; 1922)
Cinema, the Magic Vehicle. v1, p85-86.
From Caligari to Hitler. p79-81.
The Haunted Screen. p63-64.

The Vanishing American (US; Seitz, George B.; 1925)
Film Daily. Oct 5, 1925, p6.
Magill's Survey of Cinema. Silent Films. v3, p1175-76.
Motion Picture News. Nov 6, 1926, v34, p1755-56.
The New York Times. Oct 16, 1925, p18.
Photoplay. Dec 1925, v24, p4.
Selected Film Criticism, 1921-1930. p303-04.
Spellbound in Darkness. p420-21.
Variety. Oct 21, 1925, p34.
The Western: From Silents to the Seventies. p167-68.

The Vanishing Lady (FR; 1896)
Motion Pictures. p16-17.

Vanity Fair (US; 1911)
The Moving Picture World. Dec 16, 1911, p886-87.
Selected Film Criticism, 1896-1911. p103-05.

Variety (German title: Variété) (GER; Dupont, E.A.;
1925)
BFI/Monthly Film Bulletin. Jul 1979, v46, p160-61.
Dictionary of Film. p399-400.
Film Daily. Jun 27, 1926, p6.
From Caligari to Hitler. p125-27.
From Quasimodo to Scarlett O'Hara. p59-61.
The Haunted Screen. p278-84.
A History of Films. p148-49.
A History of Narrative Film. p125.
The History of World Cinema. p96-97.
Independent. Jul 24, 1926, v117, p105.
Magill's Survey of Cinema. Silent Films. v3, p1179-82.
The New Republic. Jul 28, 1926, v47, p280-81.
The New York Times. Jun 28, 1926, p15.
The New Yorker. Jul 3, 1926, v2, p34.
Photoplay. Sep 1926, v30, p55.
Selected Film Criticism, 1921-1930. p304-05.
Variety. Jun 30, 1926, p10.
Variety. Jan 20, 1926, p40.

Variety Girl (US; Marshall, George; 1947)
Commonweal. Sep 19, 1947, v46, p554.
Film Daily. Jul 15, 1947, p8.
The Films of Alan Ladd. p123.
The Films of Barbara Stanwyck. p185.
The Films of Gary Cooper. p209-10.
The Films of William Holden. p79-80.
Hollywood Reporter. Jul 14, 1947, p3.
Motion Picture Herald Product Digest. Jul 19, 1947, p3733.
The New York Times. Oct 16, 1947, p34.
Newsweek. Oct 27, 1947, v30, p96.
Starring Miss Barbara Stanwyck. p203.
Time. Nov 3, 1947, v50, p100.
Variety. Jul 16, 1947, p14.

Varsity Show (US; Keighley, William; 1937)
The Busby Berkeley Book. p111.
Film Daily. Aug 16, 1937, p7.
The Genius of Busby Berkeley. p174.
The Hollywood Musical. p128-37.
Hollywood Reporter. Aug 10, 1937, p3.
Motion Picture Herald. Aug 21, 1937, p55.
Motion Picture Herald. Jul 24, 1937, p16-17.
The New York Times. Sep 2, 1937, p17.
The New Yorker. Sep 4, 1937, v13, p60.
Rob Wagner's Script. Sep 4, 1937, v18, p12.
Variety. Aug 11, 1937, p19.

Vaudeville (US; 1900)
The George Kleine Collection Catalog. p146.

Veille d'Armes (FR; Herbier, Marcel L'; 1935)
Graham Greene on Film. p58.
The New Statesman and Nation. Mar 28, 1936, v11, p495.
The Spectator. Mar 13, 1936, v156, p467.
Variety. Jan 8, 1936, p13.

Velikii Grazhdanin *See* A Great Citizen

The Velvet Paw (US; Tourneur, Maurice; 1916)
The Moving Picture World. Sep 16, 1916, p1819, 1892.
The New York Dramatic Mirror. Apr 22, 1916, p43.
Variety. Sep 1, 1916, p24.
Wid's Daily. Aug 31, 1916, p831.

The Verdict (Also titled: Verdict) (US; Seigel, Don; 1946)
BFI/Monthly Film Bulletin. Feb 1984, v51, p62-63.
Don Siegel (Lovell). p13, 62.
Film Daily. Nov 11, 1946, p7.
The Films of Peter Lorre. p185-88.
Hollywood Reporter. Nov 5, 1946, p3.
Motion Picture Herald Product Digest. Nov 9, 1946, p3297.
The New York Times. Dec 13, 1946, p29.
Newsweek. Dec 23, 1946, v28, p93.
Variety. Nov 6, 1946, p18.

Vessel of Wrath *See* The Beachcomber

Vesyolye Rebatat *See* A Russian Jazz Comedy

Veuve Joyeuse, La *See* The Merry Widow

The Vice Squad (US; Cromwell, John; 1931)
Film Daily. Jun 7, 1931, p10.
Hollywood Reporter. Apr 27, 1931, p3.
Life. Jun 26, 1931, v97, p18.
Motion Picture Herald. May 9, 1931, p40.
The New York Times. Jun 6, 1931, p15.
The New York Times. Jun 14, 1931, p5.
The New Yorker. Jun 13, 1931, v7, p63-64.
Outlook and Independent. Jun 17, 1931, v158, p218.
Variety. Jun 9, 1931, p18.

Victoria the Great (GB; Wilcox, Herbert; 1937)
Commonweal. Oct 8, 1937, v26, p550.
Film Daily. Sep 17, 1937, p13.
Great Britain and the East. Sep 16, 1937, v49, p396-97.
The Great British Films. p39-41.
Hollywood Reporter. Sep 17, 1937, p3.
Hollywood Spectator. Nov 20, 1937, v12, p7-8.
Life. Jun 28, 1937, v2, p60.
Life. Oct 4, 1937, v3, p55-58.
Literary Digest. Oct 23, 1937, v123, p34.
London Mercury. Oct 1937, v36, p561.
Motion Picture Herald. Sep 25, 1937, p44.
National Board of Review Magazine. Nov 1937, v12, p16.
The New Masses. Nov 9, 1937, v25, p28.
The New Statesman and Nation. Sep 25, 1937, v14, p445.
The New York Times. Sep 18, 1937, p15.
The New York Times. Oct 29, 1937, p19.
The New Yorker. Oct 23, 1937, v13, p66.
Newsweek. Oct 11, 1937, v10, p26+.
Rob Wagner's Script. Nov 20, 1937, v18, p20.
Scholastic. Oct 2, 1937, v31, p27E.
Selected Film Criticism: Foreign Films, 1930-1950. p185-88.
Sight and Sound. Aut 1937, v6, p138.
The Spectator. Sep 24, 1937, v159, p499.
Stage. Sep 1937, v14, p43.
The Tatler. Sep 29, 1937, v145, p562.
Time. Nov 8, 1937, v30, p48.
Variety. Aug 25, 1937, p17.
World Film News. Nov 1937, v2, p22.

Victory (US; Tourneur, Maurice; 1919)
Exhibitor's Trade Review. Dec 6, 1919, p71.
Motion Picture News. Dec 6, 1919, p4142.
The Moving Picture World. Dec 6, 1919, p672.
The New York Times. Dec 28, 1919, sec8, p4.
Selected Film Criticism, 1912-1920. p270-71.
Variety. Nov 28, 1919, p58.
Wid's Daily. Dec 7, 1919, p3.

Vie Est a Nous, La (Also titled: Life Is Ours) (FR;
    Renoir, Jean; 1936)
Dictionary of Films. p403.
The Golden Age of French Cinema, 1929-1939. p112-14.
Hollywood Reporter. Apr 25, 1936, p11.
Jean Renoir: My Life and My Films. p125-26.
Jean Renoir: The French Films, 1924-1939. p221-33.
Jean Renoir: The World of His Films. p120-21, 204-05.
Sight and Sound. Sum 1937, v6, p85.
Variety. Nov 26, 1969, p28.

Viennese Nights (US; Crosland, Alan; 1930)
Exhibitors Herald-World. May 29, 1930, p35.
Exhibitors Herald-World. Dec 6, 1930, p28.
Film Daily. Nov 11, 1930, p10.
The New York Times. Nov 27, 1930, p32.
The New Yorker. Dec 6, 1930, v6, p109, 111.
Outlook and Independent. Dec 10, 1930, v156, p591.
Rob Wagner's Script. Mar 21, 1931, v5, p10.
Theatre Magazine. Apr 1931, v53, p48.

Time. Dec 8, 1930, v16, p42.
Variety. Dec 3, 1930, p14.

Viktor und Viktoria (GER; Schunzel, Reinhold; 1934)
Film Daily. Jan 30, 1935, p9.
The New York Times. Jan 28, 1935, p10.
Variety. Mar 6, 1934, p27.

The Violin Maker of Cremona (US; Griffith, D.W.; 1909)
A Million and One Nights. p505.
The New York Dramatic Mirror. Jun 19, 1909, p16.
Selected Film Criticism, 1896-1911. p105.

The Violin Maker of Nuremberg (US; 1911)
The Moving Picture World. Dec 9, 1911, p800, 802.
Selected Film Criticism, 1896-1911. p106-07.

The Virginian (US; 1914)
The Moving Picture World. Sep 19, 1914, p1648.
The Moving Picture World. Sep 26, 1914, p1828.
The New York Dramatic Mirror. Sep 9, 1914, p28.
Variety. Sep 9, 1914, p22.

The Virginian (US; Fleming, Victor; 1929)
The Classic American Novel and the Cinema. p184-91.
Exhibitor's Herald-World. Jan 11, 1930, p32.
Film Daily. Dec 29, 1929, p8.
The Films of Gary Cooper. p68-70.
The New York Times. Dec 23, 1929, p18.
Time. Jan 6, 1930, v15, p35.
Variety. Dec 25, 1929, p26.

The Virginian (US; Gilmore, Stuart; 1946)
The Classic American Novel and the Movies. p184-91.
Commonweal. Jul 26, 1946, v44, p360.
Film Daily. Jan 28, 1946, p6.
Hollywood Reporter. Jan 25, 1946, p3.
Motion Picture Herald Product Digest. Jan 26, 1946, p2817.
The New York Times. Apr 18, 1946, p22.
Newsweek. Apr 15, 1946, v27, p93.
Time. Apr 29, 1946, v47, p94.
Variety. Jan 30, 1946, p12.

A Virtuous Vamp (US; Kirkland, David; 1919)
Exhibitor's Trade Review. Nov 29, 1919, p2243.
Motion Picture News. Nov 29, 1919, p3976.
The Moving Picture World. Nov 29, 1919, p536.
The New York Times. Nov 17, 1919, p20.
The Talmadge Girls. p137-204.
Variety. Nov 21, 1919.
Wid's Daily. Nov 30, 1919, p23.

Visages D'Enfants (FR; Feyder, Jacques; 1924)
Cinema, the Magic Vehicle. v1, p105-06.

Visiteurs du Soir, Les (Also titled: The Devil's Envoys)
    (FR; Carné, Marcel; 1942)
Agee on Film. v1, p275-76.
Film Daily. Aug 29, 1947, p7.
Hollywood Reporter. Aug 29, 1947, p3.
The London Times. Aug 9, 1945, p8.
The Nation. Sep 13, 1947, v165, p264.
The New York Times. Aug 30, 1947, p8.
The New York Times. Aug 31, 1947, sec2, p4.
Newsweek. Sep 15, 1947, v30, p90.
Sight and Sound. Spr 1946, v15, p4-6.
Time. Sep 29, 1947, v50, p98+.
Variety. Sep 3, 1947, p16.

Viva Villa! (US; Conway, Jack; 1934)
Commonweal. Apr 27, 1934, v19, p720.
David O. Selznick's Hollywood. p132-34, 148-51.
Film Daily. Apr 12, 1934, p10.
Hawks on Hawks. p60-65.
Hollywood Reporter. Mar 26, 1934, p3.
Literary Digest. Apr 28, 1934, v117, p32.
Motion Picture Herald. Feb 10, 1934, p36.

Motion Picture Herald. Apr 7, 1934, p59.
The Nation. May 2, 1934, v138, p516+.
The New York Times. Apr 11, 1934, p25.
Newsweek. Apr 14, 1934, v3, p37.
Time. Apr 16, 1934, v23, p45.
Variety. Apr 17, 1934, p18.

Vivacious Lady (US; Stevens, George; 1938)
Commonweal. Jun 17, 1938, v28, p217.
Film Daily. May 5, 1938, p6.
The Films of Ginger Rogers. p56-58.
The Films of James Stewart. p141-45.
Hollywood Reporter. Apr 30, 1938, p2.
Hollywood Spectator. May 7, 1938, v13, p6-8.
London Mercury. Oct 1938, v38, p558.
Motion Picture Herald. May 7, 1938, p36.
The New Republic. Jun 22, 1938, v95, p188.
The New Statesman and Nation. Sep 10, 1938, v16, p380-81.
The New York Times. Jun 3, 1938, p17.
The New Yorker. Jun 11, 1938, v14, p50.
Newsweek. May 16, 1938, v11, p25.
Rob Wagner's Script. May 14, 1938, v19, p8.
The Tatler. Sep 21, 1938, v149, p516.
Variety. May 4, 1938, p15.

Vivere Pace *See* To Live in Peace

Vogues of 1938 (Also titled: Walter Wanger's Vogues of 1938; Vogues) (US; Cummings, Irving; 1937)
Film Daily. Aug 7, 1937, p4.
Hollywood Reporter. Aug 4, 1937, p3.
Motion Picture Herald. Aug 7, 1937, p45.
The New Masses. Aug 31, 1937, v24, p29.
The New York Times. Aug 20, 1937, p21.
Rob Wagner's Script. Oct 2, 1937, v18, p13.
Scribner's Magazine. Nov 1937, v102, p63.
Time. Aug 30, 1937, v30, p23.
Variety. Aug 4, 1937, p18.

The Voice of Bugle Ann (Also titled: Bugle Ann) (US; Thorpe, Richard; 1936)
Commonweal. Feb 28, 1936, v23, p497.
Film Daily. Feb 6, 1936, p9.
Hollywood Reporter. Feb 1, 1936, p3.
Lorentz on Film. p132-34.
Motion Picture Herald. Feb 15, 1936, p42.
The New York Times. Feb 27, 1936, p23.
The New Yorker. Mar 7, 1936, v12, p64.
Rob Wagner's Script. Mar 7, 1936, v15, p11.
Time. Feb 24, 1936, v27, p56.
Variety. Mar 4, 1936, p26.

The Voice of the Turtle (US; Rapper, Irving; 1948)
Commonweal. Jan 30, 1948, v47, p399.
Film Daily. Dec 29, 1947, p8.
The Films of Ronald Reagan. p153-55.
Hollywood Reporter. Dec 26, 1947, p3.
Motion Picture Herald Product Digest. Dec 27, 1947, p3993.
The New Republic. Jan 12, 1948, v118, p32.
The New York Times. Dec 26, 1948, p22.
The New Yorker. Jan 10, 1948, v23, p78.
Newsweek. Jan 12, 1948, v31, p78+.
Scholastic. Dec 1, 1947, v51, p37.
Time. Dec 15, 1947, v50, p103.
Variety. Dec 31, 1947, p10.

Voice of the Violin (US; Griffith, D.W.; 1909)
D.W. Griffith, His Biograph Films in Perspective. p86-88.
The Moving Picture World. Mar 20, 1909, p337.
Selected Film Criticism, 1896-1911. p108.

Volochayevsk Days *See* The Defense of Volochayevsk

Volochayevskiye Dni *See* The Defense of Volochayevsk

Volpone (FR; Tourneur, Maurice; 1938)
Commonweal. Dec 12, 1947, v47, p227.
Film Daily. Dec 29, 1947, p.
Fortnight. Apr 15, 1949, v6, p31.
Life. Dec 29, 1947, v23, p61.
The New Republic. Jan 5, 1948, v118, p32.
The New York Times. Dec 27, 1947, p9.
The New York Times. Jan 21, 1948, p31.
The New Yorker. Jan 3, 1948, v23, p59.
Newsweek. Nov 24, 1947, v30, p94.
Selected Film Criticism: Foreign Films, 1930-1950. p190.
Time. Dec 29, 1947, v50, p62.
Variety. Dec 24, 1947, p13.

Voltaire (US; Adolfi, John; 1933)
Canadian Magazine. Sep 1933, v80, p34.
Film Daily. Jul 28, 1933, p8.
Films in Review. Nov 1985, v36, p522.
Hollywood Reporter. Jun 8, 1933, p3.
Magill's Survey of Cinema. Series II. v6, p2622-24.
Motion Picture Herald. Jun 24, 1933, p43.
National Board of Review Magazine. Sep-Oct 1933, v8, p8-10.
New Outlook. Oct 1933, v162, p49.
The New York Times. Aug 23, 1933, p21.
The New York Times. Sep 3, 1933, p3.
The New York Times. May 21, 1933, p3.
The New York Times. Aug 20, 1933, p2.
The New Yorker. Aug 26, 1933, v9, p41.
Rob Wagner's Script. Aug 5, 1933, v9, p8.
The Spectator. Jan 5, 1934, v152, p14.
Time. Aug 21, 1933, v22, p29-30.
Variety. Aug 29, 1933, p14.
Warner Brothers Presents. p271-72.

Voyage a Travers l'Impossible, Le *See* The Impossible Voyage

Voyage dans la Lune, Le (Also titled: The Voyage to the Moon) (FR; Melies, Georges; 1902)
The Emergence of Film Art. p14-16.
Film Before Griffith. p112.
A History of Narrative Film. p15-18.
The History of World Cinema. p43-45.
Magill's Survey of Cinema. Silent Films. v2, p1183-85.
A Million and One Nights. p395.
Motion Pictures. p25-30.

Vozvrashcheniye Maksima *See* The Return of Maxim

Vredens Dag *See* Day of Wrath

Vstrechnyi *See* Counterplan

Vufku *See* Arsenal

Wachsfigurenkabinett, Das *See* Waxworks

Wagon Tracks (US; Hillyer, Lambert; 1919)
The Complete Films of William S. Hart. p114-15.
Exhibitor's Trade Review. Aug 23, 1919, p989.
Motion Picture News. Aug 23, 1919, p1685.
The Moving Picture World. Aug 23, 1919, p1176.
Variety. Aug 15, 1919, p71.
Wid's Daily. Aug 17, 1919, p23.

The Wagons Roll at Night (US; Enright, Ray; 1941)
Commonweal. May 23, 1941, v34, p111.
Film Daily. Apr 25, 1941, p9.
The Films of Humphrey Bogart. p92-94.
Hollywood Reporter. Apr 23, 1941, p3.
Humphrey Bogart: The Man and his Films. p111.
Motion Picture Herald Product Digest. Apr 26, 1941, p29.
The New York Times. May 10, 1941, p20.
Scribner's Commentator. Jul 1941, v10, p107-08.
Variety. Apr 30, 1941, p16.

Waikiki Wedding (US; Tuttle, Frank; 1937)
Film Daily. Mar 23, 1937, p7.
The Films of Bing Crosby. p83-84.
Hollywood Reporter. Mar 20, 1937, p3.
Literary Digest. Apr 3, 1937, v123, p20.
Motion Picture Herald. Apr 3, 1937, p41.
The New York Times. Mar 25, 1937, p29.
The New Yorker. Mar 27, 1937, v13, p54-55.
Time. Apr 5, 1937, v29, p53.
Variety. Mar 31, 1937, p17.

Wake Island (US; Farrow, John; 1943)
Commonweal. Sep 4, 1942, v36, p473.
Film Daily. Aug 12, 1942, p6.
The Films of World War II. p76-77.
Guts & Glory. p39-40.
Hollywood Reporter. Aug 13, 1942, p3.
The London Times. Jan 6, 1943, p8.
Motion Picture Exhibitor. Aug 26, 1942, p1078-79.
Motion Picture Herald Product Digest. Aug 15, 1942, p837.
The New York Times. Sep 2, 1942, p19.
The New Yorker. Aug 29, 1942, v18, p37.
Newsweek. Aug 31, 1942, v20, p60.
Time. Sep 14, 1942, v40, p94.
Variety. Aug 12, 1942, p8.
When Hollywood Ruled the Skies. p52-54.

Wake Up and Live (US; Lanfield, Sidney; 1937)
Film Daily. Apr 10, 1937, p7.
The Films of Alice Faye. p81-84.
Hollywood Reporter. Apr 7, 1937, p3.
Hollywood Spectator. Apr 24, 1937, v12, p12.
Literary Digest. May 1, 1937, v123, p20.
Motion Picture Herald. Apr 17, 1937, p44.
The New York Times. Apr 24, 1937, p16.
The New Yorker. Apr 24, 1937, v13, p65.
Newsweek. May 1, 1937, v9, p30.
Rob Wagner's Script. May 1, 1937, v17, p8.
Scholastic. May 8, 1937, v30, p28.
The Tatler. Sep 15, 1937, v145, p470.
Time. Apr 19, 1937, v29, p67.
Variety. Apr 28, 1937, p15.
World Film News. Oct 1937, v2, p20.

A Walk in the Sun (US; Milestone, Lewis; 1945)
Commonweal. Jan 25, 1946, v43, p382.
Film Daily. Dec 3, 1945, p14.
The Films of World War II. p236-37.
Guts & Glory. p67, 71+.
Hollywood Reporter. Nov 28, 1945, p3.
Lewis Milestone (Millichap). p130-32.
Magill's Survey of Cinema, Series I. v6, p1816-19.
Motion Picture Exhibitor. Dec 12, 1945, v35, n6, sec2, p1845-46.
Motion Picture Herald Product Digest. Dec 1, 1945, p2733.
The Nation. Jan 5, 1946, v162, p24.
The New York Times. Jan 12, 1946, p10.
The New Yorker. Jan 12, 1946, v21, p74.
Newsweek. Jan 21, 1946, v27, p98+.
Scholastic. Feb 4, 1946, v48, p37.
A Shot in the Dark. p265-68.
Sight and Sound. Apr 1951, v19, p472-73.
Theatre Arts. Jan 1946, v30, p46-47.
Time. Jan 14, 1946, v47, p90.
Variety. Nov 28, 1945, p10.

The Walking Dead (US; Curtiz, Michael; 1936)
Classics of the Horror Film. p137-39.
Film Daily. Mar 2, 1936, p6.
The Films of Boris Karloff. p116-18.
Hollywood Reporter. Feb 24, 1936, p3.
Hollywood Spectator. Mar 14, 1936, v10, p10-11.
Motion Picture Herald. Mar 7, 1936, p51, 53.
The New York Times. Mar 2, 1936, p13.
Variety. Mar 4, 1936, p26.

Walking Down Broadway (US; Foster, Norman; 1938)
Film Daily. Feb 4, 1938, p6.
Hollywood Reporter. Jan 29, 1938, p3.
Motion Picture Herald. Feb 5, 1938, p53.
The New York Times. Apr 1, 1938, p17.
Variety. Feb 2, 1938, p15.

Walking on Air (US; Santley, Joseph; 1936)
Film Daily. Aug 17, 1936, p9.
Hollywood Reporter. Aug 13, 1936, p3.
Motion Picture Herald. Aug 22, 1936, p40.
The New York Times. Sep 12, 1936, p20.
Rob Wagner's Script. Aug 29, 1936, v16, p10.
Time. Sep 21, 1936, v28, p26.
Variety. Sep 6, 1936, p17.

Walter Wanger's Vogues of 1938 *See* Vogues of 1938

Waltz Time (GB; Thiele, William; 1933)
Film Daily. Sep 29, 1933, p6.
Motion Picture Herald. Aug 12, 1933, p46.
The Nation. Oct 18, 1933, v137, p458.
The New York Times. Jul 23, 1933, p2.
The New York Times. Sep 29, 1933, p24.
The New Yorker. Oct 7, 1933, v9, p58.
Rob Wagner's Script. Dec 30, 1933, v10, p12.
Selected Film Criticism: Foreign Films, 1930-1950. p190-91.
Variety. Jun 27, 1933, p15.
Variety. Oct 3, 1933, p15.

Waltzes From Vienna (Also titled: Strauss' Great Waltz) (GB; Hitchcock, Alfred; 1934)
The Age of the Dream Palace. p214-15.
Film Daily. Apr 9, 1935, p7.
Hitchcock's British Films. p161-67.
Motion Picture Herald. Apr 27, 1935, p52.
The New York Times. Apr 8, 1935, p23.
The Spectator. Mar 9, 1934, v152, p370.
Variety. Mar 6, 1934, p14.
Variety. Apr 17, 1935, p14.

Wanderer of the Wasteland (US; Willat, Irvin; 1924)
Film Daily. July 13, 1924, p9.
Magill's Survey of Cinema. Silent Films. v3, p1186-88.
The New York Times. Jul 8, 1924, p14.
Variety. May 21, 1924, p26.

The Wandering Jew (GB; Elvey, Maurice; 1933)
Cinema Quarterly. Wint 1933-34, v2, p125.
Film Daily. Jan 12, 1935, p3.
Filmfront. Jan 28, 1934, v1, p12-13.
Hollywood Reporter. Jan 17, 1935, p7.
Motion Picture Herald. Jan 19, 1935, p63.
The New York Times. Jan 14, 1935, p11.
Selected Film Criticism: Foreign Films, 1930-1950. p191-92.
Time. Jan 21, 1935, v25, p32.
Variety. Dec 5, 1935, p17.
Variety. Jan 15, 1935, p13.

The Wandering Jew (US; Roland, George; 1933)
Film Daily. Oct 21, 1933, p4.
Motion Picture Herald. Oct 28, 1933, p59.
The New York Times. Oct 21, 1933, p11.
The Spectator. Nov 24, 1933, v151, p768.
Variety. Dec 5, 1933, p17.
Variety. Oct 24, 1933, p22.

War Brides (US; Brenon, Herbert; 1916)
Fifty Great American Silent Films, 1912-1920. p61-62.
Magill's Survey of Cinema. Silent Films. v3, p1189-92.
The Moving Picture World. Nov 18, 1916, p1066.
The Moving Picture World. Dec 2, 1916, p1343-44.
The New York Dramatic Mirror. Nov 11, 1916, p24.
The New York Dramatic Mirror. Nov 18, 1916, p25.
The New York Times. Nov 13, 1916, p11.
Photoplay. Dec 1916, v11, p63.

Selected Film Criticism, 1912-1920. p271-74.
Variety. Nov 17, 1916, p25.
Wid's Daily. Nov 16, 1916, p1101.

War on the Plains (US; Ince, Thomas H.; 1912)
The New York Dramatic Mirror. Feb 28, 1912, p37.
Selected Film Criticism, 1912-1920. p274-75.

The Ware Case (GB; Balcon, Michael; 1938)
Film Daily. Jul 31, 1939, p12.
Motion Picture Herald. Dec 31, 1938, p54, 56.
The New Statesman and Nation. Feb 11, 1939, v17, p206.
The New York Times. Jul 22, 1939, p12.
North American Review. Sep 1939, v248, p194.
The Spectator. Feb 10, 1939, v162, p216.
Variety. Dec 14, 1938, p15.

Warning Shadows (German title: Schatten eine
 Nachtliche Halluzination) (GER; Robison, Arthur;
 1922)
Cinema, the Magic Vehicle. v1, p83-84.
The Emergence of Film Art. p87.
From Caligari to Hitler. p113-14, 171-72.
The Haunted Screen. p133-37.
Variety. Dec 3, 1924, p31.

The Warrens of Virginia (US; DeMille, Cecil B.; 1915)
The Autobiography of Cecil B. DeMille. p114-15.
Fifty Great American Silent Films, 1912-1920. p26-28.
The Films of Cecil B. DeMille. p58-61.
Magill's Survey of Cinema. Silent Films. v3, p1193-96.
Motion Picture News. Feb 20, 1915, p47.
Motography. Dec 26, 1914, p876.
Motography. Mar 1915, p383.
The Moving Picture World. Feb 20, 1915, p1268.
The Moving Picture World. Feb 27, 1915, p1339.
The New York Dramatic Mirror. Feb 24, 1915, p28.
The New York Dramatic Mirror. Mar 3, 1915, p33.
Selected Film Criticism, 1912-1920. p275.
Variety. Feb 19, 1915, p25.

Washington Masquerade (US; Brabin, Charles; 1932)
Film Daily. Jul 22, 1932, p8.
The New York Times. Jul 22, 1932, p18.
The New Yorker. Jul 30, 1932, v8, p36.
Rob Wagner's Script. Dec 3, 1932, v8, p8.

Washington Merry-Go-Round (US; Cruze, James; 1932)
Film Daily. Sep 29, 1932, p6.
Judge. Dec 1932, v103, p19.
Motion Picture Herald. Oct 1, 1932, p52.
The Nation. Nov 9, 1932, v135, p466.
The New York Times. Oct 24, 1932, p18.
The New Yorker. Oct 29, 1932, v8, p51.
Time. Nov 7, 1932, v20, p38.
Vanity Fair. Dec 1932, v39, p46.
Vanity Fair. Jul 1933, v40, p45.
Variety. Oct 25, 1932, p15.

Watch on the Rhine (US; Shumlin, Herman; 1943)
Best Film Plays, 1943-44. p299-356.
Bette Davis: Her Films and Career. p121-22.
Commonweal. Sep 24, 1943, v38, p563.
Film Daily. Jul 27, 1943, p8.
The Films of World War II. p146-48.
The Great Spy Films. p31-68.
The Great Spy Pictures. p504-06.
Hollywood Reporter. Jul 27, 1943, p3.
Magill's Survey of Cinema. Series I. v4, p1820-22.
Motion Picture Herald Product Digest. Jul 31, 1943, p1454.
The New Republic. Sep 13, 1943, v109, p364.
The New York Times. Aug 28, 1943, p15.
The New Yorker. Aug 28, 1943, v19, p50.
Newsweek. Sep 6, 1943, v22, p96.
Time. Sep 6, 1943, v42, p94.
Variety. Jul 28, 1943, p8.

Waterloo Bridge (US; LeRoy, Mervyn; 1940)
Commonweal. May 31, 1940, v32, p130.
Film Daily. May 16, 1940, p12.
The Films of Robert Taylor. p82-84.
The Films of the Forties. p10-11.
The London Times. Nov 18, 1940, p6.
Magill's Survey of Cinema. Series II. v6, p2642-44.
Motion Picture Herald Product Digest. Aug 5, 1944, p2030.
The New York Times. May 17, 1940, p23.
Newsweek. May 20, 1940, v15, p45.
Time. Jun 3, 1940, v35, p73.
Variety. May 15, 1940, p16.
Vivien Leigh (Edwards). p115-16.

Waterloo Bridge (US; Whale, James; 1931)
Bette Davis: Her Films and Career. p17.
Film Daily. Aug 16, 1931, p11.
Hollywood Reporter. Jul 10, 1931, p3.
Hollywood Spectator. Sep 26, 1931, v12, p8-9, 24.
James Whale. p67-70.
Life. Oct 9, 1931, v98, p18.
Love in the Film. p85-88.
The New Statesman and Nation. Nov 21, 1931, v2, p643.
The New York Times. Sep 5, 1931, p7.
The New York Times. Sep 13, 1931, p5.
Outlook and Independent. Sep 23, 1931, v159, p118.
Rob Wagner's Script. Sep 12, 1931, v6, p8.
Rob Wagner's Script. Aug 8, 1931, v5, p11.
Time. Sep 14, 1931, v18, p49.
Variety. Sep 8, 1931, p15.

The Wave (Spanish titles: Redes; Nets; Pescados) (MEX;
 Zinnemann, Fred; Muriel, Emilio Gomez; 1935)
Architectural Record. Feb 1937, v81, p14.
Cinema, the Magic Vehicle. v1, p236.
Commonweal. May 21, 1937, v26, p104.
Dictionary of Films. p307-08.
The Documentary Tradition. p118-22.
Esquire. Jun 1938, v9, p89.
Film Daily. Apr 27, 1937, p12.
From Quasimodo to Scarlett O'Hara. p246-48.
Hollywood Spectator. Jun 25, 1938, v13, p11.
Motion Picture Herald. May 1, 1937, p37.
The Nation. May 8, 1937, v144, p545.
National Board of Review Magazine. May 1937, v12, p12.
The New Masses. Apr 27, 1937, v23, p27-29.
The New Republic. May 5, 1937, v90, p387.
New Theatre. Nov 1936, v3, p20-22.
The New York Times. Apr 21, 1937, p18.
The New Yorker. Apr 24, 1937, v13, p64-65.
Variety. Apr 28, 1937, p15.

The Wax Museum *See* Mystery of the Wax Museum

Waxworks (German title: Wachsfigurenkabinett, Das)
 (GER; Leni, Paul; 1924)
BFI/Monthly Film Bulletin. Jul 1979, v46, p161.
Cinema, the Magic Vehicle. v1, p107-08.
From Caligari to Hitler. p84-87.
The Haunted Screen. p114-18.

Way Down East (US; Griffith, D.W.; 1920)
BFI/Monthly Film Bulletin. May 1979, v46, p108-09.
Billy Bitzer: His Story. p235-36.
Exceptional Photoplays. Dec 1920, v2, p3.
Film Daily. Mar 15, 1931, p10.
Films in Review. Oct 1975, v26, p484-504.
The Films of D.W. Griffith. p150-61.
The Films of the Twenties. p41-44.
The International Dictionary of Films and Filmmakers. v1,
 p516-17.
Lillian Gish: The Movies, Mr. Griffith, and Me. p230-47.
Magill's Survey of Cinema. Silent Films. v3, p1197-1200.
The Moving Picture World. Nov 13, 1920, p224.
The New York Dramatic Mirror. Oct 9, 1920, p651.

The New York Times. Mar 16, 1931, p25.
Photoplay. Dec 1920, v19, p57-58.
Selected Film Criticism, 1912-1920. p276-79.
Spellbound in Darkness. p252-58.
Variety. Aug 20, 1920, p37.
Wid's Daily. Sep 12, 1920, p15.

Way Down East (US; King, Henry; 1935)
Esquire. Dec 1935, v4, p118.
Film Daily. Oct 31, 1935, p14.
The Films of Henry Fonda. p40-41.
The Fondas (Springer). p55-56.
Hollywood Reporter. Aug 14, 1935, p3.
Motion Picture Herald. Aug 24, 1935, p55, 58.
The Nation. Nov 20, 1935, v141, p604.
The New York Times. Oct 31, 1935, p16.
The New York Times. Feb 3, 1935, p4.
The New Yorker. Nov 9, 1935, v11, p78.
Newsweek. Nov 9, 1935, v6, p26-27.
Time. Nov 11, 1935, v26, p26.
Variety. Nov 6, 1935, p20.

The Way of All Flesh (US; Fleming, Victor; 1927)
American Silent Film. p208, 320.
Close-Up. Nov 1927, v1, p31-38.
Film Daily. Jul 3, 1927, p8.
Film Spectator. Aug 4, 1927, v3, p11.
A History of Films. p87.
The History of World Cinema. p121.
Magill's Survey of Cinema. Silent Films. v2, p431-33.
The Moving Picture World. Jul 2, 1927, p4.
The New Republic. Aug 3, 1927, v51, p283.
The New York Times. Jun 27, 1927, p25.
The New York Times. Jul 3, 1927, sec8, p3.
The New York Times. Jan 29, 1928, sec8, p6.
The New York Times. Jan 10, 1927, p20.
Selected Film Criticism, 1921-1930. p305-06.
Variety. Jun 29, 1927, p19.

The Way of Man (US; Griffith, D.W.; 1909)
The Moving Picture World. Jul 3, 1909, p11.
Selected Film Criticism, 1896-1911. p108-10.

Way Out West (US; Horne, James; 1937)
American Film Criticism. p357.
Cinema Arts. Jul 1937, v1, p97.
Fifty Classic Motion Pictures. p128-33.
Film Daily. Dec 19, 1936, p3.
The Films of Hal Roach. p66.
The Great Western Pictures. p392-93.
Hollywood Reporter. Dec 16, 1936, p3.
Hollywood Spectator. Jan 2, 1937, v11, p22.
Laurel and Hardy. p343-52.
Magill's Survey of Cinema. Series I. v4, p1823-25.
Motion Picture Herald. Jan 2, 1937, p65.
The New York Times. May 4, 1937, p29.
Rob Wagner's Script. May 8, 1937, v17, p8.
Selected Film Criticism, 1931-1940. p270.
Variety. May 5, 1937, p16.

The Way to Love (French title: Amour Guide, L') (US; Taurog, Norman; 1933)
Chevalier. p118-21.
Film Daily. Nov 11, 1933, p3.
Hollywood Reporter. Sep 19, 1933, p7.
Motion Picture Herald. Sep 30, 1933, p38.
The New York Times. Nov 20, 1933, p18.
Rob Wagner's Script. Oct 14, 1933, v10, p10.
The Spectator. Nov 17, 1933, v151, p695.
Time. Oct 23, 1933, v22, p43.
Vanity Fair. Dec 1933, v41, p49.
Variety. Nov 14, 1933, p17.

Ways of Love *See* Partie de Campagne, Une

We Are Not Alone (US; Goulding, Edmund; 1939)
Commonweal. Dec 1, 1939, v31, p137.
Film Daily. Nov 9, 1939, p8.
Hollywood Reporter. Nov 8, 1939, p3.
Hollywood Spectator. Nov 25, 1939, v14, p5-6.
Motion Picture Herald. Nov 11, 1939, p38.
The Nation. Dec 9, 1939, v149, p661-62.
National Board of Review Magazine. Jan 1940, v15, p20.
The New Republic. Dec 20, 1939, v101, p260.
The New York Times. Dec 1, 1939, p27.
The New Yorker. Dec 2, 1939, v15, p92-93.
Newsweek. Nov 20, 1939, v14, p36.
Paul Muni: His Life and His Films. p178-84.
Photoplay. Feb 1940, v54, p23+.
Rob Wagner's Script. Dec 2, 1939, v22, p16.
Time. Dec 4, 1939, v34, p83.
Variety. Nov 15, 1939, p18.

We From Kronstadt (Russian title: My iz Kronshtadta; Also titled: We Are from Kronstadt) (USSR; Dzigan, Yefim; 1936)
Cinema, the Magic Vehicle. v1, p253-54.
Dictionary of Films. p232.
The Film Criticism of Otis Ferguson. p133-35.
Graham Greene on Film. p133-34.
Hollywood Reporter. May 22, 1936, p3.
Kino. p336-37.
London Mercury. Apr 1937, v35, p625.
Motion Picture Herald. May 16, 1936, p32.
The Nation. May 27, 1936, v142, p687-88.
National Board of Review Magazine. Jun 1936, v11, p10.
The New Masses. Jun 2, 1936, v19, p28.
The New Republic. May 27, 1936, v87, p73-74.
The New Statesman and Nation. Feb 27, 1937, v13, p328.
New Theatre. Jun 1936, v3, p15, 36.
The New York Times. May 2, 1936, p11.
The New Yorker. May 9, 1936, v12, p69, 71.
Sight and Sound. Spr 1937, v6, p27.
The Spectator. Feb 26, 1937, v158, p356.
Time. May 11, 1936, v27, p56+.
Variety. May 6, 1936, p19.

We Live Again (US; Mamoulian, Rouben; 1934)
Between Flops. p95-97.
Film Daily. Sep 24, 1934, p4.
The Films of Fredric March. p123-25.
Hollywood Reporter. Sep 22, 1934, p3.
Literary Digest. Nov 17, 1934, v118, p35.
Mamoulian (Milne). p81-90.
Motion Picture Herald. Sep 29, 1934, p32.
The New Republic. Oct 24, 1934, v80, p310.
The New York Times. Nov 2, 1934, p27.
Samuel Goldwyn. p73-74.
Samuel Goldwyn Presents. p137-40.
Time. Nov 12, 1934, v24, p42.
Variety. Nov 6, 1934, p16.

We Were Strangers (US; Huston, John; 1949)
The Cinema of John Huston. p72-87.
Commonweal. May 6, 1949, v50, p95.
Film Daily. Apr 21, 1949, p8.
The Films of Jennifer Jones. p81-84.
The Films of John Garfield. p162-66.
Hollywood Reporter. Apr 22, 1949, p3.
Motion Picture Herald Product Digest. Apr 30, 1949, p4589.
The New Republic. May 9, 1949, v120, p29.
The New York Times. Apr 28, 1949, p28.
The New Yorker. May 7, 1949, v25, p103.
Newsweek. May 9, 1949, v33, p90.
Rotarian. Oct 1949, v75, p38.
Sequence. Aut 1949, n9, p127-29.
Theatre Arts. May 1949, v33, p4.
Time. May 2, 1949, v53, p92+.
Variety. Apr 27, 1949, p11.

We Who Are About to Die (US; Cabanne, Christy; 1936)
Film Daily. Oct 23, 1936, p7.
Hollywood Reporter. Oct 5, 1936, p4.
Hollywood Spectator. Nov 7, 1936, v11, p9.
Motion Picture Herald. Oct 17, 1936, p51.
The New York Times. Jan 2, 1937, p15.
The New Yorker. Jan 9, 1937, v12, p65.
Sight and Sound. Wint 1936-37, v5, p138-39.
Variety. Jan 6, 1937, p40.

The Wedding March (US; Stroheim, Erich von; 1928)
American Film. Nov 1975, v1, p72-73.
American Silent Film. p286-90.
Close-Up. Jun 1931, p138.
Close-Up. Jun 1928, p16.
The Complete Wedding March of Erich von Stroheim.
Film Daily. Oct 14, 1928, p4.
The Film Mercury. Oct 26, 1928, p6.
The Film Spectator. Mar 17, 1928, v5, p16-17.
Magill's Survey of Cinema. Silent Films. v3, p1201-05.
The New York Times. Oct 15, 1928, p26.
Selected Film Criticism, 1921-1930. p307-09.
The Silent Voice. p172-82.
Stroheim: A Pictorial Record of His Nine Films. p177-208.
Stroheim (Finler). p94-106.
Variety. Oct 17, 1928, p16.
The Wedding March.

The Wedding Night (US; Vidor, King; 1935)
Cinema Quarterly. Spr 1935, v3, p181.
Esquire. May 1935, v3, p178.
The Film Criticism of Otis Ferguson. p69-70.
Film Daily. Feb 19, 1935, p6.
The Films of Gary Cooper. p126-28.
Garbo and the Night Watchman. p91-93.
Hollywood Reporter. Feb 15, 1935, p3.
Hollywood Reporter. Mar 21, 1935, p2.
King Vidor (Baxter). p52-53.
Literary Digest. Mar 30, 1935, v119, p32.
Motion Picture Herald. Feb 23, 1935, p54.
The Nation. Mar 27, 1935, v140, p370+.
The New Republic. Apr 3, 1935, v82, p214.
The New York Times. Mar 16, 1935, p19.
The New Yorker. Mar 23, 1935, v11, p61-62.
Newsweek. Mar 23, 1935, v5, p29.
Photoplay. Apr 1935, v47, p115.
Rob Wagner's Script. Apr 13, 1935, v13, p10.
Samuel Goldwyn. p41-44.
Samuel Goldwyn Presents. p145-48.
Time. Mar 25, 1935, v25, p46.
A Tree Is a Tree. p207-09.
Vanity Fair. May 1935, v44, p46.
Variety. Mar 20, 1935, p17.

The Wedding of Palo (DEN; Dalsheim, Friedrich;
   Rasmussen, Knud; 1937)
Film Daily. Mar 5, 1937, p21.
Motion Picture Herald. Mar 20, 1937, p52.
National Board of Review Magazine. Apr 1937, v12, p15.
The New York Times. Mar 2, 1937, p17.
Variety. Mar 3, 1937, p14.

Wedding Present (US; Wallace, Richard; 1936)
Film Daily. Sep 24, 1936, p11.
The Films of Cary Grant. p98-100.
Hollywood Spectator. Sep 26, 1936, v11, p12.
Motion Picture Herald. Oct 3, 1936, p42.
The New York Times. Nov 19, 1936, p31.
Time. Oct 26, 1936, v28, p71.
Variety. Nov 25, 1936, p15.

Wee Willie Winkie (US; Ford, John; 1937)
Film Daily. Jun 28, 1937, p18.
The Films of Shirley Temple. p182-85.
Graham Greene on Film. p276-77.

Hollywood Reporter. Jun 24, 1937, p3.
Hollywood Spectator. Jul 3, 1937, v12, p10.
Literary Digest. Jul 10, 1937, v123, p19.
Motion Picture Herald. Jul 3, 1937, p44-45.
The New Masses. Aug 10, 1937, v24, p29.
The New York Times. Jul 24, 1937, p12.
Newsweek. Jul 24, 1937, v10, p26.
The Non-Western Films of John Ford. p250-52.
Rob Wagner's Script. Jul 3, 1937, v17, p10.
Saint Nicholas. Jun 1937, v64, p43.
Time. Jul 19, 1937, v30, p44.
Variety. Jun 30, 1937, p20.

Week End Husbands (US; Goodman, Daniel Carson;
   1924)
Film Daily. Feb 10, 1924, p6.
The Moving Picture World. Feb 16, 1924, p581.

Weisse Hölle vom Piz Palü, Die *See* The White Hell of
   Pitz Palu

Weisse Rausch, Der *See* The White Flame

Welcome Stranger (US; Nugent, Elliott; 1947)
Commonweal. Aug 15, 1947, v46, p428.
Film Daily. Apr 29, 1947, p6.
The Films of Bing Crosby. p169-72.
Life. Jul 7, 1947, v23, p82.
Motion Picture Herald Product Digest. May 3, 1947, p3609.
New Republic. Sep 15, 1947, v117, p36-37.
The New York Times. Aug 7, 1947, p15.
The New Yorker. Aug 16, 1947, v23, p58.
Newsweek. Jul 21, 1947, v30, p76.
Time. Aug 11, 1947, v50, p97.
Variety. Apr 30, 1947, p10.

The Well-Digger's Daughter (French title: Fille du
   Puisatier, La) (FR; Pagnol, Marcel; 1941)
Commonweal. Oct 11, 1946, v44, p623.
Film Daily. Oct 3, 1946, p9.
The Nation. Oct 26, 1946, v163, p482.
The New Republic. Nov 4, 1946, v115, p586.
The New York Times. Sep 30, 1946, p21.
The New Yorker. Sep 28, 1946, v22, p93.
Newsweek. Sep 23, 1946, v28, p94.
Theatre Arts. Oct 1946, v30, p604.
Time. Sep 23, 1946, v48, p105.
Variety. May 28, 1941, p16.

Wells Fargo (US; Lloyd, Frank; 1937)
Canadian Magazine. Feb 1938, v89, p29.
Commonweal. Dec 24, 1937, v27, p244.
Film Daily. Dec 7, 1937, p10.
The Foremost Films of 1938. p33-48.
Hollywood Reporter. Dec 3, 1937, p3.
Literary Digest. Dec 25, 1937, v124, p34.
Motion Picture Herald. Dec 11, 1937, p38.
The Nation. Jan 15, 1938, v146, p82.
The New York Times. Dec 30, 1937, p15.
The New Yorker. Jan 8, 1938, v13, p61-62.
Newsweek. Dec 27, 1937, v10, p24-26.
Rob Wagner's Script. Dec 25, 1937, v18, p5.
Saint Nicholas. Dec 1937, v65, p53.
Scholastic. Jan 8, 1938, v31, p31.
The Spectator. Jan 7, 1938, v160, p15.
Stage. Jan 1938, v15, p60-62.
Time. Jan 10, 1938, v31, p25.
Variety. Dec 8, 1937, p16.

We're Going to Be Rich (GB; Banks, Monty; 1938)
Commonweal. Jul 22, 1938, v28, p351.
Film Daily. Jul 7, 1938, p6.
The New Masses. Jul 19, 1938, v28, p30.
The New York Times. Jul 4, 1938, p10.
The New Yorker. Jul 30, 1938, v14, p39.
Newsweek. Jul 18, 1938, v12, p25.

Time. Jul 18, 1938, v32, p20.
Variety. Jul 6, 1938, p15.
World Film News. Jul 1938, v3, p127.

We're in the Money (US; Enright, Ray; 1935)
Film Daily. Aug 22, 1935, p19.
Hollywood Reporter. Jul 17, 1935, p3.
Motion Picture Herald. Jul 27, 1936, p49.
The New York Times. Aug 22, 1935, p21.
Time. Sep 2, 1935, v26, p38.
Variety. Aug 28, 1935, p12.

We're on the Jury (US; Holmes, Ben; 1937)
Film Daily. Jan 18, 1937, p12.
Hollywood Reporter. Jan 13, 1937, p3.
Motion Picture Herald. Jan 23, 1937, p38.
The New York Times. Feb 10, 1937, p18.
Time. Feb 22, 1937, v29, p25.
Variety. Feb 17, 1937, p23.

West of the Pecos (US; Rosen, Phil; 1934)
Film Daily. Dec 29, 1934, p7.
Hollywood Reporter. Nov 22, 1934, p3.
The New York Times. Dec 29, 1934, p11.
Variety. Jan 1, 1935, p18.

West of Zanzibar (US; Browning, Tod; 1928)
Faces, Forms, Films: The Artistry of Lon Chaney. p84, 116-19.
Film Daily. Jan 6, 1929, p10.
The Hollywood Professionals. v4, p44-48.
Lon of 1000 Faces ! p172-78.
Magill's Survey of Cinema. Silent Films. v3, p1206-08.
The New York Times. Dec 31, 1928, p9.
Variety. Jan 9, 1929, p11.

West Point of the Air (US; Rosson, Richard; 1935)
Film Daily. Feb 25, 1935, p3.
Hollywood Reporter. Feb 21, 1935, p3.
Motion Picture Herald. Mar 16, 1935, p39.
The New York Times. Apr 6, 1935, p10.
The New Yorker. Apr 13, 1935, v11, p63-64.
Rob Wagner's Script. Apr 27, 1935, v13, p10.
Time. Apr 15, 1935, v25, p40.
Variety. Apr 10, 1935, p17.

Western Union (US; Lang, Fritz; 1941)
Action. Nov-Dec 1976, v8, n6, p27-28.
BFI/Monthly Film Bulletin. Jun 30, 1941, n90, p74.
Commonweal. Feb 21, 1941, v30, p448.
Film Comment. Nov-Dec 1974, v10, n6, p12-17.
The Film Criticism of Otis Ferguson. p341-42.
Film Daily. Feb 7, 1941, p7.
The Films of Fritz Lang. p190-93.
Fritz Lang: A Guide to References and Resources. p78-81.
Fritz Lang (Armour). p122-25+.
Hollywood Reporter. Jan 30, 1941, p3.
The London Times. Jun 30, 1941, p8.
Magic Moments from the Movies. p103-04.
Magill's Survey of Cinema. Series II. v6, p2645-48.
Motion Picture Exhibitor. Feb 3, 1941, p684-85.
The New Republic. Feb 17, 1941, v104, p210.
The New York Times. Feb 7, 1941, p23.
The New York Times. Feb 9, 1941, sec9, p5.
The New Yorker. Feb 15, 1941, v17, p76.
Newsweek. Feb 17, 1941, v17, p66+.
Scholastic. Feb 17, 1941, v38, p32.
Scribner's Commentator. Apr 1941, v9, p107.
Time. Feb 24, 1941, v37, p95.
Variety. Feb 5, 1941, p12.

The Westerner (US; Wyler, William; 1940)
BFI/Monthly Film Bulletin. Aug 1940, v7, p34.
Camera Obscura. Sum 1979, p70-103.
Commonweal. Oct 4, 1940, v32, p491.
Film Daily. Sep 20, 1940, p5.
Film Journal. Dec 1956, n6, p12-13.

The Films of Gary Cooper. p169-73.
Hollywood Reporter. Sep 20, 1940, p3.
Kine Weekly. Jul 25, 1940, p3.
Life. Oct 7, 1940, v9, p73-74+.
The London Times. Sep 9, 1940, p6.
Magill's Survey of Cinema. Series I. v4, p1830-34.
The Making of the Great Westerns. p92-107.
Motion Picture Exhibitor. Oct 2, 1940, p613.
The New Republic. Nov 11, 1940, v103, p662.
New Statesman and Nation. Sep 14, 1940, v20, p259.
The New York Times. Oct 25, 1940, p25.
The New Yorker. Oct 26, 1940, v16, p78+.
Newsweek. Sep 30, 1940, v16, p58.
Samuel Goldwyn Presents. p212-15.
Scholastic. Oct 21, 1940, v37, p42.
Time. Oct 14, 1940, v36, p112+.
Variety. Sep 25, 1940, p15.
William Wyler: A Guide to References and Resources. p102-05.
William Wyler (Anderegg). p76-80.

The Westerners (US; Sloman, Edward; 1919)
Exhibitor's Trade Review. Aug 16, 1919, p909.
Motion Picture News. Aug 16, 1919, p1495.
The Moving Picture World. Aug 16, 1919, p1020.
The New York Times. Aug 4, 1919, p8.
Variety. Aug 8, 1919, p49.
Wid's Daily. Aug 10, 1919, p5.

Westfront 1918 (ALso titled: Four Infantry Men; Comrades of 1918; Shame of a Nation) (GER; Pabst, G.W.; 1930)
Cinema, the Magic Vehicle. v1, p176-77.
Close-Up. Aug 1930, v7, p104-11.
Dictionary of Films. p414-15.
Film Daily. Feb 22, 1931, p14.
Films and Filming. Sep 1960, v6, p12-14.
Films and Filming. Apr 1967, v13, p20.
From Caligari to Hitler. p232-35.
The German Cinema. p58-60.
G.W. Pabst (Atwell). p75-82.
Magill's Survey of Cinema. Foreign Language Films. v8, p3349-53.
National Board of Review Magazine. Apr 1931, v6, p7.
The New Statesman and Nation. Feb 13, 1932, v3, p198-99.
The New York Times. Feb 20, 1931, p18.
The New Yorker. Feb 28, 1931, v8, p59.
Scrutiny. May 1932, v1, p64-65.
Scrutiny of Cinema. p57-59.
The Spectator. Jan 16, 1932, v148, p78.
Time. Mar 2, 1931, v17, p26.
Variety. Jun 18, 1930, p55.

Westward Passage (US; Humberstone, Bruce; 1932)
Bookman. Sep 1932, v75, p460.
Film Daily. Jun 5, 1932, p10.
Judge. Jun 25, 1932, v102, p26.
Laurence Olivier: Theater and Cinema. p41-42.
Motion Picture Herald. Jun 11, 1932, p31.
The New York Times. Jun 4, 1932, p9.
The New Yorker. Jun 11, 1932, v8, p52-53.
Rob Wagner's Script. Jul 16, 1932, v7, p8.
Time. May 30, 1932, v19, p36.
Variety. Jun 7, 1932, p21.

The Wet Parade (US; Fleming, Victor; 1932)
Crime Movies (Clarens). p101-02.
Film Daily. Apr 24, 1932, p10.
The Films of Myrna Loy. p130-31.
The Great Gangster Pictures. p411-12.
Hollywood Reporter. Mar 5, 1932, p3.
Judge. May 14, 1932, v102, p22.
Judge. May 21, 1932, v102, p20.
Motion Picture Herald. Apr 30, 1932, p40.
National Board of Review Magazine. Apr 1932, v7, p8-10.

The New York Times. Apr 22, 1932, p23.
The New Yorker. Apr 30, 1932, v8, p52-53.
Rob Wagner's Script. Mar 26, 1932, v7, p10-11.
Sociology and Social Research. May 1932, v16, p498.
Time. Mar 28, 1932, v19, p51.
Variety. Apr 16, 1932, p25.

What Every Woman Knows (US; La Cava, Gregory; 1934)
Film Daily. Oct 5, 1934, p8.
Hollywood Reporter. Oct 3, 1934, p3.
Literary Digest. Nov 10, 1934, v118, p28.
Motion Picture Herald. Oct 13, 1934, p60.
The New Republic. Nov 21, 1934, v81, p46.
The New York Times. Oct 27, 1934, p20.
Time. Oct 29, 1934, v24, p58.
Variety. Oct 30, 1934, p16.

What! No Beer? (US; Sedgwick, Edward; 1933)
Film Daily. Feb 11, 1933, p4.
Hollywood Reporter. Jan 31, 1933, p3.
Motion Picture Herald. Feb 11, 1933, p30-31.
The New York Times. Feb 11, 1933, p11.
Rob Wagner's Script. Feb 18, 1933, v9, p8.
Time. Feb 20, 1933, v21, p22.
Variety. Feb 14, 1933, p21.

What Price Glory? (US; Walsh, Raoul; 1926)
BFI/Monthly Film Bulletin. Jan 1980, v47, p117.
Each Man in His Own Time. p185-95.
Film Daily. Nov 28, 1926, p5.
Guts & Glory. p24-25.
Magill's Survey of Cinema. Silent Films. v3, p1209-11.
The Moving Picture World. Nov 29, 1926, p301.
The New York Times. Nov 24, 1926, p26.
Photoplay. Feb 1927, v31, p53.
Selected Film Criticism, 1921-1930. p309.
Sight and Sound. Jan-Mar 1953, v22, p131.
Variety. Dec 12, 1926, p12.

What Price Hollywood? (US; Cukor, George; 1932)
Film Daily. Jun 22, 1932, p4.
George Cukor (Phillips). p147-50.
Judge. Aug 1932, v103, p22.
Magill's Survey of Cinema. Series I. v4, p1835-38.
Motion Picture Herald. Jun 18, 1932, p35.
The Nation. Aug 3, 1932, v135, p111.
The New York Times. Jul 16, 1932, p5.
The New Yorker. Jul 23, 1932, v8, p45.
On Cukor. p45-48.
Photoplay. Aug 1932, v42, p51.
Rob Wagner's Script. Aug 6, 1932, v7, p8.
Selected Film Criticism, 1931-1940. p270-71.
Time. Jun 27, 1932, v19, p26.
Variety. Jul 19, 1932, p24.

When Knighthood Was in Flower (US; Vignola, Robert G.; 1922)
Film Daily. Sep 17, 1922, p2.
Magill's Survey of Cinema. Silent Films. v3, p1212-14.
The New York Times. Sep 15, 1922, p17.
Photoplay. Nov 1922, p64.
Selected Film Criticism, 1921-1930. p309-10.
Variety. Sep 22, 1922, p41.

When Ladies Meet (US; Beaumont, Harry; 1933)
Commonweal. Jul 14, 1933, v18, p290-91.
Film Daily. Jun 24, 1933, p7.
The Films of Myrna Loy. p155-56.
Hollywood Reporter. May 8, 1933, p3.
Motion Picture Herald. Jun 3, 1933, p36.
The Nation. Jul 12, 1933, v137, p55-56.
New Outlook. Aug 1933, v162, p44.
The New York Times. Jun 24, 1933, p16.
The New Yorker. Jul 1, 1933, v9, p45.
Newsweek. Jul 1, 1933, v1, p31.
Pictorial Review. Sep 1933, v34, p68.

Time. Jul 3, 1933, v22, p32.
Variety. Jun 27, 1933, p14.

When My Baby Smiles at Me (US; Lang, Walter; 1948)
Film Daily. Nov 5, 1948, p8.
Hollywood Reporter. Nov 5, 1948, p3.
Motion Picture Herald Product Digest. Nov 13, 1948, p4381.
The New York Times. Nov 24, 1948, p20.
Newsweek. Dec 6, 1948, v32, p93.
Time. Nov 29, 1948, v52, p98.
Variety. Nov 10, 1948, p15.

When the Clouds Roll By (Also titled: Till the Clouds Roll By) (US; Fleming, Victor; 1919)
Classics of the Silent Screen. p28-29.
Exhibitor's Trade Review. Jan 10, 1920, p615.
His Majesty the American. p110-15.
Motion Picture News. Jan 10, 1920, p687.
The Moving Picture World. Jan 10, 1920, p289.
Variety. Jan 2, 1920, p73.
Wid's Daily. Jan 4, 1920, p3.

When the Daltons Rode (US; Marshall, George; 1940)
Commonweal. Aug 23, 1940, v32, p371.
Film Daily. Jul 29, 1940, p4.
Hollywood Reporter. Jul 26, 1940, p3.
Motion Picture Herald. Aug 3, 1940, p42.
The New York Times. Aug 23, 1940, p13.
The New Yorker. Aug 24, 1940, v16, p60.
Time. Aug 19, 1940, v36, p79.
Variety. Jul 31, 1940, p104.

When Tomorrow Comes (US; Stahl, John M.; 1939)
BFI/Monthly Film Bulletin. Nov 1981, v48, p236.
Commonweal. Sep 1, 1939, v30, p439.
Film Daily. Aug 17, 1939, p6.
Hollywood Reporter. Aug 11, 1939, p3.
Hollywood Spectator. Sep 2, 1939, v14, p9-10.
Motion Picture Herald. Aug 19, 1939, p50.
The Nation. Aug 19, 1939, v149, p205.
The New Masses. Aug 29, 1939, v32, p29.
The New York Times. Aug 17, 1939, p16.
The New Yorker. Aug 19, 1939, v15, p53.
Newsweek. Aug 28, 1939, v14, p25.
Rob Wagner's Script. Aug 26, 1939, v22, p17-18.
Time. Aug 21, 1939, v34, p41.
Variety. Aug 16, 1939, p14.

When Were You Born? (US; McGann, William; 1938)
Commonweal. Jun 24, 1938, v28, p245.
Film Daily. Jun 9, 1938, p4.
Hollywood Reporter. Jun 16, 1938, p3.
Motion Picture Herald. Jun 18, 1938, p39.
The New York Times. Jun 9, 1938, p27.
Rob Wagner's Script. Jun 25, 1938, v19, p13.
Time. Jun 20, 1938, v31, p39.
Variety. Jun 15, 1938, p14.

When You're in Love (Also titled: For You Alone) (US; Riskin, Robert; 1937)
Film Daily. Feb 18, 1937, p8.
The Films of Cary Grant. p101-03.
Garbo and the Night Watchman. p247.
Graham Greene on Film. p165-66.
Hollywood Reporter. Feb 13, 1937, p3.
Hollywood Spectator. Feb 27, 1937, v11, p9-10.
Literary Digest. Feb 27, 1937, v123, p22.
Motion Picture Herald. Feb 20, 1937, p40.
The New York Times. Feb 19, 1937, p15.
The New Yorker. Feb 27, 1937, v13, p60-61.
Rob Wagner's Script. Mar 6, 1937, v17, p10.
Scholastic. Mar 6, 1937, v30, p28.
Time. Mar 1, 1937, v29, p67.
Variety. Feb 24, 1937, p15.

Where Are My Children? (US; Weber, Lois; Smalley, Phillips; 1916)
Magill's Survey of Cinema. Silent Films. v3, p1215-17.
The Moving Picture World. Apr 29, 1916, p817.
The Moving Picture World. Jun 3, 1916, p1748.
The New York Dramatic Mirror. Apr 22, 1916, p42.
The New York Times. Apr 17, 1916, p.
Photoplay. Jun 1916, v10, p95.
Selected Film Criticism, 1912-1920. p279-80.
Variety. Apr 14, 1916, p26.
Wid's Daily. Apr 20, 1916, p524.

Where the Pavement Ends (US; Ingram, Rex; 1923)
Exceptional Photoplays. Apr 1923, v3, p1.
Film Daily. Mar 11, 1923, p2.
Magill's Survey of Cinema. Silent Films. v3, p1218-20.
The New York Times. Apr 2, 1923, p22.
Photoplay. May 1923, v23, p64.
Selected Film Criticism, 1921-1930. p310-11.
Variety. Apr 5, 1923, p36.

While New York Sleeps (US; Brabin, Charles; 1920)
Fifty Great American Silent Films, 1912-1920. p130-32.
The Moving Picture World. Aug 7, 1920, p1237.
The New York Times. Aug 24, 1920, p25.
Wid's Daily. Aug 1, 1920, p15.

While New York Sleeps (US; Humberstone, Bruce; 1938)
Hollywood Reporter. Aug 20, 1938, p3.
Hollywood Spectator. Sep 3, 1938, v13, p13-14.
Motion Picture Herald. Aug 27, 1938, p52-53.
The New York Times. Dec 22, 1938, p25.
Variety. Dec 21, 1938, p14.

Whipsaw (US; Wood, Sam; 1935)
Esquire. Mar 1936, v5, p105.
Film Daily. Jan 25, 1936, p3.
The Films of Myrna Loy. p186-88.
The Films of Spencer Tracy. p121-22.
Hollywood Reporter. Dec 3, 1935, p3.
Hollywood Spectator. Dec 21, 1935, v10, p7-8.
Motion Picture Herald. Dec 14, 1935, p59.
The New Statesman and Nation. Mar 28, 1936, v11, p494.
The New York Times. Jan 25, 1936, p18.
The New York Times. Feb 2, 1936, p5.
The New Yorker. Feb 1, 1936, v11, p46-47.
Rob Wagner's Script. Dec 21, 1935, v14, p10.
Time. Dec 23, 1935, v26, p36.
Variety. Jan 29, 1936, p16.

The Whispering Chorus (US; DeMille, Cecil B.; 1918)
Exhibitor's Trade Review. Jan 26, 1918, p663.
Exhibitor's Trade Review. Mar 30, 1918, p1373, 1389.
The Films of Cecil B. DeMille. p144-47.
Magill's Survey of Cinema. Silent Films. v3, p1221-23.
Motion Picture Classic. Jun 1918, p65.
Motion Picture News. Mar 30, 1918, p1801.
Motion Picture News. Apr 6, 1918, p2093.
The Moving Picture World. Jan 19, 1918, p394.
The Moving Picture World. Mar 30, 1918, p1869.
The Moving Picture World. Apr 6, 1918, p128.
Photoplay. Jun 1918, v18, p51.
Selected Film Criticism, 1912-1920. p282-85.
Variety. Mar 29, 1918, p46.
Wid's Daily. Mar 28, 1918, p1041-42.

Whispering Smith (US; Fenton, Louis; 1949)
Film Daily. Dec 9, 1948 , p7.
The Films of Alan Ladd. p131-36.
Hollywood Reporter. Dec 6, 1948, p4.
Motion Picture Herald Product Digest. Dec 11, 1948, p4418.
The New Republic. Feb 28, 1949, v120, p31.
The New York Times. Feb 15, 1949, p28.
Newsweek. Feb 28, 1949, v33, p79.
Rotarian. Jun 1949, v74, p51.
Variety. Dec 8, 1948, p11.

Whispers (US; Earle, William P.S.; 1920)
The Moving Picture World. Jul 10, 1920, p253.
Variety. Jul 2, 1920, p29.
Wid's Daily. Jul 4, 1920, p13.

Whistling in the Dark (US; Nugent, Elliott; 1933)
Film Daily. Jan 28, 1933, p15.
Garbo and the Night Watchman. p227-28.
Hollywood Reporter. Jan 6, 1933, p2.
Motion Picture Herald. Feb 4, 1933, p39.
The Nation. Feb 15, 1933, v136, p187.
The New York Times. Feb 5, 1933, p5.
The New Yorker. Feb 4, 1933, v8, p49.
Variety. Jan 31, 1933, p12.

The White Angel (US; Dieterle, William; 1936)
Canadian Magazine. Aug 1936, v86, p35.
Film Daily. Jun 2, 1936, p29.
Graham Greene on Film. p121.
Hollywood Reporter. May 27, 1936, p3.
Literary Digest. Jul 4, 1936, v122, p18-19.
London Mercury. Jan 1937, v35, p322.
Motion Picture Herald. Jun 6, 1936, p56.
The New Masses. Jul 14, 1936, v20, p30.
The New Statesman and Nation. Nov 28, 1936, v12, p854.
The New York Times. Jun 25, 1936, p24.
The New Yorker. Jul 4, 1936, v12, p45.
Public Health Nursing. Aug 1936, v28, p540-41.
Rob Wagner's Script. Jun 27, 1936, v15, p8.
The Spectator. Nov 27, 1936, v157, p945.
Time. Jul 6, 1936, v28, p49-50.
Variety. Jul 1, 1936, p12.
World Film News. Aug 1936, v1, p20.

White Banners (US; Goulding, Edmund; 1938)
Commonweal. Jul 1, 1938, v28, p273.
Film Daily. Jun 1, 1938, p7.
Hollywood Reporter. May 24, 1938, p3.
Motion Picture Herald. May 28, 1938, p54.
The New York Times. Jun 23, 1938, p27.
The New Yorker. Jun 25, 1938, v14, p53.
Newsweek. Jun 20, 1938, v11, p23.
Rob Wagner's Script. Jul 9, 1938, v19, p16.
Sociology and Social Research. Nov 1938, v23, p198.
Time. Jun 27, 1938, v31, p26.
Variety. May 25, 1938, p12.
World Film News. Oct 1938, v3, p267.

White Cargo (US; Barnes, A.W.; Williams, J.B.; 1930)
Exhibitors Herald-World. Mar 1, 1930, p36.
Film Daily. Mar 2, 1930, p10.
Judge. May 3, 1930, v98, p23.
The New York Times. Feb 24, 1930, p18.
The New Yorker. Mar 1, 1930, v6, p68.
Time. Mar 10, 1930, v15, p60.
Variety. Feb 26, 1930, p24.

The White Circle (US; Tourneur, Maurice; 1920)
The Moving Picture World. Jul 31, 1920, p639.
The New York Times. Aug 23, 1920, p9.
Variety. Sep 3, 1920, p42.
Wid's Daily. Aug 29, 1920, p18.

The White Cliffs of Dover (US; Brown, Clarence; 1944)
Agee on Film. v1, p94, 122.
Commonweal. May 12, 1944, v40, p80.
Film Daily. Mar 13, 1944, p14.
The Films of Elizabeth Taylor. p45-47.
The Films of World War II. p190-91.
Hollywood Reporter. Mar 9, 1944, p3.
The Nation. May 27, 1944, v158, p634.
The New Republic. Jun 26, 1944, v110, p850.
The New York Times. May 12, 1943, p15.
The New Yorker. May 13, 1944, v20, p67.
Newsweek. May 29, 1944, v23, p70.

Time. May 29, 1944, v43, p94.
Variety. Mar 15, 1944, p32.

The White Devil (GER; Wolkoff, Alexander; 1931)
Film Daily. Aug 30, 1931, p11.
Hollywood Reporter. Nov 4, 1931, p3.
Motion Picture Herald. Sep 5, 1931, p44.
The New York Times. Aug 28, 1931, p20.
The New Yorker. Sep 5, 1931, v7, p55.
Variety. Feb 26, 1930, p7.
Variety. Sep 1, 1931, p34.

The White Flame (German title: Weisse Rausch, Der;
    Also titled: The White Frenzy) (GER; Fanck,
    Arnold; 1931)
Cinema Quarterly. Spr 1933, v1, p185.
Close-Up. Mar 1932, p59-60.
Leni Riefenstahl (Berg-Pan). p64-65.
The New Statesman and Nation. Mar 4, 1933, v5, p255.
The New York Times. Jan 24, 1932, p5.
Variety. Dec 29, 1931, p167.
Variety. Mar 30, 1938, p15.

White Heat (US; Weber, Lois; 1934)
Film Daily. Jun 15, 1934, p16.
Motion Picture Herald. Jun 30, 1934, p56.
The New York Times. Jun 16, 1934, p20.
Variety. Jun 19, 1934, p27.

White Heat (US; Walsh, Raoul; 1949)
Classic Movies. p124-25.
Classics of the Gangster Film. p178-83.
Commonweal. Sep 16, 1949, v50, p560.
Crime Movies. p224-26.
Film Daily. Aug 26, 1949, p7.
The Films of James Cagney. p188-90.
Films of the Forties. p257-59.
Hollywood Genres. p108-10.
Hollywood Reporter. Aug 25, 1949, p3.
The International Dictionary of Films and Filmmakers. v1,
    p518-19.
Life. Sep 26, 1949, v27, p83-84.
Magill's Survey of Cinema. Series I. v4, p1839-41.
Motion Picture Herald Product Digest. Aug 27, 1949, p4729.
The New Republic. Sep 26, 1949, v121, p28.
The New York Times. Sep 3, 1949, p7.
The New Yorker. Sep 10, 1949, v25, p62.
Newsweek. Sep 19, 1949, v34, p80.
Rotarian. Jan 1950, v76, p41.
Saturday Review. Oct 1, 1949, v32, p28-29.
Saturday Review. Nov 5, 1949, p27-28.
Time. Sep 19, 1949, v54, p100.
Variety. Aug 31, 1949, p8.

The White Heather (US; Tourneur, Maurice; 1919)
Exhibitor's Trade Review. May 17, 1919, p1827.
Motion Picture News. May 17, 1919, p3281.
The Moving Picture World. May 17, 1919, p1070-71.
The New York Times. May 5, 1919, p11.
Variety. May 9, 1919, p53.
Wid's Daily. May 11, 1919, p15.

The White Hell of Pitz Palu (German title: Weisse Hölle
    vom Piz Palü, Die) (GER; Pabst, G.W.; Franck,
    Arnold; 1929)
BFI/Monthly Film Bulletin. Apr 1981, v49, p73.
Cinema. Dec 1930, v1, p41-42.
Film Daily. Apr 27, 1930, p13.
G.W. Pabst. p63-64.
The Haunted Screen. p308, 312.
International Photographer. Nov 1930, v2, p20-21.
The Nation. Oct 15, 1930, v131, p424.
National Board of Review Magazine. May-Jun 1930, v5, p13.
The New York Times. Sep 27, 1929, p21.
Selected Film Criticism: Foreign Films, 1930-1950. p194-95.
Variety. Dec 11, 1929, p42.

The White Parade (US; Cummings, Irving; 1934)
Film Daily. Oct 22, 1934, p8.
Hollywood Reporter. Oct 17, 1934, p3.
Motion Picture Herald. Oct 27, 1934, p40.
The New York Times. Nov 10, 1934, p19.
Time. Nov 28, 1934, v24, p28.
Variety. Nov 13, 1934, p15.

The White Rose (US; Griffith, D.W.; 1923)
Film Daily. Jun 10, 1923, p4.
The Films of D.W. Griffith. p191-94.
Magill's Survey of Cinema. Silent Films. v3, p1227-30.
The New York Times. May 23, 1923, p8.
Photoplay. Aug 1923, v24, p63.
Selected Film Criticism, 1921-1930. p312-13.
Variety. May 14, 1923, p23.

White Shadows in the South Seas (US; Van Dyke, W.S.;
    Flaherty, Robert; 1928)
The Arts. Sep 1928, p166-67.
Classics of the Silent Screen. p108-09.
Close-Up. Dec 1928, v2, p16.
Exhibitor's Herald-World and Moving Picture World. Dec 1,
    1928, p58.
Film Daily. Aug 5, 1928, p6.
The Film Spectator. Jun 23, 1928, p7-8.
Magill's Survey of Cinema. Silent Films. v3, p1231-34.
The New York Times. Aug 1, 1928, p13.
Photoplay. Aug 1928, v34, p58.
Robert Flaherty: A Guide to References and Resources. p17-20.
Selected Film Criticism, 1921-1930. p312-14.
Variety. Aug 8, 1928, p12.
The War, the West, and the Wilderness. p492-98.

The White Sister (US; King, Henry; 1923)
Film Daily. Sep 9, 1923, p8.
The Films of Ronald Colman. p37-42.
Lillian Gish. p254-59+.
Magill's Survey of Cinema. Silent Films. v3, p1235-37.
The New York Times. Sep 6, 1923, p10.
Photoplay. Nov 1923, v24, p74.
Selected Film Criticism, 1921-1930. p314.
Variety. Sep 13, 1923, p30.

The White Sister (US; Fleming, Victor; 1933)
Film Daily. Mar 20, 1933, p2.
The Films of Clark Gable. p143.
Hollywood Reporter. Feb 23, 1933, p3.
Judge. May 1933, v104, p23.
Motion Picture. May 1933, v45, p40-41+.
Motion Picture Herald. Mar 25, 1933, p19, 22.
National Board of Review Magazine. Apr 1933, v8, p10-12.
New Outlook. May 1933, v161, p47.
The New York Times. Mar 18, 1933, p9.
The New Yorker. Mar 25, 1933, v9, p49.
Newsweek. Mar 25, 1933, v1, p27-28.
Photoplay. Apr 1933, v43, p40-41.
Rob Wagner's Script. Mar 25, 1933, v9, p10.
Time. Mar 27, 1933, v21, p22.
Variety. Mar 21, 1933, p16.

The White Squadron *See* Squadrone Bianco, Lo

White Woman (US; Walker, Stuart; 1933)
Film Daily. Nov 18, 1933, p4.
The Films of Carole Lombard. p113-14.
Hollywood Reporter. Oct 14, 1933, p6.
Motion Picture Herald. Oct 28, 1933, p58.
The New York Times. Dec 3, 1933, p9.
Newsweek. Nov 25, 1933, v2, p33.
Rob Wagner's Script. Nov 4, 1933, v10, p8-9.
The Spectator. Dec 8, 1933, v151, p848.
Variety. Nov 21, 1933, p20.

White Zombie (US; Halperin, Victor; 1932)
Classics of the Horror Film. p84-87.
Commonweal. Aug 17, 1932, v16, p392.
Film Daily. Jul 29, 1932, p4.
The Films of Bela Lugosi. p74-77.
Forgotten Horrors: Early Talkie Chillers from Poverty Row.
    p53-58.
Motion Picture Herald. Aug 6, 1932, p36.
The New York Times. Jul 29, 1932, p18.
The New Yorker. Aug 6, 1932, v8, p41.
Photoplay. Sep 1932, v42, p110.
Selected Film Criticism, 1931-1940. p271.
Time. Aug 8, 1932, v20, p18.
Variety. Aug 2, 1932, p15.

Whither Germany? *See* Kuhle Wampe

The Whole Town's Talking (US; Ford, John; 1935)
BFI/Monthly Film Bulletin. May 1980, v47, p99-100.
The Cinema of Edward G. Robinson. p102-03.
Dictionary of Films. p417.
Esquire. May 1935, v3, p146.
Film Daily. Feb 15, 1935, p8.
Hollywood Reporter. Jan 17, 1935, p3.
Hollywood Reporter. Mar 8, 1935, p2.
Kiss Kiss Bang Bang. p464.
Literary Digest. Mar 16, 1935, v119, p22.
Lunatics and Lovers. p119-22.
Magill's Survey of Cinema. Series II. v6, p2662-64.
Motion Picture Herald. Jan 26, 1935, p42-43.
The Nation. Mar 20, 1935, v140, p341.
National Board of Review Magazine. Apr 1935, v10, p10.
The New Masses. Mar 19, 1935, v14, p29-30.
The New Republic. Mar 20, 1935, v82, p160.
The New York Times. Mar 1, 1935, p16.
The New York Times. Apr 14, 1935, p3.
The New Yorker. Mar 9, 1935, v11, p61.
The Non-Western Films of John Ford. p46-47.
Rob Wagner's Script. Feb 23, 1935, v13, p8.
Time. Mar 11, 1935, v25, p52.
Vanity Fair. Apr 1935, v44, p47.
Variety. Mar 6, 1935, p20.

Whom the Gods Destroy (Also titled: The Battle Cry of
    War) (US; Earle, William P.S.; 1916)
The Big V. p81-82.
The Moving Picture World. Dec 23, 1916, p1859.
The New York Dramatic Mirror. Jun 3, 1916, p26.
The New York Dramatic Mirror. Jun 10, 1916, p25.
The New York Dramatic Mirror. Dec 16, 1916, p26.
Selected Film Criticism, 1912-1920. p285-86.
Variety. Dec 8, 1916, p29.
Wid's Daily. Dec 14, 1916, p1167.

Whoopee! (US; Freeland, Thornton; 1930)
The Busby Berkeley Book. p38-39.
Cinema. Dec 1930, v1, p41.
Exhibitors Herald-World. Sep 20, 1930, p39.
Film Daily. Oct 5, 1930, p10.
The Hollywood Musical. p63-65.
Life. Oct 17, 1930, v96, p20.
Magill's Survey of Cinema. Series II. v6, p2665-67.
The New York Times. Jun 1, 1930, p4.
The New York Times. Jul 6, 1930, p4.
The New York Times. Jul 29, 1930, p3.
The New York Times. Oct 1, 1930, p26.
The New Yorker. Oct 11, 1930, v6, p75-76.
Outlook and Independent. Oct 22, 1930, v156, p315.
Samuel Goldwyn Presents. p94-97.
Selected Film Criticism, 1920-1931. p314-15.
The Spectator. Dec 20, 1930, v145, p975.
Variety. Oct 8, 1930, p22.

Why Change Your Wife? (US; DeMille, Cecil B.; 1920)
The Films of Cecil B. DeMille. p180-85.
The Moving Picture World. Feb 21, 1920, p1142-43.
The Moving Picture World. Mar 6, 1920, p1678.
The New York Times. Apr 26, 1920, p18.
Variety. Mar 12, 1920, p55.
Wid's Daily. May 2, 1920, p3.

Why Worry? (US; Newmeyer, Fred; Taylor, Sam; 1923)
Film Daily. Sep 9, 1923, p3.
Harold Lloyd. p61-67.
Harold Lloyd: The Shape of Laughter. p160-65.
Magill's Survey of Cinema. Silent Films. v3, p1238-40.
The New York Times. Sep 3, 1923, p9.
Variety. Sep 6, 1923, p23.

The Wicked Darling (US; Browning, Tod; 1919)
Motion Picture News. Feb 22, 1919, p1189-93, 1232.
Moving Picture World. Feb 15, 1919, p944.
Variety. Feb 7, 1919, p59.
Wid's Daily. Feb 2, 1919, p22.

The Wicked Lady (GB; Arliss, Leslie; 1945)
BFI/Monthly Film Bulletin. Oct 1985, v52, p323-24.
Commonweal. Dec 27, 1946, v45, p281.
Film Daily. Dec 12, 1946, p6.
The Films of James Mason. p80-81.
Fortnight. Dec 30, 1946, v1, p42-43.
Hollywood Reporter. Dec 9, 1946, p3.
Motion Picture Herald Product Digest. Dec 14, 1946, p3361.
The New Republic. Jan 13, 1947, v116, p37.
The New York Times. Dec 23, 1946, p19.
Newsweek. Jan 13, 1947, v29, p82.
Rob Wagner's Script. Feb 1, 1947, v33, p15.
Selected Film Criticism: Foreign Films, 1930-1950. p196.
Time. Dec 2, 1946, v48, p104.
Variety. Nov 28, 1945, p10.

Wife, Be Like a Rose *See* Kimiko

Wife, Doctor and Nurse (US; Lang, Walter; 1937)
Film Daily. Sep 8, 1937, p7.
Hollywood Reporter. Sep 2, 1937, p3.
Hollywood Spectator. Sep 11, 1937, v12, p16-18.
Lunatics and Lovers. p58.
Motion Picture Herald. Sep 11, 1937, p47.
The New Statesman and Nation. Nov 20, 1937, v14, p836.
The New York Times. Oct 11, 1937, p26.
The New Yorker. Oct 16, 1937, v13, p73.
Rob Wagner's Script. Sep 11, 1937, v18, p11.
Time. Sep 27, 1937, v30, p36.
Variety. Sep 8, 1937, p12, 18.

Wife, Husband and Friend (US; Ratoff, Gregory; 1939)
Commonweal. Mar 3, 1939, v29, p525.
Film Daily. Feb 27, 1939, p7.
Hollywood Reporter. Feb 10, 1939, p3.
Hollywood Spectator. Feb 18, 1939, v13, p9-10.
Motion Picture Herald. Feb 18, 1939, p43.
The New York Times. Feb 25, 1939, p19.
Rob Wagner's Script. Mar 18, 1939, v21, p16-17.
Time. Mar 13, 1939, v33, p32.
Variety. Feb 15, 1939, p12.

Wife Versus Secretary (US; Brown, Clarence; 1936)
Commonweal. Mar 13, 1936, v23, p552.
Film Daily. Feb 19, 1936, p4.
The Films of Clark Gable. p170-72.
The Films of James Stewart. p31-32.
The Films of Jean Harlow. p130-35.
The Films of Myrna Loy. p189-90.
Hollywood Reporter. Feb 14, 1936, p3.
Hollywood Spectator. Feb 29, 1936, v10, p8-9.
Love in the Film. p122-23.
Motion Picture Herald. Feb 22, 1936, p64.
The New Statesman and Nation. May 16, 1936, v11, p764.

The New York Times. Feb 29, 1936, p11.
The New Yorker. Mar 7, 1936, v12, p63-64.
Rob Wagner's Script. Mar 21, 1936, v15, p12.
Variety. Mar 4, 1936, p26.

Wild and Woolly (US; Emerson, John; 1917)
His Majesty the American. p53-63.
The Moving Picture World. Jun 16, 1917, p1836.
The Moving Picture World. Jun 30, 1917, p2117.
The New York Dramatic Mirror. Jun 23, 1917, p28.
The New York Dramatic Mirror. Jun 30, 1917, p26.
The Rivals of D.W. Griffith. p10-11.
Variety. Jun 22, 1917, p23.
Wid's Daily. Jul 5, 1917, p416.

Wild Boys of the Road (US; Wellman, William A.; 1933)
Film Daily. Sep 22, 1933, p8.
Hollywood Reporter. Sep 5, 1933, p2.
Motion Picture Herald. Sep 30, 1933, p40.
The Nation. Oct 18, 1933, v137, p458.
The New York Times. Sep 22, 1933, p14.
Newsweek. Sep 30, 1933, v2, p46.
Rob Wagner's Script. Oct 7, 1933, v10, p10.
Time. Oct 2, 1933, v22, p40.
Variety. Sep 26, 1933, p20.
We're in the Money. p100-03.
William A. Wellman (Thompson). p136-41.

Wild Geese Calling (US; Brahm, John; 1941)
Film Daily. Jul 25, 1941, p6.
The Films of Henry Fonda. p103-04.
The Fondas (Springer). p111-12.
Hollywood Reporter. Jul 23, 1941, p3.
Motion Picture Exhibitor. Aug 6, 1941, p806.
Motion Picture Herald Product Digest. Jul 26, 1941, p196.
The New York Times. Aug 30, 1941, p10.
Scribner's Commentator. Nov 1941, v11, p107.
Variety. Jul 30, 1941, p8.

Wild Girl (US; Walsh, Raoul; 1932)
Film Daily. Nov 23, 1932, p4.
Hollywood Reporter. Sep 27, 1932, p6.
Motion Picture Herald. Oct 8, 1932, p91-92.

Wild Oranges (US; Vidor, King; 1924)
Film Daily. Mar 9, 1924, p6.
Magill's Survey of Cinema. Silent Films. v3, p1241-44.
The Moving Picture World. Mar 15, 1924, p213.
The New York Times. Mar 3, 1924, p22.
Variety. May 5, 1924, p23.

Wild Orchids (US; Franklin, Sidney; 1929)
Film Daily. Apr 7, 1929, p4.
The Films of Greta Garbo. p74-78.
Magill's Survey of Cinema. Silent Films. v3, p1245-47.
The New York Times. Apr 1, 1929, p29.
Variety. Apr 3, 1929, p20.

The Wild Party (US; Arzner, Dorothy; 1929)
Film Daily. Apr 7, 1929, p5.
Film Daily. Sep 8, 1929, p8.
The New York Times. Apr 2, 1929, p28.
Variety. Apr 3, 1929, p20.

Wildflower (US; Dwan, Allan; 1914)
Allan Dwan: The Last Pioneer. p33.
Marguerite Clark. p54-57.
The Moving Picture World. Oct 24, 1914, p478, 556.
The New York Dramatic World. Oct 14, 1914, p38.

Wilson (US; King, Henry; 1944)
Agee on Film. v1, p110-13.
Best Film Plays, 1943-44. p7-88.
Chestnuts in Her Lap. p139-40.
Commonweal. Aug 18, 1944, v40, p424+.
Film Daily. Aug 2, 1944, p2.
Hollywood Reporter. Aug 2, 1944, p3.

Life. Aug 7, 1944, v17, p53-56.
The London Times. Jan 4, 1945, p6.
Magill's Survey of Cinema. Series II. v6, p2682-86.
Motion Picture Exhibitor. Aug 9, 1944, v32, n13, sec2, p1555.
Motion Picture Exhibitor. Sep 6, 1944, v32, n17, sec2, p576-77.
Motion Picture Herald Product Digest. Aug 5, 1944, p2094.
Musician. Oct 1944, v49, p190.
The Nation. Aug 19, 1944, v159, p221.
The New Masses. Sep 2, 1944, v52, p27-28.
New Movies. Oct 1944, v19, p4-5.
The New Republic. Aug 14, 1944, v111, p187.
The New Republic. Sep 11, 1944, p293.
The New York Times. Aug 2, 1944, p18.
The New York Times. Aug 6, 1944, sec3, p1.
The New York Times Magazine. Mar 26, 1944, p16-17.
The New York Times Magazine. Jun 18, 1944, p18-19.
The New Yorker. Aug 12, 1944, v20, p46.
Newsweek. Aug 14, 1944, v24, p72.
Saturday Review. Aug 12, 1944, v27, p22-23.
Scholastic. Sep 11, 1944, v45, p32.
Selected Film Criticism, 1941-1950. p253-55.
Theatre Arts. Oct 1944, v23, p591-93+.
Time. Aug 7, 1944, v44, p84+.
Variety. Aug 2, 1944, p10.

The Wind (US; Sjostrom, Victor; 1928)
Film Daily. Nov 11, 1928, p4.
The Films of the Twenties. p214-16.
The International Dictionary of Films and Filmmakers. v1, p525.
Magill's Survey of Cinema. Silent Films. v3, p1248-50.
National Board of Review Magazine. Dec 1928, v3, p9.
The New York Times. Nov 5, 1928, p26.
Photoplay. Nov 1928, v32, p52.
Selected Film Criticism, 1921-1930. p315.
Spellbound in Darkness. p472-73.

Window (US; Tetzlaff, Ted; 1949)
Commonweal. Aug 26, 1949, v50, p489.
Film Daily. May 10, 1949, p8.
Hollywood Reporter. May 10, 1949, p3.
Motion Picture Herald Product Digest. May 14, 1949, p4609.
The New Republic. Aug 15, 1949, v121, p23.
The New York Times. Aug 8, 1949, p10.
The New Yorker. Aug 13, 1949, v25, p66.
Newsweek. May 23, 1949, v33, p84-85.
Rotarian. Aug 1949, v75, p43.
Sequence. Spr 1949, n7, p39-41.
Theater Arts. Aug 1949, v33, p106.
Time. May 23, 1949, v53, p94+.
Variety. May 11, 1949, p6.

The Windsor Hotel Fire (US; 1899)
Film Before Griffith. p49.
Motion Picture News. Mar 14, 1925, p1090.
The New York Clipper. Apr 29, 1899, p178.

Wing and a Prayer (US; Hathaway, Henry; 1944)
Commonweal. Sep 15, 1944, v40, p518.
Film Daily. Jul 24, 1944, p7.
Hollywood Reporter. Jul 19, 1944, p4.
The New York Times. Aug 31, 1944, p14.
Newsweek. Sep 11, 1944, v24, p111.
Variety. Jul 19, 1944, p13.

Wings (US; Wellman, William A.; 1927)
The Academy Awards: A Pictorial History. p2-5.
American Cinematographer. Apr 1985, v67, p34-42.
The Award Movies. p140.
BFI/Monthly Film Bulletin. Dec 1978, v45, p252-53.
Film Daily. Aug 21, 1927, p8.
The Films of Gary Cooper. p37-38.
The Films of the Twenties. p170-73.
From Quasimodo to Scarlett O'Hara. p97-98.
Literary Digest. Nov 12, 1927, v95, p36-42.

Magill's Survey of Cinema. Silent Films. v3, p1251-53.
The Moving Picture World. Aug 20, 1927, p524-25.
The New York Times. Aug 13, 1927, p10.
Photoplay. Sep 1927, v32, p52.
Selected Film Criticism, 1921-1930. p315-16.
Spellbound in Darkness. p456-57.
Variety. Aug 17, 1927, p21.
Variety. Dec 17, 1980, p16.
William A. Wellman (Thompson). 58-74.

Wings in the Dark (US; Flood, James; 1935)
Esquire. Apr 1935, v3, p144.
Film Daily. Feb 2, 1935, p6.
The Films of Cary Grant. p83-84.
The Films of Myrna Loy. p182-85.
Hollywood Reporter. Jan 10, 1935, p3.
Motion Picture Herald. Jan 19, 1935, p58, 62.
The New York Times. Feb 2, 1935, p10.
The New York Times. Oct 14, 1934, p4.
Popcorn Venus. p150.
Rob Wagner's Script. Feb 16, 1935, v13, p8.
The Spectator. Feb 22, 1935, v154, p286.
Variety. Feb 5, 1935, p14.

Wings of a Serf (Russian title: Krylya Kholopa; Also
    titled: Ivan the Terrible) (USSR; Tarich, Yuri; 1926)
Cinema, the Magic Vehicle. v1, p124-25.
Film Daily. Mar 17, 1928, p6.
Kino. p214.
Variety. Mar 14, 1928, p23.

Wings of the Morning (GB; Schuster, Harold; 1937)
Esquire. Apr 1937, v7, p117.
Film Daily. Feb 2, 1937, p7.
The Films of Henry Fonda. p52-53.
The Fondas (Springer). p65-66.
Garbo and the Night Watchman. p72.
Hollywood Reporter. Jan 29, 1937, p3.
Hollywood Spectator. Feb 13, 1937, v11, p12.
Hollywood Spectator. Feb 13, 1937, v11, p13.
Literary Digest. Mar 20, 1937, v123, p28.
Motion Picture Herald. Mar 20, 1937, p52, 55.
The New Statesman and Nation. May 22, 1937, v13, p848.
The New York Times. Mar 12, 1937, p19.
The New Yorker. Mar 20, 1937, v13, p75.
Rob Wagner's Script. Feb 13, 1937, v17, p9-10.
Selected Film Criticism: Foreign Films, 1930-1950. p196-97.
The Spectator. Jun 11, 1937, v158, p1091.
Time. Mar 1, 1937, v29, p65.
Variety. Mar 17, 1937, p14.
World Film News. May 1937, v2, p23.

Wings of the Navy (US; Bacon, Lloyd; 1939)
Commonweal. Feb 17, 1939, v29, p470.
Film Daily. Jan 19, 1939, p10.
The Films of Olivia De Havilland. p127-30.
Hollywood Reporter. Jan 12, 1939, p3.
Hollywood Spectator. Jan 21, 1939, v13, p7-8.
Motion Picture Herald. Jan 21, 1939, p38.
The New York Times. Feb 4, 1939, p11.
Rob Wagner's Script. Feb 4, 1939, v20, p16.
Scholastic. Feb 4, 1939, v34, p31.
Time. Feb 13, 1939, v33, p29.
Variety. Jan 18, 1939, p12.

Wings Over Ethiopia (SWITZ; Weschler, L.; 1935)
Film Daily. Oct 14, 1935, p7.
Hollywood Reporter. Oct 3, 1935, p3.
Motion Picture Herald. Oct 26, 1935, p73.
The New Masses. Oct 22, 1935, v17, p30.
The New York Times. Oct 12, 1935, p12.
The New Yorker. Oct 19, 1935, v11, p68.
Time. Oct 14, 1935, v26, p59.
Variety. Oct 16, 1935, p22.

Winner Take All (US; Del Ruth, Roy; 1932)
Film Daily. Jun 18, 1932, p4.
The Gangster Film. p155-58.
Motion Picture Herald. Jun 25, 1932, p29.
The New York Times. Jun 18, 1932, p9.
The New Yorker. Jun 25, 1932, v8, p49.
Rob Wagner's Script. Jul 23, 1932, v7, p8-9.
Time. Jun 27, 1932, v19, p26.
Variety. Jun 21, 1932, p15.

The Winning of Barbara Worth (US; King, Henry; 1926)
BFI/Monthly Film Bulletin. Aug 1976, v43, p181.
Film Daily. Dec 12, 1926, p6.
The Films of Gary Cooper. p29-30.
The Films of Ronald Colman. p103-06.
Magill's Survey of Cinema. Silent Films. v3, p1255-56.
The Moving Picture World. Dec 4, 1926, p363.
The New York Times. Nov 29, 1926, p16.
Photoplay. Dec 1926, v31, p53.
Selected Film Criticism, 1921-1930. p316.
Variety. Oct 20, 1926, p60.

Winterset (US; Santell, Alfred; 1936)
Commonweal. Dec 4, 1936, v25, p162.
Esquire. Feb 1937, v7, p101, 111.
Film. Sep-Oct 1955, n5, p21-22.
Film Daily. Nov 17, 1936, p9.
Garbo and the Night Watchman. p110-16.
Graham Greene on Film. p141-43.
Hollywood Reporter. Nov 13, 1936, p3.
Hollywood Spectator. Nov 21, 1936, v11, p9.
Independent Woman. Dec 1936, v15, p389.
Judge. Jan 1937, v112, p32, 46.
Kiss Kiss Bang Bang. p465.
Literary Digest. Nov 28, 1936, v122, p22.
London Mercury. May 1937, v36, p71-72.
Lorentz on Film. p136-38.
Magill's Survey of Cinema. Series I. v4, p1859-61.
Motion Picture Herald. Nov 21, 1936, p46.
The Nation. Dec 19, 1936, v143, p741.
National Board of Review Magazine. Dec 1936, v11, p9.
The New Masses. Dec 15, 1936, v21, p57.
The New Republic. Jan 13, 1937, v89, p328-29.
The New Republic. Jan 27, 1937, v89, p386.
The New York Times. Dec 4, 1936, p31.
The New Yorker. Nov 28, 1936, v12, p64-65.
Newsweek. Dec 5, 1936, v8, p20.
Rob Wagner's Script. Nov 28, 1936, v16, p10.
Scholastic. Dec 5, 1936, v29, p10-11.
Scribner's Magazine. Feb 1937, v101, p78-79.
Sight and Sound. Spr 1937, v6, p21.
The Spectator. Apr 9, 1937, v158, p663.
Stage. Oct 1936, v14, p52-53.
Stage. Dec 1936, v14, p46-47.
Time. Dec 14, 1936, v28, p25.
Variety. Dec 9, 1936, p12.
World Film News. Feb 1937, v1, p26.

The Wiser Sex (US; Viertel, Berthold; 1932)
Film Daily. Mar 13, 1932, p10.
Motion Picture Herald. Mar 19, 1932, p44.
The New York Times. Mar 12, 1932, p19.
The New Yorker. Mar 19, 1932, v8, p76.
Variety. Mar 15, 1932, p14.

Witchcraft Through the Ages (Swedish title: Háxan)
    (SWED; Christensen, Benjamin; 1920)
Cinema, the Magic Vehicle. v1, p71-72.
The International Dictionary of Films and Filmmakers. v1,
    p194-95.
Magill's Survey of Cinema. Silent Films. v3, p1257-60.

With Byrd at the South Pole (US; 1930)
Close-Up. Aug 1930, v7, p115-17.
Exhibitors Herald-World. Jun 28, 1930, p29.

Film Daily. Jun 22, 1930, p14.
Judge. Sep 6, 1930, v99, p23.
Life. Jul 11, 1930, v96, p17.
Living Age. Sep 1930, v339, p100-01.
The Nation. Jul 9, 1930, v131, p49-50.
The New York Times. Jun 20, 1930, p6.
The New Yorker. Jun 28, 1930, v6, p35-36.
Outlook and Independent. Jul 2, 1930, v155, p351.
Rob Wagner's Script. Aug 2, 1930, v3, p8.
Saturday Review (London). Aug 2, 1930, v150, p143.
Time. Jun 30, 1930, v15, p23.
Variety. Jun 25, 1930, p109.
The War, the West and the Wilderness. p417-18.

Without Reservations (US; LeRoy, Mervyn; 1946)
Agee on Film. v1, p203-04.
Claudette Colbert. p139-43.
Commonweal. Jun 14, 1946, v44, p216.
The Complete Films of John Wayne. p149-50.
Film Daily. May 13, 1946, p12.
Motion Picture Herald Product Digest. May 11, 1946, p2985.
The Nation. Jun 8, 1946, v162, p701.
The New York Times. Jun 8, 1946, p17.
Newsweek. Jun 10, 1946, v27, p94.
Time. Jun 3, 1946, v47, p98.
Variety. May 8, 1946, p8.

The Wizard of Oz (US; 1910)
The New York Dramatic Mirror. Apr 2, 1910, p17.
Selected Film Criticism, 1896-1911. p112.

The Wizard of Oz (US; Fleming, Victor; 1939)
American Cinematographer. Feb 1978, v59, p190-91.
American Cinematographer. Nov 1978, v59, p1090-91.
Child Life. Sep 1939, v18, p410.
The Classic American Novel and the Movies. p165-75.
Commonweal. Aug 25, 1939, v30, p421.
Down the Yellow Brick Road.
Esquire. Nov 1939, v12, p103.
Esquire. Sep 1981, v96, p112.
The Film Criticism of Otis Ferguson. p270-71.
Film Daily. Aug 10, 1939, p6.
Films and Filming. Jan 1968, v14, p45.
The Films of the Thirties. p233-35.
Graham Greene on Film. p268-69.
The Hollywood Musical. p154-59.
Hollywood Reporter. Aug 10, 1939, p3.
Hollywood Spectator. Sep 2, 1939, v14, p10.
Hollywood Studio. 1984, n3, v17, p26-31.
The International Dictionary of Films and Filmmakers. v1, p525-27.
Judy: The Films and Career of Judy Garland. p66-72.
Life. Jul 17, 1939, v7, p28-29.
Literature/Film Quarterly. 1981, n4, v9, p241-50.
Magill's Survey of Cinema. Series I. v4, p1867-71.
The Making of the Wizard of Oz.
The MGM Years. p90-93.
Motion Picture Herald. Aug 12, 1939, p47.
National Board of Review Magazine. Oct 1939, v14, p12.
The New Republic. Sep 20, 1939, v100, p190.
The New York Times. Aug 18, 1939, p16.
The New York Times. Mar 16, 1983, p21.
The New Yorker. Aug 19, 1939, v15, p52.
Newsweek. Aug 21, 1939, v14, p23.
Photoplay. Aug 1939, v53, p21-22+.
Photoplay. Nov 1939, v53, p6.
Photoplay. Apr 1940, v54, p12.
Praxis. 1978, n4, p169-80.
Publisher's Weekly. Jul 15, 1939, v136, p158-59.
Rob Wagner's Script. Aug 26, 1939, v22, p16.
Rotarian. Aug 1949, v75, p43.
Saint Nicholas. Aug 1939, v66, p37+.
Scholastic. Sep 18, 1939, v35, p32.
Selected Film Criticism, 1931-1940. p271-73.
Soundings. 1984, n1, v67, p91-102.

The Spectator. Feb 9, 1940, v164, p179.
Studio. May 1940, v119, p177-78.
Those Fabulous Movie Years: The 30s. p162-63.
Time. Aug 21, 1939, v34, p41.
Time. May 9, 1949, v53, p103.
Variety. Aug 16, 1939, p14.
Variety. Oct 11, 1978, p46.
The Village Voice. Jan 13-19, 1982, v27, p52.

Wolf Lowry (US; Hart, William S.; 1917)
The Complete Films of William S. Hart. p69-70.
The Moving Picture World. Jun 9, 1917, p1625-26.
Variety. Jun 2, 1917, p26.
Wid's Daily. Jun 7, 1917, p360.

The Wolf Man (US; Waggner, George; 1941)
BFI/Monthly Film Bulletin. Jan 1945, n133, p7.
Film Daily. Dec 10, 1941, p6.
Film Journal. Jan-Mar 1973, v2, p6-35.
The Films of Bela Lugosi. p174-75.
The Golden Age of "B" Movies. p213-16.
Hollywood Reporter. Dec 10, 1941, p3.
Horror Films. p33-53.
Magill's Survey of Cinema. Series II. v6, p2698-2701.
Motion Picture Exhibitor. Dec 24, 1941, p914.
Motion Picture Herald Product Digest. Dec 20, 1941, p420.
The New York Times. Dec 22, 1941, p24.
Variety. Dec 17, 1941, p8.

The Woman Accused (US; Sloane, Paul; 1933)
Film Daily. Mar 11, 1933, p4.
The Films of Cary Grant. p55-58.
Hollywood Reporter. Jan 28, 1933, p3.
Motion Picture Herald. Feb 4, 1933, p39.
The New York Times. Mar 13, 1933, p18.
The New Yorker. Mar 18, 1933, v9, p63.
Rob Wagner's Script. Feb 25, 1933, v9, p8.
Time. Feb 27, 1933, v21, p35.
Variety. Mar 14, 1933, p15.

A Woman Alone *See* Sabotage

The Woman Between (US; Schertzinger, Victor; 1931)
Film Daily. Jun 21, 1931, p11.
Hollywood Reporter. Apr 13, 1931, p2.
Life. Nov 20, 1931, v98, p20.
Motion Picture Herald. Apr 25, 1931, p37.
The New York Times. Oct 24, 1931, p20.
The New Yorker. Oct 31, 1931, v7, p66.
Variety. Oct 27, 1931, p25.
Variety. Feb 11, 1931, p29.

Woman Chases Man (US; Blystone, John G.; 1937)
Film Daily. Apr 27, 1937, p10.
Graham Greene on Film. p162.
Hollywood Reporter. Apr 23, 1937, p3.
Hollywood Spectator. May 8, 1937, v12, p11-12.
Life. May 17, 1937, v2, p32-33.
Literary Digest. May 8, 1937, v123, p29.
Lunatics and Lovers. p156.
Motion Picture Herald. May 1, 1937, p30.
Motion Picture Herald. Apr 17, 1937, p12.
The New Masses. Jun 22, 1937, v23, p29.
The New York Times. Jun 11, 1937, p26.
The New Yorker. Jun 19, 1937, v13, p64.
Newsweek. Jun 19, 1937, v9, p20.
Rob Wagner's Script. May 1, 1937, v17, p9.
Samuel Goldwyn. p106-10.
Samuel Goldwyn Presents. p175-77.
The Spectator. Aug 20, 1937, v159, p312.
Stage. Apr 1937, v14, p74.
The Tatler. Aug 25, 1937, v145, p332.
Time. May 31, 1937, v29, p29.
Variety. Jun 16, 1937, p13.
World Film News. Sep 1937, v2, p25.

A Woman Commands (US; Stein, Paul L.; 1931)
Film Daily. Jan 31, 1932, p10.
Hollywood Reporter. Dec 22, 1931, p3.
Motion Picture Herald. Jan 2, 1932, p30.
The New York Times. Jan 28, 1932, p13.
Outlook and Independent. Jan 27, 1932, v160, p119.
Rob Wagner's Script. Dec 26, 1931, v6, p8.
Time. Feb 8, 1932, v19, p20.

The Woman from Monte Carlo (US; Curtiz, Michael; 1931)
Film Daily. Jan 3, 1932, p8.
Hollywood Reporter. Dec 12, 1931, p3.
Motion Picture Herald. Jan 9, 1932, p37.
The New York Times. Dec 31, 1931, p17.
Time. Jan 11, 1932, v19, p25.
Variety. Jan 5, 1932, p23.

The Woman God Forgot (Also titled: The Woman That God Forgot) (US; DeMille, Cecil B.; 1917)
The Films of Cecil B. DeMille. p136-39.
Magill's Survey of Cinema. Silent Films. v3, p127-73.
The Moving Picture World. Nov 17, 1917, p1035.
The New York Dramatic Mirror. Sep 1, 1917, p24.
The New York Dramatic Mirror. Nov 10, 1917, p18.
Selected Film Criticism, 1912-1920. p286-88.
Variety. Nov 2, 1917, p49.
Wid's Daily. Nov 8, 1917, p711.

The Woman I Love (US; Litvak, Anatole; 1937)
Canadian Magazine. Jun 1937, v87, p44.
Esquire. Jul 1937, v8, p97.
Film Daily. Apr 16, 1937, p10.
Hollywood Reporter. Apr 14, 1937, p3.
Hollywood Spectator. Apr 24, 1937, v12, p8-9.
Motion Picture Herald. Apr 24, 1937, p38.
The New York Times. Apr 16, 1937, p27.
Rob Wagner's Script. May 1, 1937, v17, p8-9.
Time. Apr 26, 1937, v29, p42.
Variety. Apr 21, 1937, p14.

The Woman in Red (US; Florey, Robert; 1935)
Film Daily. Mar 23, 1935, p4.
The Films of Barbara Stanwyck. p99.
Hollywood Reporter. Feb 15, 1935, p3.
Hollywood Reporter. Mar 29, 1935, p2.
Motion Picture Herald. Mar 30, 1935, p41-42.
The New York Times. Mar 23, 1935, p11.
Starring Miss Barbara Stanwyck. p68, 73.
Variety. Mar 27, 1935, p15.

The Woman in the Moon *See* Frau im Mond

Woman in the Window (US; Lang, Fritz; 1944)
The Cinema of Edward G. Robinson. p153-55.
Commonweal. Nov 24, 1944, v41, p152.
Film Comment. Nov-Dec 1974, v10, n6, p12-17.
Film Daily. Oct 10, 1944, p10.
Film Noir. p314-15.
The Films of Fritz Lang. p204-08.
The Films of the Forties. p136-37.
Fritz Lang: A Guide to References and Resources. p90-92.
Fritz Lang (Armour). p149-56.
The London Times. Feb 5, 1945, p8.
Magic and Myth of the Movies. p173-74.
Magic Moments of the Movies. p126-29.
Magill's Survey of Cinema. Series II. v6, p2702-04.
Motion Picture Exhibitor. Oct 18, 1944, v32, n23, sec2, p1600.
Motion Picture Herald Product Digest. Oct 14, 1944, p2137.
The New Republic. Feb 26, 1945, v112, p296.
The New York Times. Jan 26, 1945, p16.
The New Yorker. Jan 27, 1945, v20, p64.
Newsweek. Nov 27, 1944, v24, p108.
Scholastic. Dec 11, 1944, v45, p32.
Sight and Sound. Aut 1955, v25, p92-97.

Time. Nov 6, 1944, v44, p94.
Variety. Oct 11, 1944, p12.

The Woman in White (US; Godfrey, Peter; 1948)
Commonweal. Jun 18, 1948, v48, p235.
Film Daily. Apr 21, 1948, p.
Hollywood Reporter. Apr 20, 1948, p3.
Motion Picture Herald Product Digest. Apr 24, 1948, p4137.
The New York Times. May 8, 1948, p12.
Newsweek. May 10, 1948, v31, p82.
Time. May 24, 1948, v51, p100.

A Woman of Affairs (US; Brown, Clarence; 1928)
Film Daily. Jan 27, 1929, p4.
The Film Spectator. Nov 24, 1928, v6, p6.
The Films of Greta Garbo. p71-73.
The Films of the Twenties. p220-23.
The New York Times. Jan 21, 1928, p18.
Selected Film Criticism, 1921-1930. p316-18.
Variety. Jan 23, 1929, p18.

The Woman of Dolwyn (Also titled: The Last Days of Dolwyn; Dolwyn) (GB; Williams, Emlyn; 1949)
Film Daily. Aug 8, 1949, p8.
The New Republic. Sep 5, 1949, v121, p21.
The New York Times. Aug 30, 1949, p18.
The New Yorker. Sep 3, 1949, v25, p61.
Newsweek. Sep 5, 1949, v34, p67.
Sight and Sound. Sum 1949, v18, p89-90.
Variety. May 18, 1949, p8.

A Woman of Paris (US; Chaplin, Charles; 1923)
BFI/Monthly Film Bulletin. Feb 1978, v45, p33.
Charles Chaplin: A Guide to References and Resources. p71-72.
Cinema the Magic Vehicle. v1, p90-92.
Exceptional Photoplays. Oct-Nov 1923, v4, p3.
Film Daily. Oct 7, 1923, p5.
Life. Jan 24, 1924, v83, p31.
Magill's Survey of Cinema. Silent Films. v3, p1264-66.
A Million and One Nights. p651.
Motion Picture Magazine. Dec 1923, v26, p86.
Motion Picture Magazine. May 1925, v29, p52.
Motion Picture Magazine. Nov 1925, v30, p31, 88.
The New York Times. Oct 2, 1923, p7.
The New York Times. Oct 7, 1923, sec9, p4.
Photoplay. Dec 1923, v25, p73.
Selected Film Criticism, 1921-1930. p318-20.
Spellbound in Darkness. p268-74.
Variety. Sep 27, 1923, p25.

A Woman of the World (US; St. Clair, Malcolm; 1925)
Film Daily. Dec 27, 1925, p5.
Magill's Survey of Cinema. Silent Films. v3, p1267-69.
The Moving Picture World. Dec 26, 1925, p808.
The New York Times. Dec 14, 1925, p18.
Photoplay. Feb 1926, v24, p50.
Selected Film Criticism, 1921-1930. p320.
Variety. Dec 16, 1925, p44.

Woman of the Year (US; Stevens, George; 1942)
Commonweal. Feb 20, 1942, v35, p437.
Film Comment. Jul-Aug 1975, v11, p52-56.
The Film Criticism of Otis Ferguson. p414-15.
Film Daily. Jan 19, 1942, p8.
The Films of Katharine Hepburn. p105-09.
The Films of Spencer Tracy. p172-74.
The Films of the Forties. p56-57.
Hollywood Reporter. Jan 14, 1942, p3.
Life. Feb 16, 1942, v12, p47-48+.
The London Times. May 18, 1942, p8.
Magill's Survey of Cinema. Series II. v6, p2705-08.
Motion Picture Exhibitor. Jan 28, 1942, v27, n12, p936.
Motion Picture Herald Product Digest. Jan 17, 1942, p461.
Musician. May 1942, v47, p75.
The Nation. Feb 21, 1942, v44, p239.

The New Republic. Feb 16, 1942, v106, p237.
The New York Times. Feb 2, 1942, p23.
The New York Times. Feb 8, 1942, v9, p5.
Newsweek. Feb 9, 1942, v19, p64.
Reruns. p55-60.
Rob Wagner's Script. Apr 25, 1942, v27, p26-27.
Scholastic. Feb 16, 1942, v40, p28.
Selected Film Criticism, 1941-1950. p255-56.
Talking Pictures. p338-41.
Time. Feb 16, 1942, v39, p82.
Variety. Jan 24, 1942, p8.
Women's Film and Female Experience. p144-47.

The Woman on Pier 13 (Also titled: I Married a Communist) (US; Stevenson, Robert; 1949)
Commonweal. Dec 16, 1949, v51, p294.
Film Daily. Sep 26, 1949, p8.
Hollywood Reporter. Sep 19, 1949, p3.
Motion Picture Herald. Sep 24, 1949, p26.
The New York Times. Jun 6, 1950, p28.
Newsweek. Feb 6, 1950, v35, p84.
Time. Oct 17, 1949, p102.
Variety. Sep 21, 1949, p8.
The Woman on Pier 13.

Woman on the Beach (Also titled: Desirable Woman) (US; Renoir, Jean; 1947)
Commonweal. Jun 27, 1947, v46, p262.
Film Daily. May 15, 1947, p5.
Hollywood Reporter. May 14, 1947, p3.
Jean Renoir: A Guide to References and Resources. p139-41.
Jean Renoir (Durgnat). p260-70+.
Magill's Annual Survey of Cinema, 1983. p519-22.
Motion Picture Herald Product Digest. May 24, 1947, p3643.
New Republic. Jun 23, 1947, v116, p34.
The New York Times. Jun 9, 1947, p26.
Newsweek. Jun 23, 1947, v29, p84+.
Time. Jun 2, 1947, v49, p97.
Variety. Apr 23, 1947, p8.

Woman on Trial (US; Stiller, Mauritz; 1927)
Film Daily. Oct 2, 1927, p7.
The New York Times. Sep 26, 1927, p27.
Variety. Sep 28, 1927, p24.

A Woman Rebels (US; Sandrich, Mark; 1936)
Canadian Magazine. Dec 1936, v86, p38.
Esquire. Jan 1937, v7, p109.
Film Daily. Oct 28, 1936, p7.
The Films of Katharine Hepburn. p80-82.
Hollywood Reporter. Oct 28, 1936, p3.
Hollywood Spectator. Nov 7, 1936, v11, p8-9.
Independent Woman. Dec 1936, v15, p389.
Literary Digest. Nov 14, 1936, v122, p21.
Magill's Survey of Cinema, Series II. v6, p2709-10.
Motion Picture Herald. Nov 30, 1936, p45.
The New York Times. Oct 30, 1936, p27.
The New York Times. Oct 25, 1936, p4.
The New Yorker. Nov 7, 1936, v12, p70.
Newsweek. Nov 7, 1936, v8, p40.
Photoplay. Nov 1936, v50, p37.
Rob Wagner's Script. Nov 7, 1936, v16, p10.
Time. Nov 9, 1936, v28, p46-47.
Variety. Nov 4, 1936, p18.
World Film News. Jan 1937, v1, p26.

Womanhood, the Glory of a Nation (US; Blackton, J. Stuart; Earle, William P.S.; 1917)
The Moving Picture World. Apr 21, 1917, p28.
The New York Dramatic Mirror. Apr 7, 1917, p28.
Photoplay. Jun 1917, v12, p97.
Selected Film Criticism, 1912-1920. p288.
Variety. Apr 6, 1917, p22.
Wid's Daily. Apr 5, 1917, p216.

A Woman's Face (Swedish title: Kvinnas Ansikte, En) (SWED; Molander, Gustaf; 1939)
Film Daily. Sep 18, 1939, p19.
Hollywood Reporter. Nov 22, 1939, p6.
The New York Times. Sep 9, 1939, p11.
Rob Wagner's Script. Dec 2, 1939, v22, p17.

Woman's Place (US; Fleming, Victor; 1921)
Film Daily. Oct 23, 1921, p6.
Magill's Survey of Cinema. Silent Films. v3, p1274-76.
The New York Times. Oct 23, 1921, sec6, p4.
Variety. Oct 21, 1921, p36.

A Woman's Vengence (US; Korda, Zoltan; 1947)
Commonweal. Feb 20, 1948, p472.
Film Daily. Dec 18, 1947, p7.
Hollywood Reporter. Dec 16, 1947, p3.
Motion Picture Herald Product Digest. Dec 27, 1947, p3993.
New Republic. Feb 9, 1948, v118, p35.
The New York Times. Jan 30, 1948, p19.
Newsweek. Feb 23, 1948, v31, p90+.
Time. Feb 9, 1948, v51, p93-94.
Variety. Dec 24, 1947, p13 Variety & Dec 24, 1947 & p13.

The Women (US; Cukor, George; 1939)
Commonweal. Sep 22, 1939, v30, p500.
The Film Criticism of Otis Ferguson. p269.
Film Daily. Aug 29, 1939, p12.
The Films of Joan Crawford. p134-36.
The Films of Norma Shearer. p229-34.
The Films of the Thirties. p239-41.
George Cukor (Phillips). p100-04.
Hollywood Reporter. Aug 25, 1939, p3.
Hollywood Spectator. Sep 16, 1939, v14, p6.
Life. Sep 4, 1939, v7, p28-29.
The Lion's Share. p271-72.
Magill's Survey of Cinema. Series I. v4, p1872-75.
Motion Picture Herald. Sep 2, 1939, p44.
The Nation. Oct 14, 1939, v149, p422.
The New Masses. Oct 3, 1939, v33, p29-30.
The New Republic. Sep 6, 1939, v100, p132.
The New Statesman and Nation. Dec 30, 1939, v18, p956.
The New York Times. Sep 22, 1939, p27.
The New Yorker. Sep 16, 1939, v15, p61.
Newsweek. Sep 11, 1939, v14, p40.
On Cukor. p136-44.
Rob Wagner's Script. Sep 9, 1939, v22, p21.
Selected Film Criticism, 1931-1940. p273-76.
Those Fabulous Movie Years: The 30s. p174.
Time. Sep 11, 1939, v34, p58.
Variety. Sep 6, 1939, p14.

Women Are Like That (US; Logan, Stanley; 1938)
Film Daily. Apr 13, 1938, p6.
Motion Picture Herald. Apr 23, 1938, p45.
The New York Times. Apr 11, 1938, p12.
Time. Apr 18, 1938, v31, p51.
Variety. Apr 13, 1938, p15.
World Film News. Aug 1938, v3, p174.

Women in the Wind (US; Farrow, John; 1939)
Film Daily. Apr 21, 1939, p10.
Hollywood Reporter. Jan 26, 1939, p3.
Motion Picture Herald. Feb 4, 1939, p64.
The New York Times. Apr 13, 1939, p27.
Variety. Feb 1, 1939, p13.
Variety. Apr 19, 1939, p22.

Women Love Once (US; Goodman, Edward; 1931)
Film Daily. Jun 28, 1931, p10.
Hollywood Reporter. Jun 11, 1931, p6.
Judge. Jul 25, 1931, v101, p22.
The New York Times. Jun 27, 1931, p20.
The New York Times. Jul 5, 1931, p3.
Rob Wagner's Script. Aug 15, 1933, v6, p10.
Variety. Jun 30, 1931, p20.

Women Men Marry (US; Taggart, Errol; 1937)
Hollywood Reporter. Aug 31, 1937, p3.
Motion Picture Herald. Sep 11, 1937, p50.
Variety. Sep 22, 1937, p18.

Women of Glamour (US; Wiles, Gordon; 1937)
Film Daily. Mar 9, 1937, p10.
Motion Picture Herald. Mar 20, 1937, p52.
The New York Times. Mar 6, 1937, p10.
Variety. Mar 10, 1937, p15.

Women's Club *See* Club des Femmes

The Wop *See* The Italian

Words and Music (US; Taurog, Norman; 1948)
Film Daily. Dec 8, 1948, p6.
The Hollywood Musical. p299-300.
Hollywood Reporter. Dec 7, 1948, p3.
The Motion Picture Herald Product Digest. Dec 11, 1948, p4417.
The New York Times. Dec 10, 1948, p34.
The New Yorker. Dec 18, 1948, v24, p102.
Newsweek. Dec 13, 1948, v32, p91-92+.
Time. Dec 27, 1948, v52, p59.
Variety. Dec 8, 1948, p10.

The World and the Flesh (US; Cromwell, John; 1932)
Film Daily. May 8, 1932, p10.
Motion Picture Herald. May 14, 1932, p46.
The New York Times. May 7, 1932, p11.
The New Yorker. May 14, 1932, v8, p50-51.
Time. May 16, 1932, v19, p36.
Variety. May 10, 1932, p18.

The World Changes (US; LeRoy, Mervyn; 1933)
Canadian Magazine. Dec 1933, v80, p38.
Commonweal. Dec 15, 1933, v19, p178.
Film Daily. Oct 28, 1933, p5.
Hollywood Reporter. Sep 29, 1933, p2.
Motion Picture Herald. Nov 4, 1933, p38.
The New York Times. Oct 27, 1933, p22.
The New Yorker. Nov 4, 1933, v9, p59-60.
Paul Muni: His Life and His Films. p120-25.
The Spectator. Mar 30, 1934, v152, p502.
Time. Nov 6, 1933, v22, p42.
Variety. Oct 31, 1933, p17.

The World Gone Mad (US; Cabanne, Christy; 1933)
Film Daily. Apr 15, 1933, p3.
Hollywood Reporter. Jun 14, 1933, p3.
Motion Picture Herald. Apr 22, 1933, p37.
The New York Times. Apr 15, 1933, p16.
Newsweek. Apr 22, 1933, v1, p30.
Variety. Apr 18, 1933, p21.

Wormwood (US; Farnum, Marshall; 1915)
Motion Picture News. Jun 12, 1915, p67.
Motography. Jun 19, 1915, p1034.
The Moving Picture World. Jun 12, 1915, p1788.
The Moving Picture World. Jul 24, 1915, p734.
Variety. Jun 18, 1915, p1034.

The Wrath of the Gods (US; Barker, Reginald; 1914)
The Moving Picture World. Jun 6, 1914, p1458.
The Moving Picture World. Jun 20, 1914, p1665.
The New York Dramatic Mirror. Jun 10, 1914, p34.
Selected Film Criticism, 1912-1920. p288-90.
Variety. Jun 12, 1914, p21.

Wuthering Heights (US; Wyler, William; 1939)
Cinema, the Magic Vehicle. v1, p318-19.
Commonweal. Apr 21, 1939, v29, p722.
Dictionary of Films. p422-23.
The English Novel and the Movies. p67-82.
The Film Criticism of Otis Ferguson. p251-52.
Film Daily. Mar 28, 1939, p9.

The Films of the Thirties. p227-29.
From Quasimodo to Scarlett O'Hara. p295-98.
Graham Greene on Film. p219-20.
The Great Romantic Films. p68-71.
Hollywood Reporter. Mar 25, 1939, p3.
Ladies Home Journal. Jun 1939, v56, p18+.
Landmark Films. p42-47.
Laurence Olivier (Hirsch). p42-46.
Laurence Olivier: Theater and Cinema. p65-72.
Library Journal. Apr 1, 1939, v64, p283.
Life. Apr 3, 1939, v6, p39-40.
Magill's Survey of Cinema. Series I. v4, p1884-87.
Make It Again, Sam. p210-14.
Motion Picture Herald. Apr 1, 1939, p28.
The Nation. Apr 22, 1939, v148, p478.
National Board of Review Magazine. Apr 1939, v14, p16-17.
The New Masses. Apr 25, 1939, v31, p29.
The New Republic. Apr 26, 1939, v98, p336.
The New York Times. Apr 14, 1939, p28.
The New Yorker. Apr 15, 1939, v15, p79-80.
Newsweek. Apr 10, 1939, v13, p27.
North American Review. Jun 1939, v247, p385-86.
Novels Into Films. p91-114.
The Oliviers. p170-78.
Photoplay. May 1939, v53, p38-39.
Photoplay. Jun 1939, v53, 58.
Quarterly of Film, Radio and Television. Wint 1956, v11, p171-80.
Rob Wagner's Script. Apr 15, 1939, v21, p17-18.
Samuel Goldwyn (Epstein). p80-92.
Samuel Goldwyn Presents. p197-200.
Scholastic. Apr 29, 1939, v34, p33.
Selected Film Criticism, 1931-1940. p276-79.
Sequence: Film Quarterly. 1951, n13, p21.
The Spectator. May 5, 1939, v162, p760.
Stage. Apr 15, 1939, v16, p22-24.
The Tatler. May 10, 1939, v152, p240.
Those Fabulous Movie Years: The 30s. p184-85.
Time. Apr 17, 1939, v33, p49.
Variety. Mar 29, 1939, p14.
William Wyler (Anderegg). p67-76.

A Yank at Oxford (GB; US; Conway, Jack; 1938)
Around Cinemas. p151-54.
Film Daily. Jan 27, 1938, p5.
The Films of Robert Taylor. p63-66.
Hollywood Reporter. Jan 22, 1938, p3.
Life. Feb 14, 1938, v4, p22-23.
London Mercury. May 1938, v38, p68.
Lorentz on Film. p151-53.
Motion Picture Herald. Jan 29, 1938, p48, 53.
The New Masses. Mar 8, 1938, v26, p28-29.
The New Republic. Mar 23, 1938, v94, p195.
The New Statesman and Nation. Apr 9, 1938, v15, p612.
The New York Times. Feb 25, 1938, p15.
The New Yorker. Mar 5, 1938, v14, p48.
Newsweek. Feb 21, 1938, v11, p28.
Rob Wagner's Script. Feb 26, 1938, v19, p8-9.
Scholastic. Mar 19, 1938, v32, p35.
Selected Film Criticism: Foreign Films, 1930-1950. p198-99.
The Spectator. Apr 8, 1938, v160, p627.
Time. Feb 28, 1938, v31, p63.
Variety. Feb 2, 1938, p15.
World Film News. May-Jun 1938, v3, p82, 86.

Yank in London (Also titled: I Live in Grosvenor Square) (GB; Wilcox, Herbert; 1945)
Around Cinemas, Second Series. p257-59.
Commonweal. Apr 26, 1946, v44, p47.
Film Daily. Feb 19, 1946, p10.
Hollywood Reporter. Feb 20, 1946, p3.
Motion Picture Herald Product Digest. Feb 23, 1946, p2858.
The New York Times. Apr 20, 1946, p16.
The New Yorker. Apr 27, 1946, p78.
Newsweek. Apr 8, 1946, v27, p89.

Rob Wagner's Script. Oct 26, 1946, v32, p14.
Selected Film Criticism: Foreign Films, 1930-1950. p199-200.
Theatre Arts. Apr 1946, v30, p218-19.
Time. Mar 18, 1946, v47, p90+.
Variety. May 30, 1945, p16.

A Yank in the R.A.F. (US; King, Henry; 1941)
Cinema Examined. p283-95.
Film Daily. Sep 9, 1941, p5.
The Films of Tyrone Power. p118-21.
The Films of World War II. p54-56.
Hollywood Reporter. Sep 9, 1941, p3.
Life. Sep 22, 1941, v11, p86-87.
The New Republic. Nov 3, 1941, v105, p587.
The New York Times. Sep 27, 1941, p11.
Newsweek. Oct 6, 1941, v18, p59-61.
Scribner's Commentator. Dec 1941, v11, p105.
Time. Oct 13, 1941, v38, p94.
Variety. Sep 10, 1941, p8.

Yankee Doodle Dandy (US; Curtiz, Michael; 1942)
Commonweal. Jun 19, 1942, v36, p207.
Film Daily. Jun 1, 1982, p6.
The Films of James Cagney. p168-75.
The Films of World War II. p69-70.
The Hollywood Musical. p205.
Hollywood Reporter. Jun 1, 1942, p3.
Hollywood Spectator. Sep 1942, v17, p15.
The International Dictionary of Films and Filmmakers. v1, p530.
Life. Jun 15, 1942, v12, p64-66+.
The London Times. Oct 19, 1942, p8.
Magic Moments from the Movies. p117.
Magill's Survey of Cinema. Series I. v4, p1888-90.
Motion Picture Exhibitor. Jun 3, 1943, v28, n4, sec2, p1022-23.
Motion Picture Herald Product Digest. Jun 16, 1942, p699.
Musician. Aug 1942, v47, p116.
The New Republic. Jun 15, 1942, v106, p831.
The New York Times. Apr 30, 1942, p9.
The New York Times. Jun 7, 1942, v8, p3.
The New York Times Magazine. Mar 1, 1942, p14-15.
The New Yorker. Jun 8, 1942, v18, p76.
Newsweek. Jun 8, 1942, v19, p56.
Rob Wagner's Script. Aug 15, 1942, v27, p24.
Saturday Review. Jun 12, 1942, p21.
Scholastic. Jan 4, 1943, v41, p34.
Selected Film Criticism, 1941-1950. p257-59.
Time. Jun 22, 1942, v39, p86-87.
Variety. Jun 2, 1942, p8.
Yankee Doodle Dandy. 1981, p11-64.

The Yearling (US; Brown, Clarence; 1946)
Commonweal. Jan 24, 1946, v45, p375-76.
Film Daily. Nov 27, 1946, p7.
The Films of Gregory Peck. p51-55.
Fortnight. Dec 16, 1946, v1, p42.
Hollywood Reporter. Nov 27, 1946, p3.
Life. Feb 17, 1947, v22, p65-67.
Magill's Survey of Cinema. Series II. v6, p2721-23.
Motion Picture Herald Product Digest. Nov 30, 1946, p3333.
The New Republic. Jan 27, 1947, v116, p42.
The New York Times. Jan 24, 1946, p18.
The New Yorker. Feb 1, 1947, v22, p56.
Newsweek. Jan 27, 1946, v29, p89-90.
Saturday Review. Feb 22, 1946, v30, p22-24.
Selected Film Criticism, 1941-1950. p259-61.
Theatre Arts. Jan 1947, v31, p40.
Time. Jan 13, 1947, v49, p97.
Variety. Nov 27, 1946, p14.

Yellow Dust (US; Fox, Wallace; 1936)
Film Daily. Feb 25, 1936, p9.
Hollywood Reporter. Mar 2, 1936, p4.
Motion Picture Herald. Mar 28, 1936, p44.

The New York Times. Feb 24, 1936, p14.
Variety. Feb 26, 1936, p15.

Yellow Jack (US; Seitz, George B.; 1938)
Commonweal. Jun 3, 1938, v28, p161.
Film Daily. May 18, 1938, p8.
Hollywood Reporter. May 20, 1938, p3.
London Mercury. Aug 1938, v38, p359.
Magill's Survey of Cinema. Series II. v6, p2724-27.
Motion Picture Herald. May 28, 1938, p51, 54.
National Board of Review Magazine. Jun 1938, v13, p11.
The New Republic. Jun 8, 1938, v95, p131.
The New Statesman and Nation. Jul 16, 1938, v16, p114.
The New York Times. May 20, 1938, p17.
The New Yorker. May 28, 1938, v14, p59.
Newsweek. May 30, 1938, v11, p23.
Rob Wagner's Script. Jul 23, 1938, v19, p10.
The Spectator. Jul 15, 1938, v161, p104.
Stage. Jun 1938, v15, p28-29.
Time. May 30, 1938, v31, p49.
Variety. May 25, 1938, p12.
World Film News. Aug 1938, v3, p170.

Yellow Sands (GB; Brenon, Herbert; 1938)
Motion Picture Herald. Jul 23, 1938, p42-43.
The Tatler. Sep 14, 1938, v149, p470.
Variety. Jul 20, 1938, p13.
World Film News. Oct 1938, v3, p267.

The Yellow Ticket (Also titled: The Yellow Passport) (US; Walsh, Raoul; 1931)
Film Daily. Nov 1, 1931, p10.
The Films of Boris Karloff. p56.
The Films of Laurence Olivier. p60-61.
Hollywood Reporter. Oct 26, 1931, p3.
Laurence Olivier (Hirsch). p37-38.
Laurence Olivier: Theater and Cinema. p38-40.
Motion Picture Herald. Oct 17, 1931, p38.
The New York Times. Oct 31, 1931, p22.
Rob Wagner's Script. Dec 5, 1931, v6, p8.
Variety. Nov 3, 1931, p29.

Yes, My Darling Daughter (US; Keighley, William; 1939)
Commonweal. Mar 3, 1939, v29, p525.
Film Daily. Feb 15, 1939, p7.
Hollywood Reporter. Feb 2, 1939, p3.
Hollywood Spectator. Feb 18, 1939, v13, p11-12.
Life. Feb 20, 1939, v6, p23.
Motion Picture Herald. Feb 11, 1939, p40.
The New Masses. Feb 28, 1939, v30, p28-29.
The New York Times. Feb 27, 1939, p11.
Newsweek. Feb 27, 1939, v13, p25.
Photoplay. Apr 1939, v53, p52.
Rob Wagner's Script. Feb 18, 1939, v21, p16.
Time. Feb 20, 1939, v33, p67.
Time. Mar 6, 1939, v33, p31.
Variety. Feb 8, 1939, p17.

Yes or No (US; Neill, Roy William; 1920)
The Moving Picture World. Jul 3, 1920, p46.
The New York Dramatic Mirror. Jul 10, 1920, p69.
The New York Times. Jul 5, 1920, p15.
Variety. Jul 9, 1920, p26.
Wid's Daily,. Jul 11, 1920, p2.

Yeux Noirs, Les *See* Dark Eyes

Yolanda and the Thief (US; Minnelli, Vincente; 1945)
Commonweal. Nov 30, 1945, v43, p170.
Film Daily. Oct 19, 1945, p8.
The Hollywood Musical. p260, 293.
Hollywood Reporter. Oct 17, 1945, p3.
The London Times. May 27, 1946, p8.
Magill's Survey of Cinema. Series II. v6, p2731-33.
Motion Picture Exhibitor. Oct 17, 1945, v34, n24, sec2, p1815.

Motion Picture Herald Product Digest. Oct 20, 1945, p2685.
The New York Times. Nov 23, 1945, p26.
Newsweek. Dec 3, 1945, v26, p100.
Saturday Review. Jun 13, 1942, v25, p21.
Scholastic. Nov 5, 1945, v47, p30.
Starring Fred Astaire. p278-87.
Time. Dec 10, 1945, v46, p97.
Variety. Oct 17, 1945, p8.
Vincente Minnelli and the Film Musical. p155-58+.
The World of Entertainment. p162-73.

Yoshiwara (FR; Ophuls, Max; 1937)
Hollywood Reporter. Oct 20, 1937, p11.
Variety. Sep 8, 1937, p19.

You and Me (US; Lang, Fritz; 1938)
Commonweal. Jun 17, 1938, v28, p217.
Film Daily. Jun 3, 1938, p6.
The Films of Fritz Lang. p182-85.
Fritz Lang: A Guide to References and Resources. p75-77.
Fritz Lang (Armour). p22-23.
Fritz Lang (Eisner). p191-96.
Graham Greene on Film. p195-96.
The Great Gangster Pictures. p419-20.
Hollywood Reporter. May 28, 1938, p3.
Hollywood Spectator. Jun 4, 1938, v13, p8-9.
Motion Picture Herald. Jun 4, 1938, p34.
National Board of Review Magazine. Jun 1938, v13, p17.
The New Statesman and Nation. Jun 25, 1938, v15, p1064.
The New York Times. Jun 2, 1938, p19.
The New Yorker. Jun 11, 1938, v14, p50-51.
Newsweek. Jun 13, 1938, v11, p21.
Rob Wagner's Script. Jun 4, 1938, v19, p11.
The Spectator. Jul 1, 1938, v161, p16.
Variety. Jun 8, 1938, p17.
World Film News. Aug 1938, v3, p174.

You Can't Cheat an Honest Man (US; Marshall, George; 1939)
Film Daily. Feb 20, 1939, p9.
The Films of W.C. Fields. p134-39.
Hollywood Reporter. Feb 15, 1939, p3.
Hollywood Spectator. Mar 4, 1939, v13, p8-9.
Magill's Survey of Cinema. Series I. v4, p1891-93.
Motion Picture Herald. Feb 18, 1939, p42.
The New Masses. Mar 7, 1939, v30, p28-29.
The New York Times. Feb 20, 1939, p13.
The New Yorker. Feb 25, 1939, v15, p58.
Newsweek. Feb 27, 1939, v13, p25.
Rob Wagner's Script. Mar 4, 1939, v21, p16-17.
Scholastic. Mar 18, 1939, v34, p30.
Time. Feb 27, 1939, v33, p30.
Variety. Feb 22, 1939, p12.
W.C. Fields: A Life on Film. p198-205.

You Can't Get Away With Murder (US; Seiler, Lewis; 1939)
Classics of the Gangster Film. p77-80.
The Complete Films of Humphrey Bogart. p71-72.
Film Daily. Mar 29, 1939, p8.
The Gangster Film. p189-91.
The Great Gangster Pictures. p421.
Hollywood Reporter. Jan 17, 1939, p3.
Hollywood Spectator. Feb 4, 1939, v13, p14.
Humphrey Bogart: The Man and His Films. p88-90.
Motion Picture Herald. Jan 21, 1939, p40.
The New York Times. Mar 25, 1939, p19.
The New Yorker. Apr 1, 1939, v15, p68.
Variety. Jan 25, 1939, p15.

You Can't Have Everything (US; Taurog, Norman; 1937)
Commonweal. Aug 13, 1937, v26, p388.
Film Daily. Jul 28, 1937, p11.
Film Daily. Aug 4, 1937, p8.
The Films of Alice Faye. p55-58.

Hollywood Reporter. Jul 24, 1937, p3.
Hollywood Spectator. Jul 31, 1937, v12, p12-13.
Motion Picture Herald. Jul 31, 1937, p40-41.
The New Masses. Aug 17, 1937, v24, p29.
The New York Times. Aug 4, 1937, p15.
Newsweek. Aug 7, 1937, v10, p22.
Rob Wagner's Script. Aug 14, 1937, v17, p14-15.
Time. Aug 16, 1937, v30, p35.
Variety. Jul 28, 1937, p27.

You Can't Take It With You (US; Capra, Frank; 1938)
Canadian Magazine. Oct 1938, v90, p55.
Commonweal. Sep 16, 1938, v28, p534.
Dictionary of Films. p425-26.
Esquire. Mar 1939, v11, p85, 153.
The Film Criticism of Otis Ferguson. p235-36.
Film Daily. Aug 26, 1938, p9.
The Films of Frank Capra (Scherle and Levy). p157-64.
The Films of Frank Capra (Willis). p107-13.
The Films of James Stewart. p61-64.
The Foremost Films of 1938. p129-46.
Frank Capra (Maland). p101-04.
Graham Greene on Film. p203-04.
Hollywood Reporter. Aug 24, 1938, p3.
Hollywood Spectator. Sep 3, 1938, v13, p7-8.
Life. Sep 19, 1938, v5, p44-47.
London Mercury. Dec 1938, v39, p204.
Lunatics and Lovers. p144-50.
Magill's Survey of Cinema. Series II. v6, p2734-37.
Motion Picture Herald. Aug 27, 1938, p52.
The New Masses. Mar 15, 1938, v26, p28.
The New Republic. Sep 21, 1938, v96, p188.
The New Statesman and Nation. Nov 5, 1938, v16, p724.
The New York Times. Sep 2, 1938, p21.
The New York Times. Feb 24, 1939, p14.
The New York Times. Feb 25, 1939, p14.
The New Yorker. Sep 10, 1938, v14, p59.
Newsweek. Sep 12, 1938, v12, p21.
Rob Wagner's Script. Oct 1, 1938, v20, p8.
Scholastic. Oct 1, 1938, v33, p13.
Selected Film Criticism, 1931-1940. 279-80.
The Spectator. Nov 11, 1938, v161, p807.
Spotlight on Films. p106-07.
The Tatler. Nov 9, 1938, v150, p240.
Theatre Arts. Sep 1938, v22, p693.
Theatre Arts. Nov 1938, v22, p811.
Those Fabulous Movie Years: The 30s. p152-53.
Time. Sep 12, 1938, v32, p44-45.
Variety. Sep 7, 1938, p12.
We're in the Money. p144-45.

You May Be Next (US; Rogell, Albert S.; 1936)
Film Daily. Feb 25, 1936, p9.
Hollywood Reporter. Feb 19, 1936, p4.
Motion Picture Herald. Mar 28, 1936, p41, 44.
The New York Times. Feb 24, 1936, p14.
Variety. Mar 4, 1936, p27.

You Only Live Once (US; Lang, Fritz; 1937)
Crime Movies (Clarens). p160-63.
Dark Cinema. p144-46.
Esquire. Apr 1937, v7, p117.
Film Daily. Jan 27, 1937, p8.
Film Quarterly. Wint 1979-80, v33, p5-6.
The Films of Fritz Lang. p177-81.
The Films of Henry Fonda. p54-56.
The Films of My Life. p64-68.
The Fondas (Springer). p67-69.
Fritz Lang: A Guide to References and Resources. p72-74.
Fritz Lang (Armour). 107-11+.
Fritz Lang (Eisner). p177-90.
Fritz Lang (Eisner). p177-90.
Hollywood Reporter. Jan 23, 1937, p3.
Hollywood Spectator. Jan 30, 1937, v11, p11-12.
Journal of Popular Film. Fall 1978, n6, p240-41.

Judge. Mar 1937, v112, p21.
A Library of Film Criticism: American Film Directors. p246-47.
Life. Jan 25, 1937, v2, p54-56.
Literary Digest. Feb 6, 1937, v123, p24.
Magill's Survey of Cinema. Series I. v4, p1894-96.
Motion Picture Herald. Jan 30, 1937, p48.
The New Masses. Feb 16, 1937, v22, p29.
The New Statesman and Nation. Jun 5, 1937, v13, p924.
New Theatre. Apr 1937, v3, p26.
The New York Times. Feb 1, 1937, p15.
The New Yorker. Jan 30, 1937, v12, p52-53.
Newsweek. Jan 30, 1937, v9, p20.
Rob Wagner's Script. Feb 6, 1937, v16, p8-10.
Scholastic. Feb 20, 1937, v30, p22.
Sight and Sound. Sum 1955, v25, p15-21+.
Sight and Sound. Sum 1937, v6, p80-81.
The Spectator. Jun 11, 1937, v158, p1091.
Stage. Jan 1937, v14, p66.
The Tatler. Jun 16, 1937, v144, p514.
Time. Jan 11, 1937, v29, p56.
Variety. Feb 3, 1937, p14.
We're in the Money. p162-65.
World Film News. Jul 1937, v2, p24-25.

You Were Never Lovelier (US; Seiter, William; 1942)
Commonweal. Nov 6, 1942, v37, p72.
Film Daily. Oct 5, 1942, p6.
The Films of Rita Hayworth. p141-44.
The Hollywood Musical. p200, 215.
Hollywood Reporter. Oct 5, 1942, p3.
Life. Nov 9, 1942, v13, p64+.
Motion Picture Herald Product Digest. Oct 10, 1942, p945.
The New York Times. Dec 4, 1942, p31.
Newsweek. Oct 26, 1942, v20, p74.
Starring Fred Astaire. p245-56.
Time. Nov 16, 1942, v40, p99.
Variety. Oct 7, 1942, p8.

Young America (US; Borzage, Frank; 1932)
Film Daily. May 8, 1932, p10.
Motion Picture Herald. May 14, 1932, p46.
The New York Times. May 7, 1932, p11.
Variety. May 10, 1932, p18.

Young and Innocent (Also titled: The Girl Was Young) (GB; Hitchcock, Alfred; 1936)
The Art of Alfred Hitchcock. p67-74.
Cinema, the Magic Vehicle. v1, p280.
Film Daily. Jan 19, 1938, p6.
From Quasimodo to Scarlett O'Hara. p277-79.
Hitchcock: The First Forty-Four Films. p51-52.
Hitchcock's British Films. p216-31.
Hollywood Reporter. Dec 16, 1937, p10.
Hollywood Reporter. May 19, 1937, p3.
London Mercury. Mar 1938, v37, p539.
Motion Picture Herald. Dec 11, 1937, p41.
Motion Picture Herald. Oct 30, 1937, p16-17.
The Nation. Feb 12, 1938, v146, p193.
The New York Times. Feb 11, 1938, p27.
The New Yorker. Feb 12, 1938, v13, p60.
Rob Wagner's Script. May 28, 1938, v19, p9.
Selected Film Criticism: Foreign Films, 1930-1950. p57-58.
The Spectator. Feb 11, 1938, v160, p223.
Time. Feb 14, 1938, v31, p32.
Variety. Dec 8, 1937, p17.

Young and Willing (US; Griffith, Edward H.; 1943)
Film Daily. Feb 18, 1943, p4.
The Films of Susan Hayward. p83-84.
The Films of William Holden. p70-72.
Motion Picture Herald. Feb 13, 1943, p34.
Motion Picture Herald Product Digest. Feb 20, 1943, p1170.
Variety. Feb 10, 1943, p8.

Young as You Feel (US; Borzage, Frank; 1931)
Film Daily. Aug 9, 1931, p10.
Hollywood Reporter. Apr 7, 1931, p3.
Hollywood Spectator. Aug 29, 1931, v12, p24.
Life. Sep 4, 1931, v98, p21.
Motion Picture Herald. Apr 18, 1931, p42.
The New York Times. Aug 8, 1931, p16.
The New York Times. Aug 16, 1931, p3.
Outlook and Independent. Sep 2, 1931, v159, p21.
Rob Wagner's Script. Aug 1, 1931, v5, p8.
Time. Aug 17, 1931, v18, p17.
Variety. Aug 11, 1931, p19.

Young Dr. Kildare (US; Bucquet, Harold S.; 1938)
Commonweal. Nov 11, 1938, v29, p77.
Film Daily. Oct 12, 1938, p7.
Hollywood Reporter. Oct 12, 1938, p3.
Hollywood Spectator. Oct 29, 1938, v13, p16.
Motion Picture Herald. Oct 15, 1938, p36.
The New Masses. Nov 8, 1938, v29, p29.
The New York Times. Oct 28, 1938, p27.
The New Yorker. Nov 5, 1938, v14, p57-58.
Time. Nov 7, 1938, v32, p41.
Variety. Oct 19, 1938, p12.

Young Eagles (US; Wellman, William A.; 1930)
Exhibitors Herald-World. Mar 22, 1930, p38.
Film Daily. Mar 23, 1930, p10.
The Great Spy Pictures. p522.
Judge. Apr 19, 1930, v98, p25.
Life. Apr 18, 1930, v95, p27.
The New York Times. Mar 22, 1930, p22.
The New York Times. Mar 30, 1930, p5.
The New Yorker. Mar 29, 1930, v6, p53.
Outlook and Independent. Apr 2, 1930, v154, p551.
Time. Apr 28, 1930, v15, p42.
Variety. Mar 26, 1930, p39.
William A. Wellman (Thompson). p98-100+.

The Young in Heart (US; Wallace, Richard; 1938)
Canadian Magazine. Dec 1938, v90, p41.
Commonweal. Nov 18, 1938, v29, p105.
Film Daily. Nov 4, 1938, p6.
The Foremost Films of 1938. p164-81.
Hollywood Reporter. Nov 1, 1938, p3.
Hollywood Spectator. Nov 12, 1938, v13, p8-9.
Kiss Kiss Bang Bang. p466.
Life. Nov 14, 1938, v5, p54-55.
Lunatics and Lovers. p158-62.
The Nation. Nov 12, 1938, v147, p516.
The New Masses. Nov 15, 1938, v29, p30.
The New Republic. Nov 30, 1938, v97, p101.
The New York Times. Nov 4, 1938, p27.
The New Yorker. Nov 12, 1938, v14, p94.
Newsweek. Nov 14, 1938, v12, p28-29.
Photoplay. Jan 1939, v53, p54.
Rob Wagner's Script. Dec 3, 1938, v20, p17-18.
Stage. Dec 1938, v16, p58.
Time. Nov 14 1938, v32, p40.
Variety. Nov 2, 1938, p15.

Young Man of Manhattan (US; Bell, Monta; 1930)
Claudette Colbert (Quirk). p26-29.
Exhibitors Herald-World. Apr 26, 1930, p30.
Film Daily. Apr 20, 1930, p10.
The Film Spectator. Jun 7, 1930, v9, p16-17.
The Films of Ginger Rogers. p44-45.
Judge. May 17, 1930, v98, p25.
Life. May 9, 1930, v95, p18.
The New York Times. Apr 19, 1930, p15.
The New York Times. Feb 9, 1930, p7.
The New York Times. Mar 16, 1930, p6.
The New York Times. Apr 27, 1930, p5.
The New Yorker. Apr 26, 1930, v6, p83.
Outlook and Independent. Apr 20, 1930, v154, p712.

Time. Apr 28, 1930, v15, p42.
Variety. Apr 23, 1930, p36.

Young Mr. Lincoln (US; Ford, John; 1939)
American Visions. p126-36.
Cinema, the Magic Vehicle. v1, p316-17.
Cine-Tracts. 1978, n4, v2, p42-62.
Commonweal. Jun 16, 1939, v30, p218.
Esquire. Sep 1939, v12, p114.
The Film Criticism of Otis Ferguson. p257-58.
Film Daily. Jun 2, 1939, p6.
Film Heritage. Sum 1971, v6, p13-18, 32.
Film Quarterly. Wint 1973-74, v27, p37-46.
Film Quarterly. 1975, n3, v28, p33-49.
Film Reader. 1980, n4, p80-88.
Film Theory and Criticism. p695-740.
Films and Filming. Jun 1962, v8, p15.
The Films of Henry Fonda. p83-86.
The Films of John Ford. p51-58.
The Fondas (Springer). p92-94.
From Quasimodo to Scarlett O'Hara. p310-13.
Graham Greene on Film. p241-42.
Hollywood Reporter. Jun 3, 1939, p3.
Hollywood Spectator. Jun 10, 1939, v14, p5.
The International Dictionary of Films and Filmmakers. v1,
  p532-33.
John Ford (Bogdanovich). p72-74.
Life. Jun 12, 1939, v6, p72+.
Magill's Survey of Cinema. Series I. v4, p1897-1903.
Motion Picture Herald. Jun 3, 1939, p36.
Movies and Methods. p493-29.
National Board of Review Magazine. Jun 1939, v14, p26.
The New Masses. Jun 20, 1939, v31, p30.
The New Republic. Jun 21, 1939, v99, p189.
The New York Times. May 31, 1939, p26.
The New Yorker. Jun 10, 1939, v15, p74.
Newsweek. Jun 12, 1939, v13, p34.
Photoplay. Aug 1939, v53, p55.
Photoplay. Apr 1940, v54, p12.
Quarterly Review of Film Studies. 1978, n3, v3, p405-16.
Rob Wagner's Script. Jun 10, 1939, v21, p16.
Screen. Aut 1972, v13, p5-47.
Screen. Aut 1973, v14, p29-43.
Selected Film Criticism, 1931-1940. p280-82.
Sight and Sound. Spr 1955, v24, p206-08.
The Spectator. Sep 22, 1939, v163, p408.
The Tatler. Sep 6, 1939, v153, p420.
Time. Jun 12, 1939, v33, p78.
Variety. Jun 7, 1939, p12.
The Velvet Light Trap. 1973, n3, p23-24.

Young Pushkin (USSR; Naroditsky, Arcady; 1937)
Film Daily. Dec 17, 1937, p9.
The Nation. Jan 1, 1938, v146, p754.
The New Masses. Dec 28, 1937, v26, p27.
The New York Times. Dec 16, 1937, p35.
Variety. Dec 22, 1937, p17.

Young Tom Edison (US; Taurog, Norman; 1940)
Commonweal. Mar 29, 1940, v31, p494.
Film Daily. Feb 13, 1940, p7.
Hollywood Reporter. Feb 9, 1940, p3.
Motion Picture Herald. Feb 9, 1940, p5-8.
Motion Picture Herald. Feb 14, 1940, p6.
The New York Times. Mar 15, 1940, p27.
Newsweek. Mar 4, 1940, v15, p41.
Scholastic. Mar 4, 1940, v36, p34.
Time. Mar 18, 1940, v35, p86+.
Variety. Feb 14, 1940, p18.

The Younger Generation (US; Capra, Frank; 1929)
Film Daily. Jun 2, 1929, p8.
The New York Times. Mar 11, 1929, p22.
Variety. Mar 20, 1929, p12.

Your Uncle Dudley (US; Forde, Eugene; 1935)
Film Daily. Nov 14, 1935, p12.
Film Daily. Nov 14, 1935, p12.
Hollywood Reporter. Nov 9, 1935, p3.
Hollywood Spectator. Nov 23, 1935, v10, p11-12.
Motion Picture Herald. Nov 23, 1935, p72.
The New York Times. Dec 12, 1935, p3.
Rob Wagner's Script. Dec 14, 1935, v14, p10, 12.
Time. Dec 16, 1935, v26, p44.
Variety. Dec 18, 1935, p12.

You're a Sweetheart (US; Butler, David; 1937)
Film Daily. Dec 14, 1937, p11.
The Films of Alice Faye. p89-92.
Hollywood Reporter. Dec 11, 1937, p3.
Motion Picture Herald. Dec 18, 1937, p50.
The New York Times. Dec 25, 1937, p10.
Rob Wagner's Script. Jan 15, 1938, v18, p8.
The Spectator. Feb 25, 1938, v160, p311.
Time. Jan 3, 1938, v31, p29.
Variety. Dec 15, 1937, p17.
World Film News. Apr 1938, v3, p38.

You're in the Army Now *See* O.H.M.S.

Yours for the Asking (US; Hall, Alexander; 1936)
Film Daily. Aug 20, 1936, p7.
Hollywood Reporter. Jul 29, 1936, p4.
Motion Picture Herald. Aug 8, 1936, p39, 42.
The New York Times. Aug 20, 1936, p14.
Rob Wagner's Script. Aug 22, 1936, v15, p10.
Variety. Aug 26, 1936, p20.

Youth in Revolt (FR; Benoit-Levy, Jean; 1939)
Film Daily. May 24, 1939, p7.
Motion Picture Herald. May 27, 1939, p34.
The New York Times. May 16, 1939, p27.

The Youth of Maxim (Russian title: Yunost Maxima; Also
  titled: Part I of the Maxim Trilogy) (USSR;
  Kozintsev, Grigori; Trauberg, Leonid; 1935)
Cinema, the Magic Vehicle. v1, p226-27.
Dictionary of Films. p427-28.
Eighty Years of Cinema. p106-07.
The Film Criticism of Otis Ferguson. p75-76.
Film Daily. Apr 20, 1935, p4.
The International Dictionary of Films and Filmmakers. v1,
  p287.
Kino. p320-23.
Motion Picture Herald. May 11, 1935, p54.
The Nation. May 1, 1935, v140, p518+.
National Board of Review Magazine. Jun 1935, v10, p9.
The New Masses. May 7, 1935, v15, p29-30.
The New York Times. Apr 20, 1935, p16.
The New Yorker. May 4, 1935, v11, p58-59.
Rob Wagner's Script. Jun 15, 1935, v13, p8.
Theatre Arts Monthly. Jun 1935, v19, p408.
Time. Apr 29, 1935, v25, p54.
Variety. Feb 12, 1935, p39.

Youth Takes a Fling (US; Mayo, Archie; 1938)
Commonweal. Oct 28, 1938, v29, p21.
Film Daily. Sep 27, 1938, p6.
Hollywood Reporter. Sep 22, 1938, p3.
Motion Picture Herald. Oct 1, 1938, p38-39.
The New York Times. Oct 17, 1938, p12.
The New Yorker. Oct 22, 1938, v14, p57.
Rob Wagner's Script. Oct 1, 1938, v20, p10.
Time. Oct 17, 1938, v32, p32.
Variety. Sep 28, 1938, p14.

Youthful Folly (US; Crosland, Alan; 1920)
The Moving Picture World. Mar 13, 1920, p1724.
The Moving Picture World. Apr 3, 1920, p136.
Variety. Apr 2, 1920, p94.
Wid's Daily. Apr 4, 1920, p16.

Zaza (US; Porter, Edwin S.; Ford, Hugh; 1915)
Exhibitor's Trade Review. Sep 28, 1918, p1423.
Motion Picture News. Sep 25, 1915, p11.
Motion Picture News. Oct 2, 1915, p54.
Motion Picture News. Oct 16, 1915, p85.
Motion Picture News. Sep 7, 1918, p1568-69.
Motography. Oct 23, 1915, p859-60.
The Moving Picture World. Oct 16, 1915, p464.
The Moving Picture World. Oct 23, 1915, p688.
The Moving Picture World. Oct 5, 1918, p119.
The Moving Picture World. Oct 12, 1918, p281.
Variety. Oct 8, 1915, p21.

Zaza (US; Dwan, Allan; 1923)
Allan Dwan: The Last Pioneer. p65-66.
Film Daily. Sep 23, 1923, p4.
The Films of Gloria Swanson. p147-53.
Magill's Survey of Cinema. Silent Films. v3, p1277-80.
A Million and One Nights. p85.
The New York Times. Sep 17, 1923, p18.
Photoplay. Dec 1923, v25, p72.
Selected Film Criticism, 1921-1930. p320-21.
Variety. Sep 20, 1923, p23.

Zaza (US; Cukor, George; 1938)
Claudette Colbert (Quirk). p106-07.
Film Daily. Jan 4, 1939, p7.
George Cukor (Phillips). p44-46.
Hollywood Reporter. Dec 29, 1938, p3.
Hollywood Spectator. Jan 7, 1939, v13, p10-11.
Motion Picture Herald. Jan 7, 1939, p36.
The New York Times. Jan 5, 1939, p17.
The New Yorker. Jan 7, 1939, v14, p43.
On Cukor. p131-35.
Rob Wagner's Script. Jan 28, 1939, v20, p17-18.
The Spectator. Feb 17, 1939, v162, p261.
Time. Jan 16, 1939, v33, p26.
Variety. Jan 4, 1939, p14.

Zemla *See* Earth

Zemlya *See* Earth

Zemlya Zhazhdyat *See* The Soil is Thirsty

Zenobia (US; Douglas, Gordon; 1939)
Film Daily. Mar 14, 1939, p6.
Hollywood Reporter. Mar 11, 1939, p3.
Hollywood Spectator. Mar 18, 1939, v13, p9-10.
Motion Picture Herald. Mar 18, 1939, p48-49.
The New York Times. May 15, 1939, p15.
Photoplay. Jun 1939, v53, p58.
Rob Wagner's Script. Sep 30, 1939, v22, p16.
Variety. Mar 15, 1939, p16.

Zero for Conduct (French title: Zéro de Conduite) (FR; Vigo, Jean; 1933)
Cinema Quarterly. Wint 1935, v3, p86-88.
Classics of the Foreign Film. p88-89.
Dictionary of Films. p429-30.
The Essential Cinema. p141-56.
The Film and the Public. p127-28.
Film Criticism and Caricatures, 1943-1953. p57-58.
Film Heritage. Fall 1973, v9, p11-22.
The Films of Jean Vigo. p53-95.
The Golden Age of French Cinema, 1929-1939. p104-08, 130-31.
The Great French Films. p50-52.
Hollywood Quarterly. Apr 1947, v2, p261-63.
The International Dictionary of Films and Filmmakers. v1, p535-36.
Jean Vigo (Sales-Gomes). p95-147.
Magill's Survey of Cinema. Foreign Language Films. v8, p3501-05.
The Nation. Jul 5, 1947, v165, p23-25.
The Nation. Jul 12, 1947, v165, p51.

The New Statesman and Nation. Jan 23, 1937, v13, p119.
The New York Times. Jun 23, 1947, p14.
Saturday Review. Apr 12, 1952, v35, p58.
Sight and Sound. Jul-Sep 1953, v23, p21-13.
The Spectator. Sep 13, 1946, v177, p263.
Tower of Babel. p17-25.
The Velvet Light Trap. Sum 1973, n9, p5-7.
The Village Voice. Mar 29, 1962, v7, p13.
World Film News. Feb 1937, v1, p28.

Ziegfeld Follies (US; Minnelli, Vincente; 1946)
Commonweal. Apr 19, 1946, v44, p16.
Film Daily. Jan 11, 1946, p16.
The Hollywood Musical. p268.
Hollywood Musicals. p224-27.
Judy: The Films and Career of Judy Garland. p131-35.
Life. Mar 25, 1946, v20, p88-90.
Motion Picture Herald Product Digest. Aug 25, 1945, p2628.
The New York Times. Mar 23, 1946, p8.
The New Yorker. Mar 30, 1946, v22, p59.
Starring Fred Astaire. p265-78.
Theatre Arts. May 1946, v30, p283.
Time. Mar 25, 1946, v47, p98.
Variety. Aug 15, 1945, p15.
Vincente Minnelli and the Film Musical. p46-49, 158-59+.

Ziegfeld Girl (US; Leonard, Robert Z; 1941)
The Busby Berkeley Book. p133-38.
Commonweal. May 16, 1941, v34, p86.
Film Daily. Apr 1941, p7.
The Films of Hedy Lamarr. p134-43.
The Films of Lana Turner. p94-101.
The Hollywood Musical. p184-86.
Hollywood Reporter. Apr 15, 1941, p3.
The London Times. Sep 1, 1941, p8.
Motion Picture Exhibitor. Aug 30, 1941, p737-38.
Motion Picture Herald Product Digest. Feb 22, 1941, p62.
The New York Times. Apr 25, 1941, p17.
Newsweek. Apr 28, 1941, v17, p65+.
Scribner's Commentator. Jul 1941, v10, p105.
Time. May 5, 1941, v37, p92+.
Variety. Apr 23, 1941, p6.

Zimlia *See* Earth

Zoo in Budapest (US; Lee, Rowland V.; 1933)
Cinema Quarterly. Aut 1933, v2, p45-46.
Film Daily. Apr 12, 1933, p3.
Hollywood Reporter. Apr 3, 1933, p3.
Love in the Film. p100-02.
Motion Picture Herald. Apr 22, 1933, p35.
The Nation. May 17, 1933, v136, p568.
National Board of Review Magazine. May 1933, v8, p9.
The New Statesman and Nation. Jun 24, 1933, v5, p845.
The New York Times. Apr 28, 1933, p15.
The New Yorker. May 6, 1933, v9, p57.
Newsweek. May 6, 1933, v1, p30.
Rob Wagner's Script. May 6, 1933, v9, p11.
Time. Apr 17, 1933, v21, p27.
Variety. May 2, 1933, p12.
Vogue. Jun 1, 1933, v81, p70.

ZuiderZee *See* The New Earth

Zwei Herzen im 3/4 Takt (Also titled: Two Hearts in Waltz Time) (GER; Bolvary, Geza von; 1930)
Film Daily. Sep 14, 1930, p13.
Judge. Feb 7, 1931, v100, p22.
The Nation. Nov 12, 1930, v131, p536.
National Board of Review Magazine. Nov 1930, v5, p6.
The New York Times. Oct 13, 1930, p31.
The New Yorker. Jul 18, 1931, v7, p48.
The New Yorker. Oct 25, 1930, v6, p77.
Rob Wagner's Script. May 23, 1931, v5, p10.
Selected Film Criticism, 1930-1950. p179-80.
Theatre Magazine. Mar 1931, v53, p47.

Variety. Apr 2, 1930, p35.
Variety. Oct 15, 1930, p29.

Zwei Menschen (Also titled: Two Souls) (GER;
    Waschneck, Erich; 1931)
Film Daily. Dec 27, 1931, p10.
Motion Picture Herald. Feb 6, 1932, p40.

The Nation. Jan 20, 1932, v134, p82.
National Board of Review Magazine. Feb 1932, v7, p14.
The New York Times. Dec 23, 1931, p27.
Outlook and Independent. Jan 6, 1932, v160, p23, 29.
Variety. Dec 29, 1931, p167.

Director Index

Abbott, George
The Cheat
Manslaughter
The Sea God

Adolfi, John
Alexander Hamilton
The King's Vacation
The Man Who Played God
The Millionaire
The Show of Shows
Sinners' Holiday
A Successful Calamity
Voltaire

Alberini, Filoteo
Presa di Roma

Alexandre, Robert
Monastery

Alexandrov, Grigori
A Russian Jazz Comedy

Allégret, Marc
Fanny
Gribouille
Orage
Razumov

Allen, Lewis
The Uninvited

Ames, Winthrop
Snow White

Amkino
Spain in Flames

Amy, George
Kid Nightingale
She Had to Say Yes

Anderson, John Murray
The King of Jazz

Apfel, Oscar C.
Brewster's Millions
The Ghost Breaker
The Heart Bandit
The Man from Home
Ready Money
The Squaw Man
The Unafraid

Archainbaud, George
The Big Brain
Her Jungle Love
The Lost Squadron
The Silver Horde
Some Like It Hot
State's Attorney
Thanks for the Memory

Arliss, Leslie
The Man in Grey
Saints and Sinners
The Wicked Lady

Armand, Denis
Dark Rapture

Arnshtam, L.
Three Women

Arzner, Dorothy
The Bride Wore Red
Christopher Strong
Craig's Wife
Merrily We Go to Hell
Nana
Paramount on Parade
Sarah and Son
The Wild Party

Asquith, Anthony
A Cottage on Dartmoor
French Without Tears
The Lucky Number
Moscow Nights
Pygmalion
Shooting Stars
Tell England
Underground

Auer, John H.
The Crime of Dr. Crespi
S.O.S.—Tidal Wave

Avery, Charles
A Submarine Pirate

Bacon, Lloyd
Action in the North Atlantic
Boy Meets Girl
Broadway Gondolier
Brother Orchid
Cain and Mabel
Captain Eddie
Cowboy from Brooklyn

Devil Dogs of the Air
Espionage Agent
Ever Since Eve
The Famous Ferguson Case
Fifty Million Frenchmen
Fireman, Save My Child
Footlight Parade
Forty-Second Street
The Frisco Kid
Gold Diggers of 1937
Home Sweet Homicide
I Wonder Who's Kissing Her
  Now?
In Caliente
Indianapolis Speedway
Invisible Stripes
The Irish in Us
It Happens Every Spring
Knute Rockne, All American
Larceny, Inc.
Manhattan Parade
Marked Woman
Mary Stevens, M.D.
Moby Dick
Mother Is a Freshman
The Office Wife
The Oklahoma Kid
The Picture Snatcher
Racket Busters
San Quentin
The Singing Fool
A Slight Case of Murder
Submarine D-1
The Sullivans
Wings of the Navy

Badger, Clarence
Doubling for Romeo
Hands Up!
It
No, No, Nanette
A Poor Relation
She's a Sheik
Shooting of Dan McGrew

Baggot, King
Human Hearts
The Notorious Lady
Tumbleweeds

Baker, George D.
Revelation

Balcon, Michael
The Ware Case

Ballin, Hugo
Baby Mine

Balshofer, Fred J.
The Masked Rider

Banks, Monty
Smiling Along
We're Going to Be Rich

Barkas, Geoffrey
Tell England

Barker, Reginald
The Bargain
Civilization
The Coward
The Girl from Outside
The Great Divide
The Italian
The Typhoon
The Wrath of the Gods

Barnes, A.W.
White Cargo

Barrymore, Lionel
Madame X
The Rogue Song
Ten Cents a Dance

Barthelet, Arthur
Sherlock Holmes

Barton, Charles
Car 99
The Last Outpost

Baum, L. Frank
The Magic Cloak of Oz
The Patchwork Girl of Oz

Baxter, John
Love on the Dole

Beal, Frank
The Inside of the White Slave
  Traffic

Beaudine, William
Her Bodyguard
Little Annie Rooney
Make Me a Star
Penrod and Sam

Sparrows
Three Wise Girls

Beaumont, Harry
Beau Brummel
The Broadway Melody
Dance, Fools, Dance
Enchanted April
Faithless
The Floradora Girl
The Great Lover
Our Blushing Brides
Our Dancing Daughters
Should Ladies Behave?
When Ladies Meet

Becker, Jacques
Antoine et Antoinette
Goupi Mains Rouge

Beebe, Ford
Flash Gordon's Trip to Mars

Behrendt, Hans
Danton

Bell, Monta
The King on Main Street
Man, Woman, and Sin
The Snob
The Torrent
Young Man of Manhattan

Bennett, Chester
The Painted Lady

Bennett, Compton
The Seventh Veil
That Forsyte Woman

Benoit-Levy, Jean
Ballerina
Maternelle, La
Mort du Cygne, La
Youth in Revolt

Berger, Ludwig
Playboy of Paris
The Thief of Bagdad
Trois Valses
The Vagabond King

Berkeley, Busby
Babes in Arms
Dames
Fast and Furious
Footlight Parade
The Gang's All Here
Garden of the Moon
The Go-Getter
Gold Diggers of 1935
Hollywood Hotel
I Live for Love
Men Are Such Fools
She Had to Say Yes
Stage Struck
Strike Up the Band
Take Me Out to the Ball
  Game
They Made Me a Criminal

Bernard, Raymond
Miracle of the Wolves
Misérables, Les
Otages, Les

Bernhardt, Curtis
The Beloved Vagabond
Doctor and the Girl
My Reputation
Possessed
A Stolen Life

Berry, John
From This Day Forward
Miss Susie Slagle's

Berthelet, Arthur
Men Who Have Made Love to
  Me

Beyfuss, Alexander E.
Salomy Jane
Salvation Nell

Biberman, Herbert
Meet Nero Wolfe

Billon, Pierre
Courrier-Sud
Second Bureau

Binyon, Claude
Family Honeymoon
The Saxon Charm

Bischoff, Sam
The Last Mile

Blackton, J. Stuart
The Beloved Brute
The Glorious Adventure
Humorous Phases of Funny
  Faces
Womanhood, the Glory of a
  Nation

Blystone, John G.
Block-Heads
The County Chairman
Gentle Julia
Great Guy
Little Miss Nobody
The Magnificent Brute
Music for Madame
She Wanted a Millionaire
So This Is London
Swiss Miss
Tol'able David
Too Busy to Work
Woman Chases Man

Boese, Carl
The Golem

Boleslavski, Richard
Clive of India
The Garden of Allah
The Last of Mrs. Cheney
Men in White
Metropolitan

Misérables, Les
The Painted Veil
Rasputin and the Empress
Storm at Daybreak
Theodora Goes Wild

Bolvary, Geza von
Raub der Mona Lisa, Der
Zwei Herzen im 3/4 Takt

Borzage, Frank
Bad Girl
Big City
Desire
Disputed Passage
A Farewell to Arms
Flirtation Walk
Green Light
Hearts Divided
History Is Made at Night
Humoresque
Land O' Lizzards
Lazybones
Liliom
Little Man, What Now?
Living on Velvet
Magnificent Doll
Mannequin
Man's Castle
The Mortal Storm
Prudence on Broadway
The River
Secrets
Secrets
Seventh Heaven
The Shining Hour
Shipmates Forever
Smilin' Through
Song O' My Heart
Stranded
Street Angel
They Had to See Paris
Three Comrades
Young America
Young as You Feel

Bosworth, Hobart
John Barleycorn
The Sea Wolf

Brabin, Charles
The Beast of the City
The Bridge at San Luis Rey
Driven
The Great Meadow
The Mask of Fu Manchu
Sporting Blood
Washington Masquerade
While New York Sleeps

Brahm, John
The Brasher Doubloon
Broken Blossoms
Girls' School
Let Us Live
The Lodger
Penitentiary
Rio
Singapore
Wild Geese Calling

Brecher, Irving
The Life of Riley

Brenon, Herbert
Beau Geste
The Case of Sergeant Grischa
Dancing Mothers
A Daughter of the Gods
The Fall of the Romanoffs
Ivanhoe
A Kiss for Cinderella
Laugh, Clown, Laugh
Living Dangerously
Lummox
Neptune's Daughter
The Passing of the Third Floor
  Back
Peter Pan
The Spanish Dancer
12:10
War Brides
Yellow Sands

Bretherton, Howard
Ladies They Talk About

Brook, Clive
On Approval

Brower, Otto
Paramount on Parade

Brown, Clarence
Ah, Wilderness!
Anna Christie
Anna Karenina
Chained
Conquest
The Eagle
Edison, the Man
Emma
Flesh and the Devil
A Free Soul
The Goose Woman
The Gorgeous Hussy
The Human Comedy
Idiot's Delight
Inspiration
Intruder in the Dust
Letty Lynton
National Velvet
Night Flight
Of Human Hearts
Possessed
The Rains Came
Romance
Smouldering Fires
The Son-Daughter
Song of Love
They Met in Bombay
The White Cliffs of Dover
Wife Versus Secretary
A Woman of Affairs
The Yearling

Brown, Harry Joe
I Love That Man
Sitting Pretty

Brown, Karl
Stark Love

Collins, John H.
Blue Jeans

Colombier, Pierre
Roi S'Amuse, Le

Comfort, Lance
Bedelia
Old Mother Riley, Detective

Connelly, Marc
The Green Pastures

Conway, Jack
Alias Jimmy Valentine
Arsene Lupin
Boom Town
Dragon Seed
Hell Below
Honky Tonk
The Hucksters
Lady of the Tropics
Let Freedom Ring
Libeled Lady
Lombardi, Ltd.
Love Crazy
Never Give a Sucker a Break
The New Moon
Red Headed Woman
Saratoga
A Tale of Two Cities
Too Hot to Handle
The Unholy Three
The Unholy Three
Untamed
Viva Villa!
A Yank at Oxford

Cooper, Merian C.
Chang
The Four Feathers
Grass
King Kong

Cornelius, Henry
Passport to Pimlico

Corrigan, Lloyd
The Beloved Bachelor
Follow Thru
Murder on a Honeymoon
Night Key
No One Man

Costello, Maurice
Mr. Barnes of New York

Courville, Albert de
Seven Sinners

Coward, Noel
In Which We Serve

Cowen, William
Oliver Twist

Crabtree, Harold
Caravan

Crane, Frank
Thaïs

Crichton, Charles
Dead of Night

Crisp, Donald
Don Q., Son of Zorro
The Navigator

Cromwell, John
Abe Lincoln in Illinois
Algiers
Ann Vickers
Anna and the King of Siam
Banjo on My Knee
Dead Reckoning
Double Harness
The Enchanted Cottage
For the Defense
I Dream Too Much
In Name Only
Jalna
Little Lord Fauntleroy
Made for Each Other
The Mighty
Of Human Bondage
Of Human Bondage
The Prisoner of Zenda
Rich Man's Folly
The Silver Cord
Since You Went Away
So Ends Our Night
Son of Fury
Spitfire
Street of Chance
Sweepings
The Texan
To Mary—With Love
Tom Sawyer
Unfaithful
The Vice Squad
The World and the Flesh

Crosland, Alan
The Beloved Rogue
Big Boy
Don Juan
General Crack
The Jazz Singer
On with the Show
Song of the Flame
Three Weeks
Viennese Nights
Youthful Folly

Cruze, James
Beggar on Horseback
The City That Never Sleeps
The Covered Wagon
Gangs of New York
The Great Gabbo
Hollywood
I Cover the Waterfront
Mr. Skitch
Old Ironsides
Once a Gentleman
The Pony Express
Prison Nurse
Sailor Be Good
Sutter's Gold
Washington Merry-Go-Round

Cukor, George
Adam's Rib
A Bill of Divorcement
Camille
David Copperfield
Dinner at Eight
A Double Life
Gaslight
Girls About Town
Holiday
Keeper of the Flame
Little Women
Our Betters
The Philadelphia Story
Rockabye
Romeo and Juliet
The Royal Family of
   Broadway
Susan and God
Sylvia Scarlett
Tarnished Lady
Two-Faced Woman
What Price Hollywood?
The Women
Zaza

Cummings, Irving
Belle Starr
Cameo Kirby
The Cisco Kid
Curly Top
The Dolly Sisters
Down Argentine Way
Everything Happens at Night
Flesh and Blood
Girls' Dormitory
Hollywood Cavalcade
In Old Arizona
Just Around the Corner
Lillian Russell
Little Miss Broadway
Louisiana Purchase
The Mad Game
Merry-Go-Round of 1938
My Gal Sal
The Poor Little Rich Girl
The Story of Alexander
   Graham Bell
Vogues of 1938
The White Parade

Curtiz, Michael
The Adventures of Robin
   Hood
Alias the Doctor
Angels With Dirty Faces
Black Fury
Bright Lights
British Agent
Cabin in the Cotton
Captain Blood
Captains of the Clouds
Casablanca
The Case of the Curious Bride
The Charge of the Light
   Brigade
Daughters Courageous
Dive Bomber
Doctor X
Dodge City
Female
Flamingo Road
Four Daughters

Four Wives
Four's a Crowd
Front Page Woman
The Gamblers
Gold Is Where You Find It
Good Time Charlie
Goodbye Again
The Kennel Murder Case
The Keyhole
Kid Galahad
Life With Father
The Mad Genius
Mammy
Mildred Pierce
Mission to Moscow
Mystery of the Wax Museum
Night and Day
Noah's Ark
Passage to Marseilles
The Perfect Specimen
Private Detective 62
The Private Lives of Elizabeth
   and Essex
Romance on the High Seas
Roughly Speaking
Santa Fe Trail
The Sea Hawk
The Sea Wolf
Stolen Holiday
The Third Degree
This Is the Army
Twenty Thousand Years in
   Sing Sing
Under a Texas Moon
The Unsuspected
The Walking Dead
The Woman from Monte
   Carlo
Yankee Doodle Dandy

Cutts, Graham
The Rat
The Sign of the Four

Czinner, Paul
As You Like It
Dreaming Lips
Escape Me Never
A Stolen Life
Traumende Mund, Der

Dali, Salvador
Chien Andalou, Un

Dalrymple, Ian
Storm in a Teacup

Dalsheim, Friedrich
The Wedding of Palo

Daly, William Robert
Uncle Tom's Cabin

Daroy, Jacques
Generals Without Buttons

D'Arrast, Harry
Topaze

D'Arrast, Harry D'Abbabie
Raffles

Heidi
High Tension
Hollywood Party
Human Cargo
An Innocent Magdalene
Josette
Manhandled
A Modern Muskateer
Panthea
The Poisoned Flume
The Pretty Sister of Jose
Rebecca of Sunnybrook Farm
Robin Hood
Sands of Iwo Jima
Soldiers of Fortune
Suez
That I May Live
The Three Musketeers
Wildflower
Zaza

Dyott, G.M.
Savage Gold

Dzigan, Yefim
We From Kronstadt

Earle, William P.S.
Whispers
Whom the Gods Destroy
Womanhood, the Glory of a
    Nation

Eastman, Max
Tsar to Lenin

Edwards, Harry
Tramp, Tramp, Tramp

Edwards, Henry
The Man Who Changed His
    Name

Edwards, J. Gordon
Cleopatra
Du Barry
Her Double Life
The Queen of Sheba
Romeo and Juliet

Edwards, Walter
Mrs. Leffingwell's Boots
A Pair of Silk Stockings

Eggert, Konstantin
Gobsek

Eisenstein, Sergei
Alexander Nevsky
Battleship Potemkin
Bezhin Meadow
October
The Old and the New
Romance Sentimentale
Strike
Thunder Over Mexico

Ekk, Nikolai
Nightingale
The Road to Life

Elliott, Clyde
Bring 'Em Back Alive

Eltinge, Julian
The Countess Charming

Elvey, Maurice
The Clairvoyant
The Lodger
Sally in Our Alley
Transatlantic Tunnel
The Wandering Jew

Emerson, John
His Picture in the Papers
Macbeth
The Social Secretary
Wild and Woolly

Engel, Erich
The Affair Blum

Enright, Ray
Angels Wash Their Faces
Back in Circulation
China Clipper
Dames
Earthworm Tractors
Going Places
Gold Diggers in Paris
Gung Ho
Hard to Get
On Your Toes
Play Girl
Ready, Willing and Able
The Silk Express
The Spoilers
Swing Your Lady
Tracked by the Police
The Wagons Roll at Night
We're in the Money

Epstein, Jean
Auberge Rouge, L'
Belle Nivernaise, La
Coeur Fidele
Fall of the House of Usher

Epstein, Marie
Maternelle, La

Ermler, Friedrich
Counterplan
A Great Citizen
Peasants

Erskine, Chester
The Egg and I
Frankie and Johnny

Fanck, Arnold
Avalanche
The White Flame

Farnum, Marshall
Wormwood

Farrow, John
Alias Nick Beal
The Big Clock

California
China
Five Came Back
Full Confession
My Bill
Red, Hot and Blue
Reno
Sorority House
Two Years Before the Mast
Wake Island
Women in the Wind

Feher, Friedrich
The Robber Symphony

Fejos, Paul
Lonesome

Fenton, Leslie
Saigon
Tell No Tales

Fenton, Louis
Whispering Smith

Ferguson, Norman
The Three Caballeros

Fernandez, Emilio
The Pearl

Feyder, Jacques
Atlantide, L'
Carnival in Flanders
Crainquebille
Daybreak
Gens du Voyage, Les
Grand Jeu, Le
The Kiss
Knight Without Armor
Pension Mimosas
Visages D'Enfants

Figman, Max
The Hoosier Schoolmaster

Film Historians, Inc.
Spain in Flames

Fitzmaurice, George
Arsene Lupin Returns
As You Desire Me
The Avalanche
Bella Donna
Cytherea
Dark Angel
The Devil to Pay
The Emperor's Candlesticks
Forever
Lilac Time
Live, Love and Learn
Mata Hari
One Heavenly Night
Petticoat Fever
The Son of the Sheik
Strangers May Kiss
Suzy
The Unholy Garden

Flaherty, Robert
Elephant Boy
Louisiana Story
Man of Aran
Moana
Nanook of the North
Tabu
White Shadows in the South
    Seas

Fleischer, Dave
Gulliver's Travels

Fleischer, Rich
So This is New York

Fleming, Caryl S.
Beating Back

Fleming, Victor
Abie's Irish Rose
Adventure
Bombshell
Captains Courageous
Common Clay
Dr. Jekyll and Mr. Hyde
The Farmer Takes a Wife
Gone With the Wind
A Guy Named Joe
Mantrap
Reckless
Red Dust
Rough Riders
Test Pilot
Tortilla Flat
Treasure Island
The Virginian
The Way of All Flesh
The Wet Parade
When the Clouds Roll By
The White Sister
The Wizard of Oz
Woman's Place

Flood, James
Everybody's Old Man
Life Begins
Midnight Madness
The Mouthpiece
Off the Record
Scotland Yard Commands
Shanghai
Wings in the Dark

Florey, Robert
Bedside
The Cocoanuts
Disbarred
Ex-Lady
The Florentine Dagger
God Is My Co-Pilot
Hollywood Boulevard
Hotel Imperial
The House on 56th Street
King of Alcatraz
King of Gamblers
The Magnificent Fraud
Murders in the Rue Morgue
The Woman in Red

Flynn, Emmett J.
A Connecticut Yankee in King
  Arthur's Court

Ford, Eugene
Inspector Hornleigh

Ford, Francis
The Campbells Are Coming

Ford, Hugh
Bella Donna
The Eternal City
Seven Keys to Baldpate
Such a Little Queen
Zaza

Ford, John
Air Mail
Arrowsmith
The Black Watch
Born Reckless
The Brat
Cameo Kirby
Drums Along the Mohawk
Flesh
Fort Apache
Four Men and a Prayer
Four Sons
Four Sons
The Fugitive
The Grapes of Wrath
How Green Was My Valley
The Hurricane
The Informer
The Iron Horse
Judge Priest
Just Pals
The Long Voyage Home
The Lost Patrol
A Marked Man
Marked Men
Mary of Scotland
Men Without Women
My Darling Clementine
The Outcasts of Poker Flat
Pilgrimage
The Plough and the Stars
The Prisoner of Shark Island
Seas Beneath
She Wore a Yellow Ribbon
Stagecoach
Steamboat 'Round the Bend
Straight Shooting
Strong Boy
Submarine Patrol
They Were Expendable
Three Bad Men
Three Godfathers
Tobacco Road
Wee Willie Winkie
The Whole Town's Talking
Young Mr. Lincoln

Forde, Eugene
The Lady Escapes
Your Uncle Dudley

Forde, Walter
King of the Damned
Rome Express

Forman, Tom
Shadows

Forst, Willi
Mazurka

**Fosco, Piero (Pastrone,
Giovanni)**
Cabiria

Foster, Lewis R.
Manhandled

Foster, Norman
Charlie Chan in Panama
Journey Into Fear
Look Out, Mr. Moto
Mr. Moto Takes a Vacation
Rachel and the Stranger
Thank You, Mr. Moto
Think Fast, Mr. Moto
Walking Down Broadway

Fox, Wallace
Yellow Dust

Foy, Bryan
The Home Towners
The Lights of New York

Franck, Arnold
The White Hell of Pitz Palu

Franklin, Carl
Gretchen, the Greenhorn
Let Katy Do It

Franklin, Chester M.
Sequoia
The Toll of the Sea

Franklin, Sidney
The Actress
The Barretts of Wimpole
  Street
The Dark Angel
Devil May Care
Dulcy
The Forbidden City
The Good Earth
Gretchen, the Greenhorn
The Guardsman
Her Sister from Paris
A Lady of Scandal
The Last of Mrs. Cheyney
Let Katy Do It
Private Lives
Quality Street
Reunion in Vienna
Smilin' Through
Two Weeks
Wild Orchids

Fraser, Harry
Dark Manhattan

Freeland, Thornton
Accused
The Amateur Gentleman
Be Yourself

Brewster's Millions
Flying Down to Rio
Jericho
Love Affair
Whoopee!

Freund, Karl
Mad Love
Madame Spy
The Mummy

Fric, Marc
Janosik

Friedlander, Louis
The Raven

Fristch, Gunther von
Curse of the Cat People

Froelich, Carl
Luise, Konigin von Preussen

Gable, Martin
The Lost Moment

Gaillord, Robert
Mr. Barnes of New York

Gallone, Carmine
My Heart Is Calling You
Scipio Africanus

Gance, Abel
Grande Amour de Beethoven,
  Une
J'Accuse
Louise
Lucrezia Borgia
Napoleon
Roue, La
That They May Live

Gandera, Felix
Double Crime sur la Ligne
  Maginot

Gardner, Cyril
Perfect Understanding
The Royal Family of
  Broadway

Garmes, Lee
Angels Over Broadway

Garnett, Tay
Bad Company
Bataan
Cheers for Miss Bishop
China Seas
A Connecticut Yankee in King
  Arthur's Court
The Cross of Lorraine
Destination Unknown
Eternally Yours
The Joy of Living
Love Is News
Okay America
One Way Passage

The Postman Always Rings
  Twice
Prestige
Professional Soldier
Slave Ship
S.O.S Iceberg
Stand-In
Trade Winds

Gaskill, Charles
The Breath of Araby

Gasnier, Louis
Gambling Ship
Slightly Scarlet

Gasnier, Louis J.
Kismet

Gavronsky, M.
Beethoven Concerto

Genina, Augusto
Squadrone Bianco, Lo

Gering, Marion
The Devil and the Deep
Jennie Gerhardt
Ladies of the Big House
Madame Butterfly
Pick Up
Rose of the Rancho
Rumba
Thunder in the City

Gibbons, Cedric
Tarzan and His Mate

Gilliat, Sidney
The Notorious Gentleman

Gilliatt, Sidney
Dulcimer Street

Gilmore, Stuart
The Virginian

Gish, Lillian
Remodeling Her Husband

Goddard, Charles L.
The Exploits of Elaine

Godfrey, Peter
The Girl from Jones Beach
That Hagen Girl
The Two Mrs. Carrolls
The Woman in White

Goldblatt, M.
Gypsies

Goodman, Daniel Carson
Week End Husbands

Goodman, Edward
Women Love Once

Jacoby, Georg
Tales from the Vienna Woods

Jacque, Christian
Pearls of the Crown

Jason, Leigh
The Bride Walks Out
The Flying Irishman
The Mad Miss Manton
That Girl from Paris

Jessner, Leopold
Backstairs

Jones, Edgar
Dimples

Jones, F. Richard
Bulldog Drummond
Extra Girl
The Gaucho
Mickey

José, Edward
Fires of Faith
My Cousin
Poppy
Resurrection

Julian, Rupert
The Kaiser, the Beast of Berlin
The Phantom of the Opera
Three Faces East

Kane, Joseph
Billy the Kid Returns
The Man from Music
   Mountain
Springtime in the Rockies
Under Western Stars

Kanin, Garson
Bachelor Mother
The Great Man Votes
A Man to Remember
My Favorite Wife
Next Time I Marry
They Knew What They
   Wanted
Tom, Dick, and Harry

Kaufmann, George S.
The Senator Was Indiscreet

Kazan, Elia
Boomerang
Gentleman's Agreement
Pinky
The Sea of Grass
A Tree Grows in Brooklyn

Keaton, Buster
Battling Butler
The General
Go West
The Navigator
One Week
Our Hospitality

Seven Chances
Sherlock Jr.

Keene, James
Richard III

Keighley, William
Babbitt
The Bride Came C.O.D.
Brother Rat
Bullets or Ballots
Each Dawn I Die
The Fighting Sixty-Ninth
G Men
George Washington Slept Here
God's Country and the
   Woman
The Green Pastures
Ladies They Talk About
The Man Who Came to
   Dinner
The Prince and the Pauper
The Right to Live
Secrets of an Actress
The Singing Kid
Special Agent
Valley of the Giants
Varsity Show
Yes, My Darling Daughter

Kellino, Roy
I Met a Murderer

Kelly, Gene
On the Town

Kent, Charles
The Life of Moses

Kenton, Erle C.
The Devil's Playground
Island of Lost Souls

Kenyon, Jack
The Last Stand of the Dalton
   Boys

Killy, Edward
Saturday's Heroes
Seven Keys to Baldpate

King, Henry
Alexander's Ragtime Band
A Bell for Adano
The Black Swan
The Captain from Castile
Chad Hanna
The Country Doctor
I Loved You Wednesday
In Old Chicago
Jesse James
Lightnin'
Lloyds of London
Margie
Merely Mary Ann
One Hour Before Dawn
One More Spring
The Prince of Foxes
Ramona
Romola
Seventh Heaven

The Song of Bernadette
Stanley and Livingstone
State Fair
Stella Dallas
Tol'able David
Twelve O'Clock High
Twenty-Three and a Half
   Hours' Leave
Way Down East
The White Sister
Wilson
The Winning of Barbara
   Worth
A Yank in the R.A.F.

King, Louis
Bulldog Drummond Comes
   Back
Bulldog Drummond's Revenge
Charlie Chan in Egypt
Mrs. Mike
Persons in Hiding
Smoky
Tom Sawyer, Detective

Kirkland, David
A Virtuous Vamp

Kirkwood, James
Cinderella
The Dawn of a Tomorrow
A Dream or Two Ago

Knopf, Edwin H.
Paramount on Parade
Slightly Scarlet

Kolker, Henry
Disraeli

Korda, Alexander
Catherine the Great
Lilies of the Field
Marius
The Private Life of Don Juan
The Private Life of Helen of
   Troy
The Private Life of Henry
   VIII
Rembrandt
Reserved for Ladies
That Hamilton Woman
Vacation from Marriage

Korda, Zoltan
Drums
Elephant Boy
Four Feathers
Jungle Book
The Macomber Affair
Sahara
Sanders of the River
A Woman's Vengence

Koster, Henry
The Bishop's Wife
First Love
Inspector General
One Hundred Men and a Girl
The Rage of Paris

Three Smart Girls
Three Smart Girls Grow Up

Kozintsev, Gregori
The Return of Maxim

Kozintsev, Grigori
The New Babylon
The Youth of Maxim

Kraemer, F.W.
The Dreyfus Case

Krasna, Norman
Princess O'Rourke

La Cava, Gregory
The Age of Consent
Bed of Roses
Fifth Avenue Girl
Gabriel Over the White House
Gallant Lady
The Half-Naked Truth
My Man Godfrey
The Primrose Path
Private Worlds
She Married Her Boss
Smart Woman
So's Your Old Man
Stage Door
What Every Woman Knows

Lachman, Harry
Aren't We All?
Dante's Inferno
The Devil Is Driving
The Man Who Lived Twice
Our Relations
The Outsider

Lamont, Charles
Ma and Pa Kettle

Lamprecht, Gerhard
Emil and the Detectives

Land, Robert
I Kiss Your Hand, Madame

Landers, Lew
Pacific Liner
Twelve Crowded Hours

Lanfield, Sidney
Always Goodbye
Hold 'Em Yale
The Hound of the Baskervilles
Hush Money
King of Burlesque
Let's Face It
Moulin Rouge
My Favorite Blonde
One in a Million
Red Salute
Second Fiddle
Sing, Baby, Sing
Sorrowful Jones
Swanee River
Thin Ice
Wake Up and Live

I Cover the War
The Phantom of the Opera

Lubitsch, Ernst
Angel
Anne Boleyn
Bluebeard's Eighth Wife
Cluny Brown
Design for Living
Eternal Love
Flamme, Die
Forbidden Paradise
Heaven Can Wait
If I Had a Million
Kiss Me Again
Lady Windermere's Fan
The Love Parade
Madame Dubarry
The Man I Killed
The Marriage Circle
The Merry Widow
Monte Carlo
Ninotchka
One Hour With You
Paramount on Parade
The Patriot
Rosita
The Shop Around the Corner
The Smiling Lieutenant
So This Is Paris
The Student Prince
That Lady in Ermine
That Uncertain Feeling
Three Women
To Be or Not to Be
Trouble in Paradise

Ludwig, Edward
Adventure in Manhattan
The Fighting Seabees
The Last Gangster
The Man Who Reclaimed His
   Head
Swiss Family Robinson
That Certain Age

Lumiere, Louis
Arroseur Arrose, L'
Lumiere First Program
Sortie des Ouvriers de l'Usine
   Lumiere

Lund, O.A.C.
The Dollar Mark

Luske, Hamilton
Pinocchio

Lynwood, Burt
Shadows of the Orient

MacArthur, Charles
Crime Without Passion
The Scoundrel
Soak the Rich

MacDonald, David
The Brothers
Christopher Columbus
This Man in Paris
This Man Is News

MacDonald, J. Farrell
The Patchwork Girl of Oz

MacFadden, Hamilton
Charlie Chan Carries On

Machaty, Gustav
Ecstasy

MacKendrick, Alexander
Tight Little Island

MacKenna, Kenneth
The Spider

Maggi, Luigi
The Last Days of Pompeii

Mamoulian, Rouben
Applause
Becky Sharp
Blood and Sand
City Streets
Dr. Jekyll and Mr. Hyde
The Gay Desperado
Golden Boy
High, Wide and Handsome
Love Me Tonight
The Mark of Zorro
Queen Christina
The Song of Songs
We Live Again

Mankiewicz, Joseph L.
Dragonwyck
The Ghost and Mrs. Muir
House of Strangers
The Late George Apley
A Letter to Three Wives
Somewhere in the Night

Mann, Anthony
The Great Flamarion
Reign of Terror

Marcin, Max
Gambling Ship
King of the Jungle

Marin, Edwin L.
Abilene Town
A Christmas Carol
Everybody Sing
Fast and Loose
Hold That Kiss
I'd Give My Life
Listen, Darling
Maisie
Married Before Breakfast
A Study in Scarlet
The Sweetheart of Sigma Chi
The Sworn Enemy

Marischka, Hubert
Liebe im 3/4 Takt

Marshall, George
Battle of Broadway
The Blue Dahlia
The Crime of Dr. Forbes

Destry Rides Again
The Goldwyn Follies
Hold That Co-ed
In Old Kentucky
Incendiary Blonde
Life Begins at Forty
Love's Lariat
A Message to Garcia
Monsieur Beaucaire
Music Is Magic
Nancy Steele Is Missing
The Perils of Pauline
Star Spangled Rhythm
Variety Girl
When the Daltons Rode
You Can't Cheat an Honest
   Man

Marston, Theodore
Mortmain

Martin, E.A.
The Heart of Texas Ryan

Martin, Francis
Tillie and Gus

Marton, Andrew
School for Husbands

Mason, Herbert
His Lordship

Mate, Rudolph
D.O.A.

May, Joe
Paris-Mediterranée

Mayo, Archie
The Adventures of Marco Polo
Angel on My Shoulder
The Black Legion
Bordertown
Bought
Call It a Day
The Case of the Lucky Legs
Charley's Aunt
Crash Dive
Ever in My Heart
Give Me Your Heart
Go Into Your Dance
I Married a Doctor
Illicit
It's Love I'm After
The Life of Jimmy Dolan
The Mayor of Hell
Moontide
My Man
Night After Night
A Night in Casablanca
On Trial
The Petrified Forest
Street of Women
Svengali
They Shall Have Music
Two Against the World
Under Eighteen
Youth Takes a Fling

McCarey, Leo
The Awful Truth
Belle of the Nineties
The Bells of St. Mary's
Duck Soup
Going My Way
Indiscreet
The Kid from Spain
Let's Go Native
Love Affair
Make Way for Tomorrow
Mighty Like a Moose
The Milky Way
Once Upon a Honeymoon
Ruggles of Red Gap

McCarey, Ray
Let's Make a Million

McCay, Winsor Z.
The Sinking of the Lusitania

McDonald, Frank
Bulldog Drummond Strikes
   Back
Freshman Year
Isle of Fury

McGann, William
Alcatraz Island
Man of Iron
Penrod and Sam
Two Against the World
When Were You Born?

McGowan, Robert F.
Too Many Parents

McKenna, Kenneth
Always Good-Bye

McLeod, Norman Z.
Alice in Wonderland
Early to Bed
Finn and Hattie
Horse Feathers
It's a Gift
The Kid from Brooklyn
Lady Be Good
Merrily We Live
The Miracle Man
Monkey Business
The Paleface
Pennies from Heaven
Remember?
The Secret Life of Walter
   Mitty
There Goes My Heart
Topper
Topper Takes a Trip
Touchdown

Meins, Gus
Babes in Toyland
The Hit Parade

Melford, George
East of Borneo
Pettigrew's Girl
The Sea Wolf
The Sheik

Ophuls, Max
Caught
The Exile
Liebelei
The Reckless Moment
Tendre Ennemie, Le
Yoshiwara

Oswald, Richard
Hauptmann von Koepenick,
  Der
The Living Dead

Ozep, Fedor
Betrayal
Karamazov

Pabst, G.W.
Atlantide, L'
The Diary of a Lost Girl
Don Quixote
Drame de Shanghai, Le
The Joyless Street
Kameradschaft
The Love of Jeanne Ney
Mademoiselle Docteur
A Modern Hero
Pandora's Box
Secrets of a Soul
The Three Penny Opera
Westfront 1918
The White Hell of Pitz Palu

Pagnol, Marcel
César
Femme du Boulanger, La
Harvest
Heartbeat
Merlusse
The Well-Digger's Daughter

Parker, Albert
Arizona
The Black Pirate
Eyes of Youth
Sherlock Holmes

Pascal, Gabriel
Caesar and Cleopatra
Major Barbara

Pastrone, Giovanni
The Fall of Troy

Paton, Stuart
Elusive Isabel

Pearce, Perce
Bambi

Pearson, George
The Better 'Ole

Perret, Léonce
Lest We Forget
Madame Sans Gene

Petrov, Vladimir M.
Peter the First

Petrov-Bytov, P.P.
Cain and Artem
Pugachev

Physioc, Wray
The Gulf Between

Pichel, Irving
The Bride Wore Boots
Hudson's Bay
The Man I Married
The Moon Is Down
O.S.S.
The Pied Piper
She
The Sheik Steps Out
Tomorrow Is Forever

Pick, Lupu
New Year's Eve
Shattered

Pierson, Arthur
The Fighting O'Flynn

Piriev, Ivan
Anna
The Country Bride

Platt, George Foster
Deliverance

Ploquin, Raoul
Avocate d'Amour

Poh, Richard
Sable Cicada

Pollard, Harry
Fast Life
Show Boat

Polonsky, Abraham
Force of Evil

Pommer, Erich
The Beachcomber
F.P.1 Antwortet Nicht

Popkin, Leo C.
Reform School

Porter, Edwin S.
Bella Donna
The Count of Monte Cristo
The Dream of a Rarebit Fiend
The Eternal City
The Ex-Convict
The Gay Shoe Clerk
A Good Little Devil
The Great Train Robbery
Hearts Adrift
In the Bishop's Carriage
The Kleptomaniac
The Life of an American
  Fireman
Life of an American
  Policeman
Personal
The Prisoner of Zenda

Rescued from an Eagle's Nest
Sherlock Holmes Jr.
Such a Little Queen
Tess of the Storm Country
Zaza

Potter, H.C.
Beloved Enemy
Blackmail
The Cowboy and the Lady
The Farmer's Daughter
Hellzapoppin'
Mr. Lucky
Romance in the Dark
The Shopworn Angel
The Story of Vernon and Irene
  Castle
The Time of Your Life

Powell, Frank
All on Account of the Milk
A Fool There Was

Powell, Michael
Black Narcissus
Colonel Blimp
The Edge of the World
49th Parallel
I Know Where I'm Going
The Lion Has Wings
One of Our Aircraft Is Missing
The Red Shoes
Stairway to Heaven
The Thief of Bagdad
U-Boat 29

Powell, Paul
Pollyanna

Pratt, John H.
The Jungle

Preminger, Otto
Centennial Summer
Daisy Kenyon
Danger—Love At Work
The Fan
Forever Amber
Grosse Liebe, Die
Laura
That Lady in Ermine

Preobrazhenskaya, Olga
Grain

Pressburger, Emeric
Black Narcissus
Colonel Blimp
I Know Where I'm Going
One of Our Aircraft Is Missing
The Red Shoes
Stairway to Heaven

Ptushko, Alexander
A New Gulliver

Pudovkin, Vsevolod
Deserter
The End of St. Petersburg
Mother
Storm Over Asia

Raizman, Yuli
The Soil Is Thirsty

Raizsman, Yuli
The Last Night

Rapper, Irving
The Adventures of Mark
  Twain
The Corn Is Green
Deception
Now, Voyager
One Foot in Heaven
Rhapsody in Blue
The Voice of the Turtle

Rappoport, Herbert
Professor Mamlock

Rasmussen, Knud
The Wedding of Palo

Ratoff, Gregory
Adam Had Four Sons
Barricade
Black Magic
The Corsican Brothers
Day-Time Wife
Hotel for Women
Intermezzo, a Love Story
Lancer Spy
Rose of Washington Square
Wife, Husband and Friend

Rawlins, John
Arabian Nights

Ray, Albert
A Shriek in the Night

Ray, Nicholas
Knock on Any Door
They Live by Night

Raymond, Jack
The Rat
A Royal Divorce

Reed, Carol
Bank Holiday
The Fallen Idol
A Girl Must Live
Laburnum Grove
Night Train
Odd Man Out
The Stars Look Down
Talk of the Devil
The Third Man

Reed, Luther
Hit the Deck
Rio Rita

Reed, Roland
Men Make Steel

Reed, Theodore
Double or Nothing
Tropic Holiday

Redskin
The Road to Singapore
Road to Zanzibar
Safety in Numbers
The Sheriff's Son
The Slim Princess
Something to Sing About
The Woman Between

Schmidthof, V.
Beethoven Concerto

Schneider, Evgeni
Gypsies

Schoedsack, Ernest B.
Chang
Dr. Cyclops
The Four Feathers
King Kong
The Last Days of Pompeii
Mighty Joe Young
The Most Dangerous Game

Schunzel, Reinhold
Amphitryon
Balalaika
The Ice Follies of 1939
Rich Man, Poor Girl
Viktor und Viktoria

Schuster, Harold
Dinner at the Ritz
So Dear to My Heart
Wings of the Morning

Schwab, Laurence
Follow Thru

Scott, Sherman
Beasts of Berlin

Scott, Sidney
Charlie's Aunt

Seaton, George
Apartment for Peggy
Chicken Every Sunday
Miracle on 34th Street
The Shocking Miss Pilgrim

Sedgwick, Edward
The Cameraman
Dough Boys
Free and Easy
Hook and Ladder
Parlor, Bedroom and Bath
The Passionate Plumber
Pick a Star
Saturday's Millions
A Southern Yankee
Speak Easily
Spite Marriage
What! No Beer?

Seigel, Don
The Verdict

Seiler, Lewis
Career Woman
Charlie Chan in Paris
Crime School
Dust Be My Destiny
Frontier Marshall
The Great K and A Train
    Robbery
Guadalcanal Diary
King of the Underworld
Star for a Night
You Can't Get Away With
    Murder

Seiter, William
You Were Never Lovelier

Seiter, William A.
Allegheny Uprising
The Case Against Mrs. Ames
A Chance at Heaven
Dimples
Diplomaniacs
Girl Crazy
Going Wild
Hot Saturday
If You Could Only Cook
In Person
Life Begins in College
The Moon's Our Home
One Touch of Venus
Orchids to You
Professional Sweetheart
The Richest Girl in the World
Roberta
Room Service
Sally, Irene and Mary
Sons of the Desert
Stowaway
Sunny
Susannah of the Mounties
Thanks for Everything
This Is My Affair
Three Blind Mice

Seitz, George B.
Between Two Women
The Docks of San Francisco
Exclusive Story
A Family Affair
The Hardys Ride High
Judge Hardy and Son
The Last of the Mohicans
Life Begins for Andy Hardy
Love Finds Andy Hardy
Out West With the Hardys
Six Thousand Enemies
The Thirteenth Chair
The Three Wise Guys
Thunder Afloat
The Vanishing American
Yellow Jack

Selwyn, Edgar
The Mystery of Mr. X
The Sin of Madelon Claudet
Skyscraper Souls

Sennett, Mack
Hypnotized
I Surrender Dear

Mabel at the Wheel
Tillie's Punctured Romance

Seton, Marie
Time in the Sun

Shane, Maxwell
City Across the River

Sharpsteen, Ben
Dumbo

Sharpstein, Ben
Pinocchio

Shaw, Harold
The Fool's Awakening

Sherman, George
The Bandit of Sherwood
    Forest
Calamity Jane and Sam Bass

Sherman, Lowell
Bachelor Apartment
Broadway Thru a Keyhole
False Faces
The Greeks Had a Word for
    Them
High Stakes
Morning Glory
Night Life of the Gods
The Royal Bed
She Done Him Wrong

Sherman, Vincent
Across the Pacific
The Adventures of Don Juan
The Hard Way
The Hasty Heart
Mr. Skeffington
Nora Prentiss
Old Acquaintance
The Return of Doctor X
Saturday's Children

Shumlin, Herman
Confidential Agent
Watch on the Rhine

Sidney, George
Anchors Aweigh
Bathing Beauty
Cass Timberlaine
The Harvey Girls
The Red Danube

Sidney, Scott
Tarzan of the Apes

Siegal, Don
The Big Steal

Siegmann, George
Spirit of '76

Simon, S. Sylvan
Four Girls in White
The Road to Reno

Spring Madness
These Glamour Girls

Sinclair, Robert
Dramatic School

Sinclair, Robert B.
Joe and Ethel Turp Call on
    the President

Siodmak, Richard
Cry of the City

Siodmak, Robert
Cobra Woman
Criss Cross
The Dark Mirror
The Killers
Mr. Flow
The Spiral Staircase
Tempest

Siodmark, Robert
The Great Sinner

Sirk, Douglas
Hitler's Madman
Sleep My Love
Slightly French
Thieves Holiday

Sjostrom, Victor
The Divine Woman
The Girl from the Marsh
    Croft
He Who Gets Slapped
A Lady to Love
A Man There Was
The Scarlet Letter
Sir Arne's Treasure
Under the Red Robe
The Wind

Sloane, Paul
Down to Their Last Yacht
Here Comes the Band
The Woman Accused

Sloman, Edward
Alias the Deacon
Caught
His People
His Woman
The Lost Zeppelin
Murder by the Clock
Puttin' on the Ritz
Surrender
There's Always Tomorrow
The Westerners

Smalley, Phillips
The Dumb Girl of Portici
The Flirt
Where Are My Children?

Smallwood, Roy C.
Camille

Smiley, Joseph
The Battle of Shiloh

Smiley, Joseph W.
Threads of Destiny

Smith, David
Black Beauty
Captain Blood

Smith, G.A.
Grandma's Reading Glass
Mary Jane's Mishap

Smith, Noel
Secret Service of the Air

Somnes, George
The Torch Singer

Soyuzfilmnews
Abyssinia

Springsteen, R.G.
The Red Menace

Stahl, John M.
Back Street
The Eve of St. Mark
Father Was a Fullback
The Foxes of Harrow
Her Code of Honor
Holy Matrimony
Imitation of Life
The Keys of the Kingdom
A Lady Surrenders
Leave Her to Heaven
A Letter of Introduction
Magnificent Obsession
Memory Lane
Only Yesterday
Parnell
Seed
Strictly Dishonorable
When Tomorrow Comes

St. Clair, Malcolm
Are Parents People?
Born Reckless
Crack-Up
Dangerous Nan McGrew
Dangerously Yours
Gentlemen Prefer Blondes
The Grand Duchess and the
    Waiter
Montana Moon
Quick Millions
Safety in Numbers
Time Out for Romance
A Woman of the World

Steger, Julius
Cecilia of the Pink Roses

Stein, Paul
The Common Law
Her Private Affair
One Romantic Night
Sin Takes a Holiday

Stein, Paul L.
Mimi
A Woman Commands

Stephani, Frederick
Flash Gordon

Sternberg, Josef von
An American Tragedy
Blonde Venus
The Blue Angel
The Case of Lena Smith
Crime and Punishment
The Devil Is a Woman
Dishonored
The Docks of New York
The King Steps Out
The Last Command
Morocco
The Salvation Hunters
The Scarlet Empress
Sergeant Madden
Shanghai Express
The Shanghai Gesture
Thunderbolt
Underworld

Stevens, George
Alice Adams
Annie Oakley
The Cohens and Kellys in
    Trouble
A Damsel in Distress
Gunga Din
Kentucky Kernals
Laddie
The More the Merrier
Penny Serenade
Quality Street
Swing Time
Talk of the Town
Vivacious Lady
Woman of the Year

Stevenson, Robert
Back Street
Forever and a Day
Jane Eyre
King Solomon's Mines
Nine Days a Queen
To the Victor
Tom Brown's School Days
The Woman on Pier 13

Stiller, Mauritz
The Atonement of Gösta
    Berling
Hotel Imperial
Sir Arne's Treasure
The Temptress
Woman on Trial

Stoloff, Benjamin
The Affairs of Annabel
The Devil Is Driving
Goldie
Happy Days
Sea Devils
Super-Sleuth

Stone, Andrew L.
The Girl Said No
The Great Victor Herbert
Say It in French
Stolen Heaven

Storm, Jerome
Bill Henry
The Busher
The Egg Crate Wallop

Strayer, Frank R.
Blondie
Blondie on a Budget
Dance, Girl, Dance

Stroheim, Erich von
Blind Husbands
The Devil's Pass-Key
Foolish Wives
Greed
The Merry Widow
Merry-Go-Round
Queen Kelly
The Wedding March

Stroyeva, Vera
Revolutionists

Sturges, Preston
The Beautiful Blonde From
    Bashful Bend
Christmas in July
The Great McGinty
The Great Moment
Hail the Conquering Hero
The Lady Eve
The Miracle of Morgan's
    Creek
The Palm Beach Story
The Sin of Harold Diddlebock
Sullivan's Travels
Unfaithfully Yours

Sutherland, Edward
Champagne Waltz
Diamond Jim
Dixie
Every Day's a Holiday
Fireman Save My Child
The Flying Deuces
Follow the Boys
The Gang Buster
International House
June Moon
Mississippi
Mr. Robinson Crusoe
Murders in the Zoo
Palmy Days
Paramount on Parade
Poppy
Sky Devils
The Social Lion
Too Much Harmony

Swickard, Charles
Hell's Hinges

Taggart, Errol
Women Men Marry

Tarich, Yuri
Wings of a Serf

Taurog, Norman
The Adventures of Tom
    Sawyer
A Bedtime Story
The Big Broadcast of 1936
Big City
Boys Town
The Bride Goes Wild
Broadway Melody of 1940
College Rhythm
Fifty Roads to Town
Finn and Hattie
Girl Crazy
Huckleberry Finn
Lucky Night
Mad About Music
Mrs. Wiggs of the Cabbage
    Patch
The Phantom President
Presenting Lily Mars
Reunion
Rhythm on the Range
Skippy
Strike Me Pink
The Way to Love
Words and Music
You Can't Have Everything
Young Tom Edison

Taylor, Sam
Coquette
Devil's Lottery
Exit Smiling
For Heaven's Sake
The Freshman
Girl Shy
Hot Water
Kiki
My Best Girl
The Taming of the Shrew
Tempest
Why Worry?

Taylor, William Desmond
Anne of Green Gables
The Diamond From the Sky
He Fell in Love with His Wife
His Majesty, Bunker Bean
Huckleberry Finn
Johanna Enlists
Tom Sawyer

Tennyson, Pen
Convoy

Tetzlaff, Ted
Fighting Father Dunne
Window

Thiele, William
Drei von der Tankstelle, Die
The Jungle Princess
London by Night
Waltz Time

Thomas, Augustus
The Jungle

Thomson, Frederick
The Christian
The Goose Girl
Nearly a King

Wallace, Richard
Adventure in Baltimore
Blossoms on Broadway
Innocents of Paris
It's in the Bag
John Meade's Woman
Kick In
The Little Minister
The Masquerader
A Night to Remember
The Road to Reno
Seven Days Leave
The Shopworn Angel
Thunder Below
Tomorrow and Tomorrow
Tycoon
The Under-Pup
Wedding Present
The Young in Heart

Walsh, Raoul
Artists and Models
Big Brown Eyes
The Big Trail
The Bowery
The Cock-Eyed World
College Swing
Colorado Territory
Dark Command
Desperate Journey
Evangeline
Every Night at Eight
Fighter Squadron
Gentleman Jim
Going Hollywood
High Sierra
Hitting a New High
The Honor System
In Old Arizona
Klondike Annie
The Man Who Came Back
Me and My Gal
O.H.M.S.
One Sunday Afternoon
Pursued
The Regeneration
The Roaring Twenties
Sadie Thompson
Saint Louis Blues
Spendthrift
The Strawberry Blonde
They Died with Their Boots
  On
They Drive by Night
The Thief of Bagdad
What Price Glory?
White Heat
Wild Girl
The Yellow Ticket

Walters, Charles
The Barkleys of Broadway
Easter Parade
Good News

Wangenheim, Gustav
Kampf, Der

Waschneck, Erich
Zwei Menschen

Waszynsky, Michael
The Dybbuk

Watt, Harry
Night Mail

Webb, Kenneth
The Stolen Kiss

Webb, Millard
The Sea Beast

Weber, Lois
The Blot
Captain Courtesy
The Dumb Girl of Portici
The Flirt
Hypocrites
Idle Wives
It's No Laughing Matter
A Midnight Romance
Shoes
Where Are My Children?
White Heat

Wegner, Paul
The Golem

Weine, Robert
Crime and Punishment
Power of Darkness

Welles, Orson
Citizen Kane
The Magnificent Ambersons
The Stranger

Wellman, William A.
Battleground
Beau Geste
Beggars of Life
Buffalo Bill
Call of the Wild
Central Airport
College Coach
The Conquerors
Dangerous Paradise
Frisco Jenny
The Great Man's Lady
The Hatchet Man
Heroes for Sale
Lady of Burlesque
The Light That Failed
Lily Turner
Looking for Trouble
Love Is a Racket
Men With Wings
Night Nurse
Nothing Sacred
Other Men's Women
The Ox-Bow Incident
The President Vanishes
The Public Enemy
The Purchase Price
Roxie Hart
Safe in Hell
Small Town Girl
So Big
A Star Is Born
The Star Witness
The Story of G.I. Joe

Wild Boys of the Road
Wings
Young Eagles

Werker, Alfred L.
The Adventures of Sherlock
  Holmes
The Affairs of Annabelle
Blue Skies
The House of Rothschild
Kidnapped
Lost Boundaries
Love in Exile
News Is Made at Night
Repeat Performance
Up the River

Weschler, L.
Wings Over Ethiopia

West, Raymond B.
Civilization
The Cup of Life
Rumpelstiltskin

West, Roland
Alibi
The Bat
The Bat Whispers

Whale, James
The Bride of Frankenstein
By Candlelight
Frankenstein
The Great Garrick
The Impatient Maiden
The Invisible Man
Journey's End
A Kiss Before the Mirror
The Man in the Iron Mask
The Old Dark House
One More River
Port of Seven Seas
Remember Last Night?
The Road Back
Show Boat
Sinners in Paradise
Waterloo Bridge

Whelan, Tim
The Divorce of Lady X
Farewell Again
The Mill on the Floss
The Murder Man
The Perfect Gentleman
Sidewalks of London
The Thief of Bagdad
Troopship

White, Jules
Sidewalks of New York

Whitman, Phil
The Girl from Calgary

Whorf, Richard
It Happened in Brooklyn
Till the Clouds Roll By

Wiene, Robert
The Cabinet of Dr. Caligari
A Scandal in Paris

Wilcox, Herbert
Bitter Sweet
The Blue Danube
Dawn
Forever and a Day
Irene
Magic Night
Nell Gwyn
Nurse Edith Cavell
Piccadilly Incident
Sixty Glorious Years
The Three Maxims
Victoria the Great
Yank in London

Wilde, Ted
The Kid Brother
Speedy

Wilder, Billy
Double Indemnity
The Emperor Waltz
Five Graves to Cairo
A Foreign Affair
The Lost Weekend
The Major and the Minor

Wiles, Gordon
Women of Glamour

Willat, Irvin
Behind the Door
Wanderer of the Wasteland

Williams, Emlyn
The Woman of Dolwyn

Williams, J.B.
White Cargo

Williamson, James
Attack on a China Mission

Wills, J. Elder
Big Fella
The Song of Freedom

Wilson, Fred McLeod
Lassie Come Home

Wing, Ward
Samarang

Wise, Robert
The Body Snatcher
Curse of the Cat People
The Set-Up

Withey, Chet
Romance

Wolbert, William
The Light of Victory

Year Produced Index

1882
Animals in Motion

1894
Autour D'Une Cabine
Sioux Indian Dance

1895
Arroseur Arrose, L'
Sortie des Ouvriers de l'Usine
   Lumiere

1896
American Biograph First
   Program
Edison First Program
The Kiss
Lumiere First Program
The Vanishing Lady

1898
Battlefield Scenes
A Chess Maniac
Elopement on Horseback
Excursion

1899
Astor Battery on Parade
Cinderella
Jeffries-Sharkey Fight
Love and War
The Windsor Hotel Fire

1900
The Adventures of Happy
   Hooligan
Dressing Room Scenes-Adolf
   Zinc
Grandma's Reading Glass
Vaudeville

1901
Attack on a China Mission
Mary Jane's Mishap

1902
The Life of an American
   Fireman
The Magic Lantern
Voyage dans la Lune, Le

1903
Chicago-Michigan Football
   Game
The Gay Shoe Clerk

The Great Train Robbery
Uncle Tom's Cabin

1904
The Impossible Voyage
The Land Beyond the Sunset
The Mermaid
Personal
The Story of the Kelly Gang

1905
How Jones Lost His Roll
Life of an American
   Policeman
Presa di Roma
President Roosevelt's
   Inauguration
Rescued by Rover
Revolution in Russia
Scenes and Incidents, Russo-
   Japanese Peace Conference
The Seven Ages

1906
The Dream of a Rarebit Fiend
The Ex-Convict
Humorous Phases of Funny
   Faces
The Kleptomaniac

1907
Rescued from an Eagle's Nest

1908
The Adventures of Dolly
After Many Years
Antony and Cleopatra
As You Like It
The Assassination of the Duke
   de Guise
Balked at the Altar
The Bank Robbery
A Drunkard's Reformation
For Love of Gold
Julius Caesar
The Last Days of Pompeii
The Merry Widow
The Redman and the Child
Richard III
Romeo and Juliet
Samson and Delilah
Sherlock Holmes
Song of the Shirt
The Taming of the Shrew

1909
The Battle in the Clouds
Camille
A Corner in Wheat
The Curtain Pole
A Fool's Revenge
The Heart of a Race Tout
Hiawatha
In Old Kentucky
Incidents in the Life of
   Napoleon and Josephine
Launcelot and Elaine
Leatherstocking
The Life of Moses
Lines of White on a Sullen Sea
The Lonely Villa
The Merry Wives of Windsor
A Midsummer Night's Dream
Nero
Pippa Passes
The Prince and the Pauper
Princess Nicotine
The Redman's View
Resurrection
Tosca, La
The Violin Maker of Cremona
Voice of the Violin
The Way of Man

1910
All on Account of the Milk
The Burlesque Queen
Doctor Jekyll and Mr. Hyde
The Fall of Babylon
Francesca da Rimini
Frankenstein
The Fugitive
Gold Is Not All
The House with Closed
   Shutters
The Lad from Old Ireland
The Life of Moses
Othello
Ramona
1776
Simple Charity
The Song of the Wildwood
   Flute
A Summer Idyl
That Chink at Golden Gulch
The Thread of Destiny
The Twisted Trail
Uncle Tom's Cabin
The Vampire
The Wizard of Oz

1911
The Battle
The Battle of Trafalgar
Cinderella
The Colleen Bawn
A Country Cupid
David Copperfield
The Deluge
A Doll's House
Enoch Arden, Part 1
Enoch Arden, Part 2
The Fall of Troy
Fighting Blood
Gunga Din
Hamlet
Help Wanted
His Trust
His Trust Fulfilled
The Lonedale Operator
Mr. Jones at the Ball
The Poisoned Flume
Romeo and Juliet
Rory O'More
The Scarlet Letter
She
Sherlock Holmes Jr.
A Tale of Two Cities, Part I
A Tale of Two Cities, Part II
A Tale of Two Cities, Part III
Thais
The Two Orphans
Vanity Fair
The Violin Maker of
   Nuremberg

1912
Conquete du Pole, A La
A Dash Through the Clouds
The Delhi Dunbar
Dr. Jekyll and Mr. Hyde
From the Manger to the Cross
The Kerry Gow
The Last Stand of the Dalton
   Boys
The Massacre
The Muskateers of Pig Alley
The New York Hat
Oliver Twist
The Painted Lady
Queen Elizabeth
Richard III
An Unseen Enemy
War on the Plains

1913
The Adventures of Kathlyn
Anthony and Cleopatra

Devil Dogs of the Air
The Devil Is a Woman
Diamond Jim
The Dictator
Dr. Socrates
Doubting Thomas
Enchanted April
Escapade
Escape from Yesterday
Escape Me Never
Every Night at Eight
The Farmer Takes a Wife
A Feather in Her Hat
First a Girl
The Flame Within
The Florentine Dagger
Folies Bergere
Four Hours to Kill
The Frisco Kid
Front Page Woman
Frontier
G Men
The Gay Deception
The Ghost Goes West
The Gilded Lily
The Girl From 10th Avenue
The Glass Key
Go Into Your Dance
Gobsek
Goin' to Town
Gold Diggers of 1935
The Golem
Golgotha
The Good Fairy
The Goose and the Gander
Hands Across the Table
Here Comes the Band
Hold 'Em Yale
Hortobagy
I Dream Too Much
I Found Stella Parish
I Live for Love
I Live My Life
If You Could Only Cook
In Caliente
In Old Kentucky
In Person
The Informer
The Irish in Us
It's in the Air
Jalna
Janosik
Kimiko
Koenigsmark
Laddie
The Last Days of Pompeii
The Last Outpost
Liebesmelodie
Life Begins at Forty
The Little Colonel
The Littlest Rebel
Lives of a Bengal Lancer
Living on Velvet
Love in Bloom
Love Me Forever
Loves of a Dictator
Mad Love
Magnificent Obsession
Man of Iron
The Man on the Flying
   Trapeze
The Man Who Broke the Bank
   at Monte Carlo
Mark of the Vampire

Mary Burns, Fugitive
Metropolitan
A Midsummer Night's Dream
Mimi
Misérables, Les
Mississippi
Moscow Nights
The Murder Man
Murder on a Honeymoon
Music Is Magic
Mutiny on the Bounty
The Mystery of Edwin Drood
Naughty Marietta
A New Gulliver
A Night at the Opera
Night Life of the Gods
No More Ladies
Oil for the Lamps of China
One More Spring
Orchids to You
Our Little Girl
Page Miss Glory
Paris in Spring
The Passing of the Third Floor
   Back
Peasants
Pension Mimosas
The Perfect Gentleman
Peter Ibbetson
Private Worlds
The Raven
Reckless
Red Salute
Remember Last Night?
Rendezvous
The Right to Live
Roberta
Ruggles of Red Gap
Rumba
Sanders of the River
Sans Famille
The Scarlet Pimpernel
The Scoundrel
Second Bureau
Sequoia
Seven Keys to Baldpate
Shanghai
She
She Married Her Boss
Shipmates Forever
So Red the Rose
Song of Ceylon
Special Agent
Splendor
Star of Midnight
Steamboat 'Round the Bend
Storm Over the Andes
Stranded
The Student of Prague
Sweet Adeline
Sweet Music
Sylvia Scarlett
A Tale of Two Cities
Thanks a Million
The Thirty-Nine Steps
The Three Musketeers
Top Hat
Transatlantic Tunnel
Triumph des Willens
The Triumph of Sherlock
   Holmes
Under the Pampas Moon
Vanessa: Her Love Story
Veille d'Armes

The Wave
Way Down East
The Wedding Night
We're in the Money
West Point of the Air
Whipsaw
The Whole Town's Talking
Wings in the Dark
Wings Over Ethiopia
The Woman in Red
Your Uncle Dudley
The Youth of Maxim

1935-51
The March of Time

1936
Abyssinia
Accused
Adventure in Manhattan
After the Thin Man
Alibi, L'
The Amateur Gentleman
Amphitryon
And So They Were Married
Anna
Anthony Adverse
Anything Goes
As You Like It
Baltic Deputy
Banjo on My Knee
Belle Équipe, La
Beloved Enemy
The Beloved Vagabond
The Big Broadcast of 1937
Big Brown Eyes
Bonheur, Le
Born to Dance
The Bride Walks Out
Broken Blossoms
Bullets or Ballots
Cain and Mabel
The Calling of Dan Matthews
Camille
Captain Blood
Captain January
Career Woman
The Case Against Mrs. Ames
Castle in Flanders
Ceiling Zero
César
Champagne Waltz
The Charge of the Light
   Brigade
China Clipper
Club des Femmes
Colleen
College Holiday
Come and Get It
The Country Doctor
Craig's Wife
The Crime of Dr. Crespi
The Crime of Dr. Forbes
Desire
The Devil Doll
The Devil Is A Sissy
Dimples
Dodsworth
Dracula's Daughter
Dubrovsky
Early to Bed
Earthworm Tractors
The Eternal Mask

Everybody's Old Man
Everything Is Thunder
Exclusive Story
The Ex-Mrs. Bradford
Flash Gordon
Follow the Fleet
Frankie and Johnny
Fury
The Garden of Allah
The Gay Desperado
The General Died at Dawn
Gentle Julia
Girls' Dormitory
Give Me Your Heart
Go West, Young Man
God's Country and the
   Woman
Gold Diggers of 1937
The Golden Arrow
The Gorgeous Hussy
Grain
Grande Amour de Beethoven,
   Une
Great Guy
The Great Ziegfeld
The Green Pastures
Gypsies
Hearts Divided
High Tension
His Brother's Wife
His Lordship
Hollywood Boulevard
Homme du Jour, L'
Human Cargo
I Married a Doctor
I'd Give My Life
Intermezzo
The Invisible Ray
Isle of Fury
It Had to Happen
It's Love Again
The Jungle Princess
Kampf, Der
King of Burlesque
King of the Damned
The King Steps Out
Klondike Annie
Laburnum Grove
Ladies in Love
The Lady Consents
The Last of the Mohicans
The Legion of Terror
Libeled Lady
Little Lord Fauntleroy
Little Miss Nobody
Living Dangerously
Lloyds of London
Love Before Breakfast
Love in Exile
Love on the Run
The Lower Depths
The Magnificent Brute
Man Hunt
The Man Who Could Work
   Miracles
The Man Who Lived Twice
The Marriage of Corbal
Mary of Scotland
Mayerling
Mazurka
Meet Nero Wolfe
Merlusse
A Message to Garcia
The Milky Way

Snow White and the Seven
    Dwarfs
Something to Sing About
Souls at Sea
Spain in Flames
The Spanish Earth
Springtime in the Rockies
Stage Door
Stand-In
A Star Is Born
Stella Dallas
Storm in a Teacup
Submarine D-1
Super-Sleuth
Swing High, Swing Low
Tales from the Vienna Woods
Talk of the Devil
Thank You, Mr. Moto
That Certain Woman
That I May Live
That They May Live
There Goes the Groom
They Gave Him a Gun
They Won't Forget
Thin Ice
Think Fast, Mr. Moto
The Thirteenth Chair
The Thirteenth Man
This Is My Affair
Thoroughbreds Don't Cry
Thunder in the City
Time Out for Romance
The Toast of New York
Top of the Town
Topper
Tovarich
True Confession
Tsar to Lenin
Under the Red Robe
Varsity Show
Victoria the Great
Vogues of 1938
Waikiki Wedding
Wake Up and Live
Way Out West
The Wedding of Palo
Wee Willie Winkie
Wells Fargo
We're on the Jury
When You're in Love
Wife, Doctor and Nurse
Wings of the Morning
Woman Chases Man
The Woman I Love
Women Men Marry
Women of Glamour
Yoshiwara
You Can't Have Everything
You Only Live Once
Young Pushkin
You're a Sweetheart

1938
Abus de Confiance
The Adventures of Chico
The Adventures of Marco Polo
The Adventures of Robin
    Hood
The Adventures of Tom
    Sawyer
The Affairs of Annabel
Alexander Nevsky
Alexander's Ragtime Band
Algiers

Always Goodbye
The Amazing Dr. Clitterhouse
Angels With Dirty Faces
Arsene Lupin Returns
Artists and Models Abroad
Avocate d'Amour
Ballerina
Bank Holiday
Battle of Broadway
The Beachcomber
The Beloved Brat
Bête Humaine, La
The Big Broadcast of 1938
Billy the Kid Returns
Blockade
Block-Heads
Blondie
Bluebeard's Eighth Wife
Boy Meets Girl
Boys Town
Break the News
Breaking the Ice
Bringing Up Baby
Brother Rat
The Buccaneer
Carefree
Champs Élysees
The Childhood of Maxim
    Gorky
A Christmas Carol
The Citadel
City Streets
Cocoanut Grove
College Swing
The Country Bride
The Courier of Lyons
The Cowboy and the Lady
Cowboy from Brooklyn
Crime School
The Crowd Roars
Dark Rapture
Dawn Patrol
The Defense of Volochayevsk
Disparus de Saint-Agil, Les
The Divorce of Lady X
Doctor Rhythm
Double Crime sur la Ligne
    Maginot
Dramatic School
Drame de Shanghai, Le
Drums
The Duke of West Point
The Dybbuk
Equipage, L'
Everybody Sing
Fast Company
Femme du Boulanger, La
The First Hundred Years
Five of a Kind
Flash Gordon's Trip to Mars
Fools for Scandal
Four Daughters
Four Men and a Prayer
Four's a Crowd
Freshman Year
Gangs of New York
Gangster's Boy
Garden of the Moon
Generals Without Buttons
Gens du Voyage, Les
Girl of the Golden West
Girls' School
Give Me a Sailor
Go Chase Yourself

Going Places
Gold Diggers in Paris
Gold Is Where You Find It
The Goldwyn Follies
A Great Citizen
The Great Waltz
Hard to Get
Having Wonderful Time
Her Jungle Love
Hold That Co-ed
Hold That Kiss
Holiday
Hotel du Nord
I Am the Law
I Met My Love Again
If I Were King
I'll Give a Million
In Old Chicago
Jezebel
Josette
Le Jour se Lève
The Joy of Living
Just Around the Corner
Katia
Kentucky
Kidnapped
King of Alcatraz
The Kreutzer Sonata
The Lady Vanishes
A Letter of Introduction
Liebe im 3/4 Takt
Listen, Darling
Little Miss Broadway
Little Tough Guy
Lord Jeff
Love Finds Andy Hardy
Mad About Music
The Mad Miss Manton
The Man from Music
    Mountain
A Man to Remember
Marie Antoinette
Marusia
Men Are Such Fools
Men Make Steel
Men With Wings
Merrily We Live
Mioche, Le
Mort du Cygne, La
Mother Carey's Chickens
My Bill
My Lucky Star
Next Time I Marry
Of Human Hearts
Olympiad
Out West With the Hardys
Pacific Liner
Paradise for Three
Paris Honeymoon
Penitentiary
Poet and Tsar
Port of Seven Seas
Prison Nurse
Prison Without Bars
Professor Beware
Professor Mamlock
Pugachev
Puritan, Le
Pygmalion
Quai des Brumes
Racket Busters
The Rage of Paris
Rebecca of Sunnybrook Farm
Return to Life

Rich Man, Poor Girl
Ride a Crooked Mile
The Road to Reno
Roi S'Amuse, Le
Romance in the Dark
Room Service
A Royal Divorce
Safety in Numbers
Sailing Along
Sally, Irene and Mary
Say It in French
Scandal Street
Secrets of an Actress
Service DeLuxe
Sharpshooters
The Shining Hour
The Shopworn Angel
Sidewalks of London
Sing, You Sinners
Sinners in Paradise
The Sisters
Sixty Glorious Years
A Slight Case of Murder
The Slipper Episode
Smiling Along
South Riding
Spawn of the North
Spring Madness
Stablemates
Start Cheering
Stolen Heaven
Storm Over Bengal
Straight, Place and Show
Submarine Patrol
Suez
Sweethearts
Swing Your Lady
Swiss Miss
Tarnished Angel
Tendre Ennemie, Le
The Terror of Tiny Town
Test Pilot
The Texans
Thanks for Everything
Thanks for the Memory
That Certain Age
There Goes My Heart
There's Always a Woman
There's That Woman Again
This Man Is News
Three Blind Mice
Three Comrades
Three Loves Has Nancy
To the Victor
Tom Sawyer, Detective
Too Hot to Handle
The Toy Wife
Trade Winds
Troopship
Tropic Holiday
Under Western Stars
Up the River
Valley of the Giants
Vivacious Lady
Volpone
Walking Down Broadway
The Ware Case
We're Going to Be Rich
When Were You Born?
While New York Sleeps
White Banners
Women Are Like That
A Yank at Oxford
Yellow Jack

The Primrose Path
Rebecca
Remember the Night
The Return of Frank James
The Road to Singapore
Road to Zanzibar
Santa Fe Trail
Saturday's Children
The Sea Hawk
The Shop Around the Corner
Strike Up the Band
Susan and God
Swiss Family Robinson
They Drive by Night
They Knew What They
    Wanted
The Thief of Bagdad
This Thing Called Love
Tin Pan Alley
Tom Brown's School Days
Waterloo Bridge
The Westerner
When the Daltons Rode
Young Tom Edison

1941

Adam Had Four Sons
Back Street
Ball of Fire
Belle Starr
Billy the Kid
The Birth of the Blues
Blood and Sand
Blossoms in the Dust
Blues in the Night
The Bride Came C.O.D.
Buck Privates
Caught in the Draft
Charley's Aunt
Cheers for Miss Bishop
The Chocolate Soldier
Citizen Kane
The Corsican Brothers
The Devil and Daniel Webster
The Devil and Miss Jones
Dive Bomber
Dr. Jekyll and Mr. Hyde
Dumbo
Eagle Squadron
The Flame of New Orleans
49th Parallel
The Great Lie
Hellzapoppin'
Here Comes Mr. Jordan
High Sierra
H. M. Pulham, Esq.
Hold Back the Dawn
Hold That Ghost
Honky Tonk
How Green Was My Valley
Hudson's Bay
I Wake Up Screaming
I Wanted Wings
In This Our Life
Johnny Eager
King's Row
Ladies in Retirement
Lady Be Good
The Lady Eve
The Little Foxes
Louisiana Purchase
Love Crazy
Love on the Dole
Major Barbara

The Maltese Falcon
Man Hunt
The Man Who Came to
    Dinner
Meet John Doe
Mr. and Mrs. Smith
Mister V
My Favorite Blonde
My Gal Sal
Never Give a Sucker an Even
    Break
One Foot in Heaven
Out of the Fog
Penny Serenade
Rage in Heaven
The Sea Wolf
Sergeant York
The Shanghai Gesture
Smilin' Through
So Ends Our Night
Somewhere I'll Find You
The Strawberry Blonde
Sullivan's Travels
Sun Valley Serenade
Suspicion
Swamp Water
That Hamilton Woman
That Uncertain Feeling
They Died with Their Boots
    On
They Met in Bombay
This Above All
Tobacco Road
Tom, Dick, and Harry
Two-Faced Woman
The Wagons Roll at Night
The Well-Digger's Daughter
Western Union
Wild Geese Calling
The Wolf Man
A Yank in the R.A.F.
Ziegfeld Girl

1942

Across the Pacific
Arabian Nights
Bambi
The Black Swan
Captains of the Clouds
Casablanca
Cat People
Desperate Journey
Gentleman Jim
George Washington Slept Here
Goupi Mains Rouge
The Great Man's Lady
The Hard Way
Hitler's Children
Holiday Inn
I Married a Witch
In Which We Serve
Journey for Margaret
Journey Into Fear
Jungle Book
Keeper of the Flame
Larceny, Inc.
Lucky Jordan
The Magnificent Ambersons
The Major and the Minor
The Male Animal
Mrs. Miniver
The Moon and Sixpence
Moontide
My Sister Eileen

Next of Kin
A Night to Remember
Now, Voyager
Once Upon a Honeymoon
One of Our Aircraft Is Missing
Ossessione
The Ox-Bow Incident
The Palm Beach Story
The Pied Piper
The Pride of the Yankees
Reap the Wild Wind
The Remarkable Andrew
Reunion in France
Road to Morocco
Roxie Hart
Saboteur
Son of Fury
Spitfire
The Spoilers
Star Spangled Rhythm
Strangers in the House
Take a Letter Darling
Tales of Manhattan
Talk of the Town
Ten Gentlemen from West
    Point
Tennessee Johnson
This Gun for Hire
To Be or Not to Be
To the Shores of Tripoli
Tortilla Flat
Visiteurs du Soir, Les
Woman of the Year
Yankee Doodle Dandy
You Were Never Lovelier

1943

Above Suspicion
Action in the North Atlantic
Adventures of Tartu
Air Force
Bataan
Cabin in the Sky
China
Claudia
Colonel Blimp
The Constant Nymph
Corvette K-225
Crash Dive
The Cross of Lorraine
Day of Wrath
Destination Tokyo
Dixie
Du Barry Was a Lady
Five Graves to Cairo
Flight for Freedom
For Whom the Bell Tolls
Forever and a Day
Frankenstein Meets the
    Wolfman
The Gang's All Here
Girl Crazy
Guadalcanal Diary
Gung Ho
A Guy Named Joe
Hangmen Also Die
Heaven Can Wait
Hello, Frisco, Hello
Hitler's Madman
Holy Matrimony
The Human Comedy
I Walked With a Zombie
Jack London
Lady of Burlesque

Lassie Come Home
Let's Face It
Madame Curie
The Man in Grey
Mission to Moscow
Mr. Lucky
The Moon Is Down
The More the Merrier
The North Star
Old Acquaintance
Old Mother Riley, Detective
The Outlaw
The Phantom of the Opera
Presenting Lily Mars
Princess O'Rourke
Sahara
Shadow of a Doubt
So Proudly We Hail!
The Song of Bernadette
The Story of Dr. Wassell
Thank Your Lucky Stars
This Is the Army
This Land Is Mine
Wake Island
Watch on the Rhine
Young and Willing

1944

The Adventures of Mark
    Twain
Arsenic and Old Lace
Bathing Beauty
The Bridge of San Luis Rey
Buffalo Bill
The Canterville Ghost
Casanova Brown
Cobra Woman
Cover Girl
Curse of the Cat People
Double Indemnity
Dragon Seed
The Eve of St. Mark
The Fighting Seabees
Follow the Boys
Frenchman's Creek
Gaslight
Going My Way
The Great Moment
Hail the Conquering Hero
The Hairy Ape
Henry V
Home in Indiana
I'll Be Seeing You
It Happened Tomorrow
Jane Eyre
The Keys of the Kingdom
Kismet
Lady in the Dark
Laura
Lifeboat
The Lodger
Meet Me in St. Louis
Memphis Belle
Ministry of Fear
The Miracle of Morgan's
    Creek
Mr. Skeffington
Murder, My Sweet
National Velvet
None But the Lonely Heart
On Approval
Passage to Marseilles
See Here, Private Hargrove
Since You Went Away

So Dear to My Heart
So This is New York
A Song is Born
Sorry, Wrong Number
A Southern Yankee
State of the Union
The Street With No Name
That Lady in Ermine
The Three Musketeers
The Time of Your Life
The Treasure of the Sierra
     Madre
Unfaithfully Yours
The Voice of the Turtle
When My Baby Smiles at Me
The Woman in White
Words and Music

1949
Act of Violence
Adam's Rib
Adventure in Baltimore
The Adventures of Don Juan
The Affair Blum
Alias Nick Beal
All the King's Men
Always Leave Them Laughing
And Baby Makes Three
Anna Lucasta
Any Number Can Play
The Barkleys of Broadway
Battleground
The Beautiful Blonde From
     Bashful Bend

Beyond the Forest
Bicycle Thief
The Big Steal
Bitter Rice
Black Magic
The Blue Lagoon
Bride for Sale
Calamity Jane and Sam Bass
Caught
Champion
Chicken Every Sunday
Christopher Columbus
City Across the River
Colorado Territory
Command Decision
A Connecticut Yankee in King
     Arthur's Court
Criss Cross
D.O.A.
Dancing in the Dark
Doctor and the Girl
Down to the Sea in Ships
The Fallen Idol
Family Honeymoon
The Fan
Father Was a Fullback
The Fighting O'Flynn
Flamingo Road
The Forbidden Street
The Fountainhead
The Girl from Jones Beach
The Great Gatsby
The Great Sinner
Gun Crazy
The Hasty Heart

The Heiress
Holiday Affair
Home of the Brave
House of Strangers
I Was a Male War Bride
In the Good Old Summertime
Inspector General
Intruder in the Dust
It Happens Every Spring
Jolson Sings Again
Kind Hearts and Coronets
Knock on Any Door
A Letter to Three Wives
The Life of Riley
Little Women
Look for the Silver Lining
Lost Boundaries
Ma and Pa Kettle
Madame Bovary
Manhandled
Mighty Joe Young
Mrs. Mike
Mr. Belvedere Goes to College
Mother Is a Freshman
My Foolish Heart
Neptune's Daughter
On the Town
Once More My Darling
Passport to Pimlico
Pinky
Portrait of Jennie
The Prince of Foxes
The Reckless Moment
The Red Danube
Red, Hot and Blue

The Red Menace
The Red Pony
Reign of Terror
Saints and Sinners
Samson and Delilah
Sands of Iwo Jima
The Set-Up
She Wore a Yellow Ribbon
Slattery's Hurricane
Slightly French
Sorrowful Jones
The Stratton Story
Take Me Out to the Ball
     Game
That Forsyte Woman
They Live by Night
Thieves Highway
The Third Man
Three Godfathers
Tight Little Island
Tulsa
Twelve O'Clock High
Under Capricorn
We Were Strangers
Whispering Smith
White Heat
Window
The Woman of Dolwyn
The Woman on Pier 13

Country Produced Index

Madame Dubarry
Maedchen in Uniform
Mazurka
Metropolis
Morgenrot
New Year's Eve
Niebelungen
Nosferatu
Olympiad
Pandora's Box
Raub der Mona Lisa, Der
Rebell, Der
Savoy Hotel 217
Secrets of a Soul
Shattered
Siegfried
The Spiders
Spies
The Student of Prague
The Student of Prague
Tempest
Testament des Dr. Mabuse, Das
The Three Penny Opera
Trapeze
Traumende Mund, Der
Triumph des Willens
Vampyr, ou L'Étrange Adventure de David Gray
Vanina
Variety
Viktor und Viktoria
Warning Shadows
Waxworks
Westfront 1918
The White Devil
The White Flame
The White Hell of Pitz Palu
Zwei Herzen im 3/4 Takt
Zwei Menschen

Great Britain
Accused
Action for Slander
The Adventures of Chico
The Amateur Gentleman
Aren't We All?
Atlantic
Attack on a China Mission
Bank Holiday
The Battle in the Clouds
Be Mine Tonight
The Beachcomber
Bedelia
Bedlam
The Beloved Vagabond
The Better 'Ole
Big Fella
Bitter Sweet
Black Narcissus
Blackmail
Blithe Spirit
The Blue Danube
The Blue Lagoon
Break the News
Brewster's Millions
Brief Encounter
Broken Blossoms
The Brothers
Caesar and Cleopatra
Caravan
Catherine the Great
Christopher Columbus
The Clairvoyant

Colonel Blimp
The Constant Nymph
Convoy
A Cottage on Dartmoor
Dark Journey
Dawn
Dead of Night
The Dictator
The Divorce of Lady X
Doctor Syn
Dreaming Lips
The Dreyfus Case
Drums
Dulcimer Street
The Edge of the World
Elephant Boy
Elstree Calling
An Englishman's Home
Escape Me Never
Evensong
Evergreen
Everything Is Thunder
The Fallen Idol
Farewell Again
Fire Over England
First a Girl
The Forbidden Street
49th Parallel
Four Feathers
F.P.1 Antwortet Nicht
French Without Tears
Frieda
Gangway
The Ghost Goes West
A Girl Must Live
The Good Companions
Goodbye, Mr. Chips
Grandma's Reading Glass
The Great Barrier
Great Expectations
The Hasty Heart
Head Over Heels in Love
Henry V
Hindle Wakes
His Lordship
I Know Where I'm Going
I Met a Murderer
I See a Dark Stranger
I Was a Spy
In Which We Serve
Inspector Hornleigh
The Iron Duke
It's Love Again
Jamaica Inn
Jericho
Jungle Book
Juno and the Paycock
Kind Hearts and Coronets
King of the Damned
King Solomon's Mines
Knight Without Armor
Laburnum Grove
The Lady Vanishes
Let George Do It
The Lion Has Wings
Living Dangerously
The Lodger
The Lodger
Love in Exile
Love on the Dole
Loves of a Dictator
The Lucky Number
Magic Night
Major Barbara

Man of Aran
The Man Who Changed His Name
The Man Who Could Work Miracles
The Man Who Knew Too Much
The Manxman
The Marriage of Corbal
Mary Jane's Mishap
Men Are Not Gods
Michael and Mary
The Middleman
The Mikado
The Mill on the Floss
Mimi
Mister V
Moonlight Sonata
Moscow Nights
Murder!
My Heart Is Calling You
Nell Gwyn
Next of Kin
Nicholas Nickelby
Night Mail
Night Train
Nine Days a Queen
The Notorious Gentleman
Number Seventeen
Odd Man Out
O.H.M.S.
Oliver Twist
On Approval
One of Our Aircraft Is Missing
The Outsider
Pagliacci
The Passing of the Third Floor Back
The Passing of the Third Floor Back
Passport to Pimlico
Piccadilly Incident
Power
Prison Without Bars
The Prisoner of Zenda
The Private Life of Don Juan
The Private Life of Henry VIII
Pygmalion
The Rat
The Red Shoes
Rembrandt
Rescued by Rover
Reserved for Ladies
Rhodes
Rich and Strange
The Ring
The Robber Symphony
Rome Express
A Royal Divorce
Sabotage
Sailing Along
Saints and Sinners
Sally in Our Alley
Sanders of the River
The Scarlet Pimpernel
School for Husbands
The Secret Agent
Seven Sinners
The Seventh Veil
Sidewalks of London
The Sign of the Four
The Silent Witness
Sing As We Go

Sixty Glorious Years
The Skin Game
Smiling Along
Song of Ceylon
The Song of Freedom
South Riding
Spitfire
Stairway to Heaven
The Stars Look Down
A Stolen Life
Storm in a Teacup
Talk of the Devil
Tell England
There Goes the Bride
The Thief of Bagdad
Things to Come
The Third Man
The Thirty-Nine Steps
This Man in Paris
This Man Is News
The Three Maxims
Thunder in the City
Tight Little Island
To the Victor
Transatlantic Tunnel
The Triumph of Sherlock Holmes
Troopship
12:10
U-Boat 29
Under the Red Robe
Underground
Vacation from Marriage
Victoria the Great
Waltz Time
Waltzes From Vienna
The Wandering Jew
The Ware Case
We're Going to Be Rich
The Wicked Lady
Wings of the Morning
The Woman of Dolwyn
A Yank at Oxford
Yank in London
Yellow Sands
Young and Innocent

Hungary
A Chess Maniac
Hortobagy

Italy
Anthony and Cleopatra
Bicycle Thief
Bitter Rice
Cabiria
The Fall of Troy
Germany, Year Zero
The Last Days of Pompeii
The Last Days of Pompeii
Nero
Open City
Ossessione
Paisan
Presa di Roma
Quo Vadis?
Re Burlone, Il
Scipio Africanus
Shoe Shine
Squadrone Bianco, Lo
To Live in Peace

Rio Rita
Riptide
The River
The River
The Road Back
The Road to Glory
Road to Morocco
The Road to Reno
The Road to Reno
The Road to Singapore
Road to Utopia
The Road to Yesterday
Road to Zanzibar
Roadhouse Nights
The Roaring Twenties
Roberta
Robin Hood
Rockabye
The Rogue Song
Roman Scandals
Romance
Romance
Romance in Manhattan
Romance in the Dark
The Romance of Happy Valley
The Romance of Rosy Ridge
Romance on the High Seas
Romeo and Juliet
Romeo and Juliet
Romeo and Juliet
Romeo and Juliet
Romeo and Juliet
Romola
Room Service
Rope
Rory O'More
Rosalie
The Rosary
Rose Marie
Rose of the Rancho
Rose of the Rancho
Rose of Washington Square
Rosita
Rough Riders
Roughly Speaking
Roxie Hart
The Royal Bed
The Royal Family of
  Broadway
Ruggles of Red Gap
Rulers of the Sea
Rumba
Rumpelstiltskin
Saboteur
Sadie Thompson
Safe in Hell
Safety in Numbers
Safety in Numbers
Safety Last
Sahara
Saigon
Sailor Be Good
Saint Louis Blues
A Sainted Devil
Sally
Sally, Irene and Mary
Sally of the Sawdust
Salome
Salomy Jane
The Salvation Hunters
Salvation Nell
Samarang
Samson and Delilah
San Antonio

San Francisco
San Quentin
Sands of Iwo Jima
Santa Fe Trail
Sarah and Son
Saratoga
Saratoga Trunk
Satan Met a Lady
Saturday Night
Saturday's Children
Saturday's Heroes
Saturday's Millions
Savage Gold
The Saxon Charm
Say It in French
A Scandal in Paris
Scandal Street
Scaramouche
Scarface: Shame of a Nation
Scarlet Dawn
Scarlet Days
The Scarlet Empress
The Scarlet Letter
The Scarlet Letter
The Scarlet Letter
Scarlet Street
Scenes and Incidents, Russo-
  Japanese Peace Conference
Scotland Yard Commands
The Scoundrel
The Sea Beast
Sea Devils
The Sea God
The Sea Hawk
The Sea of Grass
The Sea Wolf
The Sea Wolf
The Sea Wolf
The Search
Seas Beneath
Second Fiddle
Second Honeymoon
The Secret Life of Walter
  Mitty
The Secret of Dr. Kildare
Secret Service of the Air
The Secret Six
Secrets
Secrets
Secrets of an Actress
See Here, Private Hargrove
Seed
The Senator Was Indiscreet
Sentimental Journey
Sentimental Tommy
Sequoia
Sergeant Madden
Sergeant York
Service DeLuxe
Service for Ladies
The Set-Up
The Seven Ages
Seven Chances
Seven Days Leave
Seven Keys to Baldpate
Seven Keys to Baldpate
Seven Years Bad Luck
1776
Seventh Heaven
Seventh Heaven
Sex
Shadow of a Doubt
Shadows
Shadows of the Orient

Shall We Dance
Shanghai
Shanghai Express
The Shanghai Gesture
Sharpshooters
She
She
She Done Him Wrong
She Had to Say Yes
She Married Her Boss
She Wanted a Millionaire
She Wore a Yellow Ribbon
The Sheik
The Sheik Steps Out
The Sheriff's Son
Sherlock Holmes
Sherlock Holmes
Sherlock Holmes
Sherlock Holmes
Sherlock Holmes Jr.
Sherlock Jr.
She's a Sheik
The Shining Hour
Shipmates Forever
The Shocking Miss Pilgrim
Shoes
Shooting of Dan McGrew
Shooting Stars
The Shop Around the Corner
Shopworn
The Shopworn Angel
The Shopworn Angel
Shore Acres
Should Ladies Behave?
Shoulder Arms
Show Boat
Show Boat
The Show of Shows
Show People
The Showoff
A Shriek in the Night
Sick Abed
Sidewalks of New York
The Sign of the Cross
The Silent Enemy
The Silk Express
The Silver Cord
Silver Dollar
The Silver Horde
Simple Charity
The Sin Flood
The Sin of Harold Diddlebock
The Sin of Madelon Claudet
Sin Takes a Holiday
Since You Went Away
Sing, Baby, Sing
Sing, Sinner, Sing
Sing, You Sinners
Singapore
The Singing Fool
The Singing Kid
The Single Standard
The Sinking of the Lusitania
Sinners' Holiday
Sinners in Paradise
Sinners in the Sun
Sioux Indian Dance
Sister Kenny
The Sisters
Sitting Pretty
Sitting Pretty
Six Hours to Live
Six Thousand Enemies
Skippy

Sky Devils
Skyscraper Souls
Slattery's Hurricane
Slave Ship
Sleep My Love
A Slight Case of Murder
Slightly French
Slightly Scarlet
The Slim Princess
Small Town Girl
Smart Money
Smart Woman
Smash Up—The Story of a
  Woman
Smashing the Spy Ring
Smilin' Through
Smilin' Through
The Smiling Lieutenant
Smoky
Smouldering Fires
The Snake Pit
The Snob
Snow White
Snow White and the Seven
  Dwarfs
So Big
So Dear to My Heart
So Ends Our Night
So Proudly We Hail!
So Red the Rose
So This Is Africa
So This Is London
So This is New York
So This Is Paris
Soak the Rich
The Social Lion
The Social Secretary
Soldiers of Fortune
Some Like It Hot
Something to Sing About
Somewhere I'll Find You
Somewhere in the Night
Son of Frankenstein
Son of Fury
Son of the Gods
The Son of the Sheik
The Son-Daughter
A Song is Born
Song O' My Heart
The Song of Bernadette
Song of Love
The Song of Songs
The Song of the Eagle
Song of the Flame
Song of the Shirt
Song of the South
The Song of the Wildwood
  Flute
A Song to Remember
Sons of the Desert
Sorority House
Sorrowful Jones
The Sorrows of Satan
Sorry, Wrong Number
S.O.S Iceberg
S.O.S.—Tidal Wave
So's Your Old Man
The Soul of Kura-San
Souls at Sea
Souls for Sale
A Southern Yankee
The Southerner
The Spanish Dancer
The Spanish Earth

The Yearling
Yellow Dust
Yellow Jack
The Yellow Ticket
Yes, My Darling Daughter
Yes or No
Yolanda and the Thief
You and Me
You Can't Cheat an Honest
  Man
You Can't Get Away With
  Murder
You Can't Have Everything
You Can't Take It With You
You May Be Next
You Only Live Once
You Were Never Lovelier
Young America
Young and Willing
Young as You Feel
Young Dr. Kildare
Young Eagles
The Young in Heart
Young Man of Manhattan
Young Mr. Lincoln
Young Tom Edison
The Younger Generation
Your Uncle Dudley
You're a Sweetheart
Yours for the Asking
Youth Takes a Fling
Youthful Folly
Zaza
Zaza
Zaza
Zenobia
Ziegfeld Follies
Ziegfeld Girl
Zoo in Budapest

West Germany
The Affair Blum

Books Consulted

A Nous la Liberté and Entr'Acte: Films by René Clair. René Clair. New York: Simon & Schuster, 1970.

Abel Gance. Steven P. Kramer and James M. Welsh. Boston: Twayne Publishers, 1978.

About John Ford. Lindsay Anderson. New York: McGraw-Hill Co., 1983.

The Age of the American Novel. Claude-Edmonde Magny. New York: Frederick Ungar, 1972.

Agee on Film. James Agee. New York: Grosset & Dunlap, 1967.

America in the Dark: Hollywood and the Gift of Reality. David Thomson. New York: William Morrow, 1977.

American Film Criticism: From the Beginnings to Citizen Kane. Stanley Kauffmann. New York: Liveright, 1972.

American Film Genres. Stuart M. Kaminsky. Dayton, OH: Pflaum Publishing Co., 1974.

American Silent Film. William K. Everson. New York: Oxford University Press, 1978.

America's Favorite Movies. Rudy Behlmer. New York: Frederick Ungar, 1982.

Anthony Mann. Jeanine Basinger. Boston: Twayne Publishers, 1979.

Around Cinemas. James Agate. New York: Arno Press & The New York Times, 1946, rpr. 1972

Around Cinemas. Second Series. James Agate. London: Home & Van Thal, Ltd., 1948.

The Art of Alfred Hitchcock: Fifty Years of His Motion Pictures. Donald Spoto. Garden City, NY: Doubleday & Co., 1979.

The Art of Walt Disney. Christopher Finch. New York: Harry N. Abrams, Inc., 1973.

Australian Silent Films: A Pictorial History, 1896-1929. Eric Reade. Melbourne: Lansdowne Press, 1970.

Authors on Film. Edited by Harry M. Geduld. Bloomington, IN: University of Indiana Press, 1972.

Authorship and Narrative in the Cinema: Issues in Contemporary Aesthetics and Criticism. William Luhr and Peter Lehman. New York: G. P. Putnam's Sons, 1977.

Awake in the Dark. Edited by David Denby. New York: Vintage, 1977.

Basil Rathbone: His Life and His Films. Michael B. Druxman. South Brunswick, NJ and New York: A. S. Barnes and Company, 1972.

Beauty and the Beast. Jean Cocteau. New York: New York University, 1970.

Before My Eyes: Film Criticism and Comments. Stanley Kaufmann. New York: Harper & Row Publishers, 1980.

Behind the Screen: The History and Techniques of the Motion Picture. Kenneth Macgowen. New York: Dell Publishing Co., Inc., 1965.

Best Film Plays, 1943-44. Edited by John Gassner and Dudley Nichols. New York: Garland Publishing, 1977.

Bette Davis: Her Films and Career. Gene Ringgold. Secaucus, NJ: The Citadel Press, 1985.

Between Flops: A Biography of Preston Sturges. James Curtis. New York: Harcourt, Brace, Jovanovich, 1982.

Beyond Formulas: American Film Genres. Stanley J. Solomon. New York: Harcourt, Brace, Jovanovich, 1982.

The Bicycle Thief. Vittorio De Sica. New York: Simon & Schuster, 1970.

The Big Book of B Movies: Or, How Low Was My Budget. Robin Cross. New York: St. Martin's Press, 1981.

The Big V: A History of the Vitagraph Company. Anthony Slide. Metuchen, NJ: The Scarecrow Press, 1976.

Billy Wilder. Bernard F. Dick. Boston: Twayne Publishers, 1980.

Billy Wilder. Axel Madsen. London: Secker & Warburg in Association with the British Film Institute, 1968.

Billy Wilder in Hollywood. Maurice Zolotow. New York: G. P. Putnam's Sons, 1977.

Biograph Bulletins, 1896-1908. Compiled with an Introduction and Notes by Kemp R. Niver. Edited by Bebe Bergsten. Los Angeles: Locare Research Group, 1971.

The Blue Angel. Josef von Sternberg. New York: Simon & Schuster, 1968.

The Blue Dahlia. Raymond Chandler. Edited with an Afterward by Matthew J. Bruccoli. Carbondale, IL: Southern Illinois Press, 1976.

The Bright Side of Billy Wilder, Primarily. Tom Wood. Garden City, NY: Doubleday, 1970.

Burt Lancaster: A Pictorial Treasury of His Films. Jerry Vermilye. New York: Falcon Enterprises, Inc., 1971.

The Busby Berkeley Book. Tony Thomas and Jim Terry with Busby Berkeley. Greenwich, CT: New York Graphic Society, 1973.

Caligari's Children. S. S. Prawer. New York: Oxford University Press, 1980.

David Lean and His Films. Alain Silver and James Ursini. London: Leslie Frewin, 1974.

David O. Selznick's Hollywood. Written and Produced by Ron Haver. Designs by Thomas Ingalls. New York: Alfred A. Knopf, 1980.

The Detective in Film. William K. Everson. Secaucus, NJ: The Citadel Press, 1972.

Dickens and Film. A. L. Zambrano. New York: Gordon Press, 1977.

Dictionary of Films. George Sadoul. Translated, Edited, and Updated by Peter Morris. Berkeley, CA: University of California Press, 1972.

Directors in Action. Bob Thomas. Indianapolis, IN: Bobbs-Merrill, 1973.

The Disney Films. Leonard Maltin. New York: Crown Publishers, Inc., 1973

The Disney Version. Richard Schickel. New York: Simon & Schuster, 1968.

Double Exposure: Fiction into Film. Joy Gould Boyum. New York: New American Library, 1981.

Douglas Sirk. Michael Stern. Boston: Twayne Publishers, 1979.

Dreams and Dead Ends. Jack Shadoian. Cambridge, MA: MIT Press, 1977.

Each Man in His Own Time. Raoul Walsh. New York: Farrar, Strauss & Giroux, 1974.

Eighty Years of Cinema. Peter Cowie. South Brunswick, NJ and NY: A. E. Barnes, 1977.

Eisenstein: Three Films, Battleship Potemkin, October, and Alexander Nevsky. Sergei Eisenstein. Edited by Jay Leyda and Translated by Diana Matias. New York: Harper & Row, Publishers, 1974.

The Emergence of Film Art. Lewis Jacobs. New York: Hopkinson and Blake, 1982.

The English Novel and the Movies. Edited by Michael Klein and Gillian Parker. New York: Frederick Ungar, 1981.

Ernst Lubitsch: A Guide to References and Resources. Robert Carringer and Barry Sabath. Boston: G. K. Hall & Co., 1981.

Ernst Lubitsch's American Comedy. William Paul. New York: Columbia University Press, 1983.

Faces, Forms, Films: The Artistry of Lon Chaney. Robert G. Anderson. South Brunswick, NJ and New York: A. S. Barnes, 1971.

Faulkner and Film. Bruce Kawin. New York: Frederick Ungar, 1977.

Fifty Classic British Films. 1932-1982: A Pictorial Record. Anthony Slide. New York: Dover Publications, Inc., 1985.

Fifty Great American Silent Films, 1912-1920: A Pictorial Survey. Anthony Slide and Edward Wagenknecht. New York. Dover Publications, Inc., 1980.

The Fifty Worst Films of All Time (and how they got that way). Harry Medved and Randy Dreyfuss. New York: Popular Library, 1978.

Film and Literature: An Introduction. Morris Beja. New York: Longman, 1971.

Film and Literature: Contrasts in Media. Fred H. Marcus. Scranton, PA: Chandler Publishing Co., 1971.

The Film and the Public. Roger Manvell. Baltimore, MD: Penguin Books, 1955.

Film Art: An Introduction. David Bordwell and Kristin Thompson. Reading, MA: Addison-Wesley, 1979.

Film as Film: Critical Responses to Film Art. Joy Gould Boyum and Adrienne Scott. Boston: Allyn and Bacon, 1971.

The Film Career of Billy Wilder. Steve Seidman. Boston: G. K. Hall & Co., 1977.

The Film Career of Buster Keaton. George Wead and George Lellis. Boston: G. K. Hall & Co., 1984.

The Film Criticism of Otis Ferguson. Edited by Robert Wilson. Philadelphia: Temple University Press, 1971.

Film Culture Reader. Edited by P. Adam Stickney. New York: Praeger, 1970.

Film Noir: An Encyclopedic Reference to the American Style. Edited by Alain Silver and Elizabeth Ward. Woodstock, NY: The Overlook Press, 1979.

Film Propaganda: Soviet Russia and Nazi Germany. Richard Taylor. New York: R & N Imports, 1979.

Filmguide to Henry V. Harry M. Geduld. Bloomington, IN: Indiana University Press, 1973.

Filmguide to The Grapes of Wrath. Warren French. Bloomington, IN: Indiana University Press, 1973

The Filming of the West. Jon Tuska. Garden City, NY: Doubleday, 1976.

The Films of the Second World War. Roger Manvell. New York: A. S. Barnes and Company, 1974.

The Films in My Life. François Truffaut. Translated by Leonard Mayhew. New York: Simon and Schuster, 1978.

The Films of Alan Ladd. Marilyn Henry and Ron De Sourdis. Secaucus, NJ: The Citadel Press, 1981.

The Films of Alfred Hitchcock. Robert A. Harris and Michael S. Lasky. Secaucus, NJ: The Citadel Press, 1976.

The Films of Alice Faye. W. Franklyn Moshier. San Francisco: Published by the Author, 1972.

The Films of Anthony Asquith. R. J. Minney. South Brunswick, NJ and New York: A. S. Barnes & Co., 1976.

The Films of Anthony Quinn. Alvin H. Marill. Secaucus, NJ: The Citadel Press, 1975.

The Films of Barbara Stanwyck. Homer Dickens. Secaucus, NJ: The Citadel Press, 1984.

The Films of Bela Lugosi. Richard Bojarski. Secaucus, NJ: The Citadel Press, 1980.

The Films of Bette Davis. SEE *Bette Davis: Her Films and Career.*

The Films of Bing Crosby. Robert Bookbinder. Secaucus, NJ: The Citadel Press, 1977.

The Films of Boris Karloff. Richard Bojarski and Kenneth Beale. Secaucus, NJ: The Citadel Press, 1974.

The Films of Carole Lombard. Frederick W. Ott. Secaucus, NJ: The Citadel Press, 1972.

The Films of Carl-Theodor Dreyer. David Bordwell. Berkeley: University of California Press, 1981.

The Films of Cary Grant. Donald Deschner. Secaucus, NJ: The Citadel Press, 1973.

The Films of Cecil B. DeMille. Gene Ringgold and DeWitt Bodeen. Secaucus, NJ: The Citadel Press, 1974.

The Films of Charlie Chaplin. Gerald D. McDonald, Michael Conway, and Mark Ricci. New York: Bonanza Books, 1977

The Films of Clark Gable. Gabe Essoe. New York: The Citadel Press, 1970.

The Films of D. W. Griffith. Edward Wagenknecht and Anthony Slide. New York: Crown Publishers, Inc., 1975.

The Films of Doris Day. Christopher Young. Secaucus, NJ: The Citadel Press, 1977.

The Films of David Niven. Gerard Garrett. Secaucus, NJ: The Citadel Press, 1976.

The Films of Elizabeth Taylor. Jerry Vermilye and Mark Ricci. Secaucus, NJ: The Citadel Press, 1976.

The Films of Errol Flynn. Tony Thomas, Rudy Behlmer, and Clifford McCarty. New York: The Citadel Press, 1969.

The Films of Frank Capra. Victor Scherle and William Turner Levy. Secaucus, NJ: The Citadel Press, 1977.

The Films of Frank Capra. Donald C. Willis. Metuchen, NJ: The Scarecrow Press, 1974.

The Films of Frank Sinatra. Gene Ringgold and Clifford McCarty. Secaucus, NJ: The Citadel Press, 1980

The Films of Fredric March. Lawrence J. Quirk. New York: The Citadel Press, 1971.

The Films of Fritz Lang. Frederick W. Ott. Secaucus, NJ: The Citadel Press, 1979.

The Films of Gary Cooper. Homer Dickens. New York: The Citadel Press, 1970.

The Films of Gene Kelly: Song and Dance Man. Tony Thomas. Secaucus, NJ: The Citadel Press, 1974.

The Films of Ginger Rogers. Homer Dickens. Secaucus, NJ: The Citadel Press, 1975.

The Films of Gloria Swanson. Lawrence J. Quirk. Secaucus, NJ: The Citadel Press, 1984.

The Films of Gregory Peck. John Griggs. Secaucus, NJ: The Citadel Press, 1984.

The Films of Greta Garbo. Michael Conway, Dion Mc Gregor, and Mark Ricci. New York: The Citadel Press, 1968.

The Films of Hal Roach. William K. Everson. New York: Museum of Modern Art, 1971.

The Films of Hedy Lamarr. Christopher Young. Secaucus, NJ: The Citadel Press, 1978.

The Films of Henry Fonda. Tony Thomas. Secaucus, NJ: The Citadel Press, 1983.

The Films of Howard Hawks. Donald C. Willis. Metuchen, NJ: The Scarecrow Press, 1975.

The Films of Ingrid Bergman. Lawrence J. Quirk. New York: The Citadel Press, 1970

The Films of James Cagney. Homer Dickens. Secaucus, NJ: The Citadel Press, 1972.

The Films of James Mason. Clive Hirschhorn. London: LSP Books, 1975.

The Films of James Stewart. Ken D. Jones, Arthur F. McClure, and Alfred E. Twomey. South Brunswick, NJ and New York: A. S. Barnes and Company, 1970.

The Films of Jean Harlow. Michael Conway and Mark Ricci. Secaucus, NJ: The Citadel Press, 1965.

The Films of Jean Vigo. William G. Simon. Ann Arbor, MI: UMI Research Press, 1981

The Films of Jeanette MacDonald and Nelson Eddy. Eleanor Knowles. South Brunswick, NJ and New York: A. S. Barnes and Company, 1975.

The Films of Jennifer Jones. W. Franklyn Moshier. San Francisco: Published by the Author, 1978.

The Films of Joan Crawford. Lawrence J. Quirk. New York: The Citadel Press, 1968.

The Films of John Garfield. Howard Gelman. Secaucus, NJ: The Citadel Press, 1975.

The Films of John Wayne. SEE *The Complete Films of John Wayne.*

The Films of Josef von Sternberg. Andrew Sarris. New York: Museum of Modern Art, 1966.

The Films of Katharine Hepburn. Homer Dickens. New York: The Citadel Press, 1971.

The Films of Kirk Douglas. Tony Thomas. Secaucus, NJ: The Citadel Press, 1972.

The Films of Lana Turner. Lou Valentino. Secaucus, NJ: The Citadel Press, 1976.

The Films of Laurence Olivier. Margaret Morley. Secaucus, NJ: The Citadel Press, 1978.

The Films of Leni Riefenstahl. David B. Hunton. Metuchen, NJ: The Scarecrow Press, 1978.

The Films of Mae West. Jon Tuska. Secaucus, NJ: The Citadel Press, 1973.

The Films of Marlene Dietrich. Homer Dickens. New York: The Citadel Press, 1968.

The Films of Montgomery Clift. Judith M. Kass. Secaucus, NJ: The Citadel Press, 1979.

The Films of Myrna Loy. Lawrence J. Quirk. Secaucus, NJ: The Citadel Press, 1980.

The Films of Nancy Carroll. Paul L. Nemcek. New York: Lyle Stuart, Inc., 1969.

The Films of Norma Shearer. Jack Jacobs and Myron Braum. South Brunswick, NJ: A. S. Barnes and Co., 1976.

The Films of Olivia de Havilland. Tony Thomas. Secaucus, NJ: The Citadel Press, 1983.

The Films of Orson Welles. Charles Higham. Berkeley, CA: University of California Press, 1970

The Films of Peter Lorre. Stephen D. Youngkin, James Bigwood, and Raymond G. Cabana, Jr. Secaucus, NJ: The Citadel Press, 1982.

The Films of Rita Hayworth: The Legend and Career of a Love Goddess. Gene Ringgold. Secaucus, NJ: The Citadel Press, 1974.

The Films of Robert Taylor. Lawrence J. Quirk. Secaucus, NJ: The Citadel Press, 1975.

The Films of Ronald Colman. Lawrence J. Quirk. Secaucus, NJ: The Citadel Press, 1977.

The Films of Ronald Reagan. Tony Thomas. Secaucus, NJ: The Citadel Press, 1980.

The Films of Sherlock Holmes. Chris Steinbrunner and Norman Michaels. Secaucus, NJ: The Citadel Press, 1978.

The Films of Shirley Temple. Robert Windeler. Secaucus, NJ: The Citadel Press, 1978.

The Films of Spencer Tracy. Donald Deschner. New York: The Citadel Press, 1979

The Films of Susan Hayward. Eduardo Moreno. Secaucus, NJ: The Citadel Press, 1979.

The Films of the Forties. Tony Thomas. Secaucus, NJ: The Citadel Press, 1975.

The Films of the Thirties. Jerry Vermilye. Secaucus, NJ: The Citadel Press, 1982.

The Films of the Twenties. Jerry Vermilye. Secaucus, NJ: The Citadel Press, 1985.

The Films of Tyrone Power. Dennis Belafonte with Alvin H. Marill. Secaucus, NJ: The Citadel Press, 1979.

The Films of W. C. Fields. Donald Deschner. Secaucus, NJ: The Citadel Press, 1973.

The Films of William Holden. Lawrence J. Quirk. Secaucus, NJ: The Citadel Press, 1973.

The Films of World War II. Joe Morella, Edward Z. Epstein, and John Griggs. Secaucus, NJ: The Citadel Press, 1973.

The First Twenty Years: A Segment of Film History. Kemp R. Niver. Edited by Bebe Bergsten. Los Angeles: Renovare Co., 1979.

Focus on Chaplin. Donald W. McCaffrey. Englewood Cliffs, NJ: Prentice-Hall, 1971.

Focus on Citizen Kane. Edited by Ronald Gottesman. Englewood Cliffs, NJ: Prentice-Hall, 1971.

Focus on Howard Hawks. Joseph McBride. Englewood Cliffs, NJ: Prentice-Hall, 1972.

Focus on Orson Welles. Edited by Ronald Gottesman. Englewood Cliffs, NJ: Prentice-Hall, 1976.

The Fondas: The Films and Careers of Henry, Jane and Peter Fonda. John Springer. New York: The Citadel Press, 1970.

Foremost Films of 1938. Frank Vreeland. New York: Gordon Press.

Frank Capra. Charles J. Maland. Boston: Twayne Publishers, 1980.

The Fred Astaire & Ginger Rogers Book. Arlene Croce. New York: Vintage Books, 1977.

French Cinema. National Cinema Series. Georges Sadoul and Roger Manville, Editors. Bala Cynwyd, PA: Ayer Press, 1953 rpr. 1972.

French Cinema: The First Wave, 1915-1929. Richard Abel. Princeton: Princeton University Press, 1984.

Fritz Lang. Robert A. Armour. Boston: Twayne Publishers, 1977.

Fritz Lang. Lotte H. Eisner. New York: Oxford University Press, 1977.

Fritz Lang: A Guide to References and Resources. E. Ann Kaplan. Boston: G. K. Hall & Co., 1981.

From Caligari to Hitler: A Psychological History of the German Film. Siegfried Kracauer. Princeton, NJ: Princeton University Press, 1947.

From Quasimodo to Scarlett to O'Hara: A National Board of Review Anthology, 1920-1940. Edited by Stanley Hochman. New York: Frederick Ungar, 1982.

G. W. Pabst. Lee Atwell. Boston: Twayne Publishers, 1977.

Garbo: A Portrait. Alexander Walken. New York: Macmillan Publishing Co., Inc., 1980.

George Cukor. Gene D. Phillips. Boston: Twayne Publishers, 1982.

George Kleine Collection of Early Motion Pictures in the Library of Congress. Library of Congress Motion Picture, Broadcasting, and Recorded Sound Division, Washington, D.C.: The U.S. Government Printing Office, 1980.

Gold Diggers of 1933. Edited with an Introduction by Arthur Hove. Madison, WI: Wisconsin Center for Film and Theater Research by the University of Wisconsin Press, 1980.

The Golden Age of "B" Movies. Doug McClelland. Nashville, TN: Charter House, 1978.

The Golden Age of French Cinema, 1929-1939. John W. Martin. Boston: Twayne Publishers, 1983.

Graham Greene: The Films of His Fiction. Gene B. Phillips. New York: Columbia University Teachers College, 1974.

The Great Adventure Films. Tony Thomas. Secaucus, NJ: The Citadel Press, 1976.

The Great British Films. Jerry Vermilye. Secaucus, NJ: The Citadel Press, 1978.

Great Film Directors: A Critical Anthology. Les Braudy and Morris Dickstein, Editors. New York: Oxford University Press, 1978.

The Great Films: Fifty Golden Years of Motion Pictures. Bosley Crowther. New York: G. P. Putnam's Sons, 1967.

The Great French Films. James Reid Paris. Secaucus, NJ: The Citadel Press, 1983.

The Great Gangster Pictures. James Robert Parish and Michael R. Pitts. Metuchen, NJ: The Scarecrow Press, Inc., 1976.

The Great Movies. William Bayer. New York: Grosset and Dunlap, 1973.

The Great Romantic Films. Lawrence J. Quirk. Secaucus, NJ: The Citadel Press, 1974.

The Great Spy Films. Leonard Rubenstein. Secaucus, NJ: The Citadel Press, 1979.

The Great Spy Pictures. James Robert Parish. New York: The Scarecrow Press, 1974.

Guts & Glory: Great American War Movies. Lawrence H. Suid. Reading, MA. Addison Wesley Publishing Company, 1978.

Halliwell's Hundred: A Nostalgic Choice of Films from the Golden Age. Leslie Halliwell. New York: Charles Scribner's Sons, 1982.

Harold Lloyd: The King of Daredevil Comedy. Adam Reilly. New York: Macmillan Publishing Co., Inc., 1977.

Harold Lloyd: The Shape of Laughter. Richard Schickel. Boston: New York Graphic Society, 1971.

The Haunted Screen. Lotte H. Eisner. Berkeley, CA: University of California Press, 1973.

Hawks on Hawks. Howard Hawks. Berkeley, CA: University of California Press, 1982.

Hemingway and Film. Gene D. Phillips. New York: Frederick Ungar, 1980.

Hemingway and the Movies. Frank M. Laurence. New York: De Capo Press, 1981.

Henry V. By William Shakespeare: Produced and Directed by Laurence Olivier. London: Lorrimer Publishing, 1984

High Sierra. Edited with an Introduction by Douglas Gomery. Madison, WI: Wisconsin Center for Film and Theater Research by the University of Wisconsin Press, 1979.

His Majesty the American. John C. Tibbetts and James M. Welsh. South Brunswick, NJ and New York: A. S. Barnes and Company, 1977.

A History of Films. John L. Fell. New York: Holt, Rinehart and Winston, 1979.

A History of Narrative Film. David A. Cook. New York: W.W. Norton & Company, 1981.

The History of World Cinema. David Robinson. New York: Stein and Day, 1973.

Hitch: The Life and Times of Alfred Hitchcock. John Russell Taylor. London: Faber & Faber, Ltd., 1978.

Hitchcock. Francois Truffaut, with the Collaboration of Helen G. Scott. New York: Simon & Schuster, 1984.

Hitchcock: The First Forty-Four Films. Eric Rohmer and Claude Chabrol. Translated by Stanley Hochman. New York: Frederick Ungar, 1979.

Hollywood Genres: Formulas, Filmmaking, and the Studio System. Thomas Schatz. New York: Random House, 1981.

The Hollywood Hallucination. Parker Tyler. New York: Simon and Schuster, 1970.

The Hollywood Musical. Clive Hirschhorn. New York: Crown Publishing, Inc., 1981.

The Hollywood Musical Goes to War. Allen L. Woll. Chicago: Nelson-Hall, 1983.

The Hollywood Social Problem Films. Peter Roffman and Jim Purdy. Bloomington, IN: Indiana University Press, 1981.

Hollywood: The Pioneers. Kevin Brownlow. Photographs Selected by John Kobel. New York: Alfred A. Knopf, 1979.

Hooray for Captain Spaulding! Richard J. Anobile. New York: Avon Books, 1973.

Horror Films. R. H. W. Dillard. New York: Monarch, 1976.

The Horror People. John Brosnan. New York: New American Library, 1976.

Howard Hawks. Leland A. Poague. Boston: Twayne Publishers, 1982.

Howard Hawks. Robin Wood. Garden City, NY: Doubleday & Co., 1968.

Howard Hawks: Storyteller. Gerald Mast. New York: Oxford University Press, 1982.

Humphrey Bogart. Alan G. Barbour. New York: Pyramid Publications, 1973.

Humphrey Bogart: The Man and His Films. Paul Michael. New York: Bonanza Books, 1965.

I Am a Fugitive from a Chain Gang. John E. O'Connor. Madison, WI: Wisconsin Center for Film and Theater Research by the University of Wisconsin Press, 1981.

I Lost It at the Movies. Pauline Kael. Boston: Little, Brown and Company, 1954.

An Illustrated History of the Horror Film. Carlos Clarens. New York: A Paragon Book, 1967.

In the Dark: A Primer for the Movies. Richard M. Barsam. New York: Viking, 1977.

Ingrid Bergman. Curtis F. Brown. New York: Pyramid Publications, 1973.

The International Dictionary of Films and Filmmakers. Edited by Christopher Lyon. Chicago: St. James Press, 1984.

Introduction to the Art of the Movies. Lewis Jacobs. New York: Noonday Press, 1960.

The Italian Cinema. Vernon Jarratt. New York: Arno Press & The New York Times, 1972.

The Italian Cinema. Pierre Leprohon. Translated by Roger Greaves and Oliver Stallybrass. New York: Praeger Publishers, 1966.

Italian Cinema: From Neorealism to the Present. Peter Bondanella. New York: Frederick Ungar, 1983.

James Whale. James Curtis. Metuchen, NJ: The Scarecrow Press, 1982.

Jean Renoir. Andre Bazan. Translated by W. W. Halsey and William H. Simon. New York: Simon & Schuster, 1974.

Jean Renoir. Raymond Durgnat. Berkeley, CA: University of California Press, 1974.

Jean Renoir: A Guide to References and Resources. Christopher Faulkner. Boston: G. K. Hall & Co., 1979

Jean Renoir: The French Films, 1924-1939. Alexander Sesonske. Cambridge, MA: Harvard University Press, 1980.

Jean Vigo. P. E. Salles Gomes. Berkeley, CA: University of California Press, 1971.

Jesse Matthews: A Biography. Michael Thornton. London: Hart-Davis MacGibbon, 1974.

John Ford. Peter Bogdanovich. Berkeley, CA: University of California Press, 1968.

John Wayne and the Movies. Allen Eyles. South Brunswick, NJ: A. S. Barnes & Co., 1976.

Joseph Losey. Foster Hirsch. Boston: Twayne Publishers, 1980.

Joseph L. Mankiewicz. Bernard F. Dick. Boston: Twayne Publishers, 1983.

Journey Down Sunset Boulevard: The Films of Billy Wilder. Neil Sinyard and Adrian Turner. Ryde, Isle of Wight: BCW Publishing, 1979.

Judy: The Films and Career of Judy Garland. Joe Morella and Edward Z. Epstein. New York: The Citadel Press, 1969.

Keaton. Rudi Blesh. New York: Macmillan, 1966.

Kind Hearts and Coronets. London: Lorrimer Publishing, 1984.

King Vidor. John Baxter. New York: Monarch Press, 1976.

King Vidor on Film Making. King Vidor. New York: David McKay Co., Inc., 1972.

Kino. Revised Edition. Jay Leyde. Princeton, NJ: Princeton University Press, 1983.

Ladd: The Life, the Legend, the Legacy of Alan Ladd. Beverly Linet. New York: Arbor House, 1979.

The Lady Vanishes. Frank Launder and Sidney Gilliat. London: Lorrimer Publishing, 1984.

Landmark Films: The Cinema of Our Century. William Wolf with Lillian Kramer Wolf. New York: Paddington Press, Ltd., 1979

Laurel & Hardy. John McCabe, Al Kilgore and Richard W. Bann. New York: E. P. Dutton, 1975.

Laurence Olivier. Foster Hirsch. Boston: Twayne Publishers, 1979.

Laurence Olivier: Theater and Cinema. Robert L. Daniels. New York: A. S. Barnes and Company, Inc., 1980.

Law and Ehrlinger Present Famous Plays in Pictures. Kemp R. Niver. Edited by Bebe Bergsten. Los Angeles: Locare Research Group, 1976.

Living Images: Film Comment and Criticism. Stanley Kauffman. New York: Harper & Row Publishers, 1975

Lorentz on Film: Movies, 1927-1941. Pare Lorentz. New York: Hopkinson and Blake, 1975.

Lon of a 1000 Faces! Forrest J. Ackerman. Beverly Hills, CA: Morrison, Raven-Hill Co., 1983.

The Lubitsch Touch: A Critical Study. Third Revised and Enlarged Edition. Herman G. Weinberg. New York: Dover Publications, Inc., 1977.

Lunatics and Lovers: The Golden Age of Hollywood Comedy, from Dinner at Eight to The Miracle at Morgan's Creek. Ted Sennett. NY: Limelight Editions, 1985.

Macao. Bernard C. Schoenfeld and Stanley Rubin. New York: Frederick Ungar, 1985.

The Magic and Myth of the Movies. Parker Tyler. New York: Simon and Schuster, 1947.

Magic Moments from the Movies. Elwy Yost. Garden City, NJ: Doubleday, 1978.

The Magic World of Orson Welles. James Naremore. New York: Oxford University Press, 1978.

Magill's Cinema Annual, 1982-1985. Edited by Frank N. Magill. Englewood Cliffs, NJ: Salem Press, 1982–85.

Magill's Survey of Cinema. Foreign Language Films. Edited by Frank N. Magill. Englewood Cliffs, NJ: Salem Press, 1985.

Magill's Survey of Cinema. English Language Films. Series I and II. Edited by Frank N. Magill. Englewood Cliffs, NJ: Salem Press, 1980–81.

Magill's Survey of Cinema. Silent Films. Edited by Frank N. Magill. Englewood Cliffs, NJ: Salem Press, 1982.

Make It Again, Sam: A Survey of Movie Remakes. Michael B. Durxman. South Brunswick, NJ: A. S. Barnes, 1975.

The Making of Citizen Kane. Robert L. Carringer. Berkeley, CA: University of California Press, 1985.

The Making of Henry V. Clayton C. Hutton. London: Eagle Lion Film Distributors, Ernest J. Day, 1944.

The Making of the Great Westerns. William R. Meyer. New Rochelle, NY: Arlington House, 1979.

Mamoulian. Tom Milne. Bloomington, IN: Indiana University Press, 1969.

Mank: The Wit, World, and Life of Herman Mankiewicz. Richard Meryman. New York: Morrow, 1978.

Masters of Menace: Greenstreet and Lorre. Ted Sennett. New York: E.P. Dutton, 1979.

Meeting at the Sphinx. Marjorie Denas. London: McDonald, 1946.

The MGM Years. Laurence B. Thomas. New York: Columbia House, 1972.

Mickey Mouse: 50 Happy Years. Edited by David Bain and Bruce Harris. New York: Harmony Books, 1977.

Mildred Pierce. Edited with an Introduction by Albert J. LaValley. Madison, WI: The Wisconsin Center for Film and Theater Research by the University of Wisconsin Press, 1980.

A Million and One Nights: A History of the Motion Picture through 1925. Terry Ramsaye. New York: Simon and Schuster, 1986.

A Mirror for England: British Movies from Austerity to Affluence. Raymond Durgnat. New York: Praeger Publishers, 1971.

The Modern American Novel and the Cinema. Edited by Gerald Perry and Roger Shatzhin. New York: Frederick Ungar, 1978.

Motion Pictures: The Development of an Art. Revised Edition. A. R. Fulton. Norman, OK: University of Oklahoma Press, 1980.

Movies and Methods: An Anthology. Edited by Bill Nichols. Berkeley, CA: University of California Press, 1976.

The Movies Begin: Making Movies in New Jersey, 1887-1920. Paul Spehr. Newark, NJ: The Newark Museum in Cooperation with Morgan and Morgan, Inc., 1977.

The Movies on Your Mind. Harvey R. Greenberg. New York: Saturday Review Press-Dutton, 1975.

The Moving Image: A Guide to Cinematic Literacy. Robert Gessner. New York: E. P. Dutton, 1976.

Murnau. Lotte H. Eisner. Berkeley: University of California Press, 1973.

My Autobiography. Charles Chaplin. New York: Simon and Schuster, 1964.

My Darling Clementine. John Ford, Director. Robert Lyons, Editor. New Brunswick, NJ: Rutgers University Press, 1984.

The Name Above the Title: An Autobiography. Frank Capra. New York: The Macmillan Company, 1971.

Sherlock Holmes on the Screen: The Motion Picture Adventures of the World's Most Popular Detective. Robert W. Pohle, Jr. and Douglas C. Hart. South Brunswick, NJ and New York: A. S. Barnes and Company, 1977.

The Silent Clowns. Walter Kerr. New York: Alfred A. Knopf, 1979.

Sound & the Cinema: The Coming of Sound to American Film. Evan W. Cameron. Salem, NY: Redgrave Publishing Co., 1980.

Souvenir Programs of Twelve Classic Movies, 1927-1941. Edited by Miles Krueger. New York: Dover, 1977.

The Spanish Civil War in American and European Films. Marjorie A. Valleau. Ann Arbor, MI: UMI Research Press, 1982.

Stanley Donen. Joseph Andrew Casper. Metuchen, NJ: The Scarecrow Press, 1983.

Stanley Kramer: Film Maker. Donald Spoto. New York: G. P. Putnam's Sons, 1978.

Starring Fred Astaire. Stanley Green and Burt Goldblatt. New York: Dodd, Mead, 1973.

Starring Miss Barbara Stanwyck. Ella Smith. New York: Crown Publishers, Inc., 1985.

Storytelling and Mythmaking: Images from Film and Literature. Frank McDonnell. New York: Oxford University Press, 1979.

Stroheim. Joel W. Finler. Berkeley, CA: University of California Press, 1967.

Stroheim: A Pictorial Record of His Nine Films. Herman G. Weinberg. New York: Dover Publications, Inc., 1975.

Sublime Marlene. Thierry de Navacelle. Translated by Carey L. Smith. New York: St. Martin's Press, 1982.

Surrealism and American Feature Films. J. H. Matthews. Boston: Twayne Publishers, 1979.

Surrealism and the Cinema. Michael Gould. South Brunswick, NJ and New York: A. S. Barnes & Co., 1976.

Swordsmen of the Screen. Richard Jeffrey. London: Routledge & Kegan Paul, 1977.

Talking Pictures: Screenwriters in the American Cinema, 1927-1973. Woodstock, NY: Overlook Press, 1974.

Theater and Film. Roger Manvell. Rutherford, NJ: Fairleigh Dickinson University Press, 1979.

To Have and Have Not. Edited with an Introduction by Bruce F. Kawin. Madison, WI: The Wisconsin Center for Film and Theater Research by the University of Wisconsin Press, 1980.

A Tree Is a Tree. King Vidor. New York: Garland Publishing Company, Inc., 1977.

Twenty-Five Thousand Sunsets: An Autobiography. Herbert Wilcox. London: The Bodley Head, 1967.

Unholy Fools: Wits, Comics, Disturbers of the Peace. Penelope Gilliat. New York: Viking Press, 1973.

Val Lewton: The Reality of Terror. Joel E. Siegel. New York: Viking Press, 1973.

Vincent Price Unmasked. James Robert Parish and Steven Whitney. New York: Drake Publishers, Inc., 1974.

Vincente Minnelli and the Film Musical. Joseph Andrew Casper. South Brunswick, NJ and New York: A. S. Barnes & Company, 1971.

Vintage Films. Bosley Crowther. New York: G. P. Putnam's Sons, 1977.

Visions of War: Hollywood Combat Films of World War II. Kathryn Kane. Ann Arbor, MI: UMI Research Press, 1982.

Vivien Leigh. John Russell Taylor. New York: St. Martin's Press, 1984.

W. C. Fields: A Life on Film. Ronald J. Fields. New York: St. Martin's Press, 1982.

Walt Disney: A Guide to References and Resources. Elizabeth Leebron and Lynn Garlley. Boston: G. K. Hall & Co., 1979.

Walt Disney's Fantasia. Deems Taylor. New York: Simon & Schuster, n.d.

The War, the West, and the Wilderness. Kevin Brownlow. New York: Alfred A. Knopf, 1979.

The Western: From Silents to the Seventies. Revised Edition. George N. Fenin and William K. Everson. New York: Penguin Books, 1977.

The Western Films of John Ford. J. A. Place. Secaucus, NJ: The Citadel Press, 1974.

When Hollywood Ruled the Skies: The Aviation Film Classics of World War II. Bruce W. Orriss. Hawthorne, CA: Aero Associates, 1984.

Why a Duck? Richard F. Anobile. New York: Avon Books, 1974.

William A. Wellman. Frank T. Thompson with a Foreword by Barbara Stanwyck. Metuchen, NJ: Scarecrow Press, 1983.

William Wyler. Michael A. Anderegg. Boston: Twayne Publishers, 1979.

William Wyler: A Guide to References and Resources. Sharon Kern. Boston: G. K. Hall & Co., 1979.

Women and Their Sexuality in the New Film. Joan Mellen. New York: Horizon Press, 1973.

Women in Film Noir. Edited by Ann E. Kaplan. London: The British Film Institute, 1978.

Women's Films and Female Experience. Andrea S. Walsh. New York: Praeger, 1984.

Women's Pictures: Feminism and Cinema. Annette Kuhn. London: Routledge & Kagan Paul, 1982.

The World of Enlightenment. Hugh Fordin. New York: Avon Books, 1976.

Yankee Doodle Dandy. Edited with an Introduction by Patrick McGilligan. Madison, WI: The Wisconsin Center for Film and Theater Research by the University of Wisconsin Press, 1981.

You Must Remember This. . .: The Filming of Casablanca. Charles Francisco. Englewood Cliffs, NJ: Prentice-Hall, 1980.